COST MANAGEMENT

STRATEGIES FOR BUSINESS DECISIONS

COST MANAGEMENT

STRATEGIES FOR BUSINESS DECISIONS

International Edition

Marc Wouters, Frank H. Selto,
Ronald W. Hilton, Michael W. Maher

McGraw-Hill Higher Education

London Boston Burr Ridge, IL Dubuque, IA Madison, WI New York San Francisco
St. Louis Bangkok Bogotá Caracas Kuala Lumpur Lisbon Madrid Mexico City Milan
Montreal New Delhi Santiago Seoul Singapore Sydney Taipei Toronto

Cost Management: Strategies for Business Decisions
International Edition
Marc Wouters, Frank H. Selto, Ronald W. Hilton, Michael W. Maher
ISBN-13 9780077132392
ISBN-10 0077132394

Mc Graw Hill **McGraw-Hill Higher Education**

Published by McGraw-Hill Education (UK) Limited
Shoppenhangers Road
Maidenhead
Berkshire
SL6 2QL
Telephone: 44 (0) 1628 502 500
Fax: 44 (0) 1628 770 224
Website: www.mcgraw-hill.co.uk

British Library Cataloguing in Publication Data
A catalogue record for this book is available from the British Library

Library of Congress Cataloguing in Publication Data
The Library of Congress data for this book has been applied for from the Library of Congress

Acquisitions Editor: Leiah Batchelor
Development Editor: Stephanie Frosch
Senior Production Editor: James Bishop
Marketing Manager: Alexis Thomas

Text Design by HL Studios
Cover design by Adam Renvoize
Printed and bound in Singapore by Markono

ISBN-13 9780077132392
ISBN-10 0077132394

The McGraw·Hill Companies

Dedication

To my parents, Ricky and Cor, examples in personal and professional life. To my wife and daughter, Susanne and Anouk, for all their love and support. And to my students who make teaching and research rewarding.

Marc Wouters

To my first accounting teachers: Bill Bruns, Bill Felix, Bob May, Kasi Ramanatham and Gary Sundem, who inspired me by their intellectual curiosity, creativity and consistently high standards.

Frank Selto

Brief Table of Contents

About the Authors xviii

Preface xx

Conversion Guide xxii

Acknowledgements xxiv

Guided Tour xxv

Technology to Enhance Learning and Teaching xxviii

PART 1: Setting the Strategic Foundation: The Importance of Analysing and Managing Costs

1 Cost Management and Strategic Decision Making: Evaluating Opportunities and Leading Change 2

2 Product Costing Concepts and Systems 46

3 Cost Estimation 84

PART 2: Activity-based Management

4 Activity-based Costing Systems 140

5 Customer Profitability and Activity-based Management 186

6 Managing Quality and Time to Create Value 226

PART 3: Planning and Decision Making

7 Cost Management and Short-term Decision Making 284

8 Strategic Investment Decisions 344

9 Budgeting and Financial Planning 418

PART 4: Product Costing and Cost Allocation

10 Job and Order Costing 476

11 Joint Product and Process Cost Systems 530

12 Managing and Allocating Support Service Costs 574

PART 5: Performance Measurement and Management

13 Analysis and Management of Cost Variances 624

14 Organizational Design, Responsibility Accounting and Evaluation of Divisional Performance 696

15 Transfer Pricing 746

16 Strategy, Balanced Scorecards and Incentive Systems 786

Glossary 839

Index 850

Detailed Table of Contents

About the Authors xviii

Preface xx

Conversion Guide xxii

Acknowledgements xxiv

Guided Tour xxv

Technology to Enhance Learning and Teaching xxviii

PART 1: Setting the Strategic Foundation: The Importance of Analysing and Managing Costs

1 Cost Management and Strategic Decision Making: Evaluating Opportunities and Leading Change 2

Strategic Role of Cost Management 4
- Characteristics of Cost Management 4
- Characteristics of Cost Management Analysts 5

Cost Management in a Decision-making Framework 7
- Stage I: Setting Goals and Objectives 7
- Stage II: Gathering Information 8
- Stage III: Evaluating Alternatives 10
- Stage IV: Execution and Tracking Costs 10
- Stage V: Obtaining Feedback 11

Strategic Decision Making (More about Stage I) 11
- 'Where Do We Want to Go?' 12
- 'How Do We Want to Get There?' 13
- Eight Elements of Leading and Managing Change 17

Evaluation of Plans and Outcomes 19
- Benefit-Cost Analysis (More about Stage III) 19
- Benefit and Cost Variances (More about Stage V) 21

Ethical Standards 23
- Ordinary People Face Ethical Dilemmas 23
- Codes of Ethics 24
- Sarbanes-Oxley Act 24
- Internal Controls to Protect Assets and Provide Quality Information 24
- Internal Auditing to Assure Compliance 25

Sustainability and Environmental Strategic Decisions 26

Chapter Summary 28

Key Terms 28

Review Questions 29

Critical Analysis 29

Exercises 30

Problems 33

Cases 39

Solutions to You're the Decision Maker 42

Endnotes 43

References 44

2 Product Costing Concepts and Systems 46

Cost Management and Cost Concepts 48

The Role of Cost Management at Sacs Chameaux SA 49

Concepts and Measures of Cost 50
- Applying Concepts of Cost to Decision Making 51
- Cash or Out-of-pocket Cost 52
- Variable, Committed and Fixed Costs 53
- Sunk and Accrual Costs 55

Reporting Product Costs, Period Costs and Expenses 56

Cost Analysis 58
- Costs of Manufacturing 60
- Direct Costs 61
- Indirect Costs 61
- Non-manufacturing Costs 62
- Stages of Production and the Flow of Costs 62

Detailed Table of Contents (continued)

Schedule of Costs of Goods Completed and Sold 64
- Financial Modelling 64
- Statement of Cost of Goods Completed and Cost per Unit 65

Chapter Summary 67
Key Terms 68
Review Questions 68
Critical Analysis 69
Exercises 69
Problems 73
Cases 78
Solutions to You're the Decision Maker 82
Endnotes 83
References 83

3 Cost Estimation 84

Reasons for Estimating Costs 86
- Cost Management 87
- Decision Making 87
- Planning and Standard Setting 88

Cost Estimation 88
- Cost Object (Vertical Axis) 89
- Cost Drivers (Horizontal Axis) 89
- Cost Pattern (the Shape of the Line) 90
- Cost-estimation Methods 93

Account Analysis Method 93
- Application of Account Analysis to C.C. Catering 94

Statistical Cost Estimation Using Linear Regression Analysis 95
- Simple Model for Linear Regression Analysis 95
- Application of Linear Regression Analysis to C.C. Catering 96
- High-low Method 100

Use of Multiple Regression Analysis to Estimate Cost-driver Rates 101
- Application of Multiple Regression Analysis to C.C. Catering 101
- Cautionary Note about Using Regression 104

Engineering Method 105
- Application of the Engineering Method to C.C. Catering 106

Comparison of the Methods and Estimates 108
- Choice of Cost Equation 109
- Problems with Forecasting 109

Application of the Methods to C.C. Catering 110
- C.C. Catering's Hybrid Cost Estimation Model 110
- Use of the Results 111
- Appendix 3A 113
- Technical Notes on Regression 113

Appendix 3B 116
- Learning Curves 116

Chapter Summary 120
Key Terms 120
Review Questions 120
Critical Analysis 121
Exercises 122
Problems 128
Cases 134
Solutions to You're the Decision Maker 136
Endnotes 137
References 137

Part 2: Activity-based Management

4 Activity-based Costing Systems 140

PML Background 143
- PML's Competitive Situation 143
- PML's Products and Processes 143
- PML's Costing System Options 144
- PML's Costing System Team 144

Traditional Costing System 145
- Under-costing and Over-costing Products: Cost of Dinner Example 145
- Refining a Traditional Costing System 145
- Traditional Cost System Example 146

Activity-based Costing System 147
- Step 1: Identify and Classify Activities Related to Products 148
- Step 2: Estimate the Costs of Activities 151
- Step 3: Calculate a Cost-driver Rate for Each Activity Cost Pool 152
- Step 4: Assign Activity Costs to Products 156

ABC Profitability Measures 158
- Comparisons of ABC Product Profitability 158
- MegaBurger Novelty Toy Analysis 160

Unit-level ABC Costing 162
- Cost and Information Differences 163

Activity-based Costing in Service and Merchandising Companies 164

Costs and Benefits of Activity-based Costing 164

Chapter Summary 166

Key Terms 166

Review Questions 166

Critical Analysis 167

Exercises 168

Problems 171

Cases 180

Solutions to You're the Decision Maker 182

Endnotes 184

References 184

5 Customer Profitability and Activity-based Management 186

Importance of Customer Profitability 188
- Measurement of Customer Profitability 188
- Qualitative Considerations 189

Activity-based Costing: Foundation of Process Improvement 190

PML's Initial ABC Customer Profitability Analysis 191

PML's Improved Customer Profitability Analysis 192
- Administrative Cost Analysis 192
- Identification of Alternative Actions 195

Combination of ABC and Target Costing = Cost Reduction Goal 196

Extension of ABC to Activity-based Management (ABM) 197

Step 5: Customer-perceived Value 198
- Sources of Non-value-added Activities 198
- Identifying and Measuring Value-added Activities 199
- Measures of Value-added Activities 200

Step 6: Performing the Measurement Activity 200

Step 7: Process Improvement Using Activity-based Management 201
- Eliminating Non-value-added Activities: A Competitive Necessity, but Risky 201

PML's ABM Analysis 201
- Working from the Activity List 202
- Estimating the Benefits of ABM 203
- Identification of Process Improvement Opportunities 203
- Asking the Question, 'Why?' 204
- Estimating the Cost of Saved Resources in Exhibit 5.9 205

Implementation of Activity-based Costing and Management 205
- Should All Organizations Adopt ABC and ABM? 206
- Can You Be Sure that ABC and ABM Will Be Successful? 206
- Scope of the ABC/ABM Project 206
- Resources Necessary 206
- Resistance to Change 207
- Information to Be Gathered 208
- Analysis Team's Responsibility for Information Analysis and Decision Making 208

PML's Customer Decisions 208

Chapter Summary 209

Key Terms 209

Review Questions 210

Critical Analysis 210

Detailed Table of Contents (continued)

Exercises 211
Problems 213
Cases 217
Solutions to You're the Decision Maker 222
Endnotes 224
References 224

6 Managing Quality and Time to Create Value 226

TCSI Background 228
Importance of Quality 228
Methods for Improving Quality 229
- Total Quality Management (TQM) 229
- Return on Quality (ROQ) 229
- Comparison of the Views of Quality 230
- Conflict between TQM and ROQ 230

Dimensions of Quality 231
- Product Attributes 231
- Customer Service Before and After the Sale 231

How Organizations Measure Quality 232
- Variation Causes Poor Quality 232
- Diagnostic Information 234
- Customer Satisfaction 239
- Trade-offs between Quality and Price 239
- Identifying Costs of Quality 239
- Controlling Quality 240
- Failing to Control Quality 240
- Measuring Costs of Quality 241
- Reporting Costs of Quality 241

Corporate Integrity and Quality 243
- Ethical Behaviour and Reputation 243
- Quality Awards and Certificates 243

Managing Time in a Competitive Environment 244
- New Product Development Time 244
- Customer Response Time and Cycle Time 244
- Costs of Time 245
- Time-driven Activity-based Costing and Management 245

Management of Process Productivity and Efficiency 247
- Measuring Productivity 247
- Measuring Average Cycle Time 248
- Measuring Throughput Efficiency 248

Managing Process Capacity 249
- Measuring Capacity 250

Managing Quality + Time + Productivity + Capacity = JIT or Lean Process Management 250
- Contrasts of JIT/Lean and Traditional Processes 251
- JIT/Lean Success Factors 253

Job and Project Management 256
- Project Cost and Time Budgets 256

Appendix 6 258
- Construction and Use of Control Charts 258

Chapter Summary 261
Key Terms 261
Review Questions 262
Critical Analysis 262
Exercises 263
Problems 268
Cases 275
Solutions to You're the Decision Maker 278
Endnotes 279
References 280

Part 3: Planning and Decision Making

7 Cost Management and Short-term Decision Making 284

Introducing Financial Modelling 286
- Different Kinds of Financial Models 287
- Objectives of Financial Modelling 287
- Only the Future and Only Differences are Relevant 288

Using Cost-Volume-Profit (CVP) Planning Models 289
- Basic Cost-Volume-Profit Model 289
- Cost-Volume-Profit Model and the Break-Even Point 290
- Basic CVP Model in Graphical Format 290
- CVP and Target Income 291
- Operating Leverage 292
- Set-up of Computer Spreadsheet Models 293

Modelling Taxes, Multiple Products and Multiple Cost Drivers 295
- Modelling Taxes 295
- Modelling Multiple Products 296
- Multiproduct Profit-planning and Decision-making Models 297
- Modelling Multiple Cost Drivers 299
- Profit-Planning and Decision-making Models with Multiple Cost Drivers 300

Using Sensitivity and Scenario Analysis 303
- Sensitivity Analysis: What If? 303
- Scenario Analysis (Best, Worst and Most Likely Cases) 305

Modelling Scarce Resources 306
- Profit from a Single Scarce Resource Maximization 307

Pricing Decisions 308
- Influences on Prices 308
- Special-order Price Decisions 312

Appendix 7A 314
- Theory of Constraints 314

Appendix 7B 316
- Linear Programming 316

Chapter Summary 321
Key Terms 321
Review Questions 321
Critical Analysis 322
Exercises 324
Problems 329
Cases 337
Solutions to You're the Decision Maker 340
Endnotes 341
References 342

8 Strategic Investment Decisions 344

Many Decisions are Investment Decisions 346
Section I: Investment Decisions and Discounted Cash Flows 347
Understanding Investment Alternatives 347
Discounted Cash Flow Analysis 350
- Estimating Cash Flows for DCF Analysis 350
- Illustration of ShadeTree Roasters' Replacement Decision 351
- Importance of the Discount Rate 352
- Discounting Future Cash Flows 355
- Computing the Net Present Value and Payback Period 356
- Computing the Internal Rate of Return 358
- Comparing Investment Alternatives 360

Application of DCF to Other Common Decisions 363
- Replacement of Equipment 363
- Outsourcing or Make-or-Buy Decision 364
- Add or Drop a Product, Service or Business Unit 367

Choice of the Best Alternative Using Both Financial and Non-financial Information 370
Section II: Strategic Investment Decisions 371
Strategic Investments 371
- Uncontrollable External Factors 372
- Information about External Events 372
- Identification of Uncontrollable Future Events 373
- Expected Value Analysis 374
- Internal Information 376
- Forecasts of ShadeTree's Investment Information 377

Future Actions of Competitors 379
Real Option Value Analysis 381
- Value of Deferring Irreversible Decisions 382
- Value of the Option to Wait 385

Legal and Ethical Issues in Strategic Investment Analysis 386
- Internal Ethical Pressures 386
- Roles of Internal Controls and Audits 387

Detailed Table of Contents (continued)

Appendix 8A 388
- Analysis of ShadeTree Roasters' Decision to Invest Now, Years 1–6 388

Appendix 8B 389
- Analysing Real Option Trees by Rolling Backward and with Imperfect Information 389

Chapter Summary 393
Key Terms 393
Review Questions 393
Critical Analysis 394
Exercises 395
Problems 400
Cases 406
Solutions to You're the Decision Maker 411
Endnotes 415
References 415

9 Budgeting and Financial Planning 418

Strategic Planning: Achieving and Maintaining a Competitive Advantage 420
- What Is a Strategic Plan? 420

What are the Key Purposes and Types of Budgeting Systems? 421
- Planning 421
- Facilitating Communication and Co-ordination 421
- Allocating Resources 421
- Managing Financial and Operational Performance 422
- Evaluating Performance and Providing Incentives 422
- Organizations Use Many Types of Budgets 422

Master Budget as a Planning Tool 422
- Sales Budget: The Starting Point 422
- Operational Budgets: Meeting the Demand for Goods and Services 425
- Budgeted Financial Statements: Completing the Master Budget 426
- Master Budget for Non-profit Organizations 426
- International Aspects of Budgeting 426
- Activity-based Budgeting 427
- Zero-base Budgeting for Discretionary Costs 428

Illustrating the Master Budget 429
- Sales Budget 429
- Production Budget 429
- Direct Material Budget 430
- Direct Labour Budget 432
- Manufacturing Overhead Budget 432
- Selling, General and Administrative (SG&A) Expense Budget 434
- Cash Receipts Budget 435
- Cash Payments Budget 436
- Cash Budget: Combining Receipts and Payments 438
- Budgeted Schedule of Cost of Goods Manufactured and Sold 439
- Budgeted Statement of Income 440
- Budgeted Statement of Financial Position 440
- Assumptions and Predictions Underlying the Master Budget 442
- Financial Planning Models 442

Responsibility for Budget Administration 443
Behavioural Implications of Budgets 444
- Budgetary Slack: Padding the Budget 444
- Participative Budgeting 445
- Ethical Issues in Budgeting 445

Appendix 9 447
- Inventory Management 447

Chapter Summary 451
Key Terms 451
Review Questions 452
Critical Analysis 452
Exercises 453
Problems 458
Cases 467
Solutions to You're the Decision Maker 471
Endnotes 472
References 473

Part 4: Product Costing and Cost Allocation

10 Job and Order Costing 476

Background for Creazioni di Vetro 478
Alternative Product-costing Systems 479
  Choices Among Major Types of Product Costing Systems 479
  Widespread Use of Job-order Costing 480
Basic Cost-flow Model 481
  Cost Flows and Jobs 481
  Simple Cost-flow Examples 481
Managing and Using Cost-flow Information 482
  The Process of Tracking Job-order Costs 483
  Product-costing System Design Issues 484
  Recording Job-order Costs 484
Manufacturing Overhead Costs 487
Use of Predetermined Overhead Rates 488
Manufacturing Overhead Variance 490
  Disposition of the Manufacturing Overhead Variance 491
  Prorating a Materially Large Variance 492
  Periodic Operating Income 493
Job-order Costing Information and Decision Making 494
  Income-reporting Effects of Alternative Product-costing Methods 495
  Comparison of Absorption and Variable Costing 495
  Evaluation of Absorption and Variable Costing 496
  Broadening Job-order Costing's Relevance to the Value Chain 498
  Job-order Costing in Service Organizations 499
Ethical Issues for Managing and Reporting Job Costs 500
  Misstating the Stage of Completion 500
  Charging Costs to the Wrong Job 500
  Misrepresenting the Cost of a Job 501
  Preventing Improprieties by Understanding Contracts 501
Appendix 10 502
  Throughput Costing 502
Chapter Summary 503
Key Terms 503
Review Questions 504
Critical Analysis 504
Exercises 505
Problems 513
Cases 523
Solutions to You're the Decision Maker 526
Endnotes 528
References 529

11 Joint Product and Process Cost Systems 530

Joint Product Processes 532
  The Importance of Split Off 532
  Joint Process: One Input - More Than One Output 532
The Joint Product Decision: Which Outputs to Produce? 533
  Estimation of Profits from Joint Products 533
  Decision Whether to Sell Products at Split-off or After Further Processing 535
Allocating Joint Costs for Internal and External Reporting 538
  Distinguishing between Main and By-products 538
  Joint Cost Allocation Methods 539
Process Costing Systems 541
  Allocation of Process Costs to Products 541
  Example 1: Process with No Opening WIP Inventory or Spoilage 541
  Example 2: Process with Opening and Closing WIP and Spoilage 544
Appendix 11A 548
  Other Economic Value Methods to Allocate Joint Costs 548
Appendix 11B 549

Detailed Table of Contents (continued)

Process Cost Allocations to Products Using First-in, First-out (FIFO) Costing 549
Appendix 11C 552
Operation Costing 552
Chapter Summary 555
Key Terms 555
Review Questions 556
Critical Analysis 556
Exercises 558
Problems 562
Cases 566
Solutions to You're the Decision Maker 571
Endnotes 572
References 572

12 Managing and Allocating Support Service Costs 574

Service Cost Challenge 576
Internal or Outsourced Support Services? 576
Management of Internal Support Service Costs 577
Distinguishing Between Support Service and Production Departments 578
Deciding Who Pays for Internal Support Service Costs 579
Allocating Service Costs for Decision Making 580
Allocating Service Costs for Pricing 581
Allocating Service Costs for Cost-based Contracting 581
Allocating Service Costs for Influencing Behaviour 582
Allocating Service Costs for Required Reporting 582
Cost Allocations of Internal Support Service Costs 583
Cost Allocation Process Steps 583
Step 1: Identify the Categories and Amounts of Costs to Be Allocated to Internal Customers 584
Choice of Cost Pools 584
Costs of Resources Used versus Costs of Resources Supplied 584
Step 2: Choose the Appropriate Cost Allocation Base(s) 585
Choice of Plausible and Justifiable Allocation Bases 586
Step 3: Select and Use an Appropriate Method to Compute Cost Allocation Rates and Cost Allocations of Service Department Costs 587
Cost Allocations Using the Direct Method 588
Application of the Direct Method to the City of Storhavn 588
Summary of the Direct Method 590
Benefits and Limitations of the Direct Method 590
Second-stage Cost Allocations in the Public Works Department 591
Cost Allocations Using the Step Method 592
Application of the Step Method to the City of Storhavn 593
Benefits and Limitations of the Step Method 596
Step 4: Determine Whether the Cost Allocations Achieve the Desired Results 596
Accuracy of Cost Allocations 597
Consistency of Cost Allocation 597
Behavioural Effects of Cost Allocations 598
Costs and Benefits of Cost Allocations 599
Ethical Issues 600
Appendix 12 601
Reciprocal Method 601
Chapter Summary 606
Key Terms 606
Review Questions 606
Critical Analysis 607
Exercises 608
Problems 611
Cases 615
Solutions to You're the Decision Maker 618
Endnotes 621
References 622

Part 5: Performance Measurement and Management

13 Analysis and Management of Cost Variances **624**

Use of Standard Costing Systems for Control 626
- Management by Exception 626
- Setting Standards 627
- Perfection versus Practical Standards: A Behavioural Issue 628
- Use of Standards by Non-manufacturing Organizations 629

Cost Variance Analysis for Direct Manufacturing Costs 629
- Direct Material and Direct Labour Standards 629
- Standard Costs Given Actual Output: Flexible Budget and Volume Variance 630
- Actual Material Costs and Labour Costs 630
- Price and Quantity Variances in General 631
- Direct Material Variances 632
- Direct Labour Variances 633
- Multiple Types of Direct Material and Direct Labour 634
- Allowance for Defects or Spoilage 634

Cost Variance Analysis for Flexible Overhead Budgets 635
- Flexible Overhead Budget 635
- Choice of Activity Measure 636
- Overhead Cost Variances 638
- Fixed Overhead Variance 640
- Using the Overhead Cost Performance Report in Cost Management 641

Activity-based Flexible Budget 642

Significance of Cost Variances: When to Follow Up 644
- Size of Variances 645
- Recurring Variances 645
- Trends 645
- Controllability 646
- Favourable Variances 646
- Costs and Benefits of Investigation 646

Behavioural Effects of Standard Costing 646
- Which Managers Influence Cost Variances? 647
- Interaction among Variances 648

Changing Role of Standard Costing Systems in Today's Manufacturing Environment 649
- Standard Costing: Its Traditional Advantages 649
- Impact of Information Technology 650
- Adaptation of Standard Costing Systems 650
- Kaizen Costing 652

Accounting for Cost Variances 653

Appendix 13A 656
- Production Mix and Yield Variances 656

Appendix 13B 659
- Sales Variance Analysis 659

Chapter Summary 667

Key Terms 667

Review Questions 668

Critical Analysis 669

Exercises 669

Problems 675

Cases 686

Solutions to You're the Decision Maker 690

Endnotes 692

References 693

14 Organizational Design, Responsibility Accounting and Evaluation of Divisional Performance **696**

Decentralized Organizations and Responsibility Accounting 698
- Centralization versus Decentralization 698
- Benefits and Costs of a Decentralized Organization Structure 699

Detailed Table of Contents (continued)

Responsibility Accounting 700
- Standard Cost Centre 700
- Discretionary Cost Centre 700
- Revenue Centre 701
- Profit Centre 701
- Investment Centre 701

Illustration of Responsibility Accounting 702
- Corporate Level 702
- Division Level 703
- Plant Level 704
- Department Level 704
- Work Centre Level 704

Performance Reports 705
- Budgets, Variance Analysis and Responsibility Accounting 706

How Responsibility Accounting Affects Behaviour 707
- Does It Provide Information or Place Blame? 707
- Is There Really Cost or Revenue Controllability? 707
- How Can Desired Behaviour be Motivated? 707
- Responsibility Accounting, Internal Controls and Sarbanes-Oxley 708

Performance Measurement in Investment Centres 708
- Cost of Capital 709
- Return on Investment as a Performance Measure 710
- Why ROI Can Provide the Wrong Investment Incentives 712
- Residual Income as a Performance Measure 714
- Economic Value Added (EVA) as a Performance Measure 716

Measuring Invested Capital and Operating Income for EVA, ROI and RI Performance Measures 717
- Measuring Invested Capital 717
- Measuring Investment Centre Operating Income 720
- Market Value versus Historical-cost Accounting 721
- Measuring Operating Income and Invested Capital: Summary 722

Alternatives to Accounting Performance Measures 724
- Share Price Performance 724
- Non-financial Performance Measures 724
- Viewing an Investment Centre as a Collection of Investments 725
- Performance Measurement in Non-profit Organizations 725

Internal Transactions and Transfer Prices 726

Chapter Summary 726

Key Terms 727

Review Questions 727

Critical Analysis 728

Exercises 728

Problems 732

Cases 739

Solutions to You're the Decision Maker 743

Endnotes 744

References 745

15 Transfer Pricing 746

Impact of Transfer Pricing on Organizations 748
- The Organization as a Whole 748
- The Divisional Perspective 750
- Creating Behavioural Congruence 753

Transfer Pricing Methods 753
- General Transfer Pricing Rule 753
- Market-based Transfer Price 756
- Cost-based Transfer Prices 758
- Negotiated Transfer Prices 760
- Informational Difficulties in Implementing Transfer Pricing Methods 760

Undermining of Divisional Autonomy 761
- Remedy for Motivational Problems of Transfer Pricing and Profit Centres 762

International Transfer Pricing Practices and Regulations 764

Multinational Transfer Pricing 764
Segment Reporting and Transfer Pricing 766
Chapter Summary 767
Key Terms 768
Review Questions 768
Critical Analysis 769
Exercises 769
Problems 773
Cases 778
Solutions to You're the Decision Maker 782
Endnotes 783
References 784

16 Strategy, Balanced Scorecards and Incentive Systems 786

Van Coenink Bankiers: Ahead of the Competition 788
Leading Performance Indicators to Communicate, Motivate and Evaluate 788
Leading Indicators 788
Communicating Strategy to Employees: Strategy Maps 789
Motivating Employees and Evaluating Performance 790
Modern Origin and Use of Balanced Scorecards 790
Balanced Scorecard's Strategic Performance Measures 791
Implementation of a Balanced Scorecard 792
Organizational Learning and Growth 792
Business and Production Process Performance 794
Customer Performance 795
Financial Performance 797
Benefits and Costs of a Balanced Scorecard 799
Benefits of a Balanced Scorecard 799
Costs of a Balanced Scorecard 801
Balanced Scorecard Implementation at VCB 802
Fundamental Principles of Incentive Systems 805
Measurement of Performance 805
Compensation Based on Measured Performance 806
Features of Performance-based Incentive Systems 808
Absolute or Relative Performance 808
Formula-based or Subjective Performance 810
Financial or Non-financial Performance 811
Narrow or Broad Responsibility of Performance 813
Current or Deferred Rewards 813
Salary, Bonus or Share Rewards 814
Incentive Plans in Non-profit Organizations 817
Ethical Aspects of Incentives and Compensation 817
Summary of VCB's Incentive System 818
Balanced Scorecard-based Incentives at VCB 819
Chapter Summary 820
Key Terms 821
Review Questions 821
Critical Analysis 822
Exercises 823
Problems 825
Cases 829
Solutions to You're the Decision Maker 835
Endnotes 836
References 837

Glossary 839

Index 850

About the Authors

Marc Wouters

Photo: Petra van Vlier

Marc Wouters has been Professor of Management Accounting at the Karlsruhe Institute of Technology (KIT) in Germany since 2011. He has enthusiastically worked with students in management as well as in engineering, and he has received several teaching awards. Before joining KIT, Marc Wouters was Professor of Management Accounting at the University of Twente and Associate Professor at Eindhoven University of Technology in the Netherlands. He worked at Ernst & Young Management Consultants, and at the University of Maastricht. He held visiting positions at Stanford University, School of Engineering, the University of Colorado at Boulder, Nanyang University of Technology in Singapore, Monash University in Melbourne, and HEC Paris. Marc Wouters has a Master's and PhD degree in industrial engineering from the Eindhoven University of Technology, Netherlands and a Master's degree in economics from Tilburg University.

Professor Wouters' research and teaching focuses on management accounting in operations and innovation, typically with colleagues from other disciplines and with case companies. He has published in a variety of journals, such as: *MIT Sloan Management Review*, *Accounting, Organizations and Society*, *Accounting Horizons*, *Accounting and Business Research*, *Management Accounting Research*, *Contemporary Accounting Research*, *Interfaces*, *Journal of Operations Management*, *R&D Management*, *Research-Technology Management*, *European Journal of Operational Research*, *International Journal of Operations and Production Management*. Marc Wouters has served on editorial boards of several journals, such as *Contemporary Accounting Research*, *Accounting, Organizations and Society*, the *European Accounting Review*, and the *British Journal of Management*.

Frank H. Selto

Professor Selto has been on the faculty at the University of Colorado at Boulder, USA since 1985, where he has taught accounting at the undergraduate and graduate levels and served as Division Chair of Accounting and Information Systems. He served as a research fellow for six years at the University of Melbourne. Selto has taught at the University of Denver, the University of Colorado at Denver, and the University of Washington. He holds MBA and PhD degrees in accounting from the University of Washington and BS and MS degrees in mechanical engineering from Gonzaga University and the University of Utah, respectively. Prior to earning his MBA and PhD degrees, he worked as a mechanical engineer and served as an officer in the US Army Corps of Engineers.

Active in the American Accounting Association and its Management Accounting Section, Professor Selto was the editor of the Education Research section of *The Accounting Review* and has served on the editorial boards of *The Accounting Review*, *Journal of Management Accounting Research*, *Management Accounting Research*, and *Accounting Horizons*. A researcher of management accounting and management control, Selto has published articles in the *Journal of Accounting Research*, *Accounting, Organizations and Society*, *Journal of Cost Management* and *Journal of Management Accounting Research*, one of which was recognized as a Notable Contribution to the Management Accounting Literature.

Ronald W. Hilton

Ronald W. Hilton is a Professor of Accounting at Cornell University, USA. With bachelor's and master's degrees in accounting from The Pennsylvania State University, he received his PhD from The Ohio State University. A Cornell faculty member since 1977, Professor Hilton also has taught accounting at Ohio State and the University of Florida, where he held the position of Walter J. Matherly Professor of Accounting. Prior to pursuing his doctoral studies, Hilton worked for Peat, Marwick, Mitchell and Company and served as an officer in the United States Air Force.

Michael W. Maher

A Professor of Management at the University of California–Davis, USA, Professor Maher previously taught at the University of Michigan, the University of Chicago, and the University of Washington. He also worked on the audit staff at Arthur Andersen & Co. and was a self-employed financial consultant for small businesses. He received his BBA from Gonzaga University (which named him Distinguished Alumnus in 1989) and his MBA and PhD from the University of Washington, and he earned the CPA from the state of Washington.

Preface

This book is a comprehensive, international and broad textbook on cost management. It is designed for use in courses at undergraduate and graduate levels in the United Kingdom, Ireland, Mainland Europe, the Middle East, Asia, Africa, Australia and New Zealand. The book is written not only for management and accounting students, but it is also relevant and usable for students in engineering and related study programmes. Our philosophy is that 'Costs don't just happen', and we believe that with a proactive approach toward costs, students can grow into cost managers who can add value to organizations.

The book is a completely rewritten, international edition of the very successful fourth edition of *Cost Management* by Hilton, Maher and Selto. Major improvements include:

- **Diverse and truly international examples of organizations.** Examples used throughout the book are from all over the world. This applies to the chapters' focus companies, the 'Cost Management in Practice' examples, the organizations mentioned as illustrations in the text, and the organizations pictured in the end-of-chapter material. We know of many great companies and we have not limited ourselves to the usual and sometimes worn examples often mentioned in US-centred textbooks.

  Each chapter is built around a focus company, based closely on the practices and experiences of an actual organization, whose story continues through the chapter. They represent manufacturing, retail, not-for-profit and service firms in many different countries.
- **Completely restructured and rewritten text.** The book has been rewritten, restructured and also shortened significantly, from 21 to 16 chapters. The overall structure has been improved by developing better links between chapters. We realize that instructors want flexibility to structure their own course, and we chose a modular design so that instructors can customize their class-topic sequence.
- **Integral use of spreadsheets.** All the way through the book, spreadsheet software is used for explaining the techniques and making the applications more realistic. These are also widely used in the end of chapter items to help students build their financial modelling skills. Also Excel templates are provided for instructors to assign to students – they nudge students toward good solutions and are easier to grade or critique.
- **Research connected.** We provide more and updated summaries of research studies that address important cost management issues – the Research Insight boxes. We also included many more references to recent research findings in endnotes. While much academic research may not be directly applicable tomorrow, research is valuable for making us think more critically and creatively about the applicability of cost management techniques.
- **Intuitive explanation of accounting.** It is not an introductory textbook, and students are assumed to have an understanding of basic accounting concepts, such as assets, liabilities, revenues and cash flows. However, they do not need any prior knowledge of journal entries or T-accounts. In fact, in Chapters 10, 11 and 13 where the accounting treatment of particular events is explained, we use a very intuitive approach to explain accounting entries. We show directly how events impact the balance sheet and profit and loss account. We avoid T-accounts for good pedagogical reasons, and nobody needs to unnecessarily worry about debits and credits.

Terminology

We have selected accounting terminology that we believe resonates most clearly with an international audience.

- 'Profit' and 'income' are used interchangeably (but we do not use 'earnings').

- We use 'balance sheet' interchangeably with its formal name 'statement of financial position'; we also use 'income statement' or 'profit and loss account' interchangeably with the formal name 'statement of income'.
- 'Shareholders' is used throughout because that term is common in many parts of the world. ('Stockholders' is used in the USA and Canada.)
- We use 'inventory' for goods that a company owns (called 'stock' in the UK), 'accounts receivables' (not 'debtors'), and 'accounts payable' (not creditors).
- We talk about 'profit before tax' and 'profit after tax', and we avoid 'net profit'.
- A key detail, sometimes confusing for students, is the distinction between operating profit and simply profit. The operating profit is the profit from normal business operations, before subtracting the cost of debt (interest), and before subtracting taxes. Operating profit is also called EBIT (Earnings before Interest and Taxes). The operating profit minus the cost of debt is the profit before tax. After subtracting taxes, the profit after tax is available for shareholders. Some of this may be paid out in the form of dividends, and what is left in the company becomes part of equity, as retained earnings.
- We always mean operating profit or EBIT unless we explicitly include interest or are explicitly in a tax-related circumstance, as in computing cash flows after tax (Chapter 8), using financial performance measures for performance evaluation (Chapter 14), and transfer pricing (Chapter 15). It is always important to know which measure one wants to use.

Assessment Material

Cost Management is known for its comprehensive and reliable end-of-chapter material, and we have built on that strength in this new textbook by providing:

- A wide choice of questions etc., partly in the book and partly online that reinforce and extend the chapters' pedagogy.
- Review Questions that are mostly written at a **basic** level; Critical Analysis questions and Exercises that are **intermediate**, and the Problems and Cases that are **advanced**.
- End-of-chapter material that has an entirely international flavour.
- Use of spreadsheets for many more items.

Cost management is not the sole responsibility of finance and accounting professionals. On the contrary, cost management analysts have various backgrounds, ranging from accounting and finance, to engineering, marketing and sales, and broad managerial experience. Cost management analysts use financial information, in combination with non-financial information, to improve processes, performance and profit. Cost management analysts use data available in their organizations, as well as information from the outside. Some of the financial data will have been produced for other purposes and according to financial accounting rules. However, cost management analysts are not constrained by these financial accounting rules. Not that their life is easy: they have to add value in the eyes of decision makers. Their challenge is to help make better decisions and achieve real improvements.

Marc Wouters, Karlsruhe, Germany
Frank Selto, Boulder, Colorado, USA

Conversion Guide

The numerous rewrites, additions and replacements make a direct comparison of this new book with the fourth edition of *Cost Management* by Hilton, Maher and Selto difficult. However, it may be useful to show relationships between chapters and to point out some of the major changes.

This book	Topic	4th Edition	Remarks
1	Introduction	1, 13	This chapter contains many new examples, and the decision-making framework from the previous Chapter 13 has been completely rewritten and is now introduced in Chapter 1 to lay out the structure of the entire book. The focus company is now located in Germany.
2	Product Costing Concepts and Systems	2	The new focus company is located in France, and as a supplier to a large outdoor products company it is pressured to manage its costs significantly downward. This chapter has been drastically changed to focus on using cash and accrual cost concepts to manage costs to a financial goal. The chapter now includes an introduction to financial modelling, which is used throughout the text.
3	Cost Estimation	11	The new focus company is located in South Africa. The chapter has been restructured to provide more intuition on cost behaviour for the remainder of the book. It contains many new examples.
4	Activity-based Costing Systems	4	This chapter improves the pedagogy of building activity-based costing, and relocates the focus company to the UK. Chapter 4 now also introduces and applies time-driven ABC. The chapter includes reference to current research, which indicates that ABC is still an important costing system.
5	Customer Profitability and Activity-based Management	5, 6	Chapter 5 combines and updates two chapters by using customer profitability as the cost management motivation for applying activity-based management. This novel approach streamlines the text and marries two important cost management methods, which must work closely together.
6	Managing Quality and Time to Create Value	7	This chapter is a refinement from the previous edition, with new international practice examples and research findings that improve our understanding of managing quality and time.
7	Short-term Decision making	12, 13	Chapter 7 includes many new examples and a rewritten section on pricing, a topic previously included in Chapter 13.
8	Strategic Investment Decisions	14, 13	Chapter 8 has been drastically rewritten and it contains many new applications of discounted cash flow (DCF) methods to decisions discussed in the previous Chapter 13, however not in a DCF context. It is emphasized that many decisions can be conceptualized as investment decisions. A new appendix on real options has been added.

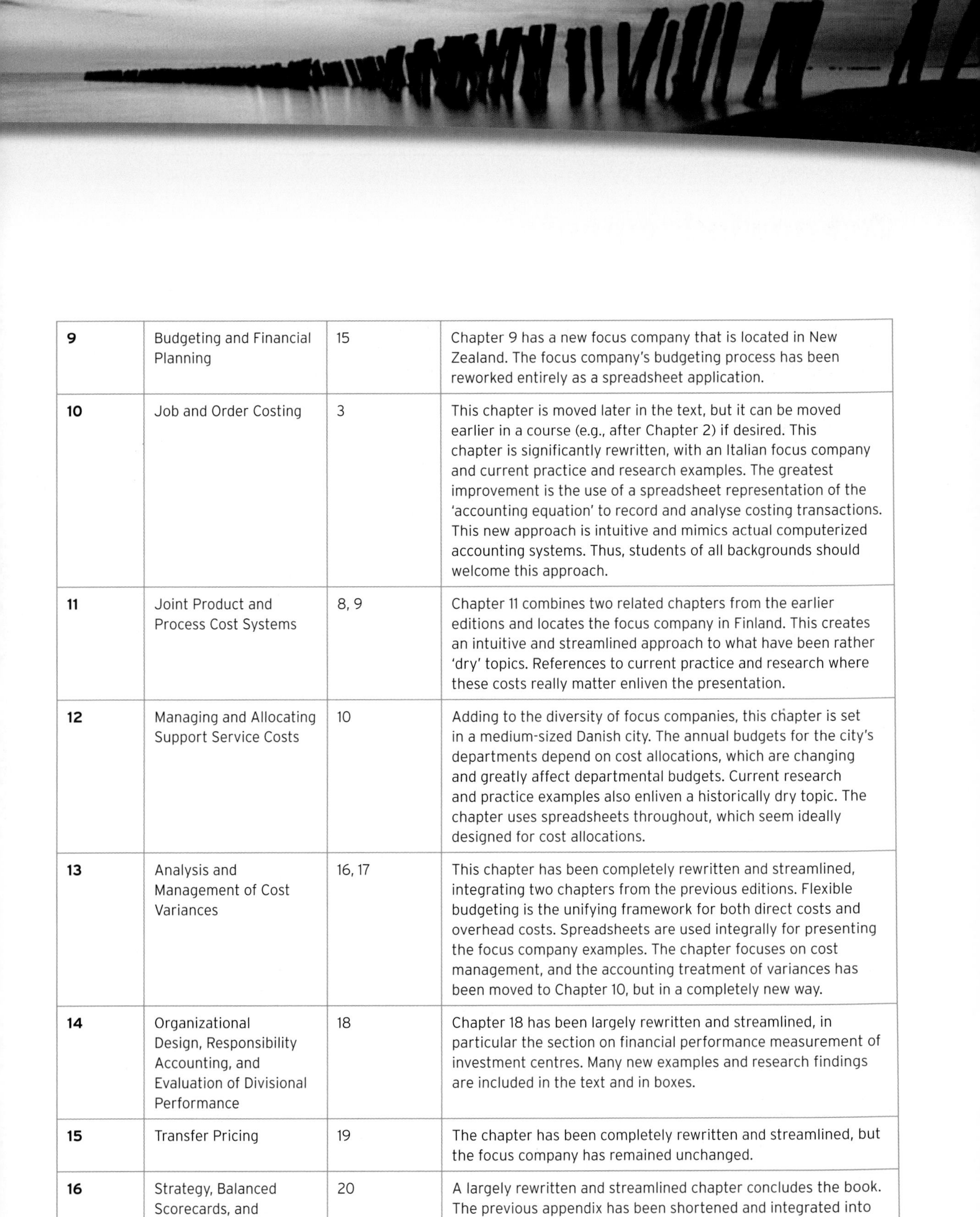

9	Budgeting and Financial Planning	15	Chapter 9 has a new focus company that is located in New Zealand. The focus company's budgeting process has been reworked entirely as a spreadsheet application.
10	Job and Order Costing	3	This chapter is moved later in the text, but it can be moved earlier in a course (e.g., after Chapter 2) if desired. This chapter is significantly rewritten, with an Italian focus company and current practice and research examples. The greatest improvement is the use of a spreadsheet representation of the 'accounting equation' to record and analyse costing transactions. This new approach is intuitive and mimics actual computerized accounting systems. Thus, students of all backgrounds should welcome this approach.
11	Joint Product and Process Cost Systems	8, 9	Chapter 11 combines two related chapters from the earlier editions and locates the focus company in Finland. This creates an intuitive and streamlined approach to what have been rather 'dry' topics. References to current practice and research where these costs really matter enliven the presentation.
12	Managing and Allocating Support Service Costs	10	Adding to the diversity of focus companies, this chapter is set in a medium-sized Danish city. The annual budgets for the city's departments depend on cost allocations, which are changing and greatly affect departmental budgets. Current research and practice examples also enliven a historically dry topic. The chapter uses spreadsheets throughout, which seem ideally designed for cost allocations.
13	Analysis and Management of Cost Variances	16, 17	This chapter has been completely rewritten and streamlined, integrating two chapters from the previous editions. Flexible budgeting is the unifying framework for both direct costs and overhead costs. Spreadsheets are used integrally for presenting the focus company examples. The chapter focuses on cost management, and the accounting treatment of variances has been moved to Chapter 10, but in a completely new way.
14	Organizational Design, Responsibility Accounting, and Evaluation of Divisional Performance	18	Chapter 18 has been largely rewritten and streamlined, in particular the section on financial performance measurement of investment centres. Many new examples and research findings are included in the text and in boxes.
15	Transfer Pricing	19	The chapter has been completely rewritten and streamlined, but the focus company has remained unchanged.
16	Strategy, Balanced Scorecards, and Incentive Systems	20	A largely rewritten and streamlined chapter concludes the book. The previous appendix has been shortened and integrated into the main text. Much more attention is given to measurement properties of performance measures. Many new examples are included. The focus company is now located in the Netherlands.

Acknowledgements

We thank Mark Selto for his excellent work in helping to prepare the end-of-chapter materials of all chapters in this book. We also thank the following reviewers for all of their challenging and constructive criticisms to the draft chapters of this major revision. We think the text is far better for the valuable assistance we have received.

Anne-Catherine Moursli, *IESEG School of Management, France*
Tom McLean, *Northumbria University, England*
Bhagwan Moorjani, *University of Westminster, England*
Christof Beuselinck, *Tilburg University, Netherlands*
Mostafa Jazayeri, *MMU Cheshire at Crewe, England*
Christian Hofmann, *Munich School of Management, Germany*
Dr. Mohamed Basuony, *Ain Shams University Cairo, Egypt*
Sophie Hoozee, *IESEG School of Management, France*
Lana Liu, *Newcastle University, England*
Christian Lukas, *Friedrich-Schiller-University Jena, Germany*
John Aston, *Brunel University, England*
Hanne Nørreklit, *Norwegian School of Economics, Norway*
Johan A.M. de Kruijf, *University of Twente, Netherlands*
John Currie, *National University of Ireland Galway, Ireland*
Samuel Hinds, *University of Surrey, England*
Androniki Triantafylli, *The University of Manchester, England*
Harshini Pushpika Siriwardane, *Nanyang Technological University, Singapore*
Peter Clarke, *University College Dublin, Ireland*
Margaret Stewart, *University of Strathclyde, Glasgow, Scotland*

Every effort has been made to trace and acknowledge ownership of copyright and to clear permission for material reproduced in this book. The publishers will be pleased to make suitable arrangements to clear permission with any copyright holders whom it has not been possible to contact.

Guided Tour

Learning Objectives

After completing this chapter, you should be

LO 1 Understand how cost manageme

LO 2 Structure business decision-maki criteria and expected outcomes.

LO 3 Describe and understand steps i

LO 4 Apply benefit–cost and variance strategic plans.

LO 5 Understand the importance of e identify measures taken to main

LO 6 Include sustainability and envir

Learning Objectives

Learning Objectives appear at the beginning of each chapter and are repeated in the margin of the text where they are addressed. Also, each end-of-chapter assignment lists its learning objective.

Company Documents and Logos

Chapters begin with a company document that introduces issues to be discussed in the chapter. These companies are fictional but based on practices of real companies. Each chapter is built around a focus company whose story continues through the chapter. Each time the focus company is presented in the chapter, its logo is shown so you see its application to the text topic.

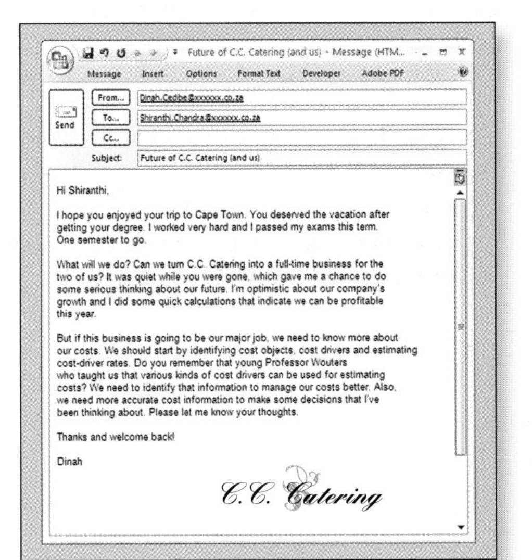

Future of C.C. Catering (and us) - Message (HTM...

Message | Insert | Options | Format Text | Developer | Adobe PDF

From... Dinah.Cedibe@xxxxxx.co.za
To... Shiranthi.Chandra@xxxxxx.co.za
Cc...
Subject: Future of C.C. Catering (and us)

Hi Shiranthi,

I hope you enjoyed your trip to Cape Town. You deserved the vacation after getting your degree. I worked very hard and I passed my exams this term. One semester to go.

What will we do? Can we turn C.C. Catering into a full-time business for the two of us? It was quiet while you were gone, which gave me a chance to do some serious thinking about our future. I'm optimistic about our company's growth and I did some quick calculations that indicate we can be profitable this year.

But if this business is going to be our major job, we need to know more about our costs. We should start by identifying cost objects, cost drivers and estimating cost-driver rates. Do you remember that young Professor Wouters who taught us that various kinds of cost drivers can be used for estimating costs? We need to identify that information to manage our costs better. Also, we need more accurate cost information to make some decisions that I've been thinking about. Please let me know your thoughts.

Thanks and welcome back!

Dinah

C.C. Catering

Key Terms

For each term's definition, refer to the indicated p

accuracy,	10
benefit–cost analysis,	20
competitive advantage,	14
cost management,	4
cost management system,	5
criteria,	8
decision alternatives,	8
decision-making framework,	7
decision usefulness,	9
extended value chain,	15
financial and non-financial criteria,	9
financial quantification,	9

Key Terms

Key terms are highlighted throughout the text and they are listed at the end of each chapter. They are also defined in the glossary at the end of the book.

Guided Tour (continued)

1.1 Cost Management in Practice

Singapore Airlines

Singapore Airlines (SIA) is considered to be one of the leading companies not only for the quality of its services, but also for its cost-effective operations. SIA manages its two main assets - planes and people - so that its service is better than rivals' and its costs are lower.

The airline invests heavily in areas of the business that touch the customer in order to enhance SIA's premium positioning. SIA replaces its fleet more frequently than do competitors, it spends more on training, and staffs each flight with more cabin crew members. As a consequence, SIA spends less on the price per aircraft, fuel, maintenance and repair. The airline keeps salaries low by offering employees bonuses of up to 50 per cent depending on SIA's profitability; also, the airline's reputation attracts younger workers.

Everything behind the scenes is subject to rigorous cost control. It spends less on sales and general administration and on back-office technologies. It outsources many such processes to low-cost providers. The company's headquarters is atop an old hangar at Changi Airport, and it is not very luxurious. For its training programmes, SIA uses its own facilities instead of sending employees to resorts. Hard-bargaining local managers negotiate hotel rates for crew members at SIA's destinations. The people and organizational culture are the linchpins of getting a dual strategy of excellent service and low cost right, and this culture is deeply rooted in an organization's history.

Cost Management in Practice

This feature highlights the cost management practices of real companies.

You're the Decision Maker

You're the Decision Maker scenarios get you involved in the decisions that the focus company needs to make. Suggested solutions are at the end of each chapter.

4.1 You're the Decision Maker

Refining a Traditional Cost System

The example company implemented the suggested refinements to

	Refinements to overhead
Machining overhead	€10,0
Normal machine hours	6
Machine overhead rate	€16.
Process overhead	€10,0
Normal direct labour cost	€5,0
Process overhead rate	2

a. Does this refined cost system change the cost of an 'average' p
b. Measure the cost of a product that's only difference is its use c
c. Measure the cost of a product that's only difference is its use c
d. Do these differences in cost matter? Explain.

(Solutions begin on page xxx.)

3.1 Research Insight

Product Variety and Costs

Several studies have shown that cost drivers other than product v that greater variety of products increases a company's costs, all els increase revenue. Some of the reasons are that customers prefer o purchases if there are more products from which to choose. Wheth product line justify the additional costs is an issue for financial ana

Professors Ittner, Larcker and Randall studied whether it was considering both the costs and revenues implied by a broader prod found that greater product variety increased this company's cost: that greater product variety also increased the company's revenu increased costs, they found, however, 'the revenue gains from hi offset by increased costs . . . on average, the firm offered greater might have been more profitable if it had offered less product vari efits that can accrue to the company from having a broad product

Research Insights

Research Insight boxes provide research findings relevant to the chapter topics.

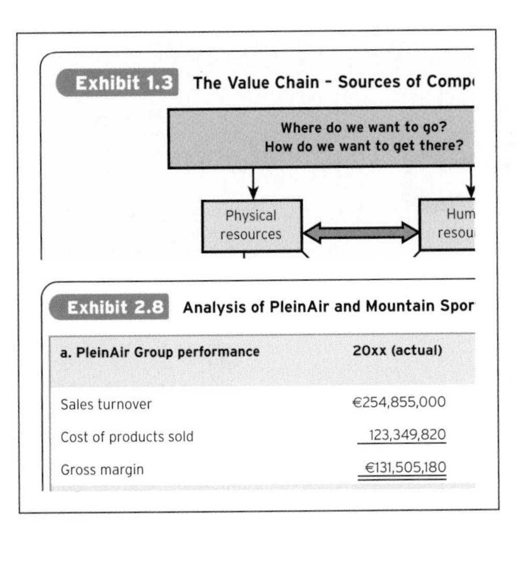

Figures, Tables and Excel Spreadsheets

Each chapter provides a number of figures and tables to help you to visualize key theories and studies. Many Excel spreadsheets help you get comfortable examining data in the format you are likely to see in your future jobs.

Chapter Summaries

Chapter Summaries briefly review and reinforce the main topics you will have covered in each chapter, to ensure you have acquired a solid understanding of the key topics.

Chapter Summary

This first chapter has two purposes. One is to explain illustrate how cost management supports strategic de porting and encouraging ethical decision making, not because it is the most effective and efficient way to do

Strategic decisions are among the most important mine the organization's future activities and performa nities and responding to threats to competitive advan nation and the best route to that destination.

Cost management is (1) an organizational *comm* reduced cost, (2) a professional *attitude* of cost manage all costs, and (3) a reliable set of *techniques* that increas interpretations and analyses of alternative courses o management analysts need broad knowledge of the o ties interact. Benefit–cost analysis is a common and compute variances between expected and actual bene

This chapter provides a framework for decision mak tion necessary to make good business decisions. The de

Stage I	Setting goals and objectives
Stage II	Gathering information
Stage III	Evaluating alternatives
Stage IV	Execution and tracking costs
Stage V	Obtaining feedback.

Review Questions

1.1 Review and define each of the chapter's ke

1.2 What is the primary objective of cost man

1.3 List and briefly describe each of the five st

1.4 Distinguish between an organization's goa

1.5 Describe a conflict that might occur betwee

Critical Analysis

1.16 'Cost accounting and cost management re agree or disagree? Explain.

1.17 The manager of a telecommunications cor relevant to business decisions, but costs ar manager correct? Explain.

1.18 Where to place the city's new shelter for ho that a new shelter is needed but 'not in my the shelter and the publisher of the local ne continues meetings and hearings to find a s making this difficult decision? Be as specific

End-of-Chapter Assessment Material

Each chapter includes an extensive selection of assignment material including Review Questions, Critical Analysis, Exercises, Problems and Cases.

Technology to Enhance Learning and Teaching

Visit www.mcgraw-hill.co.uk/textbooks/wouters today!

Online Learning Centre

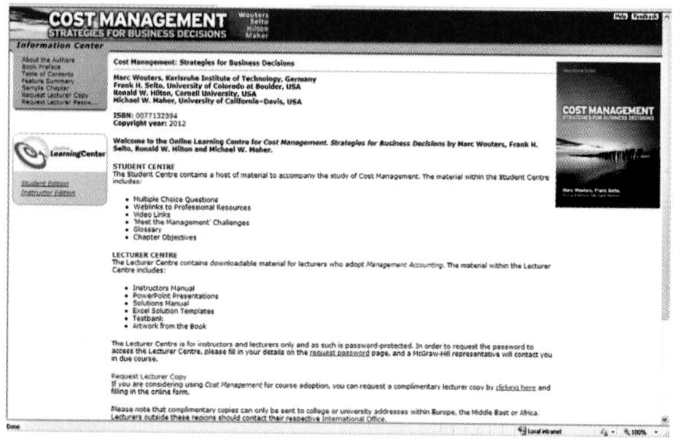

Students- Helping you to Connect, Learn and Succeed

We understand that studying for your module is not just about reading this textbook. It's also about researching online, revising key terms, preparing for assignments, and passing the exam. The website above provides you with a number of **FREE** resources to help you succeed on your module, including:

- Multiple Choice Questions
- Web Links to Professional Resources
- 'Meet the Management' Challenges
- Glossary
- Chapter Objectives

Lecturer Support- Helping You to Help Your Students

The Online Learning Centre also offers lecturers adopting this book a range of resources including:

- Instructor Manual
- PowerPoint Slides
- Solutions Manual
- Excel Solution Templates
- Testbank
- Artwork from the Book
- Video Links

To request your password to access these resources, contact your McGraw-Hill representative or visit www.mcgraw-hill.co.uk/textbooks/wouters

Test Bank available in McGraw-Hill EZ Test Online

A test bank of hundreds of questions is available to lecturers adopting this book for their module through the EZ Test online website. For each chapter you will find:

- A range of multiple choice, true or false, and essay questions
- Questions identified by type, difficulty, topic and learning objective to help you to select questions that best suit your needs

McGraw-Hill EZ Test Online is:

- **Accessible** anywhere with an Internet connection – your unique login provides you access to all your tests and material in any location
- **Simple** to set up and easy to use
- **Flexible**, offering a choice from question banks associated with your adopted textbook or allowing you to create your own questions
- **Comprehensive**, with access to hundreds of banks and thousands of questions created for other McGraw-Hill titles
- **Compatible** with Blackboard and other course management systems
- **Time-saving** – students' tests can be immediately marked and results and feedback delivered directly to your students to help them to monitor their progress.

To register for this FREE resource, visit www.eztestonline.com

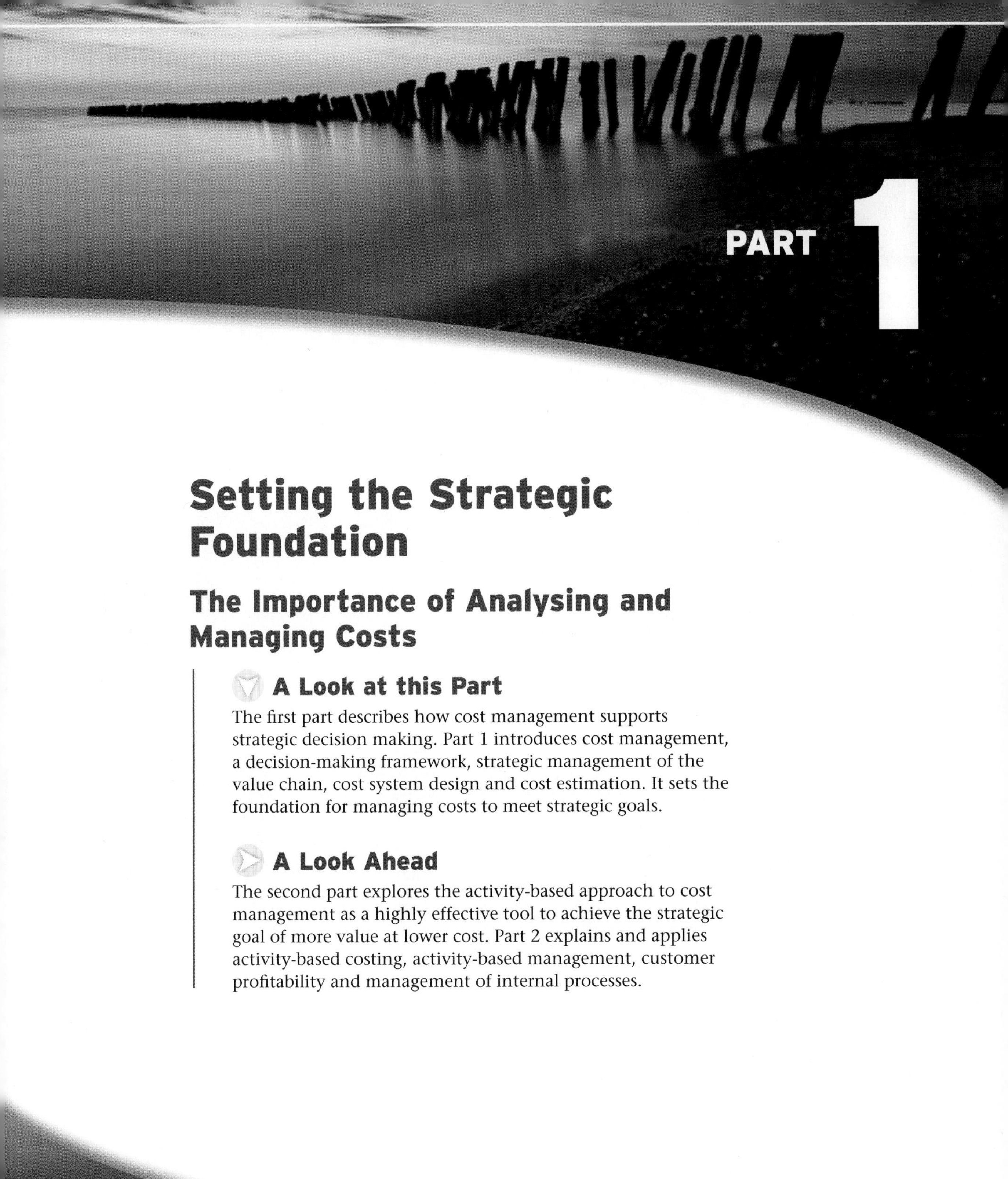

PART 1

Setting the Strategic Foundation

The Importance of Analysing and Managing Costs

A Look at this Part

The first part describes how cost management supports strategic decision making. Part 1 introduces cost management, a decision-making framework, strategic management of the value chain, cost system design and cost estimation. It sets the foundation for managing costs to meet strategic goals.

A Look Ahead

The second part explores the activity-based approach to cost management as a highly effective tool to achieve the strategic goal of more value at lower cost. Part 2 explains and applies activity-based costing, activity-based management, customer profitability and management of internal processes.

CHAPTER 1

Cost Management and Strategic Decision Making

Evaluating Opportunities and Leading Change

© lisegagne

Learning Objectives

After completing this chapter, you should be able to:

- **LO 1** Understand how cost management supports strategic planning and decision making.
- **LO 2** Structure business decision-making problems into objectives, alternative actions, criteria and expected outcomes.
- **LO 3** Describe and understand steps in strategic decision making.
- **LO 4** Apply benefit–cost and variance analysis to help evaluate an organization's strategic plans.
- **LO 5** Understand the importance of ethical behaviour and decision making, and identify measures taken to maintain such behaviour.
- **LO 6** Include sustainability and environmental concerns in strategic decisions.

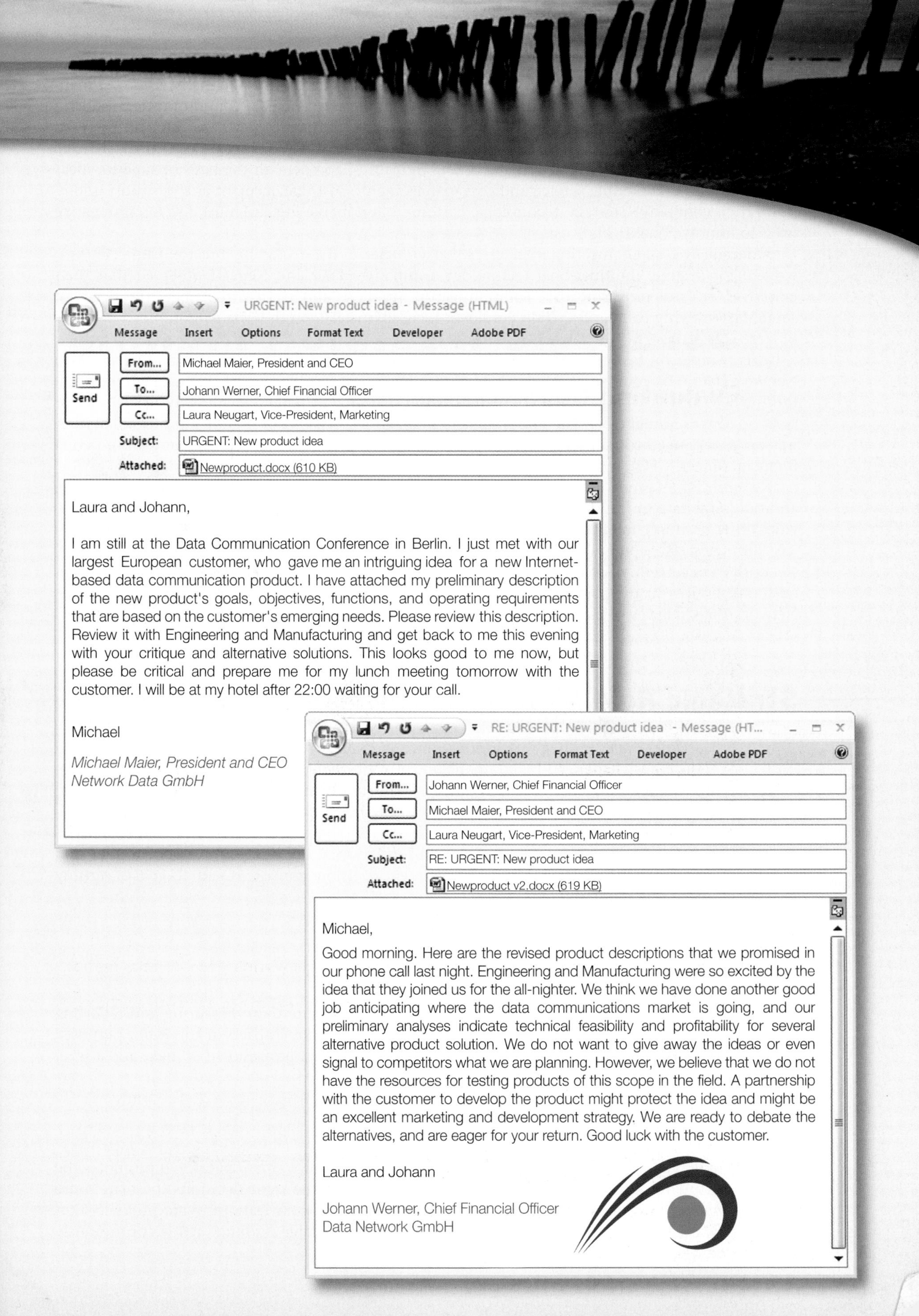
URGENT: New product idea - Message (HTML)

Message Insert Options Format Text Developer Adobe PDF

Send
From... Michael Maier, President and CEO
To... Johann Werner, Chief Financial Officer
Cc... Laura Neugart, Vice-President, Marketing
Subject: URGENT: New product idea
Attached: Newproduct.docx (610 KB)

Laura and Johann,

I am still at the Data Communication Conference in Berlin. I just met with our largest European customer, who gave me an intriguing idea for a new Internet-based data communication product. I have attached my preliminary description of the new product's goals, objectives, functions, and operating requirements that are based on the customer's emerging needs. Please review this description. Review it with Engineering and Manufacturing and get back to me this evening with your critique and alternative solutions. This looks good to me now, but please be critical and prepare me for my lunch meeting tomorrow with the customer. I will be at my hotel after 22:00 waiting for your call.

Michael

Michael Maier, President and CEO
Network Data GmbH

RE: URGENT: New product idea - Message (HT...

Message Insert Options Format Text Developer Adobe PDF

Send
From... Johann Werner, Chief Financial Officer
To... Michael Maier, President and CEO
Cc... Laura Neugart, Vice-President, Marketing
Subject: RE: URGENT: New product idea
Attached: Newproduct v2.docx (619 KB)

Michael,

Good morning. Here are the revised product descriptions that we promised in our phone call last night. Engineering and Manufacturing were so excited by the idea that they joined us for the all-nighter. We think we have done another good job anticipating where the data communications market is going, and our preliminary analyses indicate technical feasibility and profitability for several alternative product solution. We do not want to give away the ideas or even signal to competitors what we are planning. However, we believe that we do not have the resources for testing products of this scope in the field. A partnership with the customer to develop the product might protect the idea and might be an excellent marketing and development strategy. We are ready to debate the alternatives, and are eager for your return. Good luck with the customer.

Laura and Johann

Johann Werner, Chief Financial Officer
Data Network GmbH

Network Data GmbH, a small data communication company in Munich, Germany, uses cost management to support its strategy of innovation and high growth. The data communication industry changes rapidly, and competition is fierce among agile companies, such as **Alcatel-Lucent, Ericsson, Siemens, NEC, Brocade, Cisco Systems, and RAD Data Communications**. Companies in this industry (and other evolving industries) compete on the basis of superior ideas and technology, marketing, service and cost management. Cost management analysts must understand their company's strategy, technology, customers and marketing and must develop innovative ways to improve quality and cost.

A decade ago, an engineering manager, Michael Maier, and a marketing director, Laura Neugart, worked for a large, multinational technology company. Maier and Neugart observed that their employer was not providing data communication products and services that meet the needs of small, fast-growing companies. Their employer focused, instead, on the data communication needs of large companies.

This two-person team saw a potentially lucrative data communication market and left to form Network Data. The company's mission was to provide quick, flexible and reliable data communication devices and services to small companies with good growth potential. An early realization for Network Data's founders was the importance of managing costs. One of their first professional hires was an experienced cost management analyst, Johann Werner, who joined the company as chief financial officer (CFO).

Network Data's products include fibre-optic, data communication switches that route incoming and outgoing data to the right users via the Internet or internal networks. Network Data also provides other products, including software solutions to data sharing and communication, and services (consulting on data communication and reporting) to optimize the use of its switches and software. Network Data currently has more than 300 full-time employees and has tripled its sales from products and services in the past four years. Because data communication needs are growing rapidly, Network Data believes its market and profitability also will grow.[1]

Strategic Role of Cost Management

LO 1
Understand how cost management supports strategic planning and decision making.

Network Data's strategy of innovation and high growth in the data communication industry is challenged by competition from nearly every corner of the world. To meet this competition, the company must be constantly aware of its strengths, weaknesses, opportunities and threats. Because the company is small, it cannot afford major mistakes in its products, services or customers. CFO Johann Werner and his team of analysts develop financial and non-financial information about alternative opportunities and uses of resources to help Network Data make decisions consistent with its goal of earning long-term, competitive profits.

Characteristics of Cost Management

Cost management is important to organizations because it is more than measuring and reporting costs that have occurred. Cost management is focused on the future impacts of current or proposed decisions. **Cost management** is an organizational *commitment*, a professional *attitude*, and a *set of techniques* to create more value at lower cost.

Commitment

First, cost management is an organizational commitment to improvement because it promotes the idea of continually finding ways to help organizations make the right decisions to create more *customer value* at lower cost.[2] Efficient companies (such as Network Data) provide products that customers want by using the minimum of the organization's scarce resources while continuously seeking to improve value and costs.

Attitude

Second, cost management represents a proactive professional *attitude* that all costs of products and operations result from management decisions. In other words, *costs do not just happen*. Therefore, cost management analysts do not simply document decisions and record costs. Instead, they are active partners in management decisions to develop and improve products and improve efficiency.

Techniques

Third, cost management is a set of reliable techniques that use diverse performance measures to assess the impacts of decisions. These techniques may be used individually to support a specific decision or together to support the overall management of the organization. A **cost management system** is the set of cost management techniques that function together to support the organization's goals and activities.

The focus of this book is to demonstrate how the cost management commitment, attitude and techniques work together. They combine to develop measures of value, costs, quality, time and profits that allow managers to evaluate and predict the impacts of their decisions. Many chapters in this book focus on specific techniques to measure the impacts of decisions on costs. This reflects organizations' strong historical and continuing interest in controlling costs. However, the book also focuses on measuring causes or drivers of costs, such as management decisions about capacity, technology, quality, learning and customers, among others. All of these factors are integral to a well-designed strategy, and all affect costs and profitability.[3]

Career Perspectives

An organization's chief financial officer (CFO) is responsible for managing the firm's financial resources and the financial personnel. Increasingly, CFOs also manage human and information resources. CFOs typically are trained in accounting and finance as undergraduates or as graduate students and often are professionally certified (for example, certified public accountant, certified management accountant or certified financial manager). Several professional organizations that can provide information about financial management careers and certification include the **American Institute of CPAs** (www.aicpa.org), **Institute of Management Accountants** (United States) (www.imanet.org), **Society of Management Accountants** (Canada) (www.cma-canada.org), **Institute of Chartered Accountants** (Australia) (www.icaa.org.au), **Chartered Institute of Management Accountants** (Great Britain) (www.cimaglobal.com), **Institute of Cost and Works Accountants of India** (www.icwai.org), **International Controller Association** (Internationaler Controller Verein, for German-speaking countries) (www.controllerverein.com), and the **Dutch Association of Registered Controllers** (Vereniging van Registercontrollers, Netherlands) (www.vrc.nl). More general accounting associations are www.icaew.org and www.accaglobal.com.

The modern financial and cost manager is hardly the stereotypical image of a cost accountant but of a successful business consultant. A more common title than 'cost accountant' is 'financial analyst', 'cost analyst' or 'internal business consultant' and a few companies use the term 'cost management analyst'. These titles and the tasks they represent demonstrate a dramatic evolution in accountants' jobs from preparers of reports to proactive managers and consultants. The role of financial managers in many companies is changing to focus on, among other things, customer profitability, process improvement, performance evaluation and strategic planning. The most important qualities needed include a strong work ethic, understanding the business, and problem-solving, interpersonal and listening skills.

Sources: Groysberg et al. (2011); Cooper (2006); Garg et al. (2003); and Siegel et al. (2006a, 2006b).

Characteristics of Cost Management Analysts

Network Data has computerized most of the cost accountant's data-intensive, recording work. The company also redesigned its information system to make data widely available throughout the company. Because of changes in information technology and increased competition, most organizations now need cost management analysts with integrity and broad knowledge of the business who work well in cross-functional teams more than they need cost accountants who measure and report costs of past operations.

© *Yuri_Arcurs*

Cost management analysts bring a commitment, an attitude and techniques to the table that help create more value at lower cost.

Cost management teams transform cost accounting and other data into information for decisions that support strategies, improve products and services, and the use of resources that systematically reduce costs. These analysts are the most reliable sources of information on the impacts of planned and actual management decisions at Network Data. This reliable information is especially important for effective strategic decision making in a rapidly changing, globally competitive industry such as data communication.

Cost management is not the sole responsibility of finance and accounting professionals. On the contrary, cost management analysts have various backgrounds, ranging from accounting and finance, to engineering, marketing and sales, and broad managerial experience. Cost management analysts use financial information, in combination with non-financial information, to improve performance, profit and processes. Cost management analysts use data that is available in their organizations, as well as information from the outside. Some of the financial data will have been produced for other purposes and according to financial accounting rules. However, cost management analysts are not tied by these financial accounting constraints. Not that their life is easy: they have to add value in the eyes of decision makers. Their challenge is to help make better decisions and achieve real improvements.

1.1 Cost Management in Practice

Singapore Airlines

Singapore Airlines (SIA) is considered to be one of the leading companies not only for the quality of its services, but also for its cost-effective operations. SIA manages its two main assets - planes and people - so that its service is better than rivals' and its costs are lower.

The airline invests heavily in areas of the business that touch the customer in order to enhance SIA's premium positioning. SIA replaces its fleet more frequently than do competitors, it spends more on training, and staffs each flight with more cabin crew members. As a consequence, SIA spends less on the price per aircraft, fuel, maintenance and repair. The airline keeps salaries low by offering employees bonuses of up to 50 per cent depending on SIA's profitability; also, the airline's reputation attracts younger workers.

Everything behind the scenes is subject to rigorous cost control. It spends less on sales and general administration and on back-office technologies. It outsources many such processes to low-cost providers. The company's headquarters is atop an old hangar at Changi Airport, and it is not very luxurious. For its training programmes, SIA uses its own facilities instead of sending employees to resorts. Hard-bargaining local managers negotiate hotel rates for crew members at SIA's destinations. The people and organizational culture are the linchpins of getting a dual strategy of excellent service and low cost right, and this culture is deeply rooted in an organization's history.

Companies in Asia besides SIA, such as **Banyan Tree**, **Haier**, **Samsung**, and **Toyota** seem to be more surprisingly to combine service excellence, continuous innovation and cost leadership.

Source: Heracleous and Wirtz (2010).

Cost Management in a Decision-making Framework

Cost management in this text builds on a *decision-making framework*. Understanding and making recommendations for decision making have occupied philosophers and scientists for hundreds, if not thousands, of years. The literature is vast, and even a brief excursion into this field of human behaviour can be both fascinating and confusing.[4] It is safe to say that great diversity of opinion exists about how humans *do* and *should* make decisions. We cannot hope to resolve all the unknowns and controversies here, but we can provide some guidance about systematic decision making. What follows is a benefit–cost framework of decision making with five stages within which we consider the role of cost management.[5] One objective of this framework is to reinforce that cost management is a purposeful activity – more value creation at lower cost – and a proactive attitude – decisions drive costs; costs do not just happen.

LO 2
Structure business decision-making problems into objectives, alternative actions, criteria and expected outcomes.

Exhibit 1.1 presents the **decision-making framework** formally. In this chapter we discuss Stage I: setting goals, and we introduce the other stages. Note that, as shown in Exhibit 1.1, other parts of the text consider types of information that support all five stages in more detail. One of the most important parts of this framework is the feedback to all other parts of the process. Feedback is critical to managers' and workers' sustained learning and retraining; it is the essence of a 'learning organization' to learn from its successes and failures and to improve future decisions.

Stage I: Setting Goals and Objectives

Stage I is about setting goals and objectives. Organizations exist to achieve specific goals, such as generating superior returns to shareholders, offering the best customer service, providing meaningful employment, or eradicating hunger or disease. Without a clear set of goals, an organization's members have no clear guidance for their actions and decisions. Many organizational problems can be traced to the lack of either clear goals or clearly communicated goals. Network Data, the focus organization of this chapter, clearly directs its activities and decisions to achieve the goal of providing quick, flexible and reliable data communication devices and services to small companies with good growth potential.

Most organizational goals are abstract in nature (achieving the 'best customer service', for example). Although these goals provide essential guidance, successful organizations also provide tangible objectives or benchmarks by which to measure progress toward their goals. That is, **tangible objectives** are benchmarks capable of being measured in some manner. Network Data provides specific guidance to its employees by translating its goal of providing an innovative telecommunication service and products to high-growth customers into tangible objectives:

Exhibit 1.1 Decision-making Framework (and Links to the Parts of This Text)

Stage I: Setting goals and objectives
(Chapter 1 of the text)
- Strategic decision making
- Selecting goals
- Specifying tangible objectives

↓

Stage II: Gathering information
(Chapter 2, 3 and Part 2 of the text)
- Generating feasible decision alternatives
- Measuring decision alternatives on various criteria
- Understanding activities and cost drivers

↓

Stage III: Evaluating alternatives
(Part 3 of the text)
- Anticipating the future outcome(s) of each action
- Choosing the best alternative(s)
- Budgeting resources and activities, financial planning

↓

Stage IV: Execution and tracking costs
(Part 4 of the text)
- Implementing the best alternative
- Accumulating actual cost and assigning them to products and services

↓

Stage V: Obtaining feedback
(Part 5 of the text)
- Evaluating actual outcomes
- Setting transfer prices
- Measuring managerial financial performance

- Timely release of new services and products
- Revenue growth of these new services and products
- Acquisition of new high-potential customers.

For example, when making business decisions, Network Data's managers ask themselves, 'Will this action lead to revenue growth of our latest products?' In other words, these tangible objectives provide *criteria* for decision making. **Criteria** are the attributes on the basis of which the decision maker compares the decision alternatives and makes a decision. Without tangible objectives, direction and progress toward goals is unclear, and there is not enough guidance to support decision making about specific decision alternatives.

The remainder of this chapter will discuss Stage I in more detail. But first we will introduce the other stages of our decision-making framework.

Stage II: Gathering Information

In this stage analysts collect information to understand the *decision alternatives* through which organizational goals and objectives can be achieved. **Decision alternatives** are the considered alternative courses of action about which a decision is made. Cost management does not happen on paper or in spreadsheets, but through real improvements in how an organization charts and executes its strategy. Information is gathered for two purposes: to identify decision alternatives, and to understand how each decision alternative helps to meet the organization's objectives.

Identifying decision alternatives

A key requirement for cost management is that smart and feasible decision alternatives are developed. There would be no point in selecting the 'best' course of action from a set of inferior decision alternatives. Organizations often identify alternatives by thoroughly seeking information from, among others:

- *Employees*, who know their work best and often have excellent suggestions for improvement.
- *Customers*, who can articulate their unmet needs and visions of the future.
- *Competitors*, who are seeking the same competitive edge and already have made changes that this organization can imitate or improve.
- *Non-competitors*, who use 'best practices' that might be transferrable to this organization.
- *Universities*, which seek to push beyond the boundaries of scientific, engineering and social practices and exist to create and disseminate knowledge.
- *Consultants*, who observe best practices and can help adapt them to this organization.
- The *Internet*, which is a continually evolving repository of vast and growing knowledge.

For example, when deciding on which new products to develop, Network Data will gather information from suppliers and industry reports on the specifications of components that are being developed. Network Data will study so-called technology roadmaps that lay out longer-term developments in the industry, it will investigate which requirements its customers have and what kinds of new services they would like, and it will carefully look at the functionality and performance of their competitors' products.[6]

Of course, managers could spend all of their time searching for and evaluating alternatives, which is a form of 'analysis paralysis' and ignores the fact that information about decisions in a competitive world must be timely to be useful. Knowing when to cut off the search for more alternatives usually is a matter of management judgement, weighing the value of possibly finding a better alternative against the cost of delaying decisions.

Scrutinizing the decision alternatives on various criteria

Managers must understand to what extent the decision alternatives help to meet the organization's objectives. This is the basis for the evaluation of these decision alternatives. Decision alternatives are analysed on the basis of criteria that are based on the organization's objectives. For example, after Network Data's managers have listed possible new products to develop (but the company cannot develop all), they will gather more information on specific criteria such as development cost, development lead time, revenues, contribution margin, learning and risk.

Obviously, information on both **financial and non-financial criteria** will be gathered which differ regarding the unit of measurement. *Financial criteria* have a monetary unit of measurement, such as euros, dollars, rupees, pounds, or any other currency. Examples are acquisition price, material cost or labour cost. Non-financial criteria fall into two categories. *Quantitative, non-financial* criteria have a non-monetary but still quantitative unit of measurement. Examples include criteria regarding delivery time, production speed, process yield or size tolerances. *Qualitative, non-financial* criteria are expressed in words instead of numbers, such as a description of a supplier's innovative capabilities or testimonials from a supplier's other customers. Managers can assess whether the difference in non-financial criteria is worth the difference in financial criteria. For example, Network Data's managers compare two possible new products. Cost analysts estimate a difference between the initial development costs, which is a financial criterion. They also expect a difference between both development lead times, measured in weeks. This is non-financial, quantitative information. The product with the shorter development lead time also has a higher initial development cost, and managers can judge whether the shorter lead time is worth the higher cost.

Sometimes a criterion is first non-financial and can be converted into a financial criterion. Suppose cost management analysts also have estimates of higher revenues from one month earlier product introduction, which they can use to change a shorter development lead time into the financial benefit this is estimated to generate. Now the different criteria are directly comparable, which simplifies decision making tremendously. We call this **financial quantification**: translating a non-financial criterion into a financial criterion.

Information quality

Information gathering requires time and is otherwise costly. Managers need to find a balance for the required **information quality**, the dimensions of which are decision usefulness, subjectivity, objectivity, accuracy, timeliness, cost and relevance for current decisions. **Decision usefulness** is the overriding consideration: does it help managers make sufficiently better decisions to justify the cost of the information?

Cost management relies heavily on measurements of various kinds. All measurement inherently involves subjectivity and objectivity. **Subjectivity** describes the degree of disagreement about what to measure, how to measure it, what the observed measure is, or whether the measurement is important. **Objectivity**, the degree of consensus about measurement, is the mirror image of subjectivity. Clearly, some measures are more subjective or objective than others; that is, all measures conceptually reside somewhere on a continuum from subjective to objective.

The numbers in the financial statements of Network Data (and other companies) are considered to be objective measurements prepared with great care. Nonetheless, considerable judgement about financial statement measures and disclosures still exists. Closer to the subjectivity end of the spectrum is the measurement of Network Data's product or service quality perceptions, which reside in and vary among individuals. Subjective measures can be useful, however. For example, perceptions of the quality of products or services can vary among Network Data's customers, but Network Data's management believes that gathering these more subjective measures is essential because they can presage potential opportunities or problems. Similarly, many find value in the number of stars or 'thumbs up' awarded to restaurants and movies.

Information pertinent to a decision problem must also be accurate or it will be of little use. **Accuracy** is precision in measurement. For example, the estimated development cost and the unit cost Network Data incurs if it were to develop a new product is useful for decisions about whether to develop and sell it. However, if the cost figures are inaccurate because of erroneous calculations or incomplete records, the usefulness of the figures is greatly diminished.

Information is useful if it is timely; that is, **timeliness** means that information is available in time to fully consider it when making a decision. For example, information about alternative products that Network Data could develop is not very useful if it cannot be prepared before a deadline to decide which products Network Data should announce to its customers.

The **relevance** of information refers to whether it is pertinent to a decision; that is, knowing the information or different values of the information can influence choice. Because different decisions typically require different information, an important issue is deciding what information is relevant to the specific situation. The most timely, accurate, objective information is useless if it is irrelevant to the decision.

Relevant costs and benefits occur in the future *and* differ for feasible alternatives. Costs that differ for alternatives are also called differential costs. Some highly accurate information might not be useful to a decision maker. Costs that are *in the past* and cannot be changed anymore are *not* relevant for decision making. These are also called **sunk costs**. For example, Network Data has already spent considerable money on a new product and now it considers whether or not to continue developing this product further. The money spent is irrelevant for the decision on how to move forward, which should be based on future costs and benefits. These 'sunk costs' cannot be changed any more and, therefore, should not be considered when deciding on which way to go.[7]

Costs that are in the future and *are the same for all decision alternatives* will not influence the comparison and are also *not* relevant for decision making. For example, Network Data will incur considerable costs next year to buy new servers and software that are needed for product development. This investment will be made regardless of whether the current product development project is continued or not. So, we can leave it out of the analysis for decision making. Of course, buying the new servers and software is a separate investment decision that needs to be analysed, but we do not need to consider this for the continuation decision.

Similarly, non-financial information that is the same for all decision alternatives is irrelevant for the decision. That means that the financial quantification of non-financial information should also be focused on those non-financial criteria that are different between alternatives. For example, Network Data will need to obtain certification for new products. It is yet uncertain how much this will cost, but it is clear that the cost will be the same for all new products. We do not need to investigate how much this cost will be for the purpose of deciding whether or not the product will be continued. Of course, we may need to find out for other purposes.

Data gathering should be focused on information that managers will find useful and that is relevant for comparing decision alternatives.

Stage III: Evaluating Alternatives

Once alternatives have been identified and information about every alternative has been gathered, the next stage of decision making is to evaluate the alternatives. Which decision alternative is preferred, given the goals and objectives of the organization? This is the topic in Part 3 of the text, and there is a nice example about Network Data later in this chapter. Evaluating alternatives is done by aggregating (e.g., adding up) the information that has been gathered in Stage II. Financial information is easiest to add up, so that is why we like financial information. Network Data can add up the expected cost of developing a new product, producing, servicing and selling it, to find out what the total effect is.

Non-financial information is harder to factor in, unless it can be translated into financial information. But not everything that matters can be made financial. Managers need to also consider non-financial criteria. There are ways to aggregate non-financial information for evaluating decision alternatives, and this is called multi-criteria decision making.

Stage IV: Execution and Tracking Costs

The next stage of decision making is to put the selected alternative into practice, and to keep track of the actual costs and revenues. For example, Network Data tracks inventory costs in detail. Inventory of electronic components is particularly expensive. Not only because of working capital tied up in inventories, but also because of price erosion. The purchase price of electronics components is frequently reduced because of competition, technological improvement that increases production efficiency, and the introduction of new product types. As a result, an organization must revalue its inventory. So it is important to carry less inventory, and to buy the components later and maybe even at a lower price.

Part 4 of the book focuses on costing systems, which accumulate the costs of processes and assign them to the products and services that constitute the organization's output. There are different types of costing systems: job and order costing, process costing, and service centre costing systems. It is important for cost management analysts to know about product costing in detail, because they are usually preparing the costing reports. They also need to understand product costing to be able to find or construct the data they need for specific decisions.

Stage V: Obtaining Feedback

The final stage – although that is not really true, because decision making continues and we go back and forth between the different stages – is to obtain feedback. This means that the actual outcomes are analysed for improving future decisions and for holding managers accountable. This is the topic in Part 5 of the book, and there is a nice example about Network Data later in this chapter.

At the operational level, the financial focus is on costs. The actual costs for the actual production are compared to its standard costs. Differences between the actual costs and the standard cost (or 'allowable costs') are called variances. What are the causes of significant variances and what can be learned?

Strategically, the focus is on financial performance of the entire organization, or financial performance of decentralized units within the organization. These units may also purchase goods and services from each other. In such cases, the transfer price influences the financial performance of both units (the transfer price determines the allocation of the overall profit to the selling unit and the buying unit).

Finally, measuring financial performance may not be enough to understand early and concretely what is happening in the organization. Strategic performance measurement models may also contain non-financial performance measures.

Strategic Decision Making (More about Stage I)

LO 3 Describe and understand steps in strategic decision making.

An organization's **strategy** can be described as its overall plan or policy to achieve its goals. To develop a strategy, managers answer two basic questions: (1) Where do we want to go? and (2) How do we want to get there?[8] One cost management role is to provide 'financial reality' to the answers to these questions and to the development of a successful strategy by focusing the organization on providing more value at lower cost.

Strategic decision making determines 'where' and 'how' by choosing and implementing actions that will affect an organization's future abilities to achieve its goals. For example, strategic decisions might include launching an innovative product line to meet an emerging market or organizing to be the lowest-cost producer of an existing product. Some have argued that observed strategic decision making, which informs us about how these decisions are made, really is taking actions to implement past decisions or rationalizing past decisions that have been implemented. We take an explicitly *intentional* view of strategic decision making. In other words, we will describe what we believe strategic decision makers intend to do although implementations might falter.[9] Recent research shows that the way organizations answer the two strategic questions separates success from mediocrity or failure. We will follow Network Data's decision making to understand how it has continued to be successful in its highly competitive industry.

'Where Do We Want to Go?'

Network Data's answer to the first question is a strategy to achieve high growth and profitability by making innovative data communication products for growing markets and customers that themselves have high growth potential. This strategy can be successful if Network Data quickly develops innovative products that capture shares of growing markets, but it will be successful only if the company develops products and serves customers profitably. It is sadly possible to be innovative, to grow rapidly and to go bankrupt. Network Data's strategy is important in technology, science and fashion-driven industries, but it is not the only successful one for all organizations and industries. Furthermore, organizations and industries have life cycles, and certain strategies can be more appropriate at different times and for different parts of the organization.

Before examining how Network Data can reach its destination, we first discuss four major types of strategic destinations, or 'missions'. Exhibit 1.2 shows four common types of strategic missions along the important dimensions of rewards and risk: build, hold, harvest and divest.

Rewards for profit-seeking firms generally mean financial incentives in the form of profits, cash flow and share price appreciation, although many profit-seeking firms also seek non-financial rewards such as improved social responsibility. Governmental and non-profit organizations might seek rewards such as improved health care and improved environmental quality. *Risks*, on the other hand, can be defined as the possible variations in incentives, which might turn out to be very high

Exhibit 1.2 Major Categories of Strategic Missions

REWARDS (vertical axis: Low, Medium, High) vs. RISK (horizontal axis: Low, Medium, High)

Build (high rewards, high risk)
- Need to achieve growth
- New market potentially high
- Important to early entrance
- Focus on capturing market share

Hold
- Need to maintain growth
- Market continuing
- Need to be major player
- Focus on protecting market share

Harvest
- Need to maintain cash flow
- Mature market
- Need to maintain volume
- Focus on cutting costs

Divest (low rewards, low risk)
- Need to exit at lower cost
- Market declining or bad fit
- Need to minimize losses
- Focus on finding a buyer quickly

or very low. High-risk strategies might offer very high rewards, but they also can result in very low or negative returns. Conversely, the possible rewards for low-risk strategies might have very little variation but are usually also low. For example, investors who kept large share investments in 2008 hoped for continuing the very high returns of previous years, but the market bubble burst and losses resulted. Conversely, investors who kept or switched to money-market investments in 2008 were not expecting high returns, but their low positive returns were better than the losses many suffered when the market bubble burst.

The build strategy requires the organization to achieve high rates of sales growth. An organization pursues the build strategy by identifying new markets and customers with high growth potential. For example, Network Data, which follows this strategy, seeks new data communications opportunities by working closely with key customers who have large, novel communication problems that seem likely to emerge in other organizations. By quickly finding solutions to these problems, Network Data can be the first to offer them to others. Being first – and being right about the problem and the solution – means that Network Data can attract new customers, capture a large share of a new growing market, and earn high rewards. The build strategy is risky because the potentially high rewards will attract competitors who also want to be first and right. If Network Data is late or wrong, the company could quickly lose its customers, reputation and investment in new products and services.

The hold strategy means that the organization needs to maintain its current rate of growth, which generally reflects the overall market growth for a continuing market. For example, an automobile retailer that pursues a hold strategy works to maintain its retail sales growth at a rate that is at least equal to the regional population growth. To thrive with this strategy, an organization usually must be a major competitor so that activities by other major competitors do not threaten its survival. The organization must guard its market share to maintain steady growth. This strategy is less risky than the build strategy because the firm understands its market and competitors fairly well. Rewards are also lower because competition drives down profits.

A firm that follows a harvest strategy needs to maintain its cash flow, so some call this the 'cash cow' strategy. Firms that follow the harvest strategy usually operate in mature markets, which no longer experience much growth and might be on the verge of decline. Sometimes larger firms control harvest *business units* (somewhat autonomous divisions) that provide cash to fund new build business units. Harvest firms need to maintain sales volume while cutting costs, particularly in anticipation of declining sales. Lower risks and rewards are more typical in harvest firms than in either hold or build firms, but harvest firms can perform valuable functions as sources of internally generated cash.

Sometimes, or at the end of an organization's life cycle, the best strategy is to divest, and the organization needs to exit the business at the lowest cost. The divest strategy can result from a realization that a business unit is a bad fit with the rest of the organization, as, for example, when in the USA **Quaker Oats** determined that its purchase of the **Snapple** beverage business had been a mistake, when the Dutch company **Ahold** sold **US Foodservice** as part of a major strategic review after several accounting scandals, or when **Philips** decided to sell its semiconductor division, which became **NXP** as a separate company. In other situations, an organization might have reached the end of its life, and liquidation is the best course of action. As another example, **Montgomery Ward** was a major US retailer for many decades but reached a time when it could no longer compete, and it was liquidated. Although rewards can be low in a divest strategy, the risks of continuing operations can be substantial. The more quickly a buyer can be found, the better, because each day of failed operations raises the possibility of having to abandon resources before they can be sold to others.

'How Do We Want to Get There?'

Successful strategic decision making involves choosing the destination and the best route to it. A myriad of possible routes to a destination exist, and it is easy to take a wrong turn along the way. Finding the best route can be more successful when managers (1) understand sources and threats to competitive advantages and (2) use effective decision-making techniques.

Sources of competitive advantages

Organizations such as Network Data face fierce competition and seek a **competitive advantage**, which is a resource, process or value chain that enables the organization to provide more value, perhaps at lower cost, than its competitors. A competitive resource might be extremely talented employees or control of natural resources. A **process** is a related set of tasks, manual or automated, that transforms inputs into identifiable outputs. A competitive process can be the innovative use of a proprietary database of customers' buying habits or a patented process to produce a valuable chemical, which are costly or difficult to imitate.

A **value chain** is the relation of an organization's processes that links ideas, resources, suppliers and customers; a competitive value chain does so in a superior way. Decisions to change all or parts of the value chain are usually strategic because they affect the organization's ability to meet its goals. Exhibit 1.3 shows a generic value chain that links all major processes that most organizations perform in some way.

Exhibit 1.3 **The Value Chain - Sources of Competitive Advantage**

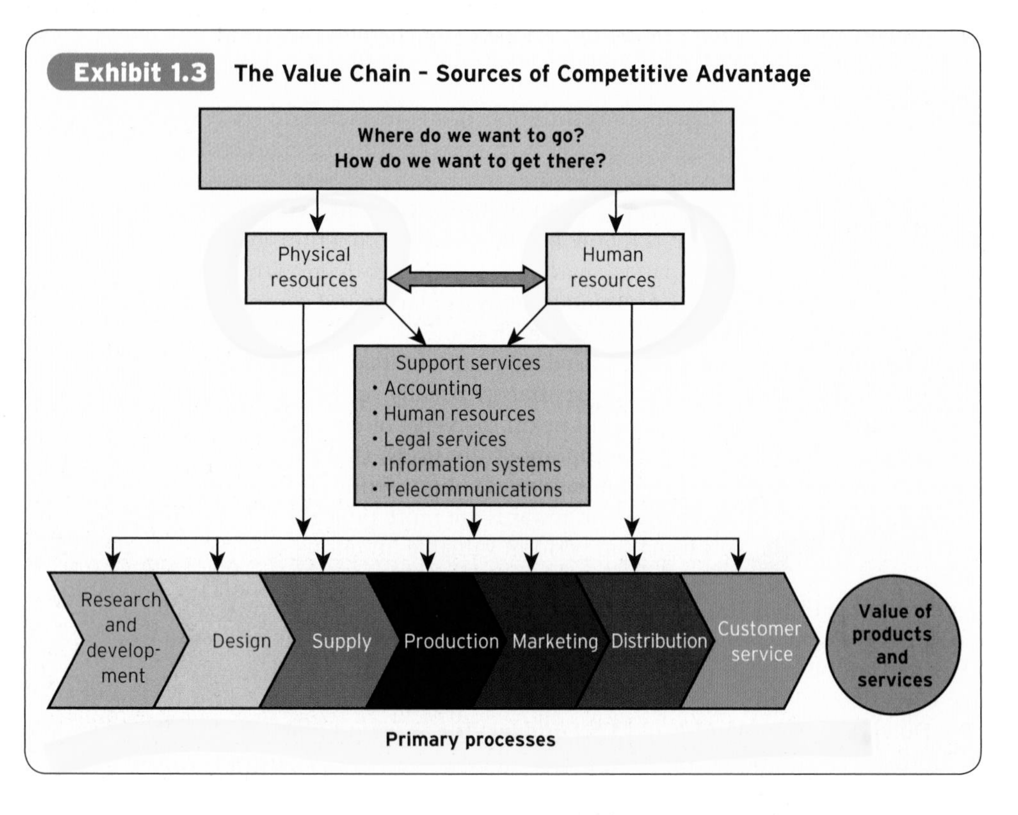

The value chain begins by obtaining physical and human resources and ends by providing products or services that customers value. Each part of the value chain describes a process that an organization performs, and each process in the chain should focus on improving customer value. The value chain also shows that managers must decide how to apply the organization's valuable (and scarce) physical and human resources to each linked process. The complete value chain includes the following processes, which are exemplified by Network Data.

Research and development (R&D)

Network Data has extensive R&D operations to develop innovative telecommunication devices and software applications.

Design

Network Data incorporates its new telecommunication ideas into the designs of innovative communications hardware and software.

Supply
Network Data has strong relations with its external suppliers who work closely with it to control the quality and timing of supply shipments. Some external suppliers have become part of Network Data's **extended value chain**, which encompasses the ways companies obtain their resources and distribute their products and services, possibly using the services of other organizations.

Production
Network Data assembles its own fibre-optic devices and writes its own software applications.

Marketing
Network Data successfully markets its products and services using both traditional, face-to-face presentations and Internet-based information (for example, websites) and solicitations.

Distribution
Network Data contracts with land-based delivery companies for local and regional deliveries and with air-delivery companies that can deliver products anywhere in the world.

Customer service
Network Data guarantees the performance of its products and services and moves quickly to resolve customer problems or complaints.

Support services
Some companies would not identify support functions, such as accounting, human resources, legal services, information systems and telecommunications, as critical parts of the value chain. However, Network Data recognizes that these are important processes that it must perform, either by itself or by *outsourcing* the work to firms that specialize in these services. **Outsourcing** is acquiring goods or services from an outside provider.

In general, a resource, a process or an entire value chain can be a continued source of competitive advantage if it is valuable, rare, difficult to imitate and without substitutes. Otherwise, these items would be freely available to competitors; all competitors could have them; and they could not provide any unique advantages. Organizations can find competitive advantages either by (1) creating new knowledge, which relies on supporting human innovation and experimentation, or (2) imitating others' ideas and implementing them in a superior way. Either creation or imitation can provide advantages, but sometimes the outcomes are unintentional. For example, the recorded music industry (firms, artists and musicians) relies heavily on profiting from controlling the distribution of new music. However, Internet-based music trading practices can easily and cheaply distribute recorded music. These superior distribution practices have led to new distribution channels, such as **iTunes** and **AmazonMP3**, in order to protect the profits from producing and selling recorded music from being eliminated.

Michael Porter[10] identified three basic ways to use resources, processes and value chains to create competitive advantages based on (1) low-cost production, (2) product differentiation or (3) market focus. Becoming the low-cost producer requires making investments to reduce operating costs to earn higher profits at market prices or lowering prices to attract more customers. Differentiating products means providing goods with superior features that command premium prices and that competitors cannot copy. Organizations can also narrow or broaden their market focus to serve either the special needs of select (niche) customers or the broad needs of a wider (mass) market. The narrow approach requires detailed information about specific customers and an ability to customize products to meet their needs. The broad approach necessitates understanding marketwide needs and trends. Exhibit 1.4 displays the sources of competitive advantages and threats to those advantages, which we discuss next.

1.1 Research Insight

Outsourcing the Value Chain

Research on outsourcing components of the value chain has identified several characteristics of firms and their operations that could lead to more outsourcing. Firms now focus their resources on those parts of the value chain

that are most important to their goals and outsource other operations.[11] Some observers predict that, in 10 to 20 years, many firms will have outsourced every part of the value chain except the few key components that are unique and sources of competitive advantage. Information services (information technology, Internet services) and traditional support services (legal, logistics, human resources, payroll, accounting transactions and tax) are most likely to be outsourced: companies seeking to reduce costs or gain access to specialized information (information technology, foreign markets) are more likely to outsource parts of the value chain.

Outsourcing is now happening on a more global scale than before by companies such as **Microsoft**, **Siemens**, **Intel**, **Toshiba**, **Boeing** and **Airbus**. India is renowned for offering IT services to customers all over the world. Even in strategic functions such as product development, global outsourcing is increasing. Companies outsource to, for example, Taiwan, China, South Korea, Russia and the Czech Republic to make use of lower costs, available expertise and large talent pools in engineering.

Because outsourcing can result in loss of control and internal expertise, trust and reliable measurement of outsourcing performance are essential. Providing outsourced services is one of the fastest growing businesses in the world.

Sources: Widener and Selto (1999); Eppinger and Chitkara (2006); and Ding et al. (2010).

Exhibit 1.4 **Competitive Advantages, Sources and Threats**

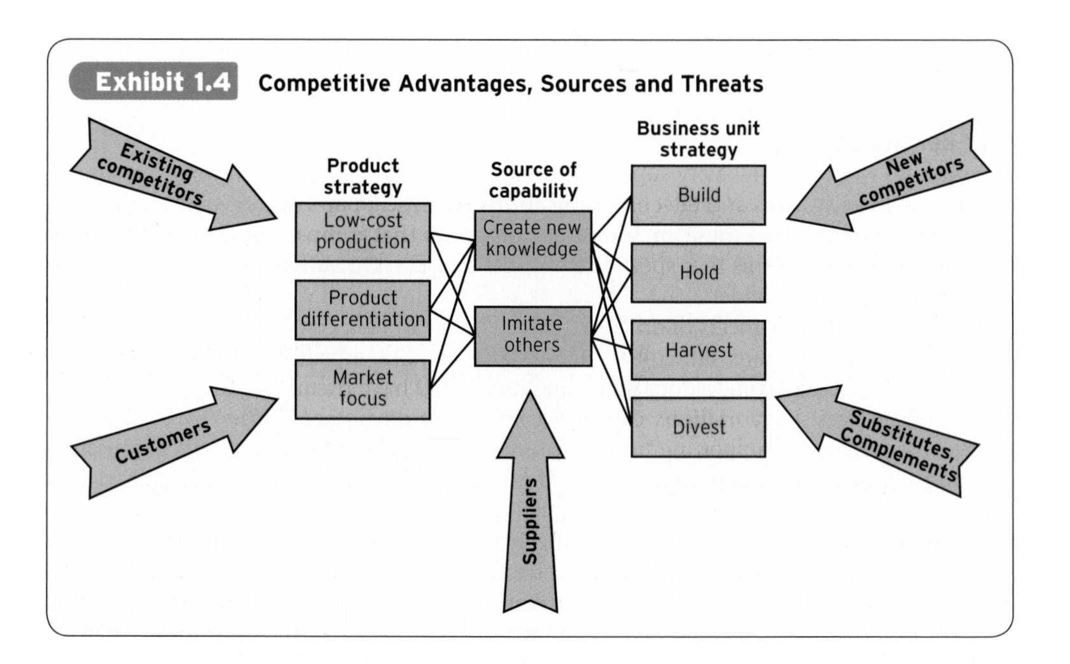

Threats to competitive advantages

The nature of competition means that competitors continually try to outperform each other. Therefore, no competitive advantage lasts forever. Michael Porter (1985) identifies five competitive forces that describe the sources of threats to competitive advantages. These forces determine how long a competitive advantage can last.

- The first force refers to the combined basis, intensity, breadth and competence of *existing competitors*, who vie for the same customers and market share. Most of Network Data's competitors are trying hard to identify new problems and solutions, but a few attempt to copy Network's solutions in a less costly way. Network Data protects its innovations with copyrights and patents, but skilful imitators can find legal ways to produce similar products.
- The second force involves the difficulty and likelihood of entry to the market by *new competitors*, who are attracted by success and high profits. Network Data maintains close relations with its customers and guards its patents and highly paid scientists and engineers, all of which would be costly and difficult for newcomers to imitate or hire.

- The third force reflects the demand and stability of *customers*, whose needs and financial stability also are affected by competitive forces and can change overnight. Network Data manages its relations with customers closely so that the company knows about their critical needs and changes as quickly as possible.
- The fourth force refers to the reliability, quality and breadth of *suppliers*, who also face competitive forces and can change their focus or experience difficulties. For a while, Network Data cultivated close relations with just a few suppliers to facilitate on-time deliveries of high-quality goods. When one supplier unexpectedly declared bankruptcy, Network expanded its set of suppliers and used improved technology to manage its relations with them.
- The fifth force includes the availability and likelihood of *substitute* or *complementary* products, technologies and services that can render current advantages obsolete. Network Data made its first big advance in the industry when it correctly predicted that optical data communication switches would quickly replace copper-wire switches. The company knows that technological breakthroughs are the rule in its industry and invests in R&D and in smaller, highly innovative firms that might be the sources of these breakthroughs. Complementary improvements in data storage devices also drive Network Data's R&D and sales.

1.2 Cost Management in Practice

Competition from and in Emerging Markets

Established firms are facing strong competition from emerging giants such as Brazil's AmBev (which has merged with Belgium's Interbrew to form **InBev**); China's **Galanz**, **Lenovo**, **Heier** and **Huawei Technologies**; India's **Dr Reddy's Laboratories**, **Tata Group**, and South Africa's **SABMiller**. These are emerging giants that compete with established firms both in emerging markets as well as in established markets. Vice versa, emerging markets may provide attractive new strategic possibilities for established firms.

In local markets (such as in Argentina, Brazil, Chile, China, India, Indonesia, Mexico, South Africa and Turkey) these companies better understand the needs of customers. For instance, **Jollibee Foods** thrives because it realizes that Filipinos like their burgers to have a particular soy and garlic taste; **Nandos** is growing in South Africa by providing cooked chicken that suits local palates; and **Pollo Campero** is doing the same in Guatemala. Over the past ten years, these companies have profitably battled American giants like **McDonald's** and **KFC**.

In established markets, these companies capitalize on their strong home positions to become formidable competitors. For example, **Haier** became a leader in China's white goods market, in the teeth of competition from **GE**, **Electrolux** and **Whirlpool**, mainly because it was able to develop products tailored to the needs of Chinese consumers. By 1991, the company had become China's biggest manufacturer of refrigerators. It first expanded to other emerging markets, and then Germany became the first Western market for Haier-branded refrigerators in 1997, and two years later, Haier entered the United States, setting up a design centre in Boston, a marketing operation in New York, and a manufacturing facility in South Carolina. In the US market, the Chinese giant has focused on price-sensitive segments and established partnerships with American retailers such as **Best Buy**, **Home Depot** and **Wal-Mart**. Indian information technology majors such as **Tata Consultancy Services**, **Infosys Technologies**, **Wipro** and **Satyam Computer Services** have excelled in recent years at catering to the global demand for software and services.

Sources: Khanna and Palepu (2006); Raman (2009).

Eight Elements of Leading and Managing Change

Kotter has identified elements in a process for implementing change.[12] The following sections identify these elements and Network Data's implementation of them to implement strategic plans, such as the launch of an innovative product line consistent with its build strategy.

1. Identify a need for change

Sometimes external threats force organizations to change, and at times unforeseen opportunities make change attractive. Consistently successful managers and organizations always expect and anticipate change and always look for opportunities to improve. Importantly, they also assess the impact of not changing. Research indicates that thriving firms keep moving, not aimlessly but always to create competitive advantages.[13] Some managers say they find opportunities by 'measuring everything' and continually evaluating trends and changes in their performance and the performance of their customers and competitors. A **performance measure** is an indicator that allows a person to determine the level of performance according to a critical attribute (for example, profit, quality) and to compare performance to expectations (see the next section of this chapter).

Providing the right measures of performance for making these evaluations is a primary role of cost management and a primary focus of this text. Frequent face-to-face meetings that develop and use the appropriate performance measures also allow managers to identify alternative actions, debate them objectively, and identify opportunities and threats quickly and accurately.

The opening Email messages between Network Data's top managers show that they quickly identify opportunities for change consistent with the firm's strategy. Furthermore, they usually generate multiple, alternative actions to meet those opportunities and count on debates among informed team members to choose the best course of action.

2. Create a team to lead and manage the change

Teams have replaced individual decision makers in many organizations, including Network Data. A few years ago, different people and functions within organizations performed separate parts of cost management but did not communicate effectively with each other. These people usually operated in separate functional roles that often impeded co-operation among functional areas. Functional roles usually are narrowly defined jobs that focus on specific types of activities, such as accounting or manufacturing. Persons restricted to functional roles often were most interested in parts of business issues that fit their own expertise. In some companies, people operating in these different functional areas rarely spoke with each other, and their actions were not necessarily consistent with organizational goals.

People from different training and backgrounds at Network Data work in small, cross-functional, diverse teams to make decisions, such as developing new products. They are assigned to specific departments such as accounting, engineering or marketing, but they spend most of their time and efforts in team activities. Cost management is an integral part of a cross-functional and innovative approach to management decision making. Anyone who is preparing to become a cost management analyst must be ready to work in cross-functional teams in which critical skills are leadership and effective communication. Most successful organizations have learned to create cross-functional, diverse teams that are more likely to be innovative in their solutions and discovery of opportunities.

3. Create a vision of the change and a strategy for achieving the vision

Network Data's strategy is to provide innovative telecommunication services and products to high-growth customers. This vision is widely shared within the company because its employees are frequently involved in team decisions and are accustomed to open but disciplined debates about choosing the best route to their 'build' strategy. It seems natural to employees to question and debate whether new products and processes are consistent with the company's overall strategy. It is very difficult to predict financial outcomes of alternative decisions, but teams create alternative scenarios of future outcomes that reflect their understanding of the impacts of internal and external events on achieving the organization's goals.

4. Communicate the vision and strategy for change and have the change team be a role model

Network Data constantly communicates its vision and strategy and encourages input from employees. Team members are well suited and trained to gather employees' input and include it in their analyses and recommendations. Giving credit for others' suggestions increases the chances that they will participate again in the future. An important behaviour to model is to fearlessly compare planned and actual outcomes, which encourages learning and improved decision making.

5. Encourage innovation and remove obstacles to change

Diverse teams almost guarantee innovations. CEO Michael Maier reserves the right to make final decisions, but he gives authority to the diverse teams to develop new product opportunities. Top managers eliminate any political or 'turf' issues that might derail or delay new product decisions by emphasizing common goals and refusing to accept obvious turf-based arguments for or against an idea.

6. Ensure that short-term achievements are frequent and obvious

Analysing the new-product proposal is an example of an effort that could have an obvious impact on the company. Network Data's approach to new-product development is to break its large problems into smaller ones that teams can analyse and solve in a short amount of time. To keep the decision making on schedule, Network Data also requires each team to commit to a schedule that can be changed but only after management approval. Even projects that do not meet their original objectives are treated as successes because the company learns why something did not work. This is valuable information that helps to prevent future failures.

7. Use successes to create opportunities for improvement in the entire organization

By making sequential parts of the process visible, the company can point to many examples of employee contributions to significant improvements in products and processes. Network Data uses this practice to make future improvements even more likely and, importantly, encourage employees to recommend improvements even if they are small.

8. Reinforce a culture of more improvement, better leadership, and more effective management

The climate of striving for improvements permeates Network Data. Employees know that opportunities for improvement always exist and that managers take their recommendations seriously. Treating occasional failures as opportunities for learning rather than reasons for assigning blame is important for motivating team members to be creative and honest in their appraisals.

Evaluation of Plans and Outcomes

Some plans that seemed wonderful on paper or in the team meeting room fail to meet expectations. Others greatly exceed expectations. The success of an individual plan is important, but understanding why and how a plan or project failed or succeeded can help organizations learn to make better future decisions. Two levels of analysis are important to evaluating the success or failure of a plan. The first level is **operational performance analysis**, which measures whether the performance of current operations is consistent with expectations. The second level is **strategic performance analysis**, which measures whether a strategic decision has met expectations.

LO 4
Apply benefit-cost and variance analysis to help evaluate an organization's strategic plans.

Generally, operational performance analysis considers performance measures within relatively short time periods (for example, days, weeks or months), but strategic performance analysis can consider years of performance. For example, a particular plan might not meet current operational performance expectations (for example, this month's lower-than-expected profit from a new product), but longer-term performance can indicate that the strategic decision was correct (for instance, with the exception of this month, a new product's performance in the past year has met or exceeded expectations). Another distinction between operational and strategic performance is the level of the results that are analysed. For example, an operational performance measure could reflect the quality of parts made in a particular department, but a strategic performance measure could reflect the reputation of quality for an entire product line or company.

Benefit–Cost Analysis (More about Stage III)

We will analyse data for a new product that Network Data recently completed to illustrate the important practice of comparing plans to actual results. This type of comparison can be used to evaluate either operational or strategic performance. A Network Data analyst based her reasoning on benefit–cost analysis of pertinent information about the product's performance. **Benefit–cost analysis** measures the effects of a plan by comparing its expected benefits and costs, which can be *quantitative* and *qualitative*. **Quantitative information** is expressed in euros, dollars or another currency (financial information) or in other quantities relating to size, frequency, and so on (non-financial information). **Qualitative information** is descriptive, expressed in words instead of numbers, and based on characteristics or perceptions, such as relative desirability, rather than quantities. Part 3 of this book focuses on benefit–cost analysis.

An organization must be concerned with both the quantitative and qualitative costs and benefits. In some cases (for example, concerns about employee morale and customer perception of service quality), qualitative information can outweigh quantitative information (such as cost savings) in making a decision. For example, a company might find an opportunity to reduce its costs in the short run, but doing so would violate its strategy. The company must weigh qualitative factors against the quantitative benefits and costs. The initial analysis of the new product was based on the quantitative and qualitative information shown in Exhibit 1.5, which shows that the company expected the product to recover its costs of development and production within two years. The company also expected normal sales growth, completion time, quality and customer satisfaction. Furthermore, Network Data expected that anticipated lay-offs might adversely affect overall employee morale. The analysis in Exhibit 1.5 compares the plan for introducing a new product to 'doing nothing', and organizations also compare the costs and benefits of alternative plans. For example, Network Data might be able to either develop the new product itself or, alternatively, give suppliers significant development responsibility. In such cases, both plans (and 'do nothing') may be compared based on their benefits and costs.

Exhibit 1.5 **Expected Benefits and Costs Two Years after Introducing a New Product**

Benefits of new product	Expected amount	Comments and explanations
Sales	€1,500,000	Based on estimated customer demand and annual sales growth
Personnel cost savings	80,000	Process improvements indicate fewer personnel required to service customers after sale
Total financial benefits	€1,580,000	
Annual sales growth (per cent)	20%	Normal sales growth for this type of product
Time to completion (months)	15	Normal completion time for product of this complexity
Product quality (number of defects)	10	Normal number of defects detected by customers for this type of product
Customer satisfaction (score out of 100)	95	Normal satisfaction for this type of product and related services
Costs of new product	**Expected amount**	**Comments and explanations**
Development costs	€300,000	Based on product complexity and time to completion
Production costs	600,000	Based on estimates from design plans and similar products
Service costs	130,000	Normal service costs for this type of product
Total financial costs	1,030,000	
Net financial benefits	€550,000	Product expected to recover costs of development and production within this time frame
Effects of personnel reductions	n/a	Personnel lay-offs could cause morale problems and higher than desired turnover of other personnel

Benefit and Cost Variances (More about Stage V)

After several years of experience with the new product, analysts compared the earlier expectations with actual results, as show n in Exhibit 1.6. The differences between a plan's actual and expected quantities are called **variances**. Part 5 of this book focuses on this topic. Because few predictions are perfect, some variances are normal. Managers can evaluate the quantitative aspects of this type of comparison by considering the causes of the exceptionally large variances. These explanations are shown in the qualitative section of Exhibit 1.6.

CFO Johann Werner's review of the analysis in Exhibit 1.6 told him that the original plan was faulty, and he recommended a complete review of the new product and its development process. His reasons were that (1) revenues were lower than expected by €300,000 which was mostly attributable to an inaccurate assessment of the competition and lower product quality and (2) most of the lower cost realized was attributable to lower product volume. In fact, other costs – development and service costs – were higher than expected and attributable to lower product quality. The lower product quality itself probably was the result of the decision to rush the product's development to meet a

Exhibit 1.6 Benefits and Costs of Introducing a New Product

Benefits of new product	Expected amount	Actual amount	Variance	Comments and explanations
Sales to date	€1,500,000	€1,200,000	€(300,000)	Sales lower than expected because of competition and lower product quality
Personnel cost savings to date	80,000	60,000	(20,000)	One fewer person laid off in order to meet higher than expected service calls
Total financial benefits to date	€1,580,000	€1,260,000	€(320,000)	
Annual sales growth (per cent)	20%	17%	–3%	Sales growth lower because of stronger competition and lower product quality than expected
Time to completion (months)	15	12	(3)	Product release date accelerated to meet competition
Product quality (number of defects)	2	23	21	Higher than expected defects caused by skipped quality testing to meet accelerated release date
Customer satisfaction (score out of 100)	95	89	(6)	Lower customer satisfaction because of increased defects and extensive calls for customer service
Costs of new product	**Expected amount**	**Actual amount**	**Variance**	**Comments and explanations**
Development costs	€300,000	€360,000	€60,000	Higher costs because of accelerated development schedule
Production costs to date	600,000	500,000	(100,000)	Lower costs because of lower production volume
Service costs to date	130,000	155,000	25,000	Higher costs because of lower quality and more service calls
Total financial costs to date	1,030,000	1,015,000	(15,000)	
Net financial benefits to date	€550,000	€245,000	€(305,000)	
Effects of personnel reductions	n/a	n/a		Adverse effects have been observed on remaining personnel, but moderated by keeping one more person than expected to correct customer-detected defects

competitive threat, but that backfired. The loss of customer satisfaction probably contributed to lower than expected sales growth and could have affected the sales of other products. This latter result might have had a much greater adverse impact on the company than any other factor. Although adverse effects on personnel morale were lower than expected, the reason again was the poor quality that necessitated keeping more personnel than planned.

Although it might be difficult to admit that a decision of this magnitude had been wrong, the company must learn from the mistake. The results of learning from this painful review were renewed commitments to improving the product development process and to enhancing the quality of the company's products. Years of hard work and close contact with customers were necessary to overcome the adverse effects of that early decision on Network Data's reputation. That mistake was not repeated, and the new product development process emerged stronger than ever. As a result, Network Data's reputation for innovation and quality is unmatched in the industry.

1.2 Research Insight

Cost Management through New Product Development

A significant portion of product costs are determined by decisions that are made during product development, for example decisions about specifications, materials used and design. Target costing is a detailed technique to manage costs during product development.[14] It is best suited for products for which the sales price is a key competitive dimension. Market prices, sales and distribution costs in the supply chain, and required profit margins define a target product cost. For larger products such as cars, the overall target cost is broken down to components. Throughout the different stages of product development, the cost of the product is estimated and if it exceeds the target, it needs to be redesigned. The cost estimations become more accurate as product development proceeds.

However, target costing is less suitable to manage costs when technology is a key consideration and costs are determined by decisions that are not made at the product level. While target costs are also watched, other cost management techniques are also required. For example, parallel cost teams work outside the main team to develop solutions for reducing costs. The main team's attention is taken by technology and lead-time challenges and cannot also pay full attention to costs. Another approach is to have strategies at the level of a portfolio of products, such as working with product platforms and enforcing component commonality. Furthermore, modular designs and other product features can reduce costs in the supply chain. The key point is that often costs cannot be managed only at the level of individual product development projects.

Sources: Davila and Wouters (2004).

1.1 You're the Decision Maker

Benefit-Cost Analysis of Introducing a New Product

Refer to the information in Exhibit 1.6.

a. Explain how you think Network Data compared the expected costs and benefits in the analysis even though some are quantitative but others are qualitative.

b. Is it possible that the qualitative or non-quantified costs or benefits of this decision could be more important than those that are quantified? Explain with an example from Exhibit 1.6.

c. Explain the possible linkages among development time, sales, product quality and customer satisfaction that are reflected in Exhibit 1.6.

d. If personnel are laid off or dismissed to realize cost savings, does Network Data have any ethical obligations to those employees? Could the way that Network Data treats those employees affect retained or future employees? Explain.

(Solutions begin on page 42.)

Ethical Standards

LO 5
Understand the importance of ethical behaviour and decision making, and identify measures taken to maintain such behaviour.

Cost management analysts must maintain high standards of ethical behaviour because they can control the information on which strategic decisions are based and justified. Unethical behaviour can lead to wasted resources, lost time, ruined reputations and perhaps legal penalties for all involved. Individuals can be pressured to misstate information or results regarding strategic decisions because of:

- *Bias from personal commitment to a decision.* This bias can be caused by a manager's unwillingness to look sufficiently far ahead or admit that a strategy might be a failure. The manager will continue to be pressured to misstate information, unwilling to face the fact that a failing strategy should be terminated.
- *Fear of loss of prestige, position, or compensation from a failed strategy.* The pressures to succeed or not admit failure can be very strong in any type of organization. Some organizations have an 'up or out' advancement policy that rewards only managers who continue to succeed financially. A manager might give in to the temptation to misstate strategic information or might force analysts to do so, perhaps rationalizing that it is only to buy a little time until the market or the industry turns around. This dangerous practice usually leads to continued misstatements that ultimately cannot be sustained.
- *Greed and intentional behaviour to defraud an organization or its stakeholders.* Some people seek opportunities to defraud others. Trust is very important in business, but it has been and will be abused. No contract can be written to anticipate every contingency, natural or criminal. The best defences against fraud are to work with people who have earned trust and to use an effective system of controls. As former President Ronald Reagan used to say, 'Trust but verify.' When markets inevitably turn down or when predicted events do not occur, powerful managers have pressured analysts to misstate information in order to sustain their image and income.

Unfortunately, these practices are too widespread to ignore. Cost management analysts must be vigilant to undue pressures to misstate information.

Ordinary People Face Ethical Dilemmas

Many students think that businesspeople who are unethical are sleazy characters. In fact, most are hard-working people who were surprised that they got caught up in unethical activities.[15] Even people who commit organizational crimes are surprised. A former federal prosecutor told us, 'Most businesspeople who commit crimes are very surprised that they did what they did.'[16] For example, a few years ago, numerous executives of companies in the dynamic random access memory (DRAM) market, such as **Samsung** and **Infineon**, were charged with price-fixing. (DRAM is the type of memory used in most personal computers.) Many of these executives did gaol time for an activity that was intended to benefit their companies, not themselves. Most of them did not realize that exchanging information with competitors was illegal. Companies and executives in various other industries have also been punished for price fixing, such as air cargo companies (**British Airways, Quantas, SAS Cargo Group, Northwest** and others), LCD displays (such as **LG Display** and **Sharp**), and beer (**Heineken** and others).

On the other hand, people have taken great risks to blow the whistle on unethical behaviour and stand up for what is right. During the wave of corporate scandals after the turn of the century, two accountants distinguished themselves for their courage in bringing unethical behaviour to light. These two accountants, Cynthia Cooper at **WorldCom** and Sherron Watkins at **Enron**, along with an **FBI** agent, were named Persons of the Year by *Time* magazine. Although these accountants have been publicly applauded for their courage and integrity, they were heavily criticized for not being team players when they brought their concerns to top management. But they held their ground and would not back down. They provide an example in courage for all of us who might be called upon by circumstances to blow the whistle on unethical practices where we work.

Codes of Ethics

Network Data and many other organizations have ethical codes that describe approved and prohibited practices. These ethical codes educate and support employees who want to behave ethically but either would not know what to do or might be pressured to act unethically. The codes also form grounds for termination of employees who violate them. Network Data has learned from the sad experiences of others that condoning ethical violations is prohibitively costly in the long run. Thus, the company has fully supported employees who adhere to the code and has dismissed several employees, including one in a management position, who violated it.

Network Data's ethical code advertises the company's ethical policy to future employees and can help attract the right employees. Prospective employees who want to work for an ethical company will be attracted to Network Data, and those who do not will find other places to work.

Although many organizations have ethical codes, cost management analysts also can subscribe to the code of ethics developed by professional organizations, such as the Institute of Management Accountants (IMA), the Chartered Institute of Management Accountants (CIMA), the International Federation of Accountants (IFAC), and other organizations mentioned in this chapter. The IMA code stresses the importance of integrity, competence and credibility of management accountants. The IMA's code also stresses resolution of ethical conflicts, and IMA provides guidance to members and other professionals, see www.imanet.org. The IFAC's code focuses more on auditors. It is based on the accountant's responsibility to act in the public interest, and places much weight on convergence of international and national ethical standards, including auditor independence requirements, see www.ifac.org.

Regulators have allowed self-regulation of industries and professions that have shown strong enforcement of their own codes of ethics and business practices. A successful legal defence against alleged wrongdoing might be based on the fact that employees followed the company's or industry's code of ethics. The accounting scandals of recent years, despite the existence of accountants' ethical codes, have seriously harmed the public's image of the accounting profession and business in general. More regulation and legal scrutiny are the natural but unfortunate result of these scandals.

Sarbanes–Oxley Act

The Sarbanes–Oxley Act 2002 (SOX) was a regulatory response to widespread unethical behaviour in companies such as **Enron, WorldCom** and **Tyco** in the United States, **Ahold** and **Baan Company** in the Netherlands, **Parmalat** in Italy, and **Lernout & Hauspie** in Belgium. Although SOX is US regulation, it affects many companies that do business with the United States. Two parts of this law are particularly important for cost management.

1. The chief executive officer (CEO) and chief financial officer (CFO) are responsible for signing off on their company's financial statements and indicating that the financial statements do not omit material information. This signing makes them personally responsible for the financial statements. They cannot 'pass the buck' to lower-level managers and employees. CEOs and CFOs are taking this requirement very seriously because misrepresentation of their company's financial results could mean substantial fines and prison time. Consequently, cost managers are expected to be particularly diligent in measuring costs and other financial data accurately. This requirement has increased the sophistication of accounting systems and the intensity of internal and external audits in a number of companies.
2. The CEO and CFO must indicate that they are responsible for the company's system of internal controls over financial reporting, which are discussed next in more detail.

Internal Controls to Protect Assets and Provide Quality Information

Companies set up internal control systems to deal with problems such as financial fraud. At a general level, internal controls provide management with reasonable assurances that their company's assets are protected and that the company's accounting is reliable. More specifically, **internal control** is a process designed to provide reasonable assurance that an organization will achieve its objectives in the following categories:

- Effectiveness and efficiency of operations
- Reliability of financial reporting
- Compliance with applicable laws and regulations.

In practice, internal controls are detailed methods of protecting assets and ensuring that information is reliable. One of the key internal controls is separation of duties, which means that no one person has control over the entire transaction. With separation of duties, one person cannot prepare the payroll, authorize the payroll cheque, prepare the payroll cheque, sign the payroll cheque, and distribute the payroll cheque to the employees. Similarly, one person does not make the sale, prepare the invoice, deposit the cash payment, and reconcile the bank statement to the company's books. Of course, employees can collude to beat the internal control system. Two or three employees can work together to handle all parts of a transaction. Only two or three high-level employees orchestrated many well-known financial frauds.

Companies use many types of internal controls in addition to separation of duties. Some examples follow.

- Setting limits on the amount of expenditures (for example, no more than €100 per person for an expense account dinner).
- Requiring management authorization for the use of a company's assets (for example, use of a company car).
- Reconciling various sets of books (for example, reconciling accounts receivable with the collections of cash from customers).
- Prohibiting particular behaviours (for example, prohibiting a company's purchasing agents from accepting gifts from present and prospective vendors).
- Rotating personnel and requiring employees to take vacations (for example, requiring the person who reconciles bank statements with the company's cash accounts to rotate duties so somebody different can verify that the cash on the books is actually in the bank).

Internal controls are not only good business practice but also legally required for publicly traded companies. As noted, SOX requires top executives to indicate that they are responsible for the system of internal controls, and the company's external auditor must attest to management's assessment. However, 25 years before SOX was enacted, the Foreign Corrupt Practices Act 1977 required that publicly traded companies have adequate internal controls. The SEC has brought more than 600 cases of violation of the internal controls provision of the Foreign Corrupt Practices Act.

The Foreign Corrupt Practices Act and SOX have caused many organizations to improve their internal controls. These laws also improve documentation of internal controls. They might improve investor confidence in companies' internal controls. These benefits come at a cost, however. Consider separation of duties. Suppose one person handled a transaction before SOX, but two people handle it after SOX. That added separation of duties creates better controls but comes at a cost. An open question is: do those benefits justify the costs of investing in better internal controls?

Internal Auditing to Assure Compliance

Internal auditors generally play either or both of two roles in companies: consultants and/or watchdogs. As consultants, internal auditors learn best practices from their work in various parts of their company and bring that information to the attention of managers in other parts of the company. As watchdogs, internal auditors check whether employees follow good internal control procedures and look for fraud.

By reviewing internal controls and ensuring that controls are working, internal auditors are often a company's first defence against fraud. One of the best-known fraud detections was that of **WorldCom**'s internal auditor, Cynthia Cooper, described earlier as one of the *Time* magazine's Persons of the Year. Cooper worked as the vice president of Internal Audit at WorldCom. After conducting a thorough investigation in secret, she informed WorldCom's board that the company had covered up $3.8 billion in losses through phony bookkeeping.

At **General Electric**, internal auditing is known to be a great training ground where new employees learn about many different operations in the company. Historically, many of General Electric's top finance people put in several years in internal auditing to start their careers.

Internal auditors usually report to top management and have access to the audit committee of the board of directors. It is important for internal auditors to report to a level higher than the controller. Much of their audit work examines accounting systems for which controllers are responsible. If internal auditors reported to the controller, they would be auditing their own boss.

1.2 You're the Decision Maker

Ethical Considerations

Competitive and personal pressures sometimes tempt individuals to act unethically to gain an advantage. Put yourself in the place of CFO Johann Werner and describe how you would respond to each of the following independent situations.

a. An acquaintance who is a technical employee of a close competitor calls you at home to say, 'You know that I've wanted to work for Network Data for several years, and I'm calling to explore options. I've been working on a new data communication product that I think you will find interesting. I just put some of my cost projections on your front porch. Please call me back when you've had a chance to look at them.'

b. You have received a 'cold call' from a company that specializes in competitive intelligence, which the salesperson describes as periodic updates on market conditions and competitors' actions and gathering timely information about specific competitors. You are offered a steeply discounted three-month trial without future obligations unless you agree that the information is valuable.

c. Your staff's initial analysis of a new product indicates possibly higher costs and more uncertainty about future demand for the product than expected. If the combination of higher costs and lower demand actually occur, the product will be a financial failure. In private conversation, the manager of the new product argues that the company's future could depend on getting this product quickly to market, and you agree. The manager urges you to not distribute the pessimistic analysis but to wait until his group can develop the product further and its costs are better understood.

(Solutions begin on page 42.)

Sustainability and Environmental Strategic Decisions

LO 6
Include sustainability and environmental concerns in strategic decisions.

Sustainability is an ambiguous concept. For the purpose of this text, it is sufficient to note that **sustainability** means that an organization should not affect the environment such that that there are long-term negative economic, ecological or social consequences. Not only should the organization consider consequences for customers and shareholders, but also for other stakeholders who are affected by its actions, such as employees, the community and future generations. In any case, sustainability is fundamentally *not* only about creating long-term 'sustainable' business and conditions for existence *for the organization itself*.

Firms and other organizations impact sustainability through their hiring and supply practices, production processes, and through their products when these are used by customers. These organizations may consider sustainability insufficiently because of what economists call 'externalities'. Prices may not reflect the wider costs (or benefits) for other stakeholders who are not directly involved in the transaction. For example, manufacturing that causes air pollution imposes costs on the whole society.

Legislators intervene in different ways. First, they directly influence conditions for transactions, for example by imposing rules for allowable pollution levels. Second, they influence market prices by giving subsidies on investments in low-pollution technology, or by implementing a policy of guaranteed prices, also called a feed-in tariff. These offer long-term contracts to renewable energy producers, which typically ratchet down over time to stimulate more efficient technology investments. Furthermore, governments influence market prices by imposing special taxes for high pollution. Third, legislators create markets for externalities, such as tradable emission rights. These are challenging interventions to get right. For example, legislators need to understand what level of taxation will lead firms to make decisions that are good for sustainability.

Faced with such rules, subsidies, taxes and market prices, organizations can make their decisions in the 'normal' way. Investment analyses and cost accounting systems can incorporate sustainability concerns that legislators have arranged. Also, there are the 'normal' and sometimes difficult issues for valuing assets (such as emission rights) and liabilities (for example, pending disputes about cleaning a production site, or accruing for future environmental costs).

But what about sustainability issues that are not imposed on organizations through rules, subsidies, taxes and market prices? Will organizations adjust their processes, products and services voluntarily in order to improve sustainability? They may if customers like products that are seen as more sustainable. For example, firms such as German **Siemens** and **BMW** have announced significant R&D investments in 'green' products. Firms can make sustainability part of its mission, and develop and implement strategies. This is quite similar to earlier 'megatrends' such as quality and IT. Firms then need to make the strategies more concrete and provide goals and incentives for managers.[17]

There are also initiatives, mostly voluntary, to enhance reporting on sustainability. For example, the Global Reporting Initiative has developed a series of performance indicators to measure economic, environmental (such as energy, water, biodiversity, emissions) and social (such as labour conditions, human rights, corruption and privacy) dimensions.[18] There are also overall indicators that aggregate many different sustainability aspects, such as the 'ecological footprint'. There are many important issues that need to be solved in a cost-effective manner. At a practical level, models are needed to estimate how the organization's decisions will impact costs and sustainability indicators. For example, if the firm invests in cleaner production technology, how much will the sustainability indicators improve, and at what cost? And measurement systems are needed to capture the data for actually measuring the indicators and costs, which heretofore have not been measured. Sustainability reports can also be subject to auditing, but how this works and who will provide assurance services (financial audit firms, engineering consulting firms, or other assurance firms) is not so clear yet.[19] More fundamentally, it is not necessarily true that reporting makes a lot of difference for what firms actually do. There are political issues involved in deciding on what is reported, and it is doubtful that firms will voluntarily disclose that their activities would be *un*sustainable. There is a danger that sustainability reporting is only a ritual.

© manfredxy

Guaranteed prices for electricity made it profitable for companies, farmers and consumers in Germany to invest in renewable energy such as solar panels.

1.3 Cost Management in Practice

Sustainable Development and the Lafuma Group

The **Lafuma Group** is a French company active on the outdoor market, with products such as backpacks, sleeping bags, tents, clothing and footwear. Its brands such as Lafuma, Millet and Eider are sold in Europe, Asia and North America.

The company has made sustainable development part of its mission. It recognizes that all of its activities have an impact on the environment *'and this impact must be kept to a minimum. The Group's commitment to preserving the environment finds its meaning in the nature of the outdoor products themselves and is an essential component in its corporate development model.'* Sustainability is part of the business strategy. It focuses the company's innovation and helps to differentiate the products and brands in the market.

'We are convinced that ecology and economy go hand-in-hand. This has meant adopting a new approach to value analysis. It means that we consume fewer materials and less energy; we reduce our waste and produce products that are longer-lasting, more versatile, safer and more comfortable, and at the same time we improve productivity.'

Lafuma reports the CO_2 emissions from production, logistics, administration and management activities. Lafuma also reports initiatives in product design, recycling, transportation, and solar roofing of its headquarters.

Sources: Lafuma Group, Annual Report 2009; www.pure-leaf-project.com.

Chapter Summary

This first chapter has two purposes. One is to explain what cost management is, and the second is to illustrate how cost management supports strategic decision making. Of paramount importance is supporting and encouraging ethical decision making, not only because it is the right thing to do, but also because it is the most effective and efficient way to do business in the long run.

Strategic decisions are among the most important ones an organization makes because they determine the organization's future activities and performance. Strategic decisions include finding opportunities and responding to threats to competitive advantages as well as selecting the organization's destination and the best route to that destination.

Cost management is (1) an organizational *commitment* of seeking increased customer value at reduced cost, (2) a professional *attitude* of cost management analysts that management decisions cause all costs, and (3) a reliable set of *techniques* that increase value and reduce cost. To provide information, interpretations and analyses of alternative courses of action that managers are contemplating, cost management analysts need broad knowledge of the organization's activities and the ways those activities interact. Benefit–cost analysis is a common and powerful technique, particularly when used to compute variances between expected and actual benefits and costs.

This chapter provides a framework for decision making that explicitly describes the types of information necessary to make good business decisions. The decision-making framework was defined as follows:

Stage I	Setting goals and objectives
Stage II	Gathering information
Stage III	Evaluating alternatives
Stage IV	Execution and tracking costs
Stage V	Obtaining feedback.

In applying this framework, managers must consider the trade-offs involved between the cost and the quality of information, which is described by dimensions of subjectivity, accuracy, timeliness and relevance. In many cases, non-financial information also is critical to making the best decisions.

Cost management analysts are valued members of the management team because they understand how managing the organization's value chain affects cost, quality and customer value. They are also trusted sources of objective information. Companies use cost management teams to evaluate alternative uses of resources. Successfully managing change requires an understanding that its management will affect the success not only of a particular change but also of future changes. Successful companies often use a formal process to lead and manage change, such as Kotter's eight-step process.

Key Terms

For each term's definition, refer to the indicated page, or turn to the glossary at the end of the text.

accuracy,	9	information quality,	9
benefit–cost analysis,	20	internal control,	24
competitive advantage,	14	objectivity,	9
cost management,	4	operational performance analysis,	19
cost management system,	5	outsourcing,	15
criteria,	7	performance measure,	18
decision alternatives,	8	process,	14
decision-making framework,	7	qualitative information,	20
decision usefulness,	9	quantitative information,	20
extended value chain,	15	relevance,	10
financial and non-financial criteria,	9	relevant costs and benefits,	10
financial quantification,	9	strategic decision making,	11

strategic performance analysis,	19	tangible objectives,	7
strategy,	11	timeliness,	9
subjectivity,	9	value chain,	14
sunk costs,	10	variances,	21
sustainability,	26		

Review Questions are mostly written at a ***basic*** *level; Critical Analysis questions and Exercises are* ***intermediate****, and Problems and Cases are* ***advanced****.*

Review Questions

1.1 Review and define each of the chapter's key terms.

1.2 What is the primary objective of cost management?

1.3 List and briefly describe each of the five stages of the decision-making framework.

1.4 Distinguish between an organization's goals and tangible objectives.

1.5 Describe a conflict that might occur between accuracy, timeliness, relevance and cost of information.

1.6 What is the difference between financial information, quantitative non-financial information, and qualitative information?

1.7 What criteria must be satisfied for information to be relevant?

1.8 Give two examples of sunk costs and explain why these amounts might be both useful to and irrelevant in decision making.

1.9 What is the concept of the value chain, and why is it important for cost management?

1.10 What is strategic decision making? Give examples of several strategic decisions.

1.11 How do organizations create and maintain competitive advantages?

1.12 What are cross-functional teams, and why are they important?

1.13 What are the eight steps of leading and managing change?

1.14 How do companies use benefit–cost analysis to make important decisions?

1.15 What is the value of ethical standards to individuals? To an organization? To society?

Critical Analysis

1.16 'Cost accounting and cost management really are the same functions and operations.' Do you agree or disagree? Explain.

1.17 The manager of a telecommunications company once commented, 'Not all future costs are relevant to business decisions, but costs are not relevant unless they occur in the future.' Is the manager correct? Explain.

1.18 Where to place the city's new shelter for homeless people has resulted in overwhelming recognition that a new shelter is needed but 'not in my neighbourhood'. As winter approaches, the director of the shelter and the publisher of the local newspaper have accused the city of 'analysis paralysis' as it continues meetings and hearings to find a suitable location. Can you suggest a feasible approach to making this difficult decision? Be as specific as you can.

1.19 With our high fixed costs, high variable costs, and competitive markets, there really is little we can do to increase our profits. Should you accept this argument without question? Explain.

1.20 Assume that you are a vice president of the largest department store in the region. The store president has called you in to give you a challenging assignment: 'Though we are the largest store, only 10 per cent of the region's residents are our customers. Find out why the other 90 per cent are not.' Why could this be a critically important assignment? How would you organize a team to find the answers?

1.21 Respond to the following statement: Benefit–cost analysis is completely different in non-profits because they have no profit to measure the value of alternatives.

1.22 Refer to Exhibit 1.5. How could Network Data determine whether it has a competitive advantage in new product development? What would it mean to employees of Network Data if it does or does not have an advantage?

1.23 'If every manager minimizes the cost of the process he or she supervises, overall costs of the company will decrease.' Do you think this would be a wise strategy? Why or why not?

1.24 Some years ago, **General Motors** installed industrial robots worth billions of dollars in its automobile assembly lines, believing that the robots would increase the efficiency of its manufacturing processes and improve profitability. In fact, General Motors lost many billions of dollars more despite the fact that it was able to make automobiles more quickly using the robots. What reasons can you think of to explain this paradox?

1.25 For many years, department stores prospered because they enhanced the process of shopping, which for many people was a break from the routine of housework and child care and was an opportunity to obtain information about available products and services. What changes have occurred in recent years that might explain the rise in shopping in 'virtual stores' via the Internet? What do these changes imply for the retail processes of traditional department stores?

1.26 'I understand the possible value of strategic planning, but I really consider it to be a luxury. I am doing all that I can just to keep the doors open and meet the next payroll.' What advice would you offer this harried CEO of a small manufacturing company?

1.27 One of your fellow classmates remarks, 'I thought this was an accounting class. If I wanted to study strategic decision making, I would take a management class. When do we get to crunch numbers?' How would you explain the importance to accounting students of understanding strategic decision making?

Exercises

Exercise 1.28 [LO 2] Decision Making

Consider the following decision-making problem and structure it using the framework presented in this chapter:

'I don't know where to begin. Right now, I feel that throwing a dart at a dartboard will give me just as much insight into how to make this decision as any other method. Can you help? I am paying my way through college using savings from my summer job. I get a small allowance from my parents, but they can't afford to send much. I find that I don't have enough money to pay my bills and have any left over for entertainment or new clothes. I am afraid that I will be broke before the year is over and have to drop out of school. I don't mind having to budget, but do I have to abandon any hope for a life, too?'

Exercise 1.29 [LO 2] Decision Making

Consider the following decision-making problem and structure it using the framework presented in this chapter:

'We employ 20 full-time internal auditors who review internal operations for quality and efficiency and do much of the compliance work prior to our annual audit by a Big 4 firm. The auditors report directly to me as the CFO. I know that many similar firms have outsourced the internal audit function to Big 4 firms or others that specialize in internal auditing. They do so primarily for cost savings, but I am concerned about loss of control, quality and sensitive information that might be leaked to competitors. We also use internal auditing as a management-training programme, where fast-track managers get wide exposure to all parts of the company. How do we get that training if we outsource internal auditing?'

Exercise 1.30 [LO 1] Cost Management Techniques

New Zealand recently transformed many of its government agencies into private corporations. This is a difficult process that many developing and former communist and socialist countries have been implementing. Match the following general techniques of cost management with the management decisions in these new corporations that were most likely to be assisted by using the techniques.

Cost management technique

a. Learning about how operations work
b. Organizing resources into efficient activities and operations
c. Measuring actual and expected costs of activities, products and services
d. Identifying profitable products, services, customers and distribution
e. Identifying opportunities for improvements in the value of products and services
f. Communicating effectively
g. Motivating and evaluating personnel

Management decision

— The design of incentive bonuses of up to 12 per cent of salary by **Electricity Corporations (ECNZ)** for middle managers based on meeting difficult profit goals
— The use of seminars called 'What If I Owned the Business?' by **Television Corporation (TVNZ)** to introduce staff to issues of competition
— ECNZ's decision to restructure into four major operating divisions: Production, Marketing, Power Transmission, and Construction
— The decision by **Coal Corporation (CoalCorp)** to evaluate every job currently performed to determine which is essential to the goal of profitability
— TVNZ's new focus on estimating the costs of television programming and production
— The decision by **Public Works Corporation (WORKS)** to sell its poorly performing Property and Computing Services divisions
— TVNZ's analysis of the programming and advertising practices of its new commercial rival, TV3.

[Adapted from Spicer et al., 1996.]

Exercise 1.31 [LO 1] Team Work

Select the decision-making team that most likely would be best for each of the following operations or decisions. Explain your choices.

Type of team

a. Individual (no team)
b. Small doubles tennis team whose members have special skills that complement each other's strengths and weaknesses
c. Large soccer team whose members have assignments but work closely together
d. Large swimming team whose members have individual responsibilities and normally do not interact but share in team outcomes

Operation or decision

— Word-processing centre of a large university where most of the work is preparing exams, copying articles, and preparing promotional materials
— Development of a new business curriculum to meet specific educational needs
— Design of advertising campaign to counter a rival's new product announcement
— Development of a new video game for **Nintendo Wii**
— Writing a new cost-management textbook
— Completion of a complex project with a short, rigid deadline
— Completion of an application to graduate school
— Competition in a collegiate intramural volleyball league

Exercise 1.32 [LO 2] Information Dimensions

Give an example of an information item at each extreme level for the following information dimensions.

	Example of information at	
Information dimensions	**Very high level**	**Very low level**
Subjectivity	?	?
Accuracy	?	?
Timeliness	?	?
Cost	?	?
Relevance	?	?

Exercise 1.33 [LO 3] Strategic Decision Making

Review the elements of strategic missions in Exhibit 1.2. Assume that you are managing a small business that sells coffee, espresso and possibly various other drinks in a university's engineering centre. Consider the possibility that the business mission could be any of the four basic types. First, for each mission, describe several decisions you must make. Second, try to arrange these decisions in roughly the order you must make them, from the earliest to the latest or ongoing decisions. Third, describe the information you will need to make these decisions.

Exercise 1.34 [LO 5] Internal Controls

One of the authors of this book has a favourite sandwich shop. After observing the sandwich shop's operations, this author observed that two employees were involved in every sandwich production and sale. The person who made the sandwich did not ring up the sale or take the money from the sale.

Required

a. What type of internal control does this example provide? Why is the shop manager/owner providing that internal control?
b. Is there an even better internal control?
c. Could the employees get around the current internal control?

Exercise 1.35 [LO 4] Benefit-Cost Analysis

Quantorus Corporation manufactures disk drives for computers by assembling parts and components from hundreds of suppliers. Cost management analysts have been analysing costs to produce disk drives and have determined that a large proportion of the cost is caused by detecting and replacing faulty components received from suppliers. Most faulty components currently cannot be detected until they are assembled into products that then fail performance tests. Following are estimated annual costs of three alternative decisions to manage this aspect of operations.

Alternatives for supply of disk drive components	Cost per year (thousands)
1. Continue current supply and assembly operations to detect and replace faulty components	€2,331
2. Thoroughly inspect incoming components before they are assembled	€1,708
3. Develop close relationships with a few selected suppliers that will guarantee the performance of all components	€1,387

Required

a. Describe and explain other possible costs and benefits of each alternative.
b. How do you think cost management analysts might have developed these cost estimates?
c. Which alternative do you recommend? Why?

Exercise 1.36 [LO 1] Strategic Decision Making and Cost Management

Find a recent article in a professional magazine, such as *Strategic Finance, Management Accounting (UK), Journal of Cost Management*, or *Harvard Business Review*, that describes accounting and finance support of strategic decision making at a specific organization.

Required

a. Prepare an outline of the article that identifies the following:
- The definition of *strategic decision making* used in this article
- The strategic 'problem' or opportunity that motivated the decision making
- Areas of operations where this organization focused its strategic efforts
- Sources of information to support this organization's strategic decision making
- Whether strategic decision making was a success, and how 'success' was defined and measured.

b. Present your own evaluation of the success of this strategic decision-making support.

Exercise 1.37 [LO 3] Value Chain Analysis

Match the following operations with appropriate elements of an organization's value chain.

Value chain element
a. Research and development
b. Design
c. Supply
d. Production
e. Marketing
f. Distribution
g. Customer service

Operation or decision
— **Dell Computer's** replies to customers' questions via Email
— Electronic ordering link between **Container Industries plc**, and a division of **DuPont Corp.** that supplies raw plastic pellets to Container Industries
— Purchase of McData Corp. by Brocade Inc. to acquire its data communications technology
— Pickup of **StorageTek Corp.'s** packaged disk drives by **United Parcel Service** for delivery to customers
— Development of animation for **Yahoo!** home pages
— **RCA's** outsourcing of the assembly of its portable CD players to a company in Mexico
— Updating **Canterbury New Zealand's** electronic Internet catalogue of sport and casual clothing

Exercise 1.38 [LO 4] Non-financial Factors

Consider the quantitative costs and benefits of two alternatives. What must be the value of the qualitative factors if the less profitable alternative is chosen?

Cost or benefit	Status quo	Alternative
Revenues	$50,000	$50,000
Costs	$30,000	$40,000
Quality	Medium	Very high
Meets production schedules	Medium	High

Problems

Problem 1.39 [LO 4] Benefit-Cost Analysis

Lillis Ltd is considering outsourcing its accounts receivable function, a support service in the finance department. Lillis's cost management analyst expects annual benefits that include personnel cost savings of £230,000, facilities savings of £100,000, other support service cost savings of £75,000, and no loss of service quality. The analyst also estimated annual costs of the decision to include the contract cost to DeGama Enterprises of £150,000, training costs of new personnel of £35,000, and contract administration costs of £15,000.

Required

a. Based on the quantifiable benefits and costs of the decision, would you recommend that Lillis outsource its accounts receivable function? What qualitative factors should Lillis also consider?

b. Lillis did outsource the accounts receivable function and measured actual benefits to include personnel cost savings of £170,000, facilities cost savings of £1,200,000, and support service cost savings of £100,000. Actual costs included £150,000 for the outsourced service, £40,000 for training costs, and £17,000 for contract administration. Furthermore, customer billing complaints were lower than in previous years; sales growth was lower; and employee turnover in other support service areas was higher. Prepare an analysis similar to the one in Exhibit 1.6.

c. On balance, do you agree with the outsourcing decision? Why or why not?

Problem 1.40 [LO 4] Benefit-Cost Analysis

Consider the following data on last year's accounting operations that were obtained by Clean Air Systems Inc. (CAS), from an industry trade association that gathers and reports data from all members of the association anonymously.

Accounting operation	CAS cost per year	CAS cost per transaction	Association cost per transaction
Accounts receivable	$50,000	$12.00	$8.00
General ledger	23,000	7.00	4.00
Accounts payable	35,000	9.00	5.00
Payroll	20,000	6.00	2.50
Credit and collections	9,000	11.00	6.00

Required

a. How many of each type of transaction did CAS perform that year?

b. In every case, the association average cost per transaction was less than CAS's cost. How might other companies operating in the same industry have lower accounting transaction costs?

c. If CAS could process accounts receivable transactions at the association's average cost, how much would it save each year at the same levels of transactions?

d. Security Detection Devices Corporation (SDDC) is a comparably sized competitor of CAS and has the same number of accounting transactions per year as CAS. SDDC, however, processes each accounting transaction for 20 per cent less than the association average. What total cost advantage does SDDC have over CAS just in the area of accounting costs per year? What is the importance to CAS of knowing this cost advantage?

e. Why do many companies compare their performance against their own industry and the best in the world?

Problem 1.41 [LO 4] Benefit-Cost Analysis and Outsourcing

ValOil Corporation is a large oil and gas producer headquartered in Norway. Historically, most of its operations have been on the Norwegian Continental Shelf. However, in the past decade, ValOil expanded its operations to 14 foreign locations where it operates alone or in conjunction with foreign companies or governments. ValOil currently maintains a large department of 73 highly trained tax specialists who report to the chief financial officer and assist in planning the tax impacts of management decisions for domestic and foreign operations. The tax department also prepares its many, complex tax returns. ValOil is considering eliminating its internal tax department and outsourcing all of its tax planning and tax return preparation to a large international business services firm. A cost management team has prepared the following preliminary calculations:

ValOil tax operation	Current costs (in kroner)
Information systems	4,200,000kr
Tax planning	7,800,000
Tax return preparation	15,000,000

Required

a. What is the most that ValOil Corporation should pay for tax services from an external provider if all but the information systems costs could be saved?

b. What considerations in addition to cost should be important to ValOil's decision to outsource its tax services?

c. Evaluate a business services company's offer to provide tax planning and return preparation services for 21 million kr per year. This offer is contingent, however, on ValOil's acceptance of another offer from the business services company to improve ValOil's tax information systems at a one-time cost of 12 million kr. This improvement should reduce annual costs of the information system by 2.4 million kr per year for the next five years and greatly improve the accuracy and responsiveness of the system. (Ignore the time value of money.)

Problem 1.42 [LO 4] Cost Reduction

MicroStorage Technology (MST) is developing a new touch-screen mobile device.

Required

a. Given the following information, compute MST's cost-reduction target.

Expected market price	$200
Required return on sales	25%
Product life	2 years
Currently feasible cost	$30,000,000
Expected average annual sales, units	75,000

b. If MST believes it can reduce the cost of the device by no more than 18 per cent, is this a feasible product for MST? Why or why not?

Problem 1.43 [LO 4] Cost Reduction

Misericórdia Hospital is a private hospital in Brasilia, Brazil that serves an ageing population. The hospital administrator, Maria Palmeira, believes that insurance companies and government-provided health care will move to fixed payments for specific procedures, which will put increasing pressure on hospitals to control costs. A common procedure performed at Misericórdia Hospital is hip-replacement surgery. Palmeira has asked the hospital's CFO to prepare information on the current costs of hip replacements at Misericórdia so that they can explore the financial viability of this (and other) procedures. Consider the following information gathered by the CFO (monetary units given in Brazilian reais, R$):

Expected charge reimbursement (sales price)	R$60,000
Required return on charges (return on sales)*	30%
Current average cost per hip replacement	R$54,000

*To cover profit goals and other support service costs.

Required

a. Build a spreadsheet to analyse whether hip-replacement surgeries are financially viable.

b. A cross-functional team of administrators, surgeons, nurses and support personnel analysed the hospital's hip-replacement procedure and estimated that, through better scheduling and post-operative care, Misericórdia could reduce hospital stays from an average of nine days to five days with no loss of quality of care. In fact, because elderly patients would be hospitalized for shorter periods, they would be less likely to contract respiratory infections. Improvements in the procedure can result in a reduction of the average cost of a hip replacement by R$20,000. If this were accomplished, what is the expected return on charges for a hip replacement? Build a spreadsheet to analyse this question.

[Adapted from Evans et al., 1997]

Problem 1.44 [LO 2] Decision Making

Obtain a copy of the article 'The environmental impacts of genetically modified plants: challenges to decision making', by Sandra Batie, *American Journal of Agricultural Economics,* vol. 85, no. 5 (2003) 1107–1111. Work in small groups to develop a 15-minute presentation that completes the following requirements.

Required

a. Using the decision-making framework presented in Exhibit 1.1, describe decision making about the management of genetically modified plants.

b. Describe the major risk factors that create uncertainty about decision making with regard to genetically modified plants.

c. (Optional) Provide an update of decision making about genetically modified plants incorporating more recent developments.

Problem 1.45 [LO 2] Decision Making

Obtain a copy of the article 'Unlocking the benefits of world trade' by Jeffrey Schott, *The Economist,* 1 November 2003. Work in small groups to develop a 15-minute presentation that completes the following requirements.

Required

a. Use the decision-making framework presented in Exhibit 1.1 to describe the reported decision making at the global trade talks in Cancun, Mexico, in September 2003.

b. Describe the major factors that impeded decision making at the Cancun talks.

c. Describe how you would measure costs and benefits of alternative decisions, such as elimination of agricultural subsidies or tariffs on manufactured clothing.

d. Summarize the status of decision making at the end of the Cancun talks.

e. (Optional) Provide an update of decision making for global trade, incorporating more recent developments.

Problem 1.46 [LO 5] Ethical Issue

Paul Richards recently joined Toxic CIC as assistant controller. Toxic processes chemicals to use in fertilizers. During his first month on the job, Richards spent most of his time getting better acquainted with those responsible for plant operations. In response to his questions as to the procedure for disposing of chemicals, the plant supervisor responded that Richards was not involved in the disposal of waste and would be wise to ignore the issue. Of course, this just drove him to investigate the matter further. He soon discovered that Toxic was dumping toxic waste in a nearby public landfill late at night. He also learned that several members of management appeared to be involved in arranging for this dumping. He was unable, however, to determine whether his superior, the controller, was involved. Richards considered three possible courses of action. He could discuss the matter with the controller, anonymously release the information to the local newspaper, or discuss the situation with an outside member of the board of directors whom he knows personally.

Required

a. Does Richards have an ethical responsibility to take a course of action? Why or why not?
b. What course of action do you recommend? Why?

[CMA adapted]

Problem 1.47 [LO 5] Ethical Issue: Fraud

Your friend works for a large company. She confides in you about a problem with her boss, who is asking customers to sign a sales agreement just before the end of the year, indicating that a sale has been made. Her boss then tells these customers that they will have 30 days to change their minds with no penalty. Thirty days is well into the next year. If they do not change their minds, then her boss sends the merchandise to them. If they change their minds, her boss agrees to cancel the orders, take back the merchandise, and cancel the invoices. Her boss gives the sales agreements to the accounting department, which prepares an invoice and records the sales. One of the people in accounting keeps the invoices and shipping documents for these customers in a desk drawer until either the customers change their minds, in which case the sale is cancelled, or the merchandise is sent at the end of the 30-day waiting period.

Your friend likes the company, and she wants to keep her job. What would you advise her to do?

Problem 1.48 [LO 4] Benefit-Cost Analysis: Internal Order

Marseille Division is part of a large corporation. It normally sells to outside customers but, on occasion, sells to another division of its corporation. When it sells internally, corporate policy states that the price must be cost plus 25 per cent. Marseille received an order from Lyon Division for 4,000 units. Marseille's planned output for the year had been 23,000 units before Lyon's order, but its capacity is 30,000 units per year. The costs for producing the planned 23,000 units follow:

	Total	Per unit
Materials	€30,000	€1.30
Labour	€120,000	€5.22
Other manufacturing costs	€85,000	€3.70
Total costs	€235,000	€10.22

Based on these data, Marseille's controller, who was new to the corporation, calculated that the unit price for Lyon's order should be €12.77 (€10.22 × 125 per cent, rounded). After producing and shipping the 4,000 units, Marseille sent Lyon an invoice for €51,080. Shortly thereafter, Marseille received a note from Lyon's buyer stating that this invoice was not in accordance with company policy. Because Andover would incur the labour and 'other' costs regardless of whether it accepted Lyon's order, the unit cost should have been only €1.30 to cover Marseille's materials costs. The price paid would be €1.63 (€1.30 × 125 per cent, rounded) per unit, and the total payment to Marseille should be €6,522.

Required

(*Note:* These questions do not require quantitative answers.)

a. What are the costs and benefits of internally 'sourcing' products and services? Which can be quantified and which cannot?
b. If the corporation asked you to review the current intercompany policy, what policy would you recommend? Why? (*Note:* You need not limit yourself to Lyon Division's calculation or to current policy.)

Problem 1.49 [LO 4] Benefit-Cost Analysis: Add a Product Line

Aroma Caffè Ss operates a small coffee shop in the downtown area. Its profits have been declining, and management is planning to expand and add gelato to the menu. The annual gelato sales are expected to increase revenue by €30,000. The cost to purchase ice cream and cones from the manufacturer is €15,000. The present manager will supervise the coffee shop and gelato shop. Due to expansion, however, the labour costs and utilities would increase by 30 per cent. Rent and other costs will increase by 25 per cent.

AROMA Caffè Ss Annual income statement before expansion	
Sales revenue	€60,000
Costs	
Food	15,000
Labour	14,000
Utilities	4,000
Rent	5,000
Other costs	2,000
Manager's salary	24,000
Total costs	€64,000
Operating profit (loss)	€(4,000)

Required

a. Build a spreadsheet to analyse whether management should open the gelato shop. Show an analysis of the costs and benefits of adding gelato.

b. Build a spreadsheet to solve requirement to analyse the decision to expand if you learn that the large chain Grom will open a gelato franchise down the road. Aroma's gelato sales could drop by one-third. Use the following hints.

Hint 1: Follow these steps to build a flexible spreadsheet (also see Chapter 7):

1. Place all facts, assumptions, and estimates in a 'data input' section of the spreadsheet. For example, place each number used in the spreadsheet in a separate, labelled cell. This is the only place you should enter any numbers.
2. Write the relations among the spreadsheet's numbers (or 'parameters') as algebraic formulas using the numbers' cell addresses (not the numbers themselves) in a separate section of the spreadsheet. For example, expected total revenues could be calculated with a formula containing the cell addresses of current revenue 1 expected revenue from the expansion (e.g., 5 B3 1 C3).
3. Steps 1 and 2 allow the spreadsheet to easily and flexibly reflect any changes you make in the parameters, such as the expected sales level, which appear only in the data input section.

Hint 2: You must make assumptions about how the possible drop in gelato sales will affect revenues and costs. Make these assumptions explicit in the data input section and in the formulas. For example, enter the possible drop in sales, 21/3, in the data input section and use that number in any formulas related to sales.

Problem 1.50 [LO 4] Benefit-Cost Analysis: Add a Project

Change Management plc is a consulting firm that helps companies adapt organizational structures to current industry trends. Recently, one of its officers was approached by a representative of a high-tech research firm that offered a six-month contract to Change Management for some help in reorganizing the company. Change Management reported the following costs and revenues during the past year.

CHANGE MANAGEMENT plc Annual income statement	
Sales revenue	£1,750,000
Costs	
Labour	650,000
Equipment lease	105,000
Rent	130,000

Supplies	70,000
Officers' salaries	420,000
Other costs	48,000
Total costs	£1,423,000
Operating profit	£327,000

If Change Management decides to take the six-month contract to help the company reorganize, it will hire two part-time consultants at £180,000 (salaries and benefits) and add support staff at a cost of £45,000. Equipment lease will increase by 12 per cent because the company must buy certain computer equipment. Supplies and other costs will increase by an estimated 15 per cent. The existing building has space for the new consultant. In addition, management believes that no new officers will be necessary for this work and that officers' salaries will not change.

Required

a. What costs would be incurred as a result of taking the contract?
b. If the contract will pay £250,000 for the six months, should Change Management accept it?
c. What considerations, other than costs, are necessary before making this decision?

Cases

Case 1.51 [LO 1, 4] Analyse a Strategic Decision

You have recently been hired as a new cost management analyst by Corporate Express, the world's largest supplier of office supplies to large corporations. Corporate Express takes orders from its customers via the Internet, processes those orders with office supply manufacturers, and delivers the supplies to the corporate employees who ordered them. Corporate Express's customers do not need to hire anyone whose job is to order, receive or distribute supplies, nor do customers need supplies inventories or warehouses. Large customers (such as **Coca-Cola** and **Hewlett-Packard**) save millions of dollars per year by outsourcing their office supply tasks to Corporate Express.

The vice president of marketing is concerned that the company's policy to serve only large companies does not fit its strategic goals. She believes it might be worthwhile to offer limited services to small, rapidly growing businesses because they could graduate to the full line of services offered to large companies. As a first step, the VP has asked you to analyse the costs and benefits of serving small and large customers.

You have developed the following information:

Annual average data	One large company	One small company
Number of orders per year	3,000	300
Sales value of supplies per order in euros	€1,000	€700
Cost of supplies to Corporate Express as a percentage of sales	80%	75%
Processing cost per order	€30	€30
Delivery cost per order as a percentage of sales	8%	8%
Cost to create and maintain Internet access per customer per year	€2,500	€2,500

Required

a. Build a spreadsheet to compute the annual profit generated from an average large or small company.
b. Build a spreadsheet to analyse whether it would be worthwhile to add 10 small customers to replace one large customer. Why or why not? What would your recommendation be if the sales value of supplies per order of a typical small customer increased to €750? to €800? Explain.

c. If other characteristics of small firms differ from those of large ones, would this change your evaluation? Give an example.

d. Do you recommend that Corporate Express consider this business alternative further?

Case 1.52 [LO 1, 4] Analyse Support Services in the Value Chain

Many companies use the services of *internal auditors*, who perform various investigative and consulting tasks within organizations, such as reviewing divisional financial statements and making recommendations to improve operating performance (e.g., improving quality and customer service). In the past, this has provided both career paths for professional internal auditors and valuable training for new managers, who benefit from seeing firsthand many of the company's operations. In recent years, however, many companies have begun to outsource their internal auditing services.

Consider this recent discussion between the new chief financial officer (CFO) and the long-time director of internal auditing (DIA) at Jeans 'R Us, a large manufacturer of casual and fashion denim clothing, which has experienced serious declines in profitability.

CFO: We need to look very hard at all of our support services and consider whether we can afford them. We need to talk seriously because I think that outsourcing internal auditing will save the company millions of dollars. In our current situation, we need to save costs wherever we can.

DIA: I think you are being short-sighted. I believe our staff can provide the best possible service to management because it understands our business. An external provider of internal audit services just will not appreciate the unique aspects of our business and our culture.

CFO: I understand that internal audit has had a long tradition here, but based on our budget constraints, I think we have no choice but to use an outside service. The service provider we are considering has a worldwide staff with wide-ranging expertise that we can utilize. You know that many of our manufacturing plants are foreign operations and require the auditors to be fluent in speaking and writing the local language and to understand the local culture. Furthermore, all of our data communications rely on information technology that changes every year. To keep internal auditing staff with these talents at Jeans 'R Us will just be too costly. And what about all of the travel expenses in the internal audit department?

DIA: I'm sorry, but you don't appreciate that internal audit is a strength of the company that has been built over the years by a trust between the internal auditors and the operational and financial management. You cannot replace that level of trust and understanding with outsourced internal auditors whose only loyalty is to the fee they will collect. Internal audit is a 'partner' promoting valuable improvements, and top management has always supported it in that way. If you outsource internal audit, you will change the climate of co-operation and trust and free flow of information that you need. In the long run, you will end up paying a lot more for inferior service. Outsourcing internal audit will be a serious mistake. If you insist on this approach, I will go straight to the board of directors. By the way, you know that internal audit reports to the board each year on whether it can rely on the company's financial statements.

Required

a. Describe the possible costs and benefits of outsourcing internal auditing at Jeans 'R Us.

b. What pressures are motivating the arguments of both the CFO and the DIA?

c. How do you interpret the DIA's last comment?

d. Can you recommend a course of action that might satisfy the CFO, DIA and board of directors?

Case 1.53 [LO 1, 3] Cost Management Support of Strategy

Interview with Jamie O'Connell, president, CEO, and cofounder of Datacom Inc., a leading designer and manufacturer of storage area network (SAN) switching devices.[20]

Author: How did you decide to drop other products and direct Datacom's resources toward the design and manufacture of these behind-the-scenes network switches? This was a major strategic decision, wasn't it?

O'Connell: This was a huge decision. We have staked the future of the company on it, but let's be clear about strategic decision making at Datacom. Before we made this decision, we – and I do mean all of us at Datacom – spent months understanding our strengths and weaknesses, our competitors' strengths and weaknesses, our customers' future needs, our business partners, and the future of data-network technology. *I* did not make this decision, *we* made the decision to focus on these very important, high-value switches.

Author: Is it really possible to involve everyone? Can you trust everyone with the responsibility of this kind of decision?

O'Connell: Yes and yes. Of course it takes time, but who knows our capabilities and customers better than our own employees? And anyone who won't take responsibility for shaping the future of this company should look for another job. In this competitive and dynamic industry, we need the help and input of everyone. This decision affects every employee, shareholder, business partner, their families, and the community. True, the ultimate decision was up to the board of directors and me, but we could not and did not make this decision in a vacuum. That would have been irresponsible.

Author: Can you talk a bit about the role of cost management personnel and the information that supported this decision?

O'Connell: One of the great strengths of our company is a finance group that understands the company's business and technology. I think that is essential in a technology-driven company of our size. Not only that, they truly understand cost management and how to effectively support our strategic decision making. These are not your typical green eyeshade bean counters. The CFO, in particular, brings what I call the 'reality of finance' to our analysis of the future of data-storage technology. Most of us are engineers by background, and we tend to focus on the technology more than the business. We would not have made our decision to focus on SAN switches so confidently and responsibly without the daily use of cost management insight and information. We might not have predicted the future of technology and the market perfectly, but we understood beforehand, as well as we could, our alternatives and their impacts on this company and its stakeholders. This was vital, strategic information. Without it, we might as well be playing the lottery with the company's resources. Current events are proving that we chose correctly, and we are positioned to be worldwide leaders in this rapidly growing market.

Required

a. CEO O'Connell of Datacom Inc. referred to various elements of making strategic decisions. How can cost management information support each of these elements?

b. What quantitative and non-quantitative costs and benefits might be relevant to Datacom's strategic decisions?

c. How can organizations choose which processes to perform and which to outsource to business partners?

Case 1.54 [LO 5] Responsibility for Unethical Action

The following story is true except that all names have been changed and the time period has been compressed. Charles Austin graduated from a prestigious business school and took a job with a public accounting firm in Atlanta. After five years of normal progress through the ranks of the accounting firm, a client hired him. This client was a rapidly growing company that produced software for the health care industry. Charles started as assistant controller and was promoted to controller after four years – a timely promotion. Charles had learned a lot and was prepared to be controller.

Within a few months of his promotion to controller, the company's chief financial officer (CFO) abruptly quit. Upon submitting her resignation, she walked into Charles's office and said, 'I have given Holmes (the company president) my letter of resignation. I'll be out of my office in less than an hour. You will be the new chief financial officer, and you will report directly to Holmes. Here is my card with my personal cell phone number. Call me if you need any advice or if I can help you in any way.'

Charles was in over his head in his new job. His experience had not prepared him for the range of responsibilities required of the company's CFO. Mr Holmes, the company president, was no help. He gave Charles only one piece of advice: 'You have lots of freedom to run the Finance Department however you want. There is just one rule: don't ever cross me. If you do, you'll never work again in this city.' Charles believed his boss could follow through on that threat because he was so well connected in the Atlanta business community.

The end of the company's fiscal year came shortly after Charles's promotion to CFO. After reviewing some preliminary financial amounts, Mr Holmes stormed into Charles's office and made it clear that the results were not to his liking. He instructed Charles to 'find more sales'. Charles was shocked, but he did as he was told. He identified some ongoing software installation work that should not have been recorded as revenue until the customer signed off on the job. Charles recorded as revenue the work done as of year-end, even though the customer had not signed off on the job. He sent an invoice to the customer for the amount of the improper revenue, and then called her to say that the invoice was an accounting error and she should ignore it.

Next year, Charles's work life was better, but his personal life was not. He went through a costly divorce that resulted in limited time spent with his two small children. Now he was particularly concerned about not crossing his boss because of the threat that if he did, he would never again work in Atlanta. He could not bear to look for a new job that would take him away from his children. Furthermore, it would be difficult to find a job anywhere that came close to paying the salary and benefits that his current job did. With high alimony and child support payments, Charles would feel a dire financial strain if he had to take a cut in pay.

The company struggled financially during the year. Clearly, the company would not generate the level of revenues and income that Holmes wanted. As expected, he again instructed Charles to find some way to 'dress up' the income statement. It did not matter to Holmes whether what Charles did was legal or not.

Charles had exhausted all legitimate ways of reducing costs and increasing revenues. He faced an ethical dilemma. He could resign and look for a new job, or he could illegitimately record non-existent sales. He now understood why the former CFO had resigned so abruptly. He wished that he could talk to her, but she was travelling in Australia and could not be contacted. The board of directors would be no help because members would take the president's side in a dispute.

After considering his personal circumstances, Charles decided to record the illegitimate sales as the president had instructed. Charles knew that what he did was wrong. He believed that if the fraud was discovered, Holmes, not he, would be in trouble. After all, Charles rationalized, he was just following orders.

Required

a. Can you justify what Charles did?

b. What could Charles have done to avoid the ethical dilemma that he faced? Assume that the company president could have made it impossible for Charles to work in Atlanta in a comparable job.

c. What if the Securities and Exchange Commission discovered this fraud? Would Charles's boss get in trouble? Would Charles?

Solutions to You're the Decision Maker

1.1 Benefit-Cost Analysis of Introducing a New Product, p. 22

a. Probably the best decision-making environment exists when cost management analysts clearly communicate the confidence they have in their measurements and team members discuss the importance of all costs and benefits. Identifying quantified and non-quantified costs and benefits is a good first step. The next step is to use your preliminary analysis to begin a discussion within the team about the reasonableness of the estimates and whether the non-quantified items are important. Starting with a preliminary analysis usually is better than starting a team meeting with a 'blank sheet'. On the other hand, you need to be careful because some team members who are less quantitatively inclined might not think to challenge your preliminary figures or ask 'what if' questions but could treat these estimates as the unshakeable truth. Although the estimates might be reasonable first guesses, they could be quite inaccurate. All team members need to challenge and ultimately feel comfortable with what the numbers do and do not say.

b. Not all costs and benefits can be measured easily or with enough accuracy to justify attaching dollar values to them. Some cost management analysts believe that people pay attention only to measurable costs and benefits, so they might argue the value of trying to measure all of them. On the other hand, others believe

that attaching highly inaccurate dollar figures to some costs or benefits reduces the confidence that managers have in all numbers. Therefore, some non-quantified or qualitative costs or benefits might be more important than the quantified ones and can lead to proper decisions that contradict the numbers.

Measures of the future costs and benefits will be somewhat subjective because the future is uncertain, and specific measures depend on assumptions about future changes (organizational structure, market demand, technological change, etc.). Organizations usually rely on accountants, financial analysts or cost management analysts to develop these measures. They base their measures on their understanding of the way the organization has acquired and used resources in the past and the way changes will affect the resources needed. They rely on information from their own organization and from sources outside that help them predict the effects of changes. This is a complex topic that is covered in more detail in subsequent chapters of this text.

c. Everything really is connected. For example, the accelerated development and production schedule might have caused lower quality because critical steps were skipped or abbreviated. Lower product quality probably is responsible for lower customer satisfaction and a resulting loss of current sales. Importantly, Network Data might lose future sales opportunities, making the company more vulnerable to competitors. Loss of good customers can outweigh the net benefits getting products to market quickly.

d. Outsourcing and downsizing decisions often result in costs that the organization might not recognize. If reassigned employees need training, they will not be fully productive for some time. These costs must be considered. Most large organizations have formal severance policies that specify the terms of dismissal (e.g., notice, pay, benefits). The organization usually is legally obligated to live up to these terms. Do organizations have ethical obligations that extend beyond their legal obligations? One point of view is that employees joined the organization knowing what its severance policy is and should not expect more than it specifies. In fact, if managers give more, they might be betraying their responsibility to owners and other contributors because they are the ones paying the cost of the additional severance benefits, perhaps unknowingly. Another view is that, depending on the economic climate and the availability of jobs, the organization might 'owe' loyal employees assistance in finding other employment. A more pragmatic perspective is that the organization can enhance its reputation with potential employees and reduce morale problems with retained employees by treating its dismissed employees generously. Thus, it could be in the best interests of the organization (and its owners) to provide more than the contractually agreed-on severance benefits.

1.2 Ethical Considerations, p. 26

a. This person sounds like trouble with a capital 'T'. First, he or she appears to be offering proprietary information. Accepting it would be the same as accepting a stolen stereo or worse. Second, why would you ever consider hiring such an unethical, mercenary person? You should expect the same behaviour in the future. Most certainly, you should not call this person but should call your company's security department to remove the information from your porch immediately. Consider whether you should identify whom you believe left the information because you might expose yourself to legal actions if that person is involved in a crime.

b. Competitive intelligence (CI) is a growing activity and field of work. At one end of the spectrum is theft of proprietary information or illegal corporate espionage. The other end is legal but uninteresting rehashing of readily available public information. Neither of the extremes is worth purchasing. In between can lie insightful gathering and analyses of public but obscure information that can be quite valuable and difficult for most organizations to duplicate. After assuring yourself of the legality of the company's practices and conferring with your co-executives, you might well consider this trial offer by giving the CI company specific objectives for its information and analysis activities.

c. If the manager is asking you to bury the pessimistic analysis until the project has been approved, you clearly would be acting unethically. Instead, you should report all relevant analyses and indicate the likelihood of both good and bad news. On the other hand, if the manager is asking for deferral of the decision until you can analyse more information, you might want to consider this to prevent a mistaken denial of a good project. You and other executives must balance the value of waiting for more information against the value of acting now.

Endnotes

1 The firm's founders and employees own 90 per cent of the corporation's share. An investment firm that specializes in supporting small, high-technology companies owns the other 10 per cent. The current owners hope to publicly sell shares of the firm in the next several years to obtain additional capital for the firm and liquidity for the owners.

2 Customers demonstrate value by the prices they are willing to pay, see Anderson et al. (2010). Constituents of non-profit organizations express value by supporting preferred organizations with donations of money, time and other resources. Constituents of government organizations express value preferences by voting, lobbying or supporting political candidates.

3 Readers should know that cost management fits within the larger scope of *management control systems*, which can be defined as 'anything that management does to control, direct, or evaluate the organization's people and activities'. Several excellent management control systems texts exist, but these do not provide detailed coverage of cost management.

4 A modern coverage of decision making is found in Kleindorfer et al. (1993); and Gilboa (2011).

5 This framework is adapted from Kleindorfer et al. (1993), Simon (1993) and Shank (1989).

6 In the semiconductor industry, technology roadmaps and cost-of-ownership calculations are used to co-ordinate investments in the industry; see Miller and O'Leary (2007). This involves firms that develop and manufacture products (e.g., computers, phones, cameras), components (e.g., microprocessors, memory), equipment (such as lithographic equipment), and subsystems (such as lenses and lasers), but also universities, government agencies, national laboratories and science foundations.

7 People are often more inclined to continue a course of action if they have already spent more resources on it. For example, they may want to continue the project just because they have already spent so much money. This is called 'escalation of commitment', see Tan and Yates (2002). The right question to ask is: will continuing in the future bring in more than the investments that still need to be made?

8 Eisenhardt (1999).

9 For a scholarly discussion of these points, see Hendry (2000).

10 Porter (1985).

11 Chapter 7 contains a cost–benefit analysis of an outsourcing decision.

12 This process is adapted from Kotter (1995).

13 Brown and Eisenhardt (1998).

14 Chapter 5 explains a few principles of target costing.

15 This is also called 'bounded ethicality', see Kern and Chugh (2009); Tenbrunsel et al. (2010).

16 Author's confidential interview with an attorney formerly employed as a prosecutor for the US Department of Justice.

17 See Lubin and Esty (2010).

18 See Lamberton (2005) for more information.

19 See O'Dwyer et al. (2011).

20 Datacom is the disguised name of a real company with approximately 200 employees and $200 million sales. SANs are high-capacity, high-speed configurations of date-storage devices, such as disk drives, that are accessible to computer networks through Datacom's fibre-optic switches.

References

Anderson, J.C., M. Wouters and W. van Rossum (2010) 'Why the highest price isn't the best price', *MIT Sloan Management Review,* Winter, pp. 69–76.

Batie, S. (2003) 'The environmental impacts of genetically modified plants: challenges to decision making', *American Journal of Agricultural Economics*, vol. 55, no 5, pp. 1107–1111.

Brown, S.L., and K.M. Eisenhardt (1998) *Competing on the Edge: Strategy as Structured Chaos*, Harvard Business School Press, Boston, MA.

Cooper, P. (2006) 'Adapting management accounting knowledge needs to functional and economic change', *Accounting Education*, vol. 13, no. 3, pp. 287–300.

Davila, T., and M. Wouters (2004) 'Designing cost-competitive technology products: improving product development through cost management', *Accounting Horizons*, vol. 18, no. 1, pp. 13–26.

Ding, R., H.C. Dekker and T. Groot (2010) 'An exploration of the use of interfirm cooperation and the financial manager's governance roles: evidence from Dutch firms', *Journal of Accounting & Organizational Change*, vol. 6, no. 1, pp. 9–26.

Drucker, P. (1995) *Managing in a Time of Great Change,* Dutton, New York.

Eisenhardt, K.M. (1999) 'Strategy as strategic decision making', *Sloan Management Review*, Spring, pp. 65–72.

Eppinger, S.D., and A.R. Chitkara (2006) 'The new practice of global product development', *MIT Sloan Management Review,* Summer, pp. 22–30.

Evans, J., Y. Hwang and N. Nagarajan (1997) 'Cost reduction and process reengineering in hospitals', *Journal of Cost Management*, vol. 11, no. 3, pp. 20–27.

Garg, A., D. Ghosh, J. Hudick and C. Nowacki (2003) 'Roles and practices in management accounting today. Results from the 2003 IMA-E&Y survey', *Strategic Finance,* July, pp. 1–6.

Gilboa, I. (2011) *Making Better Decisions: Decision Theory in Practice*, John Wiley & Sons, Chichester.

Groysberg, B., L.K. Kelly and B. MacDonald (2011) 'The new path to the C-Suite', *Harvard Business Review,* March, pp. 60–68.

Hendry, J. (2000) 'Strategic decision making, discourse, and strategy as social practice', *Journal of Management Studies,* vol. 37, no. 7, pp. 955–977.

Heracleous, L., and J. Wirtz (2010) 'Singapore Airlines' balancing act', *Harvard Business Review,* July–August, pp. 145–149.

Kern, M.C., and D. Chugh (2009) 'Bounded ethicality', *Psychological Science*, vol. 20, no. 3, pp. 378–384.

Khanna, T., and K.G. Palepu (2006) 'Emerging giants', *Harvard Business Review,* October, pp. 60–69.

Kleindorfer, P., H. Kunreuther and P. Schoemaker (1993) *Decision Sciences: An Integrative Approach*, Cambridge University Press, Cambridge.

Kotter, J.P. (1995) 'Why transformation efforts fail', *Harvard Business Review*, March–April, pp. 59–67.

Lamberton, G. (2005) 'Sustainability accounting – a brief history and conceptual framework', *Accounting Forum*, vol. 29, pp. 7–26.

Lubin, D.A., and D.C. Esty (2010) 'The sustainability imperative', *Harvard Business Review*, May, pp. 42–50.

Miller, P., and T. O'Leary (2007) 'Mediating instruments and making markets: capital budgeting, science and the economy', *Accounting, Organizations and Society*, vol. 32, pp. 701–734.

O'Dwyer, B., Owen, D and Uneman, J. (2011) 'Seeking Legitimacy for New Assurance forms: The case of Assurance on Sustainability Reporting' (January 18). Accounting, Organization and Society, available of SSRN: http://ssrn.com/abstract=1742822

Porter, M. (1985) *Competitive Advantage*, The Free Press, New York.

Raman, A.P. (2009) 'The new frontiers', *Harvard Business Review*, July–August, pp. 130–137.

Schott, J. (2003) 'Unlocking the benefits of world trade', *The Economist*, 1 November.

Shank, J. (1989) 'Strategic cost management: new wine or just new bottles?' *Journal of Management Accounting Research*, vol. 1, pp. 47–65.

Siegel, G., J.E. Sorensen and S.B. Richtermayer (2006a) 'Are you a business partner?' *Strategic Finance,* September, pp. 1–5.

Siegel, G., J.E. Sorensen and S.B. Richtermayer (2006b) 'Becoming a business partner', *Strategic Finance,* October, pp. 1–5.

Simon, H. (1993) 'Strategy and organizational evolution', *Strategic Management Journal*, vol. 14, pp. 131–142.

Spicer, B., D. Emanuel and M. Powell (1996) *Transforming Government Enterprises: Managing Radical Organisational Change in Deregulated Environments*, Centre for Independent Studies, St Leonards, Australia.

Tan, H.-T., and J.F. Yates (2002) 'Financial budgets and escalation effects', *Organizational Behavior and Human Decision Processes*, vol. 87, no. 2, pp. 300–322.

Tenbrunsel, A.E., K.A. Diekmann, K.A. Wade-Benzoni and M.H. Bazerman (2010) 'The ethical mirage: a temporal explanation as to why we are not as ethical as we think we are', *Research in Organizational Behavior*, vol. 30, pp. 153–173.

Widener, S., and F. Selto (1999) 'Management control systems and boundaries of the firm', *Journal of Management Accounting Research*, vol. 11, pp. 45–74.

CHAPTER 2

Product Costing Concepts and Systems

Learning Objectives

After completing this chapter, you should be able to:

LO 1 Understand and apply the concepts of cost and opportunity cost.

LO 2 Understand and explain the concept and measurement of out-of-pocket or cash cost.

LO 3 Understand and explain variable cost, committed cost, fixed cost, sunk cost and the accounting or accrual cost.

LO 4 Understand and explain product cost, period cost, expense, direct cost and indirect cost.

LO 5 Analyse the product costs of typical manufacturing, retail and service firms for decision making and evaluations.

LO 6 Prepare a schedule of cost of goods manufactured and sold using a flexible financial model.

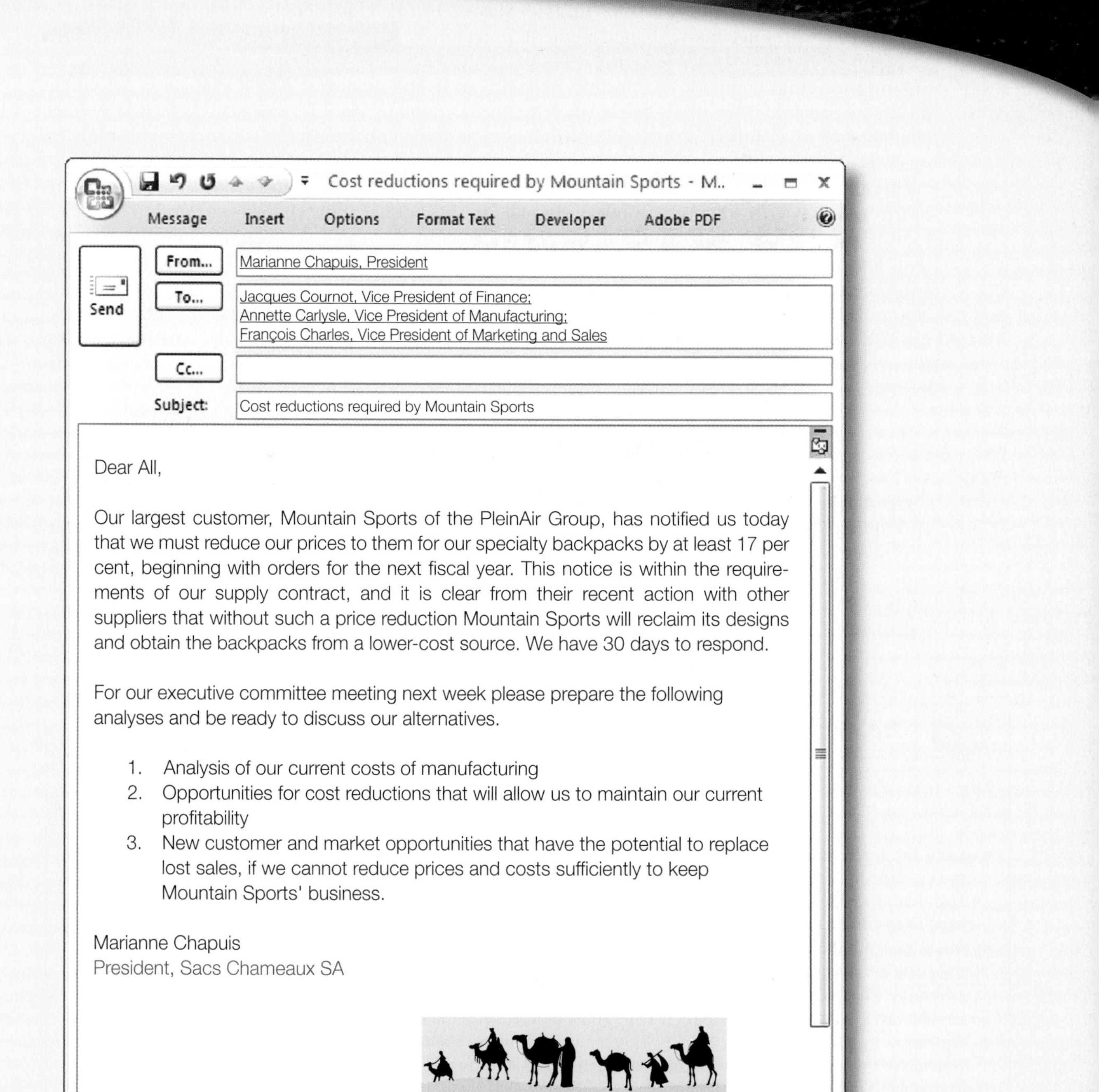

Dear All,

Our largest customer, Mountain Sports of the PleinAir Group, has notified us today that we must reduce our prices to them for our specialty backpacks by at least 17 per cent, beginning with orders for the next fiscal year. This notice is within the requirements of our supply contract, and it is clear from their recent action with other suppliers that without such a price reduction Mountain Sports will reclaim its designs and obtain the backpacks from a lower-cost source. We have 30 days to respond.

For our executive committee meeting next week please prepare the following analyses and be ready to discuss our alternatives.

1. Analysis of our current costs of manufacturing
2. Opportunities for cost reductions that will allow us to maintain our current profitability
3. New customer and market opportunities that have the potential to replace lost sales, if we cannot reduce prices and costs sufficiently to keep Mountain Sports' business.

Marianne Chapuis
President, Sacs Chameaux SA

Cost Management and Cost Concepts

Information technology and open markets create worldwide competition. All organizations must learn to produce high-quality goods and services, and to do so either at the lowest possible cost or in a distinctive way that others cannot imitate. Success in this global environment demands that a company has an effective cost management programme. Cost management helps organizations compete by identifying and validating ways to create more value for customers at lower cost. An organization finds competitive solutions by configuring and managing its value chain of activities, processes and functions more efficiently. Our focus company, Sacs Chameaux SA, faces a serious challenge to its viability, and we will introduce how the company uses cost management tools to meet its cost-reduction challenge.

Recall that the basic cost management goal is to create more value at lower cost. The second part of this goal (lower cost) concerns many chapters in this book. In this chapter we develop the basic tools to measure cost, which after all must be done before one can assess whether business alternatives lower or increase costs from the status quo. Some costs are relatively easily traced to products or processes; we will call these **direct costs**, and they typically include (direct) materials and labour. Other costs may be needed to build and deliver a product to customers, but they are more difficult or are impossible to trace to products and processes; we will call these **indirect costs** (or overhead or **burden**). Indirect costs are often common infrastructure or support costs such as building rent or supervisory salaries. In general, total costs may be expressed as:

Total costs = Direct costs + Indirect costs

Cost analysis uses a form of this general equation, but the types of costs described within the direct and indirect categories will meet specific needs and conditions. You will find that different measures of cost exist for different reporting and decision-making needs.[1] Assigning these different costs to business units and their products presents challenges to cost analysts and to the managers that they support. We will illustrate these costing challenges in this chapter in the context of Sacs Chameaux, but these examples and lessons can be applied to nearly every organization and situation.

2.1 Cost Management in Practice

Firms that have met the challenges of global competition successfully by using tools of cost management include the following:

- **EasyJet**, **Ryan Air** and **Flybe** (western Europe) enjoy the cost savings from being low-cost, no-frills airlines and the benefits of partnering with others in the travel industry to increase the value of their no-frills approach. These airlines have identified what bargain flyers really value (that is, what these flyers will pay for), and they have used cost management to design services and schedules that meet passengers' needs at lowest cost.
- **Royal Dutch Philips** (the Netherlands) uses cost management techniques to understand and successfully control the costs of using many outsourced suppliers for global services and products that Philips formerly provided internally. Philips has identified the valued characteristics of outsourced items and ensures through detailed contacts that outsourcing providers deliver quality, timeliness and innovation - at lower cost.
- **Whirlpool Sweden's** engineers have learned how assemblers, maintenance technicians and customers value Whirlpool's (and competitors') products. They design microwave ovens for ease of manufacturability and assembly to reduce the development time, number of parts, defects and assembly time of its products, which improves performance, reliability and ease of repair.

This list could be many times longer but, as these examples show, cost management activities help organizations in various ways to be successful in achieving their goals. In each case, these organizations are using cost management to identify the activities and processes they can perform better than their competitors (and outsource the rest) and to build durable advantages. It is clear that cost management spans multiple, traditional business disciplines, and a successful cost management analyst must work effectively with accounting, finance, marketing, manufacturing and logistics specialists.

The Role of Cost Management at Sacs Chameaux SA

The opening memorandum from the president of Sacs Chameaux to the company's executive officers requests urgent cost analyses, cost reduction opportunities and alternative market opportunities. Ordinarily these are recurring strategic and operational activities, but the current context is urgent because sales to its major customer are at risk. Therefore, the entire company is at risk. Before participating in the analysis, however, let's learn more about the chapter's focus company, Sacs Chameaux.[2]

Sacs Chameaux manufactures specialty backpacks that alpinists and hiking enthusiasts have praised for their functional design, minimal weight and durability for more than 20 years. Sacs Chameaux started by selling a small number of backpacks under its own name, but soon the design and quality of its products attracted the attention of the Mountain Sports division of the PleinAir Group. Sacs Chameaux now sells almost all of its products to Mountain Sports, which then sells the backpacks through its own retail stores and discount factory outlets under the Mountain Sports label.

M. Dupuis has learned from colleagues in the industry that the Mountain Sports division's profitability is lagging behind the rest of the PleinAir Group, and has been ordered to improve its financial performance by at least 17 per cent or face serious restructuring imposed by top management. The managers of the Mountain Sports division decided to require all of its suppliers who are facing contract renewals to reduce prices by at least 17 per cent, or be replaced. So far this year, more than half of Mountain Sports' domestic suppliers have been replaced with lower cost Asian or North African suppliers.

Sacs Chameaux has been profitable every year since its founding. The company's continued success is from four factors: (1) reliable, durable, and functional products; (2) a successful marketing approach that focuses directly on the needs of alpinists, mountaineers, and (now) its major customer; (3) capable employees from the top management team to the product assemblers; and (4) a strong commitment to ethical and effective management practices (including a commitment to cost management).

Sacs Chameaux's value chain in Exhibit 2.1 depicts its internal processes: product design, in-bound logistics (purchasing and material handling), production, marketing, distribution and customer service. Although some companies perform nearly all of their value-chain activities, Sacs

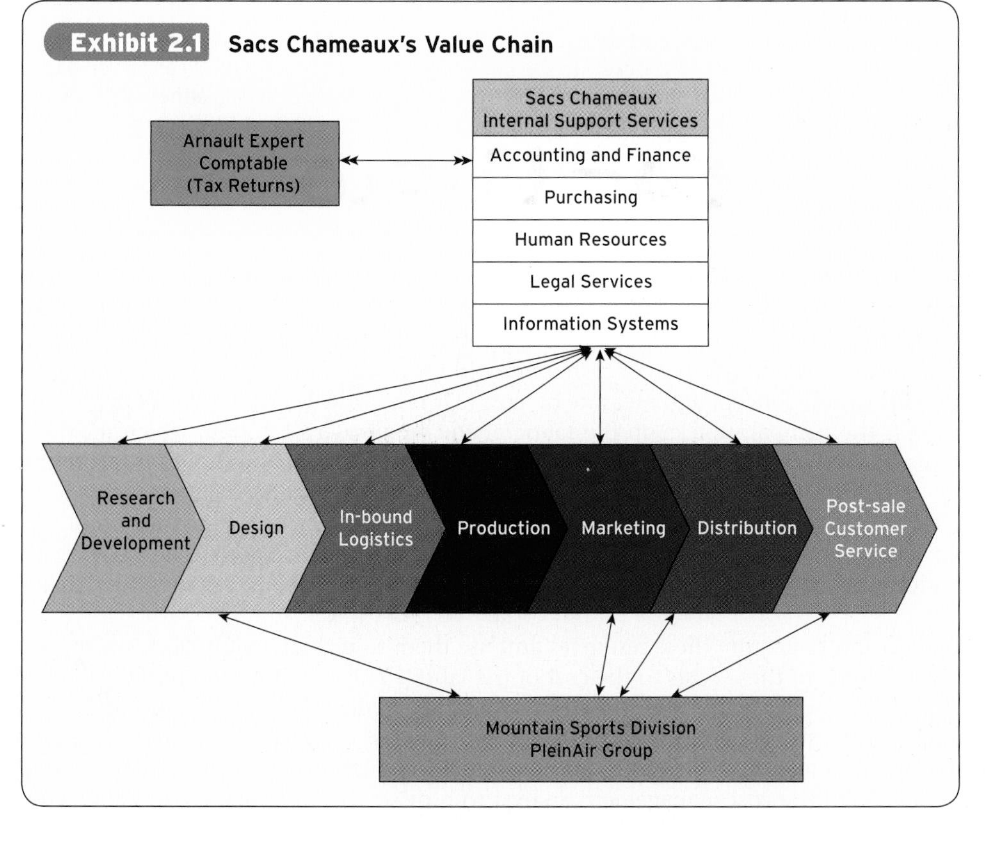

Chameaux, like most companies, outsources some services to others who can do them more efficiently. One of the service firms in Sacs Chameaux's value chain is Arnault Expert Comptable, a professional accounting firm, which Sacs Chameaux uses for preparation of its tax returns.[3] Also integrated in the value chain is Sacs Chameaux's primary customer, PleinAir Group's Mountain Sports Division. Sacs Chameaux collaborates with Mountain Sports to design its backpacks and focuses most of its marketing, distribution and post-sale service on Mountain Sports. Sacs Chameaux has not outsourced its manufacturing processes because design for manufacturability and control of costs and quality are what it does best. Maintaining its advantages does not just happen, however, and Sacs Chameaux must work diligently to manage its quality and costs – especially now.

Concepts and Measures of Cost

LO 1
Understand and apply the concepts of cost, opportunity cost, committed cost, fixed cost, variable cost and sunk cost.

An important first step in studying cost management is to gain an understanding of the meaning of the concept of 'cost'. At a basic level, a **cost** is the sacrifice made, measured by the value of the resources given up, to achieve a particular purpose. Costs can have different definitions and values for different purposes. For example, a cost can be a **cash** or **out-of-pocket cost**, the incremental money price paid, when deciding whether it is worthwhile to buy incremental resources needed now. A cost can be an accounting or **accrual cost**, which is a historical measure of the value of resources used, when reporting results of operations or estimating long-run costs. A cost can be an **opportunity cost**, which is the highest foregone value that could be obtained from the sacrifice of a resource, for example, when considering the foregone value of lost leisure time compared to working. Cost management employs cash, accrual and opportunity costs (and other definitions of cost), depending on (a) the availability of reliable information and (b) the needs of managers who must make cost-based decisions.

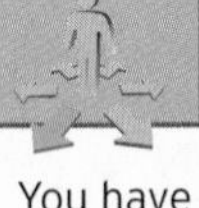

2.1 You're the Decision Maker

You have won a free ticket to see Radiohead in concert (which has no resale value). Lady Gaga is performing on the same night and is your next-best alternative activity. Tickets to see Lady Gaga that night cost €40. On any given day, you would be willing to pay up to €50 to see her show. Assume there are no other costs of seeing either performer. Based on this information, what is the opportunity cost of seeing Radiohead? (a) €0, (b) €10, (c) €40, or (d) €50.[4] What is the accounting cost of seeing Radiohead?

(Solutions begin on p. 82.)

If we look carefully, we find that a 'cost' can have more complexities that are not immediately obvious, for example, the cost of acquiring raw materials. Consider the cost to purchase, €8 per square metre, charged by the wholesale supplier of the nylon fabric that Sacs Chameaux uses in its backpacks.[5] We could observe the transaction of cash (or credit) for fabric, and €8 per square metre is an apparently straightforward concept and measure of 'cost'. Or is it? Now we learn that €8 per square metre is the cost if the company picks up the fabric at the wholesaler's location, which is 20 km away. To measure all of the resources given up to obtain the fabric it seems we should measure the cost of picking up the fabric. We proceed by identifying the resources that Sacs Chameaux uses for this purpose. The company employs several drivers and owns several trucks for the pick up of raw materials from suppliers and delivery of finished products to Mountain Sports. The decision to acquire these additional resources results in real sacrifices and costs for labour, vehicles, fuel, insurance, and so on.

Doesn't the decision to acquire these resources and use them to pick up nylon fabric mean that we should attribute some of these costs to the cost of the fabric? This is getting complicated.[6] Some would say 'yes', others would say 'no' and still others would say, 'It depends on how you want to use the cost information'. Cost management is consistent with the last response, 'it depends', and uses different meanings and measures depending on the context in which 'cost' is used. Understanding these differences enables the cost management analyst to provide the appropriate cost data to the managers who need it. The purpose of this chapter is to guide you through the various meanings and measures of costs.

Applying Concepts of Cost to Decision Making

Let us explore further the cost of Sac Chameaux's nylon fabric for both how and why we can measure the cost per square metre differently, specifically knowing that the company must reduce its costs to keep its primary customer. Consider the data in Exhibit 2.2, which contains Sac Chameaux's costs of resources related to the acquisition of nylon fabric. We will use this data to construct different costs of nylon fabric for different contexts.

Exhibit 2.2 Resources and Costs Related to Acquiring Nylon Fabric

Costs of nylon fabric		
Wholesale cost to buy nylon fabric	€8.00	per square metre
Nylon fabric required per backpack	1.00	square metre
Annual (20xx) usage of nylon fabric	24,500	square metres
Cost for delivery by wholesaler	€50.00	per order, up to 1,000 sq. m
Costs of delivery trucks (2)		
Purchase cost (each)	€25,000	per truck (purchased 5 years ago)
Useful lives (each), years	10	years
Useful lives (each), kilometres driven	400,000	km over useful life in years
Annual maintenance (each)	€2,000	per year
Annual licence and insurance (each)	€3,000	per year
Fuel usage	6.00	km per litre
Fuel cost	€1.35	per litre
Costs of truck drivers (2)		
Annual salary (each)	€30,000	per year
Annual benefits (each)	€15,000	per year

To know how best to use this data for cost management purposes, we first need to know the decision context. Suppose the decision alternatives are whether Sacs Chameaux should (a) pay the wholesale supplier to deliver the *next* fabric order or (b) pick up the *next* order itself. To meet the needs of its primary customer, Sacs Chameaux must assure itself that the transaction of obtaining fabric materials supports its goal of creating more value for its customer at the lowest cost. Receiving the wrong fabric, or the right fabric damaged or late, will make it difficult to meet Mountain Sports' on-time delivery requirements and will increase Sacs Chameaux's costs. We have seen that the company must reduce its total costs, so reliability of transport is important.

Choosing between delivery or pick up seems like a straightforward business problem, but we need several key pieces of information to decide properly. The first information is the answer to the qualitative question: *Are the two methods of obtaining the order (pick up or delivery) equally reliable?* Can Sacs Chameaux be sure that the ordered goods will arrive on time and without damage? For purposes of our discussion, let's assume that the answer is 'yes, either will be reliable' (an answer of 'no' might rule out an option). The second information is the answer to the quantitative question: *Is one method (pick up or delivery) less costly?* To answer this question, we need to determine which of the costs in Exhibit 2.2 will be affected by the decision and compare the costs of the two methods.

Exhibit 2.2 contains quite a diversity of costs that we will use to build a dictionary or taxonomy of costs that we will view from the perspective of managers at Sacs Chameaux as they choose whether to pick up the next fabric order or pay to have it delivered.

Cash or Out-of-pocket Cost

LO 2
Understand and explain the concept and measurement of the out-of-pocket or cash cost and the accounting or accrual cost.

Because the decision at hand applies to the next fabric order, the appropriate cost information to support this decision is the **cash** or **out-of-pocket cost**, which is the incremental cost paid by cash or credit to achieve a particular purpose: The calculations are shown in Exhibit 2.3.

a. *The delivered cost of the order charged by the wholesaler*: The wholesaler has quoted a cost of €50 to deliver an order for up to 1,000 square metres of fabric to Sac Chameaux's location. Larger orders require multiple deliveries. Thus, the *cash cost* of the next delivered 500 square metre order is €8/sq. m × 500 sq. m + €50 = €4,050. No other costs must be paid to acquire this order; therefore, other costs are irrelevant to the delivery alternative.

b. *The out-of-pocket or cash cost incurred by Sacs Chameaux to pick up the order*: The wholesaler will charge €8 per square metre, or €8 × 500 = €4,000, but Sacs Chameaux will incur another cash cost, that of the fuel consumed by the company's truck, which has the same capacity as the wholesaler's truck. The wholesaler is 20 km away, so the fuel cost will be the fuel consumed multiplied by the fuel's cost per litre, ((2 × 20 km)/ 6 km/litre) × €1.35/litre = €9. Thus, the total *cash cost* to pick up the next order is €4,009. As before, this decision applies to the next order, and the other costs will not change (more on this a bit later).

Exhibit 2.3 **Out-of-pocket (Cash) Cost of Nylon Fabric**

Quantity purchased	500	square metres
Purchase price	€8.00	per square metre, Exhibit 2.2
Wholesaler's delivery price for orders up to 1,000 square metres	€50.00	per order
Kilometres driven to pick up (return)	40	km
Fuel usage	6.00	km per litre, Exhibit 2.2
Fuel cost	€1.35	per litre, Exhibit 2.2
a. Delivery by wholesaler		
Purchase cost of fabric order	€4,000.00	= 500 sq. m × 8.00 per sq. m
Delivery cost	€50.00	
Total cost for delivered fabric order	€4,050.00	
b. Pick up by Sacs Chameaux		
Purchase cost of fabric order	€4,000.00	
Fuel cost to pick up fabric order	€9.00	= (40 km/6 km per litre) × 1.35 per litre
Total cost of fabric order, with pickup	€4,009.00	
Cost difference	€41.00	more for delivered order

Variable, Committed and Fixed Costs

LO 3
Understand and explain variable cost, committed cost, fixed cost and sunk cost.

The cash-cost analysis in Exhibit 2.3 analyses only Sacs Chameaux's fabric and pick-up or delivery costs. Each additional square metre purchased will cost an incremental €8, and each order picked up or delivered will cost either €9 or €50, respectively. These are **variable costs**, which vary in direct proportion to production values, such as the fabric purchase and pick-up or delivery activities. The analysis in Exhibit 2.2 also assumes that the other costs are not out-of-pocket costs, and can be ignored for the next order because they will not change, regardless of the delivery alternative chosen. Rather, the other costs are **committed costs** that are incurred because of policies or contractual obligations. In the example of the cost of acquiring nylon fabric, Sacs Chameaux has committed to owning two trucks and employing two salaried truck drivers. Picking up one more or one less order from the wholesaler will not relieve Sacs Chameaux from incurring these committed costs. However, these costs do not simply happen and are not committed forever. Committed costs reflect management decisions, and any decision can be changed – at some cost. Other committed costs could include lease obligations, licences and various taxes. In contrast, 'discretionary costs', such as some costs for advertising, remodelling or charitable giving, could be changed quickly and easily. This is a difference of degree; that is, both committed and discretionary costs can be changed, but changing committed costs is more difficult. Exhibit 2.4 details the costs to purchase, pick up or have delivered orders of different amounts of fabric. Note how the costs change with increasing order sizes.

Exhibit 2.4 **Fabric Costs**

	Prices per unit of activity		
	€8.00	€9.00	€50.00
Square metres ordered	Fabric purchase cost	Fabric pick-up cost	Fabric delivery cost
1	€8	€9	€50
2	16	9	50
3	24	9	50
4	32	9	50
5	40	9	50
6	48	9	50
7	56	9	50
8	64	9	50
9	72	9	50
10	80	9	50
100	800	9	50
200	1,600	9	50
300	2,400	9	50
400	3,200	9	50
500	4,000	9	50
1,000	8,000	9	50
2,000	16,000	18	100
3,000	24,000	27	150

Exhibits 2.5 (a) and 2.5 (b) graph the fabric purchase and delivery costs. The total purchase cost in 2.5a displays the linear, proportional behaviour of a variable cost because the purchase of each unit of fabric (a square metre) adds the purchase price of €8 to the total. More precisely in this case, fabric can be ordered in fractional amounts, and the total variable cost is the amount ordered multiplied by €8. Some resources, as we will soon see, must be purchased in whole units, so the next graph will not be as smooth.

Exhibit 2.5b graphs delivery costs that are variable with respect to the number of fabric orders placed by Sacs Chameaux, which are shown in the lower *x*-axis. Each order adds €50 to the total delivery cost, and fractional orders obviously cannot be placed (note that pick-up costs would display similar behaviour). This gives rise to the lumpy, or 'step-cost' nature of Exhibit 2.5b.

Exhibit 2.5b displays a different cost behaviour than 2.5a because the upper *x*-axis, which is the quantity of fabric ordered, is not the only determinant of delivery cost. This exhibit shows that the delivery cost does not vary for orders between 1 and 1,000 square metres, and is constant at higher levels for higher increments of 1,000 square metres. The total delivery cost does not change with respect to the quantity ordered *within each 1,000 square metre range*. This is a **fixed cost** that is a matter of the scale of decision-making and the divisibility of the resource, which does not change in total within a defined range of underlying productive activity, such as ordering the

SACS CHAMEAUX

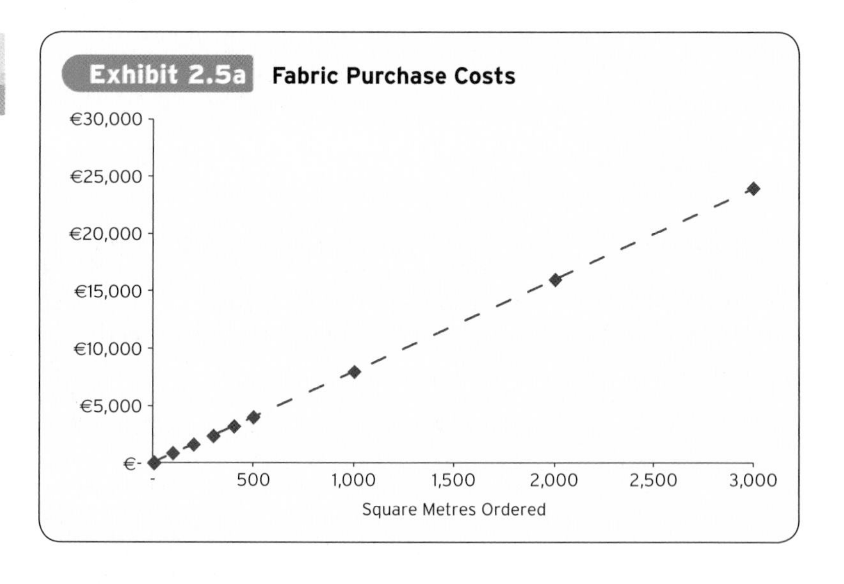

Exhibit 2.5a **Fabric Purchase Costs**

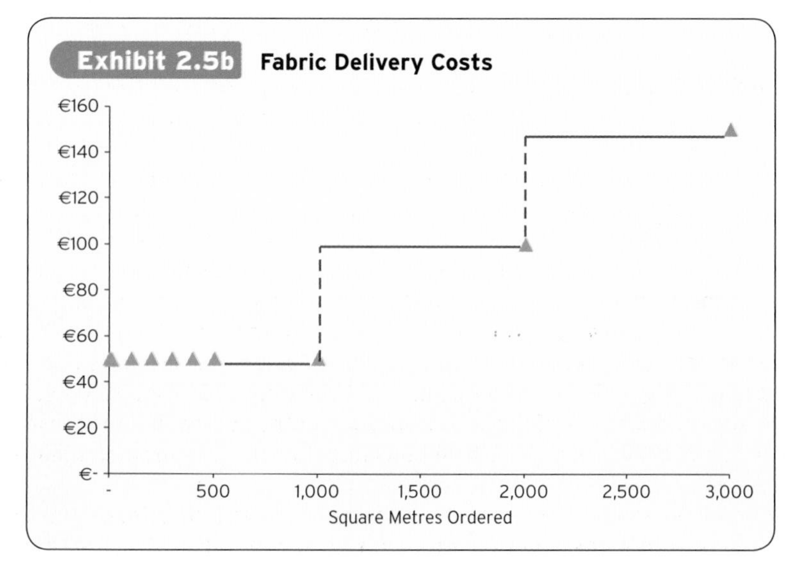

Exhibit 2.5b **Fabric Delivery Costs**

needed amount of fabric. Thus, a fixed cost reflects a capacity decision, such as which size of delivery truck to purchase or hire, a decision that reflects the normal range of fabric-order quantities. In this case, the truck size must reflect that most orders are less than 1,000 square metres of fabric.

Decisions cause costs – and we stress again that costs do not just happen – but no resource decisions are irreversible. Because all future costs are variable with respect to some decision, no future cost really can be truly fixed. It might be costly to change a resource cost in the future (e.g., replace a small truck with a larger one, renegotiate or nullify a resource contract), but it can be changed. For example, labour can be a committed cost in many countries and for many organizations with unionized labour or strong employment policies. This commitment to employment means that conducting more or fewer productive activities (such as picking up orders) might not affect the cost paid for labour. If this is so, spending for labour resources is not different from spending for other physical capacity resources. Again, the decision to acquire the capacity can be changed, but at a cost. Acquiring and using capacity resources complicates Sacs Chameaux's decision whether to pick up or pay for the delivery of all future fabric orders.

The analysis in Exhibit 2.3 shows that picking up the *next* order is less costly by €41 than paying to have it delivered. One might ask whether this conclusion is valid for all future orders or only for the next order? This question creates a decision context with a larger, more complicated set of resources to consider. We need to determine which resources would be affected if Sacs Chameaux considered paying the wholesaler to deliver all future orders, and what costs would be incurred or saved to switch from picking up to delivery.

Sunk and Accrual Costs

We have seen that the cash costs of a fabric order include the purchase price of €8 per square metre plus either the fuel cost to pick up of €9 per order or the delivery cost of €50 per order. We also have determined that the costs of truck drivers and non-fuel truck costs in Exhibit 2.2 are committed costs that appear to be fixed in nature. Maintenance, licence and insurance costs for Sacs Chameaux's trucks might be more flexible, but still would be largely fixed annual costs. Because of union contracts, Sacs Chameaux probably could not change drivers' annual salaries and benefits to variable, hourly wages. If the company wanted to change its capacity decisions to hire salaried drivers and own trucks by terminating the drivers and selling the trucks, it easily could eliminate the truck-related costs. However, the company would face union opposition and severance costs if it scaled back or eliminated the driver-related costs. The uncertainties of managing these costs and 'what if?' issues are interesting and challenging. The only certainty in these cost data is that the €25,000 purchase price of each truck is irrelevant to the decision to pick up or pay for delivery. The historical price paid for each truck is a **sunk cost** that cannot be changed by any future decision.[7]

The complete analysis, which we defer to Chapter 8, of the more complicated decision whether to indefinitely continue resources related to picking up fabric orders or to pay the wholesaler for each delivery should consider (a) several alternative scenarios and (b) the effects over a long period of time (e.g., the ordering activity over the life of a truck). These are common and important complications in cost management analysis. As it happens, sometimes managers use an accounting measure of cost that incorporates a wide variety of accounting costs across time – not always wisely for many decisions, however. We turn to this accounting cost measure next.

A short cut for the complete cost implications of the opportunity cost of picking up or delivering fabric is the accounting or **accrual cost**, which is an average cost. This average, accrual cost for the pick up of fabric can be computed by dividing the total cost of resources used during an extended time period (e.g., a year) divided by a measure of the resources used to pick up orders. The total accrual cost includes the previously calculated, out-of-pocket fuel costs plus the previously left-out committed costs for trucks and drivers. Exhibit 2.6 presents one reasonable approach to measuring the purchase and pick-up cost of a 500 square metre order.

Costs committed to picking up fabric are costs of trucks and drivers. The cost of purchasing a truck can be spread or amortized over the useful life of the truck. The analysis in Exhibit 2.6 uses

Exhibit 2.6 Accrual Cost of an Order for Nylon Fabric

Annual uses of committed resources		
Delivery trucks (each)		
Annual amortization of purchase cost	€2,500	straight-line depreciation, Exhibit 2.2
Annual maintenance, licence and insurance	€5,000	Exhibit 2.2
Truck drivers (each)		
Annual salary and benefits	€45,000	Exhibit 2.2
Total annual costs of committed resources	€52,500	
Normal annual kilometres available	40,000	kilometres, Exhibit 2.2
Committed cost per kilometre	€1.3125	per kilometre driven
Kilometres driven to pick up fabric order (return)	40	km
Accrued, committed cost of fabric order	€52.50	
Out-of-pocket (cash) cost of fuel to pick up order	9.00	fuel from Exhibit 2.3
Total cost to pick up an order	61.50	
Out-of-pocket (cash) cost of fabric order	4,000.00	purchase price from Exhibit 2.3
Total accrual cost of fabric order	€4,061.50	

an annual, straight-line or equal measure of the purchase cost. The cost of a driver includes salary and benefits. Because these resources can be used for other purposes, finding a common measure of activity, such as kilometres driven annually, is a more flexible measure than the number of orders picked up. Dividing the total cost of a truck and a driver by the normal kilometres driven in a year yields an average committed cost of €1.3125 per kilometre. The distance driven to pick up a fabric order is 40 kilometres, so the accrual cost of committed resources is €52.50 per order. Adding the previously computed, cash fuel cost of €9.00 measures the total accrual cost of an order at €61.50, which is greater than the wholesaler's cost to deliver of €50. This does not mean, however, that Sacs Chameaux should outsource the pick-up of fabric to the wholesaler because we have not considered all of the complexities and scenarios of such a switch. We will defer these important considerations until Chapter 8, which addresses the time-impact of decision making.

Reporting Product Costs, Period Costs and Expenses

LO 4
Explain product cost, period cost, expense, direct cost and indirect cost.

The primary function of cost management is to help managers create more customer value at lower cost. Rather than spend scarce time and funds to create new cost information, reusing information prepared for financial or tax reporting might be a less costly short cut, because this information normally is already available. Reusing accounting cost information has the advantage of lower cost, but the disadvantage of possibly obscuring key information details, The concept of cost used most often for financial and tax reporting is accrual cost. It is important for cost management to understand when one may safely use accrual cost and when one should not. For this key insight we need to explore a typical **cost accounting system**, which accumulates and reports accrual costs for external reporting.

Both financial and tax reporting are concerned with the timing when the costs to acquire resources are recognized as *expenses*.[8] An **expense** is the measure of the cost incurred when a resource is consumed or sold for the purpose of generating revenue. Expenses are matched to revenues to measure income. The terms 'product cost' and 'period cost' reflect the business transactions that cause their conversion into expenses.

A **product cost** is a cost assigned to goods that were either purchased or manufactured for resale. Product cost is the historical cost of the inventory of manufactured or purchased goods until the goods are sold. In the period of the sale, the costs of products sold are recognized as an expense called **costs of sales**. The cost of product inventory acquired by a retailer or wholesaler from a manufacturer for resale consists of the purchase cost of the inventory plus any shipping charges. The product cost of manufactured inventory includes all manufacturing costs. Product costs are added to the values of inventories (or stocks as they are known in the UK), until the goods are sold and the product costs are expensed as cost of sales. For example, the labour cost of a production employee at Sacs Chameaux is included as a product cost of the backpacks manufactured. To that, the company would add materials costs (fabric, zippers, other hardware) and other costs of the manufacturing facility (e.g., depreciation, maintenance, supervision). The accumulated costs of the inputs to production that are used on products become the products' cost.

For external reporting purposes, any cost that is not a product cost is a **period cost**. These costs are recognized as expenses during the time period in which they are incurred rather than with units of purchased or produced goods. Thus, period costs are *not* included in the cost of inventory. Common period costs include administrative costs, marketing costs and other costs of doing business that cannot be associated strongly with manufacturing processes. Exhibit 2.7 illustrates the

Exhibit 2.7 Product Costs, Period Costs and Cost of Sales

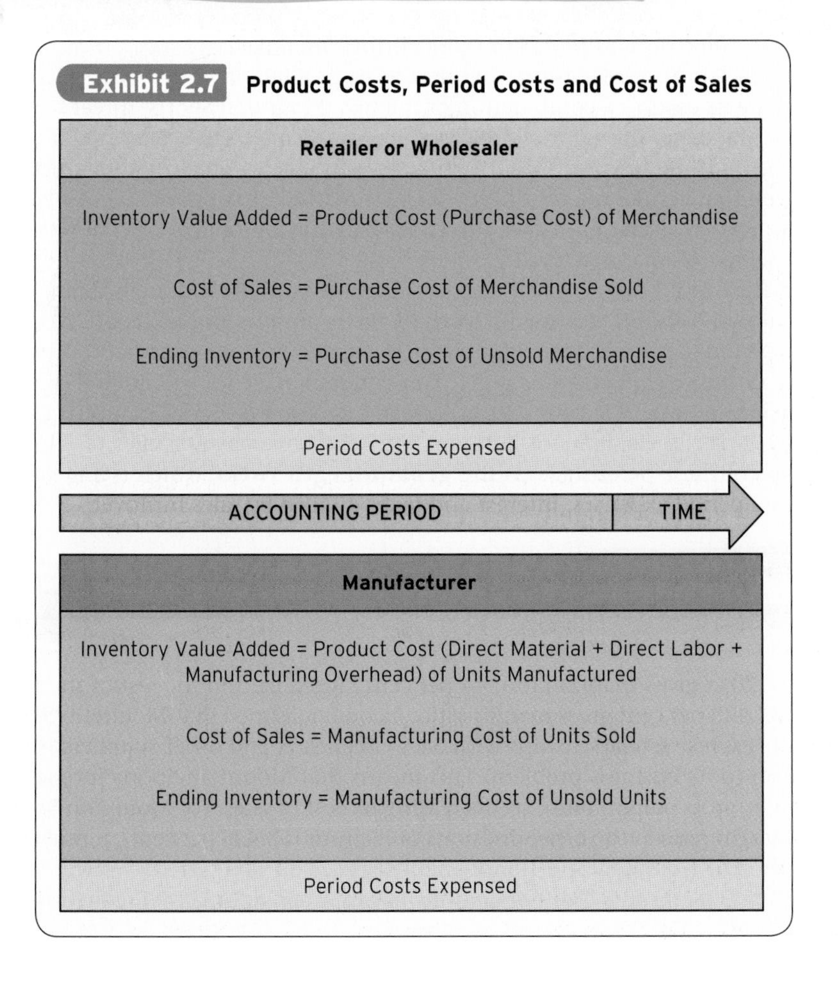

relationship between product costs cost-of-sales expense and period costs for a retailer, such as the Mountain Sports division, and for its supplier, a manufacturer such as Sacs Chameaux.

Reporting the relationship between cash outflows and costs can be complicated by the somewhat arbitrary boundaries of reporting periods. For example:

- The cash outflow and cost take place in the same period, such as when Sacs Chameaux pays for and receives nylon-fabric orders from its suppliers within the same reporting period (say, a month).
- The cash outflow occurs earlier, but the cost is capitalized (e.g., nylon fabric is put into inventory), and the cost follows in a later period when the nylon fabric is used to make backpacks.
- The cash outflow occurs later, but cost is charged to an earlier period because an accrual was created, such as when Sacs Chameaux creates a provision for future warranty cost for products sold to Mountain Sports.

Cost Analysis

LO 5
Analyse the product costs of typical manufacturing, retail and service firms for decision making and evaluations.

Recall the value chain in Exhibit 2.1. Our focus company is linked to its suppliers and customers by transactions and the strategies of each firm in its extended value chain. Their separate strategic goals might be in tension. In particular the competitive necessity for Mountain Sports to improve its profitability by 17 per cent has led it to require that its suppliers, Sacs Chameaux included, must reduce their prices by 17 per cent. All firms at all times should be managing their costs; however, Sacs Chameaux now has an urgent need to manage costs quickly and effectively or find another major customer. Let's analyse how the costs and profits of these entities are linked.

Mountain Sports Division can improve its profitability by increasing its sales turnover, reducing its costs or a combination of the two. Mountain Sports' threat to seek lower cost suppliers if Sacs Chameaux does not reduce its prices by 17 per cent seems credible in this age of global competition. Jacques Cournot, VP of Finance, was able to obtain public information about the PleinAir Group that verifies the credibility of the threat. His analysis of PleinAir is in Exhibit 2.8, which reflects typical gross margins (sales turnover less cost of products sold) of retail or wholesale companies that sell goods manufacture by others.[9]

Cournot's analysis used the actual 20xx sales turnover and gross margin figures for the entire group and its major divisions that were disclosed by PleinAir in its annual report. Note that PleinAir did not disclose period expenses for the divisions, so Jacques cannot construct complete statements of income for all of the group's business units. This is not an issue for this analysis because Cournot is most interested in Mountain Sports' cost of sales, which is partly Sacs Chameaux's sales turnover.

Cournot expressed the elements of gross margin as a percentage of sales to allow profitability comparisons. One of these percentages is the **gross margin ratio**, which is a measure of income contributed before period expenses, interest and taxes divided by sales turnover:

Gross margin ratio = Gross margin/Sales turnover
Gross margin ratio = (Sales turnover – Cost of sales)/Sales turnover

Mountain Sports' 20xx gross margin ratio, 44 per cent lagged behind the rest of the PleinAir group, which earned a 53.423 per cent gross margin ratio. Jacques reasoned that Mountain Sports was using the leverage of its exclusive relationships with Sacs Chameaux and other suppliers to obtain a cost-reduction solution to its business problem. This meant that Mountain Sports intended to improve its profitability (i.e., gross margin ratio) by decreasing its cost of sales. For Mountain Sports to achieve the same gross margin ratio as the other divisions of PleinAir (53.423 per cent), it must reduce its cost of sales by 17 per cent (rounded up). Hence the insistence on reduced sales prices for its products purchased from Sacs Chameaux. The calculations of Mountain Sports' cost reductions are based on

Exhibit 2.8 **Analysis of PleinAir and Mountain Sports**

a. PleinAir Group performance	20xx (actual)	Percentage of sales (actual)	
Sales turnover	€254,855,000	100%	
Cost of products sold	123,349,820	48.400%	
Gross margin	€131,505,180	51.600%	
b. Other divisions performance			
Sales turnover	€205,542,000	100%	
Cost of products sold	95,734,540	47.577%	
Gross margin	€109,807,460	53.423%	
c. Mountain Sports Division performance			
Sales turnover	€49,313,000	100%	
Cost of products sold	27,615,280	56.000%	
Gross margin	€21,697,720	44.000%	
d. Mountain Sports performance requirement	**20xx (adjusted)**	**Percentage of sales (adjusted)**	**Improvement required**
Sales turnover (same as 20xx)	€49,313,000	100%	
Cost of sales	22,968,368	46.577%	–16.827%
Gross margin	€26,344,632	53.423%	

maintaining its 20xx sales turnover, achieving the rest of the Group's gross margin ratio, but reducing cost of sales, as follows:

$$\textbf{Mountain Sports' Desired cost of sales} = (1 - 0.53423) \times €49{,}313{,}000$$
$$= €22{,}968{,}368$$
$$\textbf{Percentage cost reduction} = (22{,}968{,}368 - 27{,}615{,}280)/27{,}615{,}280$$
$$= -16.827\%$$
$$= -17\% \text{ (rounded)}$$

Cournot next analysed Sacs Chameaux's 20xx results to see the impacts of accepting a 17 per cent reduction of sales prices on its 20xx operations. Of course, gross margin and **operating income** (gross margin less period expenses) would be lower; in fact, without cost reductions this would cause the company's first loss in 20 years. Jacques expected that the company's officers and owners would prefer to maintain prior levels of profitability (he certainly did), which meant that Sacs Chameaux must reduce its cost of sales and period expenses. Jacques' prospective ('pro forma') analysis is in Exhibit 2.9.

Sacs Chameaux's 20xx actual operating results and income were consistent with the performance of recent years. The gross margin ratio of 60 per cent and **return on sales ratio** (operating income/sales) were what the company's officers and owners considered to be consistent with their opportunity costs of effort and capital. To maintain those ratios with a 17 per cent reduction in sales prices on the same units sold (nearly all to Mountain Sports), Sacs Chameaux would need to effect 17 per

Exhibit 2.9 Sacs Chameaux Cost Improvement Required

Sacs Chameaux performance	20xx (actual)	Changes required	20xx (adjusted)
Sales units	20,130		20,130
Sales turnover	€2,856,000	–17%	€2,370,480
Cost of sales	1,142,400	–17%	948,192
Gross margin	1,713,600		1,422,288
Period expenses	1,245,000	–17%	1,033,350
Operating income	€468,600		€388,938
Gross margin ratio	60%		60%
Return on sales ratio	16%		16%
Cost reductions required			
Cost of sales	€(194,208)		
Per unit manufacturing cost	€(9.65)		
Period expenses	€(211,650)		

cent reductions in cost of sales (in total €194,208) and period expenses (in total €211,650). Jacques believed that sufficient reductions might be achieved by the following actions:

1. Improve the efficiency of internal manufacturing processes by reducing wasted time, effort and materials.
2. Improve the efficiency of internal business services similarly or by purchasing services from other sources (i.e., outsourcing more than tax services).
3. Reduce costs of purchased materials and services by negotiating reduced purchase prices from suppliers (such as the fabric wholesaler and Arnault Expert Comptable).

Failing these, the officers and owners might have to reassess their opportunity costs.

2.2 You're the Decision Maker

1. Compute a statement of income like Exhibit 2.9 that features:
   - **a.** A 17 per cent reduction in sales turnover on the same units as sold in 20xx
   - **b.** No reductions in either cost of sales or period expenses.
2. Explain how the impact of the price reduction being forced by Mountain Sports might cascade through all of Sacs Chameaux's internal processes and suppliers. What are the likely outcomes to all concerned?

(Solutions begin on p. 82.)

Costs of Manufacturing

More detailed analysis of the reported manufacturing costs will yield more information about how Sacs Chameaux can achieve its required cost reductions. A manufacturing company such as Sacs Chameaux has a more complex statement of income than do service or retail companies. Whereas the retailer *purchases* the goods for sale, the manufacturer *makes* them. Sacs Chameaux purchases materials (for example, fabric and thread), hires employees to convert the materials into finished products, and then offers the products for sale. These additional activities add to the complexity of Sacs Chameaux's cost structure and financial reports.

An important aspect of cost incurrence is the ease with which the cost of a resource can be traced to a decision or set of decisions, such as deciding to manufacture a product or provide a service. Cost analysts often ask, 'If we make this particular decision, what resources must we obtain or use, and what will they cost?' The acquisition and use of all resources is caused by management decisions, but the ease of tracing the costs of these resources to specific decisions is important for analysing the cost effects to those decisions of the organization.

Manufacturing costs include **direct costs**, which are the costs of resources that are physically observed being used to create specific products. These include direct materials and direct labour, which are easily traced to products being made. Manufacturing costs also include **indirect costs** that cannot be feasibly traced to object, such as products.

Direct Costs

Direct materials are resources such as raw materials, parts and components that one can observe being used to make a specific product. For example, observing the use of fabric, thread, buckles and other fasteners that Sacs Chameaux uses to make backpacks is easy; therefore, the costs of these resources are all direct material costs. The cost of raw material that is *observably used in* or *traced to* production equals the direct material cost.

Direct labour is the cost of compensating employees who convert direct material into a finished product. The cost of fringe benefits for direct labour personnel, such as employer-paid health-insurance premiums, workers' compensation, and the employer's pension contribution, are also included in direct labour cost. These costs are just as much a part of the employees' compensation as are their regular wages and salaries.

Indirect Costs

Manufacturing overhead cost is an indirect cost that includes resources necessary for the manufacturing process, but which cannot be easily traced to specific units of product. Manufacturing overhead includes indirect material, indirect labour and other manufacturing costs that are shared resources for multiple products or cannot be traced. **Indirect material cost** includes all materials that either (1) are not a part of the finished product but are necessary to manufacture it or (2) are part of the finished product but are insignificant in cost. ('Insignificant in cost' means that the cost of collecting information about the use of these materials exceeds the value of the information collected.) Some examples include lubricants for Sacs Chameaux's production machinery and cleaning materials, repair parts and light bulbs for the production area. **Indirect labour cost** is the wages of production employees who do not work directly on the product yet are required for the manufacturing facility's operation. These employees include supervisors, maintenance workers, purchasing managers and material-handling employees. When all of labour cost is a small part of total manufacturing costs, some companies include labour with overhead and term the total indirect cost as a **conversion cost**.

Manufacturing overhead also includes *other manufacturing costs*, such as depreciation on the factory building and equipment, insurance on the factory building and equipment, heat, light, power and other support costs incurred to keep the manufacturing facility operating. Increasing the automation of manufacturing processes has resulted in dramatic increases in these other manufacturing costs. Support departments represent a significant source of manufacturing overhead costs and include supplier relations, machine maintenance, production scheduling, engineering, purchasing, material handling and quality assurance. Notice that many of the indirect labour employees mentioned earlier actually work in a support department. Note that the costs of outsourced support for production also should be counted as part of overhead costs.

Other manufacturing overhead costs also include overtime premiums and the cost of idle time. An **overtime premium** is the extra hourly compensation paid to an employee who works beyond the time normally allowed by regulation or labour contracts. **Idle time** is time that an employee does not spend productively because of events such as equipment breakdowns or new set-ups of production runs. Idle time is an unavoidable feature of most manufacturing processes. The costs of employees' overtime premiums and idle time are classified as overhead so that they can be spread across all products rather than being associated with a particular product or batch of products.

Non-manufacturing Costs

Non-manufacturing costs include selling and administrative costs, which are not used to produce products. Sacs Chameaux also incurs selling costs to obtain customer orders and provide finished products to customers. **Selling costs** include costs such as sales commissions, sales personnel salaries, and the sales departments' building occupancy costs. Sacs Chameaux also incurs **administrative costs,** which are the costs incurred to manage the organization and provide staff support, including executive and clerical salaries; costs for legal, computing and accounting services; and building space for administrative personnel.

2.1 Research Insight

The calculation of divisional profits, as in the case of Sacs Chameaux, is fraught with practical and theoretical measurement difficulties, as we shall see later, and particularly in Chapters 14 and 15. These difficulties almost always centre on the shares of central administrative and sunk costs that are apportioned (or 'allocated') to divisions. Despite the difficulties, the use of divisional profits to make decisions about divisions and evaluate divisions' performance is globally widespread. Surveys, such as the one conducted by R.C. Skinner, confirm the practice but also seek to explain variations in how divisional profits are computed. Some firms do and others do not allocate central costs to divisions. Reasons for allocating full accrual costs include (a) the belief that these costs are the best estimates of future cash costs, (b) full accrual costs promote shared decision making between central and divisional managers, (c) full accrual costs lead divisions to press central administrators to improve internal service efficiency, and (d) profits thus computed promote inter-divisional performance comparisons. Reasons for not including central costs include (a) uncontrollability of these costs by divisional managers, and (b) irrelevance of allocated sunk costs for divisional decision making.

Source: Skinner (1990).

Period costs are non-manufacturing costs that are expensed in the period incurred for external reporting purposes. For cost management purposes, however, one often wants to associate non-manufacturing costs with specific products or organizational subunits. For example, the PleinAir Group allocates the central costs of advertising, promotion and supplier management to its business divisions, including Mountain Sports, so that divisions can measure the total costs of their products. Chapter 4 presents activity-based costing, which is a method to observe how most, if not all, costs of the value chain are used to manufacture products (or serve customers and provide services). Chapter 10 describes multiple methods for allocating costs to organizational subunits.

Sometimes distinguishing between manufacturing costs and non-manufacturing costs is conceptually difficult. For example, are the salaries of staff in the human resources department that handle factory payrolls manufacturing or non-manufacturing costs? What about the costs of offices for the manufacturing vice president and her staff? Some of these costs have no clear-cut classification, so companies usually set their own guidelines and follow them consistently. This can make comparing the reported results of different companies difficult, however, particularly because firms rarely disclose these practices.

Stages of Production and the Flow of Costs

Suppose that we are able to tour Sacs Chameaux's Savoie production facility. We would encounter the following stages of production:

- We would observe the ordering and delivery of raw materials (e.g., nylon fabric, straps and fasteners) from suppliers. Payment (cash or credit) might be made with the order or upon delivery. Credit purchases create an accounts-payable liability to the supplier, which later cash payments extinguish.

- We might see **raw materials inventory**, which are costs of materials that have not yet been put into production. Some firms try to minimize inventory levels with frequent, timely deliveries.
- Next we would find **work in progress (WIP) inventory**, which is the cost of partially completed products in process.
- Finally, past the end of the production process, perhaps in storage or in a shipping area, we would find **finished goods inventory**, which is the cost of products ready for sale or delivery to customers. Some firms try to minimize finished goods inventory by quickly selling and delivering completed products to customers.

Each inventory or stock account typically has a beginning inventory amount, transfers-in and transfers-out during the period, and an ending inventory based on what is still on hand at the end of the period. Recall that costs added to inventory accounts are called product costs. Exhibit 2.10 illustrates how a basic cost accounting system (below) mirrors the production process (above) at Sacs Chameaux's Savoie factory.

Exhibit 2.10 Sacs Chameaux's Production Process and Cost Accounting System

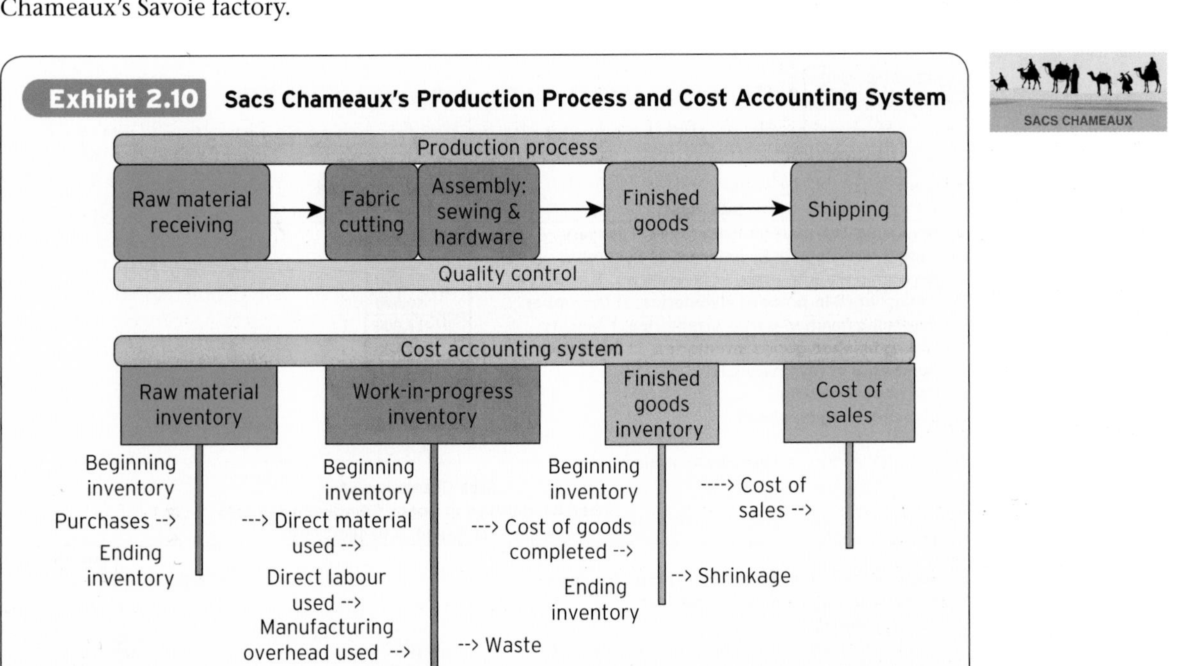

The cost accounts record and collect the costs of resources as they flow through the process. As products are built, their costs accumulate in the Work-in-progress inventory account. As products are completed, they and their costs flow to the Finished goods inventory account. Finally, when products are sold, customers take possession and the product costs are expensed as cost of sales. The firm's accounting system guarantees that the balancing relation for any inventory account is always:

$$\textbf{Beginning balance} + \textbf{Transfers-in} - \textbf{Transfers-out} = \textbf{Ending balance}$$

$$\mathbf{BB + TI - TO = EB}$$

Work-in-progress transfers-out include cost of goods completed and waste. **Waste** is the cost of unrecovered resources applied to defective products that cannot be sold. Similarly, transfers-in to finished goods include cost of goods completed, and transfers-out include cost of sales and **shrinkage**, which is the cost of unrecovered stolen or mis-shipped finished products. Both waste and shrinkage are considered period costs so that these costs are not buried in costs of goods completed or cost of sales. The costs of any backpacks that are finished but have not yet been sold to customers are included in the Finished goods inventory account at the end of an accounting period.

Schedule of Costs of Goods Completed and Sold

LO 6
Prepare a schedule of cost of goods completed and sold using a flexible financial model.

Sacs Chameaux's statement of income for 20xx is shown in the first numerical column of Exhibit 2.9. This is a typical statement of income for a manufacturer. Sacs Chameaux has a business imperative to reduce its costs sufficiently to support a 17 per cent reduction in its sales turnover. We are now interested in exploring its cost of goods completed and sold for indications of ways to reduce these costs. To proceed, we will construct a detailed statement of costs of goods completed and sold. This statement quantifies or realizes the stylized cost accounting system in the lower portion of Exhibit 2.10, and is shown in Exhibit 2.11. This statement derives the original cost of sales figure of €1,142,400 in the 20xx statement of income of Exhibit 2.9.

SACS CHAMEAUX

Exhibit 2.11 **Statement of Costs of Goods Completed and Sold**

	A	B	C	D	E
1	Sacs Chameaux, SA				
2	Manufacturing data input				
3	Data input	20xx			
4	Beginning raw-material inventories, 1 January	€ 20,000			
5	Ending raw-material inventories, 31 December	15,000			
6	Beginning work-in-process inventories, 1 January	15,000			
7	Ending work-in-process inventories, 31 December	10,000			
8	Beginning finished-goods inventories, 1 January	22,000			
9	Ending finished-goods inventories, 31 December	14,600			
10	Purchases of raw materials	240,000			
11	Use of direct labour	300,000			
12	Manufacturing overhead	585,000			
13					
14	Financial Analysis				
15	Sacs Chameaux, SA				
16	Schedule of Costs of Goods Completed and Sold				
17	For the Year Ended 31 December 20xx				
18					Formulas
19	Beginning work-in-process inventory, January 1			€15,000	= B7
20	Manufacturing costs during the year:				
21	Direct material:				
22	Beginning raw-material inventories, January 1	€ 20,000			= B5
23	Add: Purchases of raw materials	240,000			= B11
24	Raw materials available for use	260,000			= B22+B23
25	Less: Ending raw-material inventories, December 31	15,000			= B6
26	Direct materials used		€ 245,000		
27	Direct labour used		300,000		= B12
28	Manufacturing overhead used		585,000		= B13
29	Total manufacturing costs incurred			1,130,000	= SUM(C26:C28)
30	Total cost of work in process during the year			1,145,000	= D19+D29
31	Less: Ending work-in-process inventory, December 31			10,000	= B8
32	*Cost of goods completed during the year*			1,135,000	= D30–D31
33	Beginning finished-goods inventory, January 1			22,000	= B9
34	Finished-goods inventory available for sale			1,157,000	= D32+D33
35	Less: Ending finished-goods inventory, December 31			14,600	= B10
36	*Cost of sales*			€1,142,400	= D34–D35

Financial Modelling

Observe that Exhibit 2.11 was created with spreadsheet software. Virtually everyone who conducts financial analyses uses this software (typically the ubiquitous Microsoft Excel). Thus, it is important for future analyses that we introduce basic financial modelling techniques now. Future chapters will use more complex techniques, but they are variations on the basic techniques we will now use. Sound spreadsheet analysis is an important, indispensable skill.

Before explaining the accounting analysis in Exhibit 2.11, let's focus on the construction of this spreadsheet. This spreadsheet is a **financial model**, which is a flexible calculation of financial outcomes that exploits (some of) the vast power of current spreadsheet software, such as Microsoft Excel. We will use these models on many occasions in this textbook, so it is necessary to set some expectations for their construction and use. First, notice that the financial model has two related but separate sections: data input and financial analysis. The data input section contains all the numerical 'facts' or parameters of the model. It is very important that this is the *only* place where these parameters exist as numbers. This is for two reasons: (1) entering these data only once reduces the opportunities for data-entry errors, and (2) referring to these parameters by cell location everywhere else creates a model that is flexible and reliable. For example, column E of the spreadsheet displays the formulas used to compute the figures in the financial analysis section of the model (note that displaying formulas this way is not typical of actual models). For this exposition the cells that refer directly to data input parameters are highlighted. If one wanted to change any of the parameters, say for analysing the outcomes in a different time period, one only needs to change a parameter in the data input section without worrying where the parameter might be used. The entire spreadsheet model will recalculate automatically to reflect this data change. Flexibility and reliability are especially important in models that are more complex than Exhibit 2.11.

Statement of Cost of Goods Completed and Cost per Unit

Let's analyse the construction of 20xx's statement of goods completed and sold in Exhibit 2.11, which throughout uses a form of the inventory balancing equation introduced previously, BB + TI – EB = TO.

Work in progress

The first financial outcome that we want to compute is the accrual cost of goods completed, which is the 'transfer-out' of the Work-in-progress (WIP) inventory, so we begin the statement with the opening WIP inventory balance. This is computed in cell D19 by reference to the data input section (= B7). During the period 20xx, raw materials were added. We compute the direct materials transferred into production (cell C26) by starting with the opening Raw materials (RM) inventory balance (B22), adding purchases (B23), and subtracting the closing Raw materials inventory balance (B25). This transfer-out must be the total materials used to produce backpacks, which might include waste (we will discuss waste later in this text).

$$\textbf{Cost of direct materials used, } TO_{RM} = BB_{RM} + TI_{RM} - EB_{RM}$$
$$\textbf{Cost of direct materials used} = €20{,}000 + 240{,}000 - 15{,}000 = €245{,}000$$

We next add to direct materials the other product costs consumed (transferred-in) to build products during 20xx: Direct labour (cell C27) and Manufacturing overhead (cell C28). This sum is the total product cost incurred in 20xx (cell D29), which is added to the opening WIP balance to measure the total cost of products in process during 20xx (D30). We subtract the closing WIP balance (D31) to obtain the *cost of goods completed* in 20xx (D32).

$$\textbf{Cost of goods completed, } TO_{WIP} = BB_{WIP} + TI_{WIP} - EB_{WIP}$$
$$\textbf{Cost of goods completed} = €15{,}000 + (245{,}000 + 300{,}000 + 585{,}000) - 10{,}000 = €1{,}135{,}000$$

We have solved the WIP balancing equation, BB + TI – EB = TO, in the typical statement format to find the cost of goods completed as €1,135,000. For the 20,000 backpacks completed, this averages to €56.75 per backpack.

Cost of goods completed	€1,135,000
Units produced	÷ 20,000
Cost per unit	€56.75

Achieving a 17 per cent reduction means cutting $0.17 \times €56.75 = €9.65$ from the average cost of each backpack, or approximately €193,000 in total from 20xx's annual product costs consumed.

Finished goods

The calculation of 20xx's cost of sales (€1,142,400; shown first in Exhibit 2.9) also follows the format of BB + TI – EB = TO within the Finished goods (FG) inventory account. This is accomplished in rows 32 through 36. Note that the transfer-out from the WIP inventory, cost of goods completed (cell D32), is the transfer-in for the Finished goods inventory. The transfer-out from finished goods is the *cost of sales* in cell D36. If any shrinkage were detected, it would be shown separately.

$$\textbf{Cost of sales, } \mathbf{TO_{FG} = BB_{FG} + TI_{FG} - EB_{FG}}$$
$$\textbf{Cost of sales} = \mathbf{€22{,}000 + 1{,}135{,}000 - 14{,}600 = €1{,}142{,}000}$$

The average cost of the 20,130 backpacks sold to Mountain Sports in 20xx was €56.75, which because these units include partially completed backpacks from the previous year's ending WIP indicates that Sacs Chameaux's production costs are quite stable. In a way, that is bad news for cost cutting, because it might be easier to prevent a recurrence of a short-term spike in costs. It appears that solving the company's cost-reduction problem must entail structural changes in the costs of resources used (direct materials, direct labour and manufacturing overhead). Where would you begin?

2.2 Research Insight

A common structural change in production processes is to 'outsource' some or all parts of the process to other manufacturers that might be more efficient. Firms that outsource expect lower total costs without reductions in quality and on-time deliveries. Thus, the decision to outsource is often called the 'make or buy' decision, for which the comparison of the cost to make versus the cost to buy is crucial. The cost to buy is a cash cost, but the cost to make is often an accrual cost. Is this comparing apples to oranges? A 2006 survey by Brierly et al. revealed that practice varies - some practising experts use only direct manufacturing costs, but others use total accrual costs - contrary to the authors' expectations. These authors call for more research to explain why many practitioners appear to believe that sunk accrual costs are appropriate for this decision. Perhaps (as in Research Insight 2.1) the decisions faced by respondents vary as to their short or long-term nature. This issue is covered in detail in Chapter 7.

Source: Brierly et al. (2006).

2.3 You're the Decision Maker

Place yourself in the position of Jacques Cournot, the VP of Finance, who will analyse the cost results in Exhibit 2.11 for opportunities to reduce total production costs by 17 per cent, or a total of €192,237 retrospectively from 20xx's production.

a. Which product costs in Exhibit 2.11 can Sacs Chameaux reduce for the next year?
b. By how much would the average cost of a backpack need to be reduced?
c. What strategies would you recommend for the process(es) of achieving cost reductions in the costs identified in part (a)?
d. If the costs in part (a) can be reduced, would you recommend revaluing the next year's beginning inventories? Why? How?

(Solutions begin on p. 82.)

Chapter Summary

Cost management helps an organization's management create more value at lower cost by efficiently managing the organization's value chain of activities, processes and functions. An important step in studying cost management is to gain an understanding of the various concepts of cost and the types of costs that organizations incur and the way that the organizations actively manage those costs. Moreover, the ability to view different managerial situations from the appropriate decision-making perspective is important. An important cost concept is *cost behaviour*, which refers to the way in which costs respond to changes in decisions and activities. Another key concept is the difference between cash or out-of-pocket cost and accrual cost. The former reflects cost behaviour and timing, while the latter reflects average costs that show up in financial statements for external reporting.

Exhibit 2.12 summarizes relations among various concepts of cost that are oriented toward measuring the cost of a product (the exercise could be broadened to the cost of a business unit or a project). Spend a few moments reflecting on the related concepts of costs in this exhibit. The central concept, 'cost' should be measured as 'opportunity cost', but managers often must substitute measures of 'cash' or 'accrual' cost, which are useful but have different shortcomings compared to the ideal measure of opportunity cost. The choice between cash or accrual cost then leads to considerations of 'fixed' or 'variable' costs, which might be 'committed'. A 'sunk' cost is a special type of cost that is historical and unchangeable, but may become part of accrual cost measurement. Fixed and variable costs may be 'direct' or 'indirect' depending on whether their consumption can be feasibly observed and measured. These costs combine to become 'product' or 'period' costs depending on whether one wants to attach them to a product or to the operations of the period. (Recall that direct material, direct labour and manufacturing overhead are product costs for external reporting; other costs are period costs.) When products are sold, their costs become a cost of sales expense. When time expires, period costs become period expenses.

Exhibit 2.12 Summary of Related Cost Concepts

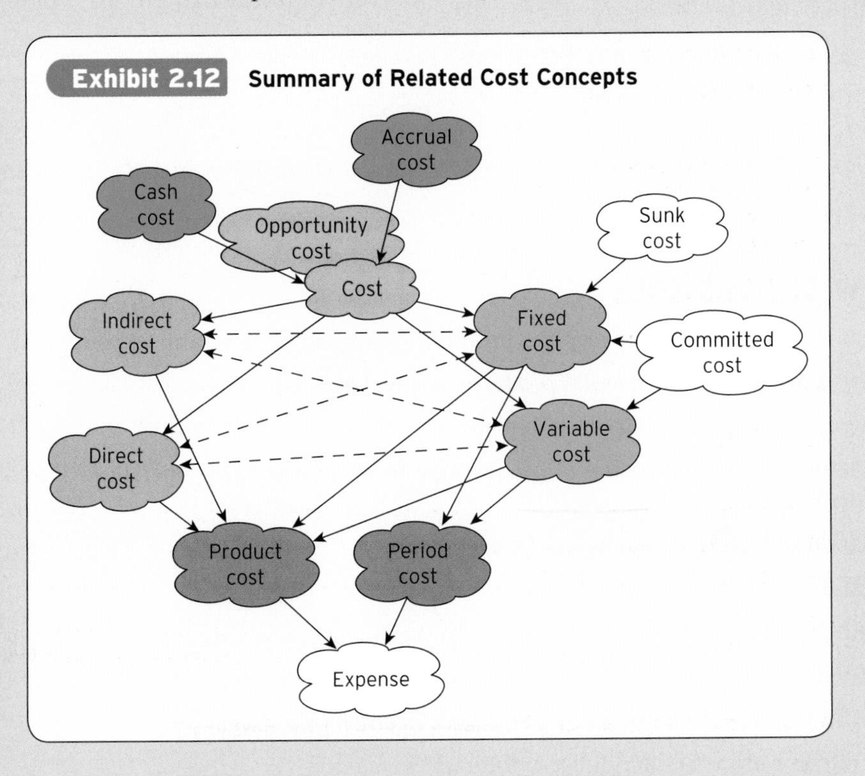

Cost accounting systems track the flow of costs using period expense accounts and three product accounts: *Work-in-Progress inventory, Finished goods inventory* and *Cost of sales;* the last is an expense on the statement of income. A manufacturing company has a more complex cost of sales statement than do service or retail companies. Whereas the retailer purchases goods for sale, the manufacturer makes them, and the statement reflects the tracking of all product costs through the product accounts.

Key Terms

For each term's definition, refer to the indicated page, or turn to the glossary at the end of the text.

accrual cost, 50, 55
administrative costs, 62
burden, 48
cash or out-of-pocket cost, 50, 52
committed cost, 53
conversion cost, 61
cost, 50
cost accounting system, 57
cost of sales, 57
direct cost, 48, 61
direct labour, 61
direct material, 61
expense, 57
financial model, 65
finished goods inventory, 63
fixed cost, 54
gross margin ratio, 58
idle time, 61
indirect costs, 48, 61
indirect labour cost, 61
indirect material cost, 61
manufacturing overhead cost, 61
operating income, 59
opportunity cost, 50
overtime premium, 61
period costs, 57, 62
product cost, 57
raw materials inventory, 63
return on sales ratio, 59
selling cost, 62
shrinkage, 63
sunk cost, 55
variable cost, 53
waste, 63
work-in-progress inventory, 63

Review Questions are mostly written at a ***basic*** *level; Critical Analysis questions and Exercises are* ***intermediate****, and Problems and Cases are* ***advanced****.*

Review Questions

2.1 What is the difference between the meanings of the terms 'cost' and 'expense'?

2.2 What is the difference between product costs and period costs?

2.3 Why is cost of sales an expense? Explain.

2.4 What are the three categories of product cost in a manufacturing operation? Describe each element briefly.

2.5 What does the term 'variable cost' mean?

2.6 What does the term 'fixed cost' mean?

2.7 Distinguish between material resources, conversion resources and operating resources.

2.8 Distinguish between production and non-production resources. Give examples of each.

2.9 Explain the concept of classifying resources as direct or indirect.

2.10 Is a resource always either direct or indirect? Explain.

2.11 Define and give an example of each of the following costs:

a. Opportunity cost

b. Cash cost

c. Product cost

d. Period cost

e. Direct cost

f. Indirect cost

2.12 Is a committed cost the same as a fixed cost? Explain.

Critical Analysis

2.13 Evaluate this statement: Issues of product costing are irrelevant for service organizations since they cannot build up inventories of services, and all costs for providing services are expensed in the period they are used.

2.14 Evaluate this statement: Issues of product costing are unimportant for virtual organizations that outsource their production operations.

2.15 Prepare a diagram that illustrates how the following resources – headquarters, facilities, division managers, information systems personnel – can be considered both direct and indirect in a company that has four operating divisions, each of which provides multiple services.

2.16 Respond to this comment from an economist friend: You cost management analysts use an overabundance of cost terms to cover up the fact that you really do not understand opportunity costs. You create jobs for yourselves based on unintelligible jargon. Not that that's a bad thing.

2.17 A colleague challenges you: What do you mean that there is no such thing as a *fixed cost?* Pick up any microeconomics or cost accounting book, and you will see the term used all the time. We have lots of fixed costs in our organization, don't we? What about your salary and the depreciation of your computer? Why do you want to replace *fixed cost* with *committed cost?*

2.18 Individually or as a group, prepare written arguments for and against the following proposition. (Be prepared to present your arguments.) The company needs to use accrual costing for financial and tax reporting. We make so many products in so many places that it would be too expensive to develop a separate accounting system based on cash or opportunity costs in addition to the system we are required to have. Our divisions should maintain minimum inventories to avoid committing scarce resources to products that might become obsolete. The way to keep divisions from making more than they can sell is to charge them interest on any inventories they maintain. If divisions want to tie up the company's resources in inventory, then they should pay the company at least the interest it could be earning if the treasurer had the same amount of cash.

2.19 Evaluate this criticism of the financial management of processes: All this emphasis on operating income, regardless of how you measure it, contributes to our continuing, short-term outlook. If we focus only on operating income, managers will do whatever they can to increase that measure, regardless of long-term impacts. This is what is wrong with modern business. We need to look beyond this period's operating income and focus on the long term.

Exercises

Exercise 2.20 [LO 6] Statement of Cost of Sales

The following items appeared in the records of Zodiac Cooperative for the last year:

Supervisory and indirect labour	€127,000
Supplies and indirect materials	14,000
Work-in-progress inventory, 1 January	135,000
Work-in-progress inventory, 31 December	142,000
Administrative costs	304,000
Depreciation, manufacturing	103,000
Direct labour	482,000
Finished goods inventory, 1 January	160,000
Finished goods inventory, 31 December	147,000
Heat, light and power (plant)	87,000

Marketing costs	272,000
Miscellaneous manufacturing costs	12,000
Plant maintenance and repairs	74,000
Raw material purchases	313,000
Raw material inventory, 1 January	102,000
Raw material inventory, 31 December	81,000
Sales revenue	2,036,000

Required

Build a spreadsheet to prepare a statement of income with a supporting schedule of cost of sales.

Exercise 2.21 [LO 3] Direct Labour: Variable or Fixed Cost

Recent articles in the business press have reported that many employers are treating direct labour as a true variable cost. Employees are hired and laid off regularly as the employer's needs dictate. One article referred to this practice as 'tapping and zapping employees'. Another article made reference to the new 'just-in-time workforce'.

Required

As a group, discuss whether direct labour is a fixed or a variable cost. What are the pros and cons of management treatment of direct labour as a variable cost? Are there ethical issues here?

Exercise 2.22 [LO 1, 4] Basic Concepts

Indicate whether each of the following costs incurred in a manufacturing operation is fixed or variable (F or V) and whether it is a period cost or product cost (P or R) under accrual costing.

a. Sales commissions
b. Office rent for sales personnel
c. Salaries for sales supervisors
d. Office rental for cost management staff
e. Administrative office heating and air conditioning
f. Transportation-in costs on materials purchased
g. Assembly-line workers' wages
h. Property taxes on office buildings for administrative staff
i. Salaries of the company's top executives
j. Overtime pay for assembly workers.

Exercise 2.23 [LO 1, 3, 4] Basic Concepts

Indicate whether each of the following costs incurred in a manufacturing operation is included in direct costs (D), conversion costs (C), or both (B).

a. Assembly-line worker's salary
b. Direct material used in production
c. Indirect material used in production
d. Factory heating and air conditioning
e. Production supervisor's salary
f. Transportation-in costs on materials purchased.

Exercise 2.24 [LO 1, 4] Basic Concepts

Indicate whether each of the following costs incurred in a manufacturing operation is fixed or variable (F or V) and whether it is a period cost or product cost (P or R) under accrual costing.

a. Utilities in cost management analysts' office
b. Factory security personnel
c. Factory heating and air conditioning
d. Power to operate factory equipment
e. Depreciation on furniture for company executives.

Exercise 2.25 [LO 4, 5] Statements for a Merchandising Company

DigiTech sells computers. On 1 January of this year, it had a beginning product inventory of €500,000, including transportation-in costs. It purchased €2,600,000 of product, had €260,000 of transportation-in costs, and had marketing and administrative costs of €1,600,000 during the year. The ending inventory of product on 31 December of this year was €300,000, including transportation-in costs. Sales revenue was €5,000,000 for the year.

Required

Build an Excel spreadsheet to prepare a statement of income with a supporting schedule of cost of sales.

Exercise 2.26 [LO 6] Statements for a Manufacturing Company

The following balances appeared in the accounts of Osaka Machine Tool Company during the current year. (¥ denotes Japanese yen.)

	1 January	31 December
Raw material inventory	¥328,000	¥366,000
Work-in-progress inventory	¥362,000	¥354,000
Finished goods inventory	¥146,000	¥150,000

During the year, ¥1,732,000 of direct material was used in production, and the year's cost of sales was ¥6,000,000.

Required

Prepare a schedule of cost sales, and fill in the following missing data.

a. Cost of raw material purchased during the year
b. Cost of goods manufactured during the year
c. Total manufacturing costs incurred during the year.

Exercise 2.27 [LO 6] Statements for a Manufacturing Company

The following information appears in Rotterdam Communication Company's records for last year:

Sales revenue	€418,000
Administrative costs	87,500
Manufacturing building depreciation	54,000
Indirect materials and supplies	12,600
Sales commissions	29,000
Raw material inventory, 1 January	36,800
Direct labour	71,200
Raw material inventory, 31 December	38,000
Finished goods inventory, 1 January	21,800
Finished goods inventory, 31 December	17,000
Raw material purchases	44,600
Work-in-progress inventory, 31 December	26,200
Supervisory and indirect labour	28,800
Property taxes, manufacturing plant	16,800
Plant utilities and power	47,000
Work-in-progress inventory, 1 January	30,800

Required

Build a spreadsheet to prepare a statement of income with a supporting schedule of cost of sales.

Exercise 2.28 [LO 1, 2] Statements for a Manufacturing Company

The following information appears in Billund Toy Company's records for last year (DKK million):

Sales revenue	9,930 DKK
Administrative costs	1,970

Manufacturing building depreciation	1,175
Indirect materials and supplies	215
Sales commissions	680
Raw material inventory, 1 January	820
Direct labour	1,630
Raw material inventory, 31 December	900
Finished goods inventory, 1 January	445
Finished goods inventory, 31 December	390
Raw material purchases	1,015
Work-in-progress inventory, 31 December	555
Supervisory and indirect labour	620
Property taxes, manufacturing plant	370
Plant utilities and power	1,150
Work-in-progress inventory, 1 January	660

Required

Build a spreadsheet to prepare a statement of income with a supporting schedule of cost of sales.

Exercise 2.29 [LO 3, 5] Cost Behaviour for Decision Making

Scafell Pike Company manufactured 1,000 units of product last year and identified the following costs associated with the manufacturing activity (variable costs are indicated with V, fixed costs with F):

Direct material used (V)	£69,000
Direct labour (V)	134,400
Supervisory salaries (F)	61,200
Indirect materials and supplies (V)	15,500
Plant utilities (other than power to run plant equipment) (F)	19,200
Power to run plant equipment (V)	14,700
Depreciation on plant and equipment (straight-line, time basis) (F)	9,600
Property taxes on building (F)	14,000

Per unit variable costs and total fixed costs are expected to remain unchanged next year.

Required

Calculate the per-unit variable cost and the average total cost per unit if 1,400 units are produced next year.

Exercise 2.30 [LO 3] Cost Behaviour

Refer to the information in the preceding exercise.

Required

Construct graphs of total fixed and variable costs.

Exercise 2.31 [LO 6] Operating Profit

Or de Paris Mustard Company produces a specialty mustard product, which it sells over the Internet for €22 per case. The company produced 120,000 units (cases) and sold 104,000 units last year. There were no beginning inventories or ending Work-in-progress inventories last year. Manufacturing costs and selling and administrative costs for last year follow:

Direct material	€780,000
Direct labour	450,000
Manufacturing overhead (variable)	180,000

Manufacturing overhead (fixed)	180,000
Selling and administrative (variable)	140,000
Selling and administrative (fixed)	120,000

Required

Build a spreadsheet to complete requirements (a) and (b).

a. Compute the per unit product (manufacturing) accrual cost.
b. Compute the operating profit using accrual costing.

Problems

Problem 2.32 [LO 3-5] Unknown Account Balances

Each of the following columns is independent and for a different company. Use the data given, which refer to one year for each company, to find the unknown account balances.

	Company		
Account	1	2	3
Sales revenue	€70,100	€1,088,000	€3,359,900
Raw material inventory, 1 January	8,000	24,600	45,000
Raw material inventory, 31 December	12,400	20,000	(d)
Work-in-progress inventory, 1 January	12,560	11,600	(e)
Work-in-progress inventory, 31 December	12,560	12,000	85,200
Finished goods inventory, 1 January	2,800	254,200	334,480
Finished goods inventory, 31 December	4,600	(b)	367,400
Purchases of raw material	(a)	262,000	248,400
Cost of goods manufactured during the year	58,000	679,200	1,518,220
Total manufacturing costs	58,000	679,600	1,526,800
Cost of sales	56,200	760,000	(f)
Gross margin	13,900	328,000	1,874,600
Direct labour	23,200	173,000	(g)
Direct material used	15,000	(c)	234,200
Manufacturing overhead	19,800	240,000	430,600

Problem 2.33 [LO 3, 5, 6] Impact of a Decision on Statements of Income

You have been appointed manager of an operating division of Espoo Technology SE, a manufacturer of products using the latest developments in microprocessor technology. Your division manufactures the chip assembly, CH-1. On 1 January of this year, you invested €1 million in automated processing equipment for the chip assembly. At that time, your expected statement of income for this year was as follows:

Sales revenue	€1,590,000
Operating costs:	
Variable (cash expenditures)	190,000
Fixed (cash expenditures)	750,000
Equipment depreciation	150,000
Other depreciation	125,000
Total operating costs	€1,215,000
Operating profit (before taxes)	€375,000

On 15 November of this year, a sales representative for Hasegawa Machine Company approaches you. Hasegawa wants to rent to your division a new assembly machine that would be installed on 31 December for an annual rental charge of €230,000. The new equipment will enable your division to produce a higher quality product with a sales price 10 per cent higher. Therefore, your division's annual revenue will be 10 per cent higher. (There will be no change in variable costs.) The new machine would decrease fixed cash expenditures by 5 per cent. You will have to write off the cost of the automated processing equipment this year because it has no salvage value. Equipment depreciation shown on the statement of income is for the automated processing equipment.

Your bonus is determined as a percentage of your division's operating profit before taxes. Equipment losses are included in the bonus and operating profit computation.

Ignore taxes and any effects on operations on the day of installation of the new machine. Assume that the data given in your expected statement of income are the actual amounts for this year and next year if you keep the current equipment.

Required

a. What is the difference in this year's divisional operating profit if the new machine is rented and installed on 31 December of this year?
b. What would be the effect on next year's divisional operating profit if the new machine is rented and installed on 31 December of this year?
c. Would you rent the new equipment? Why or why not?

Problem 2.34 [LO 6] Schedules of Cost of Goods Manufactured and Sold; Statement of Income

The following data refer to Ferruccio Fashions Company for the year 20x2:

Sales revenue	€945,000
Work-in-progress inventory, 31 December	30,000
Work-in-progress inventory, 1 January	40,000
Selling and administrative expenses	145,000
Income tax expense	80,000
Purchases of raw material	180,000
Raw material inventory, 31 December	25,000
Raw material inventory, 1 January	40,000
Direct labour	200,000
Utilities: plant	40,000
Depreciation: plant and equipment	60,000
Finished goods inventory, 31 December	50,000
Finished goods inventory, 1 January	20,000
Indirect material	11,000
Indirect labour	16,000
Other manufacturing overhead	78,000

Required

Build a spreadsheet to complete requirements (a) through (c).

a. Prepare Ferruccio Fashions' schedule of cost of goods manufactured for the year.
b. Prepare Ferruccio Fashions' schedule of cost of sales for the year.
c. Prepare Ferruccio Fashions' statement of income for the year.

Problem 2.35 [LO 3] Fixed and Variable Costs; Forecasting

UK Electronics CIC incurred the following costs during 20x1. The company sold all of its products manufactured during the year.

Direct material	£2,900,000
Direct labour	1,950,000

Manufacturing overhead:	
Utilities (primarily electricity)	140,000
Depreciation on plant and equipment	230,000
Insurance	150,000
Supervisory salaries	300,000
Property taxes	220,000
Selling costs:	
Advertising	195,000
Sales commissions	90,000
Administrative costs:	
Salaries of top management and staff	369,000
Office supplies	40,000
Depreciation on building and equipment	75,000

During 20x1, the company operated at about half of its capacity due to a slowdown in the economy. Prospects for 20x2 are slightly better. The marketing manager forecasts a 20 per cent growth in sales over the 20x1 level.

Required

Categorize each of the preceding costs as most likely variable or fixed. Forecast or predict the 20x2 amount for each cost item.

Problem 2.36 [LO 2-4] Characteristics of Costs

The following terms are used to describe various characteristics of costs.

1. Opportunity cost
2. Out-of-pocket cost
3. Sunk cost
4. Direct cost
5. Conversion cost
6. Average cost

Required

Choose one of the terms to characterize each of the following amounts.

a. The cost to build an automated assembly line in a factory was €800,000 when the line was installed three years ago.
b. The management of a high-rise office building using 2,500 square feet of space in the building for its own management functions but could be rented for €250,000.
c. The direct material and direct labour cost incurred by a mass customizer such as **Dell** to produce its most popular line of laptop computers.
d. The cost of feeding 500 children in a public school cafeteria is £800 per day, or £1.60 per child per day.
e. The cost of product inventory purchased two years ago, which is now obsolete.
f. The cost of direct labour and manufacturing overhead incurred in producing frozen fish fillets.
g. The €1,000 cost of offering a computer workshop for a group of 20 students, or €50 per student.

Problem 2.37 [LO 3] Variable Costs; Graphical and Tabular Analyses

Tungsten Metallwerk AG incurs a variable cost of €40 per kilogram for direct material to produce a special alloy used in manufacturing aircraft.

Required

a. Draw a graph of the firm's direct material cost, showing the total cost at the following production levels: 10,000 kilograms, 20,000 kilograms and 30,000 kilograms.
b. Prepare a table that shows the unit cost and total cost of direct material at the following production levels: 1 kilograms, 10 kilograms and 1,000 kilograms.

Problem 2.38 [LO 3] Fixed Costs; Graphical and Tabular Analyses

SkyAide SA manufactures a special fabric used to upholster the seats in small aircraft. The company's annual fixed production cost is €100,000.

Required

a. Graph the company's fixed production cost showing the total cost at the following production levels of upholstery fabric: 10,000 m^2, 20,000 m^2, 30,000 m^2 and 40,000 m^2.
b. Prepare a table that shows the unit cost and the total cost for the firm's fixed production costs at the following production levels: 1 m^2, 10 m^2, 10,000 m^2 and 40,000 m^2.
c. Prepare a graph that shows the unit cost for the company's fixed production cost at the following production levels: 10,000 m^2, 20,000 m^2, 30,000 m^2 and 40,000 m^2.

Problem 2.39 [LO 6] Reconstructed Financial Statements

The following data appeared in Dublin Flooring's records on 31 December of last year:

Sales revenue	€812,500
Direct material used	191,050
Work-in-progress inventory, 31 December	12,300
Raw material inventory, 31 December	42,500
Raw material purchased during the year	180,000
Finished goods inventory, 31 December	45,000
Indirect labour	16,000
Direct labour	195,000
Plant heat, light and power	22,600
Building depreciation (7/9 is for manufacturing)	40,500
Administrative salaries	24,900
Miscellaneous factory cost	16,950
Selling costs	19,300
Maintenance on factory machines	6,050
Insurance on factory equipment	9,500
Distribution costs	800
Taxes on manufacturing property	6,550
Legal fees on customer complaint	4,100

On 1 January, last year, the Finished goods inventory account had a balance of €40,000, and the Work-in-progress inventory account had a balance of €12,950.

Required

Build a spreadsheet to prepare a schedule of cost of sales and a statement of income.

Problem 2.40 [LO 5] Unknown Account Balances

Each of the following columns is independent and for a different company. Use the data given, which refer to one year for each example, to find the unknown account balances.

	Company		
Account	**1**	**2**	**3**
Finished goods inventory, 1 January	€1,900	(d)	€17,200
Finished goods inventory, 31 December	300	€4,400	28,400
Work-in-progress inventory, 1 January	2,700	6,720	82,400
Work-in-progress inventory, 31 December	3,800	3,100	76,730
Raw material inventory, 1 January	(a)	3,500	16,000

Raw material inventory, 31 December	3,600	2,900	14,100
Purchases of raw materials	16,100	12,000	64,200
Cost of goods manufactured during the year	(b)	27,220	313,770
Total manufacturing costs	55,550	23,600	308,100
Cost of sales	56,050	27,200	302,570
Gross margin	(c)	16,400	641,280
Direct material used	15,300	(e)	66,100
Direct labour	26,450	3,800	124,700
Manufacturing overhead	13,800	7,200	(g)
Sales revenue	103,300	(f)	943,850

Problem 2.41 [LO 3-5] Cost Concepts

The following data pertain to the Photon Gizmo manufactured by Geneva Gizmos AG:

Sales price	CHF 175 per unit
Fixed costs:	
Selling and administrative	CHF 20,000 per period
Manufacturing overhead	CHF 15,000 per period
Variable costs:	
Selling and administrative	CHF 5 per unit
Manufacturing overhead	CHF 30 per unit
Direct labour (manufacturing)	CHF 10 per unit
Direct material (manufacturing)	CHF 40 per unit
Number of units produced and sold during the period	1,000 units

Required

a. How much is the variable *manufacturing cost* per unit?
b. How much is the *variable cost* per unit?
c. How much is the *accrual cost* per unit?
d. How much is the *direct cost* per unit?
e. How much is the *conversion cost* per unit?
f. How much is the *profit margin* per unit?
g. How much is the *gross margin* per unit?
h. If the number of units increases from 1,000 to 1,200, which is within the company's relevant range of activity, will the *fixed manufacturing cost* per unit decrease, increase, or stay the same? Why?

Problem 2.42 [LO 1, 4] Cost Concepts

Items (a) through (e) are to be based on the following data pertaining to Atlántico's manufacturing operations:

Inventories	1 November	30 November
Raw material	€9,000	€8,500
Work-in-progress	4,500	3,000
Finished goods	13,500	18,000

Additional information for the month of November:

Raw material purchased	€22,000
Direct labour costs	14,000
Manufacturing overhead	20,000
Selling and administrative expenses	11,000
Sales revenue	99,000

Required

Calculate the following amounts for the month of November:

a. Direct costs
b. Conversion costs
c. Total manufacturing costs
d. Cost of goods manufactured
e. Cost of sales

[CPA adapted]

Cases

Case 2.43 [LO 2-5] Cost Data for Managerial Purposes

Florida Fruits Inc. agreed to sell 40,000 cases of Fang, a dehydrated fruit drink, to **NASA** for use on the international space station at 'cost plus 10 per cent'. The company operates a manufacturing plant that can produce 120,000 cases per year, but it normally produces 80,000. The costs to produce 80,000 cases are as follows:

	Total	Per case
Direct material	$960,000	$12.00
Direct labour	1,520,000	19.00
Supplies and other costs that vary with production	640,000	8.00
Costs that do not vary with production	440,000	5.50
Variable selling costs	160,000	2.00
Administrative costs (all fixed)	160,000	2.00
Total	$3,880,000	$48.50

Based on these data, company management expects to receive $53.35 (that is, $48.50 × 110 per cent) per case for those sold on this contract. After completing 10,000 cases, the company sent a bill (invoice) to the government for $533,500 (that is, 10,000 cases at $53.35 per case).

The president of the company received a call from a NASA representative, who stated that the per-case cost should be as follows:

Material	$12
Labour	19
Supplies and other costs that vary with production	8
Total	$39

Therefore, the price per case should be $42.90 (that is, $39 × 110 per cent). NASA ignored selling costs because the contract bypassed the usual sales channels.

Required

What price would you recommend? Why? Write a memo to management explaining your reasoning. (*Note:* You need not limit yourself to the costs selected by the company or by the NASA representative.)

Case 2.44 [LO 2, 4, 5] Cost Analysis for Decision Making

Le Vin Plus Ordinaire is a start-up winery that purchases excess grapes at a discount from established wineries in several regions of France. Le Vin owns a small fleet of trucks that picks up grapes from wineries and delivers wine to its distributor. On average the return distance of a pick up or delivery is 100 km. Consider the data below to complete the required analyses.

Costs of excess grapes		
Average discount price paid to growers for grapes	€2,000	per metric ton
Annual purchases of grapes	500	metric tons
Average cost for delivery by vineyard	€100.00	per delivery, up to 2 metric tons
Costs per delivery truck		
Purchase cost	€30,000	per truck (purchased 2 years ago)
Useful life, years	10	years
Useful life, kilometres driven	300,000	km over complete useful life
Annual maintenance	€2,100	per year
Annual licence and insurance	€3,200	per year
Fuel usage	7.00	km per litre
Fuel cost	€1.40	per litre
Costs of a truck driver		
Annual salary	€28,000	per year
Annual benefits	€14,000	per year

Required

a. Compute the out-of-pocket or cash cost to make an average pick up of 1.5 metric tons of grapes.
b. Compare the cash cost to the average delivery price charged by a vineyard.
c. Should Le Vin Plus Ordinaire continue to own and operate its trucks? Explain.
d. Le Vin Plus Ordinaire is considering whether to get rid of its trucks and rely on deliveries from vineyards.
  i. Compute the accrual cost to pick up 1.5 metric tons of excess grapes from a vineyard that is 50 km distant.
  ii. Is the accrual cost of the pick-up a reliable guide to whether Le Vin should continue to own and operate its trucks? Explain.
  iii. What qualitative considerations should Le Vin also consider before switching to deliveries by vineyards?

Case 2.45 [LO 2, 4, 5] Cost Analysis for Decision Making

The Green Thumb Landscaping Company prepares lawns and gardens in the spring, mows lawns and tends ornamental gardens in the summer, rakes leaves in the autumn, and clears snow in the winter. Green Thumb is located centrally but performs jobs for customers along the Front Range of the Rocky Mountains in Colorado USA, along an approximately 100 mile corridor.

Green Thumb owns all the necessary vehicles and equipment, which are billed to customers by the mileage driven to and from the job and by the hours of services provided, respectively. A vehicle that carries the service crew and its equipment cost $40,000 to purchase and typically is driven 20,000 miles per year (400,000 miles over its lifetime) and costs $6,000 per year for depreciation, insurance, etc. Fuel in the US costs approximately $4.00 per gallon, and Green Thumb's vehicles average 16 miles per gallon of fuel. Equipment on average has a useful life of 4,000 hours of use, and equipment for an entire crew costs approximately $5 to operate per hour. The purchase cost for equipment for an entire crew is approximately $10,000.

The company hires workers at an hourly rate of $20 per hour, including taxes and benefits. The company employs 4 crews year round. The company has 'home office' costs for salaries and facilities of approximately $200,000 per year.

Required

a. Compute the out-of-pocket cost(s) of completing jobs.
b. Compute the accrual cost(s) of completing jobs. Should you include a portion of home office costs? Why or why not? If so, how?
c. Compute the out-of-pocket cost to complete a job that is 40 miles distant and will take 40 hours of work.
d. Compute the accrual cost to complete a job that is 40 miles distant and will take 40 hours of work.
e. If the company has idle time, what is the opportunity cost of taking a job that is 50 miles distant and that will take 10 hours of work?

Case 2.46 [LO 1] Inventory Turnover

Campus Bookstore is a profit-making organization that reports to the Student Council. Marta Nováková, a part-time student employee, noticed that the managers at the bookstore seemed unconcerned about the costs of carrying large inventories. For example, several times a year the manager of the General Merchandise Department (one of six departments) bought large quantities of product (clothing, gift items, etc.) with the university and sports team logos to get quantity discounts. The General Merchandise manager also had argued successfully for more warehouse space for the products, for which the bookstore pays rent to the university. Inevitably, several months later, the manager would mark down the unsold products to purchase cost or less to make room for the next purchase. This seemed very inefficient to Nováková, and she began to analyse the bookstore's purchases and sales for the past year. She gathered the following data.

Department	Cost of sales	Average inventory	Percentage of warehouse space	Average number of days items were purchased in advance of sale
New textbooks	€5,730,972	€840,475	25%	63
Used textbooks	1,258,007	180,600	12	37
Trade books	563,686	370,500	10	86
Supplies	662,560	251,700	8	71
General merchandise	883,251	640,600	25	94
Computers	2,246,600	402,000	20	28
Total store	€11,345,076	€2,685,875	100%	66.3

63.2

Required

a. Compute inventory turnover ratios (i.e., cost of sales ÷ average inventory) for each department and the bookstore as a whole. What would these ratios tell Nováková about the management of inventories at Campus Bookstore? Is it reasonable to compare these ratios across departments? Why or why not?
b. A privately owned store in the university commercial area sells licensed (general) products with the university's logo and reported to Nováková that its inventory turnover ratio for the past year was 5.30. Is that a legitimate benchmark for Campus Bookstore? Why or why not?
c. What are the benefits and costs to the bookstore of its methods for purchasing and inventory?
d. What information would Nováková need to place a dollar figure on all of those costs?
e. Nováková has learned that the manager of the General Merchandise Department is a close personal friend of the bookstore manager and receives incentive prizes from suppliers for ordering large quantities of products. What are her ethical responsibilities?

Case 2.47 [LO 4-6] 'I Enjoy Challenges'; Effect of Changes in Production and Costing Method on Operating Profit

(This classic case is based on an actual company's experience.) Brassinni Company uses an accrual cost system to apply all production costs to units produced. The plant has a maximum production capacity of 40 million units but produced and sold only 10 million units during year 1. There were no beginning or ending inventories. Brassinni Company's statement of income for year 1 follows:

BRASSINNI COMPANY	
Statement of income	
For the year ending 31 December, Year 1	
Sales (10,000,000 units at €6)	€60,000,000
Cost of sales:	
Direct costs, material and labour	
(10,000,000 at €2).	€20,000,000

Manufacturing overhead	48,000,000
Cost of sales	68,000,000
Gross margin	(8,000,000)
Selling and administrative costs	10,000,000
Operating profit (loss)	€(18,000,000)

The board of directors is concerned about the €18 million loss. A consultant approached the board with the following offer: 'I agree to become president for no fixed salary. But I insist on a year-end bonus of 10 per cent of operating profit (before considering the bonus).' The board of directors agreed to these terms and hired the consultant as Brassinni's new president.

The new president promptly stepped up production to an annual rate of 30 million units. Sales for year 2 remained at 10 million units. The resulting Brassinni Company accrual-costing statement of income for year 2 follows:

BRASSINNI COMPANY Statement of Income For the year ending 31 December, Year 2	
Sales (10,000,000 units at €6)	€60,000,000
Cost of sales:	
Cost of goods manufactured:	
Direct costs, material and labour	
(30,000,000 at €2)	60,000,000
Manufacturing overhead	48,000,000
Total cost of goods manufactured	108,000,000
Less: Ending inventory:	
Variable (20,000,000 at $2)	40,000,000
Indirect (20/30 × $48,000,000)	32,000,000
Total ending inventory	72,000,000
Cost of sales	36,000,000
Gross margin	24,000,000
Selling and administrative costs	10,000,000
Operating profit before bonus	14,000,000
Bonus	1,400,000
Operating profit after bonus	€12,600,000

The day after the statement was verified, the president took his cheque for €1,400,000 and resigned to take a job with another corporation. He remarked, 'I enjoy challenges. Now that Brassinni Company is in the black, I'd prefer tackling another challenging situation.' (His contract with his new employer is similar to the one he had with Brassinni Company.)

Required

a. Step back, and look at this overall situation. In general, what do you think is going on here? More specifically, how would you evaluate the company's year-2 performance?

b. If you valued inventory at only variable cost, what would operating profit be for year 1? For year 2? (Assume that all fixed production costs and non-product costs are unchanged.) Compare those results with the accrual statements.

c. Comment on any ethical issues you see in this scenario.

Case 2.48 [LO 5, 6] Analysis of Costing; Import Decisions

Cotierre imports designer clothing manufactured by subcontractors in Mexico. Clothing is a seasonal product. The goods must be ready for sale prior to the start of the season. Any goods left over at the end of the season usually must be sold at steep discounts. The company prepares a dress design and selects fabrics approximately six months before a given season. It receives these goods and distributes them at the start of the season. Based on past experience, the company estimates that 60 per cent of a particular lot of dresses will be unsold at the end of the season and will be marked down to one-half of the initial retail price. Even with the markdown, a substantial number of dresses will remain unsold and will be returned to Cotierre and destroyed. Although a large number of dresses must be discounted or destroyed, the company needs to place a minimum order of 1,000 dresses to have a sufficient selection of styles and sizes to market the design.

Recently, the company placed an order for 1,000 dresses of a particular design for $25,000 plus import duties of $5,000 and a $7 commission for each dress sold at retail, regardless of the price. Return mailing and disposing of each unsold dress cost $3 after the end of the markdown period.

Required

a. Compute the accrual cost of each dress in this lot of dresses.

b. Suppose that the company sells 30 per cent of the dresses in this lot for $75 each during the first accounting period. What is the accrual value of the ending inventory? What is the operating profit or loss for the period, assuming no other transactions and that the season has not ended, so that the number of dresses subject to markdown or to be returned is unknown?

c. During the second period, 10 per cent of the 1,000 dresses were sold at full price, and 30 per cent were sold at the half-price markdown. The remaining dresses were returned and disposed of. What is the operating profit or loss for the period, assuming no other transactions?

d. Suggest a method to account for these dresses that would more closely relate revenues and costs.

Solutions to You're the Decision Maker

2.1 Opportunity Cost, p. 50

The opportunity cost of seeing Radiohead is the value of what you must sacrifice to attend their concert - the value to you of attending the Lady Gaga concert, €50, less the €40 you would have to pay for a ticket. If you did not get the correct answer of €10, you have company. Only 21.6 per cent of the professional economists surveyed chose that answer. The accounting cost is €0, because that is the observed transaction price.

Source: Ferraro and Taylor (2005).

2.2 Cost Reductions, p. 60

a. Sacs Chameaux statement of income

Sacs Chameaux, without cost reductions	20xx (adjusted)	Percentage change
Sales turnover	€2,370,480	–17%
Cost of sales	1,142,400	0%
Gross margin	1,228,080	–28%
Period expenses	1,245,000	0%
Operating income	(16,920)	–104%

b. The required cost reduction could ripple through the entire industry 'supply chain' to the most basic supplier. Sacs Chameaux may try to reduce its costs, and try to persuade its suppliers (e.g., the fabric wholesaler, Arnault Expert Comptable, and so on) to reduce sales prices. These suppliers may in turn pressure their suppliers to reduce their prices. Eventually, all participants in the chain may seek the lowest cost supplies and suppliers, who might be located externally to their firms and in low-cost regions of the world. One could get anxious and expect that one day there will be (low) world prices for everything. We can probably relax a bit because the world is not static, and innovations will always keep the supply chains in flux.

2.3 Sacs Chameaux's Opportunities for Cost Savings, p. 66

a. All of the costs to be added (direct material, direct labour and manufacturing overhead) may be changeable next year. None of the 20xx ending inventory balances can be changed; they are sunk costs.

b. A backpack would have to lose an average of 17% or €9.65 (= 194,208/20,130) based on 20xx production costs.

c. Some organizations levy uniform cost reductions across all departments, but that usually is unwise. Some costs might be easier than others to cut, and cutting some costs might adversely affect the quality of the product to a greater or lesser degree. The company should look to cut activities and costs that do not affect the quality of the product or the timeliness of filling orders. Many of these may be found in manufacturing overhead and period expenses. Perhaps more 'back office' services can be outsourced more cheaply, but assuming this will be true is not safe. It may be neither wise nor possible to cut direct labour or direct materials without harming quality, but these should be investigated for obvious waste and streamlining.

d. If production costs are reduced, one certainly could, for internal and customer bargaining purposes, revalue the beginning inventories for purposes of computing and demonstrating potentially sufficient cost savings. One could investigate whether writing down the inventories and taking a period loss is wise and allowed for external reporting.

Endnotes

1 You may jump to the end of this chapter to view Exhibit 2.12 to see an abstraction of the many possibilities, but don't be dismayed – we will work through the complications. The key is to understand why one is measuring cost in the first place, then settle on a definition of cost.

2 Sacs Chameaux SA is a fictional company that is based loosely on the experiences of Millet, which was acquired by the Lafuma Group in 1995.

3 Other external entities that are part of the extended value chain include materials suppliers, energy utilities, legal services and labour unions. The figure does not include these entities for economy of presentation.

4 Adapted from a 2005 study by Ferraro and Taylor.

5 If €8 is a competitive market price, this also is a market-based measure of opportunity cost. However, not all markets are competitive, and some participants may recognize opportunities to use inputs to generate even higher values.

6 But wait, we are not done with the complexity surrounding the cost of the nylon fabric. The previous measure of cost relied on observed transactions that exchanged resources (e.g., fabric for cash). Not all transactions are mediated by observed exchanges. For example, the cost of the nylon fabric reflects its production costs, which includes the costs of hydrocarbon materials usually obtained from oil, but this portion of cost is incomplete. The market price for oil fluctuates, but so far it does not include the unobserved environmental cost associated with the production and use of oil. Likewise, the cost of the fuel used by Sac Chameaux's trucks does not include the environmental and social costs of resulting emissions. These interesting pressures on the meaning and measurement of the 'true' cost of human activities are controversial and constantly evolving. For example, the cost of extracting oil, from which nylon is made, from deep-water wells might resemble the 'true' cost if insurance rates adjust to account for damages like those experienced by British Petroleum's 2010 blowout in the Gulf of Mexico. Similarly, participants in the Kyoto Protocol trade carbon credits to mitigate environmental costs of harmful emissions from fossil fuel, and in the process measure the costs of these emissions. The full treatment of these costs is beyond the scope of this text.

7 We defer to Chapter 8 the related discussion of tax effects from gains or losses on sales of resources or depreciation of historical purchase prices of long-lived capacity resources.

8 The timing of expenses can also be important to managers when a firm's or their performance is measured by periodic income. This important topic, which reflects complications of managers' incentives, is discussed in Chapter 14.

9 The statements in Exhibit 2.7 also resemble those of service firms, except that gross margin is computed as sales turnover minus cost of *services provided.*

References

Brierly, J.A., C.J. Cowton and C. Drury (2006) 'The application of costs in make-or-buy decisions: an analysis', *International Journal of Management*, vol. 23, no 4, pp. 794–800.

Ferraro P.J. and L.O. Taylor (2005) 'Do economists recognize an opportunity cost when they see one? A dismal performance from the dismal science', *Contributions to Economic Analysis and Policy*, vol. 4, no. 1, www.bepress.com/bejeep/contributions/vol4/issl/art7

Skinner, R.C. (1990) 'The role of profitability in divisional decision making and performance evaluation', *Accounting and Business Research*, vol. 20, no. 78, pp. 135–141.

CHAPTER 3

Cost Estimation

Learning Objectives

After completing this chapter, you should be able to:

LO 1 State the reasons that companies estimate relations between costs and cost drivers.

LO 2 Understand basic decisions about cost estimation.

LO 3 Use and interpret account analysis for cost estimation.

LO 4 Use and interpret linear regression for cost estimation.

LO 5 Use and interpret the high-low method for cost estimation.

LO 6 Use and interpret multiple regression for cost estimation.

LO 7 Use and interpret the engineering method for cost estimation

LO 8 Compare different cost estimation methods in a benefit–cost framework.

LO 9 Understand how regression works and identify potential statistical problems with regression analysis (Appendix 3A).

LO 10 Estimate and use learning curve cost predictions (Appendix 3B).

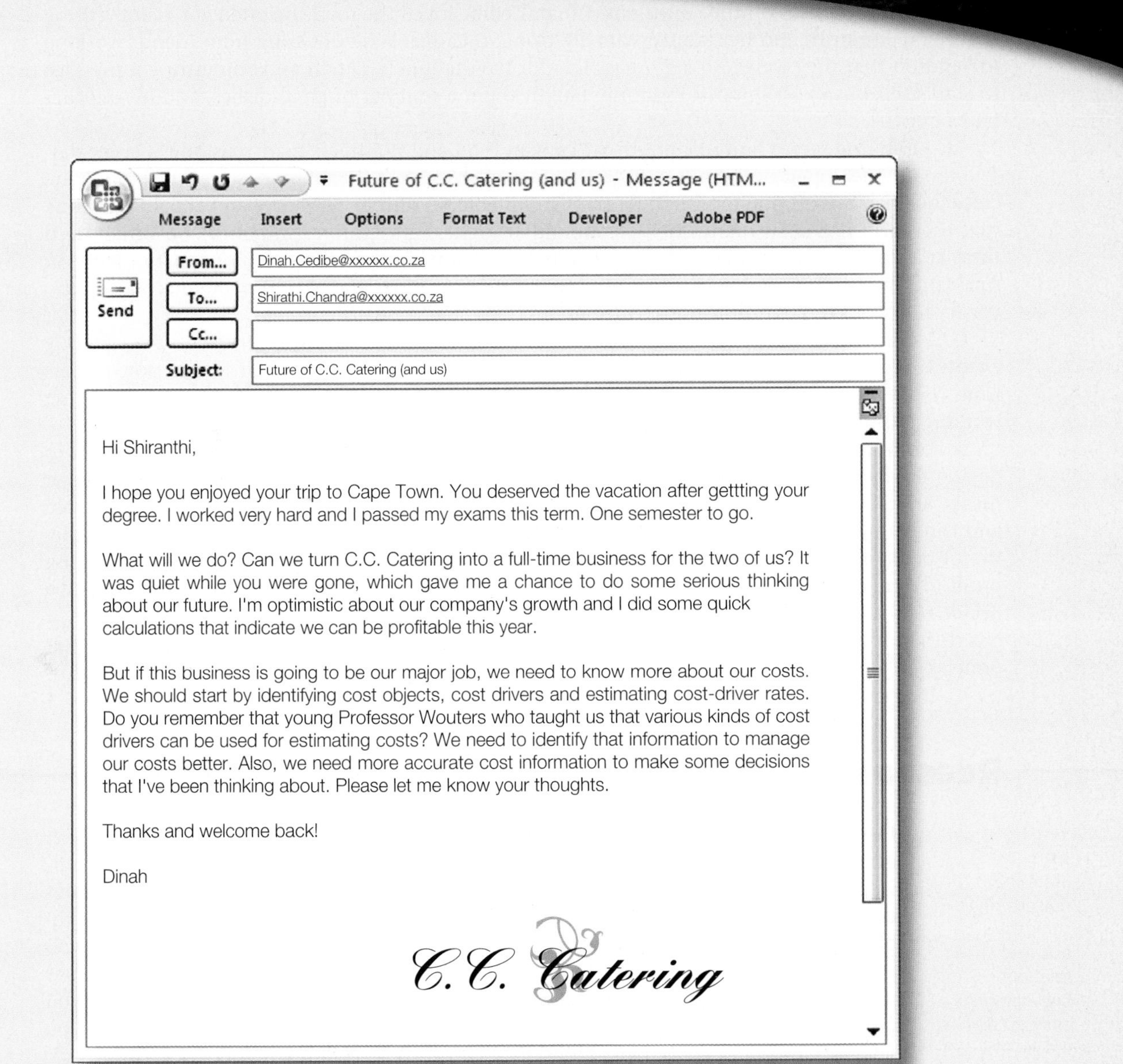

Future of C.C. Catering (and us) - Message (HTM...

Message Insert Options Format Text Developer Adobe PDF

Send

From... Dinah.Cedibe@xxxxxx.co.za

To... Shirathi.Chandra@xxxxxx.co.za

Cc...

Subject: Future of C.C. Catering (and us)

Hi Shiranthi,

I hope you enjoyed your trip to Cape Town. You deserved the vacation after gettting your degree. I worked very hard and I passed my exams this term. One semester to go.

What will we do? Can we turn C.C. Catering into a full-time business for the two of us? It was quiet while you were gone, which gave me a chance to do some serious thinking about our future. I'm optimistic about our company's growth and I did some quick calculations that indicate we can be profitable this year.

But if this business is going to be our major job, we need to know more about our costs. We should start by identifying cost objects, cost drivers and estimating cost-driver rates. Do you remember that young Professor Wouters who taught us that various kinds of cost drivers can be used for estimating costs? We need to identify that information to manage our costs better. Also, we need more accurate cost information to make some decisions that I've been thinking about. Please let me know your thoughts.

Thanks and welcome back!

Dinah

C.C. Catering

Shiranthi Chandra and Dinah Cedibe had started their own company, a restaurant and catering service, called C.C. Catering. The company is located in Sandton in Johannesburg, South Africa, close to the offices of investment banks, financial consultants, and the Johannesburg Stock Exchange (JSE). The city has become the new financial centre of South Africa and Johannesburg's premier business centre. Sandton is also home to the Sandton Convention Centre, one of the largest convention centres on the continent. Dinah Cedibe loved the food she often got when visiting her friend Shiranthi and her family, who are from Sri Lanka. When hearing from friends working in Sandton that they longed for more variety for having lunch, Dinah and Shiranthi got the idea to start their business. Shiranthi's family taught them a number of great dishes, and her mother helps out.

C.C. Catering serves fantastic South Sri Lankan food and it attracts many customers every day. The restaurant is open only for lunch. It is very small and has only about 25 seats which are quite close together. That is fine for lunch, but not so suitable for dinner. Shiranthi and Dinah also think that there will not be as many clientele around at night. Furthermore, Shiranthi and Dinah need time at night for their catering business and their study at the University of Johannesburg in Auckland Park. C.C. Catering provides food to business meetings and also to numerous official university functions (e.g., administrative meetings).

C.C. Catering provided Shiranthi and Dinah with good part-time work. In fact, C.C. Catering eventually provided them with enough opportunity and fun that they so far turned down offers from public accounting firms and industry. They are about to graduate and they are considering working full-time in the catering service.

Shiranthi and Dinah take a small monthly management salary of R5,000 each, in addition to paying themselves R50 per hour for each hour worked to obtain customers, prepare meals, deliver meals, and perform other non-management aspects of the operations.[1] At present, both Shiranthi and Dinah own minivans for delivering meals. The company reimburses them at R2.00 per kilometre for deliveries. At the end of each fiscal year (30 June), they decide how much of the operating profit to put back into the business and share the rest 50–50. Shiranthi Chandra and Dinah Cedibe decide that if they want to stay in the catering business, it is now time to turn from growing their business to focusing on managing costs and creating profits. One crucial input for that is to better understand what is driving their costs.

Reasons for Estimating Costs

LO 1
State the reasons that companies estimate relations between costs and cost drivers.

Cost estimation is the process of estimating the relations between **cost objects**, which is anything that the cost analyst may want to estimate the cost of, such as products, services, projects, activities, organizational entities, or inputs to products, and the **cost drivers**, which are measures of workload or output, that explain those costs. For example, suppose you are trying to reduce your own personal transportation costs (that is, you are a personal cost management analyst). You normally drive your car 15,000 kilometres per year, including commuting. If you use public transportation for commuting, you could reduce the annual travelling distance to 10,000 kilometres. How much would you save in automobile costs if you reduced driving by 5,000 kilometres per year? The answer to that question is not easy because, as you know, some costs are related to the number of kilometres driven and others are not. The costs of road tax are probably not related to the kilometres driven, whereas the cost of using toll roads and fuel are. Repairs and depreciation costs are related to kilometres driven but perhaps not proportionately.

In general, the impact of decisions can be quite clear for a specific out-of-pocket, variable, direct cost, such as the fuel cost of the car, or when C.C. Catering rents a tent, tables and chairs for an event.[2] Market prices are usually available, and we understand exactly what is driving the cost level. But in many other cases, some form of cost estimation is needed to understand how costs behave. Direct cost can be a mix of fixed and variable costs, and a blend of cash costs and accrual costs. And it is usually not evident what is causing indirect costs. Cost management analysts use the organization's own historical data and apply the analysis methods presented here. Organizations estimate costs primarily for three reasons:

1. To manage costs.
2. To make strategic and operational decisions.
3. To plan and set standards.

Cost Management

As we will emphasize throughout this book, costs do not just happen; they are caused by activities. The challenge for cost management analysts is to identify the activities that cause costs, to estimate the relation between costs and their causes, and to manage the activities that cause those costs, as shown in Exhibit 3.1. This chapter deals with the middle part of the process shown in Exhibit 3.1, the relation between activities and costs. Companies must manage costs to be successful. Many companies have gone out of business because they did not manage costs. Many factories have shut down because managers did not manage costs effectively. Some countries, counties and cities have faced the equivalent of bankruptcy because of poor cost management.

Exhibit 3.1 Estimating the Relation between Activities and Costs

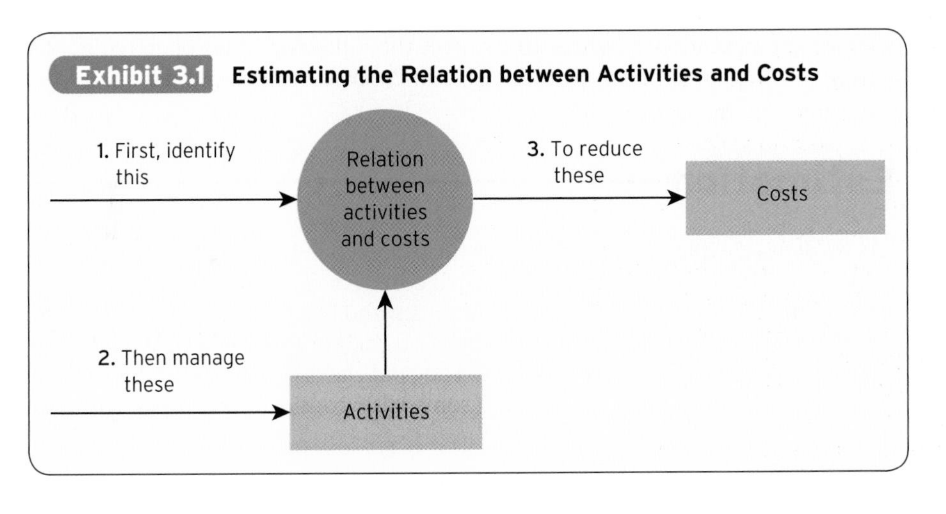

For C.C. Catering, estimating the relation between costs and activities will help Shiranthi Chandra and Dinah Cedibe understand how to make the production process more efficient. If they find, for example, that the costs of delivering and setting up each catering job are high, then they should focus on ways to reduce delivery and set-up costs. If such costs are not significant, then they should turn their attention to better opportunities for cost management.

Decision Making

In deciding between alternative actions, managers must know the costs that each alternative is likely to incur. These are examples of typical questions that require cost estimates for decision making:

- **University of Barcelona** (in Spain) administrators ask: 'What will happen to total costs if we expand the student health centre?' Decision: If estimated total costs do not increase much, the university expands the health centre.
- Managers at **Accenture** ask: 'How much will it cost to perform the Department of Motor Vehicles information systems job?' Decision: If the cost of the job plus an adequate margin is below the price that Accenture can charge, then it does the job.
- Managers of **Starbucks** ask: 'How much will it cost for us to make display racks compared to the cost of buying them?' Decision: If it costs Starbucks less to buy the racks than to make them, then it buys them.
- C.C. Catering is currently opened only for lunch. Shiranthi and Dinah are considering opening longer hours and hiring additional staff. To decide whether to do so, they should know the cost of preparing extra meals to compare with the additional revenues from longer opening hours.

These are just a few of the numerous decisions that require the knowledge of the estimated costs of the alternatives being considered. Of course, cost comparison is not the only basis for decision making, but it is a major one – *the* major one in many instances. We discuss decision making in more detail in later chapters.

Planning and Standard Setting

In planning an organization's future, managers specify the activities that they expect people in the organization to perform. Cost estimation assigns a cost to those activities. By knowing the costs of activities, managers know how much cost the organization will likely incur, which is helpful for preparing pro forma financial statements and estimating cash flows. Cost estimation also helps set standards for employee performance by estimating what the costs should be for performing particular activities.

At C.C. Catering, Shiranthi Chandra and Dinah Cedibe have estimated the costs of meal preparation to plan their activities. They decide to use the different cost estimation methods for estimating the total costs for the next month, when they expect the following levels of activities: 2,100 meals sold, 30 catering jobs, 2 new products introduced, and 2 new customers attracted.

Cost Estimation

LO 2
Understand basic decisions about cost estimation.

As we defined earlier, cost estimation is the process of estimating the relations between cost objects and the cost drivers that cause their costs. For example, consider estimating the cost of catering for an event. Suppose that Shiranthi and Dinah have data on 30 different events, their total costs, and the number of guests on each of these events. Would the number of guests drive the total costs of an event? They put the data in a figure with two axes, such as shown in Exhibit 3.2. Let's go through some basic considerations about cost estimation:

- What cost object is on the vertical axis?
- What cost driver is on the horizontal axis?
- What shape do we expect the cost function to have?
- Which cost estimation method will be used?

Exhibit 3.2 Simple Model

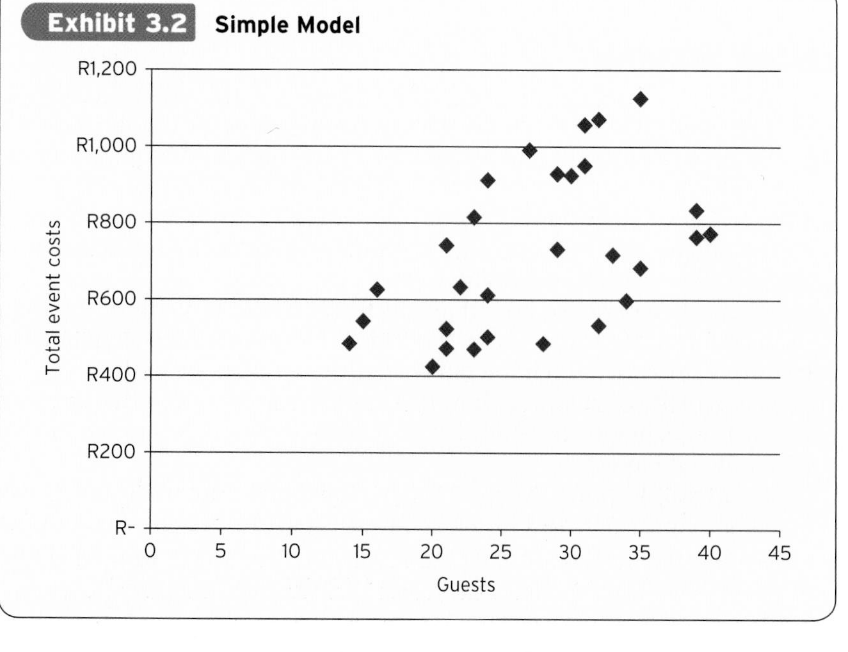

Cost Object (Vertical Axis)

A first consideration is the *cost of what* needs to be estimated. For example, the cost object may be an event (as in our example), or a department, a product, a building project, a road, a party, etc. This depends on the purpose of the cost estimation. If C.C. Catering wants to estimate the cost of an event for quoting a price, then the event is the logical object for cost estimation. Or if, for example, another company will use the data for planning which products to produce and sell, cost management analysts need data for those products. If we want to estimate the cost of a building project to support an investment decision, that building is going to be the object of the cost estimation.

It is also important to consider at what level of detail costs are going to be estimated. Very detailed analysis is a lot of work, but very aggregate investigations may not be meaningful. For example, consider estimating the cost of catering an event. In Exhibit 3.2 there seems to be only a rough relationship between the cost of the event and the number of guests because the data points are widely scattered. However, estimating the cost of 'an event' may not be detailed enough. On further investigation, suppose there are *two types of events*, namely events where only snacks are provided and events with catering of a complete meal for dinner. When separately identifying these two types of events, it becomes clear that the number of guests is a clear predictor of the costs of two types of events (cost driver). This is shown in Exhibit 3.3. Instead of estimating the cost of general events as the cost object, it is better in this case to estimate the cost of two different cost objects: events with snacks provided and events with dinner catering.

Cost Drivers (Horizontal Axis)

The second consideration is what is likely to drive costs. Many different factors could be good predictors of total costs, such as the number of guests, as we just saw, but also the quantity of produced units of a product, the volume of kilograms or litres produced, the area of square metres of an office building, or the length of a luxury yacht in metres.

There are also other kinds of cost drivers that have less to do with quantities but more with how activities are executed. For example, each time C.C. Catering orders food ingredients from their wholesaler, the company pays a fixed fee for packaging and shipping (within certain ranges of size and weight). So this cost depends on the number of orders placed, basically regardless of the quantity

Exhibit 3.3 The Costs of Two Types of Events Separately Estimated

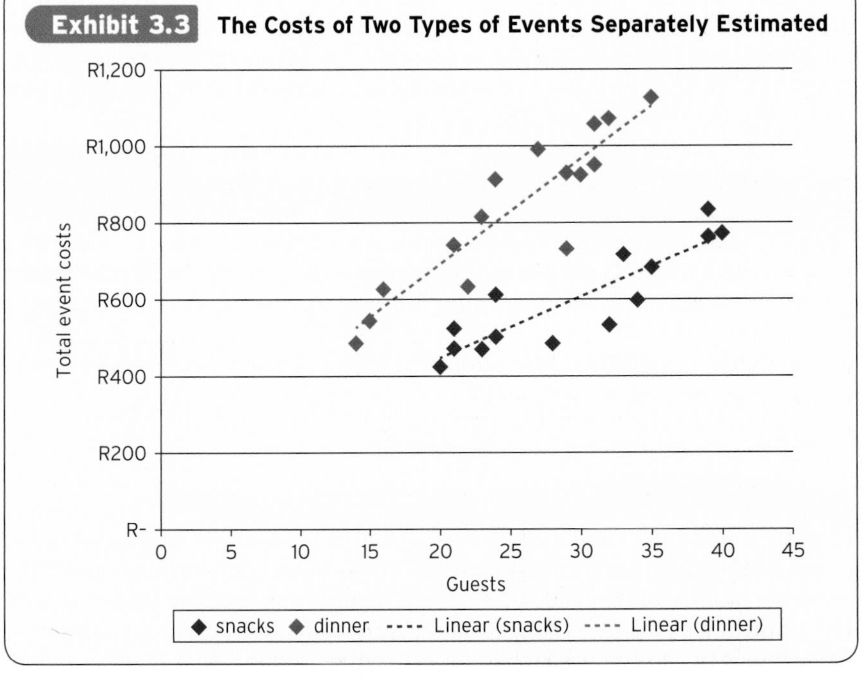

ordered. In other companies costs could, for example, be driven by the number of times a production batch is started, because each start-up involves costs for cleaning machines, fitting new tools, calibrating the machines, etc. These start-up costs will depend on the number of start-ups but will be independent of the quantity produced.

Yet other cost drivers reflect product variety and complexity of activities. For example, Shiranthi and Dinah spent quite some time and money on developing new recipes and expanding the menu. These costs depend on how many different kinds of dishes are offered, not on the quantity cooked. We also know that complex menus with many different kinds of items can make running the kitchen less efficient and creates problems having enough fresh ingredients available (or lowers the quality if there is too much in inventory and the ingredients are not fresh anymore).

Furthermore, costs could be estimated based on *several cost drivers*. For example, the combination of number of guests and the duration of a party together might be a good predictor of the costs of drinks during the party. Or the combination of process time and temperature might provide a good estimation of the cost of producing a chemical material.

So the cost management analyst has to consider which and how many cost drivers to investigate.

Cost Pattern (the Shape of the Line)

The third consideration is which cost pattern to look for. How do we think the shape of the line will look? Costs follow many patterns in the real world. Unlike the simple, straight-line model presented previously, some costs increase in steps and in curvilinear patterns as cost-driver levels increase.[3] We also talked about this in Chapter 2.

Step cost

Exhibit 3.4 shows the idea of step costs. A **step cost**, also called a **semi-fixed cost**, is a cost that increases in steps as the amount of the cost-driver volume increases. Many labour costs are step costs. In Exhibit 3.4, the costs are for delivery people for C.C. Catering. One delivery person can handle the delivery, set-up, and clean-up for 50 meals in the two-hour period. In this example, the step increments are the number of delivery people for each two-hour food delivery period. The cost driver is the number of meals. If the number of meals to be delivered is less than 50, the company hires one delivery person for a two-hour period. If the number of meals is in the 51–100 range for a particular job, management increases the number of delivery people to two, and so forth as Exhibit 3.4 shows.

Step costs are common when people are hired in time increments, such as hourly, daily or monthly. Examples include nurses in hospital departments where the number of nurses increases in steps as the number of patients increases; servers in restaurants; service personnel at rental car counters; and teachers at universities. In our experience, managers often ignore these steps, assuming that the step costs are either purely fixed or variable. Research shows, however, that managers can make erroneous decisions by treating step costs as if they are linear.[4]

Managers also rely on the concept of *relevant range* to deal with step costs. The **relevant range** is the range of workload or output (so cost-driver levels) over which the company expects to operate and over which assumed cost patterns are reasonably accurate. Such patterns would not necessarily be accurate outside the relevant range, however. For example, assume that C.C. Catering does not usually deliver more than 50 meals per job. Management could assume that 1 to 50 meals per job constitute the relevant range, as shown in Exhibit 3.4. As long as only one delivery person is needed, food delivery labour is a fixed cost. However, if the number of meals for a job increases to 75 – outside the relevant range – then the assumption that food delivery labour is fixed and, therefore, does not vary with volume is no longer valid.

Mixed costs

Costs can also be **mixed costs**, which have both a fixed and variable component. Some utilities offer products (e.g., electricity, water) for a fixed cost up to a particular volume (which can be zero) after which they charge per unit. Exhibit 3.5 shows the mixed cost for C.C. Catering's cellular telephone plan that charges R400 per month for up to 600 minutes per month of airtime and then charges R1.00 per minute for each minute used over 600. Compensation costs sometimes are mixed, as when a person earns a percentage bonus in addition to a salary for generating profits over a threshold.

Exhibit 3.4 Step Costs: Costs of Delivery Labour

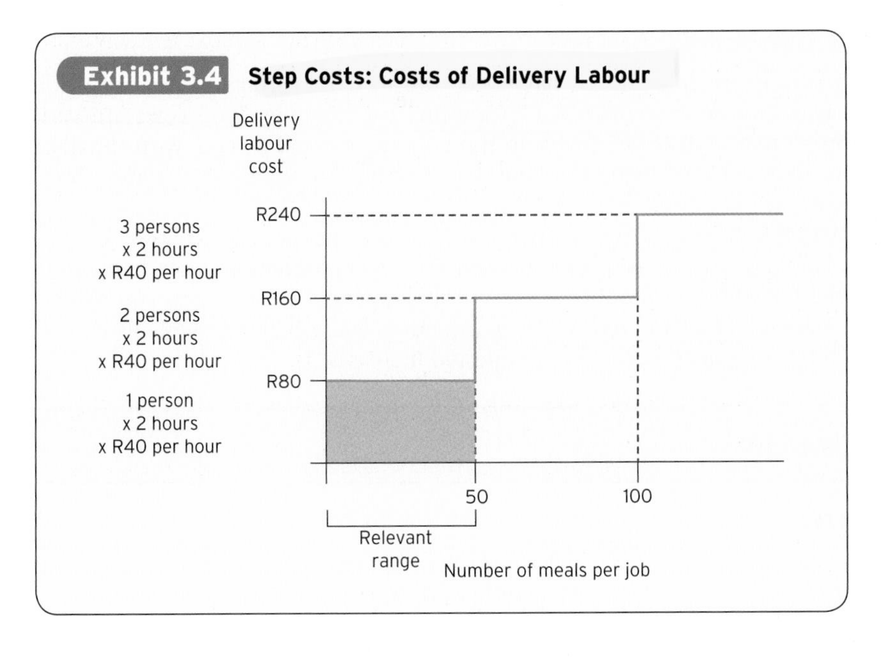

C.C. Catering

Exhibit 3.5 Mixed Costs: Cellular Telephone

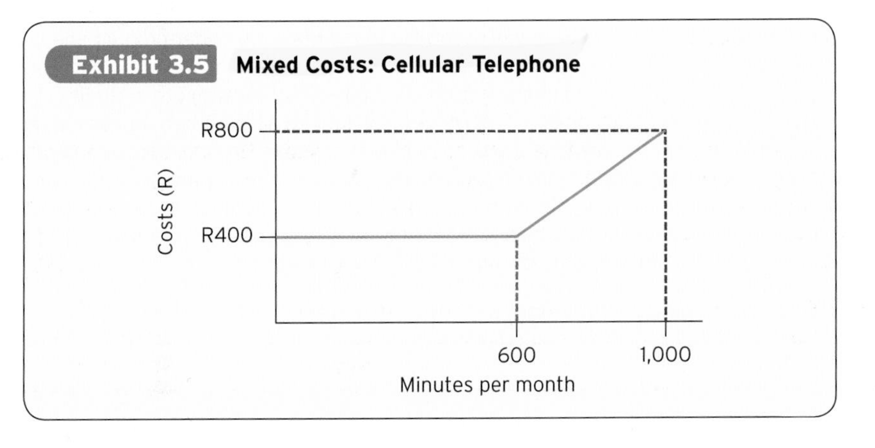

C.C. Catering

Exhibit 3.6 Non-linear Cost Behaviour

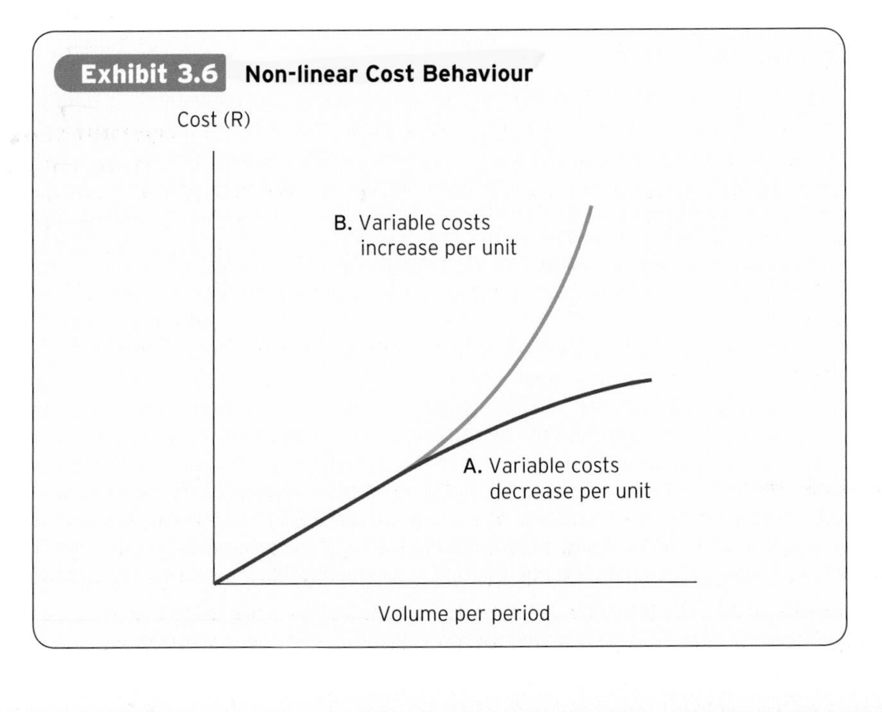

C.C. Catering

Non-linear cost behaviour

The cost behaviour patterns presented so far have been linear, that is straight lines or sections of straight lines. Costs can also be curved. At C.C. Catering, for example, food costs are variable. Suppose the company receives a discount based on the volume of bread it buys, with the discount increasing as the volume purchased increases. Line A in Exhibit 3.6 represents variable costs that decrease per unit as volume per period increases.

Line B represents variable costs that increase per unit as volume per period increases. An example of such a cost is the cost of energy in steel plants. If volume of steel production is low, companies use the most energy-efficient methods to produce steel. As volume per period increases, companies find it necessary to use less energy-efficient methods. Consequently, energy can be a variable cost whose rate increases as the volume of steel production per period increases.[5]

3.1 Research Insight

Product Variety and Costs

Several studies have shown that cost drivers other than product volume can affect total costs. These studies indicate that greater variety of products increases a company's costs, all else equal. However, greater variety of products can also increase revenue. Some of the reasons are that customers prefer one-stop shopping and are more likely to make related purchases if there are more products from which to choose. Whether the additional revenues from maintaining a broad product line justify the additional costs is an issue for financial analysis.

Professors Ittner, Larcker and Randall studied whether it was profitable to maintain a broader product line after considering both the costs and revenues implied by a broader product line in a company that produces backpacks. They found that greater product variety increased this company's costs, a result consistent with other studies. They found that greater product variety also increased the company's revenues. Taking into account both increased revenues and increased costs, they found, however, 'the revenue gains from higher sales volumes and broader product lines were offset by increased costs . . . on average, the firm offered greater product variety than optimal'. In short, the company might have been more profitable if it had offered less product variety. Of course, the company might obtain future benefits that can accrue to the company from having a broad product line today (e.g., dominance of the market might drive out competition). At the root of this analysis are reliable estimates of costs and their drivers.

Sources: For example, see Anderson (1995); Banker et al. (1995) and Ittner et al. (1997).

3.1 Cost Management in Practice

Short-run or Long-run Incremental Cost?

The European Commission study of 'Sustainable Surface Transport' estimated the long-run incremental costs (LRIC) of various types of surface transportation infrastructure in Europe (roads, railways, airports and maritime ports). LRIC is distinguished from short-run incremental cost by whether capacity can be varied. Thus, in the short run, relatively fewer costs can be changed; these include mainly operating costs, such as maintenance. The long run is defined as when all relevant costs can be varied; these include costs of expansions of roadways, railway lines, airport runways and port quays.

The European Commission has encouraged competition in the provision of transport services (as earlier in telecommunications). Because the existing infrastructure assets are limited and inflexibly located and to permit competition for services, current infrastructure owners must grant others access to roads, railways, airports and port quays - at a reasonable price. The European Commission has abandoned using historical costs as the basis for access prices and now requires the use of 'forward looking' LRIC plus a reasonable mark-up as the price basis. However, estimating LRIC is notoriously difficult, because nearly all aspects of the estimates are based on judgements and forecasts. For example, if a railway owner (e.g., an EU member country) were to grant access to a rival rail company, it would have to estimate both the 'long-run time period' over which to estimate costs, and the costs of expansion, track renewal, congestion and environmental damage over that time period. Inevitably the time period is debatable and these costs will be measured as long-run *average* costs. Estimated average costs might be below the unobservable, 'true' LRIC, which would indicate unobserved overuse or congestion. The optimal social solution is to charge some amount more than LRIC, in excess of short-run incremental costs and observed average costs. Or it could be that the long-run average cost is more than the ephemeral LRIC, which would indicate excess capacity.

In the latter case, the social optimum is to charge only the short-run incremental costs because no infrastructure investments are needed to expand services. Not surprisingly, negotiations over these access prices based on LRIC are complex, complete with duelling cost analysts, economists and lawyers. Reportedly it took British Telecom 10 years to develop satisfactory estimates of LRIC as the basis for setting telecom access prices.

Sources: Lindberg (2009); Shetty (1998); and Independent Regulators Group (2000).

Cost-estimation Methods

The fourth consideration is which cost estimation method will be used. There are different types of specific methods of cost estimation, which will be discussed in the remainder of this chapter. Going from using less to more historical data, we discuss the following methods commonly used in practice:

- Account analysis
- Linear regression analysis
- High-low method[6]
- Multiple regression analysis
- Engineering estimates.

Results are likely to differ from method to method. Consequently, organizations often apply more than one approach to compare and verify results. Managers and analysts who bear ultimate responsibility for all cost estimates frequently apply their own best judgement as a final step in the estimation process. Estimation methods, therefore, should be seen as ways to help management to arrive at the best estimates possible – not as the final answer themselves. The weaknesses of cost estimation methods as well as their strengths require attention.

Account Analysis Method

LO 3
Use and interpret account analysis for cost estimation.

The **account analysis** method is based on going through the organization's costs accounts to identify and isolate the costs of various cost objects. Sometimes the organization's information system allows objective classification of costs towards the required cost objects (e.g., projects, buildings, activities). However, many traditional information systems report costs by cost category (e.g., labour, depreciation, material) and functions (e.g., administration, manufacturing and marketing). It might be possible to subjectively cut and sort many months of functional costs into the required cost accounts, but this can be a formidable task for even a small organization. Other times the systems cannot provide the information needed for cost objects that are new, or greatly changed. So the account analysis method will vary greatly, depending on the circumstances, and the results may also vary from highly subjective to quite accurate. An advantage of this method, however, is that cost management analysts scrutinize available information, perhaps to get first estimates or to understand how to apply other cost estimation methods. It is often a natural starting point to investigate the organization's available cost accounts.

The account analysis method follows three steps:

1. Identify the objects for which costs need to be estimated.
2. Gather cost and cost-driver amounts for each cost account for each time period.
3. Compute the average cost-driver rate for each cost account.

Note that each cost account might contain both fixed and variable costs, but usually insufficient account data exist to reliably separate these components. Thus, account analysis computes *average costs per unit of cost driver*, which might generate inaccurate cost estimates, especially when levels of workload or output change considerably from one period to the other. These estimates probably are better than no estimates at all, however.

Application of Account Analysis to C.C. Catering

Assume that Shiranthi Chandra and Dinah Cedibe anticipated the possible value of analysing costs and they have recorded costs in a large number of different cost accounts that makes it possible to link cost to different kinds of cost drivers:

Cost account	Cost driver
Meal preparation and serving	Meals sold
Dealing with new customers	New customers
Managing jobs and events	Jobs
Developing new meals	New meals
Remaining costs that could not be classified above	Fixed per month

Shiranthi and Dinah recorded the past three months of costs as objectively as possible, along with cost-driver amounts, and computed average cost-driver rates. Exhibit 3.7 presents this information. Cost estimates can be derived from the past three months of account analysis.

$$\begin{aligned}\textbf{Estimated total costs} = \ & \textbf{R17,567} + \textbf{R14.60} \times \textbf{Meals sold}\\ & + \textbf{R1,525} \times \textbf{New customers}\\ & + \textbf{R201.82} \times \textbf{Jobs}\\ & + \textbf{R1,200} \times \textbf{New products}\end{aligned}$$

As said earlier, Shiranthi and Dinah will use the different cost estimation methods for estimating the total costs for the next month, when they expect the following cost-driver levels: 2,100 meals sold, 30 catering jobs, 2 new products introduced and 2 new customers attracted. Based on the account analysis, the costs for next month are estimated to be R59,732.

Exhibit 3.7 Account Analysis

Cost driver amounts				
Month	**Meals sold**	**New customers**	**Jobs**	**New products**
Feb	1,295	0	27	0
Mar	1,197	1	35	0
Apr	2,058	7	48	3
Total	4,550	8	110	3

Sorting costs into different accounts						
Month	**Meal preparation**	**Dealing with new customers**	**Managing jobs and events**	**Developing new meals**	**Remaining costs**	**Total costs**
Feb	R21,400	R0	R4,200	R0	R15,280	R40,880
Mar	17,400	1,700	8,500	0	16,640	44,240
Apr	27,650	10,500	9,500	3,600	20,780	72,030
Total	R66,450	R12,200	R22,200	R3,600	R52,700	R157,150

Average cost driver rates					
	Meals sold	**New customers**	**Jobs**	**New products**	**Fixed monthly costs**
Cost driver rates	R14.60	R1,525	R201.82	R1,200	R17,567

3.1 You're the Decision Maker

Using Account Analysis

Explain why the account analysis performed by Shiranthi Chandra and Dinah Cedibe might be unreliable for estimating future costs.

(Solutions begin on page 136.)

Statistical Cost Estimation Using Linear Regression Analysis

LO 4 Use and interpret linear regression for cost estimation.

This section discusses the use of linear regression analysis to estimate the relation between costs and cost drivers. **Linear regression analysis** (or **regression analysis**, in short), is a statistical method used to create a linear equation relating independent (or X) variables to dependent (or Y) variables. Regression uses data from the past to estimate the relation between costs of objects, which are the dependent variables, and cost drivers, which are the independent variables and will be valid in the future. In particular, this technique will enable you to estimate the cost-driver rates that will be used in examples in the next chapters.

The objective of cost estimation is to establish the existence of a plausible correlation relationship between cost drivers and the cost to be estimated. These cost drivers are X terms or independent variables of a regression equation. **Independent variables** are the cost drivers that the cost management analyst believes are strongly correlated with the dependent variable costs. The cost to be estimated is the dependent variable, or the Y term. **Dependent variables** are correlated with independent variables. The distinction between dependent and independent variables should make sense because costs do not just happen, they *depend* on cost drivers. We refer to the Y term as TC because the Y variable is always some measure of total cost (TC) in our analyses. Depending on the context, TC can refer to the total costs of the organization, total overhead costs of the organization, or some other measure of total cost.

Regression generates an equation or, visually, a line that best fits a set of data points. In addition, regression techniques provide information that helps a manager to ascertain how well the estimated regression equation describes the relationship between costs and cost drivers.

Computer spreadsheet software has regression capabilities, and more powerful statistical packages such as Minitab, SAS and SPSS are designed to run regressions. We leave descriptions of the computational details to statistics courses. Instead, we deal here with regression from the standpoint of cost management analysts and managers who must use and interpret regression analyses. (Appendix 3A discusses some of the more technical considerations that might interest those who might perform or use these analyses.)

Simple Model for Linear Regression Analysis

The linear regression model with one cost driver is a useful way to get a basic understanding about how to apply regression analysis to cost management. Later we shall discuss a more complex model.

In a simple model with one cost driver and costs divided simply into fixed and variable components, cost management analysts estimate the following cost equation:

$$TC = F + VX$$

where:

TC = **total costs**
F = **fixed costs that do not vary with the cost driver**
V = **variable costs per cost driver**
X = **the independent variable or cost driver**

The regression model is called **simple linear regression** because it has only one independent variable.

Although regression programs accept any data for the Y and X terms, entering numbers that have no plausible relation will give you misleading estimates. The following are some relationships between costs and cost drivers that make economic sense:

Costs (dependent variables)	Cost drivers (independent variables)
Costs to operate an automobile	Number of kilometres driven
Costs to teach students	Number of students taught
Costs to operate C.C. Catering	Number of meals sold

As you can see, picking cost and cost-driver relationships often requires common sense.

Application of Linear Regression Analysis to C.C. Catering

Shiranthi Chandra and Dinah Cedibe followed five steps during their linear regression analysis to find an explanation of total costs. The steps were to:

1. Identify plausible cost drivers (X variables).
2. Gather relevant data.
3. Plot data in a scattergraph and correct data, if necessary.
4. Perform the regression analysis.
5. Interpret the regression results.

We now describe these steps:

Step 1: Identify a plausible relation between costs and their drivers

The first, and perhaps most important, task is to identify the cost drivers. If an organization's structure, technology, processes and supply markets have been stable, it is reasonable to use data from the past to estimate cost-driver rates. However, if the past relation is no longer valid, then it is necessary to adjust the cost-driver rates to reflect current conditions.

Over time, the cost and cost-driver relationship could change, making the past data inappropriate for estimating the future. This is a problem particularly for many high-tech companies and companies that have products with short life spans.

Although the use of past data has limitations, in many cases it can be reliable for estimating future costs. Using past data can be relatively inexpensive for cost management analysts and managers because many data are available in the records. Cost estimations based on *past* data show *past* relationships between costs and cost drivers. Past relations between costs and cost drivers can be a meaningful starting point for estimating the future relation between costs and cost drivers as long as decision makers recognize the limitations of using past data, which might not completely reflect the future.

Shiranthi and Dinah pooled their knowledge to identify several plausible cost drivers. They believed that the number of meals sold was the most important (all meals prepared are sold).

Relevant range of activity

As discussed earlier in this chapter, the limits within which a cost projection is valid represent the relevant range for that estimate. For example, if C.C. Catering has been producing between 800 and 2,600 meals per month, the relevant range of its cost estimates is valid between 800 and 2,600 meals. If C.C. Catering expects to produce between, say, 4,000 and 7,000 meals per month in the future, the cost estimates obtained from data for 800 to 2,600 meals might not be valid. We say that producing outside the 800 to 2,600 meal range is *outside the relevant range.*

Step 2: Gather relevant data

For the second step of the analysis, Shiranthi and Dinah collected from company records the dataset that appears in Exhibit 3.8. These data are the total costs of operating the company and the number of meals sold each month for the past 16 months. It is important to note that these data were generated during an extended period of stable prices and consistent catering processes. Sometimes activities are greatly changed or new, and consistent cost and cost-driver data are not available. In these cases, cost management analysts might feel uncomfortable using only historical data to estimate future costs and also or only use other cost estimation methods, which are described later in this chapter. Note that besides the number of meals and total costs, the datasheet also contains other data. We shall use these later.

Although many specialized statistical software packages exist, Shiranthi and Dinah entered the data into a spreadsheet because they use it for financial modelling (see Chapter 7) and because it has convenient graphing and statistical analysis capabilities.

Exhibit 3.8 Input Data from Company Records

Input data from the company's records					
Month	**Meals**	**New customers**	**Jobs**	**New products**	**Total costs**
Jan, last year	896	0	30	0	R47,040
Feb	1,415	0	28	0	46,480
Mar	1,134	0	38	0	50,890
Apr	1,981	6	32	2	88,200
May	2,541	6	40	2	80,990
Jun	1,668	2	28	1	58,800
Jul	1,722	6	38	1	76,160
Aug	1,848	7	31	2	71,260
Sep	2,534	5	30	2	91,350
Oct	1,988	3	40	0	64,400
Nov	1,356	4	38	1	58,800
Dec	1,155	4	30	0	56,000
Jan, this year	882	0	35	0	35,770
Feb	1,295	0	27	0	40,880
Mar	1,197	1	35	0	44,240
Apr	2,058	7	48	3	72,030

Step 3: Plot data in a scattergraph and correct data, if necessary

After checking for data-entry errors, Shiranthi and Dinah used the spreadsheet software's chart 'wizard', a step-by-step menu, for the third step to prepare a scattergraph with total costs as the *Y* variable and meals as the *X* variable. The **scattergraph** plots costs against cost-driver levels and appears as Exhibit 3.9. Observe several things about this graph. First, note that the data lie in an upward-sloping pattern, which suggests a positive relation between total costs and meals, as expected.

Second, note that none of the data points lies an unusual distance from the general upward trend. Some scatter is always expected (indeed, no scatter is suspect), but any points that lie much farther away from others indicate possible data-entry errors, measurement errors, or effects of other cost drivers that are not modelled in a linear regression. These data points, sometimes called *outliers*, should be investigated. The investigation might uncover errors that can be corrected, but, if the data are correct, they should not be discarded even if they appear to have a bad fit with the other data. Instead, the cost management analyst should seek to find other cost drivers of the data. A truly unusual event can lead to unusual costs, such as a rare labour strike or a 100-year storm. This probably means that the unusual data point(s) should be removed from the dataset for linear regression analysis but not discarded. Cost management analysts could learn about the impacts of uncontrollable events that can affect decision making about contracts, negotiations, insurance coverage, and the like from these data. In the case of Exhibit 3.9, Shiranthi and Dinah would have preferred that the data lie closer together but found no errors or evidence of unusual events.

Step 4: Perform the regression analysis

Shiranthi and Dinah completed the fourth step of the linear regression analysis by using the spreadsheet software's data analysis tool. They selected the 'regression' menu item, and with the regression wizard chose the column of total costs as the *Y* variable (dependent) and the column of meals as the *X* variable (independent). Exhibit 3.10 shows information that resulted from the regression output. (*Note:* Appendix 3A presents more details about typical regression choices and regression output.) This abbreviated output contains the most important output details for this stage of our discussion.

Step 5: Interpret the regression results

The fifth step of the analysis is the interpretation of the regression results. The first number of importance is labelled '*R*-square' of the regression, which is 0.7843. The ***R*-square** (R^2) is the proportion of

Exhibit 3.9 Scatterplot of Total Costs and Meals

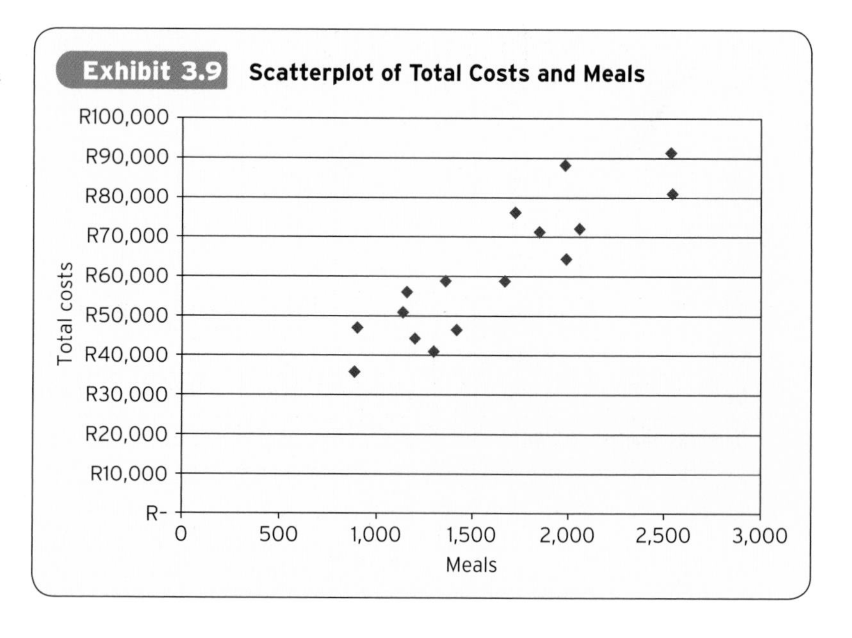

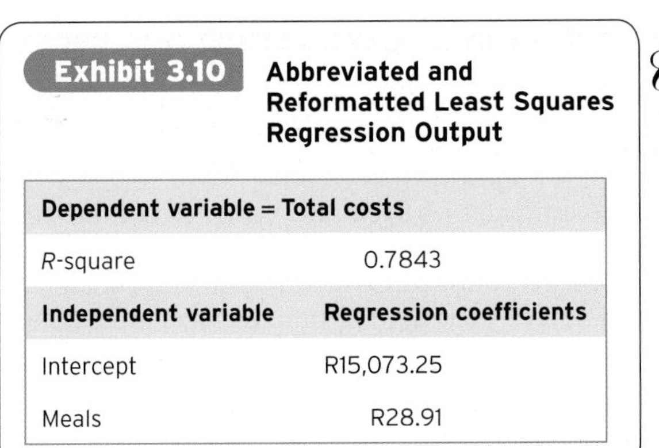

Exhibit 3.10 Abbreviated and Reformatted Least Squares Regression Output

Dependent variable = Total costs	
R-square	0.7843
Independent variable	**Regression coefficients**
Intercept	R15,073.25
Meals	R28.91

C.C. Catering

the variation in the Y or dependent variable (total costs in Shiranthi and Dinah's case) that is explained by the X or independent variable (the number of meals in this case). The *R*-square can vary between 0.00 and 1.00. An *R*-square value of 0.00 indicates no relation – none of the variance in Y is explained by X. However, a value of 1.00 indicates a perfect relation – 100 per cent of the variation in Y is explained by X. *R*-square usually lies between the extremes, and it measures how well the regression fits the data. Values close to 1.00 give the cost management analyst confidence that he or she has found a reliable cost driver. Shiranthi and Dinah believed that the *R*-square value of 0.7843 (78.43 per cent) confirmed their belief that the number of meals sold drives total costs. Because *R*-square is not 1.00 (100 per cent), they realized that other cost drivers might exist. We describe their investigation of this possibility later.

The second set of important numbers in Exhibit 3.10 is labelled 'Regression coefficients' for 'Intercept' and 'Meals'. These numbers, or coefficients, are the components of the linear cost equation sought by Shiranthi and Dinah. Every straight line has an intercept and a slope. The coefficient for the intercept, R15,073, is where the line intersects the Y axis, as shown in Exhibit 3.11. Shiranthi and Dinah reasonably interpreted this figure as an estimate of monthly fixed costs. However, they realized that the intercept is measured at a level of zero meals sold, which is well outside the relevant range of data. Therefore, the safest interpretation of the intercept is that it is an estimate of the intercept *within* the relevant range (between 882 and 2,541 meals in this case). This estimate might not be reliable at meal levels much outside the relevant range. The coefficient for meals is the slope of the line, which measures the rate of change of Y with a single unit change of X (again, within the relevant range). One can interpret this figure, R28.91, as the meal cost-driver rate or the variable cost per meal sold.

C.C. Catering's cost estimation equation based on this regression result is:

Estimated total costs = R15,073 per month + R28.91 × Number of meals sold

Exhibit 3.11 Scatterplot with Regression Line

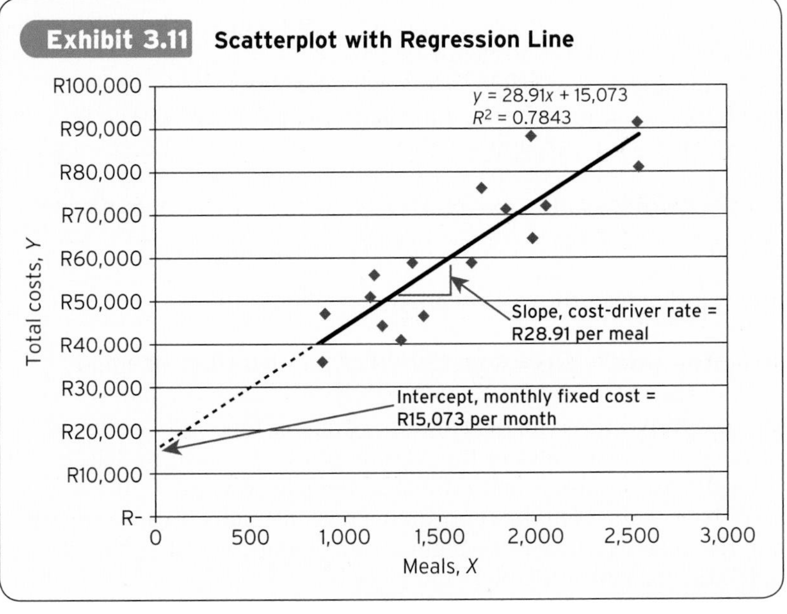

C.C. Catering

Based on the expected cost-driver levels for next month, estimated total costs are computed as follows:

Estimated total costs = R15,073 per month × R28.91 × 2,100 meals sold
= R75,784

Recall that these estimates of fixed and variable costs are reliable *only* within the relevant range and assume that the number of meals sold is the only cost driver. Both estimates might be measured inaccurately if other cost drivers exist. Shiranthi and Dinah later made more precise estimates using more cost drivers. Nevertheless, their simple model provides enough information for a basic discussion of regression analysis. The simple model is also useful as a first approximation of how the company's total cost depends on workload and output.

High-low Method

LO 5
Use and interpret the high-low method for cost estimation.

The **high-low method** estimates a cost function using only the costs at the highest and lowest level of workload and output. The high-low method is a simple 'back of the envelope' way to get estimates of the slope and intercept of a straight line using just two points of data. The high-low method has generally been replaced by the use of spreadsheets and regression analysis. Nevertheless, some people still use it, and it occasionally appears on professional examinations such as the CPA exam. We explain it here so you will not be caught unaware if you hear or read the term 'high-low method'. However, we regard it as inferior to the regression method because it uses only two data points, even when more data are available.

The following explains how to compute the cost function using the data from C.C. Catering. First, compute the *slope* of the straight line between the highest and lowest cost-driver level (i.e., number of meals) at C.C. Catering. Using the data in Exhibit 3.8,

- The highest number of meals was 2,541 in May, with a cost of R80,990;
- The lowest number of meals was 882 in January, with a cost of R35,770.
- The difference is 1,659 meals and R45,220,
- So the slope is R45,220 ÷ 1,659 meals = R27,26 per meal. (This compares with the estimate of R28.91 per meal in the regression results in Exhibits 3.10 and 3.11.)

Second, compute the *intercept* using either the lowest cost-driver level or the highest cost-driver level.

- The variable cost per unit × lowest cost-driver level equals the total variable cost = R27.2574[7] × 882 meals = R24,041 at the lowest level.
- The total fixed and variable cost is R35,770 at the lowest level.
- So the intercept, fixed cost, must be the difference of R35,770 – R24,041 = R11,729.
- Similarly, the variable cost per unit × highest cost-driver level = R27.2574 × 2,541 meals = R69,261.
- The actual cost is R80,990, so the fixed cost must be the difference of R80,990 – R69,261 = R11,729.

Therefore, the high-low estimate of the cost equation is:

Estimated total costs = R11,729 + R27.26 × Number of meals

Based on the expected cost-driver levels for next month, estimated total costs are R68,975. Comparing these high-low estimates to the estimates in the regression results shown in Exhibit 3.10 indicates that the estimated fixed costs are lower and estimated variable costs per unit are lower using the high-low method. We have more confidence in the regression results because regression incorporates all input data in the analysis whereas the high-low method incorporates only two points in the analysis even though more data are available.

Use of Multiple Regression Analysis to Estimate Cost-driver Rates

Multiple regression is a linear regression method that uses more than one independent variable. Using multiple regression analyses, cost management analysts might learn more about cost behaviour than they do from linear regression. Furthermore, multiple regression has potentially greater explanatory power; that is, more of the variation in the dependent variable (total costs) can be explained by including more independent variables (cost drivers). Multiple regression requires gathering more data, which can be costly if the organization does not have a good information system.

LO 6
Use and interpret multiple regression for cost estimation.

Application of Multiple Regression Analysis to C.C. Catering

As noted earlier in this chapter, some organizations use many cost drivers. Analysts face a cost–benefit trade-off in choosing the number of cost drivers. More cost drivers require more data but probably provide better information. For example, as shown in Research Insight 3.2, researchers using multiple regression found that, for the companies studied, the volume of output and the complexity of operations increased costs, whereas introducing total quality management and other quality improvements reduced costs. These insights would be impossible to obtain from linear regression results.

Generally, we find diminishing marginal returns by using multiple cost drivers. At some point, the additional information from an additional cost driver is not worth the effort required to get the data. Furthermore, because of the phenomenon known as *information overload*, decision makers sometimes have trouble processing large amounts of data. Therefore, a limited number of cost drivers can prove to be an advantage by reducing the amount of information to consider.

The steps in performing multiple regression are the same as for linear regression, with an addition to the fifth step: Choose the best cost estimation model.

3.2 Research Insight

Analysis of Manufacturing Overhead Costs

Based on a study of 31 manufacturing plants in three industries - electronics, automobile components and machinery - researchers used linear regression analysis to identify drivers of manufacturing overhead costs. Their approach treated manufacturing overhead cost as the dependent variable and possible measures of inputs and outputs as the independent variables. Each plant was a separate data point, so there were 31 observations in total. The researchers' model had an adjusted-R^2 of 0.78. These researchers found a strong relationship between overhead costs and both volume- and complexity-independent variables.

The researchers also found that plants implementing new manufacturing methods, namely, just-in-time production, total quality management and the use of work teams for problem solving on the shop floor, had lower overhead costs than those that had not implemented these new manufacturing methods, all other things being equal. This result is particularly interesting to the question whether improved quality increases or decreases costs.

Source: Banker et al. (1995).

Step 1: Identify plausible cost drivers

After thinking carefully about C.C. Catering's production processes, its cost hierarchy, and the data that they could get from the company's records, Shiranthi Chandra and Dinah Cedibe decided to use the following cost drivers:[8]

- *Units.* A unit is a meal sold. The cost related to meals sold includes materials such as the plastic meal containers and the food in each meal. Unit costs also include labour required to prepare meals.

- *Jobs (or batches).* If C.C. Catering takes an order for, say, 30 meals to be delivered to the dean of students' conference room for a lunch meeting, that order is one job. If the dean of students placed such an order six times in a month, C.C. Catering counts that as six different jobs.
- *New products.* C.C. Catering sometimes changes its menu, deletes existing meals, and adds new ones to keep the menu fresh for existing customers and to attract new customers. For example, suppose the company adds a Dhal (lentil) Curry to its menu. It would incur the costs to experiment with various ingredients, develop a recipe that workers could easily follow in preparing the meal, and revise its menus and advertising copy.
- *New customers.* C.C. Catering conducts marketing to attract new customers. Once signed on, the company performs a credit check on the new customer, sets up billing files, and obtains delivery instructions for its drivers. Shiranthi and Dinah decided that the activity of obtaining new customers creates costs that should be estimated.

The cost drivers that you choose in practice depend on the specific activity. For example, a service company such as Starbucks might not use a cost driver for the number of customers. Starbuck's customer-related costs from selling a drink are captured in the cost of selling that drink. So, cost drivers such as the number of units of a particular drink sold include customer-related costs. However, a utility company could have substantial customer-related costs because it collects information about usage, prepares bills, collects and deposits payments received, and maintains account records for each customer.

Step 2: Gather Relevant Costs

When estimating the costs for each cost driver, cost managers must collect total cost information for each time period, for example, total costs for each month. They also must collect information about the level of each cost driver for each time period. To estimate the costs for each of its four cost drivers, C.C. Catering must collect the information already shown in Exhibit 3.8. Shiranthi and Dinah obtained this information from the records for each month for 16 months beginning in January of the previous year.

Step 3: Plot and correct the data if necessary

Exhibit 3.12 shows the scatterplot of *total costs versus new customers*. As you can see, this cost driver shows a positive relation with total costs, as expected. Notice also that the relation appears to be less clear than between total costs and meals, which is why if using only a single cost driver as we did

Exhibit 3.12 Scatterplot of Total Costs and New Customers

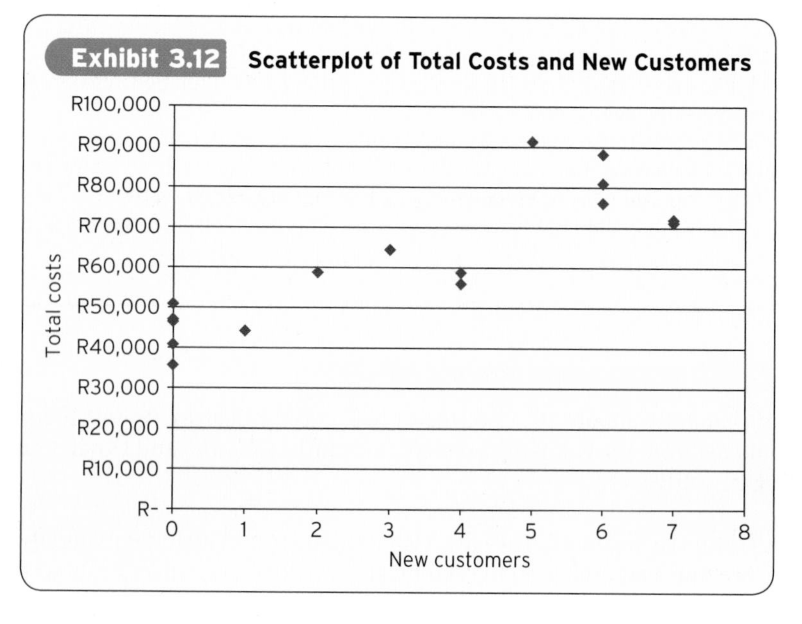

before, meals makes more sense. To save space, we do not reproduce the other two additional scatterplots (total costs versus jobs, and total costs versus new products). Shiranthi and Dinah found no evidence of errors, and all the cost drivers show positive relations with total costs.

Step 4: Perform the regression analysis

Shiranthi and Dinah used the spreadsheet software's regression wizard as before but selected multiple columns of *X* variables. (Note that in spreadsheet software, the columns of *X* variables must be next to each other.) They selected several combinations of cost drivers and compared the results in the next step.

Step 5: Interpret the regression results and choose the best model

Shiranthi and Dinah used the software to perform many multiple regressions. The first regression used all four cost-driver quantities for each month: numbers of meals, new customers, new products and jobs. They tested other multiple regressions that used combinations of two or three cost drivers. Thankfully, the software does most of the work because the last analysis task is to choose among the many possible multiple regressions for the best model. Shiranthi and Dinah and other cost management analysts choose from among multiple regressions using two criteria: economic sense and statistical superiority.

First, an acceptable model must make economic and intuitive sense, consistent with step 1 of the analysis. Consider the summary information from several of the multiple regressions as shown in Exhibit 3.13, which also displays the linear regression results for comparison. Multiple regression 1 contains all of the cost drivers, but not all of the *X* variable coefficients make economic sense. This multiple regression estimates fixed costs to be R34,822 per month, which is higher than the linear regression estimate, but this is not a cause for concern because we must look at the regression equation in its entirety. The estimated variable cost per meal is R17.63, which is lower than the linear regression, but this model has more cost drivers, so all the variation does not need to be explained by the number of meals.

Multiple regression 1 estimates the cost of each new customer to be R3,159.33, which we assume includes all customer-related costs. So far, we might wonder about the size of these coefficients, but they all have positive relations with total costs, which make economic sense. Now look at the negative coefficients for the numbers of new products and jobs. A naïve interpretation of these coefficients is that making new products and taking more jobs actually *reduces* costs by R341.27 job and R35.13 per job. It is difficult to tell an economically sensible story about these negative coefficients. As it turns out, the most likely explanation is a statistical problem with the *X* variables, which are supposed to be independent but which actually bring redundant information to the model. When supposedly independent variables are actually highly correlated, this is referred to as *multicollinearity*, which is explained in more detail in Appendix 3A. If this is the case, a model can be improved by

Exhibit 3.13 **Regression Results (abbreviated and reformatted)**

	Regression coefficients		
Independent variables	**Linear regression**	**Multiple regression 1**	**Multiple regression 2**
Intercept	R15,073	R34,822	R23,900
Meals	R28.91	R17.63	R17.79
New customers		R3,159.33	R2,829.91
Jobs		R – 341.27	
New products		R – 35.13	
R-square	0.784	0.888	0.877
Adjusted *R*-square	0.769	0.847	0.858

Dependent variable = Total costs

removing one or several independent variables which are highly correlated with others. So, for C.C. Catering, the most straightforward solution is to omit the two variables for the number of new products and jobs and re-estimate the regression with the remaining *X* variables.

Multiple regression 2 is the re-estimated model with only meals and new customers as independent variables. Notice that the intercept coefficient is reduced to R23,900 per month because it does not have to compensate for the negative impacts of the omitted variables. The coefficients for meals and new customers remain positive and are more or less the same size as in the first multiple regression, R17.79 and R2,829.91, respectively. Shiranthi and Dinah interpreted this stability as a good sign because these estimated cost-driver rates are not affected by other variables.

Second, the best model should make economic sense and should have superior statistical properties. As just discussed, multiple regression 2 makes economic sense. Note that *R*-square in Exhibit 3.13 is accompanied by 'adjusted *R*-square', which we discuss next. **Adjusted *R*-square** serves the same purpose as the *R*-square presented in the earlier discussion of linear regression, but it assesses a statistical penalty for each added independent variable. Because it is more conservative, most cost management analysts use adjusted *R*-square, not the *R*-square, to judge the statistical quality of a multiple regression. (Appendix 3A considers other statistical criteria that cost management analysts often use.) As it turns out, the adjusted *R*-square of multiple regression 2 is the highest of all the multiple regressions that Shiranthi and Dinah considered. Therefore, they judged multiple regression 2 as the best statistical description of C.C. Catering's total costs.

The results of multiple regression 2 can be written as the following equation:

Estimated total costs = R23,900 + R17.79 × Meals sold
+ R2,830 × New customers

Information regarding the numbers of new products or jobs is not necessary for estimated total costs. Estimated total costs for next month when expectations about workload and output are 2,100 meals, 2 new customers, 30 jobs, and 2 new products are R66,919.

Cautionary Note about Using Regression

Regression analysis has an aura of scientific analysis about it. In fact, it is only as good as the thought process and the quality of the data that go into developing the model. Collecting appropriate data also is complicated by the following problems:

- *Insufficient data.* A good rule of thumb is to use at least 30 data points, but this often is impractical. See the next point.
- *Inconsistent data.* Organizations and processes change, and so do information systems. These changes can limit the amount of data available that are from a consistent underlying process and are measured consistently.
- *Missing data.* Misplaced source documents or the failure to record a transaction can result in missing data.
- *Outliers.* Observations of extreme cost-driver relationships might unduly affect cost estimates. For example, in 2011 a tsunami affected operations in many companies in Japan for several months, resulting in high one-time costs.
- *Allocated and discretionary costs.* Fixed costs are often allocated on a volume basis, resulting in costs that might appear to be variable. Discretionary costs also might be budgeted so that they appear variable (e.g., advertising expense budgeted as a percentage of revenue), but they typically are authorized and spent as fixed amounts.
- *Inflation.* During periods of inflation, historical cost data do not accurately reflect future cost estimates.
- *Mismatched time periods.* The time periods for the dependent and independent variables might not match (e.g., running a machine in February and receiving and recording the energy bill in March).

Managers should be aware of problems in the data. No substitute exists for using experience to understand how costs and cost drivers are related.

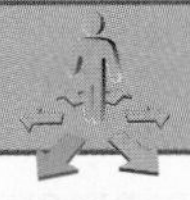

3.2 You're the Decision Maker

Using Multiple Regression Analysis

Although the numbers of jobs and new products in Multiple regression 1 (Exhibit 3.13) are not economically plausible drivers of total costs, are they of no management value? Apply this to C.C. Catering.

(Solutions begin on page 136.)

3.2 Cost Management in Practice

Estimates of Long-run Incremental Cost (LRIC)

The European Commission's Cost Allocation of Transport Infrastructure Cost project estimated the LRIC of one year of railway maintenance and track renewal costs in Britain as part of the total LRIC of railway usage. The unit of analysis was the maintenance delivery unit (MDU), of which there were 51 in Britain. The study was restricted to this narrow scope of analysis because suitable data were not available for a more thorough time-series and cross-sectional analysis of all relevant railway infrastructure costs (welcome to the real world of cost analysis!). The study's authors note the limitations of scope and time, but argue persuasively that some data analysis should be better than none.

The study estimates a linear multiple regression of MDU maintenance cost, C, as a function of alternative measures of railway traffic in the MDU's region (e.g., tons of cargo moved per km of track), MDU infrastructure (e.g., length of track), and MDU input prices (e.g., average labour cost per hour). The best fit of the data yielded an adjusted R^2 of 0.366 and several coefficients that were statistically significant (e.g., railway traffic and length of track). The authors were disappointed in this result but presented a preliminary estimate of maintenance LRIC as €8.12 per thousand tons per km travelled. If valid, this would be well under the 'true' access price that should be charged, given that many other costs were omitted.

This study illustrates the importance and difficulties of applying the methods of Chapter 3 to cost estimation. One lesson is that one should be suspicious of very high R^2 and very statistically significant coefficients that reportedly result from the analysis of real data. Sadly, this scepticism has been justified in a number of cases where researchers doctored data to produce illegitimately improved statistical results, presumably to please the funders of the research.

Source: Wheat and Smith (2009).

Engineering Method

LO 7 Use and interpret the engineering method for cost estimation.

Statistical methods and account analyses rely on data from the past. By contrast, the engineering method works with the present and future. Analysts make **engineering estimates** of costs, first by measuring the work involved in the activities that go into a product and then by assigning a cost to each of those activities. Analysts prepare a detailed step-by-step analysis of each activity required to make a product, together with the costs involved. These analyses are becoming more complete and the resulting cost estimations more accurate, as the design of products and services is further developed. When the design has been determined only roughly, the engineering estimate still has a considerable margin, but towards the phase that the detailed design has been drawn, cost estimates become very specific and accurate.[9]

Cost management analysts usually can obtain engineering estimates of the materials required for each unit of production from drawings and product specification records. Employees in the company's accounting and purchasing departments have data on the cost of materials that analysts can use to price the materials required to make a product. They can perform time-and-motion studies or review labour time records to ascertain the time required to perform each step. Labour records also provide typical wage rates for various jobs. Coupling those wage rates plus benefits with the time required to perform activities gives the estimated labour cost. Other costs are estimated similarly. For example, cost management analysts can estimate the size and cost of a building based on regional construction costs and space requirements. They can estimate the necessary number of supervisors and support personnel based on a direct labour-time estimate.

Photo: ABB

The cost of a building a power plant can be estimated more accurately as the design is becoming more detailed and final.

The engineering approach has an advantage over other cost estimation methods because it details each step required to perform an operation. Another advantage to this approach is that it does not require data from prior activities in the organization. Hence, it can be used to estimate costs for totally new activities and products.

The engineering approach can identify non-value-added activities, which are covered in more detail in Chapter 5. For example, if an engineering estimate indicates that 8,000 square metres of floor area are required for an assembly process but the company has been using 12,500 square metres, managers could find it beneficial to rearrange the plant to make floor space available for other uses. Or, if an engineering estimate indicates that the optimal production run is 1,000 units per set-up but the company has been running only 100 units per set-up, the managers might change production scheduling to get the optimal production run length.

A difficulty with the engineering approach is that it can be quite expensive to use because it analyses each process step. Another consideration is that engineering estimates are often based on optimal conditions. Therefore, when evaluating performance, bidding on a contract, planning expected costs, or estimating costs for any other purpose, it is wise to consider that the actual work conditions will often be less than optimal.

Application of the Engineering Method to C.C. Catering

To use the engineering method for C.C. Catering, Shiranthi and Dinah estimated the following costs.

Unit costs

To estimate unit costs, Shiranthi and Dinah started with the food ingredients required for a typical meal, such as chicken, shrimp, vegetables (such as lentils), rice, coconut milk, spices and herbs, and flat bread. Furthermore, they listed materials needed, such a plastic containers, plates, utensils and napkins. They considered waste; for example, they figured that 3 per cent of chicken and shrimp would be wasted.

To estimate labour costs, they timed themselves in preparing meals under ideal conditions. That was their estimate of the shortest time required to prepare meals. They also timed untrained workers to estimate the longest time for meal preparation. Considering these data, using their experience with the learning effects, and estimating how far along the learning curve the average workers were (see Appendix 3B), they estimated labour time per meal. They multiplied that by the sum of the average wage rate, payroll taxes, and benefits per hour to obtain the preparation cost per meal. To make the analysis comparable to work with multiple regression and account analysis, they used input prices that were in effect on average over the previous 16 months. Based on this work, they estimated the cost per meal to be R18.60.

Job costs

Job costs were mostly labour costs. Preparing a job included taking the order, shopping for food, instructing the meal preparation crew, delivering the meals to the customer's location, overseeing serving, and cleaning up. Some of these costs were made for several jobs at the same time. For example, one of the employees did a shopping trip for four jobs. In this case, they allocated the costs equally to each job – one-fourth of the time and one-fourth of the travelling distance to each job. They estimated job costs to average R205.00 per job, considering the fact that job costs would be less for jobs having 50 or fewer meals and more for jobs having 51 to 100 meals, as we discussed in the section on step costs earlier in this chapter.

New-product costs

New-product costs included labour to develop and test new meals for the menu, materials used to prepare new meals for testing (including those that were rejected), supervision and labour time to teach the meal preparation crew to prepare new meals, and the costs to print new menus. Shiranthi and Dinah's estimate of new product costs was R1,175 per new product.

New-customer costs

New-customer costs included the costs of advertising time spent in marketing the company's products, time spent talking to prospective customers, and time spent in setting up a new customer's account in C.C. Catering's computer system. They estimated new customer costs to be R1,450 per new customer.

Monthly fixed costs

To estimate the monthly fixed costs, Shiranthi and Dinah included the base salaries that they received, rent on the facilities, utilities and other administrative costs. They estimated these costs to be R16,900 per month.

The engineering analysis cost estimation equation can be written as follows:

$$\begin{aligned}\textbf{Estimated total costs} = {} & \textbf{R16,900} + \textbf{R18.60} \times \textbf{Meals sold} \\ & + \textbf{R1,450} \times \textbf{New customers} \\ & + \textbf{R205.00} \times \textbf{Jobs} \\ & + \textbf{R1,175} \times \textbf{New products}\end{aligned}$$

Using this equation, estimated costs for next month are R67,360.

3.3 Cost Management in Practice

Cost Analysis by Reverse Engineering

Competitors and industry analysts followed **Apple's** release of the iPad 2 closely. Competitors were particularly interested in the function and costs of the new product, but did not have historical data that it could analyse. One group, DigiTimes Systems, disassembled its first-day purchase to create the direct materials cost of this new product and reported the bill of materials (BOM) online (http://www.digitimes.com/news/a20110314PR200.html).

The exhaustive BOM listed every iPad 2 part and its current market price. The summary for the 32GB-GSM model included:

Function	Cost
Display/Touch Screen	US$127.00
Memory	65.70
Mechanical/Electro-Mechanical	35.00
Battery	25.00

Baseband/RF/PA	18.70
Apps Processing	14.00
User Interface	11.90
Power Management	10.20
BT/FM/GPS/WLAN	9.00
Boxes, literatures and accessories	5.80
Camera	4.30
Total	**US$326.60**

A selling price at the time of US$729 left a comfortable margin to cover direct labour, manufacturing overhead and profit. DigiTimes Systems estimated what might be a too-low US$ 10 for 'other manufacturing costs', which would make the iPad 2 a comfortably profitable product for Apple (US$402.40 or 55.2 per cent of sales). Industry reports were that the iPad 2 has greatly outsold competitive products.

3.4 Cost Management in Practice

Building Cost-effective Solar Power

Worldwide consumption of electric power might double by the year 2040. Most observers agree that this demand cannot be met by burning fossil fuels except at great economic and environmental cost. Many look to the conversion of solar energy to electricity as an important part of an alternative, cleaner response to growing demand. But is solar energy a competitive source of electricity? Currently many governments provide subsidies to encourage cost-effective production of electricity from wind and direct solar energy, but subsidies probably cannot continue indefinitely. The subsidies and the prospect of building clean and profitable solar power plants are encouraging dramatic innovations that promise to generate electricity profitably, without subsidies.

For example, eSolar is a California-based firm that is developing and installing utility-scale solar power plants (46 to 500 megawatts) that are expected to be cost effective because of the company's prefabricated, modular designs. The inter-connectable modules are built under controlled conditions in a factory, shipped safely to a prepared site anywhere in the world and installed flexibly and quickly.

eSolar's design deviated from conventional installations that also concentrated light to create very high temperatures. Those use large, parabolic mirrors, while eSolar uses flat mirrors, which are much cheaper. However, flat mirrors need to be smaller, so more are needed and each needs to be mounted on a device that tracks the sun and keeps the mirror's reflection directed at the same point. Cost estimation was crucial to understand whether it would be more economical to have more mirrors that are cheaper per unit.

On the basis of its expected efficiency, eSolar has attracted investors such as General Electric and Google, and this young company already has secured contracts to install large modular plants in India, China, North America and Africa.

Sources: www.esolar.com and Sweet (2011).

Comparison of the Methods and Estimates

LO 8 Compare different cost estimation methods in a benefit-cost framework.

Cost management analysts must decide when the use of a more sophisticated and, therefore, more costly, cost estimation method is important. As with other managerial decisions, they should evaluate the costs and benefits of various cost estimation techniques. Avoid complexity just for the sake of complexity and simplicity just for the sake of simplicity. Common sense and experience (and this chapter) should guide you.

Benefits of cost estimation methods can include improved accuracy and descriptiveness. Regression and account analysis have a disadvantage because they rely on past data, which might not be the best basis for predicting the future. Engineering estimates, on the other hand, rely on anticipated activities and costs and therefore are likely to provide more relevant information.

Costs can be more difficult to predict, but they include the costs of measuring, gathering and maintaining the data necessary for the analysis now and in the future. Specifically, account analysis requires breakdowns of cost data that are expensive to obtain. Account analysis requires the cost data to be divided into categories that correspond to the cost drivers (e.g., units, jobs, new products, new customers and facility-level costs for C.C. Catering). Engineering estimates are costly because they require identifying and assigning a cost to each activity required to produce a product. In contrast, regression requires only total cost data for each observation (i.e., each month for C.C. Catering). If one has the capability to work with statistical software packages and if relevant data are available, regression analysis is usually the least costly method.

Each cost estimation method might yield a different estimate of the costs that are likely to result from a particular management decision. This underscores the advantages of using multiple methods to arrive at a final estimate. By observing the range of cost estimates from different methods, management might be better able to decide whether to gather more data.

Choice of Cost Equation

Sometimes cost management analysts prepare several alternative cost estimation equations. These alternatives could result from the use of alternative cost estimation methods: regression, account analysis or engineering. Or they could result from the choice of several cost equations from using one method. For example, analysts frequently prepare several alternative cost equations using regression analysis by using various sets of independent variables. How should one select among several possible cost equations?

We recommend using the following criteria to select between alternative estimated cost equations.

- *Economic plausibility and relevance.* This is the most important criterion. The independent variables should be plausible. The cost equation should make sense. It is always possible to find some association among variables that are not logically related, enter data, and print out a sophisticated-looking result.[10] Be sure the cost drivers are reasonable causes of future costs and cost-driver rates are relevant for future activities.
- *Goodness of fit.* All other things equal, how well the variation in the independent variables explains variation in the dependent variables is important in regression analysis. R^2, or adjusted R^2, is one estimate of goodness of fit. For account analysis and engineering methods, which do not have an R^2, one typically uses good sense and judgement to assess goodness of fit.
- *Significance of the independent variables.* Are the independent variables significant? Appendix 3A discusses a statistical test used in regression. For account analysis and engineering estimates, one uses good sense and judgement to assess the significance of independent variables. Good sense and good judgement are valuable characteristics of successful cost management analysts.

Problems with Forecasting

For all methods, we have to keep in mind that predicting is difficult, especially about the future. Many factors can conspire to impede the accuracy of forecasting cost-driver levels and the associated costs. These are some important factors that affect the forecasting ability of all cost estimation models:

- Changes in markets for inputs and products caused by new technologies, products and competitors' actions.
- Changes in political climate, laws and government regulations, which can restrict or open certain resources and markets.
- Weather and natural disasters, which can dramatically affect resources, costs and schedules.
- Changes in processes and cost drivers, often as results of cost management activities motivated by past cost estimation.

- Changes in cost-driver levels that differ greatly from the immediate past or from the normal range of cost-driver levels and that can affect the use or overuse of capacity.

Because they usually cannot avoid these factors, cost management analysts often test the sensitivity of their forecasts to possible changes in these factors. This is known as *sensitivity* or *scenario analysis*, which is covered in Chapter 7.

Application of the Methods to C.C. Catering

When they were finished, Shiranthi Chandra and Dinah Cedibe compared the costs from each of the four estimation methods, which appear in Exhibit 3.14. Shiranthi remarked that the four methods gave different cost estimates for next month's total costs. 'Doing all four methods gives us more information than had we done only one, but which should we use? Because we compute different total cost estimates, we need to find and resolve the sources of the differences before we decide which to believe'.

Dinah noted, 'The regression analyses were the easiest and the most objective, but they rely entirely on past data, which we thought were stable. Perhaps our costs and processes have changed more than we thought. Account analysis helped us to look at patterns of costs as we were able to construct them with our current accounting system, but we had to make some judgements about how to classify some costs, which regression analysis did more objectively. I like the way account analysis focuses on major activities, but I also suspect that the past three months had unusually low meal costs. If we had an ABC cost system, we probably could track all of our costs better over time. I'm not sure we can afford that yet, however.'

'I think I like the process of the engineering analysis the best because it required me to work through exactly how the company prepares meals, manages jobs, develops new products, and so forth. I learned that we can do some things better. For example, I think we can cut down on meal costs by better training our employees, which also could reduce employee turnover and hiring costs.'

Shiranthi said, 'I agree with the value of engineering analysis, but I am surprised that the multiple regression analysis found that job management and new product development activities are redundant to new customer activities. I interpret this to mean that attracting new customers depends on our visibility from taking more jobs and by our reputation for developing new products to keep our menu fresh. I think we should take what we think is the best information from each cost estimation method and use a hybrid approach to estimate future costs.'

C.C. Catering's Hybrid Cost Estimation Model

Shiranthi Chandra and Dinah Cedibe scrutinized the information in Exhibit 3.14 and debated the merits of each method's cost-driver rate estimates. Based on past information, the various cost estimates, and the expectations for improvements they would make during the next few months, they settled on the following estimates for next year's cost-driver rate estimates:

Exhibit 3.14 Comparison of Estimated Cost-driver Rates and Total Costs for Next Month

Cost estimation method	Monthly fixed costs	Unit rate, per meal	Customer rate, per new customer	Batch rate, per job	Product rate, per new product	Estimated total cost, next month
Account analysis	17,567	14.60	1,525	201.82	1,200	R59,732
Linear regression	15,073	28.91				R75,784
High-low method	11,729	27.26				R68,975
Multiple regression	23,900	17.79	2,830			R66,919
Engineering analysis	16,900	18.60	1,450	205.00	1,175	R67,360

- *Unit rate: R18.00 per meal.* Shiranthi and Dinah reasoned that the engineering estimate was a bit high considering the improvements they planned, but the account estimate was too low because it was based on unusually low costs during the past several months. The multiple regression estimate was nearly the same, which was partly coincidental, but it showed that the R18.00 per meal should be achievable.
- *Customer rate: R1,300 per new customer.* They believed that job and new product activities contribute to attracting new customers, so both thought they could reduce the amount spent explicitly on acquiring new customers. The savings also could be used to manage jobs more carefully to increase customer loyalty.
- *Batch rate: R210 per job.* They hoped to improve their job management by being more efficient with orders and deliveries, which they felt should lead to cost savings. However, the estimate chosen was more than that from account analysis because they wanted employees to spend more time serving existing customers to improve customer satisfaction.
- *Product rate: R1,250 per new product.* Because Shiranthi and Dinah realized the importance of new products to their business, they decided to spend a bit more on this activity than either account or engineering analysis estimated.
- *Monthly fixed costs: R24,000 per month.* Improvements in meal preparation, job management, and new product development would require improvements in space, equipment and training. Shiranthi and Dinah planned to finance these improvements with a bank loan, and they were confident they could obtain a loan with favourable terms. The improvements and interest payments would increase monthly facility costs beyond any of the cost estimates.

The hybrid cost estimation equation can be written as follows:

$$\begin{aligned}\textbf{Estimated total costs} = \textbf{R24,000} &+ \textbf{R18.00} \times \textbf{Meals sold} \\ &+ \textbf{R1,300} \times \textbf{New customers} \\ &+ \textbf{R210} \times \textbf{Jobs} \\ &+ \textbf{R1,250} \times \textbf{New products}\end{aligned}$$

Because Shiranthi and Dinah realized that all of these changes could not be implemented immediately, they did not use this equation to estimate next month's costs, but they did use it to estimate the next year's costs, as described next.

Use of the Results

Shiranthi and Dinah's comments and insights from comparing the cost estimation results underscore the importance of using multiple methods to estimate costs. One should never blindly use only one method because each method can add unique information. Shiranthi and Dinah found the cost estimation process to be generally useful and, in some cases, surprising. They used their hybrid cost estimation model to predict or forecast future costs based on expected future activities. This was a valuable exercise because it helped them quantify and organize both financial and physical resources to meet C.C. Catering's future needs.

Meal preparation

C.C. Catering had sold just over 20,000 meals over the past year at R50 per meal. After some market research, Shiranthi and Dinah decided to keep this price at this level, while many other lunch places were increasing their prices, which they believed would make them more competitive and could increase the number of meals sold to 23,000 meals for the year, bringing in estimated revenues of R1,150,000. They expected to reduce costs by improving the efficiency of meal preparation. Considering all this, they estimated next year's meal preparation costs to be R18.00 per meal × 23,000 meals = R414,000.

Dealing with new customers

With the new pricing policy, better retention of existing customers, and an emphasis on developing customers who order more meals per job, they expected growth in their customer base. They estimated they would attract 60 new customers over the next year. Estimated customer management costs would be R1,300 per new customer × 60 new customers = R78,000.

Managing jobs and events

Shiranthi and Dinah expected the number of jobs to increase somewhat from last year because of competitive meal prices and better job management. They estimated the number of jobs to be 500 over the next 12 months and the costs to be R210 per job × 500 jobs = R105,000.

Developing new meals

Shiranthi and Dinah knew that new products are important to the business and they would start to introduce at least one new product every month. They predicted they would introduce about 20 during the next 12 months. Estimated product costs were R1,250 per new product × 20 new products = R25,000.

Fixed monthly costs

Using their cost estimate of R24,000 per month, Shiranthi and Dinah estimated facility costs to be R24,000 per month × 12 months = R288,000.

Altogether, they estimated their revenues, costs and profits for the next 12 months to be as follows:

Revenues	R1,150,000
Costs	
Meal preparation	R414,000
Dealing with new customers	78,000
Managing jobs and events	105,000
Developing new meals	25,000
Monthly fixed costs for the whole year	288,000
Total costs	R910,000
Operating profit before tax	R240,000

3.3 Research Insight

Sticky Costs

Cost management analysts usually expect that cost estimates apply to predicting costs when activities increase or decrease. However, an area of recent research indicates that some costs can be 'sticky'; that is, costs do not always increase or decrease proportionally over time with activity increases or decreases. This stickiness could be caused by a number of factors, including:

- Non-linear cost behaviour, which results in more or less change in cost than a linear cost estimation model would predict.
- Large changes in activity, which violate the assumption that a linear model is applied to predicting the effects of small changes in activity levels and which bump up against capacity constraints that are difficult to relax.
- Large reductions in activities imply the need for reduced spending, which managers find personally difficult or unpleasant to accommodate.
- Industry differences, which indicate the relative ease or difficulty of changing costs. For example, companies in an industry that requires large, inflexible investments in equipment and machinery, such as manufacturing, might have stickier costs because management is less able to adjust resources than a firm, say, in the retailing industry, which has relatively less committed cost.

Sources: See these selected studies: Anderson et al. (2003); Balakrishnan et al. (2003) and Subramanium and Weidenmeir (2003).

Appendix 3A

Technical Notes on Regression

LO 9 Understand how regression works and identify potential statistical problems with regression analysis.

This appendix discusses technical issues that often arise when using regression analysis. The proper name for the technique used in this chapter is 'least squares regression'. You should not view Appendix 3A as a substitute for courses and books that deal with these issues in much more depth. The purpose here is to alert you to issues of concern. The old adage that a little knowledge is a dangerous thing applies in a big way to regression analysis. You should always consult an expert in statistics when using regression analysis (just as statisticians should consult cost experts when using costs in their statistical analyses). Teamwork pays.

How least squares regression works

Consider the scattergraph in Exhibit 3.15, which reflects the data from Exhibit 3.8 and regression results from Exhibit 3.10. First look at the horizontal line labelled Mean Y = R61,456, which is the (rounded) average total cost for the 16 months of data. Shiranthi Chandra and Dinah Cedibe *could* use the average as the estimate of total costs each month, but this ignores the expected cost-driver relation between total costs and meals served (or any other cost driver). For example, now look at the circled actual data point, Y = R88,200 and X = 1,981 meals. The total estimation error ('Total error' on the graph) from the average is R88,200 – R61,456 = R26,744, approximately a 30 per cent error. Obviously, the caterers can estimate actual costs more accurately using the relation between total costs and meals.

Exhibit 3.15 Scattergraph of Total Costs and Meals

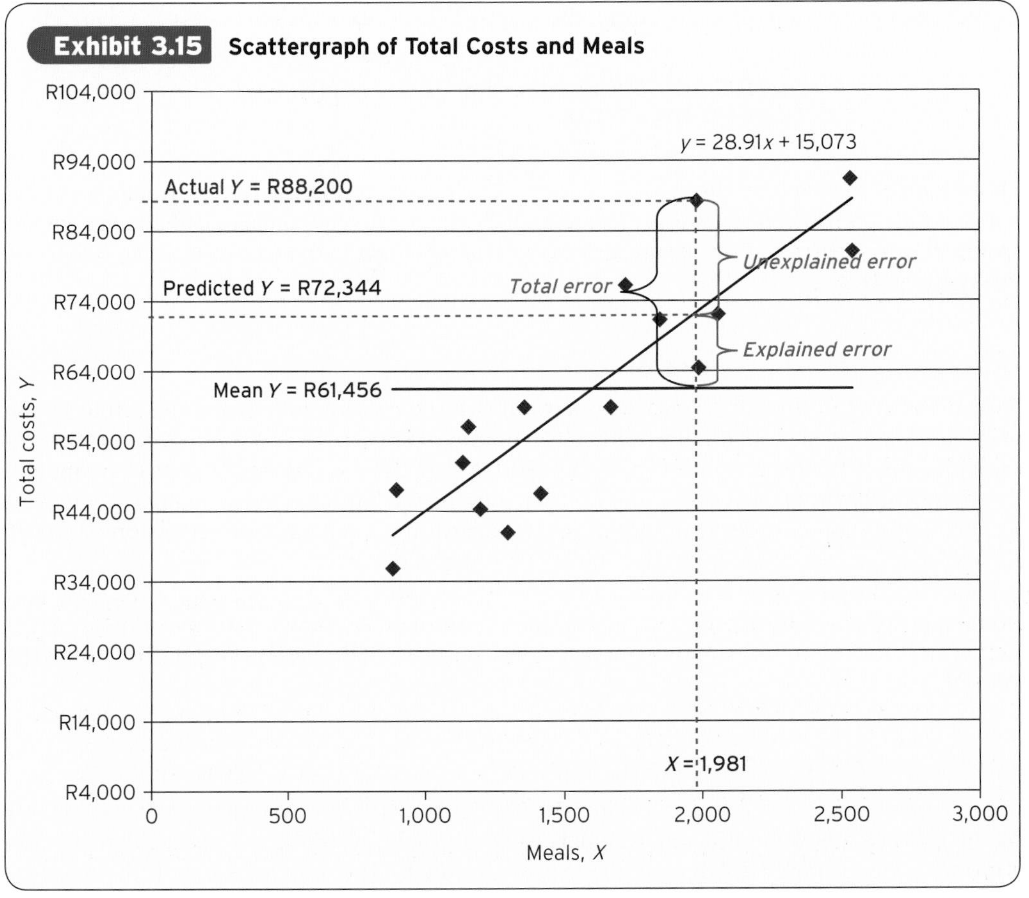

Next look at the diagonal line, which is the least squares regression line that Shiranthi and Dinah estimated earlier in the chapter: Estimated $Y = 28.91\,X + 15{,}073$. Notice how much closer this line is to the actual data point than the average cost. The line estimates total costs, Y = R72,344. It has explained part of the total error from the average ('Explained error' on the graph). The remainder of the error ('Unexplained error' on the graph) is also called a 'residual' and equals R88,200 – R72,344 = R15,856. This error indicates that the regression line does not estimate this actual total cost perfectly. This time, however, the error is smaller – only about 18 per cent.

Least squares regression uses calculus to find the line (intercept and slope(s)) that minimizes the sum of the squared, unexplained estimation errors. Why squared errors? The reason is that the sum of the unsquared errors about the average is, by definition, equal to zero, and one could not improve on that. Squaring the errors makes them all positive and facilitates certain statistical statements about coefficients and the fit of the line to the data. Most statistics texts explain the mathematics of least squares regression in detail. We now turn to somewhat technical discussions about the statistical outcomes of least squares regression.

Confidence in the coefficients

It is reasonable for managers to ask whether the coefficients of the independent variables are significantly different from zero. That is, do changes in the independent variables result in significant changes in the dependent variable? The ***t*-statistic** is used to test for the significance of the coefficients. This t is simply the coefficient divided by its standard error. The standard error is a measure of the uncertainty about the coefficient; the larger the standard error, the more the dispersion of coefficient values and the more uncertainty about its value.

Recall that for C.C. Catering, we estimated the relationship between the variation in the number of meals and the variation in total monthly costs in the linear regression. The coefficient was the cost-driver rate for meals, which was R28.91. Although we did not report it in the text, the standard error of that coefficient was 0.405. Therefore, the t-statistic for the coefficient is:

$$t = \text{coefficient} \div \text{Standard error of the coefficient}$$
$$= 28.91 \div 0.405 = 7.134$$

where both figures are given by the computer output of the regression. As a rule of thumb, a t of 2.0 or better is usually considered statistically significant. With $t > 2.0$, cost management analysts generally assume that the regression results are not due to chance. Clearly, the cost-driver rate, R28.91, is statistically significant.

Assumptions about the residuals

The differences between the estimated Y values (found on the regression line) and the actual Y's are called estimation errors or *residuals*. If a residual is random, its expected value is zero for any observation. The three important assumptions about the residuals are that (1) they are normally distributed, (2) they are independent of each other, and (3) their variance is constant over the range of independent variables. Violation of these assumptions makes statistical inferences about regression estimates questionable (e.g., are the cost-driver rates statistically significant?).

We mention these assumptions because they are often violated for cost data. Consequently, you should be careful about the inferences you draw from regression analyses. You should consult statistics books for more information about how to deal with violations of the following assumptions.

Residuals are normally distributed

Drawing inferences about the estimated value Y (total costs in the text examples) or the cost-driver rates in the text examples requires the residuals to be normally distributed around the regression line. If residuals are normally distributed, the expected value for the residual is zero. If the residuals are not normally distributed, the residual for any observation may be statistically related to that for another observation.

Residuals are independent

A common condition in which residuals are not independent occurs when observations are related to each other over time. This is known as *serial correlation* or *autocorrelation*. Serial correlation does not affect the accuracy of the regression coefficients, but it affects the standard errors of the coefficients. This effect on the standard errors affects the *t*-statistics and significance tests discussed earlier. The presence of serial correlation might be tested using the Durbin–Watson statistic, which is provided by regression software packages such as SAS and SPSS (not in spreadsheet software).

Variance of residuals is constant

The assumption of constant variance implies that the residuals are not affected by the level of the independent variable. For example, this means that the residuals are not systematically higher if the cost-driver volume is higher. Constant variance is known as *homoscedasticity*. Non-constant variance is known as *heteroscedasticity*. As with serial correlation, heteroscedasticity does not affect the accuracy of the regression coefficients, but it affects the standard errors of the coefficients, which affects the *t*-statistics and confidence intervals discussed earlier.

For linear regressions, one can ascertain whether heteroscedasticity is present by plotting the residuals over different values of Y. If the scatter of residuals is not constant over these Y values, the residuals are likely to be heteroscedastic. In some cases, the problem can be cured by transforming the variables (X's and/or Y's) to their logarithms or square roots or by constructing a regression with a new set of variables.

Multicollinearity

If more than one predictor variable is used, as in multiple regression, the interpretation of the coefficients as variable costs is somewhat more hazardous. This was the problem in the C.C. Catering example when multiple regression used all of the cost-driver activities.

The following correlation matrix describes how the variables in Exhibit 3.8 are related to each other. The highlighted figures in the matrix show that meals, new products, and new customers are highly related ($R > 0.7$), which violates the assumption that the variables are independent.

Correlations (R) among variables	Meals	New customers	Jobs	New products	Total costs
Meals	1.000				
New customers	0.746	1.000			
Jobs	0.289	0.415	1.000		
New products	0.778	0.857	0.389	1.000	
Total costs	0.886	0.863	0.252	0.810	1.000

Including all cost-driver activities in a multiple regression often results in coefficients that do not make economic sense individually, as Exhibit 3.13 showed.

The overlapping or redundant explanatory power among the two predictors is referred to as **multicollinearity**, which is the high correlation between two or more independent variables in a multiple regression equation. It does not affect the Y estimate, but it does affect the interpretation of the contribution that each of the X's is making to the prediction of Y. With multicollinearity, one can still estimate total costs from the cost equation, but one must question the accuracy of the particular cost-driver rates.

Appendix 3B

Learning Curves

LO 10
Estimate and use learning curve cost predictions.

A particular type of non-linear cost behaviour relates to the time required to learn to do a job. You may recall the first time that you used a spreadsheet program on a computer. While you might have been slow at first, your efficiency improved as you gained more experience. In practice, experience – or learning – obviously affects direct labour costs; therefore, it affects costs related to direct labour. For example, if the amount of labour required to do a job decreases because of the learning effect, the supervision of the labour to do the job also decreases.

The **learning phenomenon** is a systematic relation between the amount of experience in performing a task and the time required to perform it. This can occur when companies introduce new production methods, make new products (either goods or services), or hire new employees. For example, the effect of learning on the cost of aircraft manufacturing is well known by manufacturers such as the Brazilian company **Embraer**, the Canadian company **Bombardier Aerospace**, the US company **Boeing**, and the European company **Airbus**.

The idea embodied in the learning phenomenon is that the greater the cumulative level of workload or output, the greater the experience. The greater the experience, the lower the average number of labour hours required. The learning phenomenon partly explains why some firms seek to increase market share. They gain more cumulative experience and have lower average costs than competitors have.

The **learning curve** is the mathematical or graphic model of the systematic relation between the amount of experience in performing a task and the time required to perform it. Suppose we apply an 80 per cent learning rate to C.C. Catering for a new employee who is preparing meals. We use the symbol s for this learning rate, and it means that for every doubling of the cost-driver volume (meals, in this case), the time required is multiplied by factor s. In other words, the unit time required to prepare the second meal is 80 per cent of the time required for the first meal; the unit time for the fourth meal is 80 per cent of the time required for the second meal, and the time required for the eighth meal is 80 per cent of the time for the fourth meal, and so on.

This idea can be used to formulate a mathematical relation with the learning phenomenon. We use the following symbols:

x = the number of units of the cost-driver volume produced
s = learning rate (for every doubling of the production volume, the time required is multiplied by this factor, whereby $s \leq 1$)

Notice that after 2 units, the volume has doubled once; after 4 units, the volume has doubled twice, after 8 units, the volume has doubled three times, and so on. If the volume has doubled once, the original time required is multiplied by s; if the volume has doubled twice, the original time required is multiplied by s^2; if the volume has doubled three times, the original time required is multiplied by s^3. In general, the number of times the volume x has doubled equals $\log_2(x)$, and so we get the following equation:

$$Y = as^{\log_2(x)}$$

where:

Y = number of labour hours per unit required for the xth unit of cost-driver volume[11]
a = time required for the first unit of the cost-driver volume produced

Assume the new employee prepares the first meal in 2.00 direct labour minutes ($a = 2$ minutes). Using the 80 per cent learning rate a, the number of labour minutes for this new meal-preparation employee at C.C. Catering appears in Exhibit 3.16. This exhibit shows both the time for each following meal, as well as the *average* time per meal. Furthermore, Exhibit 3.16 shows the total time needed for all meals. There is a curvilinear nature of the relation between cost-driver level (i.e., meals prepared) and labour minutes, which shows initial learning effects that become increasingly smaller as employees learn how to prepare meals more efficiently.

Exhibit 3.16 **Labour Minutes and Quantity Produced**

C.C. Catering

Time required first unit = 2.00 minutes, s = 80%					
x	$\log_2(x)$	$s^{\log_2(x)}$	Time required for unit x	Average time required unit 1 through x	Total time required
1	0.00	1.00	2.00	2.00	2.00
2	1.00	0.80	1.60	1.80	3.60
3	1.58	0.70	1.40	1.67	5.00
4	2.00	0.64	1.28	1.57	6.28
5	2.32	0.60	1.19	1.50	7.48
6	2.58	0.56	1.12	1.43	8.60
7	2.81	0.53	1.07	1.38	9.67
8	3.00	0.51	1.02	1.34	10.69
9	3.17	0.49	0.99	1.30	11.68
10	3.32	0.48	0.95	1.26	12.63
11	3.46	0.46	0.92	1.23	13.55
12	3.58	0.45	0.90	1.20	14.45
13	3.70	0.44	0.88	1.18	15.33
14	3.81	0.43	0.86	1.16	16.18
15	3.91	0.42	0.84	1.13	17.02
16	4.00	0.41	0.82	1.12	17.84

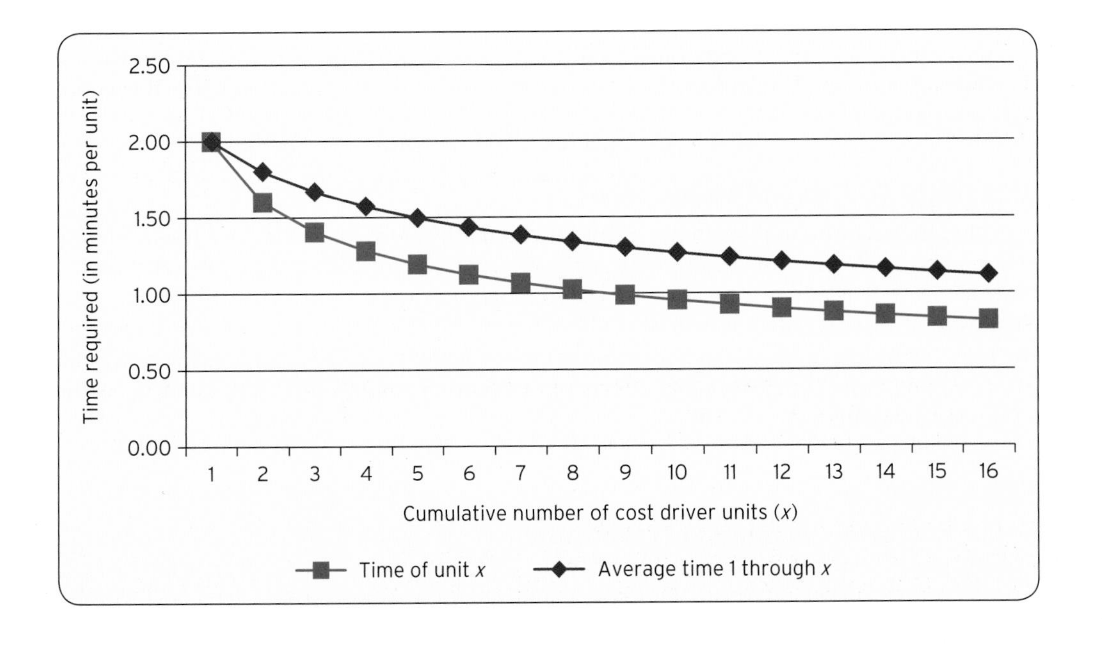

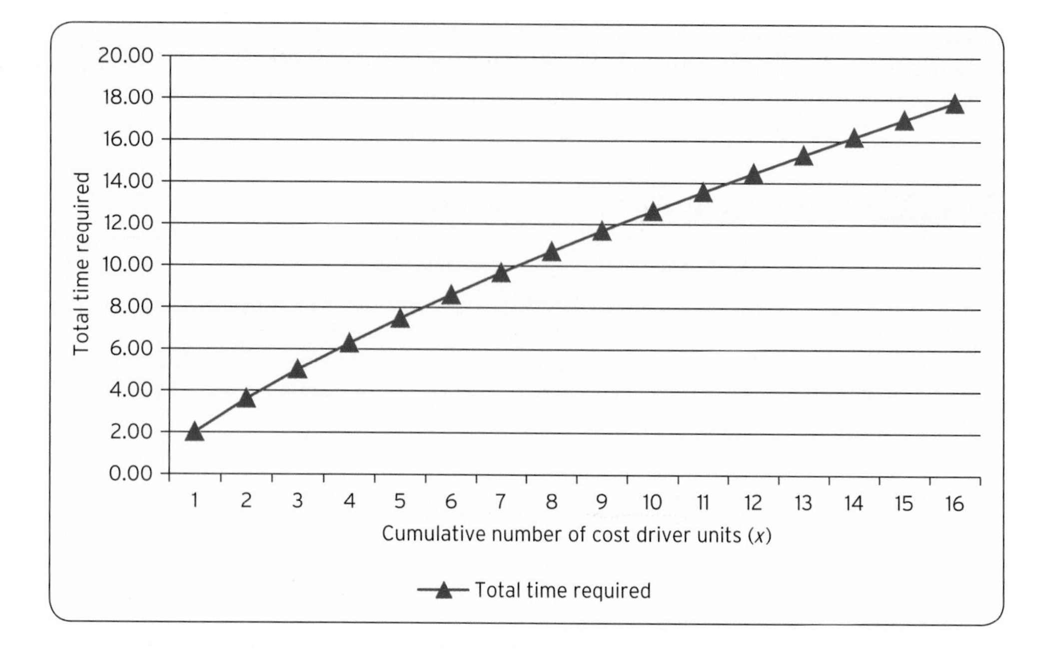

By convention, the equation for the learning curve is often written differently, namely as follows:

$$Y = ax^b$$

where:

$$b = \frac{\log(s)}{\log(2)}.$$

This equation is not so intuitive to see,[12] but it is easier to work with, because it contains x to the power of a constant (constant for a given s, for example when $s = 80$ per cent, $b = -0.322$).[13]

The learning function is curvilinear, as shown in Exhibit 3.16. The function is linear when expressed in logarithmic form, because taking the log of the learning function yields:

$$\log Y = \log a + b \log x$$

The function is linear when plotted on a log-log chart as shown in Exhibit 3.17. Thus, cost management analysts often use linear regression to estimate the learning rate, b, after taking the log of each variable (Y and x). The percentage rate of learning, s, is found by solving the equation $b = \log(s) \div \log(2)$ for s.

Applications to Cost Management

The learning phenomenon applies to time; thus, it could affect any costs that are a function of time. The phenomenon affects most professional activities such as consulting, legal, medical and engineering work, as well as any overhead costs related to labour time.

When estimating costs, decision makers should consider the potential impact of learning. The learning phenomenon can affect costs used in cost management, decision making and performance evaluation. Failing to recognize learning effects can have some unexpected consequences, as shown in the following examples.

Decision making

Assume that **Northrop Grumman LITEF GmbH** in Germany was considering the production of a new navigational system for **Airbus**. Airbus indicates it will pay €50,000 per unit for the system. Northrop Grumman LITEF engineers and cost management analysts estimate the cost to produce

Exhibit 3.17 **Labour Minutes and Quantity Produced – Logarithmic Scales**

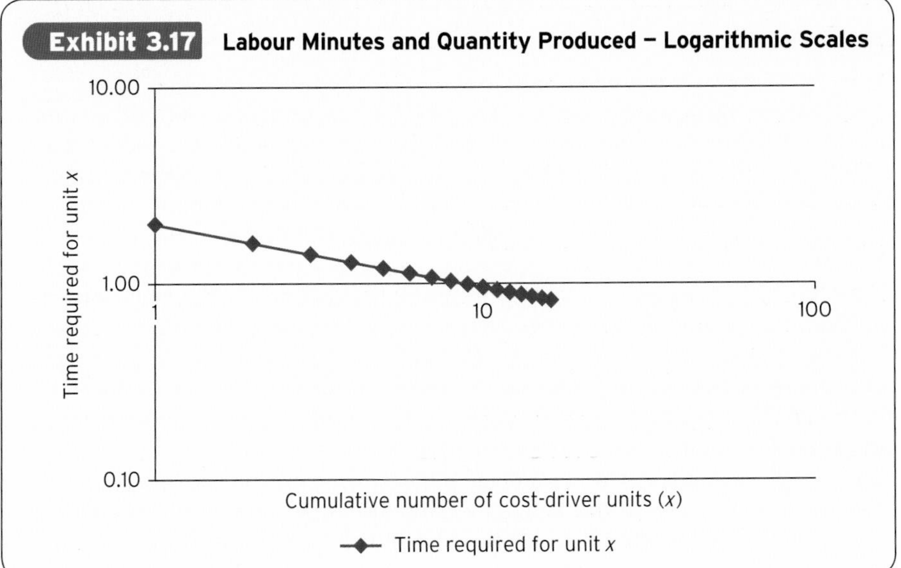

the first four units of the device to be €60,000 per unit. At first, the company decided not to produce it because the unit cost exceeded the unit price. Airbus assured Northrop Grumman LITEF that it would order 75 units of the device. After considering the learning phenomenon for the device, the company realized that the average cost per unit would drop to €40,000 for 40 units. For four units, the device was unprofitable. For 40 units, it was profitable because of the learning effect. The suppliers and Airbus then agreed not to agree on a price considering the cumulative average cost for an entire order or run, in this case 75 planes.

Performance evaluation

Elite University (not its real name) has developed labour time and cost standards for some of its clerical activities that are subject to the learning curve phenomenon. Management observed that time spent on these activities systematically exceeded the standard. Upon investigating the problem, management found high personnel turnover, which meant that the activities were performed by inexperienced people. As a result, the university never experienced the expected benefits of the learning curve. After making changes in personnel policy, the university reduced turnover and staffed the jobs with more experienced people. The time spent on clerical activities no longer exceeded standards.

3.4 Research Insight

Estimating the Learning Curve

Professor Eelke Wiersma studied the Royal Dutch Mail service to understand factors that affect how mature organizations move further down the learning curve. Most studies of the learning curve focus on new firms or new projects where initial learning often is steep. Little is known empirically about how mature organizations continue to learn, apart from fostering systems thinking, personal development, mental models of change, shared visions and team learning, as encouraged by Peter Senge. Wiersma finds that other factors, which might be or might not be related to Senge's cultural attributes, affect learning curve rates as presented in this chapter. He finds that higher proportions of temporary employees, who bring diverse values and workplace norms, are associated with higher learning rates. He finds that postal units that operate with excess capacity, and thus have the time to learn, experience higher learning rates. Postal units with a wider variety of related services also have higher learning rates. While the observed learning rates were statistically significant, they tended to be rather low (in the order of 3 per cent). Nonetheless, critics of government services might themselves be surprised to learn that learning is possible even there.

Sources: E. Wiersma (2007) and P. M. Senge (1990).

Chapter Summary

Cost estimation is the process of estimating the relation between costs and the cost drivers that cause those costs. Companies estimate costs for three purposes: to manage costs, to make decisions, and to plan and set standards. The simplest cost behaviour pattern is the breakdown of costs into fixed and variable components. More complex cost patterns include step costs (also known as *semi-fixed costs*), mixed costs and learning curves.

The three major methods of cost estimation are as follows: statistical methods using regression analysis, account analysis and engineering estimates. Regression analysis is a statistical method used to relate independent variables (known as *cost drivers* in our application) to dependent variables (known as *costs* in our application). Linear regression has one independent variable; multiple regression has more than one independent variable. Using the account analysis method, a cost management analyst separates costs from the accounting records into categories that correspond to the cost drivers. In the chapter example, that means the analyst separates monthly costs for C.C. Catering into unit-level costs, job-level costs, new-product costs, new-customer costs and facilities-level costs.

Whereas regression and account analysis rely on past data, engineering estimates use data from current practices. Cost management analysts (who can be engineers) make engineering estimates by first measuring the work involved in the activities that go into a product and by then assigning a cost to each of those activities. Regression analysis usually requires fewer data than account analysis because it does not require costs to be divided into categories that correspond to cost drivers. Engineering estimates are probably the most costly method because they require time-consuming effort to identify activities and assign costs to them. Probably the most informative estimate of cost behaviour results from using more than one of the methods because each has the potential to provide information that the others do not.

Key Terms

For each term's definition, refer to the indicated page, or turn to the glossary at the end of the text.

account analysis, 93
adjusted *R*-square, 104
cost-drivers, 86
cost estimation, 86
cost objects, 86
dependent variables, 95
engineering estimate, 105
high-low method, 100
independent variables, 95
learning curve†, 116
learning phenomenon†, 116
linear regression analysis, 95
mixed costs, 90
multicollinearity*, 115
multiple regression, 101
R-square, 98
regression analysis, 95
relevant range, 90
scattergraph, 98
simple linear regression, 96
step (semi-fixed) costs, 90
t-statistic*, 114

**Term appears in Appendix 3A.*

†Term appears in Appendix 3B.

*Review Questions are mostly written at a **basic** level; Critical Analysis questions and Exercises are **intermediate**, and Problems and Cases are **advanced**.*

Review Questions

3.1 For what reasons do companies estimate the relationship between costs and cost drivers?

3.2 Which method of cost estimation is least based on company records?

3.3 True or false: The relevant range is usually the range of observations included in a data set for cost estimation purposes.

3.4 Under what conditions is the engineering method preferred to other estimation methods?

3.5 What problems might you encounter if you simply enter data into a regression program to compute cost estimates?

3.6 When using cost estimation methods based on past data, what are the trade-offs between gathering more and fewer data?

3.7 Give an example of a step cost other than the examples mentioned in the text.

3.8 (Appendix 3A) What is the purpose of the *t*-statistic?

3.9 (Appendix 3A) True or false: Violations of assumptions that residuals are independent and are homoscedastic means that the cost drivers are correlated.

Critical Analysis

3.10 The following costs are labelled fixed or variable according to a typical designation in accounting. Under which circumstances would any of these costs behave in a manner opposite to that listed?

a. Direct labour – variable.
b. Equipment depreciation – fixed.
c. Utilities – variable.
d. Supervisory salaries – fixed.

3.11 Discuss the objectivity/subjectivity trade-off that apparently is a key difference between multiple regression analysis and account analysis. Is one always more objective or subjective than the other? Explain.

3.12 An associate of yours states, 'I would never use the results of regression because the past is a poor predictor of the future'. How would you respond?

3.13 Explain the objection to using past data to estimate future costs. Is the past always irrelevant to predicting the future? Explain. How might you reasonably adjust cost estimation results based on past data to estimate future costs?

3.14 (Appendix 3B) The fast-food restaurant **McDonald's** is known for high employee turnover, high quality and low costs. Using your knowledge of the learning phenomenon, how does McDonald's get high quality and low costs when it has so much employee turnover?

3.15 Your colleague says, 'I understand that multiple regression computes the best cost-driver rates for the production cost data we have. I also see how we can use those cost-driver rates to trace costs to products, similar to ABC analysis. However, aren't we still stuck with allocating the facility-level cost arbitrarily for absorption costing purposes? What have we gained by using multiple regression?' Respond.

3.16 Search the Internet for applications of simple or multiple regression analysis to business, economic, governmental or scientific purposes. Describe five of the most interesting applications in a brief report.

3.17 A friend comes to you with the following problem: 'I provided my boss with a cost equation based on account analysis. He was unhappy with the results. He told me to do more work and not return until I had a lower cost estimate for one of the cost drivers – the number of set-ups. My analysis covered the last 12 months, January through December of last year. I found that by including the 12 months before that, January through December of the year before last, I was able to get a lower estimated cost-driver rate for number of set-ups. My boss was happy with my new results. Do you think that what I did was unethical?' How would you respond?

3.18 After performing a regression analysis and giving the results to your boss, you discover an error in the data. Because of a formatting error, you understated costs by three digits. For example, $100 should have been $100,000. When you told your boss about the error, your boss said that the analysis had already been passed on to a top executive who was going to use it in a presentation to the board of directors tomorrow. Your boss does not want to tell the top executive about the error. Should you?

3.19 In doing cost analysis, you realize that there could be errors in the accounting records. For example, maintenance costs were recorded as zero in December. However, you know that maintenance was performed in December. You find that maintenance costs were about double the normal monthly amount in the next month, January. You suspect that maintenance costs were not recorded in December, the last month of the year, so the department's costs would appear to be below budget. The apparent error could affect regression analysis because you are using both December and January in your analysis. Should you report your concerns about the way maintenance costs were recorded? If so, to whom would you report your concerns?

3.20 Assume that you are performing multiple regression for an international company. What potential problems might you encounter when using data from multiple countries?

Exercises

Exercise 3.21 [LO 2] Cost-behaviour Patterns

Label each of the following graphs as to cost pattern: variable, fixed, step, mixed.

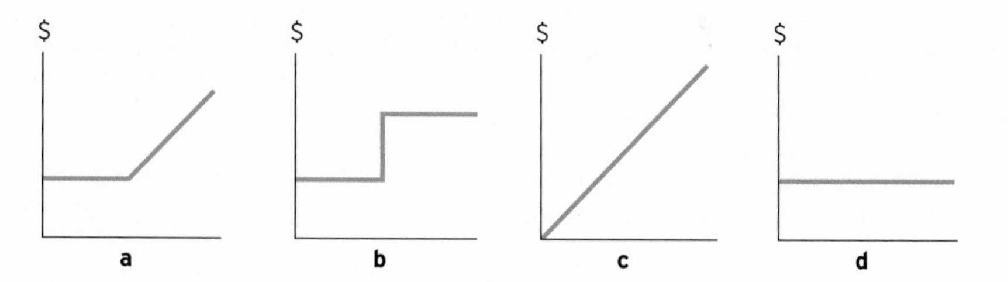

Exercise 3.22 [LO 2] Cost-behaviour Patterns

Select the following graph that best matches the description of each of the following cost items.

a. A telephone bill where the amount charged has two components: (1) a fixed amount for the first 60 minutes per month and (2) a variable cost for usage greater than 60 minutes per month. The horizontal axis is the number of telephone minutes.

b. Insurance on an automobile for which the insured pays a fixed amount for the first 15,000 kilometres per year, and then the rate increases in a step as the car is driven more than 15,000 kilometres per year. The horizontal axis is the number of kilometres driven per year.

c. Wages paid to strawberry pickers paid €2.75 per crate picked. The horizontal axis is the number of crates of strawberries picked.

d. The salary of a college professor who is paid the same salary regardless of the number of students taught. The horizontal axis is the number of students taught.

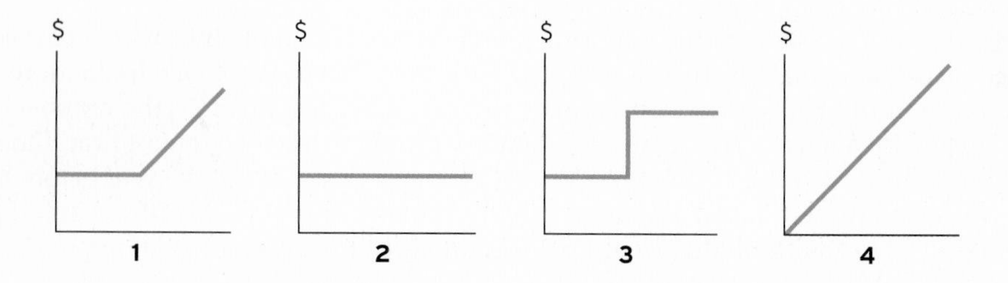

Exercise 3.23 [LO 10] Learning Curves (Appendix 3B)

Assume that **General Electric**, which manufactures high-technology instruments for spacecraft, is considering the sale of a navigational unit to a government agency in India that wishes to launch its own communications satellite. The government agency plans to purchase eight units for a total of $2,500,000, although it would also consider buying 16 units for a total of $4,500,000. General Electric requires a margin of 40 per cent of sales to cover administrative costs, contribute to basic research, and make a profit. For example, the sale of eight units must cost no more than $1,500,000 to produce [(1.00 – 0.40) × $2,500,000]. General Electric has started a chart for this product assuming the production costs are subject to an 80 per cent cumulative learning curve.

Cumulative number of units produced	Average production cost per unit	Total production costs
1	$400,000	$400,000
2	$320,000	$640,000
4	?	?
8	?	?
16	?	?

Required

a. Complete the chart by filling in the cost amounts for volumes of 4, 8 and 16 units.
b. Should General Electric sell eight units? Should it sell 16 units?

Exercise 3.24 [LO 4] Linear Regression

Aliéné SARL has developed a regression equation to analyse the behaviour of its maintenance costs (*C*) as a function of machine hours (*MH*). The following equation was developed using 30 months of data:

$$C = €12,000 + €2.25MH$$

Required

a. Using this cost equation, what are the estimated total maintenance costs at an activity level of 500 machine hours?
b. What problems might arise from using these data?

[CPA adapted]

Exercise 3.25 [LO 4] Linear Regression

Use the regression results for C.C. Catering in Exhibit 3.10.

Required

a. What are the estimated total costs for a month in which 2,800 meals will be sold?
b. What are the estimated fixed costs for a month in which 2,800 meals will be sold?
c. What are the estimated total variable costs for a month in which 2,800 meals will be sold?
d. What might be a problem with using the results in Exhibit 3.10 if C.C. Catering plans to sell 7,000 meals in a month?

Exercise 3.26 [LO 4] Linear Regression

Use the regression results for C.C. Catering in Exhibit 3.10.

Required

a. What are the estimated total costs for a month in which 2,100 meals will be sold?
b. What are the estimated committed costs for a month in which 2,100 meals will be sold?
c. What are the estimated total variable costs for a month in which 2,100 meals will be sold?
d. What might be a problem with using the results in Exhibit 3.10 if C.C. Catering plans to sell 8,000 meals in a month?

Exercise 3.27 [LO 6] Multiple Regression

Use the best multiple regression results for C.C. Catering in Exhibit 3.13.

Required

What are the estimated total costs in a month in which there are:

a. 2,750 meals sold
b. 28 jobs
c. 1 new product
d. 4 new customers

Exercise 3.28 [LO 6] High-low Method

Luigi's Limo Service operates a fleet of limousines. Management wants to estimate the fixed and variable costs per kilometre. A recent trade publication indicated that variable costs should be no more than €0.30 per kilometre. To check his costs against those indicated in the trade journal, Luigi collected the following data for his limousine fleet for last month:

Limousine Number	Costs	Kilometres
1	€3,500	12,400
2	3,400	11,800
3	3,200	10,600
4	3,800	11,500
5	3,500	11,800
6	4,000	13,200
7	3,200	9,800
8	3,000	9,200
9	4,200	11,700
10	3,900	12,300

Required

a. Use the high-low method to estimate the fixed and variable portions of overhead costs based on kilometres driven.
b. What is the estimated total cost of driving one limousine 12,000 kilometres?
c. Luigi has heard that the high-low method has a major limitation compared to linear regression. What is it?

Exercise 3.29 [LO 4] Linear Regression

Refer to the data for Luigi's Limousine Service in Exercise 3.28.

Required

Using miles as the cost driver, build a spreadsheet to derive the linear regression results and estimated total cost for Luigi's Limousine Service.

Exercise 3.30 [LO 5] High-low Method

Allu Arjun, the owner of Concrete Alkapuri Ltd, wishes to estimate the committed and variable costs for the production of concrete pipe sections. Allu collected the following data from the accounting records:

Month	Concrete pipe production costs	Number of sections produced
1	INR 128,520,000	8,600
2	140,625,000	9,800
3	149,400,000	12,600
4	150,187,500	12,500
5	159,300,000	14,800
6	185,962,500	15,200
7	135,900,000	9,800
8	158,962,500	10,200
9	180,000,000	14,700
10	145,980,000	13,300

Required

a. Use the high-low method to estimate the committed and variable portions of overhead costs based on number of sections produced.
b. What is the estimated total variable cost for a month in which 3,000 sections are produced?
c. Allu has heard that the high-low method has a major limitation compared to linear regression. What is it?

Exercise 3.31 [LO 4] Linear Regression

Refer to the data for Concrete Alkapuri Ltd in Exercise 3.30.

Required

Using sections of concrete pipe produced as the cost driver, build a spreadsheet to derive the linear regression results for Concrete Alkapuri.

Exercise 3.32 [LO 4] Interpretation of Regression Results

SicherBank AG is planning to offer a new debit card for which it expects to charge €1 per transaction. The following cost estimates have been made assuming 800,000 transactions during the first month that the card is used.

Direct labour is €450,000 (the labour rate is €20 an hour × 22,500 estimated direct labour hours)

Overhead costs have not yet been estimated for the new product, but 12 months of data on total production activities and overhead costs have been analysed for similar products using simple linear regression. The following results were derived from the linear regression and provide the basis for overhead cost estimates for the new product:

SUMMARY OUTPUT
Dependent variable = Studio costs

Regression statistics	
R-square	0.8803
Standard error	6,175.0321
Observations	12
Independent variable	**Coefficients**
Intercept	112,153.335
Direct labour hours	5.496

Required

a. What percentage of the variation in overhead costs is explained by the independent variable?
b. What is the total overhead cost for an estimated activity level of 22,500 direct labour hours per month?
c. Will the €1 per transaction charge cover the costs of direct labour and overhead, assuming 800,000 transactions?

[CMA adapted]

Exercise 3.33 [LO 4] Interpretation of Regression Results

Silhouettes Dance Studio estimates studio (non-instruction) costs based on student hours of instruction, where 1 student receiving a private lesson for 1 hour is '1 student hour'. Data were gathered for the past 24 months and entered into a regression program. The following output was obtained:

SUMMARY OUTPUT Dependent variable = Overhead costs	
Regression statistics	
R-square	0.1609
Standard error	612.0926
Observations	24
Independent variable	**Coefficients**
Intercept	1,451.784
Direct labour hours	2.551

The company is planning to operate at a level of 300 student instruction hours per month during the coming year.

Required

a. Use the regression output to write the cost equation.
b. Based on the cost equation, compute the estimated studio cost per month for the coming year.

Exercise 3.34 [LO 3] Account Analysis Method

Farout Cards makes and produces greeting cards. Every month, it produces from 5 to 15 new products in batches. At the end of the month, the company destroys the master copy of all existing cards so that it produces new card products each month. The costs of designing the card, including design and art work, are product-level costs. The costs of materials, ink and other printing costs are unit-level costs. The costs of setting up the production run are batch-level costs. All other costs are facility-level costs. Farout's accounting records report the following production costs for last December:

Unit-level costs	£26,500
Batch-level costs	10,000
Product-level costs	22,000
Facility-level costs	28,000

Production was 100,000 units for 10 different new products produced in 100 batches.

Costs for this coming December are expected to increase over last December's costs as follows: the unit-level costs, 20 per cent per unit; the batch-level costs, 10 per cent per batch; the product-level costs, 10 per cent per product; and the facility-level costs, 10 per cent for the month.

Required

Build a spreadsheet to solve the following requirements:

a. What is the unit-level cost per unit for last December?
b. What is the estimated unit-level cost per unit for this coming December?

c. What are the estimated facility-level costs for this coming December?
d. If Farout expects to produce 120,000 units for 12 new products in 100 batches this coming December, what will be its estimated total costs for the month?

Exercise 3.35 [LO 3] Account Analysis Method

EXO Sport AB manufactures protective gear for outdoor action sports. Every month, it produces several new products in batches. The costs of design, including paying designers and testers are product-level costs. The costs of materials and packaging are unit-level costs. The costs of setting up the production run are batch-level costs. All other costs are facility-level costs. EXO Sport's accounting records report the following production costs for January of this year (monetary values given in Swedish kronor, kr):

Unit-level costs	960,000 kr
Batch-level costs	240,000
Product-level costs	1,080,000
Facility-level costs	300,000

Production was 50,000 units for two new products, produced in 50 batches.

Costs for June of this year are expected to increase over the costs for January of this year as follows: the unit-level costs, 5 per cent per unit; the batch-level costs, 4 per cent per batch; the product-level costs, 4 per cent per product; and the facility-level costs, 5 per cent for the month.

Required

a. What are the unit-level cost per unit, the batch-level cost per batch, and the product-level cost per product for January of this year?
b. What are the estimated facility-level costs for June of this year?
c. If in June of this year, EXO Sport expects to produce 60,000 units for three new products in 100 batches, what will be its estimated total costs for the month?

Exercise 3.36 [LO 3] Account Analysis

Use the account analysis results for C.C. Catering in Exhibit 3.7.

Required

What are the estimated total costs in a month in which there are:

a. 2,500 meals sold
b. 32 jobs
c. 5 new products
d. 12 new customers

Exercise 3.37 [LO 9] Interpretation of Regression Data (Appendix 3A)

Unsafe Insurance Company needs to forecast its personnel department costs. The following output was obtained from a regression program used to estimate the department's costs as a function of the number of employees:

SUMMARY OUTPUT	
Dependent variable = Personal costs	
Regression statistics	
R-square	0.7255
Standard error	612.0926
Observations	24

Independent variable	Coefficients	Standard error	*t*-statistic
Intercept	8,421. 441	2,687.979	3.133
Employees	492.703	164.949	2.987

Monthly data for the past two years were used to construct these estimates. Cost relationships are expected to be the same for the coming period (monetary values should be given in euros).

Required

a. What are the estimated personnel costs for 3,645 employees?
b. (Appendix 3A) How confident are you that a significant cost-driver relation exists?

Problems

Problem 3.38 [LO 3, 4] Interpretation of Regression Results: Linear Regression

Your company, Regional-Express-Lieferung (REL), makes special deliveries to real estate and law firms. It is estimating its costs for the coming period.

The controller's office estimated overhead costs at €4,000 per month for fixed costs and €7 per delivery for variable costs. Your nemesis on the staff, Nicholas Witt, suggested that the company use the regression approach. Witt has already done the analysis on a home computer and reports the 'correct' cost equation as:

Monthly overhead = €18,005.55 + €6.30 per delivery

When asked for the data used to generate the regression, Witt produces the following list:

Month	Overhead costs	Number of deliveries
1	€85,716	11,430
2	91,134	12,180
3	115,560	15,660
4	84,618	11,250
5	99,924	12,780
6	125,124	14,730
7	95,778	12,510
8	110,394	15,060
9	116,658	15,450
10	90,072	11,970
11	92,448	12,630
12	110,880	15,300
13	109,872	14,580

The company controller is somewhat surprised that the cost estimates are so different. You have therefore been assigned to check Witt's equation.

Required

Build a spreadsheet to analyse Witt's results and state your reasons for supporting or rejecting his cost equation.

Problem 3.39 [LO 4] Interpretation of Regression Results

Lerner Inc. is accumulating data to prepare its annual profit plan for the coming year. The behaviour pattern of the maintenance costs must be determined. The accounting staff has suggested using regression to derive an equation in the form of $y = a + bx$ for maintenance costs. Monthly data regarding maintenance hours and costs for the preceding year were entered into the regression analysis.

Total hours of maintenance for the year	4,800
Total costs for the year	$43,200
Regression results:	
Intercept	$684.65
b coefficient	$7.2884
R^2	0.79724

Required

a. In a regression equation expressed as $y = a + bx$, what is the letter b best described as?
b. What is the letter y in the regression equation best described as?
c. What is the letter x in the regression equation best described as?
d. Based on the data derived from the regression analysis, what are the estimated costs for 360 maintenance hours in a month?
e. What is the percentage of the total variance that can be explained by the regression equation?

[CMA adapted]

Problem 3.40 [LO 6] Multiple Regression, Activity-based Costing

The accounting department of Insecurity Protection, a company that provides security services, is analysing the costs of its accounting services. Analysts have selected the following cost drivers: number of pay cheques processed, customer accounts maintained, and special analyses.

The cost data and level of cost-driver activity for the past 16 months follow:

Month	Special analyses	Customer accounts	Pay cheques processed	Accounting service costs
1	1	320	1,029	$62,580
2	3	330	993	69,420
3	3	315	1,268	64,210
4	2	230	1,028	62,150
5	1	228	984	60,800
6	-	216	712	50,950
7	1	187	762	51,500
8	1	140	739	54,650
9	-	125	708	51,200
10	2	301	1,232	63,500
11	1	230	978	57,850
12	2	217	929	58,260
13	3	226	1,059	62,260
14	2	150	942	55,000
15	4	300	1,299	71,620
16	4	330	1,283	65,400
Totals	30	3,845	15,945	$961,350

Required

a. Build your own spreadsheet. Using regression analysis, find the best cost estimation equation.

b. Assuming the following levels of cost-driver volume for a month, what is the accounting department's estimated costs of doing business based on the multiple regression results?

   i. 1,000 pay cheques processed

   ii. 250 customer accounts maintained

   iii. 2 special analyses

c. Insecurity Protection is considering outsourcing the processing of all pay cheques. Compared to your answer in requirement (b), how much would the accounting department save per month by outsourcing all payroll processing (before considering the cost of outsourcing)?

Problem 3.41 [LO 3] Account Analysis

Refer to Problem 3.40.

Required

a. Before proceeding to requirement (b) of this problem, indicate the information required to perform account analysis for Insecurity Protection's accounting department cost estimation that is not in Problem 3.40.

b. Now assume that Insecurity Protection's accounting department had the following total costs for each cost driver for the 16 months reported in Problem 3.40.

Total cost of pay cheques processed	$180,000
Total cost of maintaining customer accounts	110,000
Total cost of performing special analyses	60,000
Total facilities-level costs (total for 16 months)	610,000
Total costs	$960,000

What are the cost-driver rates for (1) pay cheques processed, (2) customer accounts maintained, and (3) special analyses performed?

c. Assuming the following level of cost-driver volumes for a month, what is the accounting department's estimated costs of doing business using the account analysis approach?

   i. 1,000 pay cheques processed

   ii. 250 customer accounts maintained

   iii. 2 special analyses

d. Insecurity Protection is considering outsourcing the processing of all pay cheques. Compared to your answer in requirement (c), how much would the accounting department save by outsourcing payroll (before considering the cost of outsourcing)?

Problem 3.42 [LO 7] Engineering Estimates

Refer to Problems 3.40 and 3.41. Insecurity Protection Services hired an engineering consulting firm to perform an engineering estimate of the accounting department's costs. The firm identified the following cost estimates based on information for the current period:

Facilities costs (per month)	$40,000
Payroll processing	5.00 per pay cheques
Customer account maintenance	50.00 per account
Special analyses	2,500 per analysis

Required

a. Assuming the following level of cost-driver volume for a month, what is the accounting department's estimated costs of doing business?

   i. 1,000 pay cheques processed
   ii. 250 customer accounts maintained
   iii. 2 special analyses

b. Insecurity Protection Services is considering outsourcing the processing of all pay cheques. Compared to your answer in requirement (a), how much would the accounting department save by outsourcing payroll (before considering the cost of outsourcing)?

Problem 3.43 [LO 6] Multiple Regression, Activity-Based Costing

Analysts for Fuzhou Deluxe Optics Ltd, a maker of sunglasses, have selected the following cost drivers: number of units produced, batches of sunglasses, customer orders processed, and new products designed to explain operating costs. The cost data and levels of cost-driver activity for the past 18 months follows. (Monetary values given in Chinese yuan, ¥.)

Month	Units	Batches	Customer orders	New products	Costs
1	35,100	693	252	4	¥10,502,400
2	28,900	670	240	2	10,463,400
3	37,200	550	185	1	9,362,400
4	26,800	535	116	1	8,101,200
5	31,800	535	120	0	7,263,000
6	29,000	577	105	0	7,803,600
7	32,500	610	110	2	9,543,600
8	31,400	660	126	2	9,602,460
9	42,500	737	160	3	10,203,000
10	38,000	631	185	4	10,203,600
11	51,200	756	233	4	12,723,600
12	46,900	729	245	5	12,992,990
13	41,500	780	260	5	12,601,200
14	49,700	726	235	4	12,003,600
15	44,000	645	255	3	11,883,600
16	49,300	710	169	2	11,403,900
17	30,100	600	172	3	10,501,560
18	39,850	589	170	3	9,391,800
Total	685,750	11,733	3,337	48	¥186,550,910

Required

a. Build your own spreadsheet. Using regression analysis, find the best cost estimation equation.

b. Assuming the following level of cost-driver volume for a new plant for one month, what is the estimated cost using the multiple regression results?
   i. 30,000 units produced
   ii. 500 batches
   iii. 150 customer orders
   iv. 3 new products

c. Fuzhou Deluxe Optics is considering a plan to reduce the number of batches by 100 per factory per month. Compared to your answer in requirement (b), how much would each factory save per month by reducing the number of batches by 100 per month?

Problem 3.44 [LO 3] Account Analysis

Refer to Problem 3.43.

Required

a. Before proceeding to requirement (b) of this problem, indicate the information in addition to that provided in Problem 3.43 required to perform account analysis.

b. Now assume that Fuzhou Deluxe Optics had the following breakdown of costs:

Facilities cost	¥43,200,000
Unit-level cost	41,400,000
Batch-level cost	48,000,000
Customer-order cost	37,200,000
New-product cost	15,600,000
Total costs	¥185,400,000

What are the cost-driver rates using account analysis?

c. What are the estimated costs for a month assuming the following level of cost-driver volumes using the account analysis approach?

i. 30,000 units produced
ii. 500 batches
iii. 150 customer orders
iv. 3 new products

Problem 3.45 [LO 7] Engineering Estimates

Refer to Problems 3.43 and 3.44. Fuzhou Deluxe Optics hired an engineering consulting firm to perform an engineering estimate of sunglass production costs. The consulting firm identified the following monthly cost estimates based on information for the current period:

Facilities costs	¥240,000
Unit-level costs	54 per unit produced
Batch-level costs	3,000 per batch
Customer order costs	9,000 per customer order
New-product costs	360,000 per new product

Required

Assuming the following level of cost-driver volume for a month, what is the estimated cost using the engineering estimates?

a. 30,000 units produced
b. 500 batches
c. 150 customer orders
d. 3 new products

Problem 3.46 [LO 3, 4] Methods of Cost Estimation: Account Analysis

Hospital Millennium Medische has prepared a schedule of actual overhead costs for its blood test unit for the past year.

Activities			Overhead costs								
Month	Tests	Technician hours	Total overhead	Supplies	Indirect labour	Building occupancy	Utilities	Equipment cost	Equipment maint.	Data processing	Technical support
1	4,134	1,654	€49,306	€1,332	€9,385	€18,200	€1,405	€14,200	€1,152	€1,632	€2,000
2	4,552	1,894	50,107	1,788	9,396	18,200	1,494	14,200	1,317	1,712	2,000
3	5,367	2,100	59,632	1,588	9,433	23,200	1,734	17,450	1,370	1,857	3,000
4	4,403	1,753	49,676	1,286	9,396	18,200	1,499	14,200	1,197	1,898	2,000
5	4,550	1,774	49,557	1,415	9,388	18,200	1,350	14,200	1,152	1,852	2,000
6	5,558	2,019	58,266	1,872	9,456	21,700	1,530	17,450	1,308	1,950	3,000
7	5,519	2,059	58,803	2,070	9,440	21,700	1,698	17,450	1,377	2,068	3,000
8	5,816	2,069	58,632	1,824	9,459	21,700	1,650	17,450	1,392	2,157	3,000
9	4,570	1,928	49,822	1,458	9,419	18,200	1,338	14,200	1,236	1,971	2,000
10	4,994	1,950	58,294	1,914	9,426	21,700	1,529	17,450	1,372	1,903	3,000
11	4,531	1,786	49,634	1,677	9,406	18,200	1,290	14,200	1,090	1,771	2,000
12	4,560	1,815	50,293	1,890	9,407	18,200	1,596	14,200	1,194	1,806	2,000
Total	58,554	22,801	$642,022	€20,114	€113,011	€237,400	€18,113	€186,650	€15,157	€22,577	€29,000

In the past, the overhead costs have been related to the number of tests. Following management instructions, data were gathered on past costs and past test levels and technician hours.

Required

Prepare a cost estimation equation using the account analysis approach in which the only independent variable is the number of tests. (*Hint:* Make a scattergraph of each cost with tests as the X variable.)

Problem 3.47 [LO 10] Learning Curves (Appendix 3B)

Herbe Cosmo SARL manufactures artificial playing surfaces for indoor and outdoor sports fields. The company plans to manufacture TrueFeel, a product that requires a substantial amount of direct labour on each unit. Based on the company's experience with other products that required similar amounts of direct labour, management believes that a learning factor exists in the production process used to manufacture TrueFeel.

Each unit of TrueFeel requires 5 square metres of direct material at a cost of €150 per square metre, for a total material cost of €750. The standard direct labour rate is €12 per direct labour hour. Variable manufacturing overhead is assigned to products at a rate of €18 per direct labour hour. In determining an initial bid price for all products, the company marks up variable manufacturing costs (= direct materials + direct labour + variable overhead) 30 per cent. (That is, the bid = 130 per cent of variable manufacturing costs.)

Data on the production of the first two lots (16 units) of TrueFeel follow:

1. The first lot of eight units required a total of 400 direct labour hours.
2. The second lot of eight units required a total of 360 direct labour hours.

Based on prior production experience, Herbe Cosmo estimates that production time will show no significant improvement after the first 32 units. Therefore, a standard (for planning purposes) for direct labour hours will be established based on the average number of hours per unit for units 17 through 32.

Required

a. What is the basic premise of the learning curve?

b. Based on the data presented for the first 16 units, what learning rate appears to be applicable to the direct labour required to produce TrueFeel? Support your answer with appropriate calculations.

c. Calculate the standard for direct labour hours that Herbe Cosmo should establish for each unit of TrueFeel.

d. After the first 32 units have been manufactured, Herbe Cosmo was asked to submit a bid on an additional 96 units. What price should Herbe Cosmo bid on this order of 96 units? Explain your answer.

e. Knowledge of the learning curve can be a valuable management tool. Explain how management can apply this tool in planning and controlling business operations.

[CMA adapted]

Problem 3.48 [LO 10] Learning Curves (Appendix 3B)

Krylon Company has purchased 800 pressure gauges annually from CO_2 Inc. The price of these gauges has increased each year, reaching $1,000 per unit last year. Because the purchase price has increased significantly, Krylon management has asked for a cost estimate of manufacturing gauges in its own facilities.

A team of employees from the engineering, manufacturing and accounting departments have prepared a report for management that includes the following estimate for an assembly run of 100 units. Additional production employees will be hired to manufacture the pressure gauges. However, no additional equipment or space is needed.

The report states that total costs for 100 units are estimated at $240,000 as shown here, or $2,400 per unit.

Materials	$10,000
Direct labour consisting entirely of hourly production workers (varies with production volume)	25,000
Labour-related overhead that varies closely with direct labour (varies with production volume)	50,000
Overhead not related to labour (e.g., building rent)	75,000
General and administrative costs to support the production	80,000
Total costs	$240,000

The current purchase price is $1,000 a unit, so the report recommends a continued purchase of the product.

Required

a. Before considering the learning curve effects, was the recommendation to continue purchasing the gauges correct? Explain your answer and include any supportive calculations you consider necessary.

b. Assume that Krylon could experience labour-cost improvements on the pressure gauge assembly consistent with an 80 per cent learning curve. An assembly run of 100 units represents the initial lot or batch for measurement purposes. Should Krylon produce or purchase 800 pressure gauges in this situation? Explain your answer.

[CMA adapted]

Cases

Case 3.49 [LO 1, 4] Regressions Run from Published Data

Obtain 11 years of data from the published financial statements of a company. Using the first 10 years of data, perform a regression analysis in which the dependent variable is cost of sales and the independent variable is revenue (some companies call it *sales*). Now use the results from the regression on the first 10 years of data to estimate the cost of sales for year 11. How far off were you in estimating cost of sales for year 11? Estimate the cost of sales for year 5. How far off were you in estimating cost of sales for year 5?

Required

Prepare a report that describes your work and discusses reasons that your estimate of cost of sales is different than the actual cost of sales for year 11. You will be able to find the data on the Internet. Also, Moody's, Standard & Poor's and Value-Line are good sources of financial data.

Case 3.50 [LO 4, 6] Data Correction and Regression Analysis

Optical Storage Technology Inc. (OST) manufactures CD and DVD drives for personal and business computers in 18 locations in North America. Several years ago OST implemented quality and time-based management practices throughout its manufacturing divisions (see Chapter 7 for discussions of quality and time management), and by now few differences in performance should remain. Divisions report key operational and financial measures directly to OST headquarters, whose financial staff each month review the data and look for unusual activity or costs. The analysts also provide forecasting information for budgeting and evaluation purposes. The following table contains several key performance measures for the 18 divisions for last month.

	Operating performance measures			Financial performance
Division	Defects per month	First-time pass rate, %	Average cycle time per unit (minutes)	Manufacturing overhead cost
1	149	71.10	80.60	€46,920
2	141	65.80	83.13	48,720
3	124	67.20	76.83	42,360
4	143	61.90	81.67	47,280
5	124	63.50	77.75	43,620
6	158	80.00	79.10	47,520
7	170	86.20	81.08	49,740
8	142	60.80	82.20	50,760
9	183	77.40	86.88	55,260
10	151	68.10	84.80	4,866
11	152	65.80	82.20	50,760
12	131	71.10	78.90	45,540
13	164	65.70	82.20	50,820
14	146	62.40	84.08	49,740
15	160	64.20	86.10	50,580
16	158	72.20	84.63	52,380
17	149	82.30	77.92	45,840
18	172	69.70	81.60	49,500

Required

a. Review the preceding data and consider making any needed corrections using one of the following common data-correction practices:

(1) Obtain the correct figure(s) from the divisions.

(2) If data in part (1) cannot be obtained, delete entire division(s) that have errors, which is conservative, but costly when data are scarce.

(3) Replace the incorrect figure(s) with the average value of the variable (without the error), which saves data but has no other justification.

b. In your opinion, how did performance across divisions compare last month? What assumptions are necessary to make cross-divisional comparisons? What additional data would you like to have? Explain.

c. Use regression analysis to find the best simple or multiple regression equation that explains manufacturing overhead costs across divisions. Describe how you performed the analysis and how you selected the best model.

d. Analysts have collected performance data for six divisions from the month just ended. Use these data to test the predictive ability of three of your models, including the best model by following the following steps:

(1) Use each regression equation and the operating performance data to estimate manufacturing overhead costs.

(2) Subtract estimated overhead costs from actual overhead costs; call this difference the *estimation error.*

(3) Across models, compare either the average (mean) of the absolute value of estimation errors or the square root of the mean squared errors for each model.* Which model has the lowest average estimation error? Does this result surprise you? Why or why not?

Division	Average defects per month	First-time pass rate, %	Average cycle time per unit (minutes)	Actual manufacturing overhead cost
1	146	73.00	81.00	€47,088
2	150	68.00	79.00	46,950
3	118	80.60	75.00	42,150
4	134	63.00	80.00	46,338
5	131	78.20	76.00	43,230
6	149	68.90	82.00	48,576

* Both are common measures of estimation accuracy. Absolute values can be computed with the ABS() function in spreadsheet software; then compute the mean. The root mean squared error (RMSE) for each model can be computed by squaring the prediction errors, computing the mean squared error, and computing the square root. Clearly, this is spreadsheet-friendly work.

Solutions to You're the Decision Maker

3.1 Using Account Analysis, p. 95

Shiranthi Chandra and Dinah Cedibe's account analysis was time consuming because C.C. Catering's accounting system was not designed to record costs by cost driver; that is, it was a traditional, functional accounting system. Because Shiranthi and Dinah had to record costs and cost drivers manually, it was a tedious effort that probably could benefit from a thorough system design. They did what seemed to be reasonable in addition to all of the other activities they must perform, so their classifications of costs might be unreliably subjective. Additionally, they chose the most recent three months because that was as soon as they could do the task. They did not have the time to recreate past months' costs according to the expected cost drivers. The choice of months was convenient but might not represent normal operations. In particular, the most recent months might have had lower meal preparation costs because of customer demands for lower-cost meals or unusually low input prices. Although account analysis can be a useful exercise and can provide motivation to design and install a more descriptive system, this method is prone to errors caused by the necessity of hasty analysis and selection of atypical time periods. If Shiranthi and Dinah are pleased with using the results of their analyses, they know more about how costs and cost drivers should be recorded in the future.

3.2 Using Multiple Regression Analysis, p. 105

It is true that the best multiple regression equation uses only the numbers of meals sold and new customers as cost-driver activities to estimate total costs. The other activities do not appear to contribute information about total costs given the current relation among activities. Estimating costs is not the only management activity, however, so Shiranthi and Dinah would be wise to continue to be concerned about all of its activities, including the numbers of jobs and new products that the company undertakes. They need to schedule, monitor and evaluate their effectiveness and efficiency in performing all major activities if the business is to continue to succeed. If they mistakenly stopped managing these activities and concentrated only on the numbers of meals and new customers, you can expect that the previous synergistic relations among the business's activities would break down, and the company might lose profitable customers.

Endnotes

1. At the time of writing this text, the exchange rate is about €0.10 or $0.15 for 1 South African rand.
2. We refer back to Chapter 2 on the cost terminology.
3. For example, Noreen and Soderstrom (1994) found that department overhead costs in a large sample of hospitals are not proportional to the activities in the departments. Their results imply that at least some overhead costs increase in steps and that at least some overhead costs are curvilinear.
4. See Maher and Marais (1998).
5. This, too, often exhibits step-cost behaviour, with different slopes at different levels of use. So it can be a matter of scale of the chart whether costs are modelled as non-linear in a 'smooth' way or with small, stepwise changes.
6. This method actually uses less historical data than linear regression, but we present it in this order, because it is a simplified variation on linear regression analysis.
7. We use four digits to avoid errors due to rounding.
8. In Chapter 4, you will see that these cost drivers line up well with the activity-based cost (ABC) hierarchy. That is, C.C. Catering has unit-level costs driven by the number of meals sold, batch-level costs driven by the number of jobs, product-related costs driven by the number of new products introduced, and customer-related costs driven by the number of new customers each month.
9. For more information on engineering cost estimations, see for example Sullivan et al. (2009).
10. To make this point, we know of an analyst who performed a regression analysis with the telephone numbers of department heads as the independent variable and department costs as the dependent variable. This analyst reported the results, tongue-in-cheek, only to find that some managers took the results seriously.
11. Sometimes this learning curve formula is defined differently, whereby y = average number of labour hours per unit required for the 1 through Xth unit.
12. One equation can be rewritten into the other as follows: $Y = ax^{\frac{\log(s)}{\log(2)}} = ax^{\log_2(x)} = as^{\log_2(x)}$
13. Generally, $\log(s)$ means $\log_{10}(s)$ unless another base is mentioned.

References

Anderson, M., R. Banker and S. Janikiraman (2003) 'Are selling, general, and administrative costs "sticky"?' *Journal of Accounting Research*, vol. 41, no. 1, pp. 47–63.

Anderson, S.W. (1995) 'Measuring the impact of product mix meterogeneity on manufacturing overhead cost', *The Accounting Review*, vol. 70, no. 3, pp. 363–387.

Anderson, S.W., and W.N. Lanen (2007) 'Understanding cost management: what can we learn from the evidence on sticky costs?' Rice University at University of Michigan Working Paper.

Balakrishnan, R., M. Peterson and N. Soderstrom (2003) 'Does capacity utilization affect the "stickiness" of cost?' *Journal of Accounting, Auditing, and Finance*, vol. 19, no. 3, pp. 283–299.

Banker R.J., G. Potter and R.G. Schroeder (1995) 'An empirical analysis of manufacturing overhead cost drivers', *Journal of Accounting and Economics*, vol. 19, no. 1, pp. 115–137.

Independent Regulators Group (2000) 'Principles of implementation and best practice regarding FL-LRIC cost modelling', 24 November, accessed at: www.erg.eu.int/doc/publications/call_input_lric/vodafone_final.doc.

Ittner, C., D.F. Larcker and T. Randall (1997) 'The activity-based cost hierarchy, production policies and firm profitability', *Journal of Management Accounting Research*, vol. 9, pp. 143–162.

Lindberg, G. (2009) 'Cost allocation of transport infrastructure cost', European Commission Sixth Framework Programme Priority 1.6.2, June.

Maher, M.W., and M.L. Marais (1998) 'A field study on the limitations of activity-based costing when resources are provided on a joint and indivisible basis', *Journal of Accounting Research*, vol. 36, no. 1, pp. 129–142.

Noreen, E., and N. Soderstrom (1994) 'Are overhead costs strictly proportional to activity? Evidence from hospital service departments', *Journal of Accounting and Economics*, vol. 17, no. 1–2, pp. 255–278.

Senge, P.M. (1990) *The Fifth Discipline: The Art and Practice of the Learning Organization*, Currency Doubleday, New York.

Shetty, V. (1998) 'Grasping the nettle', *Communications International*, vol. 25, nos. 9, p. 86.

Subramanium, C., and M. Weidenmeir (2003) 'Additional evidence on the stickiness of costs', Texas Christian University Working Paper.

Sullivan, W.G., E.M. Wicks and C.P. Koelling (2009) *Engineering Economy*, 14th Edition, Pearson Prentice Hall, Upper Saddle River, New Jersey.

Sweet, C. (2011) 'GE announces investment in solar-thermal company eSolar', *Wall Street Journal (Deals India)*, 7 June.

Wheat, P., and A. Smith (2009) 'Sustainable Surface Transport, D8 – Rail Cost Allocation for Europe, Annex 1E – Renewal Costs in Great Britain', European Commission Sixth Framework Programme Priority 1.6.2, January.

Wiersma, E. (2007) 'Conditions that shape the learning curve', *Management Science*, vol. 53, no. 12, pp. 1903–1915.

PART 2

Activity-based Management

A Look Back

Part 1 introduced cost management. It discussed managing the value chain, designing the cost system and estimating product costs.

A Look at this Part

Part 2 builds cost management tools to help understand production processes. The topics in this part are recent innovations in the field of cost management. Chapter 4 discusses activity-based costing. Chapter 5 discusses activity-based management with an application to customer profitability analysis. Chapter 6 discusses the management of activities to increase quality, decrease time and enhance customer value.

A Look Ahead

Part 3 discusses process costing and cost allocation.

CHAPTER 4

Activity-based Costing Systems

© billberryphotography

Learning Objectives

After completing this chapter, you should be able to:

LO 1 Describe how traditional costing could lead to under-costing and over-costing some products.

LO 2 Apply the steps used in an activity-based costing system.

LO 3 Classify five different levels of resources and activities used in production processes.

LO 4 Measure the costs to supply various activities and calculate cost-driver rates for each using practical capacity.

LO 5 Measure the costs of products (goods and services) using cost-driver rates.

LO 6 Analyse the profitability of products.

LO 7 Distinguish between ABC unit-level costing and ABC full costing of goods and services.

LO 8 Apply activity-based costing to service and merchandising companies.

Precision Moulding Ltd

The following is the transcript of a recent conference call between Tomás Siñese, Vice President of Logistics for MegaBurger International and Melody Fairchild, President and Chief Executive Officer of Precision Moulding Ltd (PML) and other PML executives. MegaBurger International is one of the world's largest fast-food restaurant chains. PML is a mid-sized UK-based company that specializes in plastic-injection moulding of plastic toys, containers and parts for other products.

Tomás Siñese, MegaBurger: Good morning, Melody. Thank you for getting your staff together on such short notice.

Melody Fairchild, PML: My pleasure. Let me introduce you to the rest of the team. Chad Norris is vice president of manufacturing, Alex Lewis is chief financial officer and Michele Chia is our vice president of marketing.

Tomás Siñese, MegaBurger: Hello, all. Thanks for joining us. Let me outline what we are proposing. We need someone to supply promotional novelty toys, such as action figures and movie tie-ins, to our European region. We hope that PML can do the job. You have a good reputation for quality products, ethical business practices and community service. PML is the type of company with which we like to be associated.

We want you and our current supplier in the region to submit bids for this business. Quite frankly, we've been disappointed with our current supplier's business practices and we're prepared to offer you the business if you show that PML can supply a quality product, with on-time delivery and at a reasonable price.

Melody Fairchild, PML: Tomás, our record for quality and on-time delivery is superb. I believe you've already checked with our current customers to verify that. We're confident that we can exceed your expectations. Before we submit a bid to you, we need to know details about products and distribution to fully evaluate this opportunity.

Tomás Siñese, MegaBurger: Melody, you should be receiving a fax with product and delivery specifications. This includes our expected sales and distribution, and, as you know, this is very sensitive information. I must have your agreement that this information stays within PML.

Melody Fairchild, PML: Agreed. When do you need our response?

Tomás Siñese, MegaBurger: We need your bid within 90 days. I'll be travelling for the next few weeks, but my assistant will know how to contact me if you need more information. Any questions now?

Melody Fairchild, PML: No, this is clear. We just received your fax. If we have any questions about it, I'll be in touch. Have a safe trip.

P M L

This chapter elaborates the product costing methods that were discussed in Chapter 2. In some cases, particularly when products are varied, complex and customized, a simple approach to costing treats all products similarly and introduces what might be large cost distortions; that is, the costs of products do not accurately reflect the resources consumed to produce them. This chapter focuses on a more complex, accurate and, yes, costly product-costing system that an estimated 30–40 per cent; of commercial firms have adopted. This chapter focuses on activity-based costing (ABC), which seeks to create product costs that accurately reflect the economics of production and consumption of resources.

ABC costing may use five different cost categories that reflect different levels of production activities and that sum to total production costs.

- **Unit-level cost:** The cost of resources dedicated to an activity that is performed for every unit of product (e.g., architectural plans for a unique building).
- **Batch-level cost:** The cost of resources dedicated to an activity that is performed for every batch of multiple units that receive simultaneous processing (e.g., architectural plans for a tract of identical apartments or flats).
- **Product-level cost:** The cost of resources dedicated to an activity that is performed for every product line of units produced (e.g., advertising for consumer electronics separate from lighting).
- **Customer-level cost:** The cost of resources dedicated to an activity that is performed for every unique customer served (e.g., each wholesale customer of a suppler).
- **Facility-level cost:** The cost of resources dedicated to an activity that is performed for a production facility (e.g., factory).

To contrast the traditional and ABC approaches, consider how each computes product costs *from the same total production cost*:

Costing method	Cost elements	Examples
Traditional Product costs	= Cost of direct materials used	€10 traced to each unit
	+ Cost of direct labour used	€24 traced to each unit
	+ Costs of indirect resources used	€20,000 per period for idle labour, machine set-ups, equipment depreciation, co-ordination with customers, factory depreciation, supervision, etc.
ABC product costs	= Unit-level activity cost	€34 materials and labour
	+ Batch-level activity cost	€2,000 machine set-ups
	+ Product-level activity cost	€5,000 depreciation of equipment for different products
	+ Customer-level activity cost	€6,000 co-design and modifications for specific customers
	+ Facility-level activity cost	€7,000 for factory depreciation, supervision, etc.

At a minimum, one can see that the ABC approach splits total production cost into more categories that reflect 'higher levels' of product aggregation. More importantly, the ABC approach determines the different types of activities performed to make different products and assign costs accordingly, which can lead to large differences in activity-based product costs, compared to the traditional approach. The costing can affect information for decision making, too, because costs in a higher ABC-level category either are fixed with changes in lower levels, or are lumpy step costs with changes in lower levels.

This chapter seeks to demonstrate the more complex ABC approach, but also to fairly discuss the benefits and costs of this more complex costing system. It might not be suitable for all organizations, at all times.

PML Background

'What an opportunity! Can we win this business? Do we want to win this business? Can we profitably supply novelty toys to MegaBurger? I don't know at this time, but we'd better figure it out!' Fairchild exclaimed to her executive team after she hung up the phone.

The small novelty toys are more complex than any product PML has made. MegaBurger also has very high expectations for quality and on-time deliveries. Winning this bid could mean a large increase in PML's sales and create future opportunities to partner with MegaBurger, which is a global giant. Fairchild was eager to expand PML's customer base because she believed the company was too dependent on just two customers. However, she knew that if PML did not evaluate this opportunity realistically, the company could suffer large losses on the MegaBurger business. Such a mistake could mean disaster for the company's employees and shareholders.

PML's Competitive Situation

PML Ltd, founded in 1981, had become one of the dominant manufacturers of plastic injection-moulded products in its geographical region. It emphasized consistent quality, quick order turnaround, reliable distribution and reasonable prices with a high level of service. PML outsourced certain parts of its value chain to suppliers and machine shops that have been reliable business partners since the early 1980s. Melody Fairchild, the current chief executive officer (CEO), believes that decisions such as selective outsourcing have allowed the company to focus on its primary competitive advantages, which are careful design, quality production and a high level of customer service.

PML was a mid-sized company that, although profitable, could ill afford to make mistakes by doing unprofitable work. To prepare its bid for the MegaBurger business, PML had to have good estimates of the costs to produce the novelty toys. Management needed accurate cost information so it could propose a product price that would ensure the business's profitability.

PML's Products and Processes

PML's current plastic products range from relatively simple items, such as reusable 1- and 4-litre beverage containers for a national discount retail chain, to complex products, such as plastic baby carriers and strollers. The simple beverage containers require blowing liquefied plastic into a mould, sometimes combining it with different colours for different types of drinks (e.g., green for ginger ale). The more complicated baby-care products, which are under exclusive contract for an international firm, have multiple, complex parts that require complicated moulds and precise control over colours, injection pressures and temperatures. PML's ability to make these complex products attracted MegaBurger's attention.

The company purchases small plastic pellets that are heated to make liquid plastic, which is put through a process known as 'injection moulding' that moulds the plastic into the desired shapes. See Exhibit 4.1 for the steps involved in the production process:

- Purge or clean the system before each production run to prevent contamination by dirt or leftover plastic and colour.
- Set up the machine to ensure that order data are recorded properly and that machine settings are correct for the product.
- Begin the production run to verify production data and ensure that the machine is operating properly; then start the full-scale operation of the run.
- Perform the actual production run.
- Remove products from the mould and visually inspect them to ensure that they meet visual quality standards.
- Recycle defective products to reduce waste and prevent defective products from reaching customers.
- Place good products in inventory (or stock) in preparation for delivery to customers.
- End the production run so that the machinery and work area are left in a safe, clean condition.

PML

Exhibit 4.1 Injection-moulding Process at PML

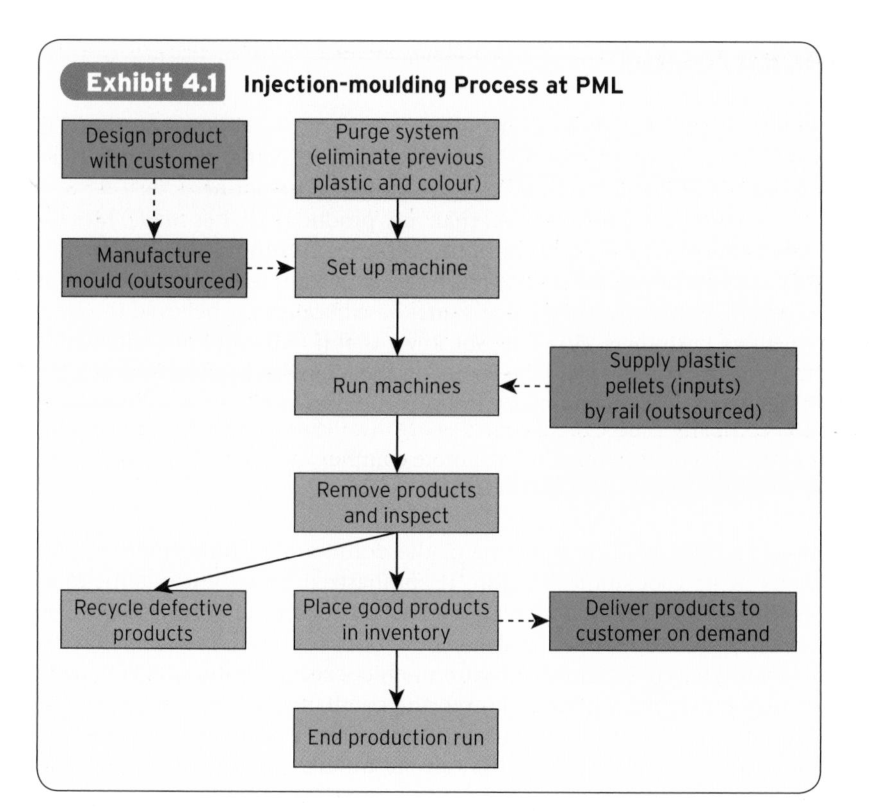

PML's Costing System Options

PML could use a simple cost system, such as the one discussed in Chapter 2, or a more complex cost system, such as the one discussed in this chapter. In choosing among alternative cost systems, PML managers must assess the costs and benefits of their choices. The simpler system requires less effort and time but provides less accurate cost estimates. The more complex system requires more effort and time but provides more accurate cost estimates. In general, company managers will weigh the benefits of having more accurate cost estimates against the time and effort required to obtain them.

PML's Costing System Team

Melody Fairchild, the CEO, knew that reliable cost information was critically important to PML as it prepared its bid for the MegaBurger business. Accordingly, she asked her chief financial officer (CFO), Alex Lewis, to form the best team possible to prepare the bid for MegaBurger. He already had some top-notch employees in mind. These included a recently hired finance department employee, who had just received her Bachelor of Commerce degree with top honours, and a production supervisor with 20 years of experience in the industry, mostly with other companies. The final team member was a product design engineer who did a good deal of consulting with customers. The team would collect information from other company employees in all areas, including human resources and information technology.

The team's goal was to measure the costs of existing products as accurately as possible and then to use this information to estimate the costs of the novelty toys for MegaBurger. Team members knew that MegaBurger's novelty toys would require many of the same activities already being used for existing PML products. Thus, team members believed that using data for existing products and adjusting these data would be appropriate for estimating the costs of the MegaBurger toys.

Traditional Costing System

LO 1
Describe how traditional costing could lead to under-costing and over-costing products.

The traditional cost system that many companies use does not assign indirect product costs, such as supervisors' salaries and utilities, directly to the product. Instead, using a traditional cost system, companies allocate indirect costs to the product according to a volume measure, such as how many direct labour hours or machine hours are used (we will illustrate this shortly). The advantage of a traditional cost system is its simplicity and ready access of needed data. However, the resulting cost data are typically not as accurate as those that more complex and expensive cost systems provide.

Nevertheless, a traditional cost system can be sufficient to meet managers' cost information requirements, particularly if (a) the proportion of indirect costs is relatively low compared to direct costs, (b) product diversity is low, or (c) the accuracy of cost information is not critical to the company's success. Managers of organizations using a traditional cost system might decide rationally that the costs to implement a more complex cost system are higher than its potential benefits.

Under-costing and Over-costing Products: Cost of Dinner Example

Suppose that you go to dinner with a friend to celebrate the end of finals week at school. You order an entrée (£8) and a cup of specialty coffee (£3). Your friend orders an appetizer (£6), a salad (£5), an entrée (£10) and dessert with coffee (£8). You agree to evenly split the bill at the end of the evening, which means each of you will pay £20. Is this £20 a fair cost of your meal? It is not; your meal was over-costed because you simply took an average of the entire cost of the two dinners. If you were to track the cost of your meal more precisely, your cost would be £11 (£3 + £8) and the cost to your friend would be £29.

A similar problem arises with a traditional cost system. Many companies have found that a traditional system tends to assign costs to products based on the volume of units produced rather than the actual resource usage by different products. As a result, products that are more complex to build and consume more resources (for example, more inspections, machine set-ups, materials) are not necessarily allocated the costs that they consume. Instead, many of these costs of complexity could be inaccurately assigned to simpler products. Thus, the complex products are under-costed and the simple products are over-costed. Note the similarity of this problem and the shared dinner bill. A simple average of the total meal cost over-costed your simple meal and under-costed your friend's more complex meal.

Refining a Traditional Costing System

Clearly, a traditional costing system has some weaknesses, including the problems of inaccuracy and under-costing and over-costing products. A refined costing system should make for more accurate costing of goods and services and less cost distortion. Three relatively low-cost steps could refine a traditional costing system to improve cost information for reporting and decision making.

1. Trace as many costs directly to the product as feasible by simply improving the use of existing documentation. For example, when you and your friend split the dinner tab, you could use the itemized bill to easily track menu-item costs to each of you, thereby resulting in a more accurate measurement of individual diner's costs.
2. Categorize indirect costs (e.g., taxes and tips on the meal), which are not easily traced to the product, into functional cost pools. A **cost pool** is a group of individual cost items that are grouped together because they have a similar function. For example, one may group together all indirect costs related to machine usage, such as costs for machine maintenance and the energy to run the machines, into a single manufacturing overhead cost pool.

   Continue this categorization until all indirect costs have been appropriately grouped into pools. Consistent with financial reporting, most companies do not allocate general and administrative (period) costs to products. However, firms could do so for internal decision-making purposes if they perceive these costs varying with production.

3. Use cost allocation to assign indirect costs to products. In general, **cost allocation** is a systematic process of assigning indirect costs to products or organizational units (e.g., departments). Select an appropriate **cost allocation base**, which is a measure that reflects the indirect cost to be allocated, for each cost pool established in item 2. Ideally, the allocation base has an observable relationship to the cost pool and readily available data. Divide the indirect cost amount by the amount of the cost allocation base to obtain the **cost allocation rate**. Multiply the cost allocation rate by the amount of the cost allocation base that represents each product to measure the indirect cost allocated. For example, one could allocate costs from an indirect cost pool to products according to a volume measure of products' uses of the machines (e.g., direct labour hours units produced, machine hours used). We illustrate a traditional cost system next.

Traditional Cost System Example

A manufacturing firm has traditionally allocated all indirect product costs based on direct labour cost used, with the following typical result.

Direct labour (average)	0.5 hours per unit at	€20.00 per hour	€10.00 per unit
Direct materials (average)	6 parts per unit at	€4.00 per part	€24.00 per unit
Manufacturing overhead	€20,000 per period		
Normal production volume	500 units		
Normal direct labour cost	€5,000		
Volume-based allocation rate	400% of direct labour cost = €20,000/€5,000		
Average cost per unit			
Direct labour	€10.00		
Direct materials	24.00		
Manufacturing overhead	40.00 = 400% × €10		
Total	€74.00		

Production managers have observed that some products use more machine capacity than others and they suggest that manufacturing overhead should be split into two cost pools: machining overhead allocated by machine hours and process overhead allocated by direct labour cost.

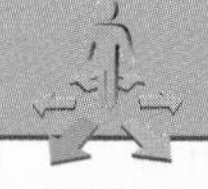

4.1 You're the Decision Maker

Refining a Traditional Cost System

The example company implemented the suggested refinements to its traditional cost system, with the following result:

Refinements to overhead allocation	
Machining overhead	€10,000 per period
Normal machine hours	600 hours
Machine overhead rate	€16.67 per machine hour
Process overhead	€10,000
Normal direct labour cost	€5,000
Process overhead rate	200% of direct labour cost

a. Does this refined cost system change the cost of an 'average' product? Why or why not?
b. Measure the cost of a product that's only difference is its use of four machine hours.
c. Measure the cost of a product that's only difference is its use of one-half a machine hour.
d. Do these differences in cost matter? Explain.

(Solutions begin on page 182.)

Managers might find that such a refined cost system works sufficiently well for product costing and decision making. However, if products are diverse in their resource usage on many dimensions and if customers require varying, specific product characteristics, such relatively simple refinements might not be sufficient to support the firm's product decisions. One indication of a possible need for a cost-system upgrade rather than a simple revision is when indirect costs are a large multiple of volume-based direct costs, as in the previous example.

Activity-based Costing System

LO 2
Discuss the four steps used in an activity-based costing system.

Activity-based costing (ABC) is a costing method that, first, *traces* costs to activities, which act as activity-cost pools and second, assigns these costs to goods and services based on how much each good or service uses the activities. An **activity** is any discrete task (e.g., assembly, testing) that an organization undertakes to make or deliver a good or service. We use the term **trace** (or **track**), to refer to accurately estimating, insofar as feasible, the costs of **resources used**, which are resources consumed to perform a specific activity. Activity-based costing is commonly used to improve a traditional costing system. The key to using ABC for cost management is that managers can reduce the cost of goods and services by modifying the activities required to produce the goods and services. In nearly all cases that we know, ABC is used to establish product costs for managerial decision-making purposes, such as whether to continue offering a product, not for inventory or stock valuation for external reporting.

Activity-based analysis uses four steps to measure the cost of goods and services. Exhibit 4.2 and the following text briefly summarize those four steps of ABC analysis. Much of this chapter is devoted to discussing each of the steps in greater detail.

Step 1: *Identify and classify the activities related to the company's products.* Activities in all areas of the value chain (product design, production, marketing, distribution, etc.) must be included. Analysts identify these activities in an **activity dictionary**, which is a list of activities performed by an organization to build its products. The activity dictionary can be obtained in a number of different

Exhibit 4.2 Visual Representation of an ABC System

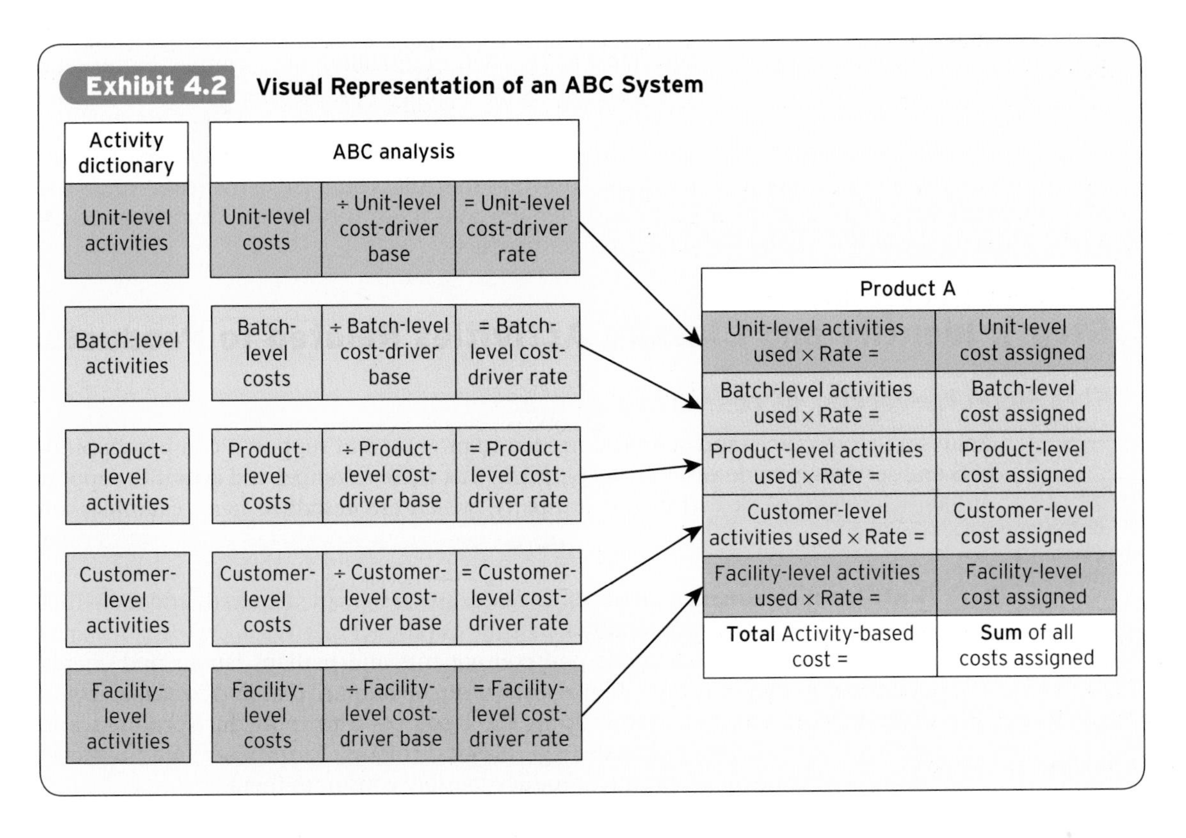

ways, such as observing or interviewing the employees who perform the activities or adapting activities identified in ISO certification processes. As activities are identified, they are classified as unit level, batch level, product level, customer level or facility level. We discuss these classifications shortly.

Step 2: *Estimate the cost of each activity identified in step 1.* Track the costs to specific activities that consume resource costs. Each separate activity becomes a cost pool in this first stage of tracing ABC costs. These traced costs are for both *human resources*, such as employee labour for production and machine maintenance and *physical resources*, such as the cost of materials, machinery and building occupancy. The required information may include employee data from personal interviews and financial data from the accounting system. Then calculate the total cost in each activity cost pool.

Step 3: *Calculate a cost-driver rate for each activity cost pool.* The activity cost data from step 2 is used to calculate a *cost-driver rate* that the company can use for assigning costs from activity pools to goods and services. A **cost driver** (or cost-driver base) is plausible explanation of the cost to perform an activity. For example, a cost of 'operating a machine' is likely driven by the number of hours it is run.[1] A **cost-driver rate** is the cost of resources consumed to perform an activity *per unit of the cost driver*. This rate should be a quotient of the cost (numerator) and a **cost-driver base** (denominator) that are plausibly linked. Thus, choosing a cost-driver rate for the cost of the activity 'operate a machine' based on machine hours used is a sensible choice.

Note that a cost-driver rate almost always is computed as an average cost; that is, a method from Chapter 3 is used to estimate the average cost per unit of an activity. An alternative is to directly observe or 'meter' costs, such as tracing the cost of power consumed by a computer-controlled machine. Thus, the cost of some activities might be metered rather than estimated. The metering approach to activity costing would be more accurate than using average cost-driver rates, but is not feasible for all activities.

Step 4: *Assign activity costs to products.* The cost-driver rates prepared in step 3 are used to assign activity costs to goods and services. For example, if a particular product uses 1.5 machine hours in production and the rate from step 3 is £50 per hour, the product is assigned £75 based on its machine usage. We use the term 'assign' from now on to mean that ABC applies costs to products regardless of the origin of the cost-driver rate (averaged or metered).

Upon completing these four steps, a company can calculate the costs to provide existing goods and services, which can be used to understand better their profitability. For example, Exhibit 4.2 shows that the total cost of the hypothetical product is the sum of all the assigned activity costs. The activity-based costing data could also be used to estimate the costs of future products.

After discussing the costing-system alternatives, PML's team decided to use an activity-based costing (ABC) system and at this point they became known as the 'ABC Team'. First, the team would use ABC to identify the cost of existing products and then it would adjust this cost information as necessary to estimate the cost to produce the MegaBurger products.

Step 1: Identify and Classify Activities Related to Products

Five-level hierarchy of resources and activities

LO 3
Identify five different levels of resources and activities used in production processes.

Analysing all resources and activities needed to produce and support a company's products and services is made easier by recognizing that these resources and activities support different levels of work within the company, which are described here. Examples are based on PML's business.

1. **Unit-level resources and activities** are resources acquired and activities performed specifically for individual units of product or service. *Unit-level resources* could include materials, parts and components and perhaps labour and energy resources if they are traceable to each unit of output. *Unit-level activities* could include work efforts that transform the resources into individual products and services. At PML, the materials (e.g., plastics, colours) for products are unit-level resources because each product produced visibly consumes them.

2. **Batch-level resources and activities** are the resources acquired and the activities performed to make a group, or batch, of similar products. *Batch-level activities* usually include the work performed to set up the production machinery to produce a certain batch (i.e., group) of products or to test quality control for a batch of product. *Batch-level resources* include the cost of labour to set up and test machines. The costs of batch-level resources and activities are directly traceable to certain batches but are assigned indirectly to the individual units produced by dividing the batch activity cost by the units produced in the batch. PML must load materials and set up machines for each batch of product to be made.
3. **Product-level resources and activities** are the resources acquired and the activities performed to produce and sell a specific type of good or service. *Product-level resources* could include specialized equipment, software and personnel that would not be needed except to provide that particular product. *Product-level activities* could include the design or advertisement of a particular product. The costs of product-level resources and activities are directly traceable to specific types of goods or services but are indirectly related to batches or individual units produced. PML uses specific moulds and machines for its different products; thus, the costs of these resources are product-level costs.
4. **Customer-level resources and activities** are the resources acquired and the activities performed to serve specific customers. Companies that serve general markets may not have many or any customer-level costs. However, *customer-level resources* could include specialized equipment, software and personnel dedicated to serving specific customers. *Customer-level activities* could include consulting with customers and making special distribution arrangements for specific customer requirements (e.g., using an air-freight service instead of normal ground service because of a particular customer's needs). The costs of customer level activities are directly traced to specific customers, but are indirectly assigned to units of products sold to customers. PML consumes design and engineering resources to meet its customers' changing needs. Furthermore, PML provides warehousing services for some customers.
5. **Facility-level resources and activities** are the resources acquired and the activities performed to provide the general capacity to produce goods and services. *Facility-level resources* could include land, buildings, costs of management and, in some cases, the labour force, which some companies by policy or by regulation maintain without laying people off (or hiring new employees) because of changes in products, customers, batches and units of output. *Facility-level activities* could include the activities of plant or store managers, research and development and company-wide advertising versus product-specific advertising.

   Facility-level resources and activities are directly related to the scale, scope and location of operations but are indirectly assigned to customers, products, batches or individual units produced. The cost of the space occupied by PML is in this category.

Objectives of classifying resources and activities

The objectives of classifying resources and activities into the five categories are to enable (1) accurate descriptions of how the organization performs its work, (2) tracing the costs of resources acquired to specific activities performed and (3) ultimately assigning activity costs to goods and services by the activities they require.

Methods for identifying and classifying activities

Organizations generate their activity lists in a variety of ways, including these:

- *Top-down approach.* Some organizations use ABC teams of people from the top levels of management. This top-down approach can generate an activity dictionary quickly and inexpensively.[2] A variation of this approach is to slightly modify a predefined (or boilerplate) activity dictionary, for example, based on ISO 9000 quality certification documentation.
- *Interview or participative approach.* This approach relies on the inclusion of operating employees on the team and/or interviews with them. For example, PML's ABC team could interview production personnel to identify and understand the activities involved to produce the

product. This approach is likely to generate a more accurate activity dictionary than is the top-down approach. People doing jobs usually know more about their jobs than their supervisors do. One danger associated with the interview or participative approach, however, is that employees might not disclose their activities truthfully if they are concerned about the possible effects of giving higher-level managers specific information about what they actually do. Another danger is that employees might not recall their work processes accurately.

PML's activity list

We now return to PML to describe how the ABC team performed step 1 of the ABC process, identifying and classifying activities related to the company's products. The ABC team began by establishing a list of its activities in the production process from its documentation prepared for ISO 9000 certification.[3]

See Exhibit 4.3 for the information for ISO 9000 certification used to list PML's activities. The ABC team organized this list according to the categories just discussed (unit, batch, etc.). Exhibit 4.3

P M L

Exhibit 4.3 **PML Ltd, Activity and Resource List**

Activity/resource number description

1. Unit level

1.1 Acquire and use materials for containers

1.1.1 Medium-grade plastic pellets

1.1.2 Colours

1.2 Acquire and use materials for baby-care products

1.2.1 High-grade plastic pellets

1.2.2 Fasteners

1.2.3 Colours

2. Batch level

2.1 Set up manually controlled injection-moulding machines (*detailed sub-activities omitted*)

2.1.1 Set up manually controlled injection-moulding machines

2.1.2 Perform quality control of batches of products produced on manually controlled machines

2.2 Set up computer-controlled injection-moulding machines

2.2.1 Set up computer-controlled injection-moulding machine

2.2.2 Perform quality control of batches of product produced on computer-controlled machines

3. Product level

3.1 Design and manufacture moulds (outsourced)

3.2 Use manually controlled injection-moulding machines

3.2.1 Machine depreciation

3.2.2 Machine maintenance

3.2.3 Machine operation-labour

3.3 Use computer-controlled injection-moulding machines (detailed sub-activities omitted)

4. Customer level

4.1 Consult with customers

4.2 Provide warehousing for customers

5. Facility level

5.1 Manage workers

5.2 Use main building

5.2.1 Lease building

5.2.2 Use utilities

5.2.3 Maintain building

includes only major categories of PML's total list to keep the list short; note that Exhibit 4.3 refers to 'detailed sub-activities omitted' in several places.

The first digit in the left column of the activity dictionary or list in Exhibit 4.3 is the most general activity (e.g., 1.), and the third digit represents the most detailed activity shown. Everything listed under activity 1 refers to unit-level activities and resources; everything listed under activity 2 refers to batch-level activities and resources and so forth for activities 3 through 5. Activity/Resource 1.2.2 refers to the materials fasteners, which are part of activity 1.2, acquire and use materials for baby-care products, which are part of activity 1, 'unit-level' activities.

As you will note, the activity is actually the *acquisition* of the material and its *use* in producing the product. At PML, the activities' acquisition and use of the materials to produce the product can be stated in the amount paid for the materials, the cost of inspecting and storing them and other costs related to acquiring them and getting them ready to be used in the production process.

In interviewing production workers, PML's ABC team asked a question such as, 'What do you do to prepare to produce a batch of beverage containers?' A production-line employee might respond, 'I set these dials and insert the specified colours every time we start a new batch of beverage containers.'

Step 2: Estimate the Costs of Activities

The next step in the ABC process is to trace or estimate the costs of the activities that were identified in step 1. PML's ABC team proceeded to estimate the human resources consumed by asking all employees to indicate how much time they spent on each activity in an average week and then identified the physical resources that supported various activities. Physical resources were tracked to activities by invoices for direct materials and indirect resources consumed by productive activities.

LO 4
Measure the costs to supply various of activities and calculate cost-driver rates using practical capacity.

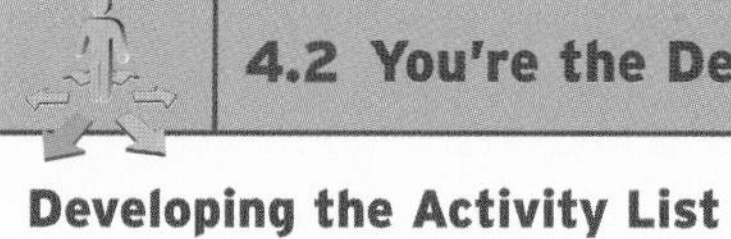

4.2 You're the Decision Maker

Developing the Activity List

Refer to Exhibit 4.3 and the preceding discussion. Put yourself in the role of a member of the ABC team preparing PML's list of activities.

a. If you were developing PML's activity list, would you regard the list in Exhibit 4.3 as complete (not considering the sub-activities omitted)? Do certain types of activities seem to be missing? Explain.
b. Suppose that people are reluctant to acknowledge that they perform some types of unproductive activities. How should a company's management deal with this problem?

(Solutions begin on page 182.)

PML's use of the employee activity data sheet

Let's look, for example, at how a production supervisor, Margaret Smythe, provided information on her activity data sheet. Ms Smythe's activity data sheet appears as Exhibit 4.4. Before completing this activity data sheet, Smythe indicated which detailed activities from the list in Exhibit 4.3 that she performed. Using the data Smythe provided, the ABC team customized a blank sheet for her by filling in her department, name, title and the list of activities she had identified. The team emailed the customized sheet to Smythe, who added her estimates of the number of hours per typical week that she spent on each activity. After adding this information, she emailed the sheet back to the team, which computed the cost of her time on activities (multiplying Smythe's hours by the hourly salary and benefits; £30 per hour). The ABC team collected data from all of PML's employees or from the employees' supervisors in the same way.

Exhibit 4.4 Employee Activity Data Sheet

Name Margaret Smythe
Title Supervisor
Wages and benefits per hour £30

Activity number	Activity description	Hours per week	Cost
2.2.1	Set up computer-controlled machine	20	£600
2.2.2	Perform quality control of batches of product produced on computer-controlled machines	6	180
4.1	Consult with customers	8	240
5.1	Manage workers	6	180
	Total hours and cost	40	£1,200

Activity data sheet combined with accounting information

For each activity, the ABC team combined the information collected from employees with data from the accounting and other records. For example, for the activity 'provide warehousing for customers' (4.2), the team collected data about the costs to lease warehouse space and insure the products in the warehouse and about employee time spent performing warehousing activities (e.g., moving products from place to place).

Step 3: Calculate a Cost-driver Rate for Each Activity Cost Pool

Cost-driver rates

An appropriate cost-driver base should:

- arguably have a plausible relationship that describes the activity and its costs;
- be measurable;
- predict or explain the activity's use of resources with reasonable accuracy;
- be based on the resource's **practical capacity** to support activities, which is the most a resource can be used for normal operations.

What drives the cost of setting up the plastic-injection moulding machines? An appropriate cost-driver base might be the number of batches produced (the more batches produced, the more set-up costs incurred). This rate is calculated by dividing the activity cost by the estimated level of activity in the cost-driver base. For example, if PML spends £60,000 per year on set-up activities related to maintaining a machine and produces 200 batches of product each year, the cost-driver rate for set-up cost is £300 per batch.

Practical, normal and theoretical capacity

Imagine that a warehouse has a **theoretical capacity** of 600 cubic metres (m^3), which is the most that the resource could be used for any purpose (e.g., storage wall to wall, floor to ceiling). However, suppose that some of this capacity, 100 m^3, is unusable or it would block access to the warehoused goods. Thus, the warehousing **practical capacity**, which is the amount of the resource that could be used for normal purposes, is 500 m^3. This should be the basis for assigning the costs of warehousing, because the theoretical capacity cannot be used. If the total cost to operate the warehouse is £10,000, the warehousing cost-driver rate is £20 per m^3 (£10,000 ÷ 500 m^3).

The user of the warehouse may decide to use some of the warehouse as **reserve capacity,** which is a set-aside of capacity for flexible or unexpected storage needs. **Normal production capacity** is the *practical* capacity less the *reserve* capacity, but we argue that it should not be the basis for assigning capacity costs. This set-aside should be charged as a period cost at the normal cost-driver rate because the reserve capacity has an opportunity cost.

Differences between resources supplied (theoretical capacity) and resources used (capacity costs applied to products) generally occur because managers have committed to supply a certain level of resources before using them, which are **resources supplied** Knowing the difference between resources used and supplied helps managers to identify unused capacity, which helps them reduce it or use it in creative ways.

PML currently uses 300 m^3 of the 500 m^3 warehouse to store baby-care products with the remaining 200 m^3 unused. For this month, analysts should assign £6,000 (£20 per $m^3 \times 300\ m^3$) to baby-care products and £2,000 (£20 per $m^3 \times 100\ m^3$) to each of 'reserve capacity' cost and 'unused capacity' cost. The total resources supplied equal 500 m^3, but the cost of only the 300 m^3 used by baby-care products should be assigned to them.

Our objection to using *normal* capacity for decision-making is that it can obscure over-investment in resources that are chronically under-used. On the other hand, normal capacity could equal practical capacity when no reserve capacity is established. In this example, the £2,000 cost of the reserved capacity could be considered the cost to maintain the storage buffer, which is a form of insurance. The £2,000 cost of the unused capacity is an indication of the opportunity cost of excess warehousing capacity, which if it persists might show that the company should reduce its warehousing resources.

Measurement of cost-driver rates for PML's activities

PML's ABC team gathered the activity-cost information from all staff as described previously. Then the team analysed the cost and activity data (using methods presented in Chapter 3) and decided to use

Exhibit 4.5 Activity List and Cost-driver Bases

Activities resources	Cost-driver bases
1. Unit level	
1.1 Acquire and use materials for containers	Number of units of beverage containers produced
1.2 Acquire and use materials for baby-care products	Number of units of baby-care products produced
2. Batch level	
2.1 Set up manually controlled machines	Number of batches of beverage containers
2.2 Set up computer-controlled machines	Number of batches of baby-care products
3. Product level	
3.1 Design and manufacture moulds (outsourced)	Number of moulds required for each product type
3.2 Use manually controlled machines	Number of different product types (i.e., containers)
3.3 Use computer-controlled machines	Number of different product types (i.e., baby-care products)
4. Customer level	
4.1 Consult with customers	Number of consultations
4.2 Provide warehousing for customers	Number of cubic metres
5. Facility level	
5.1 Manage workers	Amount of salaries and benefits of production workers
5.2 Use main building	Number of m^2 of floor space used by each product

the cost drivers shown in Exhibit 4.5. To simplify the presentation, we condense the activity list in Exhibit 4.3 according to common cost drivers as shown in Exhibit 4.5. This allows us to work with fewer categories of activities in assigning costs to goods and services for product costing purposes. For example, the unit level for materials for baby-care products condenses the individual items – high-grade plastic, fasteners and colours – into one category that we call 'materials for baby-care products'.

The following explains the cost drivers for the five activity levels in Exhibit 4.5.

1. *Unit level.* The cost of materials to make both types of products is driven by the number of units produced. In effect, the materials costs vary directly and proportionately with the volume of output. Materials costs are variable, direct and out-of-pocket costs of production.
2. *Batch level.* Batches are groups of the same units. For example, a batch of baby-care products could be 1,000 identical baby seats; a batch of containers could be 100,000 green 1-litre ginger ale bottles with particular lettering. Each batch of units requires the machines to be set up according to design specifications, just as building a house requires following the architect's design specifications. The number of batches produced drives the costs of setting up the machines and of performing quality-control inspections on batches. A substantial portion of PML's batch-level costs is made of labour costs. Labour costs at PML are largely committed, fixed costs. Although labour cannot be traced to individual units of product (i.e., they are indirect costs to units produced), the uses of labour can be traced to batch and higher-level activities. For example, some labour cost is a direct, variable cost of the decision to produce another batch.
3. *Product level.* Activity 3.1, design and manufacture moulds, refers to the moulds used in machines to shape the liquefied plastic as desired. This activity comprises designing and making the moulds for specific products and remaking them to satisfy changing customer requirements. PML outsources this activity to a company that specializes in these activities for plastic products. The outside company owns the moulds and leases them to PML.

   The cost of activities 3.2 and 3.3 includes the depreciation, maintenance and operating costs of using the machines, which are dedicated to specific product lines (currently containers or baby-care products). These operating costs include costs for space and the use of labour for regular maintenance of both types of machines. These labour costs are indirect costs of batches and volumes of units produced, but are direct to the types of products made by PML.
4. *Customer level.* Activity 4.1, consult with customers, refers to customer consultations about product designs, orders, changes in orders and complaints. The cost of these consultations is composed almost entirely of labour costs. Activity 4.2, provide warehousing for customers, refers to dedicating the warehouse space for customers' products that have been completed but not delivered, using personnel to move items in and out of it and to provide its security.
5. *Facility level.* Activity 5.1 refers to the management of production workers who work on batch- and product-level activities. Activity 5.2 refers to the use of the existing factory building to produce either containers or baby-care products. Occupancy costs include the lease of the building space, the cost of heating and lighting it, insurance and taxes on it and its contents and maintenance.

Exhibit 4.6 contains the information the ABC team used to compute the predetermined cost-driver rates for the five activity levels. Note that the numbers are calculated for a typical or normal month. As in many companies that use ABC, the ABC team wanted to derive cost-driver rates that would be generally useful and not affected by minor variations across months (e.g., utilities costs). This is especially important for companies like PML that have large committed costs for labour and facilities. Transforming committed, fixed costs into variable, transaction-based costs is a key motivation for outsourcing production. For example, this explains why PML has outsourced its design and production of moulds to a company that specializes in these activities. Perhaps if PML needed to design or change its moulds more frequently, the company might internalize these activities by hiring design engineers and by purchasing the mould fabrication equipment. We address this type of decision in more detail in Chapter 8.

The method that the ABC team used to calculate cost-driver rates is to divide each total activity cost by the quantity of the appropriate cost-driver base. By using these predetermined rates based on a normal month, the ABC team saved the time and effort of computing 'actual' cost-driver rates for

Exhibit 4.6 Computing Predetermined Cost-driver Rates for a Typical Month

	A	B	C	D	E	F	G
1	Activity/Resource	Cost-driver base	Estimated activity cost	Practical activity volume		Predetermined cost-driver rate (C ÷ D)	
2	1. Unit Level						
3	1.1 Acquire and use materials for containers	Units of beverage containers produced	£500,000.00	2,000,000	units	£0.25	per unit
4	1.2 Acquire and use materials for baby-care products	Units of baby-care products produced	£400,000.00	40,000	units	£10.00	per unit
5	2. Batch Level						
6	2.1 Set up manually controlled machines	Number of batches of beverage containers	£120,000.00	100	batches	£1,200.00	per batch
7	2.2 Set up computer-controlled machines	Number of batches of baby-care products	£60,000.00	200	batches	£300.00	per batch
8	3. Product Level						
9	3.1 Design and manufacture molds	Number of molds required	£10,000.00	5	molds	£2,000.00	per mold
10	3.2 Use manually controlled machines	Product type (containers)	£150,000.00	1	product type	£150,000.00	per product type
11	3.3 Use computer-controlled machines	Product type (baby-care)	£40,000.00	1	product type	£40,000.00	per product type
12	4. Customer Level						
13	4.1 Consult with customers	Number of consulations	£4,000.00	40	consulations	£100.00	per consulation
14	4.2 Provide warehousing for customers	Number of cubic meters of storage	£7,000.00	500	m^3	£14.00	per m^3
15	5. Facility Level						
16	5.1 Manage workers	Salaries and benefits of production workers	£3,000.00	$15,000	production labor cost	20%	of production labor cost
17	5.2 Use main building	Square meters of building usage by each product	£48,000.00	1,500	m^2	£32.00	per m^2
18	Estimated typical total unit-level activity costs *(C3 + C4)*		£900,000.00				
19	Estimated total typical batch, product, customer, facility-level costs *(sum of C6 to C17)*		£442,000.00				
20	Estimated typical total cost of manufacturing activities *(C18 + C19)*		£1,342,000.00				
21							
22	Note: Shaded cells are data inputs; unshaded cells are computed.						

every month (and made ABC costs compatible with financial reporting). If the normal month is representative, normal rates are likely to be close to the actual rates and most differences will average out over the course of a year. PML's chief financial officer, Alex Lewis, decided that computing predetermined rates infrequently or when major changes in processes or resources are obvious was an efficient use of his staff's time.

Sources of information in Exhibit 4.6:

Column (A) activities are from Exhibits 4.3 and 4.5. Column (B) cost-driver bases are from Exhibit 4.5.

The ABC team reviewed accounting records, interviewed operating personnel and collected employee activity data sheets, such as that in Exhibit 4.4, to develop Column (C), the total costs in a typical month for each activity.

The ABC team developed Column (D), the normal activity volume for each cost-driver base, by interviewing operating personnel and reviewing various records.

Column (F), the predetermined cost-driver rate, is, as indicated, Column (C) divided by Column (D) and is the cost per unit of activity for each cost-driver base.

Few companies assign *all* of their costs to products. For example, companies generally do not assign the chief executive's salary or other administrative costs to products. An allocation of such period costs to products usually is completely arbitrary and does not reflect a particular product's use of resources. Furthermore, we recommend against assigning the cost of unused capacity to products. For example, the cost of unused factory building capacity and employee time paid for but not used in production should not be charged to products. These are costs of the period that should be attributed to the company's capacity decisions and policies. As is common practice, PML's ABC team did not assign administration costs or costs of unused capacity to products.

Before discussing step 4, 'assign activity costs to products', we should note that many companies pause at this point and use the information obtained from steps 1 through 3 that identify their activity costs. These companies focus on costly, but low-valued activities and then seek to modify processes by redesigning or eliminating them. This is called activity-based management, the topic of Chapter 5. PML does use activity-based management, as we shall see, but first used step 4 in the ABC process to assign activity costs to products.

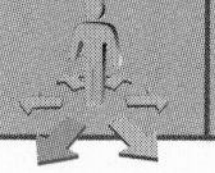

4.3 You're the Decision Maker

Using ABC Cost-Driver Rates

Review Exhibit 4.6 and the preceding discussion.

a. Does the cost-driver rate for activity 1.1 reflect the same cost behaviour as the one for activity 2.1? Explain.

b. Suppose that you are PML's CEO and decide to stop providing warehousing services for customers. Would PML really save the £7,000 per month for activity 4.2? Why or why not?

c. What other factors, besides saving costs, would you consider in deciding whether to stop providing warehousing services?

(Solutions begin on page 182.)

Step 4: Assign Activity Costs to Products

PML example

LO 5
Assign activity costs to goods and services.

Recall the set-up example in which we established a cost-driver rate for set up of the moulding machine. This rate is used to assign set-up costs to batches of product at a rate of £300 per batch. If the company makes 10 batches of containers, it assigns £3,000 to containers for set-up costs.

Exhibit 4.7 demonstrates how PML's ABC team determined the cost of products for the month of October. Exhibit 4.7 applies the *cost-driver rates for a typical month* from Exhibit 4.6 to the *actual cost-driver activity volumes* for October.

Column (A) of Exhibit 4.7 shows the activities that we have been discussing. Column (B) shows the cost-driver rate that is related to a particular activity. We derived these rates in Exhibit 4.6.

Sources of information in Exhibit 4.7:

Column (A) activities are from Exhibits 4.3, 4.5, and 4.6.
Column (B) cost-driver rates are from Exhibit 4.6, column (F).

Exhibit 4.7 Assigning Costs to Products for the Month of October

	A	B	C	D	E	F	G
1	Activity/Resource	Predetermined cost-driver rates (from Exhibit 4-6, col. F)		Actual activity volume in October		Cost of container products (B X D)	Cost of baby-care products (B X D)
2	1. Unit Level						
3	1.1 Acquire and use materials for containers	£ 0.25	per unit	1,800,000	units	£ 450,000.00	
4	1.2 Acquire and use materials for baby-care products	£10.00	per unit	30,000	units		£ 300,000.00
5	2. Batch Level						
6	2.1 Set up manually controlled machines	£ 1,200.00	per batch	90	batches	108,000.00	
7	2.2 Set up computer-controlled machines	£ 300.00	per batch	160	batches		48,000.00
8	3. Product Level						
9	3.1 Design and manufacture moulds - containers	£ 2,000.00	per mold	1	molds	2,000.00	
10	- baby-care products	£ 2,000.00	per mold	4	molds		8,000.00
11	3.2 Use manually controlled machines	£150,000.00	per product type	1	product type	150,000.00	
12	3.3 Use computer-controlled machines	£ 40,000.00	per product type	1	product type		40,000.00
13	4. Customer Level						
14	4.1 Consult with customers - containers	£ 100.00	per consultation	2	consultations	200.00	
15	- baby-care products	£ 100.00	per consultation	40	consultations		4,000.00
16	4.2 Provide warehousing for customers - containers	£14.00	per m³	230	m³	3,220.00	
17	- baby-care products	£14.00	per m³	60	m³		840.00
18	5. Facility Level						
19	5.1 Manage workers - containers	20%	of production labour cost	£ 4,000.00	production labour cost	800.00	
20	-baby-care products	20%	of production labour cost	£ 10,000.00	production labour cost		2,000.00
21	5.2 Use main building - containers	£ 32.00	per m²	465	m²	14,880.00	
22	-baby-care products	£ 32.00	per m²	650	m²		20,800.00
23							
24		Total cost summary:					
25		Total cost assigned to each product in October				£ 729,100.00	£ 423,640.00
26		Total cost assigned to manufacturing activities in October					£ 1,152,740.00
27		Reconciliation of actual and normal non-direct materials costs:					
28		Total batch, product, customer, facility costs assigned *(sum of F6 to G22)*					£ 402,740.00
29		Total normal batch, product, customer, facility costs *(Exhibit 4-6 C19)*					442,000.00
30		Cost of unused manufacturing manufacturing resources in October					£ 39,260.00

The ABC team created Column (D), the actual cost-driver volume for the month of October, by interviewing operating personnel and from company records. The cost-driver volume in October is a bit different from that in a 'typical' month, which is to be expected in ABC analyses.

Columns (F) and (G), the cost of each product, were computed by multiplying the cost-driver rates in column (B) by the actual cost-driver volumes in October in column (D). Column (F) and column (G) show the product costs for containers and baby-care products, respectively.

Column (D) of Exhibit 4.7 presents the actual cost-driver volumes for the month of October. (Note that these volumes differ slightly from the typical month shown in Exhibit 4.6.) Columns (F) and (G) in Exhibit 4.7 present the activity costs for each of the two products – containers and baby-care products. Columns (F) and (G) show the total ABC costs for October computed using predetermined cost-driver rates and actual cost-driver volumes for October. The unit costs for the two products can be computed using the total ABC costs for the month and the monthly production volumes from the top of Column (D):

Container cost per unit = £729,100 ÷ 1,800,000 units = £0.41 per unit
Baby-care cost per unit = £423,640 ÷ 30,000 units = £14.12 per unit

Note the term 'cost assigned to each product' where the amounts in Exhibit 4.7 are totalled (row 25). The ABC team appropriately excluded from the exhibit amounts of certain period costs, including particular administrative costs of running the company that were not directly related to production (e.g., the salaries of the CEO and CFO) and the cost of unused parts of the main building because that space was not used to produce either product.

Note also that unit-level costs in Exhibit 4.6, rows 3 and 4, are direct costs with respect to units produced. The supply of these resources should match their use each month. For batch-, product-, customer- and facility-level activities, however, the supply of resources exceeds the use of resources, partly because of policies to maintain reserve capacity. Consider the section 'Reconciliation of actual and normal costs' at the bottom of Exhibit 4.7 (rows 26–29). In the month of October, PML actually assigned £402,740 of all actual batch-, product-, customer- and facility-level costs to products. (See cell G28.) In a normal month, PML incurs the cost of batch, product and facility-level activities in the amount of £442,000 (G29), which is taken from Exhibit 4.6, cell C19. The difference, £39,260, is unused manufacturing capacity. Unused manufacturing capacity is caused by differences between actual and practical activity volumes. As described earlier, this cost may be partly the cost of maintaining buffer capacities. This cost may be expensed in a period as part of cost of goods sold if it is immaterial or included in other operating expenses. In the case of PML, this amount appears to be immaterial.

4.1 Cost Management in Practice

Use of Activity-based Costing

Activity-based costing has maintained a high profile as a cost management innovation for more than two decades. Enough time has passed to assess whether it is a passing fad. Studies of company practices indicate that a large number of companies, as well as some organizations in the public sector, are using ABC. However, some firms have tried it and dropped it in favour of more traditional, accrual-costing methods, as discussed in Chapters 2, 10 and 13. ABC systems arguably are 'extra' investments in costing that should be justified by observed benefits exceeding the extra costs. Numerous surveys of practice over the past ten years have sought to identify reasons why firms have adopted or dropped ABC. We consider the results of several relatively recent surveys of practice.

Al-Omri and Drury received survey responses from 176 UK firms (out of 1,000 large firms surveyed) about the sophistication of their costing systems, with ABC-type systems as the most complex and direct or cash-costing as the simplest. The responding firms reported costing systems as follows:

- ABC systems (29 per cent; $N = 51$).
- Traditional accrual costing systems (35 per cent; $N = 62$).

- Direct costing systems (23 per cent; $N = 40$).
- No formal costing systems (13 per cent; $N = 23$).

Results indicated that higher levels of cost system sophistication were positively associated with the strategic importance of cost information, intensity of the competitive environment, size of the firm, extent of the use of JIT/lean production techniques (discussed in Chapter 5), extent of use of other innovative management accounting techniques (such as total quality management, discussed in Chapter 6) and the type of business sector. Although ABC has its roots in manufacturing companies, the study found that the financial services companies surveyed were more likely to use ABC than were manufacturing companies. Surprisingly, no association was found between the level of cost system sophistication and the percentage of indirect costs, product diversity and quality of information technology. It is likely that IT sophistication has removed many of the earlier technical barriers to implementing ABC and the impacts of ABC on decision making dominate its use or non-use.

Case study research by Abernethy et al. indicates why product diversity and cost structure used in the previous study may not have captured their potential impacts on cost system design. They found high product diversity was accompanied with investment in robotic manufacturing technology that managed high product diversity. The effect of this investment was to convert the costs associated with high product diversity into facility-level costs, thus reducing the significance of batch or product-level costs. Facility-level costs cannot be specifically identified with the individual products. Thus, in conditions of advanced manufacturing technology, high levels of product diversity may not be associated with more sophisticated costing systems - and vice versa. Similarly the impact of cost structure (i.e., a high proportion of indirect costs) on cost system sophistication may be related to the level of batch-level and product-level costs rather than total indirect costs (that incorporate facility-level costs).

Stratton et al. analysed survey responses from 348 international manufacturing and service organizations and found that (a) ABC was used nearly as often as other costing methods, across all stages of the value chain but most heavily in service areas, (b) cost systems were most beneficial in profit-based planning and decision making, but least beneficial for accurately assigning indirect costs for reporting purposes, (c) ABC users generally were more satisfied with their cost information than non-ABC users, (d) ABC was particularly more useful for customer profitability studies (covered here in Chapter 5).

Sources: Al-Omiri and Drury (2007), Abernethy et al. (2001) and Stratton et al. (2009).

ABC Profitability Measures

LO 6
Analyse the profitability of products and customers.

The information presented in Exhibit 4.7 is important for measuring both product and customer profitability. Measures of profitability are central to managing products and customers and deciding whether to drop either products or customers.

Comparisons of ABC Product Profitability

See Exhibit 4.8 for a profitability report for PML's two products sold during October. Assume that the average selling price for containers and baby-care products was £0.40 and £32.00 per unit, respectively. The costs assigned to products in Exhibit 4.8 come from Exhibit 4.7, as shown in parentheses at each of the five levels of cost.

Observe that the £39,260 of unused manufacturing capacity (D15) is expensed because CFO Lewis judged the amount to be immaterial and partly used for buffer capacity during the period. If CFO Lewis decided that this cost would materially affect the decisions by users of the information, this would be a strong indication that the cost-driver rates were inaccurate and should be revised. The 'administrative costs not assigned to products' at the bottom of Exhibit 4.8 (row 16) are the general and administrative costs and unused main building space mentioned earlier that the ABC team did not assigned to products.

PML's management team was pleased with the ABC team's work but was somewhat disappointed with the results for October. CEO Fairchild stated, 'The good news is that we are profitable; the bad news is that we still lag our competitors. Our operating income was £202,000 on total turnover of

Exhibit 4.8 ABC Profitability Reports for October

		Container products	Baby-care products	Total
1	ABC product profitability			
2	Actual product volumes sold, units	1,800,000	30,000	
3	Actual sales prices per unit	£0.40	£32.00	
4				
5	Revenues	£720,000.00	£960,000.00	£1,680,000.00
6	Costs assigned to products			
7	1. Unit level *(Exhibit 4-7, F3 or G4)*	450,000.00	300,000.00	750,000.00
8	2. Batch level *(Exhibit 4-7, F6 or G7)*	108,000.00	48,000.00	156,000.00
9	3. Product level *(Exhibit 4-7, F9+F11 or G10+G12)*	152,000.00	48,000.00	200,000.00
10	4. Customer level *(Exhibit 4-7, F14+F16 or G15+G17)*	3,420.00	4,840.00	8,260.00
11	5. Facility level *(Exhibit 4-7, F19+F21 or G20+G22)*	15,680.00	22,800.00	38,480.00
12	Total costs assigned to products	729,100.00	423,640.00	1,152,740.00
13	Revenues minus costs traced to products	-£9,100.00	£536,360.00	£527,260.00
14	Return on sales before administrative costs	-1.26%	55.87%	31.38%
15	Cost of unused manufacturing capacity *(Exhibit 4-7 C29)*			39,260.00
16	Administrative costs not assigned to products			286,000.00
17	Operating income			£202,000.00
18				
19	Note: Shaded cells are data inputs; unshaded cells are computed.		Return on sales	12.02%

£1,680,000 – a return on sales of 12.02 per cent. The industry average is approximately 20 per cent return on sales, so we are behind our peers. Clearly, we have work to do to improve those operating income numbers.'

Lewis added, 'The ABC team's work has given us the tools to identify interesting problems. Look at the container products. Revenue minus costs assigned to products is negative £9,100 compared to baby-care products that generated £536,360 on roughly similar sales turnover. We need to get deeper into the container activities, particularly at the batch and product levels, to find opportunities to reduce costs without harming product quality or deliveries. We also need to look at administrative costs, particularly how they are used to serve our customers.'

Fairchild commented, 'The research on activity-based costing states that highly complex business often turns out to be very costly while low-complexity business turns out to be less expensive. We seem to have the opposite situation here. What we thought was a low-complexity container business is barely profitable, but the apparently more complex baby-care products business is more profitable. I am not sure yet what is at work, but we need to learn from this before we jump into the MegaBurger business.'

The ABC results surprised management. Before developing the ABC information, the company had allocated all labour and overhead to products at 49.1 per cent of each product's materials costs. This allocation procedure indicated that both product lines were profitable. The container business, which was the company's initial ('legacy') product line, previously did appear less profitable than the newer baby-care products, but still contributed to the bottom line – or so it seemed. The information in Exhibit 4.8 compares the traditional costing approach and the ABC operating income results. CEO Fairchild remarked, 'If this analysis is correct and I think it is, the time has come to seriously consider dropping the container product line. This is sad because many people in the company, including myself, grew up with this product and change will be difficult.'

Let's be sure of the source of the different results. Fairchild, Lewis and the ABC Team are convinced that the ABC system is more accurate and reliable because it uses more detailed activity information that better reflects how PML's resources are supplied and used. Compare rows 10 and 20 of Exhibit 4.9. This comparative analysis demonstrates that the traditional costing system, which used a predetermined manufacturing overhead rate based on direct material cost, in row 10 understates the costs of container products and overstates the costs of baby-care products relative to the more accurate ABC system in row 20. Now compare cells D13 and D23. The traditional measure of **under-applied overhead cost**, which is normal overhead cost less overhead applied to products, in D13 overstates the cost of excess overhead relative to the more accurate ABC measure of costs of unused capacity cost in D23.

Exhibit 4.9 Profitability Reports Comparing Traditional Costing to ABC

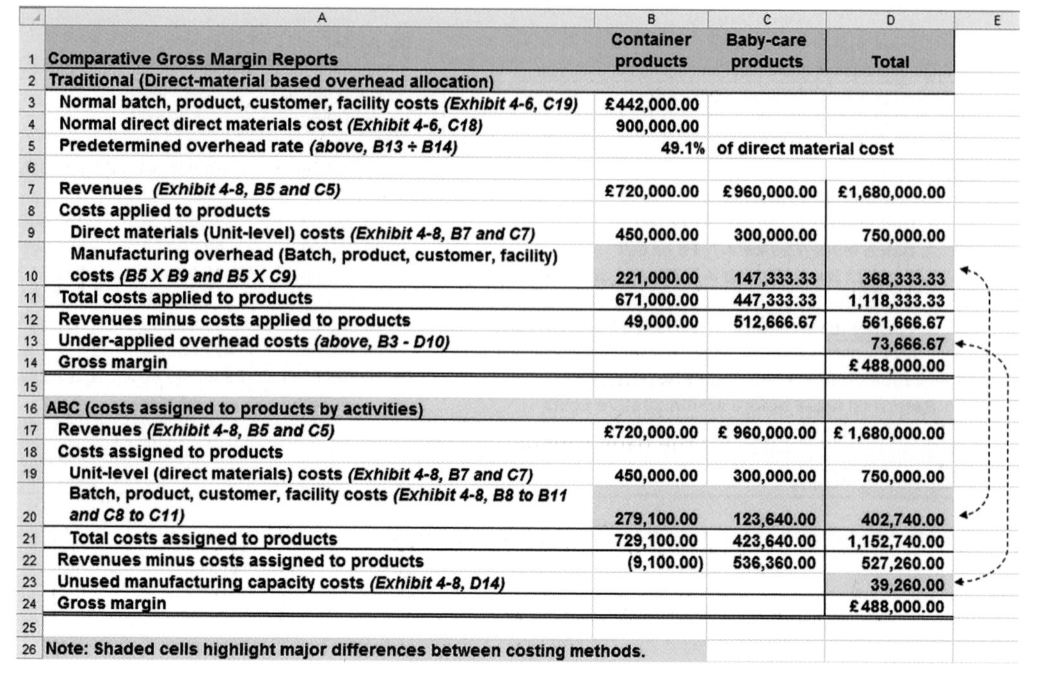

	A	B	C	D
1	Comparative Gross Margin Reports	Container products	Baby-care products	Total
2	Traditional (Direct-material based overhead allocation)			
3	Normal batch, product, customer, facility costs *(Exhibit 4-6, C19)*	£442,000.00		
4	Normal direct direct materials cost *(Exhibit 4-6, C18)*	900,000.00		
5	Predetermined overhead rate *(above, B13 ÷ B14)*	49.1%	of direct material cost	
6				
7	Revenues *(Exhibit 4-8, B5 and C5)*	£720,000.00	£960,000.00	£1,680,000.00
8	Costs applied to products			
9	Direct materials (Unit-level) costs *(Exhibit 4-8, B7 and C7)*	450,000.00	300,000.00	750,000.00
10	Manufacturing overhead (Batch, product, customer, facility) costs *(B5 X B9 and B5 X C9)*	221,000.00	147,333.33	368,333.33
11	Total costs applied to products	671,000.00	447,333.33	1,118,333.33
12	Revenues minus costs applied to products	49,000.00	512,666.67	561,666.67
13	Under-applied overhead costs *(above, B3 - D10)*			73,666.67
14	Gross margin			£488,000.00
15				
16	ABC (costs assigned to products by activities)			
17	Revenues *(Exhibit 4-8, B5 and C5)*	£720,000.00	£960,000.00	£1,680,000.00
18	Costs assigned to products			
19	Unit-level (direct materials) costs *(Exhibit 4-8, B7 and C7)*	450,000.00	300,000.00	750,000.00
20	Batch, product, customer, facility costs *(Exhibit 4-8, B8 to B11 and C8 to C11)*	279,100.00	123,640.00	402,740.00
21	Total costs assigned to products	729,100.00	423,640.00	1,152,740.00
22	Revenues minus costs assigned to products	(9,100.00)	536,360.00	527,260.00
23	Unused manufacturing capacity costs *(Exhibit 4-8, D14)*			39,260.00
24	Gross margin			£488,000.00
25				
26	Note: Shaded cells highlight major differences between costing methods.			

Armed with this information, CEO Fairchild met with Elizabeth Forney, Director of Marketing, to determine whether pricing was a cause of container unprofitability. Forney confirmed that the £0.40 average market price per unit for containers was competitive. She expected this price to increase within the next six months because of instability in world oil prices, but this would also increase PML's raw materials and fuel costs. Fairchild decided to keep producing container products for the near term and to monitor the relation between their selling price and product costs over the next several months. If the ABC profitability results continue, PML very well could decide to find a way to eliminate this product line.

In PML's case, since beverage containers and baby-care products are sold to separate, individual customers, Exhibit 4.8 can also be used as a *customer profitability* report. It shows that the customer purchasing baby-care products generates a higher level of profitability than the customer purchasing containers. Chapter 5 provides more details on measuring and managing customer profitability.

MegaBurger Novelty Toy Analysis

Activity-based costing information for existing products can be helpful for estimating the costs of new products if the activities used to make these new products are similar to those used to make the existing products. CEO Fairchild asked CFO Lewis whether the MegaBurger business would be profitable. Lewis directed the ABC team to estimate costs of the new products by modifying its ABC results.

To answer the key question about profitability, Lewis and his team matched MegaBurger's product specifications to the activity list and cost drivers for existing products (Exhibits 4.6 and 4.7). The team then decided that producing novelty toys would be more similar to making complex baby-care products with several notable exceptions:

- PML must use a higher grade (and cost) of plastic and a bigger palette of colours, although smaller amounts of both per unit for the toys.

- The product moulds for the toys must be more precise and more costly. A small error or blemish would be very noticeable in such a small product that children (and collectors) look at very carefully.
- PML would have more consultations with customers for the toys.
- MegaBurger expects its toy suppliers to warehouse the completed products and ship them directly to its restaurants on demand. This is similar to the baby-care company's requirements except that the MegaBurger project requires more complex inventory controls and distribution to many locations. PML would have to lease additional warehouse space and improve its processes to meet MegaBurger's needs. These would result in higher cost of warehousing.
- If PML retains the container product line, more production space is required for the toys. Some space could be obtained in an adjacent building and the remainder could be obtained from the presently unused space.

PML's application of the cost information from activity-based costing to assess the product profitability of one of MegaBurger's products is shown in Exhibit 4.10. PML's ABC team started with the cost-driver rates for the baby-care product in Column B and then adjusted those rates to reflect what it thought changes should be for the MegaBurger product (Column D). Column E presents the adjusted cost-driver rates. Column F shows the cost-drivers expected for an initial volume of 20,000 units per month. (Each 'unit' contains eight different novelty toys.) Column G shows each activity's expected cost. Work through this exhibit to see how PML adjusted its activity-based cost information for existing products (column B) to obtain estimated costs of the new product (column G).

PML's analysis indicated that the estimated revenues on the MegaBurger job would exceed estimated product costs by £149,300 per month as shown at the bottom of Column G. The return on sales ratio (before administrative costs) predicted that the MegaBurger business at this scale would be far more profitable than its container business, but not as profitable as the baby-care business. On the basis of the analysis reported in Exhibit 4.10, Fairchild decided that the company had the knowledge and technical capability to be a reliable supplier for MegaBurger. Based on the team's analysis, Fairchild, Lewis and the ABC team were all excited about the prospect of securing the contract with MegaBurger and proving their capabilities as a supplier. Still, the management team felt compelled to analyse the company's activities and uses of resources more carefully (as we shall see in Chapter 5).

P M L

Exhibit 4.10 **Application of ABC Cost Information to Estimate New Product Costs**

	A	B	C	D	E	F	G
1	Activities	Cost-driver rates for existing baby-care products (Exhibit 4-6)		Adjustments to rates for new products	Adjusted cost-driver rates. B X (1+D)	Monthly level of activity	Estimated monthly costs and revenues E X F
2	*1. Unit-level*						
3	1.1 Acquire and use materials	£10.00	per unit	20%	£12.00	20,000	£240,000.00
4	*2. Batch-level*						
5	2.1 Setup and quality control for computer-controlled injection moulding machines	£300.00	per batch	0%	£300.00	16	4,800.00
6	*3. Product-level*						
7	3.1 Design and manufacture of moulds	£2,000.00	per mould	100%	£4,000.00	8	32,000.00
8	3.2 Use equipment in production	£40,000.00	per product type	0%	£40,000.00	1	40,000.00
9	*4. Customer-level*						
10	4.1 Consult customers	£100.00	per consultation	100%	£200.00	40	8,000.00
11	4.2 Provide additional warehousing	£14.00	per m^3	50%	£21.00	280	5,880.00
12	*5. Facility-level*						
13	5.1 Manage workers	20%	of production labour cost	100%	40%	$6,000	2,400.00
14	5.2 Use main building	£32.00	per m^2 occupied	0%	£32.00	550	17,600.00
15		Total monthly costs					350,680.00
16		Monthly revenue per MegaBurger contract			£25.00	20,000	500,000.00
17		Monthly excess of revenue over ABC costs					£149,320.00
18							
19				Return on sales before admin. costs			29.86%

4.4 You're the Decision Maker

Making Product Decisions with ABC

Consider the information in Exhibit 4.7. You are an analyst who will recommend whether to introduce a new product line. Assume that PML obtains sufficient additional capacity to offer a new product line that has the following characteristics per month:

- Produce 100,000 units in 15 batches each month.
- Uses the same amount of medium-grade plastic and colours per unit as beverage containers and requires two moulds.
- Is made on a new, computer-controlled injection-moulding machine that costs £20,000 per month to use.
- Ships products to customers directly from production (no warehousing). However, 2,000 square metres of space for production are needed at a cost of £3 per square metre per month.
- Provides three customer consultations per month.
- Incurs production labour costs of £4,500.

Any cost items not specifically listed are the same per month as for the beverage containers reported in Exhibit 4.7.

a. Estimate the costs of this product using activity-based costing.
b. What additional information would you need before deciding whether to recommend this product?

(Solutions begin on page 182.)

Unit-level ABC Costing

LO 7
Distinguish between ABC unit-level costing and ABC full costing of goods and services.

This chapter has so far discussed the **ABC full costing** method, which assigns as many costs as can be applied to products. For example, Exhibit 4.7 reports the results of assigning costs to production using ABC full costing. An alternative to this approach is **ABC unit-level costing,** which assigns only the costs of unit-level resources to products. Thus, unit-level costing separates costs that are used incrementally for each unit produced.

Financial managers have different opinions about the relative merits of ABC full costing and ABC unit-level costing. Full costing approximates the long-run average costs over the time span when all resources can or must be changed. In this relatively long period, sales turnover must be sufficient to at least cover total costs. Unit-level costing is close to the out-of-pocket cost analysis first presented in Chapter 2. This type of analysis assumes that all of the batch and higher-level resources shown in Exhibit 4.6 have accrual and committed costs. As discussed in Chapter 2, management can change committed costs, but probably not freely. Accrual costs that are allocations of sunk costs cannot be changed, except by changing the allocation base or method.

The concept of ABC unit-level costing is to assign only the costs clearly and certainly driven by specific units to these units. Materials used to make products certainly qualify for this assignment. One can imagine complications to this rather simple portrayal of a manufacturing process. For example, it seems likely that the number of batches is related to the total quantity of units of products made, in the manner of a step cost (also introduced in Chapter 2). One might be tempted to average batch costs over the number of units produced. Another complication might be when labour costs are committed but can be easily traced to units of product. One might be tempted to assign this committed cost to units produced. Fortunately, financial managers may use professional judgement to determine how ABC costs should be assigned to products or periods because the determining factor is whether the ABC information is useful for the decisions that managers must make. Managers may have less discretion if they seek to use ABC costs for external reporting, however and ABC full costing probably would be preferred for that purpose.

Exhibit 4.11 ABC Unit-level Costing Profitability Report

	A	B	C	D
1	ABC product profitability	Container products	Baby-care products	Total
2	Actual product volumes sold, units	1,800,000	30,000	
3	Actual sales prices per unit	£0.40	£32.00	
4				
5	Revenues	£720,000.00	£960,000.00	£1,680,000.00
6	Costs traced to products			
7	1. Unit level *(Exhibit 4-7, F3 or G4)*	450,000.00	300,000.00	750,000.00
8	Revenues minus costs traced to products	270,000.00	660,000.00	930,000.00
9	Return on sales before non-unit-level costs	37.50%	68.75%	55.36%
10	Higher-level activity costs			
11	2. Batch level *(Exhibit 4-6, C6 + C7)*			180,000.00
12	3. Product level *(Exhibit 4-7, F9+F11 or G10+G12)*			200,000.00
13	4. Customer level *(Exhibit 4-7, F14+F16 or G15+G17)*			11,000.00
14	5. Facility level *(Exhibit 4-7, F19+F21 or G20+G22)*			51,000.00
15	Administrative costs not related to production			286,000.00
16	Total higher-level and administrative costs			728,000.00
17	Operating income			£202,000.00
18				
19			Return on sales	12.02%

Exhibit 4.11 shows how ABC unit-level costing analysis is computed using the data in Exhibits 4.6 and 4.7. Note that in Exhibit 4.11 only the unit-level costs – materials – are assigned to units of product. All other resources, called 'higher-level resources', are period costs in this example of ABC unit-level costing analysis.

Cost and Information Differences

You should verify the following per-unit cost comparisons of ABC unit-level costing and ABC full costing at PML:

	Containers	Baby-care products
ABC unit-level costing cost per unit (from Exhibit 4.11)	£0.25 per unit	£10.00 per unit
ABC full costing per unit (from Exhibit 4.7)	£0.41 per unit	£14.12 per unit

The per-unit costs for each product using each method differ dramatically because they are different costs for different purposes. The full costing approach says, in effect, that a firm has costs because it produces units and it must cover all costs from sales turnover. Therefore, all costs related to the production (and sale) of the units should be assigned to units.

The unit-costing approach says, however, that resources supplied for higher-level activities, such as batch-level and product-level activities, are not caused by the current production and sale of each unit. Therefore, these higher-level resources should not be applied to the units.

One cost approach is not wrong and the other right. Rather, each approach is suited to different types of decisions. In the long run, firms must make the correct production decisions. Firms also must make correct capacity decisions that incur committed costs and that must be covered by sales turnover. ABC full costing seems better suited to support long-term decisions. Furthermore, ABC full costing separates the costs of resources supplied from the costs of resources used by assigning costs via cost-driver rates and by charging unused capacity costs to the period. For short-run decisions, when capacity cannot be changed easily, ABC unit-level costing seems more appropriate to support incremental production decisions.

Activity-based Costing in Service and Merchandising Companies

LO 8
Apply activity-based costing to service and merchandising companies.

Many service and merchandising companies also have benefited from using an ABC system. For example, many banks and other financial institutions use ABC to decide how to charge fees for debit cards, credit cards, cheque, cash and automatic payment services. The analysis is very similar to that described here for PML. The primary differences are the nature of the resources and the heavy reliance on information technology to gather, analyse and report ABC information.

Service and merchandising organizations (including non-profit and governmental organizations) implement ABC as described earlier in this chapter; no changes are necessary. Any organization – manufacturing, merchandising or service – must follow these four steps presented earlier in the chapter and briefly reviewed here for a service organization.

Step 1. *Identify and classify the activities related to the company's products.* A bank can identify activities such as processing ATM transactions, processing car loans, opening customer current accounts and maintaining investment accounts. As activities are identified, they are classified as unit-level, batch-level, product-level, customer-level or facility-level activities.

Step 2. *Estimate the cost of activities identified in step 1.* A bank could estimate the cost of employee time spent processing ATM transactions and ATM machine maintenance costs to the activity processing ATM transactions.

Step 3. *Calculate a cost-driver rate for each activity.* With the activity cost data from step 2, the bank can then calculate a cost-driver rate that will allow the company to assign activity costs to goods and services. This rate's base should have some plausible link to the cost. For example, the cost associated with running an ATM machine is likely to be driven by the number of transactions it processes. Thus, the rate for this activity could be based on the number of transactions.

Step 4. *Assign activity costs to products.* The bank then uses the cost-driver rates identified in step 3 to assign activity costs to goods and services. For example, if a particular customer uses an ATM machine eight times a month and the rate per ATM transaction from step 3 is £0.50, £4.00 in costs are assigned to the customer (£0.50 × 8).

Costs and Benefits of Activity-based Costing

This chapter's discussion of activity-based costing implies that implementing it adds value to an organization. This is likely to be true for companies that have complex production processes producing many different products or services in highly competitive markets. This is the reason that many companies, such as **Daimler** and **IBM,** have implemented ABC.

We should remember, however, that implementing ABC is costly. Costs include those to develop and implement the system, to provide additional record keeping, to change the computer system, to maintain the system and perhaps to hire consultants. Therefore, managers must choose carefully when to implement an ABC system. In response to the costs of developing and maintaining an ABC system, some firms have implemented what some have called **time-driven ABC**, which uses the time to complete an activity as its summary cost driver. Thus, time-driven ABC simplifies the search for appropriate cost drivers to only time. However, each major activity still constitutes a cost pool, with its own total cost and total time consumed; hence it still can be considered a form of ABC. This simplification of ABC is discussed further in Chapter 6.

Several 'red flags' indicate problems with an organization's costing system and the likely need to refine it. Some of these problems follow:

- Indirect costs are large in proportion to direct costs and are allocated to goods and services using one or two cost pools (and therefore one or two cost-driver rates). Some analysts believe that a cost allocation rate of 300 per cent or more of direct labour costs (a common allocation base) is a sign that ABC should be considered.

- Goods and services are complex and require many different processes and inputs that use common allocation bases differently.
- Generic high-volume goods and services show losses or small profits while complex low-volume goods and services show large profits.
- Different departments within the company believe that the costs identified for producing goods and providing services (as calculated by accounting) are not accurate and often are misleading.
- The company loses bids it thought were priced relatively low and wins those it thought were priced relatively high.
- The company has not changed its costing system despite major changes it has made to its operations.

Although all companies should not implement an ABC system, a firm that experiences several of these problems should seriously consider adopting ABC.

4.1 Research Insight

Does ABC Improve Firm Performance?

The ultimate test of ABC is whether it increases organizational performance, not whether it provides more precise cost measures. Adam Maiga and Fred Jacobs analysed data from 691 US manufacturing plants and found that the extent of ABC use is significantly and positively associated with cost, quality and cycle-time improvements (Chapter 6 discusses the management of quality and time). Furthermore, quality improvement has a significant positive impact on cost improvement, cycle-time improvement and profitability. Cycle time is significantly and positively associated with cost improvement and both are associated with enhanced profitability. Additional analysis shows that the direct relationship between extent of ABC use and manufacturing plant profitability is not significant; rather, dimensions of plant operational performance intervene in the relationship between extent of ABC use and profitability. This is an important result that effectively rules out an alternative explanation that profitable firms simply are those that can afford to implement ABC. The results of this study support the credible argument that ABC helps firms to improve operational performance dimensions of cost, quality and time to complete products, which then improve profitability. Their model, which is strongly supported by data, is shown below.

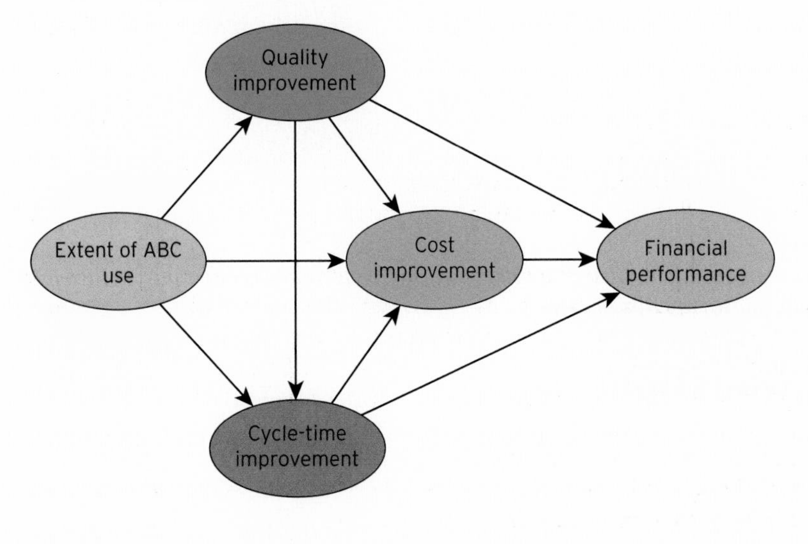

Source: Maiga and Jacobs (2008).

Chapter Summary

The theme of this book is that managers' decisions drive an organization's costs. To manage costs, managers and employees must understand how those decisions affect the efficiency of work being accomplished. Activity-based costing assigns the costs of resources to activities, which are the basic elements of an organization's work. By learning what activities the organization uses to produce goods and services, managers can assign the organization's costs to the products via the activities performed. We assign these costs using these steps:

1. Identify and classify the activities related to the company's products.
2. Estimate the cost of the activities identified in step 1.
3. Calculate a cost-driver rate for each activity.
4. Assign activity costs to products.

ABC can provide data related to a company's processes. These data can be used in various ways to benefit the company. ABC data can identify expensive and inefficient processes that could have been unnoticed in the past. The company can then change these processes to make them more efficient, often reducing their costs and increasing customer satisfaction. ABC data also can be used to establish more accurate cost information for goods and services.

Key Terms

For each term's definition, refer to the indicated page, or turn to the glossary at the end of the text.

ABC full costing, 162
ABC unit-level costing, 162
activity, 147
activity-based analysis, 147
activity-based costing (ABC), 147
activity dictionary, 147
batch-level cost, 142
cost allocation, 146
cost allocation base, 146
cost allocation rate, 146
cost driver (or cost-driver base), 148
cost-driver rate, 148
cost pools, 145
customer-level cost, 142
facility-level cost, 142
normal production capacity, 153
practical capacity, 152
product-level cost, 142
reserve capacity, 153
resources supplied, 153
resource used, 147
theoretical capacity, 152
time-driven ABC, 164
trace (or track), 147
under-applied overhead cost 159
unit-level cost, 142

Review Questions are mostly written at a ***basic*** *level; Critical Analysis questions and Exercises are* ***intermediate****, and Problems and Cases are* ***advanced****.*

Review Questions

4.1 How are indirect costs allocated to products using traditional costing systems?

4.2 What are the three key elements of refining a traditional costing system?

4.3 What is the ideal relation between allocation bases (cost drivers) and costs?

a. Simple

b. Plausible correlation

c. Complex

d. What top management wants

4.4 Why don't most companies allocate the general and administrative costs of the business to products?

4.5 Fill in the missing words: An activity is any discrete ____ that an organization ____ to make or deliver a ____ or service.

4.6 Briefly describe the five levels of resources and activities.

4.7 Describe how to calculate the cost of an activity.

4.8 Why is employee participation in identifying activities important, but problematic?

4.9 Describe how to calculate the activity-based cost of a product.

4.10 Why would organizations compute cost-driver rates for a 'normal' month instead of for each month of the year?

4.11 What 'red flags' indicate that companies have problems with their costing systems?

4.12 Is there any fundamental difference in applying ABC to goods versus services? Explain.

4.13 What conditions are necessary for using activity-based costs of existing services to estimate costs of new services to be valid?

Critical Analysis

4.14 Explain why over-costing and under-costing products can occur with traditional costing systems.

4.15 Why might a company adopt activity-based costing, then stop using it, but consider that its adoption had been a success?

4.16 In developing an activity list, why might employees not want to reveal realistic information about time spent on their activities?

4.17 Should management ever decide to assign general and administrative costs to products? Explain.

4.18 It has been said that the use of profit margins to select products is 'a snare, a trap, and a delusion' because a firm will never drop a product that has a positive profit margin for fear of losing even a small amount of profit.[4] Explain the meaning of this argument. How might the use of activity-based costing (unit level or full cost) improve the product selection process?

4.19 It has been suggested that ABC should be used to measure the costs of 'people-intensive' processes but not 'machine-intensive' processes.[5] People-intensive processes have adaptable resources, employee-paced workflows and salary-oriented costs. Examples include engineering and customer service. Machine-intensive processes have machine-paced work flows, depreciation-oriented costs and employee tasks that depend on technology. Examples include automated painting and robotic assembly. Contrast how ABC full or unit-level costing treat these types of processes. Make an argument either for or against this proposition.

4.20 Some believe that universities are among the organizations most resistant to change. However, some universities are beginning to analyse the profitability of their major departments and colleges by applying ABC concepts. Develop an exhibit that shows major university activities and resources (without numbers, unless of course you have ready access to them).

4.21 Evaluate this comment: 'Historical costs are only the starting point for predicting future costs. ... Many types of costs, such as inventory or stock, book value of equipment and allocation of fixed [higher-level resource] costs are not relevant for decision making.'[6]

4.22 One implication of ABC systems could be that using less of a cost-driver base reduces consumption of resources, which reduces costs. Therefore, this logic continues, managers should seek to reduce the quantity of all cost-driver bases used. A prominent critic of ABC has stated that activity-based prescriptions for improved competitiveness usually entail steps that lead to doing less of what should not be done in the first place. '[F]ocus on reducing variation and lead time in the work itself and costs will take care of themselves ... get busy with the improvement process.'[7] Can these views be reconciled? Explain.

Exercises

Exercise 4.23 LO 2 Cost-driver Identification

Place the following activities involved in a university's admission process in chronological order and match each to its most likely cost driver. (Cost-driver bases may be used more than once.)

Activities	Possible cost-driver bases
1. Processing applications	a. Number of acceptances
2. Enrolling students	b. Number of applications
3. Receiving applications	c. Number of inquiries
4. Receiving and responding to student inquiries	
5. Accepting students	

Exercise 4.24 [LO 2] Cost-driver Identification

Volkswagen developed ABC costs of the wheel-building process at one of its plants.[8] The process involves melting aluminium, pouring the melted aluminium into moulds (casting), testing, finishing/polishing, painting and packaging wheels.

Required

Match each activity with its most likely cost-driver base. (Cost-driver bases may be used more than once.)

Activities possible	Cost-driver bases
1. Melting aluminium	a. Number of wheels
2. Casting aluminium	b. Number of set-ups
3. X-ray testing	c. Number of casting hours
4. Drilling bolt holes	d. Number of kilograms melted
5. Finishing surfaces	
6. Chrome plating	
7. Painting	
8. Packaging	
9. Setting up machines	
10. Shipping	

Exercise 4.25 [LO 32] Different Levels of Activities and Resources

Match each of the following resources and activities with the most likely activity level.

Resource and description	Activity level
1. Production management salaries and support for managers	a. Unit
2. Marketing research salaries and support for marketing research to identify new product opportunities	b. Batch

3. Labour hourly as needed to meet production levels	c. Product
4. Set-up labour set up equipment and software for production runs	d. Customer
5. Utilities-electrical power for operating computing equipment used by set-up workers	e. Facility
6. Legal department salaries and facilities to support legal staff who prepare contracts for each customer	
7. Equipment equipment specifically designed to produce one product line	
8. Materials purchased for product manufacturing	
9. Supplies purchased to support customer-service representatives	
10. Software programs to control computerized equipment; revised for each batch of product	

Exercise 4.26 [LO 3] Different Levels of Activities and Resources

Match each of the following activities and resources with the most likely activity level for a social services agency.

Resources and activities	Activity level
1. Caseworkers - personnel who interview and service clients by type of service (child, homeless and elderly citizen)	a. Unit
2. Supplies - materials for office personnel	b. Batch
3. Library - regulations, research and court documents to support child, homeless and elderly citizen services	c. Product
4. Information technology - desktop and mobile computing equipment and personnel to develop and maintain information system	d. Customer
5. Management - salaries and support for administrators	e. Facility
6. Building - offices of employees	
7. Automobiles - transportation for caseworkers to meet clients	
8. Utilities - building's electrical power, natural gas, phone and sanitation services	

Exercise 4.27 [LO 3] Different Activity and Resource Levels

Match each of the following activities to the most likely activity level for a bank. Suggest a feasible cost-driver base for each and explain why you think that your chosen cost-driver bases are feasible.

Activity	Activity level
1. Sales calls - existing commercial customers	a. Unit
2. Sales calls - new commercial customers	b. Batch
3. Commercial loan negotiation	c. Product
4. Commercial loan review	d. Customer
5. Customer file maintenance	e. Facility
6. Community involvement	
7. Employee relations	
8. Commercial loan customer service	
9. Consumer loan customer service	

10. Consumer loan review
11. Customer deposit/withdrawal processing
12. Commercial deposit/withdrawal processing

Exercise 4.28 [LO 42] Resources Supplied versus Resources Used

Information about two activities for Atlantique, SA follows:

		Resources used	
	Resources supplied	Cost-driver rate	Cost-driver activity
Energy	€8,000	€15 per machine hour	500 machine hours used
Marketing	5,000	€20 per sales call	200 sales calls made

Required

Compute the unused capacity for each activity.

Exercise 4.29 [LO 4] Resources Supplied versus Resources Used

Selected information about several activities for Geïntegreerde Systemen NV, follows:

		Resources used	
	Resources supplied	Cost-driver rate	Cost-driver activity
Material	€50,000	€5	9,000
Energy	7,000	15	420
Set-ups	3,400	50	60
Purchasing	3,000	40	75
Customer service	3,500	50	60
Long-term labour	12,000	45	210
Administrative	20,000	50	380

Required

a Compute the unused capacity for each activity.

b Write a short report stating why managers should know the difference between resources used and resources supplied. Give examples of how managers could use the preceding information on resources used and resources supplied.

Exercise 4.30 [LO 1, 6] Benefits of Activity-based Costing

Many companies recognize that their cost systems are inadequate for today's global market. Managers in companies selling multiple products are making important product decisions based on distorted cost information because many cost systems are designed to focus on inventory or stock valuation.

Required

If management should decide to implement an ABC system, what benefits should it expect?

[CMA adapted]

Exercise 4.31 [LO 1, 5] Benefits of Activity-based Costing

Security Ltd has just completed a major change in its method to inspect its product. Previously, 10 inspectors examined the product after each major process. The salaries of these inspectors were charged as direct labour to the operation or job. To improve efficiency, Security's production manager recently bought a computerized quality-control system consisting of a microcomputer, 15 video cameras, peripheral hardware and software. The cameras are placed at key points in the production process, take pictures of the product and compare these pictures with a known 'good' image supplied by a quality-control engineer. This new system allows Security to replace the 10 quality control inspectors with only two quality control engineers.

The company president is concerned. She was told that the production process is now more efficient, yet she notices a large increase in the factory overhead rate. The computation of the rate before and after automation follows:

	Before	After
Estimated overhead	£1,900,000	£2,100,000
Estimated direct labour	£1,000,000	£700,000
Predetermined overhead rate	190%	300%

Required

Prepare a report that states how an ABC system might benefit Security Ltd and alleviate the president's concern.

[CMA adapted]

Exercise 4.32 [LO 1-7] Research Report

Search your library or the Internet for a recent article on an organization's actual experiences using activity-based costing.

Required

Prepare a short report that includes:

a. A description of the organization (economic sector, size, international scope, etc.).
b. The reasons the organization used ABC.
c. The operations that were the focus of the analysis.
d. The impact(s) of ABC on organizational performance.

Exercise 4.33 [LO 1-7] International Issues

ABC in its modern form was developed largely in the United Kingdom and United States. As a result, ABC might reflect certain cultural norms about business management that are common to these countries but are not worldwide practice. At least one article has contrasted US and French approaches to business that could account for relatively fewer applications of ABC in France than in either the United States or United Kingdom. These factors allegedly include the language, opening of the European Union, pre-existence of a complex French full-cost method, management style, class and corporate barriers and contractual basis for performance evaluation in the United States versus importance of honour and rank in France.

Required

As an individual or (ideally, an internationally diverse) group project, evaluate how these factors could affect the adoption of ABC. If internationally diverse group members are available, contrast US/UK characteristics with those of another country.

Problems

Problem 4.34 [LO 1, 4-6] Limitations of Traditional Costing Methods

Mitsu Corporation produces two types of flat-screen televisions. The standard televisions are designed for durability. The company recently began producing the higher-quality, high-grade model to appeal to dedicated watchers. Since the introduction of the high-grade product, profits have steadily declined. Management believes that the accounting system might not be accurately allocating costs to products.

Management has asked you to investigate the cost-allocation problem. You find that manufacturing overhead is currently assigned to products based on the direct labour costs in the products. For your investigation, you have data from last month. Last month's manufacturing overhead was ¥240,000,000 based on the production of 3,600 standard units and 1,200 high-grade units. Direct labour and direct material costs were as follows:

	Standard	High grade	Total
Direct labour	¥140,000,000	¥52,000,000	¥192,000,000
Direct material	116,000,000	104,000,000	220,000,000

Management believes that overhead costs are plausibly related to three cost drivers. The cost drivers and their costs for last month were as follows:

		Activity level		
Cost-driver base	Costs assigned	Standard	High grade	Total
Number of production runs	¥88,000,000	45	10	55
Quality tests performed	132,000,000	10	20	30
Shipping orders processed	36,000,000	100	50	150
Total manufacturing overhead	¥256,000,000			

Required

a. How much of the overhead will be assigned to each product if these three cost-driver bases are used to allocate overhead? What is the total cost per unit produced for each product?

b. How much of the overhead was assigned to each product if direct labour cost had been used to allocate overhead? What is the total cost per unit produced for each product? Is total overhead cost affected by the choice of traditional or ABC costing for overhead?

c. How might the results from using activity-based costing in requirement (a) help management understand Mitsu's declining profits?

Problem 4.35 [LO 4-7] Activity-based Costing in a Service Environment

Groene Garden Care BV, is a lawn and garden care service. It originally specialized in serving small residential clients but recently started contracting for work on office building grounds. Since Gerhard Groene (owner) believes that commercial lawn care is more profitable, he is considering dropping residential services altogether.

Employees worked a total of 20,000 hours last year, 13,000 on residential jobs and 7,000 on commercial jobs. Wages and benefits amounted to €16 per hour for all work done. Materials are included in overhead. All overhead is allocated on the basis of labour hours worked, which also is the basis for customer charges. Groene can charge €30 per hour for residential work but only €25 per hour for commercial work.

Required

Build a spreadsheet to solve requirements (a) and (b).

a. If overhead for the year was €130,000, what were the profits of commercial and residential service using labour hours as the allocation base?

b. Overhead consists of costs of transportation, equipment use and supplies, which can be traced to the following activities:

			Activity level	
Activity	Cost-driver base	Cost	Commercial	Residential
Transportation	Number of clients serviced	€17,000	15	45
Equipment use	Equipment hours	36,000	3,800	2,200

Supplies	Area serviced in square metres	77,000	140,000	80,000
Total overhead		€130,000		

Recalculate profits for commercial and residential services based on these cost-driver bases. Is the total overhead cost affected by the choice of traditional or ABC methods for assigning overhead costs to products?

c. What recommendations do you have for management regarding the profitability of these two types of services?

Problem 4.36 [LO 1, 4-6] Limitations of Traditional Costing Methods

Cehi d.d. produces headlamps for campers, hikers and other people who want the convenience of a light at night without carrying a flashlight. It currently allocates overhead costs using direct labour hours, but the controller has recommended an activity-based costing system using the following data:

			Activity level	
Activity	**Cost-driver base**	**Cost**	**Single bulb product**	**Dual bulb product**
Production set-up	Number of set-ups	€64,500	12	18
Materials handling and requisition	Number of parts per unit	16,950	10	20
Packaging and shipping	Number of units shipped	30,000	50,000	100,000
Total overhead		€111,450		

Required

a. Compute the amount of overhead to be allocated to each product under activity-based costing.

b. Compute the amount of overhead to be allocated to each product using direct labour hours as the allocation base. Assume that the number of direct labour hours required to assemble each unit is 0.5 per unit for the single bulb product and 1.0 per unit for the dual bulb product. The company produced 50,000 units of the single bulb product and 100,000 units of the dual bulb product.

c. Should the company follow the controller's recommendations? Is the total overhead cost affected by the choice of traditional or ABC methods for assigning overhead costs to products?

Problem 4.37 [LO 1, 7] Comparison of Traditional Costing and Activity-based Costing: Service Organization

Assume that you manage a business that provides services to both state government agencies and private organizations. Contracts for both groups are awarded on the basis of competitive bids. Your contracts with government agencies provide for reimbursement of costs plus a set percentage mark-up above cost for negotiated levels of service. Your contracts with private organizations are based on fees for levels of service. The relative profitability of the two types of contracts based on average cost information using hypothetical numbers follows:

Costs and revenues	Government contract	Private contract	Total
Costs	€2,000	€2,000	€4,000
Sales revenues:			
Cost × 140%	2,800	NA	2,800
Negotiated fee	NA	3,000	3,000
Profit	€800	€1,000	€1,800

You recently completed an ABC analysis that indicates that government contracts are much less costly than estimated previously:

Costs and revenues	Government contract	Private contract	Total
ABC costs	€1,000	€3,000	€4,000
Sales revenues:			
Cost × 140%	1,400	NA	1,400
Negotiated fee	NA	3,000	3,000
Profit	€400	€0	€400

Required

If you used the preceding ABC analysis for contracting, overall profitability would be much less. How should you use this information?

Problem 4.38 [LO 1, 4-5] Limitations of Traditional Costing Methods

Prague Glass & Crystal Company manufactures three types of glassware: unleaded glass, low-lead crystal and high-lead crystal. Glass quality increases with higher lead content, which allows for more detailed cutting and etching. Unleaded glass production is highly automated, but cutting and etching crystal products require a varying degree of labour, depending on the pattern's intricacy. Prague Glass & Crystal applies all indirect costs according to a predetermined rate based on direct labour hours. A consultant recently suggested that the company switch to an activity-based costing system and prepared the following cost estimates for year 5 for the recommended cost drivers (monetary units given in Czech koruny, Kč):

Activity	Recommended cost-driver base	Estimated costs	Estimated cost-driver units
Order processing	Number of orders	42,000 Kč	200 orders
Production set-up	Number of production runs	130,000	50 runs
Material handling	Number of kilograms of materials used	90,000	75,000 kilograms
Machine depreciation and maintenance	Number of machine hours	88,000	8,000 hours
Quality control	Number of inspections	20,000	50 inspections
Packing	Number of units	50,000	250,000 units
Total estimated overhead		420,000 Kč	

In addition, management estimated 4,000 direct labour hours for year 5.
Assume that the following activities occurred in January of year 5:

	Unleaded glass	Low-lead crystal	High-lead crystal
Number of units produced	18,000	7,500	2,800
Direct material costs	12,000 Kč	9,000 Kč	6,000 Kč
Direct labour hours	150	150	200
Number of orders	5	4	3
Number of production runs	1	2	2
Number of kilograms of material used	4,000	1,500	1,000
Number of machine hours	570	150	90
Number of inspections	1	1	1
Number of units shipped	18,000	7,500	2,800

Actual direct labour costs were 16 Kč per hour.

Required

Build a spreadsheet to solve requirements (a), (b) and (c).

a. (1) Compute a predetermined overhead rate for year 5 for each cost driver using the estimated costs and estimated cost-driver units prepared by the consultant. (2) Also compute a predetermined overhead rate for year 5 using direct labour hours as the allocation base.

b. Compute the production costs for each product for January using direct labour hours as the allocation base and the predetermined overhead rate computed in requirement (a,2).

c. Compute the production costs for each product for January using the cost drivers recommended by the consultant and the predetermined rates computed in requirement (a,1). (*Note:* Do not assume that total overhead applied to products in January will be the same for activity-based costing as it was for the labour hour-based allocation.)

d. Management has seen your numbers and wants to know how you account for the discrepancy between the product costs using direct labour hours as the allocation base and the product costs using activity-based costing. Write a brief response to management.

Problem 4.39 [LO 1, 4-6] Limitations of Traditional Costing Methods

Michaux SA manufactures three bicycle models: racing, mountain and children's. The racing model, the Ultra-léger, is made of a titanium-aluminium alloy. The mountain bike, the Cime, is made of aluminium. The steel-framed children's bike is the Fileur. Because of the different materials used, production processes differ significantly among models in terms of machine types and time requirements. Once parts have been produced, however, assembly time per unit required for each bike type is similar. For this reason, Michaux allocates overhead on the basis of machine hours. Last year, the company produced 1,000 Ultra-légers, 5,000 Cimes and 5,000 Fileurs and had the following revenues and expenses:

MICHAUX SA
Statement of income

	Ultra-léger	Cime	Fileur	Total
Sales	€4,000,000	€12,000,000	€5,000,000	€21,000,000
Direct costs:				
Direct material	2,000,000	4,000,000	200,000	6,200,000
Direct labour	300,000	900,000	600,000	1,800,000
Variable overhead:				
Machine set-up	______	______	______	130,000
Sales order processing	______	______	______	120,000
Warehousing	______	______	______	170,000
Energy and machine maintenance	______	______	______	225,000
Shipping	______	______	______	170,000
Contribution margin	______	______	______	12,185,000
Fixed overhead:				
Plant administration				185,000
Other fixed overhead				1,500,000
Gross profit				€10,500,000

Michaux's CFO hired a consultant to recommend cost allocation bases. The consultant recommended the following:

		Activity level		
Activity	Cost-driver base	Ultra-léger	Cime	Fileur
1. Machine set-up	Number of production runs	50	30	50
2. Sales order processing	Number of sales orders received	500	1,000	1,500

3. Warehousing	Number of units held in inventory	1,000	2,500	5,000
4. Energy and machine maintenance	Number of machine hours	15,000	15,000	20,000
5. Shipping	Number of units shipped	1,000	6,000	10,000

The consultant found no basis for allocating the plant administration and other fixed overhead costs and recommended that they not be allocated to products.

Required

Build a spreadsheet to solve requirements (a) and (b).

a. Using machine hours to allocate production overhead, complete the statement of income for Michaux SA (see activity 4 for machine hours.) Do not attempt to allocate plant administration or other fixed overhead.
b. Complete the statement of income using the bases recommended by the consultant.
c. How might ABC help Michaux's management make better decisions?
d. After hearing the consultant's recommendations, the CFO decided to adopt ABC but expressed concern about not allocating some overhead (plant administration and other fixed overhead) to the products. In the CFO's view, 'Products have to bear a fair share of all overhead or we won't be covering all of our costs.' How would you respond to this comment?

Problem 4.40 [LO 4, 5, 8] Cost-driver Rate Computation and Cost Assignment to Services: Missing Information

The ABC team at Fonetiska Produktioner ABm a Swedish concert-planning company, has pieced together the following data for its concert-planning service (monetary values given in Swedish kronor, kr):

- Unit-level actual activity (total number of band members in all bands) is 50; predetermined cost-driver rate is unknown; total unit cost assigned to the product in March is 50,000 kr.
- Batch-level activity is 10 concerts ('batches' of music); cost of batches assigned to the product is 600,000 kr (predetermined cost-driver rate is unknown).
- Product-level activity is 1 product; predetermined cost-driver rate is 20,000 kr.
- Customer-level activity (number of consultations with customers) is unknown; predetermined cost-driver rate is 250 kr per consultation; total customer-level cost assigned to the product in March is 12,500 kr.
- Facility-level activity is 2,500 hours of management and high-level staff support; cost of management and staff support assigned to the product in March is 100,000 kr (predetermined cost-driver rate is unknown).

Required

Prepare a table with the following table column headings: Activity/resource, Predetermined cost-driver rate, Actual activity volume in March and Cost of concerts in March. All activity levels are for the month of March.

Problem 4.41 [LO 1, 2, 4-6, 8] Product Profitability in a Service Organization

An ABC team at Córdoba Centro de Cirugía (CCC), an outpatient surgery centre that performs 25 different types of surgeries, identified the following data for a typical month (excluding costs of surgeons and anaesthesiologists). The ABC team learned that surgeries are not performed in batches, so there are no batch-level activities or resources.

Activity/resource	Cost-driver base	Activity cost in a typical month	Activity volume in a typical month
1. Unit level			
1.1 Acquire and use medical supplies	Number of surgeries	€200,000	2,000
1.2 Acquire and use surgical nursing staff	Number of hours of surgery	180,000	3,000

1.3 Clean operating room and set up for surgery	Number of surgeries	100,000	2,000
1.4 Provide recovery room care	Number of hours of patient time in recovery room	150,000	5,000
2. Product level			
2.1 Maintain information for each surgery type	Number of types of surgeries performed	50,000	25
2.2 Provide special equipment for eye surgery	Number of eye surgeries	20,500	1
2.3 Provide hip replacement parts	Number of hip surgeries	25,000	50
3. Customer level			
3.1 Conduct pre-surgery visit with patient	Number of pre-surgery patient visits	100,000	4,000
3.2 Make post-surgery calls to patients	Number of calls	15,000	5,000
3.3 Conduct post-surgery visits with patients	Number of post-surgery visits	180,000	6,000
4. Facility level			
4.1 Provide supervision	Cost amount of activities 1.2, 1.3, and 1.4	64,500	€430,000 for activities 1.2, 1.3 and 1.4 (Supervision costs = 15% of the costs of activities 1.2, 1.3 and 1.4.)
4.2 Use operating rooms	Number of hours of use	525,000	3,000
4.3 Use recovery rooms	Number of patient hours in recovery room	150,000	3,000

CCC's management wants you to compute the total cost and unit cost for 2 of the firm's 25 different products, eye surgery and hip replacement, for the month of March. The activity levels for the month of March follow. (*Note:* March is not necessarily a typical month.)

	Eye surgery	**Hip replacement**
1.1 Use medical supplies	30 surgeries	44 surgeries
1.2 Use surgical nursing staff	40 hours of surgery	60 hours of surgery
1.3 Clean operating room and set up for surgeries	30 surgeries	44 surgeries
1.4 Provide recovery room care	400 hours of patient time in the recovery room	50 hours of patient time in the recovery room
2.1 Maintain information for each type of surgery performed	1 type of surgery	1 type of surgery
2.2 Provide special equipment for eye surgery	1 type of eye surgery	NA
2.3 Provide replacement parts for hip surgeries	NA	44 parts (1 per surgery)
3.1 Conduct pre-surgery visit with patient	60 visits	70 visits
3.2 Make post-surgery calls	70 calls	100 calls
3.3 Conduct post-surgery visits with patients	80 visits	120 visits
4.1 Provide supervision	See cost of activities 1.2, 1.3 and 1.4.	See cost of activities 1.2, 1.3 and 1.4.
4.2 Use operating rooms	45 hours	60 hours
4.3 Use recovery rooms	50 hours	75 hours

Required

Build a spreadsheet to solve requirements (a), (b) and (c).

a. Compute the cost-driver rate for each cost-driver base.
b. Using ABC, compute the cost of each product, eye surgery and hip surgery, given the activity level for the month of March. Compute both the total cost and unit cost for each product for the month of March.
c. Assume that the company's traditional costing system had assigned product-level, customer-level and facility-level costs to surgeries amounting to €565 per surgery. Using this traditional costing approach, compute the cost of eye surgery and hip surgery given the activity level for the month of March. Be sure to add unit-level costs to the €565 per surgery. Compute both the total cost and unit cost for each product for the month of March.
d. Comparing the ABC and traditional costing systems, do the unit costs of the two products differ significantly? If so, what causes the differences?

Problem 4.42 [LO 1, 2, 4-6, 8] Information Misreported: Traditional versus Activity-based Costing

Refer to Problem 4.41. You have just discovered an error in data reporting for eye surgeries. The number of hours of surgery during March was 45, not 40.

Required

a. Using this new information, re-compute the total and unit costs for eye surgeries in March using both ABC and traditional costing systems.
b. Does this new information significantly affect the cost numbers using either traditional costing or ABC systems?
c. Does this new information affect the cost computations for hip replacement surgeries using either ABC or traditional costing systems?

Problem 4.43 [LO 7] Comparison of Unit-based and ABC Full Costing

Refer to Problem 4.41. Management of Córdoba Centro de Cirugía wants to compare the unit-based cost of eye surgery and hip surgery to its full cost.

Required

a. Compute the total costs of each product for the month of March using the unit-based cost approach.
b. Repeat requirement (a) but compute the unit cost of eye surgery and hip surgery (divide your results in requirement (a) by the number of units produced in March).
c. Write a brief memo that explains the differences in results between this problem and problem 4.41.

Problem 4.44 [LO 1, 2, 4-6, 8] Product Profitability in a Merchandising Company: Traditional versus Activity-based Costing

Omni Athletic plc, a sporting goods store, prides itself on its service to customers. Sales personnel, who are paid a commission based on sales, spend a lot of time with customers, helping them pick the best products. Management is concerned about the cost of two products: tennis rackets and fishing rods. The company's ABC team has developed the following data for a typical month for 600 products. These amounts exclude the cost of the product itself.

Activity/resource	Cost-driver base	Activity cost in a typical month	Activity volume in a typical month
1. Unit level			
1.1 Sell goods on commission	Sales £	€25,000	€250,000
2. Batch level			
2.1 Process purchases	Number of purchase orders	8,000	200

3. Product level			
3.1 Provide product-level advertising	Number of promotions	20,000	200
3.2 Provide product-inventory record-keeping	Number of products	2,000	500
4. Customer level			
4.1 Accept customer returns	Number of returns	6,000	600
5. Facility level			
5.1 Supervise sales personnel	Cost of sales personnel	4,000	€25,000 for activity 1.1 (supervision costs = 16% of activity 1.1 costs.)
5.2 Use building	Square metres of shelf space used by products	28,000	8,000

Omni Athletic's management wants you to compute the total cost and unit cost of the 20 tennis rackets and 10 fishing rods for the month of June, which had the following level of activities:

	Tennis rackets	Fishing rods
1.1 Sell goods on commission	€2,000 in sales	€1,000 in sales
2.1 Process purchases	2 purchase orders	3 purchase orders
3.1 Provide product-level advertising	2 promotions	2 promotions
3.2 Provide product-inventory record-keeping	1 product	1 product
4.1 Accept customer returns	5 returns	2 returns
5.1 Supervise sales personnel	See your computations for activity 1.1	See your computations for activity 1.1
5.2 Use building	80 m^2	60 m^2

Required

Build a spreadsheet to solve requirements (a), (b) and (c).

a. Compute the cost-driver rates for each cost-driver base.
b. Using ABC, compute the cost of each product given the activity level for the month of June. Compute both the total cost and unit cost for each product for the month of June. (Omni Athletic sold 20 tennis rackets and 10 fishing rods in June.)
c. Assume that the company's traditional costing system had assigned the batch-level, product-level, customer-level and facility-level costs at a rate of €9 per unit sold. Using this traditional costing approach, compute the cost of each product given the activity level for the month of June. Be sure to add the unit-level costs to the €9 per unit sold. Compute both the total cost and unit cost for each product for the month of June.
d. After comparing ABC and traditional costing systems, determine whether the unit costs of the two products differ significantly. If they do, what causes the differences?

Problem 4.45 [LO 2, 3, 4] Activity Analysis

Intellig provides the following data for a one-week period for the assembly of two different circuit boards A and B used by two different computer manufacturing customers.

- Material costs used and supplied for 4,000 units of board A produced and shipped, €32,000; 2,000 units of board B produced and shipped, €32,000.
- Labour supplied (a unit-level cost) for production of both boards, €16,000; usage based on number of parts assembled: 20 parts for each board A, 40 parts for each board B.
- Packaging and shipping provided on a per-unit basis, €10,000 shipping, €6,000 for materials and €14,000 for labour (€30,000 total).

- Batch set-up labour cost used for five batches of board A, €1,000; two batches of board B, €1,200.
- Batch set-up materials used and supplied for seven batches, €2,800.
- Facility-level equipment for both products, €20,000, traced by equipment usage: 60 per cent to product A and 40 per cent to product B.
- Custodial and security service (facility-level cost) for the manufacturing area, €5,000 traced 50 per cent to board A and 50 per cent to board B.

Required

Resources and activities are unit level, batch level or facility level. Compute cost-driver rates for each activity/resource. What is the cost per unit of these manufacturing activities for the week?

Problem 4.46 [LO 5, 6] Profitability Analysis

Refer to Problem 4.45.

Required

Intellig receives a sales price of €25 each for board A and €30 each for board B. Compute the profits for each type of board. Should Intellig discontinue either product? Why or why not?

Problem 4.47 [LO 2-4, 8] Activity Analysis in a Service Organization

Hometown Marketing Solutions is a provider of telemarketing surveys and sales for various organizations. The basic unit of service is a completed telephone survey or a sales call. Assume that all telemarketing labour is paid hourly. Supervisory labour is salaried. The following are data from a recent month (monetary values given in Indian rupees, INR):

- Hourly telemarketing labour to complete 20,000 surveys and 80,000 calls, INR 6,750,000; completed surveys take 8 minutes each; sales calls 4 minutes each.
- Long-distance phone charges for 10 per cent of surveys, INR 360,000.
- Preparation of scripts for surveys, INR 225,000 and sales pitches for calls, INR 225,000.
- Training telemarketing labour to conduct surveys, INR 585,000.
- Automated dialling equipment that serves all calls, INR 540,000.
- Occupancy costs, INR 450,000.
- Two supervisors, INR 360,000.
- Human Resources Department, INR 270,000.

Trace automated dialling equipment, occupancy costs, supervisors and human resources costs 50 per cent to surveys and 50 per cent to telemarketing calls.

Required

Resources and activities are unit level, product level, or facility level. Compute cost-driver rates for each activity/resource. What is the cost per unit of all marketing activities for the week?

Problem 4.48 [LO 5-7] Profitability Analysis

Refer to Problem 4.47.

Required

Hometown Marketing Solutions is paid INR 180 per completed survey and INR 80 per completed sales call. Prepare a report showing the profit of each service. Should Marketing Solutions discontinue either service? Why or why not?

Cases

Case 4.49 [LO 1-6, 8] Activity-based Costing in Health Care

Ciara Daly, the administrator of St Bridget's Hospital, Dublin, is exploring whether ABC can be applied to her hospital's operations. She is meeting with your consulting team to seek your advice and to determine whether to hire you to lead an ABC pilot project that, if successful, could be extended to the rest of the hospital.

Daly: I'm not too sure whether ABC is right for our situation, but I believe I should explore it at least. I think ABC is primarily for manufacturing companies, but there might be legitimate parallels between a hospital and a factory.

You: (Provide a brief response to these concerns that might encourage Whelan to hire you.)

Daly: That seems reasonable, though I'm not sure that we want to tell our board of directors and the general public that St Bridget's Hospital will be run like a factory. That's not the image we want to project. Nonetheless, I think we should proceed. I suggest that you analyse a typical nursing station and show me what analyses you can produce from an ABC perspective.

You work with nursing staff and the administrator's office to gather the following information:

Nursing activity	Personnel	Annual cost
Providing supervision	1	€93,000
Delivering nursing care	5	248,000
Cleaning, changing linens and garments	3	72,500
Total annual costs		€413,500
Total patient days (one patient in the hospital for one full day)		2,900
Average nursing cost per patient day		€142.59

All patients receive approximately the same level of cleaning and changing linens and garments, but the level of nursing care varies. Nursing staff suggested that patient days should be weighted by the level of care required. Using this input, you categorized the patients served by this nursing station in the past year as follows. Weights approximate the intensity of care needed.

Nursing care level	Number of patients	Patient days	Weight	Weighted patient days
Level 1 (needs typical nursing care)	400	800	1	800
Level 2 (needs more than typical nursing care but not intensive care)	300	900	2	1,800
Level 3 (needs most intensive nursing care)	300	1,200	3	3,600
Totals	1,000	2,900		6,200

Required

Prepare a report in memorandum form that explains the following: → separate by sections

a. The objective of your ABC analysis. → paragraph
b. The reason that the average cost per patient day is misleading.
c. The sources of your data and the feasibility of collecting them in the future.
d. The confidence you have in that data to support your analysis and conclusions.
e. The method of tracing operating costs of the nursing station to its activities.
f. The calculations of activity costs per unit and examples of nursing station costs of different patients.
g. The implications of your analysis for managing St Bridget's Hospital's nursing stations.

Case 4.50 [LO 1-7] Choice of Cost System

Prodigieux SA's tooling business unit (TBU) manufactures metal and carbon-fibre parts for the company's major products. TBU's principal focus in recent years has been to schedule its resources properly, but its manager is concerned that the current method of costing the unit's work is causing other business units to send it work that does not use TBU's strengths to the company's overall advantage. TBU computes a combined labour and overhead cost per labour hour and charges each job based on the number of labour hours used. This labour-based charge is added to materials cost to calculate the total job cost.

TBU works for internal customers exclusively and there is no consideration to allow it to seek outside work. Other business units are allowed to use external suppliers, however and are encouraged but not required to use TBU, which has 19 work centres, each of which uses computer-controlled machines and processes.

TBU uses two basic types of machines: (1) 6 multi-axis (M) machines, which allow complex parts to be rotated in multiple directions while being completed without removing the part and (2) 14 single-axis (S) machines, which are used for parts that do not have to be rotated more than once to be completed. The (M) machines were just purchased to replace 6 (S) machines. Overhead on (M) machines is three times as expensive as (S) machines. Each machine is considered a work centre and is available 6,000 hours (three shifts) per year.

TBU's employees are highly skilled and are among Prodigieux SA's highest paid hourly workers. They are qualified to work on either type of machine and any type of job. As a practical matter, employees tend to work on machines and jobs that interest them most, but TBU management encourages workers to diversify their efforts. TBU employees are available 2,000 hours per year.

Stainless steel (SS) and aluminium (A) parts are machined from metal stock. Carbon-fibre (CF) parts are made by laminating carbon fibre and plastic resins. Carbon-fibre materials are much more expensive and require more labour.

Last year's labour cost and overhead (which includes the costs of management and equipment but excludes materials costs) follow:

Labour (1,000 employees)	€120,000,000
Overhead	
Equipment (20 work canters)	240,000,000*
Management and engineering	20,000,000
Total	€380,000,000

*Based on 20 (S) machines.

The following are the data for and characteristics of five representative jobs:

Job	Equipment	Machine hours	Materials type	Weight (kg)	Materials cost	Labour hours
1	M	7.50	SS	300	€30,000	25.00
2	S	10.00	CF	200	100,000	160.00
3	M	8.75	A	350	28,000	20.00
4	S	12.50	A	500	40,000	120.00
5	S	5.00	SS	200	20,000	60.00

Required

a. Compute the costs of each job using the current cost system.
b. Recommend an alternative cost system that recognizes additional differences among jobs.
c. Re-compute the job costs using your alternative cost system.
d. Explain differences in decision making at TBU.
e. Identify TBU's internal customers that might be influenced by the use of the alternative cost system.

Solutions to You're the Decision Maker

4.1 Refining a Traditional Cost System, p. 146

a. Average product - no difference

Direct labour	€10.00	
Direct materials	24.00	
Machining overhead	20.00	at 600/500 = 1.2 machine hours
Process overhead	20.00	
Total	€74.00	

b. Machine-intensive product - large difference

Direct labour	€10.00	
Direct materials	24.00	
Machining overhead	66.67 at 4 machine hours	
Process overhead	20.00	
Total	€120.67	

c. Machine-light product-large difference

Direct labour	€10.00
Direct materials	24.00
Machining overhead	8.33 at 0.5 machine hour
Process overhead	20.00
Total	€62.33

d. These differences could affect decisions about products (their costs, prices, profitability) and productive capacity. For example, the machine-intensive product might be greatly underpriced, but increasing its price might lose customers. If the product offerings were to shift to more machine-intensive products, more machining capacity might be needed.

4.2 Developing the Activity List, p. 151

a. Aside from a reasonable level of detail (which is missing for many types of activities), the list includes few activities that might indicate process inefficiencies. For example, employees could have idle time when machines need repair or during a break in production (due to excess capacity). All employees are not likely to be productively employed every hour for which they are paid. While they might be uneasy about admitting unplanned breaks and idle time, they and management should realize that these activities exist in most organizations. Including them in the activity list improves the analysis of the organization's work.

b. To answer the question, management or high-level staff might estimate how much time and resources are spent on the omitted activities. This is a questionable practice, however, because of its top-down nature. Upper-level managers or staff are unlikely to be able to identify these problem areas with much precision and a blanket assumption that they exist throughout the organization could do more harm to employee relations than good. It is preferable for individuals who do the actual work to identify these unproductive activities and help the organization to minimize them. As noted in part (a), employees might not want to recognize them because they might be blamed for the unproductivity. The organization should promote honesty by not assigning blame but by encouraging and rewarding employees to identify and fix problems. Many firms do this by implementing a 'suggestions for improvement programme.'

4.3 Using ABC Cost-driver Rates, p. 156

a. The cost-driver rates have similar but different meanings. Both refer to the incremental cost of performing one more unit of activity. However, the cost-driver rate for activity 1.1 is a unit-level activity for the acquisition and use of materials and, therefore, is easily traced to each unit of product 1. The cost-driver rate for activity 2.1 is a batch-level activity not easily traced to particular units but more easily traced to batches of product.

b. PML might save this amount but only if eliminating the activity really eliminates the need and the spending for the resource (i.e., the warehouse and its employees).

c. Although eliminating this service could save cost in the short run, it could also result in losing a customer. If so, then eliminating warehousing could lose benefits that are far greater than the costs that would be saved.

4.4 Making Product Decisions with ABC, p. 162

a. You may choose to replicate the Excel spreadsheet in Exhibit 4.7, as shown below.

	A	B	C	D	E	F
1	Activity/Resource	Predetermined cost-driver rates (from exhibit 4-6, col. F)		New product activity volume		Cost of new product (B × D)
2	1. Unit Level					
3	1.1 Acquire and use materials	£0.25	per unit	100,000	units	£25,000.00
4	2. Batch Level					
5	2.2 Set up computer-controlled machines	£300.00	per batch	15	batches	4,500.00
6	3. Product Level					
7	3.1 Design and manufacture moulds	£2,000.00	per mould	2	moulds	4,000.00
8	3.3 Use computer-controlled machines	£20,000.00	per product type		product type	
9	4. Customer Level					
10	4.1 Consult with customers	£100.00	per consultation	3	consultations	300.00
11	4.2 Provide warehousing for customers	£14.00	per m^3	-	m^3	-
12	5. Facility Level					
13	5.1 Manage workers	20%	of production labour cost	£4,500.00	production labour cost	900.00
14	5.2 Use main building	£32.00	per m^2	180	m^2	5,760.00
15						
16			Total cost assigned to new products			£40,460.00

b. The selling price and additional information regarding whether PML is at practical capacity for all levels of resources prior to making this new product could be helpful. If it is not, PML might devote unused resource capacity to this new product. For example, PML could have unused building space available for the new product. If that were the case, PML would not have to spend as much as indicated by the costs computed in part (a).

Endnotes

1 In the ABC literature, authors sometimes refer to 'cost drivers' when they mean the bases used to trace or assign costs. We use the term 'cost drivers' to mean the decisions managers make about the structure and use of resources that drive costs. This is consistent with the economics and strategy literature that gave birth to ABC. See Porter (1985). To avoid confusion with the economic basis for ABC, we use the term 'cost-driver base' to mean the base used to trace or assign costs. Another term for the base used to trace costs is 'activity base'.

2 Carlson and Young (1993). A company executive claimed that approximately 200 to 300 activities are sufficient to describe all of the processes of its medium-sized (less than 1,000 employees) organizations.

3 The International Organization for Standardization (ISO) based in Geneva administers ISO 9000 certification of companies who either desire or are required by customers to certify the quality of their processes. Many books, articles and Internet sites are devoted to this certification. Go to www.isonet.com.

4 Quoted in Kee (1995).

5 Campbell et al. (1997).

6 Boyd (1997).

7 Johnson (1992).

8 Adapted from Gurowka (1996).

References

Abernethy, M.A., A.M. Lillis, P. Brownell and P. Carter (2001) 'Product diversity and costing system design: field study evidence', *Management Accounting Research*, vol. 12, pp. 261–280.

Al-Omiri, M., and C. Drury (2007) 'A survey of factors influencing the choice of product costing systems in UK organizations', *Management Accounting Research*, vol. 18, pp. 399–424.

Boyd, L. (1997) 'Cost information: the use of cost information for making operating decisions', *Journal of Cost Management*, May/June, pp. 42–47.

Campbell, R., P. Brewer and T. Mills (1997) 'Designing an information system using activity-based costing and the theory of constraints', *Journal of Cost Management*, January/February, pp. 16–25.

Carlson, D., and S.M. Young (1993) 'Activity-based total quality management at american express', *Journal of Cost Management*, Spring, pp. 48–58.

Gurowka, J. (1996) 'ABC, ABM and the Volkswagen saga', *CMA Magazine*, May, pp. 30–33.

Johnson, H.T (1992) 'It's time to stop overselling activity-based concepts: start focusing on total customer satisfaction instead', *Management Accounting*, September, pp. 26–35.

Kee, R. (1995) 'Integrating activity-based costing with the theory of constraints to enhance production-related decision making', *Accounting Horizons*, December, pp. 48–61.

Maiga, A., and F. Jacobs (2008) 'Extent of ABC use and its consequences', *Contemporary Accounting Research*, vol. 25, no. 2, pp. 533–566.

Porter, M., (1985). *Competitive Advantage*, The Free Press, New York.

Stratton, W.O.D., R.A. Desroches Lawson and T. Hatch (2009) 'Activity-based costing: is it still relevant?' *Management Accounting Quarterly*, vol. 10, no. 3, pp. 31–40.

CHAPTER

5

Customer Profitability and Activity-based Management

Banana Stock/Picture Quest/DAL

Learning Objectives

After completing this chapter, you should be able to:

- **LO 1** Understand the importance of customer profitability analysis.
- **LO 2** Measure customer profitability using ABC.
- **LO 3** Use activity-based costing with target costing.
- **LO 4** Extend ABC costing to activity-based management (ABM).
- **LO 5** Identify and measure the costs of activities that add value or do not add value in organizations.
- **LO 6** Use ABM to identify opportunities for process improvements.
- **LO 7** Understand how to implement ABC and ABM.

Precision Moulding Ltd

The scene is a meeting of executives of Precision Moulding Ltd. (PML) including Melody Fairchild, chief executive officer; Alex Lewis, chief financial officer; Chad Norris, vice president of manufacturing; and Michele Chia, vice president of marketing. The meeting occurred one year after PML began supplying MegaBurger Corporation with promotional plastic toys. MegaBurger is one of the world's largest fast-food chains, and PML is a leading supplier of plastic products in its geographical region.

Melody Fairchild (CEO): We need to decide whether to maintain our current product lines: containers, baby-care products, and toys for MegaBurger. Our business was somewhat profitable last year but not at the level we would like. We must increase our income on the container and MegaBurger businesses, or they are simply not worth our continued efforts.

Chad Norris (Manufacturing): We've already shown that we're capable of meeting MegaBurger's quality standards, but we need to work closely with our production personnel to make the process more efficient to reduce costs. My gut feeling is that we can do it, but everyone will have to work hard.

Alex Lewis (Finance): I think Chad's group is up to improving the novelty toy business, but I have great concerns whether the container business can be salvaged. There is just not much profit in that business, and the market is turning against plastic beverage containers that are not likely to be recycled.

Michele Chia (Marketing): As you know, our industry is a small world. Given our success with MegaBurger last year, a dozen other companies have invited us to consider bidding on their business. The reputation of being a MegaBurger supplier is already creating new business opportunities for us. The opportunity cost of the container business is growing daily.

Melody Fairchild (CEO): I agree with Michele that the potential for new business is terrific, but let's first focus on MegaBurger. Chad, I want you to work closely with Alex and the ABC team that we established last year when we first considered bidding for the MegaBurger job. That team should recommend improvements in the production processes necessary to reduce costs. Then, let's take what we have learned and resolve the container business. Michele, I want you to research other container-market opportunities to see whether we have any value to add there.

Thanks for your input. Keep me advised.

This chapter focuses on an important application of ABC, which is to add more value at lower cost by improving the activities uses to make and deliver products. Some argue that ABC analysis of an existing process is just the starting point of the more important cost-management process of activity-based management (ABM), which seeks to eliminate activities that customers do not value (i.e., will not pay for). This chapter builds an understanding of when ABM can be most powerfully applied to understanding how to improve the serving of different customers, more profitably and with higher **customer value**, which reflects the degree to which products and services satisfy customers' expectations about price, function and quality. **Customer profitability analysis** is an application of ABM to processes that serve customers and sometimes is part of a larger management strategy called **customer relations management** where the qualitative and quantitative focus of the organization is firmly fixed on the customer. As with ABC in general, if little variation exists in the serving of different customers, customer profitability analysis adds little beyond basic ABC and ABM, which still can be an important cost-management tool.

This chapter adds explicit focus on **customer-level costs**, which are costs incured to serve specific customers, in the ABC total cost equation, which can apply to every organization:

$$\begin{aligned}\textbf{Total cost} = {} & \Sigma_i\alpha_i \times \textbf{Unit-level activity}_i + \\ & \Sigma_j\beta_j \times \textbf{Batch-level activity}_j + \\ & \Sigma_k\gamma_k \times \textbf{Product-level activity}_k + \\ & \Sigma_m\delta_m \times \textbf{Facility-level activity}_m + \\ & \Sigma_n\varepsilon_n \times \textbf{Customer-level activity}_n\end{aligned}$$

Notice that each organization can perform multiple activities of each type, and each will have a 'variable' cost for each unit of activity performed. Specifically, an organization may perform certain activities that are unique to each customer or customer-type, including product design, manufacture, certification, delivery and post-sale service.

We return to our focus company of Chapter 4, Precision Moulding Ltd (PML). This manufacturer of plastic containers and baby-care products also supplied plastic novelty toys to all MegaBurger fast-food restaurants in the European region last year. The products, although small, are more complex than PML's other products, and MegaBurger has very high expectations for quality and on-time deliveries. Delivering these products successfully last year resulted in a large increase in sales and the near certainty of continued business with MegaBurger. Although PML met MegaBurger's quality standards and on-time delivery expectations PML has not found MegaBurger's business to be sufficiently profitable. Furthermore, its 'legacy' container business has not improved in profitability.

Importance of Customer Profitability

LO 1
Understand the importance of customer profitability analysis.

Customer profitability analysis identifies the costs and benefits of serving specific customers or customer types to improve an organization's overall profitability. It is a relatively new but increasingly popular cost management tool, which has two primary objectives:

- Measure customer profitability.
- Identify effective and ineffective customer-related activities.

Measurement of Customer Profitability

The first objective of customer profitability analysis is to measure the profitability of existing customers or customer types. Most organizations measure profitability according to organizational boundaries (e.g., regions) or product line. These profit measures facilitate management of production-oriented operations. Operating profits, however, usually do not focus on sales or customer-service activities, which can constitute the majority of general and administrative operating costs – which many organizations overlook when they implement ABC.

Many organizations seek to increase market share and customer satisfaction without understanding the costs of doing so. Some organizations incur significant costs to satisfy customers but often do not know whether these efforts result in revenues that exceed their costs. Customer profitability analysis seeks to identify profitable and unprofitable customers. This information helps the organization to ensure that it retains its profitable customers. It can either drop unprofitable customers or find ways to serve them more profitably.

Some studies have found that only 20 per cent of a company's customers contribute to profits; the remaining 80 per cent generate losses. See Exhibit 5.1 for an example of customer profitability analysis that reflects the historical experience of many organizations that are just beginning to use this technique. The chart shows that a small percentage of customers generated significant profits and the majority generated small profits and significant losses. In this example, the top seven customers (20 per cent of 34 total customers) contributed 155 per cent of the total profit and more than half of the customers generated losses!

Profit from top 7 customers	£381,147
Total company profit	245,941
Profit from top 7 customers	155.0%

Exhibit 5.1 Chart of Customer Profitability, Ranked from High to Low

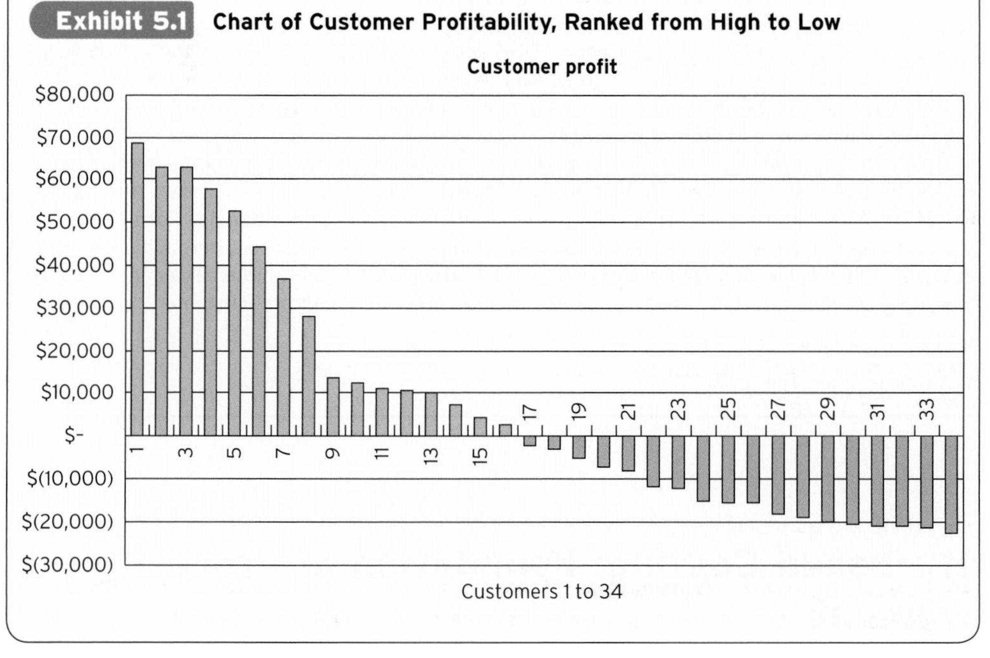

Qualitative Considerations

The quantitative factors of customer profitability are important, but companies should not fail to consider qualitative reasons for retaining marginal or even unprofitable customers, including these:

- Status of being a supplier to a leading company, which can lead to referrals to other (more profitable) customers.
- Potential for an unprofitable customer to become profitable by serving it more efficiently and by helping it succeed.
- Use of an unprofitable customer for entry into a new and profitable market by learning how to serve this market.

- Opportunity to receive transfers of knowledge from innovative but unprofitable companies about their cutting-edge needs or product applications.
- Ability to economize on customer-service activities for customers that partner with the organization or share processes with it.

Similarly, a company might *decline* to serve some profitable customers whose business practices or goals are inconsistent with its own. For example, many organizations decline to serve customers with poor environmental or human rights records. Conversely, companies might choose to serve unprofitable customers who promote the goals they wish to support.

5.1 Cost Management in Practice

Profits and Service Quality: Chicken or Egg?

Calls from **Charles Schwab's** (USA) top-rated clients, which have large asset accounts and trade frequently, are answered within a few seconds, but those from less-valued customers might not be answered for 10 minutes or more. Similarly, after estimating that answering phone calls from investors costs $13 per call, **Fidelity Investments Worldwide** (USA) directs low-profit callers to its website or an automated phone system for self-service.

An increasing number of companies such as **DHL International** (Germany) have made a deliberate decision to differentiate services by customer profitability. DHL's multi-year effort used its detailed customer-related ABC information to perform customer analyses. With that information DHL designed negotiation, pricing and service-level activities to use with global customers. Companies also may use this information to segment their customers into an 'A-list', who frequently buy premium products and services and are treated like royalty, and a 'B-list' who tend to shop based on price and convenience - and get basic services.

Some critics argue that these customer-segmenting practices resemble invisible 'redlining', a controversial form of customer discrimination that some laws prohibit. Some companies clearly are using customer profitability analysis to discriminate among customers. Alternatively, others, such as **Capital One Financial Corp** (USA) are letting customers choose among alternative products priced according to service levels. This approach allows customers to choose services, which is the opposite of discrimination. Furthermore, after setting prices at profitable levels, this customer-led approach must be less costly to implement than full-blown customer profitability analysis.

Sources: Brady (2000); Bellis-Jones Hill Group (n.d).

Activity-based Costing: Foundation of Process Improvement

LO 2
Measure customer profitability using ABC.

Chapter 4 described how PML followed the four ABC steps to estimate the cost of the products for MegaBurger. The ABC team first matched MegaBurger's product and service specifications to the activities and cost-driver rates derived from PML's activity analysis of its current products. These activities and cost-driver rates are shown in columns A and B of Exhibit 4.10 in Chapter 4, which is reproduced here as Exhibit 5.2. Column D of Exhibit 5.2 indicates the adjustments that were necessary to accurately estimate the cost to produce the MegaBurger products as calculated in E through G. The data in Exhibit 5.2 is based on the previous year's analysis, before PML actually produced any products for MegaBurger. After producing the MegaBurger products for a year, the ABC team had the new task of reviewing actual results and confirming that the estimates had been accurate. However, the team suspected that process improvements had to be made to enable the company to improve the profitability business with MegaBurger and its other customers. The cost management tool of customer profitability analysis is designed to begin this type of analysis.

Exhibit 5.2 Application of ABC Cost Information to Estimate Novelty Toy Costs

	A	B	C	D	E	F	G
1	Novelty toy activities (adapted from baby-care products)	Cost-driver rates for existing baby-care products (Exhibit 4-6)		Adjustments to rates for new products	Adjusted cost-driver rates B × (1+D)	Monthly level of cost-driver activity	Estimated monthly costs and revenues E × F
2	*1. Unit-level*						
3	1.1 Acquire and use materials	£10.00	per unit	20%	£12.00	20,000	£240,000.00
4	*2. Batch-level*						
5	2.1 Set-up and quality control of computer-controlled machines	£300.00	per batch	0%	£300.00	16	4,800.00
6	*3. Product-level*						
7	3.1 Design and manufacture of moulds	£2,000.00	per mould	100%	£4,000.00	8	32,000.00
8	3.2 Use equipment in production	£40,000.00	per product type	0%	£40,000.00	1	40,000.00
9	*4. Customer-level*						
10	4.1 Consult customers	£100.00	per consultation	100%	£200.00	40	8,000.00
11	4.2 Provide additional warehousing	£14.00	per m³	50%	£21.00	280	5,880.00
12	*5. Facility-level*						
13	5.1 Manage workers	20%	of production labour cost	100%	40%	$6,000	2,400.00
14	5.2 Use main building	£32.00	per m² occupied	0%	£32.00	550	17,600.00
15		Total monthly costs					350,680.00
16		Monthly revenue per MegaBurger contract			£25.00	20,000	500,000.00
17		Monthly excess of revenue over ABC costs					£149,320.00
18							
19	Note: Shaded cells are data inputs; unshaded cells are computed.			Return on sales before administrative cost			29.86%

PML's Initial ABC Customer Profitability Analysis

Because PML's products are closely aligned with specific customers, the team easily sorted product-line revenues by customer: containers for the large discount store (BigMart), baby-care products for the baby-products retailer (BabyCo), and novelty toys for MegaBurger. These data are reproduced from Chapter 4 in Exhibit 5.3. Companies that sell multiple products to multiple customers cannot sort out profit margins by customer this easily. However, most firms have the necessary data from sales invoice databases and costing systems (ABC or traditional cost systems). Cross-tabulating many customers and product sales can be a time-consuming task, but it is usually feasible (especially if the data are available electronically). Note that for this example, the cost of unused capacity is changed from Chapter 4 to reflect that some of the previously unused capacity (cell F18) was switched to the

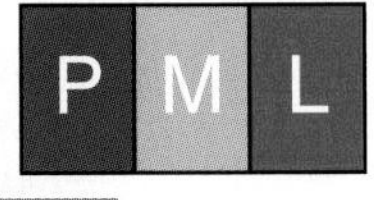

Exhibit 5.3 PML's Initial Customer Profit Margin Analysis: Before Administrative Costs

	A	B	C	D	E	F
1	ABC customer profitability before administrative costs			Customers		
2	Actual product volumes sold, units	Sales price	BigMart	BabyCo	MegaBurger	Total
3	Container products	£0.40	1,800,000	-	-	1,800,000
4	Baby-care products	£32.00	-	30,000	-	30,000
5	Novelty toys	£25.00	-	-	20,000	20,000
6						
7	Revenues		£720,000.00	£960,000.00	£500,000.00	£2,180,000.00
8						
9	Costs assigned to products					
10	1. Unit level		450,000.00	300,000.00	240,000.00	990,000.00
11	2. Batch level		108,000.00	48,000.00	4,800.00	160,800.00
12	3. Product level		152,000.00	48,000.00	72,000.00	272,000.00
13	4. Customer level		3,420.00	4,840.00	13,880.00	22,140.00
14	5. Facility level		15,680.00	22,800.00	20,000.00	58,480.00
15	Total costs assigned to products		729,100.00	423,640.00	350,680.00	1,503,420.00
16	Customer profit margin before administrative costs		-£9,100.00	£536,360.00	£149,320.00	£676,580.00
17	Return on sales before administrative costs		-1.26%	55.87%	29.86%	31.04%
18	Cost of unused manufacturing capacity					20,000.00
19	Administrative costs not assigned to products or customers					286,000.00
20	Operating income					£370,580.00
21	Return on sales after administrative costs					17.00%

production of novelty toys; unused buffer capacity remains. Note also the large, unassigned general and administrative cost (cell F19) that will be the object of later analyses.

Let's examine the calculation of PML's revenues earned from each customer, because these calculations would be repeated for each of the ABC costs for each product. The similar cost calculations are hidden in Exhibit 5.2 for clarity of presentation. We compute the sales turnover for BigMart (cell C7) by the products of sales prices and sales quantities for each of the three products:

$$\textbf{BigMart Revenues} = £0.40 \times 1{,}800{,}000 + £32.00 \times 0 + £25.00 \times 0 = £720{,}000$$

We can compute unit- and higher-level costs in just the same manner. Exhibit 5.3 shows that BigMart is an unprofitable customer, whereas BabyCo is very profitable and MegaBurger is not as profitable. This initial customer-profitability analysis raises the questions: should PML retain its container business with BigMart? Can PML make its MegaBurger business more profitable? Can PML retain BabyCo as a customer? Are administrative costs used differently to serve its customers? The team realized that they should answer the last question first, because administrative costs are quite large and, if accurately assigned to customers, could affect relative profit margins.

PML's Improved Customer Profitability Analysis

Exhibit 5.3 presents PML's initial customer profitability analysis, which did not assign administrative costs to products or customers. The ABC team next turned to the task of making these assignments.

Administrative Cost Analysis

A large, unexamined category of cost at PML and at many firms is administrative costs. These often escape ABC analysis, because they usually are not associated with specific products. That is, they usually are treated as period costs and expenses. However, careful analysis often can assign large portions of administrative costs to the service of specific customers or groups of customers. While this information would not be reported externally, if it is reasonably accurate, it can be valuable for making the types of customer decisions facing PML.

We now discuss how PML's ABC team identified and analysed customer-related costs that often are expensed in total as period costs. The steps to assigning these costs to customers emulate the ABC steps for products, but applied to customers:

Step 1. Identify and classify the activities related to the company's *customers*.
Step 2. Estimate the cost of activities identified in step 1.
Step 3. Calculate a cost-driver base and rate for the activity.
Step 4. Assign activity costs to *customers* using the appropriate cost-driver rates from step 3.

Exhibit 5.4 presents the team's analysis of PML's *unassigned* administrative costs from Exhibit 5.3, row 19 (£286,000), including:

- Selling costs, £38,000 (B3)
- Marketing costs, £48,000 (B4)
- Distribution costs by truck, £40,000 (B5)
- Distribution costs by courier, £22,000 (B6)
- Finance and human resources, £42,000 (B7)
- General administration costs, £78,000 (B8)

Selling costs include the costs of all personnel, databases, equipment, and facilities devoted to supporting sales activities. Unlike many sales-oriented organizations, PML's four sales personnel are salaried, serve all customers, and are not paid on commission (i.e., compensated with a percentage of sales). However, PML's sales personnel do keep logs of telephone calls, emails and visits with customers. After interviewing the sales personnel, the ABC team estimated the duration of each of these sales activities and estimated a total time spent with each customer. The cost-driver activity

Exhibit 5.4 PML's Analysis of Administrative Resources and Costs

	A	B	C	D	E	F
1	ABC analysis of administrative costs					
2	Administrative activities	Cost	Cost-driver base		Cost-driver rate	
3	Selling	£ 38,000.00	640	Hours available	£ 59.38	per hour
4	Marketing	48,000.00	320	Hours available	150.00	per hour
5	Distribution - Trucks	40,000.00	720	Hours available	55.56	per hour
6	Distribution - PackageXpress	22,000.00	£ 500,000.00	Sales turnover	4.4000%	of sales turnover
7	Finance and human resources	42,000.00	£ 2,180,000.00	Sales turnover	1.9266%	of sales turnover
8	General administration	96,000.00	£ 2,180,000.00	Sales turnover	4.4037%	of sales turnover
9	Total	£ 286,000.00				
10	Assignment of administrative costs	Assigned to customers			Resource usage and cost assignment	
11	Administrative costs	BigMart	BabyCo	MegaBurger	Resources used, costs assigned	Unused resources, unassigned costs
12	Selling					
13	Hours traced to customers	185.00	200.00	160.00	545.00	95.00
14	Cost assigned	£ 10,984.38	£ 11,875.00	£ 9,500.00	£ 32,359.38	£ 5,640.63
15	Marketing					
16	Hours traced to customers	120.00	80.00	110.00	310.00	10.00
17	Cost assigned	£ 18,000.00	£ 12,000.00	£ 16,500.00	£ 46,500.00	£ 1,500.00
18	Distribution - Trucks					
19	Hours traced to customers	410.00	260.00		670.00	50.00
20	Cost assigned	£ 22,777.78	£ 14,444.44		£ 37,222.22	£ 2,777.78
21	Distribution - PackageXpress					
22	Sales turnover			£ 500,000.00	£ 500,000.00	£ -
23	Cost assigned			£ 22,000.00	£ 22,000.00	£ -
24	Unassigned Administrative costs					
25	Finance and human resources					£ 42,000.00
26	General administration					£ 96,000.00
27	Total costs assigned or unassigned	51,762.15	38,319.44	48,000.00	£ 138,081.60	£ 147,918.40
28	Total administrative costs					£ 286,000.00

level selected was the total personnel hours available for selling activities in a month (640 hours = 4 personnel × 40 hours × 4 weeks).

CFO Lewis and the ABC team also have been greatly influenced by the relatively new application of ABC, called 'time-driven ABC', which argues that many if not all administrative processes are driven by available and used time. Robert Kaplan and Steven Andersen have popularized this development, which has been used in other forms since the 1980s.[1] This simplified approach to ABC is not universally accepted, however. Using time as the denominator in cost-driver rates might be convenient, but it might not be the most accurate description of the consumption of resources. For example, the number of different parts or components (SKUs) of products for customers might measure the complexity of serving customers better than time. Likewise, the number of shipping pallets or containers might be a better measure of distribution costs than time to deliver products. These are empirical issues that vary across circumstances and that must be traded off for the cost of more precise analysis and measurement.

Multiplying the computed cost-driver rate of £59.38 per hour (cell E3) by the number of selling hours traced to each customer (rows 13 and 14) assigned £10,984 to BigMart, £11,875 to BabyCo, and £9,500 to MegaBurger. These assignments left £5,640 as the cost of unused (unassigned) selling resources for the month (cell F14). The cost-driver rate £59.38 per hour probably does not capture the use of selling resources with perfect accuracy, but it is indicative of the uses of selling resources for customers. This is an example of using information that is approximately right, which might be better than not assigning any costs to customers, which undoubtedly is 100 per cent wrong.

This rationale might not be completely satisfying to those that expect more precision in measurement, but another perspective is that Exhibit 5.4 is a first draft of a cost management process that most likely will be revised with more experience. Nonetheless, PML has serious customer and product decisions to make soon, and top managers might be unwilling to wait for perfect information. This means that the analysis team must put forth a credible effort the first time. Products, customers, employees and profits are at stake.

Marketing costs include the costs of personnel, databases, equipment and facilities dedicated to providing market research, marketing strategy and marketing plans. The two-person marketing department designs advertising and promotion materials and campaigns and provides training and information support for sales personnel. It also responds to customer needs forwarded from salespeople and major account managers. The results of the examination of marketing resources and activities are also reported in Exhibit 5.4, rows 15–17. Dividing the £48,000 cost by the 320 marketing hours available computes the cost-driver rate of £150 per hour (cell E4). The cost management team interviewed marketing management staff members to estimate their time devoted to each customer, which formed the basis for assigning marketing costs to customers (row 17). Unassigned marketing costs totalled £1,500 (cell F17).

Distribution costs include the costs of packing, shipping, and delivering products or services to customers. PML distributes products to customers using a company-owned, maintained and operated fleet of trucks (lorries) to serve BigMart's and BabyCo's distribution centres in the UK and a private delivery service, PackageXpress, to serve MegaBurger locations throughout Europe. The truck fleet keeps careful time and distance records of deliveries of products to BigMart and BabyCo for billing, insurance and for the UK Department of Transport, which oversees the safety of drivers and vehicles. Thus, the ABC team was able to gather accurate time records for assigning distribution costs to two of its customers. The cost-driver rate of £55.56 per hour (cell E5) multiplied by the hours of delivery service used to serve BigMart and BabyCo (row 19) computes their assigned distribution costs (row 20).

Billing invoices provided by PackageXpress indicated that private delivery of goods cost PML 4.40 per cent of sales turnover, which the team judged would be a reliable cost-driver rate for deliveries to MegaBurger locations. MegaBurger's distribution costs are in rows 21–23. Note that this cost is 'metered' to measure actual costs, so no cost is unassigned.

This analysis raised the issue whether PML should use PackageXpress for all of its deliveries (i.e., outsource all distribution resources). If the same cost-driver rate of 4.40 per cent of sales turnover applies for deliveries to BigMart (sales turnover = £720,000) and BabyCo (sales turnover = £960,000), the outsourced distribution costs would be £31,680 and £42,240, respectively, and £73,920.00 in total. This is considerably more than the distribution resources assigned or supplied to serve these customers (£40,000), so outsourcing does not appear to offer cost savings in this case.

Finance and human resources costs are costs of administrative functions that perform required internal and external reporting and analyses (such as PML's ABC analyses). *General administration costs* are the other administrative costs that must be covered in some way by customer sales. Presumably, all activities of a profit-seeking organization such as PML are (or should be) performed to facilitate or support sales to customers. Because some administration functions and activities are several steps removed from customer-related activities, tracing their costs to customers is usually difficult. The ABC team could not develop an unambiguous cost driver for finance, human resources or general administration costs in the time available. In the end, the team decided that an accurate tracing of these costs would not be possible without expending an unjustifiable amount of effort. The team initially recommended assigning general administration costs using each customer's sales turnover as the activity level. CFO Lewis, however, was concerned about the assignment of costs for the administrative activities of Finance and Human Resources (£42,000) and General Administration (£96,000). During a meeting with the ABC team, he observed,

> *In my experience, administrative cost assignments that are based on relative sales turnover raise red flags about accuracy and reliability. I understand and agree that the MegaBurger distribution cost-driver rates are reasonably accurate, but I am not sure about the Finance and Human Resources and General Administration. Of course, I understand the arithmetic, but these cost-driver rates seem more convenient than accurate. If we cannot generate reliable, defensible assignments for these costs to customers, I prefer to treat them as costs of the period. I do not want your hard and excellent work to be dismissed by sceptics because we over-extended our ABC knowledge for two categories of cost. Does this make sense? Good. Please finish the analysis without these questionable assignments for presentation to the executive group.*

5.1 Research Insight

Effects of Customer Profitability Analysis

Marketing researchers have recently investigated the impacts of customer-profitability analysis. Raaij et al. (2003) analysed the experiences of a multinational firm that produced and sold professional cleaning products. The initial results were alarming to the company, and examples cited include, 'A relatively small customer in industrial laundry

was granted such high discounts that a price increase of nearly 60 per cent was needed to make the account profitable again. In another case, a customer with the habit of placing a large number of very small orders was asked to change its ordering behaviour to bring the relationship costs in line with sales revenues. The customer ignored these requests and is no longer served by the firm'. Furthermore, 20 per cent of the customers were responsible for 95 per cent of the firm's profits - and vice versa!

Homburg et al. (2008) analysed survey responses to 310 firms with business-to-business and business-to-customer relationships to find that acting on customer profitability analysis resulted in higher average customer profitability and higher returns on sales because of improved relationships with high-profit customers and reductions of marketing and selling costs to low-profit customers.

Niraj et al. (2001) find similar results in more complex supply-chain relationships, but Lind and Strömsten (2006) suggest that the implementation of customer profitability analysis can vary according to the dominant types of relationships between businesses and their customers. For example, firms can measure profits by customer segment for purely transactional relationships. High levels of organizational co-ordination indicate a need for periodic (e.g., quarterly), customer-level accounting. Relationships that require high technical and organizational co-ordination appear to indicate 'lifetime' customer-level accounting. These are areas of current research, but all indications are that customer profitability analysis is an important cost management tool.

Sources: Homburg et al. (2008); Lind and Strömsten (2006); Niraj et al. (2001); and Raaij et a. (2003).

Identification of Alternative Actions

The information in Exhibit 5.5, which accounts for all costs assigned to customers and the computed returns on sales for the three customers (BigMart: –8.45 per cent, BabyCo: 45.55 per cent, and MegaBurger: 13.93 per cent), led CFO Alex Lewis to propose four alternative courses of action to improve customer profitability. The alternatives were:

- Continue the status quo; do nothing – this was not acceptable, but the status quo always needs to be visibly included.
- Increase the efficiency of serving MegaBurger – this is the immediate issue facing the company, and the topic of the remainder of this chapter.
- Decrease administrative activity costs for all customers, without harming the profitable relationship with BabyCo – the profit situation certainly would not be improved if reducing costs led to BabyCo's dissatisfaction and loss as a customer. BabyCo contributes 92.4 per cent of the total customer margin and 134.4 per cent of total profits.

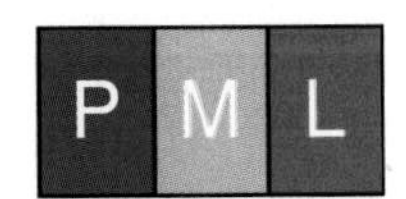

Exhibit 5.5 PML's Customer Profit Margin Analysis

	A	B	C	D	E	F
1	ABC customer profitability after administrative costs			Customers		
2	Actual product volumes sold, units	Sales price	BigMart	BabyCo	MegaBurger	Total
3	Container products	£ 0.40	1,800,000	-	-	1,800,000
4	Baby-care products	£ 32.00	-	30,000	-	30,000
5	Novelty toys	£ 25.00	-	-	20,000	20,000
6						
7	Revenues		£ 720,000.00	£ 960,000.00	£ 500,000.00	£ 2,180,000.00
8						
9	Costs traced to customers					
10	1. Unit level		450,000.00	300,000.00	240,000.00	990,000.00
11	2. Batch level		108,000.00	48,000.00	4,800.00	160,800.00
12	3. Product level		152,000.00	48,000.00	72,000.00	272,000.00
13	4. Customer level		3,420.00	4,840.00	13,880.00	22,140.00
14	5. Facility level		15,680.00	22,800.00	20,000.00	58,480.00
15	Administrative costs		51,762.15	38,319.44	48,000.00	138,081.60
16	Total costs traced to customers		780,862.15	461,959.44	398,680.00	1,641,501.60
17	Customer profit margin after assigned administrative costs		-£ 60,862.15	£ 498,040.56	£ 101,320.00	£ 538,498.40
18	Return on sales after assigned administrative costs		-8.45%	51.88%	20.26%	24.70%
19	Cost of unused manufacturing capacity					20,000.00
20	Administrative costs not traced to products or customers					147,918.40
21	Operating income					£ 370,580.00
22	Return on sales after administrative costs					17.00%

5.1 You're the Decision Maker

Trade-offs between Accuracy and Timeliness

The PML ABC team clearly made trade-offs between the accuracy and the timeliness of cost management information during its analysis of administrative costs.

a. What types of resources does PML probably devote to its truck fleet? What other costs and benefits should the company consider before deciding whether to retain the fleet or outsource all distribution activities?

b. The team had proposed to assign general administration costs on the basis of other administrative costs assigned, but CFO Lewis disagreed. Do you think his was a justifiable decision? Explain.

(Solutions begin on page 222.)

- Drop BigMart as a customer and the unprofitable container product business – this appears to be a way to improve profitability, but one should not assume that eliminating this business would also eliminate all of the costs assigned to BigMart.[2]

Combination of ABC and Target Costing = Cost Reduction Goal

LO 3 Use activity-based costing with target costing.

CFO Lewis wanted to assess whether it was feasible to improve the efficiency of serving MegaBurger. His next step was to calculate the magnitude of the profit deficit of the current MegaBurger contract using the current production and administrative processes. He calculated the toys' **target cost**, which is the highest cost of a good or service that meets both customer needs and company profit goals. Exhibit 5.6 presents PML's target costing analysis, based on the current contract with MegaBurger. The sales revenue estimate shown at the top of column B of £500,000, taken from Exhibit 5.5. PML's management has set a 40 per cent return on sales (ROS) target for the MegaBurger business (before unassigned administrative costs). This ROS might seem high, but recall that the baby-care customer margin exceeds 50 per cent. Furthermore, customer margins must cover PML's administrative and other opportunity costs that have not been assigned to

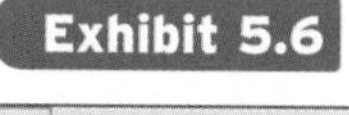

Exhibit 5.6 Target Costing Analysis of MegaBurger Promotional Toys

	A	B
1	Target cost reduction analysis	
2	Target cost calculation	
3	Expected monthly revenue from MegaBurger contract (Exhibit 5.5)	£500,000.00
4	Required rate of return on sales (before administrative costs)	40.00%
5	Less required return per month (B4 x B3)	£200,000.00
6	Target cost per month (B3 - B5)	£300,000.00
7		
8	Currently feasible customer costs per month	Total estimated cost (Exhibit 5.5)
9	Unit-level resources and activities	£240,000.00
10	Batch-level resources and activities	4,800.00
11	Product-level resources and activities	72,000.00
12	Customer-level resources and activities	13,880.00
13	Facility-level resources and activities	20,000.00
14	Assigned administrative costs	48,000.00
15	Total currently feasible customer costs per month	£398,680.00
16	Currently feasible customer profit margin	£101,320.00
17		
18	Monthly cost reduction target (B22 - B6 or B5 - B23))	£98,680.00
19	Per cent cost reduction target (B24 ÷ B22)	24.75%

each customer. Subtracting the monetary amount of the required ROS from the contracted monthly revenue gives a target cost of £ 300,000 per month, as shown near the top of Exhibit 5.6 (cell B6).

The total monthly costs for all levels of resources and activities consumed by the MegaBurger contract, £398,680, shown in cell B15, is the **currently feasible cost**, which is the total cost *without* improving the efficiency of production or administrative processes. Normally, the target cost and currently feasible cost are computed and compared for the duration of a project or contract. But in this case we can obtain the same key information by computing the costs for a normal month.

With monthly revenue of £500,000 and currently feasible, monthly ABC product costs of £398,680 (B15), PML would earn a monthly product margin of £101,320 (B26), which is short of the required ROS by £98,680 (B25). If prices are not changeable (which in this case they are not), PML must make up the shortfall by reducing ABC costs by 24.75 per cent (B19). Subtracting the monthly total target cost of £300,000 (B6) from the currently feasible cost of £398,680 (B15), which is the **cost reduction target** of £98,680 (B18) for the month, which is 24.75 per cent of the currently feasible cost. Target costing has helped the ABC team to quantify the goal for the ABM analysis of process improvement.

Although a cost reduction of 24.75 per cent seems large, the ABC team realized that if they could find and remove this much inefficiency from a new product's processes they perhaps could make at least as much improvement to the older products and processes. Furthermore, PML's top management would strongly endorse spreading this learning throughout the company.

5.2 You're the Decision Maker

Using Target Costing

Review Exhibit 5.6.

a. Two alternative ways for PML to reduce costs are (1) to seek a higher price from MegaBurger and (2) accept a lower return on sales (ROS). What total revenue (sales-dollar) amount would justify the business without reducing costs or reducing the 40 per cent return on sales? Alternatively, what (lower) return on sales would justify the business without reducing costs or increasing the total revenue? Would you recommend either of these alternatives? Why or why not?

b. Some cost-driver rates of the target-costing analysis in Exhibit 5.6 are taken directly from the original ABC analysis of existing products. Several cost-driver rates are notably different, however, to reflect the team's expectations of differences in the products. Do you think it is advisable to directly apply cost-driver rates from the experience of making existing products to new products? Why or why not?

c. *Team focus.* Assume that you are PML's customer-service manager and a member of its cross-functional team analysing the MegaBurger toy cost information. If costs must be reduced to make PML's profit goal feasible, does it make sense to recommend that all areas of the company find ways to reduce costs by 24.75 per cent? Why or why not? As an alternative, does it make more sense to focus cost-reduction efforts on the largest costs?*

(Solutions begin on page 222.)

*This is the so-called Willie Sutton rule of cost reduction. Willie Sutton was a notorious bank robber. After he was captured, he was asked why he robbed banks. He replied, 'Because that's where the money is'.

Extension of ABC to Activity-based Management (ABM)

LO 4 Extend ABC costing to activity-based management (ABM).

To continue supplying MegaBurger and to retain its container business, PML must increase its profits; to do that, it must improve its production and customer processes. As described in Chapter 4, *activity-based costing (ABC)* focuses on (1) understanding the way resources are used in current processes and (2) accurately measuring product costs using those processes. By itself, however, ABC does not result in the process improvements that might be necessary to achieve desired efficiency. Thus, ABC stops short of being a comprehensive cost management system. This chapter continues to develop questions raised in Chapter 4 concerning how to build a cost management system that increases the understanding of the uses of resources and that promotes process improvements. To illustrate these concepts, we observe how PML was able to use activity-based management to submit another bid to MegaBurger for a three-year, renewable relationship and to make a hard decision about its legacy container business.

Activity-based management (ABM) evaluates the costs and values of process activities to identify opportunities for improved efficiency.[3] ABM combines activity-based costing analysis and value-added analysis to make process improvements that improve customer value and reduce wasted resources. ABM extends basic ABC analysis.

The four ABC steps applied to the MegaBurger novelty toy business resulted in Exhibit 5.2, which computed cost-driver rates for products and, when applied to all of PML costs and revenues, the customer profit-margin analysis in Exhibit 5.5. But these important analyses identified profit problems with several products without pinpointing solutions. ABM extends ABC by adding these steps:

Step 5: Identify activities as value-added or non-value-added.
Step 6: Score each activity as high or low value-added as perceived by the customer.
Step 7: Identify process opportunities to enhance value-added activities and to reduce or eliminate non-value-added activities.

Step 5: Customer-perceived Value

LO 5
Identify and measure the costs of activities that add value or do not add value in organizations.

The main objective of performing customer profitability analysis is to quantify the effects of continuing profitable or unprofitable customer-related activities. This analysis provides the information that organizations can use to decide which activities to enhance or eliminate that will increase total profitability, decrease or eliminate customer dissatisfaction, and clarify its view of what customers value and will pay for. Enhancing customer activities include simplifying cumbersome order processes, consolidating many small orders into fewer large ones, and teaching customers to minimize costs by eliminating numerous changes to their orders.

Value-added activities enhance the value of products and services in the eyes of the customer while meeting the company's goals. In other words, the outcomes of value-added activities are what customers are willing to pay for. Note that customers could be either internal or external to the organization, but the ultimate test of customer value is the *external* customer's perception because they are the ones that contribute real revenues. **Non-value-added activities** do not contribute to customer-perceived value. Eliminating these activities by redesigning processes would not reduce customer value. In fact, eliminating these activities might permit a price decrease, which would delight customers.

PML must improve its processes to reduce its costs. An appropriate place to start is to identify activities as value-added or non-value-added. The company's goal is to eliminate non-value-added activities while making value-added activities more efficient.

Sources of Non-value-added Activities

All organizations have some non-value-added activities that can be reduced or eliminated. These are the most likely sources of the non-value-added activities:

- Building excess products to build up inventory (or stock).
- Waiting for processing.
- Spending time and effort to move products from place to place.
- Transporting workers to work sites.
- Building defective products.

5.2 Cost Management in Practice

Examples of Value-added and Non-value-added Activities

The following are more examples of both types of activities from some of the many US companies that have used ABM:[4]

Company (process)	Value-added activities	Non-value-added activities
Pacific Bell* (accounts receivable)	Processing payments	Reprocessing payments to correct errors
Dayton Extruded Plastics* (manufacturing)	Extruding window frames	Setting up machines
Tektronix* (product development)	Making new products	Making engineering changes
Stockham Valves and Fittings* (manufacturing)	Improving tooling	Moving and storing products
Qwest† (sales and marketing)	Making customer calls	Processing orders and quotes, taking orders
Weyerhaeuser ‡ (payroll)	Paying employees accurately and on a timely basis	Making data entries

Sources:
*Turney (1992).
†Convey (1991). NB: Qwest has been acquired by Century Link.
‡Pederson (1991).

Identifying and Measuring Value-added Activities

The test for whether an activity adds customer value is met by answering two questions:

1. Would an external customer encourage the organization to do more of that activity?
2. Would the organization be more likely to reach its goal by performing that activity?[5]

If both answers are yes, the activity adds value. If either answer is no, the activity adds no value and consumes scarce resources, perhaps unnecessarily. Answering these two questions also leads to two related questions:

3. How should an organization measure activities as value-added or non-value-added?
4. Who should be responsible for performing the measurement activity?

5.2 Research Insight

The Customer Is Always Right, But Is It Always Worth It?

An economic perspective of customer service predicts that if service is valued but freely offered, customers will demand more of it than they would be willing to pay for. Many commercial firms attest that they are 'customer focused' and seek to delight, not merely satisfy, customers. If their actions match their claims, can they do so profitably? In fact, maximizing customer satisfaction can be a recipe for unprofitable operations. On the other hand, some organizations identify efficient ways to provide services, thus keeping customer satisfaction high and service costs low.

What drives customer profitability? Does increased customer satisfaction lead to increased profitability? Academic research seeks objective evidence of a link between customer satisfaction and profitability. The evidence suggests that profits show a positive relation with, but decreasing marginal returns from, increases in customer satisfaction. As one study put it, 'The customer is always right, but is it always worth it?'

Sources: Anderson et al. (1994); Banker et al. (2002); Ittner and Larcker (1998); and Rust and Zahorik (1993).

Measures of Value-added Activities

Some activities, such as delivering goods and service on time, obviously add value. Other activities, such as rewriting faulty software code or reworking faulty products, obviously add no value because they should not have to be performed. Customers would not willingly pay for them, and if prices are unnecessarily higher because of them, customers will look elsewhere. The value-added/non-value-added dichotomy is important, but it could be too restrictive.

Other activities are necessary because of current technology, policy or regulatory requirements. For example, customers probably do not care whether an organization spends its resources to file its periodic tax returns. Filing tax returns is necessary but customers would not rate it as value-added. Most would agree, however, that eliminating this activity would be a mistake.

Many companies identify the value of their activities on a scale from 1 to 5 or 1 to 10, with the higher end representing more added value. The narrower the scale, the more likely the organization is to misclassify an activity because the categories might not fit well. The wider scale, however, could make distinguishing levels of value more difficult for individuals and lead to softer decisions about retaining or eliminating activities. Although practices vary, a five-point scale could provide the right amount of detail for measuring levels of value-added in most cases. On a five-point scale, an activity that is necessary but does not add value from the customer's perspective could be rated 3 while obviously value-added or non-value-added activities would be rated as a 5 or 1, respectively. Activities rated 2 or 4 are in an ambiguous zone and often are the subjects of difficult discussions to clarify their customer value.

Step 6: Performing the Measurement Activity

Ideally, someone who is objective and knowledgeable about what customers value and what the organization must do to meet its goals should measure value. It is unlikely, however, that one person could measure value reliably and without bias – intentional or not. It might not be possible for even a group or team to do so without input from others, such as internal and external customers. The reasons are numerous:

1. *Everyone's knowledge is limited.* For example, the sales manager might believe he or she knows what customers want and are willing to pay for, but customers are diverse, and their preferences could change over time. Asking a single customer might not generate representative answers. Furthermore, external customers might not communicate their desires directly to the company; they just might shop elsewhere if they are not satisfied. Another possibility is that customers could have different values, and the organization would have to decide whether to satisfy only one or many types of customer. Some level of market research and knowledge is essential to understanding what customers value. This reinforces the benefit of using cross-functional teams.
2. *Everyone's responses are potentially biased.* The warehouse supervisor could argue that inventory or stock management and warehousing are crucial to ensuring customer value. Partly the supervisor's response reflects that providing and managing product inventories is part of the business routine. Because some current jobs involve managing inventory and the warehouse, the supervisor might be unwilling to jeopardize those jobs even though he or she is responsible to the management and shareholders. Thus, the supervisor could be tempted to provide misleading information that would protect employees' jobs. Alternatively, an upwardly mobile supervisor might tell cost managers what he or she thinks they want to hear: that jobs can be cut without harming processes. Although inventory and warehouse operations could seem necessary because of current processes, they are non-value-added activities unless they are performed at the request of customers. The customer could care very little whether the company even has an inventory. Instead, the customer just wants the product on time and with the expected quality.

In practice, analysts or market researchers measure value-added activities using anything from a single person's beliefs to sophisticated surveys of internal and external customers. If the organization cannot justify expending many resources to measure its activities, the benefits of doing so might not be expected to be significant. If that is the case, the organization could be better off using its resources on more beneficial activities.

Step 7: Process Improvement Using Activity-based Management

LO 6
Use ABM to identify opportunities for process improvements.

The next ABM stage is to redesign processes to eliminate wasteful spending on non-value-added activities. This includes such simple redesigns as eliminating wasteful, time-consuming travel of parts and assemblies, eliminating redundant processing or paperwork. Process redesign also includes much more complex changes such as redesigning products and processes for improved manufacturability. This might entail reducing the number of different parts needed, reorienting the locations of parts for ease of assembly, and pre-qualifying suppliers so that defective materials and parts do not enter the production process.[6] If the organization can eliminate non-value-added activities by redesigning processes, the resources that these activities waste could either be saved to reduce spending or applied to value-added activities to increase their effectiveness. Thus, simply eliminating non-value-added activities could create short-term benefits, and redesigning processes to eliminate the need for such activities can generate long-term benefits.

Eliminating Non-value-added Activities: A Competitive Necessity, but Risky

In a competitive environment, an organization should waste as few resources on non-value-added activities as possible because waste is unnecessary and because competitors are continuously striving to create more customer value at lower cost. It is important, however, to thoroughly examine the **risks**, which are exposures to loss, of eliminating activities that at first sight seem non-value-added. For example, in recent years many banks eliminated most levels of approval for consumer and commercial loans because the multiple approval layers almost never affected the decision of granting the loans. The multiple approvals appeared to merely use scarce resources and delay final approval, and the delays greatly annoyed customers. Online applications and waivers of background checks replaced multiple levels of risk assessments of loan applications, and some banks offered nearly instant loan decisions. We now know that eliminating these so-called non-value-added approval activities contributed to the collapse of housing markets worldwide and the Great Recession of 2008–2009 (and its continuing aftershocks in many countries). The lesson is that one should eliminate activities only after discerning that financial and related operating risks are not thereby increased.

When risks are not adversely affected, organizations have incentives to reduce non-value-added activities because they could apply the freed-up resources to value-added activities or distribute them to their customers, employees and owners (via price reductions, wages and dividends). Note that individuals in the organization might derive benefits from the non-value-added activities, such as extra on-the-job perquisites, that indirectly add customer value (e.g., through better customer service attitudes). Otherwise, the organization might be better off using the resources for value-added activities. Organizations with few non-value-added activities should be better able to compete than organizations that have allowed wasteful practices to become part of their culture.

PML's ABM Analysis

PML's vice president of marketing formed a team of sales and marketing personnel to measure value-added activities. She did not include external customers because she felt it was unwise to expose all of PMLs activities to customers – a common concern. Her team used a five-point scale (5 = highest value, 1 = lowest value) to measure customer value. These ratings were used to evaluate and improve existing processes.

Working from the Activity List

A small part of PML's activity list appears in Exhibit 5.7 for computer-controlled injection moulding of novelty toys in a typical month. The entire activity list formed the basis of the thorough ABM analysis of the company's business, but that is too voluminous to present here. The complete value-added analysis measures the costs and value of the activities in all parts of the organization's value chain. Although evaluating activities to a fine level can be a formidable task, it could be necessary to find sources of wasted resources.

Notice in Exhibit 5.7 that many of PML's activities to set up and control computer-controlled machines are rated as low-valued activities. If PML could save these resources or redirect them to higher-valued activities, it could either reduce its costs or apply the saved cost to increase its effec-

Exhibit 5.7 Set-up and Quality Control of Computer-controlled Machines for Novelty Toys

	A	B	C	D	E	F	G
1		Novelty Toys: ABC set-up data for normal month					Value-added data
2	Activity	Activity description	Level 1 Activity cost	Level 2 Activity cost	Level 3 Activity cost	Level 4 Activity cost	Customer value
3	2.1	Set up and quality control of computer-controlled machines	£4,800.00				
4	2.1.1	Program machine		£1,500.00			5
5	2.1.2	Perform quality control of batches produced		£2,100.00			
6	2.1.2.1	Observe start of batch			£100.00		2
7	2.1.2.2	Remove pieces and visually inspect			£300.00		2
8	2.1.2.3	Recycle defective pieces			£200.00		1
9	2.1.2.4	Place good pieces in inventory			£1,200.00		
10	2.1.2.4.1	Trim excess plastic				£500.00	1
11	2.1.2.4.2	Place trimmings in recycle bags				£500.00	1
12	2.1.2.4.3	Place good piece in bin or box				£200.00	2
13	2.1.2.5	Record defects for batch			£300.00		3
14	2.1.3	Log out completed order		£100.00			2
15	2.1.4	Move completed order to warehouse		£800.00			4
16	2.1.5	Register completed order in inventory		£100.00			2
17	2.1.6	End production run		£200.00			2

Note to Exhibit 5.7: Costs of activities that have sub-activities are summarized in the unshaded cells. For example, the £1,200 cost of Level 3 activity 2.1.2.4 (cell E9) is the sum of Level 4 activity costs in cells F10 to F12. To avoid double counting, only un aggregated cells are valued from 1 to 5.

tiveness in generating customer value. This is the main intent of activity-based management: *Use ABC information to improve processes by reducing cost while increasing customer value.*

One can see how this analysis in Exhibit 5.7 might help PML. For example, 'Activity 2.1.3 Move completed order to warehouse' is rated 4 on the customer value scale, indicating that PML providing warehousing services for MegaBurger should have value that the customer is willing to pay for (perhaps the customer does not pay enough for the trouble; hence the rating of 4 not 5). Still, PML can review this process to find a way to reduce the cost of this activity. For example, perhaps the distance travelled to the storage area could be reduced.

Customers do not willingly pay for the activities that add little or no value (scores 1, 2 and 3), so PML should seek ways to eliminate or minimize them. For example, activity '2.1.2.3 Recycle defective pieces' should not have to be done at all – why does a computerized moulding machine create defective pieces? Is this caused by defective software code, or substandard plastic, or a defective mould? If these causes can be eliminated, the recycling cost will be saved for every batch of product. Likewise, every low valued activity should be scrutinized.

Estimating the Benefits of ABM

The most direct use of the information presented in Exhibit 5.7 is simply to cross-tabulate the activities by value and by cost. These rankings can clearly identify potential benefits of improvement. Summing the costs of an activity, for example, 2.1, by adding the cost of all the activities rated from 1 to 5 as shown in column F of Exhibit 5.7 yields the summary information shown in Exhibit 5.8. (Note that this table was created using Excel's Pivot Table, which is a very powerful summarization tool – perhaps overkill for this simple analysis). Exhibit 5.8 shows that the activities rated 3 and lower consume about 52 per cent of the resources. PML's ABC team needs to work with process engineers to determine how to reduce these activities that consume many resources but generate little value for customers. For example, if PML could eliminate just the activities rated 1 by redesigning the set-up process, the company's set-up cost would decline by 25 per cent. A competitor with a similar process that could eliminate all of these low-value-added activities could have a large cost advantage over PML.

Exhibit 5.8 **Comparisons of Activity Values and Costs: PML's Activity 2.2: Set Up Computer-controlled Machines**

	A	B	C
1	Sum of activity cost		
2	by customer value	Total	Percentage
3	5	£ 1,500.00	31%
4	4	800.00	17%
5	3	300.00	6%
6	2	1,000.00	21%
7	1	1,200.00	25%
8	**Grand Total**	**£ 4,800.00**	**100%**

5.3 You're the Decision Maker

Using Value-added Analysis

a. Based on the information in Exhibits 5.7 and 5.8 for PML, where would you start to evaluate potential improvements for existing activities?
b. Which activities, if any, would you recommend eliminating and why?

(Solutions begin on page 222.)

Identification of Process Improvement Opportunities

From the value-added analysis, the analysis team learned that the company was spending a large proportion of cost on low-value activities. Team members closely observed several activities, among them the activity '2.1 Set-up and quality control of computer-controlled machines', to find precisely where the company could make improvements. Improving this activity should result in quicker set-ups and fewer mistakes. The result of the analysis of activity 2.1 appears in Exhibit 5.9, which contains activity cost and duration measures, both before and after process improvements that were made possible by asking questions.

P M L

Exhibit 5.9 Improvement of Activity '2.1 Set-up and Quality Control of Computer-controlled Machines'

	A	B	C	D	E	F	G
1	Novelty Toys: Set-up activity cost and duration data for a typical month				Before process improvements	After process improvements	
2	Activity	Activity description	Activity cost	Customer value	Elapsed time (minutes)		Activity cost
3	2.1	Set up and quality control of computer-controlled machines					
4	2.1.1	Program machine	£1,500.00	5	450	420	£1,400.00
5	2.1.2	Perform quality control of batches produced					
6	2.1.2.1	Observe start of batch	£100.00	2	150	120	£80.00
7	2.1.2.2	Remove pieces and visually inspect	£300.00	2	450	300	£200.00
8	2.1.2.3	Recycle defective pieces	£200.00	1	300	30	£20.00
9	2.1.2.4	Place good pieces in inventory					
10	2.1.2.4.1	Trim excess plastic	£500.00	1	750	-	£ -
11	2.1.2.4.2	Place trimmings in recycle bags	£500.00	1	750	-	£ -
12	2.1.2.4.3	Place good piece in bin or box	£200.00	2	300	150	£100.00
13	2.1.2.5	Record defects for batch	£300.00	3	450	120	£80.00
14	2.1.3	Log out completed order	£100.00	2	150	-	£ -
15	2.1.4	Move completed order to warehouse	£800.00	4	1,200	900	£600.00
16	2.1.5	Register completed order in inventory	£100.00	2	150	-	£ -
17	2.1.6	End production run	£200.00	2	240	200	£166.67
18		Total activity cost	£4,800.00				£2,646.67
19		Cost savings from improvements	£2,153.33				
20		Percentage reduction in cost	-44.9%				

Asking the Question, 'Why?'

Anyone who has been around young children knows that they often repeatedly ask adults the question, 'Why?' This is a rational process of exploration that adults have rediscovered in seeking to find why the performance of non-value-added activities persists in organizations. Asking 'Why?' often enough (some believe that asking it five times in sequence is enough) most likely will identify the root cause of performing the activity. Identifying and changing that root cause almost always eliminates the need for a non-value-added activity and often leads to additional benefits because of linkages among processes.

The ABC team examined each of the activities used to make novelty toys. The results are in Exhibit 5.9. For example, in consultation with engineers, operators and the mould supplier, the analysis team asked why employees do such things as activity '2.1.2.4.1 Trim excess plastic' from moulded products. These reasons were identified successively after asking, 'Why?'

1. The product's appearance and function require the removal of the excess.
2. Under high-injection pressure, plastic leaks from the edges of the mould.
3. High pressure is required to mould the products properly.
4. The design of the moulds permits leakage.
5. The moulds are based on old designs.

The company could require the supplier to rework or replace current moulds with improved designs to completely eliminate the need to trim the excess plastic and recycle excess trim. This would reduce the labour time by 750 minutes and prevent loss of good material, which had been given to the recycler in exchange for its removal.

The team also examined record-keeping activities and persuaded Chad Norris, the vice president of manufacturing, to install a **bar-coding system**, which creates unique bar codes for each batch and order and allows the company to mark and track all batches and orders electronically.

This benefited the entire company by eliminating non-value-added record-keeping activities and the need to correct recording errors. The team expected the bar-coding system to create resource savings for virtually all of its product lines.

As a result of this and similar analyses, production teams were able to reduce the time of many processes while increasing product quality and customer service. PML was able to offer more customer value while consuming fewer resources and to transfer that knowledge to the production of all of its products.

Estimating the Cost of Saved Resources in Exhibit 5.9

Operators of computerized injection-moulding machines at PML, on average, earn £40 per hour (including benefits). Before process improvements, the cost of the activity '2.1.2.5 Record defects for batch' for a typical month was:

(450 minutes/60 minutes per hour) × £40 per hour = £300

After process improvements from improvement of moulds, the reduction of defective products, and bar coding, the cost of this activity was reduced to

(120 minutes/60 minutes per hour) × £40 per hour = £80

This represents a savings of £220 every month from just one sub-activity. PML's ABC team estimated that all of the improvements to this set-up activity would save £2,153 per month (cell C19 of Exhibit 5.9, or a savings of 44.9 per cent (cell C20) of the unimproved cost. The team could not find this much improvement in every production activity, but many could be improved substantially. The analysis team estimated that if PML implemented all of its process improvement recommendations, the company could reduce the manufacturing costs of each of its products by at least 25 per cent. This is time-consuming work, but the results in Exhibit 5.9 show that impressive cost reductions are possible from asking deceptively simple questions like 'Why?'

Implementation of Activity-based Costing and Management

LO 7
Understand how to implement ABC and ABM.

Activity-based costing and activity-based management offer feasible ways to evaluate and improve process efficiency, and the resulting benefits could well exceed the costs of implementation. Remember that ABC improves the accuracy of product costs given current processes.[7] ABM, however, identifies opportunities for improving processes, which should result in more customer value at lower cost. Thus, although not all organizations might need more accurate product costs, most could benefit from process improvements.

Some ABC critics have faulted it for generating, in some cases, product costs that are not materially different from traditional, functional costs. They argue, therefore, that ABC is too expensive for the benefits it offers. These same critics, however, usually do not consider the benefits of extending ABC to ABM and making significant process improvements. Some ABM advocates argue that ABC product costs are merely a by-product of ABM. The resulting process improvement efforts can be much more important to the organization's long-term success than knowing current product costs accurately. Activity-based techniques are conceptually appealing, but they are not trivial to implement.

Observers of ABC and ABM implementation have identified a number of factors that appear to influence whether it will be successful or unsuccessful. It appears that not all companies that have considered ABC or ABM have implemented it fully or successfully. Some firms have tried ABC and apparently have found that the cost to implement ABC alone exceeded the expected benefits.

Should All Organizations Adopt ABC and ABM?

It seems intuitive that companies facing the most price competition are the most eager to consider ABC and ABM as ways to improve the accuracy of their costs, identify the most profitable products, and identify opportunities for process improvement. Also, firms that produce many different, complex products from common facilities might obtain more benefits from ABC than firms that have simpler processes and product offerings.

Not surprisingly, ABC applications began in manufacturing firms facing global competition in industries such as electronics, machinery, construction equipment and automobile manufacturing. These industries also have pioneered ABM as a way to improve processes and profitability. As service and regulated firms have been exposed to more competition, they also have implemented ABC and ABM. Many recent applications have been in the administrative departments, such as purchasing, finance, administration and distribution in all types of organizations. Although not all firms have adopted or will adopt ABC or ABM, these methods appear to have had a lasting impact on cost management practices, particularly in multi-product firms facing intense price competition.

Can You Be Sure that ABC and ABM Will Be Successful?

No, but one thing is clear from the experiences of many ABC and ABM implementations: spending significant effort to plan the project is crucial, even before the first item of data is collected. Most of the success of ABC or ABM can be attributed to good planning. Major planning issues, which we discuss in more detail, include:

- Scope of the ABC/ABM project
- Resources to plan and implement the project
- Resistance to change
- Information to be gathered
- Analysis team's responsibility for information analysis and decision making.

Scope of the ABC/ABM Project

A small pilot project, which has a high chance for success, is a prudent way to introduce ABC or ABM to an organization. A **pilot project** is a limited-scope project intended to be a small-scale model of a larger, possibly system-wide project. A general-use, or system-wide project that has not been pilot-tested has less hope of succeeding because the organization's complexities will overwhelm the learning and development that must take place first. Management must also anticipate the linkages across departments, groups and processes as well as the data-gathering and reporting requirements of a full-scale implementation.

Resources Necessary

Any ABC or ABM project is a significant undertaking that requires sufficient management commitment, personnel and time, and technology resources.

Management commitment

Unless management is committed to the effort and to implementing the (credible) pilot project recommendations, ABC or ABM is unlikely to have a significant benefit for the organization. Analysts must educate top managers to appreciate the benefits and costs of ABC/ABM. The challenge for analysts is to communicate clearly and effectively what ABC/ABM can and cannot be expected to do. Overselling ABC or ABM as the cure for all of an organization's business problems will lead to disappointment. ABC/ABM are valuable diagnostic and decision-making aids, but they do not replace good decision-making or motivated employees.

Personnel and time

Even pilot ABC/ABM projects require a three- to four-person cross-functional team and at least four to six months of full-time effort. Starving the project limits the team to considering only a few activities and might require it to take planning and data-analysis shortcuts that will lessen the confidence in its recommendations.

Technology resources

Spreadsheet technology (as used throughout this book) is indispensible for pilot projects and applications in small companies, but this small-scale technology can be clumsy to use as a system for large organizations. If the intent is to develop a large ABC/ABM system, most consultants argue that it is most efficient to begin with existing commercial software rather than develop in-house software that will be difficult to create and maintain. Consultants might be biased in this regard because, after all, selling their services and products is their business. Real-world evidence indicates that successful ABC implementation does not depend greatly on using either commercial software or consultants.

Resistance to Change

ABC and ABM analyses often indicate opportunities for dramatic changes in organizations. Believing that everyone in the organization will agree with the need for the analyses, or the recommendations that follow, to revise processes is a mistake. Fear, distrust and cynicism, which should be expected when jobs are affected, could motivate some of this resistance.

Preventing resistance to change

Progressive organizations prevent or minimize resistance to change by (1) education and training, (2) widespread sponsorship and participation, and (3) incentives to encourage and reward change. Therefore, advance work is necessary to prepare personnel at all levels of the organization for the analysis and changes that probably will result. It seems obvious, for example, that gaining affected employees' full participation will be difficult if they believe that ABC/ABM places their jobs in jeopardy (i.e., identifies them as non-value-added personnel).

One bottom-up approach is to educate employees about the competitive necessity of ABC/ABM, give them a voice and influence in the analysis, and assure them that they will have meaningful jobs in the redesigned organization. The alternative is to implement a top-down approach, using a team or a consultant to devise the solution and impose it on the organization. One should expect more resistance to change in this approach, but a shorter development phase.

In some organizations, employees might be suspicious of the advertised benefits of ABM because management has a track record of trying the latest 'good idea' without considering its effect on people. Employees in these organizations might regard ABM as just another management fad and, if they resist long enough, the company will replace it with yet another attempt to change processes. In this situation, a pilot project that demonstrates objectively to suspicious employees what ABM can do might be imperative.

Effects of culture

Companies with culturally diverse employees should be especially sensitive to different attitudes about the roles of individuals versus groups in promoting and accepting changes such as ABC and ABM. UK and US companies often have been criticized for assuming that their management approaches will translate naturally to other cultures. For example, a bottom-up approach might not work at all in a culture where employees regard criticizing existing processes as disloyal to their managers and the company. There is much to learn about implementing ABC and ABM in international companies and those with employees from different cultures.[8]

Information to Be Gathered

ABC and ABM require information that is not normally available from an organization's accounting system. Observations, interviews or surveys of the organization's employees provide the needed information. It is important to realize that perfect accuracy is neither attainable nor desirable because the costs to obtain perfect information are prohibitive. Nonetheless, concerns about obtaining accurate activity and resource information lead many organizations to hire either consultants or experienced employees to conduct this part of the analysis.

Middle managers and support staff could resist changes that require them to give up power and control. For example, one PML recommendation, which is common at other companies, was that production teams should be able to perform minor repairs and adjustments to equipment without having to wait for an engineer or technician. At first, engineers and technicians resisted because they feared that they would first train employees to make the repairs and adjustments and then watch their own jobs disappear. PML overcame their resistance by redesigning engineers' and technicians' jobs to focus on improving designs and preventing equipment problems rather than on correcting designs and problems afterward.

Analysis Team's Responsibility for Information Analysis and Decision Making

Although top managers ultimately have the responsibility for authorizing and effecting major changes, the study team is best prepared to analyse the data and make recommendations for several reasons. First, the team is intimately familiar with the data, their strengths and their weaknesses. Second, empowering and requiring the team to make recommendations gives them control and accountability for the entire project and motivates them to gather and analyse the data carefully and consider a wide range of opportunities for change.

Whether the team should make its recommendations directly to top management depends on the organization's culture and needs. In some organizations, it could be important for the team to solicit and receive input from many individuals and departments before it issues its final recommendations to management. This allows the team to obtain even more information and to 'float trial balloons' to gauge the effectiveness of its proposals. In other organizations, however, top management might need to impose major changes and be more involved in developing recommendations for change. In the case of PML, top management strongly encouraged the ABM analysis because they saw it as an effective way to support decisions about whether to continue current product lines that are tied closely to current customers.

PML's Customer Decisions

Recall that the profitability analysis in Exhibit 5.5 provided an estimate of future customer profit margins based on PML's current processes. PML's ABC team realized that although the first year's business with MegaBurger was profitable, the profits did not meet the company's target return on sales of 40 per cent before unassigned administrative costs. Target costing analysis in Exhibit 5.6 quantified the cost savings that were needed to achieve the required return. Soon after the ABC/ABM team presented its analyses of the current production and administrative processes used to fulfil the MegaBurger contract, PML's executive committee met to decide whether to bid on a contract renewal. The following is a transcript from this meeting with Melanie Fairchild (CEO), Alex Lewis (CFO and team leader), Chad Norris (VP of Manufacturing), and Michele Chia (VP of Marketing).

Fairchild: Welcome, everyone. I know we are concerned about hitting the 40 per cent target on the MegaBurger business. What is our plan of attack?

Lewis: Our team has done a tremendous amount of work to identify areas for potential cost savings. Its target-cost analysis shows that a 24.75 per cent decrease in costs is necessary to meet the 40 per cent return on sales target. The team believes that this is a difficult but attainable goal. One example of potential savings is in our injection-moulding process. We can streamline the process and redesign the moulds currently used to reduce the need for trimming the products as they come out of the mould. We estimate a 45 per cent cost savings in this activity, and we believe that we can find similar savings elsewhere.

Norris: Our manufacturing employees agree that many processes can be improved in addition to the moulds that Alex just mentioned. The manufacturing department is now offering a cash bonus to all employees who make a suggestion for a process improvement that is ultimately implemented. Not surprisingly, we have been flooded with ideas, some of which will reduce costs substantially.

Chia: Based on this information, I believe we have the capability to reach the 40 per cent return-on-sales target. I recommend that we move forward with MegaBurger. I am eager to begin the contract negotiations.

Fairchild: I agree. Good work everyone! Based on your efforts, I think we can look forward to working with MegaBurger for several years and to hitting our target of 40 per cent return on sales as soon as possible. Let's go on this. Now tell me about plans for the container business with BigMart.

Lewis: I know this is a hard decision, but my recommendation is to divest ourselves of this business. The product still has a life, perhaps, but not with us. Our analysis shows that it cannot carry its weight, even before considering administrative costs.

Norris: I see the numbers, too, and I cannot dispute them. However, I insist that we treat our long-time employees well; after all, they have grown up with this business. We cannot just shutter that part of the plant and bid them adieu.

Fairchild: Of course, we cannot simply cut them away. Chad and Alex, I would like you to analyse whether we can sell that part of the business to a private-equity group and those employees in a manner that is favourable to them, but is no more costly to us than if we paid severance costs. Key issues are whether we really will save the costs you have assigned to this business and whether we can redeploy those costs to grow our more profitable businesses. Let's do nothing and signal nothing to employees until we have more complete information.

Chapter Summary

ABC provides important information about the uses of resources given current processes but stops short of identifying opportunities for decreasing costs and increasing value. Activity-based management (ABM) uses ABC information and perceived customer values to improve the organization's efficiency and consequently create more value at lower cost. Organizations should redesign processes to reduce or eliminate activities that add no value and either save those resources or reapply them to value-added activities. Implementing ABM (and ABC) could be difficult, but prior planning is essential to doing so effectively. Factors to be considered include the project's scope, necessary resources, resistance to change, information to be gathered, and the analysis team's responsibilities for information analysis and decision making.

Key Terms

For each term's definition, refer to the indicated page, or turn to the glossary at the end of the text.

activity-based management (ABM), 198
bar-coding systems, 204
cost reduction target, 197
currently feasible cost, 197
customer-level costs, 188
customer profitability analysis, 188
customer relations management, 188
customer value, 188
non-value-added activities, 198
pilot project, 206
risks, 201
selling costs, 192
target cost, 196
value-added activities, 198

Review Questions are mostly written at a ***basic*** *level; Critical Analysis questions and Exercises are* ***intermediate****, and Problems and Cases are* ***advanced****.*

Review Questions

5.1 What do ABC and ABM have in common, and how do they differ?

5.2 How can ABC and target costing be used together to motivate ABM?

5.3 How are product-line and customer profitability measures similar and different?

5.4 Describe how customer profitability analysis can be related to ABC and ABM.

5.5 Describe typical qualitative factors to consider when evaluating alternatives to improve customer profitability.

5.6 What are alternatives to reducing process costs to meet target costs?

5.7 What are examples of value-added and non-value-added activities?

5.8 What is the relationship between non-value-added activities and waste?

5.9 Does eliminating non-value-added activities necessarily reduce cost and waste?

5.10 What are the questions to ask to determine whether an activity adds customer value?

5.11 Why might individuals resist ABM?

5.12 Must ABM information be 100 per cent accurate to be useful? Explain.

Critical Analysis

5.13 Is it fair to assume that all individuals in an organization welcome the opportunity to improve processes by eliminating non-value-added activities? Explain.

5.14 A business writer praised a major e-commerce supplier for its 'extraordinary commitments to product and service innovation and customer service'. The article argued that these commitments are paying off by citing as proof higher than average contribution margins and growth in sales over the past three years. Evaluate this evidence of a pay-off from R&D and customer service expenditures.

5.15 A global shipping company segments customers into 'good', 'bad', and 'ugly' categories. It gives preferential treatment to good customers, who spend much and demand little service or marketing; charges higher shipping charges to bad customers, who spend little but are expensive to serve; and discourages ugly customers, who spend little with poor prospects of increases, from using its services. Is this practice of segmenting and differential pricing evidence of illegal or unethical behaviour? Explain.

5.16 At your company's monthly marketing strategy meeting, the director of customer satisfaction happily reports that 80 per cent of customers are at least 'satisfied' and half of those are 'delighted' with the company's products and services. This is good news because delighted customers are much more likely to be repeat customers. The director argues that with effort, it is possible to reach a customer satisfaction level of 90 per cent by focusing on the 20 per cent who are dissatisfied. Furthermore, a 50 per cent overall delighted rating is within reach. Everyone turns to you for approval to attempt to achieve these higher goals. What is your response?

5.17 'The cost of repairing all these defective products is killing us. We should hire more highly qualified employees who won't make so many mistakes and who can figure out how to improve our processes so that mistakes are less likely'. Write a memo explaining the trade-offs involved with this recommendation.

5.18 'Come on, be serious. Some of these activities that you have identified as non-value-added just cannot be eliminated. We have to send monthly reports to corporate headquarters, and we need to file tax return information quarterly. This ABM analysis doesn't seem to work in the real world'. Respond to this comment.

5.19 Your company wants to downsize its employment by 25 per cent, but it cannot unilaterally dismiss employees who are performing well. The company is considering whether to offer a buyout plan to its 2,000 workers. What are the risks, trade-offs and implications associated with this decision to downsize the workforce?

5.20 Your boss sent the following e-mail this morning: 'Today I am announcing a 10 per cent reduction in spending in every department, effective immediately. We must improve profitability, and this is the quickest way to improve the bottom line. I assure you that every department will share the pain equally. I am not asking anyone to work harder, but all of us will have to work smarter'. Explain why the announced across-the-board cuts in resource spending might not improve but actually worsen profitability.

Exercises

Exercise 5.21 [LO 2] Customer Profitability

British Motors sells two products, the Panthera, a sports car, and the Wanderer, an off-road vehicle, to two types of customers, urban and rural. Using the following information, prepare a customer profitability statement:

British Motors product profitability	Total	Panthera	Wanderer
Contribution margin ratio	44.44%	40.0%	50.0%
Sales revenues	£36,000,000	£20,000,000	£16,000,000
Customer sales to:			
Sales of:		Urban	Rural
Pantheras	100%	80%	20%
Wanderers	100%	30%	70%
Operating costs traced to customers	£8,500,000	£5,000,000	£3,500,000

Exercise 5.22 [LO 2] Return on Customer Sales

Refer to Exercise 5.21. British Motors desires to increase its total return on sales to 30 per cent. What amount of target cost reduction is required to meet this profitability target at the same level of sales?

Exercise 5.23 [LO 2] Customer Profitability

Precision Aerosol sells two products, spray paint and spray adhesive, to two types of customers, art supply stores and hardware stores. Using the following information, prepare a customer profitability statement:

Precision Aerosol product profitability	Total	Paint	Adhesive
Contribution margin ratio		70.0%	60.0%
Sales revenue	$20,000,000	$11,000,000	$9,000,000
Customer sales to:			
Sales of:		Art	Hardware
Spray paint	100%	30%	70%
Spray adhesive	100%	50%	50%
Operating costs traced to customers	$6,000,000	$2,000,000	$4,000,000

Exercise 5.24 [LO 2] Return on Customer Sales

Refer to Exercise 5.23. Precision Aerosol desires to increase its return on sales to 40 per cent. What amount of target cost reduction is required to meet this profitability target at the same level of sales?

Exercise 5.25 [LO 2] Customer-level Cost

Melbourne Enterprises (ME) wishes to trace its distribution costs to each of its four customer types, alpha, beta, gamma and delta. ME delivers some shipments itself and outsources the delivery of others. Use the following information to estimate distribution costs per customer:

ME customer delivery	Total	Alpha	Beta	Gamma	Delta
Shipments per year	190,000	60,000	35,000	75,000	20,000
Delivered by ME		80%	90%	25%	80%
Outsourced delivery		20%	10%	75%	20%
ME distribution costs	$8,000,000				
Outsourced shipment costs	500,000				
Total distribution costs	$8,500,000				

Exercise 5.26 [LO 2] Customer-level Costs

Vis à Vis Promotions (VVP) is interested in tracing its promotion design costs to each of its three major customer types, groceries, drug stores and discount stores. VVP designs some promotions itself and outsources the other designs. Use the following information to estimate promotion design costs per customer:

VVP Customer Designs	Total	Groceries	Drug stores	Discount stores
Promotions per year	450	100	200	150
Designed by VVP		75%	80%	90%
Outsourced design		25%	20%	10%
VVP design costs	€200,000			
Outsourced design costs	40,000			
Total design costs by customer	€240,000			

Exercise 5.27 [LO 3] Target Costing and ABC

Review the information in Exhibits 5.2 and 5.6 for PML. Assume that the sales price of £25 per unit remains the same but that the total units to be sold each month increases to 25,000 (from the original proposal of 20,000 units). (Assume that the only costs that will change are the costs driven by unit-level activities.)

Required

How much will this impact the monthly cost-reduction target?

a. In monetary terms?
b. As a percentage of currently feasible costs?

Exercise 5.28 [LO 3] Target Costing and ABC

Review the information in Exhibits 5.2 and 5.6 for PML. Assume that the total number of units to be sold each month remains the same but that the sales price increases to £30 per unit (from the original sales price of £25 per unit).

Required

How much will this impact the monthly cost-reduction target

a. In monetary terms?
b. As a percentage of currently feasible costs?

Exercise 5.29 [LO 3] Target Costing and ABC

Review the information in Exhibits 5.2 and 5.6 for PML. After further discussion, PML's management is willing to lower the required return on sales (ROS) to 30 per cent (from the original 40 per cent).

Required

How much will this impact the monthly cost-reduction target

a. In monetary terms?
b. As a percentage of currently feasible costs?

Problems

Problem 5.30 [LO 4,5] Activity and Value-added Analyses

Beständigkeit KGaA, an insurer of small businesses in Germany, has a claims-processing department that receives, processes and refers casualty and property loss claims to insurance adjusters for resolution. Approximately half of the claims arrive by standard mail; the other half are split evenly between e-mail and claims phoned in by policyholders.

Required

a. The following activities and sub-activities of Beständigkeit's claims process are not in a logical order. Arrange them into a numbered, logical sequence or process (e.g., 1.0, 1.1, . . ., 2.0, 2.1, . . .).

Claims-processing activity	Claims-processing sub-activity	Annual time (hours)
Receive claims	Take phone call	1,000
Check information	Read e-mail	400
Analyse claim	Sort e-mail by claim type	100
Forward claim to adjuster	Open mail	600
	Sort mail by claim type	300
	Refer phone call by claim type	800
	Verify completeness of information on written claim	700
	Compare coverage in policy to casualty or loss claim	800
	Log in claim	600
	Verify accuracy of policy information on written claim	1,000
	Return incorrect claims to policyholders	500
	Review incorrect claims with policyholders	500
	File multiple copies of claims	1,200
	Send claim and policy copy to adjuster	400
	Package copy of claim and policy for shipment to adjuster	600
	Log out claim	500

Problem 5.31 [LO 2, 3] Customer-level Costs and Profitability

Metropole Kreditlinie AG (MK) wishes to trace its service costs to each customer type, rated A, B or C. 'A' customers are believed to be the most profitable, 'B' customers might become profitable, and 'C' customers are unprofitable. MK offers commercial loans, consumer loans and credit cards. Its customer representatives sell services and manage customer accounts. In addition, a staff and a facility support marketing, promotions and transactions for all customers at an annual cost of €800,000.

Required

a. Use the following additional information to trace service costs to customers:

MK service cost information	Total	A	B	C
Number of customers	6,500	3,000	2,500	1,000
Customer representatives	32	15	12	5

Average salary/year		€40,000	€30,000	€25,000
Support service staff effort	100%	60%	30%	10%
Support service staff cost	$800,000			

Problem 5.32 [LO 2, 3] Customer Profitability

FilmStroom.nl provides videos online that customers download for a fee. The company segments its customers into premium members, who make numerous downloads, and standard members, who make occasional downloads. It offers premium members a 10 per cent discount on the cost of downloads but requires standard members to pay full price. FilmStroom.nl devotes one full-time customer representative per 1,000 premium members and one per 10,000 standard members. Customer representatives receive salaries and a bonus of one tenth of 1 per cent of customer revenue (after 10 per cent discount, if applicable). FilmStroom.nl estimates that it spends three times as much on total promotions for premium members to encourage their loyalty. General and administrative cost, which is not traced to customers, is €3,000,000 per year.

Customer service resources	Total	Premium	Standard
Number of customers	200,000	50,000	150,000
Average sales salary/year		€30,000	€30,000
Promotion costs	€2,400,000		
Average revenue per customer (before discount)	€200	€50	

Required

Build a spreadsheet to estimate FilmStroom.nl's profitability for each category of customer and for the entire company.

Problem 5.33 [LO 2, 3] Customer Profitability

Lightwave Manufacturing Assembly SA provides outsourced manufacturing assembly for electronic products companies. It currently has two major customers, Bell and Toshi, for which Lightwave assembles and delivers products on a just-in-time basis. Lightwave incurs annual warehousing and delivery costs solely to serve its customers. Warehousing costs are found to be proportional to the number of orders. Half of annual general and administrative costs are related to processing and managing customer orders; the remainder is not traced to customers.

Customer and administrative resources	Total	Bell	Toshi
Annual number of orders	3,500	2,000	1,500
Average cost of goods sold per order		€10,000	€5,000
Order price mark-up		60%	60%
Average deliveries per order		5	12
Warehousing costs per year	€800,000		
Delivery costs per year	5,000,000		
General administrative costs	2,000,000		

Required

Build a spreadsheet to calculate Lightwave's profitability for each customer and for the entire company.

Problem 5.34 [LO 3] Activity-based Costing and Target Costing

Refer to the information in and format of Exhibits 5.2 and 5.6. PML is considering producing one product similar to the MegaBurger novelty toys but for another customer. It will ship the product to the customer immediately upon completion. The estimates for this new product follow. Assume that PML can add capacity as needed at costs comparable to those in Exhibits 5.2 and 5.6. PML requires a 30 per cent return on sales for new business.

Number of units per month	16,000
Sales price per unit	£20
Product life	3 years
1. Unit-level costs	
1.1 Acquire and use materials	16,000 units per month; £12 per unit
2. Batch-level costs	
2.1 Set up manually controlled machines	8 batches per month; £500 per batch
3. Product-level costs	
3.1 Design and manufacture moulds	3 moulds for the 1 product (to last 3 years); £4,000 per mould per month
3.2 Use manually controlled injection-moulding machines	£40,000 per month
4. Customer-level costs	
4.1 Consult with customers	8 consultations per month, £200 each
4.2 Provide warehousing for customers	150 cubic metres, £5 per cubic metre
5. Facility-level costs	
5.1 Manage workers	£5,000 per month
5.2 Use building space	£10,000 per month

Required

a. Build a spreadsheet to calculate the monetary and percentage target-cost reduction for the three-year life of the new product.

b. As the manager responsible for making the decision, would you recommend that the company produce this product? Explain.

Problem 5.35 [LO 4, 5] Value-added Analysis

You have been hired as a consultant for Elias Svensson, whose company designs websites. Svensson has asked for your advice in assessing customers' perceptions of the value of its products. You collect the following information about Svensson's design of a website for a small co-op grocery store. (Monetary units given in Swedish kronor, kr.)

Number	Activity description	Cost	Value (5 = highest value)
1	Marketing and design		
1.1	Prepare contract with the customer (the grocery store)	24,000 kr	4
1.2	Perform marketing research for customer	54,000	5
1.3	Svensson purchases hardware, software, and infrastructure for the customer's site	30,000	4
1.4	Program and construct site	60,000	5
1.5	Svensson performs payroll services, personnel administration, and other management functions for itself	90,000	2
1.6	Svensson provides office space for its workers	30,000	1

Required

a. Explain the sources of the customer values. Do you agree with all of the customer values? Why or why not?

b. Create a table similar to Exhibit 5.8 for these activities, and prepare a memo to Svensson's management summarizing your results.

Problem 5.36 [LO 2-4] Activity-based Management and Process Improvements

Felicidad Medina is an entrepreneur considering starting a property management business in the busy resort town of Torremolinos, Spain. She intends to subcontract her services through Propiedades Costa del Sol (PCD), a large existing company that manages the majority of the area's vacation rentals. She will have to pay PCD a monthly subcontractor's fee of €40 per customer. The current competitive price in the area is €200 per month, and she currently generates a 20 per cent (pre-tax) return on sales in her other businesses. She expects customer replacement of 10 per cent per month (10 per cent of customers will leave to be replaced by an equal number of new customers). She has estimated the following activities as necessary to operate the business for an estimated 50 customers.

Activity	Cost
Advertising and promotion	€1,600 per month
Bill collecting	1,200 per month
Initial deep-clean	120 per new customer
Property assessment	20 per new customer
Subcontractor's fee	40 per customer per month
Building occupancy	1,400 per month
Equipment utilization	1,500 per month
Invoicing and billing	10 per customer per month
Business planning and analysis	1,100 per month

Required

Form small groups to respond to the following items. Build a spreadsheet to solve requirements (a) and (b).

a. Is this proposed business expected to meet Medina's financial goal of achieving a 20 per cent return on sales? What, if any, cost reductions are necessary?

b. Prepare a short presentation outlining process improvements you would recommend to make the business more profitable.

Problem 5.37 [LO 2, 6] ABM and Process Improvements

St Bridget's Hospital, Dublin is expanding facilities at its Tallaght campus. St Bridget's plans to hire 25 additional technical staff. The process to hire and train a new technical member of staff (e.g., a laboratory or clinic technician) typically involves at least six individuals: the budget director, human resources (HR) director, HR analyst, laboratory/clinic director and new and existing technicians. All of these individuals are salaried. Normal annual salaries are as follows:

- Budget director €86,400
- HR director 72,960
- HR analyst 48,000
- Laboratory/Clinic director 96,000
- Laboratory/Clinic technician 51,840

Assume that all individuals normally work a 40-hour week, 48 weeks per year. An activity analysis (performed by the budget director) identified the following activities and normal efforts applied by each individual to the activities for recruiting and hiring one new technical staffmember (see the table below). During orientation and training existing laboratory and clinic technicians will train new staff for 40 hours. All new staff will be paid at the regular technician rate during this time. Note that hiring typically involves filling only one or two positions at a time, and hiring 25 in a short period is unusual.

Recruiting activities (per new employee)		
Recruiting and hiring activity	Personnel	Hours
1. Review need to open or retain position	HR director	4
	Budget director	2

2. Revise job description	HR analyst	5
3. Assess labour trends and compensation	HR director	2
	Budget director	1
	HR analyst	4
4. Prepare and post job advertisement	HR analyst	6
5. Screen applications, verify credentials	HR analyst	4
6. Schedule personal interviews	HR analyst	2
7. Conduct personal interviews	Lab/Clinic director	1
	Lab/Clinic technician	2
	HR director	1
8. Select finalist and make offer	Lab/Clinic director	1
	HR director	1
9. Process new employee	HR analyst	2
10. Orientation and training for new employee	HR analyst	4
	Lab/Clinic director	2
Existing	Lab/Clinic technician	40
New	Lab/Clinic technician	40
Total hours		124
11. Relocation expenses for new employee		€1,000

Required

a. Compute the activity-based costs to recruit and hire one new laboratory technician and the total cost of hiring 25 new technicians.

b. Should the cost of recruiting and hiring 25 technical staff be equal to 25 times the cost to recruit one? If not, explain and recommend how recruiting for 25 technical staff could be made less costly.

c. If St Bridget's did not recruit and hire any new technical staff, how much of the recruiting activity costs could be saved? Explain.

d. Laboratory and clinic customers are physicians, nurses and patients. Which of these recruiting activities do you think would be rated by them as 'high value' or 'low value' activities? That is, which activities are most or least likely to affect the quality of services they receive? Explain your choices.

e. How much cost in total could be saved if recruiting could be redesigned to eliminate all 'low value' activities?

Bonus: use Excel's Pivot Table to answer part e.

Cases

Case 5.38 [LO 5, 6] Re-engineering the Accounting Function

An alternative to using ABM to identify opportunities for process improvement is to use benchmarking information to identify where an organization falls short of competitors and best practices. At 2 per cent of sales, Cummins Engine's overall accounting costs were twice as high as companies with world-class accounting functions, and the company was determined to improve. More detailed benchmarking information revealed that accounts payable costs and payroll costs were four and three times higher, respectively, than best practices. These areas seemed to offer the opportunity for great improvement. Cummins created a cross-functional team to analyse these transaction processes and make recommendations for improvement that would increase the quality of transaction processing and achieve best-practice costs (i.e., cost reductions of 75 per cent).

Cummins Engine's top management was fully committed to the project. It provided resources to the project team that enabled it to educate Cummins' finance and operating personnel around the world about the project's methods and objectives. Management also committed to no forced lay-offs of personnel whose jobs would be affected by resulting process changes.

In the early part of the project (the 'baseline' phase), the team recognized that accounts payable, cash disbursement, and procurement processes should be integrated and located at a single site rather than at 50 sites within the United States alone, and that new software and hardware would be required. The team began with a pilot study, however, so that it could understand the complexities of the project before launching a worldwide implementation. The pilot study allowed the team to identify tangible objectives for the new system that included:

- Electronic data interchange (EDI)
- Linkage between procurement, accounts payable, and cash disbursement
- Use of client-server technology
- Outsourcing of non-value-added activities such as cheque printing
- Improvement of process quality measures involving statistical quality-control techniques
- Software compatible with Cummins' data architecture at a competitive price and with a user-friendly graphical interface.

Project implementation was phased in over a three-year period with inflexible target dates for each phase and continuous communication with affected finance and operating personnel. The workforce in accounts payable was reduced by 80 per cent, costs reached best-practice levels and errors were reduced dramatically. (The workforce reduction occurred through attrition, assigning employees to other areas, and early retirement plans.)

Required

Form small groups to prepare a report that answers the following questions:

a. What are the differences between the activity-based management approach and the benchmarking approach used by Cummins Engine to identify opportunities for process improvement? What are the relative advantages and disadvantages of the benchmarking approach to identifying opportunities?
b. What interests, skills and knowledge would be required for members of a project team such as the one at Cummins to analyse accounts payable?
c. What are specific steps that Cummins Engine took to ensure the success of the accounts payable project?
d. Does the Cummins project appear to be perfect, or can you recommend improvement(s) and/or identify area(s) of concern if you were to copy this approach at another organization?

[Adapted from Compton et al. (1998).]

Case 5.39 [LO 2, 6] Effects of Changing Cost Drivers

TransGlobe Airways (TGA) is an embattled US airline fighting to gain market share from its much larger, traditional competitors, such as United Airlines, Delta and American Airlines, as well as successful discount airlines such as Southwest Airlines. TGA's current share of the US market is approximately 5 per cent. The executive vice president of marketing, Jack Moore, believes that TGA must improve its customer satisfaction before it can improve its competitiveness. Surveys of TGA's customers indicate that they are most dissatisfied with these areas:

- In-flight meal quality
- Attitudes of ticket counter and in-flight personnel
- Storage space for carry-on luggage
- Legroom in the economy sections of TGA's airplanes
- Charges for movies and drinks on long flights
- First-class seating availability for frequent fliers who want to upgrade from economy.

In an executive committee meeting, Moore insists that TGA must begin immediately to retrain personnel to interact well with customers, offer better meals and free movies, and begin remodelling planes to increase first-class seating, legroom in economy and storage space for carry-on luggage. He is confident that these measures will increase market share dramatically and lead to future profitability.

You are a cost management analyst with TGA whom the chief financial officer invited to attend this executive committee meeting and then asked to prepare estimates of the impacts of making changes to

TGA's structural cost drivers. You recall reading a recent *Wall Street Journal* article indicating that the most important reasons business travellers choose one airline over another are ticket prices and flight schedules.

Required

a. Prepare a brief, narrative analysis of the possible impacts of these structural changes on customer satisfaction, market share and profitability.
b. Make alternative recommendations for improving TGA's profitability.

Case 5.40 [LO 5, 6] Banking Processes

Ogden Bank has been in the consumer-lending business for more than 100 years. Competitors recently have taken a considerable portion of its market share. In addition, its remaining customers have complained that the bank's loan-approval process is too slow and that finding out the status of a loan application is difficult. The traditional procedure for consumer loan approval is summarized here:

- A loan applicant picks up a standard loan application at the bank, completes it, and mails it to the bank. A mail clerk delivers applications along with regular mail.
- The loan application is delivered to a loan-processing clerk, who logs it in, attaches a routing/status form to the front page, and files it in a folder of outstanding loan applications. At the end of the day or when the folder is full, the clerk delivers the contents to a credit analyst.
- The credit analyst enters data from the application into a computer program, records the results on the status form, and sends the application through interoffice mail to a consumer-lending specialist.
- The consumer-lending specialist approves or rejects the loan application and customizes the loan if necessary according to the particular applicant's needs. From here, all applications go to a pricing specialist via interoffice mail.
- The pricing specialist determines the appropriate interest rate to charge approved applicants by using a computer program written for this purpose. The rate is recorded on the status form of approved applications, which are forwarded to another clerical group.
- These clerks prepare letters informing applicants of the bank's decisions along with a note stating the loan terms of approved applications.
- After the legal department reviews all of this material, clerks mail the bank's decision to the applicants along with a promissory note to be signed and returned to those who are approved.

This process takes four weeks on average, during which time applicants could find alternative financing but could almost never determine the status of their application with Ogden Bank. The bank has engaged you to analyse its loan approval process and make recommendations for improvement.

Required

a. Prepare a brief memo explaining how Ogden Bank could benefit from using ABM and what steps and resources would be necessary to successfully implement it.
b. Suggest and explain at least three ways in which Ogden Bank could reduce the cycle time of its loan application process.
c. Suggest and explain at least three ways in which Ogden Bank could improve its communication, internally and externally, about its processes and possible process changes.
d. What are the potential risks involved in the streamlining of the loan application system?

[CMA adapted]

Case 5.41 [LO 1-3] Customer Profitability

Zürcher Privatbank, AG recently spent CHF500,000 to develop and implement a customer profitability analysis system that calculates the monthly profitability of each of its 40,000 customers. This system also maintains extensive customer-level information about banking and demographic history. Zürcher Privatbank offers the following services to its customers. (Monetary values given in Swiss francs, CHF.)

Note: Many customers use multiple services.

Service	Average annual profit per account
Current account	CHF 1,000
Savings account	80
Safety deposit	40
Certificate of deposit account	600
Consumer loan	800
Home equity line of credit	1,000

Zürcher Privatbank plans to use its customer profitability information to identify opportunities to market and cross-sell other services, such as home equity lines of credit, to current and savings account customers. In small groups, prepare a report or presentation that answers the following requirements.

Required

a. Explain what information you want from the customer profitability analysis system to identify current and savings account customers most likely to be interested in other banking services.

b. Consider the following two current account customers with equal and above average profitability. Does selling a home equity loan to each have equal expected profitability? Explain.

Annual customer information	Ms Kasser	Mr Stockli
Profit from current account	CHF 110	CHF 110
Average current account balance	CHF 14,000	CHF 8,300
Number of cheques written	220	80
Number of ATM transactions	100	30
Number of returned cheques	0	3
Overdraft fees paid	0	2

Case 5.42 [LO 1-4] Customer Profitability Analysis

Innsbruck Treue Brokerage (ITB) offers online securities trading and other services, such as financial planning and portfolio management. It is considering following the lead of competitors that segment their customers and focus marketing efforts. ITB believes that its customers can be segmented by the equally important attributes of account balance, trading frequency and purchase of other services. These represent major uses of resources to serve customers and drivers of revenue. The following data are from a random sample of 30 ITB customers.

	Random sample of customers		
Customer	Account balance	Trades/Year	Other services
1	€29,396	135	0
2	85,679	30	1
3	11,027	41	6
4	50,512	31	0
5	20,960	164	13
6	17,674	13	11
7	18,026	10	3
8	32,546	49	11
9	13,738	172	4
10	4,370	20	2
11	42,881	135	1
12	23,988	38	8
13	35,950	24	6
14	26,398	12	0

15	28,470	11	19
16	42,749	92	0
17	604	14	1
18	54,789	120	2
19	86,367	171	17
20	22,192	3	1
21	17,517	40	8
22	72,023	171	3
23	23,609	52	5
24	25,076	8	1
25	65,984	59	16
26	50,003	107	4
27	897	6	0
28	3,455	47	10
29	51,743	138	9
30	31,791	30	3

Required

Complete the following in small groups.

a. Use this information to develop numerical scores for each customer attribute by classifying customers into no more than four categories within each attribute (e.g., scoring = 1, 2, 3, or 4). (*Hint:* Enter the data into a spreadsheet, such as Excel, and then plot each customer attribute and look for 'natural' cut-offs for categories. *Note:* This is somewhat subjective but critically important to this type of analysis. *Hint*: 'Cluster analysis' is potentially a more objective approach.)

b. Add individual attribute scores to obtain overall scores. Use overall scores to segment customers into no more than three categories (A = best, B = middle, and C = worst). You must judge where to make cut-offs here, too.

c. Express any concerns you have about this classification process. How can you improve it or validate it?

d. For each customer type (A, B and C), estimate for the entire customer population the percentage of each type, average account balance, average number of trades and average number of other services purchased. (*Hint:* This is easily done with Excel's Pivot Table function wizard [look under the Data menu].)

e. ITB charges customers for other services based on the extent and quality of services used. Interest on account balances and trading fees are the same for each customer type. Fill in the following table and estimate ITB's customer-level revenues.

Customer revenue data	A	B	C
Customer sample percentages	?	?	?
Customer population (1,000,000)	?	?	?
Average account balance	?	?	?
Average annual trades	?	?	?
Average other services	?	?	?
Account revenue (spread)	2%	2%	2%
Trading fee per trade	€3	€3	€3
Other fees per service	€200	€100	€50

f. Use this additional information to estimate ITB's uses of resources to manage each customer service. Intensity of service means that ITB uses three times as many service resources to provide 'other' services for A customers than for C customers.

Customer cost data		A	B	C
Intensity of service per unit of service:				
Account management per account		1	1	1
Trading management per trade		1	1	1
Other services management per service		3	2	1
General and administrative		3	2	1
Service costs:				
Account management	€250,000,000			
Trading management	310,000,000			
Other services management	440,000,000			
General and administrative	360,000,000			

g. Estimate overall and customer profitability.

ITB has identified two alternatives to improve its overall profitability:

1. Drop unprofitable customers; although this will lose those customers' margins, it will save 15 per cent of overall committed management costs.
2. Change fees to induce unprofitable customers to either leave or become more profitable and induce more customers to increase their revenue-generating activities. Marketing research indicates changes in the percentage of types of customers as follows. Other customer characteristics, service intensities and costs remain unchanged.

Customer revenue data	Total	A	B	C
Customer sample	100.0%	45.0%	50.0%	5.0%
Account revenue (spread)	NA	1.5%	2.0%	3.0%
Trading fee per trade	NA	€2.50	€3.00	€4.00
Other fees per service	NA	€180.00	€120.00	€150.00

h. Measure the profit impact of each alternative.
i. Prepare a report that makes and evaluates recommendations for profit improvement.

Solutions to You're the Decision Maker

5.1 Trade-offs between Accuracy and Timeliness, p. 196

a. The direct resources devoted to the fleet include the purchase and maintenance of the trucks, fuel and garage and office facilities as well as the salaries, including benefits, of the drivers, dispatchers and mechanics. Indirect resources likely include a percentage of marketing management, sales and administration, and general and administrative efforts. Before deciding whether to retain the fleet, PML should consider the value of its flexible response to customer orders supplied by the fleet and the company identity provided by its logo on the trucks.

b. To the extent that the other administrative work performed for different customers is diverse, the team's expedient measure misstates administration costs across customers. This seems dangerous because others will recognize this and worry that other expediencies are hidden in the analysis.

5.2 Using Target Costing, p. 197

a. The required higher price must yield a 40 per cent return on sales (ROS) given the currently feasible cost. This new total revenue can be computed as follows (solving for 'revenue'):

Revenue − (ROS% × Revenue) = Currently feasible cost

Inputting the known data:

Revenue – (0.40 × Revenue) = £350,680 (from Exhibit 5.3)
0.60 × Revenue = £350,680
Revenue = £350,680/0.60
Revenue = £584,467

Thus, the total annual revenue of £584,467 is required to make 40 per cent ROS given the currently feasible cost of £350,680. At 20,000 units per month, this equates to a £29.22 sales price per unit (versus the previous £25.00 sales price per unit in the original proposal).

If the alternative is to accept a lower ROS at MegaBurger's stated price, the equation is the same but solves for a different variable, ROS. The revenue of £500,000 appears in the information in Exhibit 5.3.

Revenue – (ROS × Revenue) = Currently feasible cost

Inputting the known data, and solving for ROS:

£ 500,000 – (ROS × 500,000) = £350,680
– (ROS × £500,000) = £350,680 – £500,000
(ROS × £500,000) = –350,680 + £500,000
ROS = (£500,000 – £350,680)/£340,000
ROS = 0.2986 = 29.86% (as shown in Exhibit 5.3)

MegaBurger is not likely to agree to pay a higher price for the product since it can choose from other suppliers. Accepting a lower ROS could be feasible in the short run to get the business, but if PML really believes that a 40 per cent return on sales is appropriate, it should agree to a lower ROS only if it can be sure that it can improve processes sufficiently and quickly to get to a 40 per cent ROS.

b. If products are sufficiently similar and will use similar processes, the cost-driver rates probably can be used at least as starting points for estimating the costs of new products. PML's ABC team apparently compared the attributes of the new product with those of existing products and modified cost-driver rates as necessary. An organization should not blindly apply cost-driver rates from current products and processes, but they can provide a valid basis.

c. Managers might argue in favour of equal percentage, across-the-board cuts to 'share the pain equitably'. This approach is not likely to benefit the entire organization because it ignores the causes of waste - non-value-added activities - that might occur anywhere in the organization and disproportionately in some areas.[9] Scrutinizing only the highest cost activities for opportunities to cut costs could be expedient but also could allow waste to persist in many smaller activities. Ideally, PML should identify and try to reduce all non-value-added activities. In practice, many organizations undertake these cost-cutting exercises in times of crisis or short-lived opportunity and believe they cannot afford the time necessary to thoroughly investigate all processes. Thus, they tend to attack the highest cost processes first. One wonders why organizations do not conduct these analyses without the motivation and time pressure of a crisis.

5.3 Using Value-added Analysis, p. 203

a. A number of different approaches can be used. PML could first look at activities with a cost above a certain dollar amount (for example, all items above £ 300) and then select the items that customers ranked as lowest values, or it could start with high-cost activities first, regardless of scores.

Most companies start with the high-cost activities first, thinking that the highest potential for cost savings is within these activities. Even if the customer value-added ranking is relatively high (that is, customers perceive an activity as value-added), there might be room for making the process more efficient.

b. Answers will vary, depending on the approach used [see solution to part (a)]. If PML starts with the lowest value scores first, regardless of the cost, the three activities (recycle defective pieces: £200; trim excess plastic: £500; place trimmings in recycle bags: £500) rated 1 are prime candidates for elimination. Because value scores of 1 and 2 represent activities that add little (if any) value as perceived by the customer, PML could start by examining the highest cost activities first within these value scores (trim excess plastic: £500 and remove pieces and visually inspect: £300).

Regardless of the proposed approach, PML should remember that the goal is to minimize or eliminate all non-value-added activities and to make all value-added activities as efficient as possible.

Endnotes

1 Kaplan and Anderson (2006). Details of time-driven ABC is covered in Chapter 6.

2 This important consideration is part of the topic of 'relevant costing', which is covered in Chapters 7 and 8.

3 ABM is a popular business approach to process redesign. Other process redesign business approaches include quality function deployment (QFD), which focuses on improving quality, and business process re-engineering (BPR), which generally seeks radical changes to processes. Many believe that ABM is superior to QFD because it focuses on the concept of customer-based value, which is broader than quality. ABM has proved to be more enduring than BPR, probably because ABM embraces continuous improvement rather than BPR's radical change, which sounds more exciting but has proven more difficult to design and to implement. Engineering approaches to process redesign, which could be applied to business processes, often involve computer modelling and simulation of activities that can be described mathematically. See also Kaplan (1992).

4 Note that many European companies are cited as also using ABM effectively. However, in publications they are typically referred to as 'a manufacturing company', 'a large bank', and so on.

5 It should be apparent that one firm's non-value-added activity can be another's value-added activity. For example, a manufacturing firm might perceive little customer value from preparing and filing its periodic tax returns. However, the manufacturing firm's tax preparer derives great value from preparing and filing the return.

6 The relationships of process improvement, time reductions and quality management are obvious. We defer explicit discussions of managing quality and time to Chapter 6.

7 For a thorough discussion of ABC implementation, see Anderson and Young (2001). For additional discussion of ABC/ABM implementation issues, see Selto (1995) and Shields and McEwen (1996).

8 For example, see Brewer (1998).

9 Markels and Murray (1996).

References

Anderson, E.W., C. Fornell and D.R. Lehmann (1994) 'Customer satisfaction, market share and profitability: findings from Sweden', *Journal of Marketing*, vol. 58, no. 3, pp. 53–66.

Anderson, S.W., and S.M. Young (2001) *Implementing Management Innovations: Lessons Learned from Activity-Based Costing in the U.S. Automobile Industry*, Kluwer Academic Boston.

Banker, R.D., G. Potter and D. Srinivasan (2002) 'An empirical investigation of an incentive plan that includes nonfinancial performance measures', *The Accounting Review*, vol. 75, no. 1, pp. 65–92.

Bellis-Jones Hill Group (n.d.) 'DHL – customer profitability in action', available at www.bellisjoneshill.co.uk/media/DHL-Customer_Profitability_in_Action.pdf (accessed 8 November 2011).

Brady, D (2000) 'Why service stinks', *BusinessWeek*, 23 October.

Brewer, P (1998) 'National culture and activity-based costing systems: a note', *Management Accounting Research*, June, pp. 241–260.

Compton, T., L. Hoshower and W. Draeger (1998) 'Reengineering transaction processing systems at cummins engine', *Journal of Cost Management*, May/June, pp. 6–12.

Convey, S (1991) 'Eliminating unproductive activities and processes', *CMA Magazine*, pp. 20–24.

Homburg, C., M. Droll and D. Totzek (2008), 'Customer prioritization: does it pay off, and how should it be implemented?' *Journal of Marketing*, vol. 72 (September), pp. 110–130.

Ittner, C.D., and D.F. Larcker (1998) 'Are non-financial measures leading indicators of financial performance? An analysis of customer satisfaction', *Journal of Accounting Research*, vol. 36 (supplement), pp. 1–35.

Kaplan, R.S. (1992) 'In defense of activity-based cost management', *Management Accounting*, November, pp. 58–63.

Kaplan, R.S., and S. Anderson (2006) 'Time-driven activity-based costing', Harvard Business School Working Paper, available at http://hbswk.hbs.edu/item/5436.html (accessed 14 March 2011).

Lind, J., and T. Strömsten (2006) 'When do firms use different types of customer accounting?' *Journal of Business Research*, vol. 59, pp. 1257–1266.

Markels, A., and M. Murray (1996) 'Call it dumbsizing: why some companies regret cost-cutting', *Wall Street Journal*, 14 May, p. A1.

Niraj, R., M. Gupta and C. Narasimhan (2001), 'Customer profitability in a supply chain', *Journal of Marketing*, vol. 65 (July), pp. 1–16.

Palmer, C. (1997) 'Dial tones for deadbeats', *Forbes*, 3 November, pp. 81–82.

Pederson, R.B (1991) 'Weyerhaeuser: streamlining payroll', *Management Accounting* (US), October, pp. 38–41.

Raaij, E.M. van, M.J.A. Vernooij and S. van Triest (2003) 'The implementation of customer profitability analysis: a case study', *Industrial Marketing Management*, vol. 32, no. (7), pp. 573–583.

Rust, R.T., and A.J. Zahorik (1993) 'Customer satisfaction, customer retention, and market share', *Journal of Retailing*, vol. 69, no. 2, pp. 193–215.

Selto, F. (1995) 'Implementing activity-based management', *Journal of Cost Management*, Summer, pp. 36–49.

Shields, M., and M. McEwen (1996) 'Implementing activity-based costing systems successfully', *Journal of Cost Management*, Winter, pp. 13–22.

Stiles, R., and S. Mick (1997) 'What is the cost of controlling quality? Activity-based accounting offers an answer', *Hospital & Health Services Administration*, Summer, p. 193.

Turney, P. (1992) 'Activity-based management', *Management Accounting*, January, pp. 20–25.

CHAPTER 6

Managing Quality and Time to Create Value

Learning Objectives

After completing this chapter, you should be able to:

LO 1 Evaluate the similarities and differences of total quality management and return-on-quality approaches to managing quality.

LO 2 Measure and analyse the dimensions of quality with commonly used diagrams, charts and reports.

LO 3 Understand and explain the importance of managing process time.

LO 4 Measure and manage productivity and capacity.

LO 5 Evaluate how just-in-time methods create benefits by combining management of quality, time, productivity and capacity.

LO 6 Understand how to construct and use control charts (Appendix 6).

Dedication to Quality and Customer Response Time Overcomes Sceptical Bankers

Fast-growing U.S. firm sets the pace in the customer service industry

By Harley Earl, Business Correspondent, Dissociated Press

Chicago: The concept of the company was revolutionary – some thought it audacious. The first loan officer to review Chicago-based TCSI's (Transformation Customer Services Inc.) embryonic business proposal was less than diplomatic. Rhonda Cooper, the company's dynamic CEO, remembers his exact words as, 'That is just about the craziest idea I have ever heard. There is no way that I would authorize lending you what you ask, even with your personal assets as collateral. I strongly believe that this is a flawed business concept. First of all, I cannot believe that any business would outsource its customer service representatives – its front-line with the customer – to anyone. Second, if it were to outsource customer service, why would it use you? You have no track record. You don't know a company's business, customers or competitors. And that raises a third concern – what if you do know their competitors? How could any business be sure that sensitive customer information would not leak to the competition? I'm sorry, but you have come to the wrong place, Ms Cooper. Have you considered a fast-food franchise?'

'I almost punched him out,' a laughing Ms Cooper recalls, still visibly affected by the banker's lack of vision.

Although that initial refusal hurt deeply, Ms Cooper took away the message that her company would have to communicate clearly and demonstrate that TCSI would and could provide the highest quality service.

Ten years after that shaky start, Ms Cooper's company provides services to many large and mid-sized companies in the United States, Europe and the Pacific Rim. TCSI has been one of the fastest growing service companies on the NASDAQ-AMEX exchange. Depending on the vagaries of the market, TCSI's common stock currently is worth nearly US$1 billion. Not bad for a start-up that began in a renovated school annex with two employees, one phone line and two personal computers.

TCSI employees and managers are relentless in their pursuit and maintenance of quality because a slip in quality of service could give competitors the opening they are looking for. 'We have no intention of losing any of our valued clients to competitors or our competitive edge based on quality and customer response time,' pledges Ms Cooper. 'We religiously measure and manage the quality of our personnel, processes, and services because we know that people pay attention to what gets measured and evaluated.'

With a keen sense of irony, Ms Cooper recently signed a contract to provide a full range of customer services for a large bank holding company that recently bought the very bank that had refused to loan her start-up capital 10 years ago. 'I noticed that my original, would-be banker is no longer with the bank. Too bad, I would have liked to ask him how I could help him improve his customer service.'

TCSI Background

Transformation Customer Services Inc., (TCSI) is based closely on a company that literally was created in the founder's garage to provide outsourced customer service. The company has grown to become an international leader in providing the highest quality customer service for its global clients, which include some of the world's best-known companies. TCSI operates customer-service call centres and product warranty claims for its clients. The secret of the TCSI's success is no secret at all – TCSI succeeds because of its uncompromising dedication to quality service and to its careful, consistent employee training, monitoring and feedback. TCSI knows that complaints by its client's customers reduce its chances for success, through penalties or loss of performance incentives and risk of non-renewal of service contracts. Thus, TCSI is proactive about managing quality quantitatively.

This chapter discusses the methods and measures that TCSI and other companies concerned about the efficiency of their processes and the quality of their goods and services use to stay ahead of the competition. The chapter describes ten important cost management tools: histograms, control charts, run charts, cause-and-effect diagrams, scatter diagrams, flowcharts, Pareto charts, cost-of-quality reports, overall equipment effectiveness and financial analysis. They are useful tools for monitoring process quality, time, efficiency and capacity and for preventing mistakes in meeting customer needs. The chapter also discusses how just-in-time methods combine concerns for managing and evaluating quality, time, efficiency and capacity.

Many organizations use measures of quality, time, productivity and capacity to evaluate performance. The measurement details presented in this chapter are very important to later chapters that discuss how to use these measures.

Importance of Quality

You undoubtedly have experienced poor-quality service or defective products and, as a result, you might have decided never to deal with that particular organization again. As a result of poor quality, the company lost you as a customer, which concerns organizations and motivates them to provide quality products and services. Many top executives believe that the most important changes in their companies' strategies in recent years have been to improve customer satisfaction and product quality. In today's globally competitive environment, improving quality is clearly a high priority for all organizations.

6.1 Cost Management in Practice

Strategic Effects of Quality

The effects of quality, good or bad, on the fortunes of companies are not limited to any economic sector or region. The **Warsaw Marriott Hotel** (Poland), in contrast, is now rated by guests as among the top five in the international chain by stressing quality in its hiring and training activities.

Dautel is a mid-sized company that manufactures large parts and structures for trucks in the southern state of Baden-Wurttemberg, Germany. Like many manufacturers, **Dautel** sought lower costs by outsourcing the production of cut-metal products, in this case, to suppliers in Romania. **Dautel** found to its dismay that the lower quality of the outsourced parts overshadowed the lower costs, and the company has returned production to Germany. Some observe that returning manufacturing is a key to the German economy's resurgence. Furthermore, strict quality and cost controls in Germany have reduced costs of formerly outsourced production, in many cases, below the outsourced costs.

Caterpillar Inc. purchased the France-based remanufacturing firm **Eurenov SA** and its facilities in Chaumont, France and Radom, Poland. 'Euronov is a strong strategic fit for our company,' said Steve Fisher, general manager of Caterpillar Remanufacturing Services. 'They're a cost effective, highly flexible operation that is focused squarely on the customer.' **Euronov** rebuilds automotive and industrial engines, transmissions and other used parts to new-part specifications. Similarly, **Caterpillar** purchased the UK remanufacturer, **Wealdstone Engineering Ltd**, which also has strong customer relationships and reputation for high quality remanufacturing. The acquisitions positioned

Caterpillar to greatly expand its European presence by building on **Euronov's** and **Wealdstone's** reputations for high quality and strong customer relationships.

Silicon Graphics Inc., the USA computer company behind the dinosaurs of the classic movie, *Jurassic Park*, did not pay attention to the quality of its lower-end products and missed lucrative Internet opportunities taken over by high-quality, low-cost personal computers. European winemakers, long used to world leadership, lost significant market share to North and South American and Australian competitors that offered higher quality wine at lower prices. European wine prices crashed in the 1990s as consumers worldwide reacted to their uneven quality. Some European winemakers took extended visits to Australian wineries to learn how to improve the quality of their products. The result of increased quality has been a resurgence of French and Italian wine sales.

Sources: Hof (1997); Simpson (1997); Tietz (2007); PRNewswire (2004, 2005).

Methods for Improving Quality

LO 1
Evaluate the similarities and differences of total quality management and return-on-quality approaches to managing quality.

Should organizations try to improve their quality – at any cost? Several years ago, that was the prevailing belief. However, there are now two somewhat competing approaches to improving product and service quality:

1. Total quality management.
2. Return on quality, a traditional view of quality that is re-emerging.

Total Quality Management (TQM)

Total quality management (TQM) is the view that improvements in quality, as defined by customers, always result in improved organizational performance because improving quality improves efficiency as problems are identified and eliminated. Furthermore, the quest for improved quality is never finished. TQM advocates, inspired by W. Edwards Deming, argue that customers seek the highest quality products and are willing to pay a premium for them.[1] Thus, TQM advocates have claimed that 'quality is free' or, more precisely, that improving quality more than pays its own way by creating higher profits.

The TQM perspective assumes that quality can and should always be improved, with exceeding customers' quality expectations being the goal. Since customers define quality, customer satisfaction and product or service quality are closely linked. Quite naturally, adopters of TQM assume that increased customer satisfaction and product and service quality are the leading indicators of improved profits.

Return on Quality (ROQ)

Return on quality (ROQ) is the view that assumes a trade-off between the costs and benefits of improving quality. Although ROQ advocates believe quality is extremely important, they argue that the highest profits are obtained at an optimum quality level of products and services, which maximizes profits rather than quality.[2] The optimum quality level almost always is lower than the **maximum quality level,** which is total delight of the customer or zero defects, depending on one's definition of quality. Total delight occurs when a customer receives a product or service that far exceeds his or her expectations of quality. A **defect** is an attribute (tangible or intangible) that falls short of customer expectations.

According to the ROQ view, at some point, the cost of improving quality must exceed the benefits of increased revenues. In other words, the ROQ approach argues that there can be too much quality, too few defects and too much customer satisfaction because costs of improved quality could increase at a higher rate than revenues. Even if the ROQ approach is more profitable, however, it might not be the basis of an effective marketing campaign. Furthermore, ROQ might lead to complacency with current levels of quality, whereas TQM is relentless in its search for continuous improvement.

Exhibit 6.1 contrasts the TQM and ROQ views of quality. As the left graph shows, the TQM view implicitly assumes that the maximum profit is achieved at the maximum quality level because total revenues from increasing quality always should grow faster than total costs. ROQ, on the other hand, assumes that less-than-maximum quality maximizes profits. Regardless of the approach, the difference between total revenues and total costs represents profit. The right graph shows that ROQ assumes that the total revenue and total cost lines converge at high levels of quality and even may cross, reducing profits. Accordingly, beyond the ROQ optimum level of quality, profits actually decline. Note that the TQM revenue and cost lines in Exhibit 6.1 might not be straight lines, but the difference between them is assumed to increase with increases in quality.

Exhibit 6.1 TQM versus ROQ Views of Quality

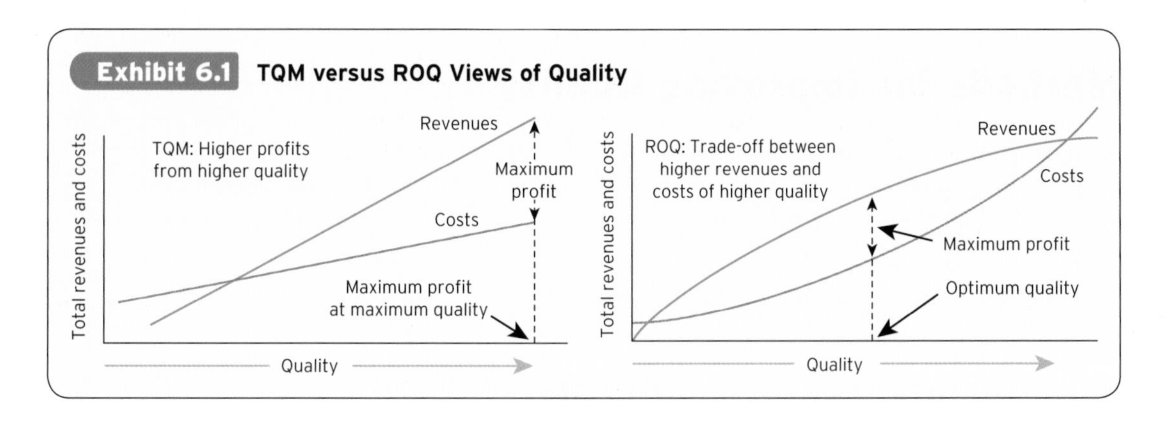

Comparison of the Views of Quality

The ROQ view of quality for many years was the traditional view, but the TQM movement eclipsed it in the 1980s as quality became a primary source of global competitive advantage. The ROQ view of quality and customer satisfaction has regained prominence in recent years as many companies have achieved parity in quality and in response to observing the fate of some winners of prestigious quality awards. A number of companies that have strenuously and successfully improved quality and received prizes for their efforts have seen profits drop alarmingly, and some have been forced to declare bankruptcy. Improved quality might not have been the root cause of financial decline in these companies, but ROQ advocates point out that improved quality, indicated by quality awards, did not prevent failure in these companies and does not guarantee success in other companies.

Conflict between TQM and ROQ

At the extremes of the two views, TQM and ROQ do conflict because ROQ's 'optimum' quality is usually less than TQM's 'maximum' quality. Martin Freeman, CFO at TCSI, prefers a middle position:

TCSI believes strongly in providing high-quality customer service and uses TQM tools to measure quality. But that does not mean TCSI would bankrupt the company to do *everything* service partners or their customers might want. If service partners are willing to pay for higher quality service, the company will do its best to provide it, knowing that our competitors will be trying to do the same. On the other hand, we do not take out the calculator every time we consider a quality issue. Since quality service is our whole business, sometimes TCSI decides to increase quality to meet its goals and competition. TCSI pays attention to the numbers but also relies on judgement in the final analysis.

6.1 Research Insight

Return on Quality

The TQM versus ROQ debate could be characterized as a difference in assumptions about the behaviour of *marginal revenues* (the revenue earned from additional sales of products or services) and *marginal costs* from additional increases in quality. TQM argues that marginal revenues will exceed marginal costs, but ROQ argues that at some point, the marginal cost of increasing quality will exceed the marginal revenues earned. Chris Ittner and David Larcker used survey data to find that a quality-oriented strategy and management participation in quality were associated with higher performance in a sample of North American, German and Japanese auto and computer manufacturers. The bottom-line question for organizations and researchers is, 'Do firms that manage for higher quality *sustain* higher profits?' This is an exceedingly difficult question to answer because a short-term increase in profits might not be sustained in the long term as competitors react with their own quality-related initiatives.

Financial research supports this concern. One study found that many companies, once rated as excellent for quality, experienced below-average share price returns just a few years later. This indicates that gains from quality must be sustained by continued efforts to outdo the competition; otherwise, competitors quickly catch up. Additionally, profits could be affected by many influences that are contemporaneous with quality efforts, such as other value-chain activities to develop new products, advertise and reconfigure supplier and distributor relations.

Sources: Ittner and Larcker (1997); and Coy (1995).

Dimensions of Quality

Customer-focused quality is a broad focus on meeting or exceeding customer expectations rather than a focus on only one of the dimensions of quality (as discussed later). TCSI measures its quality on two generally accepted quality dimensions: (1) *product* or *service attributes* and (2) *customer service* before and after the sale. TCSI believes that, to succeed in measuring and managing quality, it must understand customers' expectations on these two dimensions of quality.

Product Attributes

A product's attributes refer to its tangible and intangible features. Tangible features, in general, include performance, adherence to specifications, and functionality. Tangible features of TCSI's services include the following:

- Promptness of responses to customer inquiries
- Accuracy of responses
- Resolution of customer inquiries
- Other criteria specific to each client.

Intangible features of products include reputation, taste, appearance, style and appeal, which could be as important as tangible features to some customers. TCSI relies on its reputation for providing quality services as a major selling point to potential clients and a major factor in retaining current clients.

Customer Service Before and After the Sale

Customers' perceptions of service before and after the sale influence whether they will become new customers and remain repeat customers. Customer service features include (among other activities):

- Provision of presale information
- Proper treatment of customers by salespeople
- On-time delivery to the customer after the product or service is ordered

- Follow-up with customers after the sale
- Timeliness and accuracy of resolution of questions and complaints
- Warranty and repair services.

How Organizations Measure Quality

LO 2
Measure and analyse the dimensions of quality with commonly used diagrams, charts and reports.

Determining customers' expectations and providing superior service are possible only if organizations are able to measure quality and provide helpful feedback to their members. To ensure that TCSI meets or exceeds customers' quality expectations on the two quality dimensions, the company first uses measures that indicate clients' and their customers' evaluations of service quality. Second, to measure the quality the company has delivered, TCSI also measures the satisfaction of clients and their customers with its services. TCSI uses measures similar to those used by other service and manufacturing companies that manage quality carefully.

How does TCSI know whether its quality is either sufficient or a problem? First, the company needs to identify indicators of customer-defined quality. If indicators show that the quality of products is deteriorating, the warning could, in turn, trigger an investigation to determine the cause so that the problem can be corrected before it becomes too large. Second, the company needs diagnostic information to suggest what the problem is and, perhaps, a way to solve it.

Variation Causes Poor Quality

Quality experts believe that variations in product features are a primary source of poor quality. Variability increases the chance for product features to disappoint customers. Most leading indicators of quality measure some form of variation in process outcomes. For example, one of the attributes of TCSI's services that the company monitors is average length of time to resolve a customer complaint. TCSI believes that an optimum length of time exists; taking too much time frustrates the customer, but spending too little time increases the chance that the company will not understand and, therefore, will not react properly to the customer's true complaint.

Leading and lagging indicators of quality

Organizations usually seek to measure the quality of products while in process before exposing them to customers. **Leading indicators of quality** measure the features that customers value while manufacturing the product and before shipment or while providing a service but before completion. **Lagging indicators of quality** measure features of products after exposure or use by customers. Lagging indicators can be important, but, because damage could already be done by poor quality, they are not as valuable as leading indicators.

Histograms

A **histogram** is a chart that displays a frequency distribution of tangible or intangible process outcomes, including the range and degree of concentration of outcomes around an average value. A wider range, with less concentration, means more variation and increased likelihood that the customer received poor-quality service. Conversely, a narrower range, with tighter concentration, improves the likelihood that customers received good or high-quality service.

Exhibit 6.2 contrasts histograms of response times before and after improvements to TCSI's complaint resolution process. We discuss how cost management analysts diagnosed the problem and worked with cross-functional teams to make improvements later. Panel A of Exhibit 6.2 shows the range and concentration of response times during a week before improvements. Some variation is expected because not all complaints are the same. However, in response to customer satisfaction surveys, TCSI decided that response times varied too much, which led the company to improve technology and employee training. Panel B reflects the effects of process improvements and shows a much tighter concentration (and lower average) of response times during a week after process improvements.

Exhibit 6.2 Histograms of Customer-Response Times, Before and After Process Improvements

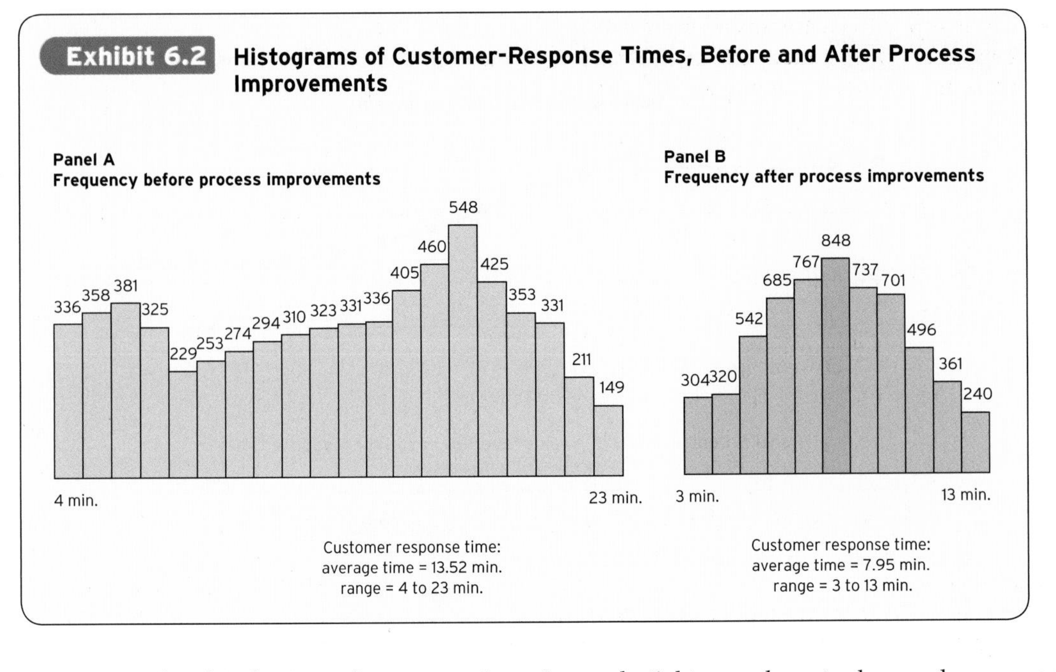

Because the distribution of response times is much tighter and centred on a lower average response time after process improvements, customers who call TCSI are more likely to have their problems resolved quickly and to be more satisfied with TCSI's service.

Run and control charts

a **run chart** shows trends in variation in product or service attributes over time by reflecting measures of important quality features taken at defined points in time. Employees use run charts to identify persistent trends in important attributes that are adverse or beneficial to quality. Panel A of Exhibit 6.3 shows that TCSI's weekly, average customer-response time appears to be permanently lower after the company introduced process improvements in week 7. This chart reinforces the value of the decision to improve processes and provides some justification for more of the same effort.

A **control chart** also describes variation in product or service attributes over time by measuring important quality features. Additionally, it compares attributes to **upper** and **lower control limits**, which are the maximum- and minimum-desired levels of product or service features. A low level of variation in product or service features is desirable, but deviations that fall either above the upper control limit or below the lower control limit are unacceptable defects because (a) the product or service will not perform reliably or (b) customers will be disappointed by worse-than-expected intangible features.[3] Cost management analysts usually prepare and analyse periodic charts such as those in Exhibit 6.3. Many organizations give individuals or teams direct responsibility for measuring product and service attributes as they perform their work so that they can detect any defects immediately and correct them before further processing or before shipping them to customers.

Organizations use summary control charts to distinguish between acceptable variations in quality and variations in performance that require further investigation. For example, TCSI evaluates each customer representative's average response time on a weekly basis. Employees whose average response times stray out of the acceptable region receive counselling or additional training. Employees whose performance is exceptionally good receive recognition for their work.

The control chart of one employee's weekly average response times (panel B of Exhibit 6.3) was within the control limits except during week 11 when the average time exceeded the upper control limit. The chart also shows that this employee's average times were trending toward the upper control limit during weeks 9 and 10. Although the average response time in week 9 does not look unusual by itself, the even higher time in week 10 signals a possible upward trend. Some organizations might intervene at this time even though the control limits have not been violated. By week 11, the employee had exceeded the upper limit, and the supervisor counselled the employee to understand the causes of poor quality and to obtain improved performance.

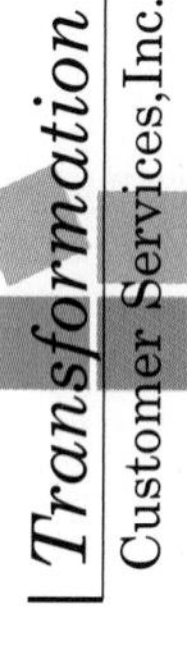

Exhibit 6.3 Run and Control Charts of Average Customer Response Time

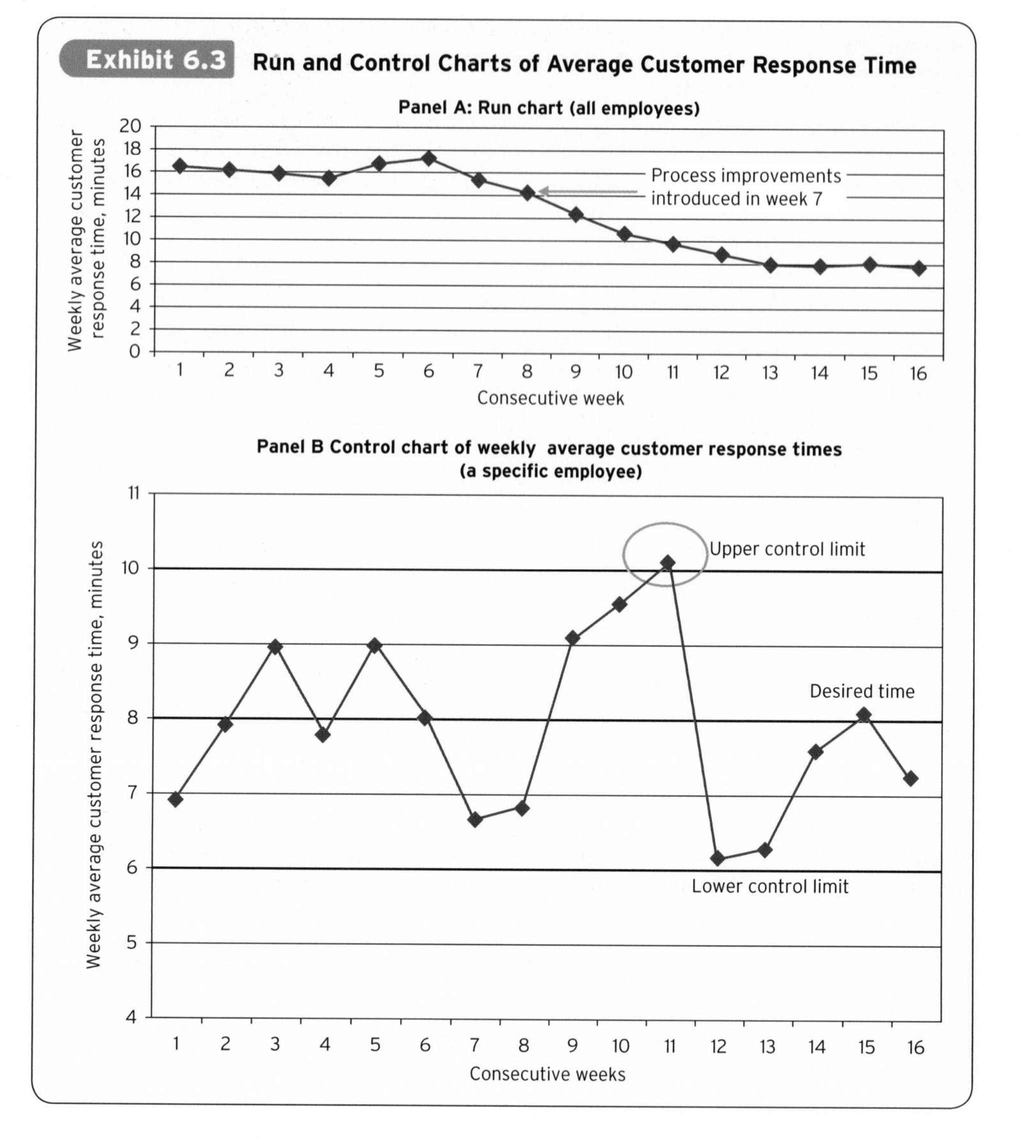

Diagnostic Information

Leading indicator information identifies potential quality problems but usually does not diagnose their causes. Cost management analysts, often with team members from production and customer service, use a number of tools, including cause-and-effect diagrams, scatter diagrams, flow charts and Pareto charts, to diagnose the causes of problems and to identify possible solutions.

Cause-and-effect diagrams

Cause-and-effect analysis involves formulating diagnostic signals that identify potential causes of product or service defects. It first defines the defect, for example, *excessive and variable customer response time*, and then the causes that could contribute to the problems. The potential causes of these problems in customer response time can be deficiencies in:

- Human resources (e.g., inadequate training or staffing)
- Physical resources (e.g., insufficient capacity or availability)
- Procedures (e.g., inadequate or out of date)
- Information technology (e.g., unavailable or incorrect information)
- Communication (e.g., failure to communicate changes in procedures or objectives).

These causes often can be identified by asking the question 'Why?' until the root cause of the problem is identified. As the causes are identified, the organization can develop and implement corrective measures.

TCSI's customers informed the company through customer satisfaction surveys that they were dissatisfied with both the length and variability of the time required to get a satisfactory response to their inquiries. TCSI was able to identify and correct causes of the problem by asking involved employees why response times were so long and variable. TCSI used a 'fishbone', or Ishikawa, cause-and-effect diagram to analyse this problem. Exhibit 6.4 shows the information developed by a team of customer-service employees that answers the question. The defect, on the right of the diagram, was due to a number of related causes and sub-causes, which are shown as 'bones' on the diagram. For example, one of the causes identified by asking 'Why?' was employee mistakes (Human Resources on the diagram). A second question – 'Why did employees make mistakes?' – yielded two causes: employee training and employee turnover. A third – 'Why weren't employees properly trained?' – yielded the cause (too little) time. A fourth – 'Why was employee turnover so high?' – yielded the causes (too little) pay and (too much) pressure. TCSI researched each major bone of the diagram similarly to find causes of the defect.

Combining all information in Exhibit 6.4, the team determined that the most important root cause of the problem was complex product information that changed faster than employees could be trained to become familiar with it. TCSI's solution was to develop a centrally maintained, 'intelligent' service database that allowed customer representatives to quickly diagnose and correct callers' service problems. TCSI's clients became responsible for entering changed and new product information directly into the database so the information that TCSI employees work with is always current.

The high cost of developing and maintaining this artificial-intelligence tool is justified by the large reduction in the time necessary to serve customers. In addition, the tool reduced stress and conflict in the workplace as well as employee turnover and discomfort. TCSI was able to find and develop a sophisticated information technology solution to its customer response time problem. Although this system did not eliminate all customer and product information errors, the company believed that this solution generated a positive return on quality (ROQ); that is, the benefits of increased sales from improved quality exceeded the costs of improving quality.

Exhibit 6.4 Cause-and-effect Diagram

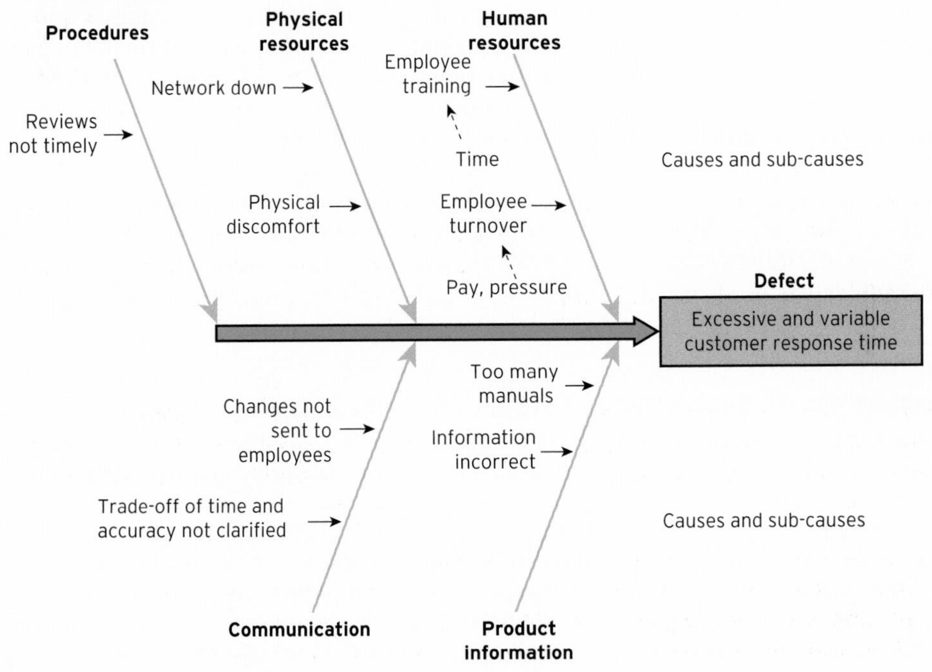

Transformation
Customer Services, Inc.

Scatter diagrams

A **scatter diagram** is a plot of two measures that could be related. Such a plot helps analysts to diagnose the cause and effect between outcomes and the activities that might drive them. That is, changes in a value-added or non-value-added activity could cause or be associated with changes in a quality measure. Scatter diagrams are useful for diagnosing whether a suspected cause of a quality problem is really responsible. If plotted points hug a diagonal line, quality and other measures are more likely related. Knowing which of the two variables causes the other suggests a solution for the problem: change the cause to eliminate the problem.

As panel A of Exhibit 6.5 shows, the quality measure, customer-response time, appears to be closely related to one suspected cause, frequency of incorrect information. Panel A indicates that as frequency of incorrect information increases, so does customer-response time. Thus, a reduction in the number of times TCSI's representatives received incorrect information resulted in a reduction in its customer response time.

Transformation Customer Services, Inc.

Exhibit 6.5 Scatter Diagrams

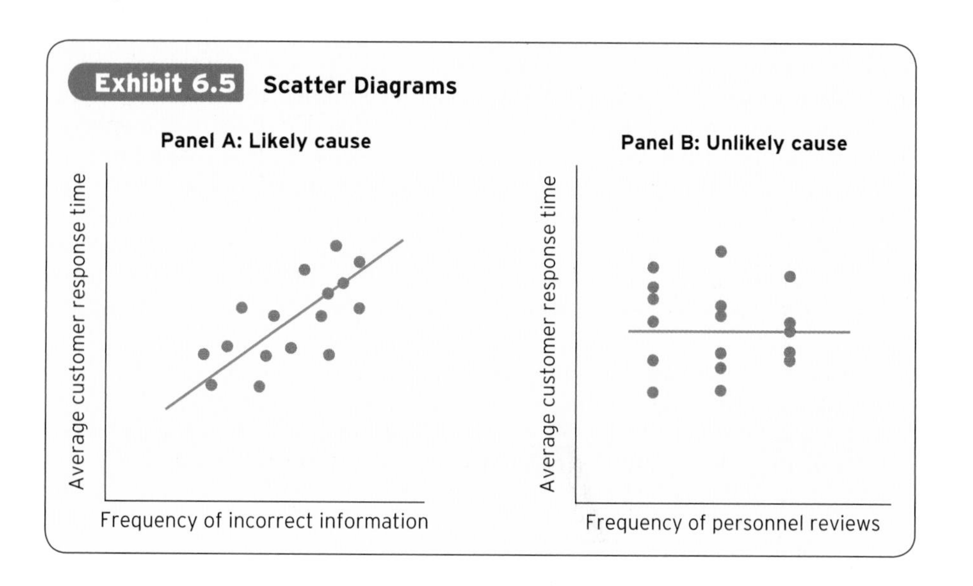

Panel B, however, does not reflect any discernable relationship between customer response time and another suspected cause of the problem, frequency of personnel reviews. The frequency of personnel reviews does not appear to affect customer response time, which indicates that TCSI does not need to devote more resources to conducting frequent personnel reviews to reduce customer response time. TCSI could have other reasons for frequent reviews, however.

A drawback to relying on scatter diagrams to diagnose causes of quality problems is that the organization must have sufficient reliable information on both quality measures and suspected causes. If sufficient data are not available, as is sometimes the case when processes or quality management efforts are new, the other diagnostic methods we discuss could be more helpful for identifying causes of quality problems.

Flowcharts

A **flowchart** reflects cause-and-effect and sequential linkages among process activities. Knowing which activities cause or precede others in producing a product or offering a service can help diagnose where quality problems arise. Cost management analysts also might prepare flowcharts to support systems analysis and auditing activities. The flowchart of the actual (not the ideal) customer response process shown in Exhibit 6.6 helped the TCSI cost management team discover that the root cause of excessive customer-response time resulted from working with incorrect product information provided by the client. Comparing the actual process to an ideal process can highlight where improvements can be made. Identifying and eliminating non-value-added activities in processes often improves not only the efficiency of the process but also the quality of the product or service.

Transformation Customer Services, Inc.

Exhibit 6.6 Customer Response (to Phone Call) Activities Flowchart

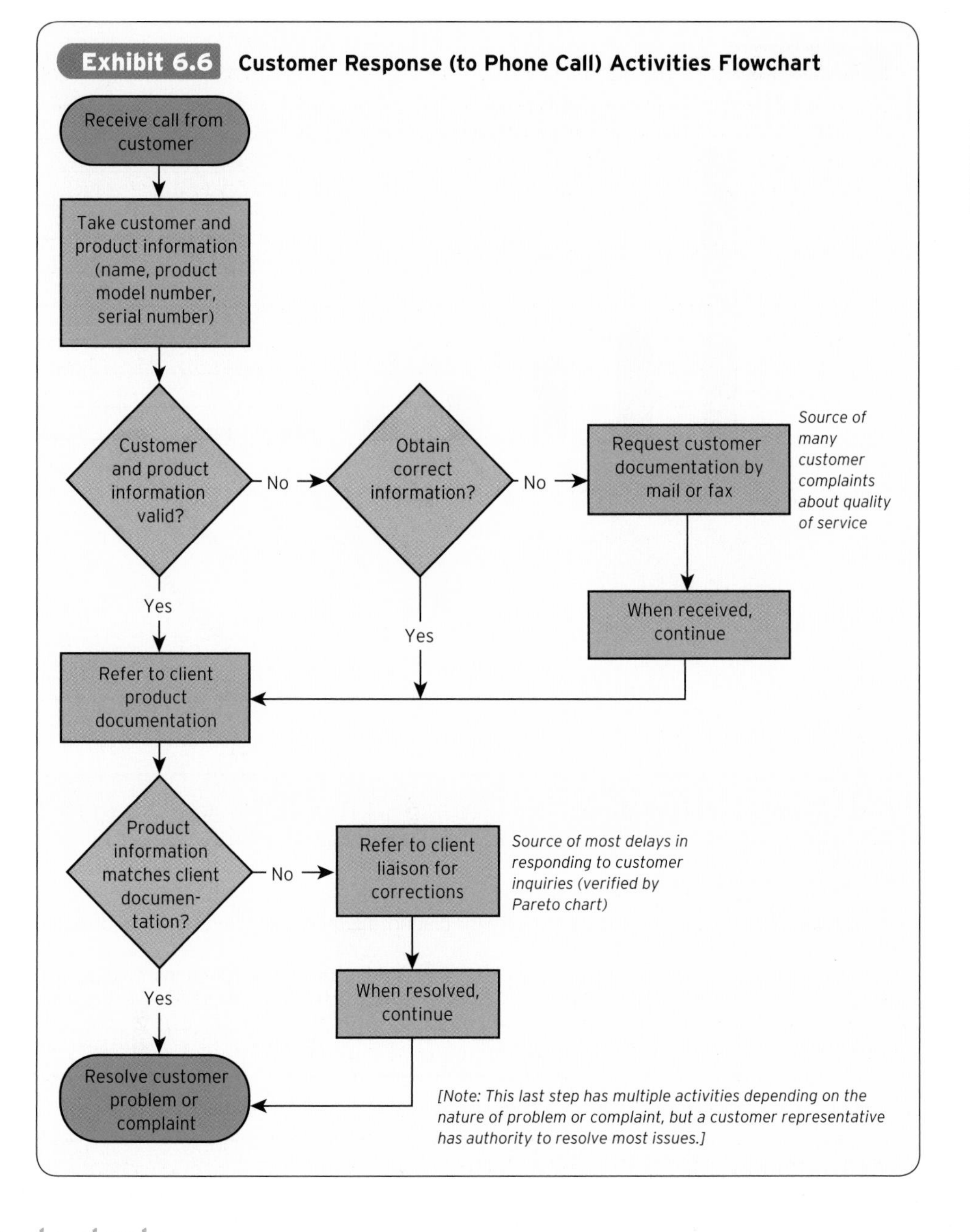
Receive call from customer
Take customer and product information (name, product model number, serial number)
Customer and product information valid?
No
Obtain correct information?
No
Request customer documentation by mail or fax
Source of many customer complaints about quality of service
When received, continue
Yes
Yes
Refer to client product documentation
Product information matches client documen-tation?
No
Refer to client liaison for corrections
Source of most delays in responding to customer inquiries (verified by Pareto chart)
When resolved, continue
Yes
Resolve customer problem or complaint
[Note: This last step has multiple activities depending on the nature of problem or complaint, but a customer representative has authority to resolve most issues.]

Pareto charts

A **Pareto chart** (named after the Italian economist Wilfredo Pareto) prioritizes the causes of problems or defects as bars of varying height, in order of frequency or size. Pareto charts help analysis teams focus on the causes that could offer the greatest potential for improvement. Focusing on correcting the most frequent causes of quality problems, identified by Pareto charts, could show analysis teams where to focus initial efforts to make the most improvement in quality. Exhibit 6.7 is a Pareto chart for the causes of excessive customer response time at TCSI before process improvements. This chart confirmed what customer representatives had told the analysis team: incorrect client information was responsible for most delays. Nonetheless, the Pareto chart identified other common causes of delays that TCSI could also correct, such as incorrect customer information and insufficient employee training.

Organizations need both leading indicator and diagnostic information about activities to identify problems that require attention. However, timely diagnostic information can be expensive to collect, so analysts might rely on leading indicators to signal the need to collect diagnostic information.

Exhibit 6.7 **Pareto Chart**

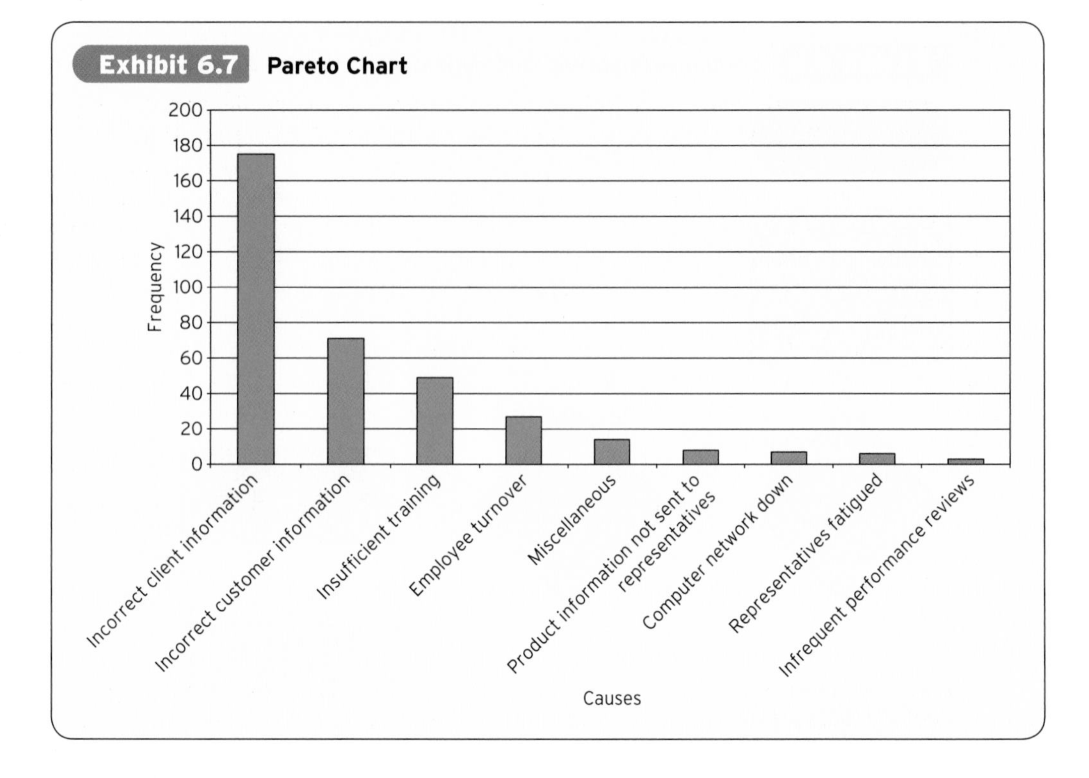

6.1 You're the Decision Maker

Using Diagnostic Quality Information

a. Do you think it is reasonable to delegate the responsibility for diagnosing quality problems to individuals in the departments where quality problems occur?

b. Would it always be better to use a cross-functional team (e.g., across departments or functions) to diagnose quality problems?

(Solutions begin on page 278.)

6.2 Research Insight

ERP Systems: Process Efficiency and Quality Management

Modern Enterprise Resource Planning (ERP) systems provide access to much more data than in the past for measuring process quality, time, efficiency, and so on. ERP systems and modules for quality management (and others) give managers more data and tools which can be modified for specific needs. Often the problem is not lack of data, but lack of knowing which data to retrieve, when, and in what format. ERP quality management modules permit the analyst to mirror organizational and reporting (responsibility) structures or to create new slices of the data that cut across normal timing and structural boundaries, such as plants, regions, product lines and customers. Reflecting the current responsibility structures reinforces the importance of the designed accountability for quality problems (e.g., who must detect and fix quality problems), but data cut this way might miss important changes or problems that span or cut across responsibility lines. The ability to 're-draw' the organization with ERP data presents opportunities for improving quality (and other management concerns) but also might create management difficulties if responsibilities are diffused.

Sources: Dechow and Mouritsen (2005); Quattrone and Hopper (2005); and Chapman (2005).

Customer Satisfaction

Customer satisfaction is the degree to which customers' expectations of product attributes, service and *price* have been or will be met. Organizations measure customer satisfaction both as leading indicators of future sales and diagnostic tools to discover causes of unexpectedly low or high sales.

The most common methods of measuring customer satisfaction are phone or online surveys by which companies ask current or potential customers to rate attributes of products or services and customer service on a multiple-point scale. Many organizations outsource the actual measurement of customer satisfaction to benefit from both survey firms' expertise and the ability to generate more valid measures. TCSI market researchers, however, conduct their own customer satisfaction surveys because TCSI believes this is an area of its expertise. Other common measurement tools are to (1) ask focus groups of customers to evaluate real or proposed products or services and (2) use phantom, or unknown, shoppers, who really are employed by the agency evaluating the product or service and who report their experiences.

As an example of survey questions that TCSI asks clients and their customers, consider how clients and customers rate the *accuracy* of the customer services they have received from TCSI. Was it:

— Much better than expected?
— About as expected?
— Worse than expected?

By asking similar questions about all attributes of its services, TCSI is able to identify its strengths and problem areas as well as what clients and their customers really want. TCSI also uses customer satisfaction ratings to evaluate the performance of its employees and business units. Many organizations believe that strong links exist between meeting quality goals, customer satisfaction and the organization's goals (e.g., profitability). These organizations might reinforce the importance of these linkages by tying customer satisfaction ratings to incentives for employees. Tying incentives to leading indicators of performance is covered in Chapter 16.

Trade-offs between Quality and Price

Market forces set competitive prices. Customers evaluate product attributes and customer service (i.e., quality) based on what is available at a comparable price from other sources. Customers buy the product or service that gives them the preferred mix of quality and price. If two products provide the same quality, the customer most likely chooses the product with the lower price. Likewise, if an organization offers superior product quality, it might be able to charge higher prices and/or increase its market share. Thus, trade-offs are always made between the various dimensions of a product's quality and its price. Decisions about the dimensions of quality are important cost and revenue drivers for any organization.

Costs of products are leading indicators of an organization's ability to meet market prices or offer competitive bid prices. Therefore, organizations that manage quality and the quality/price trade-off also monitor costs and leading indicators of costs (e.g., changes in cost drivers).

Identifying Costs of Quality

The **costs of quality (COQ)** are the costs of activities to *control quality* and the costs of activities to correct a *failure to control quality.* Costs to control quality are associated with leading indicators of imminent quality and customer value, and costs to correct failures could be leading indicators of future decreased sales.

COQ could be most valuable as a communication tool to inform employees at all levels of the magnitude and general sources of quality problems. Organizations that spend most of their quality-improvement efforts on activities controlling quality usually spend less effort correcting quality failures after they have occurred. Organizations that spend most of their efforts on activities to correct quality failures usually have serious quality problems and excessive costs of poor quality.[4]

Controlling Quality

The two general activities to control quality are prevention activities and appraisal activities. **Prevention** activities seek to prevent defects in the products offered to customers. Examples of prevention activities include the following:

- *Supplier certification.* Using only materials suppliers that can guarantee high quality.
- *Product design for manufacturability.* Designing products that can be made without defects.
- *Quality training.* Training employees to improve product quality.
- *Quality evaluations.* Measuring or evaluating employees on their quality capabilities and performance to indicate or motivate improvements.
- *Process improvement.* Evaluating and improving processes to remove causes of defects.

TQM advocates argue that the most efficient use of quality resources is on prevention activities. Preventing poor quality, they argue, is the only value-added quality activity and the most profitable way to control quality. Indeed, if one were to include all the activities that prevent poor quality, the list might include the vast majority of a successful organization's expenditures. ROQ advocates agree that preventing defects is effective but also argue that preventing *all* defects could be prohibitively expensive. Some non-value-added quality activities in conjunction with activities that prevent defects could yield the most profitable level of quality. This is perhaps a narrow view of prevention activities, that some quality experts think is myopic; that is, focusing on achieving overall lower costs requires emphasis on prevention activities.[5]

Appraisal activities (also called *detection* or *inspection* activities) inspect inputs and attributes of individual units of product or service to detect whether they conform to specifications or customer expectations and include the following:

- *Inspecting materials.* Inspecting production materials upon delivery.
- *Inspecting machines.* Ensuring that machines are operating properly within specifications.
- *Inspecting processes.* Manually inspecting the production process.
- *Performing automated inspection.* Using equipment to monitor the production process.
- *Employing statistical process control.* Using employees to inspect every unit for defects as they complete their productive activities (e.g., using control charts).
- *Sampling at end of process.* Inspecting the attributes of a sample of finished products to ensure quality.
- *Testing at end of process.* Testing the performance of all or a sample of finished products under the same or simulated conditions experienced by customers.
- *Field-testing.* Testing products in use at customer sites.

Appraisal activities usually are recognized as non-value-added because customers do not pay for inspection – they pay for a high-quality product. Quality experts believe that appraisal activities can be avoided by placing more emphasis on preventing defects. To TQM advocates, an ideal process by design produces zero defects. ROQ advocates, as you can imagine, argue that this ideal process can, in fact, be unprofitable and that some (small) number of defects is optimal. (Saying this openly might not be effective marketing, however.) Therefore, if preventing all defects is not feasible, some testing or appraisal is necessary. The earlier that testing can find defects, however, the lower the cost of defects is likely to be.

Failing to Control Quality

Failing to control quality causes internal failure and external failure activities. Organizations universally regard these as non-value-added activities.

Internal failure activities are required to correct defective processes, products and services that are detected before delivering them to customers. These include the following:

- *Disposing of scrap.* Recycling or dumping materials wasted in the production process.
- *Performing rework.* Correcting defects before the product or service is sold.
- *Re-inspecting/Retesting.* Performing quality control testing after rework.
- *Delaying processes.* Reducing production because defective items are processed by scarce resources and must be scrapped or reworked – loss of irreplaceable scarce time.

Internal failures are non-value-added activities that can be quite costly – especially from lost processing time. Although lost processing time can be the most costly, its complete cost is difficult to measure because it can affect future sales.

External failure activities are required to correct defective products or services after they have been delivered to customers. They include:

- *Warranty repairs.* Repairing defective products.
- *Field replacements.* Replacing defective products at the customer's site.
- *Product liability settlements.* Responding to liabilities resulting from product failure.
- *Customer-complaint resolution.* Replacing products or services or adjusting billing to accommodate legitimate customer concerns about products or services received.
- *Restoration of reputation.* Engaging in marketing activities to improve the company's image tarnished from poor product quality.
- *Lost sales.* Opportunity costs from decreases in sales resulting from poor-quality products (current and potential customers will go to competitors).

External failures could be the most costly of all quality activities because of their effects on the organization's reputation. Although the out-of-pocket costs of these activities can be large, they can be small compared to the opportunity costs of future sales. Because external failure costs have such harmful potential, TQM advocates argue that nearly every activity to prevent an external failure is cost effective. This argument is difficult to refute because the opportunity costs of forgone sales can be very high but are difficult to measure objectively.

Measuring Costs of Quality

Organizations that use ABC and ABM have the activity-based information necessary to compile cost-of-quality information. The only additional step beyond ABM is classifying activities according to the cost-of-quality category, as described earlier. Simply sorting the activity-cost data by cost-of-quality classification yields the cost of the quality measures.

Reporting Costs of Quality

Organizations usually sort costs by quality activity and express them as a percentage of sales. Some companies with serious quality problems might spend as much as 30 to 40 per cent of sales on correcting poor quality. Companies with excellent quality might spend much less than 10 per cent of sales for corrective activities. In general, enhancing prevention activities should increase value while decreasing or eliminating the need for inspection, internal failure and external failure activities.

An example of a quarterly COQ report prepared by cost management analysts for one of TCSI's business units (i.e., call centres) appears in Exhibit 6.8. This report indicates that TCSI spent the most on value-added quality training and process evaluations (prevention). As is typical in companies with excellent quality, this was the largest amount spent on any of the four quality activity categories. But this understates all of the spending on activities that enhance good quality at TCSI, which include all hiring, training and customer-relations activities, among others. The point of this report is to focus on explicit quality activities.

More than half of the business unit's cost of quality was non-value-added. Customers would not willingly pay for the performance of appraisal, internal failure and external failure activities. CFO

Transformation Customer Services, Inc.

Exhibit 6.8 Cost-of-Quality Report: First Quarter

		Amounts	Percentage of sales
Sales		$1,765,000	100%
Prevention activities:			
Training	$32,829		
Process evaluation	21,886	$54,715	3.10%
Appraisal activities:			
Performance measurement	24,092		
Performance reviews	10,325	34,417	1.95%
Internal failure activities:			
Wasted time	3,883		
Revision of incorrect information	15,532	19,415	1.10%
External failure activities:			
Redoing customer service	6,142		
Resolving complaints with TCSI service	9,213	15,355	0.87%
Total costs of quality		$123,902	7.02%

Freeman instructed the business unit manager to find ways to reverse that percentage while increasing quality of service.

TCSI believes that COQ information is not sufficient by itself to manage quality since it does not measure the quality of services delivered to customers or their satisfaction with services received. However, Freeman uses the COQ information prepared by his staff as one indication of the company's success in managing quality. He looks to see that most of the quality activities are for preventing mistakes, not correcting those that could have been avoided. Note that TCSI does not explicitly measure the opportunity cost of lost business. It uses qualitative indicators of forgone sales from customer satisfaction surveys and measures of customer retention (repeat sales).

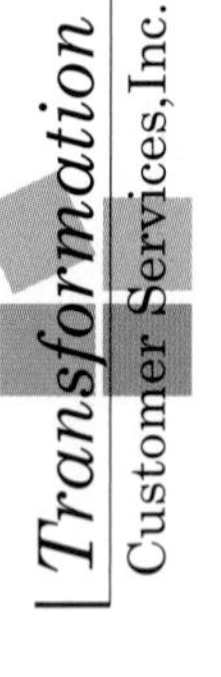

Exhibit 6.9 Relative Proportions of Quality Costs at TCSI

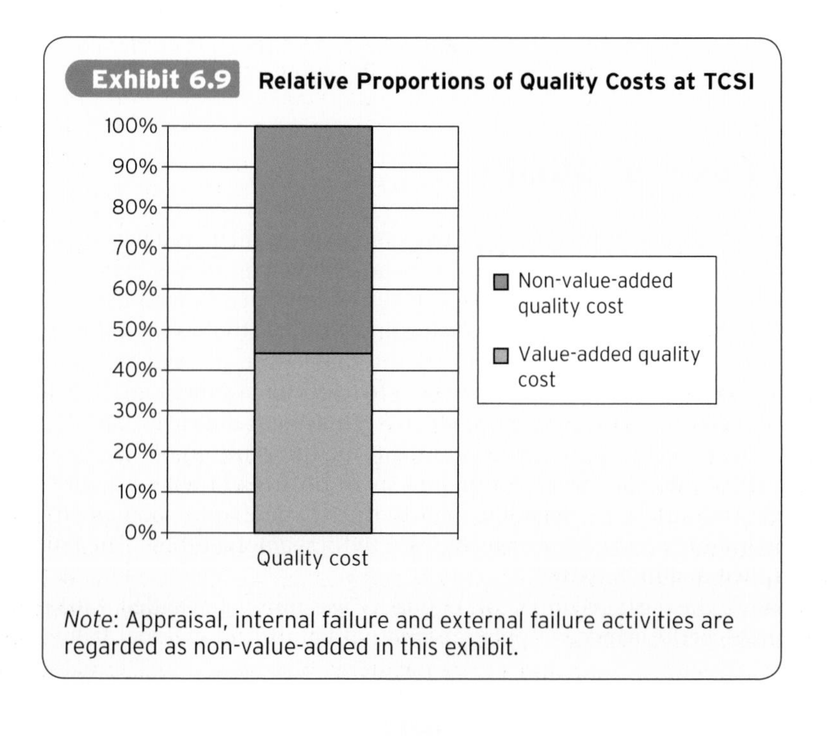

Note: Appraisal, internal failure and external failure activities are regarded as non-value-added in this exhibit.

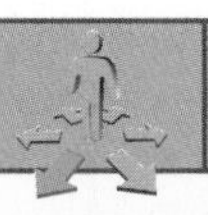

6.2 You're the Decision Maker

Evaluating the Cost of Quality

Some observers ask this question about COQ: are we really making a difference, or is COQ just another report? Evaluate these claims about the value of COQ.

a. COQ allows the organization to focus on the reduction or elimination of non-value-added costs of quality.
b. COQ is a better measure of performance than traditional operating income because costs of quality are not buried in FIFO cost of sales.
c. COQ provides a target (e.g., 4 per cent of sales for total COQ) that really measures the progress of quality improvements in concrete terms.

Source: Adapted from Brinkman and Appelbaum (1994).

(Solutions begin on page 278.)

Corporate Integrity and Quality

At a recent World Economic Forum, 1,500 corporate top executives were asked to indicate the most important measures of their companies' success. Less than 20 per cent indicated that profitability was the most important measure. Another 27 per cent said that quality of their products was the most important measure, and 24 per cent stated that reputation and integrity of the companies' brands was most important.[6]

Ethical Behaviour and Reputation

Some companies' managers make decisions to cut costs to improve short-term profits. **Bridgestone Tires** (Japan) and its North American subunit, **Firestone**, and **Ford Motor Company** (USA) are examples of companies that apparently made decisions to cut development, design and appraisal costs for tyres used on the Ford Explorer in the late 1990s and early 2000s. External failures that included many failed tyres, rollover accidents, and lost lives impaired their reputations and lost business. In many cases, the economic consequences of external failures that cost lives paled in comparison to the outcomes of decisions to save a few dollars on each unit of product. Both Firestone and Ford have dedicated significant resources to quality improvement since this unfortunate episode.

By contrast, **Johnson & Johnson** earned a positive reputation for its 1982 decision to remove all Tylenol from shelves after somebody unrelated to the company had put poison in some capsules of the medicine. Johnson & Johnson's managers did not make excuses or pass the buck; they got right to the business of protecting consumers. In the end, ethical choices paid off for Johnson & Johnson and the company's actions are often cited as exemplary crisis management.

Quality Awards and Certificates

Quality has become so important to success that currently many prestigious, internationally recognized awards are given to companies for quality by nearly every country and many professional organizations. For example, The **European Quality Award** (EQA) examines the impact of quality on a company, its customers and the company's social and environmental community. The **Malcolm Baldrige National Quality Award,** created by the United States Congress in 1987, recognizes US firms with outstanding records of quality improvement and quality management. The **Deming Prize,** created in Japan by the Japanese Union of Scientists and Engineers long before the Baldrige Quality Award, is awarded to companies around the world that excel in quality improvement.

The International Organization for Standardization, based in Europe, developed **ISO 9000,** which is a family of international standards for quality management. The ISO standards first gained popularity in Europe but are now global guidelines for the design, development, production, final inspection and testing, installation, and servicing of products, processes and services. To be certified, a company must document its quality systems and pass a rigorous third-party audit of its manufacturing and customer-service processes.

Organizations proudly display their quality awards and certificates as evidence of their commitment to product and service quality. Many organizations have adopted Baldrige or Deming prize criteria as their internal quality management guidelines even if they do not seek to win a prize for their efforts. TCSI, for example, has adopted criteria from both the Baldrige and Deming awards and has earned ISO 9001 certification.

Managing Time in a Competitive Environment

LO 3
Understand and explain the importance of managing process time.

TCSI and other successful organizations realize that competitive markets continuously demand shorter:

- new product and service development time;
- customer response time;
- cycle time.

Accordingly, TCSI focuses on improving the three dimensions of time in all of its business units. This requires that all major business unit activities have time-measurement objectives. Improvements in response time can require simplifying and shortening work processes and almost always require improvements in quality. Poor quality, which requires inspection, testing and rework, is a major cause of the excessive use of time. Eliminating the causes of poor quality, therefore, can shorten process time dramatically. Furthermore, some argue that quality and time are inextricably linked, because one cannot truly decrease processing time without increasing quality. Simply decreasing processing time is likely to increase defective products that increase failure costs.

New Product Development Time

New product (including services) **development time** is the period between the first consideration of a product and its initial sale to the customer. Firms that respond quickly to customer needs for new products can develop an advantage over competitors. For example, **Honda** and **Toyota** are examples of companies that early on identified consumers' demands for fuel-efficient, reliable autos. Early development has given Honda and Toyota a competitive advantage for many years. Likewise, TCSI was one of the first companies to recognize the market's need for outsourced customer services and continues to try to anticipate new market opportunities.

Customer Response Time and Cycle Time

Customer response time is the amount of time between a customer's placing an order for a product or requesting service and delivering the product or service to the customer. The shorter the response time, the more competitive the company is on this dimension. The components of customer response time appear in Exhibit 6.10. Improvements can be possible in all components. For example, many companies have reduced order-receipt time by incorporating electronic ordering (via wide area networks or the Internet). Electronic ordering also reduces chances for human errors in the ordering process. Organizations minimize order-waiting time by carefully scheduling **bottleneck resources,** which are the constraining factors limiting production or sales, and by keeping some reserve capacity for unexpected but valuable orders. Companies also minimize order-delivery time by using overnight delivery services or, in the case of services, delivering them electronically. Most dramatic improvements in customer response time could be made possible by eliminating non-value-added and poor-quality-related activities in **production cycle time** (or simply 'cycle time'), which is the elapsed time between starting and finishing a production process, including any time to correct mistakes.

Exhibit 6.10 Customer Response Time

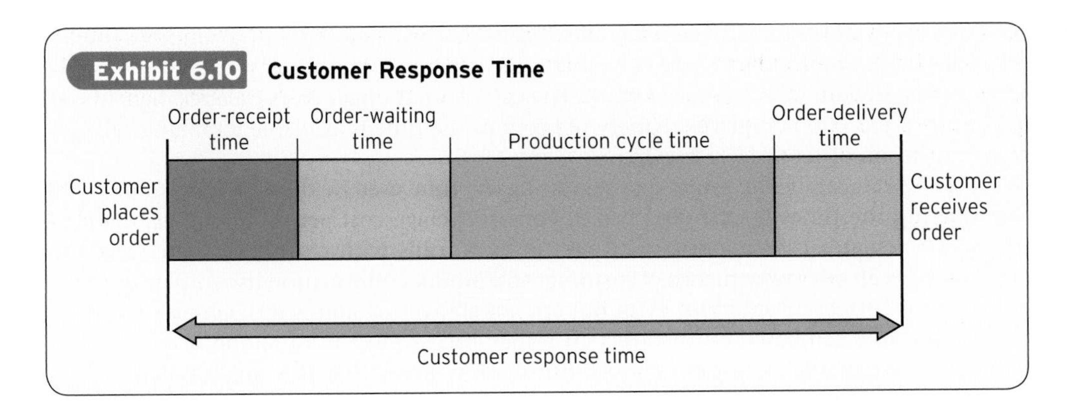

Costs of Time

The old adage, 'Time is money', has never been more true. Longer process times mean both higher out-of-pocket costs for human and physical resources and higher costs of forgone opportunities. In fact, time can be the scarcest resource of all. Individuals and organizations with good ideas can always obtain more money, but adding capacity and capability without improving processes and quality can perpetuate inefficiencies that reduce competitiveness. Attractive alternatives can be ignored because of insufficient time to analyse opportunities.

Some manufacturing companies allocate overhead costs to business units and products using cycle time as the cost-driver base. Although this allocation approach might not accurately measure the use of support resources or the opportunity costs of wasted time, it does get employees' attention. If evaluations and incentives are based on costs or profits, allocations based on cycle time also should motivate employees to improve processes to reduce cycle time. These organizations can use only costs or profits as the basis for performance evaluation since measured profits are improved with cycle time reductions, and cycle time can be reduced and revenues maintained or increased only by improving quality. Since some measures are leading indicators of quality, however, relying only on current profits to motivate employees could lead to myopic behaviour, such as ignoring the future effects of current actions. Some organizations rely on multiple, non-financial measures (e.g., the balanced scorecard) that are leading indicators of future profits to motivate employees to improve all areas of performance, not just current profits.

Time-driven Activity-based Costing and Management

According to users of activity-based costing (ABC) systems, discussed in Chapter 4, maintaining ABC systems can be quite costly, particularly when the system uses many different cost drivers. Some analysts have proposed using **time-driven ABC,** which is a method of ABC that uses time as the cost driver to replace some or all of the multiple cost drivers in an ABC system.[7] If the time to complete an activity is a sufficiently accurate measure of its resource consumption, using a single cost driver, time, can significantly reduce the costs of using an ABC system.

One can compute the time-driven cost-driver rate as equal to:

$$\frac{\textbf{Total cost supplied to perform activity(ies) during a period}}{\textbf{Total time used to perform activity(ies) during a period}}$$

If process improvements reduce the time needed to complete an activity, either more of the (value-added) activity can be performed with the supplied capacity (creating more value), or capacity can be reduced (saving costs).

Consider the example of TCSI's service calls. TCSI operates a call centre that employs the equivalent of 16 full-time employees to take customer calls by phone. The employees staff the call centre 13 weeks per quarter, and 56 hours per week. The call centre's direct costs (salaries, benefits, equipment, etc.) are $353,000 per quarter. Ninety per cent of the time is available for taking calls, and 10 per cent is spent on other tasks or breaks.

The cost of a call can be determined by summing the time used by the activities from Exhibit 6.6 and multiplying the times by the observed (metered) average cost per minute of calling capacity. Exhibit 6.11 calculates the time for two types of calls: calls with correct customer and product information and call both with incorrect customer and product information (two other combinations of correct and incorrect information exist, but are not shown for simplicity). Observe that the time cost to respond to a call based on incorrect customer and product information is more than twice that for a call that can rely on initially correct information. Recall that TCSI analysts determined that faulty information was a primary cause of poor quality service.

Transformation Customer Services, Inc.

Exhibit 6.11 Time-driven ABC Analyses of Calling Costs

	A	B	C	D	E
1	**Customer service call costs**	Quarterly			
2	Call centre's direct costs	$353,000			
3	Call centre availability, minutes	628,992			
4	Call centre cost per minute	$0.5612			
5					
6		**Correct customer & product information**		**Incorrect customer & product information**	
7	**Customer call activities**	**Time**	**Cost**	**Time**	**Cost**
8	Receive call from customer	0.25	$0.14	0.25	$0.14
9	Take customer & product information	1.00	0.56	1.00	0.56
10	Validate	0.25	0.14	0.50	0.28
11	*Obtain correct information*	-	-	4.00	2.24
12	Refer to product documentation	0.50	0.28	0.50	0.28
13	Validate as current	0.25	0.14	0.25	0.14
14	*Obtain correct documentation*	-	-	5.00	2.81
15	Resolve customer issue	5.00	2.81	5.00	2.81
16	Totals	7.25	$4.07	16.50	$9.26

6.3 You're the Decision Maker

Benefits of Quality Improvements

a. Verify the call centre's available capacity in minutes.

b. Exhibit 6.2, Panel B shows that the average time to process a call (after improving calling technology) is 7.95 minutes per call. If the call centre processed 78,013 calls in a quarter, and assuming only the two types of calls shown in Exhibit 6.11, what percentage and quantity of calls involved incorrect information?

c. If all incorrect customer and product information could be eliminated,

 i. How many calls could be processed with the existing call centre capacity?

 ii. Or, approximately how much cost could be saved while serving the same number of calls?

d. Discuss whether time-driven ABC's relatively low-cost approach represents an innovation or a re-packaging of venerable concepts. Do you think that this approach offers tools for improving customer-perceived value to the same degree of a full ABC approach, as discussed in Chapters 4 and 5?

(Solutions begin on page 278.)

In an actual cost system, all calls would be charged at the overall average cost of $353,000 ÷ 78,013 calls = $4.52 per call. This simple calculation obscures the great difference in resources needed for responding to calls with incorrect customer and product information. A traditional ABC system would set up separate cost pools for correct information and incorrect information calls, but this is a more complex accounting task than the time-driven ABC approach, which only requires accounting for the call centre's direct costs and the two types of calls processed. It is likely that in this case (but perhaps not every case), the costs per type of call would not be materially different between the two ABC methods, so the cost-benefit test would favour the time-driven approach.

Management of Process Productivity and Efficiency

LO 4
Measure and manage efficiency and capacity.

Process efficiency – the ability to transform inputs into *throughput* at the lowest cost – depends on having all employees work toward a common goal. **Throughput** is the amount of goods and services produced and delivered to customers during a period of time measured in dollar terms or physical measures. Managers need to know how well they are managing the organization's processes and activities. Employees can help identify inefficient or wasteful processes and activities to make improvements that meet customers' needs at lower cost.

Organizations manage two types of processes: production and business. **Production processes** directly result in the production of products or services provided to external customers. Examples of production processes include **Mold-Masters'** (Canada) machining aluminium stock into plastic-injection moulds, **DataPlay's** (USA) manufacturing miniature hard drives for **MP3** music players, and TCSI's providing outsourced customer services for its clients. **Business processes** support or enable production processes. Examples of business processes include the materials ordering processes that **Mold-Masters** uses to ensure that the correct aluminium stock is on hand at just the right time for machining.

Common measures of efficiency of both production and business processes include, in addition to quality:

- **Productivity**, a ratio of outcomes of a process divided by the amount of resources necessary to complete the process
- **Average cycle time**, the total processing time for all units divided by good units produced
- **Throughput time ratio**, the ratio of time spent adding value to total cycle time.

Exhibit 6.12 shows that measures of throughput and average cycle time are summary measures of efficiency, affected by quality and productivity. A low cycle time – from receipt of an order of a unit of existing product (or service) to its packaging and shipment (delivery) to the customer – and high throughput are possible only if processes are productive, and processes are productive only if they are of high quality.

Exhibit 6.12 Relations among Process Efficiency Measures

Measuring Productivity

Many possible measures exist to determine *productivity*, the ratio of the outcomes of a process divided by the amount of resources (physical units or cost) necessary to complete the process. **Total factor productivity** is the value of goods and services (measured as sales revenue) divided by the total cost to provide them. This diagnostic tool is especially useful when benchmarked

Transformation Customer Services, Inc.

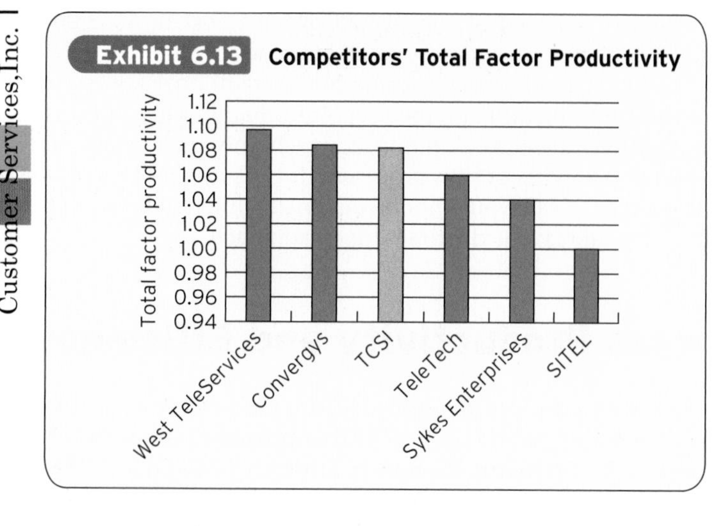

against that of competitors. For example, as shown in Exhibit 6.13, TCSI compared its total factor productivity for a recent year to that of its competitors in the industry by dividing each company's total sales by its total operating expenses. This type of information is available for many of the world's companies at **Hoover's Online** (www.hoovers.com) and from other financial databases. TCSI's total factor productivity is not the highest in the industry, and the company encourages employees to analyse all business and productive processes for ways to create more value at lower cost. Many employee suggestions for improvement (discussed earlier) focus on ways to reduce waste and improve the use of scarce resources.

More specific productivity measures compare outcomes valued by customers to the scarcest or most valuable resources used to achieve those outcomes, for example, sales revenue per employee. Last year, TCSI's sales revenue was $42,700 per employee. Is this good or bad? Productivity measures are meaningful only when compared over time or benchmarked against those of competitors. The historical trend of TCSI's sales revenue per employee shown in Exhibit 6.14 is increasing, which reflects improving sales productivity.

Transformation Customer Services, Inc.

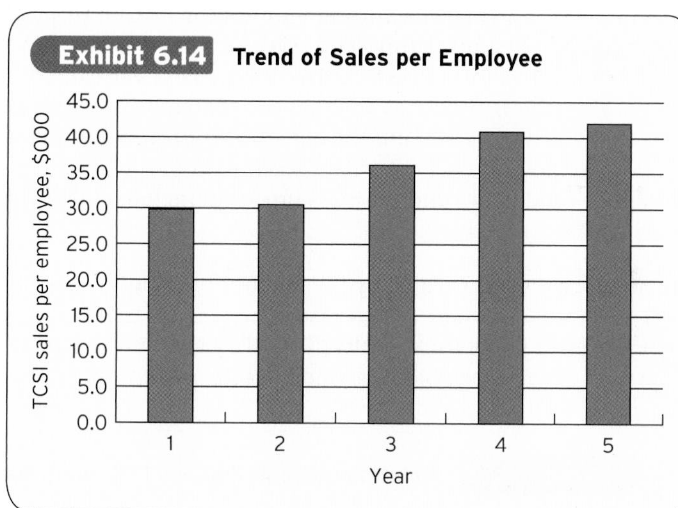

Measuring Average Cycle Time

Cycle time at TCSI includes the time elapsed from the start of a customer service call to its end. This definition of cycle time captures all processes that TCSI controls to deliver what customers expect: a quality service response in the shortest possible time.

In nearly all cases, customers and suppliers prefer short cycle times, which require a higher-quality product and fewer resources consumed by it. Therefore, low cycle times mean that organizations are delivering more customer value at lower cost, which is not possible without high quality and productive processes.

To be most useful, average cycle time should include the average time necessary to complete and deliver *all* good units and dispose of units that have to be reworked or scrapped because of defects, which is non-value-added time.

Measuring Throughput Efficiency

Not all of the time a service or product spends in process is productive; that is, value is not added to it every minute of its cycle time. **Throughput efficiency** is the relation of throughput achieved to the resources used. The throughput time ratio measures throughput efficiency as follows:

$$\textbf{Throughput time ratio} = \frac{\textbf{Value-added time}}{\textbf{Total processing time}}$$

In words, the throughput time ratio is the ratio of time spent adding customer value to products divided by total cycle time (also known as the 'ratio of work content to lead time').

The highest possible value of this ratio is 1.00 or 100 per cent, a theoretical ideal. Nonetheless, the closer an organization comes to a 100 per cent throughput ratio, the more efficient its processes are, and the more quickly it can fill customers' orders. In some organizations, only 5 per cent (or less) of its total product or service cycle time is spent adding value; if so, at least 95 per cent of the time is wasted by waiting for processing or correcting mistakes. Efficient companies have achieved throughput time ratios of much more than 50 per cent by eliminating unnecessary delays and defects.

TCSI computes its throughput time ratio for service calls each week. See Exhibit 6.15 for analysis of a recent week. Value-adding time (cell B5) includes receiving customers' calls, giving advice, and ensuring that problems have been resolved. Time spent without adding customer value (B6) includes the time customers spend waiting on hold, searching for correct information as well as reworking earlier defective or incomplete advice – activities that use scarce resources without creating anything for which customers are willing to pay. The average cycle time (B10) is the total processing time (B9) divided by the service calls completed (good units produced) during that time period (B4). A defective service call requires one or more return calls by the customer to resolve a problem. These calls are few, but the time spent on them is not counted as productive. The throughput time ratio (B11) is the time spent adding value (B5) divided by total processing time (B9). Higher ratios (over time or across competitors) indicate better uses of the scarcest resource of all – time. TCSI's nearly 79 per cent ratio shows that the company appears to be managing service-call time reasonably well, but perhaps with room for improvement.

Exhibit 6.15 Analysis of Throughput Time

	A	B	C
1	**Quarterly analysis of throughput time**		
2			
3	**Process input data**		
4	**Service calls completed**	**78,013**	**service calls**
5	**Time adding value**	**487,976**	**minutes**
6	**Time not adding value**	**132,332**	**minutes**
7			
8	**Throughput analysis**		
9	**Total processing time (B5 + B6)**	**620,308**	**minutes**
10	**Average cycle time (B9/B4)**	**7.95**	**minutes**
11	**Throughput time ratio (B5/B9)**	**78.7%**	

Transformation Customer Services,Inc.

Managing Process Capacity

Process capacity is a measure of a process's *ability* to transform resources into valued products and services, usually expressed as a rate of processing inputs or generating outputs per time period. For example, the commuting capacity of a highway could be expressed in terms of the number of commuter vehicles entering the city per hour. Using this definition, one might incorrectly conclude that widening the highway or increasing its speed limit would increase the commuting capacity of vehicles in the city. This logic is flawed, however, because the perspective of capacity is too narrow. The capacity of the *entire* commuting process – or the manufacturing or service process – must be considered. Therefore, widening a highway or increasing its speed limit without providing for additional destination *parking* would not increase commuting capacity; instead of waiting on the highway, commuters will be looking for parking places. A process- or system-wide perspective is necessary to manage capacity.

Measuring Capacity

Five common measures – theoretical, practical, normal, buffer and excess capacity – influence how organizations manage process capacity. The *theoretical capacity* of a process is the maximum possible rate of transformation of inputs into outputs if the process were fully used, with no downtime or unused capacity. Most organizations, however, operate processes at less than theoretical capacity (e.g., at 80 per cent of theoretical capacity) for a number of reasons, including the following:

- Planned downtime usually is necessary for scheduled maintenance or improvements to equipment and procedures.
- Unplanned downtime caused by breakdowns in equipment or delays in supply of inputs can make it impossible to operate at theoretical capacity.
- Some capacity can be reserved for unforeseen needs and the ability to be flexible.
- Demand for the output of the process might be less than the theoretical (inflexible) capacity.

The *practical capacity* of a process is its *theoretical capacity* less planned downtime for scheduled maintenance or improvements. Practical capacity arguably should reflect expected demand for the output of the process. *Normal capacity* is an average level of usage that often is less than practical capacity. **Buffer capacity** is an amount of capacity that may be intentionally reserved for unexpected demand. **Excess (or unused) capacity** is the amount (if any) by which practical capacity exceeds the demand plus buffer capacity. Note that organizations sometimes allow processes to operate in excess of practical capacity to meet urgent needs. In the long run, however, skipping maintenance and planned improvements will lead to breakdowns and reduced capacity. Exhibit 6.16 shows relations between measures of capacity for a process with theoretical and practical capacities in excess of demand. Persistent unused capacity indicates wasted resources; negative unused capacity can indicate lost opportunities.

Exhibit 6.16 Measures of Capacity

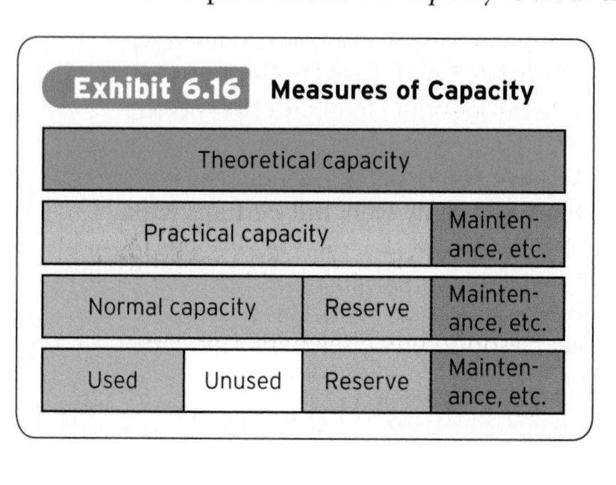

Managing Quality + Time + Productivity + Capacity = JIT or Lean Process Management

LO 5
Evaluate how just-in-time methods create benefits by combining management of quality, time, productivity and capacity.

All firms face the strategic problem of balancing the costs of inventories and/or capacity, flexible production and missed sales opportunities. Inventories create costs of production, maintenance, security, obsolescence and forgone other uses of capital. Capacity also incurs capital, maintenance and opportunity costs of excess capacity. Flexible production can reduce the need for inventories and respond quickly to customers' needs, but at a greater capital cost. Finally, the cost of satisfying all sales opportunities might be too high – the profits from some sales might not cover the costs of inventories or flexible production.[8] Although most firms find hybrid forms of managing this problem, we contrast two extremes: just-in-time and traditional manufacturing.

Just-in-time (JIT) or **lean processes** purchase, make and deliver services and products just when needed, without wasted time or effort.[9] JIT/lean processes have many benefits. Organizations that use JIT find that it reduces, or potentially eliminates, inventory carrying costs. **Inventory carrying costs** are costs of obsolescence, receiving, handling, storing and insuring inventory. JIT/lean also requires high-quality processes. Defective products are incompatible with JIT/lean because, in theory, no inventory is in reserve to keep production processes operating. Thus, defects trigger investigations of processes to eliminate their causes. Without wasteful efforts needed to correct defects, JIT/lean processes also have short cycle times. The JIT/lean philosophy – avoiding waste and non-value-added activities – is closely linked to activity-based management (the topic of Chapter 5). Furthermore, all types of organizations may apply JIT/lean management principles.

6.2 Cost Management in Practice

Benefits of Lean Processes

Many organizations report dramatic improvements in performance as a result of focusing on time management. For example, **Mold-Masters Ltd** (Ontario, Canada) has expanded its lean manufacturing of plastic-injection moulds into Germany and China. Companywide implementation of lean principles has caused floor-space savings of more than 20 per cent, a nearly 20-percentage reduction in product delivery times and total financial savings of 3 per cent. Furthermore, the company sees room for significant further improvements as it doubles output in both locations. Because of the increased product quality that lean manufacturing requires, Mold-Masters is able now to offer a 10-year warranty on all of its complete plastic-injection systems, covering in excess of 3 billion parts.

Source: Grace (2007).

Contrasts of JIT/Lean and Traditional Processes

Service-based companies such as TCSI are ideally situated to implement the JIT/lean philosophy because they can focus on improving quality and eliminating waste without the encumbrances of physical plants, inventories and entrenched production processes. Manufacturing companies also can gain from applying the JIT/lean philosophy to their management of physical resources. For example, manufacturers should realize that customers do not care whether the manufacturer maintains inventories or has the largest, most efficient forklifts to move parts and materials from one manufacturing activity to the next. As far as customers are concerned, these are non-value-added activities that only waste resources and increase costs. Nor are customers interested in paying for the manufacturer to fix defective products. They prefer defect-free products, and if a competitor offers defect-free products at a lower cost, the customer has an obvious reason to buy elsewhere. Concerns for eliminating the waste caused by non-value-added activities and unnecessary defects converge in the solution offered by JIT/lean manufacturing.[10] We now compare the filling of the same order by a traditional manufacturer and a JIT/lean manufacturer.

Traditional 'push' manufacturing

A traditional manufacturer begins the manufacturing cycle by forecasting total orders for a time period. Considering beginning and ending inventory levels yields the required production level. Based on the forecasted level of production and materials inventories, the manufacturer orders materials and then schedules production at each defined activity of the process. Thus, forecasting and scheduling activities push production through the process. For example, a traditional manufacturer of personal computers does the following:

- Forecasts sales (by model) well in advance of the start of production to accommodate purchasing and production lead times.
- Orders all components (circuit boards, disk drives, DVD or CD-ROM drives, processor chips, and so on).
- Prepares a production schedule and gives orders to all functional groups (motherboard assembly, storage device assembly, final assembly, etc.) to assemble the required number of parts, components and computers.
- Upon receiving a customer order, ships products from finished goods inventory if the product is available, or if the product is not available, either places it on back order status to be filled as soon as possible or expedites a special order.

Why is this approach to manufacturing possibly inefficient? First, sales forecasting drives it, and sales forecasting can be an inaccurate guide to production scheduling. Employees in every functional activity are motivated to meet production schedules regardless of overall sales. If sales are less than forecasted, the company invests too much in unused parts and unsold finished goods inventory, which consumes resources unnecessarily and can result in obsolete inventories. If sales are more than forecasted, the company must either back-order its sales, which could result in dissatisfied customers and lost sales, or rush orders for parts and expedite production beyond what was planned, which could greatly increase costs. Thus, pushing production through the company motivates adherence to production schedules and inhibits flexibility, regardless of the impact on throughput – the result of sales to customers.

Second, the traditional manufacturer usually does not balance the timing of receiving materials and of all production activities with capacity. Not considering capacity can result in a temporary, wasteful build-up of inventories if this is merely a matter of timing, or a permanent build-up of inventories if managers are covering their quality problems by ordering too many materials or overproducing. Thus, push production also can reduce the motivation to improve quality and can reinforce the motivation to overuse capacity.

JIT 'pull' manufacturing

Although a JIT/lean manufacturer also uses long-term sales forecasting to determine its scale of operations and capacity, JIT production is 'pulled' through the process by customer orders rather than pushed by a master production schedule. For example, consider how **Dell Computer Corporation** pulls an order through its production process in a sequence almost the reverse of that of the traditional manufacturer:

- A customer places an order for a computer with specific features.
- The sales order triggers a production order.
- The production order triggers the ordering and assembly of individual components, which are started immediately and designated for the specific order.
- The requirements for components trigger orders to suppliers, which ship parts immediately.
- The customer receives the ordered computer approximately one week later.

A traditional manufacturer could be just as *flexible* to customer orders by forecasting sales perfectly, which is not possible, or by investing in large enough inventories to avoid all back orders, which could be prohibitively costly. Obviously, the JIT approach is flexible to customer needs and requires lower inventory levels than traditional methods – only as much as is necessary to process each order. JIT production is not trivial to design, implement or manage, however.

Overall equipment effectiveness

The effects of lean operations should be observable in more efficient capacity use. **Overall equipment effectiveness (OEE)** is a summary measure of the use of process capacity to create good (defect-free) output.[11] Organizations of all types can use this summary OEE measure as a means to compare how well similar subunits are managing their capacities or how well a specific subunit is managing capacity over time. Consider TCSI's use of a call centre's customer service capacity in Exhibit 6.17.

Note that OEE does not prescribe that all organizations should operate at an OEE ratio of 100 per cent, even if this ideal were possible. For example, the poorest measure in Exhibit 6.17 is 'performance', which is plagued by longer than desired actual cycle time. Recall that this discrepancy has been traced to faulty customer or product information. Eliminating these sources of excess process time might be prohibitively expensive, but tools of cost management could be employed (e.g., ABM from Chapter 5 and decision making from Chapters 7 and 8) to evaluate the costs and benefits of preventing poor quality from faulty information.

Manufacturing inventory analysis

Cost management also can add value by measuring the costs of balancing inventory, flexibility and missing sales. Often these costs have the most communication impact when they are benchmarked against more efficient competitors. Revealing these cost disadvantages should induce companies to consider adopting a JIT/lean production approach, which should result in improved financial outcomes. Consider the summary information in Exhibits 6.18 and 6.19 that contrast the production

Exhibit 6.17 Overall Equipment Effectiveness

	A	B	C	D
1	Overall equipment effectiveness			Source
2	Availability = Operating time/Planned operating time			
3	Operating time	620,308	minutes	Exhibit 6.15
4	Planned operating time	628,992	minutes	Exhibit 6.11
5	Availability =B3/B4	98.6%		
6	Performance = Ideal cycle time/Actual cycle time			
7	Ideal cycle time	7.25	minutes per call	Exhibit 6.11
8	Actual cycle time	7.95	minutes per call	Exhibit 6.15
9	Performance =B7/B8	91.2%		
10	Quality = Good units/Total units			
11	Good calls completed	76,921		TCSI records
12	Total calls completed	78,013		Exhibit 6.15
13	Quality =B11/B12	98.6%		
14	OEE = Availability x Performance x Quality			
15	OEE=B5*B9*B13	88.7%		
16				
17	Actual good calls completed	76,921		
18	÷ Maximum calls	86,758	=B4/B7	
19	OEE	88.7%		

performance of three computer manufacturers: **Hewlett-Packard,** a relatively traditional manufacturer, and two more efficient competitors, **Dell** and **Apple**. Dell openly states that it has competitive advantages because of its flexible, JIT manufacturing approach. Observe that Dell's employees generate 1.6 times the sales revenue per employee, as do Hewlett-Packard's employees. This indicates that Dell uses human resources with greater effectiveness. But Apple's sales productivity is twice that of Dell. Both Dell and Apple manage their costs more effectively than Hewlett-Packard, too; they have much lower inventory levels and much higher inventory turnover ratios, reflecting more efficient production and supply processes than Hewlett-Packard. These convey significant advantages, particularly in competitive markets.

JIT/Lean Success Factors

How is the JIT/lean manufacturer able to reliably produce and deliver its products? Manufacturers that apply JIT/lean principles find that the following six factors are essential. Furthermore, all of them appear to be necessary; an organization probably cannot implement JIT/lean successfully without implementing *all* of its components, at least to some degree.

1. *Commitment to quality.* All employees must be involved in the quality process. Defects cause delays and require buffer inventories. Employees must be able and motivated to take preventive actions. However, if defects occur, the sooner employees can detect a defect, the sooner they can correct it, minimizing lost time and resources.
2. *Creation of flexible capacity or predictable orders.* Short set-up times and the ability to customize products is necessary to respond to unique orders. Mass-production can benefit from JIT/lean if producers are able to stabilize orders through advance or long-term purchase agreements.
3. *Achievement of reliable supplier relations.* Suppliers must be reliable, providing on-time deliveries of high-quality materials. Unreliable suppliers necessitate buffer inventories. Developing strong supplier relationships often means reducing the number of suppliers, which also results in savings in support services that manage suppliers and orders.
4. *Development of smooth production flow.* Unbalanced production leads to delays at bottlenecks and the need for excess buffer inventories. Organizing production activities to respond to individual orders can mean configuring activities into 'cells' that focus on completing a unique order rather than linear assembly lines best suited to producing large batches of identical items.

Exhibit 6.18 **Inventory Management at Three Computer Manufacturers**

Qualitative and quantitative data from 2010 Forms 10-K filed with the US Securities and Exchange Commission	Manufacturer Production Method		
	Dell/JIT	**Hewlett-Packard/ Traditional**	**Apple/Hybrid-Outsourced**
Qualitative statements	'Dell's flexible, build-to-order manufacturing process enables Dell to turn over inventory every five days on average, and reduce inventory levels. This allows Dell to rapidly introduce the latest relevant technology more quickly than companies with slow-moving, indirect distribution channels, and to rapidly pass on component cost savings directly to customers.'	'After we develop a product, we must be able to manufacture appropriate volumes quickly and at low costs. To accomplish this, we must accurately forecast volumes, mix of products and configurations that meet customer requirements.... we must adequately address quality issues associated with our products and services, including defects in our engineering, design and manufacturing processes.... If we have excess or obsolete inventory, we may have to reduce our prices and write down inventory.'	'The Company orders components for its products and builds inventory in advance of product shipments. Because the Company's markets are volatile and subject to rapid technology and price changes, there is a risk the Company will forecast incorrectly and produce or order from third parties excess or insufficient inventories of particular products or components. The Company's operating results and financial condition in the past have been and may in the future be materially adversely affected by the Company's ability to manage its inventory levels...'
Revenue (millions USD)	61,490.00	126,030.00	65,230.00
No. of employees (average, 000)	96.00	324.60	49.40
Sales per employee (millions USD)	640.52	388.26	1,320.45
Cost of goods sold (millions USD)	50,098.00	98,089.00	39,541.00
Inventories (average, millions USD)	1,176.00	6,297.00	753.00
Inventory turnover, times per year	42.60	15.58	52.51

5. *Maintenance of a well-trained, motivated, flexible workforce.* In a production cell environment, workers must be well trained and cross trained to use various machines and work on different areas of their production cell. Furthermore, they must be able and motivated to correct problems as they occur to keep the production process operating.
6. *Achievement and improvement of short cycle and customer-response times.* Short customer-response times enable companies to respond quickly to customer needs. Eliminating non-value-added time and activities results in shorter cycle times. For example, unnecessary paperwork or travel and movement of parts and assemblies waste time.

Organizations could benefit from JIT even if they cannot implement its components perfectly. In many areas of the world, for example, instantaneous resupply of materials is not possible, so many nearly JIT companies maintain some inventories. They still benefit from applying JIT principles to eliminate waste in other activities even though they still have inventories.

Exhibit 6.19 Comparative Sales and Production Performance

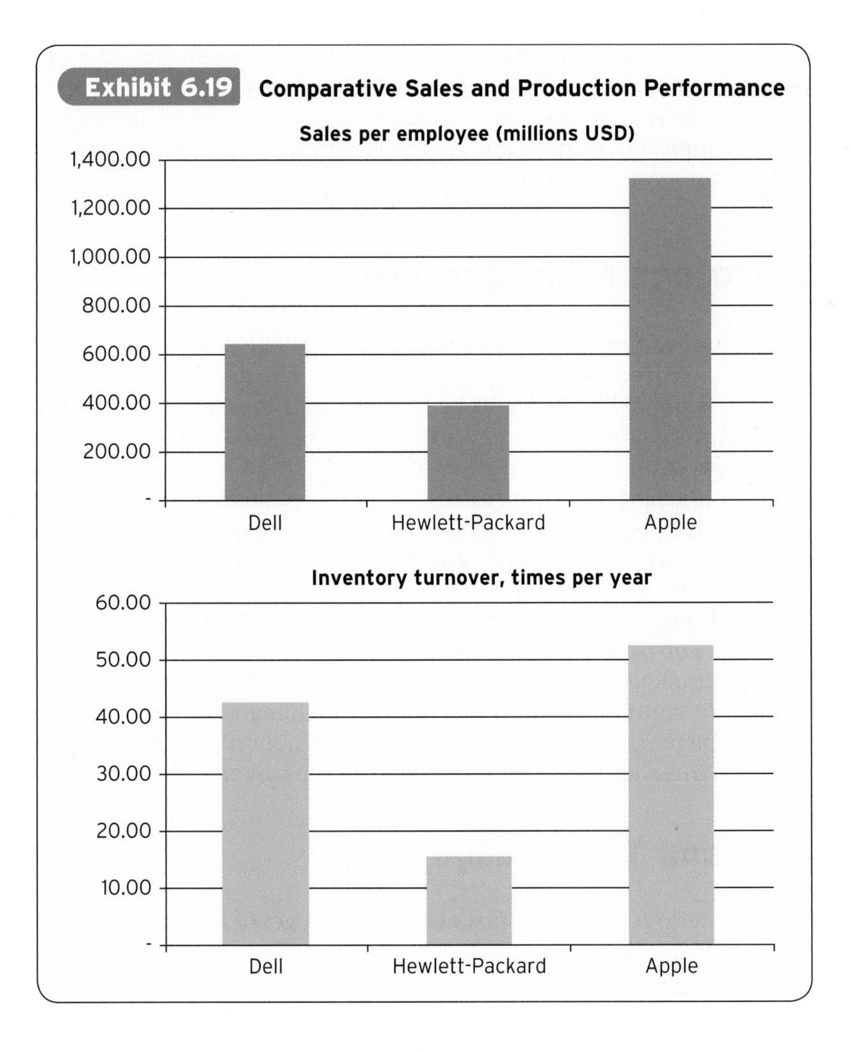

6.3 Research Insight

Benefits of JIT

Verifying average economic benefits derived from adopting JIT is difficult. The majority of self-reports are the apparent successes. Firms would be reluctant to disclose that they had failed at JIT.

A recent study using financial statement data demonstrates how difficult it is to isolate the effects of a single organizational factor such as JIT. The study did find that firms declaring that they had adopted JIT - though we do not know whether they adopted some or all of its components and how widely they adopted JIT - on average had significantly higher inventory turnover ratios afterward than did comparable firms that apparently did not adopt JIT. This confirms that JIT has a beneficial effect on the use of scarce resources.* However, this effect apparently did not extend to improvements in return on assets (ROA) because all firms in the study on average experienced declines in ROA.

Although the logic of JIT is compelling, we cannot be sure that adopting JIT results in improved profitability for all firms. More research is necessary to isolate contemporaneous and complementary effects. Some research on JIT processes indicates that firms do not and should not adopt management techniques in isolation, and it could be that the way firms bundle JIT with other techniques determines organizational performance.

Sources: Balakrishnan et al. (1996) and Selto et al. (1995).

* This finding is supported by some studies, such as that by Billesbach and Hayen (1994) but not supported by others, such as that by Procter (1995), which could not find evidence of average improvements in inventory turnover ratios that could be attributed to JIT.

The cost management analyst also fills a valuable role in JIT manufacturing organizations by identifying other areas for improvement and by monitoring performance in the preceding six components of JIT production using the same type of lead-indicator and diagnostic tools useful for managing quality. For example, measuring and reporting defects, causes of defects, cycle times and employee capabilities support the management of both quality and time.

Job and Project Management

LO 6
Understand how companies manage long-term projects and their costs.

Managing jobs and projects requires attention to quality, customer satisfaction, costs and adherence to schedules. When jobs fall behind schedule or costs become higher than expected, some individuals might be tempted to compromise quality or even to cheat. Neither behaviour is usually successful because reputations for quality and honesty generate more opportunities than short-sighted opportunism does. This section discusses the methods for tracking and ensuring successful project management over time.

Complex jobs (for example, bridges, shopping centres and complicated lawsuits) often take months or years to complete and require the work of many different departments, divisions or subcontractors. These projects are more difficult to evaluate than short jobs that can be evaluated relatively quickly (typically within a reporting period). Consider the job of painting a small house. The painter might estimate the costs and bid on the job accordingly. A week later, when the job is complete, the painter can compare estimated costs to actual costs and evaluate the job's profitability. In contrast, consider a contractor building a hospital, which will take more than two years to complete. The contractor must find a way not only to bid on the project but also to evaluate it at critical intervals to update and anticipate the cost and timing changes.

Project Cost and Time Budgets

The manager of a long-term project must first establish a budget of costs to be incurred throughout the project at various stages of completion. The stage of completion usually appears in reports as a percentage of completion for the entire project or as the completion of certain critical steps in the project. Then, as the project progresses, the manager evaluates two critical areas: (1) the planned cost of work completed to date versus the actual cost of work completed to date and (2) the planned percentage or stage of completion since the project began versus the actual percentage or stage of completion. The two graphs in Exhibit 6.20 are examples of useful information for evaluating the progress of project costs and schedules.

Exhibit 6.20 shows that the project is 40 per cent complete (the horizontal axes of panels A and B). The budget line indicates that, for this stage of completion, costs should be $0.9 million, as shown in panel A. The actual cost line indicates, however, that actual costs were $1.4 million. Thus, at the 40 per cent stage of completion, the project has a cost overrun of $500,000.

Although we know that cost overruns have occurred, we do not know whether the project is on schedule. Panel B of Exhibit 6.20 shows that the project should be 23 per cent complete by month 8. Because the contractor is 40 per cent complete by month 8, the project is approximately four months ahead of schedule. The trade-off of earlier completion for a higher cost might be acceptable to the customer. Given the complex nature of projects, however, revising budgeted costs and budgeted percentages or stages of completion throughout the project to reflect these changes might be desirable. (Most major projects require changes due to their inherent uncertainty.) Thus, the graphs in Exhibit 6.20 need updating to reflect revised cost and time budgets to allow managers to evaluate the project by comparing actual results against the revised budget, which reflects current expectations.

Project scheduling

Many companies engaged in large, complex projects use a project scheduling aid called a 'Gantt chart' (named after its developer, Henry Gantt). A **Gantt chart** depicts the stages required to complete a project and the sequence in which the stages are to be performed. A Gantt chart for building a custom home is shown in Exhibit 6.21; it shows the eight major construction activities (corresponding to the

Exhibit 6.20 Project Percentage of Completion Charts

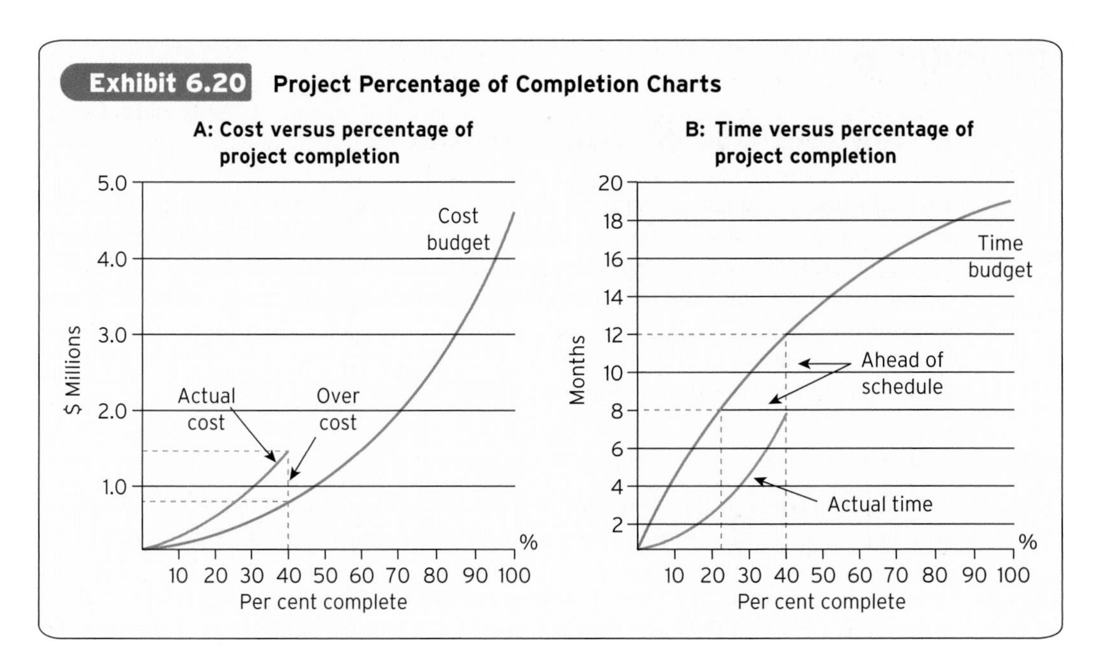

home builder's job-costing system) and reflects planned and actual start-and-finish dates by week for the project's duration. The coloured bars describe the original building plan by each activity. For example, the builder planned to start the permitting process in the first week of May and complete that activity by the end of the third week. The actual completion of each activity is shown in the grey bars below the plan. As shown, the permitting activity took two weeks longer than expected, which delayed excavation because it could not commence without the proper permits. Because many building activities are sequential, the permitting delay affected the entire building plan. The chart shows that the project finished only one week later than planned. More important, the builder was able to notify the customer about the delay early and to manage the building process so that only a week was lost. The Gantt chart allowed the builder to visualize what to expect and what to modify over the life of the project soon enough to favourably affect its cost and timing.

Exhibit 6.21 Gantt Chart for Building a Custom Home

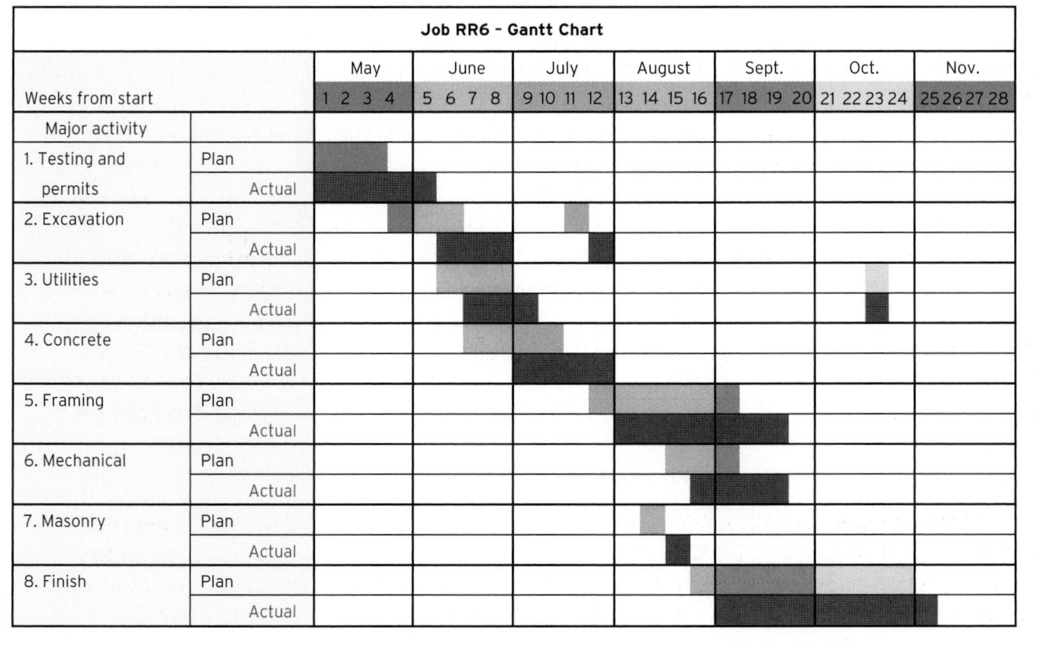

Appendix 6

Construction and Use of Control Charts

LO 6
Understand how to construct and use control charts.

Control charts display measures of important product or service attributes for individual items or for a sample of items to disclose attribute measures and variation in the production process. Organizations use control charts for several purposes, including process control, assurance sampling, and inspection activities. In most cases, control charts provide multiple benefits such as (1) causing employees to directly monitor the quality of their work, (2) detecting defects quickly and at the source, and (3) providing a common, objective means of communicating the quality of a process or product.

Statistical Control

Organizations could base control charts on historical data of attributes achieved or on desired levels of the attributes. For example, historically, the response process time for one of TCSI's customer service representatives has averaged 7.95 minutes over the past 16 weeks, as appears in Exhibit 6.22. Using this historical performance, TCSI could prepare a **statistical control chart**, which displays attributes, for example, customer response times, against the historical parameters of the *mean* (7.95 minutes) and *variation*.[12] Variation usually is displayed as an interval based on the historical *range* of outcomes (high to low) or 2 or 3 *standard deviations* above and below the mean (e.g., between 10.70 and 5.19 minutes). Some experts recommend basing variation on range because it is easier to both compute for small samples and explain to employees than standard deviation. Because using the range to set the allowable interval requires access to special tables (available in all texts on quality control), we show intervals using standard deviation.

Target Control

Alternatively, TCSI could prepare a control chart based on specified or target levels of product attributes. For example, suppose that market and customer service research reveals that properly

Exhibit 6.22 Weekly Average Customer Response Time

Week	Average response time
1	6.89
2	7.89
3	9.60
4	7.77
5	9.70
6	8.07
7	6.62
8	6.84
9	9.13
10	9.63
11	10.13
12	5.45
13	6.29
14	7.79
15	8.12
16	7.26

Statistical control parameters	
Overall mean	7.95 min.
Standard deviation (SD)	1.378 min.
2 SDs	2.755 min.
UCL = Mean + 2 SD	10.70 min.
LCL = Mean −2 SD	5.19 min.
Target control parameters	
Target mean	7.50 min.
Target deviation	2.00 min.
UCL = Mean + 2.00	9.50 min.
LCL = Mean − 2.00	5.50 min.

responding to a customer inquiry should take 7.5 minutes and that variation of plus or minus 2.0 minutes is within the range of acceptable service. In an ideal situation, the natural variation of a process is less than specified or target levels, but many quality problems result from natural process variation exceeding the target variation. Redesigning a process to reduce its natural variation can be more economical than imposing stricter target control levels that result in many defects, causing high levels of internal and external failure.

A control chart based on target-attribute parameters might classify a different set of outcomes as defects than would a statistical control chart. Exhibit 6.23 shows two sets of controls, statistical in **blue** and target in **red**. The horizontal lines in the middle of the chart reflect either the statistical (**blue**) or target (**red**) value of the attribute. The upper lines of the chart reflect the statistical (**blue**) or target (**red**) upper control limits (UCL). To give speedy customer service, customer response times should not exceed the appropriate UCL level. The lower lines reflect the statistical (**blue**) or target (**red**) lower control limits (LCL). To fully consider the customer's inquiry, customer response time should not fall below the appropriate LCL.[13]

Exhibit 6.23 Control Chart of Weekly Average Customer Response Times (Specific Employee)

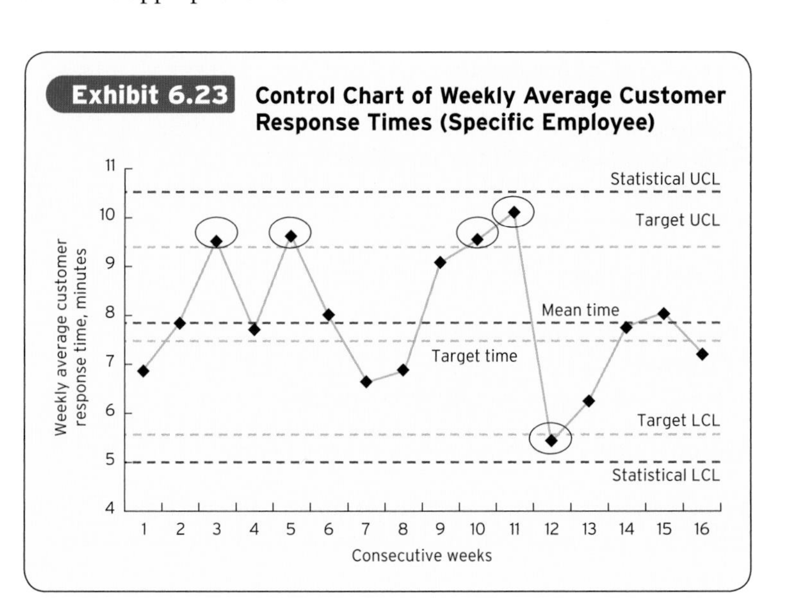

The circled observations identify customer response times that exceed or fall below *target* control limits. The statistical control limits, in contrast, do not identify any violations of control limits. Whether to use the tighter target limits rather than the looser statistical limits depends on the organization's estimates of the relative costs of:

- Intervening when a violation is detected (correctly or incorrectly) using tight limits. These costs include finding and correcting causes of defects, rework, delays and even lost sales.

- Not intervening when a violation (from the customer's perspective) occurs but is not detected using loose limits. These costs include internal and external failures, which could be large.

Auditors face the same situation when deciding to perform additional auditing tests based on results of sampling transactions. For example, does a low level of confirmed account balances signal an out-of-control accounting system, or is this a chance occurrence? Considering the costs of making errors, auditors want to be able to assure users of the financial statements (and themselves!) that the financial statements fairly present the organization's status and performance.

Patterns of Variation

A process can be out of control (exhibiting undesirable variation) even if attribute measures do not violate control limits. Attribute measures could exhibit runs, cycles, extreme jumps, or concentrations at control limits, which can signal the need for intervention or opportunities for improvement. A **run** refers to sequential values above or below the mean or values sequentially increasing or decreasing. Based on an approximately 1 per cent statistical probability of a run occurring by chance, a statistically out-of-control process can be identified using the following rules of thumb:[14]

- *Seven successive values* on the same side of the mean or target.
- *Four or more successive values* outside 1 standard deviation from the mean or target.
- *Two or more successive values* outside 2 standard deviations from the mean or target.

Causes of runs include the following:

- Worker fatigue
- Wear and deterioration of tools and equipment
- Changes in environmental conditions
- Accumulation of waste, scrap, and excess parts that cause congestion
- Learning and improved use of resources

The following can cause cyclical behaviour:

- Recurring conditions (night/day, heat/cold)
- Rotation of employees, equipment or suppliers
- Rotation of testing and inspection
- Periodic maintenance or training.

Causes of extreme jumps include:

- Changes in tools, equipment or set-ups
- Change of employees
- Changes or errors in testing or reporting procedures.

The following can cause values concentrated near control limits:

- Major differences in the quality of resources (human and physical)
- Mistakenly plotting outcomes from different processes on the same chart.

Benefits of Control Charts

Cost management analysts, industrial engineers, quality control specialists, managers and employees in all types of organizations throughout the world have found that control charts are simple, versatile and inexpensive tools for managing the quality of their products and services. If these charts are based on sound statistical evidence and compelling market research, control charts are reliable guides for controlling processes, preventing defects and measuring quality performance.

Chapter Summary

Managers in all organizations understand that product quality is one of the critical success factors for organizations. Some managers adopt the total quality management (TQM) philosophy, which argues that organizations must constantly seek improved quality. Other managers have the return-on-quality (ROQ) view that there is a trade-off between cost and quality so that the best quality level might be less than total quality. These costs of quality include prevention, appraisal, internal failure and external failure. Managers recognize trade-offs among these categories. For example, increased prevention resources can reduce internal and external failure costs.

On-time product delivery is also a critical success factor for organizations. Reducing the length of time between order and delivery of the product to the customer increases customer satisfaction. The just-in-time (JIT/lean) philosophy is a natural fit with TQM and time management. With JIT/lean, there is little or no room for product defects.

TCSI and other companies have been successful because they understand the informational and organizational requirements for managing quality, time, productivity and capacity. These requirements include:[15]

1. *Employee responsibility and authority.* Employees, not just managers, should collect and use information to get feedback and solve problems.
2. *Leading-indicator and diagnostic information.* Cost management information should be more detailed and focused on activities than that produced by traditional accounting systems. Instead of reporting just the cost of defects, for example, the information system should also report the types and causes of defects.
3. *Problem-solving information.* The information should include problem-solving information such as that coming from quality control charts. Financial reports would indicate a decline in revenues, for example, but not its causes. Control charts, however, could show an increase in customer complaints as a likely cause of the revenue decline.
4. *Timely information.* The information should be available quickly (for example, daily or 'real time') so workers can get quick feedback.
5. *Appropriate evaluations and rewards.* Evaluations and rewards should be based on performing activities that lead to high quality and customer satisfaction. This reflects that you get what you reward.

Key Terms

For each term's definition, refer to the indicated page, or turn to the glossary at the end of the text.

Term	Page	Term	Page
appraisal (also called *detection* or *inspection*),	240	Gantt chart,	256
average cycle time,	247	histogram,	232
bottleneck resources,	244	internal failure,	240
buffer capacity,	250	inventory carrying costs,	250
business processes,	247	ISO 9000,	243
cause-and-effect analysis,	234	just-in-time (JIT),	250
control chart,	233, 258	lagging indicators of quality,	232
costs of quality (COQ),	239	leading indicators of quality,	232
customer-focused quality,	231	lean processes,	250
customer response time,	244	lower control limit,	233
defect,	229	Malcolm Baldrige National Quality Award,	243
Deming prize,	243	maximum quality level,	229
European Quality Award,	243	new product development time,	244
excess (or unused) capacity,	250	overall equipment effectiveness (OEE),	252
external failure,	241	Pareto chart,	237
flowchart,	236	prevention,	240

process capacity,	249	statistical control chart,*	258
production cycle time,	244	throughput,	247
production processes,	247	throughput efficiency,	248
productivity,	247	throughput time ratio,	247
return on quality (ROQ),	229	time-driven ABC,	245
run,*	260	total factor productivity,	247
run chart,	233	total quality management (TQM),	229
scatter diagram,	236	upper control limit,	233

**Term appears in Appendix 6.*

*Review Questions are mostly written at a **basic** level; Critical Analysis questions and Exercises are **intermediate**, and Problems and Cases are **advanced**.*

Review Questions

6.1 Why do advocates of TQM expect to earn higher profits?

6.2 What are the similarities and differences between TQM and ROQ?

6.3 What is the major difference between tangible and intangible product features that affect management of quality?

6.4 How are process and product variations leading indicators of quality?

6.5 How do leading indicators of quality differ from diagnostic information about quality?

6.6 How does customer satisfaction differ from quality?

6.7 Is cost of quality a leading indicator or diagnostic information? Explain.

6.8 How do organizations make trade-offs among the four types of quality activities?

6.9 Is COQ more consistent with TQM or ROQ? Explain.

6.10 How are managing quality and managing time related?

6.11 Is JIT possible without high-quality processes? Explain.

6.12 What is cycle time? How is it measured?

6.13 What is throughput efficiency? How is it measured?

6.14 Explain the concepts of process capacities. Use an example from the chapter to describe the capacity of a specific process.

6.15 Explain why overall equipment efficiency (OEE) is indicative of efficient use of capacity, but does not prescribe 100 per cent efficiency.

Critical Analysis

6.16 An engineer argues, 'Quality means the product will perform faultlessly.' A marketing manager retorts, 'No, quality is whatever the customer says it is.' Are these views conflicting? Explain.

6.17 Two years after **Wallace Co.** won the Malcolm Baldrige Quality Award, this small oil and gas company filed for bankruptcy. Explain how this could have happened.

6.18 Contrast these statements. **FedEx:** 'We're trying to isolate quality improvements that just don't add any value . . . to the customer.' **Hewlett-Packard:** 'Asking what quality is worth is like asking what my left lung is worth.'

6.19 In its marketing activities, **United Airlines** stresses the importance of on-time flight departures and dealing with customer complaints. **Qantas Airlines** stresses its safety record and in-flight service. Are both airlines concerned with quality? Explain.

6.20 **United Parcel Service** (UPS) (www.ups.com) assumed that on-time delivery was the most important feature of its service and stressed (literally) its importance to UPS employees. UPS managers were confused as to why the company was not gaining market share even though customers rated the company's on-time delivery very high. Explain this apparently contrary result.

6.21 **Toyota** is credited with refining the practice of JIT. In Japan, it benefits greatly by having most of its suppliers in close proximity because suppliers are able to provide parts and materials almost instantaneously. A Fortune 500 manufacturing company in the centre of the United States, which is separated by long distances from most suppliers, instituted JIT practices within local operations but found it necessary to maintain a large, computerized, central warehouse. How could this company benefit from JIT even though it must maintain a costly inventory warehouse?

6.22 **Motorola** (www.motorola.com) has employed its Six Sigma approach to managing quality for many years. ('Six Sigma' refers to the probability of a defect occurring based on the area under a normal probability curve that is 6 standard deviations from the mean. This probability is 0.0000002 per cent, or only 2 defects, per million events.) The company uses these six steps:

- Identify the product you create or the service you provide.
- Identify the customer(s) for your product or service and determine what they consider important.
- Identify what you need to satisfy the customer.
- Define the process for doing the work.
- Mistake-proof the process and eliminate wasted effort.
- Ensure continuous improvement by measuring, analysing and controlling the improved process.

Is Motorola's approach to quality more closely aligned with TQM or ROQ? Explain.

6.23 Allegheny Industries' top executives are evaluated on the basis of annual profits and earnings per share. Middle managers are evaluated on the basis of cycle time and product quality. Are these evaluations consistent? Does it matter? Explain.

6.24 Assume that a manufacturer measures cycle time for only the products that pass through its processes without defects. Do you think this is necessarily a bad practice? What incentives might motivate such a practice?

6.25 Is it possible for a company to increase the throughput efficiency of one process to the point where an additional increase could reduce the company's overall profitability? If so, give an example.

6.26 Respond to this comment: I think the way you have measured practical capacity is just an excuse to keep from trying to use our processes more efficiently. We should be trying to get as close to theoretical capacity as possible. Isn't that what is meant by 'continuous improvement'? Otherwise, aren't we wasting resources?

Exercises

Exercise 6.27 [LO 1] Standards of Quality

How do the European Foundation for Quality Management (EFQM) Excellence Award (www.efqm.org), the Deming Prize (www.deming.org/demingprize/index.html), and ISO 9000 (www.iso.org) differ?

Exercise 6.28 [LO 2] Costs of Quality

Fermeture SA manufactures zippers. The following table presents its financial information for one year:

Sales	€800,000
Material inspection	15,000
Scrap	14,000
Employee training	20,000
Returned goods	7,000
Finished goods inspection	18,000
Processing customer complaints	6,000

Required

a. Classify these items into prevention, appraisal, internal failure, or external failure costs.
b. Prepare a cost-of-quality report for the year.

Exercise 6.29 [LO 2] Costs of Quality

Wanborough Ltd manufactures air conditioners. The following represents financial information for two years:

	Year 1	Year 2
Sales	£3,000,000	£2,600,000
Costs:		
Process inspection	19,000	20,000
Scrap	18,000	21,000
Quality training	180,000	135,000
Warranty repairs	60,000	56,000
Testing equipment	40,000	51,000
Customer complaints	24,000	31,000
Rework	150,000	176,000
Preventive maintenance	135,000	101,000
Materials inspection	62,000	51,000
Field testing	100,000	121,000

Required

a. Classify these items into costs of prevention, appraisal, internal failure or external failure activities.
b. Calculate the ratio of the prevention, appraisal, internal failure and external failure costs to sales for year 1 and year 2.
c. Construct a cost-of-quality report for year 1 and year 2.

Exercise 6.30 [LO 2] Costs of Quality

AwaSan Corporation manufactures computer printers. The following represents its financial information for two years (monetary values given in Japanese yen, £):

	Year 1	Year 2
Sales	¥168,000,000	¥156,000,000
Costs:		
Process inspection	¥1,200,000	¥1,120,000
Scrap	1,120,000	1,200,000
Quality training	13,600,000	8,000,000

Warranty repairs	2,880,000	3,200,000
Testing equipment	5,600,000	5,600,000
Customer complaints	1,680,000	2,000,000
Rework	10,240,000	12,000,000
Preventive maintenance	8,800,000	6,240,000
Materials inspection	4,400,000	3,280,000
Field testing	6,080,000	8,160,000

Required

a. Classify these items into costs of prevention, appraisal, internal failure or external failure activities.
b. Calculate the ratio of the prevention, appraisal, internal failure and external failure costs to sales for year 1 and year 2.
c. Construct a cost-of-quality report for year 1 and year 2.

Exercise 6.31 [LO 5] Overall Equipment Effectiveness

Centaurus Telecom SA operates a customer call centre in Costa Rica, where it employs two work shifts of 24 employees each. The call centre operates 7 days per week. Each work shift lasts 8 hours, and each employee gets paid breaks totalling one hour. Breaks are staggered so that the call centre is available to customers for the full 8 hours per shift.

During a recent week, the first shift had actual operating time of 1,045 hours. Calling records showed that the actual time to complete a call averaged 5.7 minutes, but the expected time per call was 4.5 minutes. During this week, the first shift completed 11,000 calls, of which 1,300 were repeat calls from customers whose problems were not resolved during the first call. Repeat calls are counted as defective calls.

Required

Compute the first shift's overall equipment effectiveness.

Exercise 6.32 [LO 5] Overall Equipment Effectiveness

Refer to Exercise 6.31. During a recent week, the second shift at Centaurus had actual operating time of 1,117 hours. Calling records showed that the actual time to complete a call averaged 4.6 minutes, close to the expected time per call of 4.5 minutes. During this week, the second shift completed 13,600 calls, of which 3,300 were repeat calls from customers whose problems were not resolved during the first call. Repeat calls are counted as defective calls.

Required

Compute the second shift's overall equipment effectiveness.

Exercise 6.33 [LO 5] Overall Equipment Effectiveness

Continuation of Exercises 6.31 and 6.32.

Required

a. Compare the OEE performance of Centaurus Telecom's first and second shifts at its Costa Rica call centre. What are the strengths and weaknesses of the two shifts?
b. Call operators are paid the equivalent of €7 per hour, including wages and benefits. How much of the cost of the call centre's capacity is lost to inefficiency and poor quality?
c. Are the OEE and monetary figures directly comparable in terms of likely impacts on customers? Explain.

Exercise 6.34 [LO 5] Overall Equipment Effectiveness

Vesuvius SpA manufactures high-technology fasteners for Boeing Corp.'s 787 Dreamliner. Following are data from a recent 8-hour work-shift at Vesuvius' Naples plant.

Work-shift length	8	hours
Paid breaks	1.5	hours
Unplanned downtime	45	minutes
Ideal fabrication rate	50	parts per minute
Total parts produced	19,400	parts
Defective parts produced and scrapped	1,460	parts

Required

a. Compute the work-shift's OEE.
b. Prepare a brief narrative description of the OEE analysis to explain the individual components and overall outcome.

Exercise 6.35 [LO 2, 6] Quality and Time Control (Appendix 6)

Prepare a run chart from the following, sequential weekly cycle-time data from the manufacture of computer tape storage devices. Use the historical mean of cycle time and a 2 standard-deviation upper and lower control limit. What does this chart indicate?

Week	Average cycle time in hours	Week	Average cycle time in hours
1	133.4	10	165.3
2	158.8	11	128.1
3	121.9	12	103.3
4	120.3	13	102.5
5	125.8	14	101.4
6	133.1	15	118.9
7	140.7	16	127.8
8	122.8	17	132.2
9	135.7	18	135.5

Exercise 6.36 [LO 2] Quality Control

Prepare a Pareto chart using the following data on causes of adjustments to domestic and foreign customers' billings during the month of January. What does this chart indicate?

Causes of defects	Frequency
Correction of incorrect prior adjustments	10
Miscellaneous	30
Product did not perform	12
Product prices disputed	115
Product returned	15
Product shipped by wrong priority	70
Product shipped to wrong location	30
Shipments to foreign locations	64
Wrong product shipped	20

Exercise 6.37 [LO 1] Quality Versus Cost

Mont Blanc Waters has discovered a problem involving its mix of flavour to seltzer water that costs the company €10,000 in waste and €5,000 in lost business per period. There are two alternative solutions. The first is to lease a new mix regulator at a cost of €8,000 per period, which would save €3,000 in waste and €5,000 in lost business. The second alternative is to hire an additional employee to manually monitor the existing regulator at a cost of €6,000 per period, saving €3,500 in waste and €4,000 in lost business per period.

Required

Prepare a memo that evaluates the two alternatives. Which alternative should Mont Blanc Waters choose?

Exercise 6.38 [LO 1] Quality Versus Cost

CBM Cycling has discovered a problem involving welding its bicycle frames that costs the company €6,000 in waste and €5,000 in lost business per period. There are two alternative solutions. The first is to lease a new automated welder at a cost of €2,500 per period, which would save €2,000 in waste and €4,000 in lost business. The second alternative is to hire an additional employee to manually weld the frames at a cost of €3,000 per period, which would save €1,500 in waste and €4,000 in lost business per period.

Required

Form small groups and prepare an analysis of the two alternatives. Which alternative should CBM choose?

Exercise 6.39 [LO 3] Managing Time

Search your library or the Internet for a research study that investigates the costs and/or benefits of adopting JIT or other time-based process management methods. Prepare a one-page summary that describes the study's objective, its source(s) of data and its conclusion. Prepare two questions that, if you could, you would pose to the author(s) about the study.

Exercise 6.40 [LO 4] Productivity

Consider the following information:

	Year 5	Year 4	Year 3	Year 2	Year 1
Number of employees	11,120	11,500	12,100	11,600	11,800
Sales revenue (€ millions)	€3,085	€2,987	€2,814	€2,438	€2,213
Operating income (€ millions)	€501	€497	€521	€471	€425
Sales per employee	?	?	?	?	?
Total factor productivity	?	?	?	?	?

Required

Using the preceding information, build a spreadsheet to compute 'sales per employee' and 'total factor productivity'. What appears to have happened?

Exercise 6.41 [LO 3] Cycle Time

Consider the following information:

	January	February	March	April
Units completed	95	66	54	86
Processing time, minutes	147.6	141.5	160.4	152.9
Waiting time, minutes	2432.8	1892.9	2115.3	1489.8

Required

Build a spreadsheet to compute the average cycle time per unit and the throughput efficiencies for each month.

Problems

Problem 6.42 [LO 4] Remanufacturing Costs and Benefits

DuPuis manufactures and distributes carpets made with synthetic fibres created from petroleum products. DuPuis' vice president of finance, Alphonse Benoit, is aware that one of its primary competitors, DuPont, has implemented a remanufacturing process of existing carpet fibre to new carpet specifications and performance. DuPont encourages its large customers, such as hotels, to recycle carpets by selling them carpet with full warranties but with remanufactured fibres at a price less than carpet with wholly new fibres. To get this discount, the customer must trade in old carpet when it purchases a replacement. Benoit believes that DuPuis must meet the competitive challenge posed by DuPont's new programme and sees an opportunity to improve the company's financial and environmental performance. Old, replaced carpet fibre is commonly discarded in a landfill.

Benoit has asked you, as a new financial analyst at DuPuis, to analyse alternative processes for new and remanufactured carpet fibres. You have gathered the following information related to the remanufacture of one type of fibre, which you believe is representative of DuPuis' products. The company carries no inventories.

Data input	New	Remanufactured
Sales volume per year, square metres	4,000,000	4,000,000
Sales price per square metre	€11.50	€7.00
Direct material cost per square metre	€4.75	€0.85
Direct labour cost per square metre	€0.08	€0.02
Machine hours per square metre	0.06	0.01
Cycle time per unit, hours	0.90	0.40
Manufacturing overhead per year	€3,600,000	€600,000
Total direct labour cost per year	€320,000	€80,000
Total machine hours per year	240,000	40,000
Total cycle time per year, hours	3,600,000	1,600,000

Required

a. Prepare estimates of cost per unit and total cost of goods sold per year using direct labour cost as the manufacturing overhead allocation base for new and remanufactured carpet fibre.

b. Prepare estimates of cost per unit and total cost per year using normal machine hours as the manufacturing overhead allocation base for new and remanufactured carpet fibre.

c. Prepare estimates of cost per unit and total cost per year using normal cycle time as the manufacturing overhead allocation base for new and remanufactured carpet fibre.

d. Prepare six annual gross margin estimates for sales of carpets with new and remanufactured carpet fibre using each of the overhead allocation bases. Write a short memo to Benoit explaining your cost estimates, recommending which process to implement, and identifying other factors that Benoit and DuPuis should consider before implementing either of the processes.

[Adapted from Hindo, 2006]

Problem 6.43 [LO 4] Remanufacturing Costs and Benefits

Roly Poly Equipment Company (RPEC) manufactures and distributes heavy construction equipment worldwide. RPEC's assistant controller, Bryana Wong, is aware that one of its primary competitors, Caterpillar, has implemented a remanufacturing process, which refinishes recycled engine parts to new part specifications and performance. Caterpillar encourages its customers (equipment-repair companies) to recycle these parts by selling remanufactured parts with new-part warranties at a price much less than new parts if the customer returns an old part prior to purchasing a replacement. Wong believes that Roly Poly must meet the competitive challenge posed by Caterpillar's new programme and sees an opportunity to improve the company's financial and environmental performance.

Wong has asked you, as a new financial analyst at Roly Poly, to analyse alternative processes for new and remanufactured parts. You have gathered the following information related to the remanufacture of an engine's fuel-injection case, a part commonly discarded and replaced during a major engine repair. The company carries no inventories.

Data input	New	Remanufactured
Sales volume per year, units	3,000,000	3,000,000
Sales price per unit	$6.00	$4.00
Direct material cost per unit	$1.20	$0.10
Direct labour cost per unit	$0.50	$0.10
Machine hours per unit	0.10	0.05
Cycle time per unit, hours	0.12	0.08
Manufacturing overhead per year	$1,800,000	$500,000
Total direct labour cost per year	$1,500,000	$300,000
Total machine hours per year	300,000	150,000
Total cycle time per year, hours	360,000	240,000

Required

a. Prepare estimates of cost per unit and total cost of goods sold per year using direct labour cost as the manufacturing overhead allocation base for new and remanufactured parts.

b. Prepare estimates of cost per unit and total cost per year using machine hours as the manufacturing overhead allocation base for new and remanufactured parts.

c. Prepare estimates of cost per unit and total cost per year using cycle time as the manufacturing overhead allocation base for new and remanufactured parts.

d. Prepare six annual gross margin estimates for sales of new and remanufactured parts using each of the overhead allocation bases. Write a short memo to Wong explaining your cost estimates and recommending which process to implement.
[Adapted from Hindo, 2006]

Problem 6.44 [LO 3, 4] Capacity and Cycle Time

Use the following data to supply information now represented by question marks. Practical capacities are 80 per cent of theoretical capacities.

	A	B	C	D
Number of 40-hour work shifts per week	2	2	3	1
Number of identical assembly lines	4	?	5	4
Available hours per week	?	480	?	?
Average cycle time per unit (hrs)	3	6	?	?
Throughput time ratio	25%	?	50%	20%
Value-adding cycle time (hrs)	?	2	?	?
Theoretical capacity in units	?	?	200	?
Practical capacity in units	?	?	?	1,000

Problem 6.45 [LO 3, 4] Capacity and Cycle Time

Use the following data to supply information now represented by question marks. Practical capacities are 80 per cent of theoretical capacities.

	A	B	C	D
Number of 40-hour work shifts per week	4	3	3	2
Number of identical assembly lines	4	?	5	3
Available hours per week	?	360	?	?
Average cycle time per unit (hrs)	?	10	?	?
Throughput time ratio	40%	?	30%	25%
Value-adding cycle time (hrs)	?	2.5	?	?
Theoretical capacity in units	?	?	500	?
Practical capacity in units	?	?	?	200

Problem 6.46 [LO 3, 5] Time-based Activity-based Costing

Antyczne Skarby Sprzętu (AS Sprzętu) manufactures and sells furniture hardware (knobs, hinges, etc.) to builders of replica antique furniture and restorers of true antiques. AS Sprzętu has five individuals who stock manufactured items and pick them for shipping to customers. The company employees refer to these activities as 'stocking' and 'picking'. Dawid Kowalski, the company's chief financial officer, has analysed the stocking and picking process and developed the following information about the cost of AS Sprzętu's current process of stocking inventory and picking products to ship (monetary units given in Polish zloty, PLN).

Inventory-stocking department costs:	
Payroll (labour + benefits)	PLN 344,000 per year
Depreciation of equipment based on usage	16,800
Rent and utilities	70,000
Supplies and other	30,000
Total department costs	PLN 460,800
Number of employees	5
Practical capacity use	80%
Work week (net of breaks and unavoidable lost time between activities)	32 hours
Work year	50 weeks

All of these costs would be eliminated if the stocking and picking activities were not needed or were outsourced.

Kowalski also has worked with the stocking and picking employees to identify their activities. He asked them to keep a journal to track their activities and time spent for a week. The average number of minutes and the activities for the week of observations follow:

Ordering activities	Start stock or pick	Add new or delete old inventory line item	Time to place or pick item	Fill a special order	Process a return
Inventory processing times, minutes	6	15	2	25	10

Required

a. Use the cost data to compute the cost per minute of the stocking and picking activities.

b. Use the average cost per minute and the activity processing times to assign costs to each of the following recent orders.

Recent actions	Add/delete item 1 = Yes 0 = No	Items placed or picked	Special order 1 = Yes 0 = No	Return 1 = Yes 0 = No
1. Pick order, 6 items	0	6	0	0
2. Stock 1 new item	1	1	0	0
3. Stock 5 returned line items	0	5	0	1
4. Pick 11 existing line items, special order	0	11	1	0
5. Pick and delete 7 new line item	7	7	0	0

c. Kowalski is considering whether to replace two-thirds of the current stock and pick processing capacity with an online ordering system. What are the factors that Kowalski should consider when making this decision?

[Adapted from Bruggeman et al., 2005]

Problem 6.47 [LO 2, 3] Quality and Time Control

Prepare a flowchart of the following medical appointment process at a Naval medical centre.

Prepare appointment book.
Open appointment book.
Is the appointment on shore or aboard ship?
If aboard ship, tell patient to call the appointment centre by 1500 hours (3 p.m.) to make own appointment for next working day.
If on shore, issue next available appointment to patient.
Remind patient to call 24 hours in advance to confirm appointment.
Did patient call 24 hours in advance?
If no, cancel appointment and give appointment to new patient.
If yes, give patient confirmation number.
If yes, does patient show up for appointment?
If yes, mark appointment book 'patient showed'.
If no, mark appointment book 'failure: Patient did not show'.
If no, place standby patient in appointment.
If no, issue failure report to commanding officer.

Required

a. What is a defect in this process?
b. What does this flowchart indicate about possible sources of defects?
c. Can you recommend changes in the process to reduce defects?

Problem 6.48 [LO 2, 6] Quality Control

Norsk Ferries operates daily round-trip voyages between Norway, Denmark, Germany and Sweden using a fleet of three ferries, the Sea Quill, the Neptune and the Orca. The budgeted amount of fuel for each round trip is the average fuel usage, which over the last 12 months has been 620 litres. Norsk has set the upper control limit at 720 litres and the lower control limit at 540 litres. The operations manager received the following report for round-trip fuel usage by the three ferries for the period:

Number of litres of fuel per round-trip			
Trip	Sea Quill	Neptune	Orca
1	605	551	605
2	609	562	612

3	630	573	625
4	590	559	634
5	600	726	642
6	676	586	652
7	726	598	622
8	685	631	618
9	620	732	625
10	680	581	613

Required

a. Create quality control charts for round-trip fuel usage for each of the three ferries for the period. What inferences can you draw from them?

b. Some managers propose that Norsk present its quality control charts in monetary terms rather than in physical amount (litres) terms. What are the advantages and disadvantages of using monetary fuel costs rather than litres in the quality control charts?

Problem 6.49 [LO 5] JIT and Inventory Management

Consider the following annual information about three companies in the same manufacturing industry.

Company	A	B	C
Production method	JIT	JIT	Traditional
Sales revenue	€500,000,000	€750,000,000	€10,000,000,000
No. of employees	2,500	5,000	25,000
Cost of goods sold	€245,000,000	€400,000,000	€7,000,000,000
Inventories (average)	€7,000,000	€12,500,000	€700,000,000

Required

a. Compare the three companies' uses of human and inventory resources using revenue per employee and inventory turnover measurers.

b. Assume that you are an analyst employed by the least efficient user of inventories. At the request of the company CEO, prepare a short report that analyses the relative cost advantages and outlines the types of costs and benefits that your company should expect by adopting JIT production.

Problem 6.50 [LO 5] Quantitative and Qualitative Evaluation of JIT

Your manufacturing company is considering adopting JIT production. You have gathered the following annual data, which you believe are relevant to the decision. For this analysis, ignore any initial investment costs necessary to start JIT.

- Average inventory will decline by €500,000, from €800,000 to €300,000.
- Current inventory handling, receiving, storing and insuring costs are 15 per cent of average inventory value plus €200,000. The €200,000 will decline by €81,000 by transferring three employees to unfilled positions in another part of the company. If any of these employees leaves the company, they will not be replaced.
- Annual costs of quality should change as follows:
  - Prevention (additional training, improved supplier relations) – increase by €200,000.
  - Inspection (employee time and testing equipment) – increase by €100,000.
  - Internal failure (rework, delays) – decrease by €250,000.
  - External failure (lost sales, warranty claims) – decrease by €170,000.
- Tooling and set-up costs will increase by €80,000 per year.
- Opportunity cost of capital tied up in inventory is 12 per cent per year.

Required

a. What is your estimate of the net annual quantifiable cost or benefit from your company's adopting JIT?

b. What qualitative factors should you consider before deciding this JIT issue?

Problem 6.51 [LO 3, 4] Cycle Time and Throughput Efficiency

Insurance companies spend considerable resources on processing claims (which results in a claim denial or payment to cover a loss). Short, accurate processing is desirable because both customers and the company benefit by resolving claims satisfactorily and by using minimum resources to do so. To improve its insurance claims processing, Global Insurance Company began a pilot project in its Central Europe Region's claims office to track the time to process each new automobile loss claim during a recent quarter. Processing time begins when a company representative receives a claim and ends when the final settlement is reached. Following are annual time data related to processing these claims at the company's Central Europe Region.

Claim-processing time data

			8-hour days spent in				
Days to complete	Per cent	Number	Average processing by adjusters	Waiting for adjusters	Waiting for information	Revisions and corrections	Average cycle time in days
0-10	6%	42,000	0.29	3.54	4.21	0.20	8.24
11-20	9%	63,000	0.32	7.66	9.34	0.32	17.64
21-30	35%	245,000	0.61	9.03	13.76	0.46	23.86
31-40	20%	140,000	1.32	9.57	25.44	0.54	36.87
41-50	15%	105,000	2.53	10.43	29.59	0.69	43.24
51-60	10%	70,000	3.04	11.56	38.65	1.21	54.46
More than 60	5%	35,000	3.54	12.58	45.98	2.32	64.42
Total	100%	700,000					

Required

a. Compute the overall average cycle time and throughput efficiency ratio in total and for each stage of processing for automobile loss claims during the quarter. (*Note:* These data can be easily analysed with a computer spreadsheet.)

b. Comment on the apparent cause(s) of long cycle times and low throughput efficiencies.

c. What recommendation would you make to Global Insurance Company to improve its processing of automobile loss claims?

Problem 6.52 [LO 3] Cycle Time and Quality

You are concerned that your company is understating its cycle time and throughput efficiency by measuring the cycle time for only those products completed without any defects. Products that are reworked or scrapped (because they cannot be made serviceable) are accounted for separately and removed from cycle time statistics. To understand the impact of this practice, you have decided to track the production of a typical product, Model DAD4700, over the course of four months. Sixteen different workgroups (each composed of approximately 7 to 10 employees) work on different stages of the product (and similar products). Each of three workgroups of eight employees do nothing but analyse and rework defective products (of all types) after the regular workgroups have completed them. You have gathered the following data on the DAD4700 over the past four months. (*Note:* These data can be more easily analysed with spreadsheet software than by hand.)

Regular workgroups	January	February	March	April
Units completed without rework	200	130	112	193
Assembly time for good units, hours	1,800.5	1,320.3	1,213.2	1,845.3
Total cycle time for good units, hours	5,209.1	4,640.4	3,532.2	2,901.4
Rework workgroups	**January**	**February**	**March**	**April**
Units reworked successfully	14	8	10	14
Units scrapped	3	1	2	3
Rework time for all reworked units, hours	64.2	43.6	62.8	51.4
Total rework cycle time	166.2	150	191.3	161.3

Required

Build a spreadsheet to solve requirements (a), (b) and (c).

a. Compute the average cycle time per unit and the throughput efficiency for good units produced by regular workgroups for each month and overall.
b. Compute the total cycle time and the throughput efficiency for units reworked successfully by rework workgroups for each month and overall. (*Hint:* Recall that these defective units were completed by regular workgroups first; an assumption is necessary.)
c. Compute the cycle times and the throughput efficiencies for each month for good and reworked products combined.
d. Prepare a group comment on the practice of computing separate cycle times and throughput efficiencies for good and reworked products.
e. What is your group's opinion about having separate workgroups perform all rework of defective products?

Problem 6.53 [LO 4] Capacity Management

Michael Wilson, CFO of Manchester Electrical Corp., has asked you to estimate the benefits of changing the company's current production process to a design based on published data from an American electrical manufacturer. The American firm reported the following data for its circuit breaker assemblies made with an old process and with a new process. Manchester's current process is similar to the old American process

Production item	Old American	New American	Manchester's
Average cost of parts and materials inventory	$240,500	$20,000	£200,000
Average cost of orders in process	$112,000	$450	£100,540
Cycle time per unit	15	0.75	20
Number of employees	30	15	25
Production floor area	400	45	1,000
Output in units per day	300	350	340
Value-adding cycle time percentage	5%	66%	6%

Required

a. Assume Manchester copied the American firm's approach to managing its processes. Build a spreadsheet to determine what percentage of improvement in each production item it could expect. What new levels of each item could Manchester expect?
b. Is there a relationship between average work-in-progress inventory and cycle time? Explain.
c. Manchester Electrical has a goal to earn a 20 per cent before-tax return on all its resources. In other words, a resource costing £1,000 per year should earn £200 of profit annually before taxes. Prepare a memo to Wilson explaining that money tied up in inventory cannot be earning that return, so the 20 per cent profit that is not earned is an opportunity cost of inventory. What is the opportunity cost

of Manchester's inventory for this single product under current conditions? What is the dollar benefit of achieving reduced inventories by adopting the new production approach?

[Adapted from Barker, 1994]

Problem 6.54 [LO 4] Process Improvements

Southern Cross Electrical, located in the state of Victoria, Australia, recently implemented changes to improve its manufacturing operations. Following are average process statistics before and after changes to one of the company's processes.

Item	Previous process	Current process	Percentage change
Cost of orders in process	$ 5,568	$1,377	(75.3%)
Cycle time per unit	16 hr	2 hr	(87.5)
Labour time per unit	4.45 min.	3.4 min.	(23.6)
Distance travelled in metres through the process	11.75 m	5.5 m	(53.2)
Floor area in metres used	36 sq. m	12 sq. m	(66.7)

Required

a. Explain how each of these changes could improve Southern Cross Electrical's profitability.
b. What are possible non-financial impacts of the process changes?
c. What decisions would Southern Cross Electrical's managers have to make for the company to benefit financially from these process improvements?

Cases

Case 6.55 [LO 1-3] Quality Improvement

Órbita Bicycles SA makes bicycle frames in two processes, tube cutting and welding. The tube-cutting and welding processes have a practical capacity of 200,000 and 150,000 units per year, respectively. Committed costs of quality activities follow:

Design of product and process costs	€250,000
Inspection and testing costs	90,000

The demand is very strong. Órbita can sell all output it can produce at €600 per frame. It begins producing only 150,000 units in the tube-cutting department because of the capacity constraint on the welding process; any defective units it produces are scrapped. Of the 150,000 units started at the tube-cutting department, 1,500 units (1 per cent) normally are scrapped. (Scrap is detected at the end of the tube-cutting operation.) Full costs, based on total manufacturing costs incurred through the tube-cutting operation, equal €235 per unit:

Direct materials (variable per unit)	€200
Direct manufacturing, set-up, and materials handling labour	25
Manufacturing overhead (fixed for the year)	10
Full cost per unit	€235

The tube-cutting department sends its good units to the welding department. Unit-level manufacturing costs in the welding department are €80 per unit. Welders are very highly trained, and the welding department has no scrap. Therefore, Órbita's total sales quantity equals the tube-cutting department's output. Juan Velasquez, the company president, has had his designers develop three alternative improvements to reduce scrap in the tube-cutting department.

Alternative 1: Leaving the process unchanged but starting enough units in the tube-cutting department so that the welding department can operate at practical capacity.

Alternative 2: Using a different type of tubing that is more resistant to damage and would reduce scrap by 60 per cent. It would increase the unit-level costs per unit in the tube-cutting department by €18 but would reduce costs in the welding department by €17.

Alternative 3: Spending an additional amount on training to reduce scrap in the tube-cutting process.

Required

Form small groups to respond to each of the following items:

a. Which alternative – 1 or 2 – is more attractive financially?
b. How much would the company be willing to spend on training and how much would scrap have to be reduced to make alternative 3 as attractive as either alternative 1 or 2?
c. What other qualitative factors should Órbita consider in making the decision?

Case 6.56 [LO 1, 2, 4] Quality Management

MBNA Corporation is one of the most successful banks in the world. Like traditional banks, MBNA takes deposits and makes loans, but it has no branch banks, no commercial loans, and only a small number of current accounts. MBNA specializes in making loans to individuals through a credit card. Credit cards are commodities, but MBNA differentiates itself by the way it attracts and retains the highest-quality customers.

Each of MBNA's 14.4 million customers on average carries an account balance that is more than $1,000 (45 per cent) higher than the industry average, has average transactions that are $45 (47 per cent) higher than the industry average, and has a loan default loss that is 40 per cent lower than the industry average. Its customer retention rate is 97 per cent, compared to the industry average of 89 per cent.

One of the largest credit-card issuers in the world, MBNA states that through the use of advanced information technology, 'We can control every aspect of our customer relationships and ensure consistency and quality in the delivery of our products. Recently, MBNA's systems efficiently handled 12.5 billion online transactions, 120 million customer payments, 17 million requests for credit cards, and 192 million customer statements and letters.' MBNA monitors 70 quality measures daily and evaluates its employees on 14 of them daily.

Required

In small groups or individually, respond to the following items:

a. How does MBNA Corporation define quality?
b. Examine MBNA's homepage and describe how the company attracts its customers.
c. What are the advantages and disadvantages of controlling variation and quality of services as closely as MBNA does?
d. Prepare a written evaluation of whether MBNA's approach to managing quality is desirable in all organizations.

[Adapted from the company's website, www.mbnainternational.com, and various articles from *BusinessWeek*.]

Case 6.57 [LO 2, 3] Analysis of Development Time in the Automobile Industry

An analysis of the process of developing a new model automobile identified six major development activities, which together define a new model's product development lead time.

1. *Concept generation* – conducting marketing research and combining it with technical possibilities into a product concept to meet future market needs.
2. *Product planning* – translating the concept into product design, styling and target costs.
3. *Advanced engineering* – conducting basic research to extend technical possibilities.

4. *Product engineering* – developing parts, components, and detailed, feasible designs.
5. *Process engineering* – translating product designs into manufacturing processes.
6. *Pilot run* – testing the manufacturability of the product and process performance.

The study also revealed significant differences in both the average overall product development lead time and the individual activities for high-volume automobile manufacturers in three major regions: the United States, Europe and Japan. These differences appear in the following comparative Gantt charts, which show average time before the start of product sales for each major development activity.

Required

a. Describe the overall and specific development lead-time differences among the three types of manufacturers. What appear to be the most important differences in development lead-time?
b. How can shorter development lead times result in competitive advantages for Japanese producers?
c. What factors other than lead time do you think are important for successful development of new products?
d. Explain how you would begin to analyse a typical US product development process with the objective of significantly reducing development lead-time.

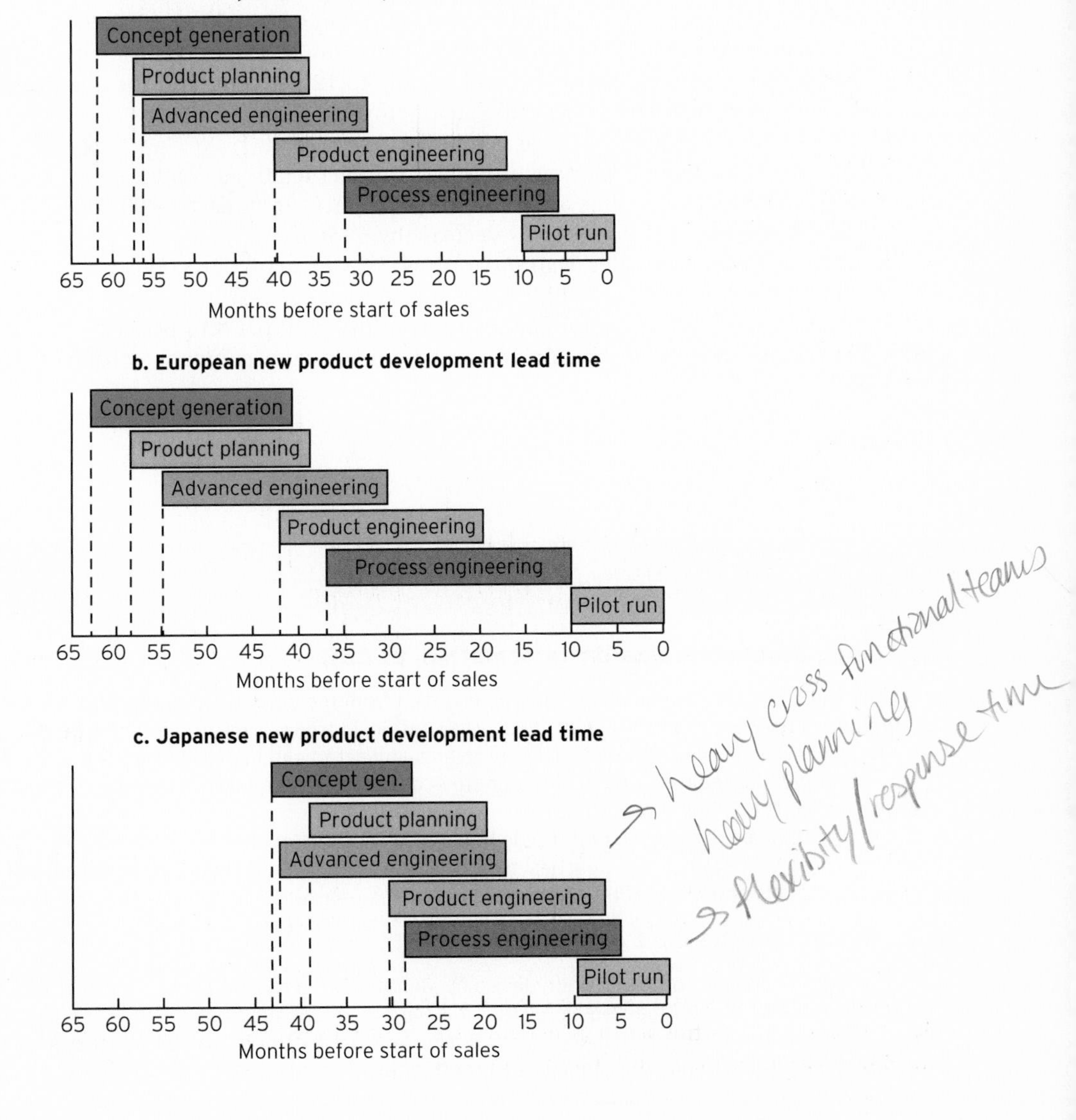

Case 6.58 [LO 1, 2, 5] Qualitative and Quantitative Evaluation of JIT Production Costs and Benefits

You are an analyst employed by a manufacturer that has traditionally produced large batches of identical items based on long-range sales forecasts. The company has maintained large buffer inventories to accommodate unforeseen fluctuations in demand and seemingly inevitable quality problems in the production process, which would result in significant rework and production delays without buffer inventory. Other members of the industry are adopting JIT production methods that are expensive to implement but are much more flexible and require fewer inventories to support production and sales. Your company is beginning to lose market share to its more flexible and efficient competitors.

Required

a. Is the decision for the company to follow its competitors and adopt JIT production something that top management should make and announce to the company as a competitive necessity?

b. Assume that you have been appointed as the leader of a team that will analyse the costs and benefits of adopting JIT and make a recommendation to top management. What type of team do you prefer, and who should be its members?

c. Given the following representative data, what is your estimate of the net annual quantifiable cost or benefit from your company's adopting JIT? (For this analysis, ignore any initial investment costs necessary to start JIT, although they can be quite large and must be considered for any final decision.)
- Average inventory will decline by €500,000, from €800,000 to €300,000.
- Current inventory carrying costs are estimated to be 15 per cent of average inventory value plus €100,000. The variable portion will decline to 12 per cent, and the committed portion used will decline to €60,000 by transferring an employee to other work.
- Costs of quality should change as follows:
- *Prevention* (additional training, improved supplier relations) – increase by €120,000.
- *Inspection* (employee time and testing equipment) – increase by €90,000.
- *Internal failure* (rework, delays) – decrease by €156,000.
- *External failure* (lost sales, warranty claims) – decrease by €185,000.
- Tooling and set-up costs will increase by €80,000 per year.
- Opportunity cost of capital tied up in inventory is 10 per cent per year.

d. What qualitative factors should you, your team and your company consider before deciding the JIT issue?

Solutions to You're the Decision Maker

6.1 Using Diagnostic Quality Information, p. 238

a. Diagnosing and improving quality cannot be divorced from the authority and responsibilities given to individuals and the way they are evaluated. In an ideal organization, individuals or groups would be able to objectively and thoroughly evaluate the causes of quality problems and act to eliminate them. Furthermore, they would be able to understand how their actions to either improve or not improve quality performance affect the rest of the organization. This is not always the case.

b. A cross-functional team can be better able to diagnose and correct quality problems than either individuals or a functional team. Both of these parties 'might not see the forest for the trees' or, because of narrow evaluation criteria (e.g., this period's profits), might have incentives to hide rather than correct quality problems.

6.2 Evaluating the Cost of Quality, p. 243

a. COQ can be a valuable communication device by identifying the magnitude and types of quality problems. If this report is visible and regarded as reliable, it is hard to ignore, for example, the very high costs of activities to correct non-value-added internal and external failures. COQ does not, by itself, suggest ways to eliminate these activities, but it does make their impact on profits clear.

b. Profits are still an important goal of profit-seeking organizations, so profit reports cannot be ignored. However, costs of quality are buried in costs of sales and general overhead. Furthermore, because of FIFO inventory valuation, it is possible that current costs of quality are hidden in inventories and will not affect profits until future periods. It is probably incorrect to say that COQ is 'better' than traditional profits since they measure different areas of performance. It is likely that COQ does add useful information about how the organization consumes resources, perhaps unnecessarily, to perpetuate quality problems.

c. Any numbers that become performance objectives have the appearance of being 'concrete' or 'hard' numbers. Some even believe that the true COQ objective is for total quality costs to be zero. What should the COQ objective be? ROQ advocates would say that some level of COQ is optimal and that it can be driven too low. Perhaps the most defensible approach is to avoid hard COQ objectives since COQ is a result of quality activities, not a measure of quality itself. One should recognize that high levels of COQ are indicative of quality problems and that competition will require improvements - but this should already be known. Quality improvements come from understanding what customers want and meeting or exceeding their expectations.

6.3 Benefits of Quality Improvement, p. 246

a. Call centre capacity = 13 weeks/quarter × 7 days/week × 8 hours/day × 60 min./hour × 16 FTE × 90per cent availability = 628,992 minutes per quarter.

b. Let x = the proportion of calls with incorrect information; $1 - x$ = the proportion of calls with correct information. The average call duration is 7.95 minutes, while a call with correct information should take 7.25 minutes and a call with both types of incorrect information should take 16.50 minutes. Solving for x means solving the following equation:

$$16.50x + 7.25(1 - x) = 7.95$$

$$x = 7.58\%$$

The quantity of calls with incorrect information= 0.0758 × 78,013 = 5,915 calls.

c. Capacity implications of eliminating incorrect information:

i. The centre could process 628,992 minutes ÷ 7.25 minutes/call = 86,757 correct information calls.

ii. If the centre only processed correct calls, the amount of time and cost that could be saved = 5,915 incorrect-information calls × (16.50 – 7.25) minutes/call = 54,714 minutes or $30,706 per quarter at $.5612 per minute. This assumes that the resources devoted to incorrect information calls would be cut, not shifted to other purposes.

Endnotes

1 For a classic discussion of quality, see Deming (1991).

2 See Rust et al. (1995). ROQ also is similar to the notion of 'reasonable assurance' in auditing – it might be uneconomical to detect all defects in financial reporting.

3 Appendix 6 presents an overview of technical details regarding the construction and use of control charts.

4 For examples of COQ reporting, see Carr (1995) and Kalagnanam and Matsumura (1995).

5 For example, see Godfrey (1996).

6 See The *Economist* (2004).

7 Kaplan and Anderson (2004). In some respects, this modification of ABC recalls developments by operations management researchers of two decades ago (e.g., Barker, 1994) and much earlier industrial engineering 'time-motion' studies.

8 See Fisher (1997).

9 See a historical summary at Wikipedia http://en.wikipedia.org/wiki/Lean_manufacturing. A highly readable account is by Womack et al. (1990). An academic chronology is found in Holweg (2007).

10 Surveys show that manufacturing firms report improvements in cycle time and quality as a result of adopting JIT, particularly those that use batch and continuous flow processes (e.g., White, 1993 and Youssef, 1995).

11 See Muchiri and Pintelon (2008). See also examples at: Wikipedia, http://en.wikipedia.org/wiki/Overall_equipment_effectiveness and a manufacturing example at http://www.oee.com/calculating_oee.html.

12 This form of control chart is called an $\bar{X}$ (X-bar) chart, since it is based on the historical mean, or X-bar. Many other forms of control chart are based on other statistical descriptions of historical or target attributes.

13 Note that control limits do not have to be symmetrical. For example, an organization might believe that the consequences of exceeding an upper limit are worse than falling below a lower limit (or vice versa) and could set the UCL closer to the mean and the LCL farther from the mean (or vice versa).

14 A 1 per cent chance can be too stringent; that is, the costs of not detecting an actual run can be high relative to the costs of intervening. Setting a less stringent criterion, say 5 or 10 per cent, leads to fewer consecutive observations signalling a run.

15 Adapted from Ittner and Larcker (1995).

References

Balakrishnan, R., T., Linsmeier and M. Venkatachalam (1996) 'Financial benefits from JIT adoption: effects of customer concentration and cost structure,' *The Accounting Review*, April, pp. 183–205.

Barker, R.C. (1994) 'Production systems without MRP: a lean time-based design', *Omega International Journal of Management Science*, vol. 22, no. 4, pp. 349–360.

Billesbach, T., and R. Hayen (1994) 'Long-term impact of just-in-time on inventory performance measures', *Production and Inventory Management Journal*, 1st Quarter, pp. 62–67.

Brinkman, S., and M. Appelbaum (1994) 'The quality cost report: it's alive and well at Gilroy Foods,' *Management Accounting* (US), September, pp. 61–65.

Bruggeman, W., P. Everaert, S.R. Anderson and Y. Levant (2005). 'Modeling logistics costs using time-driven ABC: A case in a distribution company'. Ghent University Working Paper No. 05/332.

Carr, L. (1995) 'Quality: cost of quality – making it work', *Journal of Cost Management*, Spring, pp. 61–65.

Chapman, C.S. (2005) 'Not because they are new: developing the contribution of enterprise resource planning systems to management control research,' *Accounting, Organizations and Society*, vol. 30, pp. 685–689.

Coy, P. (1995) 'Researching the nitty-gritty of quality control', *BusinessWeek*, 29 May.

Dechow, N., and J. Mouritsen (2005) 'Enterprise resource planning systems, management control and the quest for integration', *Accounting, Organizations and Society*, vol. 30, pp. 691–733.

Deming, W.E. (1991) 'A seminal thinker takes a detailed look at the quality of quality', *Automobile Magazine*, October, pp. 106–111.

Economist, The (2004) 'Two-faced capitalism', *The Economist*, 24 January.

Fisher, M.L. (1997) 'What is the right supply chain for your product?' *Harvard Business Review*, vol. 75, no. 2, pp. 105–116. Retrieved 9 November 2011, from ABI/INFORM Global (Document ID: 11223533).

Godfrey, A.B. (1996) 'Quality management: The cost of quality revisited', available at: http://www.qualitydigest.com/apr/godfrey.html (accessed 17 March 2011).

Grace, R. (2007) 'Lean initiative drives Mold-Masters', *Plastics News*, 19 November, vol. 19, issue 38.

Hindo, B. (2006) 'Everything old is new again', *BusinessWeek*, 25 September, pp. 65–70.

Hof, R.D. (1997) 'The sad saga of Silicon Graphics', *BusinessWeek*, 4 August.

Holweg, M. (2007) 'The genealogy of lean production', *Journal of Operations Management*, vol. 25, no. 2, pp. 420–437.

Ittner, C., and D. Larcker (1995) 'Total quality management and the choice of information and reward systems', *Journal of Accounting Research*, vol. 33 (supplement), pp. 1–34.

Ittner, C., and D. Larcker (1997) 'Quality strategy, strategic control systems, and organizational performance', *Accounting, Organizations and Society*, vol. 22, no. 3/4, pp. 293–314.

Kalagnanam, S., and E.M. Matsumura (1995) 'Quality: costs of quality in an order entry department', *Journal of Cost Management*, Fall, pp. 68–74.

Kaplan, R., and S. Anderson (2004) 'Time-driven activity-based costing', *Harvard Business Review*, November, pp. 131–138.

Muchiri P., and L. Pintelon (2008) 'Performance measurement using overall equipment effectiveness (OEE): literature review and practical application discussion', *International Journal of Production Research*, vol. 46, no. 13, pp. 3517–3535.

PRNewswire (2004) 'Caterpillar expands remanufacturing business with purchase of leading European automotive engine remanufactures', 16 August, available at: http://www.thefreelibrary.com/Caterpillar+Expands+Remanufacturing+Business+with+Purchase+of+ Leading. . .-a0120704739 (accessed 17 March 2011).

PRNewswire (2005) 'Caterpillar to acquire European remanufacturing company', 30 June, available at: http://www.thefreelibrary.com/Caterpillar+to+Acquire+European+Remanufacturing+Company%2c+Eurenov+S.A.-a0133672776 (accessed 17 March 2011).

Procter, S. (1995) 'The extent of JIT manufacturing in the UK: evidence from aggregate economic data', *Integrated Manufacturing Systems*, vol. 6, no. 4, pp. 16–25.

Quattrone P., and T. Hopper (2005) 'A time–space odyssey: management control systems in two multinational organisations', *Accounting, Organizations and Society*, vol. 30, pp. 735–764.

Rust, R., A. Zahorik and T. Keiningham (1995) 'Return on quality (ROQ): making service financially accountable', *Journal of Marketing*, April, pp. 58–70.

Selto, F., C. Renner and S.M. Young (1995) 'Assessing the organizational fit of a JIT manufacturing system', *Accounting, Organizations and Society*, vol. 20, pp. 665–684.

Simpson, P. (1997) 'As workers turn into risk-takers . . . one plant really turns on the steam', *BusinessWeek*, 15 December (international edition).

Tietz, J. (2007) 'Offshore doubters return work to Germany', *Spiegel Online*, 28 September, available at: http://www.businessweek.com/globalbiz/content/sep2007/gb20070928_162275.htm (accessed 17 March 2011).

White, R. (1993) 'An empirical assessment of JIT in U.S. manufacturers', *Production and Inventory Management Journal*, vol. 34, no. 2, pp. 38–42.

Wikipedia. http://en.wikipedia.org/wiki/Lean_manufacturing (accessed 7 April 2011).

Wikipedia. http://en.wikipedia.org/wiki/Overall_equipment_effectiveness.

Womack, J.P., D.T. Jones and D. Roas (1990) *The Machine that Changed the World*, Rawson Associates, New York.

Youssef, M. (1995) 'Measuring the intensity level of JIT activities and its impact on quality', *International Journal of Quality and Reliability Management*, vol. 11, no. 5, pp. 59–80.

PART 3

Planning and Decision Making

A Look Back

Part 1 and Part 2 laid the groundwork. The goals and objectives capture the organization's strategy; in other words, where it wants to go and how it wants to get there. The strategy should lead to concrete and tangible objectives for the organization, and to specific criteria for decision making. Cost estimation and cost management tools help understand processes and generate data. Specifically, Part 2 discussed activity-based management.

A Look at this Part

Part 3 includes methods of developing and using cost information for decision making. Chapter 7 shows how to develop financial and cost-volume-profit models, and it also covers pricing decisions. Chapter 8 discusses strategic issues in making capital-investment decisions. Chapter 9 covers financial planning and the development of budgets.

A Look Ahead

Part 4 discusses product costing and cost allocation. Once decisions are implemented, the actual costs are measured and allocated to products and services.

CHAPTER 7

Cost Management and Short-term Decision Making

© Matt_Brown

Learning Objectives

After completing this chapter, you should be able to:

- **LO 1** Design financial models to match strategic and operational decisions, such as profit planning or optimal use of a scarce resource.
- **LO 2** Build a basic cost-volume-profit (CVP) financial model using a computer spreadsheet.
- **LO 3** Build a financial model that reflects the effects of taxes, multiple products and multiple cost drivers.
- **LO 4** Apply scenario and sensitivity analyses to model the risk of decisions.
- **LO 5** Manage scarce resources.
- **LO 6** Analyse pricing decisions for short-term and long-term business.
- **LO 7** Apply the Theory of Constraints to manage scarce resources (Appendix 7A).
- **LO 8** Use linear programming to model decisions about the use of multiple scarce resources (Appendix 7B).

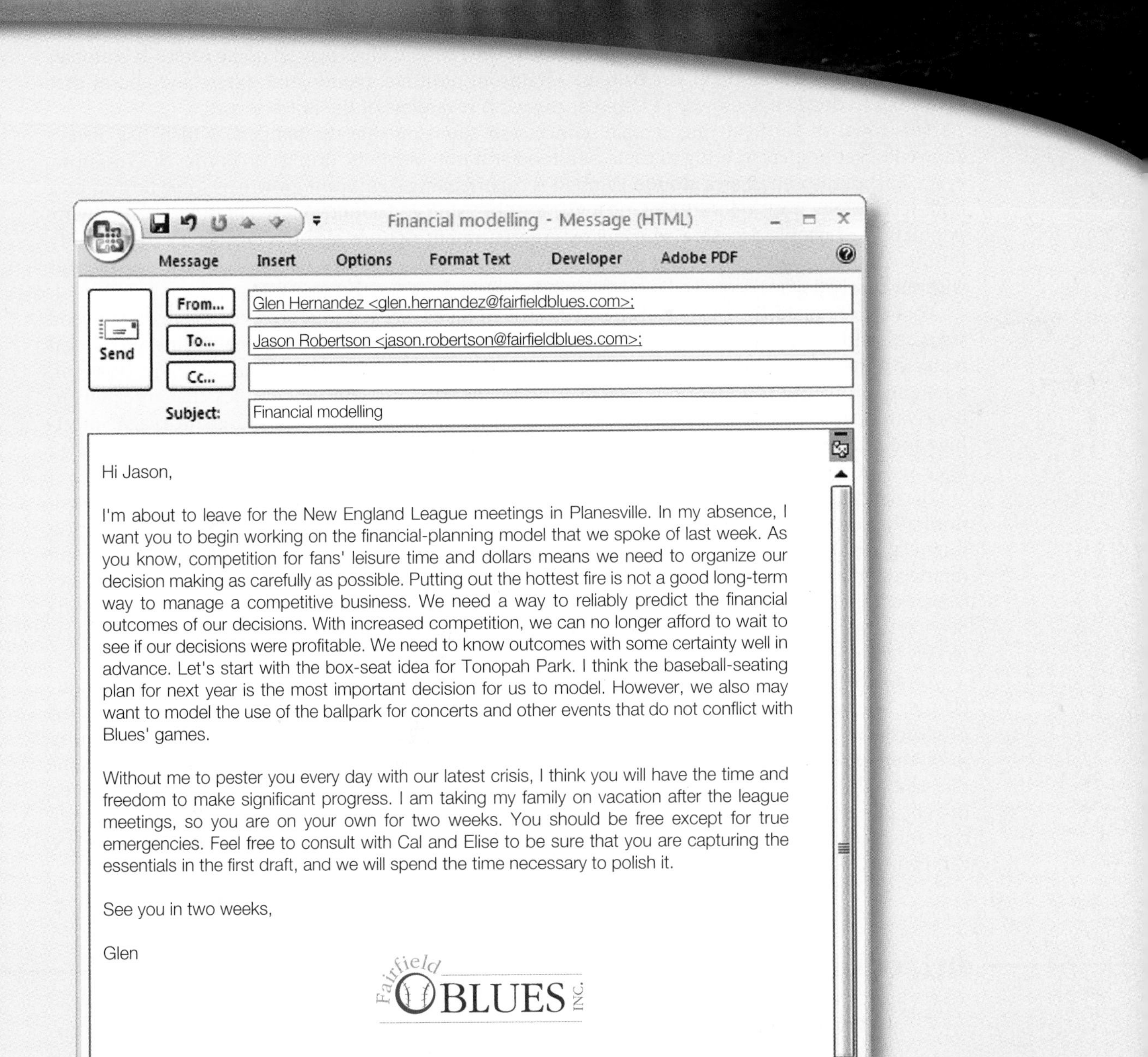
Financial modelling - Message (HTML)
Message
Insert
Options
Format Text
Developer
Adobe PDF
Send
From...
Glen Hernandez <glen.hernandez@fairfieldblues.com>;
To...
Jason Robertson <jason.robertson@fairfieldblues.com>;
Cc...
Subject:
Financial modelling
Hi Jason,
I'm about to leave for the New England League meetings in Planesville. In my absence, I want you to begin working on the financial-planning model that we spoke of last week. As you know, competition for fans' leisure time and dollars means we need to organize our decision making as carefully as possible. Putting out the hottest fire is not a good long-term way to manage a competitive business. We need a way to reliably predict the financial outcomes of our decisions. With increased competition, we can no longer afford to wait to see if our decisions were profitable. We need to know outcomes with some certainty well in advance. Let's start with the box-seat idea for Tonopah Park. I think the baseball-seating plan for next year is the most important decision for us to model. However, we also may want to model the use of the ballpark for concerts and other events that do not conflict with Blues' games.
Without me to pester you every day with our latest crisis, I think you will have the time and freedom to make significant progress. I am taking my family on vacation after the league meetings, so you are on your own for two weeks. You should be free except for true emergencies. Feel free to consult with Cal and Elise to be sure that you are capturing the essentials in the first draft, and we will spend the time necessary to polish it.
See you in two weeks,
Glen
Fairfield
BLUES
INC.

Fairfield Blues Inc., based in Fairfield, Massachusetts, USA, owns a minor league baseball team of the same name and a ballpark, Tonopah Park. The team belongs to the independent New England League, which means that the 12 member teams are not affiliated with any major league team. The league's salary cap for a 24-person team is approximately $130,000 for the six-month season; players and coaches earn from $600 to $1,200 per month. The Fairfield Blues play all home games at Tonopah Park, which opened in 1919. The ballpark retains an old-time, family atmosphere and charm that continues to draw large crowds (4,000-seat capacity) regardless of the Blues' record.

The Town of Fairfield runs a small concession stand outside the ballpark, which has always allowed ticket holders to bring in their own food and non-alcoholic drinks (no bottles or cans, however). The metropolitan area around Fairfield is experiencing significant growth as some Boston-area high-technology firms relocate seeking lower-cost housing and a more relaxed lifestyle. The growing population of people accustomed to many entertainment options also has created an opportunity for the company to promote outdoor concerts and other events at the ballpark on days or evenings without baseball games.

Four retired major-league players formed Fairfield Blues Inc. and purchased Tonopah Park several years ago with funding from their retirement accounts, friends, family, a regional airline and a local bank. In a short time, they have built the team and ballpark into a strong regional company. However, a neighbouring city recently built a large amusement park and concert complex that threatens to drain attendance from Tonopah Park. Prior to leaving for two weeks for New England League meetings and a vacation, Fairfield Blues' chief operating officer and co-founder, Glen Hernandez, emailed his assistant, Jason Robertson, about several pressing issues that needed attention.

Hernandez's email raises several interesting issues. Many young firms, Fairfield Blues included, normally first devote efforts to developing an accounting system that concentrates on preparing financial reports. External parties such as shareholders, banks and government agencies require financial reporting, and financial reports can be excellent for reviews of past operations. Young, successful companies typically outgrow their informal management styles and methods. As operations become larger and more complex, decisions become more difficult. Most firms develop financial *models* to help them organize and scrutinize their decision-making processes and options.

Recall that a model is a representation of reality. You likely have had interactions with models over the years through role-playing computer games, video games, architects' scale models of proposed real estate developments, and simulators used by driver education and pilot-training programmes. These models represent realistic conditions and simulate actual outcomes, for example, of a pilot's decision to turn, land or ascend to avoid a storm. Using models, gamers, architects, drivers, pilots and managers can learn from their decisions quickly and without the possible adverse consequences of learning from mistakes made under actual conditions. Furthermore, these people can identify opportunities for success that they might not have seen otherwise.

Introducing Financial Modelling

LO 1
Design financial models to match strategic and operational decisions, such as profit planning or optimal use of a scarce resource.

The goal of this chapter is to explain and demonstrate financial models for short-term planning decisions, such as about the mix of products to sell and produce, or about pricing. These financial models capture the relations among an organization's costs, revenues and income. For example, Fairfield Blues may use such models to find out how many tickets it needs to sell to achieve a particular target profit, or it may estimate the effects of organizing additional events. However, first a more general introduction to financial modelling is needed in this section.

A **financial model** is an accurate, reliable and flexible calculation of financial outcomes (such as costs, profit and risk) that exploits (some of the vast power of current spreadsheet software. A good financial model allows an organization to test the interactions of decisions and economic variables in a variety of settings. These models require cost management analysts to develop a set of relations that represent a company's operating and financial activities, such as the ratio of variable costs to sales, inventory turnover ratios, and the relative proportions of various products sold.

Financial models offer several benefits to users. Once the model has been developed, users can spend significant time on business analysis without being overwhelmed by the related number crunching. In addition, like the simulators just discussed, many of these models allow an organization to study the impact of a possible business action by reviewing the potential results before that action occurs. In other words, it is possible to identify a good or bad project or decision prior to committing the organization's resources to a course of action. Furthermore, valid financial models can help train inexperienced employees and increase their understanding of how their actions affect financial outcomes.

Different Kinds of Financial Models

The primary goal of this chapter is to explain and demonstrate methods of building, using and interpreting financial models. To accomplish this goal, it presents specific decision contexts faced regularly by many organizations. These decision contexts include profit planning and the optimal use of scarce resources. Common examples of financial models used by organizations of all types and sizes include these:

- *Models of relations among an organization's costs, revenues and income.* For example, a financial model of this type can compute product profitability given assumptions about quantity sold, sales price, activities and variable and fixed costs. This model also estimates the effects of short-term planning decisions about the mix of products, adding or dropping a product, the effects of adding more scarce resources, or pricing. These models typically look one year ahead. The present chapter and a number of the earlier chapters of this text use this very broad class of financial model focused on financial planning.
- *Models of relations between current investments and long-term profitability or value.* Other decisions concern significant changes, such that financial models representing the organization's current costs, revenues and income are no longer valid or adaptable. Such decisions have an impact over multiple years, involve large investments, anticipate significant changes in the environment of the organization, and consider actions of competitors. These models are based on the future cash flows that differ between alternatives. Various types of investment models (e.g., discounted cash flow and payback models) are the focus of Chapter 8.
- *Models of pro forma (or budgeted) financial statements.* This type of model shows how a firm's financial position evolves from a beginning balance sheet, to a cash flow statement, to an income statement, and finally to an ending balance sheet. The focus of these models is not a specific *decision*, as for the models in Chapters 7 and 8, but how all decisions together will impact the organization's financial results over a specific *period*. This important type of financial model is the topic of Chapter 9.
- *Specialized financial models for sophisticated decision making.* These include but certainly are not restricted to examples such as the following:
  - Models of consumer and industry demand for energy that companies such as **E.ON** (Europe), **Électricité de France** (Europe), or **Xcel Energy** (USA) use contain hundreds of variables and many equations.
  - Econometric models of the economy that the **Federal Reserve Board** and the **European Central Bank** use to estimate economic impacts of a possible change in interest rates.
  - R&D-impact models used by pharmaceutical companies such as **GlaxoSmithKline, Roche, Bayer** or **Merck & Co.** that incorporate the valuation of their R&D projects.

Objectives of Financial Modelling

Although financial models vary in complexity and purpose, they should be designed to have the following three common characteristics and objectives.

Usefulness for decision making

Decision makers must make better decisions using these models than they can without them, and the benefits of better decisions must exceed the costs of developing and using the models. Otherwise, the financial model is nothing but an elaborate (and probably expensive) toy. Unfortunately, anecdotes about resources wasted on complex, unused financial models or financial decision-support systems abound. The most common reasons for the failure of these models are (1) user lack of understanding of factors that are relevant to decisions and (2) excessive complexity.

Accurate and reliable simulation of relevant factors and relations

Decisions often hinge on the accuracy of measurements and the realism of the simulated relations among factors. The model should simulate the essential elements of business decisions, processes and the environment. Clearly, models cannot capture all of the realism of the world (or the model would be the world!). However, a useful model must reflect the essential, relevant factors that drive decisions and relations among the factors. Furthermore, reliability requires that outcomes predicted by the model should closely approximate what is observed in the real world. If a model's predictions are not reliable, managers will not and should not use the model. The model builder must be able to demonstrate that decision makers can rely on a new model to be more reliable than earlier ones, past practice, or 'gut feelings'.

Flexible and responsive analyses

Financial models can be 'back of the envelope' figures or more elaborate manual calculations. For example, your cheque book is a relatively simple, manual financial model of your cash position. Simple or not, an arithmetic error can cause you extensive grief and anxiety until you find and correct it. Think of the effort required to manually correct an arithmetic error or change a key factor in one of the **European Central Bank**'s or **Federal Reserve Board**'s complex economic models.

Complex financial modelling is not feasible today without taking advantage of the power of computer software (e.g., spreadsheets or specially designed modelling programs). Well-designed financial models allow decision makers to *easily* explore the predicted outcomes from varied decisions and assumptions about key factors. If the model is difficult to use or does not clearly show the effects of changes in decisions and key factors, decision makers probably will not use it. Before we explore building computer models, however, we first discuss some general principles of financial modelling in the context of manual profit-planning models.

Only the Future and Only Differences are Relevant

We cannot repeat this too often: financial models for decision making focus on the things that are dissimilar for future alternative courses of action. Relevant costs and benefits occur in the *future* and *differ* for feasible alternatives. Costs that differ for alternatives also are called differential costs. Some highly accurate and reliable cost information might not be relevant to a decision maker.

Suppose Fairfield considers replacing its current lawn mower because it has broken down again, although Fairfield has already spent large amounts on earlier repairs (they have highly accurate records of these repair costs!). However, the costs of these earlier repairs are irrelevant for any decision at hand, because these are in the past (sunk costs). No matter what Fairfield decides now, these past costs will not change any more.

The estimated cost of the planned repair might be irrelevant for the decision, even though this cost still lies in the future. Fairfield considers continuing to use the old mower, or replacing it, but the broken mower needs to be repaired in both cases (the dealer only takes a working mower, or the dealer repairs it and discounts the repair cost against the trading value). In that situation, the estimated repair cost is irrelevant for the decision on what to do, because it will not make any difference which alternative is preferred. What matters are only those costs that lie in the future *and* differ between decision alternatives.

We elaborate on this important characteristic of cost management information throughout this chapter. Understanding relevant costs should guide the gathering of information: focus on costs that will be different in the future.

Nevertheless, a study of the past can prove beneficial for predicting the future. In our framework, the decision-making process requires various predictions – revenues, costs, cash flows and the like – before making a decision. When making these predictions, the cost management analyst considers past experience and historical data. Although this might seem contradictory to the earlier recommendation to ignore sunk costs, understanding the past can contribute reliable information about what the future will hold. Although it is a subtle difference, sunk costs themselves are irrelevant to decisions, but analysts can use them to help estimate or predict future costs, which are relevant.

Using Cost-Volume-Profit (CVP) Planning Models

LO 2
Build a basic cost-volume-profit (CVP) financial model using a computer spreadsheet.

The most basic financial model, the **cost-volume-profit (CVP) model**, reflects the effects of changes in an organization's activities, such as sales volume, and of its prices and costs on profit. The simplest CVP model assumes that the only activity that drives profits is sales volume. The name of this basic model predates the popularity of activity-based costing, which recognizes many more potential drivers of profits than only sales volume. Nonetheless, the CVP name has stuck.[1] The basic model is worth learning and understanding because it can be extended to model the more complex profit impacts of changes in other revenue and cost drivers, demand, activity-based costs, taxation, and product or service mix. For example, basic or extended CVP models can help companies make decisions such as:

- Should **Lufthansa Cargo** should add another cargo flight between Frankfurt and Dubai?
- Can **Kansas City Public Library** cover its costs for the year if it expands its current circulation capacity and replaces some librarians with computerized 'help' and check-out functions?
- Should **Boulder Community Hospital** enlarge its current laboratory or outsource some testing to independent laboratories?
- Should Fairfield Blues, this chapter's focus company, convert some of its general admission seating to reserved box seating?

Each of these decisions concerns the effects of changing cost drivers or activities on costs, revenues and profits. These decisions are candidates for CVP modelling.

Many non-profit organizations also use forms of CVP modelling. Although legally they do not seek to generate profits, managers of non-profit organizations must plan the effects of changing cost drivers and activities on their revenue and costs. For instance, commissioners of one of the fastest-growing countries in the United States, Douglas County, Colorado, must model the effects of rapid population growth on tax revenues and the cost of providing and maintaining infrastructure such as water, sewer system, schools, roads and police protection. **Pride Industries**, a non-profit employer of handicapped individuals in the USA also uses financial modelling to determine whether revenues from its services and manufacturing operations will cover its costs.

Basic Cost-Volume-Profit Model

We apply the basic CVP model to the Fairfield Blues' seating plans for Tonopah Park.[2] Based on a review of past seasons' accounting records, Jason Robertson performed statistical analyses to estimate average fixed facility costs per season, ticket prices, and unit-level variable costs per ticket sold.[3] He found that other cost and revenue drivers either might not be important factors for profitability or can be incorporated later into a more complex model.

Robertson then updated the historical amounts to reflect expected price and cost changes and developed the following cost and price estimates for the ballpark during the six-month baseball season:

Facility cost per season (mortgage, salaries, utilities, etc.)	$450,000
Variable cost per ticket sold (programmes, custodians, etc.)	$2
Price per ticket	$7

He believed that these price and cost estimates are appropriate for typical seasonal operations for the coming year. He can easily adjust facility costs for more or fewer salaries or variable costs for more or less costly programmes. Although he can also adjust ticket prices, doing so might not reflect the team's newly competitive situation. Robertson suspects that next year's attendance might be sensitive (i.e., elastic) to changes in ticket prices. Let's next discuss how he can use these factors in a simple, manual financial planning model. Later, we will transform this manual model into a more powerful computer model.

Cost-Volume-Profit Model and the Break-Even Point

Suppose that the Fairfield Blues plans to sell 90,000 tickets during a season. The following income statement for the season shows that its estimated operating income (or operating profit) is zero:[4]

Volume, revenues, and costs	Estimated amounts
Seasonal ticket volume	90,000 tickets
Sales revenue (90,000 × $7)	$630,000
Less variable costs (90,000 × $2)	180,000
Total contribution margin	$450,000
Less facility costs	450,000
Operating income	$0

Notice that the income statement (1) is a financial model of the key revenue and cost driver (ticket sales), (2) highlights the distinction between variable costs and committed facility costs, and (3) shows the outcome of the plan to sell 90,000 tickets, which is a profit of zero. The organization has no profit or loss at this activity level; it therefore *breaks even*. This ticket volume is the organization's **break-even point,** the volume of activity that produces equal revenues and costs for the organization. If no other activities except ticket sales drive costs and revenues, the team's break-even point is 90,000 tickets per season.[5]

How can Robertson compute the Blues' break-even point if we did not already know that it is 90,000 tickets per month? He can use a *contribution-margin* approach to the basic CVP model to find the break-even point. Each ticket sells for $7, but $2 of this amount is used to cover variable costs. Thus, $5 per ticket is the **contribution margin** per ticket that in total covers the facility cost of $450,000. When enough tickets have been sold so that these $5 contributions add up to $450,000, the organization will break even. We can therefore compute the 90,000-ticket, break-even sales volume as follows:[6]

Break-even sales volume = Fixed costs per period
÷ Contribution margin per unit
Fairfield Blues' break-even volume = $450,000 per month ÷ $5 per ticket
= 90,000 tickets per month

Basic CVP Model in Graphical Format

The figures showing the break-even sales for Fairfield Blues are graphed in Exhibit 7.1.[7] Panel A shows a CVP graph, and panel B shows an alternative profit-volume graph, which condenses the revenue and cost information to a single line.

The graphs, which are also financial models, disclose more information than the break-even calculation and can be useful in presentations to illustrate the effects of changes in volume on profit. The vertical distance between the lines on the graph in panel A or the distance from the *X*-axis and the line in panel B reflects the profit or loss at a particular sales volume. If Fairfield Blues sells fewer than 90,000 tickets in a month, it will suffer a loss. The size of the loss increases as ticket sales decline. Conversely, the team enjoys a profit if sales exceed 90,000 tickets. For example, if the team sells 170,000 tickets in a season, its profit will be $400,000.

Exhibit 7.1 CVP in Graphical Format (not to scale)

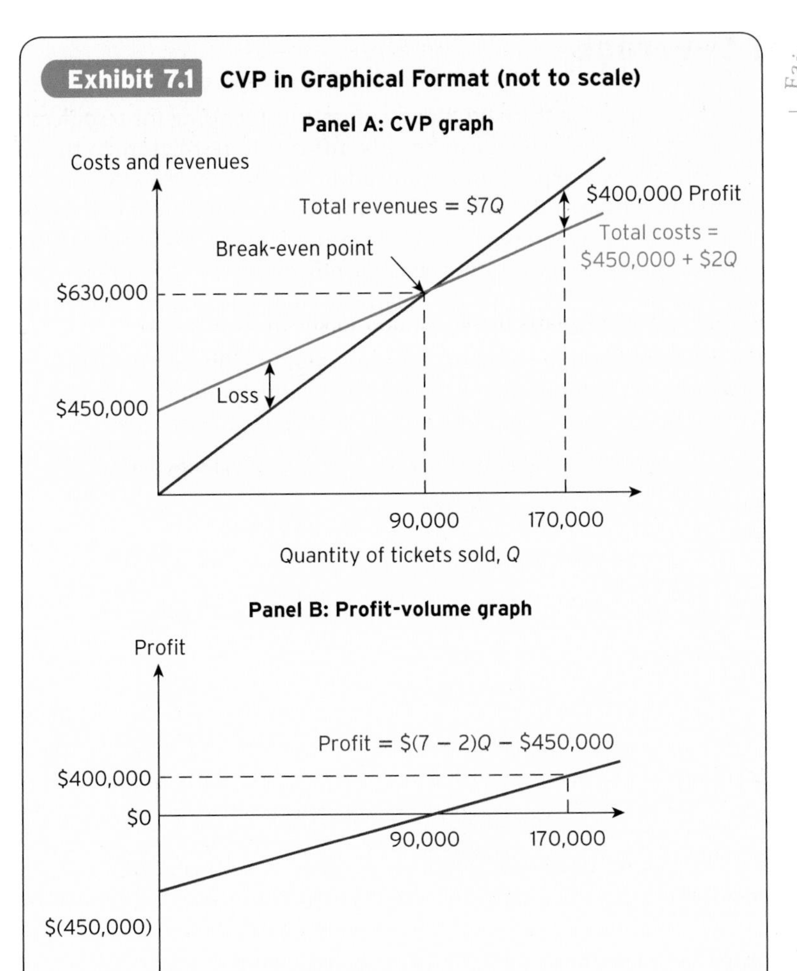

CVP and Target Income

The founders and other shareholders of the Fairfield Blues, like the owners of any other business, desire to earn a competitive return on their investment. The founders have invested some of their retirement funds in the team and ballpark, and other shareholders have contributed capital that they could invest elsewhere. In this case, the shareholders estimate that the value of the company is $4,000,000 and that they should receive a 10 per cent return on that investment value. Therefore, they believe that the company should generate a target income of $400,000, which is a 10 per cent return on their investment. The rationale is that the shareholders can sell the company, reinvest the proceeds and earn a comparable return. To be a viable investment, the Fairfield Blues must meet shareholders' opportunity costs.

Integrating the target income into the CVP model is straightforward. In the previous case, the company had to sell 90,000 tickets to cover the fixed costs and break even. Now it must go one step further: cover the fixed costs *and* earn $400,000 income. With each ticket continuing to contribute $5, the necessary calculation using either the contribution margin or equation method becomes

Target sales volume = (Fixed costs + Target income) ÷ Contribution margin per ticket
= ($450,000 + $400,000) ÷ $5
= $850,000 ÷ $5
= 170,000 tickets

Note that Exhibit 7.1 also shows the target sales volume, the quantity 170,000 that achieves the target income, to the right of the break-even point in both panels.

Operating Leverage

Most organizations, including the Fairfield Blues, commit to spending for resources such as salaries, rents, licences, interest and taxes, which can be very difficult to restructure in the short term. Large amounts of these facility costs expose an organization to the adverse effects of fluctuating sales because contribution margins are relatively small compared to committed costs. **Operating leverage** reflects the risk of missing sales targets and is measured by the ratio of the contribution margin to operating income. High levels of operating leverage reflect the risk that an organization faces from missing sales targets because facility costs are relatively high and small changes in sales can easily push the organization into a loss.[8] Conversely, low levels of operating leverage mean that facility costs are relatively low compared to the contribution margins. Consider the following example that contrasts the Fairfield Blues with a competitor that has relatively higher operating leverage.

	Fairfield Blues	Maxwell Espressos
Sales price per unit	$7.00	$9.00
Variable cost per unit	$2.00	$2.00
Contribution margin per unit	$5.00	$7.00
Expected sales quantity	170,000	170,000
Expected profitability:		
Sales revenue	$1,190,000	$1,530,000
Variable costs	340,000	340,000
Contribution margin	$850,000	$1,190,000
Facility costs	450,000	790,000
Operating income	$400,000	$400,000
Operating leverage	$850,000 ÷ $400,000 = 2.13	$1,190,000 ÷ $400,000 = 2.98

These two companies have the same levels of expected sales and equal operating incomes; at this sales level, their difference in facility costs ($790,000 – $450,000) is covered by their difference in contribution margin ($1,190,000 – $850,000). Although one might be indifferent to the two companies at this level of sales, their exposure to changes in sales is different. Fairfield Blues' operating leverage, 2.13, is lower than that of Maxwell Espressos, which is 2.98. This reflects Espressos' higher exposure to the effects of lower than expected sales. What if each company's actual sales level declined by 10,000 units to 160,000? Which company's income is hurt more? Consider the following, which shows the effects of lower sales volume for both companies:

	Fairfield Blues	Maxwell Espressos
Sales price per unit	$7.00	$9.00
Variable cost per unit	$2.00	$2.00
Contribution margin per unit	$5.00	$7.00
Actual sales quantity	160,000	160,000
Actual profitability:		
Sales revenue	$1,120,000	$1,440,000
Variable costs	320,000	320,000
Contribution margin	$800,000	$1,120,000
Facility costs	450,000	790,000
Operating income	$350,000	$330,000
Operating leverage	2.29	3.39

Because sales are lower, both companies' operating incomes naturally are lower than expected, but Espressos has taken the larger hit because its facility costs are higher than those of the Blues. Note also that unless Espressos reduces facility costs, its situation becomes riskier as reflected by its still higher operating leverage. In contrast, if its sales were expected to be consistently above the indifference point of 170,000 tickets per season, the Espressos' higher contribution margin per ticket makes it more profitable than the Fairfield Blues. Many aspects of financial models reflect this type of impact on profits. We later cover more general approaches to modelling variability and risk.

Set-up of Computer Spreadsheet Models

In concept, financial modelling does not require a computer. After all, organizations used manual financial models similar to our previous examples before computers were available. However, it is a fact of modern business that virtually all financial modelling is performed with computer spreadsheets or specialized modelling software. This software enables quicker, more flexible, and more complex modelling than was possible before. It is inconceivable that we should extend our discussion of financial modelling without recognizing the impact and value of computer software.

Computer spreadsheets such as Microsoft's Excel and Calc (the spreadsheet component of the OpenOffice.org software package) are among the most powerful and most commonly used business tools. Mastery of the fundamentals of spreadsheets is essential for anyone who undertakes any cost management analysis, particularly financial modelling. This discussion is not meant to substitute for either formal courses or diligent self-study, either of which can lead to mastery of spreadsheets. The purpose is to convey some fundamentals of building a flexible financial model.

Spreadsheets are ideally suited for financial modelling. One important key to unlocking the power of these spreadsheets is to use the spreadsheet *not* merely as a calculator but as a *model* of relations among financial and non-financial factors. Let's transform Fairfield Blues' manual profit-planning model into the computer model shown in Exhibit 7.2. The steps we perform can be extended to a more complex spreadsheet model and are outlined in the following sections.

Gathering information

First, gather all facts, assumptions and estimates that underlie the model. These include estimates of sales prices, profit targets, and so forth. Some cost management analysts call these the model's input data or 'parameters'. They are the model's cost- and revenue-driver building blocks. Fairfield Blues' profit-planning parameters include the ticket price, variable cost per ticket sold, facility costs per season, profit target and percentage of seating capacity sold per game. Note that profit targets can be expressed as absolute dollar amounts or as returns on either sales or invested capital. To facilitate

Exhibit 7.2 Computerized Profit-planning Model

	A	B	C	D
1	**Profit-planning model**			
2	**Input data**		Sales price per ticket	$7.00
3	Ballpark seating capacity per game	4,000	Variable cost per ticket	$2.00
4	Home games per season	54	Committed facility costs per season	$450,000
5	Average percentage seats sold per game	85%	Target profit	$400,000
6				
7	**Break-even analysis**		**Planned-profit analysis**	
8	Committed costs (D4)	$450,000	Planned sales volume in units (B3*B4*B5)	183,600
9	Divided by contribution margin per ticket (D2–D3)	$5.00	Sales revenues (D2*D8)	$1,285,200
10	Break-even volume in units (B8/B9)	90,000	Less variable costs (D3*D8)	367,200
11	**Target-profit analysis**		Contribution margin (D9–D10)	918,000
12	Committed costs (D4)	$450,000	Less committed costs (D4)	450,000
13	Plus target profit (D5)	400,000	Operating profit (loss) (D11–D12)	$468,000
14	Target total contribution margin (B12+B13)	$850,000		
15	Divided by contribution margin per unit (D2–D3)	$5.00		
16	Target volume in units (B14/B15)	170,000		

analysis with the model, these parameters should be located and clearly identified in a defined parameter or input-data area of the spreadsheet. Exhibit 7.2 clearly identifies the model's input-data cells. This is the only place that the parameters are located as numbers, but the analysis section of the model can use them throughout.

Modelling relations among parameters

Second, understand and describe the relations of the model's parameters. Changing a model's parameters should change its outcomes. This usually involves modelling how one parameter affects another with an algebraic relation or *formula*. For Fairfield Blues' profit-planning model, these formulas are the equations underlying the income statement and are located apart from the input data section. The model in Exhibit 7.2 has three types of CVP analyses below the data input section: break-even (cells A7 to B10), target profit (A11 to B16), and planned profit (C7 to D13). The last analysis shows expected profits at a planned level of ticket sales (183,600 tickets = 4,000-seat capacity × 54 games × 85 per cent seats sold, in this example) that might differ from either break-even volume or target volume.

Separate parameters and formulas

Third, to facilitate the analysis of the model, the formulas in the analysis sections should *never* contain the actual numerical values of the parameters. Instead, use the parameters' cell locations in all formulas where they occur. Exhibit 7.2 models the financial relationships in column B, rows 8 to 16 and column D, rows 8 to 13. Placing the cursor on any of these cells shows that *none contain numbers*. Instead, the amounts displayed in the cells are the *computed effects of formulas* that combine the model's parameters and preceding calculations, as appropriate. For this exposition, columns A and C also show these formulas, although this usually is not done because some formulas are very complex. If you highlight the cell B10, you see in the formula bar at the top of the spreadsheet that it contains the formula '= B8/B9', which models the break-even relation. Likewise, cell B16 contains the formula, '= B14/B15', which computes the target unit volume. D13 contains the formula, '= D11 – D12', which completes the calculation of the operating profit or loss at the planned sales volume.

The major benefit to separating the model's parameters and relations follows: *making a change to a parameter in the one highly visible place where it occurs as a number causes the model to recalculate outcomes by incorporating the new parameter value everywhere it is used in formulas*. Otherwise, changing a parameter requires changing every formula that uses the parameter. For large models, this can be very difficult and wastes valuable analysis time. Furthermore, someone other than the model's creator who wishes to use it might not know where to find every occurrence of the parameter and might use the model to generate inaccurate information.

© *Squaredpixels*

Building models often is a group effort, requiring input from many perspectives and functions.

Following these guidelines for constructing financial models creates powerful and flexible decision-making aids. Analysts can extend simple models to include complications of taxes, multiple products, multiple revenue and cost drivers, scarce resources and risk. You should consider replicating the model in Exhibit 7.2 on a computer so that you can better appreciate this and the following sections of the chapter.

Modelling Taxes, Multiple Products and Multiple Cost Drivers

LO 3
Build a financial model that reflects the effects of taxes, multiple products and multiple cost drivers.

Revenue and cost drivers are the building blocks of financial models, and relations between them are the mortar that holds them together. A fundamental lesson of cost management is that many decisions drive costs; costs do not just happen. Decisions also drive revenues, but not all of them are at the discretion of managers. The previous example reflected an environment in which only unit-level activity (ticket sales) appeared to drive revenues and costs because the model builder considered all other driving activities to be fixed or committed. We will now extend this and build a financial model that reflects the effects of taxes, multiple products and multiple cost drivers. With such a model Jason Roberts analyses the financial consequences of several decisions: the introduction of box-seat tickets, using the ballpark for concerts and other events. Yet other decisions are modelled later in this chapter, about the mix of products to sell when resources are scarce, and about accepting special orders.

Modelling Taxes

Profit-seeking firms pay taxes on their periodic profits, meaning that target income figures should be set high enough to meet profit requirements and cover the firm's tax obligations. The relationship between an organization's pretax income and after-tax income can be expressed in the following formula:

$$\begin{aligned}\textbf{After-tax income} &= \textbf{Before-tax income} - \textbf{Income taxes}\\ &= \textbf{Before-tax income} - (\textbf{Before-tax income} \times t)\\ &= \textbf{Before-tax income} \times (1 - t)\end{aligned}$$

where t is the average or *effective* income tax rate.

Dividing both sides by $(1 - t)$ gives:

$$\textbf{After-tax income}/(1 - t) = \textbf{Before-tax income}$$

Now we can find the desired before-tax income that will generate the desired after-tax income, given the company's effective tax rate, which will meet the profit target and cover the tax obligation.

To illustrate, we continue the previous Fairfield Blues example to show how the team can earn the desired $400,000 profit target *after tax*. Assume that the company is subject to a 20 per cent average or effective income tax rate.[9] We first convert the after-tax target profit to a before-tax amount, as follows:

$$\begin{aligned}\textbf{Before-tax income} &= \textbf{After-tax income} \div (1 - t)\\ &= \$400{,}000 \div (1 - 0.20)\\ &= \$500{,}000\end{aligned}$$

The before-tax income of $500,000 is inserted as the target income in the following calculation, now requiring Fairfield Blues to sell 190,000 tickets to generate its after-tax profit target of $500,000:

$$\begin{aligned}\textbf{Target sales volume} &= (\textbf{Fixed cost} + \textbf{Target before-tax income})\\ &\quad \div \textbf{Contribution margin per ticket}\\ &= (\$450{,}000 + \$500{,}000) \div \$5 = \underline{\underline{\textbf{190,000 tickets}}}\end{aligned}$$

Exhibit 7.3 shows Fairfield Blues' profit-planning model that Robertson modified to include the tax obligation, modelled as the average tax rate in D6. Note that the break-even analysis in Exhibit 7.3 (A7 to B10) is unchanged because at zero profit, Fairfield Blues pays no taxes. Subsequent analyses differ because of the inclusion of the tax rate. The target-profit analysis (A11 to B16) uses

Exhibit 7.3 **Profit-planning Model with an Average, Effective Tax Rate**

	A	B	C	D
1	**Profit-planning model with an average tax rate**			
2	**Input data**		Sales price per ticket	$7.00
3	Ballpark seating capacity per game	4,000	Variable cost per ticket	$2.00
4	Home games per season	54	Committed facility costs per season	$ 450,000
5	Average percentage seats sold per game	85%	After-tax target profit	$ 400,000
6			Average tax rate	20%
7	**Break-even analysis**		**Planned-profit analysis**	
8	Committed costs (D4)	$450,000	Planned sales volume in units (B3*B4*B5)	183,600
9	Divided by contribution margin per ticket (D2-D3)	$5.00	Sales revenues (D2*D8)	$1,285,200
10	Break-even volume in units (B8/B9)	90,000	Less variable costs (D3*D8)	367,200
11	**Target-profit analysis**		Contribution margin (D9-D10)	$918,000
12	Committed costs (D4)	$450,000	Less committed costs (D4)	450,000
13	Plus target profit before tax (D5/(1-D6))	500,000	Before-tax operating profit (loss) (D11-D12)	$468,000
14	Target total contribution margin (B12+B13)	$950,000	Less taxes at average tax rate (D13*D6)	93,600
15	Divided by contribution margin per unit (D2-D3)	$5.00	After-tax profit (loss) (D13-D14)	$374,400
16	Target volume in units (B14/B15)	190,000		

the before-tax profit target, B13 = D5/(1 – D6), to calculate the target volume of 190,000 tickets (B16). The planned profit analysis in cells C7 to D15 has been changed in this exhibit to reflect the effect of taxes. Note that because the average tax rate is included as an input parameter in volume and profit analyses, Robertson also can model the company's operations given changes to its average tax rate that result from different tax-planning actions. More complexities of tax planning require a more complex profit-planning model.[10] Note also that this analysis shows that expected ticket sales will not meet the company's after-tax target (see the planned profit in D15). This shortfall is a motivation for modelling the possible impacts of altering the ballpark's seating.

Modelling Multiple Products

The previous Fairfield Blues' models assume that the company has only one product: a 'general admission' seat. Most firms produce more than one product at their facilities, which adds some complexity to their profit-planning analyses.

Recall that Fairfield Blues' seasonal facility costs total $450,000 and the variable cost per ticket is $2. Suppose that the company has decided to replace some of its 4,000 general admission seats with 800 reserved box seats. These 800 seats will be more comfortable and afford a better view of the field than the ballpark's remaining general admission seating, which will now have 3,200 seats. Management has decided to reduce its general admission price to $6 per ticket and charge $15 per ticket for box seats. The construction project will result in an increase in seasonal fixed costs of $100,000 because of added depreciation.[11] Variable costs per ticket are unchanged.

Notice that 80 per cent of the available seats are general admission seats (3,200 ÷ 4,000) and 20 per cent are box seats. Assume that ticket sales for each type of seat will be in the same proportion as the number of different seats available. Therefore, if it sells 100,000 tickets per season, for example, sales should be as follows:

General admission seat tickets	$100{,}000 \times 0.8 = 80{,}000$ tickets
Box-seat tickets	$100{,}000 \times 0.2 = 20{,}000$ tickets

For any organization that sells multiple products, the relative proportion of each type of product planned or actually sold is called the **sales mix** or **product mix**. It is an important assumption in multiproduct profit planning because it is used to compute a **weighted-average unit contribution margin (WAUCM),** a tool for finding the break-even point and performing other profit-planning exercises. WAUCM is the average of the various products' unit contribution margins *weighted* by the relative proportion of each product sold. Contribution margin for general admission seats is \$4 per ticket (\$4 = \$6 – \$2) and for box seats is \$13 per ticket (\$13 = \$15 – \$2). Fairfield Blues' weighted-average unit contribution margin for the sale of regular and box seats is:

Weighted-average unit contribution margin (WAUCM) = (\$4 × 0.8) + (\$13 × 0.2) = \$5.80

The team's new break-even point in tickets is computed by replacing a single-product contribution margin with the multiproduct WAUCM in the break-even formula introduced earlier, namely:

Break-even sales volume = Fixed cost per period ÷ WAUCM per unit
= \$550,000 ÷ \$5.80
= 94,828 tickets (rounded)

(Recall that the construction of box seats increases fixed costs from \$450,000 to \$550,000.) This number of tickets, however, is a combination of regular and box seats and must be interpreted considering the sales mix. The team will break even for the month if it sells the following tickets:

General admission seat tickets	94,828 × 0.8 = 75,862 tickets
Box-seat tickets	94,828 × 0.2 = 18,966
Break-even sales volume	94,828 tickets

One may convert these sales volume figures to sales dollar figures by multiplying each product sales volume by its sales price, as follows

Break-even sales dollars = (\$6 × 75,862) + (\$15 × 18,966) = \$739,662

Observe that the break-even point of 94,828 tickets or \$739,662 is valid only for the 80:20 sales mix assumed in computing the weighted-average unit contribution margin. A shift in sales mix generally results in a different WAUCM, which changes the break-even or target income figure. Thus, the sales mix is an important input parameter for the many organizations that provide multiple products or services from common facilities.

7.1 Cost Management in Practice

Sales Mix Concept in Action

You have no doubt seen the sales-mix concept in action by observing recent trends in petrol sales. The old-fashioned petrol station has rapidly given way to the convenience store that also sells petrol. Or in some cases, petrol stations might be a partner with, say, **7-Eleven, Subway**, **Burger King**, **McDonald's** or **Spar Express**. The convenience store might also sell fresh produce and flowers, as well as provide services such as a post office, pharmacy and laundry.

What's the reason behind the change? Although petrol stations usually require expensive sites, petrol retailing is a low-margin business - 10 per cent. Convenience-store items, on the other hand, have margins of around 30 per cent. These latter goods now account for at least half of revenues, and overall profitability has increased. The next step might be for the marketers to purposely take a loss on the petrol just to attract customers who might also purchase food. This practice is already happening in some European markets.

Source: Sullivan (1996).

Multiproduct Profit-planning and Decision-making Models

Exhibit 7.4 shows Fairfield Blues' profit-planning model with the modification of two types of seating (A6 to B8) and the sales mix assumption (A9 to B11). The other addition to the model is the computation of the weighted-average unit contribution margin (WAUCM in cell B14), which is

Exhibit 7.4 **Profit-planning Model with Taxes and Multiple Products**

	A	B	C	D
1	**Profit-planning model with multiple products**			
2	**Sales input data**		**Cost input data**	
3	Ballpark seating capacity per game	4,000	Variable cost per ticket	$2.00
4	Home games per season	54	Fixed facility costs per season	550,000
5	Average percentage seats sold per game	85%	After-tax target profit	400,000
6	Sales price per ticket		Average tax rate	20%
7	Box seating	$15.00		
8	General admission seating	6.00		
9	Sales mix assumption			
10	Box seating	20.0%		
11	General admission seating	80.0%		
12				
13	**Weighted average unit contribution margin**		**Planned-profit analysis**	
14	WAUCM (B10*(B7–D3) + B11*(B8–D3))	$5.80	Planned sales volume in units (B3*B4*B5)	183,600
15	**Break-even analysis**		Sales revenues	
16	Fixed costs (D4)	$550,000	Box seating (D14*B10*B7)	$550,800
17	Divided by WAUCM (B14)	5.80	General admission seating (D14*B11*B8)	881,280
18	Break-even volume in units (B16/B17)	94,828	Total revenues	$1,432,080
19	**Target-profit analysis**		Less variable costs (D14*D3)	367,200
20	Fixed costs (D4)	$550,000	Contribution margin (D18–D19)	$1,064,880
21	Before-tax parget profit (D5/(1–D6))	500,000	Less fixed costs (D4)	550,000
22	Target contribution margin	$1,050,000	Before-tax profit (loss) (D20–D21)	$514,880
23	Divided by WAUCM (B14)	$5.80	Less taxes at average tax rate (D6*D22)	102,976
24	Target volume in units (B22/B23)	181,034	After-tax profit (loss) (D22–D23)	$411,904

computed as explained earlier. Using the WAUCM value of $5.80 allows Jason Robertson to compute the break-even volume of 94,828 tickets in cell B18. Why is the break-even ticket volume higher than before (recall that with only general admission seating, the break-even was 90,000 tickets)? The break-even volume is higher now because, although Fairfield Blues has added a new product (box seating) with a higher unit contribution margin, it also has increased fixed costs per season by $100,000. Thus, the company must sell more tickets to break even. Notice, however, that the target sales to reach the desired after-tax profit is 181,034 tickets (B24). This is a lower ticket volume than before because the higher WAUCM ($5.80 versus $5.00) requires fewer tickets to be sold above the break-even (after fixed costs are covered) to meet the same after-tax profit target.

Lower break-even and target volumes usually are desirable because they mean that fixed costs are relatively low and the operation is less vulnerable to the effects of lower sales (recall the earlier discussion of operating leverage). Does this mean that the baseball team *will* be more profitable? It does only if customers are willing to pay the higher prices for box seats *and* if they purchase tickets in accordance with the planned sales mix. Achieving the planned sales volume (D14) of 183,600 tickets *and* the assumed sales mix should result in exceeding the after-tax profit target of $400,000 by $11,904 (see D24).

So, how can Glen Hernandez use the financial model for decision making? Recall that with only general admission seats planned before-tax profit amounted to $468,000. With 20 per cent of the seats converted to box-seat tickets, planned before-tax profit will rise to $514,880 (see D22). The additional profit is $46,880, which is the result of the following differential revenues and costs: 20 per cent of the 183,600 tickets = 36,720 tickets will become box-seat tickets, each yielding a contribution margin that is $8 higher compared to the old general admission seats (the sales price is $15 instead of $7). However, 80 per cent of the 183,600 tickets = 146,880 tickets will be general admission seats, each yielding a contribution margin that is $1 lower compared to the old general admission seats (the sales price becomes $6 instead of $7). Furthermore, fixed costs will rise by $100,000 per year. The total effect, thus, equals (36,720 × $8) – (146,880 × $1) – $100,000 = $46,880. Based on this analysis, Glen Hernandez concludes that introducing box-seats is a sensible business decision.

However, this financial model only looks one year into the future. The next chapter will discuss financial models for investments considering multiple periods.

7.1 You're the Decision Maker

Effect of Sales Mix on Financial Performance

The sales mix is relevant not only for multiproduct profit planning but also for assessing an organization's actual sales and profit performance. Suppose that Fairfield Blues plans to sell 183,600 tickets next season (85 per cent of seats sold) with the assumed 80:20 sales mix and expects to exceed its after-tax income target. Suppose also that during the next season, all ticket prices and costs occurred as planned. However, the team actually sold 185,760 tickets (86 per cent of seats sold). One might expect that actual, after-tax profit should exceed the target even more because ticket volume exceeded the planned and target volumes. However, during this season when 185,760 tickets were sold, the actual sales mix was 84 per cent general admission and 16 per cent box seats, which is a departure from the 80:20 sales mix assumption.

a. What is the effect on break-even and target volumes and profit from the changes in sales volume and sales mix?
b. Explain how the changes in outcomes were caused by the actual inputs.

(Solutions begin on p. 340.)

Modelling Multiple Cost Drivers

A critique of the profit-planning model in Exhibit 7.4 reveals several limitations despite the addition of taxes and multiple products. As we just showed, for example, the sales mix must remain as predicted, or a change might influence the organization's profitability. Similarly, a company's technology, efficiency and management must remain constant because these cost and revenue drivers also affect profit-planning relations. The model is also based on straight-line, linear relations among revenues and costs, thus ignoring basic factors such as quantity discounts. Perhaps most troubling is the model's use of a single cost-driver activity, sales volume. Most organizations have multiple cost and revenue drivers that affect profits.

Cost-driver activities

Activity-based costing (Chapter 4) directs us to investigate decisions about activities performed at the unit, batch, product, customer and facility levels to identify significant cost drivers. If these activities are relevant to profit planning, financial models should include them. Models should reflect the effects of all major cost-driving activities, some of which occur at other than the unit level. For example, the number of tickets sold drives some unit-level costs of the Fairfield Blues, but decisions about seating capacity, staffing, maintenance and groundskeeping also drive the team's costs.

Revenue-driver activities

Revenues are the result of sales prices and sales volumes. Managers can set prices, but customers decide whether to pay them. In perfectly competitive markets, organizations are price takers, not price setters,[12] so modelling revenues is straightforward by multiplying the market price by the expected sales quantity, which is limited only by the organization's capacity. But if markets are less than perfect – and they often are – other factors also drive revenues. Ticket prices surely drive the team's revenues, but advertising, the quality (and cost) of the team and its competitors, and external competition for leisure time and dollars probably drive revenues, too. Because many factors driving revenues are external to the organization and because even internal ones are complex (e.g., the relation of advertising to revenues), many organizations understand revenue drivers less than they do their cost drivers. Because they represent half of the profit equation, understanding revenue drivers surely is as important as understanding cost drivers. An exploration of revenue drivers, except under conditions of perfect competition, is beyond the scope of this text. However, the final section of this chapter discusses pricing decisions in some detail.

Profit-Planning and Decision-making Models with Multiple Cost Drivers

Before we show the integration of multiple cost drivers into profit-planning models, we quickly review the nature of unit-, batch-, product-, customer-, and facility-level activities and costs. Recall the following:

- *Unit-level activities* are performed for each individual unit of product or service.
- *Batch-level activities* are performed to benefit multiple units of similar output equally and simultaneously (i.e., in batches). Batch-level activities include setting up machines to run a particular batch of units. Related costs are traced easily to specific batches but not to individual output units.
- *Product-level activities* are needed to support a specific product or service, that is, an entire product line. Such activities include new product designs, improved existing product quality and product function, product advertising, and production process monitoring.
- *Customer-level activities* are performed to meet the needs of specific customers. Examples of related costs include those attributable to unique packaging, shipping and distribution needs, and to personnel assigned to handle specific customer accounts. (Chapter 5 discusses customer-level analysis in detail.)
- *Facility-level activities* are required for an organization to have the capacity to produce goods and services. These activities are at the highest level of the activity hierarchy and tend to support all organizational processes. Typical examples include physical plant operations and top management activities.

Including these cost-driving activities changes the nature of profit-planning models. The basic CVP model assumes that revenues and variable costs vary with sales activity while other costs remain constant. However, costs can vary because of drivers other than sales activity. The following is an example of a total cost expression reflecting multiple relevant activities (recall that we model revenues assuming competitive markets):

Total cost = (Unit variable cost × Number of units) + (Batch cost × Batch activity)
+ (Product cost × Product activity) + (Customer cost × Customer activity)
+ (Facility cost × Facility activity)

Observe that this calculation no longer relies only on sales activity (e.g., the number of tickets sold) as the cost driver but introduces the impacts of multiple activities. As a result, some costs viewed as fixed under a traditional analysis are now considered variable with respect to appropriate cost-driving activities (batches, products, etc.).

Using various statistical analyses and his own knowledge of cost behaviour, Jason Robertson developed the following set of activities and costs to extend his previous financial model, now shown in Exhibit 7.5 and Exhibit 7.6. The difference between these two is that in the second model, Robertson also included costs and revenues related to offering another product at Tonopah Park: six summer concerts.

© sjoeman

The number of skier days drives revenues and costs at ski resorts.

Exhibit 7.5 Profit-planning Model with Multiple Cost Drivers

	A	B	C	D	E
1	**Profit-planning model with multiple products and cost activities**				
2	**Sales input data**		**Cost input data**	**Activity cost**	**Activity**
3	Ballpark seating capacity per game	4,000	Unit-level cost per ticket	$1.00	183,600
4	Home games per season	54	Batch-level cost - Baseball game	2,400	54
5	Concerts per summer season	-	- Concert (additional)	20,000	-
6	Average percentage seats sold per event	85%	Product-level costs - Baseball	200,000	
7	Sales price per ticket		- Concerts	-	
8	Box seating	$15.00	Customer-level cost	800	20
9	General admission seating	6.00	Facility costs per season - Tonopah Park	150,000	
10	Sales mix assumption		- Administration	79,500	
11	Box seating	20.0%	After-tax target profit per season	400,000	
12	General admission seating	80.0%	Average tax rate	20%	
13					
14	**Weighted-average unit contribution margin**		**Planned-profit analysis**		
15	WAUCM (B11*(B8-D3) + B12*(B9-D3))	$6.80	Sales revenues		
16	**Annual break-even analysis**		Box seating (B3*(B4+B5)*B6*B8*B11)	$550,800	
17	Batch-level costs (D4*E4+(D4+D5)*E5)	$129,600	Regular seating (B3*(B4+B5)*B6*B9*B12)	881,280	
18	Product-level costs (D6+D7)	200,000	Total ticket revenues	$1,432,080	
19	Customer-level costs (D8*E8)	16,000	Less unit-level costs (D3*E3)	183,600	
20	Facility-level costs (D9+D10)	229,500	Batch-level costs (D4*E4+(D4+D5)*E5)	129,600	
21	Total non-unit-level costs	$575,100	Product-level costs (D6+D7)	200,000	
22	Divided by WAUCM (B15)	$6.80	Customer-level costs (D8*E8)	16,000	
23	Break-even volume in units (B21/B22)	84,574	Facility-level costs (D9+D10)	229,500	
24	**Target profit analysis**		Total operating costs	$758,700	
25	Total non-unit-level costs costs (B21)	$575,100	Before-tax profit (loss) (D18-D24)	$673,380	
26	Target profit before-tax (D11/(1-D12))	500,000	Less taxes at average tax rate (D12*D25)	134,676	
27	Target contribution margin	$1,075,100	Profit (loss) after tax (D25-D26)	$538,704	
28	Divided by WAUCM (B15)	$6.80	Target profit after tax (D11)	400,000	
29	Target volume in units (B27/B28)	158,103	Excess (deficiency) of profit (D27-D28)	$138,704	

Exhibit 7.6 Profit-planning Model with Multiple Cost Drivers – Including Six Summer Concerts

	A	B	C	D	E
1	**Profit-planning model with multiple products and cost activities**				
2	**Sales input data**		**Cost input data**	**Activity cost**	**Activity**
3	Ballpark seating capacity per game	4,000	Unit-level cost per ticket	$1.00	204,000
4	Home games per season	54	Batch-level cost - Baseball game	2,400	54
5	Concerts per summer season	6	- Concert (additional)	20,000	6
6	Average percentage seats sold per event	85%	Product-level costs - Baseball	200,000	
7	Sales price per ticket		- Concerts	10,000	
8	Box seating	$15.00	Customer-level cost	800	20
9	General admission seating	6.00	Facility costs per season - Tonopah Park	150,000	
10	Sales mix assumption		- Administration	79,500	
11	Box seating	20.0%	After-tax target profit per season	400,000	
12	General admission seating	80.0%	Average tax rate	20%	
13					
14	**Weighted-average unit contribution margin**		**Planned-profit analysis**		
15	WAUCM (B11*(B8-D3) + B12*(B9-D3))	$6.80	Sales revenues		
16	**Annual break-even analysis**		Box seating (B3*(B4+B5)*B6*B8*B11)	$612,000	
17	Batch-level costs (D4*E4+(D4+D5)*E5)	$264,000	Regular seating (B3*(B4+B5)*B6*B9*B12)	979,200	
18	Product-level costs (D6+D7)	210,000	Total ticket revenues	$1,591,200	
19	Customer-level costs (D8*E8)	16,000	Less unit-level costs (D3*E3)	204,000	
20	Facility-level costs (D9+D10)	229,500	Batch-level costs (D4*E4+(D4+D5)*E5)	264,000	
21	Total non-unit-level costs	$719,500	Product-level costs (D6+D7)	210,000	
22	Divided by WAUCM (B15)	$6.80	Customer-level costs (D8*E8)	16,000	
23	Break-even volume in units (B21/B22)	105,809	Facility-level costs (D9+D10)	229,500	
24	**Target profit analysis**		Total operating costs	$923,500	
25	Total non-unit-level costs costs (B21)	$719,500	Before-tax profit (loss) (D18-D24)	$667,700	
26	Target profit before-tax (D11/(1-D12))	500,000	Less taxes at average tax rate (D12*D25)	133,540	
27	Target contribution margin	$1,219,500	Profit (loss) after tax (D25-D26)	$534,160	
28	Divided by WAUCM (B15)	$6.80	Target profit after tax (D11)	400,000	
29	Target volume in units (B27/B28)	179,338	Excess (deficiency) of profit (D27-D28)	$134,160	

- *Unit-level activities and costs.* Robertson assumed that the ballpark can sell 85 per cent of its seats for baseball games and concerts (total tickets computed in E3 = 204,000 = 4,000 × (54 + 6) × 85 per cent). The only unit-level costs related to games or concerts are for printing tickets and preparing game or concert programmes, which Robertson estimated per ticket to be $1 (in cell D3). He decided that the previously included variable custodial costs *used* were not supplied on a unit-level basis but were a game-level cost (see the next bullet point). Note that this lower per-unit cost increases the WAUCM of baseball games from $5.80 to $6.80 per average ticket (B15). This higher WAUCM does not magically make the team more profitable. Robertson's analysis has more accurately separated the costs that follow, which the simpler models had treated improperly as unit-level variable or committed facility costs.
- *Batch-level activities and costs.* Each game or concert is like a batch of production. For example, if Fairfield Blues sells a total of 3,900 tickets for a Saturday game, this is a 'batch' of 3,900 units. Robertson estimated the cost per game, or concert, to be $2,400 (D4), which includes wages paid to security, parking attendants, custodians, ticket takers and ushers. This batch cost is the same even if the company sold only 3,000 tickets for a game or concert. The league schedule showed that the team will have 54 games per season next year (B4 and copied in E4). Robertson began the concert planning by assuming six summer concerts next year (B5 and E5). For top regional performers, the company additionally must pay approximately $20,000 per concert, which is another batch cost (D5).
- *Product-level activities and costs.* The baseball team and concert series hosted by the ballpark are separate product lines. Robertson identified the product-level costs to be the cost of acquiring the rights to the team, advertising, hiring the players and coaches, transporting the team to away games, and purchasing baseball equipment and uniforms. He estimated this cost to be $200,000 per season (D6). He estimated that managing the inaugural concert series costs an additional $10,000 for part-time personnel and advertising (D7).
- *Customer-level activities and costs.* As a community service, Fairfield Blues rents vans and hires drivers once per week to pick up customers who are unable to drive. The drivers bring these customers to games, usually on Saturday or Sunday afternoons, and then take them home after the games. Robertson estimated the cost of this service to be $800 (D8) every time the service is performed, about 20 games per season (E8).
- *Facility-level activities and costs.* Robertson identified facility-level activities and estimated their costs in two parts, the ballpark and administration.
  - *Tonopah Park.* Robertson estimated the ballpark, including depreciation, utilities and maintenance, to cost $150,000 per season (D9).
  - *Administration.* Robertson estimated administrative activities, including payroll and marketing, to cost $79,500 per season (D10).

Before-tax profit in Exhibit 7.5 is estimated to be $673,380 (cell D25). How can we reconcile this with the expected profit in Exhibit 7.4 of $514,880 (cell D22), in other words: a difference of $158,500? Both models include the same activities and sales prices. However costs are modelled differently. In the model in Exhibit 7.4, unit-level costs are $2.00 and fixed costs are $550,000 per year. In the new model in Exhibit 7.5, the unit-level costs are $1,00, which increases the contribution margin by 183,600 tickets × $1.00 = $183,600. In the new model in Exhibit 7.5, the batch-level costs, product-level costs and customer-level costs amount to $575,100, which is $25,100 higher compared to the previous fixed costs. On balance, costs are expected to be $158,500 lower. Note that this difference in expected costs is considerable and financial models require validation with data to see which one is most accurate.[13]

The results of Robertson's model and input parameters show estimated operating income per season including the six summer concerts to be $667,700 before tax (cell D27 in Exhibit 7.6), and $534,160 after taxes (cell D27 in Exhibit 7.6). He was pleased to see that the initial plan exceeded the profit target by $134,160 (D29 in Exhibit 7.6.). By building this financial planning model, Robertson was able to anticipate this favourable outcome.

So, how can Glen Hernandez use the financial model for decision making? Recall that with only baseball games (general admission tickets and box-seat tickets) planned before-tax profit amounted to $673,380 (cell D25 in Exhibit 7.5), which is higher than the before-tax profit including the six summer concerts of $667,700. The difference is $5,680, which can be understood as follows: differential revenues are 3400 tickets per concert × 6 concerts × $6.80 WAUCM = $138,720. The differential batch-level costs are ($2,400 + $20,000) × 6 concerts = $134,400, and the differential product-level costs of \$10,000. Introducing concerts does not make a difference for the customer-level costs and the facility-level cost. Thus, the effect on the before-tax profit equals \$138,720 – \$144,400 = –\$5,680. Based on this analysis, Glen Hernandez could conclude that introducing concerts is not a sensible business decision. However, as with the decision about box-seat tickets, this financial model also looks only one year into the future. The next chapter will discuss financial models for investments considering multiple periods.

Glen Hernandez and Jason Roberts knew, however, that the outcomes of the financial models depended on the validity of the assumptions that formed the input data. Numerous alternative actual inputs must be considered. Possible variation in these parameters indicates the risk of decisions considered by the company. By focusing on the various cost-driving activities, Hernandez and Robertson now can identify different inputs that might be more likely to occur, producing different profit outcomes. We next cover several types of risk analysis, sensitivity and scenario analyses, and show the additional decision-making power of using financial planning models.

Using Sensitivity and Scenario Analysis

LO 4
Apply scenario and sensitivity analyses to model the risk of decisions.

All decisions about the future are made without knowing actual outcomes. Decisions might not translate into perfectly executed actions, and external factors might be different than those expected. This is the natural condition of risky decision making, which characterizes all business management. Financial planning models by themselves cannot reduce risks, but they can help managers understand the causes and extent of risk. They can then take actions that are most likely to result in favourable outcomes, for example by ruling out actions that are too risky or by hedging their bets.[14] In addition to operating leverage, discussed earlier, we consider two related sources of risk that can be modelled: parameter variability and alternative combinations of parameters. We present two common methods for modelling these risks more precisely: sensitivity analysis and scenario analysis.[15]

Sensitivity Analysis: What If?

Previous analyses tentatively concluded that Fairfield Blues can exceed its monthly target profit. However, numerous assumptions about its financial variables formed this conclusion. Review the data input section of Exhibit 7.6. Any of these 19 data inputs (ticket prices, activity costs, activity levels, and so on) could be wrong. That is, actual values might be different from planned ones, and actual profits, therefore, also might differ. Jason Robertson and Fairfield Blues' management could wait to find out what will actually happen: whether they actually will have sufficient profit. Alternatively, they can use several methods to assess the risk of their decision-making problem and then take actions to manage their risks.

One of the most common methods of assessing risk is *sensitivity analysis*. It tests a financial planning model for changes in outcomes (e.g., profits) caused by changes in each of the model's parameters (e.g., ticket sales). Sensitivity analysis answers the question, 'What if this parameter is changed?' The more sensitive the outcome is to a parameter change, the more risk the changes in that parameter pose. Obviously, manual sensitivity analysis is a tedious, error-prone task, and few organizations undertake it unless they use computerized financial models. This is where the power and ease of using a computerized model becomes apparent.

Robertson first determined the most likely value of each of the parameters ('base' values). Next, he determined the likely range of each parameter. A cost management analyst can determine these values and ranges by considering historical data, or, in the case of new operations, similar experiences, test cases or analysts' best estimates. Robertson then introduced a change to one of the parameters in Exhibit 7.6, first changing the parameter to the upper and then to the lower end of the range while keeping all other parameters in the exhibit at their most likely values. He then recorded the resulting profit caused by each change and repeated the analysis for all relevant parameters. Do analysts and managers always have the most reliable information they need to perform this detailed analysis? Unfortunately, no, but using informed estimates in most cases is better than performing no analysis at all. Exhibit 7.7 presents a summary of Robertson's sensitivity analysis of Fairfield Blues' financial model, which we now interpret.

Exhibit 7.7 **Summary of Sensitivity Analysis**

	A	B	C	D	E	F	G	H
1			Range			Profit		
2	**Input data**	Base	High	Low	Base	High	Low	Elasticity
3	Ballpark seating capacity per game	4,000	4,100	3,900	$534,160	$561,904	$506,416	2.08
4	Home games per season	54	60	50	534,160	633,616	467,856	1.68
5	Concerts per summer season	6	8	-	534,160	571,152	423,184	0.21
6	Average percentage seats sold per event	85%	90%	75%	534,160	599,440	403,600	2.08
7	Sales price per ticket - Box seats	$15.00	$18.00	$14.00	534,160	632,080	501,520	0.92
8	General admission seats	6.00	7.00	5.00	534,160	664,720	403,600	1.47
9	Sales mix assumption - Box seats	20%	25%	10%	534,160	607,600	387,280	0.55
10	General admission seats	80%	90%	75%	534,160	607,600	387,280	1.10
11	Unit-level cost per ticket	$1.00	$2.00	$0.80	534,160	370,960	566,800	(0.31)
12	Batch-level cost - Baseball game	2,400	3,000	2,000	534,160	508,240	551,440	(0.19)
13	- Concert (additional)	20,000	25,000	10,000	534,160	510,160	582,160	(0.18)
14	Product-level costs - Baseball	200,000	220,000	175,000	534,160	518,160	554,160	(0.30)
15	- Concerts	10,000	12,000	8,000	534,160	532,560	535,760	(0.01)
16	Customer level cost	800	500	1,000	534,160	538,960	530,960	(0.02)
17	Customer level activity	20	25	-	534,160	530,960	546,960	(0.02)
18	Facility costs per season - Tonopah Park	$150,000	175,000	130,000	534,160	514,160	550,160	(0.22)
19	- Administration	79,500	90,000	70,000	534,160	525,760	541,760	(0.12)
20	Average tax rate	20%	30%	18%	534,160	467,390	547,514	0.25

Column A of Exhibit 7.7 identifies all parameters, and column B has the most likely or base parameter values. Robertson's estimates of the highest feasible parameter values are in column C, and the lowest feasible values are in column D. Using relations from Exhibit 7.6, column E computes the estimated base profit,[16] which is the same for all parameters because all are set at their most likely or base levels. Column F computes the estimated profit if each parameter in turn is set to its *highest* value while keeping all others at base levels. Similarly, Column G computes the estimated profit if each parameter is set in turn to its *lowest* value, again keeping all others at base levels. Monthly profits range between a high of $664,720 (F8), which reflects the highest price of general admission tickets, and a low of $370,960, which reflects the highest unit-level cost (F11). Clearly, profits are sensitive to ticket prices and unit-level costs, but sorting through the mass of numbers in this summary and comparing changes in profits with respect to such different changes in inputs can be difficult. We need a way to directly compare all of these profit and parameter changes.

We can compare outcome effects by computing the **model elasticity**, the ratio of the percentage change in profit divided by the percentage change in an input parameter. This calculation is analogous to the elasticity of demand, which economists use to compare reactions of demand to changes in prices of different goods. Because elasticity is a ratio of pure percentage numbers, it is independent of the units of measurement. Thus, elasticities of profit to changes in the numbers of tickets or games are comparable. Column H shows the model elasticity for each of the parameters.

Model elasticity = Percentage change of profit ÷ Percentage change of input

For example, the model elasticity to general admission seat prices (H8) is computed as

General admission seat price elasticity = Percentage change of profit ÷ Percentage change of general admission seat price

$$\mathbf{H8 = [(F8 - E8) \div E8] \div [(C8 - B8) \div B8]}$$

$$\mathbf{1.47 = [(664{,}720 - 534{,}160) \div 534{,}160] \div [(7 - 6) \div 6]}$$

You may interpret this elasticity to indicate that a 1 per cent change in general admission ticket price should cause a 1.47 per cent change in profit.[17] An elasticity greater than 1.0 identifies a parameter with a disproportionate effect on profits (this column heading is highlighted in Exhibit 7.7). Actions to change parameters with the highest elasticity should have the greatest impacts on profits. The parameters with the greatest potential to affect profits, according to this model, are the ballpark seating capacity (row 3) and the average percentage of seats sold (row 6). With model elasticities of 2.08, the way to affect profits the most is to change either the seating capacity (temporarily or permanently) or the percentage of seats sold. Conversely, changes in parameters with low elasticity will have relatively small effects on profits. As informative as this analysis can be, it assumes that each parameter affects profits independently of the others. This is not the general case, but analysts should monitor and measure these elastic parameters carefully.

Scenario Analysis (Best, Worst and Most Likely Cases)

Robertson reasoned that some parameters should not be changed independently of others. His financial model makes it easy to change any combination of variables together, but the number of possible combinations of parameter changes is very large. Many managers assess the risk of their decision making by **scenario analysis**, which creates *realistic* combinations of changed parameters. Of all the many possible combinations, only a few are realistic; that is, they very well can happen or actually have happened in the past. By using the model to compute each scenario's profit, managers can see the different outcomes from a number of realistic sets of conditions. For example, an increase in ticket prices might be accompanied by a decrease in ticket volume. Cost management analysts commonly prepare the *best-case, worst-case* and *most likely case* for review by managers. The most likely case usually, but not necessarily, sets all parameters to their most likely or base values. The best-case scenario is the *realistic* combination of the highest prices, highest unit-volumes, and lowest costs and cost-driving activities. Conversely, the worst-case scenario is the realistic combination of lowest prices, lowest unit volumes, and highest costs and cost-driving activities. Describing these cases often requires the collective judgement of a cross-functional team because so many business interactions are involved. The range of outcomes resulting from the various cases shows how good or bad things might be, and the range of outcomes indicates the actual risks of the decision the manager faces.

Suppose that Robertson, without the help of other employees, identified best-and worst-case scenarios as shown in Exhibit 7.8 and set the model parameters to each case's values. The resulting

Exhibit 7.8 **Examples of Best, Worst and Most Likely Cases**

Input data	Best case	Worst case	Most likely
Ballpark seating capacity per game	4,100	3, 900	4,000
Home games per season	60	50	54
Concerts per summer season	8	–	6
Average percentage seats sold per event	90%	75%	85%
Sales price per ticket - box seats	$18.00	$14.00	$15.00
General admission seats	$7.00	$5.00	$6.00
Sales mix assumption - box seats	25%	10%	20%
General admission seats	75%	90%	80%
Unit-level cost per ticket	$0.80	$2.00	$1.00
Batch-level cost - Baseball game	$2,000	$3,000	$2,400
- Concert (additional)	$10,000	$25,000	$20,000
Product-level costs - Baseball	$175,000	$220,000	$200,000
- Concerts	$8,000	$12,000	$10,000
Customer level cost	$500	$1,000	$800
Customer level activity	–	25	20
Facility costs per season - Tonopah Park	$130,000	$175,000	$150,000
- Administration	$70,000	$90,000	$79,500
Average tax rate	18%	30%	20%
Scenario profit	**$1,350,322**	**$(71,138)**	**$534,160**

profits are at the bottom of the exhibit. A careful look at the combinations might lead you to label them as 'wildly optimistic' and 'hopelessly catastrophic' cases! If these are realistic scenarios, one might characterize this company's management as 'very risky'. The best case seems extremely good, and the worst case seems just as extremely bad. If Robertson were to present these scenarios to Fairfield Blues' top management, he might receive many questions about their realism. Indeed, before he considers presenting these scenarios, he should be confident that each tells a plausible story and that he can communicate this story to top management. He would be wise to consult others to develop realistic scenarios.

7.1 Research Insight

Scenario Analysis

Researchers in many fields use scenario analysis to understand the dimensions of risky decision making. For example, weather researchers use complex computer models to predict the landfall of a hurricane several days in advance, given different ocean current, air and water temperature scenarios. Research continues to improve the models' ability to predict hurricane intensity. Biologists use population dynamics models to predict the future of endangered species given alternative decisions to modify their environment. Recent modelling of Orca whales in Washington's Puget Sound examined seven likely scenarios including changes in (1) toxic chemicals, such as PCBs, (2) salmon populations, which are in decline, forcing Orcas to eat contaminated bottom fish, (3) stress from whale-watching boats, and (4) effects of capturing young whales for marine parks 20 years ago. The results indicated that 'even best-case scenarios do not look very good'.

Sources: USA Today (2005); Dunagan (2000).

7.2 Research Insight

Sales Forecasts in Retailing

Retailers such as **Carrefour**, **Tesco** and **Wal-Mart**, and suppliers in the fast-moving consumer goods such as **Nestlé**, **Unilever** and **Procter & Gamble**, face the challenge of estimating consumer demand. It is a balancing act, because they want to have enough products on the shelves in the stores and avoid too much lost sales, but they also need to manage inventories in the supply chain. Inventories are expensive because of financing, but also because of having to mark down or discard old items. Companies can share data on what is being sold to consumers (point-of-sale data) and on inventory levels at various points in the supply chain (such as in the manufacturers' and retailers' distribution centres). This provides much more 'visibility' to upstream links in the supply chain compared to when they only place orders. Furthermore, demand forecasting models have been developed that can predict consumer demands based on factors such as weather, price promotions, in-store activities and holidays. The key point is that retailers and suppliers work together to share data and knowledge, which is also difficult to implement.

Sources: Huchzermeier and Iyer (2006); Småros (2007).

Modelling Scarce Resources

LO 5
Manage scarce resources.

Choosing which goods and services to produce and sell is a basic managerial decision. For all organizations, the possible volume and mix of products is limited by available capacity (i.e., scarce resources). For instance, consider the following:

- A campus bookstore might decide to use its limited space to sell general merchandise or to increase textbook sales.
- Because of a personnel shortage, a small consulting firm must choose between working for client A or client B.
- A non-profit health clinic must choose which patients it can serve and which it must turn away.
- Sales representatives, in their limited time, must call on customers that provide the greatest profit potential.

A manager must understand and analyse the factors that limit the organization's ability to achieve its objectives. Surprisingly, the solution to improvement usually is not to make each part of the operation as efficient as possible.

Profit from a Single Scarce Resource Maximization

As an introduction to modelling scarce resources, let's observe decision making in the television commercial division of Fairfield's Channel 2, which produces TV commercials for the Fairfield Blues and other regional companies. Manager Cerise Hamilton has built the division's reputation so that it has no shortage of work. The problem is deciding which jobs to accept. Demand exceeds the available time of her two skilled editors, which she has identified is the scarcest resource for completing commercials. To maintain quality (and to retain her skilled editors), she limits maximum editing time to 100 hours per week. The issue facing Hamilton is which jobs to accept to maximize weekly profits.[18]

When an organization has a scarce resource, it wants to make the best possible use of that resource. *In the short run, Hamilton can maximize her division's profit by processing jobs that generate the most contribution margin per unit of scarce resource,* in this case, editing hours.

In a typical week, Hamilton chooses among three types of jobs: short commercial advertising, long commercial advertising, and short public service announcements. The following job data are available:

	Short commercials	Long commercials	Short public service announcements
Contribution margin value of each job	$2,500	$5,500	$1,800
Estimated editing hours per job	4	11	3

The following figures show that short commercial jobs have the highest contribution margin per editing hour, allowing Channel 2 to generate the highest profit for its scarce editing time.

Short commercial: $2,500 ÷ 4 hours = $625 contribution margin per hour

Long commercials: $5,500 ÷ 11 hours = $500 contribution margin per hour

Short public service announcements: $1,800 ÷ 3 hours = $600 contribution margin |per hour

Based on these figures, choosing to work on the short commercial jobs is the best use of the scarce editing time. Every hour spent on another job has an opportunity cost of the difference in contribution margin per hour compared to short commercials. For example, an editing hour spent on long commercials forgoes at least $125 in profit ($625 – $500). The total results for the week in the following table confirm the desirability of directing the use of scarce editing time to short commercials.

	Short commercials	Long commercials	Short public service announcements
Contribution margin value of each job	$2,500	$5,500	$1,800
Estimated editing hours per job	4	11	3
Editing-hours capacity	100	100	100
Weekly jobs completed and sold	25	9	33
Weekly throughput	$62,500	$49,500	$59,400

Appendix 7A extends the discussion of managing scarce resources to more complex situations using the Theory of Constraints.

Pricing Decisions

LO 6
Analyse pricing decisions for short-term and long-term business.

We conclude our overview of decision making in this chapter with the topic of pricing. This is a troublesome area for many organizations; determining the 'right' price for a good or service is important and can be very difficult. A company that sets its prices too high does not generate sales, resulting in total profitability below target. On the other hand, prices set too low might lead to an increase in sales activity, but the revenues might fail to cover costs. Both results miss the target profits.

For example, Fairfield's general admission seats are priced at $6.00 and the box seats at $15.00. Recall that sensitivity analysis showed that the price of the general admission seats significantly affects profit. A price per ticket of $5.00 lowers profit to $403,600, while a price per ticket of $7.00 increases profit to $664.720 – if the number of tickets sold does not change. The price of box seat tickets has less of impact on profit: a price of $14.00 per ticket generates a profit of $501,520, and a price of $16.00 gives a profit of $632,080.

Influences on Prices

Generally speaking, organizations consider several factors when determining prices: market strategy, market prices, customers, competitors, costs and a variety of legal, political and image-related issues.

Market strategy

This is the starting point for long-term pricing decisions. By market strategy, we mean what does the firm want to accomplish in this segment? What would the organization like to have happen? For example, a firm entering a new market segment may want to quickly get several leading customers, so the firm can signal that its products are serious alternatives in a market segment where these are yet unknown. This firm will use pricing to induce leading customers to try their products. As another example, a firm launching a new product generation may want its existing customer base to migrate to that new generation. Pricing for these customers may be such that it becomes attractive for them to do so. Or the firm may seek to get a larger share of the customer's purchase requirements or a more profitable mix of the customer's business. Unfortunately, when stripped of their jargon and word-speak, the 'market strategy' for many businesses is simply 'Sell more!' This is not a sufficiently well-articulated strategy. In such cases, pricing begins to substitute for actual market strategy, with price concessions and 'special' pricing being used frequently to gain business.[19]

7.3 Research Insight

Value-based Pricing

Suppliers serving business markets can base their pricing strategy on the value of their offerings for customers. **Value-based pricing** means setting a price of a market offering based on its value to a target customer. This is not a matter of charging the highest price premium possible. Rather, there are six considerations to determine value-based pricing:

- What is the market strategy for the segment? What does the supplier like to have happen? For example, the supplier could be entering a new market segment and it wants customers to try out its offering.
- What is the differential customer value that is transparent to the customer? 'Transparent' means that target customers easily understand how the supplier calculates the differential value between its offering and the next best alternative, and that the differential value can be verified with the customer's own data.
- What is the price of the next best alternative offering?
- What is the supplier's cost of the market offering?
- What pricing tactics will be used initially of eventually? Pricing tactics are price changes such as discounts that motivate customers to take actions that benefit the supplier. For example, a discount when buying a full pallet or ordering 2 weeks in advance. Sensible pricing tactics require a good understanding of the suppliers' costs.
- What is the customer's expectation of a 'fair' price?

Source: Anderson et al. (2010).

Market prices

Many products and services are offered in highly competitive markets (e.g., agricultural products, automobiles, personal desktop computers, cellular phones and service, small appliances) in which prices are readily observable. Deviating from market prices means either losing sales with prices that are too high or losing profits with prices that are too low. Setting prices in these markets requires understanding competitors' offerings and whether a product's or service's deviation from market norms (e.g., adding a higher or lower quality component) can support either higher or lower prices. In competitive markets, all producers must meet the market price. To make a profit, they must produce at a cost sufficiently below market price to survive.

Customers

An organization should consider pricing decisions for new products from the perspective of its customers. Prices that are too high will not generate the sales levels necessary to recover costs and target profits because customers will seek a less expensive or substitute product or service. They might wait for a competitor's offering. Conversely, setting prices too low could underestimate customers' willingness to pay for what might be a valuable innovation. Understanding customers' willingness to pay for the attributes and functions of a product or service is key to setting prices successfully.

Competitors

Competitors' actions also influence pricing decisions. A competitor's aggressive pricing policy can force a business to lower its prices. On the other hand, a business without a competitor has some discretion and can set higher prices to take advantage of the lack of competition. Setting high prices for items that are unprotected by patents or copyrights will generate abnormally high profits and invite competition.

International borders frequently mean little to competitive firms. Firms with overcapacity in their domestic markets (i.e., domestic supply exceeds demand at desired prices) can price aggressively in export markets. For instance, software companies such as **Microsoft** with high development costs and low unit-level costs can seek foreign markets as an outlet for their goods. In a foreign market, a firm can exploit the high development costs that it has already incurred at home and therefore charge lower prices than local competition, which must incur these costs before introducing their own new products. Managers increasingly consider both their domestic and international competition when making pricing decisions. International firms that price aggressively in foreign markets must be careful to avoid charges of 'dumping' their products at artificially low prices that discourage foreign competition. US manufacturers, for example, often complain that open markets allow foreign competitors to dump their products in the United States. Supporting those charges has been difficult because of the complexity of measuring costs and the values of other product features, such as postsale services, which might not be offered in all locations.[20]

Costs

The role of costs in price setting varies widely among organizations and industries. Managers of organizations that operate in less competitive markets might set prices at least partially on the basis of costs by adding a *mark-up* to production costs. While companies can price below cost as a promotion or 'loss leader', no profit-seeking organization can price its goods and services on average below cost for an extended period.

Managers have some latitude in determining the mark-up, but market forces usually are influential here as well. No company's management can set prices blindly at cost plus a mark-up without considering the market. If, for example, a company has a mark-up policy of 40 per cent and defines cost as \$200, the target-selling price is \$280 [$\$200 + \$200 \times 0.40$]. Managers judge the marked-up \$280 target price in light of what competitors are charging and the amount that customers are willing to pay.

Charging an excessive mark-up can increase profits in the short term, but it also invites competition to enter the market or customers to seek substitutes. If the price is deemed too high, management can lower its desired mark-up or redesign the product or service to achieve its target price. However, as Peter Drucker pointed out, cost-based pricing can be a dangerously expensive approach:

> *Most American and practically all European companies arrive at their prices by adding up costs and then putting a profit margin on top. And then, as soon as they have introduced the product, they have to start*

cutting the price, have to redesign the product at enormous expense, have to take losses – and often have to drop a perfectly good product because it is priced incorrectly.[21]

Drucker argues that target or price-led costing is a much more effective approach to pricing for almost all companies because it requires upfront knowledge of the market and customers that is incorporated into products. Although market research is costly, Drucker argues that cost-based pricing often requires much more costly fixing of pricing and product problems that never should have occurred. The analogy to managing quality is clear (see Chapter 6).

Some organizations, however, such as energy utilities in the United States, legally must base prices on costs. Managers propose prices based on marked-up costs that generally must be approved by a regulatory agency of the state or local government. Many government contracts are based on the recovery of costs, so measuring costs are of prime importance in pricing these contracts.

Many organizations consider only current production costs in production or pricing decisions when they should consider full life-cycle costs. A **product's life cycle** is the time from its initial research and development to the point at which customer support is withdrawn. The specific phases of the cycle often include the following:

1. Idea generation (early research and development)
2. Concept feasibility
3. Product design and planning
4. Prototype or working model
5. Product launch or rollout
6. Product manufacturing, delivery and service to customers
7. Product termination.

The cycle's duration varies considerably among industries, services and products. For example, the life cycle of car models is 5 to 10 years; in contrast, it can be less than one year for fad toys and fashion clothing. The realization that the great majority of a product's cost is determined well before it is produced for customers is important. Thus, many organizations can use target costing to simultaneously manage both the development and cost of the product.

Life-cycle costing tracks costs attributable to each product or service from start to finish, from cradle to grave. It provides important information for cost management and pricing. Many organizations traditionally consider only future production, sales and customer-service costs in pricing decisions. However, early activities such as research and development, product planning and concept design for new products can consume significant resources, and sales prices must cover these costs if the firm is to operate profitably. In other words, sales revenues and, thus, prices must consider and eventually cover all life-cycle costs, indeed, all value-chain costs, for the organization to meet target profits in the long term. Note that target costing explicitly considers life-cycle costs in computing target costs.

Pricing law

Organizations do not have complete freedom when they set prices for products and services. Legally, managers must adhere to laws that prohibit organizations from unfairly discriminating among their customers in setting prices. Laws such as European Union competition law also prohibit collusion, the agreement of all major firms in an industry to set their prices at the same levels. There are also national competition authorities in various European countries, such as the **Office of Fair Trading** in the UK, the **Conseil de la Concurrence** in France, and the **Bundeskartellamt** in Germany.

In the USA, antitrust laws, including the Robinson–Patman Act, the Clayton Act, and the Sherman Act, restrict certain types of pricing behaviours that often focus on deliberate attempts to reduce competition and ultimately charge higher prices. The Robinson–Patman Act in particular prohibits price discrimination, which refers to quoting different prices to different customers for the same products with the intent to harm competitors and consumers.[22] Such price differences are unlawful unless they can be clearly justified by variations in the costs incurred to produce, sell or deliver goods. Managers must keep careful records justifying these cost differences when they exist because the records can be vital to a legal defence in court challenges.

7.2 Cost Management in Practice

Pricing for the Internet

Currently, wherever data comes from, the packets of data are treated equally on the Internet, and this is called 'net neutrality'. Some telecom companies and legislators are in favour of charging different prices. Providers who are paying premium fees would get priority of their data.

Supporters of price differentiation argue that protection of net neutrality 'inhibits their ability to co-ordinate traffic flows and guarantee quality of service. Many new video and gaming service suck up a lot of bandwidth, they say, arguing that data needs to be managed and prioritized so that internet provision to users is not diminished. Furthermore, the additional revenues from preferred access fees could finance development of advanced new networks and other innovative services.'

Those who want to keep 'net neutrality' fear that the big content producers and service providers would be able to overwhelm smaller companies. Google states: 'We could easily pay any additional premiums, but that's not the point. It's a point of principle. We started out as a small company. We wouldn't be able to do the same thing now, if this passes.' Moreover, they point out that telecom companies would also be able to block or otherwise restrict the data of providers of competing services. Skype, for example, is obviously a major competitor.

Source: http://www.businessweek.com/globalbiz/content/mar2009/gb20090327_025568.htm (accessed on 29 March 2011).

Law also prohibits **predatory pricing**, which involves temporarily setting a price below cost to injure competitors that cannot sustain losses and consequently must leave the market. Predatory pricing drives out competitors and allows the 'predator' to earn abnormally high profits by charging higher prices after competitors have left the market. Note that the occasional sale or special price in a retail setting is not unlawful because the intent is to stimulate store traffic, not to drive out the competition. In determining whether a price is predatory, courts examine an organization's cost records.

Cost determination is a troublesome area, especially for manufacturers, because cost can be calculated in a variety of ways, as covered in detail in Chapters 2 and 4. Cost determination also is a problem for warehouse-type retailers such as **IKEA, Media Markt** (in Europe), **Bunnings Warehouse** (in Australia and New Zealand), **Big Bazaar** (in India), **Wal-Mart** (USA), **Home Depot** (USA) and **Office Max** (USA), but in a different way. These large retailers have such significant influence on the market that they commonly are able to obtain price concessions from their suppliers. Low costs from suppliers coupled with their low overhead means that these large businesses can sell products to the public below the cost paid by, say, the local family-owned camera shop or hardware store and still earn a sizeable profit margin. These large firms must be able to demonstrate that their low prices are justified by low costs that are themselves not the result of unfair business practices. This is one area in which a decision maker is well advised to have an accountant on the left and a lawyer on the right before setting very low prices that might be considered harmful to competition.[23]

Pricing politics and image

Political considerations can be relevant to price setting. For example, if consumers perceive that an industry reaps unfairly large profits, they might exert political pressure on legislators to tax those profits differentially or to intervene in some way to regulate prices.[24] For example, because it periodically raises retail prices, the oil and gas industry regularly attracts this type of attention.

Companies also consider their public image in the price-setting process. A firm with a reputation for top-quality goods usually sets the price of a new product high to be consistent with its image. As many have discovered, however, the same brand-name product might be available on the Internet or at a discount store or outlet mall at a fraction of the price charged by a more exclusive retailer. The wide availability of discounted merchandise prices is causing some high-end retailers, such as **Saks Fifth Avenue** (USA), **Galeries Lafayette** (Europe), **Selfridges** (UK), and **Nordstrom** (USA), to justify higher prices by offering ambience and services not offered elsewhere.

7.3 Cost Management in Practice

Revenue Management

Revenue management refers to practices whereby differential prices are offered to market segments to manage customer demand for a company's products and services. It started with **American Airlines** in the airline industry where costs are largely fixed and services are non-storable (the plane leaves with empty seats and these cannot be sold later). Revenue management is not only about adjusting the prices on a particular flight based on the bookings for it, but it is about creating market segments with different service conditions (such as the flexibility of changing the booking) and prices, and allocating capacity to those market segments. Companies in the hospitality industry, such as **Caesars Entertainment Corporation** (USA), soon also adopted revenue management practices.

More recently, we see revenue management being applied in manufacturing, for example by the German company **ThyssenKrupp**, in order to manage demand and better manage production capacity. In retailing, pricing is used to manage inventories. **Dell**, for example, adjusts the prices of product options to steer demand to components that are in inventory but have not been selling well. It is difficult to predict which product features will sell well, but Dell needs to order the components long before consumers buy their computers. Revenue management requires specialized software that is provided by many different software companies such as **JDA Software**, **Revenue Management Systems**, **R&R** and **IDeaS**.

Sources: Kopczak and Johnson (2003); Metters et al. (2008); Hintsches et al. (2010).

Special-order Price Decisions

Occasionally companies receive requests from customers for either unexpected quantities of a product or service or one-off customized products or services. Because these are unusual occurrences, usual prices might not be appropriate. The decisions to accept these *special orders* and to price them obviously are tied together. One-off, **special orders** by definition are irregular and do not have lasting implications for other products or customers. For example, an athletic team's emergency order for replacement **New Balance** shoes that were lost en route to a post-season tournament might occasion a short-term pricing decision by New Balance that would not affect the normal pricing of its shoes. We emphasize that deviations from normal pricing practices can have lasting effects if customers begin to expect the deviations to indicate changes in normal pricing.

Relevant costs of special orders

Special orders often affect only unit-level costs. Occasionally, however, a decision to accept a special order causes product-level or facility-level costs to change. For example, if to complete a one-off special order a company must purchase new equipment, secure additional supervisors, or lease more space, these costs should be considered as relevant parts of the order's total cost. The importance of identifying relevant, differential costs can be more important in pricing special orders than in regular pricing situations in which market forces provide a stronger guide to pricing.

The relevant costs required for producing and selling a good or service combine to form a firm's minimum selling price. In some cases, relevant costs might be very low, such as selling one additional seat on an already scheduled airline flight or allowing one more student to enrol in an already scheduled college course. The relevant costs in these cases are *only the differential costs incurred in the short term to fill the seat or enrol the student*. Prices often reflect this differential cost awareness (although college tuition does not, as far as we are aware). For example, a person making travel arrangements at the last minute can find steeply discounted airfares and hotel rooms on the Internet because airlines and hotels are eager to generate additional revenues that at least cover differential costs (fuel, food, cleaning, etc.) when they (1) have no prospects for charging normally higher prices and (2) can charge normal prices for most services. Obviously, they cannot afford to offer discounted prices to all customers all the time.

Fairfield normally prices its tickets for games and concerts to cover all costs plus a target profit but departs from that pricing practice in some special-order situations. For example, if it temporarily has unused resources (e.g., the ballpark is not in use) the opportunity cost at the moment is low. Fairfield might try to obtain special-order business initially at a loss to attract customers in hopes of future, regular business for renting out its facilities.

Exhibit 7.9 presents data for use in the analysis of a special-order request received by Fairfield for a concert for 2,500 people. The organizer receives the revenues from ticket sales, Fairfield organizes the event and pays the expenses and charges these to the organizer. The relevant costs for this event can be calculated using the model with multiple cost drivers in Exhibit 7.6. Unit-level costs of $1.00 per visitor are relevant for the 2,500 expected visitors to this particular concert. Batch-level costs are also relevant, because these costs are incurred for each concert. Batch-level costs include wages paid to security, parking attendants, custodians, ticket takers and ushers. The batch cost of $2,400 applies to any event, whether it is a concert or a ballgame, and it is the same for 2,500 visitors as for 4,000 visitors. Furthermore, for a concert there is the additional cost per event of $20,000. This is an average, and Fairfield needs to find out if this particular concert is different from the normal concert activity, in which case this cost should be adjusted.

Exhibit 7.9 Analysis of a Special Order

	C	D	E	F
1	**Special order cost model with multiple products and cost activities**			
2	**Cost input data**	**Activity cost**	**Activity**	**Special order cost**
3	Unit-level cost per ticket	$1.00	2,500	$2,500
4	Batch-level cost - Baseball game	2,400	1	$2,400
5	- Concert (additional)	20,000	1	$20,000
6	Product-level costs - Baseball	200,000	-	$-
7	- Concerts	10,000	-	$-
8	Customer-level cost	800	-	$-
9	Facility costs per season - Tonopah Park	150,000	-	$-
10	- Administration	79,500	-	$-

If special orders indicate new, long-term business with this concert organizer, the relevant costs should also include product-level costs that will be incurred to increase the range of facilities and services available for concerts, such as lighting, power supply, marketing and event planning. While some of these costs are for facilities, these facilities are specific for concerts, making them product-level costs. A greater number of different products, i.e., different kinds of concerts, causes these costs to go up. The current $10,000 product-level costs for concerts will not be enough if this product becomes a bigger part of Fairfield's business. Organizing more concerts, also for other organizers, may also lead to higher facility costs, for example if general facilities such as bathrooms and parking need to be upgraded.

Furthermore, long-term business should generate normal profits. Consider an airline example to add an additional base to serve growing demand; long-term differential costs include the costs to buy and maintain additional aircraft, pay salaries and operate ground facilities, among others. These costs must be recovered by prices over the years that the airline will operate flights through this new base. Because of the need to consider the effects of interest costs, the decision-making framework varies slightly for long-term decision making. This is the topic of the next chapter.

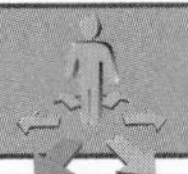

7.2 You're the Decision Maker

Alternative Analysis of Special Order

Consider that Fairfield did not have unemployed resources when the concert organizer asked to use the ballpark for a special event.

a. Does this situation affect the pricing of the special order?
b. What bid price do you recommend in this situation?

(Solutions begin on page 341.)

Appendix 7A

Theory of Constraints

LO 7
Apply the theory of constraints to manage scarce resources.

In the 1980s, Dr Eliyahu Goldratt formalized an approach to management called the **Theory of Constraints (TOC)**,[25] which seeks to improve productive processes by focusing on constrained resources. Theory of Constraints is a management method to improve productive processes in manufacturing and service organizations by measuring process capacity, identifying process constraints, using process constraints effectively, and co-ordinating other processes to the needs of bottlenecks. It argues that improving the use of constrained resources involves six steps. We next summarize these steps, and then we apply them to the Fairfield Blues.

1. *Identify the appropriate measure of value created.* In the short run, throughput is the measure appropriate for most profit-seeking firms. Other types of organizations should adopt measures of value appropriate for their goals; for example, a tax office might value the number of tax returns processed correctly the first time.
2. *Identify the organization's bottleneck.* A *bottleneck* is the *constraint* or constraining factor limiting production *or* sales. A **constraint** is a process or resource in a system that limits the throughput of the system. All productive processes have limited capacities, but most organizations have one or a few processes that limit throughput. Bottlenecks often are apparent because a backlog of parts, assemblies, casework or paperwork builds up just before the bottleneck process.
3. *Use the bottleneck properly by using it to produce or sell only the most highly valued or profitable products or services.* With a single bottleneck, the most value can be generated by producing the product or service that creates the most value (e.g., throughput) per unit of constrained capacity. This is the simple case illustrated earlier. Multiple constraints require more complex tools, such as linear programming, which is described in Appendix 7B.
4. *Synchronize all other processes to the bottleneck by producing no more of other intermediate outputs than the bottleneck can reasonably process.* Allowing all processes to produce up to their capacity wastes resources by creating unused parts, assemblies or partially completed services, which only add to inventory but do not create throughput. These excess inventories can become obsolete and usually obscure quality problems, as discussed in Chapter 6. Furthermore, some excess inventories might be defective inputs, which will waste the bottleneck capacity when processed.
5. *Increase the bottleneck's capacity or outsource the production of its output.* The only way to increase throughput is to relieve the bottleneck. In the long run, the organization can add capacity, but in the short run, outsourcing can be more profitable than forgone sales.
6. *Avoid inertia and return to step 1.* Relieving one bottleneck probably will create another one as production and sales grow. Managing by the Theory of Constraints involves always looking for ways to increase throughput. The Theory of Constraints can be applied to any productive process; it is by no means limited to manufacturing processes.

Application of the Theory of Constraints

Let's return to the management of Fairfield Blues to illustrate how Jason Robertson can help management increase the company's profitability by modelling and interpreting its constrained resources. By following the steps outlined earlier for the Theory of Constraints, Robertson can identify the company's bottleneck(s) and help develop strategies to improve profits.

Identify the appropriate measure of value created

From a seasonal perspective, ticket sales, baseball games and concerts can be part of throughput. The spending for capacity to play baseball games, promote concerts and provide facilities, however, appears to be committed for the longer term and, therefore, is not part of throughput, which is sales less spending for resources used (see Chapter 2). Ticket costs probably are directly related to the number of tickets sold, so ticket costs at $1 per ticket are part of throughput. If the team played one more game per season, however, do batch costs increase by $2,400 (the estimated batch cost per game), or is some part of that cost committed salary or depreciation that does not increase? Likewise, if Fairfield Blues decided to pick up non-driving customers for one additional game, do customer costs increase by $800, or is some of this cost committed too?

After investigating the differences between resource spending and usage, and after subtracting portions of committed costs, Robertson measured the elements of monthly throughput as follows:

Throughput element	Unit of activity	Throughput price or cost per unit of activity	Capacity	Planned usage
Box-seat price	Tickets sold, Q_B	$15	800 per event	680 per event
General admission price	Tickets sold, Q_{GA}	$6	3,200 per event	2,720 per event
Ticket cost	Tickets sold ($Q_B + Q_{GA}$)	$1	4,000 per event	3,400 per event
Game cost	Games, G	$2,400	54 per season	54 per season
Concert cost	Concerts, C	$22,400	6 per season	6 per season
Customer pickup	Pick-up games, G_P	$500	20 per season	20 per season

Total *periodic* throughput is the throughput per event multiplied by the number of events less other periodic throughput costs. The Fairfield Blues' seasonal throughput is measured by the following equation:

$$\textbf{Seasonal throughput} = (\$15 \times Q_B) + (\$6 \times Q_{GA}) - [\$1 \times (Q_B + Q_{GA})] \times (G + C) - [\$2{,}400 \times G] - [\$22{,}400 \times C] - [500 \times G_P]$$

Identify the organization's bottleneck(s)

Unlike a manufacturing plant or a bank, Fairfield Blues has no stacks of excess inventory or stacks of loan applications to identify bottlenecks. What really limits the company's monthly throughput? The place to look is the company's capacity to perform major activities: ticket sales, number of events, customer pick-up and facilities.

The preceding table shows that the only *apparent* bottlenecks are the number of events, which the league has set at 54 home games per season and the company management has set at six concerts per season. By management policy, event capacity equals event usage. Other activities appear to have some excess capacity. Well, then, why not increase the number of seasonal events? First, if the number of concerts, for example, can be increased, what is the increase in throughput? The simplest answer is that each concert adds throughput equal to the following:

$$\begin{aligned}\textbf{Throughput from each concert} &= (\$15 \times Q_B) + (\$6 \times Q_{GA}) - [\$1 \times (Q_B + Q_{GA})] \times 1 - \$22{,}400 \\ &= (\$15 \times 680) + (\$6 \times 2{,}720) - [\$1 \times (680 + 2{,}720)] - \$22{,}400 \\ &= \$720\end{aligned}$$

Second, is this the correct answer? If Fairfield Blues added another concert (or 10) each season, does each really add $720 each in throughput? If not, why not? The difficulty is that the number of concerts may not be the true bottleneck but only a visible symptom. If the number of concerts is not the constraining factor, what is? Perhaps we can understand the problem by looking at current operations a bit closer. Ticket sales do generate seasonal revenues and throughput for the company, but why is every event not a sellout? If the company does not sell out now, will adding events increase the number of tickets sold or merely cannibalize current performances?

The true bottleneck might be a marketing problem. Perhaps the events do not match the tastes of the majority of potential ticket buyers. Perhaps the local market is not large enough to support more baseball or concert fans. Perhaps the quality of the events is not sufficient to draw more customers at current prices. After applying the logic and analysis of the Theory of Constraints, many organizations are surprised to learn that their most significant bottleneck is not a production constraint but a marketing constraint – a failure to understand and meet market needs better.

Use the bottleneck(s) properly

By working with other members of the company's management team, Robertson began focusing on the company's marketing and learned the following about each marketing activity:

1. Improvements to facilities (ballpark and general management activities) and the quality of the team either were not feasible in the short run or would not increase ticket sales appreciably.
2. Advertising placed in community, club and company newsletters at a cost of $1,200 per season could increase box-seat sales by approximately 10 per event.
3. Advertising placed in neighbourhood weekly papers at a cost of $600 per season might increase general admission seat sales by 10 per event.
4. Exhibition games between the Fairfield Blues and the four local high school teams would sell 50 per cent of available seats, with net proceeds divided equally between the Fairfield Blues and the high school teams.
5. Increasing the number of concerts would not add appreciably to overall ticket sales. Six per summer season seems to be about the right number for the community.
6. Increasing the number of times that non-driving customers are picked up would not increase ticket sales appreciably at this time. Perhaps in 10 years when the population has aged, this might increase ticket sales or be necessary to maintain ticket sales.

Synchronize all other processes to the bottleneck(s)

Once company management decides on a course of action to manage a bottleneck, it must ensure the co-ordination of all activities; that is, no excess activity should exist in other areas. This might not be difficult for the Fairfield Blues, but it can be for manufacturing facilities. Historically, firms have evaluated their manufacturing departments on measures such as percentage of capacity used, unallocated overhead, percentage of downtime, or idle time. All of these measures provide the incentive to fully use productive capacity without regard to bottleneck constraints. Thus, before a firm can co-ordinate its manufacturing departments to bottleneck throughput, it should change its measures of manufacturing performance. Chapters 6 and 16 discuss this important issue in more detail from quality or time, lead indicator and compensation perspectives.

Increase the bottleneck's capacity or outsource the production of its output

In the short term, the Fairfield Blues can add a few more games and try to increase attendance at each performance. If the market can be developed to support even more ticket sales, Fairfield Blues might consider whether to increase its overall seating capacity. This is a longer-term decision that has investment implications. This type of strategic decision is covered in Chapter 8.

Avoid inertia and return to step 1

The Theory of Constraints warns that the elimination of a bottleneck causes another to pop up elsewhere, so managers must be vigilant to continue to increase value created and throughput efficiently.

Appendix 7B

Linear Programming

LO 8
Use linear programming to model decisions about the use of multiple scarce resources.

Many firms face the problem of how best to use multiple scarce resources. An example presented in the body of this chapter showed that when a single resource is constrained, management should produce the good or service that has the highest payoff per unit of scarce resource. However, the situation becomes more complicated if the organization faces decisions among multiple products with two or more scarce resources. Recall that we previously modelled multiproduct decision making by *assuming* a sales mix. A quantitative tool called 'linear programming' is designed to help find the sales mix that maximizes profits when multiple constraints exist. Linear programming, as its name implies, assumes that all model relations are linear. Non-linear methods are available when this assumption is not met. This appendix assumes some prior exposure to linear programming.

Introduction to Linear Programming Models

Linear programming shows how best to allocate multiple scarce resources among alternative courses of action in the short run when capacity cannot be increased. Linear programming finds the combination of products or services that maximizes throughput or contribution margin or minimizes cost within the limits of constrained resources. To illustrate how linear programming works, it is necessary first to describe its elements.

Objective function is a mathematical relation of inputs and outputs to be maximized or minimized. For example, the objective of the linear programming problem might be to maximize monthly throughput, revenues less throughput costs. The objective function is the equation that models throughput, for example. *Constraints* represent capacity limits of the various processes and resources. Linear programming constraints state algebraically that resources used must not exceed the resources available.

Feasible solution space is the combination of input and output values that satisfy the constraints. When more than one constraint is binding (i.e., acting as a bottleneck), maximizing the throughput per unit of constrained resource is not sufficient. Linear programming investigates the possibly numerous feasible combinations of inputs and outputs that satisfy the constraints to find the optimum point.

Optimum point is the set of inputs and outputs in the feasible solution space that maximizes or minimizes the objective function. In rare cases, multiple points are optimal.

For this discussion, we assume that linear programming problems are modelled on the computer. Our focus is on setting up the problems so they can be entered into the computer and on interpreting the output, not on the mathematical procedures used to derive the solutions. Of course, this means that the user must know enough about linear programming and the decision context to recognize an improbable solution that is the result of improperly constructing the model.

Assume that a Fairfield company called Creative Constructs Inc. makes the sets for television and theatre productions that can be staged at Tonopah Park. Over time it has developed an expertise in producing three standardized wood products from high-quality, recycled lumber (usually taken from demolished old houses and old farm buildings): armchairs (A), bookshelves (B) and cabinets (C). The demand for its products is so high that it now markets these three products commercially.

Each product must be processed through two departments (1) cutting and (2) assembly and finishing before it is sold. Exhibit 7.10 presents data about product selling prices, costs, and the rate at which each product uses scarce resources. In addition to the information provided in Exhibit 7.10, we learn that the

Exhibit 7.10 Creative Constructs' Model Parameters

	Armchairs (A) per unit	Bookshelves (B) per unit	Cabinets (C) per unit
Selling price	$14.00	$18.00	$24.00
Unit-level material cost (lumber)	6.00	7.20	10.80
Unit-level conversion cost (labour and overhead)	2.32	3.40	4.96
Contribution margins (also throughput)	$5.68	$7.40	$8.24
Material requirements in board feet	4.00	7.00	6.00
Labour requirements in hours - Cutting department	0.30	0.30	0.40
Labour requirement in hours - Assembly and finishing department	0.50	0.20	0.50
Demand	At least 100 per week	No more than 100	No constraint

company can obtain only 2,000 board feet of high-quality, recycled lumber per week. The cutting department has a maximum of 180 hours of labour available each week, and the assembly and finishing department has a maximum of 240 hours of labour available each week. No overtime is allowed.

Only variable or unit-level costs, which primarily are the costs of materials and hourly labour, are affected by the choice of which product to make. Higher-level costs, such as batch-, product-, and facility-level costs, are the same regardless of which product Creative Constructs produces and sells. The production decision is to determine which sales mix maximizes weekly profit.

Linear programming model formulation

Creative Construct's sales mix decision can be solved using linear programming models. Building a linear programming model for it requires transforming the data (in this example, in Exhibit 7.10) into equation form. Maximize total contribution margin (higher-level costs are unaffected by short-run sales mix):

$$\$5.68A + \$7.40B + \$8.24C$$

Subject to the following constraints:

Direct materials	$4A + 7B + 6C$	$\leq$ 2,000 board feet
Cutting	$0.30A + 0.30B + 0.40C$	$\leq$ 180 labour hours
Assembly and finishing	$0.50A + 0.20B + 0.50C$	$\leq$ 240 labour hours
Armchair sales	A	$\geq$ 100 units sold
Bookcase sales	B	$\leq$ 100 units sold

The direct materials constraint means that the number of board feet of lumber required for each armchair (product A) is 4, for each bookcase (product B) is 7, and for each cabinet (product C) is 6. The total of all the wood required cannot exceed the maximum of 2,000 board feet available per week. The cutting constraint similarly means that the total of all labour hours used to make A at 0.30 per unit, B at 0.30 per unit and C at 0.40 per unit cannot exceed the maximum of 180 labour hours available per week. The assembly and finishing constraint likewise states that the total assembly and finishing labour hours used to complete products A, B and C cannot exceed the 240 labour hours available per week. The sales constraints mean that the total units of A produced and sold must be at least 100 per week; sales and production of B cannot exceed 100 per week. Product C has no sales constraint.

Exhibit 7.11 displays the input of these parameters and relations into a spreadsheet model. Data inputs are in cells A1 to F9 and correspond to the preceding descriptions of the sales and production

Exhibit 7.11 Spreadsheet Linear Programming Model

	A	B	C	D	E	F
1	Data input	Armchairs	Bookcases	Cabinets		Constraint
2	Contribution margin per unit	$5.68	$7.40	$8.24		
3	Resource constraints					
4	Direct materials, board feet per unit	4.00	7.00	6.00	less than	2,000
5	Cutting, hours per unit	0.30	0.30	0.40	less than	180
6	Assembly and finishing, hours per unit	0.50	0.20	0.50	less than	240
7	Demand constraints					
8	Armchair sales, units				at least	100
9	Bookcase sales, units				no more than	100
10	Initial guess at sales levels	10	10	10		
11	Linear Programming Model	Armchairs	Bookcases	Cabinets	Total	Constraint
12	Units sold (replaced by the optimal solution)	10	10	10	30	
13	Contribution margin (B2*B12,C2*C12,D2*D12)	$57	$74	$82	$213	
14	Board feet of material used (B4*B12, etc.)	40	70	60	170	2,000
15	Cutting hours used (B5*B12, etc.)	3	3	4	10	180
16	Assembly and finishing hours used (B6*B12, etc.)	5	2	5	12	240
17	Sales of armchairs (B12)	10			10	100
18	Sales of bookcases (C12)		10		10	100

activities. An additional input is in row 10. This input, 'initial guess at sales levels', is a beginning point for the model solution. To begin the solution, you can enter any feasible number of units, even zeros, into cells B10 to D10. We entered positive numbers so that the spreadsheet displays non-zero figures computed in the other cells.

Using the spreadsheet, the model (rows 12 to 18) is entered in roughly the same format as our earlier financial planning models; each cell of the model is a formula of inputs and outputs. The number of units sold (row 12) initially is set equal to the number of guesses in row 10; these numbers can vary to create a more profitable solution. Contribution margins (CMs) in row 13 are computed by multiplying the CMs per unit in row 2 by the units sold in row 12. The sum of the product CMs is the current value of the objective function and is shown in E13.

Rows 4 through 9 display the data for the five constraints described previously. Row 14 computes the amount of lumber used for the number of units sold. Note that at the initial sales levels, the total amount of lumber used, 170 board feet (E14), is less than the constrained amount of 2,000 board feet, shown in F14. Cells E15 to E18 similarly compute the amounts of other scarce resources and of sales that are constrained for comparison with the constrained amounts in column F.

The Excel 'Tools' menu has an option called 'Solver', which is a powerful mathematical programming module (you might need to 'add in' this module). Clicking on 'Solver' generates the following window where you enter the linear programming elements as represented by the model. The 'target cell' or objective function is E13, the sum of product contribution margins. Next you specify whether to maximize or minimize the value in this cell or to force it to meet a specific value. Then you show which cells to vary to find alternative solutions, the unit sales in row 12. By clicking on the 'Add' button you can enter each of the constraints in equation form. Note the first three constraints (e.g., B12 >=0). These equations state that each unit of sales cannot be negative, which makes eminent sense, but the program must be told this explicitly. Finally, clicking on the 'Solve' button generates the optimal solution.

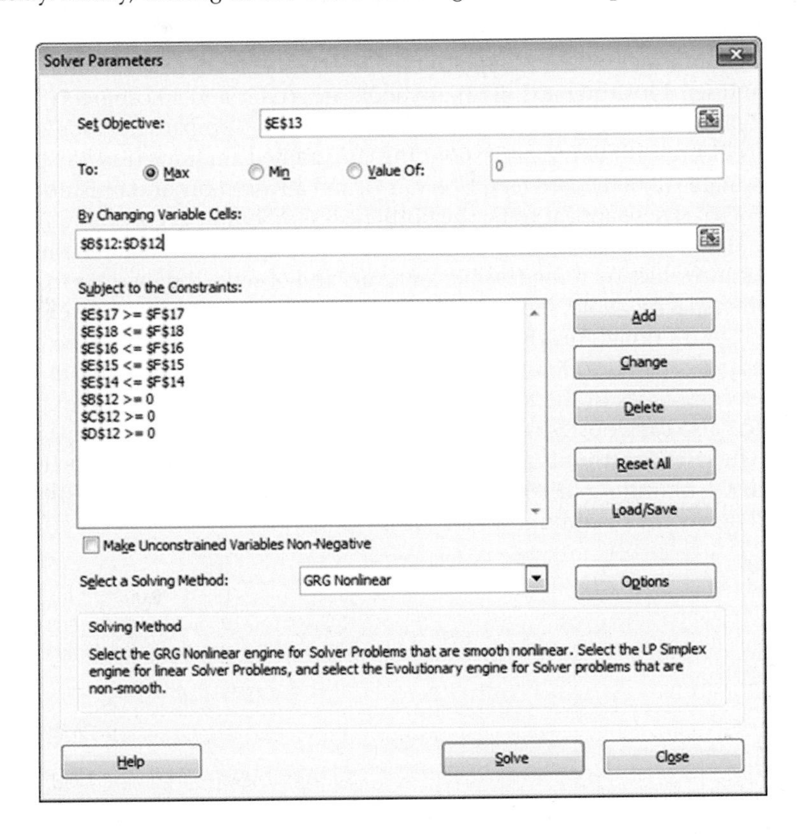

Linear programming model solution

Exhibit 7.12 is the revision of the model in Exhibit 7.11 after Solver has found the optimal solution and replaced the initial guesses in row 12 with the optimal sales levels. Note that you can produce other, more detailed reports on the properties of the solution (e.g., limits and sensitivity analyses) by

Exhibit 7.12 Linear Programming Solution

	A	B	C	D	E	F
23	Data input	Armchairs	Bookcases	Cabinets		Constraint
24	Contribution margin per unit	$5.68	$7.40	$8.24		
25	Resource constraints					
26	Direct materials, board feet per unit	4.00	7.00	6.00	less than	2,000
27	Cutting, hours per unit	0.30	0.30	0.40	less than	180
28	Assembly and finishing, hours per unit	0.50	0.20	0.50	less than	240
29	Demand constraints					
30	Armchair sales, units				at least	100
31	Bookcase sales, units				no more than	100
32	Initial guess at sales levels	10	10	10		
33	Linear Programming Model	Armchairs	Bookcases	Cabinets	Total	Constraint
34	Units sold (replaced by the optimal solution)	440	-	40	480	
35	Contribution margin (B2*B12,C2*C12,D2*D12)	$2,499	$-	$330	$2,829	
36	Board feet of material used (B4*B12, etc.)	1,760	-	240	2,000	2,000
37	Cutting hours used (B5*B12, etc.)	132	-	16	148	180
38	Assembly and finishing hours used (B6*B12, etc.)	220	-	20	240	240
39	Sales of armchairs (B12)	440			440	100
40	Sales of bookcases (C12)		-		-	100

clicking appropriate buttons after obtaining this solution. You should consult an appropriate linear programming text for the use of this additional information.

The linear programming model has replaced the initial guesses in row 12 with the optimal solution to produce and sell 440 armchairs (B12), no bookcases (C12) and 40 cabinets (D12). The weekly contribution margin generated by this solution is $2,829 (E13). Compare the total resources used by this solution (cells E14 to E18) to the corresponding constrained amounts (F14 to F18). This solution uses all lumber available (2,000 board feet, E14 = F14), and all assembly and finishing hours available (240 hours, E16 = F16). These appear to be the bottlenecks (or 'binding' constraints) at this solution. We can compare the benefit of relaxing each of these constraints by some feasible amounts (i.e., change the constraint values by some feasible amounts and observe the increase in CM) to the costs of acquiring more capacity. Note, however, that the cutting department has excess capacity (or 'slack') (E15 < F15) of 32 hours, nearly one full-time hourly employee. Thus, the available cutting time is not a binding constraint. Maintaining this level or increasing capacity in this department might be a waste of resources in the long run if this solution represents future optimal operations. Creative Constructs also can consider dropping the bookcase product line if it appears that this solution will persist. The sales constraints also appear to have no effect on this solution because armchair sales easily exceed the minimum of 100 (E17 > F17) and bookcase sales are zero (shown by dashes in C12 to C18), well below the maximum (E18 < F18).

Chapter Summary

This chapter presents an overview of financial modelling and the management of scarce resources. An understanding of financial planning or cost-volume-profit (CVP) relationships is necessary for the successful management of any enterprise. Financial modelling provides a reliable overview of the effects on profit of changes in quantities, activity costs, sales mix, sales prices and changes in bottlenecks (Appendix 7A). The basic CVP model is subject to several limitations, with one of the most troubling being the use of a single cost driver. The model can be expanded using activity-based costing to yield more realistic results. The model can be used for short-term decisions, such as about the introduction of new products and services, the mix of products to sell when resources are scarce, and pricing special orders.

Spreadsheets used in conjunction with sensitivity and scenario analyses greatly facilitate risky decision making. Any attempts to improve an organization's profitability must consider the effects of constrained resources. The Theory of Constraints offers an effective method for the short-term management of constraints (Appendix 7A). Modelling multiple constraints is possible with linear programming (Appendix 7B).

Pricing decisions are relevant for CVP models, because prices directly impact the revenue part of the model. Pricing decisions can also have long-term consequences. Organizations consider several factors when determining prices: market strategy, market prices, customers, competitors, costs, and a variety of legal, political and image-related issues.

Key Terms

For each term's definition, refer to the indicated page, or turn to the glossary at the end of the text.

break-even point, 290
constraint,* 314
contribution margin, 290
cost-volume-profit (CVP) model, 289
feasible solution space,† 317
financial model, 286
life-cycle costing, 310
linear programming,† 317
model elasticity, 304
objective function,† 317
operating leverage, 292
optimum point,† 317
predatory pricing, 311
product life cycle, 310
product mix, 296
sales mix, 296
scenario analysis, 305
special orders, 312
Theory of Constraints (TOC),* 314
value-based pricing, 308
weighted-average unit contribution margin (WAUCM), 296

**Term appears in the chapter Appendix A.*
†Term appears in the chapter Appendix B.

*Review Questions are mostly written at a **basic** level; Critical Analysis questions and Exercises are **intermediate**, and Problems and Cases are **advanced**.*

Review Questions

7.1 Review the chapter's key terms and define them.

7.2 What benefits do financial models provide to users?

7.3 What are the objectives of financial modelling?

7.4 What are the elements of a cost-volume-profit (CVP) model? Is this the best name for this type of model?

7.5 What are the advantages of computerized financial models compared to manual financial models?

7.6 Why should a financial model's parameters be located as numbers in only one place?

7.7 When is using the average tax rate desirable in modelling the effects of taxes in a financial model?

7.8 Explain the sales mix assumption in financial planning analysis. Why is this assumption made?

7.9 What is the meaning of the term 'weighted-average unit contribution margin?' What does this amount contribute toward covering?

7.10 Briefly explain how financial planning models benefit from activity-based costing (ABC).

7.11 What is sensitivity analysis? Scenario analysis? What are their purposes?

7.12 Briefly describe the proper approach to making a production decision when a single limited resource is involved.

7.13 Explain several legal influences on pricing decisions.

7.14 Explain the following assertion: 'Price setting generally requires a balance between market forces and cost considerations.'

7.15 Distinguish between price discrimination and predatory pricing.

Critical Analysis

7.16 In a strategy meeting, a manufacturing company's president said, 'If we raise the price of our product, the company's break-even point will be lower.' The financial vice president responded by saying, 'Then we should raise our price. The company will be less likely to incur a loss.' With whom do you agree and disagree? Why?

7.17 A company recently constructed a financial planning model to predict monthly cash inflows and outflows. The model is based on various financial relationships including collection patterns of receivables, inventory outflows, expense payments, and so forth, all obtained by analysing monthly data of the past three years. Before the spreadsheet model is put into use, management insists that employees perform some validity testing to ensure that the model is working properly. Suggest how the model might be tested to ensure that it is, in fact, valid.

7.18 Cost-volume-profit (CVP) analysis is an oversimplification of the real world. For this reason, it has little to offer a decision maker. Comment.

7.19 Picture the cost-volume-profit (CVP) model. Explain how the model can be used to evaluate the performance of an organization's (1) divisions and (2) divisional managers. The managers are evaluated annually for purposes of pay raises and promotions. What are the inherent dangers in using this model for evaluation purposes?

7.20 Management notes that the contribution from one product is higher than the contribution from a second product. Hence, management concludes that the company should concentrate on manufacturing the first product. Under what, if any, conditions will this approach result in maximum profits?

7.21 A sporting goods retailer is running a monthly special that prices tennis balls and golf balls to yield a negative contribution margin. What causes a negative contribution margin? What is the likely motive behind the retailer's actions?

7.22 You have built a fairly complex financial planning model for your organization. It contains many parameters and assumptions about how the parameters are related. When you presented the base-case results of the model to your planning committee, the general response was, Well, I guess we need to drop product X from the product line and that probably will mean closing the manufacturing plant in Yorkshire. You were shocked by this reaction even though the model did show product X to be unprofitable. How should you have presented your model and the results?

7.23 You and your cost management team spent months building and testing a financial planning model of your organization's operations. When you previewed the model to a long-time manager, her reaction was, I don't trust computer models any more than I trust manual election counts. Garbage in equals garbage out, as far as I am concerned. How should you use this reaction to prepare for presenting your model to the organization's chief executive?

7.24 (Appendix 7A) Proponents of the Theory of Constraints approach to managing processes argue that managers should review every task or operation performed in an organization and ask: does completing this task help the organization achieve its goal? If the answer is no, managers should find a way to eliminate the effort. Do you believe this test can be applied to every task in an organization? Should every task that fails the test be eliminated? Explain.

7.25 Respond to this comment: We are unable to meet demand for our product, yet you refuse to let us operate all our processes at least at practical capacity. I think that is a waste of equipment and personnel. What am I supposed to do, have them sweep the floors and let this expensive equipment sit idle?

7.26 One of your company's top salespersons approaches you and says, I just heard that I am not allowed in the production area anymore because you have outlawed our efforts to push customers' orders through the process. Listen, my sales performance is the best in the company because my customers know that I will fight to get their orders through this labyrinth of a plant. You are threatening my ability to work effectively for this company. There is no way that you are going to keep me off the production floor without a huge fight. I'll see you at the executive committee meeting on Wednesday. Prepare your arguments to justify your decision to outlaw the expediting of customers' orders by sales personnel.

7.27 Peter Drucker (1993) argues that one of the five deadly business sins is to base prices on costs, which means first measuring the current cost of a product or service and then 'marking it up' by adding a profit margin. He blames the disappearance of the US consumer-electronics industry in part on its practice of basing prices on costs. Can a domestic industry disappear because of its pricing practice? What is an alternative to basing prices on costs? What does this alternative require that is different from basing prices on costs?

7.28 A manager in your organization has just received a special order at a price that is below cost. The manager points to the document and says, 'These are the kinds of orders that will get you in trouble. Every sale must bear its share of the full costs of running the company. If we sell below our cost, we'll be out of business in no time.' Comment on the manager's remark.

7.29 To go from Dallas to Los Angeles for a business meeting, Nancy Wilkinson booked a flight for $950 with a departure on Wednesday and a return on Friday of the same week. The reservation agent told Nancy that if she were to return on Sunday, the ticket price would fall to $288. What factor(s) did the airline appear to focus on when setting its ticket prices? Is it likely that the airline could have been accused of price discrimination and violating the Robinson–Patman Act? Explain.

7.30 (Appendix 7A) Provide possible reactions to recommendations to implement the Theory of Constraints from the perspective of an employee in a:

a. Bottleneck process.
b. Non-bottleneck process.
c. Sales organization.
d. Customer service organization.

Exercises

Exercise 7.31 [LO 2] Cost-volume-profit

Queensland Reef Tours sells individual tickets for $75 for glass-bottom boat tours of the Great Barrier Reef. Unit-level costs, including lunch, are $15 per ticket; fixed costs total $200,000 per year.

Required

a. How many tours must be sold to break even?
b. What level of revenue is needed to earn a target income of $42,000?
c. If unit-level costs increase to $20 per tour, what decrease in annual fixed costs must be achieved to keep the same break-even point as calculated in requirement (a)?

Exercise 7.32 [LO 2] Cost-volume-profit

Delta Safety Systems manufactures a component used in aircraft radar systems. The firm's fixed costs are €5,000,000 per year. Delta's variable cost of each component is €3,000, and it sells the components for €5,500 each. The company sold 3,000 components during the prior year.

Required

a. Build a spreadsheet to compute the break-even point in units.
b. Suggest several possible actions that management can take if it wants to decrease the break-even point.
c. The sales manager believes that a reduction in sales price to €5,000 will result in orders for 1,000 more components each year. In comparison with last year's results, will the company benefit if it changes the price? Build a spreadsheet to support your answer.

Exercise 7.33 [LO 2] Cost-volume-profit and Capacity

Cleator Moor Manufacturing produced and sold 60,000 temperature gauges last year for £45 each. This level of activity amounted to 80 per cent of the firm's total productive capacity. The costs related to this level of activity follow:

	Manufacturing	Selling	Administrative	Total
Unit level	£500,000	£200,000	£0	£700,000
Facility level	£250,000	£150,000	£700,000	£1,100,000

Required

a. How many gauges must it sell to break even?
b. Compute last year's income or loss from sales of temperature gauges.
c. Considering your answer in requirement (a), at what percentage of total productive capacity must Superior operate to achieve a break-even operation?

Exercise 7.34 [LO 2] Cost-volume-profit

Choose the best answer for each of the following:

1. A firm has a negative contribution margin. To reach break-even, it must:
a. Increase unit-selling price
b. Increase sales volume
c. Decrease sales volume
d. Decrease fixed cost
e. Increase fixed cost.

2. If the firm decreases total contribution margin by a given amount, operating profit:
   - **a.** Remains unchanged
   - **b.** Decreases by the same amount
   - **c.** Decreases by more than the given amount
   - **d.** Increases by the same amount
   - **e.** Does none of the above.

3. The break-even point is increased by:
   - **a.** A decrease in variable costs
   - **b.** A decrease in fixed costs
   - **c.** An increase in selling price
   - **d.** An increase in variable costs
   - **e.** None of the above.

[CPA adapted]

Exercise 7.35 [LO 2, 3] Cost-volume-profit and Taxes

Aqua Systems Engineering provides consulting services to city water authorities. A recent income statement revealed variable costs of €750,000 on a sales level of €1,200,000. Annual fixed expenses are €300,000, and the firm's income tax rate is 20 per cent.

Required

a. Calculate the firm's break-even volume of service revenue.
b. How much before-tax income must the firm earn to make an after-tax net income of €100,000?
c. What level of revenue must the firm generate to earn an after-tax net income of €100,000?
d. Suppose the firm's income tax rate rises to 30 per cent. What will happen to the break-even level of consulting revenue?

Exercise 7.36 [LO 2, 3] Cost-volume-profit and Multiple Products

Nico's Bicycle Shop sells mountain bikes. For purposes of a cost-volume-profit analysis, the shop owner has divided sales into two categories, as follows (monetary units given in Swiss francs, CHF):

Product category	Sales price	Invoice cost	Sales commissions
High quality	CHF2,000	CHF1,000	20% of sales
Medium quality	CHF1,000	CHF500	20% of sales

The shop anticipates selling 1,000 bicycles, 700 of which will be medium quality. Annual fixed costs are CHF 100,000. Ignore taxes.

Required

a. What is the shop's sales mix?
b. What is the shop's break-even sales in Swiss francs? (*Hint:* Find the break-even sales volume first.)
c. How many bicycles of each type must the firm sell to earn a target net income of CHF 50,000?

Exercise 7.37 [LO 2, 3] Cost-volume-profit and ABC

Concord Manufacturing, which uses an activity-based costing system, sells 30,000 units per year of Glaxo containers at €45 each. Unit-level activities cost €32 per unit; facilities costs total €100,000 per year. Additional data follow:

- Batch size is 1,000 units at a cost of €2,500 per batch.
- Product-level activities consist of 500 engineering hours per year at €100 per hour.

Required

a. From an activity-based costing perspective, identify one problem associated with the basic cost-volume-profit (CVP) model.
b. Build a spreadsheet to determine Concord's annual break-even point and break-even quantity (*Hint:* Batch size is 1,000 units. Use trial and error or a solver and round up to the nearest 1,000.)
c. Build a spreadsheet to compute Concord's expected operating income before tax considering the costs mentioned above.

Exercise 7.38 [LO 2, 3] Cost-volume-profit and ABC

Penang Consulting Group, which uses an activity-based costing (ABC) system, offers a software-training seminar to companies for MYR 45,000 per seminar for 125 students; unit-level activities cost MYR 120 per student; and facility costs total MYR 600,000 per year. Additional data follow (monetary units given in Malaysian ringgits, MYR):

- Batch-level activities are MYR 12,000 per seminar (travel, etc.).
- Product-level activities consist of 1,500 product maintenance hours per year to keep the seminar up to date at MYR 180 per hour.

Required

In small groups, complete the following:

a. From an ABC perspective, identify one problem associated with the basic cost-volume-profit model.
b. Build a spreadsheet to compute Penang Consulting Group's operating income before tax considering the costs mentioned above, and an expected 100 seminars per year.
c. What is Penang's break-even seminar quantity? (*Hint:* Use trial and error or a solver and round up to the nearest whole seminar.)

Exercise 7.39 [LO 3] Cost-volume-profit

Review the information in rows 1–5 of Exhibit 7.3. Assume that Fairfield Blues takes actions to decrease its average tax rate to 15 per cent by outsourcing its tax planning. This increases facility-level costs by an average of $15,000 per season.

Required

a. Build a spreadsheet to compute the new break-even volume.
b. Compute the new target profit volume.
c. Explain the changes in these volumes.
d. Compute the new profit (loss) after tax.

Exercise 7.40 [LO 5] Scarce Resource

Quicksilver's management has been reviewing company profitability and is attempting to improve performance through better planning. The company manufactures three products in its men's belt line: leather, canvas and cotton. Selected data follow.

	Leather	Canvas	Cotton
Selling price	$50.00	$37.50	$25.00
Contribution margin	$20.00	$15.00	$10.00
Machine time required	0.5 hours	0.25 hours	0.30 hours

Machine time is limited to 120 hours per month, and demand for each product far exceeds the company's ability to produce. At the present time, Quicksilver manufactures an equal number of each product. The sales manager has urged the company to concentrate on leather belt production because of its higher selling price. Quicksilver will produce no canvas or cotton belts if it accepts this recommendation. Ignore taxes.

Required

a. If fixed costs are $2,500 per month, what profit will the company obtain by following the sales manager's recommendation?
b. What is the maximum profit obtainable and what product or product combination must be sold to obtain that maximum? (*Hint:* Compute the contribution margin of each product per unit of constrained resource.)

Exercise 7.41 [LO 5] Scarce Resource

Manufacturing cost and other data for two components, 543 and 789, used by Electronics Corporation of India (ECI) follow (monetary units shown in Indian rupees, INR):

	Component	
	543	789
Direct materials	INR20	INR400
Direct conversion cost	INR130	INR275
Sales price	INR250	INR750
Yearly demand (units)	6,000	8,000
Machine hours per unit	4	2

In past years, ECI has manufactured all of its components. However, during the coming year, the firm will have only 30,000 hours of machine time available. Ignore taxes.

Required

a. Can ECI fully satisfy demand? Show calculations to support your answer.
b. Determine the number of units of each component that ECI should make during the coming year.

[CPA adapted]

Exercise 7.42 [LO 8] Linear Programming (Appendix 7B)

Classic Corporation manufactures two models, small and large. The weekly time available for processing the two models is 100 hours in machining and 90 hours in polishing. The contribution margin is €3 for the small model and €4 for the large model. Each model is processed as follows:

	Machining	Polishing
Small	1 hour	2 hours
Large	4 hours	3 hours

Required

In small groups, complete the following:

a. Formulate the objective function and constraint equations necessary to solve for the optimum sales mix.
b. Prepare a short memo explaining how the linear programming approach differs from profit planning with an assumed sales mix.

[CPA adapted]

Exercise 7.43 [LO 7] Bottleneck Identification (Appendix 7A)

Identify which of the following insurance claim processes are most likely to be current and future bottleneck processes.

A Process	B Available hours per week	C Value-adding time (hours per claim)	D Theoretical capacity (claims per week) (D = B ÷ C)	E Practical capacity (85%) (E = 0.85 × D)	F Average demand	G Excess capacity (G = E − F)
Receive claim	50	0.10 hr	?	?	375	?
Route claim to adjuster	80	0.16 hr	?	?	375	?
Investigate and settle claim	400	1.25 hr	?	?	375	?
Issue payment and close claim	45	0.12 hr	?	?	375	?

Exercise 7.44 [LO 7] Bottleneck Identification (Appendix 7A)

Identify which of the following business processes for a small (two-person) independent telephone company are most likely to be current and future bottleneck processes.

A Process	B Available hours per week	C Value-adding time (hours per claim)	D Theoretical capacity (claims per week) (D = B ÷ C)	E Practical capacity (85%) (E = 0.85 × D)	F Average demand	G Excess capacity (G = E − F)
Advertising (ads)	6	0.50 hr	?	?	5	?
Bill collecting (bills)	8	0.20 hr	?	?	20	?
Service installations	60	0.25 hr	?	?	140	?
Credit analyses	10	0.25 hr	?	?	140	?
Purchases of phone service from Southwestern Bell	6	0.15 hr	?	?	140	?
Invoicing and billing (bills)	10	0.02 hr	?	?	1,000	?
Business planning and analysis (plans)	5	5.00 hr	?	?	2	?

Exercise 7.45 [LO 7] Theory of Constraints (Appendix 7A)

Search the periodicals in your library or on the Internet for an article about or description of an organization that applied the principles of the Theory of Constraints to improve its productive processes. Prepare either a two-page written description or analysis of that organization's experience or a five-minute oral presentation (instructor's choice). You should cover the following points:

1. Description of the organization
2. Description of the production problem
3. Steps taken by the organization
4. Results of the steps taken
5. Credibility of the article or description.

Exercise 7.46 [LO 7] Theory of Constraints (Appendix 7A)

Prepare a group response either in favour of or against the following comment: the greatest obstacle to improving the overall efficiency of an organization is the cost-accounting mentality that seeks to make each individual process as efficient as possible. Be prepared to debate your position.

Exercise 7.47 [LO 6] Pricing Methods

Customers, costs, competitors, cost-plus formulas and target-costing procedures all play a role in the pricing of goods and services. Sometimes the pricing process is relatively straightforward; on other occasions, it is more complex. The preceding factors and the procedures followed often vary from one business to the next.

Required

Form a team with three other students in your class and visit the manager or sales manager of a business: big, small, retailer, wholesaler, manufacturer, service business. Determine the relative significance of customers, costs, competitors, cost-plus formulas and target costing in the firm's pricing methods. What approach does the manager use when (1) the good or service is new, unique and untested in the marketplace and (2) the manager has little knowledge on which to base a decision? What has been the manager's biggest success and failure in pricing? Submit your findings to your instructor in a memo or email with an attached table or diagram that summarizes your findings.

Exercise 7.48 [LO 6] Pricing

Replace the question marks with information based on mark-up over cost for A–E.

	A	B	C	D	E
Unit-level cost	€12	€20	€32	€8	€60
Product-level cost per unit	€6	€22	$12	?	€24
Facility-level cost per unit	€15	€16	?	€3	€16
Mark-up percentage	25%	?	40%	100%	75%
Price per unit		€87.00	€71.40	€54.00	?

Problems

Problem 7.49 [LO 2] Cost-volume-profit Analysis

PhotoKingu transfers old home movies (VHS tape) to DVD. The current year's projected sales volume is 20,000 units. The company has been selling the service for an average of ¥800 per recorded DVD; variable costs consist of the ¥60 purchase price of the blank DVD and a ¥80 handling and packaging cost. PhotoKingu's annual committed costs for this process (equipment and labour) are ¥8,000,000.

Required

a. Build a spreadsheet to calculate PhotoKingu's break-even point for the current year in units.

b. Management is planning for the coming year when it expects unit sales volume to increase by 10 per cent, the unit purchase price of the disks to drop by 30 per cent, and committed costs to increase by 10 per cent. What is the new break-even volume in units? What volume of units and yen sales must PhotoKingu achieve in the coming year to make a profit of ¥7,000,000 if its average selling price remains at ¥800? Build a spreadsheet to solve these requirements.

[CMA adapted]

Problem 7.50 [LO 2, 3, 4] Multiple Products and Scenario Analysis

Refer to the information for Fairfield Blues presented in Exhibit 7.6, rows 1–12. Assume that you have some new information about costs and activities for next year. Namely, you learn that the cost per game should be $2,800 instead of $2,400, the cost per ticket should be $1.25 instead of $1.00, and the estimated number of tickets sold should be 195,000 instead of 204,000. Assume that all other information in rows 1–12 of Exhibit 7.6 is valid.

Required

a. Build a spreadsheet to compute the new weighted-average unit contribution margin (WAUCM) considering this new information.
b. Compute the new break-even volume.
c. Compute the new target profit volume.
d. Compute the estimated operating income for next year for Fairfield Blues.

Problem 7.51 [LO 2] Cost-volume-profit

A cost management analyst is studying two packaging systems, basic and deluxe. The basic system has variable operating costs of €5 per unit and annual committed costs of €600,000; in contrast, the deluxe system has variable costs of €2.50 and committed costs of €800,000. The company sells its products for €50 per unit, subject to a 15 per cent sales commission. Ignore taxes.

Required

Build a spreadsheet to solve the following requirements:

a. Which of the two systems will be more profitable for the firm if sales are expected to average 150,000 units per year?
b. How many units must the company sell to break even if it selects the deluxe system?
c. At what volume level will management be indifferent to the basic system and the deluxe system?
d. How do changes in unit variable costs affect the indifference volume?

Problem 7.52 [LO 2, 3] Multiple Products

Hoffmann Lawn Equipment Company manufactures a line of electric garden tools that hardware stores sell. The company's controller, Lucas Bauer, has just received the upcoming year's sales forecast for the firm's three products: weeders, hedge clippers and leaf blowers. Hoffmann has experienced considerable variations in sales volumes and variable costs over the past two years, and Bauer believes that the forecast should be carefully evaluated from a cost-volume-profit viewpoint. The preliminary budget information for next year follows.

	Weeders	Clippers	Blowers
Unit sales	60,000	60,000	80,000
Unit selling price	€75	€100	€150
Variable manufacturing cost per unit	€45	€66	€95
Variable selling cost per unit	€5	€5	€5

The committed manufacturing overhead is budgeted at €4,000,000, and the company's committed selling and administrative expenses are forecast to be €2,000,000. Hoffmann has a tax rate of 40 per cent.

Required

Build a flexible spreadsheet to solve the following requirements:

a. Estimate Hoffmann Company's budgeted net income for next year.
b. Assuming that the sales mix remains as budgeted, determine how many units of each product Hoffmann must sell to break even.
c. After preparing the original estimates, management determined that the variable manufacturing cost of leaf blowers will increase by 20 per cent and the variable selling cost of hedge clippers will increase by 40 per cent. However, management has decided not to change the selling price of either product. In addition, management recently learned that the firm's leaf blower has been rated as the best value on the market, and the company now expects to sell three times as many leaf blowers as each of the other products. Under these circumstances, determine how many units of each product Hoffmann must sell to break even.

[CMA adapted]

Problem 7.53 [LO 2, 3] Financial Planning and Activity-based Costing

Emirates Airways operates a commuter airline in the United Arab Emirates. Last year the airline flew 10,000 flights and sold 500,000 one-way tickets at AED236 per ticket. Total costs amounted to AED102,600,000. An activity-based costing study recently revealed that Emirates costs include the following components. The costs associated with number of passengers are unit-level costs. All other costs are higher-level costs. (Monetary units given in UAE dirham, AED.)

Activity cost driver	Activity cost
Kilometres flown (4,800,000 kilometres at AED5 per kilometre)	AED24,000,000
Number of passengers (500,000 passengers at AED50 per passenger)	25,000,000
Number of flights (10,000 flights at AED3,000 per flight)	30,000,000
Number of television advertisements (15 at AED200,000 each)	3,000,000
Airplane lease	12,000,000
Physical plant	5,600,000
Marketing and administrative	3,000,000
Total	AED102,600,000

Required

Complete the following requirements:

a. Assume that the projections for next year include 10 per cent increases in kilometres flown, passengers and flights. Advertisements will double. The cost-driver rates for kilometres, passengers, flights and advertisements are projected to increase by 5 per cent over the amounts listed. Costs for airplane leases, ground facilities and sales and administrative costs will increase by 7 per cent. With those projections, prepare a financial model that has a ticket price increase of AED20 per one-way ticket.

b. Management wants to consider a new ticket-pricing method. Assume that it believes it can sell 300,000 tickets for reserved seating at AED350 per ticket. In addition, it proposes to sell discount tickets on less popular flights for AED200 per ticket. Using the same cost and activity data in requirement (a), how many discount tickets must Emirates Airways sell to generate the same operating income as it did when it sold 550,000 tickets for AED256 each?

c. What happens if the number of AED350 tickets Emirates Airways can sell in requirement (b) is 10 per cent less than expected? Do you recommend that Emirates Airways add the new service in requirement (b)?

Problem 7.54 [LO 5] Managing Scarce Resources

Cerise Hamilton was having a conversation with her neighbour, a production supervisor for Avco Corporation, a metal products company. Avco's metal turning department has 90,000 machine hours to manufacture two products: S109 and T678. The following data are available:

	S109	T678
Unit contribution margin	£8	£6
Machine hours per unit	5 hours	3 hours
Maximum monthly sales	15,000 units	10,000 units

Required

Assume Cerise Hamilton's role in discussing the following issues with her neighbour.

a. Does Avco have sufficient machine time to fill all sales orders?
b. Should Avco focus on the manufacture of S109 or T678?
c. Set a production schedule for Avco that makes the most profitable use of its manufacturing time.

Problem 7.55 [LO 7] Theory of Constraints in a Non-profit Organization (Appendix 7A)

University Bookstore is a non-profit retail outlet for textbooks, computers and general merchandise (including trade books, supplies and university-licensed apparel and gifts). It is located near the main campus of Charles University in Prague, Czech Republic and controls the majority of the local market share for new and used textbooks. Other retail outlets, such as the Neoluxor and Neopalladium bookstore chain, University Drugstore (a private company), and the Alza computer store, have larger shares of the local market for other items. Marta Nováková is a full-time accounting student and part-time employee of University Bookstore who recently studied the current chapter on managing constrained resources. She observed that the bookstore's primary constraints are floor and shelf space for fast-selling items such as textbooks and market share for slow-selling items such as general merchandise. Average inventory levels and the most recent year's cost of goods sold in the three departments follow.

Department	Average inventory	Annual cost of goods sold
New and used textbooks	€1,000,000	€4,000,000
Computers	€400,000	€1,500,000
General merchandise	€1,200,000	€1,400,000

Marta approached her boss, the bookstore's general manager, and suggested that they try to improve its efficiency by managing its constraints more effectively. The general manager thanked Marta for her concern but assured her that this manufacturing technique was neither needed by nor applicable to the non-profit bookstore.

Required

In small groups, complete the following:

a. Explain how University Bookstore's constraints can be both floor space (internal) and market share (external).

b. Is Marta or her boss correct about the relevance of the Theory of Constraints to the bookstore's operations? Explain.

c. Prepare a short report with recommendations for managing the bookstore more efficiently.

Problem 7.56 [LO 2] Spreadsheet Model

Marie, your housemate and an art student, plans to start a small T-shirt printing business to partially finance her education. A generous art teacher has donated old but serviceable equipment and the use of a heated garage. Marie will produce original and custom designs per customer requests. Relevant facts about the T-shirt printing operation follow:

- Jobs will be marked up 100 per cent over the cost of materials to cover the cost of design and printing time.
- Plain, high-quality T-shirts cost €6.00 each.
- T-shirts can be printed with one or two colours, front and/or back, resulting from one to four different elements per shirt design.
- Each design element requires a separate silk screen, which costs €40, and a developing film, which costs €20.
- Each colour application (i.e., up to four per shirt, one for each design element) uses heat-sensitive paint costing €0.50 per application.
- Orders must be placed in increments of 10 between a minimum of 30 and a maximum of 50.

Required

Marie has asked you to help build a spreadsheet model that will allow her to price jobs of different sizes and complexity. Build a spreadsheet that will help her.

Problem 7.57 [LO 8] Linear Programming (Appendix 7B)

A computer spreadsheet solution of a linear programming model follows:

1	7.66 Linear Programming					
2	Data input Products	Whos	Whats	Wheres		Constraint
3	Contribution margin per unit	$8.00	$7.00	$9.00		
4	Resource constraints					
5	Direct materials, per unit	12.00	3.00	6.00	less than	500
6	Design hours per unit	1.00	2.00	3.00	less than	80
7	Machining, hours per unit	2.00	1.00	1.00	less than	80
8	Demand constraints					
9	Bangles sales, units				no more than	20
10	Beads sales, units				at least	30
11	Initial guess at sales levels	10	10	10		
12	Linear Programming Model Products	Whos	Whats	Wheres	Total	Constraint
13	Units sold (to be replaced by the optimal solution)	30	11	9	50	
14	Contribution margin	$240	$77	$81	$398	
15	Material used	360	33	54	447	500
16	Design hours used	30	22	27	79	80
17	Machining hours used	60	11	9	80	80
18	Sales of Whats		11		11	20
19	Sales of Wheres			9	9	30

Required

a. Write the linear programming objective function and constraints in equation form.
b. Explain the meaning of each cell in the linear program model section of the spreadsheet.

Problem 7.58 [LO 6] Special Order

InterMontagne Products Company is presently operating at 75 per cent of capacity, producing 150,000 units of an electronic component. The firm recently received a special order from Scott Corporation for 50,000 components with reduced function at €6 per unit. Unit-level costs for the modified component will decrease by 20 per cent, and the order will require a one-off set-up cost of €100,000. Planned production costs for 150,000 units of output follow.

Units	150,000
Unit-level costs	€300,000
Facility costs	€600,000
Total costs	€900,000
Cost per unit	€6.00

The sales manager believes that the firm should accept the order even if it results in a loss because the sale might build future markets. The production manager does not want it to be accepted primarily because it shows a loss when computed using the new average unit cost.

Required

Build a spreadsheet to solve the following requirements:

a. Is the special order profitable? Show supporting computations.
b. What other factors should be considered before accepting this special order?

[CPA adapted]

Problem 7.59 [LO 6] Cost Reduction

Feiyue Sewing Machine Company has been in operation for more than 25 years. During this time, it has shown consistent growth and has developed a strong following of satisfied customers. Min Sayre, company president, states that her business philosophy is 'a quality product at a competitive price'. Until recently, this philosophy has carried the company to its current position. The company is planning for next year's operations, and Feiyue is concerned about the projected increased foreign competition.

For the last three years, Feiyue has been manufacturing as its only product a machine that has the characteristics of both a serger and a zigzag machine, called the Sergzig. During the current year, the company expects to sell 200,000 machines at an average price of ¥3,900. To remain competitive and continue to sell 200,000 machines, Sayre believes that the company will have to reduce the selling price to ¥3,152.50 for the next year.

At the current level of sales and production, Feiyue earns 15 per cent return on sales, as shown (monetary units shown in Chinese yuan, ¥):

Sales price per unit		¥3,900
Product costs per unit:		
Materials		
Computer chip	¥422.50	
Motor	¥260	
Housing unit	¥325	
Mechanical parts	¥487.50	
Miscellaneous parts	¥130	
Assembly labor	¥520	
Testing labor	¥325	¥2,470
Product-level equipment		¥390
General administrative cost		¥455
Total product costs		¥3,315
Profit per unit		¥585
Return on sales		15%

In planning for next year, even at the reduced sales price the company wants to maintain the 15 per cent return on sales by reducing costs as follows:

- Feiyue can purchase the computer chip at ¥234 per unit by committing to a long-term purchase agreement for the year's needs with the supplier. The long-term agreement calls for the supplier to certify that all chips are defect-free.
- Feiyue can reduce the number of housing units and miscellaneous parts by 18 per cent by substituting equivalent but less expensive parts and by redesigning the housing to eliminate multiple parts.
- Because of these changes, the company can reduce assembly and testing labour and equipment and facility costs specific to the Sergzig by 20 per cent (net of redesign costs).
- All other product costs will remain the same.

Required

Build a spreadsheet to solve the following requirements:

a. List the advantages and disadvantages of Feiyue's proposed changes. Explain the risks involved with the proposed changes.

b. Based on the new data for next year, can Feiyue meet or exceed its target of 15 per cent return on sales? Show calculations.

c. Assume that competition during the next year is stronger than Feiyue anticipates and that the average selling price is only ¥3,022.50 per unit. Calculate the cost reduction necessary (relative to situation under a and b) to achieve the 15 per cent return on sales. Show calculations.

[CMA adapted]

Problem 7.60 [LO 6] Cost Reduction

DigiBooks is a new Internet retailer of electronic books for use with consoles such the Sony Reader and Apple's iPad. Based on a sales volume of 500,000 units, the projected net income for the current year is €600,000. The company will sell the electronic books for an average of €6 each. Unit-level costs consist of royalty fees of 15 per cent of sales price and a €2.75 selling cost per unit. DigiBooks currently has 5,000 titles available, each title requiring a one-time digitizing cost of €250. This digitizing cost will be paid in the first year but amortized over the life of the product. DigiBooks' annual committed facility and period costs are €400,000. Due to copyright laws DigiBooks can only sell each title for 10 years.

Required

a. If DigiBooks desires a 20 per cent return on sales, what cost reduction is required at the current year's prices and costs?

b. What cost reduction is required if there are the following changes in next year's costs and prices that result from taking no management actions, that is, maintaining the status quo:
- 5 per cent decrease in sales price
- 20 per cent increase in royalty fees
- 30 per cent increase in selling cost
- 15 per cent increase in committed costs
- 5 per cent decrease in sales quantity

c. Explain why maintaining the status quo often is a prescription for declining profitability.

[CMA adapted]

Problem 7.61 [LO 6] Special Order

Cosmos Toy Co. SE, manufactures collectible toy cars in a plant that has the capacity to produce 3,000 cars each month. Current monthly production is 80 per cent of capacity. The normal selling price is €36; unit-level costs and facility costs for the current activity level are as follows:

Unit-level costs	€28,560
Facility-level costs:	
Manufacturing	€96,000
Marketing	€78,000
Total costs	€202,560

Cosmos has just received a special order from a Japanese company for 1,100 cars at €31 each, with a target completion date in three months. Cosmos has never competed in the global marketplace. The company has hired a consultant for €5,500 each month of the contract to obtain advice on conducting business in Japan.

Required

a. Does Cosmos have sufficient productive capacity to accept the order? Explain.

b. Is the order attractive from a financial perspective? Show computations to support your answer.

c. Discuss any other considerations that Cosmos should include in analysing the order.

d. Is it beneficial for Cosmos to take a loss on this order if it desires to enter the Japanese market? Discuss briefly.

Problem 7.62 [LO 6] Special Order

Daisuke Robotics manufactures automation machinery according to customer specifications. The company operated at 75 per cent of practical capacity during the year just ended with the following results (monetary units given in thousands, Japanese Yen, ¥):

Sales revenue	¥2,400,000
Less: Sales commissions (10%)	¥240,000
Net sales	¥2,160,000

Expenses:	
Unit-level costs	¥1,288,000
Facility-level costs	¥193,200
Total costs	¥1,481,200
Income before taxes	¥678,800
Income taxes (35%)	¥237,580
Net income	¥441,220

Daisuke, which expects continued operations at 75 per cent of capacity, recently submitted a bid of ¥12,138,890 on some custom-designed machinery to APA, Inc. To derive the bid amount, Daisuke used a pricing formula based on last year's operating results (monetary units given in thousands, Japanese yen, ¥):

Estimated materials (unit level)	¥2,800
Estimated labour (unit level)	¥4,800
Facility costs at 15% of unit-level costs	¥1,140
Estimated total costs excluding sales commissions	¥8,740
Add 25% mark-up for profits and taxes	¥2,185
Suggested price (with profits) before sales commissions	¥10,925
Suggested total price: ¥10,925 ÷ .9 to adjust for 10% commission	¥12,138.89

Required

Build a spreadsheet to solve the following requirements:

a. Calculate the impact the order will have on Daisuke's net income if APA accepts the ¥12,138,890 bid.
b. Assume that APA has rejected Daisuke's bid but has stated that it is willing to pay ¥10,800,000 for the machinery. Should Daisuke manufacture the machinery for the counter-offer of ¥10,800,000? Explain your answer, and show calculations.
c. At what bid price will Daisuke break even on the order?
d. Explain how the profit performance in the coming year is affected if Daisuke's accepted all of its work at prices similar to APA's ¥10,800,000 counter-offer described in requirement (b).

[CMA adapted]

Problem 7.63 [LO 6] Life-cycle Costs

Quantorus Data Storage Company (QDS) wants to compute the life-cycle costs of equipment used in its manufacturing process. QDS will use these life-cycle costs to cost its data storage products. Although no rules govern life-cycle costing by private companies, QDS wants to account for as much of its operating and ownership costs as possible to be sure that it costs its products accurately. Analysts have obtained the following information for a piece of robotic assembly equipment.

Purchase cost	€225,000
Resale cost at replacement	€38,000
Useful life, years	3
Operating hours per year	4,200
Opportunity cost of capital	15%
Annual insurance cost	€1,400
Annual property tax	€500
Energy consumption per hour, kilowatt-hours (kwh)	65
Energy cost per kwh	€0.03
Annual scheduled maintenance cost	€11,000
Annual repair cost	€20,000
Hourly operator cost (wage + benefits)	€40

Required

Build a spreadsheet to solve the following requirements:

a. Compute the life cycle ownership, operating, and total costs per hour for the robotic assembly equipment.
b. Prepare the cost of a batch of product that has the following characteristics:

Units of product per batch	400
Direct labour hours	200
Direct labour hourly rate (wage + benefits)	€28.40
Assembly equipment hours	80
Direct materials	€45,500
Overhead rate per direct labor hour	€19.80
Overhead rate per equipment hour	€72.75
Target rate of return on sales	20%

c. The vice president of manufacturing at QDS expects that the market price for the product in requirement (b) will be very competitive, about €150 per unit, and the low-cost producer will have opportunities to gain market share. The vice president suggests eliminating the opportunity cost of equipment and the overhead rates, which represent allocations of committed costs. Recompute the cost per unit and comment on the wisdom of these cuts.

Cases

Case 7.64 [LO 1, 2] Cost-volume-profit

Virtually no organization publicizes its break-even point to external parties. Airlines are a notable exception, but only a handful disclose this key operating statistic. Access the homepages of Continental Airlines and Comair Holdings, Inc. Continental is a global carrier and one of the largest in the industry. COMAIR, on the other hand, is a much smaller entity, operating regional jets and playing a major role in Delta Connection's programme at its Cincinnati and Orlando hubs.

Required

In small groups, complete the following:

a. Learn more about these two firms by exploring their websites.
b. By reviewing key financial and operating statistics disclosed by the carriers, find the break-even load factor – the percentage of seats that must be occupied by paying passengers for the airline to break even. What break-even load factors have these carriers disclosed in recent periods?
c. Explain several underlying factors/characteristics of these carriers that likely cause their break-even points to differ.

Case 7.65 [LO 7] Managing Constraints (Appendix 7A)

The Tooling Business Unit (TBU) of the Massig Company manufactures tools, setup jigs, fixtures and prototypes used throughout the company's operations. The market value of products produced at TBU is estimated to be €1 billion annually. These products are machined and/or welded from metal parts or are made from advanced composite materials. These products are used in turn to produce the company's ultimate products and must be manufactured to exceptionally close tolerances. TBU employs approximately 1,000 highly skilled machinists, operators and toolmakers that take great pride in their skills and the high quality of their products (i.e., conformance to required tolerances).

For example, one of TBU's products is a jig that the aerospace division uses to manufacture aircraft wings. The jig has gross dimensions of 23 metres × 6 metres × 2.5 metres, which has elements (subassemblies) that are machined on a computer-numerically-controlled (CNC) machine to tolerances of one-thousandth of an inch. These are extremely close tolerances for such large fixtures.

Another critical feature of TBU's products is that they are made in very small numbers (e.g., almost never more than one or two of a kind). Because of the uniqueness of manufacturing at TBU, numerous manual and computer (i.e., software) set-ups are required during any month, and large production runs virtually are non-existent.

The production of TBU's tools and fixtures precede the production of Massig's products. Any delays in delivering them to the manufacturing divisions set back delivery dates to customers. Furthermore, because of the complexities of manufacturing, any delays are often compounded with delays from other suppliers. An added complication for TBU is that tooling designs often arrive behind schedule from internal customers, who are the product divisions, and TBU is expected to make up as much lost time as possible. Thus, TBU's objectives are to:

1. Manufacture complex parts to exacting tolerances.
2. Meet or improve scheduled delivery dates.

David Weber, a young industrial engineer and recent MBA graduate, and his new management team inherited a chaotic manufacturing situation at TBU. Thousands of orders from dozens of manufacturing divisions were being shepherded through TBU by an extensive expediting system. Each customer division placed at least one expediter at TBU. This expediter's primary objective was to see that the division's jobs moved through TBU's machining or fabricating workstations as quickly as possible. It was common for a workstation operator to halt work on one order to begin work on another at the request of a favoured or especially persuasive expediter. It also was common to find a behind-schedule order languishing at a workstation while the operator worked on another order that was not due for weeks. Because of the exacting tolerances required for most of TBU's products, these problems were most critical at its CNC workstations. The results were a large backlog of orders, many idle workstations, some overwhelmed workstations, and many unhappy customers who blamed TBU for their inability to meet their (external) customers' delivery dates.

Required

a. As David Weber, you have been charged with bringing order to TBU and improving the business unit's on-schedule performance. How do you proceed?

b. What do you recommend for managing TBU capacity?

Case 7.66 [LO 3] Managing Ski Resort Operations

Predicting the profitability of a ski resort's winter operations can be as difficult as forecasting the weather and the world political situation, as events of the 2001–2002 season confirmed. Nonetheless, modelling aspects of the operations, which can be quantified and related, can prove useful to ski resort managers as they plan for next year's activities and assess the impacts of different planning scenarios. This case relies on publicly available information to identify potentially important factors that could be included in a financial model of Vail Resorts winter ski resort operations.[26]

Vail Mountain opened for skiing in 1962 with two chairlifts, one gondola and a $5 lift ticket. During the inaugural 1962–63 season, the mountain recorded 55,000 skier days. By 1968 Vail had installed its first snowmaking systems and achieved 1 million cumulative skier days. By 2003, Vail Resorts had expanded its ownership to five major mountain resorts in Colorado, Nevada and Wyoming and had large interests in several others. In the 2000–2001 season, Vail Mountain alone recorded more than 1.6 million skier visits, and its other Colorado resorts achieved nearly 3.3 million.

The 2001–2002 season, however, was plagued by below-normal snowfall in Colorado and a general fall-off of tourism related to a weakening economy, terrorism and war. These events might have conspired to create a worst-case planning scenario than managers could have expected. Having a flexible financial planning model of resort operations would help managers assess future risks and respond quickly to events as they unfold.

Elements of Ski Resort Operations

Until recently, managers of North American ski resorts could rely on estimates of skier-visit days as the primary driver of resort revenues and variable costs. Furthermore, in Colorado, gross margin percentages at one time reliably averaged approximately 56 per cent of revenue on an average stay of seven days per skier. The average stay at a single resort, however, has declined over the years from seven days to barely four days; the decline reflects the combined effects of an ageing population, reduced vacation time, increased vacation costs, and stays at multiple resorts during a single vacation.[27]

In recent years, ski resorts have consolidated into large corporate entities, such as American Skiing (i.e., Killington and Sugarbush), Intrawest (i.e., Whistler/Blackcomb, Copper and Mammoth), and Vail Resorts (Vail, Beaver Creek, Breckenridge, Keystone and Heavenly Valley). This consolidation created management, marketing and operational efficiencies that have greatly increased competition for overall declining skier-visit days.

Increased competition has led to improved marketing analysis and differential pricing for destination (e.g., non-locals who stay overnight) and local (e.g., daily drive-in) skiers. Ticket prices paid by destination skiers for individual days have climbed steadily by approximately 10 per cent annually ($65 per day), but season passes for local individuals ($300 per season) and families ($500 per season) have declined dramatically as resorts compete for the steady cash flow from local skiers. Although destination skiers represent approximately 55 per cent of its total skier visits, Vail Resorts earns approximately 75 per cent of its operating income before tax, depreciation and amortization (EBITDA) from destination skiers. In contrast, one of its major competitors, Intrawest, earns approximately 70 per cent of its EBITDA from destination skiers, who represent only 20 per cent of its skier visits.

Resorts earn revenues from ticket sales, meals, lodging, rentals, retail sales and real estate sales. Most revenue growth has been from increases in non-ticket sales revenue. Vail's average revenue per skier visit was $99 for 2003, down from the previous year's $106. Destination skiers contribute roughly $195 per day, compared to $31 for local skiers. Additional operating data for Vail Resorts are in the following table which was extracted from Vail Resorts 10-K reports (dollar values are in millions).

Ski Resort Risk Factors

Skiing is an expensive, time-consuming, weather-dependent recreational activity. Skier visits, particularly destination visits, are affected by early season snowfall, the health of the economy, airline service, promotions and competition among resorts. Poor snowfall, an economic downturn and political conditions adversely affected Vail Resorts' 2001–2002 operations, compared to the 2000–2001 season. Therefore, the financial planning model should reflect the effects of sources of risk.

	Revenues		Operating expenses			Statistics			Balance sheet information	
Fiscal year	Mountain/resort	Lodging	Mountain	Lodging	Depreciation and amortization	Skier visits	Resort revenue per skier visit	Total assets	Long-term debt (including current maturities)	Share-holders' equity
2003[a]	$470,148	$159,849	$370,779	$150,624	$82,242	5,730	$99.18	$1,455,442	$584,151	$496,246
2002	400,478	150,928	308,896	137,259	68,480	4,732	106.53	1,449,026	602,786	504,004
2001	391,373	124,207	299,414	109,664	65,580	4,975	97.67	1,188,546	388,380	494,000
2000[b]	373,786	116,610	284,136	103,570	61,748	4,595	100.96	1,135,596	394,235	475,791
1999	424,647		346,936		53,569	4,606	90.25	1,094,548	398,186	464,300
1998[c]	350,803		242,009		45,432	4,717	74.37	958,167	318,520	449,848
1997[d]	259,038		172,715		34,044	4,273	60.62	855,949	265,062	405,666
1996	140,288		89,890		18,148	2,228	62.97	422,612	144,750	123,907
1995	126,349		82,305		17,968	2,136	59.15	429,628	191,313	167,694

Notes: a. Vail Resorts purchased Heavenly Valley in 2003.
b. Vail began reporting mountain and lodging operations separately in 2000. Prior years reported them jointly as Resort Operations.
c. Vail changed its calendar year end to July 31 in 1998. 10-month data for 1997 and 1998 follow:

Fiscal year	Mountain/resort	Lodging	Mountain	Lodging	Depreciation and amortization	Skier visits	Resort revenue per skier visit	Total assets	Long-term debt (including current maturities)	Share-holders' equity
1998	$336,547		$217,764		$36,838	4,717	$71.35	$912,122	$284,014	$462,624
1997	248,511		155,412		27,604	4,273	58.16	814,816	236,347	417,187

1998 (12-month) data are 10-month data scaled up by the same percentage increase as experienced in 1997.
d. Vail purchased Keystone and Breckinridge in 1997.

Required

a. Transform the information from (1) this case, (2) any other relevant sources, such as Vail Resorts' recent 10-K reports (be sure to properly identify them), and (3) additional assumptions you believe are necessary (explain them) into data input that form parameters for a financial planning model of Vail Resorts ski resort operations. For this case ignore non-winter, non-resort operations and any long-term investments.

b. Using the parameters from requirement (a), create a computerized financial planning model that forecasts the profitability of next season's ski resort operations.

c. Conduct sensitivity and scenario analyses that identify and illustrate financial planning risks within this model.

d. Identify qualitative factors that managers of Vail Resorts should consider in their planning along with the outcomes of using your financial planning model.

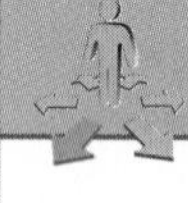

Solutions to You're the Decision Maker

7.1 Effect of Sales Mix on Financial Performance, p. 299

a. Consider the following spreadsheet, which is identical to Exhibit 7.4 except for the changed and highlighted inputs of average percentage of seats sold (B5), which affects sales volume (D14), and sales mix (cells B10 and B11). This revised model shows that the change in actual sales mix has an adverse effect on after-tax profits despite a higher-than-planned ticket volume.

b. Actual sales emphasized lower contribution-margin general admission tickets at the expense of higher contribution-margin box-seat tickets. The sales-mix change lowered the WAUCM from $5.80 to $5.44 (B13) and consequently increased both the break-even volume (B18) and target volume (B24). Because the actual ticket volume was lower than the target volume required at the actual, lower WAUCM, Fairfield Blues did not reach its after-tax target of $400,000 (see D24). This type of adverse effect can occur whenever managers increase sales or market share without regard to the contribution margins of products. Motivating managers to increase sales or market share can be counterproductive to meeting an organization's goal of profitability. Designing incentive systems is the topic of Chapter 16

	A	B	C	D
1	**Profit-planning model with multiple products**			
2	**Sales input data**		**Cost input data**	
3	Ballpark seating capacity per game	4,000	Unit-level variable cost per ticket	$2.00
4	Home games per season	54	Fixed facility costs per season	550,000
5	Average percentage seats sold per game	86%	After-tax target profit	400,000
6	Sales price per ticket		Average tax rate	20%
7	Box seating	$15.00		
8	General admission seating	6.00		
9	Sales mix assumption			
10	Box seating	16.0%		
11	General admission seating	84.0%		
12				
13	**Weighted-average unit contribution margin**		**Planned-profit analysis**	
14	WAUCM (B10*(B7–D3) + B11*(B8–D3))	$5.44	Planned sales volume in units (B3*B4*B5)	185,760
15	**Break-even analysis**		Sales revenues	
16	Fixed costs (D4)	$550,000	Box seating (D14*B10*B7)	$445,824
17	Divided by WAUCM (B14)	5.44	General admission seating (D14*B11*B8)	936,230
18	Break-even volume in units (B16/B17)	101,103	Total revenues	$1,382,054
19	**Target-profit analysis**		Less variable costs (D14*D3)	371,520
20	Fixed costs (D4)	$550,000	Contribution margin (D18–D19)	$1,010,534
21	Before-tax parget profit (D5/(1–D6))	500,000	Less fixed costs (D4)	550,000
22	Target contribution margin	$1,050,000	Before-tax profit (loss) (D20–D21)	$460,534
23	Divided by WAUCM (B14)	$5.44	Less taxes at average tax rate (D6*D22)	92,107
24	Target volume in units (B22/B23)	193,015	After-tax profit (loss) (D22–D23)	$368,428

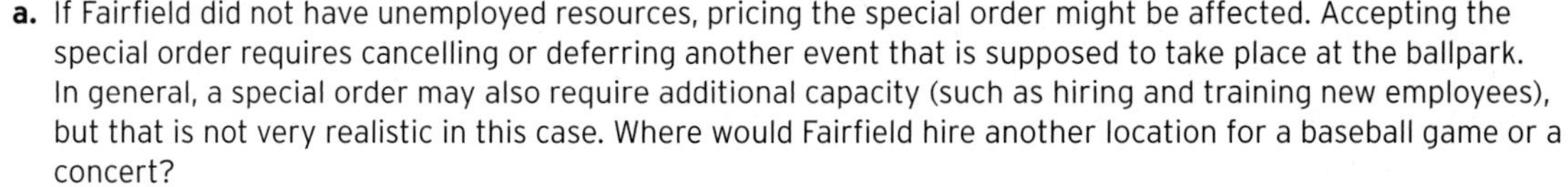

7.2 Alternative Analysis of Special Order, p. 313

a. If Fairfield did not have unemployed resources, pricing the special order might be affected. Accepting the special order requires cancelling or deferring another event that is supposed to take place at the ballpark. In general, a special order may also require additional capacity (such as hiring and training new employees), but that is not very realistic in this case. Where would Fairfield hire another location for a baseball game or a concert?

b. Fairfield will price the special order to reflect not only the cost of organizing the concert, but also the net benefits it loses by cancelling or deferring the other event. However, cancelling or deferring another event might harm its reputation. Fairfield is unlikely to take actions that would harm its good reputation, but it requires covering at least normal costs and target profits (perhaps more to cushion losses from reduced reputation effects).

Endnotes

1 A more general name for these financial planning models is CRD (cost and revenue driver) models, but CVP is widely used at this time.

2 Later in the chapter we will also model plans to promote concerts and other events at the ballpark.

3 Chapter 3 presented detailed discussions of cost estimation.

4 Income and profit are used interchangeably in practice and in this text. The *operating* income is the income from normal business operations, before subtracting the cost of debt (interest), and before subtracting taxes. It is also called earnings before interest and taxes, or EBIT. The operating income minus the cost of debt is the income before taxes (also called gross profit). Profits or losses from exceptional activities, if applicable, are also included in the income before taxes. Income before taxes minus taxes is the income after taxes (also called net profit).

5 Recall from Chapter 4 that many organizations have a hierarchy of cost-driving activities. Our early examples consider only variable and facility-level activities. For convenience, some refer to all non-variable costs as 'fixed' costs, although this can be a dangerous practice because it can incorrectly imply to decision makers that these costs cannot be changed or do not change with respect to other activities. We address this in later sections.

6 Although the expression for the break-even sales volume is quite intuitive, we will point out how it can be derived:

Operating income = Revenues − Expenses = Revenues − Variable costs − Fixed costs = (Selling price × Sales volume) − (Variable cost per unit × Sales volume) − Fixed costs = [(Selling price − Variable cost per unit) × Sales volume] − Fixed costs.

Setting operating income equal to zero because we seek the break-even point, this becomes

[(Selling price − Variable cost per unit) × Sales volume] − Fixed costs = 0,

now solving for sales volume, we have

Break-even sales volume = Fixed costs ÷ (Selling price − Variable cost per unit)

= Fixed costs ÷ Contribution margin per unit.

7 Note that 'sales volume' refers to number of units sold. We could also analyse the break-even revenues, which would refer to the revenues measured in euros (or another currency that the company uses for accounting).

8 Historically, one of the rationales behind the rate regulation of public utilities was to guarantee them an adequate return on very large committed costs in exchange for reliable public service. Guaranteed rates of return were compensation for assuming the risk associated with high operating leverage in the public interest.

9 A more nuanced modelling of taxes, for example distinguishing between average and marginal tax rates, is beyond the scope of this book. We will assume a linear relationship between profit and taxes throughout the text.

10 The complexity of tax planning is beyond the scope of this text.

11 Many organizations build financial models to reflect accounting accruals such as depreciation. However, financial models also can reflect cash flows, excluding depreciation and similar accruals. See Chapter 8.

12 In a perfectly competitive market (an ideal situation), no single participant can affect prices, supply or demand. Entry to the market has no restrictions, and prices reflect all relevant market knowledge.

13 See Chapter 3 on various models for cost estimation.

14 A *hedging action* seeks to neutralize risks, for example, by simultaneously contracting to buy and sell a desired quantity of inputs at a fixed price; gains or losses on the two contracts may offset. The company's only cost could be the cost of the contract, which is similar to buying insurance. For example, the Swiss company **Nestlé** might contract to both buy and sell coffee at a fixed price, or the American company **General Mills** might contract both to buy and sell

grain for its cereals at a fixed price. If the eventual market price is higher (or lower) than the contract price, Nestlé's and General Mills' gain on the 'buy' contract matches the loss on the 'sell' contract (or vice versa).

15 *Monte Carlo simulation analysis* is another method used when sufficient data exist to estimate parameters' probability distributions.

16 The formula in each cell of column E contains the revenue and cost relations from Exhibit 7.6 and the base parameters.

17 Because the profit calculation contains only linear relations among the variables, using either the highest or lowest parameter value and corresponding profit results in the same estimated elasticity. This is not the general economic situation, and one could compute elasticities to both high and low parameter values.

18 Hamilton could have other objectives, including diversity of creative work or maintaining a broad market presence, which might cause her to trade off some profit.

19 See Anderson et al. (2010).

20 An interesting twist to the practice of 'dumping' is the domestic backlash that prescription drug companies received recently. Under pressure from the United Nations, they agreed to sell AIDS drugs in Africa at 10 per cent or less of the domestic price only to receive scorn from domestic consumers who recoiled at the apparently high profits earned on domestic sales. See Harris (2001).

21 Drucker (1993).

22 The Robinson–Patman Act covers goods but not services.

23 For recent case law, see the 'Legal Developments' section of the *Journal of Marketing*. Also see Barton and MacArthur (2003).

24 See, for example, Cahan and Kaempfer (1992).

25 Many books and articles discuss the Theory of Constraints. The most accessible and popular source is Goldratt and Cox, *The Goal*. This book was first published in 1984 and several editions have been published since then. A concise review that probably should be read after *The Goal* is Ruhl (1996). For an analysis of the implications of the Theory of Constraints for cost management, see Noreen et al. (1995). A recent overview of the development of the Theory of Constraints is Watson et al. (2007).

26 Many large ski resort companies, such as Vail Resorts in Colorado, have made significant investments in golf courses, tennis facilities, and so on to make the summer and fall seasons important sources of income (see, for example, www.vailresorts.com). This case considers only winter operations. This case makes further simplifying assumptions by ignoring long-term investment decisions and assuming that assets in place do not change. This is almost never the case for large resorts that vie for scarce tourism dollars.

27 Rudowsky (2001).

References

Anderson, J.C., M. Wouters and W. van Rossum (2010) 'Why the highest price isn't the best price', *MIT Sloan Management Review*, Winter, pp. 69–76.

Barton, T.L., and J.B. MacArthur (2003) 'Activity-based costing and predatory pricing: the case of the petroleum retail industry', *Management Accounting Quarterly*, vol. 4, no. 3, pp. 1–7.

Cahan, S., and W.H. Kaempfer (1992) 'Industry income and congressional regulatory legislation: interest groups vs. median voter', *Economic Inquiry*, vol. 3, no. 1, pp. 47–56.

Drucker, P. (1993) 'The five deadly business sins', *Wall Street Journal*, 21 October, p. A1.

Dunagan, C. (2000) 'Report: Washington Orcas Endangered', *Scripps Howard News Service*, 18 November.

Goldratt, E., and J. Cox (1984) *The Goal,* North River Press, Great Barrington, MA.

Harris, G. (2001) 'AIDS gaffes in Africa come back to haunt drug industry in the US', *Wall Street Journal*, 23 April.

Hintsches, A., T.S. Spengler., T. Volling., K. Wittek and G. Priegnitz (2010) 'Revenue management in make-to-order manufacturing: case study of capacity control at ThyssenKrupp VDM', *BuR – Business Research*, vol. 3, no. 2, pp. 173–190.

Huchzermeier, A., and A.V. Iyer (2006) 'Supply chain management in a promotional environment', in M. Krafft and M.K. Mantrala (eds.), *Retailing in the 21st Century*, Springer, Berlin, pp. 325–344.

Kopczak, L., and M.E. Johnson (2003) 'The supply-chain management effect', *MIT Sloan Management Review*, Spring, pp. 27–34.

Metters, R., C. Queenan., M. Ferguson., L. Harrison., J. Higbie., S. Ward., B. Barfield., T. Farley., H.A. Kuyumcu and A. Duggasani (2008) 'The "killer application" of revenue management: Harrah's Cherokee Casino & Hotel', *Interfaces*, vol. 38, no. 3, pp. 161–175.

Noreen, E., D. Smith and J.T. Mackey (1995) *The Theory of Constraints and Its Implications for Management Accounting,* The North River Press, Great Barrington, MA.

Rudowsky, G. (2001) 'Staying on top of Aspen', *Rocky Mountain News*, 23 June, p. 11C.

Ruhl, J. (1996) 'An introduction to the theory of constraints', *Journal of Cost Management*, Summer, pp. 43–48.

Småros, J. (2007) 'Forecasting collaboration in the European grocery sector: observations from a case study', *Journal of Operations Management*, vol. 25, pp. 702–716.

Sullivan, R.L. (1996) 'Exxonsafeway', *Forbes*, vol. 157, no. 5, p. 106.

USA Today (2005). 'Computer's view of a hurricane', *USA Today*, 20 May, available at: www.usatoday.com/weather/whur15.htm.

Watson, K.J., J.H. Blackstone and S.C. Gardiner (2007) 'The evolution of a management philosophy: the theory of constraints', *Journal of Operations Management*, vol. 25, pp. 387–402.

CHAPTER 8

Strategic Investment Decisions

© Greg Kuchik/Getty Images/DAL

Learning Objectives

After completing this chapter, you should be able to:

- **LO 1** Distinguish alternatives for investment decisions.
- **LO 2** Build a financial model of investment decisions using discounted cash flow methods.
- **LO 3** Apply discounted cash flow methods to common investment decisions.
- **LO 4** Understand different ways of using both financial and non-financial information for investment decisions.
- **LO 5** Understand the nature of strategic investment decisions.
- **LO 6** Model the impacts of competitors' actions.
- **LO 7** Know when and how to apply real option analysis to evaluate strategic investments.
- **LO 8** Identify and evaluate ethical issues in strategic investment decisions.

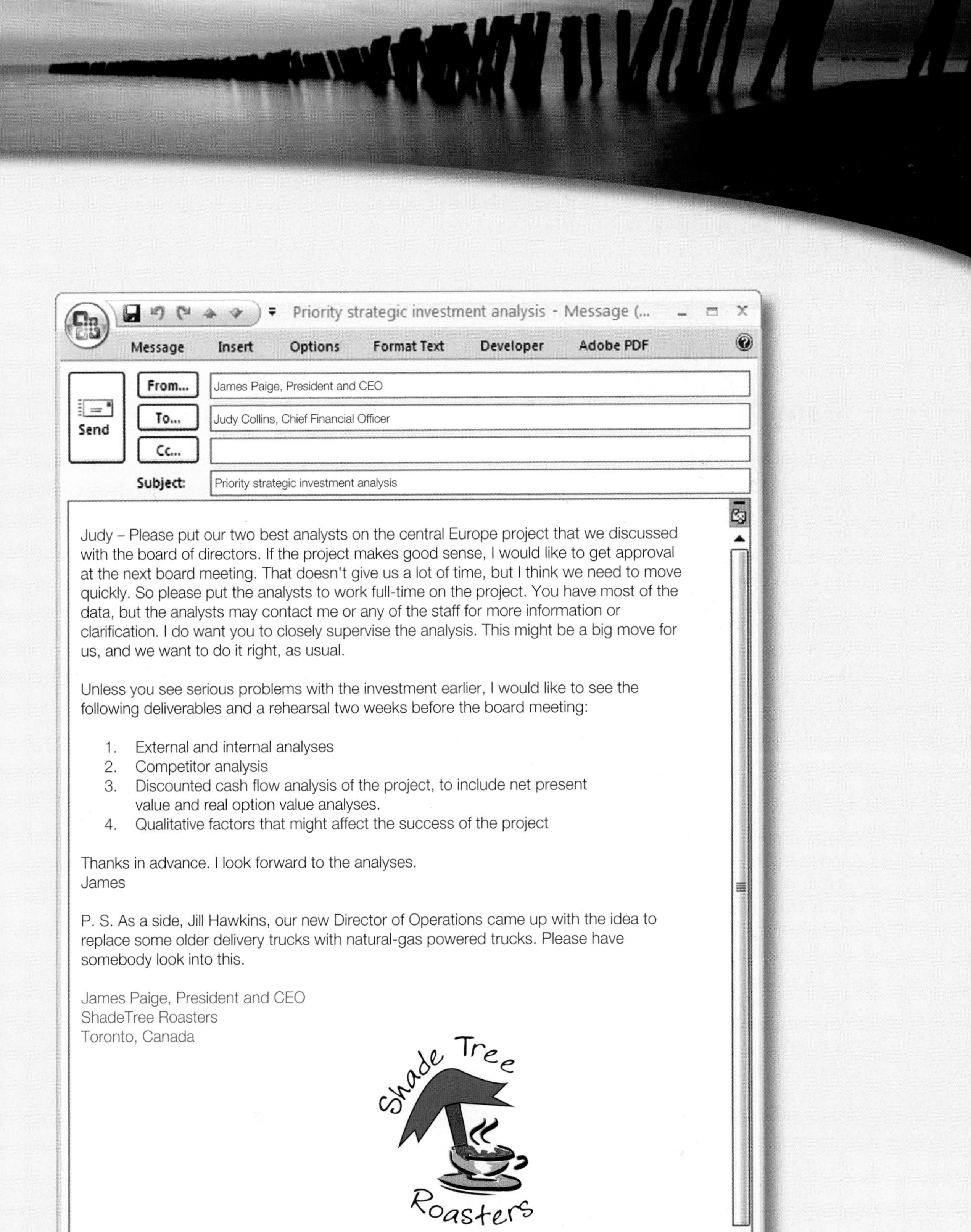

Priority strategic investment analysis - Message (...

Message Insert Options Format Text Developer Adobe PDF

Send

From... James Paige, President and CEO

To... Judy Collins, Chief Financial Officer

Cc...

Subject: Priority strategic investment analysis

Judy – Please put our two best analysts on the central Europe project that we discussed with the board of directors. If the project makes good sense, I would like to get approval at the next board meeting. That doesn't give us a lot of time, but I think we need to move quickly. So please put the analysts to work full-time on the project. You have most of the data, but the analysts may contact me or any of the staff for more information or clarification. I do want you to closely supervise the analysis. This might be a big move for us, and we want to do it right, as usual.

Unless you see serious problems with the investment earlier, I would like to see the following deliverables and a rehearsal two weeks before the board meeting:

1. External and internal analyses
2. Competitor analysis
3. Discounted cash flow analysis of the project, to include net present value and real option value analyses.
4. Qualitative factors that might affect the success of the project

Thanks in advance. I look forward to the analyses.
James

P. S. As a side, Jill Hawkins, our new Director of Operations came up with the idea to replace some older delivery trucks with natural-gas powered trucks. Please have somebody look into this.

James Paige, President and CEO
ShadeTree Roasters
Toronto, Canada

ShadeTree Roasters Inc. started as the entrepreneurial effort by two coffee-loving college classmates in Toronto, Canada. Today it is a successful, growing international company. The company sold its first bag of fresh-roasted, organic coffee to a small college shop in Toronto and now, 15 years later, sells organic coffees, teas and related specialty items in 200 of its own stores located in North America and western Europe. ShadeTree Roasters competes directly with larger companies such as **Starbucks** and is seeking future growth opportunities that have been overlooked by its larger competitors. In particular, ShadeTree is investigating the launch of a major effort in central Europe, where most coffee and tea sales are currently to restaurants and grocery markets. This chapter describes the methods that ShadeTree Roasters and other companies use and the issues they confront when considering major decisions, such as the development of a new business venture.

Many Decisions are Investment Decisions

Investments are major decisions that have long-term consequences beyond current consumption. For example, buying a coffee business is an investment, but buying a cup of coffee is not. Investments also include the decision by an airline to replace ageing aircraft with new planes or to expand ground facilities at an existing airport, the decision by a real estate developer to buy agricultural land and convert it to a new housing development, or the decision of a student to forgo current income to attend college full-time. All of these decisions have important long-term effects for the individuals or organizations who give up something now to obtain something better in the future.

Two effects of time on a decision and its outcomes distinguish an investment decision from the decisions considered in earlier chapters. First, making a decision commits resources for a lengthy period of time, and the organization will receive some of the benefits a long time into the future. The entire *investment period* should be covered in the financial model, as well as the *cost of capital*. The cost of capital is the return that the organization needs to offer to investors, who will only finance the organization's investments if they can expect an appropriate return on their investments. Second, investment decisions are characterized by management *flexibility* to modify an investment project as time and information unfold that can affect the desirability of the investment alternatives. We will model both of these investment characteristics in this chapter.

Financial accounting, economics and finance textbooks cover the basics of making investment decisions, also called 'capital budgeting decisions', using various techniques, such as **discounted cash flow (DCF)** methods. DCF methods are based on discounting future cash flows to their equivalent present values, using as the discount rate the forgone rate of interest (so an opportunity cost) available from alternative investments with an equal risk.

This chapter applies DCF methods to various kinds of decisions, such as investing in new production capacity, replacement of equipment, make-or-buy decisions, and adding or dropping a product. Why are such decisions covered in this chapter? Because any decision should be analysed based on its future cash flows, which will differ between the various alternatives being considered. We therefore consistently discuss decisions as applications of the DCF concept. There are exceptions. The previous chapter treated planning decisions about the quantity and mix of products and services. These decisions had a horizon of one year. That's why the cost management analyst did not use DCF. However, also note that the decision on the introduction of box seats in the previous chapter did include an investment, was which was depreciated over several years. With hindsight, the cost management analyst's financial model should have been based on DCF. We will now learn how DCF models can be built.

To facilitate course design by instructors, this chapter is formally divided into two sections, which can be assigned independently. Section I should be covered first. This provides a basic overview of the mechanics of the DCF method. Section II describes how to model strategic investment decisions. A *strategic* investment requires anticipating (1) changes in natural, social and economic conditions and (2) actions of competitors. ShadeTree's strategic investment project for expansion into central Europe will be discussed in Section II.

Section I: Investment Decisions and Discounted Cash Flows

This section applies to investment decisions in general. We discuss discounted cash flow (DCF) methods for modelling investment decisions. These decisions require a choice among alternative courses of action. These alternatives involve significant initial cash outflows for investing in tangible and intangible assets, and several cash inflows and savings on cash outflows during subsequent years to recover these initial investments and to obtain an economic return on the investment.

Several examples of ShadeTree's investment decisions will be used in Section I: investing in a new delivery truck, or refurbishing an existing truck; replacing coffee roasting equipment, or making no changes; expanding the warehouse, or outsourcing warehousing activities altogether; and closing a shop (so *disinvesting*) or keeping it open. The examples demonstrate varied applications of the DCF method for modelling investment decisions. The examples are investment decisions made under continuing conditions and unrelated to competitors' actions, so these are not strategic investments.

Finally, Section I addresses the choice of the best alternative using financial information as well as non-financial information that is not captured by modelling cash flows. Investments may have key consequences that cannot be adequately expressed in terms of future cash flows. Organizations consider non-financial and financial factors together when choosing the preferred course of action.

Understanding Investment Alternatives

LO 1
Distinguish alternatives for investment decisions.

Since most investment decisions consider several alternatives or many alternatives with complex options, evaluating the alternatives systematically is advisable. A useful decision aid is a **decision tree**, which diagrams decisions and alternative outcomes expected from those decisions in a 'tree, branch and limb' format. The choice of the most desirable alternative is made after considering the benefits and costs of each 'limb'. Exhibit 8.1 is a decision tree of ShadeTree's two alternative choices for investing in a new delivery truck. Although it might not be necessary for simple decisions, a decision tree can help identify and communicate the dimensions of complex decisions that managers face. Making complex decisions without such a decision aid can be confusing and prone to errors, particularly the omission of relevant factors.

To build the decision tree of ShadeTree's decision problem shown in Exhibit 8.1, follow these steps:

1. *Display the decision alternatives in the order the decisions must be made.* ShadeTree's cost-reduction alternatives shown in diamond shapes are *the status quo* or *change*. If the decision is to change, two alternatives exist: *purchase new diesel engine truck* or *switch to natural-gas powered truck*. Complex situations can have multiple layers of decisions and decision trees can be complicated. For example, after selecting the type of engine, there are alternative brands to consider.
2. *Trace the path of each decision to its ultimate outcomes and identify the set of outcomes that result from each decision path.* Exhibit 8.1 expresses outcomes in terms of ShadeTree's tangible objectives. The new diesel truck uses less diesel, has lower maintenance costs and emits less CO_2 and other gases that are bad for the environment than the refurbished truck. However, it requires a higher initial investment. The natural-gas powered truck requires the highest initial investment. The maintenance costs are in between the costs of the other alternatives, and the energy costs are the lowest. The natural-gas powered truck is more environmentally friendly than the new diesel truck and much more environmentally friendly than the refurbished diesel. Investing in a natural-gas powered truck will also allow ShadeTree to gain experience with alternative fuel vehicles.
3. *Measure the benefits and costs of each set of outcomes.* In this exhibit, we express the outcomes in qualitative terms, but we will quantify many of them in this chapter.

Exhibit 8.1 ShadeTree Decision Tree: Delivery Truck Replacement

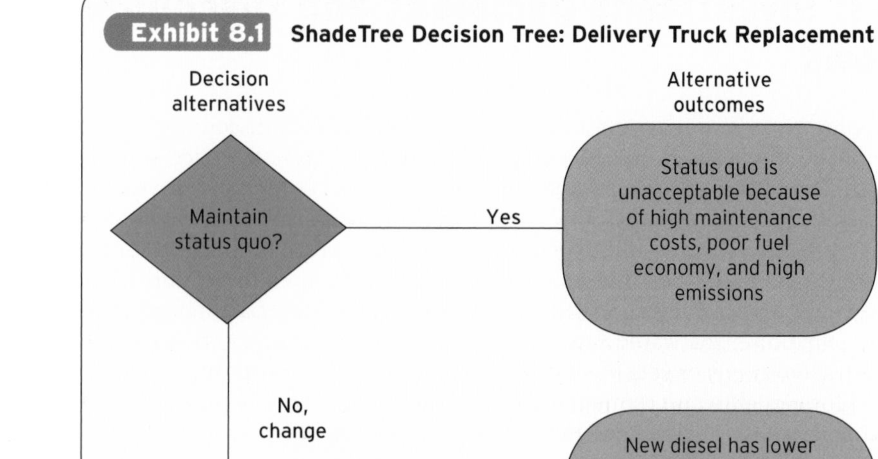

What is the status quo?

One alternative is always available and also included in Exhibit 8.1: the status quo. This is also the 'do nothing' or 'do nothing differently' alternative. However, it does not necessarily mean that nothing will change. Even without explicit management actions, the status quo may alter and this should be reflected in the decision model. For example, suppose ShadeTree's current truck needs to be refurbished because it has worn too much and it does not now meet driver safety regulations and therefore needs to have particular devices retrofitted. These costs are part of the status quo. These costs are relevant, because they are incurred in the future and they are also dissimilar for the decision alternatives.

Mutually exclusive or independent alternatives?

The decision alternatives in Exhibit 8.1 are mutually exclusive. Selection of a particular alternative excludes selection of any of the other alternatives – they cannot be combined. However, parallel to this investment decision, ShadeTree plans to replace some of its coffee roasting equipment by investing in new equipment that can produce more volume and is also more energy efficient. These equipment alternatives are independent from the delivery truck alternatives. As will be discussed later, DCF methods can be used to identify the preferred alternative, but how this is done depends on whether the decision alternatives are mutually exclusive or independent.

Discrete alternatives or optimization?

The number of decision alternatives in Exhibit 8.1 is limited. ShadeTree considers buying one truck, either diesel or natural-gas powered. But if ShadeTree would consider buying 50 new trucks, it could consider which mix of different types of trucks would best meet its goals and objectives. Strictly speaking, the number of alternatives is still limited (to 50), but it becomes an optimization problem instead of a selection from a discrete set of alternatives. That is beyond the scope of this text.

Consider opportunity costs, but don't calculate these!

Choosing one alternative from a set of mutually exclusive alternatives means blocking the remaining alternatives. This is where the notion of **opportunity costs** comes in: this is the highest forgone value that could have been obtained from other possible alternatives that are blocked by choosing a particular alternative and using a scarce resource for that. Cost analysts – and investors – should always be aware of such opportunity costs.

For example, ShadeTree owns a warehouse at a central location in Toronto. This has been bought many years ago, and its location is nowadays a popular, upcoming central area in Toronto, and the market value of the warehouse has increased considerably. If ShadeTree uses the warehouse, it cannot sell it. The company gives up the potential cash flow from selling this asset. Selling the warehouse could be an attractive alternative that deserves to be considered as well. Similarly, investors have alternative investment opportunities. Having a positive return on investment is not necessarily good enough – it should be at least equal to the return on comparable investments that are not made because the funds are invested in a particular company.

The opportunity costs become clear by explicitly comparing the alternatives, such as selling the warehouse or using it, investing in ShadeTree or investing in shares of another company. Some analysts, however, include opportunity costs in their calculation by mixing up different alternatives. For example, the sales price of the warehouse would then be treated as a cost under the alternative of using the warehouse. However, we find that way of modelling confusing and we advise against doing so. The notion of opportunity costs is crucial, but the best way to consider these in financial models is as follows:

1. *Make sure all appropriate alternatives are considered.* Don't forget any valuable mutually exclusive possible courses of action. The decision can only be as valuable as the best opportunity that is taken into account!
2. *Look at the future cash flows that differ between alternatives.* We have seen this principle of relevant information in the previous chapter, and it will also be a guiding principle in this chapter. Relevant cash flows are the basis for comparing the alternatives.

8.1 Cost Management in Practice

Power Generation and Distribution in the City of Boulder

The City of Boulder, Colorado USA faces a major decision whether to renew a 20-year contract with a large multi-state electrical utility or to create a city-owned utility that would be responsible for acquiring, distributing and servicing the power used by city residents and businesses. The decision is motivated by many city residents' desire to (a) obtain electrical power increasingly from renewable sources, whereas the large utility relies mainly on its legacy, coal-powered electricity generation plants, and (b) discontinue paying for the large utility's allegedly ill-considered, recent decisions to build new coal-powered plants rather than invest in equivalent renewable sources.

The city wishes to promote 'roof-top' solar generation in this sunny part of the country, which the large utility discourages, but this will provide only a small fraction of the total power needed. The city has enlisted the help of consultants and knowledgeable residents to model (a) the costs of about 3 to 5 different scenarios of purchasing electric power from different mixes of power sources (e.g., 20 per cent solar, 30 per cent wind and 50 per cent natural gas); and to model (b) the costs of operating the entire municipal utility itself or outsourcing some or all of the billing, distribution and service functions to private firms. Around three service alternatives will be investigated. The city will have to reimburse the utility company for the so-called 'stranded costs' of the existing network assets. These costs will be amortized over 20 years and the amortization cost will be factored into the rate charged to consumers.

The feasibility of each scenario will be measured against the criteria of meeting or beating the large utility's record of service reliability (which is high) and price per kilowatt-hour of electrical power (which is average for the region).

Discounted Cash Flow Analysis

LO 2 Build a financial model of investment decisions using discounted cash flow methods.

The purpose of Section I is to present the basic concepts and method of the discounted cash flow (DCF) method. This section may be a review for readers who already have learned the DCF method but are rusty on the concepts or as an introduction for those who are unfamiliar with the topic. Both groups should carefully read this section for development of the DCF techniques and understand how this chapter uses spreadsheets to model and computes investment decisions. Section II will apply these techniques to ShadeTree's strategic investment decisions.

We first discuss estimating current and future cash flows and explain the role of the discount rate. Then we demonstrate how the DCF method can be applied to net present value (NPV), payback period and internal rate of return (IRR) analyses.

Estimating Cash Flows for DCF Analysis

DCF methods are based on the current and future cash flows expected from a particular investment opportunity. The amounts and timing of the cash flows determine the economic value of the investment, so accurately predicting future cash flows is a key to effective investment analysis.

Project cash flows

Investment projects can have three types of cash flows that are estimated separately. These are:

- *Investment cash flows*, which are of three types:
  1. Asset acquisition, which might include
     - **a.** *New equipment costs*, including installation and start-up costs. Generally, all costs of acquiring and placing equipment into service are considered costs of the equipment. That is, these costs are *capitalized*. This topic is covered in most financial accounting texts.
     - **b.** *Future reinvestment or refurbishing costs* may be necessary to extend the life of the asset. These costs are distinct from normal maintenance and operating costs. The difference between investment and operating costs is an important topic in financial reporting. Correct classification can affect investment choice and financial reporting. Improper classifications have generated several high-profile financial frauds in recent years (e.g., **WorldCom** in the USA).
     - **c.** *Proceeds from or costs of disposing of existing assets* should be considered. Sometimes companies sell old assets for a salvage value but at other times must pay to dispose of old assets.
  2. *Tax effects from a loss or gain* on the sale of replaced assets (if any) could arise. If an asset is sold for less than its depreciated net book value, the owner generally incurs a loss that might offset other income. If an asset is sold for more than its book value, the sale generates a gain that could be taxable. These tax complications are beyond the scope of this text but are covered in detail in most financial and tax accounting texts. We will simply include the loss or gain as part of the taxable income. Note that managers might be unwilling to add that loss to periodic income even though the historical purchase price and book value are irrelevant, sunk costs.
  3. *Tax credits* and *subsidies* (if any) could be a factor. Sometimes governments encourage certain types of investments by offering subsidies or tax credits that are immediate reductions in taxes owed from periodic taxable income. Subsidies and tax credits can change from year to year and also are beyond the scope of this text.
- *Periodic operating cash flows*, which are incremental cash inflows and outflows from normal operating activities. Normally, these are revenues and expenses, but not all revenues and expenses are cash flows in the period in which these are recognized for financial reporting. For example, equipment depreciation is an expense, but it is not a cash flow in the period recognized. It does, however, reduce periodic income and tax expense.

When the operating income in a year is negative, the resulting tax is modelled as a tax income, instead of 0. Of course, government does not really pay out 'negative' taxes, but it is a useful convention, assuming that operating loss on this investment reduces the organization's total taxes. It is an approximation because a more detailed discussion of loss compensation is beyond the scope of this text.

- *Disinvestment* (or *termination*) *cash flows*, which are the anticipated costs of shutting down or terminating the investment being considered. These cash flows might include proceeds from the sale of assets, tax effects of loss or gain on the sale, and severance, outplacement and restoration costs. All potential disinvestment cash flows must be considered at the end of the project horizon, and all remaining assets (at least those that are different among decision alternatives) are sold to make decision alternatives comparable. Even if it is unclear whether these assets will actually be put on the market, disinvestment cash flows are included *as if* the assets are disinvested to have equivalent decision alternatives.

Financial cash flows are excluded

Financial cash flows (such as paying interest, repaying a loan, payment of dividend to shareholders) are *not* included. We are not considering in detail how the investments are financed and which financial cash flows will occur. Financing decisions are decoupled from investment decisions. Instead, future project cash flows are discounted to their lower present values. For example, if an organization receives CA$1,000 two years from today it will have to attract more funding compared to when it would receive the same CA$1,000 immediately. We consider this by discounting the CA$1,000 to a lower present value. How this works is discussed later in this chapter. For now, it is sufficient to note that because of this discounting, financial cash flows must be excluded. Otherwise, financing would be included twice.

Other possible differences between cash flows and accounting numbers

Cash flows are either notes and coins changing hands, or payments found on bank statements. Otherwise, it is not a cash flow. Yet, practically, revenues and expenses are usually taken as good approximations of cash flows, except for depreciation, as mentioned above. But in some situations there are other significant differences that may need to be considered when estimating project cash flows.

- Besides tangible assets such as equipment, intangible assets such as research and development are sometimes capitalized and depreciated. This means that cash outflows occur earlier than the related depreciation expenses.
- Reversely, cash outflows may occur much later than the associated expenses. For example, warranty expenses may be shown when the sales takes place (creating a provision for future warranty costs) while the cash outflows occur later when services and repairs under warranty are executed.
- Customers sometimes make significant prepayments before revenues are recognized, for example to help finance a construction project with a long completion time. Such prepayments are project cash flows that must be considered.
- Reversely, a supplier and customer may negotiate long payment periods. For example, suppliers of supermarket retail chains sometimes have to wait 60 or 90 days before receiving payment while the supermarket receives cash payments from consumers. The supplier's cash inflow is the actual payment that occurs significantly later than when it recognizes revenues from sales to the retailer.

Illustration of ShadeTree Roasters' Replacement Decision

To illustrate NPV analysis, assume that ShadeTree Roasters is planning to replace some of its coffee roasting equipment for equipment with higher capacity that is also more energy efficient. This investment is less complex than the central Europe strategic investment project and more suitable for

Exhibit 8.2 Example Input Data

	A	B	C
1	**Data input (all amounts in Canadian dollars, CA$)**		
2	New equipment cost, including installation and training	$200,000	
3	Salvage value of old equipment	-	
4	New equipment useful life	4	years
5	Salvage value of new equipment	-	
6	Annual increase in contribution margin	$30,000	
7	Annual energy cost savings	$40,000	
8	Income tax rate	40%	
9	Discount rate	8.0%	

our purposes. We will return to the strategic investment project later in this chapter. The proposed investment information appears in Exhibit 8.2.

The new equipment cost of CA$200,000 (B2 of Exhibit 8.2) is by convention a cash outflow at the end of the current year (year 0). The new equipment cost (B2, net of salvage value, B5) will be depreciated on a straight-line basis over its useful life of four years (B4). Analysts estimate that the new equipment will have a zero salvage value after four years (B5). The old equipment has no salvage value or disposal cost (B3). Note that in many cases, acquiring and disposing of assets have more complications than displayed in this example.

The annual increase in contribution margin, CA$30,000 (B6) from higher sales driven by the larger capacity of the new roasting equipment will improve operating income by that amount. The energy cost savings, CA$40,000 (B7), also will increase operating income. These combined with the straight-line depreciation expense of the new equipment, CA$50,000 [= (B2 – B5) ÷ B4], will change operating income. Subtracting taxes on this change in income at a rate of 40 per cent (B8), which is assumed to cover all federal, state and local taxes, generates the change in operating income after tax. This tax rate assumption is a major simplification of the tax impacts of investment activities, which are beyond the scope of this text.

Operating income after tax (revenues less all expenses, including taxes) understates operating cash flows because depreciation expense is deducted from income, although it is not a cash flow. Adding back depreciation restates after-tax operating income to operating net cash flow. Putting all of this information together over the five-year life of the investment generates estimates of annual net cash flows from the project that are the heart of DCF analysis. Mistakes or misstatements in these estimates can result in wrong investment decisions that can be quite harmful. On the other hand, careful estimates identify promising investment alternatives that can generate valuable cash flows and competitive advantages.

The five-year estimates of the investment's cash flows are shown in Exhibit 8.3. Work carefully through this exhibit through row 22 using the data input from Exhibit 8.2 to verify how after-tax net cash flows are computed from the input data.

Discussion of NPV analysis of the investment in Exhibit 8.3 will continue at the conclusion of the presentation of the discount rate and discounting cash flows.

Importance of the Discount Rate

The one piece of input data that we have not discussed is the discount rate of 8 per cent (Exhibit 8.2, cell B9). This is crucial information because the **discount rate** measures the opportunity cost of

Exhibit 8.3 Example Investment Net Cash Flows

	A	B	C	D	E	F
10	**Investment analysis (in CA$)**			**End of year**		
11	Initial cash flows for year:	0	1	2	3	4
12	Investment cost	$(200,000)				
13	Proceeds from old equipment	-				
14	Annual operating income items					
15	Increase in contribution margin		$30,000	$30,000	$30,000	$30,000
16	Energy cost savings		40,000	40,000	40,000	40,000
17	Depreciation expense		(50,000)	(50,000)	(50,000)	(50,000)
18	Change in operating income		20,000	20,000	20,000	20,000
19	Tax on change in income		(8,000)	(8,000)	(8,000)	(8,000)
20	After-tax change in operating income		12,000	12,000	12,000	12,000
21	Add back depreciation expense		50,000	50,000	50,000	50,000
22	After-tax operating cash flow	(200,000)	62,000	62,000	62,000	62,000

investing and is used to discount future values to their equivalent present values. Organizations should use a discount rate, so called because we will use it to 'discount' future cash flows, which measures the rate of return the company would forgo by choosing a particular investment. Choose a rate that is too high and the company might reject quite profitable investments. Choose a rate that is too low and the company might accept subpar investments and forgo better returns that it could earn elsewhere. The debate continues in finance and economics about how to choose the proper discount rate, or cost of capital. It is clear, however, that investors have other opportunities. Investors will only be willing to let the company use their money if they can expect to get the same return as on comparable investments. Comparable here means: *the same level of risk*. Investors who buy into the company's equity require the same return as on equity with the same risk. Lenders who supply debt to the company will also demand the same return as on debts that are equally risky. And so the cost of capital becomes a weighted average of the cost of equity and the cost of debt.[1] This weighted average cost of capital (WACC) applies to the whole company, and it can be adjusted upward or downward for the expected risk of the particular project, although there is no general agreement about how to properly adjust for risk.[2]

Public or governmental organizations also have difficulty choosing the proper discount rate. Because the federal government is so large and diversified, some public finance economists argue that the proper discount rate is the risk-free rate. However, others argue that because public investment displaces private investment (by taking taxes that private parties otherwise could invest), government agencies should use a higher rate comparable to private investment rates of return. The stakes can be quite high, depending on how these disputes are decided, but this interesting topic is beyond the scope of this text.

Effective discount rate and nominal rate

Suppose interest is paid every quarter at 3 per cent per quarter. The so-called nominal interest is 3 per cent × 4 quarters = 12 per cent, but the effective interest rate is higher. We only care about the effective rate. Compounding refers to how often banks and other lenders charge the interest. Compounding four times in a year at 3 per cent gives an effective interest rate of $(1 + 3 \text{ per cent})^4 - 1 = 1.1255 - 1 = 12.55$ per cent. This is understandable, because it would indeed be cheaper to pay the entire interest at the end of the year compared to paying the same absolute interest earlier at four moments throughout the year.

In general, the relationship between the nominal and the effective discount rate can be expressed as follows:

$$\begin{aligned} r &= \textbf{Effective discount rate per year} \\ r_n &= \textbf{Nominal rate per year} \\ M &= \textbf{Number of times compounding per year} \end{aligned}$$

$$r = (1 + r_n/M)^M - 1$$

For example:

$$r = (1 + 12\% \div 4)^4 - 1 = 1.03^4 - 1 = 1.1255 - 1 = 12.55\%$$

Or, when compounding every month:

$$r = (1 + 12\% \div 12)^{12} - 1 = 1.01^{12} - 1 = 1.1268 - 1 = 12.68\%$$

In the text, whenever we simply say discount rate, we always mean the *effective* discount rate.

Effective discount rates for different period lengths

Another matter is the length of the periods in the financial model. Financial models for investment decisions often use entire years. But, for example, when a lot of things happen in the start-up phase of the investment project, showing cash flows per month or quarter may be more insightful. If the effective discount rate is 16 per cent per year, the corresponding effective discount rate per quarter is not simply 16 per cent ÷ 4. Instead, we know that (1 + effective rate per quarter)^4 = 1.16. So (1 + effective rate per quarter) = $\sqrt[4]{1.16}$ = 1.378, so the effective rate per quarter is 3.78 per cent in this case.

In general, the relationship between effective discount rate of different period lengths can be expressed as follows:

$$\mathbf{r = \text{Effective discount rate per year}}$$
$$\mathbf{r_m = \text{Effective discount rate per modelling period}}$$
$$\mathbf{X = \text{Number of modelling periods in one year}}$$
$$\mathbf{r_m = \sqrt[X]{1 + r} - 1}$$

For example:

$$\mathbf{r_m = \sqrt[4]{(1 + 16\%)} - 1 = 1.378 - 1 = 3.78\% \text{ per quarter}}$$

Or, when using months as the modelling period:

$$\mathbf{r_m = \sqrt[12]{(1 + 16\%)} - 1 = 1.0124 - 1 = 1.24\% \text{ per month}}$$

Effects of inflation

Inflation reflects general price increases in an economy. The expected inflation rate can also be a component of the discount rate and future cash flows. Market rates of return (e.g., the opportunity rate of a similar investment) contain an expectation of inflation. For example, a market-based opportunity rate of 8 per cent might be composed of an expectation of a 3 per cent inflation rate and a 5 per cent rate of return on a comparable investment without inflation.[3] Adjusting DCF analysis for inflation involves adjusting the discount rate for the expected inflation rate and adjusting future cash flows for expected inflation. Therefore, if one uses a market rate, which already includes expected inflation, as the discount rate, future cash flows also should reflect expected inflation unless contractual obligations fix them. The effects of inflation are multiplied or 'compounded' over time – each year's inflation builds on the previous year's inflation. For example, assume that the expected inflation rate is 3 per cent each year and that future cash inflows without inflation are expected to be CA$12,000 per year (in current dollars). If the analysis takes place in year 0, future cash inflows should be inflated as follows:

Year 0	Year 1	Year 2	Year 3 . . .	Year N
Cash flow in current (non-inflated) dollars	$12,000	$12,000	$12,000	$12,000
Cumulative inflation at 3 per cent	$(1.03)^1$	$(1.03)^2$	$(1.03)^3$	$(1.03)^N$
	= 1.03	= 1.0609	= 1.0927	-
Inflation-adjusted Cash flows (rounded)	= $12,360	= $12,731	= $13,113	-

For simplicity, the examples and analyses in this chapter implicitly include the effects of inflation.

Effects of taxation

Profit-seeking firms pay taxes on their periodic profits, and these cash flows for taxes are part of the project cash flows. But there is another effect of taxation: it affects the discount rate. Why is that? The cost of debt financing (but not the cost of equity) is an expense that is deductible from the taxable income. This is considered as lowering the cost of capital. For example, a firm has an operating profit of CA$1,000 and an effective income tax rate t of 30 per cent. Compare two situations:

	Situation A: No debt	Situation B: $30,000 debt at 12%
Operating income	$1,000	$1,000
Interest expense	$0	$360
Before-tax income	$1,000	$640
Taxes (t = 30%)	$300	$192
After-tax income	$700	$448

Debt causes the firm to pay less taxes, CA$108 in this example. We model this as a reduction of the discount rate, so *as if* the cost of capital is reduced. The cost of debt becomes (CA$360 – CA$108) ÷ CA$30,000 = 8.4 per cent. This can also be calculated as follows $(1 - t) \times 12$ per cent $= (1 - 0.30) \times 12$ per cent = 8.4 per cent. And the cash flow for taxes is modeled without considering the effects of debt, so for the 'full' €300 in this example.

The examples and analyses in this chapter implicitly include the effect of taxation on the discount rate.

Discounting Future Cash Flows

To account for the opportunity cost of investing, DCF methods discount future cash flows to the amounts that would have to be invested now at the discount rate to yield the expected future cash flows. For example, if the discount rate is 10 per cent and the expected cash flow after one year hence is CA$110, then CA$100 must be invested now at 10 per cent to generate the future amount of CA$110. The CA$100 figure is the present value of the future CA$110 at a 10 per cent discount rate. In general, the **present value** of a future cash flow is the equivalent amount that would have to be invested today to generate the future amount at a given discount rate.

Algebraically, the relation between present and future values is expressed in the example as follows:

$$\boldsymbol{P} = \textbf{Present value, CA\$100}$$
$$\boldsymbol{F} = \textbf{Future value, CA\$110}$$
$$\boldsymbol{r} = \textbf{Discount rate, 10\%}$$

For a one-year investment,

$$P + P \times r = F$$

which can be simplified as:

$$P \times (1 + r) = F$$

You can verify this relation using the example amounts:

$$\text{CA\$100} \times (1 + 0.10) = \text{CA\$110}$$

The other way around, the relation between future and present values is expressed in this example as follows. For a one-year investment, because $\boldsymbol{P \times (1 + r) = F}$,

$$P = \frac{F}{(1 + r)}$$

You can verify this relation using the example amounts:

$$\text{CA\$100} = \frac{\text{CA\$110}}{(1 + 0.10)} = \text{CA\$110} \cdot 0.909$$

For an investment of *N* years:

$$P \times (1 + r)^N = F$$

$$P = \frac{F}{(1 + r)^N}$$

For example, assume that an expected future net cash inflow in *two* years is CA$130. To earn CA$130 in two years would require an investment of an unknown present value amount for two years and forgoing the first year's interest on that amount and the second year's interest on both the present value amount and its first year's interest. If the discount rate is 10 per cent, we can solve for the unknown present value, *P*, algebraically as follows:

Algebra	Notes
$[P \times (1 + 0.10)] \times (1 + 0.10) = \$130$	The unknown amount, *P*, will earn interest for the first year, as shown in brackets [ ], and that amount will earn interest for the second year, shown by multiplying again by 1 + *r*.
$P \times (1 + 0.10) \times (1 + 0.10) = \$130$	Removing the brackets [ ] does not affect the algebra.
$P \times (1 + 0.10)^2 = \$130$	Simplify the multiplication of identical amounts.
$P = \frac{\$130}{(1 + 0.10)^2}$	Solve for *P*.
$P = \$130 \times \frac{1}{(1 + 0.10)^2}$	Separating the fraction does not affect the algebra.
$P = \$130 \times 0.826 = \$107.38$	Finish the arithmetic and solve for P.

Thus, CA$107.38 invested today at 10 per cent would grow to CA$130 in two years. Confirm this by multiplying CA$107.38 by $(1 + 0.10)^2$. The figure 0.826 [or $1 \div (1 + 0.10)^2$] is the 10 per cent *present value factor* for an amount to be received two years from now.

Analysts use the principle of discounting cash flows to derive three measures for deciding on investments. These are the **net present value** (NPV), the **payback period**, and the **internal rate of return** (IRR). The NPV, IRR and payback period are different ways of condensing the project cash flows into one overall number that can be used for decision making. The following equation summarizes the calculations, which will be explained in this chapter:

N = Number of periods
t = any period between now (0) and the final period
r = Discount rate per period

$$NPV = \sum_{t=0}^{N} \frac{\text{Cash flow period } t}{(1 + r)^t}$$

NPV:	Calculate NPV with the equation	*N* is chosen	*r* is chosen
Payback period:	NPV = 0	Find the number of periods *N*	*r* is chosen
IRR:	NPV = 0	*N* is chosen	Find the discount rate *r*

Computing the Net Present Value and Payback Period

When a series of future cash flows is expected, compute the total present value by summing the present values of each period's cash flows. Most investments have a purchase price or investment cost that is payable now. The **net present value (NPV)** of an investment is the present value of its future cash flows less its purchase price. If the NPV is positive, the project promises returns in excess of the discount or opportunity rate and vice versa.

To compute the NPV of an investment manually, follow these steps:

1. Estimate current and future net cash flows (similar to Exhibit 8.3) and the relevant discount rate.

2. Multiply each period's future net cash flow by the appropriate present value factor for the time period and discount rate (preferably using spreadsheet software) to compute the discounted cash flows. Note that current cash flows in year 0 are multiplied by 1 plus the discount rate, raised to the 0 power, which is 1. Note also that computing present values manually can generate rounding errors, but these are almost never critical to investment decisions.
3. Sum the current and discounted future net cash flows to obtain the NPV.

Exhibit 8.4 extends Exhibit 8.3 to present the NPV analysis of ShadeTree Roasters' equipment replacement decision. Cash flows are the same as in Exhibit 8.3. Present value factors for the discount rate of 8 per cent are in row 25. Instead of using spreadsheet functions, the spreadsheet 'manually' computes present value factors in cells like C25 V_i for example cell C25 = 1/(1 + B9)^1C11. The periodic present value amounts, or discounted cash flows, are the net cash flows multiplied by the present value factors and appear in row 26. To compute the project's NPV, sum the present values of the future cash flows (C26 to F26) and the present (negative) cash flow of the project (B26). As shown in cell B28, the investment has a positive NPV of CA$5,352 and probably will be accepted as long as no serious qualitative factors are uncovered.

Most NPV analyses are completed using spreadsheet software and the software's NPV function, but it is important that you know how the arithmetic is done. Don't forget that the difficult part of NPV analysis is estimating future cash flows and the proper discount rate. Spreadsheets are important NPV tools because they simplify the arithmetic, facilitate sensitivity analysis, and reduce the opportunity for calculations errors.

Some firms report the use of the **payback period** as a secondary investment criterion when the environment is unstable. That is, if two investments have (nearly) equal NPVs, a firm prefers the investment with the shorter payback period. The payback period *with discounting of cash flows* is computed using the cumulative present values shown in row 27 in Exhibit 8.4. The starting point is the present value of year 0. In the next column, the present value of year 0 and the present value of year 1 are summed, which gives the cumulative result until year 1. Sum this with the present value of year 2 to get the cumulative result until year 2, and continue like this for subsequent years. By the end of the third year the cumulative present value is CA$40,220 negative, and by the end of the fourth year the cumulative present value is CA$5,352 positive, so the payback period is sometime in the fourth year. We can approximate the payback period as three years' present value plus a portion of the fourth year's present value of CA$45,572, as follows:

Payback period = (3 + CA$40,220 ÷ CA$45,572) years = 3 + 0.88 years = 3.88 years

Exhibit 8.4 **Example of NPV Analysis**

	A	B	C	D	E	F
10	**Investment analysis (in CA$)**			**End of year**		
11	Initial cash flows for year:	**0**	**1**	**2**	**3**	**4**
12	Investment cost	$(200,000)				
13	Proceeds from old equipment	-				
14	Annual operating income items					
15	Increase in contribution margin		$30,000	$30,000	$30,000	$30,000
16	Energy cost savings		40,000	40,000	40,000	40,000
17	Depreciation expense		(50,000)	(50,000)	(50,000)	(50,000)
18	Change in operating income		20,000	20,000	20,000	20,000
19	Tax on change in income		(8,000)	(8,000)	(8,000)	(8,000)
20	After-tax change in operating income		12,000	12,000	12,000	12,000
21	Add back depreciation expense		50,000	50,000	50,000	50,000
22	After-tax operating cash flow	(200,000)	62,000	62,000	62,000	62,000
23						
24	Net cash flow	(200,000)	62,000	62,000	62,000	62,000
25	Present value factors	1.000	0.926	0.857	0.794	0.735
26	Present values of cash flows	(200,000)	$57,407	$53,155	$49,218	$45,572
27	Cumulative present values of cash flows	(200,000)	$(142,593)	$(89,438)	$(40,220)	$5,352
28	Net present value	$5,352	Note: =SUM(B26:F26)			

Note that this is an approximation because it assumes a linear relationship between cumulative present value and time.

Firms also use the payback period *without* discounting of cash flows. Although this is theoretically incorrect, it is discussed here for completeness. The payback period for the investment in Exhibit 8.4 is 3.23 years, computed as follows:

Initial investment cost = CA$200,000
Annual (equal) net cash flow = CA$62,000 recovered per year
Payback period = Initial investment cost ÷ Annual (equal) net cash flow
Payback period = CA$200,000 ÷ CA$62,000 per year = 3.23 years

Note that this calculation of the payback period is straightforward because annual cash flows are received uniformly across years, which might not be the case. If the annual cash flows are unequal, the payback period is again computed by calculating the cumulative values of the cash flows, as done above (but then using undiscounted cash flows instead of discounted cash flows).

Computing the Internal Rate of Return

We could also evaluate the investment somewhat differently. Instead of using the chosen discount rate to calculate the NPV, we may recognize that an unknown discount rate can lead to an NPV of zero. The **internal rate of return (IRR)** is the discount rate that would create an NPV of exactly zero for an investment project. A positive NPV signals a favourable investment, but we compare a project's IRR to the discount rate: only projects with IRRs higher than the discount rate are favourable and vice versa. Sometimes the term 'hurdle rate' is used: the project's IRR must 'clear the hurdle' to be favourable. NPV and IRR methods almost always are equivalent approaches to investment analysis, but we will return to possible inconsistencies later in this chapter.

Let's first compute the IRR of an example investment that requires an initial investment of CA$111.41 and offers CA$130 after two years. Thus, the NPV relation becomes:

$$\mathbf{0 = CA\$130 \times \frac{1}{(1+r)^2} - CA\$111.41}$$

One could solve this quadratic equation for the unknown, r, but it is simpler (especially for more complex investments) to use a spreadsheet. To start, let's guess that the investment's IRR is 11 per cent. The present value factor for 11 per cent and two years is 0.812. After substituting this figure into the NPV equation, we compute (and you should verify) that

$$\mathbf{0 \neq CA\$130 \times 0.812 - CA\$111.41 = CA\$(5.85)}$$

We have discounted the future cash flow, CA$130, too much; that is, we guessed an IRR that is too high. Now let's guess that the IRR is 8 per cent. We now find (and you should verify) that

$$\mathbf{0 = CA\$130 \times 0.857 - CA\$111.41}$$

Now we have discounted the future cash flow to find that its IRR is exactly 8 per cent. If, however, the hurdle rate is 10 per cent, this is not a favourable investment project. The NPV and IRR methods give consistent investment advice for this project: Do not invest, or try to reduce the cost of the initial investment.

Using spreadsheet functions to compute NPV and IRR

Trial and error methods to compute NPV and IRR are time consuming and unnecessary when spreadsheet software – which nearly every cost management analyst uses – is available. We can use the investment information in Exhibits 8.2 and 8.3 (which are from the same worksheet) and built-in functions to readily compute the NPV and IRR for ShadeTree's equipment replacement analysis.[4]

Exhibit 8.5 NPV and IRR Computed with Spreadsheet Functions

	A	B	C	D	E	F
1	**Data input (all amounts in Canadian dollars, CA$)**					
2	New equipment cost, including installation and training	$200,000				
3	Salvage value of old equipment	-				
4	New equipment useful life	4	years			
5	Salvage value of new equipment	-				
6	Annual increase in contribution margin	$30,000				
7	Annual energy cost savings	$40,000				
8	Income tax rate	40%				
9	Discount rate	8.0%				
10	**Investment analysis (in CA$)**			**End of year**		
11	Initial cash flows for year:	**0**	**1**	**2**	**3**	**4**
12	Investment cost	$(200,000)				
13	Proceeds from old equipment	-				
14	Annual operating income items					
15	Increase in contribution margin		$30,000	$30,000	$30,000	$30,000
16	Energy cost savings		40,000	40,000	40,000	40,000
17	Depreciation expense		(50,000)	(50,000)	(50,000)	(50,000)
18	Change in operating income		20,000	20,000	20,000	20,000
19	Tax on change in income		(8,000)	(8,000)	(8,000)	(8,000)
20	After-tax change in operating income		12,000	12,000	12,000	12,000
21	Add back depreciation expense		50,000	50,000	50,000	50,000
22	After-tax operating cash flow	(200,000)	62,000	62,000	62,000	62,000
23						
24	Net cash flow	(200,000)	62,000	62,000	62,000	62,000
25	Present value factors	1.000	0.926	0.857	0.794	0.735
26	Present values of cash flows	(200,000)	$57,407	$53,155	$49,218	$45,572
27	Cumulative present values of cash flows	(200,000)	$(142,593)	$(89,438)	$(40,220)	$5,352
28	Net present value	$5,352	Note: =SUM(B27:F27)			
29						
30	**Net present value using NPV**	**$5,352**	=NPV(B9,C24:F24)+B24			
31	**Internal rate of return using IRR**	**9.196%**	=IRR(B24:F24)			

Exhibit 8.5 illustrates the use of these functions in rows 30 and 31. The syntax of the IRR function is straightforward: insert the IRR function into a cell and select the sequence of after-tax cash flows (B24:F24), *beginning* with the initial investment cost. Using the NPV function is a bit more complex. The first argument of the NPV function is the discount or hurdle rate, B9. The second argument is the sequence of after-tax *future* cash flows (C24:F24) *not* including the initial investment cost. The initial investment cost (B24) is separately added to the future cash flows that are discounted in the NPV function. The project's IRR is 9.2 per cent, which is higher than the hurdle rate of 8 per cent used to compute the positive NPV, CA$5,352. The IRR and NPV methods consistently indicate that this equipment replacement is a favourable investment.

Another useful spreadsheet function to find the IRR is Goal Seek. This function works as if the spreadsheet software does high-speed trial-and-error for you. Exhibit 8.6 shows that Goal Seek changes the value of cell B9 (Discount rate) until the value of cell B28 (the NPV) reaches 0. Goal Seek can also be used to find other critical values. For example: which annual energy cost savings are needed to have a NPV of 0 (answer: CA$37,307), or which annual increase in contribution margin is needed to have a NPV of 0 (answer: CA$27,307).

Exhibit 8.6 Using Goals Seek to Compute IRR

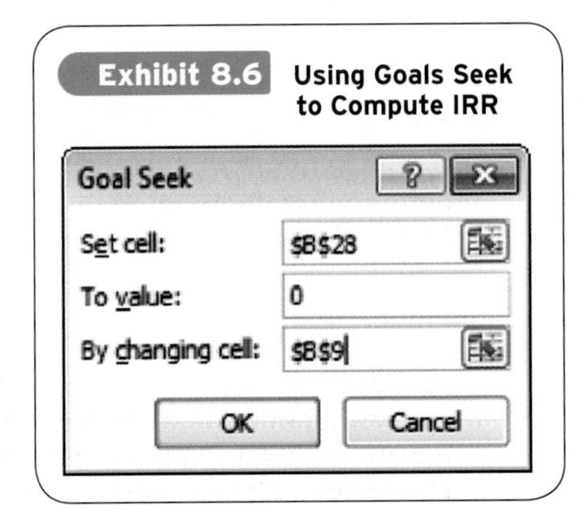

Timing of cash flows

By convention, the calculations are done so far *as if* the cash flows are all received and paid at the end of each year. This may not be realistic for cash flows that are the result of buying materials and selling goods and services. These activities usually happen throughout the year and cash flows occur throughout the year. If cash flows occur evenly throughout the year, this can be approximated by timing the total yearly cash flow in the middle of the year. For example, the cash flows of the second year are received between 1 year + 1 day and 1 year + 365 days, so 'on average' after 1½ years. Hence, the total cash flow received in the second year would be discounted by $1 \div (1 + r)^{1\frac{1}{2}}$. The cash flows can also be different throughout the year, for example because of seasonal sales, so the 'average' may not be in the middle of the year. For short model period lengths, such as months, the effect is very small.

Comparing Investment Alternatives

The NPV, IRR and payback period are three measures for aggregating the project cash flows into one overall number that can be used for decision making. How should these measures be used?

Independent investment alternatives

Independent investments can be accepted if the NPV is greater than 0 or if the IRR is greater than the discount rate. Decision alternatives are independent if each can be accepted or rejected separately. The decision make can consider each investment project individually and does not have to compare it directly to other investment projects. For example, ShadeTree considers investing in the new equipment and also whether to replace a delivery truck. These investments are independent, because ShadeTree can accept any combination (none, only new equipment, only a new delivery truck, or both).

There is no clear benchmark for the payback period to know whether an investment can be accepted, but organizations sometimes use pragmatic rules for the acceptable payback period of projects.

Mutually exclusive investment alternatives

Mutually exclusive investments must be compared among each other, because the organization can only accept one alternative. The decision alternative with the highest NPV is the preferred alternative. This alternative usually also has the highest IRR. ShadeTree compared investing in the new equipment or keeping the status quo, and these alternatives exclude each other. The investment generates a positive NPV of CA$5,352, while the NPV of the status quo is 0, so investing is the preferred alternative. Consistent with this, the project's IRR of 9.2 per cent exceeds the discount rate of 8 per cent.

Sometimes only cash *outflows* of mutually exclusive investments are considered in the calculation of NPV. This is when the investment alternatives all involve exactly the same cash inflows and only the cash outflows differ (so only the cash outflows matter for the decision at hand). ShadeTree compares three alternatives concerning the delivery truck: keep the current truck, purchase new diesel engine truck, or switch to natural gas powered truck. Cash inflows will be the same for all. While all alternatives have a negative NPV, we still follow the rule that the highest NPV (the least negative NPV) is the best. In this case one could still compare differences between alternatives, for example because of operating costs. Of course, when only cash outflows are considered, the IRR cannot be calculated (because the NPV will not reach 0).

The payback period is not suitable to compare the financial attractiveness of mutually exclusive investments, but organizations sometimes use payback as an additional consideration. Especially when the NPV and IRR are comparable, an organization may prefer the investment with the shorter payback period. When only cash outflows are considered, there is no payback period.

Inconsistent ranking of investment alternatives

NPV and IRR usually lead to the same conclusion as to which mutually exclusive alternative is the best one. However, this does not have to be the case, which means there is **inconsistent ranking**. If that occurs, the solution is simple: choose the alternative with the highest NPV even if it does not have the highest IRR. Why can NPV and IRR lead to different conclusions? Let's consider ShadeTree's investment in new equipment again, and now there is another investment alternative to be analysed, called 'EnergyPlus'. This is the same new roasting equipment but with an extra installation added to make the equipment even more energy efficient. The extra investment for this installation is CA$20,000 and the extra energy cost savings are CA$6,800 per year. Otherwise, the cash flows are the same as in the original project. Exhibit 8.7 shows the NPV calculation of the EnergyPlus project. It has a positive NPV of CA$5,490 an IRR of 9.1 per cent. Thus, EnergyPlus has a *higher NPV* than the original project's NPV of CA$5,352, but EnergyPlus has a *lower IRR* compared to the IRR of 9.2 per cent of the original project. How can this happen?

Let's consider the NPV and IRR of only the extra investment. This has an NPV of CA$138 and an IRR of 8.3 per cent. The calculation is not included because it can be done in the exact same way as for the original project and for the EnergyPlus alternative. Now you can see what is going on: the NPV of EnergyPlus is the sum of the original project's NPV and the NPV of the extension: CA$5,490 = CA$5,352 + CA$138. However, EnergyPlus's IRR of 9.1 per cent is some kind of a weighted average of the original project's IRR of 9.2 per cent and of the extra investment's IRR of 8.3 per cent. So an extension with a positive NPV (that means: it should be accepted) and an IRR that is below the IRR of the 'base project' reduces the IRR. Therefore, the IRR should not be used for deciding on investments when it conflicts with the NPV.

Note that this effect does not only occur when the investment alternatives really consist of a 'base project' and possible extension. For any comparison of two projects, the cash flow differences can create the same effect: these differential cash flows can have a positive NPV but an IRR that is in between the IRRs of the two projects.

Exhibit 8.7 **NPV Analysis of EnergyPlus Investment Alternative**

	A	B	C	D	E	F
1	**Data input (all amonts in Canadian dollars, CA$)**					
2	New equipment cost, including installation and training	$ 220,000				
3	Salvage value of old equipment	-				
4	New equipment useful life	4	years			
5	Salvage value of new equipment	-				
6	Annual increase in contribution margin	30,000				
7	Annual energy cost savings	$ 46,800				
8	Income tax rate	40%				
9	Discount rate	8%				
10	**Investment analysis (in CA$)**			**End of year**		
11	Initial cash flows for year:	**0**	**1**	**2**	**3**	**4**
12	Investment cost	$ (220,000)				
13	Proceeds from old equipment	-				
14	Annual operating income items					
15	Increase in contribution margin		$ 30,000	$ 30,000	$ 30,000	$ 30,000
16	Energy cost savings		46,800	46,800	46,800	46,800
17	Depreciation expense		(55,000)	(55,000)	(55,000)	(55,000)
18	Change in operating income		21,800	21,800	21,800	21,800
19	Tax on change in income		(8,720)	(8,720)	(8,720)	(8,720)
20	After-tax change in operating income		13,080	13,080	13,080	13,080
21	Add back depreciation expense		55,000	55,000	55,000	55,000
22	After-tax operating cash flow	(220,000)	68,080	68,080	68,080	68,080
23						
24	Net cash flow	(220,000)	68,080	68,080	68,080	68,080
25	Present value factors	1.000	0.926	0.857	0.794	0.735
26	Present values of cash flows	(220,000)	$ 63,037	$ 58,368	$ 54,044	$ 50,041
27	Cumulative present values of cash flows	(220,000)	$ (156,963)	$ (98,595)	$ (44,551)	$ 5,490
28	Net present value	$ 5,490	Note: =SUM(B27:F27)			
29						
30	**Net present value using NPV**	**$ 5,490**	=NPV(B10,C25:F25)+B25			
31	**Internal rate of return using IRR**	**9.1%**	=IRR(B25:F25)			

Comparing investment alternatives on a yearly basis

Instead of looking at the total NPV of an investment, we can also calculate the worth of project per year. ShadeTree's investment project in new equipment generates an NPV of CA$5,352 in 4 years. What would this be per year? Just dividing the NPV by 4 is wrong. Instead, we are looking for a constant cash flow per year that in 4 years has the same NPV of CA$5,352.

If the cash flow is the same per period, the present value can be calculated at once without having to separately calculate the present value of the individual cash flows. A series of the same cash flows per period is called an **annuity**, and this usually refers to yearly cash flows. But the equation below is applicable to any period, as long as the cash flow is the same in every period:

$$\begin{aligned} N &= \textbf{Number of periods} \\ t &= \textbf{Any period between now (0) and the final period} \\ r &= \textbf{Discount rate per period} \\ A &= \textbf{Cash flow per period that is the same for every year } t \end{aligned}$$

$$NPV = \sum_{t=0}^{N} \frac{\textit{Cash flow period } t}{(1+r)^t} = A\left(\frac{(1+r)^N - 1}{r(1+r)^N}\right)$$

ShadeTree uses a discount rate of 8 per cent and the investment takes 4 years, so the present value factor for the annuity equals $(1.08^4 - 1) \div (0.08 \times (1.08)^4) = 3.3121$. That means

$$\begin{aligned} \text{CA\$5,352} &= A \times 3.3121, \text{ so} \\ A &= \text{CA\$5,352} \div 3.3121 = \text{CA\$1,616} \end{aligned}$$

You can easily verify this by comparing the NPV of the separate years. The present value factors are in Exhibit 8.5.

$$\begin{aligned} \text{NPV} &= \text{CA\$1,616} \times 0.926 + \text{CA\$1,616} \times 0.857 + \text{CA\$1,616} \times 0.794 + \text{CA\$1,616} \times 0.735 \\ &= \text{CA\$5,352} \end{aligned}$$

This annuity is, for example, useful when comparing mutually exclusive investment alternatives with a different number of periods.

8.1 Research Insight

Capital Budgeting Practices

Surveys in the USA, Canada and the UK indicate that DCF techniques are commonly used for investments. Use of DCF has increased over time, and large firms use NPV more than small firms.

A survey among firms in the Netherlands found that more sophisticated practices, such as decision trees, real options valuation, and Monte Carlo simulation, were used more by larger firms and when there was more financial uncertainty (about inflation, interest and exchange rates). More sophisticated capital budgeting practices augment rather than replace more traditional capital budgeting practices (such as DCF or payback). The study also found that particular industries (the financial services industry and the building, construction and utilities industries) used sophisticated techniques more than other industries.

Actual decision making about investments is difficult. Managers are only human and they have a tendency to underweight opportunity costs (the benefits the organization would get if it uses resources in another way) and to continue projects when more money has been invested (although only future cash flows should matter). Managers who know more about, for example, customers, processes and suppliers, may also be tempted to use this information advantage when applying for investment funds in the organization.

Sources: Arnold and Hatzapoulos (2000); Graham and Harvey (2001); Ryan and Ryan (2002); Verbeeten (2006); Haka (2007).

Application of DCF to Other Common Decisions

The decision-making logic of relevant cash flows and DCF are applicable to many types of business decisions that involve identifying and comparing alternative courses of action. We now consider several common business decisions. The DCF method itself is not different, but these examples show some important nuances that need to be considered in realistic decision models.

LO 3 Apply discounted cash flow methods to common investment decisions.

Replacement of Equipment

We first consider the common decision of equipment replacement. This can be triggered by the fact that the planned useful life of equipment is reached, or by unplanned events such as when extraordinary repairs are needed or when more efficient equipment becomes available on the market. Consider the decision faced by ShadeTree's Operations Manager Jill Hawkins discussed earlier. She considers three investment alternatives: keep the current truck and refurbish it, purchase a new diesel engine truck, or switch to a natural-gas powered truck. Cash inflows will be the same for all, so these are not included in the NPV calculation. The existing truck is sold if a new truck is bought.

The NPV calculation for a new diesel truck is shown in Exhibit 8.8, and it has a negative NPV of (CA$58,798). Note that there are no tax implications from selling the existing truck because its salvage value equals the book value. Note also that operating incomes are negative, so the resulting tax

Exhibit 8.8 NPV Example for Replacement of Equipment – Diesel Truck Alternative

	A	B	C	D	E	F
1	**Data input (all amounts in Canadian dollars, CA$)**					
2		**Old truck**	**Diesel**	**Natural gas**		
3	Refurbishment or new truck investment	$7,000	$85,000	$105,000		
4	Salvage value of truck, after useful life*	$-	$20,000	$5,000		
5	Truck useful life	4	4	4	years	
6	Salvage value of old truck*	$17,000				
7	Annual maintenance costs	$4,000	$2,600	$3,300		
8	Annual energy costs	$14,000	$11,000	$6,000		
9	Income tax rate	40%				
10	Discount rate	8.0%				
11	*Salvage values equal book values here, so there are no tax effects from the sale of a disposed asset.					
12	**Investment analysis (in CA$)**			**End of year**		
13	**Alternative: New diesel truck**	**0**	**1**	**2**	**3**	**4**
14	Initial cash flows					
15	New equipment	$(85,000)				
16	Proceeds from old equipment	17,000				
17		(68,000)				
18	Annual operating income items					
19	Maintenance costs		$(2,600)	$(2,600)	$(2,600)	$(2,600)
20	Energy costs		(11,000)	(11,000)	(11,000)	(11,000)
21	Depreciation expense		(16,250)	(16,250)	(16,250)	(16,250)
22	Change in operating income		(29,850)	(29,850)	(29,850)	(29,850)
23	Tax on change in income		11,940	11,940	11,940	11,940
24	After-tax change in operating income		(17,910)	(17,910)	(17,910)	(17,910)
25	Add back depreciation expense		16,250	16,250	16,250	16,250
26	After-tax operating cash flow		(1,660)	(1,660)	(1,660)	(1,660)
27	Disinvestment cash flows					$20,000
28	Net cash flow	(68,000)	(1,660)	(1,660)	(1,660)	18,340
29	Present value factors	1.000	0.926	0.857	0.794	0.735
30	Present values of cash flows	(68,000)	$(1,537)	$(1,423)	$(1,318)	$13,480
31	Net present value	$(58,798)				

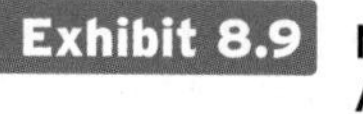

Exhibit 8.9 **NPV Example for Replacement of Equipment – Natural Gas and Current Truck Alternatives**

	A	B	C	D	E	F
32	**Alternative: Natural gas truck**					
33	Initial cash flows					
34	New equipment	$(105,000)				
35	Proceeds from old equipment	17,000				
36		(88,000)				
37	Annual operating income items					
38	Maintenance costs		$(3,300)	$(3,300)	$(3,300)	$(3,300)
39	Energy costs		(6,000)	(6,000)	(6,000)	(6,000)
40	Depreciation expense		(25,000)	(25,000)	(25,000)	(25,000)
41	Change in operating income		(34,300)	(34,300)	(34,300)	(34,300)
42	Tax on change in income		13,720	13,720	13,720	13,720
43	After-tax change in operating income		(20,580)	(20,580)	(20,580)	(20,580)
44	Add back depreciation expense		25,000	25,000	25,000	25,000
45	After-tax operating cash flow		4,420	4,420	4,420	4,420
46	Disinvestment cash flows					$5,000
47	Net cash flow	(88,000)	4,420	4,420	4,420	9,420
48	Present value factors	1.000	0.926	0.857	0.794	0.735
49	Present values of cash flows	(88,000)	$4,093	$3,789	$3,509	$6,924
50	Net present value	$(69,685)				
51	**Alternative: Current truck**					
52	Investment cash flows					
53	Refurbishment	$(7,000)				
54	Proceeds from old equipment	-				
55		(7,000)				
56	Annual operating income items					
57	Maintenance costs		$(4,000)	$(4,000)	$(4,000)	$(4,000)
58	Energy costs		(14,000)	(14,000)	(14,000)	(14,000)
59	Depreciation expense		(1,750)	(1,750)	(1,750)	(1,750)
60	Change in operating income		(19,750)	(19,750)	(19,750)	(19,750)
61	Tax on change in income		7,900	7,900	7,900	7,900
62	After-tax change in operating income		(11,850)	(11,850)	(11,850)	(11,850)
63	Add back depreciation expense		1,750	1,750	1,750	1,750
64	After-tax operating cash flow		(10,100)	(10,100)	(10,100)	(10,100)
65	Disinvestment cash flows					$-
66	Net cash flow	(7,000)	(10,100)	(10,100)	(10,100)	(10,100)
67	Present value factors	1.000	0.926	0.857	0.794	0.735
68	Present values of cash flows	(7,000)	$(9,352)	$(8,659)	$(8,018)	$(7,424)
69	Net present value	$(40,452)				

is modelled as a tax income, because it is assumed that operating loss on this investment reduces the organization's total taxes.

The NPV calculation for the other two alternatives is show in Exhibit 8.9, and these are also negative (CA$69,685) and (CA$40,452). The NPVs of the three investment alternatives are negative, because only cash outflows are included in the financial model. This is consistent with the principle that only future differences matter, and the cash inflows are the same for these three replacement alternatives. Given that ShadeTree needs the delivery truck, the alternative to refurbish and keep the existing truck has the highest NPV and should be preferred when looking strictly at financial consequences.

Outsourcing or Make-or-Buy Decision

Outsourcing is acquiring goods or services from an outside provider, and so an outsourcing or **make-or-buy decision** is any decision an organization makes about acquiring goods or services internally or externally. A restaurant that uses its own ingredients to prepare meals from scratch has chosen the 'make' alternative; one that serves meals from frozen entrées acquired from suppliers has chosen the 'buy' alternative. An electronics firm that assembles its own circuit boards 'makes', whereas one that contracts with a specialized supplier for the assembly of circuit boards 'buys'.

The outsourcing or make-or-buy decision is part of a company's value-chain strategy. Some companies meet their goals by performing all processes of the value chain to control all activities that lead to the final product or service. Others prefer to rely on outsiders for some inputs and specialize in only certain steps of the total process. Outsourcing is one of the fastest-growing business activities because many firms are choosing to concentrate on their core activities, leaving other peripheral tasks to organizations with expertise in performing them. An equipment manufacturer, for example, might outsource all printing activities to **Fuji Xerox** (in Asia) or **FedEx Kinko** (in the USA). Whether to rely on outsiders for a substantial amount of goods and services depends on relevant cost comparisons and other factors that are not so easily quantified, such as suppliers' dependability and quality.

ShadeTree's outsourcing

To analyse the outsourcing decision with our decision-making framework, let's look at ShadeTree's warehousing activities. The organization owns a warehouse in Toronto from where stores in Canada are supplied. A logistics company takes care of the distribution from this warehouse to the stores. ShadeTree considers also outsourcing the warehousing activities to the same logistics company. One reason is that ShadeTree suspects that its own costs per pallet may be higher than the rate a specialized logistics company would charge. Another reason is that the current warehouse would have to be expanded to accommodate ShadeTree's growth. So management considers whether they should do warehousing at all, especially if this now would require further investments.

Exhibit 8.10 shows project information and the NPV calculation for the outsourcing alternative. If ShadeTree outsources, it can sell the current warehouse for CA$300,000, which is far above the

Exhibit 8.10 **NPV Example for Outsourcing**

	A	B	C	D	E	F	G
1	**Data input (all amounts in Canadian dollars, CA$)**						
2	Book value of old warehouse and equipment	$50,000					
3	Income tax rate	40%					
4	Discount rate	8.0%					
5		**Outsource**	**Expand**				
6	Salvage value of old warehouse and equipment	$300,000					
7	Warehouse and equipment investment	$-	$650,000				
8	Salvage value after 5 years	$-	$400,000				
9	Project horizon	5	5	years			
10	Annual labor and other operating costs	$-	$108,000				
11	Annual energy costs	$-	$18,000				
12	Monthly outsourced storage cost per pallet	$9.85					
13	Pallets positions used on average	3,600					
14	**Investment analysis (in CA$)**			**End of year**			
15	**Alternative: Outsource**	**0**	**1**	**2**	**3**	**4**	**5**
16	Initial cash flows						
17	Proceeds from selling existing assets	$300,000					
18	Gain on sale above book value	250,000					
19	Tax effects	(100,000)					
20	Annual operating income items						
21	Outsourcing costs		$(425,520)	$(425,520)	$(425,520)	$(425,520)	$(425,520)
22	Depreciation expense		-	-	-	-	-
23	Change in operating income		(425,520)	(425,520)	(425,520)	(425,520)	(425,520)
24	Tax on change in income		170,208	170,208	170,208	170,208	170,208
25	After-tax change in operating income		(255,312)	(255,312)	(255,312)	(255,312)	(255,312)
26	Add back depreciation expense		-	-	-	-	-
27	After-tax operating cash flow		(255,312)	(255,312)	(255,312)	(255,312)	(255,312)
28	Disinvestment cash flows						$-
29	Net cash flow	200,000	(255,312)	(255,312)	(255,312)	(255,312)	(255,312)
30	Present value factors	1.000	0.926	0.857	0.794	0.735	0.681
31	Present values of cash flows	200,000	$(236,400)	$(218,889)	$(202,675)	$(187,662)	$(173,761)
32	Net present value	$(645,626)					

Exhibit 8.11 NPV Example for Outsourcing – Expand and Make Alternative

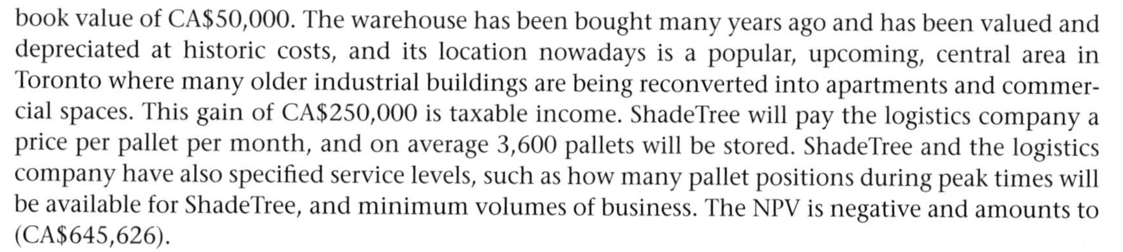

	A	B	C	D	E	F	G
33	**Alternative: Expand**						
34	Initial cash flows						
35	New construction and equipment	$(650,000)					
36	Annual operating income items						
37	Labour costs		$(108,000)	$(108,000)	$(108,000)	$(108,000)	$(108,000)
38	Energy costs		(18,000)	(18,000)	(18,000)	(18,000)	(18,000)
39	Depreciation expense		(60,000)	(60,000)	(60,000)	(60,000)	(60,000)
40	Change in operating income		(186,000)	(186,000)	(186,000)	(186,000)	(186,000)
41	Tax on change in income		74,400	74,400	74,400	74,400	74,400
42	After-tax change in operating income		(111,600)	(111,600)	(111,600)	(111,600)	(111,600)
43	Add back depreciation expense		60,000	60,000	60,000	60,000	60,000
44	After-tax operating cash flow		(51,600)	(51,600)	(51,600)	(51,600)	(51,600)
45	Disinvestment cash flows						$400,000
46	Net cash flow	(650,000)	(51,600)	(51,600)	(51,600)	(51,600)	348,400
47	Present value factors	1.000	0.926	0.857	0.794	0.735	0.681
48	Present values of cash flows	(650,000)	$(47,778)	$(44,239)	$(40,962)	$(37,928)	$237,115
49	Net present value	$(820,906)					

book value of CA$50,000. The warehouse has been bought many years ago and has been valued and depreciated at historic costs, and its location nowadays is a popular, upcoming, central area in Toronto where many older industrial buildings are being reconverted into apartments and commercial spaces. This gain of CA$250,000 is taxable income. ShadeTree will pay the logistics company a price per pallet per month, and on average 3,600 pallets will be stored. ShadeTree and the logistics company have also specified service levels, such as how many pallet positions during peak times will be available for ShadeTree, and minimum volumes of business. The NPV is negative and amounts to (CA$645,626).

The NPV calculation for the other investment alternative 'Expand and make' is shown in Exhibit 8.11. If ShadeTree continues its warehousing activities, it will have to expand the warehouse. Construction can start quickly, because there is planning permission and they already found a builder. Operating costs are estimated based on current costs. The NPV is negative and comes to (CA$820,906).

Note that the project horizon in both calculations is 5 years. This goes back to the question for how long into the future the alternatives should be compared. How long is ShadeTree realistically committed to a chosen decision alternative? In other words: when will this decision come up again? The contract with the logistics company is for two years. But that's not a very realistic horizon, because if ShadeTree keeps and expands its own warehouse, this will not be for just two years. ShadeTree's managers want to make a decision for at least the next 5 years.

At the end of this horizon, ShadeTree can still sell its warehouse, and the estimated value 5 years from today is CA$400,000. It is relevant to consider this! It does not mean that the company now decides that it certainly will sell the warehouse 5 years from now, but this represents cash flows that must be included to make the decision alternatives comparable. If ShadeTree leaves this out, a significant benefit of the alternative 'Make and expand' would be forgotten. ShadeTree will depreciate the warehouse from a book value of CA$50,000 + CA$650,000 = CA$700,000 down to CA$400,000 after 5 years (hence, the annual depreciation expense of CA$60,000), so there are no tax effects from this sale of the warehouse 5 years from now.

Comparing both investment alternatives, it is clear that in this example Outsource has the least negative NPV and is therefore more economical than Expand and make. Only operational cash outflows are considered here and not the cash inflows, because the cash inflows are the same for both alternatives.

Pitfalls of outsourcing

Although many organizations reduce operating costs by outsourcing processes, they often find that other factors can affect the decision to retain or outsource. Analysts assume that freed-up resources will be either saved or applied to higher valued activities, but does this happen? If not, the organization now pays for the outsourced activities and for resources that are idle or assigned to less valued activities – with no substantial improvements. Another assumption is that outsourced activities are of at least as high quality as the replaced activities. If not, the organization might save operating costs in the short run but end up paying more to correct quality shortfalls.

Outsourcing often is sold on the promise of access to better knowledge and technology from an external provider who specializes in certain activities. If in fact the external provider is not more advanced, the organization might pay the provider to learn how to provide better services to others or might not experience the promised improvements.

Outsourcing activities that interact with customers are particularly critical. It is important to consider that customers would not be alienated when they realize they are not dealing with the company that sold them the products. Companies that outsource processes such as billing and post-sales service also want to make sure they will not lose information from valuable customer contacts, such as their changing needs. Finally, organizations need to ensure that the outsourcing contracts and incentives are compatible with control of sensitive information and value-adding processes.

Outsourcing companies claim that they have 'firewalls' between the information provided by different customers, but a company would have little satisfaction in winning a lawsuit for breach of privacy if the outsourcing company leaked key customer or product information to a competitor. The damage could be so great that legal fees and lost opportunities would overwhelm any monetary settlement. Organizations also must be able to ensure that the outsource provider is meeting contractual obligations; therefore, outsourcing performance must be auditable, and the company must have recourse if obligations are not met.

Add or Drop a Product, Service or Business Unit

One of the most difficult decisions managers make concerns adding or dropping a product, service or business unit. These are difficult decisions because they usually have major effects on the organization's strategy and on its stakeholders. Consequently, managers do not make them lightly.

The term 'business unit' can refer to a product, a market territory, a department, a warehouse, or just about any other business segment imaginable. Products that were formerly profitable might be losing market share to newer goods and no longer adequately cover costs. On the other hand, a company can add a business unit to serve new product markets or geographic regions. In nearly all of these cases, managers must make difficult trade-offs between financial and non-financial criteria.

Making these decisions is not easy, but managers can feel comfortable that they have made them correctly by following the decision-making framework. Note that no analysis of whether to drop or add a business unit is complete without considering the status quo: the current net benefits from the resources being used by the potentially added or dropped unit. For example, computing how much can be saved by dropping an unprofitable business unit is not sufficient, managers must also consider whether the recovered resources can be used more profitably. At a minimum, for example, ShadeTree could sell its resources and invest the proceeds in low-risk, marketable securities, but this would not meet its organizational goals.

To illustrate the proper handling of these decisions, let's analyse how ShadeTree decided whether to close a large store in Montreal. This stored opened 2 years ago in a newly constructed mall close to the city's downtown area and on the shore of the river. ShadeTree signed a 5-year renting contract for a commercial space in the mall, which cannot be cancelled prematurely. The company conducted an expensive remodelling of this space and ordered custom-made furniture to make it one of its newest and best stores. These costs are capitalized and depreciated over the same 5-year period.

However, business in the new mall is not going that well, and the ShadeTree's store is also performing below expectations that were outlined in the initial business plan underlying the original investment decision. Exhibit 8.12 shows that the status quo of this operation will generate an annual loss of CA$58,000, which indicates that it does not contribute to the organization's financial success. Something will need to be done. A relevant issue is whether ShadeTree can improve overall profitability (eliminate the loss) by closing the store.

Relevant cash flows

The NPV calculation for closing the store is presented in Exhibit 8.13. The contribution margin falls back to CA$0, which shows that for now ShadeTree does not have an alternative business use for the

Exhibit 8.12 **NPV Example for Continuing the Store**

	A	B	C	D	E
1	**Data input (all amounts in Canadian dollars, CA$)**				
2		**Continue**	**Close**		
3	Book value store assets	$120,000			
4	Salvage value store assets	$-	$20,000		
5	Salvage value after 3 more years	$-	$-		
6	Contribution margin	$254,000	$-		
7	Annual store rent	$24,000	$24,000		
8	Annual labour costs store manager	$65,000	$65,000		
9	Annual other labour and operating costs	$165,000	$-		
10	Central services	$18,000	$18,000		
11	Income tax rate	40%			
12	Discount rate	8.0%			
13	**Investment analysis (in CA$)**			**End of year**	
14	**Alternative: Continue**	**0**	**1**	**2**	**3**
15	Initial cash flows	$-			
16	Annual operating income items				
17	Contribution margin		$254,000	$254,000	$254,000
18	Store rent		(24,000)	(24,000)	(24,000)
19	Labour costs store manager		(65,000)	(65,000)	(65,000)
20	Other operating costs		(165,000)	(165,000)	(165,000)
21	Central services		(18,000)	(18,000)	(18,000)
22	Depreciation expense		(40,000)	(40,000)	(40,000)
23	Change in operating income		(58,000)	(58,000)	(58,000)
24	Tax on change in income		23,200	23,200	23,200
25	After-tax change in operating income		(34,800)	(34,800)	(34,800)
26	Add back depreciation expense		40,000	40,000	40,000
27	After-tax operating cash flow		5,200	5,200	5,200
28	Disinvestment cash flows				$-
29	Net cash flow	-	5,200	5,200	5,200
30	Present value factors	1.000	0.926	0.857	0.794
31	Present values of cash flows	-	$4,815	$4,458	$4,128
32	Net present value	$13,401			

Exhibit 8.13 **NPV Example for Closing the Store**

	A	B	C	D	E
34	**Alternative: Close**				
35	Initial cash flows				
36	Proceeeds from selling existing assets	$20,000			
37	Gain or loss on sale of existing assets	(100,000)			
38	Tax effects	40,000			
39	Annual operating income items				
40	Contribution margin		$-	$-	$-
41	Store rent		(24,000)	(24,000)	(24,000)
42	Labour costs store manager		(65,000)	(65,000)	(65,000)
43	Other operating costs		-	-	-
44	Central services		(18,000)	(18,000)	(18,000)
45	Depreciation expense		-	-	-
46	Change in operating income		(107,000)	(107,000)	(107,000)
47	Tax on change in income		42,800	42,800	42,800
48	After-tax change in operating income		(64,200)	(64,200)	(64,200)
49	Add back depreciation expense		-	-	-
50	After-tax operating cash flow		(64,200)	(64,200)	(64,200)
51					
52	Net cash flow	60,000	(64,200)	(64,200)	(64,200)
53	Present value factors	1.000	0.926	0.857	0.794
54	Present values of cash flows	60,000	$(59,444)	$(55,041)	$(50,964)
55	Net present value	$(105,450)			

resources that can be recovered by closing the store operation. Thus, it shows no revenues if the store is closed. Let's leave this for now, but clearly we need to revisit this item.

If the store is closed, employment of most staff can be terminated, because these are part-time workers with temporary contracts. Yet, the store manager has a fixed contract, and ShadeTree's policy is to not fire employees with fixed contracts. Many organizations, profit-seeking firms included, have similar employment commitments and lay off employees only as a last resort. Thus, employee wages and salaries of the operation are committed facility-level costs to the organization and closing often will not result in these employee-related cost reductions.

If the store is closed, the furniture and most equipment has a very low salvage value. Only the expensive Italian coffee machine that is only 2 years old has a considerable salvage value, and the assets can be sold for CA$20,000. However, the book value of all the furniture and equipment is CA$120,000.

The store makes use of centrally supplied services, such as payroll, insurance, training, maintenance and marketing. Although the closed operation will not use central services, closing it will not reduce ShadeTree's capability (e.g., administrative personnel) to provide those services. The rest of the organization will bear these costs that also will not be saved.

The analysis shows keeping the store open provides an NPV equal to CA$13,401. This is positive despite the operating loss, because the NPV only includes the future cash flows. The initial investment is now a sunk cost. Closing the store provides a negative NPV equal to (CA$105,540). Given our assumptions, it is now better to keep the store open. While the current operations would not have warranted the original investment, that is not relevant anymore. At this point in time, looking at future cash flows, the NPV of closing the store is inferior, because selling the assets generates not much cash and quite a few cash flows are unavoidable in the future.

Unfinished business

Clearly, Exhibits 8.12 and 8.13 show that the analysis of the decision to close the store is not finished. Simply closing it (doing nothing else) would save CA$165,000 + 40,000 = CA$205,000 in annual costs but also would forgo CA$254,000 in contribution margin, thus increasing the annual operating loss by CA$49,000. The annual loss would go from (CA$58,000) to (CA$107,000). Surely this do-nothing alternative does not advance ShadeTree's goals of having profitable operations. What must ShadeTree's managers do, and what is the magnitude of the problem?

To complete the data needed for the analysis, ShadeTree must identify and analyse alternative uses of its recovered resources – in particular the commercial space and the employee resource of the store manager – in a manner similar to that shown previously in Exhibits 8.12 and 8.13. The objective of this analysis is to find the best alternative that operates profitably. We have made this point before: it all starts with finding good alternatives; otherwise it is not very useful to choose the 'best' alternative from a set of inferior alternatives. In fact, ShadeTree did find such an alternative (see You're the Decision Maker 8.1).

It is important to note that the presentation format of these data can be applied to any organization's decision making about adding or dropping a business unit, but the specifics of which benefits and costs might or might not be saved or avoided will differ across organizations.

8.1 You're the Decision Maker

Further Analysis of Dropping a Business

Complete the analysis in Exhibit 8.12 by considering the changes predicted for the following two alternatives for the store operations.

a. Replace the store manager by another, more experienced manager who can run the store more efficiently, lowering the annual operating costs to CA$150,000, and who will increase sales and the contribution margin to CA$335,000 per year. This manager receives a higher salary of CA$75,000.

b. The new manager proposes to invest in kitchen equipment and display units so the store can offer a greater variety of food items. The investment is $24,000 with no residual value after 3 years, and the contribution margin will increase to CA$355,000 per year.

(Solutions begin on page 411.)

Choice of the Best Alternative Using Both Financial and Non-financial Information

LO 4
Understand different ways of using both financial and non-financial information for investment decisions.

A comparison of quantified factors that reduce to a single profit or cost-reduction number might not make the best alternative obvious. Other factors can be just as (or more) important to decision making. To clarify the importance of non-financial information, consider how managers can put a value on the sum of the non-financial factors. For example, suppose a cost management analyst gives ShadeTree's managers the numerical analysis of the delivery truck replacement, provided in Exhibit 8.8 and 8.9. This analysis shows that refurbishing the old truck is the most economical alternative, because it gives an NPV that is CA$18,347 better than the alternative of buying a new diesel truck and CA$29,233 better than the alternative of a natural-gas powered truck.

However, there are several disadvantages of refurbishing the old truck which have not been considered thus far. These are also shown in Exhibit 8.1 at the beginning of this chapter. (1) The refurbished truck uses more diesel than a new diesel truck, which is partly included in the NPV analysis through lower energy costs, but it also means that the refurbished truck emits much more CO_2 and other gases that are bad for the environment. (2) The natural-gas powered truck is more environmentally friendly than the new diesel truck and much more environmentally friendly than the refurbished diesel. Natural gas is cost effective, clean-burning and abundant, but only the lower energy cost is part of the NPV analysis. (3) ShadeTree will not learn anything new from operating either an old or new diesel truck, but investing in a natural-gas powered truck will allow ShadeTree to gain experience with alternative fuel vehicles. Such vehicles may become much more important in ShadeTree's future strategy, so it could be good to start experimenting with using a natural-gas powered truck.

How important are these non-financial factors to ShadeTree's managers? If they decide to buy a new diesel truck, the improved environmental performance must be worth at least CA$18,347 to the organization and its stakeholders. The CA$18,347 given up by not selecting a new diesel truck is the opportunity cost of the decision, or the amount forgone by choosing one mutually exclusive alternative or opportunity over another. Similarly, if they decide to buy the natural-gas powered truck, the better environmental performance plus the learning opportunities must be worth at least CA$29,233 to the organization and its stakeholders. Or put differently, the non-financial benefits of the natural-gas powered truck compared to a new diesel truck must be worth at least CA$10,887 (which is the difference between the NPVs of these alternatives of CA$69,685 and CA$58,798).

Formal methods exist for using financial and non-financial information together. Decision alternatives are described on the basis of several factors (also called 'criteria' or 'attributes'). Recall from Chapter 1 that *financial factors* have a monetary unit of measurement, such as euros, dollars, rupees, pounds or any other currency. *Quantitative, non-financial factors* have a non-monetary but still quantitative unit of measurement. For example, emissions of CO_2 and other gases can be expressed in numbers, so this is quantitative information. *Qualitative, non-financial factors* are expressed in words instead of numbers, such as the learning opportunities that an alternative fuel vehicle will provide. Sometimes a non-financial factor is can be translated into a financial factor. For example, energy use will first be expressed as litres of diesel per 100 kilometres, and with some more information (the price of a litre of diesel, and kilometres per year) the energy use can be translated into the annual energy costs.

The key issue is how to combine the diverse factors in order to understand what is the 'overall' best alternative. It is easy if all factors are financial. Then all factors are incorporated in the NPV calculation and the best investment alternative is simply the one with the highest NPV. But this is not realistic for many investment decisions. It is also easy if one decision alternative is superior on *all* financial and non-financial factors. However, it is difficult if one alternative is better on some factors while another alternative is better on other factors. Different factors lead to different conclusions. For example, the refurbished diesel truck is preferred when looking at the NPV, but the natural-gas powered truck is preferred when looking at environmental performance. Such differences cannot be compared because their measurement units are incommensurable. In other words, this involves **multi-criteria decision-making**: alternatives differ on several criteria, typically financial as well as nonfinancial criteria, which are conflicting and have different units of measurement.

Formal methods for multi-criteria decision making fall into two categories: compensatory and non-compensatory methods.[5] The basic principle of the **compensatory methods** is that the values for all criteria must be converted into a common measurement scale. For example, ShadeTree's managers may give points for environmental performance, for learning, and for financial performance (NPV) to each alternative and compare the three alternatives on the basis of these total points. Thus, these methods involve a single dimension, and good performance on one criterion can compensate for bad performance on another criterion. Sometimes the NPV is not included this way, and the results of the multi-criteria decision-making method are shown separately from the NPVs, for example in a diagram with the NPV on one axis and the overall non-financial result on another axis.

Non-compensatory methods look in more detail at the separate criteria. These methods do not involve a single dimension, and good performance on one criterion cannot compensate for bad performance on another criterion. These methods are often most helpful in eliminating inferior alternatives from the analysis. For example, ShadeTree may define certain minimum standards for the environmental performance of its trucks. If the refurbished diesel truck would not meet these requirements, this investment alternative would be rejected.

Weighing trade-offs between quantitative and qualitative costs and benefits and considering opportunity costs in making decisions are hallmarks of management decision making. Managers' skill, experience, judgement, and ethical standards are crucial in making such difficult choices. Although the natural-gas powered truck has an unfavourable NPV compared to both diesel alternatives, we would not be surprised if ShadeTree chooses the natural-gas powered truck.

Section II: Strategic Investment Decisions

This section is about strategic investment decisions. Everything said in Section I also applies to strategic investment decisions, but there is more. First we consider that organizations need to take into account relevant future uncontrollable factors and actions of competitors for modelling strategic investments. Then we consider the impact of flexibility for modelling strategic investments. Flexibility means that management can take decisions about a strategic investment in stages and modify an investment as time and information unfold. Let's return to the central Europe strategic investment project that James Paige, ShadeTree's President and CEO, mentioned in his note to Judy Collins, CFO, at the start of this chapter.

Strategic Investments

LO 5
Understand the nature of strategic investment decisions.

A **strategic investment** is a choice among alternative courses of action and the allocation of resources to those alternatives most likely to succeed after anticipating (1) changes in *natural, social, and economic conditions* and (2) *actions of competitors*. In contrast, routine decisions are choices made under continuing conditions and are unrelated to competitors' actions. ShadeTree Roasters' proposed expansion of operations to central Europe is a strategic investment because the company must consider *both changes in the emerging economy of the region* and *actions that its competitors might take to serve the same market.*

If an organization has kept good records on past investment decisions, analysts might learn why some alternative investments were chosen but others were not. These lessons about the effects of uncontrollable events and past actions can be applied to future investment decisions.

ShadeTree Roasters must consider relevant future uncontrollable factors and competitors' actions because they can influence the future growth of the central European coffee and tea market and ShadeTree's market share. These factors in turn will affect ShadeTree's sales, costs and profits. We assume that ShadeTree cannot control the total market size and market growth, but its and competitors' actions do affect ShadeTree's market share.

8.2 Cost Management in Practice

Strategic Investments in China and India

The growth of China and India creates many opportunities for global strategic investments, especially if companies are able to make use of what both countries have to offer. Relative strengths of India are its capital market, protection of property rights and the availability of large numbers of technically sophisticated, English-speaking university graduates. Comparatively, China is strong in terms of infrastructure, welcoming foreign investments and efficient government. Companies can use these complementarities for making strategic investments.

For example, **Mahindra & Mahindra**, the Indian tractor and automobile maker, set up a joint venture with the Nanchang city government. M&M's low powered tractors are ideal in India and China, and these are designed and engineered at its facilities in India, while its Chinese company manufactures these. And the Chinese company **Huawei** invested in R&D centres in Bangalore, India, which develop software solutions for communication networks. **GE Healthcare**, for a high-end radiology system, developed particular software and hardware components in Bangalore and allocated part of the hardware manufacturing and assembly to Beijing. The ability to set up parallel groups of highly skilled engineering talent in both countries increased the efficiency of product development.

Source: Khanna (2007).

Uncontrollable External Factors

Making a successful investment decision depends on anticipating such factors as changes in climate, business cycles, consumers' income, tastes and preferences, and changes in political/legal conditions. Furthermore, choosing investments includes planning for actions if these external factors turn out to be much better or worse than expected. These factors cannot be controlled by individuals, but planning allows identifying them, assessing their impacts and developing contingency plans. Farmers, for example, decide to plant specific commodity crops such as corn or coffee after predicting favourable weather and market conditions. Many also purchase crop insurance as protection against unfavourable environmental events. They might have contingency plans, such as leasing their land or water rights to others if the weather turns unexpectedly bad. Ski resorts that invest in improvements during the summer off-season make similar decisions. Health care companies that invest in assisted-living care and nursing homes anticipate growing demand for these services from an ageing population. ShadeTree Roasters Inc., anticipates that demand for coffee and tea will grow in the emerging economies of central Europe. Furthermore, ShadeTree believes that its services and products will add value beyond what is currently available while still respecting local culture and traditions.[6]

Whether an individual or organization makes the right investment decisions can reflect some element of chance or luck, but consistent success usually reflects careful gathering and evaluation of relevant information. Consistent success is also often the result of preparing for unexpected external events that could be much better or worse than expected. Developing thorough and relevant information for investment decisions is also known as conducting a *due diligence* investigation. Investigating an investment with **due diligence** is exercising all reasonable care to identify potential problems and opportunities of a proposed investment. The most common sources of problems are legal and environmental liabilities that an organization might inherit unknowingly when purchasing an existing business or property. Operating in a different legal environment might affect the nature of contracts, environmental responsibilities and employee obligations in unforeseen ways. Likewise, a proposed investment might offer unexpected benefits by complementing current operations or opening unexpected opportunities.

We now consider the types of external information that ShadeTree Roasters has gathered and evaluated to support its decision whether to expand its operations to central Europe.

Information about External Events

Decisions have to be made, but no organization or individual has a crystal ball to forecast the future business environment. The premise of cost management, indeed of all business study, is

Exhibit 8.14 **Internal and External Sources of Information**

Organization's financial records	Interviews with knowledgeable individuals (company personnel and consultants)	Publicly available information
Past financial records have limited usefulness for predicting future events and probabilities if the organization has never operated in a similar environment.	Company personnel who can think creatively might identify future events. Experienced consultants can also be excellent sources of future events and knowledge of organizations' experiences. Groups of experienced consultants and company personnel can estimate probabilities, but individuals are notoriously weak at this task.	News, government, foundation, and industry analyses can be excellent sources of future events and probabilities. Descriptions of other organizations' experiences can be helpful.

that well-planned and modelled decisions are consistently better than random choices or choices based on hunches. As discussed in earlier chapters, decisions should be based on relevant information, which is information about future costs and benefits that differ among alternatives. Broadly speaking, relevant external information includes alternative, uncontrollable, and uncertain future events and the likelihood or odds that future events will occur.[7] Cost management analysts at ShadeTree Roasters identified the sources and potential usefulness of these sources shown in Exhibit 8.14. These sources generate information about the range of possible uncontrollable events and how likely they are to occur.

Identification of Uncontrollable Future Events

Identifying possible future events, such as changes in weather or social conditions, depends on learning from past experience, understanding current trends and anticipating future changes that depart from the past. Unless an organization is very large and operating in diverse conditions, most organizations' past financial records generally are of little use in identifying future events. Usually a company's financial records reflect one set of decisions made and only one set of uncontrollable events that occurred. If an organization has kept careful records of past expectations of possible events, the list of possibilities might be a useful starting point to generate a new list. However, analysts might rely too much on the old list and might not consider future possibilities that are more relevant. Therefore, generating a new list can be beneficial.

Organizations often use formal, group brainstorming methods (anonymous or face to face), decision-support software, or lower-tech meetings to identify the range of future events. Using a group to combine individual knowledge and critical thinking can be even more effective than relying on a very knowledgeable individual. Organizations sometimes use skilled consultants to manage the brainstorming efforts or to augment the knowledge necessary to identify future events.

Government agencies, foundations, industry associations and news organizations also can be valuable sources of analyses of past and possible future events. An added benefit of these analyses is that they are often free of charge and can be objective. Evaluating the accuracy and objectivity of these analyses and applying their findings, however, requires expertise that the organization might not have and might justify the use of knowledgeable consultants.

ShadeTree Roasters' managers used consulting services, external reports and consultant-managed brainstorming sessions that identified the following possible future events relevant to the decision to invest in central European operations.

- *Natural events.* Because ShadeTree's primary products and services are based on agricultural products, natural events, such as climate change or plant diseases, can affect the company's future operations and profitability. However, these factors affect all of the company's operations but do not affect the proposed investment relative to alternative investments in the coffee and tea business. ShadeTree is well aware of environmental change and supports research to improve the biological diversity of coffee and tea plants that might protect its future supplies. However, major climatic or biological changes could cause the company to rethink its entire business. Indeed, this chapter's approach to investment decision making could be used to completely reorient the business, but that is beyond the scope of our discussion. We assume that future natural events affect all of ShadeTree's global business equally and that the chance of a general catastrophe is small.

- *Economic events.* Per capita income in central Europe is expected to grow at an above average rate, generating more leisure time and disposable income, which should create above average growth in demand for premium coffees and teas. The social aspects of coffee and tea drinking will continue to be important in the region. Both expected developments support ShadeTree Roasters' plan to open stores in central Europe. Coffee and tea prices fluctuate, but ShadeTree has made long-term purchase commitments with growers' co-operatives to lock in current prices. ShadeTree operates in foreign countries, and the company has made currency investments, which are a form of insurance to protect against currency fluctuations.[8] Because many central European countries have joined or soon will join the European Union, ShadeTree will conduct the new regional business in euros (€).
- *Social, political, and legal events.* Population, which drives demand, is expected to mirror the rest of Europe's relatively low rate of growth. Analysts expect the influences of West European and North American culture to grow, but strong preferences for regional drinks and ambiance are also expected. The region's political climate is expected to improve for private businesses that invest regionally and hire local employees through attractive tax incentives. Most coffees and teas are grown in developing countries with histories of political, economic and legal instability. Instability could affect the company's supply source of green coffee and tea. To protect its sources and to meet its social responsibility goals, ShadeTree's long-term purchase agreements are with local co-operatives that foster environmentally and socially conscious agricultural and business practices (also known as *fair trade* practices). These agreements result in somewhat higher costs than those of some competitors, but ShadeTree expects that its business practices will resonate with Europeans' environmental and social concerns and will be a major competitive advantage for the company.

ShadeTree Roasters' analysts used the current measure of the central European non-grocery coffee and tea market size (total annual sales) of €50 million from industry and governmental analyses. The analysts applied all of the environmental information to estimate the annual sales growth of coffee and tea. Although each environmental event can have an independent effect on demand and could be considered separately, for simplicity we consider only the aggregate impact of future events on estimates of central Europe's annual market growth. ShadeTree Roasters' analysts provided three estimates of future coffee and tea market annual growth as follows:

Central Europe coffee and tea estimates	Possible annual market growth estimates (per cent)
High estimate	8%
Medium estimate	4
Low estimate	2

Expected Value Analysis

A central question confronting investment decision makers is: how likely are the relevant future events? Although decision making should focus on the most likely events, decisions should also consider less likely but catastrophic events. The key to using this type of information is not to over-weight unlikely events. For example, some people fear commercial flying and drive instead, although the odds of being in a car accident far exceed the odds of being in a commercial aeroplane crash. Good reasons might exist to drive rather than fly in certain cases, but fear of flying commercially is not justified by experience.

Three approaches to modelling the effects of likely future events include sensitivity analysis, scenario analysis and expected value analysis.

- *Sensitivity analysis* forecasts the effects of a likely change in *each* future relevant event on investment outcomes. Factors that have the most potential impact on outcomes deserve the most attention. If one or more uncontrollable factors seem likely to cause disastrous outcomes, managers might reject the investment.
- *Scenario analysis* forecasts the effects of likely *combinations* of future events on investment outcomes. Commonly considered scenarios include the most likely, best- and worst-case scenarios. If the most likely case scenario is favourable and if the worst-case scenario is neither a disaster nor judged to be very likely, managers probably would approve the investment.
- **Expected value analysis** summarizes the combined effects of relevant future events on decision outcomes, weighted by the probabilities or odds that the events will occur. Both sensitivity and scenario analyses are very popular approaches to modelling future events for investment decisions, particularly when explicit odds of future events cannot be estimated.

Because Chapter 7 covers sensitivity and scenario analyses in detail, this chapter explains and applies only expected value analysis to modelling future events relevant to strategic investment decisions. All three analyses can be applied to these decisions.

The **expected value** of a future event is the measure of each possible outcome weighted or multiplied by its probability of occurrence. ShadeTree Roasters' analysts believe that the probabilities of future annual market growth can be predicted from past experience in the region. The analysts have used government, industry and their own analyses to estimate the probabilities of market growth as follows:

Relevant future event	Probability of occurrence
Annual market growth = 8%	30%
Annual market growth = 4	40
Annual market growth = 2	30
Total probability	100%

Observe that the probabilities associated with the annual market growth estimates sum to 100 per cent because with certainty some rate of growth will occur and because for simplicity these are assumed to be the only possible outcomes.[9] The expected value of annual market growth is computed as:

$$\textbf{Expected market growth} = 8\% \times 0.30 + 4\% \times 0.40 + 2\% \times 0.30$$
$$\textbf{E[market growth]} = 2.4\% + 1.6\% + 0.6\% = \underline{\underline{4.6\%}}$$

It is possible but not likely that the actual value of the future annual growth will be precisely 4.6 per cent. However, the expected value of market growth summarizes what is known about possible values and their likelihood of occurrence. ShadeTree Roasters can use the expected value of 4.6 per cent market growth with other internal information to compute the value of the proposed investment in central Europe, as we demonstrate after discussing the gathering of internal information.

Expected value analysis depends on measures of the probability or odds of the actual occurrence of each relevant future event. Two general approaches exist to measure probabilities or odds: (1) assess the degree of belief (or confidence) about future events and (2) count the historical frequency (or distribution) of occurrence of similar past events.[10] Measuring probabilities or odds by assessing degree of belief is difficult and subjective if future events are unrelated to past events. For example, a stockbroker might believe that the Nikkei 225 index will rise tomorrow, and if asked, she might say that she is 80 per cent certain that the index will rise. However, another stockbroker might

8.2 You're the Decision Maker

Sensitivity of Expected Value Analysis

The expected market growth of 4.6 per cent is a critical assumption or parameter of ShadeTree's expansion decision.

a. Compute the expected market growth rate with the following sets of possible growth rates and probabilities.
   1. Possible growth rates = 10%, 5%, (2%); probabilities = 0.4, 0.3, 0.3
   2. Possible growth rates = 8%, 4%, 2%; probabilities = 0.2, 0.6, 0.2
   3. Possible growth rates = 10%, 5%, (2%); probabilities = 0.2, 0.2, 0.6

b. Explain how the different expected market growth rates might affect the investment decision.

(Solutions begin on page 411.)

be 80 per cent certain that the index will drop tomorrow. You might rely on one stockbroker's degree of belief if you are confident that he or she has unique information or analysis skills; otherwise, their assessments are highly subjective.

If the occurrence of past events is relevant, one could feel comfortable using historical frequencies to predict future events. For example, the weather forecast of a 70 per cent chance of rain tomorrow means that, when today's weather conditions have been observed in the past, rain occurred 70 per cent of the time the next day. Although rain is not certain tomorrow, that forecast might justifiably cause a farmer to wait a few days before cutting a hayfield and risk a ruined crop by cutting just before a rainstorm.

Internal Information

A major stage of information gathering is to predict the effects of each uncontrollable future event on planned operations and activities and on expected costs and benefits. An organization's internal financial records can be sources of relevant operating activities, costs and cost savings that might be applied to the proposed investment. For example, the results of statistical analyses of past costs might be 'engineered' for differences expected with the proposed investment activities (see Chapter 3). Activity-based costing information (see Chapters 4 and 5) can be particularly useful for planning activities and costs.

If the proposed investment is unlike past operations, an organization can use consultants and publicly available information to identify operating activities and activity costs. Consultants can be quite useful if they have experience with other organizations that have operated under similar conditions. Public information about a region's economy and infrastructure can also be useful for forecasting activities and costs. Company personnel might be able to apply tools of engineering analysis (see Chapter 3) to create new processes, activities and costs required by the proposed investment.

Evaluating an investment involves generating the following internal information forecasts:

- The resources and activities necessary to operate the investment for all levels of uncertain future events over the life of the investment: generally the people, working capital, equipment and facilities vary with different event outcomes. Expected annual and total sales activities often indicate the scale and breadth of operations that must be planned for the life of the investment.
- The resources necessary to acquire the investment: generally the purchase price and subsequent instalment payments, if any.
- The revenues, expenses and net cash flows associated with annual sales and related production activities.
- The expected value of the investment.

We now illustrate these uses of internal information by examining ShadeTree's analysis of its proposed investment in new operations in central Europe.

8.2 Research Insight

Bundling Assets

The well-known producer of construction equipment, **Caterpillar Inc.,** found that it needed to change its investment analysis procedures when it changed to high-technology manufacturing methods. Historically, the company made incremental investments in its old mass production processes. However, Caterpillar invested in high-technology production more efficiently when it made 'bundles' of related investments simultaneously instead of one at a time.

Investing in bundles of assets allowed managers to think about how assets created synergies. Sometimes an investment that appeared only marginally profitable made better sense as part of a bundle of assets. For example, a machine that reduced labour cost might have a negative net present value when examined by itself as a labour-saving device. When combined with other assets that together sped up the production process, however, the whole bundle had a higher positive net present value than without the labour-saving asset.

This approach of investing in bundles of assets is consistent with economic theory, which argues that the entire set of complementary assets is necessary to achieve economic efficiency. Lower efficiency results if an organization leaves out one or more apparently inefficient assets from the bundle. All are needed for efficient operations. This might explain why reports of widespread adoptions of manufacturing innovations, such as JIT (see Chapter 6), have not been matched by increases in profitability. Perhaps a set of investments is required, but some firms have attempted to economize by leaving out one or more of the set. A study of the Italian footwear manufacturer **Geox** also illustrates the important of complementary assets.

Sources: Miller and O'Leary (1997); Milgrom and Roberts (1995); and Camuffo et al. (2008).

Forecasts of ShadeTree's Investment Information

The information needed to evaluate ShadeTree's proposed investment is shown in Exhibit 8.15. The information is divided into internal and external information categories. Most internal information items, such as the gross margin ratio of 65 per cent in cell B5, are represented by only one estimate. This does not mean that ShadeTree's analysts know these items with certainty, which, of course, they cannot. Analysts can use expected values or sensitivity and scenario analyses (see Chapter 7) to measure the sensitivity of the predicted outcomes to changes in these figures. The information in Exhibit 8.16 is a simple set of internal data, but it is sufficient to generate the analyses of this chapter. Undoubtedly, ShadeTree's analysts would have prepared detailed estimates of the components and likely values of all of the information items, which could change over the investment's 5-year horizon. They could include all of these details in the financial model of the investment decision, but this is unnecessarily complex for our purposes.

One information item deserves more discussion. The expected market share of 20 per cent in cell C8 of Exhibit 8.15 is, of course, an estimate like the others and might turn out to be different than expected. The specific point we want to make now is that this is an estimate of market share *without a major competitor.* What if a major competitor, such as Starbucks, also decides to enter this

Exhibit 8.15 ShadeTree Roasters' Investment Information

	A	B	C	D	E	F	G
1	Internal Information (amounts in euros)			External Information			
2	Tax rate	40%		Annual market growth	Possible values	Probability	Expected value
3	Required rate of return	8%		Market growth - high	8%	30%	
4	Decision horizon	5	years	Market growth - middle	4%	40%	4.6%
5	Gross margin ratio	65%		Market growth - low	2%	30%	
6	SG&A costs - cash (000)	€5,000	per year			100%	
7	Initial investment - cash (000)	€5,500		Initial market size (annual sales)	€50,000,000		
8	Market share - with no major competitor	20%		Market share - with major competitor	10%		
9				Probability of a major competitor	40%		

Exhibit 8.16 Forecasted Investment Cash Flows and Net Present Value - No Major Competitor (€000)

	A	B	C	D	E	F	G
1	ShadeTree Roasters Expansion - no competitior, invest now	Year 0	Year 1	Year 2	Year 3	Year 4	Year 5
2	Expected market size (thousands euros)	€ 50,000	€ 52,300	€ 54,706	€ 57,222	€ 59,854	€ 62,608
3	Market share		20%	20%	20%	20%	20%
4	Sales		€ 10,460	€ 10,941	€ 11,444	€ 11,971	€ 12,522
5	Cost of goods sold		3,661	3,829	4,006	4,190	4,383
6	Gross margin		6,799	7,112	7,439	7,781	8,139
7	Committed costs						
8	Investment (cash/non-cash)	(5,500)	1,100	1,100	1,100	1,100	1,100
9	SG&A - cash		5,000	5,000	5,000	5,000	5,000
10	Total committed costs		6,100	6,100	6,100	6,100	6,100
11	Operating income before tax		699	1,012	1,339	1,681	2,039
12	Tax (savings)		280	405	536	672	816
13	Operating income after tax		419	607	803	1,009	1,223
14	Add-back non-cash expenses		1,100	1,100	1,100	1,100	1,100
15	Annual cash flows	(€ 5,500)	€ 1,519	€ 1,707	€ 1,903	€ 2,109	€ 2,323
16	Expected NPV - yrs 1-5, no competitor	€ 2,012					

new market? ShadeTree's analysts expect that this would cause a large reduction in ShadeTree's market share (see cell F8). We will consider the impacts of this possibility on both expected cash flows and decision making after illustrating the basic investment decision model, which is shown in Exhibits 8.15 and 8.16.

The analysis in Exhibit 8.16 combines the information in Exhibit 8.15 to produce the project's estimated annual cash flows, which are shown in row 15, for each year of the investment's life.[11] For example, multiplying 1 plus the expected rate of market growth (1.046) by the market size for year 0 in B2 (€50 million in the year before operations begin) yields a new estimate of market size for year 1 in the amount of €52.3 million (C2). The model computes each succeeding year's market size similarly from the preceding year. Multiplying each year's market size in row 2 by ShadeTree's expected market share (20 per cent, row 3) generates that year's estimate of sales revenues in row 4. Multiplying sales revenue by 1 minus the gross margin ratio (1 – 0.65 = 0.35) yields the cost of goods sold (row 5), and subtraction gives annual gross margin (row 6). Committed costs (beginning in row 7) include the investment outlay in year 0 of €5.5 million (B8), which ShadeTree will pay in cash before operations begin. This investment cost, which includes costs of leases, fixtures and related store facilities, will be amortized, straight-line, over the investment life (row 8). Also subtracting sales, general and administrative costs (SG&A in row 9) generates operating income before tax (row 11). Subtracting taxes at 40 per cent (row 12) results in operating income after tax (row 13).

DCF methods use estimates of cash flow, not accounting income, because cash flow can be used for consumption or reinvestment in other projects, but accounting income itself cannot.[12] The analysis in Exhibit 8.16 assumes that all but one income item is a cash flow in each year. The non-cash item is the amortization expense of the investment cost of €1.1 million per year (row 8). This expense has understated annual cash flow and is added back to operating income after tax (row 14) to measure expected annual cash flows (row 15). The model's final step is to discount the future cash flows and compute the investment's expected net present value (NPV), which is calculated in cell B16. The positive NPV of €2,012,000 indicates that the proposed investment is expected to be more profitable than required by ShadeTree's required rate of return of 8 per cent.

If non-financial aspects of the investment and competitors' actions were not concerns, ShadeTree's managers probably would approve the investment. 'Choice of the Best Alterative Using both Financial and Non-financial Information' in Section I of this chapter explained how non-financial quantitative and qualitative aspects of decisions can outweigh the financial aspects if, for example, the investment was expected to have adverse impacts on the organization's employees, customers, reputation, non-financial goals, or ability to operate in a legal or socially responsible way. Alternatively, beneficial non-financial outcomes might weigh in favour of an investment that does not meet strict DCF criteria.

8.3 You're the Decision Maker

Sensitivity and Scenario Analyses

Quite a number of assumptions or model parameters determine the positive NPV of €2,012,000 in Exhibit 8.16. Among these parameters are the size of the market in year 0, the market growth rate, and ShadeTree's market share.

a. Explain how these parameters affect expected revenues (change each separately and put others at the base levels from the text).
b. Compute year 1's gross margin if the market size is €60 million or €40 million.
c. Compute year 1's gross margin if the market growth rate is 2 per cent or 6 per cent.
d. Compute year 1's gross margin if ShadeTree's market share is 30 per cent or 15 per cent.
e. The most likely scenario uses the parameters in Exhibit 8.16. Compute year 1's gross margin under best-case and worst-case scenarios using the parameters in requirements (b)-(d).

(Solutions begin on page 411.)

8.3 Cost Management in Practice

Non-financial Benefits of Investments in Technology

Analyses of investments in new technology frequently do not show positive net present values. Technology innovations usually have a high initial cost and a long payback period. This especially is true in public sector entities where many of the benefits are non-financial. Nonetheless, pressures from taxpayers and limited budgets increasingly direct government managers to justify technology investments on the basis of future cost savings and revenue enhancements. Purely financial calculations, however, are likely to understate important non-financial impacts. For example, investments in improved Internet access for taxpayers can result in shorter wait times, improved responsiveness, improved public safety and reduced errors. While these ultimately can translate into dollars, these impacts are not easily measured and would be ignored in purely financial analyses.

Source: Doherty (2005).

Future Actions of Competitors

LO 6 Model the impacts of competitors' actions.

How would major competitors' decisions affect the expected values of investments? Few decisions depend only on unknown future uncontrollable events, such as weather or political change. The decisions of competitors in the local or global economy can also affect many investment decisions and outcomes. ShadeTree Roasters is hoping that major competitors either will not identify the same market opportunity in central Europe or will not meet emerging market demand effectively. We now add the complexity of a major competitor to the effects of previously discussed internal and external information.

The investment information in Exhibit 8.15 includes an estimate of ShadeTree's market share (10 per cent, cell F8) should a major competitor, such as **Starbucks**, enter the market effectively. Because success attracts competition, ShadeTree analysts estimate a 40 per cent probability (cell F9 of Exhibit 8.15) that a major competitor will enter the market after observing ShadeTree's start-up operations in year 0. The impacts of the competitive entry could be felt as soon as year 2, and Shade-Tree's analysts expect its market share to drop from 20 to 10 per cent. ShadeTree's analysts modified the investment model to reflect the impacts of a major competitor. The modified model is shown in Exhibit 8.17.

The only data input difference between the models in Exhibit 8.16 (without a major competitor) and Exhibit 8.17 (with a major competitor) is ShadeTree's expected market share, which is the 10 per cent figure repeated in cells D3–G3. This drop in market share dramatically changes the

Exhibit 8.17 **Forecasted Investment Cash Flows and Net Present Value with a Major Competitor (€000)**

	A	B	C	D	E	F	G
1	ShadeTree Roasters Expansion - with competitior, invest now	Year 0	Year 1	Year 2	Year 3	Year 4	Year 5
2	Expected market size (thousands euros)	€ 50,000	€52,300	€54,706	€57,222	€59,854	€62,608
3	Market share		20%	10%	10%	10%	10%
4	Sales		€10,460	€5,471	€5,722	€5,985	€6,261
5	Cost of goods sold		3,661	1,915	2,003	2,095	2,191
6	Gross margin		6,799	3,556	3,719	3,891	4,070
7	Committed costs						
8	Investment (cash/non-cash)	(5,500)	1,100	1,100	1,100	1,100	1,100
9	SG&A - cash		5,000	5,000	5,000	5,000	5,000
10	Total committed costs		6,100	6,100	6,100	6,100	6,100
11	Operating income before tax		699	(2,544)	(2,381)	(2,209)	(2,030)
12	Tax (savings)		280	(1,018)	(952)	(884)	(812)
13	Operating income after tax		419	(1,526)	(1,428)	(1,326)	(1,218)
14	Add-back non-cash expenses		1,100	1,100	1,100	1,100	1,100
15	Annual cash flows	(€5,500)	€1,519	(€426)	(€328)	(€226)	(€118)
16	NPV - yrs 1-5, with competitor	(€4,966)					

company's expected sales revenues, operating income and cash flows. The summary measure of the investment's value, the NPV in cell B16, is now a large negative number (€4,966,000). This negative NPV indicates that the expansion would be a financial disaster for ShadeTree if a major competitor enters the market a year later and has the expected effect on market share. If it proceeded and a major competitor entered, the company would waste most of its €5.5 million investment.

However, this financial disaster is not a certainty. ShadeTree's analysts estimate a 40 per cent chance that this outcome will occur. Expected value analysis weighs each expected outcome by its probability of occurrence to obtain the expected NPV of the proposed investment. Exhibit 8.18 presents the expected value analysis decision tree. The expected NPV or E[NPV] of the expansion decision is negative (€779,000) as shown in cell I73 and here:

$$\mathbf{E[NPV] = 0.4 \times (4{,}996{,}000) + 0.6 \times 2{,}012{,}000 = (€779{,}000)}$$

Expected value analysis shows emphatically that the best decision is not to expand to central Europe because the odds are that it will be a losing venture. This analysis shows that a better decision is to invest the company's capital in other projects that earn at least the required rate of return (and earn an NPV of €0; see cell D82). But is this the right decision?

Exhibit 8.18 **Expected Value Analysis Decision Tree (€000)**

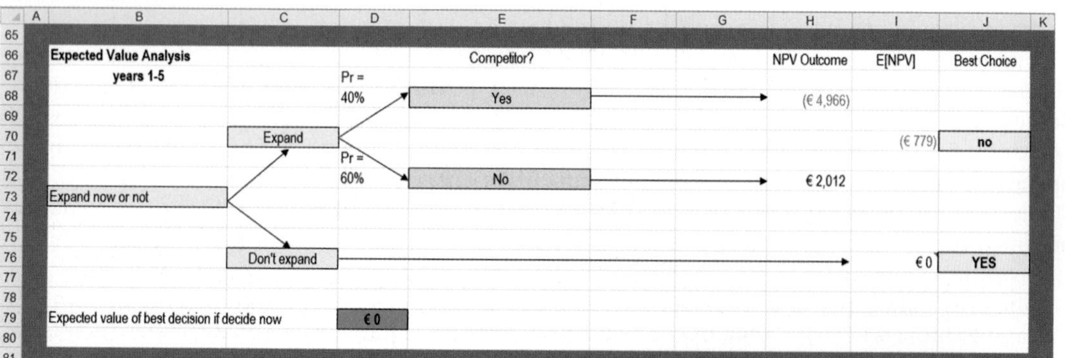

Real Option Value Analysis

LO 7 Know when and how to apply real option analysis to evaluate strategic investments.

Under common investment conditions, the preceding NPV analysis is incorrect. First, even if ShadeTree cannot recover its investment (a sunk cost), terminating the project after one year would be less costly than continuing to operate with the next four years of negative cash flows. In other words, if ShadeTree has the option of quitting at no cost after a competitor enters, the expected NPV of the project is larger because the company can avoid four years of negative cash flows. The calculation of the revised NPV, which uses only the year 0 and year 1 cash flows from Exhibit 8.17 (cells B15 and C15), is as follows:

Investment event	NPV	Probability	Weighted value
Expand without a major competitor	= €2,012,000	0.60	€1,207,200
Expand with a competitor, but terminate after 1 year *(0.9259 is the one-year present value factor for a rate of 8%)*	= (€5,500,000) + €1,519,000 × 0.9259 = (€4,093,558)	0.40	€(1,637,423)
Total expected NPV			€(430,223)

Although we will show that even this analysis is simplified, the new analysis begins to incorporate management's flexibility to terminate the project. This is an important and relatively new way of describing investments that can completely reverse this type of decision. The negative NPV apparently signals to reject the investment, but ShadeTree should make no decision until it includes more information about the company's flexibility. This flexible approach to investment analysis is called **real option value (ROV) analysis**. It combines analyses of decision trees, expected values and NPV to describe investments as a series of options to change investments. As we have seen, an investment might be terminated, but it also might be expanded, shrunk, phased in, redesigned or deferred. The decision tree part of ROV analysis describes the flexibility an organization has to change its decisions as it gains experience with the investment. ROV analysis investigates impacts of decisions to go one way or another on a decision tree. If ShadeTree could terminate the expansion once it learned that Starbucks had entered the market and cut its market share in half, shouldn't ShadeTree build that flexibility into its analysis? We now turn to modelling that flexibility.

8.3 Research Insight

Investing in High Technology

Academics and consultants have criticized traditional expected NPV analysis for high-technology investments for years because analysts tend to use:

- Discount rates that are too high and overstate the risk of the investment.
- Time horizons that are too short to capture long-term benefits of the technology.
- Only easily quantified costs and benefits that ignore the impacts on other operations and customers from improvements in quality, cycle time and flexibility to meet customers' needs.
- NPV models that do not reflect management flexibility as well as ROV analysis does.

Researchers recommend using ROV analysis for investments in such diverse fields as engineering design, biotechnology, information technology and manufacturing flexibility. For example, Jens Bengtsson has classified numerous applications of ROV analysis to flexibility of machines, processes, internal logistics, plants and products themselves. Because technology changes rapidly and is highly uncertain, traditional NPV analysis might lead to rejection of many technology investments. However, ROV analysis forces analysts to model how the organization might respond to changes. Modelling this flexibility can lead to the adoption of more technology investments, but perhaps in different forms rather than the 'all-or-nothing' investments characterized by NPV analysis. Experimental studies suggest that ROV analysis can also lead to better decision making about stopping projects, because the possibility of abandonment is given more thought when assessing the project. However, other research suggest that actually exercising the 'stop option' will run counter to many organizational pressures, as well as people's psychological tendency to continue because they have already spent more in the past.

Boeing, Kimberly-Clark, Merck/Schering-Plough and **Matsushita Electronics** are among the many firms that use real option value analysis of investments. Because ROV models can be mathematically complex and because not all decision problems can be cast into standard models, companies, consultants and researchers have also developed many different kinds of, and more pragmatic approaches to, ROV.

Sources: Adner and Levinthal (2004); Bengtsson (2001); Denison (2009); Nichols (1994); Wouters et al. (2011).

Value of Deferring Irreversible Decisions

We now turn to modelling the flexibility to defer a decision, a condition that can make the usual expected NPV analysis incorrect. Sometimes acting quickly can prevent competitors from dominating a market. However, waiting to gather more information about the investment or uncontrollable events might identify new opportunities to take or problems to avoid. For example, assume that by waiting a year, ShadeTree Roasters could learn whether its nemesis, Starbucks, will or will not decide to serve the central European market.

The first step of ROV analysis is to describe the proposed investment alternatives with decision trees. We consider two alternatives: (1) defer expansion for one year or (2) expand now. Exhibit 8.19 displays the decision tree for alternative 1: wait one year. As shown in column C, the first decision is to defer the expansion decision. ShadeTree Roasters will wait a year to learn whether Starbucks will enter the central European market. If Starbucks does not enter the market then, ShadeTree analysts believe that it will not do so in the foreseeable future.

By waiting a year, ShadeTree can convert the 40 per cent probability that Starbucks will enter the market into a 100 per cent probability of having a major competitor or not. Although we know from the previous analysis that expansion facing a major competitor would likely be a disaster, the decision tree includes space for the NPV outcome of such an expansion (cell H6) because in general analysts want to compute all relevant outcomes. Cells H8 and H12 have zero NPV values to show that analysts assume the decision not to expand will result in earning the required rate of return.

Completion of this part of the ROV analysis entails estimating the NPV values of the decision to invest with or without a major competitor (cells H8 and H12). Column I is set up to choose the best decision from each set of outcomes, with or without a major competitor. Finally, cell E14 computes the expected value of the decision to wait one year, as will be shown. Exhibits 8.20 (with a competitor) and 8.21 (without a competitor) present the NPV computations that will be placed in Exhibit 8.19's decision tree. There is one difference between these computations and the earlier

Exhibit 8.19 Real Option Value Decision Tree – Defer Decision One Year

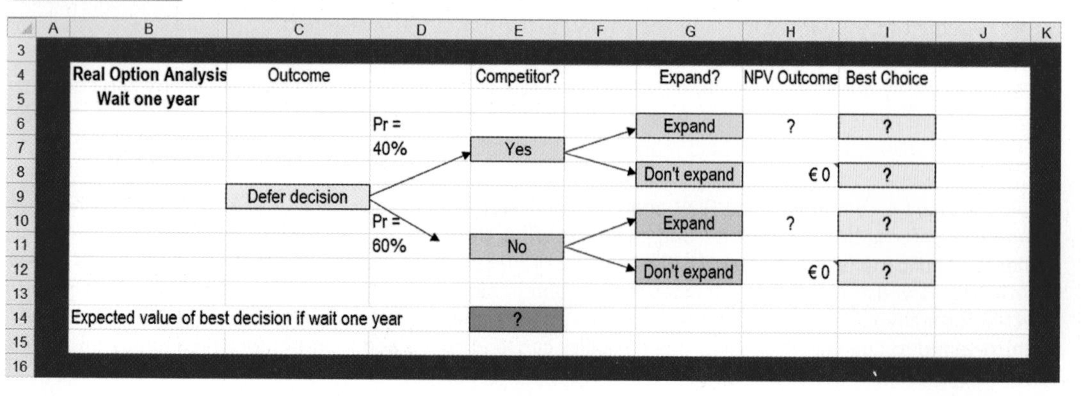

Exhibit 8.20 **Real Option Value Analysis – Wait One Year, *with* a Major Competitor**

	A	B	C	D	E	F	G	H
1	ShadeTree Roasters Expansion - with competitor, wait one year	Year 0	Year 1	Year 2	Year 3	Year 4	Year 5	Year 6
2	Market size (thousands €)	€ 50,000	€ 52,300	€ 54,706	€ 57,222	€ 59,854	€ 62,608	€ 65,488
3	Market share			10%	10%	10%	10%	10%
4	Sales			€ 5,471	€ 5,722	€ 5,985	€ 6,261	€ 6,549
5	Cost of goods sold			1,915	2,003	2,095	2,191	2,292
6	Gross margin			3,556	3,719	3,891	4,070	4,257
7	Committed costs							
8	Investment (cash/non-cash)		(5,500)	1,100	1,100	1,100	1,100	1,100
9	SG&A - cash			5,000	5,000	5,000	5,000	5,000
10	Total committed costs			6,100	6,100	6,100	6,100	6,100
11	Operating income before tax			(2,544)	(2,381)	(2,209)	(2,030)	(1,843)
12	Tax (savings)			(1,018)	(952)	(884)	(812)	(737)
13	Operating income after tax			(1,526)	(1,428)	(1,326)	(1,218)	(1,106)
14	Add-back non-cash expenses			1,100	1,100	1,100	1,100	1,100
15	Annual cash flows		(€ 5,500)	(€ 426)	(€ 328)	(€ 226)	(€ 118)	(€ 6)
16	NPV - yrs 1-6, competitor, wait	(€ 5,969)						

NPV calculation in Exhibits 8.16 and 8.17. The timing of the investment and operations has been deferred one year to years 2 to 6. Note that the analyses assume that the market will grow as expected from year 0, as before.

ShadeTree would not expand after learning of a major competitor because the NPV of expansion would be negative (€5,969,000) (see cell B16 of Exhibit 8.20) if that event occurs. The company will reinvest elsewhere and earn at least the required rate of return, which generates €0 NPV. On the other hand, ShadeTree will expand without a major competitor because the NPV would be positive, €2,619,000 (see cell B16 of Exhibit 8.22).

Exhibit 8.22 presents the completed decision tree for this part of the analysis. The decision tree shows that the best choices are not to expand if a major competitor enters the market (NPV = €0, cell H19) and to expand if a major competitor does not enter (NPV = €2,619,000, cell H21). The probability of a major competitor is 40 per cent and that no major competitor will materialize is 60 per cent. The expected NPV of the decision to wait one year (cell D28) is computed as follows from the best option choices:

$$\textbf{E[NPV, defer decision]} = €0 \times 0.40 + 2{,}619{,}000 \times 0.60 = \underline{\underline{€1{,}571{,}000}}$$

The expected NPV of deferring the decision for one year cannot be compared directly with the previous analysis of investing now because both sets of analyses should cover the same time period,

Exhibit 8.21 **Real Option Value Analysis – Wait One Year, *without* a Major Competitor**

	A	B	C	D	E	F	G	H
1	ShadeTree Roasters Expansion - no competitor, wait one year	Year 0	Year 1	Year 2	Year 3	Year 4	Year 5	Year 6
2	Expected market size (thousands euros)	€ 50,000	€ 52,300	€ 54,706	€ 57,222	€ 59,854	€ 62,608	€ 65,488
3	Market share			20%	20%	20%	20%	20%
4	Sales			€ 10,941	€ 11,444	€ 11,971	€ 12,522	€ 13,098
5	Cost of goods sold			3,829	4,006	4,190	4,383	4,584
6	Gross margin			7,112	7,439	7,781	8,139	8,513
7	Committed costs							
8	Investment (cash/non-cash)		(5,500)	1,100	1,100	1,100	1,100	1,100
9	SG&A - cash			5,000	5,000	5,000	5,000	5,000
10	Total committed costs			6,100	6,100	6,100	6,100	6,100
11	Operating income before tax			1,012	1,339	1,681	2,039	2,413
12	Tax (savings)			405	536	672	816	965
13	Operating income after tax			607	803	1,009	1,223	1,448
14	Add-back non-cash expenses			1,100	1,100	1,100	1,100	1,100
15	Annual cash flows		(€ 5,500)	€ 1,707	€ 1,903	€ 2,109	€ 2,323	€ 2,548
16	NPV - yrs 1-6, no competitor, wait	€ 2,619						

Exhibit 8.22 Real Option Value Decision Tree – Defer Decision One Year, with Calculations

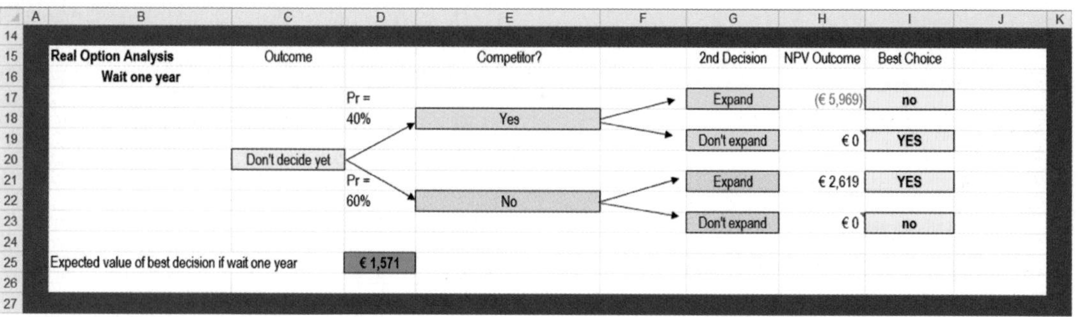

years 1 to 6. This is particularly important in this situation because the assumption of continued market growth drives the expected profitability of the investment. It is a simple matter to extend the previous analyses to a sixth year (see Appendix 8A for the spreadsheets for the decision to invest now over 6 years). Exhibit 8.23 presents the decision tree for the alternative of investing now with the results of extending operations and the analysis to a sixth year. This analysis assumes that ShadeTree could extend its operations for an additional year for an additional annual committed cost as in previous years. However, this committed cost in the sixth year is treated as a cash outlay and is not added back to operating income after tax. The company could and perhaps should model other possibilities for year 6.

The NPV outcomes in cells H31 and H33 of Exhibit 8.23 show that the entry of a competitor would be a financial disaster (as before) even if the company can terminate the operations after a year. If a competitor entered, ShadeTree's best decision would be to terminate the operation with a negative expected NPV of (€4,093,000) (cell H33). Without a major competitor, ShadeTree expects a positive NPV of €2,925,000 (cell H35) from continuing operations and would not consider terminating the project (cell H37). Extending the analysis to six years makes the investment favourable, with an overall expected NPV of €118,000 (cell D45). The expected NPV of the decision to expand now is computed as follows from the best option choices of this alternative:

$$\mathbf{E[NPV,\ expand\ now] = (€4{,}093{,}000) \times 0.40 + 2{,}925{,}000 \times 0.60 = €118{,}000}$$

This improvement in expected NPV from the first analysis in Exhibit 8.19 is the direct result of the assumed continued market growth through year 6, which makes the effects of competition less severe and the effects of lack of competition more favourable. This analysis indicates that the company could invest now profitably, but that would be wrong because the better option is to wait and gather more information.

Exhibit 8.23 Real Option Value Decision Tree – Decide Now, Years 1-6

Real Option Analysis
Decide now
1st Decision
Competitor?
2nd Decision
NPV Outcome
Best Choice
Expand now or not
Expand
Pr = 40%
Yes
Continue
(€ 5,663)
no
Terminate
(€ 4,093)
YES
Pr = 60%
No
Continue
€ 2,925
YES
Terminate
(€ 4,093)
no
Don't expand
€ 0
Expected value of best decision if decide now
€ 118

Value of the Option to Wait

© BirdImages
The option to develop real estate can have significant value.

The **real option value** of an investment is the difference between the expected NPV of one option form of the investment and the next best option. In this investment situation and others, when the investment is irreversible and relevant information can be obtained over time, deferring a decision can be more valuable than acting immediately. As the previous analyses have shown, ShadeTree's investment is more valuable if it can wait for a year rather than investing now. The real option value of waiting can be computed by comparing the NPV values of the decisions to defer or invest now.

E[value of waiting] = E[NPV, wait from Exhibit 8.22
– E[NPV, invest now, from Exhibit 8.23]
E[value of waiting] = €1,571,000 – €118,000 = €1,454,000

In other words, if ShadeTree Roasters can be assured that it will learn about its competitors' actions in the next year, the company should defer its investment decision.

The decisions to reject the investment or invest now with a 6-year horizon are incorrect. ROV analysis shows in this case that the best decision is to defer the decision and learn more about its competitors' future actions.

When trees become more complex, the calculation has to be done differently, namely by rolling backwards. Furthermore, analysts sometimes have information that is useful but not a perfect predictor of uncertain factors. For example, suppose ShadeTree can conduct market research that predicts whether a major competitor will be successful in increasing its market share at the expense of ShadeTree, but there is a possibility that the market research is not correct. Appendix 8B to this chapter explains the principles.

8.4 You're the Decision Maker

Apply Real Option Value Analysis

a. Why did ShadeTree's analysts extend the ROV analysis without a major competitor to six years? Is this a reasonable approach to the analysis? Why or why not?

b. Compute expected NPV values with the following alternative investment model outcomes. (*Hint:* Draw decision trees similar to those in Exhibits 8.22 and 8.23).

1. Defer the decision to invest one year: NPV[with competitor] = (€3,000,000); NPV[no competitor] = €6,000,000
2. Invest now: NPV[with competitor, continue] = (€2,800,000); NPV[with competitor, terminate after one year] = (€500,000); NPV[no competitor] = €6,500,000
3. Compute the real option value of waiting.
4. What does the computation in part (3) indicate is the best investment strategy?

(Solutions begin on page 411.)

Legal and Ethical Issues in Strategic Investment Analysis

LO 8
Identify and evaluate ethical issues in strategic investment decisions.

One meaning of the real option value computation is that ShadeTree Roasters would be willing to pay up to the amount of €1,454,000 to secure its option to invest in the central European market one year later. By waiting a year, ShadeTree can learn about its competitors' actions and avoid head-to-head competition, which the company expects to lose. Perhaps ShadeTree might consider spending up to this amount to guarantee its right to 20 per cent of the market. This could be done legally by setting up a joint venture with an existing company or illegally by paying bribes. Alternatively, the company could purchase additional market and industry analyses that might predict its competitors' future actions more precisely, or it could conduct questionable or illegal industrial espionage. With large money amounts at risk and the possibility of financial (or personal career) disaster, some individuals can be tempted to commit illegal or unethical acts to improve the chances of a favourable investment.

Trade unions, regulators, investors, non-government organizations, and some business executives have succeeding in influencing national laws and recent Organisation for Economic Co-operation and Development guidelines that prohibit bribery and other corrupt practices by multinational companies. However, no uniform definitions of these unethical practices exist. What is one country's bribe can be another's 'business facilitation' cost; one company's bribed official might be another's 'business intermediary' who is essential to finding new markets. Furthermore, although some European countries have stricter laws against corrupt practices than the United States has, prosecution has been rare in these countries. Worldwide enforcement of anticorruption laws may be too weak to cause improved practices.

An added complication arises when regulators attempt to prosecute executives who knew or should have known about illegal practices. US firms, for example, are required by law to have effective internal control systems, but recent events have proved that these can be subverted. Even if prosecutors cannot prove that executives ordered bribes or fraudulent investment reports, for instance, executives could be prosecuted for failing to properly supervise those who actually carried out the unethical or illegal acts. However, establishing that an executive should have known that a subordinate, who is layers away in the hierarchy, was misbehaving can be almost impossible without evidence of relevant communications between them.

Even if governments cannot define or prosecute illegal investment activities, socially conscious investors might affect business practices by using their own social investment criteria to:

- Screen for positive and negative issues such as bribery or environmental performance
- Generate shareholder advocacy on social issues
- Invest directly in their community
- Provide the financial foundation for new, socially responsible companies.

Whether these investor-driven approaches can affect ethical investment practices in a material way remains to be seen.[13]

Internal Ethical Pressures

Individuals can be pressured to misstate information or results regarding strategic investments because of:

- *Bias from personal commitment to an investment project.* This bias can begin as myopia, or not wanting to look sufficiently far ahead, or to admit that a favourite project might be a failure. After an investment is approved, this bias can continue as 'escalation to commitment', which results in throwing good money after bad rather than facing the fact that an investment should be terminated and written off.

- *Fear of loss of prestige, position or compensation from a failed investment.* The pressures to succeed and not to admit failure can be very strong in any type of organization. Some organizations have an 'up-or-out' advancement policy, and only those that continue to succeed financially are rewarded. While the best result of this pressure is that managers invest in good projects and manage them well, sometimes projects perform below expectations. A manager might give in to the temptation to misstate investment success or might force analysts to do so. This can lead to continued misstatements that ultimately cannot be sustained. The predictable results include wasted resources, lost time and ruined reputations.
- *Greed and intentional behaviour to defraud an organization or its stakeholders.* Some people, unfortunately, are ethically challenged and seek opportunities to defraud others. Trust is very important in business, but trust has been and will be abused. Anyone who has followed corporate misbehaviour over the past several years knows that greed is a powerful motivator. The combination of greed and initial financial success can lead to a sense of invincibility and entitlement to greater wealth. When markets inevitably turn down or when predicted events do not occur, powerful managers have pressured analysts to misstate investment success and outlook in order to sustain their image and income. Wealthy criminals might be able to hide their assets and escape prosecution, but analysts who connive with them likely cannot and will be ruined financially and personally.

Roles of Internal Controls and Audits

Hiring practices and codes of ethics are important to counter pressures to invest unethically. For example, many ethical codes prohibit employees from soliciting or accepting gifts from potential suppliers or outsourced service providers. This is to help ensure that evaluations of investments and other projects will not be biased by favouritism or obligations induced by gifts and the expectations of future gifts.

Many organizations have formal reporting and periodic reviews of investment projects before and after acceptance. Reporting and review elements include financial analyses to demonstrate that projects will meet or are meeting required rates of return and qualitative analyses to verify that projects meet the goals and objectives of the organization and to verify that investment managers are adhering to investment guidelines, including ethical requirements.

Internal audits are examinations of operations, programmes and financial results performed by independent investigators. Effective internal audits can be powerful reinforcements of ethical investment policies and deterrents to those tempted to violate those policies for new and existing investments. The threat and consequences of being caught at unethical investment practices might be enough to dissuade those who might be tempted to misbehave. Furthermore, internal audits of the investment process and ongoing investments also can be valuable sources of information about what worked and what did not. This information can be used to revise investment practices and improve investment decisions in the future.

Appendix 8A

Analysis of ShadeTree Roasters' Decision to Invest Now, Years 1–6

Analyses such as the ones in Exhibits 8.24 and 8.25 are easily extended to additional time periods if Chapter 7's modelling guidelines have been followed. If every cell in the exhibits is a formula that refers to either data input (e.g., the 'Input' worksheet shown in the bottom bar of this screen shot) or other results on this worksheet, one can simply copy and paste year 5's cells to any number of subsequent years. One must be careful, however, to ensure that the assumptions that govern the earlier years also apply to the later years. For example, analysts should question whether the company would be able to extend operations for a sixth year for a cash outlay at the same level of committed costs, €1,100,000, as before. If the economic life of the investment really is 5 years, additional cash investment beyond the previous annual committed costs might be necessary for a sixth year.

Exhibit 8.24 Forecasted Cash Flows and Net Present Value – No Major Competitor, Years 1–6

	A	B	C	D	E	F	G	H
1	ShadeTree Roasters Expansion - no competitor, invest now	Year 0	Year 1	Year 2	Year 3	Year 4	Year 5	Year 6
2	Expected market size (thousands euros)	€ 50,000	€ 52,300	€ 54,706	€ 57,222	€ 59,854	€ 62,608	€ 65,488
3	Market share		20%	20%	20%	20%	20%	20%
4	Sales		€ 10,460	€ 10,941	€ 11,444	€ 11,971	€ 12,522	€ 13,098
5	Cost of goods sold		3,661	3,829	4,006	4,190	4,383	4,584
6	Gross margin		6,799	7,112	7,439	7,781	8,139	8,513
7	Committed costs							
8	Investment (cash/non-cash)	(5,500)	1,100	1,100	1,100	1,100	1,100	**1,100**
9	SG&A - cash		5,000	5,000	5,000	5,000	5,000	5,000
10	Total committed costs		6,100	6,100	6,100	6,100	6,100	6,100
11	Operating income before tax		699	1,012	1,339	1,681	2,039	2,413
12	Tax (savings)		280	405	536	672	816	965
13	Operating income after tax		419	607	803	1,009	1,223	1,448
14	Add-back non-cash expenses		1,100	1,100	1,100	1,100	1,100	-
15	Annual cash flows	(€ 5,500)	€ 1,519	€ 1,707	€ 1,903	€ 2,109	€ 2,323	€ 1,448
16	Expected NPV - yrs 1-5, no competitor	€ 2,012						
17	Expected NPV - yrs 1-6, no competitor	€ 2,925						

Exhibit 8.25 Forecasted Cash Flows and Net Present Value – with a Major Competitor, Years 1–6

	A	B	C	D	E	F	G	H
1	ShadeTree Roasters Expansion - with competitior, invest now	Year 0	Year 1	Year 2	Year 3	Year 4	Year 5	Year 6
2	Expected market size (thousands euros)	€ 50,000	€ 52,300	€ 54,706	€ 57,222	€ 59,854	€ 62,608	€ 65,488
3	Market share		20%	10%	10%	10%	10%	10%
4	Sales		€ 10,460	€ 5,471	€ 5,722	€ 5,985	€ 6,261	€ 6,549
5	Cost of goods sold		3,661	1,915	2,003	2,095	2,191	2,292
6	Gross margin		6,799	3,556	3,719	3,891	4,070	4,257
7	Committed costs							
8	Investment (cash/non-cash)	(5,500)	1,100	1,100	1,100	1,100	1,100	**1,100**
9	SG&A - cash		5,000	5,000	5,000	5,000	5,000	5,000
10	Total committed costs		6,100	6,100	6,100	6,100	6,100	6,100
11	Operating income before tax		699	(2,544)	(2,381)	(2,209)	(2,030)	(1,843)
12	Tax (savings)		280	(1,018)	(952)	(884)	(812)	(737)
13	Operating income after tax		419	(1,526)	(1,428)	(1,326)	(1,218)	(1,106)
14	Add-back non-cash expenses		1,100	1,100	1,100	1,100	1,100	-
15	Annual cash flows	(€ 5,500)	€ 1,519	(€ 426)	(€ 328)	(€ 226)	(€ 118)	(€ 1,106)
16	NPV - yrs 1-5, with competitor	(€ 4,966)						
17	NPV if terminate after 1 year	(€ 4,093)						
18	NPV - yrs 1-6, with competitor, now	(€ 5,663)						

Appendix 8B

Analysing Real Option Trees by Rolling Backward and with Imperfect Information

Real option trees show multiple possible paths that an investment project can take along succeeding nodes. These nodes can either represent uncertainty or decisions. Uncertainty nodes show several possibilities (branches) and their probabilities, and the node is valued as the expected value of these possibilities. Decision nodes are controlled by the firm, and the node is valued as the maximum of its branches. Option trees are calculated by rolling backwards. Let us look at the following example.

Perfect Predictive Information

A company has a choice to develop a new technology, which requires an investment of €100. The development has a 70 per cent chance of being successful, and a 30 per cent chance of being unsuccessful. If it is unsuccessful, the project ends (without any further cash flows). If it is successful, the company can decide either to end the project (without any further cash flows), or to launch the product, which will require an additional cash outflow of €300. There are three possible market responses: Good, Normal or Bad, which yield €700, €500, and €250, respectively and the probabilities of these market responses are 30, 50 and 20 per cent, respectively. Market research can predict the market response perfectly. This market research is conducted directly after product development has been completed and before the product launch decision has to be made. Let's consider the option tree and the calculation-by-rolling-backwards for this investment project.

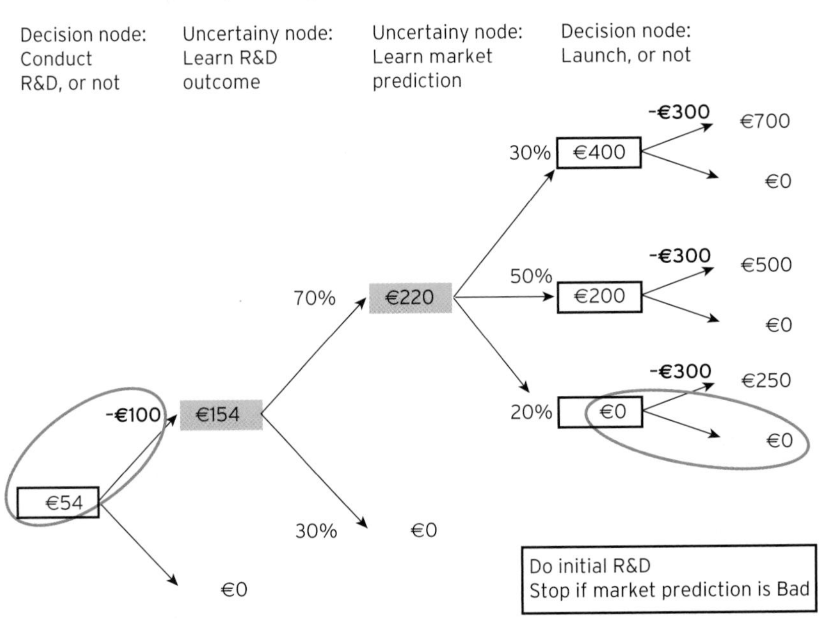

The calculation starts on the right-hand side. The value of the decision nodes is the maximum value of its branches. The first decision node has two branches, one with a value of $-€300 + €700 = €400$, and the other with a value of €0, so managers will select the branch with a value of €400. The logic is similar for the two decision nodes shown below it. One step to the left, there is an uncertainty node with three branches. The value of the uncertainty node is the expected value of its branches: $30\% \times €400 + 50\% \times €200 + 20\% \times €0 = €220$. Similarly, one step further to the left, the uncertainty node has an expected value of $70\% \times €220 + 30\% \times €0 = €154$. Finally, the initial decision node has two nodes, one with a value of $-€100 + €154 = €54$, and the other with a value of €0, so managers will select the branch with a value of €54. The recommended decisions are therefore: to start the initial R&D, to stop the project if the market predication is Bad, and to launch the product if the market prediction is Normal or Good.

In ShadeTree's proposed strategic European expansion investment, an important uncertainty is whether or not a major competitor will enter the market. The decisions involve whether to expand now or to defer the decision by one year, and then whether to expand or not after one year. A complication in these kinds of models is the discount rate. The discount rate depends on the project risk and this risk may not be the same in all branches of an option tree. There are several techniques to correct for this, but these are beyond the scope of this text.

Imperfect Predictive Information

In ShadeTree's proposed strategic European expansion investment, waiting one year will completely resolve the uncertainty about the competitor's actions. However, this may not be the case. Waiting can also reduce uncertainty without completely settling it. Similarly, suppose that the product development example introduced in this appendix, market research cannot predict the market response perfectly. The market research is conducted directly after product development has been completed and before the product launch decision has to be made. However, the actual market response is only learnt after the product launch, and the response can differ from the prediction. The option tree looks as follows:

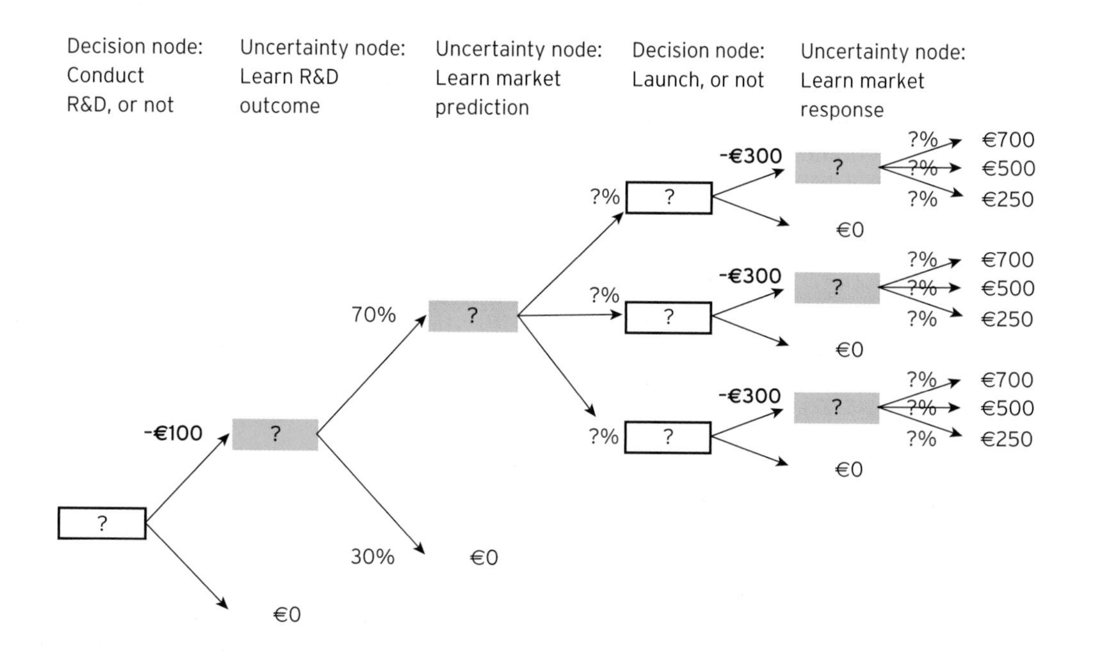

More generally, there are situations where predictive information is important but not perfect. Oil firms conduct geological surveys to predict the probability of finding oil in a particular spot, but only the actual drilling will provide the definite answer of whether there is oil. Firms also conduct laboratory tests of the functionality or performance of new products, use weather forecasts, and do consumer research. Typically, the predictive quality of such a test is expressed as the chance of a particular prediction given the actual state of the world. In our example, the market research can yield three predictions about the expected market response: 'Good', 'Normal', or 'Bad', and you have information about the nine conditional probabilities of the market prediction *given* the actual market response, for example:

- P(Good market response prediction | Good market response) = 85 per cent, so the prediction is correct,
- P(Normal market response prediction | Good market response) = 10 per cent, now the prediction is incorrect,
- P(Bad market response prediction | Good market response) = 5 per cent, now the prediction is also incorrect.

The nine conditional probabilities in as follows:

Conditional probablities of market response prediction *given* actual market response

		Market response		
		Good	Normal	Bad
Market	Good	85%	10%	5%
Response	Normal	10%	80%	5%
Prediction	Bad	5%	10%	90%

Just to be extra clear: 'Bad market response prediction' does not mean that the prediction is bad, as in 'wrong', but that a Bad market response is predicted.

However, looking at the decision tree, it is clear that the analysts need more information, namely information about (a) the probabilities of receiving the different market predictions, and (b) the conditional probabilities of a particular market response *given* a market prediction, so for example:

- P(Good market response | Good market response prediction), or
- P(Normal market response | Good market response prediction), or
- P(Bad market response | Good market response prediction).

We go through the calculations in two steps.

(a) Probabilities of receiving the different market response predictions

For example, a prediction of a Good market response can occur in combination with actually having a Good, Normal or Bad market. That is why

P (Good market response prediction) =
P(Good market response, Good market response prediction) +
P(Normal market response, Good market response prediction) +
P(Bad market response, Good market response prediction)

These probabilities can be calculated as follows, using the probabilities that are known:

- P(Good market response, Good market response prediction) = P(Good market response) × P(Good market response prediction | Good market response) = 30% × 85% = 25.5%
- P(Normal market response, Good market response prediction) = P(Normal market response) × P(Good market response prediction | Normal market response) = 50% × 10% = 5.0%
- P(Bad market response, Good market response prediction) = P(Bad market response) × P(Good market response prediction | Bad market response) = 20% × 5% = 1.0%.

And so, P(Good market response prediction) = 25.5% + 5.0% + 1.0% = 31.5%

Similarly, P(Normal market response prediction) = 44.0% and P(Bad market response prediction) = 24.5%.

(b) Conditional probabilities of a particular market response given *a market prediction*

In general, the conditional probability of event A *given* B, P(A | B) = P(A, B) ÷ P(B). Using this, for example:

- P(Good market response | Good market response prediction) = P(Good market response, Good market response prediction) ÷ P(Good market response prediction) = 25.5% ÷ 31.5% = 81.0%
- P(Normal market response | Good market response prediction) = P(Normal market response, Goodmarketresponseprediction) ÷ P(Goodmarketresponseprediction) = 5.0% ÷ 31.5% = 15.9%

- P(Bad market response | Good market response prediction) = P(Bad market response, Good market response prediction) ÷ P(Good market response prediction) = 1.0% ÷ 31.5% = 3.2%.

These probabilities are used in the option tree below.

The other six conditional probabilities are calculated in the same way and are also used in the option tree below.

Using these results, the option tree can be calculated as follows:

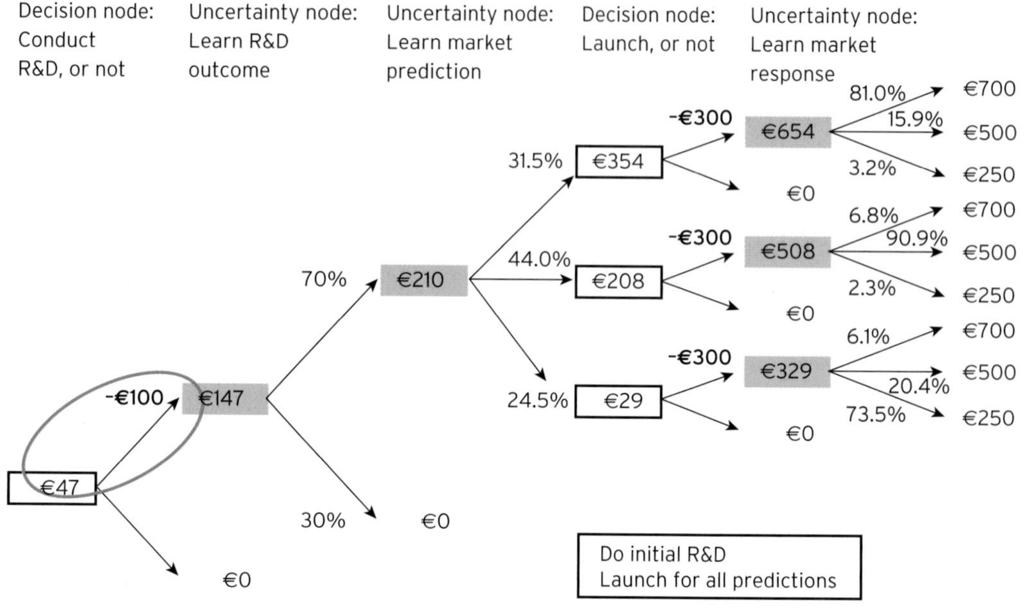

Chapter Summary

This chapter focuses on strategic investment decisions. Investment decisions are long-term commitments of capital and effort that preclude other opportunities. Thus, these decisions have opportunity costs over time, which are measured by forgone interest. Analysts use discounted cash flow (DCF) methods to evaluate alternative investments. The chapter reviews net present value (NPV) analysis, which is a common DCF method. Strategic investment analysis accounts for uncertain future events and competitors' actions. Strategic analysis also considers management flexibility to change investments as relevant information is gathered.

Real option value (ROV) analysis combines decision-tree representations of management flexibility, NPV analysis, and expected value analysis to analyse strategic investments. ROV analysis can lead to materially different investment decisions when, for example, investments are irreversible and deferred decisions can benefit from additional information that becomes available over time.

The large monetary amounts of strategic investments can provide temptations for unethical and illegal practices that most organizations forbid. Organizations use multiple internal controls to encourage ethical and legal behaviour, including hiring policies, training, reporting and reviews, ethical codes and internal audits.

Key Terms

For each term's definition, refer to the indicated page, or turn to the glossary at the end of the text.

annuity,	362	make-or-buy decision,	364
compensatory method,	371	multi-criteria decision-making,	370
decision tree	347	net present value (NPV),	356
discount rate,	352	non-compensatory method,	371
discounted cash flows (DCF),	346	opportunity cost,	349
due diligence,	372	outsourcing,	364
expected value,	375	payback period,	357
expected value analysis,	375	present value,	355
inconsistent ranking,	360	real option value,	385
internal audits,	387	real option value (ROV) analysis,	381
internal rate of return (IRR),	358	strategic investment,	371

*Review Questions are mostly written at a **basic** level; Critical Analysis questions and Exercises are **intermediate**, and Problems and Cases are **advanced**.*

Review Questions

8.1 What is the difference between a consumption decision and an investment decision?

8.2 What two types of factors affect strategic investment decisions?

8.3 Describe the strategic nature of the investments by Chinese and Indian companies described in Cost Management in Practice 8.2.

8.4 When might an organization's financial records be useful for anticipating uncontrollable future events and their likelihood of occurrence?

8.5 What are the advantages of using news, government, foundation and industry analyses of uncontrollable future events and their likelihood of occurrence?

8.6 How does expected value analysis summarize what is known about uncontrollable future events and their likelihood of occurrence?

8.7 If expected market growth can be either 10 per cent or 2 per cent with probabilities of occurrence of 30 per cent and 70 per cent, respectively, you can determine the expected value of market growth. Describe the meaning of that amount for planning and for actual future market growth.

8.8 Explain why analysts added back depreciation expense to compute operating cash flow in Exhibit 8.17.

8.9 Explain how non-financial qualitative factors might override NPV analysis of investing in improved Internet access (Cost Management in Practice 8.3).

8.10 Why should organizations try to anticipate competitors' actions as part of analysing strategic investments? Give an example.

8.11 Traditional accounting systems record only actual transactions. How can opportunity costs, which usually are not actual transactions, be important in decision making?

8.12 What is different about real option value (ROV) analysis compared to traditional net present value (NPV) analysis?

8.13 How might ROV analysis lead to accepting an investment that traditional NPV analysis says to reject?

8.14 Why might individuals misstate information or results regarding strategic investments?

8.15 Describe how internal controls and audits can support ethical investment practices.

Critical Analysis

8.16 Respond to this comment: Net present value analysis is too narrow and excludes important factors in decision making.

8.17 If an investment does not fit with an organization's strategic plan, it is probably not a good idea, even if the NPV is positive. Do you agree or disagree? Explain.

8.18 Where would real option value analysis be more useful, replacing a machine with a new model that has a 5-year life or replacing a mass-production method with a flexible, JIT production method? Explain.

8.19 Respond to this observation in the context of investment decisions: Estimating future cash flows is a nightmare compared to measuring the cost of capital.

8.20 CEO: 'It's all well and good for you to say that I should disregard sunk costs when I consider whether to sell this unprofitable operation. After we report lower-than-expected profits, you won't have to answer the angry questions from shareholders and analysts because our share price has dropped or from employees who say this is just a way to keep from paying bonuses.' Explain the CEO's rationale for not selling an unprofitable business unit. Do you agree? Why or why not?

8.21 A medium-size retailer of upscale retail goods is considering outsourcing its data-processing, human resources, billing, and legal activities. Prepare a list of the benefits and costs of these considerations.

8.22 Sometimes investments with a positive NPV have a negative impact on earnings. For example, investing in certain types of research and development could result in a large expense at the time of investment with the benefits coming years later. Suppose an executive rejects all investments that decrease current earnings, citing qualitative factors and the belief that lower earnings will depress share prices to the detriment of shareholders. What other, unspoken factors might be behind this behaviour?

8.23 The chapter describes how ShadeTree Roasters have included social causes in their strategic plans. Do you think this is a good business practice? Explain.

8.24 ShadeTree Roasters is planning an expansion to central Europe, but the chapter does not discuss contingency plans beyond terminating the investment if a major competitor enters the market. Individually or with a small group, develop a plan C that ShadeTree Roasters might implement if market growth is much lower than expected.

8.25 Expected NPV analysis does not model the risk of investments directly. Discuss how sensitivity and scenario analyses model investment risk. Some experts argue that these analyses are better for modelling risk than adding a higher risk premium to the discount rate for riskier projects. Explain why that might be the case.

8.26 Explain how ABC and NPV analyses can be used together to evaluate an investment.

8.27 Of course depreciation is a source of cash flow. There it is right on your NPV analysis. Explain.

8.28 Consider both sides of this argument. *Side 1:* Portraying all the possible combinations of different future external events can become hopelessly complex. Imagine the size of a decision tree that has 15 future events with three different levels each. Because reality can be even more complex than that, ROV analysis can never be truly useful and one might as well just use NPV analysis. *Side 2:* You are right, reality is complex, but using a simplistic approach to investment analysis does not make the world simpler; it just makes the world look that way. ROV analysis can be useful even in a very complex environment because it forces analysts to understand complexity and model its implications for investments. State and explain your side of this argument.

8.29 You are a member of a strategic planning team that is considering a decision, the success of which depends on your major competitor's actions. Your colleague suggests that the best legal way to learn about a competitor's future actions is to hire away one of the competitor's key employees. What do you think of this approach?

Exercises

Exercise 8.30 [LO 2] Decision Between Leasing and Buying

In recent years, the number of new cars leased by individuals has increased significantly. Many consumers, dealers and manufacturers find the leasing alternative preferable to bank financing or an outright purchase, especially when prices are high and vehicle sales are slow.

Required

Form small groups to visit a local automobile dealership. Talk to an employee in the financing area about the relative merits of leasing versus purchasing a new automobile. Obtain dollar amounts comparing leasing to purchasing. List the relevant costs and benefits associated with the two alternatives. Include any qualitative considerations as well. Summarize your findings in a decision-tree outline submitted to your instructor. (Do not lease or purchase an automobile as part of your assignment.)

Exercise 8.31 [LO 2] Effective Interest on a Loan

A computer company advertises its financing plan as follows: For a loan of €750, you pay a one-time fee of €49.95 and then you simply repay the loan during 10 months, each month paying €75.00. According to the advertisement, the effective interest rate is 6.66 per cent per year.

Required

a. Calculate the effective interest per year on the basis of discounting, assuming that the monthly payments start at the end of the first month. In other words: find the interest rate, such that the present value of the cash flows for a loan equals the cash payment without a loan of €750.

b. Calculate the effective interest more 'roughly' by simply relating the interest paid to the average amount of the loan. (*Hint*: this should be close to your answer above.)

c. Find out how the computer company calculated their claimed effective interest of 6.66 per cent. In other words: reconstruct their calculation, which is very wrong. Explain the two big mistakes made in their calculation.

Exercise 8.32 [LO 1] Relevant Costs

Match the cost(s) most likely to be relevant to each listed decision.

Decision	Cost
Accept a special order	a. Internal unit-level manufacturing cost
Close a plant	b. Cost to buy externally
Launch a new product	c. Opportunity cost of alternative use
Make or buy a product component	d. Cost paid for parts on hand
Outsource a business activity	e. Lease cost for facility
	f. Loss of quality reputation
	g. Loss of control
	h. Loss of employee trust

Exercise 8.33 [LO 1] Decision Tree

Prepare a decision tree to reflect the choice between repairing an old car or buying a new or used car. Identify quantitative and qualitative costs and benefits.

Exercise 8.34 [LO 1] Strategic Investments

Give at least one reason for classifying each of the following investment decisions as either routine or strategic.

a. The University of Göttingen's decision to replace existing personal computers after three years.
b. Microsoft's decision to purchase a small, innovative company that is developing new technology.
c. Southwest Airline's decision to base its airplane maintenance facilities in Mexico to take advantage of lower labour costs.
d. General Electric's decision to expand its in-house 'college'.

Exercise 8.35 [LO 5] Uncontrollable External Events

Identify two relevant, uncontrollable external events and two possible competitors' actions that might affect each of the following investment decisions:

a. **Level3's** decision to install thousands of miles of fibre-optic cable between major cities to support worldwide Internet-based communications.
b. **DaimlerChrysler's** decision to develop hydrogen fuel cell-powered vehicles.
c. **Motorola's** decision to develop *Iridium*, a satellite-based telecommunication system.
d. **Merck/Schering-Plough's** investment in *Zetia*, a drug to block absorption of cholesterol.

Exercise 8.36 [LO 3] Net Present Value

The City of Utrecht, the Netherlands is considering an investment that would expand a community centre. City analysts forecast the following net cash flows over the next 10 years, after which a major reinvestment is expected.

End of year	Net cash flow
0	€(500,000)
1	60,000
2	65,000
3	75,000
4	85,000
5	85,000
6	95,000
7	95,000

8	100,000
9	90,000
10	85,000

Required

Build a spreadsheet to solve the following requirements:

a. What is the net present value of the project if the appropriate discount rate is 10 per cent?
b. What is the net present value of the project if the appropriate discount rate is 8 per cent?

Exercise 8.37 [LO 4] Evaluating Qualitative Factors

Consider the investment decision in Exercise 8.36. What qualitative factors might be critical to evaluating this decision? If the discount rate is 10 per cent, what monetary value of the qualitative factors would make the project financially viable?

Exercise 8.38 [LO 3] Net Present Value and Leasing

Non-profit DRK Kliniken Berlin is considering opening a new hospital branch to reduce travel costs incurred by patients and staff. Because the centre depends on community support and donations and has no budget excess, it must make wise investment decisions. A financial executive who volunteers at the centre made the following estimates of cash flow savings related to the new centre over the next five years.

End of year	Cash flow savings
1	€50,000
2	55,000
3	60,000
4	65,000
5	70,000

Required

a. What is the most the clinic should commit for a 5-year lease on a building, fixtures and other start-up costs if the appropriate discount rate is 8 per cent?
b. What is the most the clinic should commit for a 5-year lease on a building, fixtures and other start-up costs if the appropriate discount rate is 4 per cent?

Exercise 8.39 [LO 4] Evaluating Qualitative Factors

Consider the investment decision in Exercise 8.38. What qualitative factors might be critical to evaluating this decision? If the lowest-cost alternative is €300,000 and if the discount rate is 8 per cent, what monetary value of the qualitative factors would make the project financially viable?

Exercise 8.40 [LO 2] Basic DCF Using Spreadsheets

Build a spreadsheet to compute a discount rate of 8 per cent per year for each requirement.

Required

a. Present value of £(6,500) now
b. Present value of £3,000 one year from now
c. Present value of £3,500 two years from now
d. Present value of £2,500 three years from now

e. Present value of £2,000 four years from now
f. Net present value of (a)–(e) using the SUM function
g. Net present value of (a)–(e) using the NPV function
h. Internal rate of return of (a)–(e) using the IRR function
i. Payback period of (a)–(e)

Exercise 8.41 [LO 2] Inconsistent Ranking of Projects

An organization considers three mutually exclusive projects. For each project, estimations are available regarding the initial capital investment, the market value of these after 20 years, and annual cash flows. These annual cash flows consist of cash outflows for operations and maintenance, and cash inflows from selling services to users. See the table below.

	Project A	Project B	Project C
Capital investment	€125,000	€160,000	€180,000
Residual value	€40,000	€50,000	€50,000
Annual O&M	€10,000	€10,000	€9,500
Annual cash inflow	€35,000	€42,000	€44,000

a. For each project, calculate the present value of the cash inflows. Use a discount rate of 10 per cent.
b. For each project, calculate the net present value (NPV).
c. For each project, calculate the internal rate of return (IRR).
d. There is inconsistent ranking. Explain this in words and also using a calculation of the NPV and the IRR of the difference between projects A and B, the difference between projects B and C, and the difference between projects A and C.

Exercise 8.42 [LO 6] Modelling Competitors' Actions

HvalKebab is planning to open a fast-food restaurant near the University of Oslo's new campus housing. HvalKebab estimates that the current neighbourhood's fast-food market is kr1,200,000 per year, which will double when the new housing is occupied next year. HvalKebab expects to capture 25 per cent of the total neighbourhood market unless MacBurger also opens a new store in the area. In that case, HvalKebab expects to gain only 10 per cent of the market. HvalKebab's gross margin ratio is 30 per cent. (Monetary units given in Norwegian krone, kr.)

Required

a. Compute HvalKebab's forecasted gross margin for next year *without* a major competitor.
b. Compute HvalKebab's forecasted gross margin for next year *with* a major competitor.

Exercise 8.43 [LO 6] Modelling Competitors' Actions

Mid-sized Virton, Belgium plans to completely renovate its ageing shopping mall. The city depends on value added (sales) tax revenues of 21 per cent of sales at the mall to fund many city services, but sales at the mall have declined to a current €90 million. Virton's plans call for 20 per cent annual growth in sales at the mall after renovation, which will take one year unless the neighbouring city of Aubange attracts a **Carrefour Hypermarket**. In that case, Virton's mall might experience only 5 per cent annual growth. The mall's sales tax revenues will decline 25 per cent from its current level during the renovation period.

Required

a. Compute Virton's value added tax revenues after the renovation *without* competition from Aubange.
b. Compute Virton's value added tax revenues after the renovation *with* competition from Aubange.

Exercise 8.44 [LO 7] Decision Tree and Expected NPV

HvalKebab (Exercise 8.42) is planning to open a new restaurant that might be affected by the entry of MacBurger into the same market area. HvalKebab could invest in the new restaurant now by buying and improving property. HvalKebab analysts believe there is a 40 per cent chance that MacBurger will enter the market. They have prepared the following NPV estimates: (Monetary units given in Norwegian Krone, kr.)

Decision and competitor's action	NPV estimate
Invest now, without a major competitor	kr90,378
Invest now, with a major competitor	(168,348)
Invest now, with a major competitor, terminate after one year	(93,336)

Required

a. Prepare a decision tree of this investment alternative similar to the one in Exhibit 8.23.
b. Compute the expected NPV of the decision to invest now.

Exercise 8.45 [LO 7] Decision Tree and Expected NPV

HvalKebab (Exercises 8.42 and 8.44) is planning to open a new store that might be affected by the entry of MacBurger into the same market area. HvalKebab could defer its decision to invest by one year to learn whether MacBurger will enter the market. HvalKebab analysts believe there is a 40 per cent chance that MacBurger will enter the market. They have prepared the following NPV estimates: (Monetary units given in Norwegian krone, kr.)

Decision and competitor's action	NPV estimate
Defer the decision, without a major competitor	kr94,272
Defer the decision, with a major competitor	(104,460)

Required

a. Prepare a decision tree of this investment alternative similar to the one in Exhibit 8.22.
b. Compute the expected NPV of the decision to defer the decision one year.

Exercise 8.46 [LO 7] Real Option Value

HvalKebab (Exercises 8.42, 8.44 and 8.45) is planning to open a new store that might be affected by the entry of MacBurger into the same market area. Assume the expected NPV of investing in the new store now is kr17,000 and the expected NPV of deferring the decision one year is kr60,000.

Required

a. What is the real option value of waiting for one year?
b. Explain the economic meaning of this amount.

Exercise 8.47 [LO 8] Ethical Investment Practices

Give at least one reason that each of the following investment activities might be unethical or illegal and one reason that each of the following investment activities might *not* be unethical or illegal.

a. Paying a fee to a third party who understands local market conditions and can streamline interactions with government regulators.
b. Restating the expected salvage value of an investment.
c. Obtaining information about a competitor's planned actions.
d. Not giving close supervision to subordinates who make investment plans or decisions.
e. Not modelling an adverse scenario of future events.

Exercise 8.48 [LO 8] Code of Ethical Investment Practices

Perform an Internet search for a company that describes how an ethical code guides its investment practices. Prepare a short memorandum to your instructor that describes the company, its ethical code, and how the code affects investment practices.

Exercise 8.49 [LO 3] Outsourcing

Locate a recent article on outsourcing practices. Complete the following requirements based on the article.

Required

a. What are the major reasons for the decision to outsource?
b. What are the major concerns about outsourcing?
c. Which business functions are outsourced?

Exercise 8.50 [LO 3] Relevant Costs

Kassel Digital Machining's performance for the first 11 months of the year has been a surprise with sales and profits somewhat above expectations. On 20 December, just prior to the holiday break, Jan Schmidt faced the decision of scrapping some old equipment and replacing it. The old equipment had a book value of €400,000 but could be sold for only €250,000. The new machinery had a cost of €1,500,000 and was expected to produce net annual savings in cash operating costs of €180,000 over a 10-year life. The investment predicts returns higher than the minimum return required by the company. Schmidt's year-end bonus is computed on the basis of company profitability.

Required

a. Discuss the conflict that sometimes arises in business between decision making and performance evaluation.
b. Should Schmidt acquire the new machinery? Why? Show computations to support your answer. Ignore taxes and the time value of money.

Problems

Problem 8.51 [LO 3] Outsourcing

Diamant Noir, SA, has been manufacturing 5,000 units of part 10541 per month. At this level of production, the company's costs (expressed on a per-unit basis) are:

Unit-level cost	€40
Facility-level cost	15
Total cost per unit	€55

Diamant Noir can outsource the manufacture of 5,000 units of part 10541 to Mogul Company at a cost of €48 per unit to Diamant Noir. If Diamant Noir does outsource the part, it has determined that it can sell some facilities it presently uses to produce part 10541 and use the remaining facilities to manufacture a new product, RAC. Diamant Noir also has determined that facility costs can drop by one-third if it outsources part 10541 to Mogul.

Required

a. Should Diamant Noir make or buy this part?
b. How much profit must the new product RAC generate to justify the decision to outsource part 10541?
c. What other considerations are important to this outsourcing decision?

[CPA adapted]

Problem 8.52 [LO 1] Decision Tree and Benefit-Cost Analysis

Maytag Corp. recently purchased rival **Amana Appliances** and is consolidating its manufacturing and assembly processes. Maytag now wants to reduce costs for the combined businesses by moving some labour-intensive assembly operations to Mexico. The new assembly plant, with an estimated initial investment of $2 million, will receive plastic and metal parts from Maytag's manufacturing plants and will return subassemblies to Maytag's US operations for final assembly. The new operation will employ about 230 people and will be similar to Maytag's **Hoover** floor-care plant that it has operated for more than 17 years. Amana has operated assembly operations in Amana, Iowa, Florence, South Carolina, and Searcy, Arkansas.

Required

a. Use the decision-making framework in Exhibit 1.1 in Chapter 1 (and your imagination) to describe Maytag Corp.'s decision making about whether to locate a new assembly plant in Mexico.
b. Prepare a decision tree that describes Maytag Corp.'s assembly plant decision making and includes qualitative and quantitative benefits and costs.

[Adapted from Lauzon, 2001]

Problem 8.53 [LO 3] Make or Buy

South Africa Automotive Components (SAAC) purchases 200,000 pumps annually from Cemo Pumps Ltd. The pumps are used in complete fuel pump assemblies sold by SAAC. Because the price keeps increasing and reached ZAR105 per unit last year, SAAC's management has asked for a cost estimate to manufacture the pump internally. SAAC has little experience with manufacturing this specific part.

The engineering, manufacturing and accounting departments have prepared a report for management that includes the following estimate for an assembly run of 200,000 pumps. To manufacture the pumps SAAC will hire additional production employees but will need no additional equipment, space or supervision. The report estimates that total costs for 200,000 units are estimated at ZAR22,400,000, or ZAR112 per unit. The current purchase price is ZAR105 per unit, so the report recommends the continued purchase of the product. If the pumps are purchased, the currently unused space could be leased for ZAR700,000 annually. (Monetary units given in South African rand, ZAR.)

Components	ZAR8,050,000
Assembly labour*	11,550,000
Share of existing facility costs based on labour	2,800,000
Total costs	ZAR22,400,000

*Assembly labour consists of hourly production workers.

Required

a. Was the analysis prepared by SAAC's engineering, manufacturing and accounting departments and their recommendation to continue purchasing the pumps correct? Explain your answer and include any supporting calculations that you consider necessary.
b. Present several benefits and problems of dealing with outside suppliers such as Cemo Pumps Ltd.

[CMA adapted]

Problem 8.54 [LO 3] Drop a Service

Hergé College is a small liberal arts school located in Etterbeek, Belgium. It is evaluating its botany programme because the programme's tuition revenues and costs recently produced an €80,000 loss, which is typical of performance in the past few years. Tuition revenues earned totalled €320,000; operating expenses were faculty salaries, €215,000; supplies, €10,000; and other facility costs, €175,000. If the programme is dropped, the following are expected:

- Some students will change majors, but overall college enrolment will decline as other students transfer to other universities. Total lost tuition revenue is estimated at €195,000.
- Untenured faculty members with combined salaries of €170,000 can be dismissed. The tenured faculty will transfer to the biology department. In addition, 75 per cent of the programme's supplies cost can be saved.
- Other facility costs include €98,000 of general college overhead costs that are assigned to the programme and €77,000 of salaries earned by office and support personnel. One of these employees (annual salary, €22,000) will be transferred to the music school; other employees can be laid off.

- Equipment will be removed and transferred to the fine arts school at a cost of €1,100. The vacated space can be converted to a weight room and physical conditioning facility for student athletes. This new facility likely will help attract better athletes and make the college's athletic programmes more competitive.

The director of development reports that Annemarie Ficus, an alumna and supporter of the botany programme, is now sole owner of the highly successful Ficus Scientific Corporation. Ficus has designated the college as a major beneficiary of her estate.

Required

a. Should Hergé drop the botany programme? Show calculations.
b. What other factors should be considered if the decision is made to drop the programme?
c. What options might be open to Hergé if it continues the programme and the college's president mandates that 'programme losses must be eliminated within three years'?

Problem 8.55 [LO 3, 5] DCF Analysis

Wärtsilä, Oyj. is a Finnish company that manufactures large diesel and gas engines for use in powering ships and electricity generation. Wärtsilä is considering investing in a robotics manufacturing process. Purchase and installation of the process will cost an estimated €5,400,000. This amount must be paid immediately. The company expects to dismantle this production process at the end of its 7-year life and salvage the equipment for €400,000. Wärtsilä will depreciate the process equipment at €750,000 per year. Starting in year 4, the company expects significant quality improvements valued at €4 million until the end of the process in year 7. Because this investment is risky, the company believes it should use an 18 per cent discount rate. The company's effective tax rate is 40 per cent.

Required

a. Build a spreadsheet to compute the net present value of this investment.
b. Is this a routine or strategic investment? Explain.
c. What is your evaluation of the way this company models risk?

[CMA adapted]

Problem 8.56 [LO 2] DCF Analysis

Octopus' Garden plc, manufactures innovative trendy toys and gifts. Successful gifts provide a very high rate of return, averaging 16 per cent, and the company's development department has a very good success rate. Marketing research indicates that the latest new toy can be sold for three years but not after that. To meet expected demand for the new toy, Octopus' Garden needs to buy additional equipment and obtain 2,000 square metres of space. The company has 1,000 square metres of unused space, which it controls under a lease with three more years at £3 per square foot per year. Octopus' Garden can rent an additional 1,000 square metres for three years at £4 per square metre per year. The equipment will be purchased for £900,000, depreciated at £290,000 per year, and salvaged for £30,000. Sales, general and administrative (SG&A) costs are allocated to all products, although these costs are not traced to specific products. Octopus' Garden analysts have made the following income forecasts:

End of	Year 1	Year 2	Year 3
Sales	£1,000,000	£1,200,000	£700,000
Unit, batch & product costs	750,000	400,000	350,000
SG&A (allocated)	40,000	75,000	35,000
Rent of existing space	30,000	30,000	30,000
Rent of new space	40,000	40,000	40,000
Depreciation	290,000	290,000	290,000
Income before tax	£(150,000)	£365,000	(45,000)
Tax (savings) @ 28%	(42,000)	102,200	(12,600)
Income after tax	£(108,000)	£262,800	£(32,400)

Required

a. Compute after-tax net cash flows for this investment.
b. Compute the net present value of this investment. Is this a desirable project? Explain why or why not.

[CMA adapted]

Problem 8.57 [LO 1, 2] Assess the Effects of the Discount Rate in DCF Analysis

The financial staff of North American Motors used a 30 per cent discount rate to analyse a technological improvement that promised to save the company millions in quality-related costs. The financial staff recommended that top management reject the project. Production managers responded by email that they believed the new process and equipment were necessary to improve product quality, which had fallen behind that of competitors. They argued that, although quality improvements were a strategic goal of the company, the direct reduction in quality costs was only a small part of the benefits of this project. The company's reputation and sales would improve as the quality of its products improved.

Martha Flowers, chief financial analyst, replied to the production managers' arguments by stating, 'You have not quantified these so-called benefits from improved company reputation, and we don't believe it is possible to do so. Therefore, we have to evaluate this project by the numbers, and the net present value is negative. So, our recommendation is "no"'.

The production managers complained that the use of a 30 per cent discount rate was far too high. Lead production manager Art High said, 'I don't know what thin air you have been breathing, but we almost never get a 30 per cent return on investments'.

Flowers responded, 'We have audited your past technology investments and found that they almost never performed as well as you said they will. Because of your unrealistic projections, we bumped up the discount rate.'

After seeing these emails and a flurry of subsequent ones that became progressively more heated, the division president took two aspirin and called you in for advice. 'Make sense of this,' he said. 'Write a short report that communicates what's really going on here, and advise me what to do with this project.'

Required

Write the report requested by the division president.

Problem 8.58 [LO 2] Equipment Replacement, DCF Analysis and Non-financial Factors

Zug Medical Equipment AG plans to replace its customer service computing equipment now to improve service and reduce costs. The manager has made the following estimates to support the decision. (Monetary units given in Swiss Francs, CHF.)

New equipment cost, including installation and training	CHF140,000
Salvage value of new equipment at the end of its life	CHF0
New equipment useful life	4 years
Salvage value of old equipment	CHF0
Annual increase in contribution margin	CHF28,000
Annual operating cost savings	CHF18,000
Income tax rate	25%
Discount rate	10%

Required

Build a spreadsheet to create an analysis similar to the one in Exhibit 8.5 to solve requirements (a) and (b).

a. Net present value of the equipment replacement decision using the NPV function.
b. Internal rate of return of the equipment replacement decision using the IRR function.
c. Should Zug Medical Equipment replace its computing equipment? What non-financial factors might be important to this decision?

Problem 8.59 [LO 2] Equipment Replacement, DCF Analysis and Sensitivity Analysis

Construcción Pirineo (CP) prefabricates cabins and storage sheds in the mountainous regions near the city of Lleida, Spain. CP is considering replacing some of its existing manufacturing equipment now to increase its production capacity and consequent sales. The new equipment also will reduce annual energy costs. CP's CFO has estimated the following information to support the decision.

New equipment cost, including installation and training	€150,000
Salvage value of new equipment at the end of its life	0
New equipment useful life	3 years
Salvage value of old equipment (equals the old equipment's net book value)	€10,000
Annual increase in contribution margin	€30,000
Annual energy cost savings	€35,000
Income tax rate	30%
Discount rate	10%

Required

Build a spreadsheet to create an analysis similar to the one in Exhibit 8.5 to solve requirements (a)–(c).

a. Net present value using the NPV function.
b. Internal rate of return using the IRR function.
c. Lowest energy cost savings that would give the investment a zero NPV. (*Hint:* Use 'Solver' or 'Goal Seek'.)
d. What controllable and uncontrollable factors might affect the new equipment's energy cost savings?

Problem 8.60 [LO 2] Equipment Replacement, DCF Analysis and Sensitivity Analysis

HvalKebab fast-food restaurant plans to add a second cafeteria truck to service Norway's Stavanger Harbour, where growing numbers of oil workers and commercial fishermen head out to sea and return from work. The company's owner has made the following estimates related to adding a second truck. (Monetary values given in Norwegian krone, kr.)

New truck cost, including installation of kitchen equipment	kr900,000
Salvage value of new equipment	72,000
New equipment useful life	5 years
Annual increase in contribution margin	kr270,000
Income tax rate	35%
Discount rate	8%

Required

Build a spreadsheet to create an analysis similar to the one in Exhibit 8.5 to compute requirements (a)–(c).

a. Net present value of the equipment expansion decision using the NPV function.
b. Internal rate of return of the equipment expansion decision using the IRR function.
c. Increase in contribution margin that creates a zero NPV for the equipment expansion decision. (*Hint:* Use 'Solver' or 'Goal Seek'.)
d. What controllable and uncontrollable factors might affect the planned contribution margin?

Problem 8.61 [LO 7] Model Effects of Competitors' Actions in DCF Analysis

Kapsalon Patat (KP) is planning to open a fast-food restaurant near a new housing development and office park. KP estimates that the neighbourhood's fast-food market will be €450,000 per year when the new housing and offices are occupied next year. KP expects to capture 25 per cent of the total neighbourhood market unless MacBurger also opens a new location in the area. In that case, KP expects to gain only 15 per cent of the market. KP's gross margin ratio is 40 per cent. Its analysts believe there is a 50 per cent chance that MacBurger will enter the market. They have prepared the following estimates that they believe are valid for the first 4 years of the investment.

First year's market	€450,000
Annual market growth	12%
Market share without MacBurger	25%
Market share with MacBurger	15%
Gross margin ratio	40%
Opportunity (discount) rate	8%
Investment cost	€(86,000)
Tax rate	25.5%
Depreciation	€20,000
SG&A	€10,000
Probability of MacBurger entry	50%

Required

a. Prepare spreadsheet models similar to those in Exhibits 8.20 and 8.21, assuming that Kapsalon Patat can defer its investment decision one year to resolve uncertainty about MacBurger's intentions.
b. What does this analysis indicate about the possible effects of MacBurger's entry into this market?
c. On the basis of this analysis, would you recommend that Kapsalon Patat defer its decision? Explain.

Problem 8.62 [LO 7] Model Effects of Competitors' Actions in DCF Analysis (Appendix 8A)

This is a continuation of Problem 8.61.

Required

a. Build a spreadsheet models similar to those in Exhibits 8.24 and 8.25 (Appendix 8A) that permit comparisons with the models in Problem 8.61. Assume that Kapsalon Patat makes its investment decision now without resolving the uncertainty about MacBurger's intentions. Also assume that Kapsalon Patat can terminate its investment after one year and sell its assets for €63,000. It also can extend its operations through year 5 by spending an additional €25,000 at the end of year 4, which is deductible from income in year 5.
b. What does this analysis indicate about what Kapsalon Patat should do if MacBurger does enter the market in a year?
c. On the basis of this analysis, would you recommend that Kapsalon Patat invest in the new restaurant now? Explain.

Problem 8.63 [LO 7] Apply Real Option Value Analysis

This is a continuation of Problems 8.61 and 8.62.

Required

a. Prepare decision trees similar to those in Exhibits 8.22 and 8.23 that contain expected net present values of Kapsalon Patat's investment options.
b. Does this analysis indicate that it is better for Kapsalon Patat to invest now or wait a year to find more information about MacBurger's plans? Explain.
c. Compute the real option value of waiting one year on this investment decision.
d. What is the economic meaning of the amount calculated in requirement (c)?

Problem 8.64 [LO 1, 5, 6, 7] Apply Real Option Value Analysis

Unreal Networks Inc. participated with several large music industry firms in a joint venture to distribute music electronically to third parties, such as Internet service providers and computer manufacturers, who would then sell the rights to download music to consumers. Unreal Networks is considering an investment in a start-up company that uses Unreal's Internet-based audio and video technology to deliver music directly to consumers. However, the start-up company's technology was unproven, and consumer enthusiasm for paying to download music was unclear. Unreal Networks has identified two investment options: (1) buy a controlling share of the start-up company now or (2) invest a smaller amount now both to support the technology and secure a relationship with the start-up with an option to buy the company later. If Unreal buys the start-up, it will terminate participation in the current joint venture.

Unreal's analysts identified two major external events that could affect consumers' willingness to pay for downloaded music. First, **Apple Computer** was beginning a service to sell downloaded music at $0.99 per song. The success of that business could signal consumers' willingness to pay for selected music. Second, music-recording companies were planning a legal strategy to discourage unlicensed music sharing and downloading. If successful, these approaches could enlarge the market for paid downloads. Either of these events could improve the prospects for significant returns from a purchase of the start-up company; success of both would be a stronger signal.

Required

a. Draw decision trees that describe the investment options that Unreal Networks was considering. Indicate the amounts that it must measure to complete the decision trees.
b. Describe the methods you would use to measure each of the amounts identified in requirement (a).
c. How would you recommend assessing the risks of the investment options?
d. What qualitative factors might be important to this decision?

Problem 8.65 [LO 8] Evaluate Ethical Issues in Strategic Investment Analysis

One-Day Shades LLP is considering expanding its London manufacturing operations. It can either convert a warehouse that it owns outside the city, or it can expand its current plant downtown. After the board of directors approved the expansion, George Wilson, the controller, set about to determine which proposal had the higher net present value. He assigned this task to Helen Griffiths, the assistant controller. She completed her task, which indicated that the warehouse proposal had a negative net present value, but the downtown expansion proposal had a slightly positive one.

Wilson was displeased with Griffiths' report on the suburban warehouse proposal. He returned it to her, stating, 'You must have made an error. This proposal should look better.' She suspected that Wilson wanted the suburban warehouse proposal to succeed so that he could avoid his lengthy commute to the city on the days he worked at the expansion site.

She checked her figures and found nothing wrong, although she believed that estimates of property sales values at the end of the investment lives provided by the real estate department were particularly uncertain. She made minor changes to the wording of the report to that effect but left the substance of the report unchanged. Wilson was still angry and demanded a second revision. He told Griffiths to double the estimate of the suburban warehouse's salvage value because he believes that the real estate department is being too conservative and that suburban land values will increase dramatically as the region continues to grow. This change would make the suburban warehouse proposal's net present value positive and higher than that of the downtown expansion.

Required

a. Was Griffiths' first revision on the proposal for the warehouse proposal unethical? Explain.
b. Was Wilson's conduct unethical when he gave Griffiths specific instructions on preparing the second revision? Explain.
c. How should Griffiths attempt to resolve this issue? Should she discuss this issue with anyone outside the organization?

[CMA adapted]

Cases

Case 8.66 [LO 1] Benefit-Cost Analysis

Grand Coulee Dam on the Columbia River in Washington State, USA was completed in 1941 with the objectives of providing employment, inexpensive electrical power and agricultural irrigation. Since then, additional project objectives have included recreation, flood control and wildlife conservation. Beneficiaries of Grand Coulee Dam include:

- Farmers, who lobbied effectively for the project and receive water and power at subsidized prices.
- Power users, who also lobbied effectively for the project and enjoy below-market rates for electric power.
- Downstream residents, who are protected from floods.
- Recreationists, who have access to boating, lake fishing and hunting.
- Pacific Northwest residents, who have benefited from the extensive regional economic development resulting from the availability of inexpensive electric power.

Others have borne the costs of Grand Coulee Dam. These cost bearers include:

- US taxpayers who financed the project but will not see significant repayments until and beginning in 2009.
- Native Americans and Canadian First Nation members who lost traditional fishing rights and culture because the dam halted annual salmon and steelhead migrations in the Columbia River above the dam and lost reservation lands because Lake Roosevelt, created by the dam, flooded occupied and hunting lands, mostly without compensation or consultation.
- Commercial and sports fishers who lost livelihoods and recreation because the dam halted annual salmon and steelhead migrations above the dam, without compensation or consultation.
- White settlers who were displaced from lands flooded by the lake and who received little or no relocation assistance or adequate compensation and were not consulted.
- Farmers who live outside the power and irrigation district and who must pay unsubsidized prices for power and water.

Granted, this information is available with 70 years of hindsight. Nonetheless, many of the benefits and costs were disputed prior to the project, but only the benefits (along with political manoeuvring) were considered in the decision making. Furthermore, the project had no considerations of irreversible effects or provisions for re-evaluations and possible modifications.

Required

You have been hired by the World Bank to set up a process for identifying and evaluating the benefits and costs of a major hydroelectric and irrigation project in an undeveloped country.

a. What are the major categories of benefits and costs you should expect from this project? Will quantifying and comparing these benefits and costs be problematic? Explain.
b. How would you structure the decision-making process about whether to proceed with this project?
c. How would you propose to re-evaluate the success of the project after completion?

[Adapted from Ortolano and Cushing, 2002]

Case 8.67 [LO 1-4] Expected NPV Analysis

Liquid Chemical Co. – Part 1.[14] Liquid Chemical Company manufactures chemical products that require careful packing. The company has been profitable for the past decade and expects continued future profitability. The company operates a department that maintains its containers in good condition and makes new ones as needed using a special patented container lining made from a material known as GHL.

Matt Walsh, the general manager, believed the firm might save money and get equal service by buying its containers and maintenance services from an outside source. He approached Packages Inc. and asked for a quotation for making and maintaining the containers. He also asked Carol Dyer, his chief financial analyst, for a statement of the cost of operating the container department.

Packages Inc.'s quotation specified that it can supply 3,000 new containers for €1,200,000 a year and can perform routine maintenance on containers for €300,000 a year, the contract to run for a guaranteed term of 5 years and renewable from year to year thereafter. If the required quantity increases, the contract price is increased proportionally. If the required quantity decreases below 3,000 containers, however, Liquid Chemical must pay the contracted amount.

Walsh compared these figures with Dyer's cost figures for last year's container department operations. Those figures are as follows:

Materials		€725,000
Labour		
Supervisor		50,000
Workers		400,000
Department overheads		
Manager's salary (Duffy)	€80,000	
Rent on container department	45,000	
Depreciation on machinery	125,000	
Maintenance of machinery	32,000	
Other expenses	175,000	
		457,000
Total department costs		€1,632,000
Proportion of general administrative overhead		225,000
Total cost of container department for year		€1,857,000

Walsh concluded that closing the department and entering into the contract offered by Packages Inc. was optimal. However, he gave the manager of the container department, Les Duffy, an opportunity to question this conclusion before he acted on it. Even if his department were closed, Duffy's own position was not in jeopardy. There are no net cash consequences for the firm of transferring Duffy to another position because he can fill a position that would otherwise be filled by a newly hired manager paid €80,000 per year.

Duffy thought the matter over. The next morning, he spoke to Walsh and said he thought there were several factors to consider before his department was closed. 'For instance,' he said, 'what will you do with the machinery? It cost €1,000,000 four years ago, but you'd be lucky if you got €300,000 for it now, even though it's good for another five or six years.'

'Another matter,' Duffy said, 'is the expected quantity of containers we will need. The contract prices can be negotiated upward but not downward. The odds are 25 per cent that in any given year we will need only 2,000 containers, but we could just as easily need 4,000. We can save costs internally if demand drops, but we would have to eat the extra contract costs if we outsource containers and maintenance and demand drops.'

Walsh called Dyer in and reported Duffy's points. Dyer said, 'I think my figures are pretty conclusive for 3,000 containers per year. At 2,000 or 4,000 containers per year, materials and machine maintenance costs would shift proportionately, but most likely we would not save or incur additional other costs at those levels. We're also paying €90,000 a year in rent for a warehouse for other corporate purposes. If we closed Duffy's department, we'd have all the warehouse space we need without renting.'

'That's a good point,' said Walsh. 'Moreover, I don't think we can find room easily for the supervisor or any of the workers elsewhere in the firm. We are bound to spend something on outplacement and retraining. Allow €40,000 a year for five years. We also should budget an additional €25,000 for severance pay to be paid in a lump sum when or if we close the department.'

Duffy added, 'What about this €225,000 for general administrative overhead? You surely don't expect to sack anyone in the general office if I'm closed, do you?'

'Probably not,' said Dyer, 'but someone has to pay for these costs. We can't ignore them when we look at an individual department because if we do that with each department in turn, we'll finish up by convincing ourselves that word processing, accounting, administration and the like don't have to be paid for.'

'Well, I've told the people at Packages Inc. that I'd let them know my decision within a week,' said Walsh. 'I'll let you know what I decide to do before I contact them.'

Assume the company has an after-tax cost of capital of 10 per cent per year and uses an income tax rate of 30 per cent for decisions like these. Depreciation for book and tax purposes is straight-line over eight years. The machinery has a tax basis of €500,000. Any gain or loss on sale of machinery is taxed at 30 per cent. For ease of analysis, assume that all cash flows occur at the end of each year. Input data are available here or from your instructor electronically.

Data Input		
Tax rate	30%	
Hurdle (discount) rate	10%	
Decision horizon	5 years	
Materials		
Total materials (make containers, do maintenance)	€725,000 per year	
Machinery		
Machinery purchase cost	€1,000,000	
Machinery salvage value at year 0	€300,000	
Age of machinery	4 years	
Machinery depreciation, assuming zero salvage value	€125,000 per year	
Depreciable life of machinery	8 years	
Opportunity cost of facility rental	€90,000 per year	
Labour costs		
Labour	€400,000 per year	
Supervisor	€50,000 per year	
Manager	€80,000 per year	
Severance costs	€25,000 year 0	
Training and outplacement costs	€40,000 per year	
Machinery maintenance	€32,000 per year	
Other expenses	€175,000 per year	
Maintenance contract for containers	€400,000 per year	
Container contract	€1,200,000 per year	
Container demand, units per year, probability now	2,000	25%
Container demand, units per year, probability now	3,000	50%
Container demand, units per year, probability now	4,000	25%

Required

Individually or with a small group, complete requirements (a)–(c).

a. Describe Walsh's two alternative choices and the major uncontrollable, external event identified in the case.
b. Build a financial spreadsheet model of the alternative choices. Which action should be taken? Support your conclusion with a net present value analysis of the alternative costs.
c. How sensitive is your conclusion in requirement (b) to changes in the discount rate? Demonstrate and explain using sensitivity analysis.

Case 8.67 [LO 5-7] Real Option Value Analysis

Liquid Chemical Company – Part 2. Use the information and analyses from Case 8.76 to continue the case. Liquid Chemical's chief competitor is being investigated by the European Environment Agency (EEA). The competitor is facing punitive action for repeated violations. The most serious sanction against the competitor will require it to close its plant for at least three years for clean-up and retooling. Liquid Chemical's legal staff estimates the probability of this sanction to be 40 per cent. Lesser sanctions will increase the competitor's costs but will not lead to a shutdown. The EEA outcome will be known in one year. During a shutdown, total regional demand for containers will drop, and Walsh believes that Liquid Chemical should be able to negotiate 30 per cent lower costs for the 5-year outsourcing contracts for maintenance and containers. Additionally, if the competitor shuts down, Dyer estimates that the probability of Liquid Chemical's demand for only 2,000 containers per year drops to zero and the probabilities of demand for either 3,000 or 4,000 containers per year are equal. Duffy has convinced Walsh that if Liquid Chemical decides to not outsource containers and maintenance, the company should commit to continuing internal operations for the foreseeable future. Assume the following:

- Internal operations will continue for at least one year if the decision is delayed.
- The company could elect to outsource containers and maintenance after learning the competitor's status.
- Neither demand probabilities nor outsourcing costs revert to original values after a competitor shutdown.

Ms Dyer has prepared the following additional analyses.

Decide now?	Decision 1: Internal or outsource?	Competitor shutdown?	Decision 2: Internal or outsource?	Expected NPV
Yes	Internal	Yes	Internal	€4,917,039
Yes	Internal	Yes	Outsource	3,909,057
Yes	Internal	No	Internal	4,612,685
Yes	Internal	No	Outsource	4,938,313
Yes	Outsource	Yes	Outsource	5,186,906
Yes	Outsource	No	Outsource	4,905,527
No	Internal	Yes	Internal	4,917,039
No	Internal	Yes	Outsource	3,909,057
No	Internal	No	Internal	4,612,685
No	Internal	No	Outsource	4,938,313

Required

Individually or with a small group, address the following:

a. Prepare a decision tree of the decisions to decide now or wait a year.
b. Does waiting a year for the EEA ruling before making this decision have value? Demonstrate and support your answer using real option value analysis. What is your recommendation?

Case 8.68 [LO 1-7] Real Option Value Analysis

Virton, Belgium plans to remodel its ageing shopping mall. The city owns the property and depends on value added (sales) tax revenue of 21 per cent of sales at the mall to fund many city services, but annual sales at the mall have declined 5 per cent to a current €90 million. Virton's plans call for 20 per cent annual growth in sales at the mall after remodelling, which will take one year, unless the neighbouring city of Aubange attracts a Carrefour Hypermarket. In that case, Virton's mall might experience only 10 per cent annual growth. The city manager believes that if the city acts quickly, the probability that Carrefour will move to Aubange is 20 per cent, but if the city delays as much as a year, the probability rises to 75 per cent.

The mall's sales tax revenues will decline 25 per cent during the remodelling period. Because merchants and customers alike are fleeing the ageing mall, the city believes it must either remodel the mall or demolish it now and sell the land to private developers. The city's current remodelling costs will be €8 million. However, the city's district federal representative is certain that she can obtain an urban renewal grant for 40 per cent of the cost, but government approval will take one year. The city's current budget crisis makes the federal grant very attractive. Is it worth waiting for?

Virton's director of finance, Walter Baele, has consulted private developers and the city's planning and urban renewal boards to assemble the following estimates relevant to the mall remodelling.

Data Input	Amount (thousands)
Remodelling cost – now	€(8,000)
Remodelling cost – defer one year	€(5,000)
Current mall sales	€90,000 per year

Administrative costs	€1,500 per year
Net proceeds of demolition	€4,000
Discount rate	6%
Value added (sales) tax rate	21%
Current rate of sales decline	(5%) per year
Sales growth without **Carrefour**	20% per year
Sales growth with **Carrefour**	10% per year
Sales decline during remodelling	(25%) per year
Probability of **Carrefour** if delay	75%
Probability of **Carrefour** if act now	20%
Remodel life	10 years

Required

a. From the perspective of Virton, prepare a real option value (ROV) analysis of the decision either to remodel the mall now or defer a year. (*Hint:* Deferring the decision one year means you should give all alternatives equal lives.) What is your recommendation?

b. Demonstrate the sensitivity of the ROV analysis to estimates of the probabilities of **Carrefour's** actions now or later.

c. What qualitative factors might be important to the decision?

d. Make a presentation of your analysis suitable for discussion at a meeting of Virton's mayor, director of finance, planning board and urban renewal board.

Solutions to You're the Decision Maker

8.1 Further Analysis of Dropping a Business, p. 369

Both alternatives promise improved profitability and a higher NPV over de status quo and over the alternative to simply close the store. The track record of the new store manager, who will receive a higher salary, should be good enough to warrant the higher labour cost. If the manager would be unable to reduce other operational costs and improve revenues, the financial results may not be better than the status quo. The investment in kitchen equipment and display cabinets promises to be a good idea, but now it is even more important that the expectations are sound.

	A	B	C	D	E
57	**Alternative: Improve**				
58	Initial cash flows	$-			
59	Annual operating income items				
60	Contribution margin		$335,000	$335,000	$ 335,000
61	Store rent		(24,000)	(24,000)	(24,000)
62	Labour costs store manager		(75,000)	(75,000)	(75,000)
63	Other operating costs		(150,000)	(150,000)	(150,000)
64	Central services		(18,000)	(18,000)	(18,000)
65	Depreciation expense		(40,000)	(40,000)	(40,000)
66	Change in operating income		28,000	28,000	28,000
67	Tax on change in income		(11,200)	(11,200)	(11,200)
68	After-tax change in operating income		16,800	16,800	16,800
69	Add back depreciation expense		40,000	40,000	40,000
70	After-tax operating cash flow		56,800	56,800	56,800
71	Disinvestment cash flows				$-
72	Net cash flow	-	56,800	56,800	56,800
73	Present value factors	1.000	0.926	0.857	0.794
74	Present values of cash flows	-	$52,593	$48,697	$45,090
75	Net present value	$146,379			
76					

77	**Alternative: Improve II**				
78	Initial cash flows	$(24,000)			
79	Annual operating income items				
80	Contribution margin		$355,000	$355,000	$355,000
81	Store rent		(24,000)	(24,000)	(24,000)
82	Labour costs store manager		(75,000)	(75,000)	(75,000)
83	Other operating costs		(150,000)	(150,000)	(150,000)
84	Central services		(18,000)	(18,000)	(18,000)
85	Depreciation expense		(48,000)	(48,000)	(48,000)
86	Change in operating income		40,000	40,000	40,000
87	Tax on change in income		(16,000)	(16,000)	(16,000)
88	After-tax change in operating income		24,000	24,000	24,000
89	Add back depreciation expense		48,000	48,000	48,000
90	After-tax operating cash flow		72,000	72,000	72,000
91	Disinvestment cash flows				$-
92	Net cash flow	(24,000)	72,000	72,000	72,000
93	Present value factors	1.000	0.926	0.857	0.794
94	Present values of cash flows	(24,000)	$66,667	$61,728	$57,156
95	Net present value	$161,551			

8.2 Sensitivity of Expected Value Analysis, p. 376

a. The computations follow directly:

1. Expected market growth = 10% × 0.40 + 5% × 0.30 − 2% × 0.30

E[market growth] = 4.0% + 1.5% − 0.6% = 4.9%

2. Expected market growth = 8% × 0.20 + 4% × 0.60 + 2% × 0.20

E[market growth] = 1.6% + 2.4% + 0.4% = 4.4%

3. Expected market growth = 10% × 0.20 + 5% × 0.20 − 2% × 0.60

E[market growth] = 2.0% + 1.0% − 1.2% = 1.8%

b. The changes in parts (1) and (2) do not appear to change the expected growth rate dramatically. However, a small change in a growth rate can have a large absolute effect on a large market over time. If these growth rates are likely, the company should apply them to the investment model(s) to gauge their effects on expected NPV. The last expected growth rate in part (3) could result in a failed project if it actually happened. This small rate of growth probably would not justify the investment, but analysts should 'plug' it into the models to measure the effects. Another consideration not discussed in the chapter is that the range or variation in possible growth rates can be a source of risk because they could lead to more extreme cash flow outcomes. All of these sets of growth rates have wider ranges and variances. Thus, if any of these were the growth rates used instead, the project might be considered riskier than before.

8.3 Sensitivity and Scenario Analyses, p. 379

a. These parameters directly drive the company's expected revenues. The original market size is multiplied by the expected growth rate, which in turn is multiplied by the expected market share. The result is the estimated annual revenue. This linkage is perhaps the most crucial part of the investment models because they drive cash inflows. Cash outflows, as modelled, are more predictable.

b.

	Market size = €60 million		Market size = €60 million	
	Year 0	Year 1	Year 0	Year 1
Expected market size (thousands)	€60,000	€62,760	€40,000	€41,840
Market share		20%		20%
Sales		€12,552		€ 8,368
Cost of sales		4,393		2,929
Gross margin		€ 8,159		€ 5,439

c.

	Market growth rate = 2%		Market growth rate = 6%	
	Year 0	Year 1	Year 0	Year 1
Expected market size (thousands)	€50,000	€51,000	€50,000	€53,000
Market share		20%		20%
Sales		€10,200		€10,600
Cost of sales		3,570		3,710
Gross margin		€ 6,630		€ 6,890

d.

	Market share = 30%		Market share = 15%	
	Year 0	Year 1	Year 0	Year 1
Expected market size (thousands)	€50,000	€52,300	€50,000	€52,300
Market share		30%		15%
Sales		€15,690		€ 7,845
Cost of sales		5,492		2,746
Gross margin		€10,199		€ 5,099

e. Many alternative scenarios are possible, but consider that the best-case scenario can be:

Market size = €60 million; market growth rate = 6 per cent; market share = 30 per cent

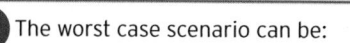

The worst case scenario can be:

Market size = €40 million; market growth rate = 2 per cent; market share = 15 per cent

	Best-case scenario		Worst-case scenario	
	Year 0	Year 1	Year 0	Year 1
Expected market size (thousands)	€60,000	€63,600	€40,000	€40,800
Market share		30%		15%
Sales		€19,080		€6,120
Cost of sales		6,678		2,142
Gross margin		€12,402		€3,978

8.4 Apply Real Option Value Analysis, p. 385

a. The analysts extended the 'no competitor' option to six years because investment alternatives must be of comparable time periods. If analysts had not included a sixth year, they are explicitly assuming that the company will generate zero net cash flow from its investment funds. At a minimum, the company should earn its required rate of return. In the chapter's case, analysts are assuming that the company could extend operations for a sixth year at the same committed cost. That might be overly optimistic, and they perhaps should model other possibilities.

b. **1.** The decision tree of the alternative to defer investment one year follows:

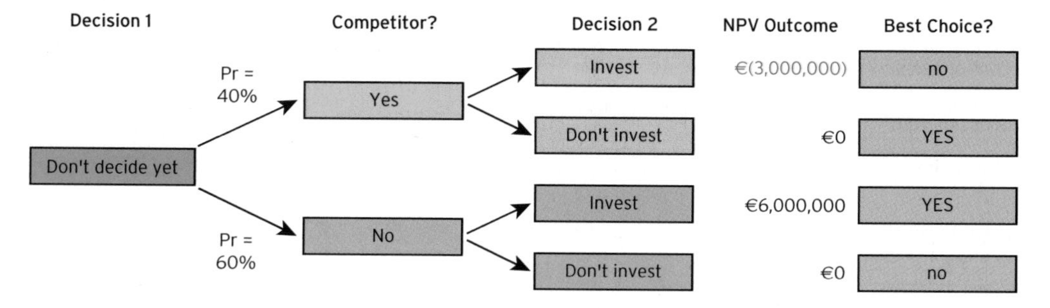

If a competitor enters, the company would not invest and would earn a zero NPV. The expected NPV of deferring the decision is

$$€0 \times 0.40 + 6{,}000{,}000 \times 0.60 = €3{,}600{,}000$$

2. The decision tree of the alternative to invest now follows:

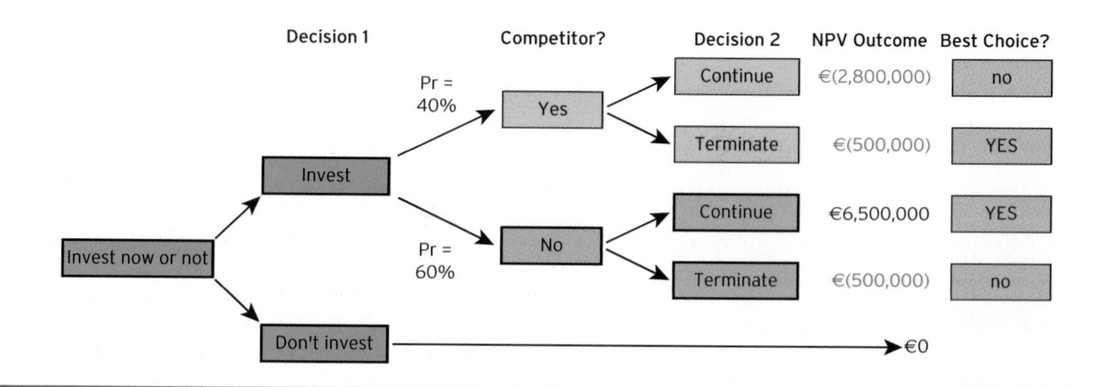

If a competitor enters, the company would terminate the project after one year.
The expected NPV of the decision to invest now is

$$(€500{,}000) \times 0.40 + 6{,}500{,}000 \times 0.60 = €3{,}700{,}000$$

3. The real option value of the decision to wait is

$$€3{,}600{,}000 - €3{,}700{,}000 = (€100{,}000)$$

4. These calculations indicate that the best strategy is to invest now rather than wait. The primary reason for this outcome is the relatively low cost of terminating the investment after one year. This means that the investment is mostly reversible. Under this condition (unlike the situation in the chapter), waiting is not beneficial. Investing now and starting the cash flows in the first year is better than deferring them a year.

Endnotes

1 Think about the cost of capital as the market price for money. This works in the same way as the market price for other resources that the company buys. For example, the company can only hire offices if it pays the market price for a particular kind of office space. Employees only want to work for the company if it pays the same as other companies for similar jobs.

2 More on the cost of capital is in Chapter 14.

3 Technically, the inflation rate and the inflation-free opportunity rate interact, but at low rates of interest, the interaction is negligible.

4 Spreadsheet software has hundreds of built-in functions. The easiest way to learn how to use them is to select the 'Function' option from the drop-down 'Insert' menu. This generates a function 'wizard' that will guide you. You also can consult the 'Help' menu from within the wizard for guidance and examples.

5 For more information on multi-attribute decision making, see Phillips and Bana e Costa (2007) and Kowalski et al. (2009).

6 ShadeTree Roasters also plans for competitors' actions, which is discussed later in this chapter.

7 The formal study of making decisions with this type of information is called *statistical decision theory*. This chapter uses a simple but realistic approach to making investment decisions under uncertainty.

8 These investments are called *hedges*.

9 Certainly, more future events are relevant to the decision, but the complication of modelling additional events is not necessary to demonstrate the lessons of the chapter. Modelling more events means the investment models must be expanded. More complicated methods also might use probability distributions or Monte Carlo simulations of possible market growth outcomes.

10 Degree of belief can be related to historical frequency, as in the application of Bayes' Theorem. See a statistics text for an explanation of Bayes' Theorem.

11 Note that Exhibit 8.16 shows amounts in thousands for clarity of presentation. Be sure to work through and understand this exhibit because all of this chapter's investment models are similar.

12 Recall that accounting income is a measure of financial performance that often deviates from cash flow.

13 See the following articles for interesting discussions related to this section: Kaminski (2003); McNamee et al. (2003); and Harrington (2003).

14 Adapted from a case by Professor David Solomons, Wharton School of the University of Pennsylvania.

References

Adner, R., and D.A. Levinthal (2004) 'What is not a real option: considering boundaries for the application of real options to business strategy', *Academy of Management Review*, vol. 29, no. 1, pp. 74–85.

Arnold, G.G., and P.D. Hatzapoulos (2000) 'The theory-practice gap in capital budgeting: evidence from the United Kingdom', *Journal of Business Finance and Accounting*, vol. 27, no. 5/6, pp. 603–626.

Bengtsson, J. (2001) 'Manufacturing flexibility and real options: a review', *International Journal of Production Economics*, vol. 74, pp. 213–224.

Camuffo, A., A. Furlan, P. Romano and A. Vinelli (2008) 'Breathing shoes and complementarities: strategic innovation in a mature industry', *International Journal of Innovation Management*, vol. 12, no. 2, pp. 139–160.

Denison, C.A. (2009) 'Real options and escalation of commitment: a behavioral analysis of capital investment decisions', *The Accounting Review*, vol. 84, no. 1, pp. 133–155.

Doherty, M. (2005) 'Mapping ROI', *The American City and County*, February, pp. 32–35.

Graham, J.R., and C.R. Harvey (2001) 'The theory and practice of corporate finance: evidence from the field', *Journal of Financial Econometrics*, vol. 60, pp. 187–243.

Haka, S.F. (2007) 'A review of the literature on capital budgeting and investment appraisal: past, present and future musings', in C.S. Chapman, A.G. Hopwood and M.D. Shields (ed.) *Handbook of Management Accounting Research*, Elsevier, Oxford, vol. 2, pp. 697–728.

Harrington, C. (2003) 'Socially responsible investing', *Journal of Accountancy*, January, pp. 52–57.

Kaminski, M. (2003) 'Global vice squad', *Wall Street Journal*, 30 June.

Khanna, T. (2007) 'China + India, the power of two', *Harvard Business Review*, December, pp. 60–69.

Kowalski, K., S. Stagl, R. Madlener and I. Omann (2009) 'Sustainable energy futures: methodological challenges in combining scenarios and participatory multi-criteria analysis', *European Journal of Operational Research*, vol. 197, pp. 1063–1074.

Lauzon, M. (2001) 'Maytag moving some assembly to Mexico', *Plastic News*, September, p. 5.

McNamee, M., N. Byrnes., and E. Thornton (2003) 'Banking's bigwigs may be beyond the law's reach', *BusinessWeek*, 19 May.

Milgrom, P., and J. Roberts (1995) 'Complementarities and fit: strategies, structure and organizational change in manufacturing', *Journal of Accounting and Economics*, vol. 19, nos. 2–3, pp. 179–208.

Miller, P., and T. O'Leary (1997) 'Capital budgeting practices and complementarity relations in the transition to modern manufacture: a field-based analysis', *Journal of Accounting Research*, vol. 35, no. 2, pp. 257–271.

Nichols, N. (1994) 'Scientific management at Merck: an interview with CFO Judy Lewent', *Harvard Business Review*, January–February, pp. 88–99.

Ortolano, L., and K.K. Cushing (2002) 'Grand Coulee Dam 70 years later: what can we learn?' *Water Resources Development*, vol. 18, no. 3, pp. 373–390.

Phillips, L.D., and C.A. Bana e Costa (2007) 'Transparent prioritization, budgeting and resource allocation with multi-criteria decision analysis and decision conferencing', *Annals of Operations Research*, vol. 154, pp. 51–68.

Ryan, P.A., and G.P. Ryan (2002) 'Capital budgeting practices of the Fortune 1000: how have things changed?' *Journal of Business and Management*, vol. 8, no. 4, pp. 355–364.

Verbeeten, F.H.M. (2006) 'Do organizations adopt sophisticated capital budgeting practices to deal with uncertainty in the investment decision? A research note', *Management Accounting Research*, vol. 17, pp. 106–120.

Wouters, M., B. Roorda and R. Gal (2011) 'Managing uncertainty during R&D projects: a case study', *Research-Technology Management*, vol. 54, no. 2, pp. 37–46.

CHAPTER 9

Budgeting and Financial Planning

Learning Objectives

After completing this chapter, you should be able to:

- **LO 1** Describe the key role that budgeting plays in the strategic planning process.
- **LO 2** Explain the purposes and types of budgeting systems.
- **LO 3** Describe a master budget, including each of its components.
- **LO 4** Prepare a master budget.
- **LO 5** Describe and evaluate a typical organization's process of budget administration.
- **LO 6** Understand the behavioural implications of budgetary slack and participative budgeting.
- **LO 7** Use the economic-order-quantity model to make inventory-ordering decisions and discuss the implications of the JIT approach for inventory management (Appendix 9).

Westport Team Wear

New Zealand

Memorandum

To: Steve Keegan, President

From: Meg Johnston, Sales Manager

CC: Bradley Roaldsson, Production Supervisor

Subject: Sales forecast for the next four quarters

I have completed the sales forecast for the next four quarters for inclusion in the annual budget and anticipate unit sales as follows:

1st quarter	10,000 units
2nd quarter	6,500 units
3rd quarter	5,500 units
4th quarter	14,000 units
Total	36,000 units

As usual, the heaviest volume is expected to be in the first and fourth quarters. The first quarter sales reflect the start of the summer sports season and the return of students to campus for the spring semester (or winter quarter). The fourth quarter sales reflect not only heavy sales during the fall semester (or quarter) but also sales during the December holiday period. As you will notice, the forecast shows a slight increase over the current year's projected sales. (Next year's sales forecast of 36,000 units represents a 3.75 per cent increase over the current year's projection of 34,700 units.) Interestingly, it appears that our volume in rugby sportswear will decrease by about 2,000 units, but this is offset by an anticipated higher volume of sales units in soccer shirts. The reasons for this are not immediately clear, and I intend to explore this issue further. More targeted advertising to build on our rugby heritage might be worth considering.

The assumptions on which the sales forecast is based include very little change in general economic conditions, a continued low rate of inflation, little change in amount of kids and adults practising sports. To support this forecast, I conducted telephone interviews with buyers from sports clubs and colleges (various sports and a representative sample of institutions in the small, medium and large college categories).

Please let me know if I can provide any further information at this time.

Westport Team Wear was established in New Zealand in 1956 to manufacture and supply sportswear. It has specialized in providing team wear to schools. Through the company's website customers can choose from the gallery of current garments and designs, and colour the jersey to the team or school colours. Customers can also place their logos, names and numbers into position. The company also sells replica jerseys of many different sports clubs, especially in rugby, such as the Bulldogs, Wallabies and Warriors.

As the memo on the preceding page indicates, Westport Team Wear is about to begin its annual budgeting, or financial planning, process. Developing a budget is a critical step in planning any economic activity. This is true for businesses, governmental agencies, and individuals. We all must budget our money to meet day-to-day expenses and to plan for major expenditures, such as buying a car or paying for college tuition. Similarly, businesses of all types and governmental units at every level must make financial plans to conduct routine operations, to plan for major expenditures and to help make financing decisions.

Before exploring Westport Team Wear's budgeting process in detail, let's step back and take a broader view of organizational planning and the role of budgeting in cost management systems.

Strategic Planning: Achieving and Maintaining a Competitive Advantage

LO 1
Describe the key role that budgeting plays in the strategic planning process.

Every enterprise has a set of goals, such as profitability, growth or public service. To achieve those goals, an organization's top management periodically (or even continuously) engages in strategic planning.[1] Achieving and maintaining a competitive advantage usually are primary goals of this strategic-planning exercise. Management often outlines the organization's **critical success factors,** the key strengths that are most responsible for making the organization successful. Critical success factors enable a company to outperform its competitors. By identifying these factors and ensuring that they are incorporated into the strategic plan, companies are able to maintain an edge over competitors. In addition, important critical success factors can be exploited to improve the company's overall competitiveness.

For example, **Southwest Airlines** (www.southwestair.com) in the US has relied on several factors to maintain its competitive edge. It keeps its prices consistently low and its routes in the short to medium range, and Southwest uses only one type of plane (keeping costs to a minimum). The company's management knows that these are among Southwest's critical success factors and has continued to increase the airline's competitiveness by building these factors into the strategic planning process. This is very similar to **Ryanair** (www.ryanair.com) in Europe and **Tiger Airways Australia** (www.tigerairways.com/au/en).

What Is a Strategic Plan?

Although a statement of strategic goals is necessary to guide an organization, it is important to also specify tangible objectives in strategic plans. These objectives make the goals, which are often a bit abstract in nature, more concrete. Tangible objectives provide measurable benchmarks ('Are we on track with the realization of our goals?') and offer specific criteria for decision making. Strategic plans also discuss the major capital investments required to maintain present facilities, increase capacity, diversify products or processes and develop particular markets. For example, a paper company's strategies included the following:[2]

- *Cost control.* Optimize the contribution from existing product lines by holding product cost increases to less than the general rate of inflation. This will involve acquiring new machinery proposed in the capital budget as well as replacing our five least efficient plants over the next five years.
- *Market share.* Maintain our market share by providing a level of service and quality comparable to our top competitors. This requires improving our quality control to reduce customer complaints and returned merchandise from a current level of 4 per cent to 1 per cent within two years.

The company's strategy was implemented by choosing tangible objectives for the next 5 years, which included sales targets for sales volumes, aggregate costs and cash flow projections. At this stage, management had not stated the plans in much detail, but the plans had been well thought out and provided a general framework for guiding management's operating decisions.

Strategic plans look many years ahead and are achieved in year-by-year steps. The guidance is more specific for the coming year than it is for more distant years. The plan for the coming year is called the *master budget*, which we will explore in detail later in the chapter. First, however, let's look more closely at the purposes of budgeting systems and the various types of budgets.

What are the Key Purposes and Types of Budgeting Systems?

A **budget** is a detailed plan, expressed in quantitative terms, that specifies how an organization will acquire and use resources during a particular period of time. A **budgeting system** comprises the procedures used to develop a budget. Budgeting systems have five primary purposes: planning, facilitating communication and co-ordination, allocating resources, managing financial and operational performance, and evaluating performance and providing incentives.

LO 2
Explain the purposes and types of budgeting systems.

Planning

The most obvious purpose of a budget is to quantify a plan of action. The budgeting process forces the individuals who constitute an organization to plan ahead. The development of a quarterly budget for a **Westin Hotel**, for example, forces the hotel manager, the reservation manager, and the food and beverage manager to plan for the staffing and supplies needed to meet anticipated demand for the hotel's services.

Facilitating Communication and Co-ordination

For any organization to be effective, each manager throughout the organization must be aware of the plans made by other managers. To plan reservations and ticket sales effectively, the reservations manager for **Lufthansa** must know the flight schedules developed by the airline's route manager. The budgeting process pulls together the plans of each manager in an organization.

© DAL

Class sizes and other activities in colleges are determined in part by budgetary considerations.

Allocating Resources

Generally, an organization's resources are limited, and budgets provide one means to allocate resources among competing uses. The city of **Melbourne,** for example, must allocate its revenue among basic safety services (such as police and fire protection), maintenance of property and equipment (such as city streets, parks and vehicles), and other community services (such as child care services and programmes to prevent alcohol and drug abuse).

Managing Financial and Operational Performance

A budget is a plan, and plans are subject to change. Nevertheless, a budget serves as a useful benchmark with which actual results can be compared. For example, **Allstate Insurance Company** can compare its actual sales of insurance policies for a year against its budgeted sales. Such a comparison can help managers evaluate the firm's effectiveness in selling insurance.

Evaluating Performance and Providing Incentives

Comparing actual results with budgeted results also helps managers to evaluate the performance of individuals, departments, divisions or entire companies. Since budgets are used to evaluate performance, they also can be used to provide incentives for people to perform well. For example, **IBM Corporation,** like many other companies, provides incentives for managers to improve profits by awarding bonuses to managers who meet or exceed their budgeted profit goals.[3]

Organizations Use Many Types of Budgets

Different types of budgets serve different purposes. A **master budget**, or **profit plan**, is a comprehensive set of budgets covering all phases of an organization's operations for a specified period of time. We examine a master budget in detail in this chapter.

Budgeted financial statements show how the organization's financial statements will appear at a specified time if operations proceed according to plan. Budgeted financial statements include a *budgeted statement of income, a budgeted statement of financial position*, and a *budgeted statement of cash flows*.

A **capital budget** is a plan for buying and selling capital assets, such as buildings and equipment. We covered capital budgeting in Chapter 8. A **financial budget** is a plan that shows how the organization will acquire its financial resources, such as issuing shares or incurring debt.

Budgets are developed for specific time periods. *Short-range budgets* cover a year, a quarter or a month, whereas *long-range budgets* cover periods longer than a year. **Rolling** (or **revolving** or **continuous) budgets** are continually updated by periodically adding a new incremental time period, such as a quarter, and dropping the period just completed.

Master Budget as a Planning Tool

LO 3
Describe a master budget, including each of its components.

The master budget, the principal output of a budgeting system, is a comprehensive profit plan that ties together all phases of an organization's operations. The master budget comprises many separate budgets, or schedules, that are interdependent. Exhibit 9.1 portrays these interrelationships in a flowchart, which shows the components of a master budget for a manufacturing firm. (Later in the chapter, we explore Westport Team Wear's master budget in detail.)

Sales Budget: The Starting Point

The starting point for any master budget is a sales revenue budget based on forecasted sales of goods or services. Airlines forecast the number of passengers on each of their routes. Banks forecast the number and euro amount of consumer loans and home mortgages to be provided. Hotels forecast the number of rooms that will be occupied during various seasons. Manufacturing and merchandising companies forecast sales of their goods. Some companies sell both goods and services. For example, **Kmart** is a large US merchandising company, but its automotive-service branch provides the firm with substantial service revenue, and the German **Karstadt** has department stores but also a travel agency (in the stores and on the Internet).

© 1001nights

Auto manufacturers rely on district sales budgets in delivering new vehicles to their dealerships.

Sales forecasting

All companies have two things in common when it comes to forecasting sales of services or goods: sales forecasting is a critical step in the budgeting process, and it is very difficult to do accurately. **Sales forecasting** is the process of predicting sales of services or goods. Various procedures are used in sales forecasting, and the final forecast usually combines information from many different sources. Many firms have a top-management-level market research staff whose job is to co-ordinate the company's sales forecasting efforts. Typically, everyone from key executives to the firm's sales

Exhibit 9.1 Components of a Master Budget for a Manufacturing Firm

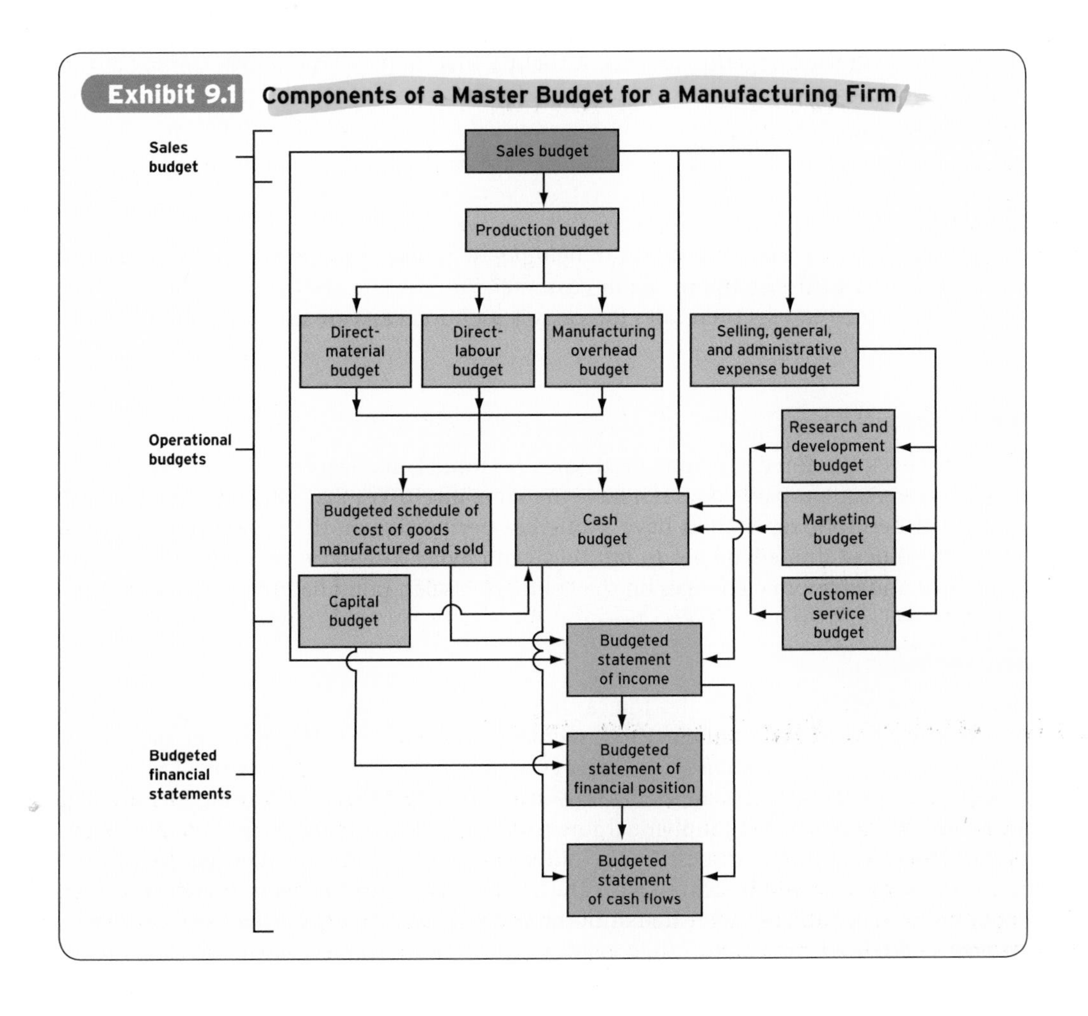

personnel is asked to contribute sales projections. These are among the major factors considered when forecasting sales:

1. *Past sales levels and trends.*
   - **a.** For the firm developing the forecast (for example, **Royal Dutch Shell**).
   - **b.** For the entire industry (for example, the petroleum industry).
2. *General economic trends.* (Is the economy growing? How fast? Is a recession or an economic slowdown expected?)
3. *Economic trends in the company's industry.* (In the petroleum industry, for example, is personal travel likely to increase, thereby implying increased demand for gasoline?)
4. *Other factors expected to affect sales in the industry.* (Is an unusually cold winter expected, which would result in increased demand for home heating oil and gas in northern climates?)
5. *Political and legal events.* (For example, is any legislation pending in China, the US Congress or in the European Union that would affect the demand for petroleum, such as new tax incentives to use alternative energy sources?)
6. *The intended pricing policy of the company.*
7. *Planned advertising and product promotion.*
8. *Expected actions of competitors.*
9. *New products contemplated by the company or other firms.* (For example, has an automobile firm announced the development of a vehicle that runs on hydrogen fuel, thereby reducing the demand for gasoline?)
10. *Market research studies.*

The starting point in the sales forecasting process is generally the sales level of the prior year. Then the market research staff considers the information just discussed along with input from key executives and sales personnel. A great deal of effort generally goes into the sales forecast since it is such a critical step in the budgeting process. A slightly inaccurate sales forecast, coming at the very beginning of the budgeting process, will throw off all of the other schedules that make up the master budget.

Sales staff

Sales personnel are in the unique position of being close to the customers, and they might possess the best information in the company about customers' immediate and near-term needs. However, they might be tempted to bias their sales forecasts if such forecasts are used as the norm for performance evaluation.

Market researchers

To provide a check on forecasts from local sales personnel, management often turns to market researchers. This group probably does not have the same incentives that sales personnel have to bias the budget. Furthermore, researchers have a different perspective on the market. They might know little about customers' immediate needs, but they can predict long-term trends in attitudes and the effects of social and economic changes on the company's sales, potential markets and products.

Delphi technique

The Delphi technique is another sales forecasting method used to enhance forecast accuracy and reduce bias in estimates. With this method, members of the forecasting group prepare individual forecasts and submit them anonymously. Each group member obtains a copy of all forecasts but is unaware of their sources. The group then discusses the results. In this way, group members address and reconcile differences among individual forecasts without involving the personality or position of individual forecasters. After discussing the differences, each group member prepares a new forecast and distributes it anonymously to the others. These forecasts are then discussed in the same manner as before. The process is repeated until the forecasts converge on a single best estimate of the coming year's sales level.

Econometric models

Another forecasting approach is to enter past sales data into a regression model to obtain a statistical estimate of factors affecting sales. For example, the predicted sales for the coming period could be related to factors such as economic indicators, consumer-confidence indexes, back-order volume, and other internal and external factors that the company deems relevant. Advocates of these econometric models contend that they can include many relevant predictors and manipulate the assumed values of the predictors to examine a variety of hypothetical conditions and then relate them to the sales forecast.

Sophisticated analytical models for forecasting are now widely available. Most companies have software packages that allow economical use of these models, after they have been estimated. Nonetheless, it is important to remember that no model removes the uncertainty surrounding sales forecasts. As in any decision, management should use cost–benefit tests to determine which forecasting methods are most appropriate.

Operational Budgets: Meeting the Demand for Goods and Services

Based on the sales budget, a company develops a set of **operational budgets**, which specify how its operations will be carried out to meet the demand for its goods or services. The budgets constituting this operational portion of the master budget are depicted in the middle portion of Exhibit 9.1, which portrays the master budget for a manufacturing firm.

Manufacturing firms

A manufacturing company develops a production budget, which shows the number of product units to be manufactured. From the production budget, a manufacturer develops budgets for the direct materials, direct labour and overhead required in the production process. These budgets provide the basis for a budgeted schedule of cost of goods manufactured and sold. A budget for selling, general and administrative (SG&A) expenses is also prepared. The SG&A budget includes budgets for research and development (R&D), design, marketing, distribution and customer service.

Merchandising firms

The operational portion of a merchandising firm's master budget is similar to that of a manufacturer, but instead of a production budget for goods, a merchandiser develops a budget for merchandise purchases. A merchandiser does not have a budget for direct materials because it does not engage in production. However, the merchandiser develops budgets for labour (or personnel), overhead, and selling and administrative expenses.

Service-industry firms

Based on the sales budget for its services, a service-industry firm develops a set of budgets that show how it will meet the demand for those services. An airline, for example, prepares the following operational budgets: a budget of planned air miles to be flown; materials budgets for spare aircraft parts, aircraft fuel, and in-flight food; labour budgets for flight crews and maintenance personnel; and an overhead budget.

Cash budget

Every business prepares a cash budget. This budget shows expected cash receipts as a result of selling goods or services and planned cash disbursements to pay the bills incurred by the firm.

Capital budget

The capital budget, which is prepared in all types of organizations, details plans for major acquisitions and disposals of assets, such as plant and equipment, vehicles and land.

Summary of operational budgets

Although operational budgets differ according to the operations of individual companies in various industries, they are also similar in important ways. In each firm, operational budgets encompass a detailed plan for using the basic factors of production (materials, labour and overhead) to produce a product or provide a service.

Budgeted Financial Statements: Completing the Master Budget

The final portion of the master budget, depicted in Exhibit 9.1, includes a budgeted statement of income, a budgeted statement of financial position (a balance sheet) and a budgeted statement of cash flows. These budgeted financial statements show the overall financial results of the organization's planned operations for the budget period.

Master Budget for Non-profit Organizations

The master budget for a non-profit organization includes many of the components shown in Exhibit 9.1. However, there are some important differences. Many non-profit organizations provide services free of charge. Hence, they have no sales budget as shown in Exhibit 9.1. However, such organizations do begin their budgeting process with a budget that shows the level of services to be provided. For example, the budget for the city of **Amsterdam** would show the planned levels of various public services. Non-profit organizations also prepare budgets showing their anticipated funding. The city of Amsterdam budgets for revenue sources such as taxes, central government funding and letting out land on long leases.

In summary, all organizations begin the budgeting process with plans for (1) the goods or services to be provided and (2) the revenue to be available, whether from sales or from other funding sources.

International Aspects of Budgeting

As the economies and cultures of countries throughout the world become intertwined, more and more companies are becoming multinational in their operations. Firms with international operations face a variety of additional challenges in preparing their budgets. First, a multinational firm's budget must reflect the translation of foreign currencies into a common currency, such as euros, British pounds or US dollars. Since almost all of the world's currencies fluctuate in their values relative to the dollar, this makes budgeting for those translations difficult. Although multinationals have sophisticated financial ways to hedge against such currency fluctuations, the budgeting task for these firms is still more challenging. Second, budget preparation is difficult when inflation (or deflation) is high or unpredictable. While Europe and the United States have experienced periods of high inflation in the past, some foreign countries have experienced hyperinflation, sometimes with annual inflation rates well over 100 per cent. Predicting such high inflation rates is difficult and further complicates a multinational's budgeting process. Finally, the economies of all countries fluctuate in terms of consumer demand, availability of skilled labour, laws affecting commerce, and so

9.1 Research Insight

Practice-based and Theoretical Approaches to Budgeting Research

Budgeting has drawn the interest of researchers for many years, both from a practice-based and a theoretical perspective. A recent example of practice-based research by Hansen et al. (2004) focused on approaches currently being employed by practitioners to address shortcomings in traditional budgeting practices. One such approach 'advocates *improving* the budgeting process and primarily focuses on the planning problems with budgeting'. The

foremost example of this approach is *activity-based budgeting* (ABB), which 'focuses on generating a budget from an activity-based model of the organization'. The ABB approach 'contends that budgeting serves primarily a planning role, and that budgeting suffers because the financial-oriented, higher-level budgeting process is not adequately connected to the underlying operational model of the organization'.

In recent years, the Consortium for Advanced Manufacturing International (CAM-I) has promoted the concept of *beyond budgeting*, which seeks to replace annual budgeting with continuous, real-time budgeting. This effort has evolved into the Beyond Budgeting Round Table (www.bbrt.org). The BBRT has identified a set of 12 principles that describe a flexible ('lean') organization that might be freer to adapt to changing conditions than one characterized by traditional, centrally controlled, annual budgeting. Proponents claim it is the wave of the future, but, while we are more cautious, we do believe that *beyond budgeting* is an exciting development that bears watching and deserves objective research. For more on *beyond budgeting*, see Research Insight 9.2.

Theoretical approaches to budgeting have employed one of three perspectives: (1) *economics*, which asks what is the economic value (and effect) of budgeting practices; (2) *psychology*, which asks what are the effects of budgeting practices on individuals' behaviour and performance; and (3) *sociology*, which asks how budgeting influences decision making and bargaining among the plurality of interests in an organization. A recent example of economics-based, theoretical research 'experimentally investigated the effects of budget-based contracts and budget levels (performance targets) on group performance'. A variety of budget-based contracts was compared to see which types of contracts result in the best overall group performance.

Sources: Hansen et al. (2004); and Fisher et al. (2003). See also Rankin et al. (2003).

forth. Companies with offshore operations face the task of anticipating such changing conditions in their budgeting processes.

Activity-based Budgeting

The process of constructing a master budget can be significantly enhanced if the concepts of activity-based costing are applied.[4] Activity-based costing uses a two-stage cost-assignment process. In stage I, overhead costs are assigned to cost pools that represent the most significant activities constituting the production process. The activities identified vary across manufacturers, but such activities as engineering design, materials handling, machine set-up, production scheduling, inspection, quality control and purchasing provide examples.

After assigning costs to the activity cost pools in stage I, cost drivers are identified that are appropriate for each cost pool. Then in stage II, the overhead costs are allocated from each activity cost pool to cost objects (e.g., manufactured goods, services and customers) in proportion to the amount of activity consumed.

Exhibit 9.2 Activity-based Costing versus Activity-based Budgeting

Activity-based Costing (ABC)	Activity-based Budgeting (ABB)
Resources ↓	Resources ↑
Activities ↓	Activities ↑
Cost objects: products and services produced, and customers served	Forecast of products and services to be produced, and customers served

Source: Kaplan and Cooper (1998).

Applying activity-based costing (ABC) concepts to the budgeting process yields **activity-based budgeting (ABB)**,[5] which is the process of developing a master budget using information obtained from an ABC analysis. Remember that ABC is a costing method that, first, traces costs to activities, which act as activity-cost pools, and, second, assigns these costs to goods and services based on how much each good or service uses the activites. Under ABB, the first step is to specify the products or services to produce and the customers to serve. Then the activities that are necessary to produce these products and services are determined. Finally, the resources necessary to perform the specified activities are quantified. Conceptually, ABB takes the ABC model and reverses the flow of the analysis, as depicted in Exhibit 9.2. As portrayed in the diagram, ABC assigns resource costs to activities and then assigns activity costs to products and services produced and customers served. ABB, on the other hand, begins by forecasting the demand for products and services as well as the customers to serve. These forecasts are then used to plan the activities for the budget period and budget the resources necessary to carry out the activities.

9.1 Cost Management in Practice

Benefits of ABB

American Express has successfully used ABB for its travel-related services in its New York operations. This relatively new system has been used to identify and implement cost reduction and process improvement initiatives. Then, an activity-by-activity analysis of each department has allowed process improvement savings to be factored into the forecasted costs for each department in the next budget cycle.

AT&T Paradyne designs and produces medium- and high-speed data communications equipment, which provides an interface between telephone networks and computers. The company's activity-based costing project ultimately led to activity-based budgeting. As ABM and ABB matured at AT&T Paradyne, the company began to experience a culture change. A key lesson learned in this case was that linking activity-based costing to the budgeting process and performance evaluation led to the integration of ABC into the management of the company.

Sources: Aldea and Bullinger (1999); and Collins (1999).

Zero-base Budgeting for Discretionary Costs

Many organizations have attempted to measure discretionary costs through a budgeting method called zero-base budgeting. Numerous companies (e.g., **Texas Instruments, Xerox** and **Control Data**) and governmental units (e.g., the **State of Georgia**) have implemented zero-base budgeting at one time or another. **Zero-base budgeting** initially sets the budget for virtually every activity in the organization to zero. To receive funding during the budgeting process, each activity must be justified in terms of its continued usefulness. The zero-base budgeting approach forces management to rethink each phase of an organization's operations before allocating resources.

Some organizations use a base budgeting approach without going to the extreme of zero-base budgeting. Base budgeting sets the initial budget for each of the organization's departments in accordance with a base package, which includes the minimal resources required for the subunit to exist at an absolute minimal level. Below this level of funding, the subunit would not be a viable entity. Any increases above the base package would result from a decision to fund an incremental package, which describes the resources needed to add various activities to the base package. The decision to approve such an incremental budget package would have to be justified on the basis of the costs and benefits of the activities included. Base budgeting has been effective in many organizations because it forces managers to take an evaluative, questioning attitude toward each of the organization's programmes.

Illustrating the Master Budget

LO 4
Prepare a master budget.

To illustrate the steps involved in developing a master budget, we focus on Westport Team Wear, a small manufacturer of sports T-shirts bearing the names and logos of sport teams of schools, universities and sports clubs in New Zealand, Australia, and around the world. Located in Westport in New Zealand, the company is wholly owned and managed by Steve Keegan, who started the firm 4 years ago. The entire business is operated in a single building. The manufacturing process is highly automated, using three machines to cut out pieces of fabric, stitch them together, and imprint names, numbers and logos. The entire production cycle for a T-shirt requires just 12 minutes (0.20 hour).

Westport Team Wear's master budget for the year 201x has just been completed. It contains the following schedules, which are displayed and explained in the following pages.[6]

Schedule	Title of Schedule
1	Sales Budget
2	Production Budget
3	Direct Material Budget
4	Direct Labour Budget
5	Manufacturing Overhead Budget
6	Selling, General and Administrative Expense Budget
7	Cash Receipts Budget
8	Cash Payments Budget
9	Cash Budget
10	Budgeted Schedule of Cost of Goods Manufactured and Sold
11	Budgeted Statement of Income
12	Budgeted Statement of Financial Position.

Sales Budget

The first step in developing Westport Team Wear's 201x master budget is to prepare the sales budget, which is displayed in Schedule 1. The **sales budget** displays the projected sales in units and the projected sales revenue. It displays the projected sales in units for each quarter, and then multiplies the unit sales by the sales price to determine sales revenue. Notice that there is a significant seasonal pattern in the sales forecast, with the bulk of the sales coming in the fall and winter. (This is the sales forecast to which Westport Team Wear's sales manager, Meg Johnston, referred in the memo at the beginning of this chapter.)

Schedule 1

Westport Team Wear
Sales Budget (in New Zealand Dollars)
For the year ending 31 December

	Quarter 1	2	3	4	Year
Sales in units	10,000	6,500	5,500	14,000	36,000
Unit sales price	$32.00	$32.00	$32.00	$32.00	$32.00
Total sales revenue	$320,000	$208,000	$176,000	$448,000	$1,152,000

Production Budget

The **production budget** shows the number of units of services or goods that are to be produced during a budget period. Westport Team Wear's production budget, displayed in Schedule 2, determines the number of T-shirts to be produced each quarter based on the quarterly sales projections in the sales budget (see Schedule 2). Schedule 2 is based on the following formula.

Sales in units + **Desired ending inventory of finished goods** = **Total units required**

Total units required − **Expected beginning inventory of finished goods** = **Units to be produced**

Focus on the second-quarter column in Schedule 2. Expected sales are 6,500 T-shirts, and management desires to have 550 finished units on hand at the end of the quarter. This is 10 per cent of the expected sales for the third quarter. However, 650 T-shirts are expected to be in inventory at the beginning of the second quarter. Thus, only 6,400 T-shirts need to be produced.

Schedule 2[7]

Westport Team Wear
Production Budget (in units)
For the year ending 31 December

	Quarter				
	1	**2**	**3**	**4**	**Year**
Sales in units (Schedule 1)	10,000	6,500	5,500	14,000	36,000
Add desired ending inventory of finished goods	650	550	1,400	1,000	1,000
Total units required	10,650	7,050	6,900	15,000	37,000
Less expected beginning inventory of finished goods	1,000	650	550	1,400	1,000
Units to be produced	9,650	6,400	6,350	13,600	36,000

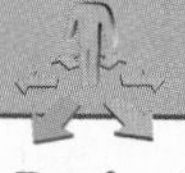

9.1 You're the Decision Maker

Revised Production Budget

Suppose you are in charge of Westport Team Wear's budgeting process. The sales manager has just informed you that the sales forecast has been increased by 20 per cent during each quarter of 201x and the first quarter of 201x+1.

a. Revise Westport Team Wear's production budget for 201x. Assume that the expected finished-goods inventory on 1 January 201x, is still 1,000 units.

b. Now put yourself in the position of Westport Team Wear's production supervisor. If the sales manager said she was only somewhat confident in the increased sales forecast, would you recommend increasing production to the levels in your revised budget? Why?

(Solutions begin on page 471.)

Direct Material Budget

The **direct material budget** shows the number of units and the cost of material to be purchased and used during a budget period. As is true for almost all manufacturers, Westport Team Wear's direct material cost is a unit-level cost. Each shirt requires 1.5 metres of fabric.[8] Westport Team Wear's direct material budget, displayed in Schedule 3, shows the total amount of material needed to make T-shirts during each quarter. The amount of fabric to be purchased each quarter, is based on the following formula.

Raw material required for production + **Desired ending inventory of raw material** = **Total raw material required**

Total raw material required − **Expected beginning inventory of raw material** = **Raw material to be purchased**

The lower portion of Schedule 3 computes the cost of each quarter's raw materials purchases. (This information also will be needed later in the budgeting process in Schedule 10.)

Production and purchasing: an important link

Notice the important link between planned production and purchases of raw material. This link is apparent in Schedule 3, and it is emphasized in the formula preceding the schedule. Let us focus on the second quarter. Since 6,400 T-shirts are to be produced, 9,600 metres of material will be needed (6,400 units times 1.5 metres per unit). In addition, management desires to have 953 metres of material in inventory at the end of the quarter, namely 10 per cent of the expected requirement of material in the next quarter.[9] Thus, total needs are 10,553 metres. Does Westport Team Wear need to purchase this much raw material? No, it does not, because 960 metres will be in inventory at the beginning of the quarter. Therefore, the firm needs to purchase only 9,593 metres of material during the quarter (10,553 metres less 960 metres in the beginning inventory).

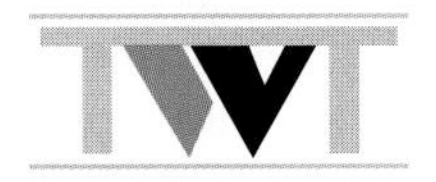

Schedule 3

Westport Team Wear
Direct Material Budget (in NZ$)
For the year ending 31 December

	Quarter				
	1	**2**	**3**	**4**	**Year**
Units to be produced (Schedule 2)	9,650	6,400	6,350	13,600	36,000
Raw material required per unit (metres of fabric)	1.50	1.50	1.50	1.50	1.50
Raw material required for production (metres)	14,475	9,600	9,525	20,400	54,000
Add desired ending inventory of raw material (metres)	960	953	2,040	1,448	1,448
Total raw material required (metres)	15,435	10,553	11,565	21,848	55,448
Less expected beginning inventory of raw material (metres)	1,448	960	953	2,040	1,448
Raw material to be purchased (metres)	13,988	9,593	10,613	19,808	54,000
Purchase cost per metre	$5.00	$5.00	$5.00	$5.00	$5.00
Total cost of raw material purchases	$69,938	$47,963	$53,063	$99,038	$270,000
Direct material used (metres)	14,475	9,600	9,525	20,400	54,000
Cost of direct material used	$72,375	$48,000	$47,625	$102,000	$270,000

Inventory management

Planned production and raw-material purchases represent a particularly critical linkage in manufacturing firms. Thus, considerable effort is devoted to careful inventory planning and management.

How did management decide how much raw material to have in inventory at the end of each quarter? Examination of Schedule 3 reveals that each quarter's desired ending inventory of raw material is 10 per cent of the *material needed for production* in the next quarter. For example, 953 metres of raw material ($0.10 \times 9{,}525$) will be in inventory at the end of the second quarter because 9,525 metres will be needed for production in the third quarter. The effect of this approach is to have a larger ending inventory when the next quarter's planned production is greater. Inventories are drawn down when the subsequent quarter's planned production is lower.

The appendix to this chapter explores various other tools used in inventory management.

Direct Labour Budget

The **direct labour budget** shows the number of hours and the cost of the direct labour to be used during a budget period. Westport Team Wear's direct labour budget is displayed in Schedule 4. Based on each quarter's planned production, this schedule computes the amount of direct labour needed each quarter and the cost of the required labour. Westport Team Wear is a small company, and owner Steve Keegan hires all of his direct labour production employees from the collegiate communities in Canterbury. College students are employed, on a part-time basis only, to meet the labour demands of a given time period. Thus, Westport Team Wear's direct labour may be adjusted up or down to meet short-term needs. As a result, direct labour for this company is a unit-level cost. As Schedule 4 shows, each T-shirt manufactured requires 0.2 hours (12 minutes) of direct labour.

A note on direct labour and the cost hierarchy

It is important to note that the position of direct labour in the cost hierarchy depends on management's ability to adjust the organization's labour force to match short-term requirements, as well as management's attitude about making such adjustments. For either strategic business reasons or ethical concerns, many companies strive to maintain a relatively stable labour force. If production employees are retained when production declines, direct labour will not be a unit-level cost. In the extreme case when employees are virtually never laid off, direct labour becomes a facility- or general operations-level cost.

Westport Team Wear's ability to easily adjust the total hours of its part-time workforce results in a unit-level designation for direct labour cost in this situation.

Schedule 4

Westport Team Wear
Direct Labour Budget (in NZ$)
For the year ending 31 December

	Quarter				
	1	**2**	**3**	**4**	**Year**
Units to be produced (Schedule 2)	9,650	6,400	6,350	13,600	36,000
Direct labour required per unit	0.20	0.20	0.20	0.20	0.20
Total direct labour hours required	1,930	1,280	1,270	2,720	7,200
Direct labour cost per hour	$28.00	$28.00	$28.00	$28.00	$28.00
Total direct labour cost	$54,040	$35,840	$35,560	$76,160	$201,600

Manufacturing Overhead Budget

The **manufacturing overhead budget** shows the cost of overhead expected to be incurred in the production process during the budget period. Westport Team Wear's manufacturing overhead budget, displayed in Schedule 5, lists the expected cost of each overhead item by quarter. At the bottom of the schedule, the total budgeted overhead for each quarter is shown. Then each quarter's depreciation is subtracted to determine the total cash payments to be expected for overhead during each quarter. This cash-disbursement information will be needed later in the budgeting process when the cash payments budget is constructed (Schedule 8).

Activity-based budgeting and the cost hierarchy

Westport Team Wear's unit-level costs include indirect material and electricity used to run the production machinery. These costs are NZ$0.25 and NZ$0.15 per unit, respectively. Batch-level costs include machine set-up, purchasing and material handling, and inspection. The cost driver for these costs is the number of production runs, and these costs are NZ$100, NZ$190 and NZ$80 per run, respectively. A run typically produces around 230 T-shirts. Westport Team Wear's only product-level cost is design. The company typically commissions two new style designs each quarter from a local freelance textile designer. Each new design costs NZ$1,700. The remaining overhead costs in Schedule 5 include all costs at the facility or general-operations level.

Benefits of ABB

Proponents of ABB believe that real, sustainable pay-offs from activity-based costing and activity-based management will not be forthcoming until an organization's budgeting process embraces the ABM approach. Utilizing ABC information in the budgeting process provides solid reasoning for budgeting costs at particular levels since the underlying ABC information is based explicitly on the relationships among cost drivers, activities and resources consumed. Moreover, the resulting budget is more useful to management because it reveals how cost levels will change if the predicted quantities of the cost drivers change. For example, what will happen to Westport Team Wear's set-up costs in the first quarter if the quantity produced is 9,650 units as reflected in the budget (see Schedule 5), but 50 production runs are used to produce these 9,650 units instead of 42 runs as specified in the budget? As mentioned above, set-up cost is in total NZ$370 per run (check also Schedule 5: NZ$15,540 ÷ 42 = NZ$230). Therefore, 50 runs would result in NZ$18,500 of set-up cost in the first quarter, and this is true even if 9,650 units are produced as forecast in the budget.

Traditional budgeting processes, which do not embrace the ABB approach, often classify costs such as set-up, purchasing and materials handling, quality control and inspection, or design engineering as *fixed costs* since they do not vary with the number of units produced. The ABB approach, however, recognizes that these costs are really *variable* if the budget analyst is careful to identify the appropriate cost driver with which each of these costs varies.

Schedule 5

Westport Team Wear
Manufacturing Overhead Budget (in NZ$)
For the year ending 31 December

	Quarter				
	1	**2**	**3**	**4**	**Year**
Unit-level costs					
Units to be produced (Schedule 2)	9,650	6,400	6,350	13,600	36,000
Indirect material cost	$2,413	$1,600	$1,588	$3,400	$9,000
Electricity for machines cost	$1,448	$960	$953	$2,040	$5,400
Total unit-level costs	$3,860	$2,560	$2,540	$5,440	$14,400
Batch-level costs					
Production runs	42	28	28	60	158
Set-up cost	$4,200	$2,800	$2,800	$6,000	$15,800
Purchasing and handling cost	7,980	5,320	5,320	11,400	30,020

Inspection cost	3,360	2,240	2,240	4,800	12,640
Total batch-level costs	$15,540	$10,360	$10,360	$22,200	$58,460
Product-level costs					
New style designs	2	2	2	2	8
Design costs	$3,400	$3,400	$3,400	$3,400	$13,600
Total product-level costs	$3,400	$3,400	$3,400	$3,400	$13,600
Facility and general operations-level costs					
Supervisory salary cost	$24,000	$24,000	$24,000	$24,000	$96,000
Insurance and property tax costs	2,400	2,400	2,400	2,400	9,600
Maintenance cost	2,600	2,600	2,600	2,600	10,400
Utilities costs	2,500	2,500	2,500	2,500	10,000
Depreciation cost	36,000	36,000	36,000	36,000	144,000
Total facility and general operations-level costs	$67,500	$67,500	$67,500	$67,500	$270,000
Total manufacturing overhead costs	$90,300	$83,820	$83,800	$98,540	$356,460
Less depreciation	36,000	36,000	36,000	36,000	144,000
Total cash payments for manufacturing overhead	$54,300	$47,820	$47,800	$62,540	$212,460

9.2 You're the Decision Maker

Revision of Manufacturing Overhead Budget

Suppose it is 15 September 201x, and the production plan has been revised for the fourth quarter so that 16,250 units will be manufactured. The fourth quarter production runs will be 325 units each. Moreover, four new design styles will be commissioned instead of two.

a. Revise the *fourth quarter* manufacturing overhead budget to reflect the changed production plan.
b. Suppose a special adjustment will need to be made on the cutting machine at the midpoint of each production run at a cost of NZ$185. Where will this cost appear in the overhead budget?

Note: Due to rounding, the numbers do not always add up. The calcuations have been performed with more decimal points than shown here.

(Solutions begin on page 471.)

Selling, General and Administrative (SG&A) Expense Budget

The **selling, general and administrative (SG&A) expense budget** shows the planned amounts of expenditures for selling, general and administrative expenses during the budget period. Westport Team Wear's selling, general and administrative expense budget is displayed in Schedule 6. This budget lists the expenses of administering the firm and selling its product.

Westport Team Wear uses activity-based budgeting for its SG&A budget. Sales commissions and freight out (i.e., shipping) are unit-level expenses, at NZ$0.60 and NZ$0.40 per unit. The cost driver for these unit-level expenses is the number of units *sold* (not the number of units *produced*). Licensing fees paid to sport clubs for permission to use their names and logos on Westport Team Wear's T-shirts are customer-level costs. Each club typically charges a licensing fee, which is fixed within broad ranges of unit sales. These costs are NZ$950 per customer, and it is estimated that three licensing fees must to be paid in every quarter. The remainder of Westport Team Wear's selling, general and administrative expenses are incurred at the facility or general-operations level.

Schedule 6

Westport Team Wear Selling, General and Administrative Expense Budget (in NZ$) For the year ending 31 December	Quarter (current year)				
	1	2	3	4	Year
Unit-level expenses					
Sales in units (Schedule 1)	10,000	6,500	5,500	14,000	36,000
Sales commissions	$6,000	$3,900	$3,300	$8,400	$21,600
Freight-out	4,000	2,600	2,200	5,600	14,400
Total unit-level expenses	$10,000	$6,500	$5,500	$14,000	$36,000
Customer-level expenses					
Licensing fees	$2,850	$2,850	$2,850	$2,850	$11,400
Total customer-level expenses	$2,850	$2,850	$2,850	$2,850	$11,400
Facility and general operations-level expenses					
Sales salaries	$2,000	$2,000	$2,000	$2,000	$8,000
Advertising	250	250	250	250	1,000
Clerical wages	2,500	2,500	2,500	2,500	10,000
Total facility and general operations-level expenses	$4,750	$4,750	$4,750	$4,750	$19,000
Total selling, general and administrative expenses	$17,600	$14,100	$13,100	$21,600	$66,400

Cash Receipts Budget

The **cash receipts budget** details the expected cash collections during a budget period. Westport Team Wear's cash receipts budget is displayed in Schedule 7. The firm collects 80 per cent of its billings during the same quarter in which the sale is made and another 18 per cent in the following quarter. Two per cent of each quarter's sales are expected to be uncollectable accounts.

Schedule 7

Westport Team Wear Cash Receipts Budget (in NZ$) For the year ending 31 December	Quarter (current year)				
	1	2	3	4	Year
Sales revenue (Schedule 1)	$320,000	$208,000	$176,000	$448,000	$1,152,000
Collections in quarter of sale	$256,000	$166,400	$140,800	$358,400	$921,600
Collections in quarter following sale	80,640	57,600	37,440	31,680	207,360
Total cash receipts	$336,640	$224,000	$178,240	$390,080	$1,128,960
Uncollectable accounts	$6,400	$4,160	$3,520	$8,960	$23,040
Accounts receivable (net), ending	$57,600	$37,440	$31,680	$80,640	$80,640

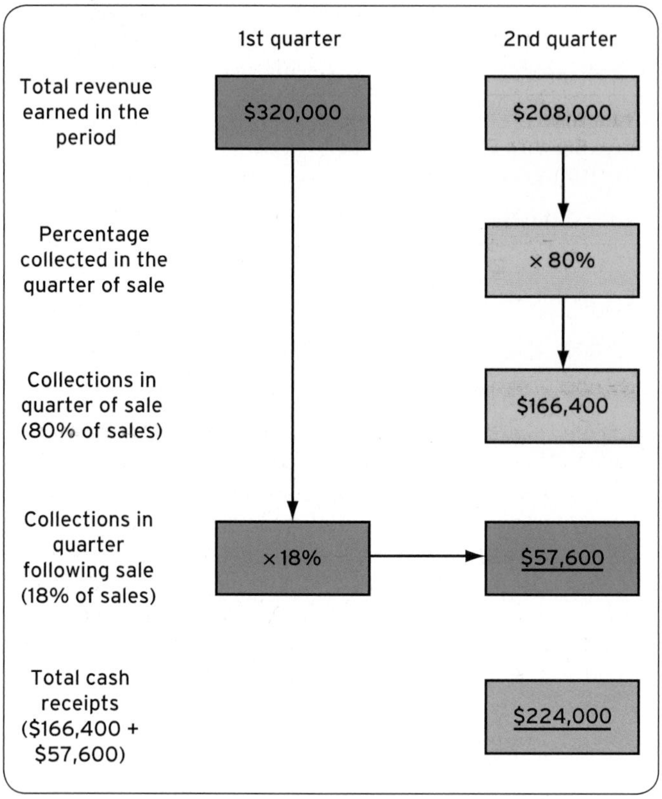

	1st quarter	2nd quarter
Total revenue earned in the period	$320,000	$208,000
Percentage collected in the quarter of sale		× 80%
Collections in quarter of sale (80% of sales)		$166,400
Collections in quarter following sale (18% of sales)	× 18% →	$57,600
Total cash receipts ($166,400 + $57,600)		$224,000

How to budget cash receipts

To understand how the cash receipts budget is prepared, let's focus again on the second quarter column. The NZ$208,000 of total revenue comes directly from Schedule 1, the sales budget (second column, last row). Since most of Westport Team Wear's sales are on account, not all of the second quarter's revenue will be collected during the second quarter. The cash that the firm will collect during the second quarter includes two components, as depicted in the following diagram.[10]

The second quarter's total cash receipts are the sum of NZ$166,400 (which relates to second quarter sales) and $57,600 (which relates to first quarter sales).

Another point to notice is that 2 per cent of each quarter's sales are not expected to be collected. Thus, the NZ$4,160 of second quarter uncollectable accounts amounts to 2 per cent of the second quarter's revenue (2% × NZ$208,000).

One final point to notice is that the amount of accounts receivables at the end of each quarter is estimated. For example, the second quarter starts with accounts receivables of NZ$57,600, which increases by the second quarter's sales of NZ$208,000 and is reduced by the cash collections in the second quarter of NZ$224,000. Furthermore, accounts receivables is reduced in the second quarter by the uncollectable amounts of NZ$4,160, resulting in accounts receivables of NZ$37,440 at the end of the second quarter.

Cash Payments Budget

The **cash payments budget** details the expected cash payments during a budget period. Schedule 8 displays Westport Team Wear's cash payments budget. The first part shows the schedule of cash payments for raw material purchases, which are made on account. The company pays for 60 per cent of its purchases on account during the quarter in which the purchase is made. The remaining 40 per cent of each quarter's purchases are paid for during the quarter following the purchase.

The other part of Schedule 8 shows all of the company's direct labour, manufacturing overhead, and selling, general and administrative expenditures. Based on the beginning level of accounts payable, the accounts payable at the end of each quarter is also calculated.

Schedule 8

TWT

Westport Team Wear
Cash Payments Budget (in NZ$)
For the year ending 31 December

	Quarter (current year)				
	1	**2**	**3**	**4**	**Year**
Cost of raw material purchases (Schedule 3)	$69,938	$47,963	$53,063	$99,038	$270,000
Cash payments for current quarter's purchases	$41,963	$28,778	$31,838	$59,423	$162,000

Cash payments for prior quarter's purchases	39,615	27,975	19,185	21,225	108,000
Total cash payments for raw material purchases	$81,578	$56,753	$51,023	$80,648	$270,000
Other cash payments					
Direct labour costs (Schedule 4)	$54,040	$35,840	$35,560	$76,160	$201,600
Manufacturing overhead costs (Schedule 5)	54,300	47,820	47,800	62,540	212,460
Selling, general and administrative expenses (Schedule 6)	17,600	14,100	13,100	21,600	66,400
Total other cash payments	$125,940	$97,760	$96,460	$160,300	$480,460
Total cash payments	$207,518	$154,513	$147,483	$240,948	$750,460
Accounts payable, ending	$27,975	$19,185	$21,225	$39,615	$39,615

How to budget cash payments

Westport Team Wear purchases raw material, direct labour and various services. The raw material purchases are made on account, which means payment is not made in cash at the time of the purchase. Let's focus on the second quarter column. The second quarter's raw material purchases on account amount to NZ$47,963. Does the company pay for all of the NZ$47,963 purchases on account during the same quarter? No, it does not. As the following diagram shows, the second quarter's actual cash payment for purchases made on account includes two components.

The second quarter's total cash payments *for purchases made on account* are the sum of NZ$28,778 (which relates to second quarter purchases on account) and NZ$27,975 (which relates to first quarter purchases on account).

We are not finished with the second quarter's cash payments yet because Westport Team Wear *also pays for some of its purchases in cash at the time of purchase.* These cash expenditures are detailed in the lower part of Schedule 8. The amounts are drawn from Schedules 4, 5 and 6, which detail expenditures for direct labour, manufacturing overhead and selling, general and administrative expenses, respectively. For example, Schedule 5 lists NZ$47,820 for cash expenditures on manufacturing overhead costs in the second quarter, and Schedule 6 lists NZ$14,100 on selling, general and administrative cash expenditures.

	1st quarter	2nd quarter
Total purchases on account in the period	$69,938	$47,963
Percentage paid in the quarter of purchase		× 60%
Payments made in the quarter of purchase (60% of purchases)		$28,778
Payments made in following quarter (40% of sales)	× 40%	$27,975
Total cash payments ($28,778 + $27,975)		$56,753

The last row in the cash payments budget (Schedule 8) shows the total cash payments during each quarter. Thus, the NZ$154,513 total payment in the second quarter is the sum of NZ$56,753 (for raw material purchases on account) and NZ$97,760 for other purchases made in cash.

One final point to notice is that the amount of accounts payable at the end of each quarter is estimated in Schedule 8. For example, the second quarter starts with accounts payable of NZ$27,975, which increases by the purchases of raw materials in the second quarter of NZ$47,963, and it is reduced by the cash payments in the second quarter of NZ$56,753. This results in accounts payable of NZ$19,185 at the end of the second quarter.

Cash Budget: Combining Receipts and Payments

The **cash budget** details the expected cash receipts and payments during a budget period. Westport Team Wear's completed cash budget is displayed in Schedule 9. The top portion pulls together the cash receipts and cash payments from operating activities detailed in Schedules 7 and 8. Below that, cash from investing activities are specified. Westport Team Wear is undertaking construction activities to expand its production facility, and needs to make the bulk of the payments to the contractor in the first quarter of this year.

The lower portion of Schedule 9 discloses the company's plans to take out a short-term bank loan on 2 January 201x. The company will repay the loan (with interest) in four instalments on the last day of each quarter in 201x. The funds for repayment will come from excess cash generated from operations during 201x.

Also shown in Schedule 9 are the interest payments on the short-term bank loan, at an interest rate of 10 per cent.

Schedule 9

Westport Team Wear
Cash Budget (in NZ$)
For the year ending 31 December

	Quarter (current year)				
	1	**2**	**3**	**4**	**Year**
Cash from operating activities					
Cash receipts (Schedule 7)	$336,640	$224,000	$178,240	$390,080	$1,128,960
Cash payments (Schedule 8)	(207,518)	(154,513)	(147,483)	(240,948)	(750,460)
Total cash from operations	$129,123	$69,488	$30,758	$149,133	$378,500
Cash from investing activities					
Payments for construction	$(185,000)	$(25,000)	$(5,000)	$(5,000)	$(220,000)
Total cash from investing	$(185,000)	$(25,000)	$(5,000)	$(5,000)	$(220,000)
Cash from financing activities					
Proceeds from bank loan for building addition	$100,000	$-	$-	$-	$100,000
Repayments of loan principal	(25,000)	(25,000)	(25,000)	(25,000)	(100,000)
Interest paid on bank loan	(2,500)	(1,875)	(1,250)	(625)	(6,250)
Total cash from financing	$72,500	$(26,875)	$(26,250)	$(25,625)	$(6,250)
Total change in cash	$16,623	$17,613	$(493)	$118,508	$152,250
Beginning cash balance	10,000	$26,623	$44,235	$43,743	10,000
Ending cash balance	$26,623	$44,235	$43,743	$162,250	$162,250

Exhibit 9.3 Calculation of Absorption Unit Cost

Westport Team Wear Budgeting Data for Schedule 10 (in NZ$)		
Units produced for the year (Schedule 2)	36,000	**Per unit**
Average direct material cost per unit (Schedule 3)	$270,000	$7.50
Average direct labour cost per unit (Schedule 4)	201,600	5.60
Average manufacturing overhead cost per unit (Schedule 5)	356,460	9.90
Absorption cost per unit		$23.00

Budgeted Schedule of Cost of Goods Manufactured and Sold

The **budgeted schedule of cost of goods manufactured and sold** details the direct material, direct labour and manufacturing overhead costs to be incurred and shows the cost of the goods to be sold during a budget period. Schedule 10 shows Westport Team Wear's budgeted schedule of cost of goods manufactured and sold.

In Schedule 10 we also see the expected beginning and ending inventories of finished goods for each quarter of 201x. For example, the beginning finished-goods inventory is valued at NZ$23,000, which is the beginning inventory of 1,000 units (Schedule 2) multiplied by the absorption cost per unit of NZ$23.00. The calculation of this absorption cost per unit is specified in Exhibit 9.3. Recall from Chapter 2 that the *accrual* cost includes the direct materials and direct labour costs and an allocation of *all* manufacturing overhead costs (i.e., overhead at the unit, batch, product and facility or general operations levels).

Schedule 10

Westport Team Wear Cost of Goods Manufactured and Sold Budget (in NZ$) For the year ending 31 December					
	Quarter (current year)				
	1	**2**	**3**	**4**	**Year**
Direct material (Schedule 3)	$72,375	$48,000	$47,625	$102,000	$270,000
Direct labour (Schedule 4)	54,040	35,840	35,560	76,160	201,600
Manufacturing overhead (Schedule 5)	90,300	83,820	83,800	98,540	356,460
Cost of goods manufactured	$216,715	$167,660	$166,985	$276,700	$828,060
Add: Beginning finished-goods inventory (Schedule 2)	$23,000	$14,950	$12,650	$32,200	$23,000
Cost of goods available for sale	$239,715	$182,610	$179,635	$308,900	$851,060
Deduct: Ending finished goods inventory (Schedule 2)	$(14,950)	$(12,650)	$(32,200)	$(23,000)	$(23,000)
Cost of sales	$224,765	$169,960	$147,435	$285,900	$828,060

Budgeted Statement of Income

The **budgeted statement of income** shows the expected revenue and expenses for a budget period, assuming that planned operations are carried out. Westport Team Wear's budgeted statement of income is displayed in Schedule 11.

Schedule 11

Westport Team Wear
Budgeted Statement of Income (in NZ$)
For the year ending 31 December

	Quarter (current year)				
	1	**2**	**3**	**4**	**Year**
Sales revenue (Schedule 1)	$320,000	$208,000	$176,000	$448,000	$1,152,000
Less: Cost of sales	224,765	169,960	147,435	285,900	828,060
Gross margin	$95,235	$38,040	$28,565	$162,100	$323,940
Other expenses					
Selling, general and administrative expenses (Schedule 6)	$17,600	$14,100	$13,100	$21,600	$66,400
Uncollectible accounts (Schedule 7)	6,400	4,160	3,520	8,960	23,040
Interest expense (Schedule 9)	2,500	1,875	1,250	625	6,250
Total other expenses	$26,500	$20,135	$17,870	$31,185	$95,690
Net income before tax	$68,735	$17,905	$10,695	$130,915	$228,250

Budgeted Statement of Financial Position

The **budgeted statement of financial position, or balance sheet** shows the expected end-of-period balances for the company's assets, liabilities and owners' equity, assuming that planned operations are carried out. Westport Team Wear's budgeted balance sheet for 31 December 201x, is displayed in Schedule 12. To construct this budgeted balance sheet, we start with the firm's balance sheet projected for the *beginning* of the budget year (Exhibit 9.4) and adjust each account balance for the changes expected during 201x.

Notice how the budgeted balance sheet pulls together information from most of the schedules constituting the master budget.

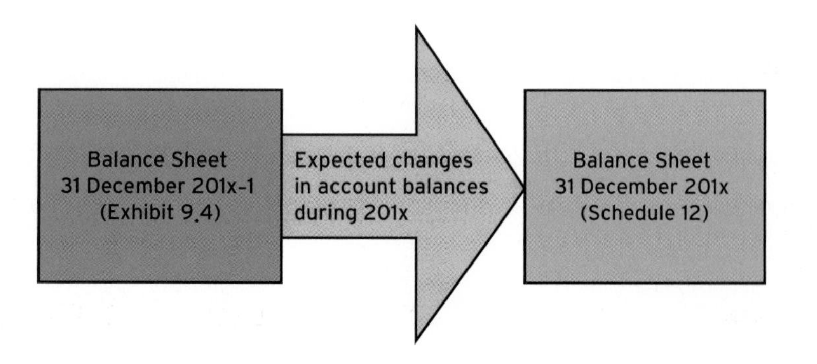

Exhibit 9.4 **Statement of Financial Position as of 31 December 201x–1**

Westport Team Wear **Budgeting Data for Schedule 12** **Beginning Balances (in NZ$)**	
Assets	
Current assets	
Cash	$10,000
Accounts receivable (net)	80,640
Inventories	
Raw material	7,238
Finished goods	23,000
Supplies	2,000
Total current assets	$122,878
Long-lived assets	
Building and equipment	720,000
Less: Accumulated depreciation	(240,000)
Total long-lived assets	$480,000
Total assets	$602,878
Liabilities and Owner's equity	
Current liabilities	
Accounts payable	$39,615
Short-term note payable	
Total current liabilities	$39,615
Long-term liabilities	
Note payable (non-interest bearing, due in 3 years)	200,000
Total long-term liabilities	200,000
Total liabilities	$239,615
Owner's equity	363,263
Total liabilities and owner's equity	$602,878

Schedule 12

Westport Team Wear
Budgeted Statement of Financial Position (in NZ$)
as of the end of each quarter and the year

	Quarter (current year)			
	1	**2**	**3**	**4**
Assets				
Current assets				
Cash	$26,623	$44,235	$43,743	$162,250
Accounts receivable (net)	57,600	37,440	31,680	80,640
Inventories				
Raw material	4,800	4,763	10,200	7,238
Finished goods	14,950	12,650	32,200	23,000
Supplies	2,000	2,000	2,000	2,000
Total current assets	$105,973	$101,088	$119,823	$275,128

Long-lived assets				
Building and equipment	905,000	930,000	935,000	940,000
Less: Accumulated depreciation	(276,000)	(312,000)	(348,000)	(384,000)
Total long-lived assets	629,000	618,000	587,000	556,000
Total assets	$734,973	$719,088	$706,823	$831,128
Liabilities and owner's equity				
Current liabilities				
Accounts payable	$27,975	$19,185	$21,225	$39,615
Short-term note payable	75,000	50,000	25,000	-
Total current liabilities	$102,975	$69,185	$46,225	$39,615
Long-term liabilities				
Note payable (non-interest bearing, due in 3 years)	200,000	200,000	200,000	200,000
Total long-term liabilities	200,000	200,000	200,000	200,000
Total liabilities	$302,975	$269,185	$246,225	$239,615
Owner's equity	431,998	449,903	460,598	591,513
Total liabilities and owner's equity	$734,973	$719,088	$706,823	$831,128

Assumptions and Predictions Underlying the Master Budget

A master budget is based on many assumptions and estimates of unknown parameters. What are some of the assumptions and estimates used in Westport Team Wear's master budget? The professional sales budget was built on an assumption about the seasonal nature of demand for sports T-shirts. The direct material budget uses an estimate of the direct material price, NZ$5.00 per metre, and the quantity of material required per T-shirt, 1.5 metres. An estimate of the direct labour required to make a T-shirt was used in the direct labour budget.

These are only a few of the many assumptions and estimates used in Westport Team Wear's master budget. Some of these estimates are much more likely to be accurate than others. For example, the amount of material required to make a T-shirt is not likely to differ from past experience unless the type of material or production process is changed. In contrast, estimates such as the price of material, the cost of utilities and sales demand are much more difficult to predict.

Financial Planning Models

Managers must make assumptions and predictions in preparing budgets because organizations operate in a world of uncertainty. One way to cope with that uncertainty is to supplement the budgeting process with a *financial planning model*. A **financial planning model** is a set of mathematical relationships that express the interactions among the various operational, financial and environmental events that determine the overall results of an organization's activities. A financial planning model is a mathematical expression of all the relationships expressed in the flowchart of Exhibit 9.1.

To illustrate this concept, focus on the following equation, which was used to budget uncollectable accounts expense in Schedule 7.

$$\textbf{Uncollectable accounts expense} = 0.02 \times \textbf{Sales revenue}$$

Suppose that Westport Team Wear's management is uncertain about this 2 per cent estimate. A financial planning model might include the following equation instead.

$$\textbf{Uncollectable accounts expense} = p \times \textbf{Sales revenue}$$

where:

$$0 \leq p \leq 1.0$$

The budget staff can run the financial planning model as many times as desired on a computer, using a different value for p each time. Perhaps the following values would be tried: 0.04, 0.045, 0.05, 0.055 and 0.06. Now management can answer the question, What if 4 per cent of sales prove to be uncollectable? In a fully developed financial planning model, the key estimates and assumptions are expressed as general mathematical relationships. Then the model is run on a computer many times to determine the impact of different combinations of these unknown variables. 'What-if' questions can be answered about unknown variables such as inflation, interest rates, the value of the dollar, demand, competitors' actions, production efficiency, union demands in forthcoming wage negotiations, and a host of other factors. The widespread availability of personal computers and electronic spreadsheet software has made financial planning models a more and more common management tool.

Chapter 7 includes a more thorough discussion of financial planning models.

9.3 You're the Decision Maker

Financial Planning Model: Uncollectable Accounts Expense

Refer again to Westport Team Wear's cash receipts budget in Schedule 7. Apply the financial planning concept to perform sensitivity analysis on the implications of different estimates of the rate of uncollectable accounts expense.

a. Prepare a table as a spreadsheet with a row for each of the following estimates of the rate of uncollectable accounts: 1, 2, 3 and 4 per cent. Also include a row for the budgeted sales revenue. Your table should have five columns, one for each quarter and one for the entire year. The entries in the table will be the budgeted uncollectable accounts expense.

b. How could this financial planning model help Westport Team Wear to manage its uncollectible accounts expense?

(Solutions begin on page 471.)

Responsibility for Budget Administration

LO 5 Describe and evaluate a typical organization's process of budget administration.

The procedures that small organizations use to gather information and construct a master budget are usually informal. At Westport Team Wear, for example, the firm's owner, Steve Keegan, co-ordinates the budgeting process. In contrast, larger organizations usually designate a **budget director** (or **chief budget officer**) who specifies the process by which budget data are gathered, collects the information and prepares the master budget.[11] This is often the organization's controller. To communicate budget procedures and deadlines to employees throughout the organization, the budget director often develops and disseminates a budget manual. The **budget manual** indicates who is responsible for providing various types of information, when the information is required, and what form the information is to take. For example, the budget manual for a large manufacturing firm might specify that each regional sales director is to send an estimate of the following year's sales, by product line, to the budget director by 1 September. The budget manual also states who should receive each schedule when the master budget is complete.

A **budget committee**, consisting of key senior executives, advises the budget director during the preparation of the budget. The authority to give final approval to the master budget usually belongs to the board of directors, or the board of trustees in many non-profit organizations. Usually the board has a subcommittee whose task is to examine the proposed budget carefully and recommend approval or any changes deemed necessary. By exercising its authority to make changes in the budget and grant final approval, the board of directors, or trustees, can wield considerable influence on the overall direction the organization takes.

9.2 Cost Management in Practice

Global Accounting Information Systems in Large Organizations

Budgeting and other accounting activities have become more efficient and faster because of enterprise resource planning (ERP) systems, data warehouse technology and 'business intelligence' software. In multinational companies, global information systems have been created. Accounting information may become more useful, for example because more performance measurement data are accessible, comparisons can be made between different parts of the organization, rolling forecasts are possible, and powerful analytical tools are available.

An example is **Toronto-Dominion Bank** (www.tdbank.com). When the bank's executives were searching for a new solution capable of handling the bank's enterprise-wide budgeting and planning function, they turned to the Internet. 'In the past, we have compiled our business plan using hundreds of spreadsheets, and our analysts have spent a disproportionate amount of time compiling and verifying data from multiple sources,' according to Toronto-Dominion's controller. 'Implementing a Webbased, enterprise-wide budgeting solution will help us develop business plans and allow our analysts to be proactive in monitoring quarterly results'.

Case studies find that these developments in accounting information systems lead to moving more management accounting activities to line managers, who are supported by management accounting specialists. However, global IT systems are sometimes also less flexible to adapt and sometimes they block particular accounting choices. Furthermore, global systems require standardization, and local managers sometimes find that it is more difficult to get site-specific information from their own systems. Still, there is not so much systematic evidence on how modern accounting information systems change budgeting and other accounting activities, and this is an important research topic.

Sources: Granlund (2001); Hornyak (1998); Kallunki et al. (2007); Rom and Rohde (2007); Scapens and Jazayeri (2003).

Behavioural Implications of Budgets

LO 6
Understand the behavioural implications of budgetary slack and participative budgeting.

In perhaps no other area of management are behavioural implications more important than in budgeting. A budget affects virtually everyone in an organization: those who prepare the budget, those who use the budget to facilitate decision making, and those who are evaluated using the budget. The human reactions to the budgeting process can have considerable influence on an organization's overall effectiveness. A great deal of study has been devoted to the behavioural effects of budgets. This discussion barely scratches the surface by briefly considering two issues: budgetary slack and participative budgeting.

Budgetary Slack: Padding the Budget

The information on which a budget is based comes largely from people throughout an organization. For example, the sales forecast relies on market research and analysis by market research staff but also incorporates the projections of sales personnel. If a territorial sales manager's performance is evaluated on the basis of whether the sales budget for the territory is exceeded, what is the incentive for the sales manager in projecting sales? The incentive is to give a conservative, or cautiously low, sales estimate. The sales manager's performance will look much better in the eyes of top management when a conservative estimate is exceeded than when an ambitious estimate is not met. At least that is the *perception* of many sales managers, and in the behavioural area, perceptions are what count most.

When a supervisor provides a departmental cost projection for budgetary purposes, there is an incentive to overestimate costs. When the actual cost incurred in the department proves to be less than the inflated cost projection, the supervisor appears to have managed in a cost-effective way.

These illustrations are examples of **padding the budget**, which means intentionally underestimating revenue or overestimating costs. The difference between the revenue or cost projection that a person provides and a realistic estimate of the revenue or cost is called **budgetary slack**. For example, if a plant manager believes the annual utilities cost will be €23,000 but gives a budgetary projection of €25,000, the manager has built €2,000 of slack into the budget.

Why do people pad budgets with budgetary slack? There are three primary reasons. First, people often *perceive* that their performance will look better in their superiors' eyes if they can 'beat the budget'. Second, budgetary slack is often used to cope with uncertainty. A departmental supervisor might feel confident in the cost projections for 10 cost items. However, the supervisor might also believe that some unforeseen event during the budgetary period could result in unanticipated costs. For example, an unexpected machine breakdown could occur. One way to deal with that unforeseen event is to pad the budget. If nothing goes wrong, the supervisor can beat the cost budget. If some negative event does occur, the supervisor can use the budgetary slack to absorb the impact of the event and still meet the cost budget.

The third reason that people pad cost budgets is that budgetary cost projections are often cut in the resource-allocation process. Thus, a vicious circle exists. Budgetary projections are padded because they will likely be cut, and they are cut because they are likely to have been padded.

How does an organization solve the problem of budgetary slack? First, it can avoid relying on the budget as a negative evaluative tool. If a departmental supervisor is harassed by the budget director or some other top manager every time a budgetary cost projection is exceeded, the likely behavioural response will be to pad the budget. In contrast, if the supervisor is allowed some managerial discretion to exceed the budget when necessary, the tendency toward budgetary padding will decrease. Second, managers can be given incentives not only to achieve budgetary projections but also to *provide accurate projections*. This can be accomplished by asking managers to justify all or some of their projections and by rewarding managers who consistently provide accurate estimates.[12]

Participative Budgeting

Most people will perform better and make greater attempts to achieve a goal if they have been consulted in setting that goal. **Participative budgeting** involves employees throughout an organization in the budgetary process. Such participation can give employees the feeling that 'this is our budget' rather than the all-too-common feeling that 'this is the budget you imposed on us'.[13]

Although participative budgeting can be very effective, it can also have shortcomings. Too much participation and discussion can lead to vacillation and delay. Also, when those involved in the budgeting process disagree in significant and irreconcilable ways, the process of participation can accentuate those differences. Finally, the problem of budget padding can be severe unless incentives for accurate projections are provided.

Ethical Issues in Budgeting

A departmental or divisional budget often is the basis for evaluating a manager's performance. Actual results are compared with budgeted performance levels, and those who outperform the budget often are rewarded with promotions or salary increases. In many cases, bonuses are tied explicitly to performance relative to a budget. For example, the top-management personnel of a division might receive a bonus if divisional profit exceeds budgeted profit by a certain percentage.

Serious ethical issues can arise in situations when a budget is the basis for rewarding managers. For example, suppose a division's top-management personnel will split a bonus equal to 10 per cent of the amount by which actual divisional profit exceeds the budget. This might create an incentive for the divisional budget officer, or other managers supplying data, to pad the divisional profit budget. Such padding would make the budget easier to achieve, thus increasing the chance of a bonus. Alternatively, there might be an incentive to manipulate the actual divisional results to maximize management's bonus. For example, year-end sales could be shifted between years to increase reported revenue in a particular year.

Budget personnel could have such incentives for either of two reasons: (1) they might share in the bonus or (2) they might feel pressure from the managers who would share in the bonus. Padding the budget or manipulating reported results to maximize one's personal gain or that of others is a serious ethical violation.

9.2 Research Insight

Beyond Budgeting

Some managers have argued that the traditional approach to budgeting is outmoded and no longer meets the needs of management in today's dynamic business environment. Adherents to this broad criticism of budgeting have come to embrace an approach they call *beyond budgeting*. Two leading proponents of the beyond budgeting approach had this to say when asked what beyond budgeting is all about.

'*Beyond budgeting* is about releasing capable people from the chains of the top-down performance contract and enabling them to use the knowledge resources of the organization to satisfy customers profitability and consistently beat the competition. With intellectual assets accounting for 80–90% of shareholder value today, people really are the organization's most valuable asset. But the way the annual budget contract works means that their energy and ingenuity are used more for negotiating the budget than for creating value for customers and shareholders. The budget contract is a relic from an earlier age. It is expensive, absorbs far too much time, adds little value, and should be replaced by a more appropriate performance management model.'*

Beyond budgeting enthusiasts suggest replacing budgets with rolling forecasts that give managers an idea where their part of the organization is heading but without tying them to specific budget targets. Then managers are freed from budgetary constraints and encouraged to optimize the use of resources and strive for the best performance possible in their sphere of influence in the organization. Hierarchical management is replaced by collaborative networking among teams, and decision making is pushed down to lower levels of management than has traditionally been the case.

The twelve principles of beyond budgeting* are as follows:

Key Performance Management Principles

- Beat the competition.
- Reward team-based competitive success.
- Make strategy a continuous and inclusive process.
- Draw resources when needed.
- Co-ordinate cross-company interactions through 'market-like' forces.
- Provide fast, open information for multilevel control.

Key Leadership Principles

- Create a performance climate based on sustained competitive success.
- Build the commitment of teams to a common purpose, clear values, and shared rewards.
- Devolve strategy to front-line teams and provide the freedom and capability to act.
- Champion frugality and challenge the value-added contribution of all resources.
- Organize around a network of teams that dynamically connect their capabilities to serve the external customer.
- Support transparent and open information systems.

Recent studies investigate the ideas behind beyond budgeting more systematically. Survey-based research in North America found a much more nuanced picture of problems with budgets than the beyond budgeting proponents claim. For example, use of the fixed performance contract is not very prevalent, and subjective considerations or allowances for non-controllable events are frequently observed in firms using the budget to evaluate performance. Furthermore, time spent on budgeting does not appear excessive. In unpredictable environments, budgets are revised quite frequently. In the majority of firms surveyed, the budget process is explicitly linked to strategy implementation. Finally, budgetary gaming behaviours are a problem in the sample firms, such as deferring necessary expenditures to future periods, and negotiating easier targets by 'sandbagging'. Overall, while problems exist with budgets, organizations are adapting their use for these problems rather than abandoning budgets altogether. See also the detailed case study by Østergren and Stensaker (2010) of the implementation of beyond budgeting principles in two divisions of a large Norwegian-based multinational oil and energy company.

Sources: *Hope and Fraser (2001, 2003a, 2003b); Libby and Lindsay (2010); Østergren and Stensaker (2010).

Appendix 9

Inventory Management

A key decision in manufacturing, retail and some service industry firms is how much inventory to keep on hand. Once inventory levels have been established, they become an important input to the budgeting system. Inventory decisions involve a delicate balance between three classes of costs: ordering costs, holding costs and shortage costs. Examples of costs in each of these categories are given in Exhibit 9.5.

LO 7
Use the economic-order-quantity model to make inventory-ordering decisions and discuss the implications of the JIT approach for inventory management.

Economic Order Quantity

It is now 201x+3 and Westport Team Wear has expanded its production capability. Owner and president, Steve Keegan, has signed a contract with a large New Zealand university to supply all its athletic T-shirts for use in its physical education programme. The colour and type of fabric is unlike the T-shirts in Westport Team Wear's regular product line. The contract calls for 24,000 shirts to be delivered each year.

Westport Team Wear's production supervisor, Bradley Roaldsson, has decided to use an economic order quantity (EOQ) decision model to determine the size and frequency with which the fabric should be ordered. The **EOQ model** is a mathematical tool for determining the order quantity that minimizes the cost of ordering and holding inventory, which is called the **economic order quantity**, or **EOQ**.

Roaldsson has determined that Westport Team Wear will need 1,200 bolts of cotton/polyester fabric per year to produce the shirts for the contract.[14] Each bolt costs NZ$145. He estimates that it costs NZ$70 to place and receive a typical order, and that the annual cost of carrying fabric in inventory is NZ$17 per bolt.

Exhibit 9.5 Inventory Ordering, Holding and Shortage Costs

Ordering costs
Time spent in finding suppliers and expediting orders
Clerical costs of preparing purchase orders
Transportation costs
Receiving costs (e.g., unloading and inspection)
Holding costs
Costs of storage space (e.g., warehouse depreciation)
Security
Insurance
Forgone interest on working capital tied up in inventory
Deterioration, theft, spoilage or obsolescence
Shortage costs
Lost sales and dissatisfied customers
Loss of quantity discounts on purchases
Disrupted production when raw materials are unavailable
Idle workers
Extra machinery set-ups

Tabular approach

Suppose that Roaldsson orders 150 bolts of fabric in each order placed during the year. The total annual cost of ordering and holding fabric in inventory is calculated as follows:

Number of orders per year
= Annual requirement ÷ Order quantity
= 1,200 ÷ 150 = 8

Annual ordering cost = 8 orders × NZ$70 per order = NZ$560

Average quantity in inventory = Order quantity ÷ 2 = 150 ÷ 2 = 75 bolts

Annual holding cost = Average quantity in inventory
× Annual carrying cost per bolt
= 75 × NZ$17 = NZ$1,275

Total annual cost of inventory policy = Ordering cost + Holding cost
= NZ$560 + NZ$1,275 = NZ$1,835

Notice that the NZ$1,835 cost does *not* include the purchase cost of the fabric at NZ$145 per bolt. We are focusing only on the costs of *ordering* and *holding* fabric inventory.

Can Roaldsson do any better than $1,845 for the annual cost of the fabric inventory policy? Exhibit 9.6, which tabulates the inventory costs for various order quantities, indicates that Roaldsson can lower the costs of ordering and holding fabric inventory. Of the five order quantities listed, the 100-bolt order quantity yields the lowest total annual cost. Unfortunately, this tabular method for finding the least-cost order quantity is cumbersome. Moreover, it does not necessarily result in the optimal order quantity. It is possible that some order quantity other than those listed in Exhibit 9.6 is the least-cost order quantity.

Exhibit 9.6 **Tabulation of Inventory Ordering and Holding Costs for Westport Team Wear**

Annual cost of inventory policy for different order quantities					
Order quantity	50	80	100	120	150
Number of orders per year	24	15	12	10	8
Annual ordering cost	$1,680	$1,050	$840	$700	$560
Average inventory	25	40	50	60	75
Annual holding cost	$425	$680	$850	$1,020	$1,275
Total annual cost of inventory policy	$2,105	$1,730	$1,690	$1,720	$1,835

Equation approach

The total annual cost of ordering and holding inventory is given by the following equation:

$$\textbf{Total annual cost} = \left(\frac{\textbf{Annual requirement}}{\textbf{Order quantity}}\right)\left(\begin{matrix}\textbf{Cost per}\\ \textbf{order}\end{matrix}\right) + \left(\frac{\textbf{Order quantity}}{\textbf{2}}\right)\left(\begin{matrix}\textbf{Annual holding}\\ \textbf{cost per unit}\end{matrix}\right)$$

The following formula for the least-cost order quantity, called the *economic order quantity* (or EOQ), has been developed using calculus:

$$\textbf{Economic order quantity} = \sqrt{\frac{\textbf{2(Annual requirement)(Cost per unit)}}{\textbf{Annual holding cost per unit}}}$$

Applying the EOQ formula in Westport Team Wear's problem yields the following EOQ for fabric: $\text{EOQ} = \sqrt{((2 \times 1{,}700 \times 70) \div 17)} = 99.41$, which is rounded to 100.

Graphical approach

Another method for solving the EOQ problem is the graphical method, which is presented in Exhibit 9.7. Notice that the ordering-cost line slants down to the right. This indicates a decline in these costs as the order size increases and the order frequency decreases. However, as the order size increases, so does the average inventory on hand. This results in increased holding costs as indicated by the positive slope of the holding-cost line. The EOQ falls at 100 units, where the best balance is struck between these two costs. Total costs are minimized at $1,690.

Timing of Orders

The EOQ model helps management decide how much each order will include. Another important decision is when to order. This decision depends on the **lead time**, which is the length of time it takes for the materials to be received after an order has been placed. Suppose that the lead time for fabric is 15 days (approximately one-half month). Westport Team Wear's use of 1,200 bolts of fabric per year, with a constant production rate throughout the year, implies that it uses 100 bolts each month. Production manager Roaldsson should order fabric in the economic order quantity of 100 bolts when the inventory falls to 50 bolts. By the time the new order arrives one-half month later, the 50 bolts in inventory will have been used in production. Exhibit 9.8 depicts this pattern of ordering and using inventory. By placing an order early enough to avoid running out of inventory, management considers the potential costs of shortages.

Safety inventory

Our example assumed that fabric usage is constant at 100 bolts per month. Suppose instead that monthly usage fluctuates between 80 and 120 bolts. Although average monthly usage still is 100

Exhibit 9.7 Graphical Solution to Economic Order Quantity Decision for Westport Team Wear

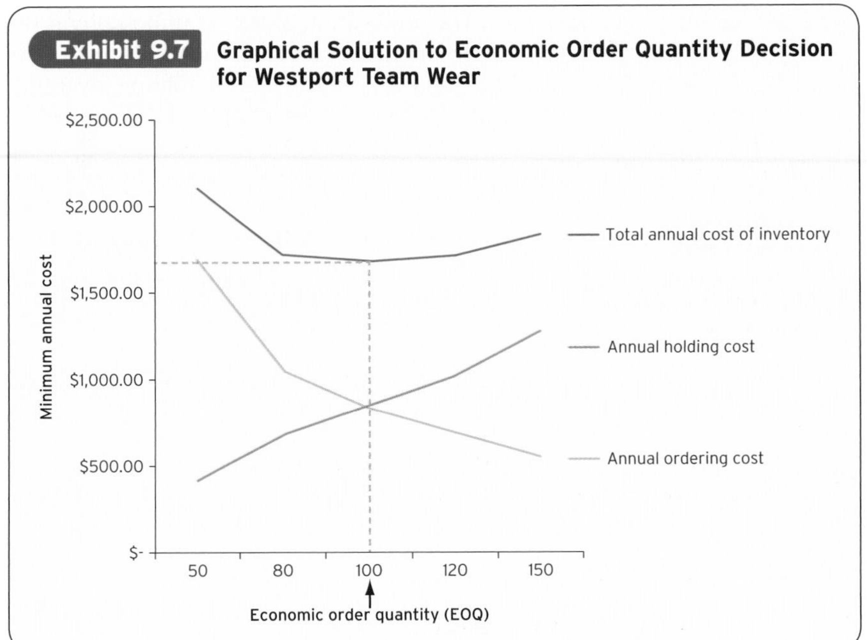

Exhibit 9.8 Ordering, Lead Time, and Usage of Inventory for Westport Team Wear

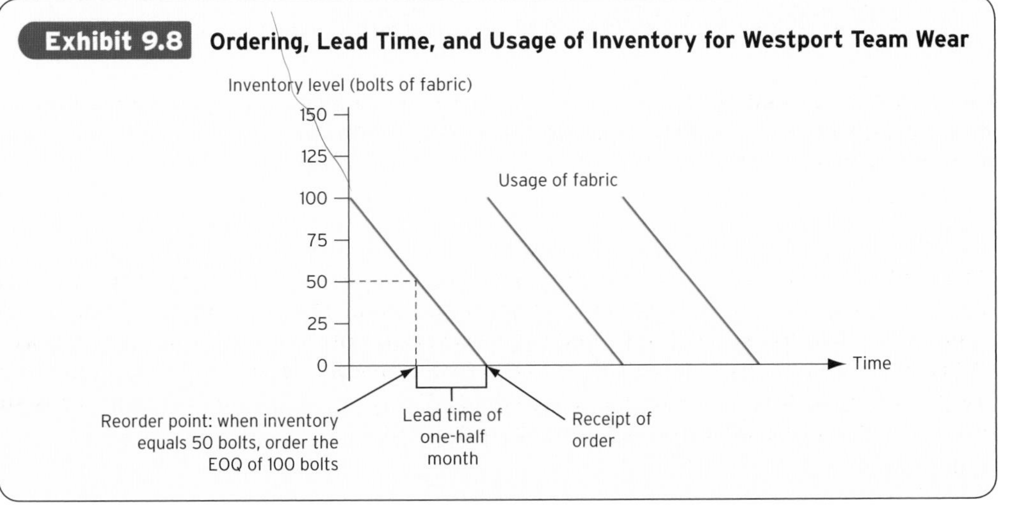

bolts, there is the potential for an excess usage of 20 bolts in any particular month. This means that the usage during the half-month lead time required to receive an order fluctuates between 40 and 60 bolts, so there is the potential for excess usage of 10 bolts during the half-month lead time. In light of this uncertainty, management might wish to keep a safety inventory of fabric equal to the potential excess usage of 10 bolts during the half-month lead time. A **safety inventory** is the potential excess usage of material when material usage fluctuates during the lead time. With a safety inventory of 10 bolts, the reorder point is 60 bolts. Thus, Roaldsson should order the EOQ of 100 bolts when fabric inventory falls to 60 bolts. During the half-month lead time, another 40 to 60 bolts of fabric will be consumed in production. Although a safety inventory increases inventory holding costs, it minimizes the potential costs caused by shortages.

Inventory Management under JIT: Implications for EOQ

The EOQ model minimizes the total cost of ordering and holding purchased inventory. Thus, this inventory management approach seeks to balance the cost of ordering against the cost of storing inventory. Under the JIT philosophy, the goal is to keep *all* inventories as low as possible. *Any* inventory-holding costs are seen as inefficient and wasteful. Moreover, JIT purchasing minimizes ordering costs by reducing the number of vendors, negotiating long-term supply agreements, making less frequent payments and eliminating inspections. The implication of the JIT philosophy is that inventories should be minimized by more frequent deliveries in smaller quantities. This result can be demonstrated using the EOQ formula, as shown in Exhibit 9.9. As the cost of holding inventory increases, the EOQ decreases. Moreover, as the cost of placing an order declines, the EOQ decreases.

Exhibit 9.9 Economic Order Quantity with Different Ordering and Holding Costs

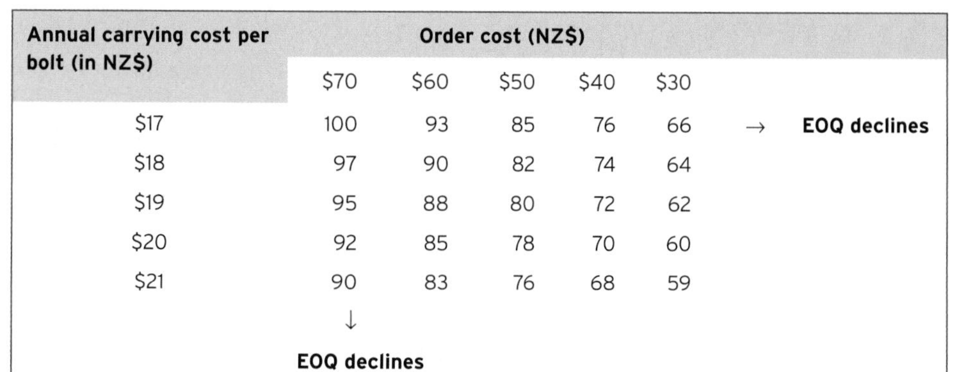

Annual carrying cost per bolt (in NZ$)	Order cost (NZ$)						
	$70	$60	$50	$40	$30		
$17	100	93	85	76	66	→	EOQ declines
$18	97	90	82	74	64		
$19	95	88	80	72	62		
$20	92	85	78	70	60		
$21	90	83	76	68	59		
	↓						
	EOQ declines						

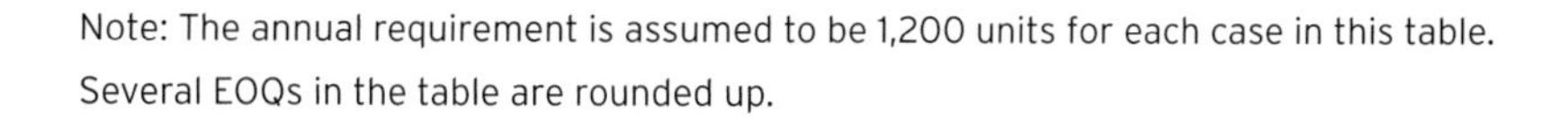

Note: The annual requirement is assumed to be 1,200 units for each case in this table.
Several EOQs in the table are rounded up.

The economics underlying the EOQ model supports the JIT viewpoint that inventory should be purchased or produced in small quantities and should be kept to the absolute minimum. However, the basic philosophies of JIT and EOQ are quite different. The EOQ approach takes the view that some inventory is necessary and the goal is to optimize the order quantity to balance the cost of ordering against the cost of holding inventory. Also implicit in this approach is the need to hold some buffer of inventory prior to bottleneck operations. (Review our discussion of this issue in Chapters 4 and 6.) In contrast, the JIT philosophy argues that holding costs tend to be higher than might be apparent because of the inefficiency and waste of storing inventory. Thus, inventory should be minimized, or even eliminated completely if possible. Moreover, under the JIT approach, orders typically vary in size, depending on needs. The EOQ model, in contrast, results in a constant order quantity.

The JIT approach to production and inventory management is much more than 'just an inventory system'. It has implications for many other issues in cost management. See Chapter 6 for additional discussion.

Chapter Summary

The *budget* is a key tool for planning, control and decision making in virtually every organization. Budgeting systems are used to force planning, to facilitate communication and co-ordination, to allocate resources, to control profit and operations, and to evaluate performance and provide incentives. Various types of budgets are used to accomplish these objectives.

The comprehensive set of budgets that covers all phases of an organization's operations is called a 'master budget'. The first step in preparing a master budget is to forecast sales of the organization's services or goods. Based on the sales forecast, operational budgets are prepared to plan production of services or goods and to outline the acquisition and use of materials, labour and other resources. Finally, a set of budgeted financial statements is prepared to show what the organization's overall financial condition will be if the organization carries out its planned operations.

Since budgets affect almost everyone in an organization, they can have significant behavioural implications. One common problem in budgeting is the tendency of people to *pad* budgets. The resulting *budgetary slack* makes the budget less useful because the padded budget does not present an accurate picture of expected revenue and expenses. Participative budgeting is the process of allowing employees throughout the organization to have a significant role in developing the budget. Participative budgeting can result in greater commitment to meet the budget by those who participated in the process.

Key Terms

For each term's definition, refer to the indicated page, or turn to the glossary at the end of the text.

activity-based budgeting (ABB), 428
budget, 421
budget committee, 443
budget director (or chief budget officer), 443
budget manual, 443
budgetary slack, 444
budgeted statement of financial position, 440
budgeted financial statements, 422
budgeted statement of income, 440
budgeted schedule of cost of goods manufactured and sold, 439
budgeting system, 421
capital budget, 422
cash budget, 438
cash payments budget, 436
cash receipts budget, 435
critical success factors, 420
direct labour budget, 432
direct material budget, 430
economic order quantity (EOQ),* 447
EOQ model,* 447
financial budget, 422
financial planning model, 442
lead time,* 449
manufacturing overhead budget, 432
master budget, 422
operational budgets, 425
padding the budget, 444
participative budgeting, 445
production budget, 429
profit plan, 422
rolling budget (revolving or continuous budget), 422
safety inventory,* 450
sales budget, 429
sales forecasting, 423
selling, general and administrative (SG&A) expense budget, 434
zero-base budgeting, 428

**Term appears in Appendix 9.*

*Review Questions are mostly written at a **basic** level; Critical Analysis questions and Exercises are **intermediate**, and Problems and Cases are **advanced**.*

Review Questions

9.1 What are the relationships among organization goals, strategic plans and a master budget for the coming period?

9.2 What is meant by the term *operational budgets?* List three operational budgets that a hospital would prepare.

9.3 Use an example to explain how a budget could be used to allocate resources in a university.

9.4 Give an example of the effect of general economic trends on sales forecasting in the airline industry.

9.5 What is the danger of relying entirely on middle-management estimates of sales, costs, and other data used in budget planning?

9.6 What is the purpose of a *budget manual?*

9.7 Describe the role of a *budget director.*

9.8 Discuss the importance of predictions and assumptions in the budgeting process.

9.9 What is the purpose of a financial planning model? Briefly describe how such a model is constructed.

9.10 Define the term *budgetary slack* and briefly describe a problem it can cause.

9.11 How can an organization help to reduce the problems caused by budgetary slack?

9.12 Explain the concept of *zero-base budgeting.*

9.13 (Appendix 9) Explain the differences in the basic philosophies underlying the JIT and EOQ approaches to inventory management.

Critical Analysis

9.14 Draw a flowchart similar to the one in Exhibit 9.1 for a service station. The service station provides automotive maintenance services in addition to selling fuel and related products.

9.15 The chief executive officer of Home Workout Equipment Corporation remarked to a colleague, 'I don't understand why other companies waste so much time in the budgeting process. I set our company goals, and everyone strives to meet them. What's wrong with that approach?' Comment on the executive's remarks.

9.16 Give three examples of how the City of Nice could use a budget for planning purposes.

9.17 A budget is also a legal limitation on expenditures of governmental agencies. If governmental employees are asked about their agencies' needs for the coming fiscal period, what types of biases are they likely to incorporate in their estimates? Why?

9.18 If a company prepares budgeted income statements and balance sheets, why is a cash budget necessary?

9.19 List the steps you would go through in developing a budget to meet your college expenses.

9.20 Surveying the accounts payable records, a clerk in the controller's office noted that expenses appeared to rise significantly within a month of the close of the budget period. The organization did not have a seasonal product or service to explain this behaviour. Can you suggest an explanation?

9.21 Briefly describe three issues that create special challenges for multinational firms in preparing their budgets.

9.22 Borealis Corporation has established a bonus plan for its employees. An employee receives a bonus if his or her subunit meets the cost levels specified in the annual budget plan. If the subunit's costs exceed the budget, its employees earn no bonus. What problems might arise with this bonus plan?

9.23 How would the use of a just-in-time inventory system affect a company's budget plans?

Exercises

Exercise 9.24 [LO 2, 3, 4] Estimate of Sales Revenue

The Bank of Bavaria (BB) has €40 million in commercial loans with an average interest rate of 6 per cent. The bank also has €30 million in consumer loans with an average interest rate of 8 per cent. Finally, the bank owns €6 million in government securities with an average rate of 7 per cent.

BB estimates that next year its commercial loan portfolio will fall to €35 million, and the interest rate will fall to 5.5 per cent. Its consumer loans will expand to €35 million with an average interest rate of 8.5 per cent, and its government securities portfolio will increase to €8 million with an average rate of 6.5 per cent.

Required

Estimate BB's revenues for the coming year.

Exercise 9.25 [LO 3, 4] Estimate of Production

Penna Pillow Company has just made its sales forecasts for the coming period. Its marketing department estimates that the company will sell 12,000 units during the coming year. In the past, management maintained inventories of finished goods at approximately two months' sales. The inventory at the start of the budget period is 600 units. Sales occur evenly throughout the year.

Required

Estimate the production level required for the coming year to meet these objectives.

Exercise 9.26 [LO 2, 3, 4] Estimate of Sales Revenue

Ujvari and Company Ltd is a large securities dealer in Frankfurt, Germany. Last year, the company made 60,000 trades with an average commission of €300. Small investors are abandoning the market, whose volume is expected to decline by 15 per cent for the coming year. The firm's volume generally changes with the market. However, in addition to market factors, the firm expects an additional 10 per cent decline in the number of trades due to unfavourable publicity.

Offsetting these factors is the observation that the average commission per trade is likely to increase by 30 per cent because trades are expected to be large in the coming year.

Required

Estimate the firm's commission revenue for the coming year.

Exercise 9.27 [LO 1, 2] City or State Budget; Use of Internet

Choose a city or state in the United States (or a Canadian city or province), and use the Internet to explore the annual budget of the governmental unit you selected. For example, you could check out the budget for Los Angeles at www.losangeles.com. Alternatively, take a look at the US federal budget at www.fms.treas.gov/annualreport/index.html.

Required

List three items in the budget that you found surprising or particularly interesting, and explain why.

Exercise 9.28 [LO 3, 4] Estimate of Production and Materials Requirements

Technoplast Company makes a line of specialized plastic tubing items. During each of the next two years, it expects to sell 300,000 units. The beginning Finished goods inventory is 75,000 units. However, the target ending Finished goods inventory for each year is 30,000 units.

Each unit requires 2 metres of plastic tubing. At the beginning of the year, 80,000 metres of plastic tubing are in inventory. Management has set a target to have tubing materials on hand equal to three months of production requirements. Sales and production occur evenly throughout the year.

Required

Compute the total targeted production of the finished product for the coming year. Compute the required purchases of tubing materials for the coming year. (Note that production in the following year should be 300,000 units of finished product.)

Exercise 9.29 [LO 3, 4] Estimate of Purchases and Cash Payments

Léman Products' management wishes to purchase goods in one month for sale in the next. On 31 January, the company has 10,000 mp3 players in inventory, although sales for the next month (February) are estimated to total 11,000 units. Sales for March are expected to equal 10,500 players, and April sales are expected to total 11,200 players.

Mp3 players are purchased at a wholesale price of €100. The supplier has a financing arrangement by which Léman pays 60 per cent of the purchase price in the month when the players are delivered and 40 per cent in the following month. Léman purchased 12,000 players in January.

Required

a. Estimate purchases (in units) for February and March.
b. Estimate the cash required in February and March to pay for the company's first-quarter purchases.

Exercise 9.30 [LO 1, 2, 6] Beyond Budgeting

Visit the website for the *Beyond Budgeting Round Table* at www.bbrt.org. Read about the new management model that some have referred to as *beyond budgeting*.

Required

Stage an in-class debate on the pros and cons of traditional budgeting. Should the traditional approach to budgeting be abandoned as some have suggested? Or does the traditional model merely need to adapt to today's competitive business environment?

Exercise 9.31 [LO 3, 4] Estimate of Purchases and Cash Payments

Party Time LLP buys plain Mylar balloons and prints different designs on them for various occasions. It imports the balloons from Taiwan, so at all times it keeps on hand an inventory equal to the balloons needed for two months' sales. The balloons cost £0.50 each and must be paid for in cash. The company has 14,000 balloons in inventory. Sales estimates, based on contracts received, are as follows for the next six months:

January	7,000
February	9,000
March	7,200
April	8,000
May	6,000
June	5,500

Required

Build a spreadsheet to complete the following requirements:

a. Estimate purchases (in units) for January, February and March.
b. Estimate the cash required to make purchases in January, February and March.

Exercise 9.32 [LO 3, 4] Estimate of Cash Collections

Jordaan Produce Company is preparing its cash budget for July. The following information is available concerning its accounts receivable:

Estimated credit sales for July	€420,000
Actual credit sales for June	300,000
Estimated collections in July for credit sales in July	25%
Estimated collections in July for credit sales in June	70%
Estimated collections in July for credit sales prior to June	€35,000
Estimated write-offs in July for uncollectible credit sales	18,000
Estimated provision for bad debts in July for credit sales in July	16,000

Required

Build a spreadsheet to calculate the estimated cash receipts from accounts receivable collections in July.

[CPA adapted]

Exercise 9.33 [LO 2, 3, 4] Use of Budgets for Financial Planning

German Sound Performance AG is a large retailer of stereo equipment. The controller is about to prepare the budget for the first quarter of 201x. Past experience has indicated that 75 per cent of the store's sales are cash sales. The collection experience for the sales on account is as follows:

80 per cent during month of sale
15 per cent during month following sale
5 per cent uncollectable

The total sales for December 201x-1 is expected to be €500,000. The controller believes that sales in January 201x could range from €300,000 to €400,000.

Required

a. Demonstrate how financial planning can be used to project cash receipts in January 201x for three different levels of January sales. Build a spreadsheet.

	Total sales in January 201x		
	€300,000	€350,000	€400,000
Cash receipts in January 201x			
From December sales on account	€	€	€
From January cash sales			
From January sales on account			
Total cash receipts	€	€	€

b. How could the controller of German Sound Performance AG use this financial planning approach to help in planning operations for January?

Exercise 9.34 [LO 3, 4] Estimate of Cash Receipts

Nozze Couture specializes in custom wedding attire. The average price of each of the bride's wedding ensembles is €3,000. For each wedding, Nozze Couture receives a 20 per cent deposit two months before the wedding, 50 per cent the month before, and the remainder on the day the goods are delivered. Based on information at hand, Nozze Couture expects to prepare outfits for the following number of weddings during the coming months:

January	6
February	4
March	3
April	5
May	6
June	14

Required

Build a spreadsheet to complete the following requirements:

a. What are the expected revenues for Nozze Couture for each month, January through June? Revenues are recorded in the month of the wedding.

b. What are the expected cash receipts for each month, January through April?

Exercise 9.35 [LO 3, 4] Estimate of Cash Receipts

Poolside Ltd manages private pools in Auckland, New Zealand. The company attempts to make service calls at least once a month to all homes that subscribe to its service. More frequent calls are made during the summer. The number of subscribers also varies with the season. The number of subscribers and the average number of calls to each subscriber for the months of interest follow:

	Subscribers	Service calls
September	80	0.5
October	100	1.0
November	240	1.8
December	280	2.2
January	300	2.0
February	260	1.7

The average price charged for a service call is $65 (NZD). Of the service calls, 20 per cent are paid in the month the service is rendered, 60 per cent in the month after the service is rendered, and 18 per cent in the second month after. The remaining 2 per cent is uncollectable.

Required

What are Poolside's expected cash receipts for November, December, January and February? Build a spreadsheet to complete this requirement.

Exercise 9.36 [LO 2, 3, 4] Preparation of Budgeted Financial Statements

Refer to the original data in the preceding exercise. Poolside's management estimates that the number of subscribers in March should fall 10 per cent below February levels, and the number of service calls should decrease by an estimated 20 per cent. The following information is available for costs incurred in February. All costs except depreciation are paid in cash. (Monetary values are given in New Zealand dollars.)

Service costs	
Variable costs	$6,136
Maintenance and repair	5,460
Depreciation (fixed)	2,860
Total	$14,456

Marketing and administrative costs:	
Marketing (variable)	$3,250
Administrative (fixed)	2,990
Total	$6,240
Total costs	$20,696

Variable cash and marketing costs change with volume. Fixed depreciation will remain the same, but fixed administrative costs will increase by 5 per cent beginning 1 March. Maintenance and repair are provided by contract, which calls for a 1 per cent increase in March.

Required

Prepare a budgeted statement of income for March. Build a spreadsheet to solve this requirement.

Exercise 9.37 [LO 7] EOQ (Appendix 9)

a. The following information relates to Sweeny Industries:

Units required per year	640,000
Cost of placing an order	$150
Unit carrying cost per year	$300

Assuming that the units will be required evenly throughout the year, what is the EOQ?

b. Ewing Company requires 102,400 units of product Q for the year. The units will be required evenly throughout the year. The cost to place an order is $200, and the cost to carry a unit in inventory for the year is $16. What is the EOQ?

[CPA adapted]

Exercise 9.38 [LO 7] Impact of Quantity Discounts on Order Quantity (Appendix 9)

Éclipse Company uses 810 tankloads a year of a specific input material. The tankloads are delivered by rail to a siding on the company property. The supplier is offering a special discount for buyers of large quantities. The schedule is as follows:

Quantity ordered (tankloads)	Percentage discount
1-19	0
20-79	2
80-149	5
150 and more	6

Ordering costs amount to €500, and carrying costs are €450 per tankload and are not affected by the discounts. Each tankload costs €1,500.

Required

Compute the optimal order quantity. (Round to the nearest whole number.)

Exercise 9.39 [LO 7] Impact of Constraints on Optimal Order (Appendix 9)

Considering the situation in the preceding exercise, suppose that the maximum storage capacity for the company is 50 tankloads.

Required

What is the optimal order? Demonstrate why.

Problems

Problem 9.40 [LO 3, 4] Budgeted Purchases and Cash Flows

Chelsea Supply Warehouse seeks your assistance in developing cash and other budget information for September October and November. On 30 August, the company had cash of £6,500, accounts receivable of £437,000, inventories of £309,400 and accounts payable of £133,055. The budget is to be based on the following assumptions.

Sales

- Each month's sales are billed on the last day of the month.
- The billings are collected as follows: 60 per cent within the discount period, 25 per cent by the end of the month, 9 per cent by the end of the second month, and 6 per cent are uncollectable.
- Customers are allowed a 3 per cent discount if payment is made within 10 days after the billing date. Receivables are recorded in the accounts at their gross amounts (not net of discounts).

Purchases

- The cost of each unit of inventory is £20.
- Of all purchases of merchandise and selling, general and administrative expenses, 54 per cent is paid in the month purchased and the remainder in the following month.
- The number of units in each month's ending inventory equals 130 per cent of the next month's units of sales.
- Selling, general and administrative expenses, of which £2,500 is depreciation, equal 15 per cent of the current month's sales.

Actual sales for July and August and projected sales for September through December are as follows:

	Pounds	Units
July	£363,000	12,100
August	375,000	12,500
September	366,000	12,200
October	354,000	11,800
November	369,000	12,300
December	366,000	12,200

Required

Using the preceding information, compute the following amounts:

a. Budgeted purchases in pounds for September.
b. Budgeted purchases in pounds for October.
c. Budgeted cash collections during September.
d. Budgeted cash payments during October.
e. Budgeted number of units of inventory to be purchased during November.

[CPA adapted]

Problem 9.41 [LO 3, 4] Preparation of a Production Budget

Dahlia's Gardenware VOF manufactures floral containers. The controller is preparing a budget for the coming year and asks for your assistance. The following costs and other data apply to container production:

Direct material per container:
1 kilogram Z-A styrene at €0.30 per kilogram
2 kilograms Vasa finish at €0.60 per kilogram

Direct labour per container:	
1/4 hour at €10.50 per hour	
Overhead per container:	
Indirect labour	€0.11
Indirect material	0.07
Power	0.10
Equipment costs	0.25
Building occupancy	0.30
Total overhead per unit	€0.83

You learn that equipment costs and building occupancy are facility-level (fixed) costs and are based on a normal production of 25,000 units per year. Other overhead costs are unit-level (variable) costs. Plant capacity is sufficient to produce 30,000 units per year.

Labour costs per hour are not expected to change during the year. However, the Vasa finish supplier has informed the company's management that it will impose a 10 per cent price increase at the start of the coming budget period. No other costs are expected to change.

During the coming budget period, management expects to sell 22,000 units. Finished goods inventory is targeted to increase from 6,000 units to 9,000 units to prepare for an expected sales increase the year after next. Production will occur evenly throughout the year. Inventory levels for Vasa finish and Z-A styrene are expected to remain unchanged throughout the year. There is no Work-in-progress inventory.

Required

Prepare a production budget and estimate the material, labour and overhead costs for the coming year. Build a spreadsheet to solve this requirement.

Problem 9.42 [LO 1-4] Preparation of Budgeted Financial Statements; Estimation of Cash Receipts

The following information is available for 20×5 for Al-Rashidi Construction Supply (monetary values given in Kuwaiti dinar, KWD):

Revenue (100,000 units)	KWD222,000
Manufacturing costs:	
Materials (unit level)	KWD 12,600
Unit-level (variable) overhead cash costs	10,680
Facility-level (fixed) overhead cash costs	24,570
Depreciation (facility level)	69,000
Marketing and administrative costs:	
Marketing (unit level, cash)	31,680
Marketing depreciation	12,300
Administrative (facility level, cash)	38,190
Administrative depreciation	5,610
Total costs	KWD204,630
Operating profit	KWD17,370

All depreciation charges are facility-level costs and are expected to remain the same for 20×6. Sales volume is expected to increase by 18 per cent, but prices are expected to fall by 5 per cent. Material costs are expected to decrease by 8 per cent. Unit-level (variable) manufacturing overhead costs are expected to decrease by 2 per cent per unit. Facility-level (fixed) manufacturing overhead costs are expected to increase by 5 per cent.

Unit-level (variable) marketing costs change with volume. Administrative cash costs are expected to increase by 10 per cent. Inventories are kept at zero. (In the following requirements, round to the nearest whole number.)

Required

Build a spreadsheet to solve the following requirements:

a. Prepare a budgeted income statement for 20x6.
b. Estimate the cash from operations expected in 20x6.

Problem 9.43 [LO 3, 4] Activity-based Overhead Budget; Sales, Production and Purchases Budgets

Electro Technology Inc., based in Singapore, manufactures two different types of housings used for electric motors. In the fall of the current year, James Li, the controller, compiled the following data. (All monetary amounts are given in terms of the national currency of Singapore, the Singaporean dollar.) On the day this problem was written, the Singaporean dollar was equivalent in value to 0.6408 US dollars.

- Sales forecast for 201x:

Product	Units	Price
Small housing	65,000	$72
Large housing	50,000	$100

- Raw-material prices and inventory levels:

Raw material	Expected inventories 1 January 201x	Desired inventories, 31 December 201x	Anticipated purchase price
Sheet metal	42,000 kg	46,000 kg	$8.25
Bar inventory	30,000 kg	34,000 kg	$6
Base	6,200 units	7,200 units	$3

- Use of raw material:

	Amount used per unit	
Raw material	Small housing	Large housing
Sheet metal	4 kg	6 kg
Bar inventory	2.5 kg	4 kg
Base	–	1.5 units

- Direct labour requirements and rates:

Product	Hours per unit	Rate per hour
Small housing	2	$17
Large housing	3	$22

- Finished goods inventories (in units):

Product	Expected 1 January 201x	Desired 31 December 201x
Small housing	25,000	30,000
Large housing	10,000	12,000

- Manufacturing overhead:

Overhead cost item	Activity-based budget rate
Purchasing and material handling	$0.30 per kilogram of sheet metal and bar inventory purchased
Depreciation, utilities and inspection	$4.25 per housing produced (either type)

Shipping	$1.10 per housing shipped (either type)
General manufacturing overhead	$2.75 per direct labour hour

Required

Build a spreadsheet to prepare the following budgets for 201x:

a. Sales budget (in dollars)
b. Production budget (in units)
c. Raw material purchases budget (in quantities)
d. Raw material purchases budget (in dollars)
e. Direct labour budget (in dollars)
f. Manufacturing overhead budget (in dollars).

[CPA adapted]

Problem 9.44 [LO 3, 4] Sales Expense Budget

Vancouver Software Company has just received its sales expense report for January, which follows:

Item	Amount
Sales commissions	$170,000
Sales staff salaries	55,000
Telephone and mailing	18,450
Building lease payment	18,000
Heat, light and water	5,600
Packaging and delivery	25,200
Depreciation	14,500
Marketing consultants	20,000

You have been asked to develop budgeted costs for the coming year. Since this month is typical, you decide to prepare an estimated budget for a typical month in the coming year, and you uncover the following additional data:

- Sales volume is expected to increase by 5 per cent.
- Sales prices are expected to increase by 10 per cent.
- Commissions are based on a percentage of selling price.
- Sales staff salaries will increase 4 per cent next year regardless of sales volume.
- Building rent is based on a 5-year lease that expires in 3 years.
- Telephone and mailing expenses are scheduled to increase by 8 per cent even with no change in sales volume. However, these costs are variable with the number of units sold, as are packaging and delivery costs.
- Heat, light and water are scheduled to increase by 12 per cent regardless of sales volume.
- Depreciation includes furniture and fixtures used by the sales staff. The company has just acquired an additional $15,000 in furniture that will be received at the start of next year and will be depreciated over a 10-year life using the straight-line method.
- Marketing consultant expenses were for a special advertising campaign that runs from time to time. During the coming year, the costs are expected to average $40,000 per month.

Required

Prepare the company's budget for sales expenses for a typical month in the coming year. (Round to nearest whole numbers.)

Problem 9.45 [LO 5, 6] Ethics; Budgetary Pressure; Management Bonuses; Budgetary Constraints

Venlige Chemical Corporation produces and distributes industrial chemicals in its Nordlige Division, which is located in Aalborg, Denmark. Nordlige's earnings increased sharply in 201x, and bonuses were paid to the management staff for the first time in several years. Bonuses are based in part on the amount by which reported income exceeds budgeted income.

Magnus Larsen, vice president of finance, was pleased with Nordlige's 201x earnings and thought that the pressure to show financial results would ease. However, Emma Madsen, Nordlige's division manager, told Larsen that she saw no reason why the 201x + 1 bonuses should not be double those of 201x. As a result, Larsen felt pressure to increase reported income to exceed budgeted income by an even greater amount. This would ensure increased bonuses.

Larsen met with Carl Poulsen of Reneste A/S, a primary vendor of Nordlige manufacturing supplies and equipment. Larsen and Poulsen have been close business contacts for many years. Larsen asked Poulsen to identify all of Nordlige's purchases of perishable supplies as equipment on Reneste's sales invoices. The reason Larsen gave for his request was that Nordlige's division manager had imposed stringent budget constraints on operating expenses but not on capital expenditures. Larsen planned to capitalize the purchase of perishable supplies and include them with the Equipment account on the balance sheet. In this way Larsen could defer the expense recognition for these items to a later year. This procedure would increase reported earnings, leading to increased bonuses. Poulsen agreed to do as Larsen had asked.

While analysing the second quarter financial statements, Simon Rasmussen, Nordlige's director of cost management, noticed a large decrease in supplies expense from one year ago. Rasmussen reviewed the Supplies Expense account and noticed that only equipment but no supplies had been purchased from Reneste, a major source for supplies. Rasmussen, who reports to Larsen, immediately brought this to Larsen's attention.

Larsen told Rasmussen of Madsen's high expectations and of the arrangement made with Poulsen of Reneste. Rasmussen told Larsen that his action was an improper accounting treatment for the supplies purchased from Reneste. Rasmussen requested that he be allowed to correct the accounts and urged that the arrangement with Reneste be discontinued. Larsen refused the request and told Rasmussen not to become involved in the arrangement with Reneste.

After clarifying the situation in a confidential discussion with an objective and qualified peer within Nordlige, Rasmussen arranged to meet with Madsen, Nordlige's division manager. At the meeting, Rasmussen disclosed the arrangement Larsen had made with Reneste.

Required

Prepare a presentation to the class covering the following issues:

a. Explain why the use of alternative accounting methods to manipulate reported earnings is unethical.

b. Is Simon Rasmussen, Nordlige's director of cost management, correct in saying that the supplies purchased from Reneste A/S were accounted for improperly? Explain your answer.

c. Assuming that Magnus Larsen's arrangement with Reneste A/S was in violation of professional codes of ethics (see Chapter 1 for references to professional organizations), discuss whether Rasmussen's actions were appropriate or inappropriate.

[CMA adapted]

Problem 9.46 [LO 1, 3, 4] Comprehensive Budget Plan

John Company LLP, a manufacturer of tea and coffee travel mugs, decided in October 201x that it needed cash to continue operations. It began negotiating for a one-month bank loan of £120,000 starting 1 November 201x. The bank would charge interest at the rate of 1 per cent per month and require the company to repay interest and principal on 30 November 201x. In considering the loan, the bank requested a projected income statement and cash budget for November. The following information is available:

- The company budgeted sales at 100,000 units per month in October 201x, December 201x and January 201x + 1, and at 80,000 units in November 201x. The selling price is £8 per unit.
- The inventory of finished goods on 1 October was 28,000 units. The Finished goods inventory at the end of each month equals 20 per cent of sales anticipated for the following month. There is no Work-in-progress inventory.

- The inventory of raw material on 1 October was 11,000 kilograms. At the end of each month, the Raw material inventory equals no less than 40 per cent of production requirements for the following month. The company purchases materials as needed in minimum quantities of 12,000 kilograms per shipment.
- Selling expenses are 12 per cent of gross sales. Administrative expenses, which include depreciation of £600 per month on office furniture and fixtures, total £40,000 per month.
- The manufacturing budget for coffee cups, based on normal production of 90,000 units per month, follows:

Material (1/4 kilogram per cup, 24,000 kilograms, £1 per kilogram)	£24,000
Direct labour	35,000
Variable overhead	22,000
Fixed overhead (includes depreciation of £5,000)	12,000
Total	£93,000

- John Company's customers are allowed a 2 per cent discount if payment is made within 10 days, and these discounts are always taken. Uncollectible accounts are projected at 1.5 per cent of gross sales.

Required

Build a spreadsheet to complete the following requirements:

a. Prepare schedules computing inventory budgets by months for the following:
 (1) Production in units for October, November and December.
 (2) Raw material purchases in pounds for October and November.

b. Prepare a projected income statement for November. Cost of goods sold should equal the variable manufacturing cost per unit times the number of units sold plus the total fixed manufacturing cost budgeted for the period. (Round amounts to the nearest pound.)

[CPA adapted]

Problem 9.47 [LO 1, 3, 4] Preparation of Budgeted Financial Statements; Estimation of Cash Receipts

Kozlov Aluminum Company has the following data from 20x5 operations, which are to be used for developing 20x6 budget estimates (monetary units given in Russian rubles, RUB):

Revenue (100,000 units)	RUB24,600,000
Manufacturing costs:	
Material (unit level)	3,990,000
Unit-level (variable) overhead cash costs	5,427,000
Facility-level (fixed) overhead cash costs	2,160,000
Depreciation (facility level)	2,670,000
Marketing and administrative costs:	
Marketing (unit level, cash)	2,850,000
Marketing depreciation	585,000
Administrative (facility level, cash)	2,703,300
Administrative depreciation	390,000
Total costs	20,775,300
Operating profits	RUB3,824,700

All depreciation charges are facility-level costs. Old manufacturing equipment with an annual depreciation charge of RUB291,000 will be replaced in 20x6 with new equipment that will incur an annual depreciation charge of RUB420,000. Sales volume and prices are expected to increase by 12 per cent and 6 per cent, respectively. On a per-unit basis, expectations are that material costs will increase by 10 per cent and unit-level (variable) manufacturing overhead costs will decrease by 4 per cent. Facility-level (fixed) overhead costs are expected to decrease by 7 per cent.

Unit-level (variable) marketing costs will change with volume. Administrative cash costs are expected to increase by 8 per cent. Inventories are kept near zero. (In the following requirements, round to nearest whole numbers.)

Required

a. Prepare Kozlov Aluminum Company's budgeted income statement for 20x6.
b. Estimate the cash from operations expected in 20x6.

Problem 9.48 [LO 3, 4] Production, Materials, Labour, and Overhead Budgets

Texas Technology's San Angelo Division produces an intricate component used in the company's product line. The division manager has been concerned recently by a lack of co-ordination between purchasing and production personnel and believes that a monthly budgeting system would be better than the present system.

The San Angelo division manager has decided to develop budget information for the third quarter of the current year as an experiment before the budget system is implemented for an entire year. In response to the division manager's request, the divisional controller accumulated the following data.

- The unit sales price of San Angelo Division's main product is $15, and management expects to sell 60,000 units during the current year. Sales through 30 June, the first six months of the current year, are 24,000 units. Actual sales in units for May and June and estimated unit sales for the next four months are as follows:

May (actual)	4,000
June (actual)	4,000
July (estimated)	5,000
August (estimated)	6,000
September (estimated)	7,000
October (estimated)	7,000

- The desired monthly ending inventory of completed components is 80 per cent of the next month's estimated sales. There are 5,000 finished units in inventory on 30 June.
- Data regarding the materials used in the component are shown in the following schedule. The desired monthly ending inventory for all raw materials is an amount sufficient to produce the next month's estimated sales.

Raw material	Units of raw material per finished component	Cost per unit	Inventory level 30 June
B42	6	$2.40	35,000 units
F68	4	$3.60	30,000 units
M03	2	$1.20	14,000 units

- Each component must pass through three different processes to be completed. Data regarding direct labour follow:

Process	Direct labour hours per finished component	Cost per direct labour hour
Forming	0.400	$16.00
Assembly	1.000	$11.00
Finishing	0.125	$12.00

- The division produced 27,000 components during the six-month period ending 30 June. The actual unit-level (variable) overhead costs incurred during this six-month period are given in the following schedule. The divisional controller believes the unit-level (variable) overhead costs will be incurred at the same rate during the last six months of the current year.

Supplies	$61,000
Electricity	19,000
Indirect labour	52,400
Other	16,100
Total variable overhead	$148,500

The facility-level (fixed) overhead costs *actually incurred* during the first six months of the year amounted to $93,500. These facility-level overhead costs are *budgeted* for the full year as follows:

Supervision	$59,000
Taxes	8,200
Depreciation	86,400
Other	32,400
Total fixed overhead	$186,000

Required

Build a spreadsheet to complete the following requirements:

a. Prepare a production budget in units for San Angelo for the third quarter of the current year, ending 30 September.

b. Independent of your answer to requirement (a), assume that San Angelo Division plans to produce 18,000 units during the third quarter ending 30 September and 60,000 units for the entire year ending 31 December.

(1) Prepare a raw material purchases budget, in units and dollars, for the third quarter, ending 30 September.

(2) Prepare a direct labour budget, in hours and dollars, for the third quarter, ending 30 September.

(3) Prepare a manufacturing overhead budget for the *six-month period* ending 31 December of the current year.

[CMA adapted]

Problem 9.49 [LO 2-5] Production and Direct Labour Budgets; Activity-based Overhead Budget

Klarheit Korporation manufactures stereo headphones in Wennebostel, Germany. Jan Meyer, director of cost management, is responsible for preparing the company's master budget. In compiling the budget data for 201x, Meyer has learned that new automated production equipment will be installed on 1 March. This will reduce the direct labour per set of headphones from 1 hour to 0.75 hours.

Labour-related costs include pension contributions of €1.40 per hour, workers' compensation insurance of €0.25 per hour, employee medical insurance of €1.00 per hour, and employer contributions to Social Security equal to 20 per cent of direct labour wages. The cost of employee benefits paid by the company on its employees is treated as a direct labour cost. The company has a labour contract that calls for a wage increase to €20.00 per hour on 1 April 201x. Management expects to have 23,500 headphone sets on hand at 31 December 201x-1, and has a policy of carrying an end-of-month inventory of 100 per cent of the following month's sales plus 50 per cent of the second following month's sales.

These and other data compiled by Meyer are summarized in the following table.

	January	February	March	April	May
Sales price per unit	€65.00	€60.00	€60.00	€60.00	€60.00
Estimated unit sales	15,000	17,000	13,000	14,000	14,000
Direct labour hours per unit	1.0	1.0	0.75	0.75	0.75

Wage per direct labour hour	€18.00	€18.00	€18.00	€20.00	€20.00
Manufacturing overhead	€3.50	€3.50	€3.50	€3.50	€3.50
Shipping and handling (per unit sold)					
Purchasing, material handling and inspection (per unit produced)	€3.25	€3.25	€3.25	€3.25	€3.25
Other manufacturing overhead (per direct labour hour)	€6.00	€6.00	€6.00	€6.00	€6.00

Required

a. Prepare a production budget and a direct labour budget for Klarheit Korporation by month and for the first quarter of 201x. Both budgets can be combined in one schedule. The direct labour budget should include direct labour hours and show the detail for each direct labour cost category.
b. For each item used in the firm's production budget and direct labour budget, identify the other components of the master budget that would also use these data.
c. Prepare a manufacturing overhead budget for each month and for the first quarter.

[CMA adapted]

Problem 9.50 [LO 7] Economic Order Quantity; Equation Approach; JIT Purchasing (Appendix 9)

Arrow Space Inc. manufactures specialized ceramic components used in the aerospace industry. The company's materials and parts manager is currently revising the inventory policy for XL-20, one of the chemicals used in the production process. The chemical is purchased in 10-pound canisters for $95 each. The firm uses 7,000 canisters per year. The controller estimates that to place and receive a typical order of XL-20 costs $175. The annual cost of storing XL-20 is $5 per canister.

Required

a. Write the formula for the total annual cost of ordering and storing XL-20.
b. Use the EOQ formula to determine the optimal order quantity.
c. What is the total annual cost of ordering and storing XL-20 at the economic order quantity?
d. How many orders will be placed per year?
e. Arrow Space's controller, Jane Turnbull, recently attended a seminar on JIT purchasing. Afterwards she analysed the cost of storing XL-20, including the costs of wasted space and inefficiency. She was shocked when she concluded that the real annual holding cost was $22.40 per canister. Turnbull then met with Doug Kaplan, Arrow Space's purchasing manager. Together they contacted Reno Industries, the supplier of XL-20, about a JIT purchasing arrangement. After some discussion and negotiation, Kaplan concluded that the cost of placing an order for XL-20 could be reduced to just $25. Using these new cost estimates, Turnbull computed the new EOQ for XL-20.
   (1) Use the equation approach to compute the new EOQ.
   (2) How many orders will be placed per year?

Problem 9.51 [LO 7] Economic Order Quantity; Tabular Approach (Appendix 9)

Refer to the *original* data given in the preceding problem for Arrow Space Inc.

Required

a. Prepare a table showing the total annual cost of ordering and storing XL-20 for each of the following order quantities: 500, 700 and 900 canisters.
b. What are the weaknesses in the tabular approach?

Problem 9.52 [LO 7] Economic Order Quantity; Graphical Approach (Appendix 9)

Refer to the *original* data given in Problem 9.50 for Arrow Space Inc.

Required

Prepare a graphical analysis of the economic order quantity decision for XL-20.

Problem 9.53 [LO 7] Economic Order Quantity; Lead Time and Safety Inventory (Appendix 9)

Refer to the *original* data given in Problem 9.50 for Arrow Space Inc. The lead time required to receive an order of XL-20 is one month.

Required

a. Assuming stable usage of XL-20 each month, determine the reorder point for XL-20.
b. Suppose that the monthly usage of XL-20 fluctuates between 400 and 800 canisters, although annual demand remains constant at 7,000 canisters. What level of safety inventory should the materials and parts manager keep on hand for XL-20? What is the new reorder point for the chemical?

Cases

Case 9.54 [LO 1-4] Comprehensive Master Budget; Acquisition of Automated Materials-Handling System

Électronique Universel SA (EU) is a small, rapidly growing wholesaler of consumer electronic products in France. The firm's main product lines are small kitchen appliances and power tools. Madeleine Arceneau, EU's general manager of marketing, recently completed a sales forecast. She believes the company's sales during the first quarter of 201x will increase by 10 per cent each month over the previous month's sales. Then Arceneau expects sales to remain constant for several months. EU's projected balance sheet as of 31 December 201x-1, is as follows:

Cash	€32,000
Accounts receivable	280,000
Marketable securities	18,000
Inventory	155,000
Buildings and equipment (net of accumulated depreciation)	625,000
Total assets	$1,110,000
Accounts payable	$177,500
Bond interest payable	12,500
Property taxes payable	3,600
Bonds payable (10%; due in 20x6)	300,000
Common shares	500,000
Retained earnings	116,400
Total liabilities and sharekholders' equity	$1,110,000

Stéphane Gaudet, the assistant controller, is now preparing a monthly budget for the first quarter of 201x. In the process, the following information has been accumulated:

1. Projected sales for December 201x are €600,000. Credit sales typically are 75 per cent of total sales. EU's credit experience indicates that 10 per cent of the credit sales is collected during the month of sale, and the remainder is collected during the following month.
2. EU's cost of goods sold generally is 70 per cent of sales. Inventory is purchased on account, and 40 per cent of each month's purchases are paid during the month of purchase. The remainder is paid during the following month. To have adequate levels of inventory on hand, the firm attempts to have inventory at the end of each month equal to half of the next month's projected cost of goods sold.

3. Gaudet has estimated that the company's other monthly expenses will be as follows:

Sales salaries	€20,000
Advertising and promotion	17,000
Administrative salaries	22,000
Depreciation	20,000
Interest on bonds	2,500
Property taxes	900

In addition, sales commissions run at the rate of 1 per cent of sales.

4. EU's president, Corrine Fornier, has indicated that the firm should invest $125,000 in an automated inventory-handling system to control the movement of inventory in the firm's warehouse just after the new year begins. This equipment purchase will be financed primarily from the firm's cash and marketable securities. However, Fornier believes that EU needs to keep a minimum cash balance of €20,000. If necessary, the remainder of the equipment purchases will be financed using short-term credit from a local bank. The minimum period for such a loan is three months. Gaudet believes that short-term interest rates will be 10 per cent per year at the time of the equipment purchases. If a loan is necessary, Fornier has decided it should be paid off by the end of the first quarter if possible.
5. EU's board of directors has indicated its intention to declare and pay dividends of €45,000 on the last day of each quarter.
6. The interest on any short-term borrowing will be paid when the loan is repaid. Interest on EU's bonds is paid semi-annually on 31 January and 31 July for the preceding 6-month period.
7. Property taxes are paid semi-annually on 28 February and 31 August for the preceding 6-month period.

Required

Work as a group to prepare Électronique Universel's master budget for the first quarter of 201x by completing the following schedules and statements.

a. Sales budget:

	201x-1	201x			
	December	January	February	March	1st Quarter
Total sales					
Cash sales					
Sales on account					

b. Cash receipts budget:

	201x			
	January	February	March	1st Quarter
Cash sales				
Cash collections from credit sales made during current month				
Cash collections from credit sales made during preceding month				
Total cash receipts				

c. Purchases budget:

	201x-1	201x			
	December	January	February	March	1st Quarter
Budgeted cost of goods sold					
Add: Desired ending inventory					

Total goods needed				
Less: Expected beginning inventory				
Purchases				

d. Cash payments budget:

	201x			
	January	February	March	1st Quarter
Inventory purchases:				
Cash payments for purchases during the current month*				
Cash payments for purchases during the preceding month†				
Total cash payments for inventory purchases				
Other expenses:				
Sales salaries				
Advertising and promotion				
Administrative salaries				
Interest on bonds‡				
Property taxes‡				
Sales commissions				
Total cash payments for other expenses				
Total cash payments				

*40 per cent of the month's purchases (Schedule c).
†60 per cent of the prior month's purchases (Schedule c).
‡Bond interest is paid every 6 months, on 31 January and 31 July. Property taxes also are paid every 6 months, on 28 February and 31 August.

e. Complete the first three lines of the summary cash budget. Then do the analysis of short-term financing needs in requirement (f). Then finish requirement (e). Summary cash budget:

	201x			
	January	February	March	1st Quarter
Cash receipts (from Schedule b)				
Less: Cash payments (from Schedule d)				
Change in cash balance during period due to operations				
Sale of marketable securities (2 Jan. 201x)				
Proceeds from bank loan (2 Jan. 201x)				
Purchase of equipment				
Repayment of bank loan (31 Mar. 201x)				
Interest on bank loan				
Payment of dividends				
Change in cash balance during first quarter				
Cash balance (1 Jan. 201x)				
Cash balance (31 Mar. 201x)				

f. Analysis of short-term financing needs:

Projected cash balance as of 31 December 201x-1	€
Less: Minimum cash balance	
Cash available for equipment purchases	€
Projected proceeds from sale of marketable securities	
Cash available	€
Less: Cost of investment in equipment	
Required short-term borrowing	

g. Prepare EU's budgeted income statement for the first quarter of 201x. (Ignore income taxes.)
h. Prepare EU's budgeted statement of retained earnings for the first quarter of 201x.
i. Prepare EU's budgeted balance sheet as of 31 March 201x. (*Hint:* On 31 March 201x, Bond interest payable is €5,000 and Property taxes payable is €900.)

Case 9.55 [LO 1-4] Preparation and Interpretation of Cash Budget for Service Organization

Liverpool Fitness Club is a non-profit health club. Its board of directors is developing plans to acquire more equipment and expand club facilities. The board plans to purchase about £25,000 of new equipment each year and wants to begin a fund to purchase an adjoining property in four or five years when the expansion will need the space. The adjoining property has a market value of about £300,000.

The club manager is concerned that the board has unrealistic goals in light of its recent financial performance. She sought the help of a club member with an accounting background to assist her in preparing the club's records, including the cash-basis income statements that follow. The review and discussions with the manager disclosed the additional information that follows the statement.

LIVERPOOL FITNESS CLUB
Statement of Income (Cash Basis)
For the Year Ended 31 October

	20x8	20x7
Cash revenue:		
Lesson and class fees	£240,000	£200,000
Annual membership fees	365,000	300,000
Miscellaneous	2,500	2,000
Total cash received	£607,500	£502,000
Cash costs:		
Manager's salary and benefits	£38,000	£38,000
Lesson and class employee wages and benefits	190,000	160,000
Regular employees' wages and benefits	180,000	180,000
Towels and supplies	16,500	16,000
Utilities (heat and light)	24,000	18,000
Mortgage interest	35,000	3,700
Miscellaneous	2,500	2,000
Total cash costs	£486,000	£417,700
Cash income	£121,500	£84,300

Additional information follows:

1. Other financial information as of 31 October 20x8:
   a. Cash in current account, £5,000.
   b. Petty cash, £400.
   c. Outstanding mortgage balance, £325,000.
   d. Accounts payable for supplies and utilities unpaid as of 31 October 20x8, and due in November 20x8, $2,500.
2. The club purchased £25,000 worth of exercise equipment during the current fiscal year. Cash of £8,000 was paid on delivery, with the balance due on 1 October which had not been paid as of 31 October 20x8.
3. The club began operations in 20x2 in rental quarters. In October 20x4, it purchased its current property (land and building) for £600,000, paying $120,000 down and agreeing to pay £30,000 plus 9 per cent interest annually on the unpaid loan balance each 1 November starting 1 November 20x5.
4. Membership rose 3 per cent during 20x8, approximately the same annual rate of increase the club has experienced since it opened and that is expected to continue in the future.
5. Membership fees were increased by 15 per cent in 20x8. The board has tentative plans to increase them by 10 per cent in 20x9.

6. Lesson and class fees have not been increased for three years. The number of classes and lessons has grown significantly each year, and the percentage growth experienced in 20x8 is expected to be repeated in 20x9.
7. Miscellaneous revenues are expected to grow in 20x9 (over 20x8) at the same percentage as experienced in 20x8 (over 20x7).
8. Lesson and class employees' wages and benefits will increase to £290,000. The wages and benefits of regular employees and the manager will increase 15 per cent. Towels and supplies, utilities, and miscellaneous expenses are expected to increase 25 per cent.

Required

a. Construct a cash budget for 20x9 for the Liverpool Fitness Club.
b. Write a memo to the health club's board of directors to accompany the budget. In the memo, identify any operating problem(s) that this budget discloses for the Liverpool Fitness Club.
c. Is the manager's concern that the board's goals are unrealistic justified? Explain your answer.

[CMA adapted]

Solutions to You're the Decision Maker

9.1 Revised Production Budget, p. 430

a. Revised budget:

Westport Team Wear
Production Budget (in units)
For the year ending 31 December

	Quarter				
	1	2	3	4	Year
Sales in units (Schedule 1)	10,000	7,800	6,600	16,800	41,200
Add desired ending inventory of finished goods	780	660	1,680	1,200	1,200
Total units required	10,780	8,460	8,280	18,000	42,400
Less expected beginning inventory of finished goods	1,000	780	660	1,680	1,000
Units to be produced	9,780	7,680	7,620	16,320	41,400

b. This is where the art of management comes into play. If the increase in sales is not very certain, management has a tough decision to make. One possible strategy is to increase production as indicated in the preceding table for the first quarter or two and to see whether the increased demand materializes and then cut back production if it does not. Another possibility is to produce quantities between those specified in the original and revised budgets.

9.2 Revision of Manufacturing Overhead Budget, p. 434

a. Revised fourth quarter budget (yellow cells are the origins of the changes in the budget):

Westport Team Wear
Manufacturing Overhead Budget (in NZ$)
For the Fourth Quarter ending 31 December

	Quarter 4
Unit-level costs	
Units to be produced (Schedule 2)	16,250
Indirect material cost	$4,063
Electricity for machines cost	2,438

Total unit-level costs	$6,500
Batch-level costs	
Production runs	50
Set-up cost	$5,000
Purchasing and handling cost	9,500
Inspection cost	4,000
Total batch-level costs	$18,500
Product-level costs	
New style designs	4
Design costs	$6,800
Total product-level costs	$6,800
Facility and general operations-level costs	
Supervisory salary cost	$24,000
Insurance and property tax costs	2,400
Maintenance cost	2,600
Utilities costs	2,500
Depreciation cost	36,000
Total facility and general operations-level costs	$67,500
Total manufacturing overhead costs	$99,300
Less depreciation	36,000
Total cash payments for manufacturing overhead	$63,300

b. The special adjustment on the cutting machine will be a batch-level cost. The appropriate cost driver is production runs.

9.3 Financial Planning Model: Uncollectable Accounts Expense, p. 443

a. This table shows the budgeted uncollectable accounts expense for different rates of uncollectable accounts.

b. Predictive information such as this is crucial for the management of uncollectable accounts expense. Management might decide, for example, to implement more restrictive credit and collection policies if the uncollectable accounts rate exceeds 2 per cent.

	A	B	C	D	E	F
1		**Estimates of uncollectable accounts expense**				
2		**Quarter 1**	**Quarter 2**	**Quarter 3**	**Quarter 4**	**Year**
3	Sales revenue (Schedule 1)	$320,000	$208,000	$176,000	$448,000	$1,152,000
4	Uncollectable rate					
5	1%	$3,200	$2,080	$1,760	$4,480	$11,520
6	2%	$6,400	$4,160	$3,520	$8,960	$23,040
7	3%	$9,600	$6,240	$5,280	$13,440	$34,560
8	4%	$12,800	$8,320	$7,040	$17,920	$46,080

Endnotes

1 Chapter 1 talked more about strategic decision making. We see this as the starting point (Stage I) in the decision-making framework that we use throughout this text.

2 The source of these strategy statements was the company's internal documents, which the company provided to the authors.

3 The relationships between budgeting, control and performance measurement are also addressed in Chapters 13 and 14.

4 Activity-based costing (ABC) is covered in Chapter 4, and more details on activity-based budgeting are in Chapter 13.

5 This section is based on the following references: Brimson and Antos (1991); Borjesson (1997); and Kaplan and Cooper (1998).

6 Companies usually produce and sell more different products than we illustrate here with the schedules of the focus company. A company such as Westport Team Wear will also carry, for example, polo shirts, track suits, shorts, jerseys, and maybe items like protective vests and even sports bags. That makes no difference for the principles and the calculations, but actual plans and financial schedules are more elaborate than needed for the purpose of this text.

7 Throughout this example, we assume that beginning inventories (finished products, fabric, etc.) in Q1 are the same as the ending inventories in Q4. This is simpler but essentially the same as when you would have additional data on these beginning levels.

8 You would expect a usage expressed in 'square metres', or m^2. However, the material requirement per shirt (and the same for the price of the fabric) refers to the length in metres from a roll of fabric of the standard width used by Westport Team Wear.

9 It is often desirable to have a buffer inventory just before a bottleneck operation.

10 How do we know collections in Q1 from sales in Q4 of the previous year? Note that we assume that the year repeats itself, so the sales in Q4 of the previous year is the same as this year's sales in Q4. This assumption is also relevant for Schedule 8.

11 This person can also be the Controller or Chief Accountant.

12 Budgetary slack is not always considered to be a bad thing for the organization. When companies follow strategies that require innovation and experimentation, they can benefit from budgetary slack because it allows managers to focus on relevant long-term and short-term objectives other than meeting budgets such as quality or customer service. In these settings, budgetary slack provides operating flexibility to increase the predictability of earnings, reduce the time spent on control tasks, reduce risks of dysfunctional behaviour, and give managers discretion to pursue multiple goals while dealing with adverse exogenous factors. See Davila and Wouters (2005); Lillis (2002); Merchant and Manzoni (1989); Van der Stede (2000).

13 Recent economic modelling research demonstrates the value of co-operation in a budgeting process. See Chen (2003). See Derfuss (2009) for a review of the literature.

14 A 'bolt' is the usual term for a roll of fabric.

References

Aldea, D.M., and D.E. Bullinger (1999) 'Using ABC for shared services, charge-outs, activity-based budgeting, and benchmarking', in S. Player and D.E. Keys (eds.), *Activity-Based Management: Arthur Andersen's Lessons from the ABM Battlefield*, pp. 138–145, John Wiley & Sons, New York.

Borjesson, S. (1997) 'A case study on activity-based budgeting', *Journal of Cost Management*, vol. 10, no. 4, pp. 7–18.

Brimson, J., and J. Antos (1999) *Driving Value Using Activity Based Budgeting*, John Wiley & Sons, New York.

Chen, Q. (2003) 'Cooperation in the budgeting process', *Journal of Accounting Research*, vol. 41, no. 5, pp. 775–796.

Collins, J. (1999) 'Advanced use of ABM: using ABC for target costing, activity-based budgeting, and benchmarking', in S. Player and D.E. Keys (eds.), *Activity-Based Management: Arthur Andersen's Lessons from the ABM Battlefield*, pp. 152–158. John Wiley & Sons, New York.

Davila, T., and M. Wouters (2005) 'Managing budget emphasis through the explicit design of conditional budgetary slack', *Accounting, Organizations and Society*, vol. 30, nos. 7–8, pp. 587–608.

Derfuss, K. (2009) 'The relationship of budgetary participation and reliance on accounting performance measures with individual-level consequent variables: a meta-analysis', *European Accounting Review*, vol. 18, no. 2, pp. 203–239.

Fisher, J.G., S.A. Peffer and G.B. Sprinkle (2003) 'Budget-based contracts, budget levels, and group performance', *Journal of Management Accounting Research*, vol. 15, pp. 51–74.

Granlund, M. (2011) 'Extending AIS research to management accounting and control issues: a research note', *International Journal of Accounting Information Systems*, vol. 12, pp. 3–19.

Hansen, S.C., D.T. Otley and W.A. Van der Stede (2004) 'Practice developments in budgeting: an overview and research perspective', *Journal of Management Accounting Research*, vol. 15, pp. 95–116.

Hope, J., and R. Fraser (2001) *Beyond Budgeting: Questions and Answers*, CAM-I Inc., Bedford, Texas.

Hope, J., and R. Fraser (2003a) 'New ways of setting rewards: the beyond budgeting model', *California Management Review*, vol. 45, no. 4, pp. 104–119.

Hope, J., and R. Fraser (2003b) 'Who needs budgets', *Harvard Business Review*, February, pp. 108–115.

Hornyak, S. (1998) 'Budgeting made easy', *Management Accounting*, October, pp. 18–23.

Kallunki, J.-P., E.K. Laitinen and H. Silvola (2011) 'Impact of enterprise resource planning on management control systems and firm performance', *International Journal of Accounting Information Systems*, vol. 12, pp. 20–39.

Kaplan, R.S., and R. Cooper (1998). *Cost and Effect*, Harvard Business School Press, Boston, MA.

Libby, T., and R.M. Lindsay (2010) 'Beyond budgeting or budgeting reconsidered? A survey of North-American budgeting practice', *Management Accounting Research*, vol. 21, pp. 56–75.

Lillis, A.M. (2002) 'Managing multiple dimensions of manufacturing performance – an exploratory study', *Accounting, Organizations and Society*, vol. 27, pp. 497–529.

Merchant, K.A., and J.F. Manzoni (1989) 'The achievability of budget targets in profit centers: a field study', *The Accounting Review*, vol. 64, pp. 539–558.

Østergren, K., and I. Stensaker (2010) 'Management control without budgets: a field study of 'beyond budgeting' in practice', *European Accounting Review*, first published on 22 January 2010 (iFirst), URL: http://dx.doi.org/10.1080/09638180903487842

Rankin, F.W., S.T. Schwartz and R.A. Young (2003) 'Management control using nonbinding budgetary announcements', *Journal of Management Accounting Research*, vol. 15, pp. 75–93.

Rom, A., and C. Rohde (2007) 'Management accounting and integrated information systems: a literature review', *International Journal of Accounting Information Systems*, vol. 8, pp. 40–68.

Scapens, R.W., and M. Jazayeri (2003) 'ERP systems and management accounting change: opportunities or impacts? A research note', *European Accounting Review*, vol. 12, no. 1, pp. 201–233.

Van der Stede, W.A. (2000) 'The relationship between two consequences of budgetary controls: budgetary slack creation and managerial short-term orientation', *Accounting, Organizations and Society*, vol. 25, pp. 483–496.

PART 4

Product Costing and Cost Allocation

A look back

The preceding part 3 covered planning and decision-making, which is based on looking ahead and estimating the consequences of future courses of action.

A look at this part

This part 4 covers the accumulation of actual costs and assigning them to products and services, once decisions are implemented. The first chapter explains job-order costing, and the second chapter in this part review process costing and joint cost allocation. The third chapter in this part is about managing and allocating support service costs.

A look ahead

The next part 5 will deal with performance measurement and management. This means that the actual outcomes will be analyzed for improving future decisions and for holding managers accountable.

CHAPTER

10

Job and Order Costing

© ra-photos

Learning Objectives

After completing this chapter, you should be able to:

- **LO 1** Explain the differences in job-order, process and operation costing.
- **LO 2** Explain how costs flow through the manufacturing accounts.
- **LO 3** Assign direct costs to production jobs or products using a job-order costing system.
- **LO 4** Record indirect, manufacturing overhead costs.
- **LO 5** Use a predetermined overhead rate to assign normal indirect resource costs to production jobs.
- **LO 6** Measure and dispose of the manufacturing overhead variance.
- **LO 7** Understand the use of job-order costing information for decision making.
- **LO 8** Measure, reconcile and interpret operating income using absorption and variable costing.
- **LO 9** Be aware of ethical considerations of managing job costs.
- **LO 10** Measure and understand throughput costing's effects on costs and operating income (Appendix 10).

creazioni di vetro
Viale Jonio 137
Roma, Italia

30 January

Sra. Diana Itturalde
Aquarium Costa Brava
Barcelona, España

Querida Sra. Itturralde:

We have completed the estimates for the two stained glass doors you are planning for the aquarium's main entry portico. Our designer has developed sketches for some beautiful stained glass panels for the doors following the guidelines you gave us during our meeting in November. Each door has six stained glass panels, featuring a variety of marine species, from dolphins and whales to angelfish and sea horses. The panel designs are, as you requested, very colourful. I think you will be pleased with them.

We have carefully estimated the costs of the doors, which cover the materials, design talent, glass workers' labour, and applied overhead, which are based on the projected labour time required for the job. As per our previous discussions, our price for your non-profit organization will be cost plus a modest 10 per cent profit margin.

I will call you next week to set up a meeting so that we can go over the design sketches and the projected job-cost figures. Naturally, we will be happy to make any modifications that you wish. Thank you for allowing us to make a contribution to your aquarium project.

Atentamente,
Paolo Benedetti
Creazioni di Vetro

This chapter describes a product costing method that is commonly used to account for the costs of specific orders or jobs; hence, the title 'job and order costing'. The application of this costing method relies on the easy and accurate observability of the use of direct materials and direct labour. Still, job and order costing also applies indirect costs, which by their very nature cannot be easily traced to products. As is common in most product costing applications, arbitrary decisions often are made to reasonably apply or allocate indirect costs. As we saw in Chapter 4, ABC presents one solution to the vexing problem of applying indirect costs, but the ABC solution tends to be complex and costly. Thus, many manufacturing and service organizations that see the need to fully cost their goods and services, rely on relatively simply but possibly inaccurate cost allocation methods to assign these indirect costs to products.

The cost allocation method presented in this chapter is perhaps the simplest possible: we use single overhead cost pools and volume-based cost-allocation bases. Of course, some organizations have built more complex cost allocation tools, both ABC and traditional, and all of the examples in this chapter could be repeated with more complex indirect cost allocation methods. We feel that this would unnecessarily complicate the discussions here. The allocation arithmetic would be identical, but repeated for each of the cost pools that one might want to use.

Background for Creazioni di Vetro

Creazioni di Vetro (CV, or 'Glass Creations') creates and markets stained glass windows, doors and freestanding art pieces for private homes, businesses and other organizations. The small, family-run business is located in Rome, Italy. Paolo and Mariana Benedetti, who studied fine arts in college, founded the business 15 years ago. Both are involved in the design and creation of the stained glass pieces. In addition, CV's employees include one other designer, five highly skilled glass workers, a framing technician, and several office personnel. Louisa Malina, CV's Controller and a certified management accountant, provides support to the firm in purchasing, production scheduling, accounting and cost management.

Roughly 75 per cent of the firm's sales revenues are earned from single, unique pieces, most of which are commissioned by private homeowners and businesses. Products sell for prices ranging from €800 for a simple, relatively small piece, to tens of thousands of euros for large, complex pieces. CV has produced stained glass pieces for religious organizations, but the majority of its products are secular in nature. The remainder of CV's products are its windows, which are produced in small batches, stored in inventory, and sold as retail items for about €400 each at arts festivals, on the firm's website, or through catalogues of specialized building materials. Among the firm's basic (or 'stock') windows are the pelican window, the blue heron window and the dolphin window. Each unit in a batch of stock windows uses the same basic design with minor modifications from batch to batch. Moreover, the units within a batch typically can be slightly different because of the different glass colours used. As the correspondence on the preceding page indicates, CV is currently developing the design and cost estimate for two elaborate, stained-glass doors to be installed in the remodelled Aquarium Costa Brava.

The owners must make some important marketing and strategic decisions to thrive in the company's competitive environment. For example, they must decide whether CV should compete with larger window manufacturers for the retail window market or concentrate on the custom design market. They must also determine how best to use the typically slow months of December and January. Should they aggressively seek more custom design work? Or should they use this period to produce basic windows for inventory to be sold later in the spring and summer months, when arts festivals are in full swing and the home building industry picks up?

During their first decade as the owners of a small business, the Benedettis focused exclusively on the artistic side of their enterprise. They were artists, after all, not businesspeople. However, they became increasingly aware of the unpredictability of the cost (and, by implication, the profit) on large, custom glass pieces. Sometimes CV bid too high on a job and lost it. Other times it bid too low and got the job but lost money on it. As Paolo once said in frustration, 'The profit margins on our various jobs seem random. We just never know what to expect.' That frustration, coupled with several lean years of the 'starving artist' syndrome, led the owners to hire Louisa Malina, a college friend who had majored in business, as the company's Controller to support their operations in a number of important business functions. The owners were becoming frustrated by spending too much time ordering materials, making estimates, and so on, and not getting enough time in the studio. They needed Malina to help develop a sound costing system and help manage costs. She installed a simple product-costing system for CV, which gave the Benedettis a much better idea of the costs of their jobs, which in turn helped them make better cost estimates for prospective jobs.

This chapter explores a cost-accounting system called 'job-order costing' (or simply 'job costing'), which traces costs to products in organizations such as CV. This chapter discusses job-order costing using CV's business. The methods illustrated apply, however, to all types of organizations – manufacturing, service, non-profit, and government – which have unique, customized or clearly identified jobs and orders.

Alternative Product-costing Systems

Cost analysts could ask themselves and their managers a number of questions regarding the nature of the information needed to support their organization's decision making. Answers to these questions have direct implications for designing a **product costing system,** which accumulates the costs of a production process and assigns them to the products or services that constitute the organization's output. One question of direct interest for cost system design is the following: are specific costs of each product and product line necessary, or are average costs across products adequate?

LO 1
Explain the differences in job-order, process and operation costing.

As analysts develop answers to this question, a certain type of costing system usually appears to be most appropriate. The most common types of product costing systems include *job-order costing* and *process costing,* as well as their hybrid, *operation costing.* In addition, other important variations of costing systems can be implemented in conjunction with job-order, process or operation costing. We address these other cost-system design variations later in this chapter.

Choices Among Major Types of Product Costing Systems

Job-order costing treats each individual job as the unit of output and assigns costs to it as the job uses resources. A job can be a single, unique product, such as CV's large art pieces, a custom home, a commercial aeroplane, a cinematic film or an audit of a public company. Alternatively, a job can be a relatively small batch of identical or very similar products, such as CV's pelican window that is produced in batches of about 20 to 25 units, or batches of printed wedding invitations, or batches of furniture suites for retail customers. Job-order costing creates and maintains separate records or accounts for each job. Job-order costing is appropriate for the following situations:

- Each unit or batch of products is distinct and clearly distinguishable from other products.
- Each unit or batch is of relatively high value, which makes the benefits of separately assigning production costs worth the cost of doing so.
- Each unit or batch of products is often priced differently, frequently in accordance with an ordering or bidding process.
- Each unit or batch of products can feasibly trace its direct costs.

CV and other producers of unique jobs can see important benefits of tracing costs to each job that justify the expenses of doing so. Job-order costing is useful for the following purposes:

- *Identifying types of jobs* that are likely to be most profitable so that the organization can specify the scope and scale of its operations.
- *Providing data to predict costs of future jobs* so that the organization chooses appropriate jobs on the basis of the expected resources needed and profitability.
- *Managing the costs of current jobs* to ensure that they stay within expectations and to provide early warning if costs will exceed expectations.

- *Renegotiating job contracts* before introducing any significant changes in jobs that will affect resources, costs or profits.
- *Reporting actual financial results* of the period's operations to demonstrate the organization's efficiency to internal and external parties such as creditors and stockholders.

Managers use their knowledge of the costs of past jobs to estimate the costs of prospective jobs. Accurate cost estimates on future jobs help them prepare competitive bids. The Benedettis know that if CV bids too high on a commissioned job, it will not be awarded the job, and if the bid is too low, the company could lose money on the job. Artists working on commissioned pieces, construction contractors, and other businesspeople who bid on jobs must have reliable estimates of the costs of prospective jobs to prepare bids that are low enough to win but high enough to make a profit.[1]

Managers compare actual job costs to the estimated (*budgeted*) job costs to help manage them. They can use job-cost information to renegotiate contracts with customers. CV has found that jobs often turn out differently than the customer originally specified. Sometimes these changes are inexpensive, and the company does the extra work as part of good customer service. Other times the changes are expensive, and the customer and the firm need to negotiate who will bear their cost. Reliable cost information helps management know (1) whether the changes are expensive or inexpensive and (2) what the changes cost so that the commissioned price or bid can be renegotiated.

To summarize, job-order costing is important for both pricing and cost management. Businesses must be able to estimate costs accurately if they are to be competitive and profitable.

Widespread Use of Job-order Costing

Many companies that produce customized products and services use job-order costing in some form. Examples include **Grupo ACS**, the global construction company; **Airbus**, the large commercial aeroplane manufacturer; **Mayo Clinic**, the world-renowned hospital where the jobs are 'cases'; **New Line Cinema**, the producer of jobs such as the movie *The Hobbit*; **Accenture** and **KPMG**, global business-services firms, whose jobs are 'clients'; and **McGraw-Hill**, the publisher of this and other leading textbooks.

In contrast, **process costing,** discussed in Chapter 11, treats all units processed during a *time period* as the output to be costed and does not separate and record costs for each unit produced. The next time you have a bottle of **Coca Cola** or **Pepsi**, consider whether the bottler tracked the cost of the specific bottle you are drinking. Not likely! It would be prohibitively costly to do so and without benefit since the bottler would not expect any cost variation among bottles of the same soft drink. Process costing is appropriate for the following types of production processes:

- Units of output that are homogeneous and indistinguishable from one another.
- Individual product units that are typically of relatively low value.
- Individual product units for which it is not feasible to trace direct costs.

Companies that use continuous processes use process costing to value many identical units of product or service (such as bottling beverages, manufacturing chemicals, grinding flour, refining oil and processing credit-card transactions).

Another product costing method is **operation costing**, which is a hybrid of job-order and process costing used by companies that continuously produce many products that have a large proportion of common inputs but that also have observable differences created for different customers. Examples include computers made by **Dell** that have many common parts but are individualized for specific customers; or shirts made from common designs and fabrics but are 'tailored' for different retail customers. As outputs become more unique and separately identifiable, job-order costing becomes more appropriate. Conversely, as separate units of output become indistinguishable, process costing is more appropriate. An organization whose output falls somewhere between the two extremes might use operation costing to value its output partly by methods of process costing and partly by methods of job-order costing. Furthermore, a company can use job-order costing for its unique products and process costing for its mass-produced products.

Basic Cost-flow Model

As your previous accounting courses probably discussed, all cost-accounting systems rely on a basic cost-flow model, which is a periodic accounting framework for recording the costs of jobs (or processes). The basic cost-flow model is an *inventory* or *stock* model or equation that measures all of the resources used to produce products for sale. The basic cost-flow model follows:

LO 2
Explain how costs flow through the manufacturing accounts.

Job cost *opening balance*		Resource *transfers in*		Resource *transfers out*		Job cost *closing balance*
OB	+	**T1**	−	**TO**	=	**CB**

Cost Flows and Jobs

The cost-flow model assigns costs of resources used to work on jobs according to the cost-flow equation, as explained here:

- At any time, every active job has an opening balance (OB) that measures the cost of resources used on the job to date. The opening balance might be zero if the job so far is only an order. (Although one could argue that human resources have been used to generate the order, the opening balance still is zero until costs are traced to the job.)
- Resources used or transferred in (TI) during the time the job is active also are assigned to measure resource use.
- Transfers out (TO) record the accumulated costs of products that are (a) transferred to another process in the organization, (b) completed and stored, or (c) sent to the customer. Transfers-out ordinarily are the costs of good products that are suitable for further processing or sale. Costs of defective products that must be scrapped or recycled should be counted as separate costs of the job or of the period.
- The closing balance (CB) for the job is the traced cost of products that are still in process at the end of an accounting period. The value also may be computed as a residual from the simple algebra of the cost-flow equation:

$$\mathbf{CB = OB + TI - TO}$$

You might use this same model if you periodically update your bank account. Alternatively, the bank's accounting system *perpetually* updates your account balance as you make deposits and withdrawals. Similarly, inventory-stock systems either periodically or perpetually update inventory balances for transfers-in and transfers-out, depending on the need and technology used.

An imbalance of the cost-flow model indicates an unintentional error, wasted resources or, perhaps, theft or fraud. One of the best features of the basic cost-flow model is its use as a powerful tool for controlling the use of all physical resources. By making the misuse of physical resources difficult, the cost-flow model becomes a *control mechanism*, which is a policy or procedure that helps the organization ensure that its goals and objectives are met.

Simple Cost-flow Examples

Examine the examples in Exhibit 10.1, and observe how to use the cost-flow equation to solve for the missing element in each column.

Cost-flow Equation (OB + TI − TO = CB)
B2: OB + €8,000 − €11,000 = €16,000

$$\mathbf{OB} = €16{,}000 - €8{,}000 + €11{,}000$$
$$\mathbf{OB} = €19{,}000$$

$$\mathbf{C3:}\ €4{,}000 + \mathbf{TI} - €61{,}000 = €1{,}000$$
$$\mathbf{TI} = €1{,}000 - €4{,}000 + €61{,}000$$
$$\mathbf{TI} = €58{,}000$$

$$\mathbf{D4:}\ €5{,}000 + €8{,}000 - \mathbf{TO} = €7{,}000$$
$$-\mathbf{TO} = €7{,}000 - €5{,}000 - €8{,}000$$
$$-\mathbf{TO} =- €6{,}000$$
$$\mathbf{TO} = €6{,}000$$

$$\mathbf{E5:}\ €3{,}000 + €65{,}000 - €48{,}000 = \mathrm{CB}$$
$$\mathrm{CB} = €20{,}000$$

Exhibit 10.1 **Cost-flow Examples**

	A	B	C	D	E
1	**Inventory entry**	**Known and unknown entries**			
2	Opening balance	= ?	€4,000	€5,000	€3,000
3	Transfers in	€8,000	= ?	8,000	65,000
4	Transfers out	11,000	61,000	= ?	48,000
5	Closing balance	16,000	1,000	7,000	= ?

We are ready to add a slight complication to the basic cost-flow model by recognizing that most organizations use several types of inventory accounts to manage job costs. Most commonly, these additional accounts include Work-in-progress (WIP) inventory and Finished goods (FG) inventory, which record transfers of costs and inventory balances as jobs are in progress and when they have been completed, respectively.

Managing and Using Cost-flow Information

LO 3
Assign direct costs to production jobs or products using a job-order costing system.

Companies such as CV that use job-order costing employ several accounts (or files) to track the costs of resources used on jobs. These accounts are the sources of data for product costing, estimating costs of future jobs and financial reporting for both internal and external purposes. The WIP inventory account collects all costs of resources used on various jobs not yet completed. Each job also has its own job-cost record or *subsidiary* inventory account. The subsidiary, **job-cost record (or file, card, sheet)** records the costs of all production-related resources used on the job to date. The accumulation of all of the job-cost records measures the total effects of activities in the WIP and FG inventory accounts.

The total cost in the WIP inventory account is the sum of the costs in all of the active (but not completed) jobs, as recorded on their subsidiary job-cost records. Similarly, the Finished goods inventory account collects total costs of all completed jobs not yet sold to customers. The *Cost of sales expense* account records the costs of finished goods (or jobs) that have been transferred out or sold to customers during a specific period. The basic cost-flow model ties these accounts together as Exhibit 10.2 shows.

Transfers in (TI) to WIP inventory include direct material, direct labour and manufacturing overhead costs. As jobs or products are completed, they and their accumulated costs are transferred out (TO) of the WIP inventory account. This cost of completed goods becomes the transfers in (TI) to the next sequential process (if there are sequential production processes) and ultimately, as Exhibit 10.2 shows, to Finished goods inventory. The transfers out of FG inventory become the transfers in to Cost of sales expense for the period.

Exhibit 10.2 Product and Cost Flows

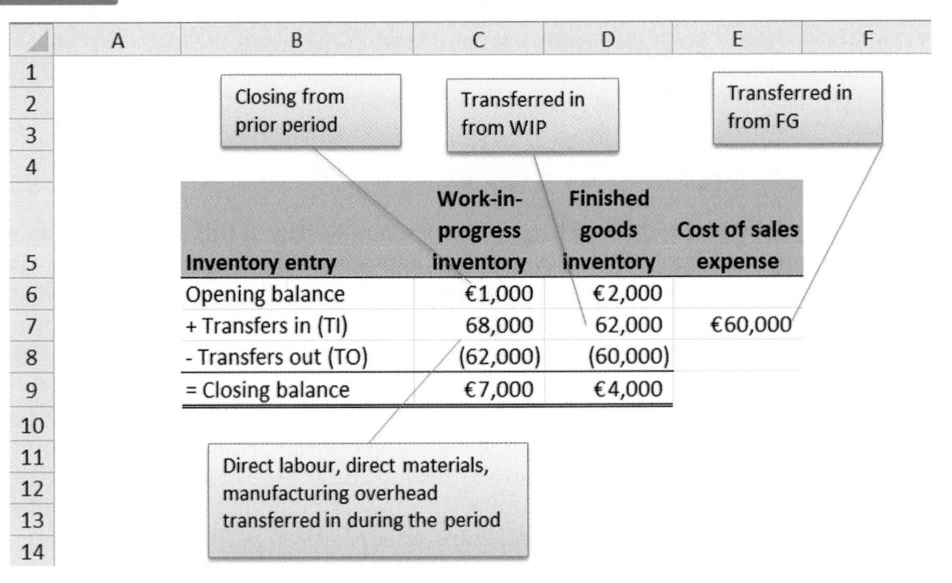

Inventory entry	Work-in-progress inventory	Finished goods inventory	Cost of sales expense
Opening balance	€1,000	€2,000	
+ Transfers in (TI)	68,000	62,000	€60,000
- Transfers out (TO)	(62,000)	(60,000)	
= Closing balance	€7,000	€4,000	

The Process of Tracking Job-order Costs

In job-shop or batch-production operations, managers estimate and manage costs by keeping separate cost records for each job or batch. The primary cost document for a job is the 'job-cost record' (also called a 'job-cost file or sheet'). See Exhibit 10.3 for a printout of the job-cost record for CV's job, S-PEL-08.01.20xy. (The numbering system reflects a stock (S) job of pelican windows (PEL) started on 8 January 20xy.) Note that this record shows detailed calculations for the direct materials, direct labour and manufacturing overhead costs charged to the job. Louisa Malina, CV's controller, compared the actual costs accumulated for the job with the estimated costs. Any significant

Exhibit 10.3 Job-cost Record for Job S-PEL-08.01.20xy

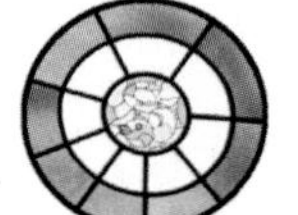

	A	B	C	D	E	F	G	H	I	J	K	L
1						Creazioni di Vetro						
2		Job number:	S-PEL-08.01.20xy			Batch number or name of customer:					PEL-08.01.20xy	
3		Date started:	8 January 20xy			Date finished:					26 January 20xy	
4		Job name:	Pelican window			Job supervisor:					Andretti	
5		Quantity:	20									
6												
7		Direct materials				Direct labour					Manufacturing overhead	
8	Date	Requisition identifier	Cost	Date	Employee identifier	Hours	Rate	Cost	Date	Direct labour Hours	Overhead rate per DL hour*	Cost
9	8 Jan xy	S-PEL-08.01.20xy	€1,000	8 Jan xy	D01:	3	€21.00	€63	26 Jan xy	113	€30	€3,390
10	13 Jan xy	S-PEL-08.01.20xy	400	12-18 Jan xy	G03:	60	22.00	1,320				
11				12-18 Jan xy	G06:	40	22.00	880				
12				18 Jan xy	F02:	10	15.00	150				
13	Total		€1,400	Total		113.00		€2,413	Total			€3,390
14						Total job cost						
15				Cost item		Expected	Variance	Actual			* Predetermined overhead rate	
16				Direct materials		€1,300	€100	€1,400			(explained later in chapter)	
17				Direct labour		2,500	(87)	2,413				
18				Manufacturing overhead		3,510	(120)	3,390				
19				Total costs applied		€7,310	€(107)	€7,203				
20												
21				Transferred to Finished goods inventory				Actual				
22				Direct materials				€1,400				
23				Direct labour				2,413				
24				Manufacturing overhead				3,390				
25				Total cost of completed job				€7,203				
26				Cost per unit				€360.15				

differences (called *variances*) are noted on the job-cost record. The comparison also provides feedback on the accuracy of the cost estimates, which is important for future pricing decisions. In this case, the variances do not seem particularly large (about 1.5 per cent of total expected cost) and may be within CV's typical experience. If so, Malina would be unlikely to inquire further.

Product-costing System Design Issues

Three design aspects of CV's product-costing system are noteworthy at this juncture. First, as noted previously, the company uses *job-order costing*. It is an appropriate method for CV because the firm's products are dissimilar, and many of them are custom jobs. Second, CV uses *absorption costing*, which also was explained as *accrual* costing in Chapter 2. Thus, the manufacturing overhead shown on the job-cost record in Exhibit 10.3 includes total manufacturing overhead as product costs. Third, CV uses a *normal costing system*, which assigns actual costs of direct material and direct labour to each production job but *applies* (or allocates) the manufacturing overhead using a *predetermined overhead rate* that is computed with the normal level of a cost driver in the denominator. This third design aspect of CV's product-costing system (i.e., normal costing and the use of a predetermined overhead rate) is explored in more detail later in the chapter. For now, it is important to realize that these three terms (job-order, absorption and normal costing) describe the type of product-costing system employed by CV.

Recording Job-order Costs

Most companies with job-shop or batch-production environments follow the basic job-order costing steps presented in this section. We show the accounting entries to record the costs incurred by CV in January 20xy, a typically slow month. Several employees take their vacations then, and during the current year, the studio worked on only three jobs.

In a job-order costing system, Work-in-progress inventory is a *control account* because cost records in the subsidiary ledger support it. Costs associated with each job are recorded on a job-cost record as shown in Exhibit 10.3. Thus, job-cost records serve as *subsidiary ledgers* to the WIP inventory account. This enables management to identify the costs for a particular job by reviewing its job-cost record.

CV's job, S-PEL-08.01.20xy, was moved to the FG Inventory on 26 January 20xy. On 31 January, it awaited shipment to various customers. Its costs are presented on the job cost record in Exhibit 10.3. Another of CV's jobs, C-05.12.20xx-D, which was in process on 1 January, had been started on 5 December of the preceding year, 20xx. (The job number used denotes that this custom (C) job was started on 5 December 20xx for customer D.) After some additional work, it was completed and installed for the customer in January. The third job, C-15.01.20xy-A (a custom job started on 15 January 20xy for customer A), was still in progress on 31 January. Therefore, the following is the status for each of these production jobs on 31 January.

Job	Status on 31 January 20xy
C-05.12.20xx-D	Sold
S-PEL-08.01.20xy	Finished but not sold
C-15.01.20xy-A	In process

Opening inventories

Exhibit 10.4 shows the opening balances in the (abbreviated) set of financial position accounts in row 3, including the Raw Material Inventory and Work-in-Progress Inventory accounts.[2] Opening Raw Material Inventory on 1 January was €5,000. Opening Work-in-Progress Inventory on 1 January had consisted of only job C-05.12.20xx-D, which had incurred the total costs of €11,700 during December, the previous month.

Work-in-progress inventory, opening balance	
Direct material	€6,500
Direct labour	2,200
Manufacturing overhead applied	3,000
Total	€11,700

There was no opening Finished goods inventory on 1 January. Other opening balances represent the company's remaining assets, liabilities and equities.

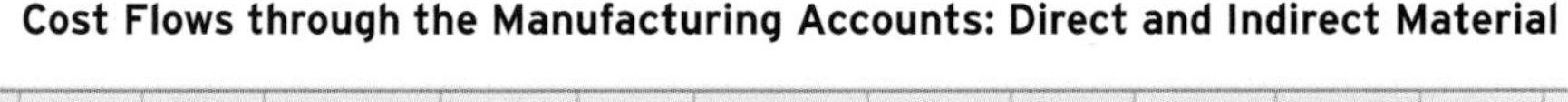

Exhibit 10.4 Cost Flows through the Manufacturing Accounts: Direct and Indirect Material

	A	B	C	D	E	F	G	H	I	J	K	L	M
1	Exhibit 10.4	ASSETS								LIABILITIES		EQUITIES	
2	Transaction	Cash	Acc'ts Rec.	Raw Mat'ls Inven.	*Manufacturing Overhead**	WIP Inven.	FG Inven.	Plant, Prop. & Equip. (Net)	PrePaid Expenses	Wages Payable	Accounts Payable	Owners' Equity	Balance Check
3	Opening	5,000	0	5,000	0	11,700	0	10,000	1,200	1,000	3,000	28,900	-
4	1			25,000							25,000		-
5	2			(7,600)	200	7,400							-
6													-
7													-
8													-
9													-
10													-
11													-
12													-
13	Closing	5,000	0	22,400	200	19,100	0	10,000	1,200	1,000	28,000	28,900	-
14		* Temporary accounts are italicized											
15	Transaction	Memorandum											
16	Opening	opening balances for all accounts (i.e., opening statement of financial position or balance sheet)											
17	1	to record purchase of raw materials											
18	2	to record actual raw materials cost used for indirect and direct materials costs											
19													
20													
21													
22													
23													
24													
25													
26	Closing	closing balances for all accounts (i.e., closing statement of financial position or balance sheet)											

Raw and direct material

In January, CV purchased €25,000 of raw material. This purchase anticipated the Aquarium Costa Brava job mentioned in the letter at the opening of the chapter and was made somewhat early to take advantage of a favourable price for glass. This purchase was recorded in row 4 of Exhibit 10.4 and explained by the memo in row 17.

When material is needed for one or more production jobs, the job supervisor, an owner, or one of the other skilled glass workers requisitions it using a **material requisition form**, which is the source document for tracing the cost of a *raw material* from Raw material inventory as *direct material* to the WIP inventory account, and to the job-cost records of the specific jobs. No additional materials were requisitioned for job C-05.12.20xx-D in January. Job S-PEL-08-01.20xy had two requisitions for material totalling €1,400 (see Exhibit 10.3, cell C13). Material of €6,000 was requisitioned for Job C-15.01.20xy-A.

Indirect materials also are drawn from the Raw material inventory. The indirect costs are not traced to specific jobs but are charged to the temporary Manufacturing overhead account for later allocation to jobs, as we shall see. The entry for the transfer of the €7,400 of raw materials to the WIP inventory and €200 to Manufacturing overhead account is in row 5 of Exhibit 10.4.[3]

Direct labour

Production employees may be paid an hourly rate or a monthly salary. Nevertheless, they record for the hours spent on each production job during the day. The company's total cost includes the employee's gross pay plus the employer's payroll taxes, the employer's contribution to pension and insurance plans, and any other benefits that the company pays for the employee. Companies generally add the benefit costs to the wage rate when assigning costs to production jobs. A company accounts for the use of labour resources by tracing labour hours to jobs, multiplied by an appropriate hourly rate, which might be a monthly salary plus benefits divided by the normal hours worked per month.

CV's controller recorded total costs of €22,413 for production employees during January. Of the €22,413 total, €16,413 was attributed to direct labour costs, including employee benefits and taxes. The €16,413 is charged (debited) to WIP inventory and assigned to the specific jobs worked on during the period. Based on the time records, the jobs were charged direct labour costs as follows: job C-05.12.20xx-D, €6,000 in January (for 285 direct labour hours of differing wage rates); job S-PEL-08.01.20xy, €2,413 (for 113 direct labour hours) as indicated in the job-cost record in Exhibit 10.3; and job C-15.01.20xy-A, €8,000 (for 380 direct labour hours, also of differing wage rates). Since design costs are easily traceable to specific custom jobs, they are included in direct labour. However, design costs for existing stock windows were long ago fully charged to past production.

The remaining €6,000 (of the €22,413 discussed earlier) is indirect labour and is charged to Manufacturing overhead. Recall from Chapter 2 that indirect labour is the cost of compensating employees such as supervisory, custodial, maintenance, security and material-handling personnel, as well as idle time and overtime premiums paid to direct labour employees. CV is a small firm and typically its employees perform a variety of activities. Sometimes an employee works directly on a specific job (classified as direct labour) and sometimes does work unrelated to any particular job, such as general clean-up of the glass studio (classified as indirect labour). The entries on row 6 of Exhibit 10.5 records the disposition of CV'S €22,413 labour costs in January.

Exhibit 10.5 **Cost Flows through the Manufacturing Accounts: Direct and Indirect Labour**

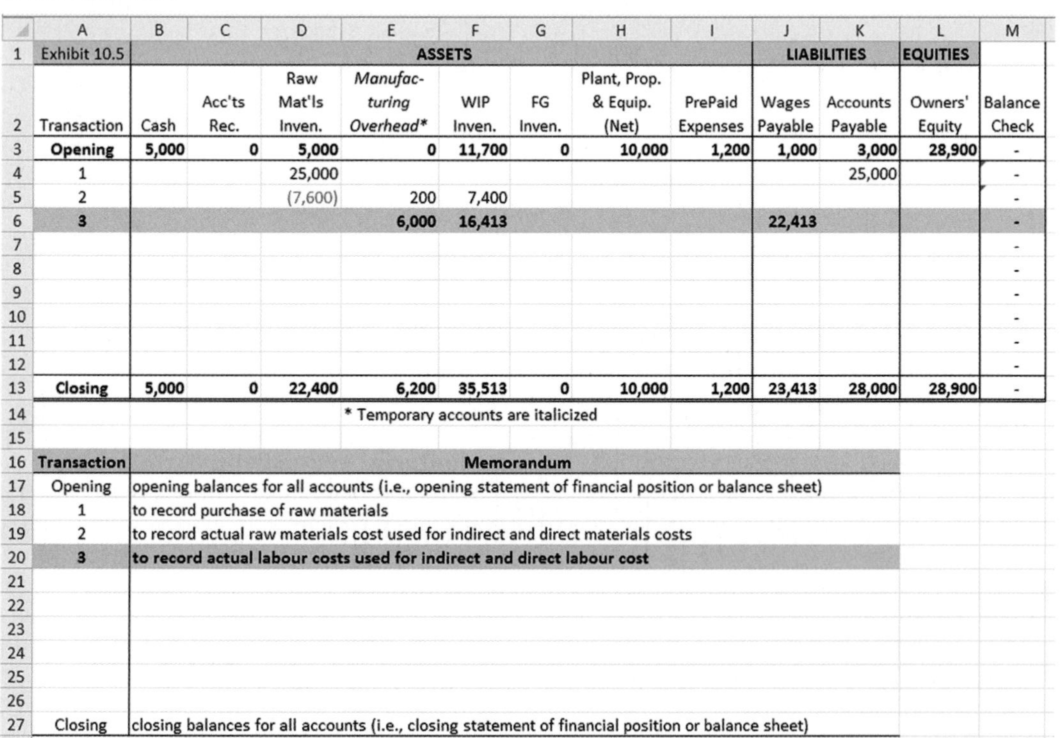

	A	B	C	D	E	F	G	H	I	J	K	L	M
1	Exhibit 10.5	ASSETS								LIABILITIES		EQUITIES	
2	Transaction	Cash	Acc'ts Rec.	Raw Mat'ls Inven.	*Manufacturing Overhead**	WIP Inven.	FG Inven.	Plant, Prop. & Equip. (Net)	PrePaid Expenses	Wages Payable	Accounts Payable	Owners' Equity	Balance Check
3	**Opening**	**5,000**	**0**	**5,000**	**0**	**11,700**	**0**	**10,000**	**1,200**	**1,000**	**3,000**	**28,900**	-
4	1			25,000							25,000		-
5	2			(7,600)	200	7,400							-
6	**3**				**6,000**	**16,413**				**22,413**			-
7													-
8													-
9													-
10													-
11													-
12													-
13	**Closing**	**5,000**	**0**	**22,400**	**6,200**	**35,513**	**0**	**10,000**	**1,200**	**23,413**	**28,000**	**28,900**	-
14					* Temporary accounts are italicized								
15													
16	**Transaction**	**Memorandum**											
17	Opening	opening balances for all accounts (i.e., opening statement of financial position or balance sheet)											
18	1	to record purchase of raw materials											
19	2	to record actual raw materials cost used for indirect and direct materials costs											
20	**3**	**to record actual labour costs used for indirect and direct labour cost**											
21													
22													
23													
24													
25													
26													
27	Closing	closing balances for all accounts (i.e., closing statement of financial position or balance sheet)											

Manufacturing Overhead Costs

LO 4
Record indirect, manufacturing overhead costs.

Accounting for manufacturing overhead is less straightforward than for direct labour and direct material. Manufacturing overhead typically is a heterogeneous pool of indirect costs. In traditional cost systems indirect costs are assigned to individual production jobs using a predetermined overhead rate. We address the process of establishing this overhead rate in the next section. At this point, however, note that CV's approach to assigning overhead is a very simple system. Louisa Malina did not believe that CV would benefit from a more complex, ABC system, such as discussed in Chapter 4.

At CV, indirect manufacturing costs, including costs such as indirect material, indirect labour, power and insurance on the studio and its equipment, are first charged to the Manufacturing overhead account. CV uses absorption or accrual costing, so it treats *all* manufacturing overhead (variable and fixed) as a product cost. These costs are combined into one control account, simply called *Manufacturing overhead*, which is a temporary asset account that transfers in indirect product costs and transfers out indirect costs to jobs or products. At the end of an accounting period this account is adjusted, as we shall see, to a zero closing balance.

As noted earlier, in January CV's controller charged indirect material costs of €200 and indirect labour costs of €6,000 to the Manufacturing overhead account as shown earlier in entries (2) and (3). Malina also charged utilities and other overhead costs of €12,000 that were paid on account. The €700 portion of prepaid insurance applicable to January is also charged to the overhead account, as is depreciation of €6,000. These items total €18,700 and in addition to indirect material and indirect labour comprise the actual overhead incurred during the period. The transaction, labelled (4) in row 7 of Exhibit 10.6, records the additional €18,700 manufacturing overhead for the month of January.

Exhibit 10.6 **Cost Flows through the Manufacturing Accounts: Manufacturing Overhead**

	A	B	C	D	E	F	G	H	I	J	K	L	M
1	Exhibit 10.6	ASSETS								LIABILITIES		EQUITIES	
2	Transaction	Cash	Acc'ts Rec.	Raw Mat'ls Inven.	*Manufacturing Overhead**	WIP Inven.	FG Inven.	Plant, Prop. & Equip. (Net)	PrePaid Expenses	Wages Payable	Accounts Payable	Owners' Equity	Balance Check
3	**Opening**	**5,000**	**0**	**5,000**	**0**	**11,700**	**0**	**10,000**	**1,200**	**1,000**	**3,000**	**28,900**	-
4	1			25,000							25,000		-
5	2			(7,600)	200	7,400							-
6	3				6,000	16,413				22,413			-
7	**4**				**18,700**			(6,000)	(700)		**12,000**		**-**
8													-
9													-
10													-
11													-
12													-
13	**Closing**	**5,000**	**0**	**22,400**	**24,900**	**35,513**	**0**	**4,000**	**500**	**23,413**	**40,000**	**28,900**	-
14					* Temporary accounts are italicized								
15													
16	**Transaction**	**Memorandum**											
17	Opening	opening balances for all accounts (i.e., opening statement of financial position or balance sheet)											
18	1	to record purchase of raw materials											
19	2	to record actual raw materials cost used for indirect and direct materials costs											
20	3	to record actual labour costs used for indirect and direct labour cost											
21	**4**	**to record actual accum depr, utillities, prepaid expenses, etc. ued for indirect production cost**											
22													
23													
24													
25													
26													
27	Closing	closing balances for all accounts (i.e., closing statement of financial position or balance sheet)											

10.1 Cost Management in Practice

Combining ABC and Job Costing in the Canadian Construction Industry

A Canadian industrial construction company reported the results of integrating ABC methods with job costing to complete a large project. The use of ABC improved job-cost estimates, management and cost control. The marriage of methods involved cross-referencing the usual construction functions (e.g., sitework, substructure, and so on) into more descriptive and detailed activities (e.g., clear site, strip topsoil, erect and strip foundation walls, and so on). The cost of each activity was generated from past experience and applied per unit of work performed (e.g., per m^2 of land cleared). The job-cost reports were more descriptive of the work done and pointed to obvious areas of cost improvement. A major benefit of the ABC/job-cost system was to estimate and control the costs of change-orders, which are common in the construction industry.

Source: Fayek (2001).

Use of Predetermined Overhead Rates

LO 5
Use a predetermined overhead rate to assign normal indirect resource costs to production jobs.

Within a year, manufacturing overhead costs incurred might be uneven. If *actual* monthly overhead costs were assigned to jobs, more overhead cost might be assigned in some months than in other months. For example, preventive maintenance costs can be higher in months when production activity is low. Utility costs in cold climates are higher in the winter than in the summer, and vice versa. In addition, a company usually will not know its actual overhead costs until the end of an accounting period, but decisions about jobs usually cannot wait. A **predetermined overhead rate**, which is the estimated fixed manufacturing overhead divided by the normal level of an appropriate cost driver, can provide a reliable estimate of actual indirect product costs over the course of a year.[4] The predetermined overhead rate is often established before the year in which it is to be used and may remain the same for an entire year. By using a predetermined overhead rate, a company *normalizes* (i.e., smoothes out) overhead applied to various production jobs.

Overhead costs are assigned to products or jobs by multiplying the rate by the amount of the cost-driver activity used. Thus, if a predetermined overhead rate is €50 per machine hour and if a job uses 20 machine hours (MH), the job is assigned €50/MH × 20 MH = €1,000 of overhead.

This approach is called a **normal costing system**, which *applies* manufacturing overhead to jobs using a predetermined overhead rate based on **normal production capacity**, which is an average of recent periods' production activity supplied. Normal costing assigns to production jobs the *actual* costs of direct material and direct labour, and *applied* manufacturing overhead. Predetermined overhead rates may be established by the following five steps, which are a simplified version of the ABC process described in Chapter 4:

Step 1. *Identify the costs to be included as indirect costs.* CV has developed a detailed list of cost items included as its manufacturing overhead. The company's total manufacturing overhead cost pool is composed of all indirect product costs.

Step 2. *Estimate and sum the annual costs for all indirect-cost items identified in step 1.* Estimated annual manufacturing-overhead costs for CV total €288,000 based on last year's actual manufacturing overhead adjusted for anticipated changes this year.

Step 3. *Select the cost driver(s).* CV's controller determined that the best cost driver to use for the company's manufacturing overhead costs is the normal number of direct labour hours. That is, annual manufacturing overhead costs are believed to be positively correlated with the number of direct labour hours used and the cost-driver data are readily available. This is typical in a labour-intensive business such as CV, but direct labour hours might not be the best choice for more capital-intensive companies.

Step 4. *Estimate the annual level of the cost driver.* Louisa Malina estimated the normal level of its cost driver to be 9,600 direct labour hours that are normal for the year. CV's practical production capacity, given its artistic talent and size, also is estimated to be 9,600 direct labour hours (DLH) during the year.

Step 5. *Compute the predetermined overhead rate.* This calculation is:

$$\textbf{Predetermined overhead rate} = \frac{\textbf{Estimated annual manufacturing overhead cost}}{\textbf{Estimated annual cost-driver level}}$$

$$= \frac{\text{€}288{,}000}{9{,}600\text{ DLH}} = \text{€}30 \text{ per DLH}$$

The Manufacturing overhead account also records the allocation or *application* of overhead costs using the predetermined overhead rate, multiplied by the cost-driver activity used. In January, CV used its predetermined overhead rate to apply manufacturing overhead to individual production jobs as follows:

	Actual direct labour hours (DLH) used in January		Predetermined overhead rate		Manufacturing overhead applied
C-05.12.20xx-A	285	×	€30 per DLH	=	€ 8,550
S-PEL-08.01.20xy	113	×	€30 per DLH	=	3,390
C-15.01.20xy-D	380	×	€30 per DLH	=	11,400
Total	778	×	€30 per DLH	=	€23,340

CV's entry to record the application of €23,340 manufacturing overhead cost to jobs using the predetermined overhead rate is labelled (5) in row 8 of Exhibit 10.7.[5]

Exhibit 10.7 Cost Flows through the Manufacturing Accounts: Applied Manufacturing Overhead

	A	B	C	D	E	F	G	H	I	J	K	L	M
1	Exhibit 10.7	ASSETS								LIABILITIES		EQUITIES	
2	Transaction	Cash	Acc'ts Rec.	Raw Mat'ls Inven.	*Manufacturing Overhead**	WIP Inven.	FG Inven.	Plant, Prop. & Equip. (Net)	PrePaid Expenses	Wages Payable	Accounts Payable	Owners' Equity	Balance Check
3	**Opening**	**5,000**	**0**	**5,000**	**0**	**11,700**	**0**	**10,000**	**1,200**	**1,000**	**3,000**	**28,900**	-
4	1			25,000							25,000		-
5	2			(7,600)	200	7,400							-
6	3				6,000	16,413				22,413			-
7	4				18,700			(6,000)	(700)		12,000		-
8	**5**				(23,340)	**23,340**							-
9													-
10													-
11													-
12													-
13	**Closing**	**5,000**	**0**	**22,400**	**1,560**	**58,853**	**0**	**4,000**	**500**	**23,413**	**40,000**	**28,900**	-
14			* Temporary accounts are italicized					Check: change in OE = profit or loss according to P&L				0	
15													
16	**Transaction**	**Memorandum**											
17	Opening	opening balances for all accounts (i.e., opening statement of financial position or balance sheet)											
18	1	to record purchase of raw materials											
19	2	to record actual raw materials cost used for indirect and direct materials costs											
20	3	to record actual labour costs used for indirect and direct labour cost											
21	4	to record actual accum depr, utillities, prepaid expenses, etc. ued for indirect production cost											
22	**5**	**to record applied manufacturing overhead cost to WIP Inven.**											
23													
24													
25													
26													
27	Closing	closing balances for all accounts (i.e., closing statement of financial position or balance sheet)											

Transfers to Finished goods inventory

When jobs are transferred from work-in-progress to finished goods, an entry is made to transfer the costs of the jobs from the WIP inventory account to the FG inventory account. For example, CV completed jobs C-05.12.20xx-D (€26,250) and S-PEL-08.01.20xy (€7,203) in January and transferred

Exhibit 10.8 **Cost Flows through the Manufacturing Accounts: Recording Completion of Products and Cost of Sales**

	A	B	C	D	E	F	G	H	I	J	K	L	M
1	Exhibit 10.8	ASSETS								LIABILITIES		EQUITIES	
2	Transaction	Cash	Acc'ts Rec.	Raw Mat'ls Inven.	*Manufacturing Overhead**	WIP Inven.	FG Inven.	Plant, Prop. & Equip. (Net)	PrePaid Expenses	Wages Payable	Accounts Payable	Owners' Equity	Balance Check
3	**Opening**	**5,000**	**0**	**5,000**	**0**	**11,700**	**0**	**10,000**	**1,200**	**1,000**	**3,000**	**28,900**	-
4	1			25,000							25,000		-
5	2			(7,600)	200	7,400							-
6	3				6,000	16,413				22,413			-
7	4				18,700			(6,000)	(700)		12,000		-
8	5				(23,340)	23,340							-
9	**6**					(33,453)	**33,453**						-
10	**7**		**38,000**				(26,250)					**11,750**	-
11	8												-
12	9												-
13	**Closing**	**5,000**	**38,000**	**22,400**	**1,560**	**25,400**	**7,203**	**4,000**	**500**	**23,413**	**40,000**	**40,650**	-
14					* Temporary accounts are italicized								
15													
16	**Transaction**	**Memorandum**											
17	Opening	opening balances for all accounts (i.e., opening statement of financial position or balance sheet)											
18	1	to record purchase of raw materials											
19	2	to record actual raw materials cost used for indirect and direct materials costs											
20	3	to record actual labour costs used for indirect and direct labour cost											
21	4	to record actual accum depr, utillities, prepaid expenses, etc. ued for indirect production cost											
22	5	to record applied manufacturing overhead cost to WIP Inven.											
23	**6**	**to record completion of jobs and transfer to FG Inven.**											
24	**7**	**to record revenues earned and the cost of the job sold to customer**											
25													
26													
27	Closing	closing balances for all accounts (i.e., closing statement of financial position or balance sheet)											

them to Finished goods inventory. The transfer of the costs of the two completed jobs (€33,453) to finished goods is labelled (6) and shown in row 9 of Exhibit 10.8.

Transfers to Cost of Sales

When finished goods are sold, their production cost is transferred from Finished goods inventory to Cost of Sales expense. CV sold job C-05.12.20xx-D, which cost €26,250, in January for a total of €38,000, the commissioned price for this custom job. The gross margin on this job is the difference, €11,750. The sales revenue and the corresponding transfer of Finished goods inventory to Cost of sales is labelled (7) in row 10 of Exhibit 10.8.

Note that the amount left as the closing balance of FG inventory (€7,203, G13) is the cost of job S-PEL-08.01.20xy, which was completed but not yet sold at the end of January.

Manufacturing Overhead Variance

LO 6
Measure and dispose of the manufacturing overhead variance.

The Manufacturing overhead account is a temporary asset account, so it is 'closed' at the end of an accounting period. *Closing* an account means that its balance is transferred at the end of the accounting period to some other account, leaving a zero balance in the closed account. You might recall from your study of financial accounting that revenue and expense accounts are closed to the Income summary (or Owners' equity) account at the end of the accounting period. Usually this closing process is not performed until the end of the period, when the books are formally *closed.* For illustrative purposes, let's assume that CV closes its Manufacturing overhead account each month.

Under normal costing, the *actual* manufacturing overhead incurred is unlikely to equal the amount of **applied overhead**, which is the amount of manufacturing overhead assigned to WIP inventory as a product cost. It is calculated by multiplying the predetermined overhead rate by the actual cost driver volume. The difference between the actual overhead and the applied overhead amounts is the **overhead variance**. Actual incurred overhead that exceeds normal applied overhead is *under-applied overhead.* In the opposite case, when normal overhead applied exceeds overhead incurred, the variance is **over-applied overhead**.

During January, CV incurred manufacturing overhead in the amount of €24,900 and applied €23,340 to WIP inventory.[6] The €1,560 difference is the *overhead variance*, which in this case is *under-applied overhead*, because in this case overhead incurred exceeds overhead applied. In most instances, these periodic under-applied or over-applied amounts tend to be relatively small and, thus, usually do not reflect material inaccuracies in the numerator or the denominator of the predetermined overhead rate.

Disposition of the Manufacturing Overhead Variance

At year's end, the manufacturing overhead variance is closed entirely to Other expenses or to Cost of sales, if the variance is judged to be an *immaterial* amount, or (2) prorated (i.e., allocated) to WIP inventory, FG inventory and Cost of sales, if the variance is judged to be *material*.[7]

Charging an immaterial manufacturing overhead cost variance should be the usual treatment if the predetermined overhead rate is reasonably accurate. The simple disposition of an immaterial variance is labelled (8) in row 11 of Exhibit 10.9.

We also expense at this time the month's selling and administrative costs. These costs do not flow through the inventory accounts because they are period costs, not product costs, and are expensed during the period incurred. CV's selling and administrative expenses (all on account) amounted to €4,000 in January. Selling expenses are labelled (9) in row 12 of Exhibit 10.9. Note that row 13 of Exhibit 10.9 can be reformatted as a 31 January statement of financial position. The Owners' equity column (L) can be formatted as the month's statement of income.

Exhibit 10.9 **Closing the Manufacturing Overhead Account and Expensing the Overhead Variance and Selling Costs**

	A	B	C	D	E	F	G	H	I	J	K	L	M
1	Exhibit 10.9	ASSETS								LIABILITIES		EQUITIES	
2	Transaction	Cash	Acc'ts Rec.	Raw Mat'ls Inven.	*Manufacturing Overhead**	WIP Inven.	FG Inven.	Plant, Prop. & Equip. (Net)	PrePaid Expenses	Wages Payable	Accounts Payable	Owners' Equity	Balance Check
3	**Opening**	**5,000**	**0**	**5,000**	**0**	**11,700**	**0**	**10,000**	**1,200**	**1,000**	**3,000**	**28,900**	-
4	1			25,000							25,000		-
5	2			(7,600)	200	7,400							-
6	3				6,000	16,413				22,413			-
7	4				18,700			(6,000)	(700)		12,000		-
8	5				(23,340)	23,340							-
9	6					(33,453)	33,453						-
10	7		38,000				(26,250)					11,750	-
11	**8**				(1,560)							(1,560)	-
12	**9**										4,000	(4,000)	-
13	**closing**	**5,000**	**38,000**	**22,400**	**0**	**25,400**	**7,203**	**4,000**	**500**	**23,413**	**44,000**	**35,090**	-
14													
15													

	Transaction	Memorandum
17	Opening	opening balances for all accounts (i.e., opening statement of financial position or balance sheet)
18	1	to record purchase of raw materials
19	2	to record actual raw materials cost used for indirect and direct materials costs
20	3	to record actual labour costs used for indirect and direct labour cost
21	4	to record actual accum depr, utillities, prepaid expenses, etc. ued for indirect production cost
22	5	to record applied manufacturing overhead cost to WIP Inven.
23	6	to record completion of jobs and transfer to FG Inven.
24	7	to record revenues earned and the cost of the job sold to customer
25	**8**	**to record closing of manufacturing overhead to cost of sales**
26	**9**	**to record periodic selling expenses**
27	Closing	closing balances for all accounts (i.e., closing statement of financial position or balance sheet)

10.1 You're the Decision Maker

Prepare a Job-cost Record

a. From the preceding information in this chapter, prepare a job-cost record similar to Exhibit 10.3 for job C-05.12.20xx-D. You will not be able to provide all the details that are in Exhibit 10.3, but you will be able to prepare the actual, completed cost of the job.

b. From the preceding information in this chapter, prepare a job-cost record similar to Exhibit 10.3 for job C-15.01.20xy-A. You will not be able to provide all the details that are in Exhibit 10.3, but you will be able to prepare the actual cost of the job as of the end of January.

(Solutions begin on p. 526.)

Prorating a Materially Large Variance

The *allocation* of a materially large variance is its allocation in proportionate amounts to WIP inventory, FG inventory, and Cost of sales – all of the product cost accounts through which the cost passed. Exhibit 10.10 recaps the overhead costs in CV's production accounts at the end of January (each containing one job, in this example) before and after allocation, as if CV had prorated the overhead variance.[8]

Exhibit 10.10 demonstrates that Cost of sales, which at month-end contains 36.6 per cent of the normally applied overhead (0.366 = 8,550/23,340, rounded), is assigned an additional €571 of under-applied overhead (€571 = 36.6% × €1,560), which adds to this expense. The other accounts would be charged similarly. When the jobs that are in WIP and FG inventories are sold, these additional amounts of overhead will be expensed as part of Cost of sales.

The difference in operating income between prorating the variance and assigning it to Cost of sales is a matter of timing. Any difference between actual and applied overhead eventually is expensed, even if a company prorates. Prorating the overhead variance merely defers expensing the portion allocated to WIP and FG inventory until the products in those accounts are sold. For managerial purposes, one must ask how useful it is to revalue Work-in-progress and Finished goods inventories to their actual cost. A large, material overhead variance could affect some cost management decisions and other decisions, such as performance-evaluation and pricing. If the variance is immaterial, allocation is not worthwhile.

The key cost management objective is to understand the causes of a materially large difference between actual and applied overhead. A persistently material overhead variance might indicate the need to revise overhead rates, impose new procedures to reduce costs, or investigate possible accounting errors.

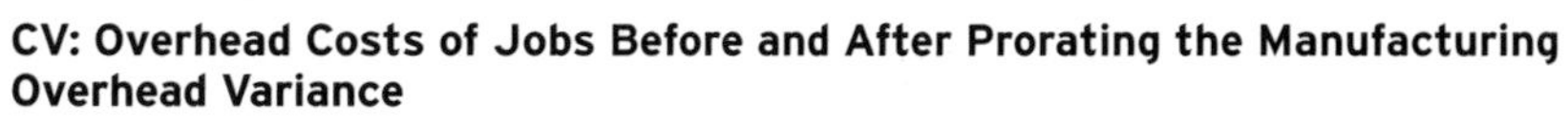

Exhibit 10.10 CV: Overhead Costs of Jobs Before and After Prorating the Manufacturing Overhead Variance

	A	B	C	D	E	F
1	Job No.	Status of job at end of the month	Manufacturing overhead applied in January	Percentage of total overhead applied in January	Prorated overhead variance to account	Total overhead applied to account
2	C-05.12.20xx-D	Cost of Sales	€8,550	36.6%	€571	€9,121
3	S-PEL-08.01.20xy	Finished Goods Inventory	3,390	14.5%	227	3,617
4	C-15.01.20xy-A	Work-in-Progress Inventory	11,400	48.8%	762	12,162
5	Total		€23,340	100.0%	€1,560	€24,900
6		Overhead incurred	24,900			
7		Overhead variance	€1,560	Under-applied		
8					= 0.366 x 1,560	

Periodic Operating Income

To illustrate the traditional form of a cost of goods completed and sold statement, we rearrange the production and sales items in Exhibit 10.10, as shown in Exhibit 10.11.

Exhibit 10.11 **Statements of Income and Cost of Goods Manufactured and Cost of Sales**

	E F G H	I	J	K	L
29	**Creazioni di Vetro**				
30	**Statement of Income**				
31	**For the Month of January**				Ex 10-9
32	Sales revenue	€38,000			=C10
33	Less: Cost of sales (see following)	27,810			
34	Gross margin	€10,190			
35	Less: Selling and administrative expenses	4,000			=K12
36	Operating income	€6,190			
37					
38	**Schedule of Cost of Goods Completed and Cost of Sales**				
39	**For the Month of January**				
40	Opening Work-in-progress inventory, 1 January			€11,700	=F3
41	Manufacturing costs during the month:				
42	Direct material:				
43	Opening Raw material inventory, 1 January	€5,000			=D3
44	Add: Purchases	25,000			=D4
45	Raw material available for use	€30,000			
46	Less: Closing Raw material inventory	22,400			=D13
47	Total raw material used	€7,600			
48	Less: Indirect material used	200			=E5
49	Direct material used in production		€7,400		
50	Direct labour used in production		16,413		=F6
51	Manufacturing overhead applied		23,340		=F8
52	Total manufacturing costs incurred			47,153	
53	Total cost of Work-in-progress			€58,853	
54	Less: Closing Work-in-progress			25,400	=F13
55	Cost of goods completed			€33,453	
56	Add: Opening Finished goods inventory January 1			0	=G3
57	Less: Closing Finished goods inventory, January 1			7,203	=G13
58	Cost of sales (unadjusted)			€26,250	
59	Add: Under-applied overhead*			1,560	=-E11
60	Cost of sales (adjusted)			€27,810	
61	*CV closes under-applied or over-applied overhead to Cost of sales.				

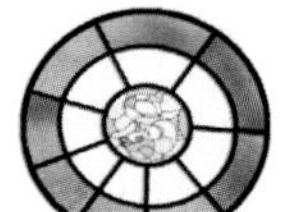

10.2 You're the Decision Maker

Tracing Cost Flows from Accounts to Statements

a. Verify that each number in Exhibit 10.11 is derived from entries shown in Exhibit 10.9.

b. What would be the adjusted Cost of sales amount in Exhibit 10.11 if the controller, Louisa Malina, judged that the manufacturing overhead variance was a material amount?

c. What would be the adjusted Cost of sales amount if the manufacturing overhead variance was *over-applied* by €4,000 for the month of January? What judgement must you make before disposing of this variance?

d. What does IAS 2 say about the proper allocation of manufacturing overhead? How might this affect reports for management? Do you agree with IAS 2? Why or why not?

(Solutions begin on p. 526.)

Job-order Costing Information and Decision Making

LO 7 Understand the use of job-order costing information for decision making

Louisa Malina, CV's controller, used the job-cost information to analyse the relative profitability of two types of jobs, stock windows and commissioned glass pieces. She made a comprehensive list of every job undertaken in the past five years, the period during which the costing system had been in place. She prepared an absorption-cost and profit table, from which two representative jobs are shown in Exhibit 10.12.

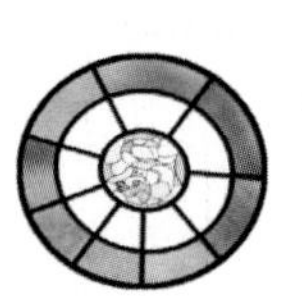

Exhibit 10.12 Comparative Jobs Costs and Profits

	A	B	C	D	E
1	Job	C-05.12.20xx-D		S-PEL-08.01.20xy	
2	Cost & Profit	Estimate	Actual	Estimate	Actual
3	Sales price	€38,000	€38,000	€400	€-
4	Units	1	1	20	20
5	Sales revenue	€38,000	€38,000	€8,000	€-
6	Direct material	6,500	6,500	1,300	1,400
7	Direct labour	7,900	8,200	2,500	2,413
8	Manufacturing OH	11,100	11,550	3,510	3,390
9	Gross margin	€12,500	€11,750	€690	n/a
10					
11	Return on sales	32.9%	30.9%	8.6%	n/a
12					
13	DL hours used	370	385	117	113
14					
15	Gross margin/DL hr	€33.78	€30.52	€5.90	n/a

The job-costing system gives CV's owners information to plan the costs of both types of new work. The analysis of job-costs showed that stock items are expected to be much less profitable than custom (commissioned) jobs. For example, the two representative jobs show that custom work generates more than three times the gross-margin return on sales (row 11) and more than five times the gross margin on each labour hour used (row 15). Moreover, custom jobs generally are relatively lower-risk jobs since a buyer already has commissioned the piece. Unfortunately, not enough commissioned work has been available during a typical year to keep the glass studio busy year-round, given its current size and talent staffing.

The Benedettis are considering whether to continue using the slow months of December and January to build an inventory of stock windows to sell in the busier spring and summer months. However, Malina's additional analysis indicated that CV would be forced to rent space in another building to store the windows inventory, to insure it, and to provide security for it. All things considered, it became apparent that inventorying stock windows might not be the best strategy. The owners concluded that the best way to increase their productivity during the slow winter months was to seek to increase their commissioned business by better advertising and by attending more professional builders' and architects conferences, which are good venues to gain exposure for their products. If they are able to increase their commissioned work, they will solve two problems simultaneously. First, they will be able to more productively employ its labour and studio resources in the December–January period. Second, they will reduce their reliance on the stock window business, thereby minimizing the effect of potentially losing that type of business to larger, mass-production competitors. This evolving strategy might not have been apparent without the information provided by CV's job-order costing system.

10.1 Research Insight

Information Technology and Job Cost Information

The information technology (IT) efforts of many organizations could focus on improving the quality of 'inside' information (e.g., improved job-cost information). Most IT improvements take advantage of declining computing costs and increasing computing speed to deliver more data to more people, but as Peter Drucker argued, IT specialists are sometimes providing the wrong 'data' and ignoring the right 'information' for today's competitive environment. To build wealth and value, today's managers need more information about external competitors, changes in markets, and profitable opportunities. The challenge for cost management and IT specialists is to understand the need for information as well as they currently understand the capability of 'technology'.

Source: Drucker (1998).

Income-reporting Effects of Alternative Product-costing Methods

LO 8
Measure, reconcile and interpret operating income using absorption and variable costing.

Operating income is a key measure used to evaluate the performance of companies and their business units. Managers watch the bottom line as they make the decisions that determine the future of their companies. The product-costing method used can significantly affect a manufacturing company's reported income by changing the timing when certain costs are recognized as expenses. This section explores three alternative product-costing methods. It begins by comparing the two traditional methods, *absorption costing* and *variable costing*. Then it examines a third method that is more recent in origin, *throughput costing*.

The most widely used product-costing method is **absorption** (or **accrual** or **full costing)**, which includes direct material, direct labour, and *both* variable and fixed manufacturing overhead in the costs of products. An alternative approach to product costing is **variable costing**, which applies direct material and direct labour costs but only variable manufacturing overhead to products.[9]

Fixed manufacturing overhead: the key to differences

The primary difference between the two methods is the timing when fixed overhead costs are recognized as expenses. Eventually, all fixed overhead cost is expensed under either absorption or variable costing, but absorption costing first assigns fixed overhead costs to products, which remain in inventories until the products are sold. Absorption costing *inventories* fixed overhead with the other product costs (i.e., direct material, direct labour and variable overhead) until the time when the products are sold. Variable costing, however, treats fixed overhead as a period expense *immediately*, as it is incurred, and does not count fixed overhead as a product cost. This difference can create large differences in periodic income between the two costing methods.

Comparison of Absorption and Variable Costing

Let us return to Exhibit 10.11, which contains CV's January operating statement of income. Louisa Malina prepared this statement using absorption costing, which she used to respond to inquiries from the company's bank and to prepare CV's income tax return.

Because absorption costing blurs the timing of outlays and expenses for fixed manufacturing overhead, Malina suspected that making the operating decisions based on absorption cost-based operating income could mislead the owners about the company's profitability and adversely affect their decision making about products and uses of resources.

The direct material and direct labour costs of jobs are identical using either absorption or variable costing. However, overhead costs are recorded differently. Accordingly, Malina prepared January's

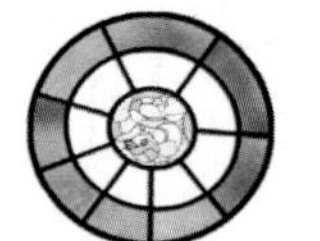

Exhibit 10.13 CV's Fixed and Variable Overhead Costs and Rates

Normal Cost and Activity	Annual	Monthly	
Variable manufacturing overhead	€96,000	€8,000	
Fixed manufacturing overhead	192,000	16,000	
Total manufacturing overhead	€286,000	€24,000	
Direct labour hours (DLH) available	9,600	600	
Variable overhead rate, per DLH	€10.00	€1000	
Fixed overhead rate, per DLH	€20.00	€2000	
Total overhead rate, per DLH	€30.00	€30.00	
Under-applied variable overhead	€1,120.00	= (800 normal hours - 776 actual hours) × €10 + €900	
Under-applied fixed overhead	€440.00	= (800 normal hours - 776 actual hours) × €20	
Total under-applied overhead	€1,560.00		

manufacturing overhead cost data in Exhibit 10.13 to support her investigation of the impacts of the two costing methods. The new data to this analysis are the estimates of the annual variable and fixed manufacturing overhead costs. For this discussion, we can be assured that Malina used an appropriate method from Chapter 3 to estimate this split from the historical data available on total manufacturing overhead and the direct-labour-hour normal capacity. Also notice that the controller has been able to split the under-applied overhead into fixed and variable components. Part of these amounts is because actual hours used were less than normal. The cause is higher spending on variable overhead than expected. (This type of analysis is covered in detail in Chapter 13.)

Malina used the actual cost data in Exhibits 10.12 and 10.13 to reconstruct the absorption cost statement of income as the left portion of Exhibit 10.14. The right portion presents the variable cost statement of income for the same period.

Examine the absorption-costing statement of incomes in Exhibit 10.14. First, notice that the direct material and direct labour recognized in Cost of sales expense and Selling expenses are the same for both methods. Second, notice that absorption costing applied fixed and variable manufacturing overhead to the job that was sold at a cost of €30/DLH, but variable costing applies only €10/DLH, which is only variable overhead. Third, the **contribution margin**, which is the difference between sales revenue and variable cost of sales that, measures the incremental profit earned toward covering fixed costs and desired profits. Fourth, variable costing expenses the entire fixed overhead amount. Finally, the considerable difference in operating income is explained by the relatively more total overhead that was expensed by variable costing.[10]

In general, if inventories increase, absorption costing will report higher operating income than variable costing. The converse also is generally true: when inventories are depleted, products that had been stored with fixed overhead attached will be expensed, and absorption costing will report lower operating profit. When inventories are constant, or minimal as in a company with JIT or lean processes the two methods will report equal or nearly equal operating profits.

Evaluation of Absorption and Variable Costing

Some managers find absorption costing to be unintuitive and confusing and prefer to use variable costing for internal income reporting. Variable costing dovetails much more closely than absorption costing with any operational analyses that require a separation between fixed and variable costs.

Product-cost information

Product costs computed under absorption costing could be more accurate measures of the full uses of production resources than those computed under variable costing because absorption costs recognize and contain fixed, indirect production costs. However, just as the overall average cost could misstate product costs by allocating indirect production costs, absorption costs could misstate the

Exhibit 10.14 CV's Absorption and Variable Cost Statement of Incomes for January 20xy

Creationi di Vetro Absorption Cost Statement of Income for the Month of January, 20xy			Creationi di Vetro Variable Cost Statement of Income for the Month of January, 20xy		
Sales revenue, = 'Ex 10-12' !C3		€38,000	Sales revenue		€38,000
Less absorption cost of goods sold			Less variable cost of goods sold		
Direct material, = 'Ex 10-12' !C6		6,500	Direct material		6,500
Direct labour hours, = 'Ex 10-12' !C7		8,200	Direct labour		8,200
Fixed and variable overhead			Variable overhead		
Direct labour hours, = 'Ex 10-12' !C13	385		Direct labour hours used	385	
Normal total overhead rate. Ex 10-13	€30.00	11,550	Normal variable overhead rate	€10.00	3,850
Normal cost of goods sold		26,250	Normal cost of goods sold		18,550
Under-applied overhead, Ex. 10-13		1,560	Under-applied variable overhead		1,120
Total absorption cost of goods sold		€27,810	Total variable cost of goods sold		€19,670
Gross margin		10,190	Contribution margin		€18,330
			Less: Fixed overhead		16,000
Less: Selling expenses. Ex 10-11		4,000	Selling expenses		4,000
Operating income		€6,190	Operating income		€(1,670)
Reconcilation of Overhead Expenses					
Difference in operating incomes		€(7,860)	Variable-cost operating income is lower. Why?		
Absorption costing overhead expensed					
Fixed and variable overhead	€11,550		385 OLH × € 30/DLH		
Under-applied overhead	1,560	€13,110			
Variable costing overhead expensed					
Variable overhead	€3,850		385 OLH × € 10/DLH		
Under-applied variable overhead	1,120				
Fixed overhead	16,000	€20,970			
Difference in overhead expensed		€(7,860)	Because variable costing expensed more (fixed) overhead		

use of indirect production resources. It is possible that CV's various product lines use indirect production resources to a different degree. Absorption costing also ignores each product line's differential use of non-production resources. Thus, absorption costing actually could distort the costs to provide products and services if they represent greatly different levels of support from indirect resources. For example, CV's custom products need much more design support than stock windows, but allocations unrelated to resource usage obscure this difference.

Pricing decisions

Many managers prefer to use absorption-costing data in cost-based pricing decisions. They argue that fixed manufacturing overhead is a necessary cost incurred in the production process. To exclude this fixed cost from the product cost of a product, as variable costing does, is to understate the product's full cost. For this reason, many companies that use cost-based pricing base their prices on absorption-costing data. Proponents of variable costing counter that a product's variable cost provides a better basis for making the pricing decision. They note that any price above a product's variable cost makes a positive contribution to covering fixed cost and profit.

Use of both costing methods

ERP accounting systems make it straightforward for larger companies to prepare statement of incomes under both absorption and variable costing. Since absorption-costing statements are required for external reporting, managers need to review the effects of their decisions on financial reports to outsiders, yet it is difficult to deny the greater benefit of variable-costing income reporting as a method for supporting operational analyses. Preparation of both absorption-costing and variable-costing data for internal management use is perhaps the best solution for firms that have the technology to do so, as long as managers use each set of statements properly.

Unit costs under absorption costing can be misleading for decision making

When fixed manufacturing costs are allocated to each unit, as they are under absorption costing, the *fixed* costs could appear as though they are *variable*. For example, allocating some of the factory insurance cost to each unit of product results in including insurance as part of the 'unit cost' even though the total insurance cost does not increase with the manufacture of another unit of product. Therefore, cost data that include unitized fixed costs could be misleading if used incorrectly. Later chapters cover this issue in detail.

Let's return to the information detailed in Exhibit 10.14. Absorption costing reflects a healthy operating profit in January for CV. However, this statement obscures the fact that a large amount of fixed overhead (€7,860) has been inventoried. When those inventoried products are sold in a future period, those fixed costs will be expensed, along with the fixed costs of other products that were produced and sold during the period. In concept, inventories could defer fixed-cost expenses indefinitely, but as a practical matter these costs will be recognized when products are eventually sold or written off. Using absorption costing, only, may obscure the necessity of using fixed, capacity-related resources productively at all times. Louisa Malina used the analysis in Exhibit 10.14 to communicate to the Benedettis that their capacity policy to maintain the labour force and keep the employees busy building stock windows in low-demand times has two effects:

1. Building low-margin stock windows exposes CV to risks of inventory obsolescence if the windows ultimately cannot be sold or must be sold at a discount.
2. Charging fixed costs to inventories just defers those costs to future periods when the stock windows eventually are sold or written off. Therefore, the current healthy profits in January overstate future profitability unless more custom work can be gained.

The Benedettis must weigh these risks against the benefits of maintaining their skilled workforce. As reported earlier, they decided that the best strategy was to replace the stock work with more profitable custom work.

Broadening Job-order Costing's Relevance to the Value Chain

CV's value chain, shown in Exhibit 10.15, includes the important business functions of research and development, design, purchasing and material handling, production, marketing, distribution, and customer service. Note that the *design* and *production* activities distinguish CV from its competitors. Nevertheless, the other functions in the value chain are also important. For example, finding the right sources of supply at the best possible prices is a key element in helping CV to be profitable. Marketing and distributing the studio's windows, doors, and other artistic pieces are increasingly more important, as just discussed. CV's owners realize that they need to expand their professional

Exhibit 10.15 CV's Value Chain

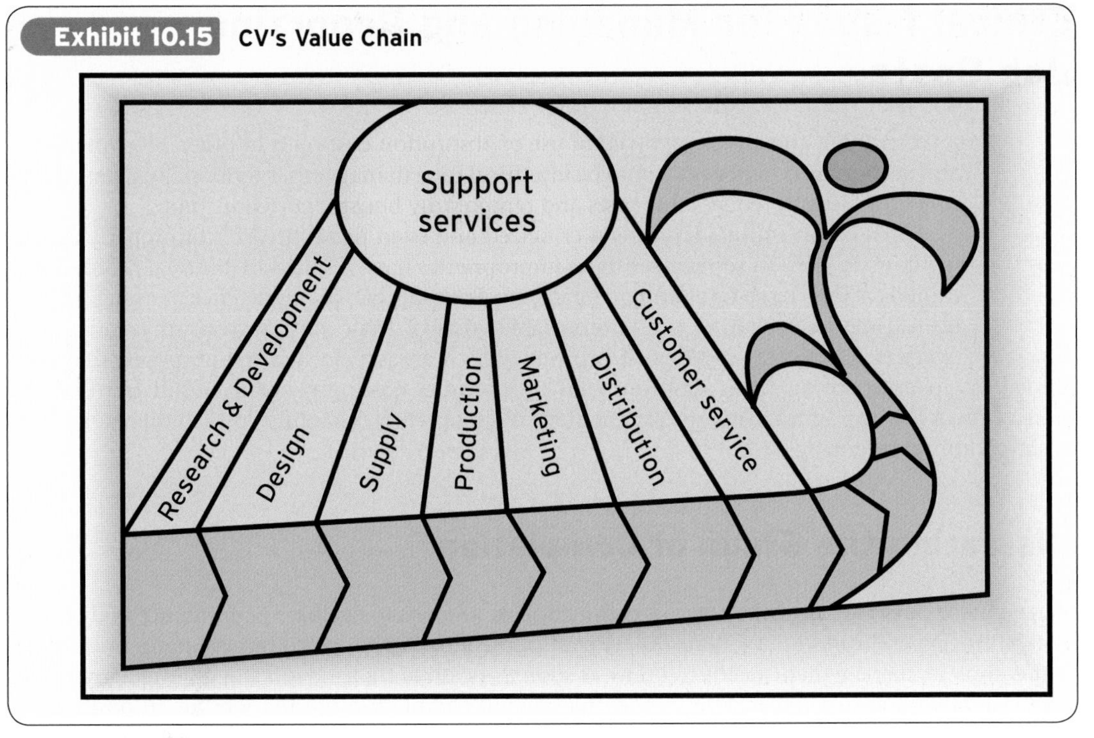

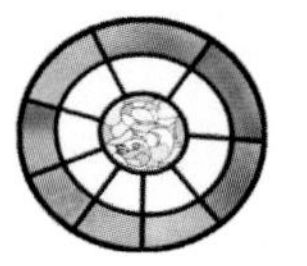

presence to enrich its distribution possibilities. Customer service assures CV's customers that any subsequent problems with the studio's glass pieces (which are exceedingly rare) or casualty damages will be attended to promptly and professionally.

Traditional product costing systems, and job-order costing systems in particular, have tended to emphasize the production activities of the value chain to the relative exclusion of the other components. Most of our discussion of CV's job-order costing system focused on the actual production costs for its stained glass pieces. Little was said about measuring or managing the costs of design, purchasing, marketing, and so forth, yet all of these functions are important contributors to the firm's costs and profitability.

What is needed to overcome this deficiency is a broader focus on *all* of the *activities* in the organization's value chain. Then a costing system can be built on those activities by measuring the costs of the resources they use and associating those costs with the values they provide to the organization. Organizations like CV might decide that it would be more efficient to re-configure or even outsource some parts of its value chain. Although traditional approaches to product costing, such as job and order costing, are important, activity-based costing and management (covered in Chapters 4 and 5) are better suited to managing the entire value chain.

Job-order Costing in Service Organizations

Job operations frequently are used in service organizations, such as architectural firms, moving companies and consulting firms. The job-order costing process is basically the same in both service and manufacturing organizations except that service firms generally use fewer direct materials than manufacturing firms do.

An architectural firm, for example, is very interested in the profitability of each job (referred to as a 'client'). Bids to obtain or retain a client typically are based on projected costs estimated using actual results for comparable jobs. Job-order costing, therefore, provides management with the information necessary to assess job profitability and to use historical cost data to estimate costs for bidding purposes. (Many firms use a more sophisticated approach, called *customer profitability analysis*, to assess the profitability of each customer or client; see Chapter 5.)

Ethical Issues for Managing and Reporting Job Costs

LO 9
Be aware of ethical considerations for managing job costs.

A word about the ethics involved in use of absorption costing is in order. Most managers and accountants believe it would be unethical for a manager to intentionally overproduce inventory just to reduce unit costs and temporarily boost reported income.

Some organizations have been criticized and even prosecuted for improperly assigning costs to jobs. In some cases these improprieties have resulted in criminal proceedings, ruined careers, large fines and prison terms. For example, major defence contractors have been caught overstating the reimbursable costs of their jobs. Several universities have overstated the costs of research projects (which are jobs for costing purposes) that were funded by government agencies. Improprieties in job-order costing generally result from one or more of the following actions: misstating the stage of completion, charging costs to the wrong jobs, or simply misrepresenting costs.

Misstating the Stage of Completion

Management needs to know the stage of completion of projects to evaluate performance and control costs. If the expenditures on a job are 90 per cent of the amount budgeted but the job is only 70 per cent complete, management needs to know as soon as possible that the job will require higher costs than estimated. Job supervisors who report the stage of completion of their jobs are in positions to affect managers' decisions based on how realistic the supervisors' estimates are. Some contracts allow for partial payments to contractors based on the percentage of the project's completion. An unethical contractor might overstate the actual percentage of completion to receive unauthorized payments.

Charging Costs to the Wrong Job

To avoid the appearance of cost overruns on a specific job, supervisors sometimes are tempted to encourage employees to charge the job's costs to other jobs that are not in danger of cost overruns. At a minimum, this practice misleads managers who rely on accurate cost information for pricing, cost control and other decisions. It also can cheat the organization or people paying for a job on a cost-plus-a-fee basis if the actual job costs based on resource usage do not total as much as claimed.

10.2 Cost Management in Practice

Fraudulent Costs in Cost-reimbursement Contracts

The scale of government contracting offers opportunities for fraudulent behaviour. Some say that the widespread use of cost-plus and cost-reimbursement contracts by governments is an open door to misrepresentations of costs of jobs, particularly when they are performed under circumstances that are difficult to observe. For example, a small US-based firm recently was successfully prosecuted for misrepresenting costs of infrastructure improvement jobs, including electrical facilities, health facilities, schools, and irrigation systems, in Afghanistan. The jobs were performed under greater-than-100 per cent cost-reimbursement contracts with the US Agency for International Development (USAID). But an investigation supported by the FBI determined that the company inflated expenses and fabricated invoices from fictitious companies. The principals of the company forfeited $3 million in proceeds and faced long prison terms and large fines.

Source: http://www.mcclatchyc.com/2010/19/100690/US-contractor-accused-of-fraud.html (accessed on 29 March 2012)

Misrepresenting the Cost of a Job

Sometimes managers know a job's correct costs but intentionally deceive a customer to obtain a higher payment. Sometimes deceiving a banker to obtain a larger loan for the job by overstating its expected cost is possible. One way to combat these potential problems is to insist on *ex post* or ongoing audits of the job's financial records to avoid such deception. Government auditors generally work on-site at defence contractors, universities and other organizations that have large government contracts.

Preventing Improprieties by Understanding Contracts

Intentional misrepresentation is not the same as agreeing to a contract that is favourable to your interests. Contracts and agreements for jobs usually result from negotiating and bargaining, and each side strives for favourable terms. Naivety in contracting could be the cause of disappointment (and learning the hard way), but lack of understanding of terms and conditions is not usually grounds to recover damages or nullify contracts.

Especially in the context of job-order costing, it is important for parties who agree to the terms for reimbursement of job costs to agree on the definitions of costs and that methods of applying costs to jobs are clearly described. For example, agreeing to reimburse a contractor for simply 'the costs of construction' is unwise without clarifying the nature and scope of eligible costs. With that liberal terminology, one would expect the contractor to interpret the costs of construction broadly. This might be acceptable to both parties, but getting a clear agreement before signing is wise. In fact, references to 'cost' as a basis for reimbursement, performance or allocations of profit should be clarified for any contract or agreement. For example, a general partner might sell limited partnerships to others who share the profits of the partnership after the general partner's costs have been covered. Without clarification about what costs are allowed to be charged to the partnership, the general partner could be tempted to allocate as many costs as possible from his or her related activities to it.

Most project contractors have learned over the years that it is far better for the job, the customer, and their reputation if:

- The contractor and the customer clearly agree on what the project's contract covers and what it does not.
- Both parties agree to all changes before the contractor executes them.
- Both parties resolve disputes amicably and without resort to legal proceedings if at all possible.

These stipulations are not always attainable, which is why contractors and sophisticated customers have capable lawyers.

Appendix 10

Throughput Costing

LO 10
Measure and understand throughput costing's effects on costs and operating income

Advocates of the *Theory of Constraints* approach to management have been advocating *throughput costing* as the best alternative to either absorption or variable costing.[11] **Throughput costing** assigns *only* out-of-pocket *spending* for direct costs as the cost of products or services. Thus, throughput costing is very similar to the cash or out-of-pocket costs of Chapter 2. Advocates of throughput costing argue that adding any other indirect, past, or committed costs to a product's accounting cost creates improper incentives to drive down the average cost per unit by making more products than can be used or sold. Since these other costs are committed and generally related to capacity, making more units with the same level of resource spending arithmetically reduces the average cost per unit and appears to make the production process more efficient. One often hears of 'spreading' fixed costs across more units as evidence of achieving economies of scale. But this is only efficient if all units of product can be sold. It is false economy if producing up to capacity only increases inventories and defers allocated costs from being recognized as expenses (or write-offs).

Throughput costing avoids the incentive to overproduce because the cost per unit depends only on out-of-pocket costs (e.g., costs of materials), not how many units are made. Costs that reflect management commitments to fixed expenditures (past or present) that reflect capacity to produce always are expensed in the period. Therefore, inventories should be small, and production should reflect demand. There is no financial reporting advantage to produce more than can be sold (except for small buffer stock concerns), because all committed costs are expensed, even more than in variable costing.[12] For example, if CV's policy is to maintain a fixed artistic and production labour force, regardless of monthly demand for stained-glass products, the cost of labour is a committed, fixed cost that is expensed, not inventoried, under throughput costing.

Louisa Malina experimented with throughput costing and decided that only direct materials qualified as a throughput cost. This reflects that the Benedettis have *committed*, at least for the time being, to provide *all* other resources (i.e., direct labour and all manufacturing-support costs included in manufacturing overhead) regardless of monthly production. Throughput costing considers all other indirect, discretionary, committed or past spending for resources to be period costs and expenses. CV's January statement of income appears as Exhibit 10.16. Notice that all costs other than the throughput cost (only direct materials in this illustration) are considered to be operating costs of the period. This is a straightforward costing system that avoids most accounting accruals, and some critics compare it to cash-basis accounting.

Note that this statement presumes that all direct labour and overhead costs that were incurred during *December* were expensed in December, when the only job sold, C-05.12.20xx-D, was started. All direct labour and overhead costs incurred in January are expensed in January. Purists might object that CV built its stock-window products in January, so the inventoried direct material costs should be expensed despite the fact that they are completed and apparently saleable. Nonetheless, Malina's throughput analysis still indicates the very high financial cost associated with building inventory in excess of demand. This is unavoidable when the company builds longer-term, custom projects that span several months, but building low-margin stock windows to keep the workforce employed is a questionable strategy.

Exhibit 10.16 CV's Throughput Costing Statement of Income

Creazioni di Vetro Throughput Cost Statement of Income For the Month of January, 20xy	
Sales revenue	€38,000
Less throughput cost of goods sold	
Direct material	6,500
Throughput margin	31,500
Period expenses	
Direct labour, Ex 10-9. F6	16,413
Manufacturing overhead. Ex 10-9, SUM(ES:E7)	24,900
Selling expenses	4,000
Total period expenses	45,313
Operating income	€(13,313)

Chapter Summary

Accounting and finance personnel work closely with their colleagues to design cost management systems that support their organization's decision making. An important consideration is the design of the *product-costing system*, which accumulates the costs of a production process and assigns them to the products that constitute the organization's output. The most common types of product-costing systems include job-order costing, process costing (a topic of Chapter 11) and operation costing.

Job-order costing, which is the topic of this chapter, treats each individual job as a unit of output and assigns costs to it as resources are used. A *job* may be a single, unique product or a relatively small batch of identical or very similar products. Job-order costing is useful for identifying types of jobs likely to be most profitable, providing data to predict costs of future jobs, managing the costs of current jobs, renegotiating job contracts, and financial reporting of actual results of the period's operations.

Companies using job-order costing employ several accounts (or files) to track the costs of resources used on jobs. These accounts are the sources of data for product costing, estimating costs of future jobs, and financial reporting for both internal and external purposes. The Work-in-progress inventory account collects all costs of resources used on various jobs that have not been completed. Each job also has its own job-cost record on which the costs of all production-related resources used on that job to date are reported. Finished goods inventory records the costs of jobs that have been completed but are not yet sold.

Companies often use *predetermined overhead rates* to assign manufacturing overhead to individual jobs. The predetermined overhead rate is usually established before the year in which it is to be used by dividing estimated overhead costs by a measure of the normal level of production activity. Predetermined overhead rates thus normalize (i.e., smooth out) the application of manufacturing overhead to jobs. The resulting product costs are called 'normal costs', and this method of applying overhead is called 'normal costing'.

The difference between the actual and the applied manufacturing overhead amounts is the *overhead variance* referred to as *over-applied* or *under-applied overhead*. At year-end, the manufacturing overhead variance is usually charged entirely to Cost of sales, if it is immaterial or prorated (i.e., allocated) to Work-in-progress inventory, Finished goods inventory, and cost of Sales if it is a material amount.

Job-order costing systems are indispensable for reporting and controlling costs of jobs, particularly when the jobs are numerous and complex. Job-order costing systems also provide valuable information as feedback for decision making and planning future operations.

Absorption and variable costing are two of the alternative product-costing methods, which differ in their treatment of fixed manufacturing overhead. *Absorption* (or *accrual) costing* applies variable and *fixed* overhead as a product cost. Therefore, the applied fixed overhead cost remains in inventory until the products are sold. *Variable costing* applies only variable costs to products and assigns fixed overhead as a period cost that is expensed during the period when it is incurred. *Absorption costing* is required for external reporting and tax purposes. However, variable costing is more consistent with operational decision making, which benefits from a separation of fixed and variable costs. Another costing alternative is *throughput costing*, in which only out-of-pocket costs required for production are inventoried as product costs. They argue that throughput costing reduces the incentive for management to produce excess inventory simply for the purpose of spreading committed costs across a larger number of units produced.

Key Terms

For each term's definition, refer to the indicated page, or turn to the glossary at the end of the text.

absorption (accrual, full) costing,	495	operation costing,	480
applied overhead,	490	over-applied overhead,	491
contribution margin,	496	overhead variance,	491
job-cost record (or file, card, sheet),	482	predetermined overhead rate,	488
job-order costing,	479	process costing,	480
material requisition form,	485	product-costing system,	479
normal costing system,	488	throughput costing,	502
normal production capacity,	488	variable costing,	495

Review Questions are mostly written at a ***basic*** *level; Critical Analysis questions and Exercises are* ***intermediate****, and Problems and Cases are* ***advanced****.*

Review Questions

10.1 What is a product-costing system and what does it do?

10.2 What are the distinguishing features of the following three product-costing methods: (a) job-order costing, (b) process costing, and (c) operation costing? Give an example of a product that would be accounted for by each method.

10.3 Describe the basic cost-flow model as an algebraic equation.

10.4 What is different about work in progress, finished goods and cost of sales?

10.5 Explain how to measure the costs of a product using normal costing.

10.6 How can overhead be over- or under-applied?

10.7 Does it matter how the overhead variance is disposed? Explain.

10.8 Describe several ways in which job-order costing can be misused.

10.9 Why is the use of direct labour as a cost driver for manufacturing overhead declining?

10.10 Explain the benefits of using a predetermined overhead rate instead of an actual overhead rate.

10.11 **(Appendix 10)** Timing is the key in distinguishing between absorption, variable and throughput costing. Explain this statement.

10.12 **(Appendix 10)** When inventory increases, is absorption costing or variable costing income higher? Why?

10.13 **(Appendix 10)** Do throughput, variable and absorption costing result in significantly different income measures in a JIT setting? Why?

Critical Analysis

10.14 Would a dentist, an architect, a landscaper and a lawyer use job-order costing or process costing? Explain.

10.15 An employee of Doughties Foods overstated inventories to make periodic profits higher. Using the basic cost-flow model, explain how overstating inventories could increase profits. If the employee did this a second and a third time, use the basic cost-flow model to show what the effect would be. How could this misrepresentation be detected?

10.16 Interview the manager of a construction company (for example, a company that does house construction, remodelling, landscaping, or street or highway construction) about how it bids on prospective jobs. Does it use cost information from former jobs similar to prospective ones, for example? Does it have a specialist in cost estimation to project the costs of prospective jobs? Write a report to your instructor summarizing the results of your interview.

10.17 Interview the manager of a campus print shop or a print shop in the local area about how the company bids on prospective jobs. Does it use cost information from former jobs similar to prospective ones, for example? Does it have a specialist in cost estimation to project costs of prospective jobs? Write a report to your instructor summarizing the results of your interview.

10.18 A co-worker states, 'I don't know why we spent so much money on that new job-costing system. I can do everything we need on a simple spreadsheet. If the CFO had listened to me, we could have saved a lot of money.' Would it have been desirable to follow your co-worker's advice? Why or why not?

10.19 Your manager tries to persuade you that all of the overhead variance should be charged to Cost of sales. This is appealing to you since you have hundreds of jobs and many overhead accounts to reconcile, and this is the least fun part of your job. Why should you consider this argument with caution?

10.20 How might job-order costing for a homebuilder be similar to and differ from that used by a consulting firm?

10.21 A government contractor had a contract with **NASA** to build a space shuttle. Under this contract, all costs of development and construction are to be reimbursed and the contractor is to be guaranteed a specific profit. At the same time, the contractor had a fixed-fee contract with the **US Air Force** to build fighter planes, which limited total reimbursement to the contractor to a fixed amount. The Air Force contract had a cost overrun that the contractor transferred to the NASA contract. Explain how this might have been accomplished and why the contractor might have thought it was desirable.

10.22 Motion picture contracts often offer some participants residual profits, which are shares of profits computed after all costs of production have been covered. Sometimes blockbuster movies never pay residual profits because they do not fully recover their costs, which could include upfront payments to movie stars and producers. If you sold your novel to a producer in exchange for residual profits that never materialized, yet the stars and producers made millions of dollars, is there anything wrong or unethical about this?

10.23 **(Appendix 10)** Explain how making more products than can be sold in a period can increase the organization's operating income. Is this a sustainable tactic to increase operating income? Would this happen in a service company, or is it an issue only in manufacturing companies? Explain.

10.24 **(Appendix 10)** In general, how would you expect a manufacturing company's statement of financial position at any particular date to be different under absorption and variable costing?

Exercises

Exercise 10.25 [LO 2] Basic Cost-flow Model

A small building-supply company, Excel Lumber, experienced the following events during the year:

- Incurred €250,000 in selling costs.
- Purchased €820,000 of building material.
- Paid €20,000 for vehicles and transportation resources.
- Incurred €400,000 of general and administrative costs.
- Took a periodic inventory at year-end and learned that building material costing €270,000 was on hand. This compared with a beginning inventory of €300,000 on 1 January.
- Determined that sales revenue during the year was €2,000,000.

All costs incurred were added to the appropriate accounts. All sales were for cash.

Required

Give the amounts for the following items in Excel Lumber's Building material inventory account:

a. Opening balance (OB).
b. Transfers in (TI).
c. Closing balance (CB).
d. Transfers out (TO).

Exercise 10.26 [LO 2] Basic Cost-flow Model

Fill in the missing items for the following inventories:

	(A)	(B)	(C)
Opening balance	€136,000	€56,800	€312,000
Closing balance	?	49,600	256,000
Transferred in	128,000	?	560,000
Transferred out	152,000	176,000	?
	(D)	**(E)**	**(F)**
Opening balance	€34,000	€14,200	€78,000
Closing balance	?	12,400	64,000
Transferred in	32,000	?	140,000
Transferred out	38,000	44,000	?

Exercise 10.27 [LO 2, 3] Basic Cost-flow Model

The following spreadsheet represents data from a division of Penumbra Fabricación SA's manufacturing records. Fill in the cells that are missing data with the most likely entries. Note that each row must balance, and each permanent account (non-italicized) should have a beginning and a closing balance. Be prepared to explain the meaning of each entry.

Penumbra Fabricaión SA						
Transaction	Raw Mat'ls Inven	*Manufacturing Overhead*	WIP Inven.	FG Inven.	*Cost of Sales*	*Entries to Miscellaneous Accounts*
OB			**9,000**			
1	27,000					(27,000)
2	(31,500)					
3			25,500			(25,500)
4						
5			(87,900)			
6				(123,000)	123,000	
7						
					(123,000)	
CB	**11,250**		**14,550**			n/a

Exercise 10.28 [LO 2-5] Assignment of Costs to Jobs

Ravenna LegnoDuro SpA, a custom manufacturer of furniture, uses job-order costing. The following transactions to support a job for a custom meeting room set – a large table plus 16 chairs – occurred in January:

a. Purchased €17,000 of raw materials on account.
b. Issued €500 of supplies from Raw material inventory.
c. Paid for the raw material purchased in transaction (a).
d. Issued €8,500 in raw material to the production department.
e. Incurred production labour costs of €12,500, which were charged to Wages Payable.
f. Paid €23,250 cash for utilities, power, equipment maintenance and miscellaneous items for the manufacturing plant.

g. Applied overhead on the basis of 185 per cent of €8,500 in material costs.
h. Recognized depreciation on manufacturing property, plant and equipment of €6,250.

Required

Prepare entries to record these transactions in the following spreadsheet. Ignore beginning and ending account balances.

	Assets								Liabilities		Equities
Transaction	Cash	Accounts receivable	Raw materials inventory	Manufacturing overhead	WIP inventory	FG inventory	Plant, property, & equipment	Accumulated depreciation	Wages payable	Accounts payable	Owner's equity
OB											
a											
b											
c											
d											
e											
f											
g											
h											
CB											

Exercise 10.29 [LO 2-5] Assignment of Costs to Jobs

Refer to the data in Exercise 10.28. The following balances appeared in the accounts of Ravenna LegnoDuro SpA for January before closing temporary accounts. During January, €32,925 was transferred from Finished goods inventory to Cost of sales.

	Opening	Closing
Material inventory	€18,525	
Work-in-progress inventory	4,125	
Finished goods inventory	20,750	€17,900

Required

Complete the entries in the spreadsheet to show the flow of costs during January from Raw material inventory purchases through cost of sales.

Exercise 10.30 [LO 2-5] Costs Traced to Jobs

Partially completed entries and additional information for Triad NV for the month of May follow:

Triad NV						
Transaction	Raw Mat'ls Inven.	Manufacturing Overhead	WIP Inven.	FG Inven.	Cost of Sales	Entries to Miscellaneous Accounts
OB	**2,000**		**4,000**	**6,000**		
1	8,000					
2						

3{DL)			6,000			
4				12,000		
5				(8,000)		
G		5,200				
CB						

Additional Information

- Labour wage rate was €24 per hour.
- Overhead is applied at 80 per cent of direct material cost.
- During the month, sales revenue was €17,500, and selling and administrative costs were €2,900.

Required

a. What was the amount of direct material issued to production during May?
b. What was the amount of manufacturing overhead applied to production during May?
c. What was the cost of products completed during May?
d. What was the balance of the Work-in-Progress inventory account at the end of May?
e. What was the manufacturing overhead variance during May?
f. What was the operating profit for May?

Exercise 10.31 [LO 3-5] Predetermined Cost-driver Rate

Maritza SA, located in Buenos Aires, manufactures cutlery. Management estimates manufacturing overhead to be ARS 44,000 and direct labour costs to be ARS 80,000 for year 1. The actual manufacturing labour costs were ARS 20,000 for job 1, ARS 30,000 for job 2, and ARS 40,000 for job 3 during year 20xy; the actual manufacturing overhead was ARS 49,000. Manufacturing overhead is applied to jobs on the basis of direct labour costs using a predetermined rate. (ARS is the currency code for Argentina's peso, although the $ is often used.)

Required

a. How much manufacturing overhead was assigned to each job during the year 20xy?
b. What was the manufacturing overhead variance for the year 20xy?

Exercise 10.32 [LO 3, 5] Overhead Application Using a Predetermined Rate

Paige Impression SCS uses a job-order costing system. The following transfers in and transfers out appeared in the Work-in-Progress account for May:

Description	Transfers In	Transfers Out
May 1	Balance	€5,000
Entire month	Direct material	30,000

Entire month	Direct labour	20,000
Entire month	Factory overhead	16,000
Entire month	To finished goods	€60,000

Paige Impression SCS applies overhead to production at a predetermined rate of 80 per cent based on direct labour cost. Job 75, the only job still in progress at the end of May, has been charged with direct labour of €2,500.

Required

What was the cost of direct material charged to job 75?

[CPA adapted]

Exercise 10.33 [LO 3, 5, 6] Overhead Variance Calculation

Jay Furniture Co. uses a predetermined cost-driver rate based on direct labour hours. For October, its budgeted overhead was $900,000 based on budgeted activity of 100,000 direct labour hours. Actual overhead amounted to $980,000 with actual direct labour hours totalling 110,000.

Required

a. Build a spreadsheet to compute the amount that overhead was over-applied or under-applied.
b. Should this variance be closed to Cost of sales? Explain.

[CPA adapted]

Exercise 10.34 [LO 3, 5, 6] Under- or Over-applied Overhead Allocated

Required

a. Refer to the information in the preceding exercise. Allocate the overhead variance as follows:

Work-in-progress inventory	10%
Finished goods inventory	25%
Cost of sales	65%

b. Restate the affected account balances for the allocated overhead variance amounts.

Exercise 10.35 [LO 3, 5] Predetermined Overhead Rate

Melodious Ltd manufactures one product and accounts for costs using a job-order costing system. You have obtained the following information from the company's books and records for the year ended 31 December, year 1:

- Total manufacturing cost during last year was £500,000 based on actual direct material, actual direct labour and manufacturing overhead applied on the basis of actual direct labour dollars.
- Manufacturing overhead was applied to work in progress at 75 per cent of direct labour dollars. Applied manufacturing overhead for the year was 33 per cent of the total manufacturing cost during the year.

Required

Compute actual direct material, actual direct labour and applied manufacturing overhead. (*Hint:* The total of these costs is £500,000.)

Exercise 10.36 [LO 3, 5, 6] Job Costs for a Service Organization

At the beginning of the month, Cuisine Design SCS had two jobs in progress that had the following costs assigned from previous months:

Job No.	Direct labour	Applied overhead
X-10	€1,280	?
Y-12	840	?

During the month, jobs X-10 and Y-12 were completed but not billed to customers. The completion costs for X-10 required €1,400 in direct labour. For Y-12, €4,000 in direct labour was used.

During the month, a new job, Z-14, was started but not finished; it was the only new job. Total direct labour costs for all jobs amounted to €8,240 for the month. Overhead in this company refers to the cost of work that is not directly traced to particular jobs, including copying, printing and travel costs to meet with clients. Overhead is applied at a rate of 50 per cent of direct labour costs for this and previous periods. Actual overhead for the month was €3,900.

Required

Build a spreadsheet to complete requirements (a)–(c).

a. What are the costs of jobs X-10 and Y-12 at (1) the beginning of the month and (2) when completed?
b. What is the cost of job Z-14 at the end of the month?
c. How much was the manufacturing overhead variance for the month?

Exercise 10.37 [LO 3, 5, 8] Straightforward Exercise on Absorption Versus Variable Costing

Haninge Ketchup Company produces ketchup, which it sells exclusively to fast-food restaurants in Sweden in 20-litre containers, which sell for kr112 each and have the following variable costs:

Direct material	kr35
Direct labour	14
Variable overhead	21

Normal fixed overhead in 20x0 was kr2,100,000. Actual production of 20-litre containers totalled 150,000, of which 125,000 were sold. The company incurred the following selling and administrative expenses:

Fixed	kr350,000 for the year
Variable	kr7 per container sold

Required

Build a spreadsheet to complete requirements (a)–(c).

a. Compute the standard accrual product cost per container of ketchup under (1) absorption costing and (2) variable costing.
b. Prepare a statement of income for 20x0 using (1) absorption costing and (2) variable costing.
c. Reconcile the income reported under the two methods.

Exercise 10.38 [LO 3, 5, 8] Comparison of Variable and Absorption Costing

The following questions are based on Bennett's Pickles and Chutneys Ltd. The company's gourmet pickles are sold to restaurants for £12 per unit (one jar). Of the 100,000 units produced, 80,000 were sold during year 1; all ending inventory was in Finished goods inventory. The company had no inventory at the beginning of the year.

Direct material (unit-level or variable cost)	£220,000
Direct labour (unit-level or variable cost)	170,000
Manufacturing overhead (unit-level or variable cost)	90,000
Manufacturing overhead (facility-level or fixed cost).	240,000
Selling and administrative (unit-level or variable cost)	80,000
Selling and administrative (facility-level or fixed cost)	128,000

Required

a. In presenting inventory on the statement of financial position at 31 December, what is the unit cost under absorption costing?
b. In presenting inventory on a variable-costing statement of financial position, what is the unit cost?
c. What is the operating profit using variable costing?
d. What is the operating profit using absorption costing?
e. What is the cost of the ending inventory using absorption costing?
f. What is the cost of the ending inventory under variable costing?

[CPA adapted]

Exercise 10.39 [LO 8] Difference in Income Under Absorption and Variable Costing

Hoffmann Lawn Equipment Company manufactures lawn mowers with a unit variable cost of €350. The mowers sell for €630 each. Budgeted fixed manufacturing overhead for the most recent year was €2,200,000. Planned production and actual production for the year were the same.

Required

Under each of the following conditions, state (a) whether income is higher under variable or absorption costing and (b) the amount of the difference in reported income under the two methods. Treat each condition as an independent case.

1. Production	11,000 units
Sales	9,000 units
2. Production	10,000 units
Sales	10,000 units
3. Production	20,000 units
Sales	23,000 units

Exercise 10.40 [LO 9] (Appendix 10) Throughput Costing

The following data pertain to Javier Tile Company. Compute throughput product cost of sales, throughput and operating income from the following data for each month.

	Month 1	Month 2	Month 3
Beginning inventory, in units	0	0	100
Units produced	500	600	400
Units sold	500	500	500
Sales	€50,000	€50,000	€50,000
Material cost	10,000	12,000	8,000
Direct conversion cost used	12,000	14,400	9,600
Indirect conversion cost	8,000	5,600	10,400
Indirect operating cost	16,000	16,000	16,000

Exercise 10.41 [LO 8] Variable Costing

Refer to the data in Exercise 10.40. Compute variable cost of sales, contribution margin and operating income. Why is operating income different from one month to the next?

Exercise 10.42 [LO 8] Absorption Costing

Refer to the data in Exercise 10.40. Compute absorption cost of sales, gross margin and operating income. Why is operating income different from one month to the next?

Exercise 10.43 [LO 8] Comparison of Income Amounts Under Absorption and Variable Costing

Heligdom Security Company sells a security system keypad for €400 per unit. This product has the following unit costs.

Direct material	€164.00
Direct labour	70.00
Manufacturing overhead (based on planned production of 5,000 units):	
Variable	31.20
Fixed	28.00
Selling and administrative costs (based on 6,500 units sold):	
Variable	20.80
Fixed	14.00

This year, 1,500 units were in beginning Finished goods inventory, 5,000 units were produced, and 6,500 units were sold. The beginning inventory was valued at €266 per unit using variable costing and at €294 per unit using absorption costing. There was no beginning or ending Work-in-progress inventory.

Required

a. Prepare a statement of income for the year using variable costing and a contribution-margin format.
b. Would reported operating profits be more, less, or the same if absorption costing were used? Support your conclusions with a statement of income using absorption costing.

Exercise 10.44 [LO 8, 10] (Appendix 10) Absorption, Variable and Throughput Costing

Information taken from SilviStrat Lumber Company's records for the most recent year is as follows:

Sales revenue	€1,500,000
Direct material used	290,000
Direct labour	100,000
Variable manufacturing overhead	50,000
Fixed manufacturing overhead	80,000
Variable selling and administrative costs	40,000
Fixed selling and administrative costs	20,000

Required

a. Assuming that Silvistrat Lumber Company uses variable costing, compute the product costs for the year.
b. Compute the year's product costs using absorption costing.
c. Now assume that the company uses throughput costing and has *committed* to spending for direct labour, variable overhead and fixed overhead in the amounts given in the problem. Under this scenario, compute the company's inventoriable cost for the year.

[CMA adapted]

Exercise 10.45 [LO 8, 10] (Appendix 10) Absorption, Variable and Throughput Costing

Penna Pillow Company's planned production for the year just ended was 10,000 units. This production level was achieved, but it sold only 9,000 units. Other data follow:

Sales revenue	€135,000
Direct material used	40,000
Direct labour incurred	20,000
Fixed manufacturing overhead	25,000
Variable manufacturing overhead	12,000
Fixed selling and administrative expenses	30,000
Variable selling and administrative expenses	4,500
Finished-goods inventory, 1 January	None

There were no work-in-progress inventories at the beginning or end of the year.

Required

a. What would be Penna Pillow Company's finished-goods inventory cost on 31 December under the variable-costing method?

b. Which costing method, absorption or variable costing, would show a higher operating income for the year? By what amount?

c. Suppose that Penna Pillow Company uses throughput costing, and the cost of direct material is its only unit-level cost. What would be the company's finished-goods inventory on 31 December?

[CPA adapted]

Problems

Problem 10.46 [LO 3, 6] Analysis of Overhead Using a Predetermined Rate

Northern Lights Corporation uses a job-order costing system for its production costs. A predetermined cost-driver rate based on machine hours is used to apply facility-level overhead to individual jobs. An estimate of overhead costs at different volumes was prepared for the current year as follows:

Machine hours	55,000	60,000	65,000
Unit-level overhead costs	$385,000	$420,000	$455,000
Facility-level overhead costs	216,000	216,00	216,000
Total overhead	$601,000	$636,000	$671,000

The expected volume is 60,000 machine hours for the entire year. The following information is for November, when jobs 50 and 51 were completed:

Inventories, 1 November	
Raw materials and supplies	$10,500
Work in progress (job 50	54,000
Finished goods	112,500
Purchases of raw materials and supplies	
Raw materials	$135,000
Supplies	15,000

Materials and supplies requisitioned for production		
Job 50		$45,000
Job 51		37,500
Job 52		25,500
Supplies		6,000
Subtotal		$114,000
Job	**Direct labour hours (DLH)**	**Production machine hours (MH)**
Job 50	2,000 DLH	3,500 MH
Job 51	3,000 DLH	3,000 MH
Job 52	3,500 DLH	2,000 MH
Labour costs:		
Production labour wages (all hours @ $8)		$68,000
Support labour wages (4,000 hours)		17,000
Supervisory salaries		36,000
Subtotal		$121,000
Building occupancy costs (heat, light, depreciation, etc.):		
Factory facilities		$6,500
Sales and administrative offices		2,500
Subtotal		$9,000
Factory equipment costs:		
Power		$3,900
Repairs and maintenance		1,400
Other		2,700
Subtotal		$8,000

Required

Build a spreadsheet to solve requirements (a)–(e).

a. Compute the predetermined cost-driver rate (combined unit and facility) to use to apply overhead to individual jobs during the year.
[*Note:* Without prejudice to your answer to requirement (a), assume that the predetermined cost-driver rate is $9 per machine hour. Use this amount in answering requirements (b) through (e).]
b. Compute the total cost of job 50 when it is finished.
c. Compute the overhead costs applied to job 52 during November.
d. Compute the total amount of overhead applied to jobs during November.
e. Compute the actual factory overhead incurred during November.
f. At the end of the year, the company had the following account balances:

Over-applied overhead	$1,000
Cost of sales	980,000
Work-in-progress inventory	38,000
Finished goods inventory	82,000

What is the most common treatment of the overapplied overhead, assuming that it is not material?

[CMA adapted]

Problem 10.47 [LO 3, 5, 7] Job-order Costing in a Service Organization

Fullkomna Cleaners has five employees and a president, Jón Stefánsson. Stefánsson and one of the five employees manage all selling and administrative duties. The remaining four employees work directly on operations. The firm has four service departments: dry cleaning, coin washing and drying, special cleaning and repairs. A time report is marked, and records are kept to monitor the time each employee spends working in each department. When business is slow, there is idle time, which is marked on the time record. (Some idle time is necessary because the company promises 60-minute service, and it must have reserve labour available to accommodate fluctuating peak demand periods throughout the day and the week.)

Some of the November operating data are as follows:

	Idle time	Dry cleaning	Coin washing and drying	Special cleaning	Repairs
Sales revenue		kr536.500	kr609.000	kr232.000	kr72,500
Direct labour (in hours)	25	320	80	125	90
Overhead traceable to departments:					
Cleaning compounds		kr58,000	kr29,000	kr46,400	kr0
Supplies		14,500	23,200	20,300	16,240
Electric usage		29,000	72,500	11,600	2,900
Rent		23,200	58,000	10,440	1,160

Additional information

- Each of the four employees working in the operating departments makes kr928 per hour.
- The fifth employee, who helps manage selling and administrative duties, earns kr162,400 per month, and Stefánsson earns kr243,600 per month.
- Indirect overhead (i.e., overhead that is not traceable to departments) amounted to kr59,392 and is assigned to departments based on direct labour hours used. Because of the idle hours, some overhead will not be assigned to a department.
- In addition to salaries paid, marketing costs for such items as advertising and special promotions totalled kr45,240.
- In addition to salaries, other administrative costs were kr18,560.
- All sales transactions are in cash; all other transactions are on account.

Required

Build a spreadsheet to complete this requirement.

Management wants to know whether each department is contributing to the company's profit. Prepare a statement of income for November that shows the revenue and cost of services for each department. No inventories were kept.

Problem 10.48 [LO 2, 3, 5, 7] Job Costs in a Service Organization

During January, Toulouse Consultants worked 1,000 hours for Nocando Fabrication, 300 hours for Les Voiles Inc. and 500 hours for Restaurant Originel. The firm bills clients at €80 an hour; its labour costs are €30 an hour. A total of 2,000 hours were worked in January with 200 hours not billable to clients. Overhead costs of €30,000 were incurred and assigned to clients on the basis of direct labour hours. Because 200 hours were not billable, some overhead was not assigned to jobs. Toulouse Consultants had €30,000 in selling and administrative costs. All transactions were on account.

Required

Build a spreadsheet to complete requirements (a) and (b).

a. What are the revenue and cost per client?
b. Prepare a statement of income for January.

Problem 10.49 [LO 2, 3, 5] Assignment of Costs Using Predetermined Cost-driver Rate

The following transactions occurred at Aérospatiale SA, a small defence contractor that uses job-order costing:

a. Purchased €71,600 in raw material on account.
b. Issued €2,000 in supplies (indirect material) from raw material inventory to the production department.
c. Paid for the raw material purchased in (a).
d. Issued €34,000 in raw material to the production department.
e. Incurred wage costs of €56,000 and associated fringe benefit costs of €28,000.
f. Analysed the Wages payable account and determined that 40 per cent represented production labour; 40 per cent manufacturing support (overhead) labour; and 20 per cent selling and administrative costs.
g. Paid for utilities, power, equipment maintenance and other overhead items for the manufacturing plant totalling €43,200.
h. Recognized depreciation of €21,000 on manufacturing property, plant and equipment.
i. Applied manufacturing overhead on the basis of 400 per cent of *production* labour costs.

Required

Compute the flow of costs during the period in spreadsheet format.

	Assets								Liabilties		Equities
Transaction	Cash	Accounts Receivable	Raw Materials Inventory	Manufacturing Overhead	WIP Inventory	FG inventory	Plant, Property, & Equipment	Accumulated Depreciation	Wages Payable	Accounts Payable	Owners' Equity
OB											
a											
b											
c											
d											
e											
f											
g											
h											
i											
CB											

The following balances appeared in Aérospatiale's accounts before closing temporary accounts:

	Beginning	Ending
Raw material inventory	€74,100	?
Work-in-progress inventory	16,500	?
Finished goods inventory	83,000	€66,400
Cost of sales	0	131,700

Problem 10.50 [LO 2, 3, 5, 7] Cost Estimation Using Alternative Cost-driver Rates

Refer to the information in Problem 10.49. Aérospatiale has determined that 65 per cent of its manufacturing overhead spending is related to jobs' use of material, and 35 per cent is related to jobs' use of production labour.

Required

a. Based on information in this problem and Problem 10.49, calculate cost-driver rates using actual material cost and production labour costs as possible cost-driver bases.

b. Aérospatiale is considering bidding on two jobs with the following budgeted characteristics:

Job	A	B
Direct-material cost	€40,000	€30,000
Production labour cost	20,000	30,000

Estimate the costs of these two jobs using (1) the original cost-driver rate of 400 per cent of production labour and (2) the cost-driver rates derived in requirement (a).

c. What are the possible outcomes if bids for the two jobs are based on the original cost-driver rate but resource costs are actually *used* in accordance with the new cost-driver rates?

Problem 10.51 [LO 2, 3, 5, 7] Cost-driver Rates

Yōshoku Frozen Foods Co. prepares, packages and distributes six frozen entrées in two different container sizes. It prepares the different entrées and different sizes in large batches. It uses a normal job-order costing system. Manufacturing overhead is assigned to batches by a predetermined rate on the basis of machine hours. The company incurred manufacturing overhead costs during two recent years (adjusted for changes using current prices and wage rates) as follows: (All values shown in thousands.)

	20xx	20xy
Machine hours worked	1,380,000	1,080,000
Manufacturing overhead costs incurred:		
Power	¥175.920	¥137,520
Heat and light	44,880	44,880
Support {indirect) labour	883.200	691.200
Employee benefits	331,200	259.200
Supplies	220.800	172.800
Supervision	229.200	210.000
Depreciation	634.400	634.400
Property taxes and insurance	240.400	240.400
Total manufacturing-overhead costs	¥ 2.760.000	¥ 2.390.400

Yōshoku expects to operate at a level of 1.15 million machine hours in 20xz.

Required

Using the data from the two previous years, write a report to management that shows the cost-driver rate used to assign manufacturing overhead to its products. Prepare a memo explaining whether it is advisable for Yōshoku Frozen Foods Co. to use an average cost-driver rate for all jobs.

[CMA adapted]

Problem 10.52 [LO 2-5] Transaction Entries in Job-order Costing

Møller Marine Pumps K/S manufactures bilge pumps for small boats in Denmark. It uses a job-order costing system. Normal costing is used, and manufacturing overhead is applied on the basis of machine hours. Estimated manufacturing overhead for the year is kr7,100,000, and management expects that 71,000 machine hours will be used.

Required

a. Calculate the company's predetermined overhead rate for the year.

b. Prepare a spreadsheet to record the following events, which occurred during April.

1. Purchased pump impellers from Marion Corporation for kr39,250 on account.
2. Processed requisition from the Gauge Department supervisor for 660 kilograms of clear plastic. The material was purchased at a cost of kr3.00 per kilogram.
3. Processed the Testing Department's requisition for 990 metres of electrical wire, which is considered an indirect material. The wire cost kr0.50 per metre when it was purchased.
4. Paid kr4,000 in cash on electric utility bill.
5. Incurred direct labour costs of kr375,000 in April.
6. Recorded April's insurance cost of kr9,000 for insurance on the cars driven by sales personnel. The policy had been prepaid in March.
7. Purchased metal tubing costing kr15,000 on account.
8. Made cash payment of kr8,500 on outstanding accounts payable.
9. Incurred indirect labour costs of kr105,000 during April.
10. Recorded depreciation of kr35,000 on equipment for April.
11. Finished job G22 during April at a total cost of kr5,500.
12. Used 6,900 machine hours during April.
13. Made sales on account for April of kr895,000. The April cost of sales was kr705,000.

Problem 10.53 [LO 2, 3, 5] Job costs in a Manufacturing Company

On 1 June, two jobs were in progress at Pintores Apuestos SC Details of the jobs follow:

Job No.	Direct material	Direct labour
P-20	€174	€64
P-43	32	84

Material inventory (for example, paint and sandpaper) on 1 June totalled €920, and €116 in material was purchased during the month. Indirect material of €16 was withdrawn from material inventory. On 1 June, the Finished goods inventory consisted of two jobs: P-12, costing €392, and P-26, costing €158. Both jobs were transferred to Cost of sales during the month.

Also during June, jobs P-20 and P-43 were completed. To complete job P-20 required an additional €68 in direct labour. The completion costs for job P-43 included €108 in direct material and €200 in direct labour.

Job P-45 was started during the period but was not finished. A total of €314 of direct material was used (excluding the €16 indirect material) during the period, and total direct labour costs during the month amounted to €408. Manufacturing overhead has been estimated at 150 per cent of direct labour costs, and this relationship has been the same for the past few years.

Required

Build a spreadsheet to complete this requirement:

Compute the costs of jobs P-20 and P-43 and the balances in the 30 June inventory accounts.

Problem 10.54 [LO 2, 3, 5] Incomplete Data; Job-order Costing

CDS Printas is a rapidly growing Turkish company that has not been profitable despite increases in sales. It has hired you as a consultant to find ways to improve the situation. You believe that the problem results from poor cost control and inaccurate cost estimation on jobs. To gather data for your investigation, you turn to the accounting system and find that it is almost non-existent. However, you piece together the following information for April: (monetary units shown in Turkish lira, TRY).

- Production
  1. Completed job 101.
  2. Started and completed job 102.
  3. Started job 103.

- Inventory values:
  1. Work-in-progress inventory:

31 March: Job 101	
Direct materialartr	TRY3,000
Labour (960 hours × TRY15)	14,400
30 April: Job 103	
Direct material	TRY2,400
Labour (1,040 hours × TRY15)	15,600

  2. Each job in Work-in-progress inventory was exactly 50 per cent completed as to labour h o u r s ; however, all direct material necessary to do the entire job was charged to each job as soon as it was started.
  3. There were no Raw material inventories or Finished goods inventories at either 31 March or 30 April.
- Actual manufacturing overhead was TRY28,500.
- Cost of sales (before adjustment for over- or under-applied overhead):

Job 101:	
Direct material	TRY3,000
Direct labour	?
Overhead	?
Total	TRY46,200
Job 102:	
Direct material	?
Direct labour	?
Overhead	?
Total	?

- Overhead was applied to jobs using a predetermined rate based on labour cost that has been used since the company began operations.
- All raw materials were purchased for cash and charged directly to Work-in-progress inventory when purchased. Raw material purchased in April amounted to TRY6,900.
- Direct labour costs charged to jobs in April totalled TRY48,000. All labour costs were the same per hour for April for all labourers.

Required

Write a report to management to show the following:

a. The cost elements (direct material, labour and overhead) of cost of sales before adjustment for over- or under-applied overhead for each job sold.

b. The value of each cost element (direct material, labour and overhead) for each job in work-in-progress inventory at 30 April.

c. Over- or under-applied overhead for April.

Problem 10.55 [LO 9] Job-order Costing and Ethics

Marcella Garcia, an accountant for a consulting firm, had just received the monthly cost reports for the two jobs she supervises: one for Arrow Space Inc. and one for the United States government. She immediately called her boss after reading the figures for the Arrow Space job.

'We're going to be way over budget on the Arrow Space contract,' she informed her boss. 'The job is only about three-fourths complete, but we've spent all the money that we had budgeted for the entire job.'

'You'd better watch these job costs more carefully in the future,' her boss advised. 'Meanwhile, charge the rest of the costs needed to complete the Arrow Space job to the government job. The government won't notice the extra costs. Besides, we get reimbursed for costs on the government job, so we won't lose any money because of this problem you have with the Arrow Space contract.'

Required

a. What should Garcia do?
b. Does it matter that Garcia's company is reimbursed for costs on the government contract? Explain.

Problem 10.56 [LO 7, 8] Variable-costing Operating Profit versus Absorption-costing Operating profit

Lake Yssel Fabricating Company (LYFC) employs an absorption-costing system for external reporting and internal management purposes. The latest annual statement of income follows:

Sales revenue	€465,000
Cost of sales:	
Beginning Finished goods inventory	€22,000*
Cost of goods manufactured	315,000
Ending Finished goods inventory	(86,000)†
Cost of sales	251,000
Gross	€214,000
Selling costs	83,000
Administrative costs	49,800
Operating profit before taxes	€81,200

*Includes €9,900 variable costs.
†Includes €60,200 variable costs.

Management is somewhat concerned that although LYFC is showing adequate income, it is short of cash to meet operating costs. The following information has been provided to assist management with its evaluation of the situation:

Schedule of Cost of Goods Manufactured	
Direct material:	
Beginning inventory	€16,000
Purchases	62,000
Ending inventory	(22,000)
	€56,000
Direct labour	125,100
Manufacturing overhead:	
Variable	39,400
Fixed (including depreciation of €30,000)	94,500
Cost of goods manufactured	€315,000

There are no work-in-progress inventories. Management reports that it is pleased that this year's manufacturing costs are 70 per cent variable compared to last year's costs when they were only 45 per cent variable.

Although 80 per cent of the selling costs are variable, only 40 per cent of the administrative costs are considered variable. The company uses the first-in, first-out (FIFO) inventory method.

Required

Build a spreadsheet to solve (a).

a. Prepare a variable-costing statement of income for the year.
b. Write a short report to management that explains why the company might be experiencing a cash-flow shortage despite the adequate income shown in its absorption-costing statement of income.

Problem 10.57 [LO 7, 8] Variable versus Absorption Costing; JIT

BESTOOL AG manufactures small electric hand tools in Wendlingen, Germany. The firm uses a standard absorption-costing system for internal reporting purposes; however, the company is considering using variable costing. Data regarding BESTOOL's planned and actual operations for 20x0 follow:

	Planned activity	Actual activity
Beginning Finished goods inventory in units	35,000	35,000
Sales in units	140,000	125,000
Production in units	140,000	130,000

	Budgeted costs		
	Per unit	Total	Actual costs
Direct material	€12.00	€1,680,000	€1,560,000
Direct labour	9.00	1,260,000	1,170,000
Variable manufacturing overhead	4.00	560,000	520,000
Fixed manufacturing overhead	5.00	700,000	715,000
Variable selling expenses	8.00	1,120,000	1,000,000
Fixed selling expenses	7.00	980,000	980,000
Variable administrative expenses	2.00	280,000	250,000
Fixed administrative expenses	3.00	420,000	425,000
Total	€ 50.00	€7,000,000	€6,620,000

The budgeted per-unit cost figures were based on BESTOOL producing and selling 140,000 units in 20x0. BESTOOL uses a predetermined overhead rate for applying manufacturing overhead to its product. A total manufacturing-overhead rate of €9 per unit was employed for absorption-costing purposes in 20x0. Any over-applied or under-applied manufacturing overhead is closed to the Cost of sales account at the end of the year. The 20x0 beginning Finished goods inventory for absorption-costing purposes was valued at the prior year's budgeted unit manufacturing cost, which was the same as the 20x0 budgeted unit manufacturing cost. There are no Work-in-progress inventories at either the beginning or the end of the year. The planned and actual unit selling price for 20x0 was €75 per unit.

Required

Was BESTOOL's 20x0 income higher under absorption costing or variable costing? Why? Compute the following amounts.

a. The value of BESTOOL's 20x0 ending Finished goods inventory under absorption costing.
b. The value of BESTOOL's 20x0 ending Finished goods inventory under variable costing.
c. The difference between BESTOOL's 20x0 reported income calculated under absorption costing and calculated under variable costing.

d. Suppose that BESTOOL had introduced a JIT production and inventory-management system at the beginning of 20x0.
   1. What would likely be different about the scenario as described in the problem?
   2. Would reported income under variable and absorption costing differ by the magnitude you found in requirement (c)? Explain.

[CMA adapted]

Problem 10.58 [LO 2, 3, 4, 8] Comparison of Absorption and Variable Costing; Actual Costing

Precision Toner Company (PTC) manufactures toner used in photocopy machines. The company's product is sold by the jug at €60 per unit. PTC uses an actual costing system, which means that the actual costs of direct material, direct labour and manufacturing overhead are entered into Work-in-progress inventory. The actual application rate for manufacturing overhead is computed each year; actual manufacturing overhead is divided by actual production (in units) to compute the application rate. Information for PTC's first two years of operations is as follows:

	Year 1	Year 2
Sales (in units)	2,500	2,500
Production (in units)	3,000	2,000
Production costs:		
Variable manufacturing costs	€21,000	€14,000
Fixed manufacturing overhead	42,000	42,000
Selling and administrative costs:		
Variable	25,000	25,000
Fixed	20,000	20,000

Precision Toner Company had no beginning or ending Work-in-progress inventories for either year.

Required

a. Prepare operating statements of income for both years based on absorption costing.
b. Prepare operating statements of income for both years based on variable costing.
c. Prepare a numerical reconciliation of the difference in income reported under the two costing methods used in requirements (a) and (b).
d. Reconcile PTC's income reported under absorption and variable costing, during each year, by comparing the following two amounts on each statement of income.
- Cost of sales
- Fixed cost (expensed as a period expense).

e. What was PTC's total income across both years under absorption costing and under variable costing? Comment on this result.

Problem 10.59 [LO 6-8] Comparison of Variable and Absorption Costing

The following questions are based on Paqui Deben SC, which produces Spanish leather belts that sell for €35 per unit. Of the 40,000 units produced, 30,000 were sold during the year. All ending inventory was in Finished goods inventory. The firm had no inventory at the beginning of the year.

Direct material (unit-level cost)	€120,000
Direct labour (unit-level cost)	200,000
Factory overhead (unit-level cost)	100,000
Factory overhead (capacity cost)	300,000
Selling and administrative (unit-level cost)	80,000
Selling and administrative (capacity cost)	128,000

Required

a. In presenting inventory on the statement of financial position at 31 December, what is the unit cost under absorption costing?
b. In presenting inventory on a variable-costing statement of financial position, what is the unit cost?
c. What is the operating profit using variable costing?
d. What is the operating profit using absorption costing?
e. What is the ending inventory (euro amount) using absorption costing?
f. What is the ending inventory (euro amount) under variable costing?

[CPA adapted]

Problem 10.60 [LO 6, 7, 8, 10] Absorption, Variable, and Throughput Costing (Appendix 10)

Jordin & Byrd Inc., which uses throughput costing, just completed its first year of operations. Planned and actual production equalled 10,000 units, and sales totalled 9,600 units at $80 per unit. Cost data for the year are as follows:

Direct material (per unit)	$12
Conversion cost:	
Direct labour	45,000
Variable manufacturing overhead	65,000
Fixed manufacturing overhead	220,000
Selling and administrative costs:	
Variable (per unit).	8
Fixed	118,000

The company classifies only direct material as a throughput cost.

Required

a. Compute the company's total cost for the year assuming that (1) variable manufacturing costs are driven by the number of units produced and (2) variable selling and administrative costs are driven by the number of units sold.
b. How much of this cost would be held in year-end inventory under (1) absorption costing, (2) variable costing, and (3) throughput costing?
c. How much of the company's total cost for the year would be included as an expense on the period's statement of income under (1) absorption costing, (2) variable costing, and (3) throughput costing?
d. Prepare the company's throughput-costing statement of income.

Cases

Case 10.61 [LO 2, 3, 5, 6] Interpreting Information from a Job-order Costing System

KinderMöbel AG manufactures furnishings for children. The company uses a job-order costing system. The company's Work-in-progress inventory on 30 November consisted of the following jobs.

Job No.	Description	Units	Accumulated cost
CBS102	Cribs (Krippen)	20,000	€900,000
PLP086	Playpens (Laufgitter)	15,000	420,000
DRS114	Dressers (Kommoden)	25,000	250,000
Total			€1,570,000

The company's 30 November Finished goods inventory, which is valued using the FIFO (first-in, first-out) method, consisted of five items.

Item	Quantity and unit cost	Accumulated cost
Cribs	7,500 units @ €64 each	€480,000
Strollers	13,000 units @ €23 each	299,000
Carriages	11,200 units @ €102 each	1,142,400
Dressers	21,000 units @ €55 each	1,155,000
Playpens	19,400 units @ €35 each	679,000
Total		€3,755,400

KinderMöbel applies manufacturing overhead on the basis of direct labour hours. The company's overhead budget for the year totals €4,500,000, and the company plans to use 600,000 direct labour hours during this period. Through the first 11 months of the year, a total of 555,000 direct labour hours were worked, and total overhead amounted to €4,273,500.

At the end of November, the balance in the Raw material inventory account, which includes both raw material and purchased parts, was €668,000. Additions to inventory and requisitions from inventory during December included the following.

	Raw material	Purchased parts
Purchases	€242,000	€396,000
Requisitions:		
Job CBS102	51,000	104,000
Job PLP086	3,000	10,800
Job DRS114	124,000	87,000
Job STR077 (10,000 strollers)	62,000	81,000
Job CRG098 (5,000 carriages)	65,000	187,000

During December, the factory payroll consisted of the following:

CBS102	12,000 hr	€122,400
PLP086	4,400 hr	43,200
DRS114	19,500 hr	200,500
STR077	3,500 hr	30,000
CRG098	14,000 hr	138,000
Indirect labour	3,000 hr	29,400
Supervision		57,600
Total		€621,100

The following list shows the jobs that were completed and the unit sales for December.

Production job no.	Items	Quantity completed	Sales items	Quantity shipped
CBS102	Cribs	20,000	Cribs	17,500
PLP086	Playpens	15,000	Playpens	21,000
STR077	Strollers	10,000	Strollers	14,000
CRG098	Carriages	5,000	Dressers	18,000
			Carriages	6,000

Required

a. Explain when it is appropriate for a company to use a job-order costing system.
b. Calculate the euro balance in the Work-in-progress inventory account as of 31 December.
c. Calculate the euro amount related to the playpens in the Finished goods inventory account as of 31 December.

[CMA adapted]

Case 10.62 [LO 2, 3, 7] Motion Picture Project Accounting

Hollywood accounting can be every bit as creative as a good movie script. At least, that is what some lawyers and journalists seem to be telling us. According to news reports, the hit movie *Forrest Gump*, which won 'best picture' honours at the 1994 Academy Awards, claimed a worldwide theatrical gross of $661 million in the first 18 months after its release. That amount excludes videocassette and soundtrack revenues, nor does it include licensing fees on *Forrest Gump* products such as wristwatches, table tenis bats, and shrimp cookbooks. Yet, according to **Paramount Studios**, the film project lost $62 million on a box office gross of $382 million during its first year.

Forrest Gump is one of many hit movies to report a loss. Other losers include *Batman, Rain Man, Dick Tracy, Ghostbusters, Alien, On Golden Pond, Fatal Attraction* and *Coming to America*. Each of these motion pictures grossed well over $100 million, but in each case, costs were reportedly higher than revenues.

How can the studios be losing so much money on their most successful projects? Sometimes what is referred to as a loss is not really a loss at all. Typically, profits are calculated based on contracts between the studios and the film's 'net profit participants'. In a typical net profit participation contract, 'profit' is gross studio revenues after deducting:

- 'Negative costs' – production costs and payments to 'gross participants' (who receive a percentage of gross studio revenues).
- Studio overhead (some of which is allocated to the film as a percentage of the gross revenue).
- Promotion and distribution costs.
- Advertising overhead (which is computed as a percentage of promotion and distribution costs).
- A distribution fee paid directly to the studio.
- Interest on the unrecovered costs (losses), whether or not the film was financed with debt.

The net profit participation contract is not the same as profit or loss for the motion picture, which is accounted for as a project or job. *Net profit participation* is a contract for compensation between the studio and certain individuals.

Winston Groom, the author of *Forrest Gump*, retained an attorney to obtain a share of the profits from the film, although Paramount reported a loss. Groom was paid $350,000 for the movie rights to the book and was entitled to 3 per cent of the film's net profits. Paramount said it expected *Forrest Gump* to eventually show a profit and advanced Groom $250,000 against his net profit participation.

At issue in the lawsuit is the way the studios calculate net profit. Critics argue that some of the costs (such as the distribution fee) are not really costs at all; instead, they are studio profits disguised as costs. Overhead allocations, such as studio overhead and advertising overhead, are based on arbitrary allocations, which, some have argued, are much higher than the actual overhead costs that are assignable to the film. In addition, whether the net profit participants should lose compensation because of cost overruns is questionable; they are largely under the control of the director, the stars and the studio.

Did Paramount ever report a profit for *Forrest Gump?* That depends on how you define 'profit' and whose perspective you take. Actor Tom Hanks and director Robert Zemeckis collected more than $40 million each, including a share of the gross. But from the point of view of the net profit participants (e.g., Winston Groom), the film might never show a profit.

Required

Build a spreadsheet to complete requirements (a) and (b).

Examine the following net profit participant statement of profit and loss.

a. What amount of box office gross revenues is required before *Forrest Gump* earns a profit according to the net profit participation contract?

b. What amount of box office gross revenues is required before *Forrest Gump* earns a profit for Paramount?
c. Is Paramount's calculation of net profit fair to the net profit participants? Explain.

Net Profit Participant Statement of Profit and Loss
Forrest Gump
During its First Year of Release (in millions)

Box office gross revenues	€382
Less: Amount retained by movie theatres (50%)	191
Studio's gross revenues	€191
Less: Negative costs:	
Production costs	€66.8
Gross profit participation (director, actors, 16% of studio gross revenues)	30.6
Studio's overhead (15% of negative costs)	14.6
Promotion and distribution costs	67.2
Advertising overhead (10% of promotion and distribution cost)	6.7
Total operating costs	€247.0
Operating profit (loss)	(56)
Less: Financing costs (3% above prime on operating loss, assume amount is fixed)	6
Net profit (loss) for distribution to net profit participants	€(62)

[Adapted from Pfeiffer et al., 1997]

Solutions to You're the Decision Maker

10.1 Prepare Job-cost Records, p. 492

a.

Creazioni di Vetro

Job number:	C-05.12.20xx-D	**Batch number or name of customer:**	D
Date started:	5 December 20xx	**Date finished:**	26 January 20xy
Job name:	Custom D	**Job supervisor:**	Andretti
Quantity:	1		

Direct Materials			Direct labour					Manufacturing Overhead			
Date	Requisition Identifier	Cost	Date	Employee Identifier	Hours	Rate	Cost	Date	Direct-labour Hours	Overhead Rate per DL hour*	Cost
Dec xx	C-05.12.20xx-A	€6,500	Dec xx		100	€22.00	€2,200	Dec xx	100	€30	€3,000
			30 Jan xy		285		6,000	30 Jan xy	285	€30	€8,550
Total		€6,500	Total		385.00		€8,200	Total			€11,550

Total Job Cost

Cost item	Expected	Variance	Actual
Direct materials			€6,500
Direct labour			8,200
Manufacturing overhead			11,550
Total costs applied	€-	€-	€-

Transferred to Finished-Goods Inventory	Actual
Direct materials	€6,500
Direct labour	8,200
Manufacturing overhead	11,550
Total cost of completed job	€26,250
Cost per unit	€26,250

b.

Creazioni di Vetro			
Job number:	C-15.01.20xy-A	**Batch number or name of customer:**	C-15.01.20xy-A
Date started:	15 Jan 20xy	**Date finished:**	
Job name:	Custom A	**Job supervisor:**	
Quantity:	1		

Direct Materials			Direct labour					Manufacturing Overhead			
Date	**Requisition Identifier**	**Cost**	**Date**	**Employee Identifier**	**Hours**	**Rate**	**Cost**	**Date**	**Direct-Labour Hours**	**Overhead Rate per DL hour***	**Cost**
15 Jan xy	C-15.01.20xy-A	€6,000	30 Jan xy		380		€8,000	26 Jan xy	380	€30	€11,400
							-				
							-				
							-				
Total		€6,000	Total		380.00		€8,000	Total			€11,400

Total Job Cost			
Cost item	**Expected**	**Variance**	**Actual**
Direct materials			€6,000
Direct labour			8,000
Manufacturing overhead			11,400
Total costs applied	€-		€25,400

Transferred to Finished-Goods Inventory	**Actual**
Direct materials	
Direct labour	
Manufacturing overhead	
Total cost of completed job	
Cost per unit	

10.2 Tracing Cost Flows from Accounts to Statements, p. 493

a. The cell addresses to the right of the amounts in Exhibit 10.11 should allow you to trace these amounts to their origins in Exhibit 10.9.

b. If the overhead variance is material, it should be prorated to WIP, FG and cost of sales. From Exhibit 10.10, we see that job which was sold, C-05.12.20xx-D, would be assigned an additional €571, not the entire €1,560. Therefore, the adjusted cost of sales would equal €26,250 + €571 = €26,821.

c. First, you must judge whether the variance is material; that is, whether the disposition of the variance would make a difference in managers' decisions. If immaterial, the variance would be charged entirely to cost of sales (CGS) expense, which would be adjusted to €26,250 – €4,000 = €22,250. If material, the variance would be prorated across WIP, FG and CGS, in the manner of Exhibit 10.10. The allocation follows, assuming the same initial applications of overhead as before, which means that less overhead had been incurred:

Jab No.	Status of Job at End of the Month	Manufacturing Overhead Applied in January	Percentage of Total Overhead Applied in January	Prorated Overhead Variance to Account	Total Overhead Applied to Account
C-05.12.20xx-D	Cost of Sales	€8,550	36.6%	€(1,465)	€7,085
S-PEL-08.01.20xy	Finished Goods Inventory	3,390	14.5%	(531)	2,809
C-15.01.20xy-A	Work-in-Progress Inventory	11,400	48.8%	(1.954)	9,446
Total		€23,340	100.0%	€(4,000)	€19,340
	Overhead Incurred	19,340			
	Variance	€(4,000)	Over-applied		

In this case CGS would be adjusted to €26,250 – €1,465 = €24,785.

d. IAS 2, para. 13 states (emphasis added): 'The allocation of fixed production overheads to the costs of conversion is based on the **normal capacity** of the production facilities. Normal capacity is the production expected to be achieved on average over a number of periods or seasons under normal circumstances, taking into account the loss of capacity resulting from planned maintenance. The actual level of production may be used if it approximates normal capacity. The amount of fixed overhead allocated to each unit of production is not increased as a consequence of low production or idle plant. **Unallocated overheads are recognized as an expense in the period in which they are incurred.** In periods of **abnormally** high production, the amount of fixed overhead allocated to each unit of production is decreased so that inventories are not measured above cost. Variable production overheads are allocated to each unit of production on the basis of the actual use of the production facilities.'

This statement has some areas of ambiguity, but managers would be expected to justify choices other than 'normal'. IAS 2 presumes that overhead variances will be immaterial; otherwise normal overhead rates should have been revised for the entire period. This could raise issues of consistency across time periods, and managers that revise overhead rates frequently could be questioned about their capacity decisions. Whether you agree or not, this is the rule for financial reporting under IFRS. Internally, one might wish to use a different approach, but the costs of maintaining multiple sets of accounting numbers might not be justified.

Endnotes

1 Economists sometimes refer to the 'winner's curse', which means that if you bid low enough to get the job, you could well have bid too low to make a profit.

2 Exhibit 10.4 and the extensions that follow represent a spreadsheet approach to recording transactions. This approach models the accounting equation (Assets – Liabilities + Equities) that is the foundation of all accounting systems. Each column functions as a ledger or T-account. Positive and negative numbers in the account columns correspond to traditional debits and credits. The advantages to this approach are (a) unambiguous presentations of the effects of transactions on the various accounts and (b) assurance that every transaction and the 'real-time' financial position (or closing balances) always balance. For simplicity, CV is presented with no cash transactions or long-term debt.

3 Each column of this spreadsheet corresponds to a general ledger account wherein transactions also can be displayed as journal entries to the T-account. For example, transaction #2 could be prepared as:

	Dr.	Cr.
Manufacturing overhead	200	
WIP inventory	7,400	
Raw mat'l inventory		7,600

This summary entry would be supplemented with entries of 1,400 and 6,000 to the subsidiary accounts or job-cost sheets of the two jobs that received materials.

4 IAS 2 requires the use of normal activity levels to allocate indirect manufacturing overhead but makes exceptions for other methods if the resulting costs are substantially the same. Fixed and variable overhead may have different normal cost drivers. Also recall that other indirect, non-product (or period) costs are expensed in total during the period.

5 Often a non-zero balance (positive or negative, but usually relatively small) is left in the Manufacturing overhead account at the end of a period; its disposition is covered later in the chapter.

6 Actual overhead:

Indirect material	€200
Indirect labour	6,000
Insurance	700
Depreciation	6,000
Utilities and other overhead	12,000
Total	€24,900

7 A variance is *material* if its disposition is likely to affect the decisions made by a user of the information. Conversely, a variance is *immaterial* if it is unlikely to affect decisions. This is a professional judgement, but some organizations have rules of thumb that specify when an amount is or is not material. Observe that direct and other indirect costs also can have cost variances that must be disposed of. This topic reappears in Chapter 13.

8 This approach to allocating a variance applies to the disposition of any materially large variance that might occur.

9 Sometimes variable costing is misleadingly called direct costing, which implies tracing only direct labour and direct materials to products. Variable costing also assigns variable overhead to products.

10 The difference in operating income measures is also explained by the net amount of fixed overhead added to (or subtracted from) stock during the period by absorption costing. Fixed cost in WIP inventory increased from €20/DLH × 100 DLH (OB) to €20 × 380 DLH (EB), or an increase of €5,600. Fixed cost in FG inventory increased from 0 (OB) to €20 × 113 DLH (CB), or an increase of €2,260. The total amount of fixed overhead added to stock was, therefore, €7,860. This is the same amount as the additional expense recognized by variable costing.

11 The seminal reference is *The Goal* (Goldratt and Cox, 1984). Also see Ruhl (1996).

12 Technically, throughput-costing advocates argue that production of inventory in excess of buffer stock should also be expensed because building excess stock reflects a policy of the period to overproduce and defer expenses. This reflects a lack of trust in accountants to properly apply 'lower of cost or market' or fair-value rules to inventory.

References

Fayek, A.R. (2001) 'Activity-based job costing for integrating estimating, scheduling, and cost control', *Cost Engineering*, vol. 43, no. 8, pp. 23–32.

Goldratt, E., and J. Cox (1984) *The Goal*, North River Press, Great Barrington, MA.

Drucker, P. (1998) 'The next information revolution', *Forbes ASAP*, 24 August, available at: www.forbes.com/asap.

Pfeiffer, G., R. Capettini and G. Whittenburg (1997) 'Forrest Gump – accountant: a study of accounting in the motion picture industry', *Journal of Accounting Education*, vol. 15, no. 3, pp. 319–344.

Ruhl, J. (1996) 'An introduction to the Theory of Constraints', *Journal of Cost Management*, Summer, pp. 43–48.

CHAPTER 11

Joint Product and Process Cost Systems

Learning Objectives

After completing this chapter, you should be able to:

LO 1 Optimize profits from a joint product process by analysing the sell-or-process-further decision.

LO 2 Use the physical measures and net realizable value joint cost allocation methods for reporting the costs of main products and by-products.

LO 3 Apply a five-step costing method to allocate process costs to finished and partially completed main products.

LO 4 Apply the five-step method to allocate process costs to prepare a production report of finished goods, work-in-progress, and spoilage using weighted-average costing.

LO 5 Use the relative sales value at split-off and constant gross margin percentage methods of joint cost allocation (Appendix 11A).

LO 6 Allocate process costs to products using first-in, first-out (FIFO) process costing (Appendix 11B).

LO 7 Explain operation costing (Appendix 11C).

Suomalainen Timber Products, *or STP, is a fictional company that is based on the experiences of several real Scandinavian companies. STP has three main products: sawn timber, wood chips sold for biofuel, or wood pulp from processed wood chips sold to paper manufacturers. The three products come from a standard source – Northern European forests of softwood trees such as Scots pine and Norway spruce. STP also thins its forests, resulting in small diameter timber and branches that can be processed further as either wood chips for biofuel or wood pulp for paper. STP's customers are companies that use sawn timber for building construction, convert wood pulp into paper, or convert wood chips to biofuel. All of STP's customers can buy their lumber, pulp, or wood chips on open, international markets from the cheapest source.*

Excerpts from Comments by the CEO of Suomalainen Timber Products' to the Executive Group:

'The global economy continues to be volatile, and we should prepare for a challenging year. Our competitors are expanding to developing countries where labour costs are lower and environmental regulations are lax. We have determined to focus on improving our traditional resources in Europe. To be successful we have to be absolutely sure that we understand our costs and our capabilities. Each of us must make every production decision count. We cannot afford to waste any of our capacity on products that do not generate the most profit. In particular, we must increase our yields by reducing waste and spoilage. I do not need to tell you that the Board and industry analysts are watching us closely. We have to make smart, tough decisions. Let's get to work.'

Suomalainen Timber Products

Joint Product Processes

Many companies that use natural resources face the problem of how to use cost information to manage processes that can produce different products. Like STP, companies such as **Stora Enso** (a direct competitor in wood products), **Royal Dutch Shell** (petroleum and chemicals), **Orsu Metals Corporation** (minerals), and **ConAgra** (meat) face the challenge of making optimal decisions for their joint product processes. A **joint production process** simultaneously converts a common input into several outputs. For example, processing timber results *jointly* in sawn timber (lumber) and wood chips that can be sold directly to biofuel manufacturers or converted into paper pulp for sale to paper manufacturers. As another example, processing crude oil can result *jointly* in gasoline of various grades, kerosene, jet fuel, asphalt and/or petrochemicals. **Joint products** are the products that jointly result from processing a common input.

The Importance of Split Off

The **split-off point** is the point at which joint products appear in the production process. For example, literally at the point of a saw blade, both lumber and scrap wood appear. In refining oil, the split-off point occurs in a 'cracking' process, which produces various petroleum products simultaneously. A **final product** is one that is ready for sale without significant further processing. For example, STP sells its lumber as final products (after inspecting, grading and packaging). An **intermediate product** is a product that might require further processing before it is saleable to the ultimate consumer, either by the producer or by another processor. Thus, an intermediate product might be a final product for one company (the producer) and input for another company that will process it further.

Joint costs are the costs to operate joint-product processes including the disposal of **waste**, the cost of unrecovered resources applied to defective products that cannot be sold. Depending on the technology used, joint-product processes primarily use resources at the batch and facility levels. In most cases, companies set up the joint product process to accommodate a specific type of input or to produce a specific type of output in a batch. Thus, an oil refiner might set up the refinery (a large, facility-level resource) to process a batch of crude oil of a particular grade and to produce specific petroleum products. STP sets up its sawmills to process uniform quality logs and to produce specific sizes and grades of lumber.

In practice, assigning joint costs to the various products for *financial reporting* involves a somewhat arbitrary cost *allocation* based on the quantities of outputs or the relative profitability or sales values of the joint products. *The sequence of decisions involved in the management and reporting of joint product processes requires, first, deciding which products to produce and, only then, determining how to allocate joint process costs.* We now describe STP's joint product decision making and costing. Note that the decisions and methods described in this chapter are generally applicable to all joint product processes.

Joint Process: One Input – More Than One Output

At STP's Metsä facility in Finland, raw timber (logs) is the common input to produce the following outputs:

1. *Grade A lumber*, which is high quality with minor or no imperfections, or *Grade B lumber*, which is rougher but with no structural imperfections. Grade A has a higher sales price, but quantities are lower and trimmings are higher than when Grade B is produced. Trimmings and ungraded lumber are considered scrap wood.
2. Scrap wood and sawdust, which are processed further into *wood chips*. Forest thinning scraps are also added to sawmill scrap for processing into wood chips.[1] At one time in the distant past, scrap wood and sawdust were burned as waste, but technology improvements and pollution concerns have made these former waste products into intermediate or final products.

Based on the quality of timber inputs, prices, costs and yields, STP management decides the grade of sawn timber to produce and whether to sell wood chips to biofuel manufacturers or to process wood chips further into wood pulp for sale to paper manufacturers. The choices are shown in Exhibit 11.1.

Exhibit 11.1 Uses of Resources and Process Capacities

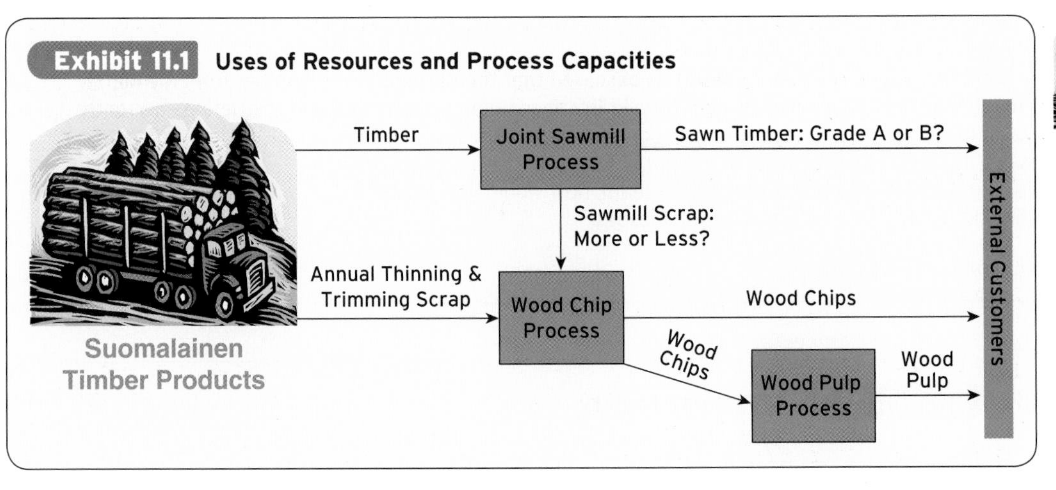

Suomalainen Timber Products

The Joint Product Decision: Which Outputs to Produce?

STP and other joint product process operators typically seek to optimize operations by selecting the quantities of final products that will maximize overall profits. In some situations, such as joint ventures among various parties that use the outputs of a process, contracts can specify the products and quantities to be made.

LO 1
Maximize profits from a joint product process by analysing the sell-or-process-further decision.

Estimation of Profits from Joint Products

Using its best estimates of sales prices and production costs, STP decides to use its mill capacity by these steps:

1. *Identify alternative sets and quantities of final products possible from the joint product process.* From joint processing of logs, STP considers two sets of sawn timber products, Grade A and Grade B Standard lumber, and wood chips as final or intermediate products.
2. *Forecast the sales price of each final product.* STP closely watches regional and international market prices and drivers of demand and prices, such as housing starts and monthly timber harvests reported by industry trade groups. The company also seeks to establish long-term customer relationships and contracts to ensure predictable sales and prices.
3. *Estimate the costs (if any) required to further process joint products into saleable products.* To produce wood chips and wood pulp, STP incurs additional costs for chipping scrap wood to uniform size and processing wood chips that might be converted to wood pulp.
4. *Choose the set of final products with the overall maximum profit.*

Exhibit 11.2 shows the data to support joint product decision making at STP's Metsä facility. Cell C4 of Exhibit 11.2 shows that the mill's monthly practical processing capacity is 11,000 cubic metres (m^3) of raw timber.

Just below the mill capacity in rows 7–10 are the forecasted sales prices of each of the four final outputs. Below that are the alternative output quantities available from each production alternative

11.1 You're the Decision Maker

Operate or Shut Down the Process?

The practical capacity of STP's Metsä facility is based on operating one 8-hour shift a day, 5 days a week, which is set partly by operating agreements with labour unions and the local government.

a. A member of the corporate controller's staff has observed that the per-unit cost of lumber from the Metsä sawmill is much higher than at sawmills operating in Brazil or China, where operating restrictions currently are less. He suggests that the company should consider selling the Metsä facility because some international operations are more efficient. Build an argument in favour of this recommendation.

b. As a member of the Metsä facility management team, how would you refute this recommendation to sell your facility? Consider both local and company-wide issues.

(Solutions begin on page 571.)

Suomalainen Timber Products

Exhibit 11.2 STP, Metsä Facility

	A	B	C
1	**Suomalainen Timber Products**		
2	**Metsä Facility**		
3	**Process Data**		
4	Sawmill practical capacity per month, m^3 raw timber		11,000
5	Altenative sets of products from use of practical capacity		
6	Forecasted sales prices		
7	Grade A lumber, per cubic metre (m^3)		€350.00
8	Grade B lumber, per m^3		€260.00
9	Wood chips, per metric ton (MT)		€115.00
10	Wood pulp, per MT		€310.00
11			
12	Alternative yields from raw timber and forest trimmings	Yield %	Quantities
13	1. Grade A lumber, yield %, m^3	50%	5,500
14	Wood chips, MT		2,000
15	Forest trimmings, MT		1,000
16	2. Grade B lumber, yield %, m^3	60%	6,600
17	Wood chips, MT		1,500
18	Forest trimmings, MT		1,000
19	Joint sawmill process cost per month		€1,540,000
20			
21	Further processing costs	Variable per Unit	Fixed per Month
22	Grade A lumber, per m^3	€15.00	
23	Grade B lumber, per m^3	€12.00	
24	Wood chips as a final or intermediate product, per MT	€9.00	
25	Wood pulp yield % from wood chips	95%	
26	Wood pulp, per MT processed and per month	€8.00	€500,000

in m^3 or metric tons (MT). STP can produce and sell either all Grade A lumber plus wood chips from sawmill scrap and forest trimmings or all Grade B lumber, also plus wood chips from sawmill scrap and forest trimmings. Note that producing Grade A lumber has a lower yield from raw timber (50 per cent) than does producing Grade B lumber (60 per cent), but consequently produces more wood chips from sawmill scrap. Wood chip inputs from forest trimming are the same for both options.

Next in cell C19 is the joint cost to process 11,000 m^3 of raw timber to make either Grade A or Grade B lumber. This joint cost of €1,540,000 per month includes all the costs of operations and waste disposal up to the point of split-off, including both obtaining the raw timber (stumpage cost) and cutting it into lumber. Each of the products from either Option 1 or Option 2 would require some additional or further processing before they could be sold or used in a subsequent process. **Further processing costs** are the costs incurred to make joint products usable or saleable after split-off. Note that wood chips that are processed into wood pulp (at a 95 per cent yield) incur variable further processing costs of €17 per MT (= €9 + €8). The fixed cost of operating the pulp process is shown in cell C25 as €500,000 per month.

Exhibit 11.3 illustrates the decision making for optimizing the production processes. This decision tree shows the outputs, fixed and variable costs, and sales prices of the alternative uses of the Metsä process capacities that are obtained from Exhibit 11.2. The decision tree also reflects the physical and cost flows through the Metsä facility. Note that the decisions whether to operate joint product sawmill or the further processing of wood chips into wood pulp cannot be made until the entire process is diagrammed and analysed. This analysis is the next step.

Decision Whether to Sell Products at Split-off or After Further Processing

Companies that operate joint processes may sell fully processed or partly processed products from various production stages. The management team must decide whether selling outputs at intermediate stages or processing them further is more profitable. In this 'sell-or-process-further' decision, the relevant economic data to consider are (1) the revenues that can be earned before or after further processing and (2) the additional costs to process further.

Joint-process costs incurred *prior* to the split-off point are not affected by the decision whether to sell outputs or process them further after the split-off point. Only the revenues from outputs sold beyond the split-off point less any costs for further processing are the relevant factors, regardless of the way the company later allocates joint costs because these are sunk costs once the process operates. It is ultimately necessary to measure whether the contribution to profits from the optimal set of products exceeds the joint process cost but only after selecting the best set of products.

The **net realizable value (NRV)** of a product is its contribution to profit *after* the split-off point and is computed as sales revenue minus further processing costs. To reiterate, a product's NRV does not include any 'upstream' joint processing costs that occur up to the point of split-off. Computing the total NRV of each alternative set of products provides a comparison of each production option's contribution to profit after split-off.

We compute the NRV after preparing a decision tree like Exhibit 11.3 and by working backwards from the alternative final products to the split-off point. In the case of the Metsä facility, four alternative sets of final products are possible. We compute the total NRV of each set of products and determine which decisions contribute most to profit – moving from right to left on Exhibit 11.3. The results of these analyses are in Exhibit 11.4, which combines the information in Exhibits 11.2 and 11.3 into NRV calculations.

Most profitable products

The analyses of Exhibit 11.4 compute that the most profitable decision is expected to be Option 1B: produce and sell Grade A lumber and process wood chips further for sale as wood pulp. Furthermore, the NRV of €2,177,550 per month for Option 1B exceeds the joint processing cost of $1,540,000 per month (from Exhibit 11.2). You should verify the calculations of all of the figures in Exhibit 11.4, paying special attention to production of wood pulp.

As long as general and administrative costs do not exceed $637,550 per month (the difference between the best NRV and the joint process cost), STP can operate the Metsä facility profitably. If relative prices or costs among the alternative products were expected to change, the optimal production decision also could change. Thus, the long-run decision how or whether to continue to operate the Metsä facility might depend on future housing construction activity (for lumber), biofuel technologies (for wood chips), and the demand for paper and packaging (for wood pulp) – as well as global competition.

Suomalainen Timber Products

Exhibit 11.3 Decision Tree of the Joint Processing Decision

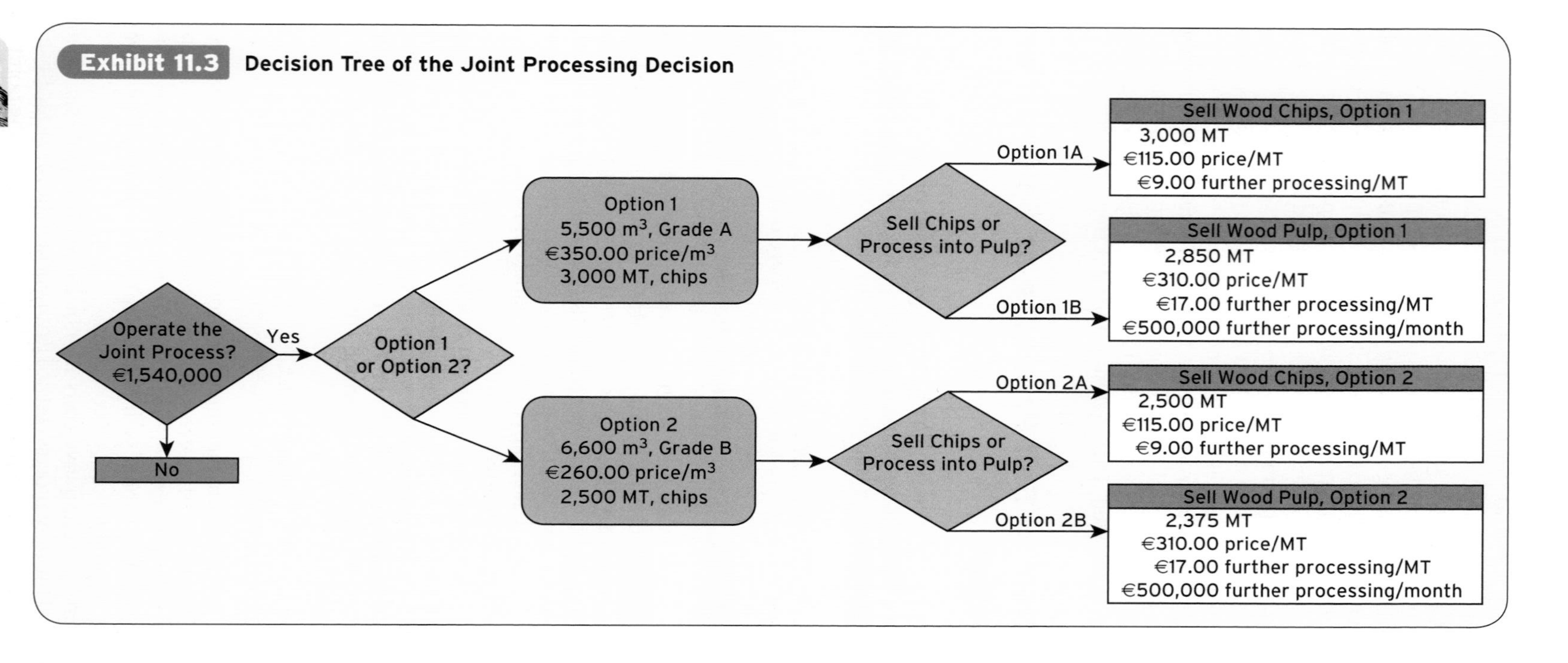

Exhibit 11.4 Metsä Facility: Analysis of Production Alternatives

Option 1A: Sales of Grade A Lumber plus Wood Chips				Costs After Split-off			
	Quantity	Price	Sales Revenue	Lumber	Wood Chips	Wood Pulp	NRV
Grade A lumber, m3	5,500	€350.00	€1,925,000	€82,500			€1,842,500
Wood chips, MT	3,000	€115.00	345,000		27,000		318,000
Total Net Realizable Value (NRV)							€2,160,500

Option 1B: Sales of Grade A Lumber plus Wood Pulp				Costs After Split-off			
	Quantity	Price	Sales Revenue	Lumber	Wood Chips	Wood Pulp	NRV
Grade A lumber, m3	5,500	€350.00	€1,925,000	€82,500			€1,842,500
Wood pulp, MT	2,850	€310.00	883,500			548,450	335,050
Total Net Realizable Value (NRV)							€2,177,550

Option 2A: Sales of Grade B Lumber plus Wood Chips				Costs After Split-off			
	Quantity	Price	Sales Revenue	Lumber	Wood Chips	Wood Pulp	NRV
Grade B lumber, m3	6,600	€260.00	€1,716,000	€79,200			€1,636,800
Wood chips, MT	2,500	€115.00	287,500		22,500		265,000
Total Net Realizable Value (NRV)							€1,901,800

Option 2A: Sales of Grade B Lumber plus Wood Chips				Costs After Split-off			
	Quantity	Price	Sales Revenue	Lumber	Wood Chips	Wood Pulp	NRV
Grade B lumber, m3	6,600	€260.00	€1,716,000	€79,200			€1,636,800
Wood pulp, MT	2,375	€310.00	736,250			540,375	195,875
Total Net Realizable Value (NRV)							€1,832,675

11.2 You're the Decision Maker

Testing the Sensitivity of the Analysis

Refer to Exhibits 11.2 and 11.4. The analysis in Exhibit 11.4 is based on the company's best estimates of quantities, revenues and costs, but actual amounts could differ. You have been asked to determine whether the recommendations could differ if these figures have errors.

a. Which figures in Exhibits 11.2 and 11.4 probably are most subject to error? Why?
b. Describe the concept of *materiality* in the context of the analysis in Exhibit 11.4.
c. Sensitivity analysis is a method of systematically testing whether a decision would change by changing one key figure in the analysis at a time and observing the change in expected outcomes. It is a way of asking 'what-if' questions about changes in figures and measuring the effects. For example, *what if* an economic slowdown reduces the price for wood pulp to €250 per metric ton? Is the decision to produce Option 1B *sensitive* to this change in price? What would be the implication for operating the wood pulp process?
d. What advice regarding the analysis would you give to managers of the Mitsä facility to help them in their product planning for the year?

(Solutions begin on page 571.)

Allocating Joint Costs for Internal and External Reporting

LO 2
Use the physical measures and net realizable value joint-cost allocation methods for reporting the costs of main products and by-products.

None of the preceding analyses involved allocating any of the $1,540,000 joint production cost to any product, but most companies do allocate these costs for various purposes – after making the optimal product decision. Organizations allocate joint costs for many reasons, including financial reporting, pricing, measuring and verifying process performance, estimating casualty losses, calculating regulated rates, specifying contractual obligations and resolving contractual disputes. Manufacturing companies are required to use joint cost allocations for financial and tax reporting to value inventories and cost of sales. For example, valuing inventories and measuring reported income for lumber and wood pulp at STP's Mitsä facility requires the allocation of joint production costs to both final products.

Although there is no precise way to trace joint process costs to joint products (as activity-based costing seeks to do in other production processes, for example), the results of allocating joint costs in different ways can affect management decision making. Although financial reporting rules allow any rational and consistent method to allocate joint costs (e.g., IAS 2, paragraph 14), the method should not be determined randomly.

11.1 Cost Management in Practice

Joint Costs in International Trade Disputes

A long-running trade dispute has existed between Canada and the United States regarding alleged 'dumping' of Canadian lumber in the United States. Dumping occurs when a manufacturer sells products at a price that is less than its 'manufacturing cost'. As one might expect, this dispute centres on whether Canadian lumber producers' manufacturing costs really are as low as claimed by the US. Early on, the US alleged that Canada set the stumpage cost of its publicly controlled timber at an arbitrarily low amount that was not comparable to market prices faced by US lumber companies. A World Trade Organization (WTO) panel agreed, but noted that US dumping laws applied only when subsidies are granted to a single industry. Canada offered similar subsidies to many industries besides lumber producers. At another time, a North American Free Trade Agreement (NAFTA) panel agreed that Canadian lumber was unfairly subsidized, but also ruled that the damages were insufficiently large to support countervailing tariffs by the US. At still another juncture, Canada agreed to pay countervailing tariffs, but owners of British Columbia sawmills argued that the tariffs would make exporting raw timber to Asia more profitable than milling lumber for the US market. This would shutter the BC sawmills and cost thousands of good paying jobs. Decisions for and against each country's position seem to be in a never-ending cycle, but joint production costs and allocations of joint costs are central to the dispute.

Sources: http://en.wikipedia.org/wiki/United_States_Canada_softwood_lumber_dispute and www.sfu.ca/~grubel/_private/Forestry%20Paper.doc

Distinguishing between Main and By-products

In practice, companies distinguish between main products and by-products before allocating joint costs because, by convention, joint costs are allocated only to *main products*. A **main product** is a joint output that generates a significant portion of the net realizable value (NRV) from the process. A **by-product** is the output from a joint production process that is minor in quantity and/or NRV when compared to the main products. Because they are deemed to be *immaterial* to reported financial results, by-products do not receive allocations of joint costs. By-products also by convention are not inventoried, but the NRV from by-products is typically recognized as 'other income' or as a reduction of joint product processing costs when the by-product is produced.[2]

As a by-product of cutting the bark off of logs, the Mitsä sawmill also produces decorative bark for landscaping. The NRV from the bark is considerably less than the NRV from any of the facility's other products. The decorative bark sells for barely more than its further processing cost, but packaging and selling the decorative bark is financially and environmentally better than disposing of the bark as waste. STP considers the bark to be a by-product of lumber production, allocates no joint cost to it, and includes its NRV as 'other income' of the period.[3]

Joint Cost Allocation Methods

The two major methods of allocating joint costs are (1) the net realizable value method and (2) the physical measures method. Other methods, such as the relative sales value at split off and relative gross margin are important for certain industries, but are used less frequently; they are discussed in Appendix 11A.

The **net realizable value (NRV) method** allocates joint costs based on the NRV of each *main product* after the split-off point. If the main products are to be sold at the split-off point without further processing, the market values or sales prices at split-off are used for this allocation base. If further processing is required, the NRV at the split-off point is computed by subtracting actual or estimated further processing costs from the sales value. Using the NRV method, joint costs are allocated to the main products in proportion to their NRVs after the split-off point.

From the previous analysis, assume that STP did choose to produce Option 1B, Grade A lumber and wood pulp. The joint cost up to the split-off point is €1,540,000. Using the NRV method, this €1,540,000 joint cost is allocated based on the relative NRVs of Grade A lumber and wood pulp, as shown in Panel A of Exhibit 11.5. And as shown in row 6 and based on the relative NRVs, 84.6 per cent of the $1,540,000 joint cost is allocated to Grade A lumber and 15.4 per cent is allocated to wood pulp.

Panel B of Exhibit 11.5 (row 17) demonstrates that the joint cost allocation has not affected the relative gross margins earned by either product. This equality is an important feature of the NRV method, because it maintains the relative profitability of the products. The profitability of neither the Grade A lumber nor the wood pulp is distorted by the allocations by using the NRV method.

The **physical measures** (or **quantities**) **method** is a joint cost allocation based on the relative volume, weight, energy content or other physical measure of each joint product that appears at the split-off point. Companies might prefer the physical measures method when the outputs can be measured comparably and the prices of their output products are highly volatile or unpredictable. This method is sometimes used when significant processing occurs between the split-off point and the first sales opportunity or when the market does not set product prices. The latter situation could arise when regulatory bodies set prices in regulated pricing situations or when cost-based contracts stipulate this method.

Many oil- and gas-producing companies allocate joint costs on the basis of the products' energy equivalents (BTU content), which are closely related to their sales values. They use this method because the products are typically measured in different physical units (e.g., natural gas by thousands

Exhibit 11.5 **Joint Cost Allocations – NRV Method**

	A	B	C	D
1	**Panel A: Joint cost allocations - NRV method**			
2	**Production Option 1B**	**Grade A Lumber**	**Wood Pulp**	**Total**
3	Sales revenue	€1,925,000	€883,500	€2,808,500
4	Less further processing costs	82,500	548,450	630,950
5	Estimated NRV	€1,842,500	€335,050	€2,177,550
6	Proportional share of NRV	84.6%	15.4%	100%
7	Joint cost allocations	€1,303,047	€236,953	€1,540,000
8				
9	**Panel B: Gross margins - NRV method**			
10	**Production Option 1B**	**Grade A Lumber**	**Wood Pulp**	**Total**
11	Sales revenue	€1,925,000	€883,500	€2,808,500
12	Cost of sales			
13	Joint cost allocations	1,303,047	236,953	1,540,000
14	Further processing costs	82,500	548,450	630,950
15	Total cost of sales	1,385,547	785,403	2,170,950
16	Gross margins - NRV method	€539,453	€98,097	€637,550
17	Proportional shares of gross margins	84.6%	15.4%	100.0%

of cubic feet, oil by barrels), although oil and natural gas often are produced simultaneously from the same well.

STP's Mitsä facility produces lumber and wood pulp according to Option 1B: 5,500 cubic metres of Grade A lumber and 2,850 metric tons of wood pulp. To use the physical measures method, one must convert the physical measures to a common metric. Mitsä production managers have found that the fibre content of one metric ton of wood pulp is equivalent to the fibre content of 2.5 cubic metres of wood. Therefore, the 2,850 MT of wood pulp is equivalent to 7,125 m^3.

As shown in Panel A of Exhibit 11.6, STP analysts using the physical measure method would allocate 43.6 per cent of the joint process costs to Grade A lumber and 56.4 per cent of the joint process costs to wood pulp (row 26).

Panel B of Exhibit 11.6 demonstrates that the physical measures method gives Grade A Specialty lumber a very high gross margin compared to wood pulp – which appears to be sold at a large loss. This happens because the physical measures method allocates a high proportion of the joint product costs to wood pulp. The gross margin calculation seems to be a misleading outcome, which would indicate on its face that STP should not sell wood pulp from the Mitsä facility. Yet we know from the previous decision-making analysis that wood pulp contributes a significant NRV to the facility's profit.

If by-products were misclassified as main products (or vice versa), the physical measures method could materially distort joint cost allocations to main products. This impropriety was alleged in the Canada–US trade dispute described in note 2. The impacts of misclassifying decorative bark as a main product are shown in Panel C of Exhibit 11.6. Decorative Bark comprises 11.2 per cent of the volume of output produced, and receives 11.2 per cent of the joint processing cost. This improper joint cost allocation, therefore, misstates the product costs of the two properly classified main products. It is likely that most cost analysts (and trade dispute mediators) would regard the percentage differences in costs as 'material' and likely to mislead users of the cost information. Misclassification is less likely and with less effect if the NRV method is used.

In general, it is much wiser to rely on net realizable values for joint product decision making than on product gross margins. Gross margins might be required for reporting purposes, but they can be greatly affected by the method used to allocate joint costs. Of course, the combined profits of the two products would be the same whatever joint cost allocation method is used. But the relative profitability of joint products can be affected by the cost allocation method that is used.

Exhibit 11.6 **Joint Cost Allocations: Physical Measures Method**

22	A	B	C	D
23	**Panel A: Joint cost allocations - Physical Measures Method**			
24	**Production Option 1B**	**Grade A Lumber**	**Wood pulp**	**Total**
25	Quantities produced, m3*	5,500	7,125	12,625
26	Proportional share of quantity	43.6%	56.4%	100%
27	Joint cost allocations	€670,891	€869,109	€1,540,000
28	** One metric ton of wood pulp is equivalent to 2.5 cubic meters of wood*			
29				
30	**Panel B: Gross margins - Physical Measures Method**			
31	**Production Option 1B**	**Grade A Lumber**	**Wood pulp**	**Total**
32	Sales revenue	€1,925,000	€883,500	€2,808,500
33	Cost of sales			
34	Joint cost allocations	670,891	869,109	1,540,000
35	Further processing costs	82,500	548,450	630,950
36	Total cost of sales	753,391	1,417,559	2,170,950
37	Gross margins - physical measures method	€1,171,609	€(534,059)	€637,550
38	Proportional shares of gross margins	183.8%	-83.8%	100.0%
39				

40	A	B	C		D
41	**Panel C: Improper Joint cost allocations - Physical Measures Method**				
42	**Production Option 1B**	**Grade A Lumber**	**Wood pulp**	**Decorative bark**	**Total**
43	Quantities produced, m3*	5,500	7,125	1,600	14,225
44	Proportional share of quantity	38.7%	50.1%	11.2%	89%
45	Joint cost allocations	€595,431	€771,353	€173,216	€1,540,000
46	Differences in allocations to main products	$75,461	$97,756		$173,216
47	Percentage differences	11.2%	11.2%		

11.1 Research Insight

Joint Cost Allocations by Not-for-Profit Organizations

Prospective donors to not-for-profit (NFP) organizations appear to rely on efficiency ratios that are reported by the organizations. A typical ratio is the percentage of raised funds that are directly applied to the organization's charitable activities, or conversely the ratio of fund-raising plus administrative costs to total organizational costs. Evidence exists that donations are higher for organizations that report higher efficiency ratios. Therefore, some critics allege that charitable organizations have incentives to misstate and do misstate the allocations of costs incurred to jointly serve charitable/educational activities and fundraising activities.

Source: Khumawala et al. (2005).

Process Costing Systems

LO 3
Apply a five-step costing method to allocate process costs to finished and partially completed main products.

A **process costing system** treats all units processed during a time period as the output for costing and does not separately record costs for individual units produced. The rationales are that every unit is identical and recording the costs of each unit would be prohibitively expensive, without observable benefits. Organizations that typically use process costing include **Coca-Cola** (cola concentrate), **Gruppo Ivas** (paint), **Royal Dutch Shell** (petrochemicals), and **Megro GmbH & Co KG** (cereal).

Recall that job-order costing records the costs incurred to make specific units of production, which are typically jobs or orders. In process costing systems, however, costs are first recorded for each department (plant or process) and then are allocated to the units (for example, litres of cola concentrate) that are completed by the department. The costs allocated to products are commonly used to help control the efficiency and capacity usage of the process and to set prices for internal and external customers. Allocated process costs are also used to identify which products might be too costly and need to be redesigned, re-priced or dropped. Process costs allocated to products are used to determine inventory values and cost of sales for financial reporting.

Allocation of Process Costs to Products

We illustrate process costing using two examples, starting from a simple situation and moving to a more complex, realistic one. These examples are adaptable to all process costing situations. These examples use just two categories of resource costs, direct materials and conversion costs, to keep the examples as simple as possible. Recall that *direct materials* are resources such as raw materials, parts and components that one can feasibly observe being made into a specific product and that *conversion costs* include direct labour and manufacturing overhead.[4]

Example 1: Process with No Opening WIP Inventory or Spoilage

We begin with a simple scenario: no opening Work-in-progress (WIP) inventory and no spoilage. As we have seen, STP's Metsä pulp plant produces wood pulp for sale to kraft (packaging) paper manufacturers. Metsä's continuous wood-pulp process typically begins with scrap wood from the sawmill and trimmings from regional forest-thinning operations. The scrap wood is continuously chipped, then mechanically ground into pulp, and finally packaged for shipment to customers.[5] At the (arbitrary) end of a month, the process costing system will record the costs incurred during the month, the number of units fully completed (metric tons of packaged wood pulp), and the units partially completed (wood chips and pulp still in process).

After a holiday break, the Pulp Plant began the next month with no opening work-in-progress inventory (no wood chips or pulp in process); it started 3,000 MT of scrap wood, and completed 2,300 units or packaged metric tons (MT) of wood pulp. Not all units placed into production during this month were completed by the end of the month. Only 2,300 of the 3,000 units started had been completed and transferred out of production, when normally a higher number of units would have been completed. This left 700 MT of product still in progress at the end of the month.

The 2,300 completed units were either sold or were placed at the end of the month in the finished goods warehouse, awaiting shipment. All direct materials had been added to the 700 units still in progress at the end of the month, but on average only 50 per cent of the conversion costs had been incurred for the 700 units in opening WIP inventory. At the end of the month, STP must calculate the cost of (1) the 2,300 completed units and (2) the 700 units still in WIP inventory and not yet completed.

Process costing allocates costs to opening WIP inventory and to units completed (transferred out of WIP inventory) in five steps. These steps are:

1. Summarize the flow of physical units.
2. Compute the equivalent number of units produced.
3. Summarize the total costs to assign to products; these are the sums of the costs in opening inventory and the actual costs incurred in the department during the period. Note that use of standard costs eliminates the need to perform steps 3 and 4, because all inventories are valued at standard cost. Variances from standards would be expensed, as explained in Chapter 13.
4. Compute costs per *equivalent unit* (to be defined later).
5. Allocate per-unit costs to goods transferred out to finished goods (completed) and to opening WIP inventory (not completed).

These steps are shown in Exhibit 11.7 and are explained in turn.

Step 1: Summarize the flow of physical units

Step 1 summarizes the flow of physical units, using the basic cost-flow model to account for units:

Opening inventory + Transfers in – Transfers out = Closing inventory

Exhibit 11.7 Process Costing with No Opening WIP Inventory or Spoilage

	A	B	C	D	E	F
1			(Step 2)			
2		(Step 1)	Degree of Completion		Equivalent Units	
3	Flow of Units	Physical units	Direct Materials	Conversion Costs	Direct Materials	Conversion Costs
4	Units to account for:					
5	Opening Work-in-progress inventory	0				
6	Units started this period	3,000				
7	Total units to account for	3,000				
8	Units accounted for:					
9	Completed and transferred out	2,300	100%	100%	2,300	2,300
10	Closing Work-in-progress inventory	700	100%	60%	700	420
11	Total units accounted for	3,000			3,000	2,720
12	Flow of Costs	Total			Direct Materials	Conversion Costs
13	Costs to account for (Step 3):					
14	Costs in opening Work-in-progress inventory	€ -			€ -	€ -
15	Current period costs	572,000			27,000	545,000
16	Total costs to account for	€572,000			€ 27,000	€ 545,000
17	Costs per equivalent unit (Step 4):*	€ 209.368			€ 9.000	€ 200.368
18	Costs accounted for (Step 5):**					
19	Costs allocated to units transferred out	€ 481,546			€ 20,700	€ 460,846
20	Costs allocated to closing Work-in-progress inventory	90,454			6,300	84,154
21	Total costs allocated	€572,000			€ 27,000	€ 545,000
22	NB: Un-shaded cells are computed by formulas.					
23	* Costs per equivalent unit = Total cost to account for ÷ Total equivalent units by cost category					
24	** Costs assigned = Cost per equivalent unit x Equivalent units by cost category					

This example has no opening inventory. Transfers in (or units started) total 3,000 units and transfers out (to finished goods) total 2,300 units. Thus, opening WIP inventory is 700 units.

Step 2: Compute the equivalent number of units produced

Step 2 applies the concept of an **equivalent units,** which represents the amount of work actually performed on units of product completed and not yet complete that is expressed as the work required to complete entire, fully completed units. This concept is one of the keys to applying process costing in a cost-effective manner. According to this concept, if five units were incomplete at the end of a month and each was 60 per cent finished at the end of the month, the work performed would be considered equivalent to the work performed to complete three whole units. Thus, for process-costing purposes, the five incomplete units equal three equivalent units.

One can estimate the average degree of completion of all units still in process at the end of a period, without tracing costs to every unit in process. Many organizations use the equivalent-unit concept. For example, university administrators often count the number of students in a department for tuition forecasting and class-scheduling purposes in terms of *full-time equivalents (FTE)*. Two half-time students are considered to be one FTE student because together they take the same number of classes as a full-time student.

Cells E9 and E10 of Exhibit 11.7 compute that all direct materials have been added to each unit transferred out or in closing inventory.

E9: 2,300 units × 100% = 2,300 equivalent units of direct material
E10: 700 units × 100% = 700 equivalent units of direct materials

Cell F9 computes that the units transferred out are also fully complete with respect to conversion costs.

F9: 2,300 units × 100% = 2,300 equivalent units of conversion cost

However, only 60 per cent of the conversion costs have been applied to the units that remain in opening inventory. Cell F10 computes the equivalent units of conversion cost in the 700 units of opening work-in-progress to be the equivalent of 420 units of conversion cost.

F10: 700 units × 60% = 420 equivalent units of conversion cost

Exhibit 11.7, row 11 computes that the wood-pulp process performed work during the month that is equivalent to 3,000 units of direct materials and 2,720 units of conversion costs.

You might wonder who provides the degrees of completion that are so essential to computing equivalent units. Ideally, someone who is objective and honest should prepare these estimates so they are not over- or underestimated to suit a biased purpose. For example, since these figures are used to derive the outcomes of a process, a manager could have a motivation to overestimate the degrees of completion to keep costs in inventory, thereby increasing income and the manager's current bonus. Or a manager might wish to underestimate the degrees of completion to charge more to cost of goods completed and sold, thereby decreasing current income and taxes, and increasing current cash flow. This example of 'earnings management' could simply defer minor effects to the next period or could escalate to serious financial fraud with the intent of misleading investors or tax authorities.

Step 3: Accumulate costs to allocate to products

Rows 13 to 16 of Exhibit 11.7 summarize the costs to be accounted in Step 3. Row 14 shows no costs of opening WIP inventory, because there was no opening WIP at the start of this month. Current period costs are accounted by direct materials and conversion costs in row 15. The pulp plant's manufacturing costs added for the month were:

Direct materials	Cell E15	€27,000
Conversion costs	Cell F15	545,000
Current period costs	Cell B15	€572,000

Because there was no cost of opening WIP inventory, these current period costs also comprise the total costs to allocate to products of the period (row 16).

Step 4: Compute costs per equivalent unit

Row 17 of Exhibit 11.7 computes Step 4 as the total production costs divided by total equivalent units, which measures costs per equivalent unit, by cost category and in total.

E17: Direct materials cost per equivalent unit = €9.00 = €27,000 ÷ 3,000 equivalent units of direct materials effort

F17: Conversion cost per equivalent unit = €200.368 = €545,000 ÷ 2,720 equivalent units of conversion effort

B17: Total cost per equivalent unit = €209.368 = €9.000 + €200.368

Step 5: Allocate costs to goods completed and to goods not completed

Rows 18 to 20 complete the process costing analysis in Step 5. These rows allocate costs incurred to units completed and transferred out and to units in opening WIP inventory. The total cost of goods completed is computed in row 19 as:

€481,546 = 2,300 equivalent units × €9.00 + 2,300 equivalent units × €200.368
= €20,700 + €480,846

Similarly, the cost of closing WIP inventory is computed in row 20 as:

€90,454 = 700 equivalent units × €9.00 + 420 equivalent units × €200.368
= €6,300 + €84,154

The total cost allocated to products (€481,546 + €90,454) equals the total costs to account for (€572,000), as shown in cells B16 and B21. This summarizes the process costs allocated to final outcomes and completes the **production cost report** for the first example.

Example 2: Process with Opening and Closing WIP and Spoilage

LO 4
Apply the five-step method to allocate process costs to prepare a production report of finished goods, work-in-progress, and spoilage using weighted-average costing.

Now that we have accounted for costs in a process costing system under a relatively simple scenario – one with no opening WIP inventory but with closing WIP inventory – we next discuss the more detailed task of accounting for costs when both opening *and closing* WIP inventory and spoilage occur.

Concepts and measurement of spoilage

If you have ever worked on a project that you discarded and then restarted from the beginning, you understand the concept of *waste* or *spoilage*. From your experience, you understand that wasted efforts do not result in productive outcomes (e.g., idle time in front of the TV does little perhaps besides switching off your brain). **Waste** is the loss of product because the technology of production does not convert all inputs to usable outputs. For example, a clothing manufacturer experiences waste when cutting patterns cannot use 100 per cent of the material. STP's wood-pulp plant creates waste because its technology results in a 95 per cent conversion of wood chips into pulp. Five per cent of the input is lost to waste, which is an undesirable but normal cost of production. Efforts to reduce waste can improve product yield and increase profitability, but perhaps some waste is inevitable.

Spoilage, however, is effort (materials and conversion) that results in defective outcomes: goods that are damaged, do not meet specifications, or are otherwise not suitable for further processing or sale as good output. Whether it is a discarded school assignment, a ruined meal, or a mis-filed scholarship application, spoilage is costly. At a minimum the time and effort expended to complete a faulty product is lost. Often the direct materials also are lost and must be discarded as waste, but recycling or reworking might save valuable materials.

Sometimes lost effort is a necessary part of learning to do the task right. However, we also expect that effort lost to waste and spoilage should decline with learning (see Chapter 3's discussion of the learning curve). By measuring the amounts and costs of waste and spoilage, managers are able to make trade-off decisions about the expected costs to reduce them, such as the costs of improved technology, training employees, using higher-quality materials, and reworking or recycling defective goods.

11.2 Research Insight

Environmental Costs

Chemical, paper, steel, oil and other companies that produce in continuous processes often have significant environmental costs. Researchers have found that while such companies generally keep good records of such visible costs as fees for permits and the cost of maintaining pollution control equipment, they do not identify disposal costs that are buried in overhead. Researchers of companies in the steel industry have found the additional 'hidden' costs to be 10 times as much as the visible costs.

Source: Joshi et al. (2001).

A controller in a small company that had pre-tax accounting income of $840,000 estimated the company's environmental costs to be $50,000. Upon further study, the company found the direct and indirect costs totalled $1,000,000, 20 times as much as the company controller had initially estimated. Accurate estimates of environmental costs enable managers to make good decisions that both benefit the environment and the bottom line. In the case of this small company, an investment in environmental improvements seemed to be unprofitable when the most that could be saved appeared to be only $50,000 per year. Realizing that hundreds of thousands of dollars could potentially be saved made it worthwhile to invest in environmental improvements.

Source: Kunes (2001).

Normal versus abnormal spoilage: is spoilage ever normal?

Normal spoilage is unsaleable products that are expected results, given the technology of regular operations of the production process. Organizations that strive to eliminate all defects (see Chapter 6 for more details) might not consider any spoilage to be *normal*, because this implies acceptance of defects. These might treat *all* spoilage as *abnormal*.

Abnormal spoilage is spoilage from unusual or unexpected operations of a process, such as an industrial accident or a logistical failure that allowed defective inputs to be used. In general, normal spoilage (if it is allowed to be labelled such) is waste that is counted as a usual cost of production. Abnormal spoilage is accounted as a loss of the period. At STP's Mitsä wood-pulp plant the 5 per cent loss of direct materials that is attributed to the plant's technology is considered to be normal spoilage and a usual cost of production. Any waste in excess of 5 per cent is considered abnormal spoilage.

Exhibit 11.8 presents the five steps of process costing applied to the typical situation when opening and closing WIP inventories and spoilage result from a month's processing of wood pulp.

11.2 Cost Management in Practice

Process Costing and Waste at Louisiana Pacific

Louisiana Pacific (USA), one of the world's largest wood products firms, has operations throughout the Western Hemisphere. The company uses process costing for most of its many processes and is vitally concerned with the costs of its outputs, which include waste that it must treat before disposing of it. At one time, costs of waste disposal were not considered to be material and were counted as normal costs of products. However, higher costs caused by environmental concerns and regulations have motivated Louisiana Pacific to monitor costs of waste from its processes and to find ways to reduce those costs.

Its Chetwynd, BC, Canada mill, for example, utilizes a state-of-the-art mechanical pulping process and a zero-effluent discharge system to produce pulp for use in its paper processes or for sale to other paper manufacturers. Its Samoa, California, mill produces bleached and unbleached kraft pulp (used by packaging manufacturers) by a chlorine-free process, thereby eliminating environmentally dangerous dioxins. Louisiana Pacific decided to sell its Ketchikan, AK, USA Pulp Company subsidiary when the combination of low pulp prices, restricted access to raw timber, and greatly increased costs of reducing and treating its process waste made the plant unprofitable.

Source: Louisiana Pacific Form 10-K.

Step 1: Summarize the flow of physical units

For the second example, assume that the Mitsä plant began a month later with 520 metric tons of WIP inventory that was 100 per cent complete by direct materials and 60 per cent complete by conversion. The plant started another 3,000 metric tons of wood chips, and by month end had completed 3,100 metric tons of wood pulp, with 220 metric tons of product in opening WIP inventory. Thus, the plant had 3,520 metric tons in process during the month (cell B6 of Exhibit 11.8) and had inventories totalling 3,320 metric tons (cells B8 + B11). This means that total spoilage for the month must equal 200 metric tons (3,520 – 3,320 MT). In equation format,

Opening inventory + Transfers in – (Transfers out) = Closing inventory
520 MT + 3,000 MT – (3,100 MT + Spoilage) = 220 MT
520 + 3,000 – 3,100 – 220 = Spoilage = 200 MT

To distinguish between normal and abnormal spoilage requires that we know (a) the normal spoilage rate and (b) when spoilage is detected in this process (the inspection point). The normal spoilage rate, which is determined by the plant's technology, is 5 per cent of metric tons processed. This normal loss of weight occurs by elimination of unusable liquids and solids as the wood chips are processed. At the

Suomalainen Timber Products

Exhibit 11.8 Process Costing with Opening and Closing WIP Inventory and Spoilage

	A	B	C	D	E	F
1			(Step 2)			
2	**Flow of units**	**(Step 1)**	**Degree of completion**		**Equivalent units**	
			Direct	**Conversion**	**Direct**	**Conversion**
3	Units to account for:	**Physical units**	**materials**	**costs**	**materials**	**costs**
4	Opening Work-in-progress inventory	520	100%	60%	520	312
5	Units started this period	3,000				
6	Total units to account for	3,520				
7	Units accounted for:					
8	Completed and transferred out	3,100	100%	100%	3,100	3,100
9	Normal spoilage (5% of units processed)*	165	100%	100%	165	165
10	Abnormal spoilage**	35	100%	100%	35	35
11	Closing Work-in-progress inventory	220	100%	60%	220	132
12	Total units accounted for	3,520			3,520	3,432
					Direct	**Conversion**
13	**Flow of costs**	**Total**			**materials**	**costs**
14	**Costs to account for (Step 3):**					
15	Costs in opening Work-in-progress inventory	€ 59,000			€ 4,900	€ 54,100
16	Current period costs	572,000			27,000	545,000
17	Total costs to account for	631,000			31,900	599,100
18	**Costs per equivalent unit (Step 4):**[b]	€ 183.625			€ 9.063	€ 174.563
19	**Costs allocated (Step 5):**					
20	Costs allocated to units completed	€ 569,239			€ 28,094	€ 541,145
21	Costs allocated to normal spoilage	30,298			1,495	28,803
22	Costs allocated to abnormal spoilage	6,427			317	6,110
23	Costs allocated to closing Work-in-progress inventory	25,036			1,994	23,042
24	Total costs allocated	€ 631,000			€ 31,900	€ 599,100
25						
26	* 5% of units processed = 0.05 x Units to account for less units in closing work in progress = 0.05 x (3,520 - 220) = 165					
27	** Abnormal spoilage = total spoilage - normal spoilage = [3520 - (3,100 - 220)] - 165 = 35					

Mitsä plant defective or abnormally spoiled product, which contains unacceptable levels of contaminants, is detected by random sampling of fully completed wood pulp. That is, any opening or closing WIP inventory might have undetected abnormal spoilage, but the actual amount will not be detected until the product is 100 per cent complete. Wood-pulp spoilage will not be accepted by customers and must be disposed of as waste.

Normal spoilage is computed as 5 per cent of the units that were inspected by the end of the month. In this case, 3,520 metric tons were placed in process, but 220 metric tons were not completed and, thus, not inspected. This means 3,300 units were inspected, of which 5 per cent or 165 metric tons would be normal spoilage (cell B9). Therefore, abnormal spoilage is the difference between total spoilage and normal spoilage, or 35 metric tons (cell B10 = 35 metric tons = 200 – 165).

Step 2: Compute the equivalent number of units produced

All units completed or spoiled were 100 per cent complete by direct materials and by conversion (rows 8–10), and their equivalent units are computed by multiplying the physical units by 100 per cent. The 220 metric tons of opening WIP inventory (row 11) were 100 per cent complete by direct materials, but only 60 per cent complete by conversion. Closing WIP equivalent units are 220 and 132 for direct materials and conversion, respectively. For the month, the Mitsä plant completed efforts equivalent to 3,520 units of direct material and 3,432 units of conversion (row 12).

Step 3: Accumulate costs to allocate to products

The costs of direct materials, conversion and in total were obtained from the plant's accounting system. The costs to allocate to this month's production activity are shown in rows 14 to 17 of Exhibit 11.8. These costs include both the current month's costs and the costs transferred into the month as opening WIP inventory. For this analysis, which is called **weighted-average process costing**,the method by which the costs and equivalent units of the current efforts applied and the costs of opening WIP are pooled and averaged. Total costs to allocate to products are €31,900 of direct material (E17) and €599,100 of conversion (F17). Appendix B to this chapter describes *FIFO process costing* wherein these costs are not pooled and are analysed separately. FIFO may be a more accurate approach to process costing when WIP inventories are large and processing costs vary over time; otherwise, the weighted-average approach is suitable.

Step 4: Compute costs per equivalent unit

Because we are using weighted-average costing in this example, we also pool the equivalent units added during the period with those transferred into the period as opening WIP. The weighted-average costs of direct materials and conversion are computed in row 18, cells E18 and F18 as:

E18: Direct material cost per equivalent unit = €31,900 ÷ 3,520 equivalent units = €9.063
F18: Conversion cost per equivalent unit = €599,100 ÷ 3,342 equivalent units = €174.563

Step 5: Allocate costs to goods completed and to goods not completed

Rows 19 to 24 complete the allocation of costs of direct materials and conversion to the month's outputs by multiplying each output's equivalent units from Step 2 by the appropriate cost per equivalent unit from Step 4. Typically, companies will measure the total cost of goods completed by adding the cost of normal spoilage, as follows:

Costs allocated to goods completed (B20)	€569,239
Costs allocated to normal spoilage (B21)	30,298
Total cost of goods completed	€599,537

Thus, the reported cost per unit including normal spoilage would increase from €183.625 (cell B18) to €193.399 (= 599,537 ÷ 3,100). STP's reporting policy is to report normal and abnormal spoilage costs prominently for internal reports, but to add normal spoilage to costs of goods completed for valuing inventories and cost of goods sold. STP also follows the typical practice to charge abnormal spoilage cost (€6,427) to expense of the period (e.g., IAS 2, paragraph 16), labelled as 'Other expense'.

Appendix 11A

Other Economic Value Methods to Allocate Joint Costs

LO 5
Use the relative sales value at split off and constant gross margin percentage methods of joint cost allocation.

The chapter discussed the typical net realizable value (NRV) method for allocating joint costs. This appendix presents two other methods also based on the economic values of joint outputs: (1) the relative sales value at split-off method and (2) the constant gross margin percentage method.

Relative Sales Value at Split-off Method

The **relative sales value at split-off method** allocates joint costs based on the relative sales values of the joint products at their split-off point. This method does not consider further processing costs after the split-off point. Recall that the revenues at the split-off point for STP's Mitsä sawmill before additional processing were as shown in Exhibit 11.9.

Suomalainen Timber Products

Exhibit 11.9 Relative Sales Value Method for Joint Cost Allocation

	A	B	C	D
1	**Relative sales value method**	**Sales revenue**	**Percentage sales value**	**Joint cost allocation**
2	Grade A Lumber	€1,925,000	68.5%	€1,055,546
3	Wood pulp	883,500	31.5%	484,454
4	Total	€2,808,500	100.0%	€1,540,000

Given these values, 68.5 per cent (= 1,925,000 ÷ 2,808,500) of the joint costs, or 1,055,546, would be allocated to Grade A lumber and 31.5 per cent would be allocated to wood pulp, or 484,584. Note that the relative sales value method does not include any further processing costs and based on *relative* values at the split-off point *before* any additional processing. This is one of the rational, consistent methods permitted by financial reporting (e.g., IAS 2).

Constant Gross Margin Percentage Method

The constant gross margin percentage method is another method of joint cost allocation that is based on the economic values of joint products. The **constant gross margin percentage method** allocates joint costs to products in such a way that the gross margin percentages as a percentage of revenue *are the same* for each joint product. Three steps are required to use this method:

1. Compute the total gross margin percentage for the outputs of the total joint process.
2. Use the total gross margin percentage calculated in step 1 to calculate the gross margin for each product.

Gross margin = Total gross margin percentage × Sales value

3. Solve for the joint costs allocated to each product by subtracting gross margins and further processing costs from the sales revenue.

Sales revenue – Further processing costs – Allocated joint costs = Gross margin

Or rearranged,

Allocated joint costs = Sales revenue – Gross margin – Further processing costs

Exhibit 11.10 shows the data provided and the calculation of the total gross margin percentage (step 1). The joint cost allocations that remain to be calculated are first denoted with a question mark. Exhibit 11.10 next shows the calculation of the gross margin dollar amount for each product

Exhibit 11.10 Joint Costs Allocated Using the Constant Gross Margin Percentage Method

	A	B	C	D
1	**Step 1: Measure total gross margin**	**Grade A Lumber**	**Wood pulp**	**Total**
2	Sales revenue	€1,925,000	€883,500	€2,808,500
3	Joint process costs	?	?	1,540,000
4	Further processing costs	82,500.00	548,450.00	630,950
5	Total gross margin			€637,550
6	Total gross margin percentage			22.70%
7				
8	**Solve for joint cost allocations**	**Grade A Lumber**	**Wood pulp**	**Total**
9	Sales revenue	€1,925,000	€883,500	€2,808,500
10	less Further processing costs	(82,500)	(548,450)	(630,950)
11	**Step 2: less Gross margins**			
12	=0.227 × 1,925,000	(436,989)		
13	=0.227 × 883,500		(200,561)	(637,550)
14	**Step 3: Equals allocated Joint costs**	**€1,405,511**	**€134,489**	**€1,540,000**

(step 2). After the gross margin dollar amount has been calculated for each product, we can solve for the joint costs to be allocated to each product (step 3).

The constant gross margin percentage method is based on a similar principle to the NRV method, except for one difference. The NRV method results in gross margin percentages that are equal as a percentage of the *net realizable values* of each joint product, whereas the constant gross margin method requires that gross margin percentages be equal as a percentage of the *revenues* of each joint product.

Appendix 11B

Process Cost Allocations to Products Using First-in, First-out (FIFO) Costing

A limitation of weighted-average costing is that it mixes current period costs with the costs of products in opening inventory, making it impossible for managers to know by how much the costs to make a product during the current period differ from prior periods. **First-in, first-out (FIFO) costing** is an inventory method that identifies the first units completed as the first ones sold or transferred out. FIFO costing separates current period costs from those in opening inventory and transfers out the costs in opening inventory in a lump sum (assuming that the units in opening inventory were completed during the current period) rather than mingling them with current period costs.

LO 6
Allocate process costs to products using first-in, first-out (FIFO) costing.

If WIP inventories are large and if production costs vary across periods, FIFO process costing generates more accurate information about the work done in the current period. If the production process is a FIFO process, the inventory numbers are more likely to reflect reality under FIFO costing than under weighted-average costing because the units in opening inventory are likely to have been produced in the current period.

Example 3: FIFO Process Costing with Opening and Closing WIP and Spoilage

To illustrate accounting for process costing using FIFO, we modify the data from Example 2 for the Mitsä wood pulp process, which includes opening and closing WIP inventory and spoilage. The data are reproduced in Exhibit 11.11, along with the revised FIFO analysis. FIFO costing uses the same five

Exhibit 11.11 **FIFO Process Costing with Opening and Closing WIP and Spoilage**

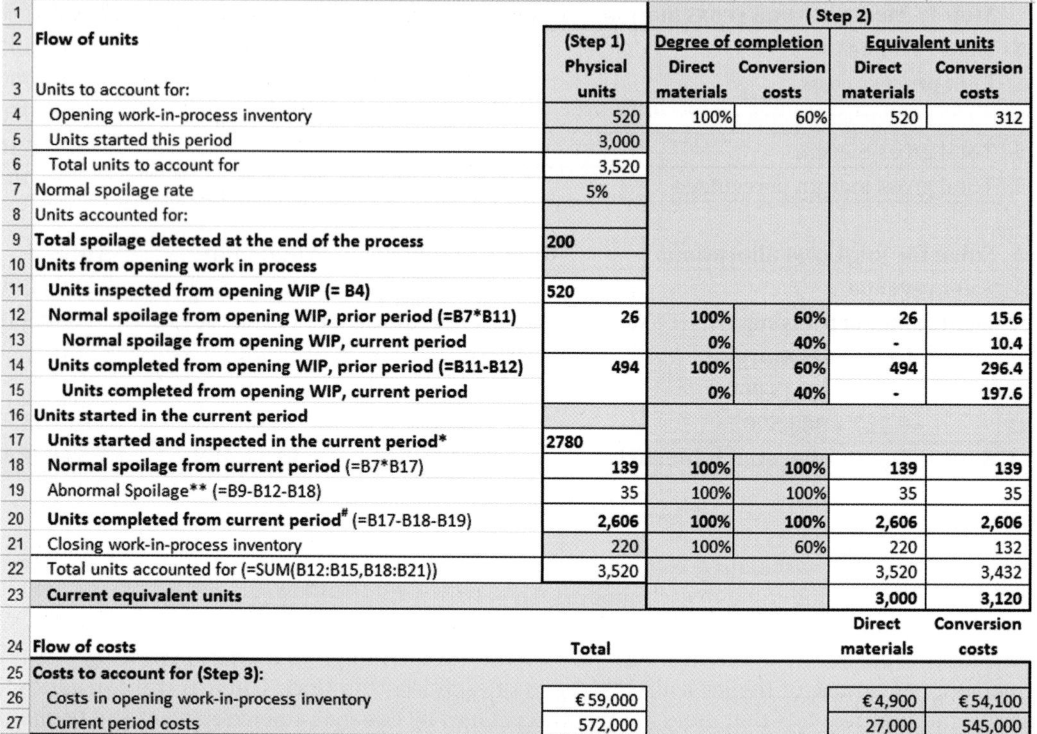

	A	B	C	D	E	F
1			(Step 2)			
2	**Flow of units**	**(Step 1)**	**Degree of completion**		**Equivalent units**	
		Physical	**Direct**	**Conversion**	**Direct**	**Conversion**
3	Units to account for:	**units**	**materials**	**costs**	**materials**	**costs**
4	Opening work-in-process inventory	520	100%	60%	520	312
5	Units started this period	3,000				
6	Total units to account for	3,520				
7	Normal spoilage rate	5%				
8	Units accounted for:					
9	**Total spoilage detected at the end of the process**	**200**				
10	**Units from opening work in process**					
11	**Units inspected from opening WIP (= B4)**	**520**				
12	**Normal spoilage from opening WIP, prior period (=B7*B11)**	**26**	**100%**	**60%**	**26**	**15.6**
13	**Normal spoilage from opening WIP, current period**		**0%**	**40%**	**-**	**10.4**
14	**Units completed from opening WIP, prior period (=B11-B12)**	**494**	**100%**	**60%**	**494**	**296.4**
15	**Units completed from opening WIP, current period**		**0%**	**40%**	**-**	**197.6**
16	**Units started in the current period**					
17	**Units started and inspected in the current period***	**2780**				
18	**Normal spoilage from current period** (=B7*B17)	**139**	**100%**	**100%**	**139**	**139**
19	Abnormal Spoilage** (=B9-B12-B18)	35	100%	100%	35	35
20	**Units completed from current period**# (=B17-B18-B19)	**2,606**	**100%**	**100%**	**2,606**	**2,606**
21	Closing work-in-process inventory	220	100%	60%	220	132
22	Total units accounted for (=SUM(B12:B15,B18:B21))	3,520			3,520	3,432
23	**Current equivalent units**				**3,000**	**3,120**
					Direct	**Conversion**
24	**Flow of costs**	**Total**			**materials**	**costs**
25	**Costs to account for (Step 3):**					
26	Costs in opening work-in-process inventory	€59,000			€4,900	€54,100
27	Current period costs	572,000			27,000	545,000
28	Total costs to account for	631,000			31,900	599,100
29	**Prior costs per equivalent unit (Step 4):** ##	**€182.821**			**€9.423**	**€173.397**
30	**Current costs per equivalent unit:**	**€183.679**			**€9.000**	**€174.679**
31	**Costs allocated (Step 5):**					
32	Costs of goods completed					
33	**Costs of units completed from opening WIP**	**90,567**			**4,655**	**85,912**
34	**Costs allocated to normal spoilage from opening WIP**	**4,767**			**245**	**4,522**
35	**Current costs allocated to units started & completed**	**478,669**			**23,454**	**455,215**
36	**Costs allocated to normal spoilage from current period**	**25,531**			**1,251**	**24,280**
37	**Total costs of goods completed**	**€599,534**			**€29,605**	**€569,929**
38	Costs allocated to abnormal spoilage#	6,429			315	6,114
39	Costs allocated to closing work-in-process inventory	25,038			1,980	23,058
40	Total costs allocated	€631,000			€31,900	€599,100
41	* Units started and inspected in the current period = 3,000 started - 220 closing WIP inventory					
42	** Abnormal spoilage = total spoilage - normal spoilage = 200 - (26 + 139) = 35					
43	# Assume that all abnormal spoilage is from the current period					
44	## Prior cost per equivalent unit = Prior period cost ÷ Prior equivalent units					
45	Currrent cost per equivalent unit = Current period cost ÷ Current equivalent units					

steps as weighted-average costing, but with important differences. These differences are highlighted in bold font in Exhibit 11.11, and are described in the following discussions of the costing steps. Briefly, the complications of FIFO process costing arise from tracking the equivalent units and costs of opening WIP inventory to states of completion or spoilage. Accounting for the current period's production is straightforward and almost identical to the previous example.

Step 1: Summarize the flow of physical units

This step identifies the flow of physical units from their origins to their stages of completion. The FIFO flow is more detailed than for weighted-average costing because of FIFO's need to track opening WIP inventory separately. Weighted-average costing did not make this distinction because there was no need to separate inventory layers. Using FIFO wood-pulp units that were completed or detected as spoiled are combinations of units from opening WIP inventory and those started in the current period. This complexity is reflected in the section of Exhibit 11.11 labelled 'Step 1'. New to this part of the worksheet (for convenience) are the normal spoilage rate (B7), total spoilage (B9), and more details about the units processed. This step tracks the 3,520 units in process from their origins as units begun in the prior period (B4) or the current period (B5). Furthermore, we split the 520 units carried over from the prior period into more detailed categories. First, 5 per cent or 26 units (B12) would normally be spoiled, and the balance, 494 units (B14), would normally be completed. Second, we track when these units were completed. These received 100 per cent of the direct materials and 60 per cent of the conversion in the previous period (E12, F12, E14, F14). In the current period, these units (rows 13 and 15) received no direct materials and the remaining 40 per cent of conversion (E13, F13, E15, F15).

Of the 3,000 units started in the current period, 220 (B21) were left as closing WIP inventory, and the balance, 2,780 units (B17), were subject to inspection at the end of the process. Normally 5 per cent, or 139 units (B18), would be detected as spoiled. Because 200 units (B9) were detected as spoiled, 35 units (B19) were counted as abnormal spoilage (200 – 26 – 139). Units completed from the current period equal 2,606 units (2,780 – 139 – 35). Note that for simplicity, abnormal spoilage is counted as a result of the current period.

Step 2: Compute the equivalent number of units produced

FIFO costing computes equivalent units differently from weighted-average costing, because FIFO costing separates what was in opening inventory from what occurred in the current period. To separate the inventory layers, FIFO computes equivalent units in several parts for both direct materials and conversion costs:

1. Equivalent units transferred in as opening WIP inventory.
2. Equivalent units to complete opening WIP inventory as either good units or spoilage.
3. Equivalent units of goods started and completed as either good units or spoilage during the current period.
4. Equivalent units of goods started during the period and remaining in closing WIP inventory.

The cells in Step 2 of Exhibit 11.11 calculate the equivalent units for all units based on their degrees of completion (columns C and D, E and F). Opening WIP units can end as either normal spoilage or good units. Because the physical units were begun in the prior period, these good and spoiled units have equivalent units of direct material added in the previous period, and equivalent units of conversion added in *both* periods – at potentially different costs. Rows 12 to 15 compute the equivalent units from both periods for both types of units from opening WIP inventory. Units in WIP received 100 per cent of the direct materials and 60 per cent of the conversion in the previous period (E12, F12, E14, F14). In the current period, as noted before, these units (rows 13 and 15) received no direct materials but did receive the remaining 40 per cent of conversion (E13, F13, E15, F15).

Computing the equivalent units for those started in the current period (rows 17 to 21) is straightforward because these units comprise but a single inventory layer. The **current equivalent units** (row 23) are equivalent units added in the current period only for the current layer of inventory, which are calculated by subtracting the equivalent units transferred into the period as opening WIP (row 4) from the total equivalent units in process (row 22).

Step 3: Accumulate costs to allocate to products

The total costs to account for using FIFO costing are the same as when using weighted-average costing. Whatever our assumption about cost flows, we account for *all* costs in the process (those in opening inventory plus those incurred during the period). These costs are shown in Step 3 of Exhibit 11.11 (rows 25 to 28).

Step 4: Compute costs per equivalent unit

The two layers of inventory can result in different costs per equivalent unit for each layer. If the costs per equivalent unit consistently are not materially different, one should rethink using the more complex FIFO method. The prior period's costs per equivalent unit (E29 and F29) are computed by dividing the prior period's costs in opening WIP inventory (E26 and F26) by the prior period's equivalent units (E4 and F4). Similarly, the current period's costs per equivalent unit (E30 and F30) are computed by dividing the current period's costs (E27 and F27) by the current equivalent units (E23 and F23).

Step 5: Allocate costs to goods completed, spoilage and to closing WIP inventory

The final cost allocation results appear in Step 5 of Exhibit 11.11. This section multiplies each outcome's equivalent units by the appropriate costs per equivalent unit. For example, the cost of units completed from opening WIP inventory (row 33) is computed as:

$$\begin{aligned}\text{€}90{,}567 &= (26 \times \text{€}9.423 + 0 \times \text{€}9.000) + (15.6 \times \text{€}173.397 + 10.4 \times \text{€}174.679)\\ &= \text{€}4{,}655 + \text{€}85{,}912\end{aligned}$$

The cost of spoilage from units in opening WIP inventory (row 34) is computed similarly. Current costs of units started and completed (row 35) or spoiled (row 36) in the current period are computed directly. The total cost of goods completed, including normal spoilage) is summed in row 37. As noted before, abnormal spoilage is treated as a cost of the current period (row 38). The cost of closing WIP inventory (row 39) is entirely from current equivalent units and current costs. Row 40 confirms that total costs incurred are fully allocated to outcomes that occur at the end of the period.

11.3 You're the Decision Maker

Should STP use Weighted Average or FIFO Process Costing?

1. Compare the costing outcomes in Exhibits 11.8 and 11.11.
2. Give arguments for and against whether STP should use weighted average or FIFO costing at the Mitsä wood pulp plant.
3. Does it appear that these analyses include all of the relevant costs?

(Solutions begin on page 571.)

Appendix 11C

Operation Costing

LO 7
Explain operation costing.

Operation costing is a hybrid of job-order and process costing, and companies use it when they produce batches of similar products with significantly different types of material. Hybrid costing is appropriate for costing the manufacture of goods that have both common characteristics and some individual characteristics. An *operation* is a standardized method of making a product that is repeatedly performed. For example, a computer assembly plant makes several models on the same assembly line. Each model has permanent memory (a hard drive) installed; installing them is an operation. However, some computers have large hard drives, others have smaller. Whether the hard drive is large or small, the computer passes through essentially the same hard drive installation operation. Companies such as **Nike** (shoes) and **Volvo** (automobiles) also use operation costing. **Van Heusen,** a shirt maker, has a cutting operation and a stitching operation for each shirt, although the materials (cotton, polyester or blend) for each type of shirt can differ.

Product Costing in Operations

The key difference between operation costing, job costing and process costing is that direct materials for each work order or batch passing through a particular operation are different although

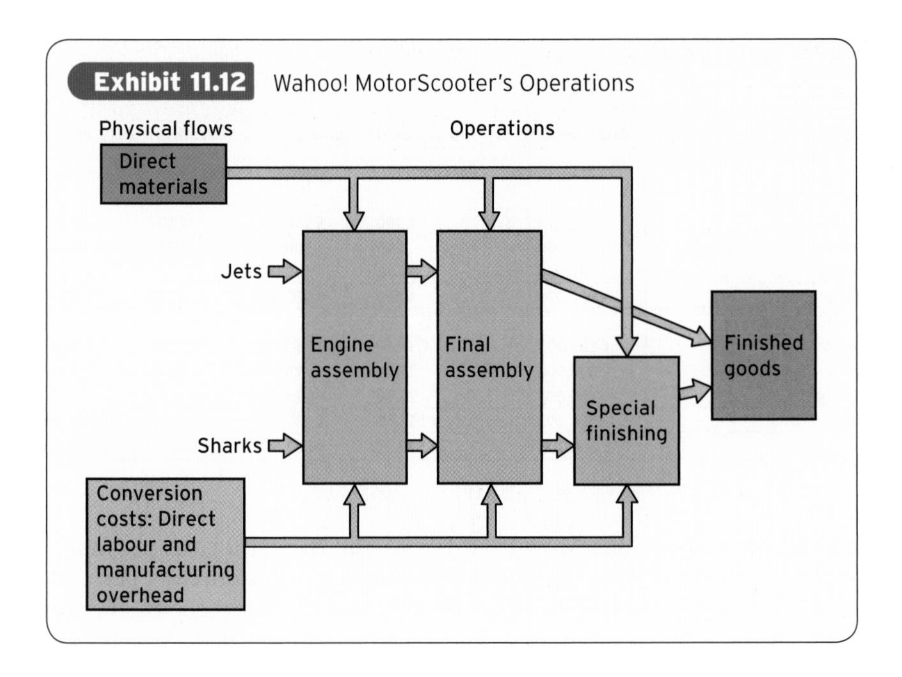

Exhibit 11.12 Wahoo! MotorScooter's Operations

conversion costs (direct labour and manufacturing overhead) are the same. For example, assume that **Wahoo! MotorScooter** makes two models of motor scooters, Jets and Sharks. The Shark has a larger engine and generally more costly direct materials than the Jet. Exhibit 11.12 shows the flow of products through departments (assume that each department has one operation). Note that Jets pass through only the first two departments where operations are identical for both types of motorcycles but Sharks pass through all three departments. Direct materials and conversion costs are added to both models in Engine Assembly and Final Assembly, but only Sharks receive Special Finishing.

Illustration of Operation Costing

Assume that Wahoo! MotorScooter's cost analysts prepared the following summary of the company's fixed conversion operations and the variable direct materials costs for each type of motor scooter shown in Exhibit 11.13.

Exhibit 11.13 **Wahoo! MotorScooter Operations**

	A	B	C	D
1	**Fixed conversion costs:**	**Monthly cost**	**Normal capacity**	**Cost per unit**
2	Engine assembly	€150,000	4,000	€37.50
3	Final assembly	300,000	4,000	75.00
4	Special finishing	50,000	2,000	25.00
5	Total conversion costs	500,000		
6				
7	**Variable direct materials costs per unit**	**Sharks**	**Jets**	
8	Engine assembly	€150	€100	
9	Final assembly	200	150	
10	Special finishing	50	-	
11	Total direct materials	€400	€250	

Exhibit 11.14 **Wahoo! MotorScooter Job Costs, March**

	A	B	C	D	E	F	G
1	**Monthly costs**	**Operations**	**Work order 101 Sharks**		**Work order 102 Jets**		**Unused conversion**
2	Units	Total	Per Unit	1,000	Per Unit	2,000	
3	Variable direct material costs:						
4	Engine assembly	€350,000	€150	€150,000	€100	€200,000	
5	Final assembly	500,000	200	200,000	150	300,000	
6	Special finishing	50,000	50	50,000	-	-	
7	Total direct materials	€900,000	€400	€400,000	€250	€500,000	
8	Allocated conversion costs:						
9	Engine assembly	€150,000	€37.50	€37,500.00	€37.50	€75,000	€37,500
10	Final assembly	300,000	75.00	75,000	75.00	150,000	75,000
11	Special finishing	50,000	25.00	25,000	-	-	25,000
12	Total conversion costs	€500,000	€137.50	€137,500	€112.50	€225,000	€137,500
13	Total costs	€1,400,000	€537.50	€537,500	€362.50	€725,000	€137,500

The three conversion operations incur fixed labour and overhead costs per month. Following accepted practice, the cost analysts computed the normal conversion costs per unit of product. Because these operations are virtually identical for each type of motor scooter, the conversion cost per unit would be the same for each type of motor scooter (if performed, of course). Observe that the direct materials costs per unit are higher for Sharks than for Jets but the conversion costs per unit are the same for the two operations that both models pass through. Using operations costing, Wahoo! MotorScooter would create a job for each type of scooter and trace specific direct materials costs, as incurred, to each job. Conversion costs would be applied to jobs based on the numbers of units of the job, regardless of the type of motor scooter. If all went as planned in March, the cost results would be as shown in Exhibit 11.14.

The company's accounting system would increase Finished goods inventory by €537,500 for Work order 101 and €725,000 for Work order 102. Expense of the period would be increased by the amount of unused conversion cost, €137,500. Because conversion operations are so similar for each product, the company can simplify its inventory accounting by treating the conversion costs as the expected results of a process costing system.

Chapter Summary

Joint product processes simultaneously produce multiple outputs. Selling or processing these outputs further depends on the net realizable values (sales less further processing costs) of joint products. Product decisions should not be made, if at all possible, based on joint cost allocations, which arise from the need to assign joint process costs to two or more products manufactured from a common input. The usual objective of joint cost allocation is to measure costs of the inputs for financial or contractual reporting. There is no exact way to trace joint costs to products, so allocations are arbitrary but not random. On the other hand, joint cost allocations might prove useful or strategically sound in some industries or situations where prices or revenues depend on discretionary choice of the allocation method. Two common methods of joint cost allocation distribute joint costs to main products based on relative net realizable value (or *estimated* net realizable value) or relative physical measures. By-products do not receive joint cost allocations and their net realizable values are counted as other income or are deducted from joint process costs.

Process costing is used when it is not possible or practical to identify costs with specific lots or batches of product. A process costing system accumulates costs for each production department but does not maintain separate records of costs for each unit produced. When comparing job and process costing, companies generally find that job costing provides more data but has higher record-keeping costs. Managers and accountants must decide whether the additional data available under job costing justify these higher costs. For companies that produce relatively homogeneous units in a continuous process, cost–benefit analysis generally favours process costing.

The two most common process costing methods are weighted-average costing and first-in, first-out (FIFO) costing (discussed in Appendix 11B). The weighted-average method makes no distinction between opening inventory and current period costs. Weighted-average costing results do not differ materially when costs do not vary much across periods.

Process costing assigns costs to closing WIP inventory and units completed using five steps:

Step 1: Summarize the flow of physical units.
Step 2: Compute the equivalent number of units produced.
Step 3: Summarize the total costs to be accounted for.
Step 4: Compute costs per equivalent unit.
Step 5: Allocate costs to goods transferred out (completed and to closing inventory and to spoiled units, if applicable).

Appendix 11A: The relative sales value at split-off method allocates joint costs based on the relative sales values of the joint products at their split-off point. The constant gross margin percentage method allocates joint costs to products in such a way that the gross margin percentages as a percentage of revenue *are the same* for each joint product.

Appendix 11C: Operation costing is a hybrid of job-order and process costing and companies use it when they produce batches of similar products with significantly different types of material. Hybrid costing is appropriate for costing the manufacture of goods that have both common characteristics and some individual characteristics.

Key Terms

For each term's definition, refer to the indicated page, or turn to the glossary at the end of the text.

abnormal spoilage,	545	further processing costs,	535
by-product,	538	intermediate product,	532
constant gross margin percentage method,*	548	joint costs,	532
current equivalent unit,#	551	joint products,	532
equivalent units,	543	joint production process,	532
final product,	532	main product,	538
first-in, first-out (FIFO) costing,#	549	net realizable value (NRV),	535

net realizable value (NRV) method, 539
normal spoilage, 545
operation costing†, 552
physical measures (or quantities) method, 539
process costing system, 541
production cost report, 544
relative sales value at split-off method,* 548
split-off point, 532
spoilage, 544
waste, 532, 544
weighted-average process costing, 547

** Term appears in Appendix 11A.*
 # Term appears in Appendix 11B.
† Term appears in Appendix 11C.

*Review Questions are mostly written at a **basic** level; Critical Analysis questions and Exercises are **intermediate**, and Problems and Cases are **advanced**.*

Review Questions

11.1 What is the nature of a joint production process?

11.2 How do joint products, intermediate products and final products differ?

11.3 What are the similarities and differences between joint costs and indirect costs?

11.4 What are the steps to follow to make decisions about producing products from joint processes?

11.5 Why might some express a preference for the net realizable value method of joint-cost allocation over the physical measures method?

11.6 When might a physical measures method for allocation be preferred?

11.7 What is the condition under which an item should be treated as a by-product rather than as a joint product?

11.8 Why are joint costs irrelevant in the sell-or-process-further decision? What costs are important?

11.9 Why are equivalent units computed for process costing?

11.10 A manufacturing company has records of its current activity in WIP inventory and its closing WIP inventory; however, the record of its opening inventory has been lost. What data are needed to compute the opening inventory? Express your answer in equation form.

11.11 How are spoilage costs similar to under-applied overhead?

11.12 (Appendix 11B) If costs change from one period to another, why do costs that are transferred out of one department under FIFO costing include units with two different costs?

11.13 (Appendix 11C) How is operation costing similar to, and different from, both job costing and process costing?

Critical Analysis

11.14 Company A and Company B are negotiating the construction and operation of a plant that will produce joint products X and Y and by-product W, which has a positive net realizable value. Company A will use all of product X and operate the plant. Company B claims that it needs only 80 per cent of product Y that will be produced. Company A has no use for the excess product Y, but a market for it exists. Prepare a written memo outlining the principles you recommend the companies use to negotiate the sharing of the plant's costs of production.

11.15 Bonzo Oil Co. and Crusty Petroleum Inc. are entering a joint venture to construct and operate an oil refinery in a foreign country. This refinery will process crude oil in a joint process that results in multiple products, such as gasoline, jet fuel, asphalt and petrochemicals that require further processing. The companies have determined to jointly create a corporation to operate the refinery and share its outputs and costs fairly. The joint venture will pay a royalty fee to the host country for each barrel of crude oil processed and will charge the costs of operations to Bonzo and Crusty. Ignore taxation, political issues and technical processing considerations (all of which, by the way, are material). Form small groups to design a costing system to allocate the costs of *receiving* crude oil, *refining* the crude oil and *distributing* the products from the refinery that is both fair and informative to Bonzo and Crusty. Be prepared to present proposals in an open forum.

11.16 (continuation of 11.15) A year later, Bonzo Oil experienced a 25 per cent decline in the sales of its products and no longer accepts its full shipments of the refinery outputs. Accordingly, Bonzo seeks to renegotiate the agreement based on the joint-costing system prepared previously. Form small groups, half representing Bonzo and half representing Crusty. Considering only your company's interests, prepare proposals to modify the joint-costing agreement. If possible, choose two representative groups to openly resolve their differences and develop a modified agreement.

11.17 Assume that your company operates a joint production process that generates three main products and one by-product. If you allocate joint costs only for financial reporting, would you ever care whether you use the NRV or the physical measures method? Explain.

11.18 Top management has decided that your division, which operates a joint production process, no longer provides a competitive return and should be shut down and all assets liquidated. Prepare an outline of the costs and benefits (to all affected parties) of the decision to shut down and liquidate your division.

11.19 Respond to this comment: 'Because joint cost allocations are arbitrary, there is no rational argument for allocating joint costs except for complying with financial or tax reporting requirements.'

11.20 Management of a large beer maker is trying to decide whether to install a job or a process costing system. The manufacturing vice president has stated that job costing gives the company the best control because it makes possible the assignment of costs to specific batches of beer. The controller, however, has stated that job costing requires too much record-keeping. Would a process costing system meet the manufacturing vice president's control objectives? Explain.

11.21 (Appendix 11B) A new member of the controller's staff in your company, a large producer of paper products, has just completed a report that urges the company to adopt the last-in, first-out (LIFO) method of process costing. The controller is concerned about the recommendation because the cost records are maintained on a FIFO basis. Indeed, the controller has not even heard of using LIFO for process cost accounting. Form small groups to prepare a report addressing the following:

a. If allowed by IFRS, would it be possible to use LIFO for process costing? What are the key issues? Would using it be desirable? Explain.

b. In your library or on the Internet (company home pages or the SEC's EDGAR database), obtain information on inventory policies of four paper manufacturers (e.g., **The Portucel Soporcel Group, MeadWestvaco, Ballarpur Industries Limited**). Describe how firms in this industry account for their process costs.

11.22 (Appendix 11B) Under which of the following conditions will the first-in, first-out (FIFO) method of process costing produce the same cost of goods manufactured as the weighted-average method?

a. When goods produced are homogeneous.

b. When there is no opening inventory.

c. When opening and closing inventories are each 50 per cent complete.

d. None of these.

[CPA adapted]

11.23 An error was made in computing the percentage of completion of the closing WIP inventory for the current year. The error resulted in assigning a *lower percentage of completion* to each component of the inventory than actually was the case. Assume that there was no opening inventory. What is the effect of this error on:

a. The computation of total equivalent units? (understate or overstate?)

b. The computation of costs per equivalent unit? (understate or overstate?)

c. Costs assigned to cost of goods transferred out for the period? (understate or overstate?)

[CPA adapted]

11.24 When computing the cost per equivalent unit, the weighted-average method considers

a. Current costs only.

b. Current costs plus costs in opening WIP inventory.

c. Current costs plus costs in closing WIP inventory.

d. Current costs less costs in opening WIP inventory.

[CPA adapted]

11.25 Explain how the concept of 'normal spoilage' could impede quality improvements in processes. If you do not distinguish between normal and abnormal spoilage, how would you identify 'unacceptable' spoilage?

11.26 Describe how an individual could manipulate reported earnings by misstating degrees of completion of closing WIP. Would it be easy to continue this manipulation for subsequent periods? Explain.

Exercises

Exercise 11.27 [LO 1] Sell or Process Further

Amazon Company processes Chemical DX-1 through a joint production process. The costs to process one batch of DX-1 are R$300,000 for materials and R$450,000 for conversion costs. This processing results in two outputs, Laudinium and Tranquil, that sell for a total of R$1,125,000. The sales revenue from Laudinium amounts to R$900,000 of the total. Joint product Tranquil can be processed further and sold for R$450,000 as T-Prime. Further processing costs for T-Prime are estimated to be R$150,000 for the batch's production. (Monetary units given in Brazilian reais, R$.)

Required

Which products should Amazon produce and sell?

Exercise 11.28 [LO 1] Sell or Process Further

Dama Roja Mining SA operates an ore-processing plant. A typical batch of ore run through the plant yields three refined products: lead, copper and manganese. At the split-off point, the intermediate products cannot be sold without further processing. The lead from a typical batch sells for €30,000 after incurring additional processing costs of €10,000. The copper is sold for €100,000 after additional processing costs of €45,000. The manganese yield sells for €40,000 but requires additional processing costs of €15,000. The cost of processing the raw ore, including its purchase, is €50,000 per batch.

Required

Which products should Dama Roja produce and sell?

Exercise 11.29 [LO 2] Net Realizable Value Method

Refer to Exercise 11.27.

Required

Using the net realizable value method, assign joint costs to Amazon's final products.

Exercise 11.30 [LO 2] Physical Measures Method

Refer to Exercise 11.27. Assume that one batch of DX-1 produces 400 units of Laudinium and 100 units of T-Prime (after additional processing).

Required

Using the physical measures method, assign joint costs to final products.

Exercise 11.31 [LO 5] Relative Sales Value at Split Off and Constant Gross Margin Methods (Appendix 11A)

Refer to Exercise 11.27.

Required

Allocate the joint costs using (1) the relative sales value at split off and (2) the constant gross margin percentage methods described in Appendix 11A.

Exercise 11.32 [LO 2] Estimated Net Realizable Value Method

Refer to Exercise 11.28.

Required

Use the net realizable value method to allocate Dama Roja's joint processing costs.

Exercise 11.33 [LO 2] Comparison of Methods

The following questions are based on Atkinson Ltd, which manufactures products X, Y and Z from a joint process. Joint process costs were £90,000. Additional information is provided:

			If processed further	
Product	Units produced	Sales value at split off	Sales values	Additional costs
X	15,000	£100,000	£125,000	£20,000
Y	5,000	40,000	60,000	16,000
Z	10,000	60,000	75,000	18,000

Required

a. Assuming that joint product costs are allocated using the physical measures (units produced) method, what were the total costs of product X (including £20,000 if processed further)?

b. Assuming that joint product costs are allocated using the net realizable value method, what were the total costs of product Y (including the £16,000 if processed further)?

[CPA adapted]

Exercise 11.34 [LO 5] Relative Sales Value at Split Off and Constant Gross Margin Percentage Methods (Appendix 11A)

Refer to Exercise 11.33.

Required

Allocate the joint costs using (1) the relative sales value at split-off method and (2) the constant gross margin percentage method described in Appendix 11A.

Exercise 11.35 [LO 2] Physical Measures Method with By-product

Mon Ami Fertilizer Corporation uses organic materials to produce fertilizers for home gardens. Through its production processes, the company manufactures Nitro, a high nitrogen fertilizer, and Phospho, a high phosphorus fertilizer. A by-product of the process is methane, which is used to generate power for the company's operations. The fertilizers are sold either in bulk to nurseries or in individual packages to home gardeners. The company allocates the costs on the basis of the physical measures method.

Last month, 315,000 units of input were processed at a total cost of €250,000. The output of the process consisted of 45,000 units of Nitro, 90,000 units of Phospho and 180,000 units of methane. The by-product methane would have cost €10,000 had it been purchased from the local gas utility. This is considered to be its net realizable value, which is deducted from the joint processing costs of the main products.

Required

Build a spreadsheet to solve this requirement. What share of the joint costs should be assigned to each main product using the physical measures method?

Exercise 11.36 [LO 2] By-products

European Leather Products processes cowhide to produce three outputs (leather, suede, dog chews). Leather and suede are considered main products, and dog chews are a by-product. During a recent month, the following events occurred:

- Produced and sold 200 units of leather and 100 units of suede. Produced 25 units of dog chews.
- Recorded €115,000 sales revenue from leather and suede. The cost of sales before accounting for the by-product was €45,000.
- These costs are charged as they are incurred against any by-product sales. (None of the by-products were in closing inventory.)
- Received €875 in revenue from the sale of the 25 units of dog chews.

Required

Prepare an analysis showing the sales revenue, other income, cost of goods sold, other relevant data and gross margins that would be reported for each of the two methods of by-product accounting described in the text.

Exercise 11.37 [LO 2] By-products

The following questions are based on Bluth Corporation, which manufactures a product that gives rise to the by-product Buster. The only cost associated with Buster is the additional processing cost of $2 for each unit. Bluth accounts for Buster sales first by deducting its separable costs from such sales and then by deducting this net amount from the cost of sales of the major product. (This is method 2 discussed in the text.) This year, 5,000 units of Buster were produced; all were sold at $10 each.

Required

a. Sales revenue and cost of goods sold from the main product were $500,000 and $250,000, respectively, for the year. What was the gross margin after considering the by-product sales and costs?
b. If Bluth changes its method of accounting for Buster sales by showing the net amount as other revenue, what would its gross margin be? Explain.
c. If Bluth changes its method of accounting as indicated in requirement (b), what are the effects of the change on the company's profits?

[CPA adapted]

Exercise 11.38 [LO 4] Equivalent Units Computation, Weighted-average Method

ManU Ltd shows the following information concerning its work in progress:

1. Opening inventory, 4,000 partially complete units.
2. Transferred out, 12,000 units.
3. Closing inventory (materials, 10 per cent complete; conversion costs, 20 per cent complete).
4. Started this month, 16,000 units.

Required

a. Compute the number of equivalent units for materials using the weighted-average method.
b. Compute the number of equivalent units for conversion costs using the weighted-average method.

Exercise 11.39 [LO 6] Equivalent Units Computation, FIFO Method (Appendix 11B)

Refer to the data in Exercise 11.38. Assume that closing inventory is 20 per cent complete with respect to materials and 15 per cent complete with respect to conversion costs.

Required

a. Compute the number of equivalent units for materials using FIFO.
b. Compute the number of equivalent units for conversion costs using FIFO.

Exercise 11.40 [LO 4] Equivalent Units Computed, Weighted-average Method

Titilleau SARL, a soft drink maker, adds materials at the opening of the process in Department A. The following information pertains to Department A's work in progress during April:

	Units
Work in progress, 1 April (60% complete as to conversion costs)	11,000
Started in April	60,000
Completed	50,000
Work in progress, 30 April (40% complete as to conversion costs)	15,000

Required

a. Compute the number of equivalent units for materials using the weighted-average method.
b. Compute the number of equivalent units for conversion costs using the weighted-average method.

[CPA adapted]

Exercise 11.41 [LO 6] Equivalent Units Computed, FIFO Method (Appendix 11B)

Department A is the first stage of Macaro Company's production cycle. The following information is available for conversion costs for the month of April:

	Units
Opening work in progress (50% complete)	40,000
Started in April	300,000
Completed in April and transferred to Department B	200,000
Closing work in progress (30% complete)	140,000

Required

Using the FIFO method, compute the number of equivalent units for the conversion costs.

[CPA adapted]

Exercise 11.42 [LO 4] Cost Per Equivalent Unit (with Spoilage) Computed, Weighted-average Method

Chimiche Innocue SpA had opening WIP inventory of €119,500 on 1 October. Of this amount, €55,000 was the cost of direct materials, and €64,500 was for conversion costs. The 21,000 units in the opening inventory were 25 per cent complete with respect to both direct materials and conversion costs.

During October, 18,000 units were transferred out, 600 were spoiled and 15,000 remained in the closing inventory. Spoiled units were 100 per cent complete with respect to materials and 50 per cent complete with respect to conversion costs when they were found to be spoiled. The units in the closing WIP inventory were 80 per cent complete with respect to direct materials and 40 per cent complete with respect to conversion costs. Costs incurred during the period amounted to €432,000 for direct materials and €518,000 for conversion costs.

Required

Build a spreadsheet to compute the cost per equivalent unit for direct materials and for conversion costs using the weighted-average method.

Exercise 11.43 [LO 4] Cost Assignment to Units Completed, Spoilage and Closing Inventory, Weighted-average Method

Refer to the data in Exercise 11.42.

Required

Build a spreadsheet to compute the costs of good units completed and transferred out, spoilage, and closing inventory using the weighted-average method.

Exercise 11.44 [LO 7] Assign Costs to Products Using Operation Costing (Appendix 11C)

The Liberty in Motion Corporation makes three products – standard manual wheelchairs, electric wheelchairs and wheelbase scooters. The company had the following work orders for the month of September:

Customer	Order quantity	Order revenue
South	40 manual, 40 electric, 10 wheelbase	€117,000
Central	100 manual, 80 electric	194,000
West	100 manual, 100 electric, 50 wheelbase	355,000

Direct materials costs are as follows:

Manual wheelchairs	€200 per unit
Electric wheelchairs	700 per unit
Wheelbase scooters	1,000 per unit

Conversion costs incurred in Work-in-progress – Basic assembly = €100 per unit for all three types. Conversion costs incurred in Work-in-progress – Special assembly = €150 per unit for electric wheelchairs and €200 per unit for wheelbase scooters. Manual wheelchairs require no special assembly.

Required

a. Compute the product costs for September for each of the three products.

b. Use a spreadsheet to show the flow of costs through inventory accounts. Assume that all products are transferred to Finished goods when completed, and then to Cost of goods sold when sold. All products in this exercise were sold in September. Use two work-in-progress accounts: Work-in-progress – Basic assembly and Work-in-progress – Special assembly.

c. Taking into account the revenue from each customer's order and the direct materials and conversion costs required to produce the products for each order, compute customer profits for each order.

Problems

Problem 11.45 [LO 1] Sell or Process Further

Norsk Trelast AS operates a sawmill facility. The company accounts for the bark chips that result from the primary sawing operation as a by-product. It sells the chips to another company at a price of kr 100 per cubic metre. Normally, sales revenue from this bark is kr3,400,000 per month. The customer loads and transports the bark at no cost to Norsk Trelast.

As an alternative, the company can rent equipment that will process the chips and bag them for sale as decorative garden mulch. Approximately 35 per cent of the bark will be graded 'large' and will sell for kr200 per cubic metre. About 55 per cent will be graded 'medium' and will sell for kr125 per cubic metre. The remainder will be sold as mulch for kr75 per cubic metre.

Costs of the equipment to process and bag the chips and the personnel to operate the equipment total kr1,120,000 per month, regardless of the amount of bark processed. (Monetary values given in Norwegian krone, kr.)

Required

Assuming a typical month, prepare a memo to Norsk Trelast's management that demonstrates whether the company should sell the bark for kr 100 per cubic metre or process it further.

Problem 11.46 [LO 1, 2] Sell or Process Further

O'Malley Corp. uses a joint process that costs €120,000 for inputs and processing per batch. Processing one batch results in the following joint outputs:

Product	Quantity	Sales price at split off	Further processing	Sales price after further processing
X	1,000,000 litres	€0.10 per litre	NA	NA
Y	500,000 litres	€0.12 per litre	€12,000	€0.15 per litre
Z	100,000 litres	NA	2,000	0.08 per litre

O'Malley Corp. allocates joint costs on the basis of volume (litres) of output.

Required

Build a spreadsheet to solve requirement (b).

a. What alternatives to sell or process further are available to O'Malley?

b. Compute the product costs for each main product in total and per unit for each alternative presented in requirement (a).

c. Illustrate how can your spreadsheet be used to demonstrate the effect of possible changes in sales prices or costs on O'Malley's decision to sell Product Y at split off or process it further?

Problem 11.47 [LO 1, 2] Net Realizable Value Method

Komfort Konfekt AG purchases cocoa beans and processes them into cocoa butter, cocoa powder and shells. The standard yield from processing each 50 kilogram sack of cocoa beans is 10 kilograms of butter, 20 kilograms of powder and 20 kilograms of shells. The butter can be sold for €14 per kilogram and the powder for €12 per kilogram at the split-off point. The shells are disposed of at a cost of €2 per batch of 10 kilogram of shells.

The cost of the cocoa beans is €50 per 50 kilograms. Conversion resources to process each 50 kilograms of beans up to the split-off point cost €100.

Required

Compute the joint cost allocated to cocoa butter and cocoa powder produced from 50 kilograms of cocoa beans using the net realizable value method.

Problem 11.48 [LO 2] Physical Measures Method

Refer to Problem 11.47.

Required

Use the physical measures method to allocate joint costs.

Problem 11.49 [LO 1, 2] Sell or Process Further

Refer to Problem 11.47. Assume that the cocoa butter could be sold either at split off or after additional processing. The additional processing costs are €1 per kilogram, at which point the butter can be sold for €16.50 per kilogram.

Required

a. Should cocoa butter be sold at split off or processed further?
b. Assume that cocoa butter is processed further and allocate the joint costs using the net realizable value method.

Problem 11.50 [LO 1, 2] Sell or Process Further

Refer to Problems 11.47 and 11.49. In addition to possibly processing cocoa butter further, assume that the cocoa shells could be processed further at a cost of €2 per batch of 10 kilograms and sold for €0.10 per kilogram as garden mulch.

Required

a. Prepare a diagram that describes the possible sets of products and by-products.
b. Allocate the joint costs to the main products using the net realizable value method.

Problem 11.51 [LO 1, 2, 3] Joint Costing in a Process-costing Context: Net Realizable Value Method

Greek Company produces three products: Alpha, Beta and Gamma. Alpha and Gamma are main products; Beta is a by-product of Alpha. Information on the past month's production processes follows:

- In process 1,120,000 units of the raw material Rho are processed at a total cost of €210,000. After processing in process 1, 65 per cent of the units are transferred to process 2, and 35 per cent of the units (now unprocessed Gamma) are transferred to process 3.
- In process 2, the materials received from process 1 are processed at an additional cost of €56,000. Sixty per cent of the units become Alpha and are transferred to process 4. The remaining 40 per cent emerge as Beta and are sold at €3.50 per unit after additional processing. The additional processing costs to make Beta saleable are €10,500.
- In process 3, Gamma is processed at an additional cost of €224,000. A normal loss of units of Gamma occurs in this process. The loss equals 15 per cent of the units processed. The remaining good output is then sold for €15.40 per unit.
- In process 4, Alpha is processed at an additional cost of €25,200. After this processing, it can be sold for €7 per unit.

Required

a. Prepare a diagram to display Greek Company's revenues, costs, products and processes.
b. Prepare a schedule showing the allocation of the €210,000 joint cost between Alpha and Gamma using the net realizable value approach. The net realizable value of by-products reduces the joint costs of the related main product.

[CPA adapted]

Problem 11.52 [LO 1, 2] Maximum Input Price: Net Realizable Value Method

Cape Town Manufacturing Company produces two joint products from its manufacturing operation. Product J sells for R308 per unit, and product M sells for R91 per unit at the split-off point. In a typical month, 42,000 units are processed; 32,000 units become product M and 10,000 units become product J after an additional R455,000 of processing costs are incurred.

The joint process has only unit-level costs. In a typical month, the conversion costs of the joint products amount to R861,000. Materials prices are volatile, and if they are too high, the company stops production. Cape Town Manufacturing requires a minimum 20 per cent return on sales. (Monetary values given in South African rand, R or ZAR.)

Required

Build a spreadsheet to solve requirement (a).

Management has asked you to determine the maximum price that the company should pay for the materials.

a. Calculate the maximum price that Cape Town Manufacturing should pay for the materials.
b. Write a brief memo to management explaining how you arrived at your answer in requirement (a).

Problem 11.53 [LO 1, 2] Joint-cost Allocation and Product Profitability

Grünchem AG produces chemicals used in the cleaning industry. During the previous month, it incurred €400,000 of joint costs in producing 90,000 units of AM-12 and 60,000 units of BM-36. Grünchem allocates joint costs based on the number of units produced. Currently, AM-12 is sold at split off for €6.00 per unit. Flanke Company has approached Grünchem to purchase all of the AM-12 monthly production after further processing, which will cost Grünchem €90,000 per month.

Required

a. What is the minimum sales price Grünchem should charge Flanke for AM-12 after further processing?
b. Assume that Grünchem has agreed to sell AM-12 to Flanke after further processing for €8.00 per unit. During the first month, Grünchem delivered 60,000 units to Flanke and had 30,000 units remaining in inventory at the end of the month. What is the operating profit generated by sales of AM-12 during the first month, and what is the cost of processed AM-12 still in inventory at the end of the month?

[CMA adapted]

Problem 11.54 [LO 3, 4] Production Cost Report (Prior Department Process Costs), Weighted-average Method

Recycle Industries of Stockholm recycles galvanized steel from automobile bodies in two processes: shredding and de-galvanizing. It processes galvanized steel auto bodies in the shredding process and sends the shredded steel to the newly developed de-galvanizing process, which removes zinc by electrolysis. Zinc, which has a relatively high value, is the principal product of the process. The company transferred 6,000 metric tons of steel to the de-galvanizing process this month. Neither process had any spoilage.

Because the galvanized steel is homogeneous and shredded in a continuous process, the company uses a process-costing accounting system to assign costs to it. The following information is available for the de-galvanizing process during the last year:

Recycle Industries
De-galvanizing process last year

			De-galvanizing process	
Physical flow (metric tons):	**Units**	**Shredding process costs**	**Direct materials**	**Conversion costs ($Canadian)**
Opening inventory	2,000	100% complete	40% complete	80% complete
Closing inventory	3,000	100% complete	80% complete	60% complete
Transferred in	6,000	100% complete		
Costs incurred (Swedish kr):				
Opening inventory		7,000,000kr	534,000kr	320,000kr
Current costs		40,000,000	2,500,000	7,840,000

Required

Prepare a production cost report using weighted-average costing.

Cases

Case 11.55 [LO 1, 2] Joint-product Decision Making and Joint-cost Allocation in a Risky Venture

Honda imported the first automobile with a galvanized (zinc-coated) body into the United States. By the 1990s, nearly every automobile manufacturer in the world used galvanized metal to extend the life of vehicles. At the same time, the use of galvanized metal for appliances and structural applications, for example, increased.

Through obsolescence and recycling, a rapidly increasing amount of galvanized scrap exists. The zinc coating on this galvanized scrap causes pollution problems due to zinc contamination when the scrap is melted to produce new iron or steel. In conjunction with the University of California–Berkeley, **Metal Recovery Technologies Inc.** (MRTI), is improving its doubly patented electrolytic process to strip pure zinc from galvanized scrap. The process originally was developed in 1991 with support from the **Argonne National Laboratory** and the **US Department of Energy.** MRTI's process uses much less energy than other methods; produces two pure joint products, zinc and highest-quality, reusable ('black') steel and prevents environmental damage from zinc and waste resulting from other methods.

The government and the company estimate that using this process to de-zinc 5 million tons of galvanized scrap (the amount recycled in the United States each year) could

- Save 50 trillion BTUs of energy.
- Save $140 million in raw materials for US iron and steel companies.
- Save $100 million in foreign exchange spending by reducing the need for zinc imports.
- Eliminate toxic zinc from waste streams.

In 1998 MRTI listed its shares on the Berlin Stock Exchange and received financing of $3 million from Geneva-based Zinc Investments Inc. With the proceeds of share sales and the Swiss financing, MRTI revamped its East Chicago, Indiana, plant to reach a commercial scale of 120,000 tons of galvanized scrap per year, which would result in expected revenues of $23 million per year (at 1998 prices) opening in the year 1999. Clouding the future is the development-stage company's financial performance, which at 31 December 1997, included a net loss of $622,500, current assets of $61,619, and current liabilities of $7,295,282. MRTI's independent auditors raised questions about the company's ability to continue as a going concern, which could affect its ability to raise additional capital.

MRTI expects the following annual costs of operations for the commercialized process:

Material cost (galvanized steel scrap and sodium hydroxide)	$6,600,000
Conversion cost (labour, power, depreciation and amortization)	12,500,000
General and administrative cost	1,800,000

The commercialized process, if successful, would separate and recover 100 per cent of the steel and zinc from the galvanized scrap and regenerate the sodium hydroxide in the electrolytic solution. The typical proportion of steel and zinc in galvanized steel is 98 per cent steel and 2 per cent zinc. The 1998 per-ton market prices for black steel and recovered zinc were $170 and $1,200, respectively.

Required

Prepare group responses to each of the following items for presentation.

a. If MRTI is successful in commercializing its electrolytic process, would the company be profitable?

b. Market prices for non-precious metals can fluctuate 20 per cent per year. Would MRTI be profitable if the prices of the scrap it uses and of the metals it produces decline by 20 per cent?

c. Using the original data in the case, compare the profitability of the two joint products using the net realizable value and physical-measures methods.

d. Under what conditions would MRTI have an incentive to use one method or the other to measure product profitability? What ethical responsibilities do MRTI's managers and auditors face?

[Adapted from Buderi (1991) and Recyclers' World (www.recycle.net).]

Case 11.56 [LO 1, 2] Joint Products from Recycling

The weight of used tyres in Europe was expected to reach 2.5 million tons by the end of 1999. Anne Forteza of **IDE Environment** argued that more intense retreading and recycling must replace the currently widespread practice of sending used tyres to landfills. She estimated that approximately one-half of used tyres are re-treadable, but the balance is sent to landfills (36 per cent), left on vehicles in scrap yards (30 per cent), exported for incineration in the United States (8 per cent), incinerated for power (22 per cent), or incinerated for disposal (4 per cent). Aside from power generation, the treatment of most non-retreadable tyres is a waste of primary materials, an expensive disposal option, and a source of environmental pollution. Legislation in France requires alternative, environmentally sound solutions to dumping used tyres. Costs of dumping used tyres in landfills currently are €220 per ton and are expected to rise dramatically in France and elsewhere if other European countries adopt similar legislation.

The **Alpha Recyclage Project (ARP)** was launched in France to demonstrate an economical and environmental treatment of non-retreadable tires. ARP will take large numbers of used tyres at no cost if they contain the usual mix of re-treadable tires (50 per cent), sort them, sell suitable tyres to re-treaders for €2 per tyre, and treat the rest. ARP uses a cryogenic method to transform the waste tyres into primary materials (30 per cent fibre, 20 per cent steel and 50 per cent reusable rubber pellets). The cryogenic method, which uses liquid nitrogen, is more expensive than mechanical grinding (the other currently feasible method) but is cleaner and results in a higher quality of rubber pellet.

Following are data regarding ARP's annual operations.

Weight of tyres collected (average of 20 pounds per tyre)	30,000 tons
Sold to re-treaders @ €2 each	15,000 tons
Cryogenic joint process costs of recycled tires	€4,500,000
General and administrative costs	€1,900,000
Market price for scrap steel	€90 per ton
Market price for scrap fibre	€300 per ton
Market price for scrap rubber pellets	€45 per ton

Required

Prepare group responses to the following items for presentation.

a. Is the ARP's process a viable process for disposing of used tyres? Why or why not?

b. ARP must report results of operations to the National Council of Car Professions (NCPA), which is sponsoring the project. ARP intends to report revenues and costs by major product.

c. Prepare an objective and factual report that shows the results of annual operation and explains them in a manner to persuade NCPA to continue to sponsor the project.

[Information taken from www.recycle.net]

Case 11.57 [LO 1, 2] Effect of Cost Allocation on Pricing and Make-versus-buy Decisions

Ag-Coop is a large farm co-operative with a number of agriculture-related manufacturing and service divisions. As a co-operative, it pays no federal income taxes. It operates a fertilizer plant, which processes and mixes petrochemical compounds into three brands of agricultural fertilizer: Greenup, Maintane and Winterizer. The three brands differ with respect to selling price and the proportional content of basic chemicals.

The Fertilizer Manufacturing Division transfers the completed product to the co-operative's Retail Sales Division at a price based on the cost of each type of fertilizer plus a mark-up. The Manufacturing Division is completely automated so that the only costs it incurs are for the petrochemical inputs plus automated conversion, which is committed for the coming period. The primary feedstock costs $1.50 per kilogram. Each 1,000 kilograms of feedstock can produce either of the following mixtures of fertilizer:

Output schedules (in kilograms)	A	B
Greenup	500	600
Maintane	300	100
Winterizer	200	300

Production is limited to the monthly capacity of the dehydrator at 750,000 kilowatt-hours. The different chemical make-up of each brand of fertilizer requires different dehydrator use as follows:

Product	Kilowatt-hour usage per kilogram
Greenup	32
Maintane	20
Winterizer	40

Monthly conversion costs are $81,250. The company is producing according to output schedule A. Joint production costs including conversion are allocated to each product on the basis of weight.

The fertilizer is packed into 50 kilogram bags for sale in the co-operative's retail stores. The Manufacturing Division charges the retail stores its cost plus a mark-up. The sales price for each product charged by the co-operative's Retail Sales Division is as follows:

	Sales price per kilogram
Greenup	10.50
Maintane	9.00
Winterizer	10.40

Selling expenses are 20 per cent of the sales price.

The manager of the Retail Sales Division has complained that the prices charged are excessive and that she would prefer to purchase from another supplier. The Manufacturing Division manager argues that the processing mix was determined based on a careful analysis of the costs of each product compared to the prices charged by the Retail Sales Division.

Required

a. Assume that joint production costs including conversion are allocated to each product on the basis of weight. What is the cost per kilogram of each product including conversion costs and the feedstock cost of $1.50 per kilogram, assuming production schedule A is used?

b. Assume that joint production costs including conversion are allocated to each product on the basis of net realizable value if it is sold through the co-operative's Retail Sales Division. What is the allocated cost per kilogram of each product, assuming production schedule A is used?

c. Assume that joint production costs including conversion are allocated to each product on the basis of weight. Which of the two production schedules, A or B, produces the higher operating profit to the firm as a whole?

d. Would your answer to requirement (c) be different if joint production costs including committed overhead were allocated to each product on the basis of net realizable value? Explain.

e. Can you recommend an approach to product planning that considers the organization's overall profitability and avoids the divisional controversy? What are the costs and benefits of your recommended approach?

[CMA adapted]

Case 11.58 [LO 3, 4] Public Policy and Process Costs

After the United States Government tightened the ban on timber sales from US federal land, an industry consultant in Oregon observed, 'For communities affected by federal timber, the outlook is dismal.' In a related development, the British Columbia, Canada, government began implementing its Forest Practices Code, which has strict standards for logging activities and reforestation responsibilities. These developments unfavourably affected a number of US wood and paper products companies that had relied heavily on timber sales from US and BC public lands. They have experienced higher material costs and have had access to lower volumes of timber. Other companies, however, have benefited from the price increases caused by the ban on federal timber sales and increased restrictions on logging in British Columbia because they have either large private timberland elsewhere or long-term supply contracts with private timber owners.

Longview Fibre Co. of Longview, Washington, was one of the companies adversely affected by these developments. For several years after the imposition of these restrictions, the company suffered higher material costs for most of its products. Since Longview Fibre was at a disadvantage compared to its competitors with unaffected sources of raw materials, the company set a goal to significantly reduce its conversion costs. Following are the data that the company disclosed in one of its financial reports for each of its major product lines: timber products (logs and lumber), paper and paperboard, and containerboard products (packaging).

Longview Fibre Co
Consolidated Statement of Income (Unaudited)
For Six Months Ended 30 April, Year 2

Net sales:		
Timber products		$79,045,000
Paper and paperboard		92,433,000
Container-board products		190,677,000
		362,155,000
Cost of sales (all products)		329,748,000
Gross profit		$32,407,000
Selling, administrative and general expenses		32,313,000
Operating profit		$94,000
Operating profit (loss) by product:		
Timber products		$37,309,000
Paper and paperboard		(11,842,000)
Container-board products		(25,373,000)
		$94,000
	30 April, Year 2	**31 October, Year 1**
Inventories:		
Finished goods	$25,445,000	$24,832,000
Work in progress	19,220,000	13,868,000
Raw materials and supplies	48,192,000	45,802,000
	$92,857,000	$84,502,000
	Sales quantity	
Six months ended 30 April, Year 2:		
Timber products, board feet	144,000,000	
Paper and paperboard, tons	177,000	
Container-board products, tons	255,000	

Required

Work in small groups to develop solutions to the following requirements and then be prepared to present them to the class.

a. Reconstruct the elements of the basic cost-flow model (OB + TI – TO = CB) for Finished goods and Work-in-progress inventories. (*Hint:* Work backwards from cost of sales.)

b. Compute the average process cost per unit sold of each of the three product lines for the period opening 30 April, Year 2. [*Hint:* Work backwards from operating profit (loss) for each product.] Assume that selling, general and administrative costs were assigned to product lines on the basis of relative revenue.

c. Average process costs per unit sold during the comparable period in year 1 follow:

Average cost per unit sold	Year 1
Timber products, per board foot	$0.23
Paper and paperboard, per ton	502.01
Container-board products, per ton	789.59

Compare the year 1 costs to the year 2 costs computed in part (b). During the year 2 period, the company's costs increased as follows: raw timber, 8 per cent; wood chips used to make paper, 36 per cent; and container board, 12 per cent. From these data, does it appear that the company achieved its goal of reducing conversion costs? Describe a likely scenario that explains the company's changes in costs and year-2 profit performance.

[Adapted from Yang (1994) and Longview Fibre Co., Form 10-Q.]

Case 11.59 [LO 3, 4] Spoilage Costs, Weighted-average Method

Wendig Sport AG is a mature firm that manufactures a variety of high quality sports clothing for high school and university sports programmes throughout Europe. During the last year, the company's profits declined. Wendig has been using cost information that was developed two years ago. To determine the causes for weakened earnings performance, Wendig's controller, Paul Austerlitz, has asked Lara Klein, senior cost analyst, to investigate product costing at one of the company's largest plants in Munich, Germany.

The Munich plant manufactures insulated warm-up jackets in a continuous, one-department process. The process first involves the partial assembly of jackets using materials packet 1 (liner, shell, hood, pocket linings, zippers), which consumes 75 per cent of the conversion costs. At this point, partially complete jackets are inspected. Jackets that pass this inspection are finished with materials packet 2 (embroidered logos, numbers and names). After the finishing process, the jackets are inspected again. Conversion costs are applied uniformly through the process, and the Munich plant uses the weighted-average process-costing method. Typical jackets cost €60 to produce and, based on desired return on sales, sell for €100 each in the competitive sports apparel market.

The following information for the most recent month was available to Klein:

Units in opening WIP inventory	700	jackets
Conversion costs	€5,200	25% complete
Materials packet 1	€14,500	
Units started	10,500	jackets
Units fully completed	8,000	jackets
Spoilage at first inspection	600	jackets
Spoilage at second inspection	250	jackets
Current costs applied during the month:		
Conversion costs	€295,000	
Materials packet 1	€287,000	
Materials packet 2	€78,500	
Units in closing WIP inventory	2,850	jackets
Conversion costs	50%	complete

Required

a. The Munich plant manager indicates to Klein that all but 200 of the spoiled jackets at the first inspection point should be regarded as normal spoilage, and Austerlitz concurs. Discuss the accounting and management implications of separating spoilage into normal and abnormal spoilage.

b. Prepare a production cost report that analyses the most recent month's process costs.

c. Given your analysis in requirement (b), what sales price is necessary to generate the desired return on sales? Alternatively, what total process cost reduction is necessary to maintain the current sales price? What is your recommendation?

[CMA adapted]

Solutions to You're the Decision Maker

11.1 Operate or Shut Down the Process?, p. 534

a. High facility-level costs and low levels of production mean high average costs. In the long run, average costs must be surpassed by enough profit to justify the capital investment in the Mitsä mill. The company should analyse and improve the mill's constraints on production (bottlenecks), which can be either internal or external. For example, the Mitsä mill might have insufficient milling capacity (human or physical capital) to operate on a scale large enough to be more profitable, particularly with constraining operating agreements. Perhaps the mill's location means that the area does not have a sufficiently large market to support its capacity. Apparently, however, labour rules are causing the mill to operate only one shift per day when other mills operate two or more shifts per day. Assuming that the mill is operating below capacity and there is ample opportunity to sell increased mill output profitably, the company needs to consider obtaining more input for the mill or putting the resources to a better use. This could mean closing the Mitsä mill - or at least threatening to do so.

b. Let's assume that you prefer to continue working at the Mitsä mill because of the community and good working conditions. You are, however, aware of the responsibility to external shareholders and creditors, and you have no intention of misleading your superiors. Your response to the possible closing of the mill should be factual and complete. Consideration of all the costs and benefits would include not only the mill's direct operating costs but also the opportunity costs of lost sales, lost goodwill and lost skilled personnel. Other costs to consider are the costs of closing the mill, retraining employees for other jobs in the company, and offering severance packages to employees who are dismissed. You might be able to identify how the company could work with labour unions and the community to achieve mutual benefits – a fair price for timber, environmentally sensitive removal of timber, replanting trees, and higher regional income from mill employment and local purchases.

11.2 Testing the Validity of the Analysis?, p. 537

a. The Mitsä mill's products are commodities whose sales prices are set in very competitive markets. Thus, the revenue half of the data is subject to external forces that the company cannot control or forecast with complete accuracy. It is not unusual for some commodity prices to vary by 20 per cent or more from year to year, depending on economic conditions. In contrast, production quantities – given timber quality and availability – are probably quite reliable estimates. Joint process and further processing costs also are likely to be known with confidence.

b. *Materiality* means the amount a figure must differ from what is expected before a decision maker would change his or her decision (e.g., the difference between the two best alternatives, which is only about €17,000). The Mitsä mill's product decision is based on the expected net realizable values of alternative product mixes. A material difference in any of the elements of NRV – sales and further processing costs – would cause the mill's managers to select a different lumber and wood chip or pulp mix.

c. If the sales price for wood pulp (only) drops as indicated, the product decision changes completely. Such a decline in price makes selling wood chips directly to biofuel manufacturers more profitable. This decision also would idle the wood-pulp process, which undoubtedly has impacts on the company and the community.

d. Managers who do not understand sensitivity analysis sometimes accept an initial analysis without asking sufficient 'what-if' questions. Cost analysts should feel an obligation to subject important product analyses to thorough sensitivity analysis to determine which parameters are most material to product decisions. The sensitivity analysis at least should compute the effects of parameters at extreme values ('best-case' and 'worst-case' levels) and most likely values – at first one at a time. Combining the worst-case or best-case values of each parameter results in the worst-case or best-case 'scenarios.' You should advise managers about which parameters are most sensitive so that they can take steps to minimize adverse effects. These actions include gaining more precise measures of parameters or negotiating long-term sales or supplier contracts to lock in quantities, prices and costs.

11.3 Should STP use Weighted Average or FIFO Process Costing?, p. 552

a. The alternative methods, weighted-average or FIFO costing, result in very similar final cost allocations, as shown below.

Comparison of weighted average to FIFO costing	Weighted average	FIFO	Difference
Cost of goods completed	€599,537	€599,534	€4
Abnormal spoilage	6,427	6,429	(2)
Ending WIP inventory	25,036	25,038	(2)
Total	€631,000	€631,000	€0

b. The choice between methods seems obvious: if the costs are not materially different, choose the simpler, weighted-average method. Why go through the more complicated information gathering and calculations of equivalent units, particularly regarding spoilage, when the costs of all outcomes are nearly identical? This seems persuasive. However, once the analysis is set up, the Excel spreadsheet does all the arithmetic. Plant managers also might be comforted knowing that they had access to more detailed information about the outcomes of the plant operations, which could be improved by conducting the analysis at least daily. In this way, spoiled wood pulp that might be traced to contaminated wood chips could be intercepted quickly.

c. It appears that the joint/process costing system employed by the Mitsä facility does not clearly account for the costs of disposing abnormal spoilage. It seems likely that the joint and further processing costs include the costs of disposing normal spoilage, but an added charge should be expensed in the period when abnormal spoilage is disposed of (in addition to the lost processing costs). Perhaps this added charge is handled in an ad hoc way, but doing so underestimates the costs of abnormal spoilage.

Endnotes

1 STP periodically thins and trims its commercial forests to reduce fire danger and to increase growth rates and wood fibre yields.

2 Inconsistent accounting for by-product net revenues has been a source of conflict between Canada and the United States in their wood-products dumping dispute. The World Trade Organization ruled on appeal in 2004 that the United States applied accounting practices that inconsistently increased alleged product margins for Canada's main lumber products. *see World Trade Organization, 2004.*

3 Because the total NRV of decorative bark is immaterial, STP as easily could count it as a reduction of the sawmill's joint processing cost.

4 Note that the simplest situation would be without opening or closing WIP inventories or spoilage. In this case, the cost per unit would simply be the total product costs added during the month divided by the total units completed (and started, of course). Very high quality JIT processes might closely approximate this simple example (one more benefit of JIT = simple process costing!). For now, ignore the typical wood pulp yield from chips.

5 If STP decided instead to sell wood chips to biofuel manufacturers, the wood-pulp plant might be idle.

References

Buderi, R. (1991) 'A power-pinching way to recycle rust-proof steel', *BusinessWeek*, 11 November.

Grubel, H. (2004) 'The Canada–US softwood lumber dispute: the basic cause and the BC government's remedy', available at: www.sfu.ca/~grubel/_private/Forestry%20Paper.doc.

Joshi, S., R. Krishnan and L. Lave (2001) 'Estimating the hidden costs of environmental regulation', *The Accounting Review*, vol. 76, no. 2, pp. 171–198.

Khumawala, S.B., L.M. Parsons and T.P. Gordon (2005) 'Assessing the quality of not-for-profit efficiency ratios: do donors use joint cost allocation disclosures?' *Journal of Accounting, Auditing and Finance*, vol. 3, pp. 287–309.

Kunes, T. (2001) 'A green and lean workplace?' *Strategic Finance*, February, pp. 71–83; reprinted in J. Edwards (ed.), *Emerging Practices in Cost Management*, Gorham & Lamont, Valhalla, NY.

World Trade Organization (2004) *United States – Final dumping determination on softwood lumber from Canada*, WT/DS264/AB/R, 11 August.

Yang, D.J. (1994) 'Splinters everywhere', *BusinessWeek*, 10 January.

CHAPTER

12

Managing and Allocating Support Service Costs

Learning Objectives

After completing this chapter, you should be able to:

LO 1 Explain the importance of managing support service costs and the reasons these costs are allocated.

LO 2 Understand how to choose cost pools and to separate the cost of resources supplied from the cost of resources used.

LO 3 Understand how to choose appropriate allocation bases.

LO 4 Allocate support service department costs using the direct method.

LO 5 Allocate support service department costs using the step method.

LO 6 Evaluate the consequences of alternative cost allocations.

LO 7 Allocate support service department costs using the reciprocal cost method (Appendix 12).

Storhavn

Storhavn is a medium-sized Danish city that is facing budgetary difficulties. Storhavn is like most Danish cities that are characterized by large financial responsibilities, elected officials and active citizens. The scene is a meeting of Director of Budget, Mette Pedersen, and her budget staff who, under the guidance of the City's Mayor, prepared the draft of Storhavn's budget for the next fiscal year. After it is approved by the City Council, Pedersen and her staff will administer the budget from the Mayor's office. She had recently presented the draft of next year's budget to an open City Council meeting the week before. It had been a long, debate-filled meeting. The city's operating funds, which are mostly derived from the national government but also from local tax revenues, are not keeping pace with growing demands for services, so the city must make difficult trade-offs. Since the meeting, the Mayor's office received many angry phone calls and letters from citizens who felt the City was using the proposed budget to take funds away from their valued programmes.

'At times I think this budget process is hopelessly complex, and no matter what we do, someone is going to be angry,' Pedersen observed. 'Who would think that something as ordinary as *cost allocations* would cause so many citizens to pack City Council meetings, write angry letters to the editor of the local paper, and make us feel like public enemies instead of public servants?

'The city of Storhavn is trying to apply principles of *lean government*,[1] and I believe what we are doing is right, but we need to communicate better the "why" and "how" of what we are doing for the citizens of Storhavn. They need to understand that we are trying to run an efficient city government, but even a lean municipality has staff and facilities that need to be supported financially.

'I thought our proposal for using a more accurate approach to allocating costs would be so obviously better than what we have been doing that we would get praise, not condemnation. I half-expected to get a medal,' she chuckled ruefully.

Pedersen is highly qualified for the technical aspects of her job, but she is learning a difficult lesson in the art and politics of budgeting. Although a city's budget negotiations might be more open than most, cost allocation issues can cause friction in nearly every organization – public or private, for-profit or non-profit. In any organization, managing the process of cost allocation can be just as important as the allocations themselves.

Service Cost Challenge

The goal of every organization should be to achieve the objectives that prompted its creation. Commercial firms are created to provide goods and services and to earn at least a competitive profit. Non-profit hospitals are created to provide superior health care for the community and at least cover their costs of operation. Cities are established to provide essential services to their citizens within budgetary limits. Providing these services requires using scarce resources and making complex trade-offs among competing uses. Making these resource trade-offs requires reliable quantitative and qualitative cost management information about relative costs and benefits of alternatives.

Nearly every organization – commercial, public, non-profit – contains two types of subunits or departments: support service and production. **Support service** (or **indirect) departments** provide services internally within the organization. Typical support service departments include human resources, finance and accounting, and legal services. **Production** (or **line) departments** provide goods and services to customers, clients or public citizens. The total resources used by the organization to provide products externally include the costs of both types of departments; thus, organizations often allocate **support service costs**, which are the costs of resources supplied to provide support services, to their production departments to be counted as indirect or overhead costs. The amounts of support service costs allocated and methods used can affect decisions in production departments. An important decision is whether to use internal services or seek them from external entities. Relatedly, production departments may object to excessive allocations when support service departments appear to have excess capacity that is being passed on. Allocations of support service costs can also affect product costs that must be recovered by revenues; thus, affecting pricing and product mix decisions. Therefore, allocations of service department costs should be made carefully, accurately and with the intent of managing support services efficiently. This chapter applies (a) the differences between support service and production departments, (b) alternative support service cost allocation methods. The chapter further discusses how support service cost allocations can affect decisions about service capacity, service outsourcing and production.

Internal or Outsourced Support Services?

© Moonboard_Images

Indian employees at a call centre provide service support to international customers. The hiring frenzy in India is the flip side of the United States and Britain, where thousands of software and back-office jobs are being cut as companies take advantage of inexpensive global communications to drive down costs. This multi-billion euro industry in India already provides more than a million jobs.

As discussed in earlier chapters, every organization must make decisions that determine how to use its resources for productive processes that provide goods and services directly to customers, clients or citizens. The organization decides whether to perform all of the productive processes itself or to outsource some or parts of them. In addition, organizations must decide how to support their productive processes, for example, by providing accounting, human resources and legal support services. These support services could be provided by the organization's internal support service departments or by outsourcing them to external providers.

Some might argue that support services are a necessary part of every organization. But are they? Many organizations are outsourcing at least some of their internal support services. Companies commonly outsource traditional accounting functions such as payroll and accounts payable that require routine, straightforward procedures. Many companies also outsource their human resources, legal, tax and internal auditing functions. Outsourcing has become a popular way to 'right size' or 'downsize' organizations. As a result, organizations that provide such services have become some of the fastest-growing industries in developed and developing economies.

Cost management analysts from finance, accounting or operations departments most often are the professionals who prepare and analyse the information to support outsourcing decisions. The required information includes the knowledge base necessary to perform a service, the sensitivity of information needed to perform a service, the relative costs of a service, and the difficulty in finding, managing and keeping reliable, high-quality service providers. Whether to outsource any support service depends on the consideration of a combination of many quantitative and qualitative factors (see also Chapter 8 for an example).

Knowledge base

Complex or unique organizations might have distinct procedures and cultures that external service providers could have difficulty understanding and supporting. On the other hand, some support service expertise could be too specialized for the organization to maintain by itself. Consider, for example, the management of information technology in foreign countries. Organizations might see advantages to outsourcing these knowledge-based services to external service providers who have specialized expertise in these foreign countries and can provide benefits from economies of scale.

Sensitive information

Some organizations compete on the basis of their knowledge of technology or complex market and political situations. These firms might be reluctant to outsource support services, such as internal auditing, that would allow outsiders and potentially competitors to obtain their strategically important knowledge.

Reliable service providers

A less expensive outsourced service is not cost effective if its reliability and quality are low and adversely affect the organization's ability to meet its objectives. For example, many large firms have outsourced their customer-service departments to other companies (e.g., **Teletech**, www.teletech.com). Customer service is a very sensitive function that, if performed poorly, can drive away customers and damage the company's reputation. A damaged reputation can be very difficult to repair.

Relative costs

Many organizations see the outsourcing of support services as a means to increase budget flexibility and reduce current and long-term costs (outsourced employees' health care and pension costs, too). This puts great pressure on internal service departments to either provide comparable (or better) services at lower cost or disappear.

Management of Internal Support Service Costs

LO 1
Explain the importance of managing support service costs and the reasons these costs are allocated.

Customers accept products only if the value of the product meets or exceeds the prices charged. Customers who have choices provide strong discipline to an organization's use of resources for its products. But most internal support service departments function without such external discipline because usually all of their customers are internal and cannot buy services from outside. How does the organization manage its support service costs in the absence of competition? There are several cost-based, management approaches, two of which are discussed here.

- *Charge internal customers nothing for support services and recover the costs of the services from general revenues.* The advantage to this approach is that it is simple and inexpensive to operate because there is no need either to measure or charge for support service costs. Its disadvantage is that as

12.1 Cost Management in Practice

Municipal Outsourcing

In 2011 two municipalities in the Netherlands signed an outsourcing agreement to reduce costs. The city of Enschede will conduct several operational activities for the much smaller, nearby municipality of Losser. This customer-municipality specifies which activities will be outsourced, and Enschede decides how the activities will be carried out in order to save costs. This agreement mainly concerns back-office activities, such as payroll, accounting and treasury activities. Citizens of Losser will not notice much change in their contacts with the municipality. Cost savings will come from lower purchasing prices when buying larger quantities, economies of scale, and lower ICT costs because no separate systems are needed for Losser (their activities are done with the software and hardware that already runs Enschede's applications). Fifty-five civil servants moved from the payroll of Losser to Enschede, and, when people leave or retire, the efficiency savings will be used to lower total salary costs. Within 5 years, an annual cost reduction of €1.2 million is expected, which will be equally divided between the two cities.

Source: Author's research.

long as internal customers perceive *any* positive value from free services, they may demand more service without regard to the costs to the organization. Thus, internal support service departments could grow dramatically but inefficiently in response to high internal demand. There is no obvious signal to organization managers that they might be using resources inefficiently to provide support services that few internal customers would want if they had to pay for them.

- *Charge the costs of support services provided to internal customers and recover at least some of the costs from them.* Because of inefficiency problems with the first approach, most organizations use **cost allocation** – a systematic method of assigning the costs of resources to a department, product, or service when directly tracing costs is not possible – to charge support service costs to internal customers. Many organizations also recover those costs from users in the form of actual payments or transfers of funds on the basis of the allocations. A user department or internal customer would accept these support services only if the value of those services meets or exceeds the costs charged to the department. If user departments are required to use only internal services, they might control spending for support services indirectly by demonstrating that the organization is spending too much for those services.[2]

This second approach is common, but it also has disadvantages. First, cost allocations are, by nature, arbitrary; they are, at best, *discretionary* and might not measure the uses of resources accurately. Second, if internal customers are required to use internal services, they might spend valuable time negotiating and lobbying over fair prices, which could be an inefficient use of time and effort.

Poorly designed cost allocations can be the subject of disputes among departments and their constituents. Furthermore, cost allocations can create incentives to use or not use the services inappropriately if the allocated costs are not closely associated with the actual consumption of resources.

The issues of efficiency, fairness and team-building within private and public organizations are analogous to, although not as socially wrenching as, those that centrally managed countries recently faced. These countries, such as the People's Republic of China, relied on cost allocations in the past and are now using many market mechanisms to measure the values of goods and services and to allocate resources. These countries are finding not only that market mechanisms are more efficient because they do not require a large bureaucracy of central planners (although they do require enforcement of contracts) but also that market solutions are challenging cultural concepts of fairness and co-operation.

Distinguishing Between Support Service and Production Departments

Mette Pedersen's staff had prepared the budget draft after co-ordinating the spending requests of all the city's departments. The city's organizational chart appears in Exhibit 12.1. This chart separates the two types of departments, support services and production. Recall that *support service departments* (or indirect departments) provide support services to each other and to the production departments.

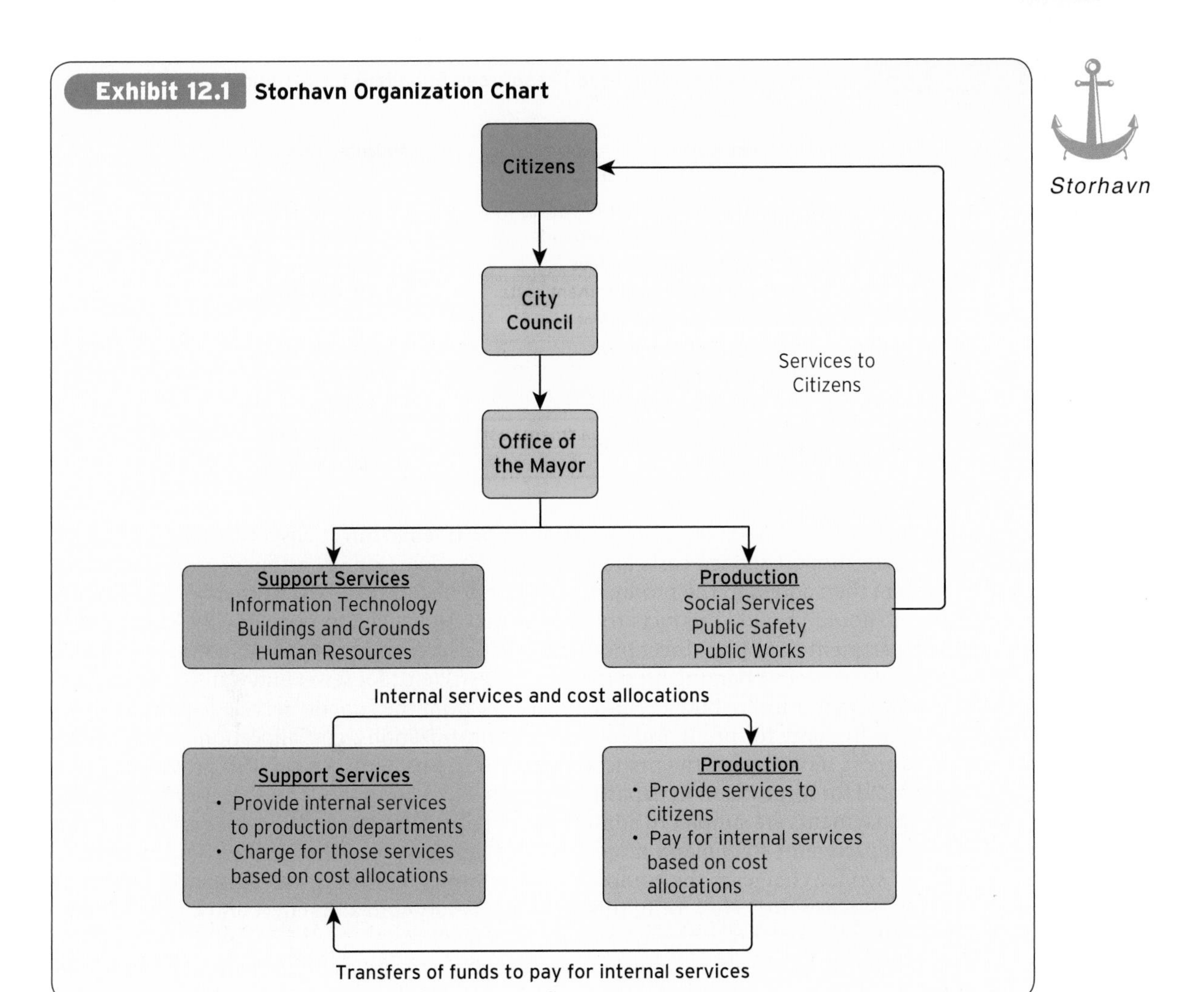

Production (or line) *departments* provide services directly to customers or the public. For example, *Public Safety* is a production department because it provides services (fire, police and emergency response) to citizens. *Public Works* is another production department that provides services (parks, roads and flood control) and products (water and sewer) to citizens. Whereas the *Human Resources* department is a support service because it provides services to other city departments, but not to citizens.

Deciding Who Pays for Internal Support Service Costs

Many production departments are supported by funds specifically designated for those purposes. For example, allocations from the Danish national government support Storhavn's internal support services and the Public Safety department. However, local tax revenues, which citizens voted for, support the city's parks. Thus, part of Pedersen's job to administer the city of Storhavn's budget is to ensure that funds are used for their intended purposes. In private, for-profit firms, top management may set aside funds for specific purposes, such as capital expenditures, environmental improvement or remediation, employee training, and so on to help ensure that lower-level managers actively pursue the related activities. In most cases, internal performance audits assure that funds were spent appropriately and with intended effects.

Support service costs are the costs of the resources supplied by a support service department that are used to provide its support services. These costs include the costs of personnel and the equipment, facilities and supplies these personnel need to provide the types and levels of support services that the organization desires. In a typical month, Storhavn spends DKK 1,450,000 on its

Exhibit 12.2 Storhavn: Costs Budgeted (Resources Supplied) for a Typical Month

	A	B	C
1	**Department**	**Budgeted cost**	
2	*Support department*		
3	S1: Information Technology	360,000	DKK
4	S2: Buildings and Grounds	840,000	
5	S3: Human Resources	250,000	
6	Total support department costs	1,450,000	DKK
7	*Production department*		
8	P1: Social Services	5,000,000	DKK
9	P2: Public Safety	2,700,000	
10	P3: Public Works	1,850,000	
11	Total production department costs	9,550,000	DKK
12	Total costs	11,000,000	DKK

support services and DKK 9,550,000 on production departments' direct costs (Exhibit 12.2). If, as occurs in Storhavn, support service costs are allocated to production departments, these allocated (indirect) costs are then added to the production departments' direct costs. Normally each production department should provide products to citizens that are judged to be worth the sum of allocated service department costs plus direct production department costs. If a production department must recoup its total costs by charging for services to citizens (e.g., for sewer and water), that department has a strong interest in the budgets and its services from the support service department.

In Storhavn, as in many for-profit and other public organizations, cost allocations compute the charges from support service departments to production departments for services provided. These services may be paid for by production departments, either as a lump sum or on a per-unit of service used. Lump-sum payments are simpler to administer, but also can have an adverse effect of motivating production departments to demand more services than they need. The greatest impediment to using per-unit of service charges is the complexity of defining, measuring and accounting for units of many different services. In its full form, this approach is very similar in effect and cost to an ABC costing system, wherein the unit of service is a unit of activity.[3]

As Pedersen learned, making these transfers is not simply a technical or mechanical process, particularly if there is a change in the allocation method, which alters the amounts that production departments pay for services from support service departments. As we shall see, Pedersen employs a hybrid cost allocation system for support service costs that is more responsive to service demand by production departments than only lump-sum payments but is less complex than payments based on an ABC costing system.

Allocating Service Costs for Decision Making

Allocating costs to activities unavoidably is done on a somewhat arbitrary basis. Some critics of cost allocation interpret the word *arbitrary* to mean 'unfounded' or 'without justification'. They argue, sometimes correctly, that arbitrary cost allocations can result in misleading information that causes poor decisions and, therefore, should be avoided. It is going too far, however, to argue that making decisions about support services, products or direct services should never depend in *any* way on cost allocations. The city of Storhavn recognizes that cost allocations are arbitrary but, like many organizations, it has established principles of cost allocation that are intended to generate useful information for City employees and citizens:

The City shall employ a cost allocation system to identify the full cost of providing goods and services to the public and to recover certain costs incurred by various departments in providing support services to other City departments. The system shall accomplish the following objectives:

a. *Complete recovery of service costs incurred with the exception of the costs of 'general governance,' which are supported by general revenues*
b. *Equitable allocation of service costs to users*

c. *Provision of incentives for service providers to deliver services efficiently and effectively*
d. *Provision of a stable cost allocation system to facilitate the organization's budgeting for service costs and revenues*
e. *Promotion of customer confidence in and acceptance of the accuracy, reasonableness, and fairness of the charges they incur*

The City believes that these principles of cost allocation will create the atmosphere of a simulated 'market' for services wherein internal customers – those who use the internal services – will negotiate (or demand!) cost allocations for support services that are reasonable measures of the value of those services. Thus, allocations of service costs are especially important in non-market situations, which are prevalent both in government and private organizations that have internal support service departments. As noted earlier, outsourcing or 'privatizing' support services is a fast-growing phenomenon that affects both public and private organizations.

12.1 You're the Decision Maker

Principles of Cost Allocation

a. Do you think it is a good idea for organizations to formally express principles of cost allocation? Would it be any more important in a public organization such as a municipality than in a private firm? Explain.
b. You are the manager of the Social Services Department (a production department with a budget of approximately DKK 5,000,000 per month). How might you react if you found out that the Information Technology Department (a support service department with a budget of approximately DKK 360,000 per month) is increasing its budget by 50 per cent over the next year?
c. Take the position of the Mayor who is responsible for both support service and production departments. Explain which of the five principles of cost allocation identified that you think is most important. How would you resolve disputes over cost allocations?

(Solutions begin on page 618.)

Cost allocations can serve many purposes that may indicate different calculations. It is possible that an organization would prepare one set of cost allocations for external reporting, for example, and another set for internal decision making, such as pricing or contracting (e.g., as in the movie business).

Allocating Service Costs for Pricing

Most of Storhavn's production departments do not charge citizens for services. However, the Public Works department charges citizens for water supply and sewer services at rates that cover its fully allocated costs of production. Thus, the Public Works department uses a second stage of allocations of its direct department costs and its shares of the service departments' costs to measure the fully allocated costs of its sub-departments. This second stage of allocation is presented after the first set of service department costs (see Exhibit 12.7).

Allocating Service Costs for Cost-based Contracting

Some organizations contract for work on a cost basis or cost-plus basis. National governments sometimes reimburse private contractors for work done on a cost-plus (a profit) basis. Government agencies, foundations and private industry also often reimburse universities for research on a direct cost-plus basis, where the 'plus' is a relatively large overhead rate that the university may use for general purposes. Obtaining complete and proper levels of reimbursement requires properly allocating all (but only) allowed costs to the government contract, research work or training activity. In many cases, the appropriate cost allocation method is prescribed in the contract.

12.2 You're the Decision Maker

Municipal Service Costs per 'Unit'

The city of Denver, Colorado, USA was faced with nearly flat tax revenues and growing demands for services. The City Council recently solicited recommendations from citizens, lawmakers and politicians for how the city might reduce its budget to correct a forecasted $30 million deficit for the next fiscal year. 'Some of the ideas are crazy, and some of them can't be done legally,' opined the city's chief financial officer. Nonetheless, some ideas appeared sensible, but others questioned whether the alleged cost savings really would materialize. For example, using the city's most recent budget the following costs of services were cited as sources of annual cost savings:

$240,000 - the cost saved by operating one less police car
$350,000 - the cost saved by operating one less branch library
$488,800 - the cost saved by operating one less recreation centre
$1,500,000 - the cost saved by operating one less fire station.

1. As an informed citizen, what questions would you ask about these estimates of cost savings?
2. Why does this matter?
3. How do you think the cost estimates were derived?
4. Any concerns about these cost estimates?
5. What do you think of the opportunity costs of each of these 'units' of service?

Source: Meyer (2011).
(Solutions begin on page 618.)

Allocating Service Costs for Influencing Behaviour

Managers often allocate costs to influence behaviour. As mentioned earlier, if costs of services are free to internal customers, one can expect the customers to demand these services as long as they perceive any benefit from them. Under this condition, one also can expect that managers of service departments will attempt to grow the size of the department almost without bounds to meet the demand for their services. On the other hand, allocating service costs to other departments for services gives managers of these other departments some market-like incentives to control their uses of support services. For example, allocating the costs of the Information Technology Department to other city departments based on services provided causes the other department managers to request information technology service only when they believe that the service is worth at least as much as it will cost their departments to obtain it.

Allocating Service Costs for Required Reporting

In general, tax regulations and external financial reporting require allocating fixed and variable manufacturing overhead to the products of manufacturing firms. Allocations of manufacturing overhead

12.2 Cost Management in Practice

Corporate Cost Allocation for Profit Awareness

An executive of Kmart, the US retail giant, reported during an interview that 'allocating corporate headquarters' costs to stores makes each store manager aware that these costs exist and must be covered by the individual stores for the company as a whole to be profitable'. Surveys of corporate cost allocation found that the great majority of companies reported allocating common headquarters' costs to business units. The studies indicated that a primary managerial reason for cost allocation was to give business unit managers incentives to generate sufficient divisional profits to cover all corporate costs.

Sources: Dean et al. (1991); and Fremgren and Liao (1981).

should not include allocations of corporate or support service department expenses.[4] However, many higher-level costs are allocated to products and services for regulatory purposes in public utilities.

Cost Allocations of Internal Support Service Costs

All cost allocations of indirect, support service costs are at least somewhat arbitrary because they cannot precisely link resource spending and resource use. For example, suppose that an organization would like to allocate its human resources (HR) department spending (e.g., salaries, depreciation and utilities) accurately to internal customers. We have seen in previous chapters that manufacturing companies routinely allocate manufacturing overhead to manufactured goods. It seems reasonable to most organizations that it similarly can allocate support service costs to internal services provided. The problems of course, are that (a) services, such as HR services, are not uniform and (b) the spending for resources is largely fixed (e.g., for salaries and facilities). Thus, organizations seeking to allocate support services must do so on a reasonable, but typically arbitrary basis. Determining the proper basis for cost allocation can be very important, but this is not the only consideration to implementing a cost allocation method that supports the organization's goals.

Suppose that an organization proposes to allocate its HR department costs to user departments proportionately based on the number of total full-time equivalent (FTE) employees in each department. These data are readily available, but they are not without ambiguity that could affect the efficacy of the allocations. For example, what if a large department with mostly long-time employees needs less service from the HR department than a smaller department that is hiring and training new employees, which consumes much of the HR department's time? If costs are allocated based on FTE, the larger department with established employees will be allocated a large share of the HR department costs even if it uses relatively little of that support service resource. Likewise, the smaller department will pay only a small share of the cost although it uses much of the resource. Is the HR cost allocation based on FTE fair? Will it cause unnecessary disputes? Does it motivate department managers to use HR services properly? Does it result in the proper level and quality of HR support services? These are difficult and very important questions, and analysts should give careful thought to the impacts of alternative bases for cost allocations. The alternative allocations that result might vary in how accurately they reflect the uses of HR resources by other departments. Another consideration is whether it is cost effective to obtain more accurate information that would allow cost allocations to more closely match the use of support services.

For most of this chapter, we assume that the organization has decided to provide internal support services using facility-level resources (recall the ABC hierarchy from Chapter 4); that is, the organization has decided to *not* outsource the services, but instead has built and maintains internal support-service departments. Furthermore, the organization has decided to allocate the costs of those resources to internal customers. These are important managerial decisions that can affect the organization's efficiency and ability to meet its goals. Once made, these decisions require implementation by cost management analysts who use a systematic and defensible method to allocate support service costs that also reinforces the organization's goals. We now consider alternative methods for allocating support service costs.

Cost Allocation Process Steps

The process of allocating service costs systematically follows several steps, each of which can affect the success of cost allocations. The steps, which are explained in detail in subsequent sections, follow:

1. Identify the categories and amounts of costs to be allocated to internal customers.
2. Choose the appropriate cost allocation base(s) for each cost category.
3. Select and use an appropriate method to compute cost allocation rates and cost allocations of service department costs.
4. Determine whether the cost allocations achieve the desired results; if they do not, begin the process again.

Step 1: Identify the Categories and Amounts of Costs to Be Allocated to Internal Customers

LO 2
Understand how to choose cost pools and to separate the cost of resources supplied for the cost of resources used.

Typically, organizations separate support-service costs by department into separate *cost pools*, which are the budgeted and actual spending amounts for distinct sets of resources, as Storhavn has done. Using separate cost pools for the service departments facilitates the management of the different types of support services and should allow more accurate cost allocations to internal customers than using only one cost pool for all support services. As shown earlier, Storhavn uses three support service cost pools – Information Technology, Buildings and Grounds, and Human Resources – which correspond to the city's organizational structure and management responsibilities.

Choice of Cost Pools

Deciding how many cost pools to use involves a cost-benefit evaluation. If the organization designs cost pools carefully, using more cost pools should benefit the organization with more accurate cost allocations that match resource use better than using fewer cost pools.[5] Better information should result in better management decisions about support service type, quantity, source and payment. However, designing and maintaining a complex cost allocation system with many cost pools can be very costly. Organizations would not willingly implement a complex cost allocation system unless the benefits from its better decisions justify the costs required to set up and maintain the system.

For the purposes of this chapter, we assume that Storhavn maintains only three support service cost pools, one for each support service department. This level of complexity is sufficient to illustrate the methods and computations of cost allocation.

12.1 Research Insight

Cost Pools and Cost Allocations

The cost allocation process just described is a 'heuristic' process in that it does not describe a process that intends to build the 'optimal' cost system. Rather the described process is intended to result in a cost allocation system that is 'good enough' to meet the decision-making needs of the organization. In other words, no feasible cost system can perfectly measure the 'true' cost of any product, let alone the cost of support-services, because the true cost is unobservable. Ramji Balakrishnan, Steve Hansen and Eva Labro have used computer simulations to estimate the amounts of error that might be caused by various heuristic approaches to cost system design (an error in their study is a costing difference relative to a benchmarked, ideal cost system). They find that grouping similar (i.e., highly correlated) resource costs into separate cost pools generally results in the smallest costing errors. Other groupings examined include grouping by the amounts of spending - high-cost activities might be in separate pools, and low-cost activities might be combined. They also find that increasing the number of cost pools beyond 12 does not result in meaningful reductions in cost errors. Grouping resource costs by major activity, such as support service department activities, might be similar to grouping cost categories by statistical correlation and size. Furthermore, using a limited number of activity-cost pools seems like a sensible (although heuristic) approach to cost-system design.

Source: Balakrishnan et al. (2011).

Costs of Resources Used versus Costs of Resources Supplied

Cost allocation assigns support service department costs to user departments based on a reasonable measure of the user departments' use of support service resources. Recall that the *use* of resources is not necessarily the same as the *supply* of resources. For example, you might spend €100 per month to acquire storage capacity for your belongings but use only 40 per cent of the space. In that case, we may distinguish between resources supplied (or money spent) of €100 per month, resources used of €40 per month (0.40 × €100), and unused capacity of €60 per month (€100 resources supplied – €40 resources used).

Before allocating support-service department costs to user departments, we should first separate resources supplied from resources used. *Only resources used should be allocated to user departments* because users should be charged for services that they use. This argument states that users should not have to pay for the support service departments' unused capacity. Repeated instances of unused capacity might signal that a service department might have excess capacity that should be eliminated by reducing spending.

Pedersen and her staff had begun the budget process by attempting to use the past several years of support service budgets and charges to separate support service department resources used from resources supplied to the departments. Unfortunately, the very reason that Pedersen decided to implement a new cost allocation system was that she could not be confident that the previous system accurately reflected resource usage by production departments. Because seemingly every citizen and every department head were clamouring for more services than the departments could provide, it seemed especially arbitrary to try to separate the amounts of resources supplied from the resources used at this time. Pedersen resolved to use future data that she believed would be more reliable to address the department capacity issues, which could result in changes in departmental spending – but not this year. Thus, the costs used for the budgeted cost allocations were from Exhibit 12.2, which contain unknown amounts of unused capacity.

Step 2: Choose the Appropriate Cost Allocation Base(s)

LO 3 Understand how to choose appropriate allocation bases.

Each cost pool should have its own appropriate cost allocation base. *Cost allocation bases* are factors that cost management analysts use to assign indirect costs to cost objects. Ideally, a cost allocation base reflects **plausible correlation** between resource spending and use, which is the combination of strong statistical correlation and economic rationale. However, determining these correlative relationships could be difficult or costly because suitable data often are not available. In other words, the methods of Chapters 3 and 4 apply to the choice of the best cost allocation base for each cost pool. If the best cost allocation base is the same for two cost pools, these cost pools could be combined.

Recall that if an organization is able to accurately measure plausible correlative relationships, it can more precisely trace costs rather than *approximately allocate* them. If it cannot identify correlative relationships between resource spending and use but still desires to allocate costs, it must use a more arbitrary and probably less accurate cost allocation base. The more closely the allocation base reflects a link between resource spending and use, the more useful allocated costs are likely to be for planning, decision making and influencing behaviour.[6] Using one of the cost allocation methods discussed later, the organization could allocate support service costs to internal customers by charging the allocation base rate for each unit of service, for example, for each new employee hired and trained.

Many organizations have sought improved cost allocation systems to allocate service department costs, and most have reported political as well as technical problems. Recall that organizations often design cost allocations explicitly to influence behaviour, and individuals often resist unexplained changes. Therefore, successful cost management analysis anticipates that changing cost allocation bases might induce changes in behaviour that also might provoke complaints. We advise cost management analysts to consider applying Kotter's approach to effect change in organizations (see Chapter 1), even for something as mundane as changing cost allocations.

In the absence of suitable, reliable data, many organizations have implemented simpler but probably less accurate approaches to choosing allocation bases and allocation rates. These organizations typically classify support service costs and choose cost allocation bases that are plausible for labour, equipment, occupancy and other related costs.

12.3 Cost Management in Practice

Use of ABC to Measure Costs

One of the earliest (and best documented) reports of using ABC to measure the costs of internal services comes from Weyerhaeuser, the international wood products firm (www.weyerhaeuser.com). Weyerhaeuser developed a comprehensive cost allocation system based on the major activities demanded of its internal service divisions. As the product divisions use internal services, they are charged according to a reasonably simple but thorough set of cost-driver rates. These rates regulate demand for services and, since internal customers have a voice in setting the rates, force the internal service departments to provide high-quality, efficient services.

Source: Johnson and Loewe (1987).

Choice of Plausible and Justifiable Allocation Bases

The organization should choose allocation bases that are reasonable and justifiable to internal customers. Pedersen conducted statistical and qualitative analyses of the work performed in each service department for other departments. For example, Pedersen's allocation base analysis recommended that support service costs should be allocated using the following cost allocation bases, which add equivalent amounts to the previous allocation bases.

Support service department	Original allocation base	Additional allocation base
Information Technology	Number of computers	**Plus 10x the number of network servers**
Buildings and Grounds	Number of square metres in building occupied	**Plus 25% of square metres of grounds and parking**
Human Resources	FTE of continuing employees	**Plus 5x the number of expected newly hired employees**

These cost allocation bases are also called **indexed cost allocation bases** because they combine multiple bases into a single index of services provided. Indexed cost allocation bases might be preferable to creating separate cost pools for each type of service activity when resources cannot be easily separated or traced to activities because they recognize that some measures are 'equivalent' to the previous allocation bases that, when added, expand the scope of work performed by each service department. For example, Pedersen estimated that installing and maintaining a network server was equivalent to ten times the resources used to service a computer on a desk. Similarly, the grounds and parking space used by each department's buildings cost approximately one-fourth as much to service as the space in the buildings. Finally, Pedersen estimated that hiring or terminating an employee consumes five times the resources as processing routine HR transactions for continuing employees.

Pedersen also recognized that the support service departments provide a number of other services that might not be related to these augmented bases (the additions are in boldface). Be aware that no feasible cost system is perfect, and the perfect should not be the enemy of the good.[7] Pedersen believed that creating separate cost pools within each department would require more tracking of resource use than would be practical at this time. Pedersen knew that many engineering, legal, accounting and consulting firms do track resources to accurately cost work done for different customers, and she was researching technologies to accomplish more accurate allocations of service department resources.

The indexed cost allocation base amounts expected for each department appear in Exhibit 12.3. Observe that the additions of the equivalent base amounts alter the measures and relative uses of service department resources. These changes might dramatically affect next year's cost allocations to production departments. We will use *subsets* of the data in this exhibit to demonstrate two different cost allocation methods as discussed in step 3 (and a third method in Appendix 12). We use subsets because each of the methods makes different assumptions about how service department costs

Exhibit 12.3 **Allocation Bases and Proportional Uses of Support Services**

	A	B	C	D	E	F	G
1	**Panel A: Information Technology**	**S1 Base: Computers**	**Percentage of original base**	**S1 Servers**	**S1 Equivalent base**	**S1 Indexed base total**	**Percentage of total base**
2	*Support department*						
3	S1: Information Technology	40	19.7%	10	10	140	28.4%
4	S2: Buildings and Grounds	13	6.4%	1	10	23	**4.7%**
5	S3: Human Resources	20	9.9%	4	10	60	**12.2%**
6	*Production department*						
7	P1: Social Services	60	29.6%	2	10	80	16.2%
8	P2: Public Safety	45	22.2%	6	10	105	21.3%
9	P3: Public Works	25	12.3%	6	10	85	17.2%
10	*Production department subtotal*	*130*		*14*		*270*	
11	Total cost allocation base	203	100.0%	29		493	100.0%
12							
13	**Panel B: Buildings and Grounds**	**S2 Base: m² Buildings**	**Percentage of original base**	**S2 m² Grounds & Parking**	**S2 Equivalent base**	**S2 Indexed base total**	**Percentage of total base**
14	*Support department*						
15	S1: Information Technology	1,800	8.0%	1,200	0.25	2,100	**7.1%**
16	S2: Buildings and Grounds	2,300	10.2%	3,000	0.25	3,050	10.3%
17	S3: Human Resources	2,700	11.9%	2,100	0.25	3,225	**10.9%**
18	*Production department*						
19	P1: Social Services	4,300	19.0%	5,100	0.25	5,575	18.8%
20	P2: Public Safety	5,500	24.3%	6,400	0.25	7,100	24.0%
21	P3: Public Works	6,000	26.5%	10,300	0.25	8,575	28.9%
22	*Production department subtotal*	*15,800*		*21,800*		*21,250*	
23	Total cost allocation base	22,600	100.0%	28,100		29,625	100.0%
24							
25	**Panel C: Human Resources**	**S3 Base: Employees**	**Percentage of original base**	**S3 Changes in employees**	**S3 Equivalent base**	**S3 Indexed base total**	**Percentage of total base**
26	*Support department*						
27	S1: Information Technology	30	7.3%	15	5	105	**12.2%**
28	S2: Buildings and Grounds	40	9.7%	10	5	90	**10.4%**
29	S3: Human Resources	18	4.4%	3	5	33	3.8%
30	*Production department*						
31	P1: Social Services	65	15.8%	5	5	90	10.4%
32	P2: Public Safety	112	27.2%	12	5	172	20.0%
33	P3: Public Works	147	35.7%	45	5	372	43.2%
34	*Production department subtotal*	*324*		*62*		*634*	
35	Total cost allocation base	412	100.0%	90		862	100.0%

Note: Numbers in boldface font in the last column are used in the discussion of the Step Method.

should be allocated. You should attach a removable tag to the page with Exhibit 12.3 because we will refer to it often.

Step 3: Select and Use an Appropriate Method to Compute Cost Allocation Rates and Cost Allocations of Service Department Costs

This section describes two commonly used methods to allocate support service costs: (1) the *direct method* and (2) the *step method*. A third method, the *reciprocal cost method*, is conceptually more accurate than the two more common methods, but it is less used at this time. Because the reciprocal method could be used more in the future as cost management analysts gain familiarity with it, we present it in Appendix 12. We illustrate each method using Storhavn's expected spending and allocation bases from Exhibit 12.3.

Cost Allocations Using the Direct Method

LO 4
Allocate support service department costs using the direct method.

The **direct method** of cost allocation charges support service costs to production departments *without making allocations among support service departments*. All support service cost allocations go directly to production departments. The direct method does not consider the work done by a service department for other service departments or for itself. Therefore, the direct method uses only the relative allocation base amounts *in the production departments*.

Application of the Direct Method to the City of Storhavn

Exhibit 12.4 describes the allocation of service department costs using the direct method. Observe that the direct method makes no allocations *among* the support service departments themselves. The direct method ignores any support service department relationship or work supplied to any other support service department. Service department costs are allocated directly to production departments.

Direct allocation of Information Technology Department costs

Pedersen and her staff proposed to allocate the DKK360,000 monthly costs of the Information Technology Department based on the number of equivalent computers in the three production departments: Social Services, which had the equivalent of 80 computers, Public Safety, which had the equivalent of 105 computers, and Public Works, with the equivalent of 85 computers, or a total of 270. The amounts of computers used in the service departments are irrelevant in the direct method, although the Information Technology Department services them. The allocation proceeds as shown in the following table, which uses departmental cost information from Exhibit 12.2 (i.e., DKK360,000) and indexed allocation base information from Exhibit 12.3 (i.e., 80, 105, 85 equivalent computers).

Direct Allocation of Information Technology Department Costs

Department	Allocation base, equivalent computers	Percentage of base	Direct cost allocation, DKK
Information Technology cost to allocate			**360,000**
P1: Social Services	80	29.6%	106,667
P2: Public Safety	105	38.9%	140,000
P3: Public Works	85	31.5%	113,333
Total	270	100.0%	360,000

= 80/270

= 0.296 x 360,000

The direct method allocates the Information Technology Department costs 29.6 per cent (80 ÷ 270) to Social Services because it had 80 of the 270 total equivalent computers, 38.9 per cent (105 ÷ 270) to Public Safety, which had 105, and 31.5 per cent to Public Works.[8] The direct method allocations are computed by multiplying the percentage of the base in each production department by the service department cost of DKK360,000. For example, the direct method would allocate DKK106,667 to Social Services (= 0.296 × DKK360,000). The direct method computes the allocations to the other production departments similarly.

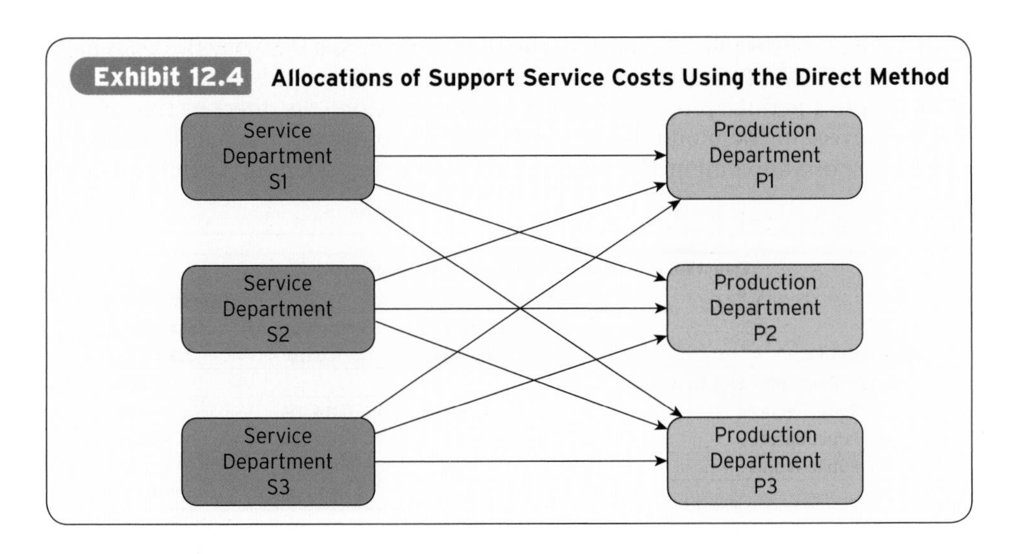

Direct allocation of Buildings and Grounds Department costs

Pedersen and her staff proposed to allocate the DKK 840,000 monthly costs of the Buildings and Grounds Department based on the number of square metres of building, grounds and parking space used. Because most of Buildings and Grounds' work was for construction, repairs and maintenance, the size of the space used was a relevant allocation base.

As before, the direct method of cost allocation allocates *none* of the Buildings and Grounds Department's costs to the other support-service departments. *All* of the Buildings and Grounds Department's monthly costs of DKK 840,000 are allocated directly to the three production departments, as shown in the following table that uses departmental cost and indexed allocation base information from Exhibits 12.2 and 12.3.

Direct Allocation of Buildings and Grounds Department Costs

Department	Allocation base, equivalent space used, m^2	Percentage of base	Direct cost allocation, DKK
Buildings and Grounds cost to allocate			**840,000**
P1: Social Services	5,575	26.2%	220,376
P2: Public Safety	7,100	33.4%	280,659
P3: Public Works	8,575	40.4%	338,965
Total	21,250	100.0%	840,000

= 5,575/21,250

= 0.262 x 840,000

The direct method allocates the Buildings and Grounds Department's costs 26.2 per cent to Social Services (5,575 of the 21,250 square metres occupied by the three production departments), 33.4 per cent to Public Safety, and 40.4 per cent to Public Works. The direct method allocation of costs multiplies the percentage of base in each production department by the service department cost of DKK 840,000. For example, Social Services would receive DKK 220,376 of the Buildings and Grounds department cost (= 0.262 × DKK 840,000). The other allocations are computed similarly.

Direct allocation of Human Resources Department costs

Finally, Pedersen and her staff proposed to allocate the DKK 250,000 monthly Human Resources costs based on the equivalent number of employees in the production departments. Departments that hired or terminated numerous employees consumed much of the Human Resources' staff time. For example, Buildings and Grounds each year hired and terminated many seasonal workers. So the change in employees was a logical addition to the allocation base.

Again, the direct method allocates *none* of the Human Resources Department's costs to the other support departments. *All* of the Human Resources Department's monthly costs of DKK 250,000 are allocated directly to the three production departments. Therefore, the direct method uses only the equivalent employees in the production departments. The proposed direct method allocations of Human Resources costs are computed similarly as before from information in Exhibits 12.2 and 12.3, as follows.

Direct Allocation of Human Resources Department Costs

Department	Allocation base, equivalent employees	Percentage of base	Direct cost allocation, DKK
Human Resources cost to allocate			**250,000**
P1: Social Services	90	14.2%	35,489
P2: Public Safety	172	27.1%	67,823
P3: Public Works	372	58.7%	146,688
Total	634	100.0%	250,000

= 90/634

= 0.142 x 250,000

The direct method allocates the Human Resources Department's costs 14.2 per cent (90 ÷ 634) to Social Services, 27.1 per cent (172 ÷ 634) to Public Safety, and 58.7 per cent to Public Works (372 ÷ 634). Therefore, Human Resources would charge Social Services DKK 35,489 (= 0.142 × DKK 250,000). Because it has the most variable workforce, Public Works would be charged the majority of Human Resources' costs (DKK 146,688).

Summary of the Direct Method

The direct method allocates support-service department costs based *only* on the relative amounts of the total cost-allocation base in the various production departments. Because support costs are allocated directly, the order of allocation – which support cost is allocated first, second, and so on? – is irrelevant. We began with the Information Technology Department, but we could have begun as easily with any of the others with the same results.

Exhibit 12.5, panel A summarizes the results of the direct method of support service cost allocations for the city of Storhavn. These are the proposed charges from each support service department to each production department and, if approved, would allow support service departments to fully recover their budgeted costs. Allocations of service costs in other organizations might not cause actual transfers of funds. But the cost allocations could be added to user departments' total overhead costs for pricing and performance evaluation purposes.

The supporting figures to panel A are obtained from the previous direct method tables and are summarized in panels B and C. Panel C displays how the support service costs flow (horizontally in this panel) entirely and directly to the production departments.

Benefits and Limitations of the Direct Method

The direct method is the simplest method to use and to communicate. The arithmetic is straightforward, and all users of the information can easily trace the computations. For these reasons, it has been the most commonly used method for many years. Many criticize the direct method because it ignores the services that one support service department provides to another. For example, Storhavn's Human Resources Department hires and trains employees for itself and other support service departments as well as for production departments. However, if support service departments are relatively small or devote most of their efforts to production departments, ignoring interactions among support service departments creates small difference in allocated costs.

If production departments are not vigilant, however, support service departments could grow and over-serve each other and pass the costs to the production departments in the form of higher

Exhibit 12.5 Summary of Cost Allocations: Direct Method

	A	B	C	D	E
38	**Panel A: Summary of Direct Method Allocations of Support-Service Department Costs**				
39		**From: Support-Service Department Allocations,**			
40	**To: Production Departments**	**Information Technology**	**Buildings and Grounds**	**Human Resources**	**Total Allocated**
41	P1: Social Services	106,667	220,376	35,489	362,532
42	P2: Public Safety	140,000	280,659	67,823	488,482
43	P3: Public Works	113,333	338,965	146,688	598,986
44	Total service department costs	360,000	840,000	250,000	1,450,000

	A	B	C	D	E	F	G	H	I
46	**Panel B: Percentages of Support-Service Department Cost Allocated to *Production* Departments**								
47		**Support-Service**	**From: Support Service Departments**			**To: Production Departments**			
48	**Support-Service Department**	**Department Costs, DKK**	**Information Technology***	**Buildings and Grounds***	**Human Resources***	**Social Services**	**Public Safety**	**Public Works**	**Totals**
49	Information Technology (S1)	360,000	-100%	n/a	n/a	29.6%	38.9%	31.5%	100%
50	Buildings and Grounds (S2)	840,000	n/a	-100%	n/a	26.2%	33.4%	40.4%	100%
51	Human Resources (S3)	250,000	n/a	n/a	-100%	14.2%	27.1%	58.7%	100%

	A	C	D	E	F	G	H	I
53	**Panel C: Direct Method of Cost Allocation**	**From: Support-Service Departments, DKK**			**To: Production Departments, DKK**			
54		**Information Technology**	**Buildings and Grounds**	**Human Resources**	**Social Services**	**Public Safety**	**Public Works**	**Totals**
55	Department costs before service department allocations (from Exhibit 10.2)	360,000	840,000	250,000	5,000,000	2,700,000	1,850,000	11,000,000
56	Allocation of Information Technology costs	(360,000)	-	-	106,667	140,000	113,333	360,000
57	Allocation of Buildings and Grounds costs	-	(840,000)	-	220,376	280,659	338,965	840,000
58	Allocation of Human Resources costs	-	-	(250,000)	35,489	67,823	146,688	250,000
59	Total allocations from support service departments	-	-	-	362,532	488,482	598,986	1,450,000
60	Total department costs after allocations	-	-	-	5,362,532	3,188,482	2,448,986	11,000,000

61 NOTES:
62 * -100% in these columns means that 100 per cent of each support service department cost is allocated to production departments.
63 n/a = not applicable. By the direct method, no costs are allocated from a support service department to another service department.
64 ** The total figures signal whether allocation percentages sum to 100% and allocations to production departments sum to service department costs.
65 The highlighted cells reflect one of the computations of cost allocations from the service departments: 106,667 = 0.296 x 360,000. All others are similar.

cost allocations. The step method of allocating support service department costs partially remedies this problem by recognizing that support service departments in fact provide services to each other and use the organization's resources to do so.

Second-stage Cost Allocations in the Public Works Department

Exhibit 12.6 presents a **second-stage cost allocation**, which is the reallocation of service department costs and direct department costs to products. Exhibit 12.6 also shows the pricing charged to citizens for water and sewer products. General revenues collected by the city cover other services (parks, etc.). The Public Works Department uses the percentages of sub-department direct costs to make this second-stage allocation. The department has found that direct cost is a more consistent allocation base than other possible bases (number of employees, payroll, etc.).

Panel A uses the percentages of sub-department direct costs to reallocate the Public Works' service department allocation of €598,986. For example, the Water department has 15 per cent of the Public Works' direct cost, and by this allocation base receives 15 per cent of the total service department allocation, or €89,848. The Water department's total cost that it must recover by user rates is €367,348. Similarly, the Sewer and Water Treatment department must cover €685,716 by user rates.

Panel B of Exhibit 12.6 computes the water consumption and treatment rates that the two sub-departments must charge to cover their expected annual costs. Storhavn citizens will be charged €1.45 per 1,000 litres of water consumed and €2.71 per 1,000 litres of water treated (these are expected to be the same amounts). These separate rates alert citizens of the costs to supply and treat water and assume that (a) costs are incurred as expected, and (b) water usage and treatment volumes occur as expected. 'Variances' or differences between actuals and expected amounts would be measured and acted on as discussed in Chapter 13.

Storhavn

Exhibit 12.6 Public Works Department Second-stage Cost Allocation

	A	B	C	D	E	F
69						
70	Panel A: Public Works sub-department costs		Direct cost, DKK	Percentage of Public Works direct costs	Allocation of Support-Service costs	Total sub-department cost, DKK
71		Parks	388,500	21%	125,787	514,287
72		Roads	555,000	30%	179,696	734,696
73		Flood control	111,000	6%	35,939	146,939
74		Water	277,500	15%	89,848	367,348
75		Sewer and Water Treatment	518,000	28%	167,716	685,716
76	Total costs		1,850,000	100%	598,986	2,448,986
77	Panel B: Calculation of user fees		Total sub-department costs, DKK	Expected water consumption, 1,000 Liters	User rates, DKK per 1,000 Liters	
78		Water	367,348	253,343	1.450	
79		Sewer and Water Treatment	685,716	253,343	2.707	

12.3 You're the Decision Maker

Effects of Alternative Cost Allocation Bases

Storhavn's Director of Budget, Mette Pedersen, proposed to used indexed cost allocation bases to better capture the diversity of support services provided to user departments. However, this caused something of an uproar.

1. Re-do the direct method cost allocations using the original, unindexed cost allocation bases (number of computers, building space occupied and number of employees).
2. Why might some user departments and citizens object to the impacts of changing cost allocation bases?

(Solutions begin on page 618.)

Cost Allocations Using the Step Method

LO 5 Allocate support service department costs using the step method.

The **step method** of cost allocation allocates support service department costs in ordered, sequential steps to production departments. The steps are:

A. Rank-order support service departments by the proportions of their total allocation bases in *other support service departments*. This creates an allocation order from the most general support service department to the least.

B. Allocate costs from the most general support service department to the less general support service departments and to production departments. The allocation basis is the allocation base in all of these other departments, excluding the base in the most general support service department.

C. Repeat and allocate costs in order from the less general support service departments until all support service department costs are allocated to production departments. The step method thus uses as many sequential allocation steps as there are support service departments.

Exhibit 12.7 illustrates the step method allocation steps graphically. The red arrows depict the first allocation step of costs from the most general support service department to the less general support service departments and the production departments. The blue arrows show the second allocation step from the next-ranked support service department to the least and to the production department. Finally, the green arrows show the (last) cost allocation step from the least general support service department to the production departments.

Exhibit 12.7 Step Method of Cost Allocation

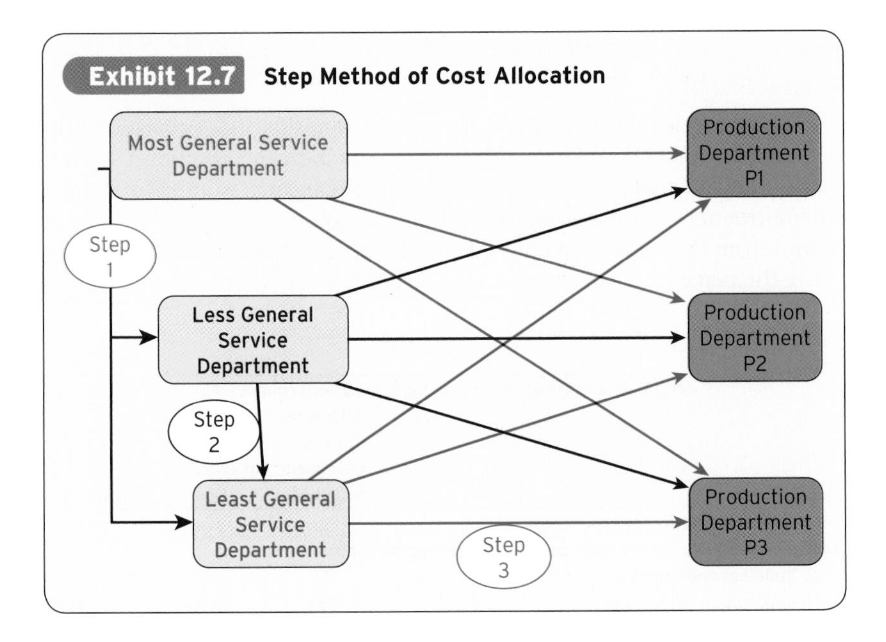

Unlike the direct method, the step method of cost allocation recognizes that support service departments provide some services to other support services, as well as to production departments. Note that once the organization makes an allocation from a more general support service department, no subsequent allocations are made back to that department. Thus, allocations from support service departments are made in only one direction: from more general support services to less general support services and production departments. Whether the step method results in materially different cost allocations depends on the costs to be allocated and on the degrees of interactions among support service departments.

Application of the Step Method to the City of Storhavn

The first task of the step method is to rank-order each support service department by the proportions of service it provides to each other support service department. Refer to the last column of Exhibit 12.3 to find these proportions. The following table contains the boldfaced figures extracted from the last column of Exhibit 12.3, which are the proportions of the indexed cost allocation bases that measure the relative amounts of service provided by support service departments to the others.

Support Service department ordering based on:	**From: Support Service Department**		
Proportion of allocation base used in other support service departments (last column of Exhibit 10.4)	**S1: Information Technology**	**S2: Buildings and Grounds**	**S3: Human Resources**
S1: Information Technology	n/a	7.1%	12.2%
S2: Buildings and Grounds	4.7%	n/a	10.4%
S3: Human Resources	12.2%	10.9%	n/a
Total proportion of allocation base	16.8%	18.0%	22.6%
Rank Order	**3**	**2**	**1**

Storhavn's Human Resources Department provides the highest proportion (22.6 per cent) of its services to the other support services departments. Therefore, it is Storhavn's most general service department. Using the step method, Storhavn first allocates Human Resources Department costs to all other departments, including Building and Grounds and Information Technology. Next, the step method allocates all of the costs now in Building and Grounds (its original department cost plus the allocation from Human Resources) to Information Technology and the production departments. Finally, the step method allocates all of the costs from Information Technology (its original department cost plus allocations from Human Resources and Building and Grounds) to production departments.

Allocation of Human Resources Department costs (the most general department)

Following the support service department order for the step method, Pedersen and her staff first allocated the Human Resources costs of DKK 250,000 to the less general support service departments and the production departments. The allocation base is the *indexed* number of employees in these 'downstream' departments. The allocation base amounts, equivalent employees, are extracted from the second column from the right in Exhibit 12.3 and placed in the second column of the following table. Multiplying the percentages of the allocation base by the HR department cost of DKK 250,000 generates the allocations to the other departments as shown.

Step 1: Allocation of S3: Human Resources Department Costs			
Departments	Allocation base, equivalent employees	Percentage of allocation base	Cost, DKK
S3: Human Resources department cost			250,000
Less general service departments and production departments:			
S2: Buildings and Grounds	90	10.9%	27,141
S1: Information Technology	105	12.7%	31,665
P1: Social Services	90	10.9%	27,141
P2: Public Safety	172	20.7%	51,870
P3: Public Works	372	44.9%	112,183
Subtotal to production departments			191,194
Totals for Human Resources	829	100.0%	250,000

Allocation of Buildings and Grounds Department costs (the second most general)

Buildings and Grounds is second in the step method order, so its costs are allocated next to the remaining departments. Recall that Buildings and Grounds' cost of resources used was DKK 840,000 before allocating costs from any other support service department. Pedersen and her staff have just allocated DKK 27,141 from Human Resources to Buildings and Grounds. So the Buildings and Grounds cost to be allocated is now increased by the DKK 27,141 allocated to it from Human Resources. The total Buildings and Grounds cost to be allocated downstream is DKK 867,141.

Note that Human Resources' use of Buildings and Grounds resources is not considered in the Buildings and Grounds' allocation because step allocations are in one direction only – from more to less general support service departments. Therefore, based on the number of equivalent square metres used by the other departments (see Exhibit 12.3, second column from the right), Pedersen and her staff computed the relative percentages of the allocation base and the resulting cost allocations, as shown next.

Step 2: Allocation of S2: Buildings and Grounds Department Costs			
Departments	Allocation base, equivalent space occupied, m^2	Percentage of allocation base	Cost, DKK
S2: Buildings and Grounds department cost			840,000
Allocation from S3: Human Resources			27,141
Total department cost to allocate:			867,141
Less general service departments and production departments:			
S1: Information Technology	2,100	9.0%	77,987
P1: Social Services	5,575	23.9%	207,037
P2: Public Safety	7,100	30.4%	263,670
P3: Public Works	8,575	36.7%	318,447
Subtotal to production departments			789,154
Total for Buildings and Grounds	23,350	100.0%	867,141

Allocation of Information Technology Department costs (the least general)

Finally, we allocate the Information Technology Department costs. Because the other two support service departments' costs have already been allocated to other departments, no costs are allocated back to them. Therefore, Information Technology costs are allocated only to the production departments. Recall that Information Technology's costs were DKK 360,000 before receiving allocation from any other support service department. Pedersen and her staff have already allocated DKK 31,665 from Human Resources plus DKK 77,987 from Buildings and Grounds to Information Technology. This sums to DKK 469,652 to allocate to the remaining, downstream production departments.

Information Technology costs are allocated based on the number of equivalent computers in the charged departments. Pedersen and her staff calculated the resource usage percentages of the allocation base as before from the data in the next-to-last column of Exhibit 12.3 and the resulting allocations as shown in the following table. At this point, all support service department costs have been allocated to production departments, and the cost allocation process is complete.

Step 3: Allocation of S1: Information Technology Department Costs

Departments	Allocation base, equivalent computers	Percentage of allocation base	Cost, DKK
S1: Informnation Technology department cost			360,000
Allocation from S3: Human Resources			31,665
Allocation from S2: Buildings and Grounds			77,987
Total department cost to allocate:			469,652
Production departments:			
P1: Social Services	80	29.6%	139,156
P2: Public Safety	105	38.9%	182,642
P3: Public Works	85	31.5%	147,853
Total for Information Technology	270	100.0%	469,652

Exhibit 12.8 summarizes Storhavn's support service costs using the step method. Panel A combines the results of the previous step method tables. Notice that the totals allocated from the less general support

Exhibit 12.8 Summary of Cost Allocations: Step Method

Panel A: Summary of Step Method Allocations of Support Service Department Costs

	Support Service Department Allocations,			
Production Departments	Step 1: Human Resources	Step 2: Buildings and Grounds	Step 3: Information Technology	Total Allocated
P1: Social Services	27,141	207,037	139,156	373,334
P2: Public Safety	51,870	263,670	182,642	498,182
P3: Public Works	112,183	318,447	147,853	578,484
Total service department costs allocated to production	191,194	789,154	469,652	1,450,000

Panel B: Percentage of Support Service Department Cost Allocated to *All User* Departments

	Support	Support Service Departments			Production Departments			
Support Service Department	Service Department Costs, DKK	Human Resources*	Buildings and Grounds*	Information Technology*	Social Services	Public Safety	Public Works	Totals
Information Technology (S1)	360,000	-100.0%	10.9%	12.7%	10.9%	20.7%	44.9%	100%
Buildings and Grounds (S2)	840,000	0.0%	-100.0%	9.0%	23.9%	30.4%	36.7%	100%
Human Resources (S3)	250,000	0.0%	0.0%	-100.0%	29.6%	38.9%	31.5%	100%

Panel C: Step Method of Cost Allocation

	Support Service Departments, DKK			Production Departments, DKK			
	Human Resources	Buildings and Grounds	Information Technology	Social Services	Public Safety	Public Works	Totals, DKK
Department costs before interdepartment allocations (Exhibit 10.2)	250,000	840,000	360,000	5,000,000	2,700,000	1,850,000	11,000,000
Step 1: Allocation of Human Resources	(250,000)	27,141	31,665	27,141	51,870	112,183	250,000
Step 2: Allocation of Buildings and Grounds	n/a	(867,141)	77,987	207,037	263,670	318,447	867,141
Step 3: Allocation of Information Technology	n/a	n/a	(469,652)	139,156	182,642	147,853	469,652
Total allocations from support service departments	-	-	-	373,334	498,182	578,484	1,450,000
Total department costs after allocations	-	-	-	5,373,334	3,198,182	2,428,484	11,000,000

* -100% in these columns means that 100 per cent of the support service department costs are allocated to other departments.
n/a = not applicable. By the step method, once costs are allocated from a support service department, no costs are allocated back to it.
The highlighted cells reflect one of the computations of cost allocations from the service departments: 31,6655 = 0.127 x 250,000. All others are similar.

Storhavn

Exhibit 12.9 Comparisons of Allocations Using the Direct and Step Methods

	A	B	C	D	E
1	Summary of Direct and Step Method Allocations of Support Service Department Costs				
2	Production Departments	Direct method allocations, DKK	Step method allocations, DKK	Differences, DKK	Percentage differences
3	P1: Social Services	362,532	373,334	(10,802)	-3.0%
4	P2: Public Safety	488,482	498,182	(9,700)	-2.0%
5	P3: Public Works	598,986	578,484	20,502	3.4%
6	Total service department costs	1,450,000	1,450,000	-	

service departments to production departments do not equal the direct costs of these departments. This is because support service department costs are allocated to less general service departments, too. Therefore, downstream service departments accumulate costs from upstream departments. Panel B repeats the appropriate allocation base use figures from Exhibit 12.3. Panel C displays how the support service department costs flow in one direction from the most general support service department (Human Resources) to the less general support service departments and the production departments.

Exhibit 12.9 compares step method allocations with direct method allocations. The differences in allocations do not seem large in absolute or relative terms, but some of the larger differences could represent adding or eliminating specific resources or services. If Storhavn used the step method, Social Services would be charged DKK 10,802 more per month for support services, but Public Works would be charged DKK 20,502 less. Even these relatively modest cost allocation differences could cause controversy when budgets are tight.

Benefits and Limitations of the Step Method

The step method might result in more plausible allocations than the direct method because it recognizes that some service departments also use other service departments. The step method is not necessarily better than the direct method, however. Many organizations use the direct method because of its comparative simplicity. An organization that already uses the direct method could find switching methods unnecessarily controversial, particularly if the differences in cost allocations for the methods are small. However, some external parties require organizations, such as many hospitals, to use the step method for cost reimbursement.

The step method does go part way in recognizing that support service departments can benefit from using the resources of other support service departments. However, as demonstrated, this use is recognized in only one direction. In fact, all of Storhavn's support service departments actually use services from each other. This means that they use **reciprocal services,** which are services provided among multiple support service departments. If its support service departments had relatively more reciprocal services, the city should consider using the *reciprocal method* of cost allocation to explicitly recognize the reciprocal, or back-and-forth nature of support services. This method is defined and described in Appendix 12.

Step 4: Determine Whether the Cost Allocations Achieve the Desired Results

LO 6
Evaluate the consequences of alternative cost allocations.

Step 3 is very important because if a service department has too many resources for its work, cost allocation rates will be higher than customers will tolerate, or unused capacity will be obvious. Thus, allocation base rates may not only affect user departments that pay them but also the service departments that charge them. Pedersen proposed to continue using the direct method for allocating support service costs. However, she created a controversy when she unveiled cost allocations based on more complex cost-driver bases that reflect multiple activities that the support service departments perform to serve each production department. This was a departure from the simpler but less accurate cost allocation bases that the city traditionally had used. Her approach seems appropriate, but Pedersen realized that even more accurate approaches cannot establish cause and effect and might not appease doubting constituencies.

Storhavn's Mayor and the City Council understood the inaccuracies and apparent inequities in the current allocation system and asked Pedersen to study alternative cost allocation bases for future years. They recommended that she present a new proposal for any changes well in advance of preparing the next budget so that the city could respond to comments from all affected departments and citizens.

12.4 You're the Decision Maker

Leading Implementation of Changes in Cost Allocation Approaches

Advise Mette Pedersen on an effective way to lead the City to an improved cost allocation process.

Hint: You might consider applying the recommendations from Chapter 1.

(Solutions begin on page 618.)

What is the most effective way for an organization to choose the method to allocate support service costs? Discussions (or arguments) about the 'best' approach to allocating support costs can waste valuable time and create dissension and lack of co-operation among departments. Awkward implementation of new cost allocations is bound to create distrust because affected departments will suspect that the motive is to 'steal' funds or profits. This could discredit the budget department and cause relations among departments to worsen.

On the other hand, discussions about cost allocations could increase information flow and co-operation if the negotiation process is open and all parties have an opportunity to participate and influence its outcome. An open evaluation of cost allocation approaches would consider accuracy, effects on departments, and relation of costs and benefits.

Accuracy of Cost Allocations

Tracing costs avoids controversy about accuracy. For example, if the HR department advertises a single job, the department could trace and charge the invoiced cost for the advertisement directly to the production department that has the vacancy, instead of including this in the overall HR costs. However, many costs are common (or joint in the terminology of Chapter 11) and cannot be traced easily to specific services performed. Thus, for all the reasons described earlier, these costs may be allocated to user departments.

One way to determine the best way to allocate support service costs is to examine how accurately each approach reflects the use of support service resource costs by departments receiving these services. **Accuracy**, which is precision in measurement, is both conceptual and empirical. The direct method does not consider any interactions among service departments, whereas the step method considers some, and the reciprocal method is more thorough in this respect (see Appendix 12). Likewise, more complex cost allocation bases might better reflect perceived cause-and-effect relationships between resource spending and use than do traditional cost allocation bases. Conceptually, combining causal cost allocation bases and the reciprocal method should be the most **accurate cost allocation** approach, which measures the cost of support service resource usage with the least error. Likewise, the combination of the direct method and convenient cost allocation bases could be the least accurate reflection of resource spending, use and provision of services. Other combinations lie somewhere between those extremes. The conceptual definition of accuracy is difficult to implement because it presumes that an ideal cost allocation approach that measures the 'true' cost is a feasible reference. Unfortunately, true cost is unobservable and unusable as a benchmark.

Consistency of Cost Allocation

Consistency of cost allocation is the degree to which cost allocation bases fully allocate spending for support services, is related to accuracy, and is easier to establish than true cost or true cause-and-effect relationships. One could simulate cost allocations to departments using alternative departmental cost allocation base amounts. The cost allocation bases that most consistently and fully allocate total support service costs to user departments are likely to be more accurate.[9] Conceptual accuracy or consistency alone might influence the choice of approach. This, however, is only one dimension to consider when choosing the appropriate approach for allocating support service costs.

12.4 Cost Management in Practice

International Tax and Customs Tariff Impacts of Service Cost Allocations

Multinational firms often allocate the costs of centrally served services (e.g., human resource services or financial services) to their foreign subunits. The firm may allocate these central service costs for all the reasons mentioned in this chapter, but faces the added complication of complying with tax and customs regulations. Domestic and foreign authorities are on the alert to be sure that the allocated services are priced properly to (a) allocate profits and income taxes consistently and fairly between the firm's domicile and foreign locations and (b) to reflect market prices of the services for customs duties. See KPMG (2011), also Chapter 15.

Behavioural Effects of Cost Allocations

Another way to compare cost allocation approaches is to examine the behavioural effects of alternative distributions of cost allocations to production (and support service) departments, similar to those shown in Exhibit 12.9. Cost allocations can have unintended effects. For example, department managers' performance evaluations might depend on their control of departmental costs, and they will be reluctant to change from cost allocations that they have understood and have accommodated in their departments' operations.

Effects of distributions of costs

Both direct and step methods allocate the same total support service cost for Storhavn, DKK 1,450,000. Any differences between methods are in the amounts allocated to particular production departments. If the differences are large, alternative cost allocations could affect performance evaluations, decision making and contracts.

Effects on performance evaluation

If performance evaluations of department managers are based on their abilities to provide services and control costs, which cost allocation method, direct or step, would they prefer? For example, consider Exhibit 12.8. Social Services and Public Safety departments would prefer the direct method, but Public Works would prefer the direct method because of the effects on departmental costs.

Effects on decision making

Cost management analysts should consider the effects of cost allocation differences on decision making in the affected departments. For example, the step method charges the Social Services Department DKK 9,858 per month more than does the direct method. Since this approximates the monthly cost of a counsellor, the department head might regard this difference as important.

Except for the effects of the amounts of support service costs allocated to production departments, the cost allocation base itself could influence departmental decision making. For example, if Storhavn allocates Human Resources Department costs more heavily on the basis of new employees, other department managers could perceive that they can reduce their costs (and transfers of funds to Human Resources) by reducing their employee turnover. However, they *should* do this only if the benefits of reducing employee turnover exceeds the costs; that is, the department should not retain unsatisfactory employees just to reduce cost allocations. This reasoning also applies to the use of other support services.

Effects on cost-plus contracts

As noted earlier, many organizations sell products on the basis of a **cost-plus contract**, which reimburses the seller for costs incurred plus a profit. Private contractors, for example, traditionally have sold products to governments on a cost-plus basis. Government agencies traditionally have reimbursed hospitals and nursing homes on a cost-plus basis for particular types of patients.

Cost-plus contracts give incentives to the supplier of the good or service to seek as much reimbursement as possible and, therefore, to allocate as much cost as possible to the product for which reimbursement is possible. For example, Madsen Construction ApS has contracts with both private companies and Storhavn. For simplicity, assume that Madsen is deciding how to allocate DKK 120,000 of support service cost between two major contracts, Company A and Storhavn. This DKK 120,000 is a common support service cost that cannot be directly traced to either contract. Madsen sells commercial jobs at a price set in the market, but the contract with Storhavn was negotiated for cost, plus a fixed profit. Thus, every dollar of support service cost that can be allocated to the Storhavn contract results in an additional dollar of revenue in cost reimbursement.

Suppose that Madsen is choosing between direct labour hours and construction equipment hours as the two possible allocation bases. The relative uses of direct labour hours and construction equipment hours follow:

	Contract	
Alternative allocation bases	**Company A**	**Storhavn**
Percentage of direct labour hours used	30%	70%
Percentage of construction equipment hours used	60%	40%

It seems likely that Madsen prefers to allocate the DKK 120,000 using direct labour hours because it could seek DKK 84,000 ($0.70 \times$ DKK 120,000) reimbursement from Storhavn using direct labour hours, but only DKK 48,000 ($0.40 \times$ DKK 120,000) from the city using construction equipment hours. Madsen would be DKK 36,000 better off (DKK 84,000 – DKK 48,000) if it could use direct labour hours as the allocation base. Of course, Storhavn, if city managers were aware of the difference, would prefer construction equipment hours for similar reasons. If the Storhavn contract does not specify how costs should be allocated, Madsen ethically can choose the most advantageous approach.

Because the support service costs cannot easily be directly attributed to a contract, allocation debates are common in cost-plus contracting. It is better to specify in the contract beforehand precisely how to define costs and how to make allocations. Thus, contracts and policies governing cost reimbursement usually try to clearly specify which costs and cost allocations are allowable.

Costs and Benefits of Cost Allocations

A third consideration in the design of cost allocations is the relation of the costs of setting up, administering and maintaining the cost allocation system and its benefits. Cost management analysts must realize that complex cost allocation systems are not only difficult and costly to design but also are costly to maintain. For example, organizations that implement an ABC approach often find that the ABC information indicates where processes can be greatly improved (this is the topic of Chapter 4). Thus, after cost management analysts lead and implement process improvements, they might recognize that the previous cost-driver base information is obsolete and requires revision. This can be a continual process of improvement, which is costly but justified if decisions and organizational performance also continue to improve.

If decisions or meeting organizational goals are unaffected by cost allocation type or improvements in the cost allocation used, however, it would be difficult to justify implementing a complex, expensive cost allocation system. An unchanged or traditional direct approach could be quite adequate in this situation.

Ethical Issues

The inherent arbitrariness of cost allocation means that usually no clear-cut way to allocate costs exists. This arbitrariness can lead to difficult ethical choices for those responsible for allocating the costs. Consider again the allocation of costs in cost-plus contracts. We have seen cases in which the contracts specified *manufacturing* cost plus a profit, yet the contractor allocated advertising, general and administrative, and similar costs to the manufacturing department's overhead. This appears to be a violation of the contract terms, but the contractor argued that *full* manufacturing cost should include the allocations of these other costs.

10.2 Research Insight

Ethical Cost Allocations

Professor Mark Wolfson analysed a classic example of the effects of ambiguous or unethical cost allocations in organizations structured as partnerships. General partners are responsible for conducting the work of the partnership, such as real estate development or oil and gas exploration, for the benefit of limited partners who share in the profits of the partnership. General managers also, however, can allocate their management costs to different partnerships that they manage to maximize their profits but perhaps at the expense of some limited partners. Dr Wolfson finds that limited partners are willing to pay more to participate in partnerships managed by general partners with reputations for ethical cost allocations (and other ethical practices). Therefore, general partners with reputations for ethical cost allocations earned higher returns, while less ethical general partners earned less.

Source: Wolfson (1985).

Many lawsuits involving contract and tax disputes have arisen because people have allocated costs in inappropriate ways, or contracts have been ambiguous. For example, a fast-growing county was sued by building contractors who argued that the total revenues collected by the county for building permits exceeded the costs to operate the county building department. Thus, the builders argued, the excess revenues amounted to an unfair tax on builders that the county used illegally to fund other programmes and services. The county counter-argued that permit revenues did not exceed the sum of both direct building department costs and costs allocated from county support services. After years of arguments and court appearances, the judge requested the opinions of outside experts on a reasonable cost allocation approach and mediated the dispute.

Appendix 12

Reciprocal Method

LO 7
Allocate support service department costs using the reciprocal method.

The step and direct methods omit all or some of the costs of support services consumed by one service department that were provided by other service departments. The reciprocal method of cost allocation addresses these technical limitations by making a reciprocal cost allocation when support service departments provide reciprocal services, that is, they provide services to each other. The **reciprocal method** recognizes and allocates the costs of all services provided by any support service department, including those provided to other support service departments. If allocation bases are plausible, this method is conceptually the most accurate approach because it reflects the actual processes by which services are exchanged among the organization's departments.

The reciprocal method first expresses the total costs of each service and production department in equation form:

Total departmental costs = Direct costs of the department + Service cost to be allocated to the department

This creates one equation for each department in which the unknown element is the total departmental cost. This set of equations (one equation for each unknown total department cost) is then solved simultaneously. Solving all of the equations simultaneously accounts for all support service department allocations, including direct costs and reciprocal services provided by support service departments to each other. This algebraic approach is also known as the *simultaneous solution method* because it solves a system of equations simultaneously.

Let us first illustrate this method with a hypothetical situation of two reciprocal departments, A and B, in a private firm. The direct cost of A is €50,000, and the direct cost of B is €100,000. Furthermore, department A uses 20 per cent of B's resources, and B uses 5 per cent of A's resources. The remainder of departmental cost is expensed. Each department's unknown total cost can be expressed in equation form, as follows:

$$A = €50{,}000 + 0.20\,B$$
$$B = €100{,}000 + 0.05\,A$$

Substituting for B in the first equation yields:

$$A = €50{,}000 + 0.20(100{,}000 + 0.05\,A) = €72{,}000 + 0.01\,A$$

Or,

$$0.99\,A = €70{,}000$$
$$A = €70{,}707$$ (a €20,707 increase over its direct cost)

Therefore,

$$B = €100{,}000 + 0.05\,(70{,}707) = €103{,}535$$ (a €3,535 increase over its direct cost)

In summary, A allocates €3,535 to B, and B allocates €20,707 to A, and the remainders to expense. The departmental allocations and expenses are shown horizontally in the following table.

Accounting for costs		Allocated from:			Allocated to:			
Department	Direct	A	B	Total cost	A	B	Expense	Total
A	50,000		20,707	70,707		(3,535)	(67,172)	-
B	100,000	3,535		103,535	(20,707)		(82,828)	-
Total	150,000						(150,000)	-

Ultimately, only the consolidated transactions affect financial statements. Thus, the total expense is no more than the total direct department costs of €150,000, as shown in the last row. However, because of the reciprocal services, the departments' contributions to expense reflect the back-and-forth resorting of direct costs. Department A's contribution to total expense is €67,172, which is greater than its direct cost, because of its relatively heavy use of Department B. Department B's contribution to total expense is lower than its direct cost at €82,828 because it uses relatively little of Department A's resources in return.

Application of the Reciprocal Method to Storhavn

In more realistic and complex situations (three or more reciprocal departments), analysts use matrix algebra to solve for the unknown total department costs. Next we set up the data for the analysis for the city of Storhavn. Using the information in the next-to-last column of Exhibit 12.4, the amounts of the cost allocation base from each support service department to all other departments follow.

	Amounts of allocation base (Exhibit 12.4):						
Service performed by:	Information Technology S1	Buildings & Grounds S2	Human Resources S3	Social Services P1	Public Safety P2	Public Works P3	Total allocation base
Information Technology S1	0	23	60	80	105	85	353
Buildings & Grounds S2	2,100	0	3,225	5,575	7,100	8,575	26,575
Human Resources S3	105	90	0	90	172	372	829
Social Services P1	0	0	0	0	0	0	0
Public Safety P2	0	0	0	0	0	0	0
Public Works P3	0	0	0	0	0	0	0

Note that, as with the direct and step methods, we do not count the service that support service departments provide to themselves, and, in this example, production departments provide no services to other departments. Next we transform these amounts into proportions, horizontally and similarly as the proportions used in the direct and step methods.

	Proportions of allocation bases and services used by:					
Service performed by:	Information Technology S1	Buildings & Grounds S2	Human Resources S3	Social Services P1	Public Safety P2	Public Works P3
Information Technology S1		0.065	0.170	0.227	0.297	0.241
Buildings & Grounds S2	0.079		0.121	0.210	0.267	0.323
Human Resources S3	0.127	0.109		0.109	0.207	0.449
Social Services P1	0	0	0	0	0	0
Public Safety P2	0	0	0	0	0	0
Public Works P3	0	0	0	0	0	0
Direct costs (Exhibit 12.2), DKK	360,000	840,000	250,000	5,000,000	2,700,000	1,850,000

= 105/829

= 23/353

We can write total cost equations for each department using the proportions of service costs, represented by the proportions of allocation bases used by each department, and its direct costs. For example, the unknown total costs, labelled **S1**, of the Information Technology Department is expressed as follows:

Total department costs = **Allocated costs** + **Direct costs** (from Exhibit 12.2)

$$\mathbf{S1} = 0\ \mathbf{S1} + 0.079\ \mathbf{S2} + 0.127\ \mathbf{S3} + 0\ \mathbf{P1} + 0\ \mathbf{P2} + 0\ \mathbf{P3} + 360{,}000$$

Where the zero terms are included for completeness to show that no costs are allocated from P1 to itself, or from Social Services, Public Safety or Public Works (although they might be in other circumstances). Similar equations are constructed for each of the other support service and production departments:

$$\mathbf{S2} = 0.065\ \mathbf{S1} + 0\ \mathbf{S2} + 0.109\ \mathbf{S3} + 0\ \mathbf{P1} + 0\ \mathbf{P2} + 0\ \mathbf{P3} + 840{,}000$$
$$\mathbf{S3} = 0.170\ \mathbf{S1} + 0.121\ \mathbf{S2} + 0\ \mathbf{S3} + 0\ \mathbf{P1} + 0\ \mathbf{P2} + 0\ \mathbf{P3} + 250{,}000$$
$$\mathbf{P1} = 0.227\ \mathbf{S1} + 0.210\ \mathbf{S2} + 0.109\ \mathbf{S3} + 0\ \mathbf{P2} + 0\ \mathbf{P3} + 5{,}000{,}000$$
$$\mathbf{P2} = 0.297\ \mathbf{S1} + 0.267\ \mathbf{S2} + 0.207\ \mathbf{S3} + 0\ \mathbf{P1} + 0\ \mathbf{P3} + 2{,}700{,}000$$
$$\mathbf{P3} = 0.241\ \mathbf{S1} + 0.323\ \mathbf{S2} + 0.449\ \mathbf{S3} + 0\ \mathbf{P1} + 0\ \mathbf{P2} + 1{,}850{,}000$$

Let us rewrite these equations to a form that is more convenient for solution by matrix algebra. First, collect all the known amounts on the left sides of the equations and all the unknowns on the right.

$$
\begin{aligned}
-360{,}000 &= -\mathbf{S1} + 0.079\,\mathbf{S2} + 0.127\,\mathbf{S3} + 0\,\mathbf{P1} + 0\,\mathbf{P2} + 0\,\mathbf{P3}\\
-840{,}000 &= 0.065\,\mathbf{S1} - \mathbf{S2} + 0.109\,\mathbf{S3} + 0\,\mathbf{P1} + 0\,\mathbf{P2} + 0\,\mathbf{P3}\\
-250{,}000 &= 0.170\,\mathbf{S1} + 0.121\,\mathbf{S2} - \mathbf{S3} + 0\,\mathbf{P1} + 0\,\mathbf{P2} + 0\,\mathbf{P3}\\
-5{,}000{,}000 &= 0.227\,\mathbf{S1} + 0.210\,\mathbf{S2} + 0.109\,\mathbf{S3} - \mathbf{P1} + 0\,\mathbf{P2} + 0\,\mathbf{P3}\\
-2{,}700{,}000 &= 0.297\,\mathbf{S1} + 0.267\,\mathbf{S2} + 0.207\,\mathbf{S3} + 0\,\mathbf{P1} - \mathbf{P2} + 0\,\mathbf{P3}\\
-1{,}850{,}000 &= 0.241\,\mathbf{S1} + 0.323\,\mathbf{S2} + 0.449\,\mathbf{S3} + 0\,\mathbf{P1} + 0\,\mathbf{P2} - \mathbf{P3}
\end{aligned}
$$

We now have six equations and six unknowns, which is a solvable system of equations. To obtain the solution, we will use matrix notation and spreadsheet software. In matrix notation, these equations can be written as follows. Note that the '–1' is implied for each department's total cost.

C		A						D
360,000		–1.00	0.079	0.127	0	0	0	S1
840,000		0.065	–1.00	0.109	0	0	0	S2
250,000	=	0.170	0.121	–1.00	0	0	0	S3
5,000,000		0.227	0.210	0.109	–1.00	0	0	P1
2,700,000		0.297	0.267	0.207	0	–1.00	0	P2
1,850,000		0.241	0.323	0.449	0	0	–1.00	P3

Or: **C** = **A D,** where **C** is the matrix of direct costs, **A** is the matrix of allocation base usage, and **D** is the unknown total department cost matrix (minus signs omitted with no impact on the analysis). The solution for the unknown **D** is found by multiplying both sides by the inverse of **A**. This matrix algebra is most easily accomplished on spreadsheet software, as described next. Note that we do not use entirely matrix functions on the spreadsheet because we want to format the output to resemble the earlier analyses).

Set up the coefficient matrix, A

Panel A of Exhibit 12.10, titled Coefficient Matrix, **A**, is reproduced from the total cost equations and the matrices just derived. For display purposes we have moved the direct costs to the right side of this matrix. This is the most important part of the analysis, on which the rest of the solution is calculated. It contains the matrix for the percentage of services used and the amount of costs to be allocated that we previously calculated. For example, column B reflects the right-hand side of the equation for S1, which you should verify. Columns B to G reflect all of the departmental equations' right-hand sides.

Compute the inverse matrix

Panel B of Exhibit 12.10, Inverse Matrix $\mathbf{A}^{-1}$, displays the output of Microsoft Excel's inverse matrix function, =MINVERSE(). See the steps under the exhibit. The inverse matrix presents the reciprocal percentage allocations of each department's costs to other departments. The negative percentages represent a support service department's costs allocated to/from other service departments. They are negative because they will be reallocated to production departments.

You will notice that for departments S1, S2 and S3, the total of the negative percentages is more than 100 per cent because of the reciprocal nature of the allocations. The service departments allocate costs to other service departments, which are allocated back to them reciprocally, bringing service departments' total costs to more than their direct costs. It is common when services are reciprocal that the allocations out of the support service departments are in excess of 100 per cent of their direct costs.

Allocate costs to departments

Panel C of Exhibit 12.10, Cost Allocations, presents the dollar amounts allocated to each department based on the reciprocal services provided to every department multiplied by each support service department's direct costs. The solution in Panel C deserves some detailed explanations.

1. The amounts summed for each column are the *fully allocated costs* of each department. These amounts reflect the reciprocal work done among the support service departments.[10]

Exhibit 12.10 **Reciprocal Method Analysis**

	A	B	C	D	E	F	G	H
1	Panel A Coefficient Matrix, A Services performed by:	Information Technology S1	Buildings & Grounds S2	Human Resources S3	Social Services P1	Public Safety P2	Public Works P3	Costs to be Accounted For, DKK
2	Information Technology S1	-1.000	0.065	0.170	0.227	0.297	0.241	360,000
3	Buildings & Grounds S2	0.079	-1.000	0.121	0.210	0.267	0.323	840,000
4	Human Resources S3	0.127	0.109	-1.000	0.109	0.207	0.449	250,000
5	Social Services P1	0.000	0.000	0.000	-1.000	0.000	0.000	5,000,000
6	Public Safety P2	0.000	0.000	0.000	0.000	-1.000	0.000	2,700,000
7	Public Works P3	0.000	0.000	0.000	0.000	0.000	-1.000	1,850,000
8								11,000,000
9	Panel B Inverse Matrix, A^{-1}	Information Technology S1	Buildings & Grounds S2	Human Resources S3	Social Services P1	Public Safety P2	Public Works P3	
10	Information Technology S1	-1.030	-0.087	-0.186	-0.272	-0.368	-0.360	
11	Buildings & Grounds S2	-0.099	-1.022	-0.141	-0.252	-0.331	-0.417	
12	Human Resources S3	-0.141	-0.122	-1.039	-0.170	-0.290	-0.540	
13	Social Services P1	0	0	0	-1	0	0	
14	Public Safety P2	0	0	0	0	-1	0	
15	Public Works P3	0	0	0	0	0	-1	
16								
17	Panel C Cost Allocations, DKK	Information Technology S1	Buildings & Grounds S2	Human Resources S3	Social Services P1	Public Safety P2	Public Works P3	Costs Accounted For, DKK
18	Information Technology S1	(370,953)	(31,429)	(66,865)	97,921	132,610	129,469	360,000
19	Buildings & Grounds S2	(82,793)	(858,229)	(118,223)	211,640	278,447	349,913	840,000
20	Human Resources S3	(35,303)	(30,495)	(259,701)	42,592	72,531	134,877	250,000
21	Social Services P1	0	0	0	5,000,000	0	0	5,000,000
22	Public Safety P2	0	0	0	0	2,700,000	0	2,700,000
23	Public Works P3	0	0	0	0	0	1,850,000	1,850,000
24	Fully Allocated Costs	(489,048)	(920,153)	(444,789)	5,352,154	3,183,588	2,464,258	11,000,000
25								
26	**Steps: Excel for Mac (steps for Excel for Windows are similar except for step 4; see Excel Help)**							
27	1. Prepare the coefficient matrix, A, (B2 to G7) from the resource use equations. (Add row and column labels for clarity)							
28	2. Add the departmental costs (H2 to H7).							
29	3. Prepare the blank inverse matrix (B10 to G15) to be filled.							
30	4. Type the formula =MINVERSE(B2:G7) into cell B10. The single value -1.030 should be computed in this cell							
31	5. Select the entire inverse matrix area B10 to G15. Press control-U, then press command-return. The inverse matrix should fill.							
32	6. Fill the cost allocation table (B18 to G23) with formulas that multiply cells from the inverse matrix and the costs to be allocated, H2 to H9. For example, B18 = B10*H2, C18 = C10*H2 and so on.Allocations to production departments are made positive for clarity. Bold borders are added for emphasis.							

2. Because each of the support service departments provides and receives reciprocal services, each of their total costs (values of resources used) exceeds its direct cost. These totals, however, represent transactions of back-and-forth work, but not normally transactions of funds because each support service department exists primarily to serve production departments and is funded at its direct cost only.

3. In contrast, the production departments receive the full amounts of the direct costs of the support service departments. These allocations are shown in the rainbow-shaded cells that horizontally sum to each support service department's direct cost (column H of Panel C). The allocated costs are shown as positive amounts for clarity.

4. The explanation of how the proper amounts get allocated fully to production departments may be described in an allocation table that more closely resembles those seen earlier in the chapter for the direct and step methods. Consider the allocation process in Exhibit 12.11, which uses the information from Exhibit 12.10 in a slightly different format. The top portion repeats the allocation base percentages from the resource use equations. The bottom portion uses these percentages and the support service departments' fully allocated costs to measure the flows from support service departments to production departments.

We begin Exhibit 12.11 with each support service department's direct cost, but we allocate the amount of its fully allocated cost to other departments. For example, Information Technology's

Exhibit 12.11 Reciprocal Method Cost Allocations

Storhavn

	A	B	C	D	E	F	G	H
34	Excerpts from Matrices A and cost allocations from support service department	Proportion of services used by:						
35		Information Technology S1	Buildings & Grounds S2	Human Resources S3	Social Services P1	Public Safety P2	Public Works P3	Totals
36	Information Technology S1	-	0.065	0.170	0.227	0.297	0.241	1.000
37	Buildings & Grounds S2	0.079	-	0.121	0.210	0.267	0.323	1.000
38	Human Resources S3	0.127	0.109	-	0.109	0.207	0.449	1.000
39	Fully allocated costs	(489,048)	(920,153)	(444,789)	5,352,154	3,183,588	2,464,258	11,000,000
40								
41	Explanations of allocations	Support service and production departments						
42	Accumulation of Costs, DKK	Information Technology S1	Buildings & Grounds S2	Human Ressources S3	Social Services P1	Public Safety P2	Public Works P3	Total costs
43	Direct costs	360,000	840,000	250,000	5,000,000	2,700,000	1,850,000	11,000,000
44	Allocation of S1	(489,048)	31,864	83,124	110,832	145,468	117,760	-
45								
46	Costs after allocation of S1	(129,048)	871,864	333,124	5,110,832	2,845,468	1,967,760	11,000,000
47	Allocation of S2	72,712	(920,153)	111,665	193,033	245,836	296,907	-
48								
49	Costs after allocation of S2	(56,336)	(48,288)	444,789	5,303,865	3,091,303	2,264,667	11,000,000
50	Allocation of S3	56,336	48,288	(444,789)	48,288	92,284	199,592	-
51								
52	Costs after allocation of S3	-	-	-	5,352,154	3,183,588	2,464,258	11,000,000
53								
54		= 0.065 x 489,048						

(S1's) direct cost is DKK 360,000, but the reciprocal method allocates S1's fully allocated cost of DKK 489,048 to all other user departments. Doing so naturally adds to the other departments' costs, but puts Information Technology temporarily in a deficit position.

Allocating the other support service departments' fully allocated costs (DKK 920,153 from S2 and DKK 444,789 from S3) also adds to the other departments' costs. This eventually leaves all of the support service departments at zero balances, because all of the support service departments' fully allocated costs have been allocated to each other, and ultimately, completely to production departments.

Comparative cost allocations using the direct, step and reciprocal methods appear in Exhibit 12.12. The allocations that result from the direct and reciprocal methods are more similar than either is to the step method. Some organizations use the direct method if allocations are not dramatically different just because it is easier to explain to managers and internal customers than the other methods. Cost management analysts, however, should consider all issues raised at the end of this chapter regarding the choice among alternative cost allocation approaches.

If Storhavn wishes to use a method that recognizes services among support service departments, the budget department probably should use the reciprocal method because it is conceptually superior and actually easier to use. The reciprocal method could be more difficult to explain, however, because the fully allocated (partially double-counted) costs from each support service department exceed departmental direct costs. The final costs allocated to the production departments, however, do total to only departmental direct costs. The partly satisfying, intuitive explanation is that the support service costs circulate among themselves before finally settling out in the production departments.

Exhibit 12.12 Comparisons of Direct, Step and Reciprocal Cost Allocations

	A	B	C	D	E	F
12	Summary of direct, step and reciprocal method allocations of support service department costs					
13	Production departments	Direct method allocations, DKK	Step method allocations, DKK	Reciprocal method allocations, DKK	Percentage differences from direct method	Percentage differences from step method
14	P1: Social Services	362,532	373,334	352,154	-2.9%	-5.7%
15	P2: Public Safety	488,482	498,182	483,588	-1.0%	-2.9%
16	P3: Public Works	598,986	578,484	614,258	2.5%	6.2%
17	Total service department costs	1,450,000	1,450,000	1,450,000		

Chapter Summary

Allocating support service costs should reflect a plausible, correlative relationship between spending for support services and the services provided to internal customers. That is, cost allocations should accurately measure the costs of support services provided. Tracing support service spending directly to internal customers is usually difficult. Many organizations use reasonable, although not completely accurate, cost allocations based on allocation bases that reasonably describe the use of service resources.

The direct and step methods are the most common methods of allocating service costs. A currently less common method is the reciprocal cost method (see Appendix 12). Cost allocation is not a purely technical exercise since allocations can have both intended and unintended consequences. Therefore, choosing how to allocate costs should not be based solely on technical merits (e.g., recognizing reciprocal services). The way to allocate service costs depends more on the behaviour of the departments and divisions that receive the allocations.

Key Terms

For each term's definition, refer to the indicated page, or turn to the glossary at the end of the text.

accuracy,	597	production (or line) departments,	576
accurate cost allocation,	597	reciprocal method*,	601
consistency of cost allocation,	597	reciprocal services,	596
cost allocation,	578	second-stage cost allocation,	591
cost-plus contract,	599	step method,	592
direct method,	588	support service costs,	576, 579
indexed cost allocation bases,	586	support service (or indirect) departments,	576
plausible correlation,	585		

**Term appears in Appendix 12.*

*Review Questions are mostly written at a **basic** level; Critical Analysis questions and Exercises are **intermediate**, and Problems and Cases are **advanced**.*

Review Questions

12.1 What factors would you consider when deciding whether to outsource a particular support service?

12.2 What are some costs of the cost allocation process itself?

12.3 What are some benefits of cost allocation?

12.4 How should a manager decide whether to allocate costs?

12.5 What are some management uses of information based on allocated costs?

12.6 What are four broad categories of common costs and a typical basis for the allocation of costs in each category?

12.7 What are the similarities and differences of allocating service costs for the direct method and the step method (and the reciprocal method, if studied)?

12.8 What criterion should be used to determine the order of allocation from support service departments when using the step method? Explain why.

Critical Analysis

12.9 Three students share a house. Having better things to do than clean the house, they hire someone to come in and clean once each week. How should they share the costs of the housekeeper? One simple solution is to share the cost equally. Suppose that one student's bedroom is twice as large as each of the other students' bedrooms. The second student has a small bedroom and uses the house only four days per week. The third student uses the house all week, has a small bedroom, and is generally acknowledged to be the cleanest of the three. Sharing the cost equally is simple, but is it fair? Form groups of three. Each should take the role of one of the roommates. Using the techniques of the chapter, develop a reasonable way to share housekeeping costs.

12.10 Respond to this comment: 'Outsourcing is based on a market economy and, therefore, is the most efficient way to obtain a service.'

12.11 Consider the following conversation between a self-proclaimed cost allocation expert and Jack, the manager of a pub.

Expert: Joe, you said you put in these crisps because some people ask for them, but do you realize what this rack of crisps is costing you?

Jack: It's not going to cost! It's going to be a profit. Sure, I had to pay £100 for a fancy rack to hold the bags, but the crisps cost 24 pence a bag, and I sell them for 40 pence. Suppose I sell 50 bags a week to start. It'll take 12½ weeks to cover the cost of the rack. After that I have a clear profit of 16 cents a bag. The more I sell, the more I make.

Expert: That is an antiquated and completely unrealistic approach, Jack. Fortunately, modern accounting procedures permit a more accurate picture that reveals the complexities involved.

Jack: Huh?

Expert: To be precise, those crisps must be integrated into your entire operation and be allocated their appropriate share of business overhead. They must share a proportion of your expenditures for rent, heat, light, equipment depreciation, decorating, salaries for your waitresses, cook...

Jack: The cook? What's he got to do with the crisps? He doesn't even know I have them.

Expert: Look, Jack, the cook is in the kitchen, the kitchen prepares the food, the food brings people in here, and the people ask to buy crisps. That's why you must charge a portion of the cook's wages, as well as a part of your own salary, to crisp sales. This sheet contains a carefully calculated cost analysis, which indicates that the crisp operation should pay exactly £2,278 per year toward these general overhead costs.

Jack: The crisps? £2,278 a year for overhead? The crisp salesman said I'd make money – put them on the end of the counter, he said, and get 16 pence a bag profit.

Expert: [with a sniff]: He's not an accountant. Do you actually know what the portion of the counter occupied by the crisp rack is worth to you?

Jack: Nothing. No stool there, just a dead spot at the end.

Expert: The modern cost picture permits no dead spots. Your counter contains 6 square metres, and your counter business grosses £60,000 a year. Consequently, the tenth of a square metre occupied by the crisp rack is worth £1,000 per year. Since you have taken that area away from general counter use, you must charge the value of the space to the occupant.

Jack: [eagerly] Look! I have a better idea. Why don't I just throw the crisps out – put them in a trash can?

Expert: Can you afford it?

Jack: Sure. All I have is about 50 bags of crisps – cost about 12 pounds – so I lose £100 on the rack, but I'm out of this crisp business and no more grief.

Expert: [shaking head] Jack, it isn't quite that simple. You are in the crisp business! The minute you throw those bags out, you are adding £2,278 of annual overhead to the rest of your operation. Jack – be realistic – can you afford to do that?

Jack: [completely crushed]: It's unbelievable! Last week I was making money. Now I'm in trouble – just because I believed selling 50 bags of crisps a week would be easy.

Expert: [with raised eyebrow]: That is the object of modern cost studies, Jack – to dispel those false illusions.

Form small groups and develop a solution to Joe's problem. Be sure to consider appropriate cost allocations, if any, and the appropriate opportunity cost of counter space.

12.12 If support service cost allocations are arbitrary and potentially misleading, should we assume that managers are foolish for using information about which services to provide based on allocated service costs?

12.13 One critic of cost allocation noted, 'You can avoid the problem of arbitrary cost allocations by simply not allocating any higher-level resource service costs to lower-level uses of resources.' Prepare a memo outlining the costs and benefits of this approach.

12.14 Explain how cost allocation in an organization could be both a technical and a political exercise.

12.15 (Appendix 12) What argument(s) could be given in support of the reciprocal method as the preferred method for allocating the costs of service departments?

12.16 Under what conditions are the results from using the direct method of allocation the same as those from the step method? Why?

12.17 Consider a company with two producing departments and one service department. The service department allocates its costs to the producing departments on the basis of the number of employees in each department. If the costs in the service department are fixed by policy for the coming period, what effect would the (unexpected) addition of employees in one production department have on the service costs allocated to the other? Comment on the reasonableness of the situation.

12.18 Prepare a short presentation to explain and comment on this argument: cost allocation can never provide an incentive to reduce service costs unless the amount allocated is tied to some controllable driver. Awareness of the service cost serves no purpose if the driver is not controllable.

12.19 The manager of an operating department just received a cost report and has made the following comment with respect to the costs allocated from one of the service departments: 'This charge to my division does not seem right. The service centre installed equipment with more capacity than our division requires. We seem to be allocated more costs in periods when other departments use less service capacity. We are paying for excess capacity of other departments when other departments cut their usage levels. Explain how this result occurred and how to solve this manager's problem.'

Exercises

Exercise 12.20 [LO 3] Alternative Allocation Bases

Kaufmann AG operates a 10,000 square metre supermarket. Each department in the store is charged a share of the cost of the building. The following information concerning two of the departments in the store is available.

Department	Meat	Dry goods
Sales revenues	€300,000	€385,000
Cost of goods sold	85,000	80,000
Salaries and other direct expenses	65,000	60,000
Allocated administrative expenses	25,000	25,000
Operating profit before building occupancy costs	€125,000	€220,000
Area occupied (square metres)	1,000	3,000

Other departments use the remaining 6,000 square metres. The total building occupancy costs are €800,000 per year.

Required

a. If area occupied is the basis for allocating building occupancy costs, what is the operating profit or loss for each of these two departments?

b. Would you allocate based on something other than square metres if you learned that the dry goods department is located in a back corner of the store? Explain.

Exercise 12.21 [LO 3] Alternative Service Cost Allocation Bases

Quality Credit Ltd of Canada produces two styles of credit reports, standard and executive. The difference between the two is in the amount of background checking and data collection. The executive report uses more skilled personnel because additional interviews and analyses are performed. The relevant figures for the previous year follow.

Allocation base	Standard reports	Executive reports
Data purchased	$30,000	$45,000
Research hours	13,500	31,500
Interview hours	2,000	6,000
Number of reports	8,000	2,000

The company wants to allocate $1,500,000 in support service costs to these two product lines.

Required

For each of the four potential allocation bases, determine the amount of support service cost allocated to each type of report.

Exercise 12.22 [LO 3] Alternative Allocation Bases

Refer to your calculations for Exercise 12.21. Your supervisor wants to know the costs to prepare a standard report and an executive report, including the cost of data, labour (which costs $40 per hour), and support services.

Required

a. For each type of report, prepare four different answers to this question: how much does it cost to produce?

b. Prepare a memo explaining to your supervisor why there are four different cost numbers for each report. Also indicate whether total costs are the same for Quality Credit Ltd regardless of the overhead allocation base used.

c. What do you recommend?

Exercise 12.23 [LO 4] Cost Allocations: Direct Method

Société Réussite has two production departments, P1 and P2, and two support service departments, S1 and S2. Direct costs for each department and the percentage of service costs used by the various departments for the month of May are as follows:

		Percentage of services used by			
		S1	S2	P1	P2
Department	Direct costs				
S1	€ 120,000		40%	30%	30%
S2	140,000	25%		45%	30%
P1	200,000				
P2	180,000				

Required

Build a spreadsheet to compute the allocation of support service department costs to producing departments using the direct method.

Exercise 12.24 [LO 4] Service Department Costs Allocated First to Production Departments and Second to Jobs

Refer to the facts in Exercise 10.23. Assume that both P1 and P2 work on just two jobs, 10 and 11, during the month of May. Costs are allocated to jobs based on the number of labour hours in P1 and of machine hours in P2. The labour and machine hours worked in each department are as follows:

		P1	P2
Job 10	Labour hours	80	10
	Machine hours	10	20
Job 11	Labour hours	10	10
	Machine hours	10	90

Required

How much of the support service department costs allocated to P1 and P2 in the direct method should be allocated to Job 10? How much to Job 11?

Exercise 12.25 [LO 5] Cost Allocation: Step Method

Refer to the data for Société Réussite (Exercise 12.23).

Required

Build a spreadsheet and the *step* method to allocate the service costs, using:

a. The order of allocation starting with S1.
b. The allocations made in the reverse order (starting with S2).

Exercise 12.26 [LO 6] Cost Allocation Comparisons

Refer to the data for Société Réussite (Exercises 12.23 and 12.25, part a).

Required

a. Compare the results of the *direct* and *step* methods. Which method is better? Explain.
b. Explain how the choice of allocation method might affect outsourcing decisions.

Exercise 12.27 [LO 7] Cost Allocation: Reciprocal Method (Appendix 12)

During the past month, the following costs were incurred in the three production departments and two service departments in ProSport Ltd:

P1	£144,100
P2	£300,400
P3	£412,000
S1	£ 81,000
S2	£ 62,500

The use of services by other departments follows:

	Percentages used by internal customers				
Service departments	S1	S2	P1	P2	P3
S1	-	35%	30%	20%	15%
S2	15%	-	15%	20%	50%

Required

Build a spreadsheet to allocate service department costs to P1, P2 and P3 using the *reciprocal* method, and present the total costs of P1, P2 and P3 after this allocation.

Problems

Problem 12.28 [LO 4] Service Cost Allocation: Direct Method

Danych SA allocates service costs to its East and West Divisions. During the past month, it incurred the following service costs (monetary values given in Polish zloty, PLN):

Computing services	PLN 465,000
Human resources	1,560,000
Custodial services	228,000

The following information concerning various activity measures and service uses by each of the divisions is available:

	East	West
Area occupied (m^2)	1,000	3,000
Payroll (for HR)	PLN 825,000	PLN 255,000
Computer time	150	80
Computer storage (GB)	350	250
Equipment value	PLN 315,000	PLN 360,000
Operating profit, before allocations	PLN 1,035,000	PLN 1,245,000

Required

Build a spreadsheet to allocate the service costs to the two divisions using the direct method and the most appropriate of these allocation bases. For computing services, use computer time only.

Problem 12.29 [LO 4] Cost Allocation: Direct Method

Metafel AG manufactures and sells T-shirts for advertising and promotional purposes. The company has two manufacturing operations, shirt-making and printing. When the company receives an order for T-shirts, the shirt making department obtains the materials and colours requested and has the shirts made in the desired mix of sizes. It sends the completed shirts to the printing department where the custom labels or designs are prepared and silk-screened onto the shirts.

To support the manufacturing activity, the company has a building that houses the two manufacturing departments as well as the sales department, payroll department, and the design and patterns staff. To aid in cost control, the company accumulates the costs of these support functions in separate service departments: (1) building occupancy, (2) human resources, and (3) design and patterns.

During the current period, the direct costs incurred by each department are as follows:

Shirt making (P1)	€52,000
Printing (P2)	28,000
Sales (P3)	17,000
Building occupancy (S1)	218,000
Human resources (S2)	147,000
Design and patterns (S3)	87,000

Building occupancy costs are allocated on the basis of the number of square metres of each department. Human resources costs are allocated on the basis of the number of full-time equivalent employees. The design and pattern costs are charged to departments on the basis of the number of designs requested by each department. For the current period, the following table summarizes the usage of services by other service cost centres and other departments:

	S1	S2	S3	P1	P2	P3
Building occupancy (S1) (m^2)	-	900	420	3,000	4,400	1,000
Human resources (S2) (employees)	5	-	7	33	17	8
Design and patterns (S3) (designs)	-	-	-	18	44	8

Required

Using the direct method for service cost allocations, what are the total costs in each of the three 'producing' departments?

Problem 12.30 [LO 5] Cost Allocation: Step Method

Refer to the facts for Problem 12.29.

Required

a. Compute the cost allocations and total costs in each production department using the step method. Which service costs should be allocated first? Second?

b. How might the choice of allocation method affect a decision whether to outsource the shirt-making activity?

Problem 12.31 [LO 3] Second Stage of Cost Allocation

Syntel Corporation's memory chip division manufactures two types of computer memory chips: the RAM-A chip is a commonly used chip for personal computer systems, and the RAM-B chip is used for specialized scientific applications. Unit-level materials costs for the RAM-A chip are $0.40 per unit and for the RAM-B are $1.25 per unit. The division's annual output is 28 million chips. Labour costs in the division total $750,000. Manufacturing overhead is composed of $1 million of corporate service cost allocated to the division on the basis of labour costs and $1.5 million of divisional overhead (supervision, materials handling and security, utilities, equipment costs and depreciation, etc.).

The company's assembly process is highly automated. As a result, the primary function for direct labour is to set up a production run and to check equipment settings on a periodic basis. Yesterday the equipment was set up to run 2,000 RAM-B units. When that run was completed, equipment settings were changed, and 75,000 RAM-A units were produced. Part of the daily cost report follows:

	RAM-A	RAM-B
Units produced	75,000	2,000
Unit-level materials used	$20,000	$1,500
Labour used	$2,700	$1,300

Required

a. Recommend how to allocate the memory chip division's overhead (centrally allocated and divisional) to the division's two products. What should influence your choice of allocation bases?

b. For yesterday's production run, what is the total manufacturing cost per unit for RAM-A and RAM-B using your recommended approach?

c. Compare your result in requirement (b) with another approach using a different cost allocation base(s). Explain the source of the difference between full costs per unit for each product.

Problem 12.32 [LO 1, 5] Step Method with Three Service Departments

Votre Tour SAS rebuilds old cars. It operates two production departments, mechanical repair and body work, and has three service departments for its plant: building occupancy, human resources and equipment maintenance. Management is concerned that the costs of its service departments are getting too high. In particular, management would like to keep the costs of each service department under €750 per unit on average. You have been asked to allocate budgeted service department costs to the two production departments and compute the expected unit costs.

The company decided that building occupancy costs should be allocated on the basis of the number of square metres used by each production and service department. Human resources costs are allocated on the basis of the number of employees; equipment maintenance costs are allocated on the basis of the dollar value of the equipment in each department. The use of each basis by all departments during the current period follows:

Allocation base	Used by				
	Building occupancy	Human resources	Equipment maintenance	Mechanical repair	Body work
Building area, m^2	500	1,200	1,000	1,400	4,500
Employees	10	6	7	40	50
Equipment value	€18,000	€360,000	€52,500	€810,000	€748,500
Budgeted departmental costs	€600,000	€787,500	€465,000	€2,250,000	€1,342,500

Required

Build a spreadsheet to solve requirement (a).

a. Using the step method, determine the allocated costs and the total costs in each of the two producing departments. The allocation order is (1) building occupancy, (2) human resources, and (3) equipment maintenance.

b. Assume that 1,250 units were processed in each of the two producing departments during the current period. Did the company meet management's standards of keeping service department costs below €750 per unit?

Problem 12.33 [LO 1, 6] Cost Allocation: Step Method with Analysis and Decision Making

Auckland Products is reviewing its operations to determine what additional energy-saving projects it might implement. The company's southern plant has three service departments and two production departments. This plant has its own electric-generating facilities powered by natural gas wells that the company owns and that are located on the same property as the plant. The service departments are natural gas, electricity generation and general administration. A summary of the use of services by other service departments as well as by the two production departments at the plant follows:

	Services provided to				
Services from	(S1)	(S2)	(S3)	(P1)	(P2)
Natural gas, S1	–	40%	–	10%	50%
Electricity generation, S2	10%	–	15%	45%	30%
General administration, S3	10%	15%	–	40%	35%
Departmental costs	$70,000	$110,000	$48,000	$600,000	$440,000

The company currently allocates the costs of service departments to production departments using the step method. The local power company indicates it would charge $150,000 per year for the electricity now being generated by the company internally. Management rejected switching to the public utility on the grounds that its rates would cost more than the $120,000 cost of the present company-owned system. (Monetary values given in New Zealand dollars, $.)

Required

a. Prepare for management an analysis of the costs of the company's own electric-generating operations. (Use the step method.) The order of allocation is S1, S2 and S3. Should Auckland Products purchase or continue to make its own electricity?

b. Indicate how your analysis would change if the company could realize $55,000 per year from the sale of the natural gas now used for electric generating. (Assume no selling costs.)

Problem 12.34 [LO 7] Cost Allocation: Reciprocal Method (Appendix 12)

Refer to Problem 12.33 and the data for Auckland Products.

Required

a. Using the reciprocal method, compute the costs of electricity generation and the costs allocated to production.
b. Explain the differences in costs for the two methods, step and reciprocal.

Problem 12.35 [LO 4, 5] Service Department Cost Allocation: Direct and Step Methods

Meuse Fabrication has three support service departments (general factory administration, factory maintenance and factory cafeteria), and two production departments (fabrication and assembly). A summary of costs and other data for each department prior to allocation of service department costs for the year ended 30 June follows:

	General factory administration	Factory maintenance	Factory cafeteria	Fabrication	Assembly
Direct materials	0	€65,000	€91,000	€3,130,000	€950,000
Direct labour	€90,000	82,100	87,000	1,950,000	2,050,000
Manufacturing overhead	70,000	56,100	62,000	1,650,000	1,850,000
Total department cost	€160,000	€203,200	€240,000	€6,730,000	€4,850,000
Direct labour hours	32,000	28,000	44,000	564,000	438,000
Number of employees	14	10	22	285	210
Square metres occupied	175	200	480	880	7,200

The costs of the service departments are allocated on the following bases: general factory administration department, direct labour hours; factory maintenance department, square metres occupied; and factory cafeteria, number of employees.

Required

Round all final calculations to the nearest euro.

a. Assume that Meuse elects to distribute service department costs to production departments using the direct method. Compute the amount of factory maintenance department costs allocated to the fabrication department.
b. Assume the same method of allocation as in requirement (a). Compute the amount of general factory administration department costs allocated to the assembly department.
c. Assuming that Meuse elects to distribute service department costs to other departments and using the step method (starting with factory cafeteria and then factory maintenance), compute the amount of factory cafeteria department costs allocated to the factory maintenance department.
d. Assume the method of allocation as in requirement (c). Compute the amount of factory maintenance department costs allocated to factory cafeteria.

[CPA adapted]

Problem 12.36 [LO 4-6] Cost Allocation for Travel Reimbursement

Your company has a travel policy that reimburses employees for the 'ordinary and necessary' costs of business travel. Employees often mix a business trip with pleasure either by extending the time at the destination or travelling from the business destination to a nearby resort or other personal destination. When this happens, an allocation must be made between the business and personal portions of the trip. However, the travel policy is unclear on the allocation method to use.

Consider this example. An employee obtained a first-class ticket for $2,340 and travelled the following itinerary:

From	To	Mileage	One-way regular fare	Purpose
Washington, DC	Salt Lake City	1,839	$1,200	Business
Salt Lake City	Los Angeles	590	300	Personal
Los Angeles	Washington, DC	2,288	1,000	Return

Required

a. Form small groups to compute the business portion of the airfare and state the basis for the indicated allocation that is appropriate according to each of the following independent scenarios:
  (1) Based on the maximum reimbursement for the employee.
  (2) Based on the minimum cost to the company.

b. Prepare a short presentation to management explaining the method that you think should be used and why. What ethical issues do you perceive and how should they be resolved? You do not have to restrict your recommendation to either of the methods in requirement (a).

Cases

Case 12.37 [LO 4-6] Cost Allocation for Rate-making Purposes

Conexo Insurance Company asked the regulatory board for permission to increase the premiums of its insurance operations. Insurance premium rates in the jurisdiction in which Conexo operates are designed to cover the operating costs and insurance claims. As a part of Conexo's expenses, its agents earn commissions based on premium revenues. Premium revenues are also used to pay claims and to invest in securities.

Administrative expenses include the costs to manage the company's investments and investment services (e.g., retirement annuities). All administrative costs are charged against premium revenue. Conexo claims that its insurance operations 'just broke even' last year and that a rate increase is necessary. The following income statement (in millions) was submitted to support Conexo's request:

Insurance income:	
Premium revenue	$600
Operating costs:	
Claims	300
Administrative	200
Sales commissions	100
Total operating costs	$600
Insurance profit (loss)	0
Investment income	100
Profits after Investment income	$100

Further investigation reveals that approximately 20 per cent of the sales commissions might be considered related to investment activities. In addition, the investment division uses 30 per cent of the support services. The state insurance commission (which sets insurance rates) believes that Conexo's insurance activities should earn about 5 per cent on its premium revenues.

Required

Form separate groups to prepare responses to the following:

a. If you were a consumer group, how would you present Conexo's income statement? (For example, how would you allocate administrative costs and sales commissions to the insurance income and investment income categories?) What ethical issues do you perceive as a consumer?

b. If you were Conexo's management, what arguments would you present in support of the cost allocations included in the income statement presented in the problem? What ethical issues do you perceive as management?

c. Meet as opposing groups to resolve the allocation issue with another student acting as the mediator.

Case 12.38 [LO 1, 6] University Instructional Cost Study

Universities seek to understand their costs of offering services, which include the broad categories of instruction, research and public service. The largest resource cost is for faculty and staff salaries, which are college- or departmental-level expenditures and, in the short run, do not vary with respect to instructional activities. Because the university faculty provides most of the university's services, measuring the costs of the three types of service requires the allocation of faculty salaries. Likewise, expenditures for physical plant and libraries support all three types of service, which requires allocations of these costs.

The method and allocation bases used can affect a university's internal decisions about funding staffing in different colleges and departments and, for public and state universities, can affect decisions by state legislatures and governing boards for appropriations and tuition levels.

Many difficulties exist in developing these cost allocations, including:

- Different sources of funding could restrict the use of funds. For example, non-state-supported funds might specify that the funds be used to support research activities only.
- Faculty might teach classes in multiple disciplines.
- Faculty might have different assignments with respect to teaching, research and public service.
- Different levels of classes (undergraduate, graduate, professional) might require different faculty and support resources.
- General administrative and library resources at the university, campus, college and department levels provide support for all three types of services.

The Office of Planning and Analysis (OPA) of the **University of Minnesota** conducted an extensive analysis of the costs of instruction at each of the university's five campuses. One objective of the analysis was to measure the cost of instruction per full-year-equivalent (FYE) student in each department, college and campus. An FYE student is the equivalent of one student taking a normal course load (30 semester credit hours) for a full academic year. The OPA followed these procedures for determining the instructional costs per FYE student:

1. *Allocations of departmental resource costs.* Courses and FYE students taught were assigned by department according to course designation (e.g., accounting courses and FYE students taught in those courses were assigned to the accounting department). Instructors and their salaries were matched with courses taught. Faculty salaries (whole or part) were assigned to departments according to the designation of classes. Salaries were added to departmental administrative costs and allocated to FYE students by dividing total departmental costs by total FYE students taught.
2. *Allocations of support service costs.* Administrative and support service costs at the university, campus and college levels were allocated on the basis of departmental budgets before allocations using the step method. Graduate school administrative costs were allocated using the direct method on the basis of the number of graduate-level credit hours taught. Library costs were allocated directly to research, instruction and public service based on historical percentages. Other service costs are allocated directly on the basis of FYE student enrolment. These departmental allocations also were divided by total number of FYE students taught.

A summary of results from the most recent OPA analysis at the college level follows:

Comparative Costs of Instruction, University of Minnesota

Campus	College	FYE student	Departmental cost per FYE student	Allocated cost per FYE student	Total cost per FYE student
Twin Cities	Architecture	381	$6,914	$3,449	$10,363
	Biology	1,252	7,006	3,219	10,225
	Education	3,312	4,765	2,916	7,681
	Human ecology	892	5,996	3,325	9,321
	Liberal arts	12,480	4,883	2,621	7,504
	Natural resources	293	4,748	2,689	7,437
	Agriculture	1,185	5,870	3,685	9,555
	Business	2,175	9,059	3,191	12,250
	Dentistry	627	12,129	8,330	20,459
	General college	699	8,303	3,562	11,865
	Public affairs	193	12,501	3,980	16,481
	Engineering	6,627	7,702	3,392	11,094

	Law	801	9,365	2,567	11,932
	Medicine	4,063	15,554	4,422	19,976
	Nursing	368	10,198	4,665	14,863
	Pharmacy	377	15,328	5,040	20,368
	Public health	632	8,441	4,127	12,568
	ROTC	22	12,314	3,300	15,614
	Veterinary	545	14,859	4,991	19,850
	Total Twin Cities	36,924	7,646	3,325	10,971
Duluth	Achievement ctr	39	3,918	2,610	6,528
	Human services	1,107	4,198	2,804	7,002
	Liberal arts	2,071	3,046	2,466	5,512
	Science & engineering	1,970	4,780	2,284	7,064
	Medicine	212	22,944	6,964	29,908
	Business & economics	668	5,268	2,920	8,188
	Fine arts	611	4,498	2,673	7,171
	Total Duluth	6,678	4,740	2,836	7,576
Morris	Academic affairs	1,861	3,663	4,016	7,679
Crookston	Academic affairs	1,043	3,540	4,393	7,934

Required

a. Critique the allocation methods used by OPA to measure cost per FYE student at the college level.

b. A Minnesota state legislator at a budget hearing argued, 'It is clear that the state could save significant funds by transferring programs from the Twin Cities campus to the Duluth campus. For example, every student in a business program that we transfer from the Twin Cities campus to Duluth would save the state $4,062. And every student in an engineering program that we transfer to Duluth would save nearly $4,030 per student. People are tired of paying high taxes to support inefficient programs. We need to be sure that taxpayers get the most for their money.' What are the pros and cons of this argument?

c. How could the OPA figures be used to support higher-education decision making? In what ways are the figures presented either helpful or misleading?

[Adapted from the University of Minnesota's Instructional Cost Study]

Case 12.39 [LO 1, 2, 4-6] Federal Highway Cost Allocation Study

The **US Department of Transportation** completed an extensive study of costs and uses of the federal highway system, the Federal Highway Cost Allocation Study (HCAS). This study led to recommendations for significant changes in user fees paid by private citizens (e.g., in fuel taxes) and commercial enterprises (e.g., licences and fuel taxes paid by highway transportation companies). The costs of highway usage include their construction and repair due to traffic and weather damage. In a major departure from previous studies, the HCAS recommended including environmental impacts, safety, congestion and noise caused by the federal highway system in the costs to be shared by highway users. Federal highway spending, not including mass transit, environmental impacts, and so on, amounted to approximately $27,102,000,000.

Private automobile traffic dominated Vehicle Miles Travelled (VMT) on federal highways as shown:

Passenger vehicles	VMT total (millions)	VMT percentage	Vehicles	Vehicle percentage
Autos	1,818,461	67.5%	167,697,897	70.0%
Pickups/Vans	669,198	24.8	63,259,330	26.4
Buses	7,397	0.3	754,509	0.3
Single-unit trucks	83,100	3.1	5,970,431	2.5
Combination trucks	115,689	4.3	1,971,435	0.8
Total	2,693,845	100%	239,653,602	100%

Required

a. Compute highway spending costs per vehicle (by type) by allocating $27,102,000,000 highway spending on the basis of (1) the number of vehicles and (2) the VMT. Would inequities be created by either of these allocations? Explain.

b. The federal HCAS recommended the following cost pools and allocation bases:

Cost Pool*	Amount	Allocation base
New construction and pavement replacement	$19.161 billion	VMTs weighted by passenger car equivalents (PCE)†
Bridge construction and replacement	3.757 billion	VMT
Highway enhancements	4.184 billion	VMT weighted by PCE
Mass transit	5.787 billion	VMT

*Not included in the previous total obligations.

†A passenger car equivalent (PCE) measures each type of vehicle's effects on highways compared to an automobile, pickup or van. On average, a bus has a PCE of 4.0, a single-unit truck has a PCE of 5.4, and a combination truck has a PCE of 10.6. One mile driven by a bus, for example, has 4 times the effect as an automobile, pickup or van.

Allocate the $27,102,000,000 highway costs to the types of vehicles using these cost pools and allocation bases. Compare them to allocations based on VMT alone.

[Adapted from a US Federal Highway Cost Allocation Study.]

Solutions to You're the Decision Maker

12.1 Principles of Cost Allocation, p. 581

a. Principles of cost allocation become more important as cost allocations become a larger part of an organization's total costs. Obviously, if most support services are outsourced, cost allocation principles seem unnecessary. In this case, market transactions take the place of bureaucratic rules and principles. On the other hand, if most support services are internal and production departments bear the costs of those services via cost allocations, it is in the organization's interest to have clear cost allocation principles and policies. Otherwise, managers will spend unproductive time mediating disputes over cost allocations.

Cost allocations might be more prevalent in public institutions because they seldom obtain or provide services through open markets (although this is changing throughout the world). Furthermore, since public organizations usually exist to provide goods and services that are not available via market transactions, monetary measures of their values are unavailable. Thus, cost allocations might be the predominant quantitative measures of services.

b. As the manager of a production department, you know that spending for support services can affect your department. First, you probably agree that information technology is important, but you might express surprise that you were not informed about this decision, which should have been discussed openly and fully as a major decision. Next, because departments like yours will pay for this increased support service spending, you might wonder what services your department can expect in return. By challenging the budget increase, you are providing a control on support service spending, but you also might wonder aloud whether your department might be better off if it could outsource information technology services. Furthermore, you might express concern about the unplanned effects on your budget and whether the city expects your department (a) to reduce its spending on other resources to pay for increased support services, (b) to increase fees charged to citizens, or (c) to seek increased funding from tax revenues or state and federal grants. You could also express concern about whether the support-service departments are more concerned with their budgets than with providing reasonable charges for fair services to others. Note that these concerns are similar to those you would have as a department or division manager in a private corporation; sales from departments such as yours must cover spending for internal services.

c. As city Mayor, you must be concerned with the efficiency with which the city provides services to its citizens. That means ensuring that the city provides the type, quality and quantity of services that citizens want and need within its budget and according to appropriate laws and regulations. Perhaps the most important principle is *provision of incentives for service providers to deliver products and services efficiently and effectively* because adhering to this principle will ensure that scarce city resources are supplied and used appropriately.

12.2 Municipal Service Costs per 'Unit', p. 582

Q1: As an informed citizen, what questions would you ask about these estimates of cost savings?
A1: Are these really incremental, avoidable, cash costs? Or are these average accounting costs?

Q2: Why does this matter?
A2: Because only those costs that will no longer be paid can be counted as saved.

Q3: How do you think the cost estimates were derived?
A3: Most likely they are the result of dividing fully allocated department costs (as we will discuss) by the 'units' of service (e.g., the number of police cars in service).

Q4: Any concerns about these estimates?
A4: The main concern is about the avoidability of what appear to be reasonable but arbitrary costs.

Q5: What do you think of the opportunity costs of each of these 'units' of service?
A5: Even if the estimates are close to the cost savings that would be realized, the cost to the city might be far higher if, for example, police were slower to respond to a crime, or fire-fighters to a fire.

12.3 Impact of Changes in Cost Allocation Bases, p. 592

a. Following are the direct method cost allocations with the original cost allocation base amounts.

Direct Allocation of Information Technology Department Costs

Production department	Allocation base, computers	Percentage of base	Direct cost allocation, DKK
Information Technology cost to allocate			360,000
P1: Social Services	60	46.2%	166,154
P2: Public Safety	45	34.6%	124,615
P3: Public Works	25	19.2%	69,231
Total	130	100.0%	360,000

= 60/130

= 0.462 x 360,000

Direct Allocation of Buildings and Grounds Department Costs

Department	Allocation base, space used, m^2	Percentage of base	Direct cost allocation, DKK
Buildings and Grounds cost to allocate			840,000
P1: Social Services	4,300	27.2%	228,608
P2: Public Safety	5,500	34.8%	292,405
P3: Public Works	6,000	38.0%	318,987
Total	15,800	100.0%	840,000

= 4,300/15,800

= 0.272 x 840,000

Direct Allocation of Human Resources Department Costs

Department	Allocation base, employees	Percentage of base	Direct cost allocation, DKK
Human Resources cost to allocate			250,000
P1: Social Services	65	20.1%	50,154
P2: Public Safety	112	34.6%	86,420
P3: Public Works	147	45.4%	113,426
Total	324	100.0%	250,000

= 65/324

= 0.201 x 250,000

The summary of the original direct method cost allocations follows next.

Direct Allocations of Support Service Department Costs				
	Support Service Department			
Production Departments	Information Technology	Buildings and Grounds	Human Resources	Total Allocated
P1: Social Services	166,154	228,608	50,154	444,916
P2: Public Safety	124,615	292,405	86,420	503,440
P3: Public Works	69,231	318,987	113,426	501,644
Total service department costs	360,000	840,000	250,000	1,450,000

b. Comparing the original with the indexed base allocations reveals large differences. Under the new allocation proposal, Public Works would receive DKK 97,342 more cost, which is a 19.4 per cent increase. This likely will have noticeable impacts on the services that Public Works can provide to Storhavn's citizens. Probably Social Services would not complain about its 18.5 per cent cost reduction, however.

Summary of Original and Indexed Cost Allocations				
Production departments	Original base	Indexed base	Differences, DKK	Percentage differences
P1: Social Services	444,916	362,532	(82,384)	-18.5%
P2: Public Safety	503,440	488,482	(14,958)	-3.0%
P3: Public Works	501,644	598,986	97,342	19.4%
Total service department costs	1,450,000	1,450,000	-	

12.4 Leading Implementation of Changes in Cost Allocation Approaches, p. 597

Before Pedersen presents the proposal in six months, the budget department must repair the damage to the credibility of its analysis as an approach that is consistent with the city's principles of cost allocation. One possible approach follows:

Steps for leading change	Possible plan
• Identify a need for change.	• Review Pedersen's analyses to verify that previous cost allocations violate the city's cost allocation principles and that improved allocation bases could improve cost allocations in significant ways.
• Create a team to lead and manage the change.	• Expand the team to include representatives from some of the support service and production departments, taking care to add skilled, articulate team members but not so many that the team becomes too large to be efficient.
• Create a vision of the change and a strategy for achieving the vision.	• Stress the importance of city efficiency in all departments and that management decisions drive costs. Stress that both accurate cost allocations and process improvements are necessary to meet growing service expectations and the public's desire for lower taxes. Prepare a description of the benefits of an ABC approach, including: • Understanding how decisions affect how work is accomplished. • Learning what activities the organization uses to produce products and services. • Choosing the most profitable uses of scarce capacity. • Measuring the consumption of the organization's resources. • Guiding process improvements.

	• Steps in the analysis, adapted from Chapter 4, are to: 1. Identify and classify the activities related to services. 2. Estimate the cost of activities identified in step 1. 3. Calculate a cost allocation rate for each activity. 4. Assign activity costs to services.
• Communicate the vision and strategy for change and have the change team be a role model.	• Meet with all department managers to describe the need and proposal for revising cost allocations. Do not be defensive but be prepared to accept criticism and suggestions for improvement. • Have a similar meeting with the city manager and council.
• Encourage innovation and remove obstacles to change.	• Obtain approval from city and department managers to allow the team to develop best solutions.
• Ensure that short-term achievements are frequent and obvious.	• Consider beginning with a pilot project in one support-service department to demonstrate the approach and 'work out the bugs'.
• Use successes to create opportunities for improvement in the entire organization	• Communicate the benefits of improvements and indicate how new knowledge about a more complex approach can benefit the entire city management
• Reinforce a culture of more improvement, better leadership, and more effective management.	• Apply the approach throughout the organization and let departments have continuing input to use and improve cost allocation information.

Endnotes

1 *Lean government* is a set of principles used by government bodies to mimic market-oriented, business practices. *Lean government* seeks to improve government efficiency without harming the value of public-service objectives; thus, it is consistent with cost management's focus on creating more value at lower cost. See Furterer and Elshennawy (2005).

2 Charging for internally provided support services is much the same issue as 'transfer pricing', which is covered in more detail in Chapter 15. Cost allocations that are charged to user departments are transfer prices 'at cost'. Chapter 15 also covers examples where the support service (or other transferring unit) is expected to generate a profit because it could sell services externally.

3 See also discussions of *Grenzplankostenrechnung* in Chapter 13.

4 Note that allocation of central administration costs to business subunits does not change the 'period cost' nature of these costs, which are expensed by subunits and not added to product costs.

5 This is effectively the message of activity-based costing (Chapter 4), which might provide better information about the uses of service resources. We note that use of ABC for cost allocation purposes might be more accurate than traditional methods, but is not common practice because of its greater complexity and costs to develop and maintain.

6 Some authors and consultants argue that one should search for cause-and-effect relationships that explain past and predict future resource use. Doing so is notoriously difficult, and some have argued in favour of relying on 'probabilistic causality', which is no more than correlation with a good story about how bases and costs might be related economically. Thus, we use the less ambitious term, plausible correlation.

7 This is related to Harold Demsetz's famous warning about committing the 'nirvana fallacy' by rejecting imperfect but feasible alternatives, because they are not perfect (Demsetz, 1969).

8 Note that the percentages are displayed here as rounded numbers. Unrounded figures are used to calculate the allocations, which also are displayed as rounded numbers.

9 This is the empirical approach used by Balakrishnan et al. (2011). A shortcoming is that this approach assumes that total support service spending is 'ideal'. So, there is no getting around making compromises to define a satisfactory approach to cost allocations.

10 Some might argue that the *fully allocated costs* are benchmarks for comparing the costs of outsourced services. That is, outsourcing services might be indicated if the contracted costs are less than the fully allocated costs. We recommend caution in using fully allocated costs for this purpose because they do not identify which of these costs are avoidable if the service is outsourced. Outsourcing also has implications for other service attributes, such as quality, timeliness and flexibility.

References

Balakrishnan, R., S. Hansen and E. Labro., (2011) 'Evaluating heuristics used when designing product costing systems', *Management Science*, vol. 57, no. 3, pp. 520–541.

Dean, G.W., M.P. Moye and P.J. Blayney (1991) *Overhead Cost Allocation and Performance Evaluation Practices of Australian Manufacturers*, The Accounting and Finance Foundation, Sydney.

Demsetz, H. (1969) 'Information and efficiency: another viewpoint', *Journal of Law and Economics*, vol. 12, pp. 1–22.

Fremgren, J.M., and S.S. Liao (1981) *The Allocation of Corporate Indirect Costs*, National Association of Accountants, New York.

Furterer, S., and A.K. Elshennawy (2005) 'Implementation of TQM and lean Six Sigma tools in local government: a framework and a case study', *Total Quality Management and Business Excellence*, vol. 16, no. 10, pp. 1179–1191.

Johnson, H.T., and D. Loewe (1987) 'How Weyerhaeuser manages corporate overhead costs', *Management Accounting*, August, pp. 20–26.

KPMG (2011) 'Compliance, efficiency, and growth in cross-border trade', available at www.kpmg.com

Meyer, J.F. (2011) 'Do you have any idea?' *Denver Post*, 26 May p. 1B.

Wolfson, M. (1985) 'Empirical evidence of incentive problems and their mitigation in oil and gas tax shelter programs', in J. Pratt and R. Zeckhauser (eds.), *Principals and Agents*, Harvard Business School Press, Boston.

PART 5

Performance Measurement and Management

A look back

The preceding part covered the accumulation of actual costs and assigning them to products and services.

A look at this part

The first chapter in Part 5 explores standard costing systems and cost variance analysis as a cost management tool. The second chapter in this part covers organizational design issues, responsibility accounting and various measures of investment centre performance. The third chapter in Part 5 covers transfer pricing. The final chapter in this part explores the use of leading and lagging measures to motivate, communicate and evaluate and includes a discussion of the balanced scorecard.

CHAPTER 13

Analysis and Management of Cost Variances

Learning Objectives

After completing this chapter, you should be able to:

- **LO 1** Discuss how companies set standards and use standard costing systems to manage costs.
- **LO 2** Explain how cost management analysts use budgets to control direct manufacturing costs, using price and quantity variances.
- **LO 3** Explain how cost management analysts use budgets to control overhead costs, using spending, quantity and fixed overhead variances.
- **LO 4** Explain why an activity-based flexible budget can provide more useful cost management information than a conventional flexible budget.
- **LO 5** Describe several methods used to determine the significance of cost variances.
- **LO 6** Discuss some behavioural effects of standard costing and the controllability of variances.
- **LO 7** Understand how standard costing can be adjusted to modern manufacturing environments.
- **LO 8** Prepare accounting entries for cost variances.
- **LO 9** Compute and interpret mix and yield variances (Appendix 13A).
- **LO 10** Compute and interpret sales variances (Appendix 13B).

2145 Yarra Drive
Melbourne, Victoria
Australia

To: Geoff Weatherby

From: Marc Wesley

Cc: Margo Hastings

Subject: June cost variance report

The cost variance report for direct material, direct labour and overhead costs for the month of June appears below. I suggest that we add a discussion of the report to tomorrow morning's staff meeting. The original budget was based on an output in June of 2,800 tents, but this report and flexible budget is based on June output of 3,000 Tree Line tents.

The unfavourable direct material and direct labour variances, while cause for concern, are not nearly as high in percentage terms as the overhead cost variances. We need to get to the bottom of these variations from standard costs, and we can begin with tomorrow morning's meeting. Before then I will analyse these costs in greater detail to see whether I can provide any insights into our June performance.

	Actual	Budget	Variance as percentage of budget	
Total material costs	AU$296,660	AU$288,000	3.01%	U
Total labour costs	112,100	108,000	3.80%	U
Total flexible overhead cost	30,480	27,000	12.89%	U
Total fixed overhead costs	32,500	30,000	8.33%	U

*U denotes unfavourable; F denotes favourable

The memorandum above includes a cost variance report intended to help the management of Koala Camp Gear Company manage the company's production costs. How do small manufacturing companies such as Koala, or large companies such as **Dell Computer** or **Volkswagen,** manage and control the many direct costs and overhead costs they incur in their production process? As Chapter 9 explained, a budget provides a plan for managers to follow in making decisions and directing an organization's activities. At the end of a budget period, the budget serves another useful purpose. At that time, managers use it as a benchmark against which to compare the results of actual operations. Did the company make as much profit as anticipated in the budget? Were costs higher or lower than expected?

Many companies use standards for preparing budgets for a period. A *standard* is a benchmark performance level. For example, many manufacturing firms set standards for the amount and price of direct materials and for the amount and rate paid for direct labour used to produce their products. At the end of the period, management compares the standards with actual results. These comparisons help management gain insight into what went right and what went wrong in the production process.

Use of Standard Costing Systems for Control

LO 1
Discuss how companies set standards and use standard costing systems to manage costs.

A budgetary control system has three basic parts: a predetermined or *standard* cost level, a measure of *actual* cost, and a *comparison* of standard and actual costs. A thermostat, a control system with which we are all familiar, has three comparable parts. First, it has a predetermined or standard temperature, which you can set at any desired level. If you want the temperature in a room to be 21 degrees Celsius, you set the thermostat at the *standard* of 21 degrees. Second, the thermostat has a thermometer, which measures the *actual* temperature in the room. Third, the thermostat *compares* the preset or standard temperature with the actual room temperature. If the actual temperature differs from the preset or standard temperature, the thermostat activates a heating or cooling device.

A cost analyst's budgetary control system works like a thermostat. First, a predetermined, or *standard cost* is set. In essence, a **standard cost** is a budget for the production of one unit of product or service. It is the cost chosen by the cost management analyst to serve as the benchmark in the budgetary control system. When the firm produces many units, the cost management analyst uses the standard unit cost to determine the total standard or budgeted or allowable cost of production.[1] For example, suppose that the standard direct material cost for one of Koala Camp Gear's tent models is $96.00, and the firm manufactures 1,000 units. The total standard or budgeted direct material cost, given actual output of 1,000 units, is $96,000 ($96.00 × 1,000).

Second, the cost management analyst measures the actual cost incurred in the production process.

Third, the cost management analyst compares the actual cost with the budgeted, or standard, cost. Any difference between the actual cost and the standard cost is called a **cost variance.** Cost management analysts then use these cost variances to control costs.[2]

Management by Exception

When operations are going along as planned, actual costs and profit are typically close to the budgeted amounts. Variances will be small. However, significant or 'materially large' cost variances can also occur. A variance is material if it is likely to affect the decisions made by a user of the information. Conversely, a variance is immaterial if it is unlikely to affect decisions.

This distinction matters for cost management purposes. Although managers do not have time to explore the causes of every variance between actual and standard costs, they do take the time to investigate the material variances to determine their cause, if possible, and take corrective action when indicated. This process of following up only on the most significant variances between budgeted and actual results is called **management by exception**.[3]

Furthermore, the materiality of variances determines their accounting treatment. Chapter 10 explained that variances that are judged to be immaterial are simply moved to Other expenses or to Cost of sales. However, materially large variances are prorated (i.e., allocated) in proportionate amounts to WIP inventory, FG inventory and Cost of sales – all of the product cost accounts through which the cost passed.

What constitutes a material variance? This question has no precise answer, since it depends on the size and type of the organization and its production process. We consider this issue later in the chapter when we discuss common methods for determining the significance of cost variances. First, however, we turn our attention to the process of setting standards.

Setting Standards

Cost management analysts typically use two methods to set cost standards: analysis of historical data and task analysis.

Analysis of historical data

One indicator of future costs is historical cost data. In a mature production process, when the firm has considerable production experience, historical costs can provide a reliable basis for predicting future costs. The methods for analysing cost behaviour that we studied in Chapters 3 and 4 are used in making cost predictions. The cost analyst often needs to adjust these predictions to reflect expected movements in price levels or technological changes in the production process. For example, the amount of leather required to manufacture a pair of the Italian shoe company **Geox** is likely the same this year as last year unless a significant change in the process used to manufacture shoes has occurred. However, the price of leather is likely to be different this year than last, and this fact must be reflected in the new standard cost of a pair of shoes.

Despite the relevance of historical cost data in setting cost standards, cost management analysts must guard against relying on these data excessively. Even a seemingly minor change in the way a product is manufactured could make historical data almost totally irrelevant. Moreover, new products also require new cost standards. For new products, such as genetically engineered vaccines, no historical cost data exist on which to base standards. In such cases, the cost analyst must turn to another approach.

Activity analysis[4]

Another way to set cost standards, called **activity analysis** or **task analysis**, is the technique of setting standards by analysing the process of manufacturing a product to determine what it *should* cost. The emphasis shifts from what the product *did* cost in the past to what it *should* cost in the future. In using this approach, the cost management analyst typically works with engineers who are intimately familiar with the production process. Together they conduct studies to determine exactly the amount of direct material that should be required and the way that machinery should be used in the production process. Time-and-motion studies sometimes are conducted to determine how long each step performed by direct labourers should take. Storyboarding sessions are sometimes used to develop a detailed process map of all the activities in a work centre.

A combined approach

Cost management analysts often apply both historical cost analysis and task analysis in setting cost standards. It might be, for example, that the technology has changed for only one step in the production process. In such a case, the cost analyst works with engineers to set cost standards for the technologically changed part of the production process. However, the accountant may be tempted to rely on the less expensive method of analysing historical cost data to update the cost standards for the remaining steps in the production process.

Participation in setting standards

Standards should not be determined by accounting staff alone. People generally are more committed to meeting standards if they are allowed to participate in setting them. For example, production supervisors should have a role in setting production cost standards, and sales managers should be involved in setting targets for sales prices and volume. In addition, knowledgeable staff personnel should participate in the standard-setting process – a team consisting of production engineers, production supervisors and cost management analysts should perform task analysis.

Employee reluctance to reveal cost-saving ideas: an ethical issue

In some cases, employees may be reluctant to reveal cost-saving ideas that they have discovered to management or to the standard-setting team. The reason for this is that when such cost-saving ideas are communicated to management, they fear that standards are then reset to a tighter (i.e., more difficult to achieve) level. One way to mitigate this behaviour is to reward employees for submitting cost-saving ideas that are implemented and result in more efficient processes.[5]

Perfection versus Practical Standards: A Behavioural Issue

How difficult should it be to attain standard costs? Should cost management analysts set standards so loosely that actual costs rarely exceed standard costs? Or, should standards be so difficult to attain that actual costs frequently exceed them? The answers to these questions depend on the purpose for which standards are used and the way standards affect behaviour.

Perfection standards

A **perfection (or ideal) standard** is one that can be attained only under nearly perfect operating conditions. Such standards assume peak efficiency, the lowest possible input prices, the best-quality materials obtainable, and no disruptions in production due to causes such as machine breakdowns or power failures. Some managers believe that a perfection standard motivates employees to achieve the lowest cost possible. They claim that since the standard is theoretically attainable, employees have an incentive to come as close as possible to achieving it.

Other managers and many behavioural scientists disagree. They believe that perfection standards discourage employees, since such high standards are so unlikely to be attained. Moreover, setting unrealistically difficult standards could encourage employees to sacrifice product quality to achieve lower costs. By skimping on the quality of raw materials or the attention to manual production tasks, employees might be able to lower the production cost. However, this lower cost could come at the expense of a higher rate of defective units, causing internal failure costs (such as for performing rework) and/or external failure costs if defective products reach customers (such as for conducting warranty repairs). Failure costs were discussed in Chapter 6.

© Francis Joseph Dean/Dean Pictures

If you were managing a car-rental agency, for what kinds of costs would you set standards?

Practical standards

Standards that are challenging but still are expected to be attained are called **practical (or attainable) standards**. Such standards assume a production process that is as efficient as practical under normal operating conditions. Practical standards allow for events such as occasional machine breakdowns and normal amounts of raw material waste. Attaining a practical standard keeps employees on their toes without demanding miracles. Most behavioural theorists believe that practical standards encourage more positive and productive employee attitudes than do perfection standards.

Use of Standards by Non-manufacturing Organizations

Service industry firms, non-profit organizations and governmental units also use standard costs. For example, airlines set standards for fuel and maintenance costs. A county motor vehicle office might have a standard for the number of days required to process and return an application for vehicle registration. Banks, insurance companies and credit card companies such as **Deutsche Bank**, **Allianz** and **American Express** have analysed their back-office processes. Many financial services can be broken into back tasks, and for each of these tasks, performance standards can be set and standard costs can be specified. Restaurant chains such as **wagamama**, **Applebee's**, **Hereford Steak Houses** or **Quanjude** and affiliated restaurants (known for trademark Quanjude Peking Roast Duck) have detailed manuals for food preparation and, based on these, standard costs for their dishes.

Cost Variance Analysis for Direct Manufacturing Costs

LO 2
Explain how cost management analysts use budgets to control direct manufacturing costs, using price and quantity variances.

To illustrate the use of standards in controlling costs, we focus on Koala Camp Gear Company, a manufacturer of camping tents based in Melbourne, Australia. Although relatively small, Koala Camp Gear has established a reputation for excellence throughout Australia, Europe and the United States. Most of the company's sales are domestic, but exports have been increasing to the United Kingdom, Germany, Switzerland, Italy and the United States. Koala recently introduced its newest product, a lightweight but durable backpacking tent trade-named the Tree Line tent. Margo Hastings, Koala's founder and CEO, plans to market the Tree Line tent aggressively in Europe and the United States.

Koala Camp Gear plans to manufacture only the Tree Line tent itself. The company will purchase aluminium tent poles and tent stakes as finished components and package them with the tent. As detailed in the memorandum at the beginning of this chapter, Koala's controller, Marc Wesley, recently set standards for the direct materials and direct labour required to manufacture the Tree Line tent as outlined in Exhibit 13.1.

Direct Material and Direct Labour Standards

Koala Camp Gear Company

Exhibit 13.1 Standard Direct Costs for Koala Camp Gear

	A	B
1	**Standard direct cost per unit (in Australian dollars):**	
2	**Material cost per unit:**	
3	Fabric in finished product (m^2)	11.000
4	Allowance for normal waste (m^2)	1.000
5	Total standard quantity required per tent (m^2)	12.000
6	Purchase price per m^2 of fabric (net of discounts)	AU$7.75
7	Transportation cost (converted to cost per m^2)	AU$0.25
8	Standard price per m^2 of fabric	AU$8.00
9	Standard material cost per unit	**AU$96.00**
10		
11	**Labour cost per unit:**	
12	Direct labour required per tent (hours)	2.000
13	Hourly wage rate	AU$15.00
14	Fringe benefits as percentage of wages	20%
15	Standard rate per hour	AU$18.00
16	Standard direct labour cost per unit	**AU$36.00**
17	Total Standard direct cost per unit	**AU$132.00**

The fabric in a tent is considered a direct material. The thread is inexpensive and is considered an indirect material, part of manufacturing overhead.[6] The standard quantity of fabric needed to manufacture one Tree Line tent is 12 square metres, even though only 11 square metres actually remain in the finished product. One square metre of fabric is wasted as a normal result of the cutting and trimming that are part of the production process. Therefore, the entire amount of fabric needed to manufacture a tent is included in the standard quantity of material.

The standard price of fabric reflects all costs incurred to acquire the material and transport it to the plant. Notice that the cost of transportation is added to the purchase price. Any purchase discounts are subtracted out from the purchase price to obtain a net price.

To summarize, the **standard direct material quantity** is the total amount of materials normally required to produce a finished product, including allowances for normal waste or inefficiency. The **standard direct material price** is the total delivered cost after subtracting any purchase discounts. For Koala Camp Gear's Tree Line tent, the standard direct material cost is AU$8.00 per square metre (cell B8), or AU$96.00 per tent (cell B9).

The standard quantity and rate for direct labour for the production of one Tree Line tent are also shown in Exhibit 13.1. The **standard direct labour quantity** is the number of labour hours normally needed to manufacture one unit of product. The **standard direct labour rate** is the total hourly cost of compensation, including fringe benefits. For Koala Camp Gear's Tree Line tent, the standard direct labour cost is AU$18.00 per labour hour (cell B15), or AU$36.00 per tent (cell B16).

Standard Costs Given Actual Output: Flexible Budget and Volume Variance

The budget for direct manufacturing costs was based on a production volume of 2,800 tents, as indicted in cell B20 of Exhibit 13.2.[7] However, during June, Koala manufactured 3,000 Tree Line tents, as indicated in cell D20 of Exhibit 13.2. Obviously, the budget for direct manufacturing costs must be adjusted to reflect the standard cost of the actual production output. Therefore, the total standard cost in Exhibit 13.2 for the direct material and direct labour inputs is based on Koala's *actual output*. This is called a **flexible budget**, which is adjusted to the actual activity level and valid for a range of activity levels within which the firm operates. The **relevant range** is the span of activity levels within which management expects the firm to operate and within which cost behaviour patterns remain relatively stable.[8]

In the case of Koala Camp Gear, the division should incur costs of $396,000 ($288,000 + $108,000) for direct material and direct labour, *given that it produced 3,000 tents*. The total standard costs for direct material and direct labour serve as the cost management analyst's benchmarks against which to compare actual direct material and direct labour costs.

The difference between the original budget and the flexible budget, simply because the budget is adjusted to the actual production volume, is called **volume variance**, and it is shown in column C.[9] It is important to understand what it means, but the volume variance is unimportant for cost control. It is the difference between the flexible budget and the actual costs that we will worry about.

Actual Material Costs and Labour Costs

The difference between the flexible budget and the actual costs is called the **budget variance**. This is the important variance for cost management purposes, and so we do not need to consider the original budget nor the volume variance anymore.

Exhibit 13.2 Budget and Flexible Budget for June for Kola Camp Gear

	A	B	C	D
19		Original budget	Volume variance	Flexible budget
20	Production volume (tents)	2,800	200	3,000
21	Total material usage (m^2)	33,600		36,000
22	Total labour hours	5,600		6,000
23	Total material costs	AU$268,800	AU$19,200	AU$288,000
24	Total labour costs	AU$100,800	AU$7,200	AU$108,000
25	Total direct costs	AU$369,600		AU$396,000

During June, Koala incurred the actual costs for direct material and direct labour as indicated in Exhibit 13.3 in column E. Compare these actual expenditures with the total standard costs for the production of 3,000 tents (column D). Koala spent more than the budgeted amount for both direct material and direct labour (AU$8,660 and AU$4,100, respectively). But why were these excess costs incurred? Could the cost management analyst provide any other analysis to help answer this question? This is where price variances and quantity variances come in the picture.

Exhibit 13.3 **Budget Variances for June for Koala Camp Gear**

	A	D	E	F
19		Flexible budget	Actuals	Budget variance
20	Production volume (tents)	3,000		
21	Total material usage (m^2)	36,000	36,400	
22	Total labour hours	6,000	5,900	
23	Total material costs	AU$288,000	AU$296,660	AU$8,660
24	Total labour costs	AU$108,000	AU$112,100	AU$4,100
25	Total direct costs	AU$396,000	AU$408,760	

Price and Quantity Variances in General

The investigation of the budget variance is called **variance analysis**, and its objective is to better understand why budget variances occurred. To this end, the variance will be broken down into several components. The **price variance** shows to what extent the variance is caused by differences between the actual price and the budgeted price, while the **quantity variance** shows to what extent the variance is caused by actual quantity used being different from the standard quantity.[10] We will discuss these variances in general, and then apply these to the material costs and labour costs of Koala Camp Gear.

The equation for the price variance is as follows:

$$\textbf{Price variance} = (P_a - P_s)\, Q_a$$

where:

$$P_a = \text{actual price}$$
$$P_s = \text{standard price}$$
$$Q_a = \text{actual quantity}$$

So P stands for price and Q for quantity, and subscripts a and s denote actual or standard.

The equation for the quantity variance is as follows:

$$\textbf{Quantity variance} = (Q_a - Q_s)\, P_s$$

where:

$$Q_a = \text{actual quantity}$$
$$Q_s = \text{standard quantity}$$
$$P_s = \text{standard price}$$

Both variances are also shown in Exhibit 13.4. The actual costs are represented by the outer box, namely the actual quantity multiplied by the actual price (Actual costs = $Q_a \times P_a$). The budgeted costs are the standard quantity times the standard price (Budget = $Q_s \times P_s$) and this is shown as the inner

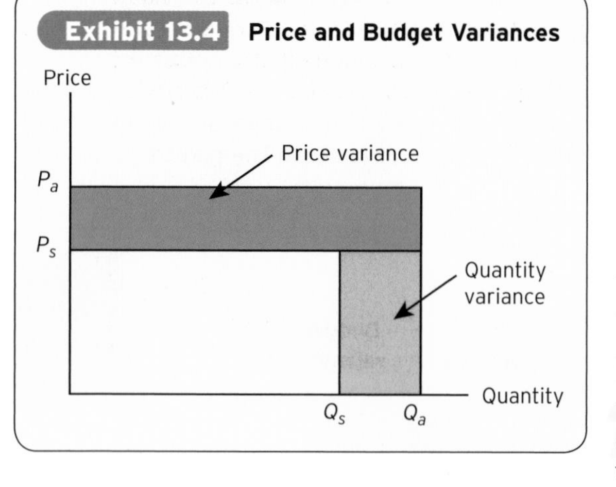

box. The total difference between the two boxes is split into two parts. The blue surface is the price variance, namely the difference in price times the actual quantity; the green surface is the quantity variance, namely the difference in quantity times the standard price.[11]

Variances are **favourable** when the actual costs are less than the budget (or when revenues exceed the flexible budget – this is relevant in Appendix 13B), and variances are **unfavourable** when the actual costs exceed the budget (or revenues are below budget).[12]

Note that the square in the upper right corner of Exhibit 13.4 is now part of the price variance. That is why the equation for the price variance is based on the actual quantity. This is done by convention. However, this surface could also be seen as part of the quantity variance, in which case the price variance would be based on the standards quantity (Q_s) and the quantity variance would be based on the actual price (P_a). In other words, alternative definitions of the variance components are possible.

Direct Material Variances

What caused Koala to spend AU$8,660 (total variance) more than the anticipated amount on direct material? First, as shown in Exhibit 13.5, the company purchased fabric at a higher price ($8.15 per square metre) than the standard price ($8.00 per square metre). Second, the company used more fabric than the standard amount. The amount actually used was 36,400 square metres instead of the standard amount of 36,000 square metres, which is based on actual output of 3,000 tents. Using this information and the general equations for price and quantity variances, we can split the total variance of AU$8,660 into the **direct material price variance** and the **direct material quantity variance**. Quantity in this case refers to the number of m² material used. Price pertains to the price per m², including the various components as shown in the calculation in Exhibit 13.1.

Exhibit 13.5 Price and Quantity Variances for Koala June for Camp Gear

	A	D	E	F	G	H	I	J	K
19		Flexible budget	Actuals	Budget variance	=	Price variance	+	Quantity variance	
20	Production volume (tents)	3,000							
21	Total material usage (m²)	36,000	36,400			=(E27-D27)*E21		=(E21-D21)*D27	
22	Total labour hours	6,000	5,900						
23	Total material costs	AU$288,000	AU$296,660	AU$8,660	U	AU$5,460	U	AU$3,200	U
24	Total labour costs	AU$108,000	AU$112,100	AU$4,100	U	AU$5,900	U	AU$(1,800)	F
25	Total direct costs	AU$396,000	AU$408,760						
26						=(E28-D28)*E22		=(E22-D22)*D28	
27	Price per m² of fabric	AU$8.00	AU$8.15						
28	Rate per hour	AU$18.00	AU$19.00						

The actual prices paid are calculated by dividing the actual cost and the actual quantity. As indicated in Exhibit 13.5, In June Koala Camp Gear used 36,400 m² for an actual cost of AU$296,660, giving an actual price of AU$8.15 per m². The standard price was shown in Exhibit 13.1 and is repeated in Exhibit 13.5, namely AU$8.00 per m².

The direct material price variance = (AU$8.15 − AU$8.00) × 36,400 = **AU$5,460** Unfavourable. This variance is unfavourable because the actual purchase price exceeded the standard price. This result is shown in Exhibit 13.5 (cell H23).

The direct material quantity variance = (36,400 – 36,000) × AU$8.00 = **AU$3,200** Unfavourable. This variance is unfavourable because the actual quantity of direct material used in June exceeded the standard quantity allowed, given actual June output of 3,000 tents. The quantity variance is based on the quantity of material actually used in production. This result is shown in Exhibit 13.5 (cell J23).[13]

Direct Labour Variances

Why did Koala Camp Gear spend AU$4,100 more than the anticipated amount on direct labour during June? We will use again the general equations for price and quantity variances, whereby quantity in this case refers to the number of labour hours used. Price pertains to the rate per labour hour, including the various components as shown in the calculation in Exhibit 13.1.

First, the company incurred a cost of $19.00 per hour for direct labour instead of the standard amount of $18.00 per hour. The actual rate per hour is calculated by dividing the actual costs and the actual number of hours. As indicated in Exhibit 13.5, In June Koala Camp Gear used 5,900 hours for an actual cost of AU$112,100, giving an actual price of AU$19.00 per hour. The standard rate was shown in Exhibit 13.1 and is repeated in Exhibit 13.5, namely AU$18.00 per hour. Second, Koala used only 5,900 hours of direct labour, which is less than the standard quantity of 6,000 hours, given actual output of 3,000 tents.

Using this information and the general equations for price and quantity variances, we can split the total variance of AU$4,100 into two components. The **direct labour rate variance** is the difference between the actual and standard hourly labour rate multiplied by the actual quantity of direct labour used. The **direct labour efficiency variance** is the difference between the actual hours and the standard hours of direct labour allowed, given actual output, multiplied by the standard hourly labour rate. Exhibit 13.5 displays the results, and the computations for these variances are explained below.

The direct labour rate variance = (AU$19.00 – AU$18.00) × 5,900 = **AU$5,900** Unfavourable (cell H24). This variance is unfavourable because the actual rate exceeded the standard rate during June.

The direct labour efficiency variance = (5,900 – 6,000) × AU$18.00 = **AU$1,800** Favourable (cell J24). This variance is favourable because the actual number of direct labour hours used in June were less than the number of standard hours allowed, *given actual June output* of 3,000 tents.

13.1 Research Insight

International Use of Flexible Budgeting to Control Costs

Standard costing systems are common throughout the world. Research has shown, for example, that standard costing is widely used in Japan, the United Kingdom and Germany, as well as in the United States. In Germany, *Grenzplankostenrechnung*, which means 'flexible standard costing', is used for cost planning and control. This approach separates a large number of cost centres.

- A cost centre needs to be the responsibility of one manager.
- The costs should be as homogeneous as possible and have at least one representative output measure (cost driver), such as machine hours.
- Each cost centre distinguishes between variable costs and fixed costs.
- The firm must be able to estimate activity volume and costs and to record actual volume and cost for the individual cost centre.
- There are monthly statements of each cost centre's actual and planned demand for resources, actual costs standard costs and different types of variances.

This method exhibits many of the features illustrated in this chapter. It is like German precision engineering applied to standard costing systems. German firms tend to place much higher emphasis on management accounting than, for example, US firms. Managers in German firms are generally more satisfied with their costing systems.

This approach functions in the same way in service organizations as in manufacturing when there are direct service activities and many repetitive processes. However, it becomes more complex when there are non-routine activities and variability of routine activities. The approach is supported by the Controlling module of the integrated information system SAP, which also has German origins. More recent extensions of *Grenzplankostenrechnung* include a more sophisticated allocation of support department costs, called *Prozesskostenrechnung*.

Sources: Krumwiede (2005, 2007); Sharman (2003) and Sharman and Vikas (2004).

Multiple Types of Direct Material and Direct Labour

Manufacturing processes usually involve several types of direct material. In such cases, direct materials price and quantity variances are computed for each type of material. Then these variances are added to obtain a total price variance and a total quantity variance, as follows:

	Price variances	**Quantity variances**
Direct material X	AU$1,500 F	AU$1,900 U
Direct material Y	2,400 U	300 U
Direct material Z	900 U	400 F
Total variance	AU$1,800 U	AU$1,800 U

F denotes a favourable variance; U denotes an unfavourable variance.

Similarly, if a production process involves several types of direct labour, rate and efficiency variances are computed for each labour type. Then they are added to obtain a total rate variance and a total efficiency variance.

When a manufacturing process involves multiple types of direct material or direct labour, additional variance analysis can be conducted to analyse the proportions with which the multiple inputs are used. This analysis is covered in Appendix 13A.

Allowance for Defects or Spoilage

In some manufacturing processes, a certain amount of defective production or spoilage is normal. This must be considered when the standard quantity of material is computed. To illustrate, suppose that 1,000 litres of chemicals are normally required in a chemical process to obtain 800 litres of good output. If total good output in February is 5,000 litres, what is the standard allowed quantity of input?

$$\textbf{Good output quantity} = 80\% \times \textbf{Input quantity}$$

Dividing both sides of the equation by 80%

$$\frac{\textbf{Good output quantity}}{\textbf{80\%}} = \textbf{Input quantity allowed}$$

Using the numbers in the illustration

$$\frac{\textbf{5,000 litres of good output}}{\textbf{80\%}} = \textbf{6,250 litres of input allowed}$$

The total standard allowed input is 6,250 litres, given 5,000 litres of good output. Of course, this level of spoilage may not be acceptable any more when the company takes sustainability seriously. The company can set sustainability goals that strive to reduce waste and to increase the proportion of good output.

13.1 You're the Decision Maker

Direct Material and Direct Labour Variances

In December, Koala Camp Gear Company produced 2,000 Tree Line tents and incurred the following actual costs for direct material and direct labour:

Purchased 25,000 sq. metres of tent fabric at AU$8.25 per sq. metre.
Used 24,500 sq. metres at AU$8.25 per sq. metre.
Used 4,200 hours of direct labour at AU$16.75 per hour.

The standard costs for tent production were the same in December as those given earlier in the chapter for June. Compute Koala's direct material and direct labour variances for December using the format for a spreadsheet shown in Exhibit 13.5.

(Solutions begin on page 690.)

Cost Variance Analysis for Flexible Overhead Budgets

LO 3 Explain how cost management analysts use budgets to control overhead costs, using spending, quantity and fixed overhead variances.

Now we turn our attention to flexible overhead costs. Unlike direct material and direct labour, manufacturing overhead costs are not traceable to individual products. Moreover, manufacturing overhead can be a pool of many different types of costs. Indirect material, indirect labour and other indirect production costs often exhibit different relationships to productive activity. In other words, in contrast to direct manufacturing costs, overhead costs are typically caused by a variety of different cost drivers, ranging from units produced, machine and labour hours, to the number of SKUs (different part numbers) and other drivers that reflect complexity of product variety and of the value chain. Moreover, different individuals in an organization are responsible for different types of overhead costs. Considering all of these issues together, controlling manufacturing overhead presents a challenge for cost management analysts.

Flexible budgets and the overhead control techniques based on them traditionally are based on a simplified view of a firm's overhead cost structure. Overhead costs are classified as variable or fixed. Variable costs change in total in proportion to changes in the company's activity, as expressed in terms of a single, volume-based measure such as machine hours, labour hours, total process time or direct material costs. Fixed costs do not change in total as the organization's activity changes.

However, some organizations have more detailed budgeting systems based on activity-based costing. This means that the budget for flexible overhead costs is based on various types of cost drivers. So there are good reasons to discuss both systems, starting with budgeting based on a single cost driver.[14]

Overhead variance analysis based on a single cost driver is similar to what we saw above regarding direct manufacturing costs. The starting point is the budget, which is adjusted to the actual level of activity. This flexible budget is then contrasted to the actual costs. The difference between the actual costs and the budget is the variance, which will also be broken down into several components.

Flexible Overhead Budget

Koala's overhead costs in the flexible budget are divided into variable and fixed costs. The activity level is expressed in *machine hours*, in this case. Exhibit 13.6 shows the various elements of the flexible overhead costs, and these amount to AU$6.00 per machine hour (cell B12). Each tent requires 1.5 machine hours, according to the standard costs. Based on these data, Exhibit 13.7 shows the budget for flexible overhead costs, both under Koala's original plan for June to produce 2,800 tents

Exhibit 13.6 Standard Flexible Overhead for Costs for Koala Camp Gear

	A	B
1	**Budgeted overhead costs (in Australian$)**	
2	**Variable overhead costs per machine hour:**	
3	Indirect material:	
4	Thread	AU$2.00
5	Strings	0.67
6	Eyelets	0.33
7	Manufacturing supplies	1.00
8	Indirect labour: maintenance	1.67
9	Utilities:	
10	Electrical power	0.20
11	Heat	0.13
12	Total variable overhead cost per hour	AU$6.00
13	**Fixed overhead costs per month:**	
14	Indirect labour:	
15	Quality assurance	AU$2,400
16	Production supervisors	7,000
17	Set-up	3,600
18	Material handling	9,600
19	Depreciation: plant and equipment	1,300
20	Insurance and property taxes	1,100
21	Engineering	5,000
22	Total fixed overhead cost per month	AU$30,000
23		
24	Note: Spreadsheet software normally carries and uses eight decimal places, but fewer are displayed for easier reading. Using fewer may create rounding errors.	

Exhibit 13.7 Budget and Flexible Budget for Overhead Costs for June for Koala Camp Gear

	A	B	C
1	Monthly flexible overhead budget		
2	Koala Camp Gear Company		
3	Machine hours required per tent	1.5	
4		**Original budget**	**Flexible budget**
5	Production volume (tents)	2,800	3,000
6		**Machine hours**	
7		**4,200**	**4,500**
8	**Variable overhead costs at budgeted machine hours:***		
9	Indirect material:		
10	Thread	AU$8,400	AU$9,000
11	Strings	2,800	3,000
12	Eyelets	1,400	1,500
13	Manufacturing supplies	4,200	4,500
14	Indirect labour: maintenance	7,000	7,500
15	Utilities:	-	-
16	Electrical power	840	900
17	Heat	560	600
18	Total variable overhead cost	AU$25,200	AU$27,000
19	**Fixed overhead costs:**		
20	Indirect labour:		
21	Quality assurance	AU$2,400	AU$2,400
22	Production supervisors	7,000	7,000
23	Set-up	3,600	3,600
24	Material handling	9,600	9,600
25	Depreciation: plant and equipment	1,300	1,300
26	Insurance and property taxes	1,100	1,100
27	Engineering	5,000	5,000
28	Total fixed overhead cost	AU$30,000	AU$30,000
29	Total overhead cost per month	AU$55,200	AU$57,000

(allowing 4,200 machine hours) and for Koala's actual production volume in June of 3,000 tents (allowing 4,500 hours). The total budgeted *variable* overhead cost increases compared to the original budget, from AU$25,200 (cell B17) to AU$27,000 (cell C17). In contrast, the total budgeted *fixed* overhead does not change with increases in activity; it remains constant at AU$30,000 per month (cell B27 and C27).

In general, the format for expressing a flexible budget is called a *formula flexible budget.* In this format, the cost management analyst expresses the relationship between activity and total budgeted overhead cost with the following formula.

$$\textbf{Total budgeted monthly overhead cost} = \left(\textbf{Budgeted variable overhead cost per activity unit} \times \textbf{Total activity units}\right) + \textbf{Budgeted fixed-overhead cost per month}$$

Koala's formula flexible overhead budget is as follows:

$$\textbf{Total budgeted monthly overhead cost} = (\$6 \times \textbf{Total machine hours}) + \$30{,}000$$

Choice of Activity Measure

Koala Camp Gear Company bases its flexible overhead budget on machine hours. Different companies use a variety of activity measures in practice. Machine hours, direct labour hours, direct labour cost, total process time, and direct materials cost are among the most common measures.

The activity measure should be one that varies in a similar pattern to the way that variable overhead varies. As productive activity increases, both variable overhead cost and the activity measure should increase in roughly the same proportion. As productive activity declines, both variable overhead cost and the activity measure should decline in roughly the same proportion. In other words, the cost management analyst needs to understand cost behaviour, and this topic is discussed in more detail in Chapters 3 and 4.

Activity measure based on input or output

Notice that the flexible budget for overhead costs in in this example is based on machine hours, which is an *input* in the production process. The machine-hour activity levels shown in the flexible budget are the standard allowed machine hours given various levels of output. If 3,000 tents are produced, and the standard allowance per tent is 1.5 machine hours, the standard allowed number of machine hours is 4,500.

Why are the activity levels in the flexible budget based on machine hours, an *input* measure, instead of the number of tents produced, an *output* measure? This has everything to do with cost behaviour. Suppose that during July, Koala Camp Gear Company manufactured 2,800 tents in total, consisting of three different tent models: 1,200 Tree Line, 900 River's Edge and 700 Valley. Some flexible overhead costs could be driven by output volume, such as indirect materials, packaging and quality assurance. Budgeting these flexible overhead costs could be based on output. However, other flexible overhead costs could vary greatly between different model tents, and total output would make little sense as a cost driver. Of course, activity-based budgeting would be the most accurate solution here, but a firm may feel that the benefits of more refined budgeting systems do not outweigh the extra costs of it. Input measures can be an approximation for flexible overhead costs that are not linearly driven by output.

The controller has assigned the following standards to the different tent models:

Product model	Units produced	Standard machine hours per unit	Total standard allowed machine hours
Tree Line	1,200	1.5	1,800
River's Edge	900	1.8	1,620
Valley	700	2.0	1,400
Total			4,820

Recall that Koala's cost management analyst estimates flexible overhead cost at AU$6.00 per machine hour. Thus, the flexible overhead cost budget cost during July is 4,820 × AU$6.00 = AU$28,920.

Impact of changing manufacturing technology

Direct labour time has traditionally been the most popular activity measure for manufacturing firms. However, as automation increases, more and more firms are switching to measures such as machine hours or process time for their flexible overhead budgets. Machine hours and process time are linked more closely than direct labour hours to the robotic technology and computer-integrated manufacturing (CIM) systems common in today's manufacturing environment.

Dollar measures can be misleading

Companies sometimes use dollar measures, such as direct labour or raw materials costs, as the basis for flexible overhead budgeting. However, such measures have significant drawbacks. Dollar measures are subject to price-level changes and fluctuate more than physical measures. For example, the direct labour *hours* required to manufacture a tent are relatively stable over time. However, the direct labour *cost* varies as wage levels and fringe-benefit costs change with price-level changes in the economy.

© *Gerenme/Thiel_Andrzej*

Increasing automation in manufacturing has resulted in direct labour becoming a less appropriate activity measure in flexible budgeting. Advanced manufacturing environments, such as flexible manufacturing systems (FMS) and computer-integrated manufacturing (CIM), have caused a shift in many companies' cost structures away from direct labour cost and toward overhead costs. Pictured here are a labour-intensive electronics assembly line and a high-tech circuit-board manufacturing robot.

Overhead Cost Variances

The flexible overhead budget is the cost management analyst's primary tool for controlling manufacturing overhead costs using this traditional cost management technique. At the end of each accounting period, the cost management analyst uses the flexible overhead budget to determine the level of overhead cost that should have been incurred, given the actual level of activity. Then the cost management analyst compares the overhead cost in the flexible budget with the actual overhead cost incurred. The analyst then computes three separate overhead variances, each of which conveys information useful in managing overhead costs.

To illustrate overhead variance analysis, we continue our illustration of Koala Camp Gear Company. From the cost accounting records, the controller determined that overhead costs of AU$62,980, as shown in Exhibit 13.8, were actually incurred during June. This consists of actual variable overhead costs of AU$30,480 plus actual fixed overhead costs of AU$32,500. Furthermore, the production supervisor's records indicate that actual machine usage in June was 4,800 hours. Notice that the actual number of machine hours used (4,800) exceeds the standard number of machine hours allowed given actual production output (4,500). We now have assembled all of the information necessary to compute Koala's overhead variances for June. (In Exhibit 13.8 we repeated from Exhibit 13.6 that the total variable overhead cost per labour hour is AU$6.00.)

What caused the company to spend $3,480 more than the budgeted amount on variable overhead? To discover the reasons behind this performance, the cost management analyst splits the overall variance in two components.

The calculation of the **variable overhead spending variance** is easiest to understand if you realize that it is quite similar to the *price variance* for direct costs that we saw earlier. It is the difference between the actual and the standard variable overhead rate, multiplied by the standard number of hours (in general, the quantity of an activity base). The following equation defines the variable overhead spending variance:

$$\textbf{Variable overhead spending variance} = (R_a - R_s)\, Q_a$$

where:

R_a = **actual variable overhead rate**[15]

R_s = **standard variable overhead rate**

Q_a = **actual quantity of the activity base**

Koala's variable overhead spending variance for June is computed as follows: **(AU$6.35 – AU$6.00) × 4,800 = AU$1,680 Unfavourable**. This variance is unfavourable because the actual variable overhead cost exceeded the expected amount after adjusting that expectation for the actual number of machine hours used.

Exhibit 13.8 Overhead Costs Variances for June for Koala Camp Gear

	A	B	C	D	E	F	G	H	I	J
35		Original budget	Flexible budget	Actuals	Variance	=	Spending variance	+	Quantity variance	
36	Production volume (tents)	2,800	3,000							
37	Machine hours	4,200	4,500	4,800						
38	Total flexible overhead cost	AU$25,200	AU$27,000	AU$30,480	AU$3,480 U		AU$1,680 U		AU$1,800 U	
39	Total fixed overhead costs	AU$30,000	AU$30,000	AU$32,500	AU$2,500 U					
40	Total overhead costs	AU$55,200	AU$57,000	AU$62,980						
42	Overhead cost per machine hour		AU$6.00	AU$6.35						

The **variable overhead quantity variance** is also easy to understand, if you realize that the calculation is quite similar to the *quantity variance* for direct costs. It is the difference between the actual and standard quantity of an activity base (or cost driver) multiplied by the standard variable overhead rate. The following equation defines the variable overhead quantity variance:

$$\textbf{Variable overhead quantity variance} = (Q_a - Q_s)\, R_s$$

where:

Q_a = **actual quantity**

Q_s = **standard quantity**

R_s = **standard variable overhead rate**

Koala's variable overhead quantity variance for June is computed as follows: = **(4,800 – 4,500) × AU$6.00 = $1,800 Unfavourable**. This variance is unfavourable because actual machine hours exceeded the standard machine hours allowed given actual output.

How to interpret the quantity variance

Recall that an unfavourable direct labour quantity variance results when more direct labour is used than the standard allowed quantity. Thus, direct labour has been used inefficiently relative to the standard. However, that is not the proper interpretation of an unfavourable variable overhead quantity variance. This variance resulted when Koala used *more machine hours* than the standard quantity given actual output. Recall that the cost management analyst had found that variable overhead cost varies in a pattern similar to the way machine hours vary. Since 300 more machine hours were used than the standard quantity allowed, the division's management should expect that variable overhead costs will be higher. Thus, this variance simply reflects an adjustment in the cost management analyst's expectation about total variable overhead cost because the company used more than the standard quantity of machine hours, *which is allowed to lead to higher variable overhead costs*. Another question is why more machine hours were used, but that has nothing to do with managing the efficiency of using overhead cost.

What is the important difference between direct labour and variable overhead that causes this different interpretation of the quantity variance? Direct labour is a traceable cost and is budgeted on the basis of direct labour hours. Variable overhead, on the other hand, is a pool of *indirect* costs that are budgeted on the basis of *machine hours*. The indirect nature of variable overhead costs causes the different interpretation.

What does the spending variance reveal?

The spending variance indicates that per unit of the activity base, the overhead costs are different than budgeted. For example, Koala was allowed to spend AU$6.00 per machine hour on variable overhead costs. Machine hours can be used as the activity base, if this factor reasonably models the total variable overhead cost. A higher actual variable overhead cost per machine hour of AU$6.35 indicates that somehow manufacturing consumed more overhead resources than standardly allowed. This may have to do with quantities or prices that we cannot separate here. For example, as part of the AU$6.00 per machine hour, the cost of thread is budgeted at AU$2.00 per machine hour. If the actual cost of thread per machine hour is AU$1.97, there is a favourable spending variance. This may be caused by fewer metres of thread being used, or the thread being cheaper per metre. As this example also illustrates, it is useful to break down the overhead costs into the different items. Reporting of variance analysis results is discussed later in this chapter.

So while the spending variance calculation closely resembles the price variance calculation for direct manufacturing costs, the interpretation of the spending variance is not the same. An unfavourable spending variance means that the total actual cost of variable overhead is higher than expected after adjusting for the actual quantity of machine hours used. An unfavourable spending variance could result from paying a higher than expected price per unit for variable overhead items. The variance also could result from using more of the variable overhead items than expected based on the flexible budget.

The *spending variance* is the real control variance for variable overhead, since the variable overhead quantity variance indicates nothing about efficient or inefficient usage of variable overhead. Managers can use the spending variance to alert them if variable overhead costs are out of line with expectations.

Fixed Overhead Variance

The actual fixed overhead costs also deviated from the budget, by an amount of AU$2,500. This is indicated in Exhibit 13.8. This variance is unfavourable, because the actual costs exceed the budget. The **fixed overhead budget variance** is simply the difference between the actual fixed overhead and the budgeted fixed overhead.

Notice that we need not specify an activity level to determine budgeted fixed overhead. This is because the fixed overhead does not change as the activity base varies.[16] Hence, budgeted fixed overhead is the same at all activity levels in the flexible budget. It is important to find out what the fixed overhead actually consisted of and why the company spent a different amount than budgeted. However, it is not possible to break this total variance into different components such as quantity and price variances to provide more insight. However, the cost analyst will break down the actual costs into different cost categories, and this may provide useful indications of what happened. That is why the overhead cost performance report can be quite detailed regarding various cost categories.

13.2 You're the Decision Maker

Overhead Variances

In October, Koala Camp Gear Company produced 3,600 Tree Line tents, used 5,700 machine hours, and incurred the following manufacturing overhead costs:

Variable overhead	AU$37,050
Fixed overhead	29,000

Koala's flexible overhead budget for December is the same as in Exhibit 13.6 given earlier in the chapter for June.

a. Compute Koala's variable overhead variances and fixed overhead variances using the format shown in Exhibit 13.8.

b. How should Koala's management interpret the fixed overhead budget variance?

(Solutions begin on page 690.)

Using the Overhead Cost Performance Report in Cost Management

The variable overhead spending and quantity variances and the fixed overhead budget variance can be computed for each overhead cost item in the flexible budget. When these itemized variances are presented along with actual and budgeted costs for each overhead item, the result is an **overhead cost performance report**. An overhead cost performance report shows the actual and flexible budget cost levels for each overhead item, together with the variable overhead spending and quantity variances and the fixed overhead budget variance. Koala's performance report is displayed in Exhibit 13.9. Management would use this report to exercise control over each of the division's overhead costs.

Notice that the performance report includes only spending and quantity variances for the variable items and only a budget variance for the fixed items. Upon receiving this report, a manager might investigate the relatively large variances for indirect material (thread), indirect labour (maintenance) and engineering.

Note that we have concentrated in this section on cost variance analysis as a tool for cost management. Equally important in affecting a company's bottom line, though, is its *sales* performance. The sales price and the sales volume of each product have a significant impact on a company's revenue, contribution margin and profit. Appendix 13 B covers *sales variance analysis*, a technique used to help management understand and manage the effects of the company's sales performance on its profitability.

Finally, cost management analysts need to keep in mind that their performance reports are intended for managers, and the usefulness depends on whether those managers believe the reports help them to better assess what is going on and to make better decisions. Managers expect the numbers to tell a story about the company. They should provide insights that complement other pieces of information that managers receive, such as reports from other analysts who may work outside in manufacturing, logistics or engineering departments, information systems that managers work with themselves, oral and other qualitative information in all kinds of meetings. More about useful reports is described in Research Insight 13.2.

Exhibit 13.9 **Overhead Costs Performance Report: Koala Gear Company**

	A	B	C	D	E	F	G	H	I	J
4		Original budget	Flexible budget	Actuals	Variance	=	Spending variance	+	Quantity variance	
5	Production volume (tents)	2,800	3,000							
6		Machine hours								
7		4,200	4,500							
8	**Variable overhead costs at budgeted machine hours:***									
9	Indirect material:									
10	Thread	AU$ 8,400	AU$ 9,000	AU$ 9,450	AU$ 450 U		AU$ (150) F		AU$ 600 U	
11	Strings	2,800	3,000	3,600	600 U		400 U		200 U	
12	Eyelets	1,400	1,500	1,750	250 U		150 U		100 U	
13	Manufacturing supplies	4,200	4,500	4,550	50 U		(250) F		300 U	
14	Indirect labour: maintenance	7,000	7,500	8,960	1,460 U		960 U		500 U	
15	Utilities:	-	-							
16	Electrical power	840	900	1,300	400 U		340 U		60 U	
17	Heat	560	600	870	270 U		230 U		40 U	
18	Total variable overhead cost	AU$ 25,200	AU$ 27,000	AU$ 30,480	*AU$ 3,480*		*AU$ 1,680*		*AU$ 1,800*	
19	**Fixed overhead costs:**									
20	Indirect labour:									
21	Quality assurance	AU$ 2,400	AU$ 2,400	AU$ 2,250	AU$ (150)					
22	Production supervisors	7,000	7,000	7,100	100					
23	Set-up	3,600	3,600	3,870	270					
24	Material handling	9,600	9,600	10,430	830					
25	Depreciation: plant and equipment	1,300	1,300	1,300	-					
26	Insurance and property taxes	1,100	1,100	1,050	(50)					
27	Engineering	5,000	5,000	6,500	1,500					
28	Total fixed overhead cost	AU$ 30,000	AU$ 30,000	AU$ 32,500	*AU$ 2,500*					
29	Total overhead cost per month	AU$ 55,200	AU$ 57,000	AU$ 62,980						
31	* Standard rates used in columns B, C, I and K are from Exhibit 13.5									
32	** Actual costs in column D are from company records.									

13.2 Research Insight

Performance Reports

A survey of US manufacturers found that 96 per cent of the responding companies' prepare periodic performance reports including variances from standard costs for management. However, 62 per cent of the respondents believed that the reports contained too much detail, and only 41 per cent of the responding production managers believed their reports to be timely. Just 37 per cent of the survey respondents believed that their performance reports enabled them to assign responsibility for the variances. A need for improvement in the performance reporting system was suggested by 71 per cent of the surveyed managers.

Useful reports contain and highlight information that is necessary for specific operating decisions or for monitoring key success factors. They eliminate uncertainties about the status and the results of activities for which the manager is responsible. Furthermore, these match the scope of data and information to the area of responsibility of the manager; provide simple, straightforward presentation of limited pieces of data; are available on a timely basis; are well organized (e.g., summary information with drill down possibilities); and have a reputation for reliability.

Managers use not only formal reports, but they combine information from various sources (such as observations, conversations, emails, phone calls, meetings, non-financial information systems and formal reports) to monitor the current status of processes, to predict whether goals will be achieved, and to respond to setbacks and other unexpected situations. Informal information is provided interpersonally (such as in meetings), rather than on paper or on screen; it is unplanned, instead of formally scheduled; and it originates voluntarily, as opposed to official operating procedures.

Useful reports also need to be consistent with how operational managers influence costs and performance. For example, a case study of cost management by site managers in a road building company demonstrated that these managers were closely involved in the planning and budgeting of a project. As a result, they formulated observable milestones to monitor actual costs and progress during project execution. If they observed that actual progress and costs were not meeting these milestones (and the budget) they employed a variety of practices to expedite the project, reduce costs or increase revenues. Identifying these management practices was key to understanding why planning and budgeting were crucial activities for these site managers. Explicating these practices was also key for understanding why the managers made limited use of a new information system for monitoring actual project costs during project execution. Instead, they used other, more practical sources of information for assessing the status of operations and for solving cost management problems.

Sources: Moscove (1998); McKinnon and Bruns (1992); Pitkänen and Lukka (2011); and van der Veeken and Wouters (2002).'

Activity-based Flexible Budget

LO 4
Explain why an activity-based flexible budget can provide more useful cost management information than a conventional flexible budget.

The flexible overhead budget shown in Exhibit 13.7, which underlies our variance analysis for Koala Camp Gear Company, is based on a single cost driver. Overhead costs that vary with respect to *machine hours* are categorized as variable; all other overhead costs are treated as fixed. This approach is consistent with traditional, volume-based product costing systems.

Under the more accurate product costing method called activity-based costing (ABC), several cost drivers are identified.[17] Costs that could appear fixed with respect to a single volume-based cost driver, such as machine hours, can be variable with respect to other appropriate cost drivers. The activity-based costing approach also can be used as the basis for a flexible budget for planning and cost management purposes. Exhibit 13.10 displays an **activity-based flexible budget** for Koala. An activity-based flexible budget is based on several cost drivers rather than a single, volume-based cost driver.

Compare the conventional flexible budget (Exhibit 13.7) and the activity-based flexible budget (Exhibit 13.10). The key difference lies in the costs that were categorized as fixed with respect to machine hours on the conventional flexible budget. These costs might be fixed with respect to machine hours, but analysis showed that they are not fixed with respect to other more appropriate cost drivers. For example, cost pool II includes quality assurance and set-up costs, which vary with respect to the number of production runs.

The activity-based flexible budget provides a more accurate prediction (and benchmarking) of overhead costs. The following table compares the budgeted cost levels for several overhead items

Exhibit 13.10 **Activity-based Flexible Budget**

	A	B	C	D
1	**Monthly Flexible Overhead Budget**			
2	**Koala Camp Gear Company**			
3				
4			**Original budget**	**Flexible budget**
5	Production volume (tents)		2,800	3,000
6	**Cost Pool I (cost driver: machine hours)**	**Cost per unit of activity**	**4,200**	**4,500**
7	Indirect material:			
8	Thread	AU$2.00	AU$8,400	AU$9,000
9	Strings	0.67	2,800	3,000
10	Eyelets	0.33	1,400	1,500
11	Manufacturing supplies	1.00	4,200	4,500
12	Indirect labour: maintenance	1.67	7,000	7,500
13	Utilities:		-	-
14	Electrical power	0.20	840	900
15	Heat	0.13	560	600
16	Total of cost pool I		AU$25,200	AU$27,000
17				
18	**Cost Pool II (cost driver: production runs)**		**12**	**13**
19	Indirect labour:			
20	Quality assurance	$200.00	$2,400	$2,600
21	Set-up	$300.00	3,600	3,900
22	Total of cost pool II		$6,000	$6,500
23				
24	**Cost Pool III (cost driver: engineering design specs)**		**12**	**15**
25	Engineering	$320.00	$3,840	$4,800
26	Total of cost pool III		$3,840	$4,800
27				
28	**Cost Pool IV (cost driver: sq. metres of material handled)**		**48,000**	**52,000**
29	Material handling	$0.20	$9,600	$10,400
30	Total of cost pool IV		$9,600	$10,400
31				
32	**Cost Pool V (facility-level costs)**			
33	Indirect labour: production supervisors	AU$7,000	$7,000	$7,000
34	Depreciation: plant and equipment	1,300	1,300	1,300
35	Insurance and property taxes	1,100	1,100	1,100
36	Total of cost pool V		$9,400	$9,400
37				
38	**Total overhead cost**		$54,040	$58,100

on the conventional and activity-based flexible budgets. The budgeted electrical power is the same on both budgets because both use the same cost driver (machine hours). Insurance and property taxes are also the same because both budgets recognize them as facility-level fixed costs. However, the other overhead costs are budgeted at different levels because the conventional and activity-based flexible budgets use *different cost drivers* for these items. The conventional budget treats quality assurance, set-up, materials-handling, and engineering costs as fixed, but the activity-based flexible budget shows that they are all variable with respect to the appropriate cost driver.

Overhead cost Item	Conventional flexible budget (Exhibit 13.7)	Activity-based flexible budget (Exhibit 13.10)
Electrical power	AU$900	AU$900
Quality assurance	2,400	2,600
Set-up	3,600	3,900
Material handling	9,600	10,400
Engineering	5,000	4,800
Insurance and property taxes	1,100	1,100

These differences are important for performance reporting. The activity-based flexible budget provides a more accurate benchmark against which to compare actual costs. Suppose that the actual quality assurance cost in August is $2,500. Using the conventional flexible budget would result in an unfavourable variance of $100 ($2,500 – $2,400). However, the activity-based flexible budget yields a favourable variance of $100 ($2,500 – $2,600).[18]

13.1 Cost Management in Practice

Activity-based Budgeting at Sierra Trucks*

Sierra Trucks Corporation, based in the Midwest of the USA, is a leading producer of heavy- and medium-duty trucks and school buses and mid-range diesel engines. It generated net sales and revenues around $12 billion in 2010. A competitive cost structure is one of the pillars for the company's growth plan.

To achieve cost competiveness, the company has made its production plants more flexible, so that assembly plants have the capability of manufacturing a greater variety of engine or truck models. The increased flexibility enables the company to build trucks closer to the customer, better utilize capacity and enhance customer service. Improved proximity reduces logistics costs. Furthermore, the company consolidated the truck and engine research and development activities in a central location for improved efficiency. The company uses product platforms to be able to launch new products while managing costs. The company also introduced new electrical and gas-powered vehicles to the market.

Sierra expands internationally through exports and co-operation with partners. For example, in India it formed a joint venture to introduce a full line-up of vehicles for the rapidly growing India market. The company is in the middle of starting a joint business in China.

Sierra began to investigate and apply activity-based costing (ABC) practices to provide management information. Early in the project, the ABC methodology had a firmly established record of success at Sierra, and the operational managers were interested in using the same logic for budgeting and decision-making purposes. They wanted to plan and predict the impact of various product mix scenarios on activities and on resources. Three types of cost behaviour were defined:

- Transaction-related activities, the cost of which vary with the number of units sold or manufactured.
- Business-line-specific activities support a business line, or group of models, and the cost of these are not related to production or sales volume. For example, the company may offer many different types of gas tank sizes and various locations for the tanks on the trucks themselves. There is a significant cost to maintaining one part number.
- Business-sustaining activities support all models and business lines.

However, the budgeting part was more difficult that the costing part. In costing, there is at least the total costs as a starting point and the question is how these can be linked to the different products. But for budgeting, total costs are not given and data that the budgeting system produces are more difficult to validate. Thus, it required a deeper understanding of cost behaviour. The company experienced that cost drivers should represent a volume number of units, number of moves, number of part numbers, and so on. When costs in the ABC model are evenly assigned or based on surcharges, that is typically not good enough for activity-based budgeting.

Furthermore, the budgeted resource consumption may be above the available capacity. Thus, the activity-based budgeting system has information on each department or activity twice: once to represent 'required' and one for 'available'.

Source: Adkins (2006).

* Sierra Trucks is a pseudonym for a real company, but this example was written anonymously.

Significance of Cost Variances: When to Follow Up

LO 5
Describe several methods used to determine the significance of cost variances.

Managers are busy people. They do not have time to investigate the causes of every cost variance. *Management by exception* enables managers to explore the causes of only significant variances. But what constitutes an exception? How does the manager know when to follow up on a cost variance and when to ignore it?

These questions are difficult to answer because to some extent the answers are part of the art of management. It also depends on where one is in the organization. Someone at the shop floor level might be very concerned with a AU$1,000 variance, but this would be immaterial at the top management level. A manager applies judgement and experience in making guesses, pursuing hunches and relying on intuition to determine when to investigate a variance. Nevertheless, there are guidelines and rules of thumb that managers often apply.

Size of Variances

The *absolute size* of a variance is one consideration. Managers are more likely to follow up on large variances than on small ones. The *relative size* of the variance is probably even more important. A manager is more likely to investigate a $40,000 material quantity variance that is 20 per cent of the standard direct material cost of $200,000 than a $60,000 labour efficiency variance that is only 2 per cent of the standard direct labour cost of $3,000,000. The *relative* magnitude of the $40,000 material quantity variance (20 per cent) is greater than the *relative* magnitude of the $60,000 labour efficiency variance (2 per cent). For this reason, cost management analysts often show the relative magnitude of variances in their cost variance reports.

Managers often apply a rule of thumb that considers both the absolute and the relative magnitude of a variance. An example of such a rule is the following: Investigate variances that are either more than $10,000 or more than 10 per cent of standard cost.

Recurring Variances

Another consideration in deciding when to investigate a variance is whether the variance occurs repeatedly or only infrequently. Suppose that a manager uses the rule of thumb just stated and the following direct materials quantity variances occur.

Month	Variance	Percentage of standard cost*
September	$6,000 F	6.0%
October	6,400 F	6.4%
November	3,200 F	3.2%
December	6,200 F	6.2%

*The standard direct material cost is $100,000.

Strict adherence to the rule of thumb indicates no investigation since none of the monthly variances is more than $10,000 or 10 per cent of standard cost. Nevertheless, the manager might investigate this variance in December, since it has *recurred* at a reasonably high level for several consecutive months. In this case, the consistency of the variance triggers an investigation, not its absolute or relative magnitude.

Trends

A trend in a variance also might call for investigation. Suppose that a manager observes the following direct labour efficiency variances.

Month	Variance	Percentage of standard cost*
September	$250 U	0.25%
October	840 U	0.84%
November	4,000 U	4.00%
December	9,300 U	9.30%

*The standard direct labour cost is $100,000.

None of these variances is large enough to trigger an investigation if the manager uses the '$10,000 or 10 per cent' rule of thumb. However, the four-month *trend* is worrisome. An alert manager will likely follow up on this unfavourable trend to determine its causes before costs get out of hand.

Trends are clearly shown on *run charts* and *control charts* which are discussed in Chapter 6. A run chart simply shows a variance or any other important measure over time. A control chart does the same, and it also includes upper and lower control limits. These are critical values, and management should follow up only if the variance goes outside these limits. The control limits are based on statistical analysis of the pattern of variance. For example, if the cost variances can be assumed to have a normal probability distribution with a mean of zero, then the critical value is set at some multiple of the distribution's standard deviation.

Controllability

Another important consideration in deciding when to investigate the causes of a variance is the manager's view of the controllability of the cost item. A manager is more likely to investigate a variance for a cost that someone in the organization can control than a variance for a cost that cannot be controlled. For example, there might be little point to investigating a materials price variance if the organization has no control over the price. This could happen, for example, if the firm has a long-term contract with a supplier of the material at a price determined on the international market. In contrast, the manager is likely to follow up on a variance that should be controllable, such as a direct labour efficiency variance or a direct materials quantity variance.

Favourable Variances

Investigation of significant favourable variances is just as important as of significant unfavourable variances. For example, a favourable direct labour efficiency variance could indicate that employees have developed a more efficient way to perform a production task. By investigating the variance, management can learn about the improved method. A similar approach might be used elsewhere in the organization.

Costs and Benefits of Investigation

The decision to investigate a cost variance is a cost–benefit decision. The costs of investigation include the time spent by the investigating manager and the employees in the department where the investigation occurs. Other potential costs include the disruption of the production process to conduct the investigation and to take corrective actions to eliminate the cause of a variance. The benefits of a variance investigation include reduced future production costs if the cause of an unfavourable variance can be eliminated. Another potential benefit is the cost savings associated with lowering the cost standards when the cause of a favourable variance is discovered. Weighing these considerations takes the judgement of skilful and experienced managers. Key to this judgement is an intimate understanding of the organization's production process and day-to-day contact with its operations.

Behavioural Effects of Standard Costing

LO 6
Discuss some behavioural effects of standard costing and the controllability of variances.

Standard costs and variance analysis help managers discern 'the story behind the story' – the details of operations that underlie reported cost and profit numbers. Standard costs, budgets and variances are also used to evaluate the performance of individuals and departments. The performance of individuals, relative to standards or budgets, is often used to help determine salary increases, bonuses and promotions. When standards and variances affect employee reward structures, they can profoundly influence behaviour.

For example, suppose that the purchasing manager of Koala earns a bonus when purchasing prices are reduced and there is favourable price variance. Such an incentive can have either positive or negative effects. The bonus might induce a manager to seek innovative ways for sourcing more efficiently. However, the bonus also might persuade the manager to buy lower-quality zippers and other materials, and this could ultimately result in lower customer satisfaction and lost sales for the company. Let's assume that the inferior quality of the material is not readily apparent and that the negative implications will not be realized until long after the products are manufactured and sold. It is a serious violation of ethical standards for the purchasing manager to buy the off-standard material. Ethical issues can easily arise when employees' performance relative to standards affects their reward system.

One aspect of skilful management is knowing how to use standards, budgets and variances to get the most out of an organization's employees. Unfortunately, there are no simple answers or formulas for success in this area. However, we do know that standard costing systems are more acceptable for employees and more beneficial for the organization if employees are held accountable by what they can control, at least to some reasonable extent. By determining which managers are in the best position to influence each cost variance, the managerial accountant can assist managers in deriving the greatest benefit from cost variance analysis.

Which Managers Influence Cost Variances?

Who is responsible for the direct materials price and quantity variances, and for the direct labour rate and efficiency variances? Answering these questions is often difficult because any one person rarely has complete control of any event. Nevertheless, it is often possible to identify the manager who is *most able to influence* a particular variance even if he or she does not exercise complete control over the outcome.

Direct material price variance

The purchasing manager generally is in the best position to influence material price variances. Through skilful purchasing practices, an expert purchasing manager can get the best prices available for purchased goods and services. To achieve this goal, the purchasing manager uses practices such as buying in quantity, negotiating purchase contracts, comparing prices among vendors and global sourcing.

Despite these purchasing skills, the purchasing manager is not in complete control of prices. The need to purchase component parts with precise engineering specifications, the all-too-frequent rush requests from the production department, and worldwide shortages of critical materials all contribute to the challenges that the purchasing manager faces.

Direct material quantity variance

The production supervisor is usually in the best position to influence material quantity variances. Skilful supervision and motivation of production employees, coupled with the careful use and handling of materials, contribute to minimal waste. Production engineers also are partially responsible for material quantity variances since they determine the grade and technical specifications of materials and component parts. In some cases, using a low-grade material results in more waste than using a high-grade material.

Direct labour rate variance

Direct labour rate variances generally result from using a different mix of employees than that anticipated when the standards were set. Wage rates differ among employees due to their skill levels and their seniority with the organization. Using a higher proportion of more senior or more highly skilled employees than a task requires can result in unfavourable direct labour rate variances. The production supervisor is generally in the best position to influence the employee work schedules.

Direct labour efficiency variance

The production supervisor is usually most responsible for the efficient use of employee time. Through motivation toward production goals and effective work schedules, employee efficiency can be maximized.

Interaction among Variances

Interactions among variances often occur, making the determination of the responsibility for a particular variance even more difficult. To illustrate, consider the following incident, which occurred at Koala Camp Gear Company during March. The purchasing manager obtained a special price on tent fabric from a new supplier. When the material was placed into production, it turned out to be a lower grade of material than the production employees were used to. The fabric was of a slightly different composition, which made the material tear easily during cutting. Koala could have returned the material to the supplier, but doing so would have interrupted production and kept the company from filling its orders on time. Since using the off-standard material would not affect the quality of the company's finished products, the production manager decided to keep the material and make the best of the situation.

The ultimate result was that Koala incurred four interrelated variances during March. The material was less expensive than normal, so the direct material price variance was favourable. However, the employees had difficulty using the material, which resulted in more waste than expected. Hence, the division incurred an unfavourable direct material quantity variance. What were the labour implications of the off-standard material? Due to the difficulty in working with the fabric, the employees required more than the standard amount of time. This resulted in an unfavourable direct labour efficiency variance. Finally, the production supervisor had to use his most senior employees to work with the off-standard material. Since these people earn relatively high wages, the direct labour rate variance was also unfavourable. To summarize, the purchase of off-standard material resulted in the following interrelated variances:

Purchase of off-standard material ⇒
- **Favourable direct material price variance**
- **Unfavourable direct material quantity variance**
- **Unfavourable direct labour rate variance**
- **Unfavourable direct labour efficiency variance**

Such interactions of variances make the assignment of responsibility more difficult for any particular variance.

Think back to our discussions of the value chain in earlier chapters. Recall that the value chain is the set of linked operations or processes that begins by obtaining resources and ends with providing products or services that customers value. The preceding discussion regarding interactions and trade-offs among variances emphasizes that variances in one part of the value chain can result from root causes in another part of the chain. For example, when Koala Camp Gear's purchasing manager bought tent fabric at a special price, and the material turned out to be below standard, several direct material and direct labour variances resulted in the production process. Thus, an incident in the supply component of Koala's value chain resulted in cost variances in the production component of the chain.

Trade-offs among variances

Does the preceding incident mean that the decision to buy and use the off-standard material was a poor one? Not necessarily. Perhaps these variances were anticipated, and a conscious decision was made to buy the material anyway. How could this be a wise decision? Suppose the amounts of the variances were as follows:

AU$(7,900)	Favourable direct material price variance
1,100	Unfavourable direct material quantity variance
1,900	Unfavourable direct labour rate variance
2,100	Unfavourable direct labour efficiency variance
AU$(2,800)	Favourable net overall variance

Koala saved money overall on the decision to use a different grade of fabric. Given that the quality of the final product was not affected, the company's management acted wisely.

13.3 Research Insight

Other Types of Variance Analyses

Variance analysis is not restricted to manufacturing, although that receives most attention in textbooks and in research. Transportation costs, for example, is another interesting area. Standard costs can be based on the optimal route planning specifying allowable kilometres and hours. The unit for measuring volume can be, for example, kilometres, pallets or full truckloads. Furthermore, there can be different ways for disaggregating the total variance. Price and quantity variances are possible, but also a mix variance reflecting the use of full truckloads versus less-than-full truckloads. And in a study by Gaffney et al. (2007), the variance analysis included a breakdown into different kinds of distribution mix variances (representing the distribution alternatives available for getting products to the final customers) and carrier charge variances.

Variance analysis can also be extended to better understand environmental costs. The cost impact of the actual versus the standard emissions per unit of output can be isolated, for example. The cost of using more than the standard quantity of inputs can be split into the costs borne by the firm and the societal costs. This can also be done for the cost of choosing a particular technology versus a more efficient technology.

In Appendix 13A, mix and yield variances in manufacturing are explained, while Appendix 13B gives more details on the computation and interpretation of sales variances. The bottom line is that you can creatively devise variance analyses for a wide variety of costs.

Sources: Gaffney et al. (2007); Wouters and Roijmans (2011); Dutta et al. (2010); Roth (2008).

Changing Role of Standard Costing Systems in Today's Manufacturing Environment

LO 7 Understand how standard costing can be adjusted to modern manufacturing environments.

Standard costing has been a widely used accounting system in manufacturing companies. For cost management purposes, standard costing simply means that there is a standard cost to which one can compare actual costs.[19] The use of standard costing is spreading to non-manufacturing firms as well. The widespread use of standard costing over such a long time period suggests that it has traditionally been perceived as advantageous. However, today's manufacturing environment is changing dramatically. Some managers are calling into question the usefulness of the traditional standard costing approach.

In this section, we will list advantages of standard costing, talk about the impact of modern information technology, and suggest several ways in which the role of standard costing is beginning to change.

Standard Costing: Its Traditional Advantages

Standard costing systems provide information that can help managers control costs. Some advantages of standard costing are:

- Computation of standard costs and cost variances enables managers to employ *management by exception*. As we discussed earlier, this approach conserves valuable management time.
- Standard costs provide a basis for *sensible cost comparisons*. As we discussed earlier, comparing budgeted costs at one (planned) activity level with actual costs incurred at a different (actual) activity level makes no sense. Standard costs enable the cost manager to compute the standard allowed cost, given actual output, which then serves as a sensible benchmark to compare with the actual cost.
- Variances provide a means of *performance evaluation* and rewards for employees.

- Since the variances are used in performance evaluation, they provide *motivation* for employees to adhere to standards.
- Use of standard costs in product costing results in *more stable product costs* than the use of actual production costs. Actual costs often fluctuate erratically, whereas standard costs change only periodically.

Like any tool, a standard costing system can be misused. When employees are criticized for every cost variance, the positive motivational effects will quickly vanish. Moreover, if standards are not revised often enough, they will become outdated. Then the benefits of cost benchmarks and product costing will disappear.

Impact of Information Technology

Standard costing can be a costly system to run. Standards must be updated, data on actual costs must be gathered, and preparing reports also requires resources. Fortunately, modern information technology can facilitate standard costing. Many businesses are adopting integrated business software packages that handle a broad range of computing needs such as customer and supplier databases, personnel and payroll functions, production scheduling and management, inventory records, financial accounting and cost management functions. Standard costing and flexible budgeting typically is included in such software packages. Among the integrated software packages in wide use are **PeopleSoft** (www.oracle.com) and the German product **SAP**, which stands for **Systems Applications and Products in Data Processing** (www.sap.com).

Integrated software contains a standard cost database. Based on the detailed production planning that is also part of these systems, standard quantities and prices of materials, standard labour costs, and standard overhead costs for the actual production can be determined.

Tracking of actual costs is also much easier with modern information technology. Bar codes are now widely used to capture important events in manufacturing processes. When raw materials arrive at the production facility, their bar code is scanned and the event is recorded. Inventory records are updated automatically. Subsequently, by scanning bar codes of raw materials and partially completed components, their movement through the production process is efficiently recorded. In *real-time shop floor data-collection systems*, production employees can record the time they begin and stop working on a particular job order by scanning the bar code on their employee ID badge and a bar code assigned to the production job order. Similarly, they can requisition materials and components and scan the job orders for which these are used.

The availability of detailed data on standard and actual costs makes it possible to prepare not only aggregate variance analysis reports, but to also drill down to specific product lines, production batches, or flexible manufacturing system (FMS) cells. Furthermore, the availability of large amounts of the company's transaction data in integrated software, such as SAP's Business Warehouse module, makes it possible for different users – not just cost management analysts – to prepare all kinds of regular and ad-hoc reports.

Standard costing systems also can be integrated with a computer-aided design (CAD) system to assist design engineers in the product design process. The standard costs of material and labour are stored in the computer database where the product design team can access them easily. This information enables a product design engineer to get a quick answer to the question, 'What will be the new product cost if certain design changes are made to the product?' If, for example, the engineer wants to know the cost of changing the exterior case on a particular computer model, this information is easily determined by accessing the cost database.[20] Car companies, such as **Mercedes Benz**, **BMW**, **Nissan**, and **Toyota**, use target costing or value engineering approaches in new product design to estimate the cost of designs and compare these against targets for different components of the product.

Adaptation of Standard Costing Systems

The rise of global competition, the introduction of JIT production methods and flexible manufacturing systems, the goal of continuous process improvement, and the emphasis on product quality are dramatically changing the manufacturing environment.[21] Some highly automated manufacturers have de-emphasized standard costing in their control systems.[22] Most manufacturing firms continue to use standard costing to some extent, even after adopting advanced manufacturing methods, but they make changes in their use of standard costing.[23]

Reduced importance of labour standards and variances

As direct labour has come to occupy an ever-diminishing role in the manufacturing environment, the standards and variances used to control labour costs also have declined in importance. The heavy emphasis of traditional standard costing systems on labour efficiency variances is giving way to variances that focus on the more critical inputs to the production process. Machine hours, materials and support department costs, product quality and manufacturing cycle times have assumed greater importance as the objects of managerial control.

Emphasis on material and overhead costs

As labour continues to diminish in importance, materials and support department costs also have assumed greater significance. Controlling the costs of materials and quality and controlling non-unit-level costs through cost driver analysis become key aspects of the cost management system.

Cost drivers

Identification of the factors that drive production costs becomes more important in the cost management system. Cost drivers such as machine hours, number of parts, engineering change orders and production runs become the focus of the cost management system. Overhead cost control becomes especially critical.

High quality and zero defects

Total quality management (TQM) programmes that typically accompany a JIT approach strive for very high quality levels for both raw materials and finished products. One result should be very low materials price and quantity variances and low costs of rework.

Shorter product life cycles

As product life cycles shorten, developing standards and revising them more frequently become necessary.

Non-financial measures for operational control

Managerial accountants traditionally have focused on financial measures of performance such as deviations from budgeted costs. Financial measures still are very important, but to an ever-greater extent, financial performance criteria are being augmented by non-financial measures. In today's advanced manufacturing environment, operational performance measures are being developed that focus directly on performance issues that management wants to improve. For example, such issues could include product quality, processing time and delivery performance.

Benchmarking

One widely used method to control costs and improve operational efficiency is *benchmarking* – the continual search for the most effective method of accomplishing a task by comparing existing methods and performance levels with those of other organizations or other subunits within the same organization. For example, hospitals routinely benchmark their costs of patient care by diagnostic-related groups (such as circulatory disorders) with the costs of other hospitals.

Total costs of ownership, and cost to serve

Outside manufacturing, firms incur a lot of costs related to sourcing of inputs from suppliers and to delivery of goods and services to customers. Modern costing systems also capture such costs more accurately. In addition to the purchase price and transportation costs, the *total cost of ownership* (TCO) may include the costs of ordering, paying bills, scheduling delivery, receiving, inspecting, handling and storing, as well as any production-line disruptions resulting from untimely or incorrect delivery.[24] *Cost to serve* (CTS) may include the costs of sales, distribution, warranty, in-store promotions, customer-specific product development, customer-specific tools and customer-support activities.[25]

Open book accounting

Companies and suppliers share more information on product costs and are transparent about cost reduction targets and profit margins.[26]

Kaizen Costing

In today's global business environment, for some companies to survive, they must continually seek to reduce production costs. If a standard costing system is used in such a competitive environment, the standards must be reduced every year or even every month. **Kaizen costing** is the process of cost reduction during the manufacturing phase of a product.[27] The Japanese word 'kaizen' refers to continual and gradual improvement through small betterment activities rather than large or radical improvement made through innovation or large investments in technology. The idea is simple. Improvement is the goal and responsibility of every worker, from the CEO to the manual labourers, in every activity, every day, all the time! Through the small but continual efforts of everyone, significant reductions in costs can be attained over time.

To help achieve the continuous cost reduction implied by the kaizen costing concept, an annual (or monthly) *kaizen cost goal* is established. Then actual costs are tracked over time and compared to the kaizen goal. Depending on the nature of the production process and the competitive environment, a company could focus its kaizen costing efforts on a particular segment of its cost structure. For example, **Sumitomo Electric Industries** (www.sei.co.jp), a Japanese company that is the world's third largest manufacturer of electrical wire and cable, concentrates its kaizen cost-reduction programme on material costs.[28] In contrast, 'at the Kyoto brewery of **Kirin** beer (www.kirin.com), cost-reduction programs typically identified four or five targets for improvement each year. This continuous change of focus helped keep the programs active'.[29]

Citizen Watch Company (www.citizenwatch.com) focuses its kaizen costing efforts on direct labour.[30] Car manufacturers such as **Honda**, **Nissan**, and **Toyota** also extend kaizen costing efforts towards their suppliers and help those companies to meet cost reduction targets.[31]

We present a typical kaizen costing chart in Exhibit 13.11.[32] Notice that the cost base, or reference point, is the actual cost performance at the end of the prior year. A kaizen goal is established for

Exhibit 13.11 Typical Kaizen Costing Chart

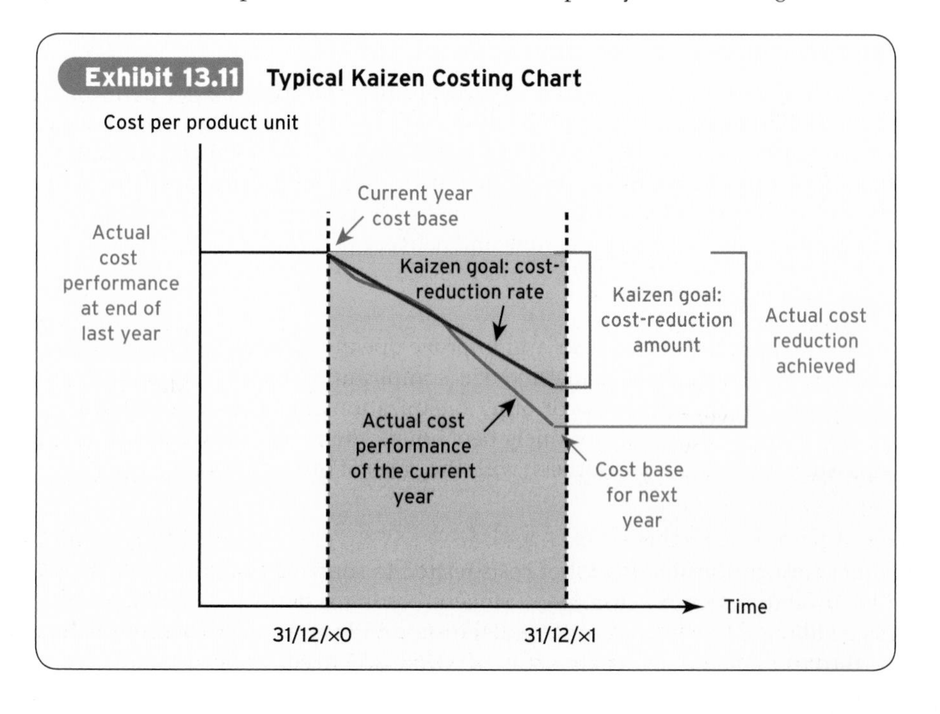

the cost-reduction rate and amount during the current year. Actual cost performance throughout the year is compared with the kaizen goal. At the end of the current year, the current actual cost becomes the cost base, or reference point, for the next year. Then, a new (lower) kaizen goal is established, and the cost-reduction effort continues.

How are kaizen costing goals met? The continual and relentless reduction of non-value-added activities and costs, the elimination of waste, and improvements in manufacturing cycle time all contribute to the effort. In addition, management takes seriously the improvement suggestions and kaizen efforts of all employees and implements them when appropriate. The result is a continually more efficient and cost-effective production process.[33]

13.2 Cost Management in Practice

Cost of Ownership

Northrop Aircraft Division (www.northgrum.com) (USA) tracks various elements of the total cost of ownership (TCO)* through its cost-based Supplier Performance Rating System (SPRS). Among the cost factors that SPRS measures are the costs Northrop incurs due to suppliers' hardware, paperwork or delivery deficiencies. Any 'nonconformance event is assigned a standard cost based on industrial engineering studies of the hours required to resolve the problem'.

Texas Instruments (www.ti.com) (USA) has developed a supplier rating system called CETRAQ, which stands for cost, environmental responsibility, technology, responsiveness, assurance of supply and quality. The company's vendors are regularly measured on these six criteria.

At a plant in Spennymore, England, owned by **Black & Decker** (www.blackanddecker.com), the company 'has integrated the cost-of-ownership concept into its activity-based costing system'. Among the TCO issues included are quality, delivery, flexibility and customer service. Also considered is a suppliers' billing reliability. 'As one Spennymore manager noted, "You can be dealing with the best company in the world in terms of quality, but if they can't get their invoices right, you're going to have trouble doing business with them"'.

Source: Carr and Ittner (1992). The information about Texas Instruments is based on an author's research in 2003.

* The *total cost of ownership* includes all costs incurred to have materials in place and ready for use in production, including the purchase price; the transportation cost; and the costs of ordering, receiving, inspecting and storing the materials.

Accounting for Cost Variances

LO 8 Prepare accounting entries for cost variances.

Our discussion of standard costing has focused on its use for controlling costs. Firms that employ standard costing systems also often use standards for product costing. When products are sold, the Cost of sales is valued at the *standard cost* including fixed overhead costs. This means that products are also valued in the Finished goods (FG) inventory at standard costs, which implies that these have been transferred to FG inventory from Work-in-progress (WIP) inventory at standard cost. However, as production was taking place, the *actual overhead costs* have been added to the Manufacturing overhead account and the *actual direct costs* have been added to the WIP inventory. So the Manufacturing overhead account and the WIP inventory is where the variances will show up. Exhibit 13.12 shows several accounts to explain this movement of actual costs and standard costs.[34] Note that the opening balance numbers have not been discussed so far and are not important right now (these have just been added to get a complete picture).

The crucial point is that after completion of production, the Manufacturing overhead account and the WIP account have not gone back to 0. Recall that the actual overhead costs are AU$30,480 + 32,500 = AU$62,980 (see Exhibit 13.8). However, the Manufacturing overhead account has only been reduced by the standard overhead cost of AU$59,143. (This amount will be explained later in this section.) The difference (variance) of **AU$3,837** needs to be settled.

Exhibit 13.12 **Journal Entries around Costing Variances**

	A	B	C	D	E	F	G	H	I	J
1		ASSETS						LIABILITIES		EQUITIES
2	Transaction	Cash	Raw Mat'ls Inven.	*Manufac-turing Overhead*	WIP Inven.	FG Inven.	Plant, Prop. & Equip.	Wages Payable	Accounts Payable	Owners' Equity
3	**BB**	**100,000**	**300,000**	**0**	**0**	**0**	**50,000**	**0**	**0**	**450,000**
4	Use of raw materials		(296,660)		296,660					
5	Use of direct labour				112,100			112,100		
6	Use of flexible overhead cost for production	(30,480)		30,480						
7	Use of fixed overhead cost for production	(31,200)		32,500			(1,300)			
8	Application of manuf overhead to WIP			(59,143)	59,143					
9	Completion of jobs and transfer to FGI				(455,143)	455,143				
10	Closing of manuf overhead to CoGS			(3,837)						(3,837)
11	Closing of WIP to CoGS				(12,760)					(12,760)
12	**EB**	**38,320**	**3,340**	**0**	**0**	**455,143**	**48,700**	**112,100**	**0**	**433,403**

Recall that the actual direct costs are AU$296,660 + 112,100 (see Exhibit 13.3) to which the standard overhead costs of AU$59,143 are added (see Exhibit 13.12). This gives a total cost on WIP of AU$467,903. However, the WIP account has only been reduced by the standard cost of AU$455,143. (This amount will be explained later in this section.) The variance of **AU$12,760** needs to be settled.

First of all, the budget variances that we have seen before are also relevant here. These are shown in the following table:

Direct material variance	8,660	U	See Exhibit 13.3
Direct labour variance	4,100	U	See Exhibit 13.3
	12,760	U	
Flexible overhead costs variance	3,480	U	See Exhibit 13.8
Fixed overhead budget variance	2,500	U	See Exhibit 13.8
Fixed overhead volume variance	(2,143)	F	
	3,837	U	

However, for the *fixed overhead costs*, we also have to consider an additional variance, namely the *fixed overhead volume variance*. How does this work? For the product costing purpose of the cost accounting system, the FGI also needs to include fixed overhead costs. To achieve this, the budgeted fixed overhead is divided by the planned activity to obtain a predetermined (or standard) fixed overhead rate.[35] For Koala, this rate is AU$7.1429 per machine hour (the budgeted fixed overhead of AU$30,000 divided by the *planned* activity of 4,200 machine hours).[36] This predetermined rate is then used to apply fixed overhead. When tents are completed, the standard number of machine hours allowed times the predetermined rate is transferred to the Manufacturing overhead account ('applied'). Suppose 2,800 tents would have been completed – as planned – then the standard amount of 4,200 machine hours means that exactly the budgeted fixed costs are applied: 4,200 hours × AU$7.1429 = AU$30,000. However, for 3,000 tents the applied fixed overhead amounts to 4,500 hours × AU$7.1429 = AU$32,143. The difference between this amount and the budget of AU$30,000 is equal to AU$2,143 and is called the fixed overhead volume variance. It is caused by the production volume being different than planned. This variance is illustrated in Exhibit 13.13. Now we can reconcile all differences, as shown in the table above.

In general, the **fixed overhead volume variance** is the difference between the budgeted fixed overhead and the fixed overhead applied. In a formula:

$$\textbf{Fixed-overhead volume variance} = \textbf{Budgeted fixed overhead} - Q_s R_p$$

Exhibit 13.13 **Budgeted versus Applied Fixed Overhead (picture not to scale)**

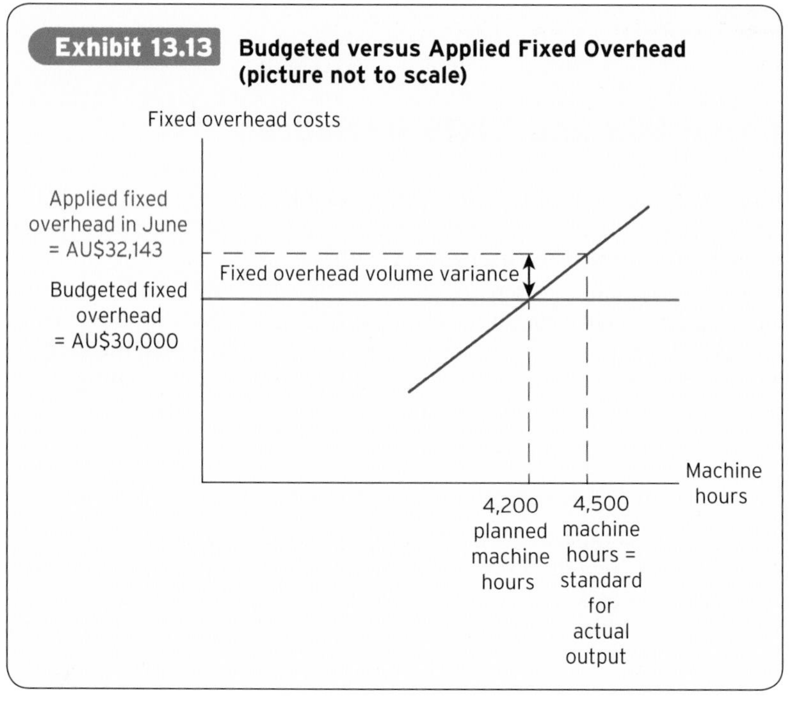

where

$$\boldsymbol{R_p} = \textbf{Predetermined fixed overhead rate}$$

$$= \textbf{Budgeted fixed overhead} \div \textbf{budgeted activity level}$$

The fixed overhead volume variance can be interpreted as a correction of the standard Cost of sales. If more activity or production has been possible for the same fixed cost, that is favourable. It means that, actually, the costs per unit were a bit lower, so profit can be adjusted upwardly. If less activity or production has been realized for the same fixed costs, that is unfavourable. The actual costs per unit were a bit higher, so profit needs to be adjusted downwardly.

Note how the predetermined rate is used to calculate the standard cost for product costing purposes. The standard overhead cost of AU$59,143 = 3,000 tents × 1.5 hour × (AU$6.00 + 7.1429) *per machine hour*. The standard direct cost is AU$132.00 *per tent* (see cell B12 in Exhibit 13.1), so for 3,000 tents this amounts to AU$396,000. Thus, the standard total cost for 3,000 tents = AU$59,143 + AU$ 396,000 = AU$455,143.

13.3 You're the Decision Maker

13.1 and 13.2 Revisited

a. Suppose that Koala's management uses a statistical control chart to plot direct cost variances and help management decide which variances to investigate. Let's assume that the cost management team has estimated that all of Koala's variances exhibit a normal probability distribution with a mean of zero and a standard deviation of AU$4,800. The critical value is 1 standard deviation. Which of Koala's December direct cost variances would you investigate? Explain.

b. Under what circumstances would there have been no fixed overhead volume variance for Koala Camp Gear's December operations?

(Solutions begin on page 690.)

Appendix 13A

LO 9
Compute and interpret mix and yield variances.

Production Mix and Yield Variances

Manufacturing processes typically involve multiple direct material inputs. Food, chemical, steel, fabric, plastic, and many other products require a mix of direct materials, some of which can be substituted for each other without greatly affecting product quality. Moreover, multiple types of direct labour often are required (e.g., machinists and assembly employees). When a manufacturing process involves multiple types of direct material or direct labour, additional variance analysis can be conducted to analyse the proportions with which the multiple inputs are used. Such an analysis assumes that some degree of substitutability exists among the inputs to the production process.

Production Mix and Yield Variances Illustrated

Let's return to Koala Camp Gear Company. Margo Hastings's nephew has convinced her that Koala should expand its product line to include certain camp foods. For its initial entry into this market, Koala has begun to produce trail mix. Variously known to outdoor enthusiasts as trail mix, this venerable food has sustained many a hiker. Koala has introduced its trail mix product under the brand name Crocodile Chomp.

Multiple direct material inputs

The three inputs to Crocodile Chomp are raisins (R), peanuts (P), and sunflower seeds (S). The standard costs and quantities for Crocodile Chomp are given in the following table. The trail mix is produced in 10 kilogram units; subsequently, each unit is divided into 20 half-kilo packages (a little over a pound).

(a) Direct material	(b) Standard price per kilogram	(c) Standard number of kilograms per unit of finished product	(d) Standard proportion (Col c ÷ 10)
R	AU$2.00	4	0.4
P	1.60	4	0.4
S	1.50	4	0.2
Total		10	

During September, Koala produced 1,000 units of Crocodile Chomp (i.e., 10,000 kilograms of trail mix). However, it purchased and consumed 10,800 kilograms of inputs, as the following table shows. The quantity purchased and the actual quantity used (Q_a) are the same, due to the perishability of the inputs.

(a) Direct material	(b) Actual price per kilogram	(c) Actual amount used	(d) Actual proportion (Col c ÷ 10)
R	AU$2.00	3,780	0.35
P	1.80	5,400	0.50
S	1.45	1,620	0.15
Total		10,800	

First, let's compute the direct material price and quantity variances for September. As the variance analysis shows in the table below, the total price variance is $999 unfavourable, and the total quantity variance is $1,230 unfavourable.

Direct material	$(P_a - P_s)\ Q_a$	Price variance	$(Q_a - Q_s{*})\ P_s$	Quantity variance
R	3,780 (AU$2.00 – AU$2.00)	0	AU$2.00 (3,780 – 4,000)	AU$440 F
P	5,400 (AU$1.80 – AU$1.60)	AU$1,080 U	AU$1.60 (5,400 – 4,000)	2,240 U
S	1,620 (AU$1.45 – AU$1.50)	81 F	AU$1.50 (1,620 – 2,000)	570 F
Total		AU$999 U		AU$1,230 U

* Q_s, the standard quantity allowed given actual output, is equal to the standard input proportion multiplied by 10,000 kilograms (the actual output produced).

Now we divide the quantity variance into a *direct material mix variance* and a *direct materials yield variance.* The **direct material mix variance** for a particular direct material is the difference between the actual and standard input proportions for that direct material multiplied by that material's standard price and multiplied by the actual total quantity of all direct materials used. The direct material mix variance is computed as follows. Notice that the total direct material mix variance is defined as the sum of the direct material mix variances for each input.

$$\textbf{Direct-material mix variance} = \textbf{Sum of direct material mix variances for each direct material used}$$

$$\textbf{Direct-material mix variance for direct material } i = \left(\textbf{Standard price of direct material } i\right) \times \left(\begin{matrix}\textbf{Actual input proportion for direct material } i \\ - \textbf{Standard input proportion for direct material } i\end{matrix}\right) \times \left(\textbf{Actual total quantity of all direct materials used}\right)$$

Using this formula, Koala's September direct material mix variances are computed as follows:

R mix variance = AU$2.00 × (0.35 – 0.40) × 10,800 = AU$1,080 F
P mix variance = AU$1.60 × (0.50 – 0.40) × 10,800 = 1,728 U
S mix variance = AU$1.50 × (0.15 – 0.20) × 10,800 = 810 F
Total mix variance = AU$162 F

Koala's September direct material mix variance is $162 favourable, which means that the mix of inputs was altered in such a way that it had a favourable impact on the total production cost. Notice that signs (F or U) are assigned to the individual input components of the mix variance in accordance with this rule: F if the actual input proportion is lower than the standard input proportion and U otherwise. During September, the actual input proportions for raisins and sunflower seeds were lower than their standard input proportions; the actual proportion for peanuts was higher than its standard. It is important to note, however, that *it is the total direct material mix variance of AU$162 F that is a meaningful measure for management's analysis, not the individual mix variance components.*

The **direct material yield variance** for a particular direct material is the difference between the actual quantity of all direct materials used and the standard quantity of all direct materials, given actual output, multiplied by that particular direct material's standard price and multiplied by that direct material's standard input proportion. Again, the total direct material yield variance is defined as the sum of the individual yield variance components for the several inputs.

$$\text{Direct material yield variance} = \text{Sum of direct material yield variances for each direct material used}$$

$$\begin{pmatrix}\text{Direct material yield variance for direct material } i\end{pmatrix} = \begin{pmatrix}\text{Standard price of direct material } i\end{pmatrix} \times \begin{pmatrix}\text{Actual quantity of all direct materials used} - \text{Standard allowed total quantity of all direct materials given actual output}\end{pmatrix} \times \begin{pmatrix}\text{Standard input proportion for direct material } i\end{pmatrix}$$

Using this formula, Koala's September direct material yield variances are computed as follows:

R yield variance = AU\$2.00 × (10,800 – 10,000) × 0.40 = AU\$640 U
P yield variance = AU\$1.60 × (10,800 – 10,000) × 0.40 = 512 U
S yield variance = AU\$1.50 × (10,800 – 10,000) × 0.20 = 240 U
Total mix variance = AU\$1,392 U

Koala's September direct material yield variance is \$1,392 unfavourable. The interpretation is that the total inputs used (10,800 kilograms) exceeded the standard quantity allowed given actual output (10,000 kilograms of input allowed for 10,000 kilograms of output). As with the mix variance, the most meaningful interpretation applies to the *total yield variance* rather than its individual components.

Notice that Koala's direct material mix variance (\$162 F) and yield variance (\$1,392U) add up to the direct material quantity variance (\$1,230 U). Koala's September direct material variances in the production of Crocodile Chomp are summarized in Exhibit 13.14.

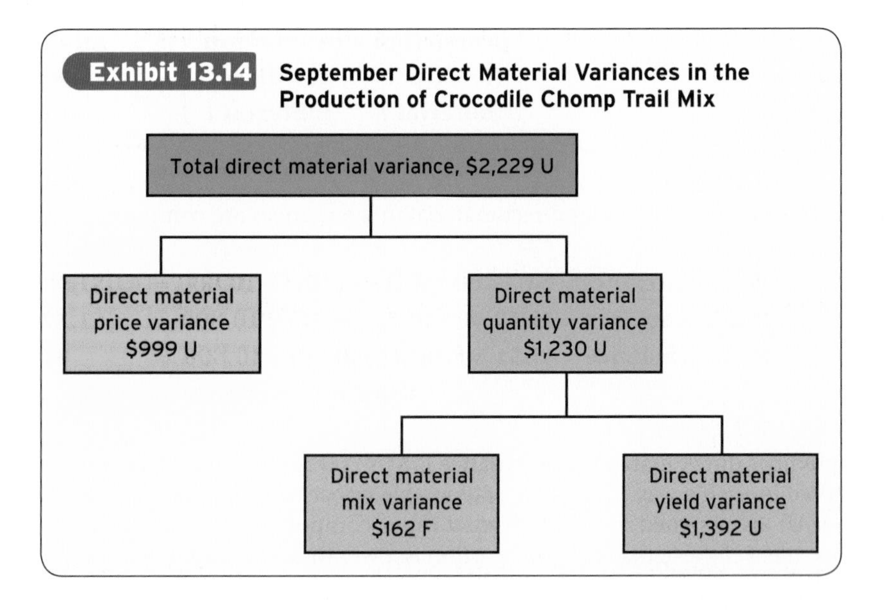

Exhibit 13.14 September Direct Material Variances in the Production of Crocodile Chomp Trail Mix

Multiple direct labour inputs

The same analysis for direct material can be applied to direct labour if a company has multiple types of direct labour input. Suppose, for example, that Koala's direct labour employees in the Crocodile Mix line include inspectors, mixers and packers, each with a different standard pay rate. Moreover, assume that there is a standard or expected input proportion for each type of direct labour. Then we can apply the same analysis to direct labour as we used for direct material. Just substitute the words 'direct labour' for 'direct material' in all of the formulas given in the preceding section. Now the total direct labour variance consists of the direct labour rate and efficiency variances, and the direct labour efficiency variance is decomposed into a **direct labour mix variance** and a **direct labour yield variance**. As with direct materials, this analysis makes sense only if some degree of substitutability exists among the various types of direct labour.

Mix and Yield Variances in Service Organizations

The concepts underlying production mix and yield variances can be applied to service organizations also. Service organizations often make substitutions among different types of labour. **Ernst & Young**, for example, might substitute partner time for staff time on a particular audit job.

Consider an audit firm that has bid a job for 1,000 hours: 300 hours of partner time at a cost of AU$60 per hour and 700 hours of staff time at a cost of AU$20 per hour. Due to scheduling problems, the partner spends 500 hours, and the staff member spends 500 hours. If the actual costs are AU$60 for partner time and AU$20 for staff time, no labour rate variance exists. However, even though the 1,000 hours required were exactly what was bid, the job cost is AU$8,000 over budget, as shown here:

Actual cost = (500 hours × AU$60) + (500 hours × AU$20)
= AU$30,000 + AU$10,000 = AU$40,000
Budgeted cost = (300 hours × AU$60) + (700 hours × AU$20)
= AU$18,000 + AU$14,000 = AU$32,000
Cost overrun = AU$8,000

We can apply the mix and yield variance analysis to help us understand this cost overrun. First, there is no yield variance because the total number of actual hours and total budgeted hours are the same. (Review the formula for the yield variance.) However, there is an unfavourable mix variance of AU$8,000, which is calculated as follows by applying the mix variance formula given earlier in the appendix.

Partner labour mix variance	**= AU$60 × (0.5* − 0.3†) × 1,000 =**	**AU$12,000 U**
Staff labour mix variance	**= AU$20 × (0.5* − 0.7†) × 1,000 =**	**4,000 F**
	Total mix variance =	**AU $8,000 U**

***The actual input proportions were 0.5 for both partner and staff time (500 ÷ 1,000).**

†The budgeted (standard) input proportions were 0.3 for partner time (300 ÷ 1,000) and 0.7 for staff time (700 ÷ 1,000).

Thus, the entire budget overrun of AU$8,000 is due to the unfavourable mix effect of substituting expensive partner time for less expensive staff time. This scenario had no rate (price) or yield effects at all.

Appendix 13B

Sales Variance Analysis

LO 10 Compute and interpret sales variances.

In this chapter, we explored cost variance analysis as a tool for cost management. In this appendix, we turn our attention to assessing a company's overall sales performance. One common method for analysing sales performance is *sales variance analysis*. This approach examines the difference (variance) between actual sales performance and budgeted sales performance by computing a set of variances, with each variance focusing on some underlying aspect of sales performance. Sales variance analysis can be carried out in either of two alternative ways:

1. *Focus on sales revenue.* The first approach to sales variance analysis analyses the difference (variance) between actual and budgeted *sales revenue*.

2. *Focus on contribution margin.* The second approach to sales variance analysis analyses the difference (variance) between actual and budgeted *contribution margin.*

Under this approach we are implicitly assuming that the organization's cost structure can be represented by the traditional (and relatively simple) cost behaviour pattern that includes only variable costs and fixed costs. *Variable costs* are those that vary in proportion to the level of a single, unit-level cost driver. A product's *unit contribution margin,* then, is the product's sales price minus its variable cost (including both variable manufacturing costs and variable selling costs). (See Chapter 2 for further discussion of fixed and variable costs.)

The next section discusses the revenue approach to sales variance analysis in more detail. After computing and interpreting all of the revenue sales variances, we conclude the section with a general discussion of the contribution margin approach to sales variance analysis.

Illustration of Sales Variance Analysis

To illustrate sales variance analysis, let's focus again on Koala Camp Gear Company, the small Australian manufacturer of camping equipment. To keep the illustration relatively simple, we focus on the company's early years when it manufactured only tents. This occurred before Koala added other product lines, such as camp foods and other camping equipment. During these early years, Koala Camp Gear Company manufactured three models of camping tents: the Tree Line (T), the River's Edge (R) and the Valley (V). Data from the year on which our illustration is based appear in Exhibit 13.15. The exhibit presents both budget data and actual data for the year of the analysis. Notice that the budgeted total sales revenue for the year was AU$9,950,000, but the actual total sales revenue achieved was AU$11,110,000. What was behind this difference (variance) of AU$1,160,000 in sales revenue?

Notice also that Koala's budgeted total contribution margin for the year was AU$1,750,000, but the company's actual total contribution margin was AU$2,227,500. This actual total contribution margin result was AU$477,500 higher than expected. How did this come about?

To help Koala's management gain insight into the answers to these questions, we now consider the sales variance analysis for the year summarized in Exhibit 13.15.

Exhibit 13.15 Data for Illustration of Sales Variance Analysis: Koala Camp Gear Company

	A	B	C	D	E	F	G	H
1	**Budget Data**							
2	**Tent model**	**Budgeted price**	**Budgeted unit variable cost**	**Budgeted unit contribution margin**	**Budgeted unit sales volume**	**Budgeted sales proportion***	**Budgeted total sales revenue**	**Budgeted total contribution margin**
3	T	AU$ 180	AU$150	AU$30	30,000	0.60	AU$ 5,400,000	AU$ 900,000
4	R	220	180	40	15,000	0.30	3,300,000	600,000
5	V	250	200	50	5,000	0.10	1,250,000	250,000
6	Total				50,000		AU$ 9,950,000	AU$ 1,750,000
7	Budgeted industry unit sales volume				1,000,000			
8	Budgeted Koala market share				5.0%			
9	**Actual Data**							
10	**Tent model**	**Actual price**	**Actual unit variable cost**	**Actual unit contribution margin**	**Actual unit sales volume**	**Actual sales proportion***	**Actual total sales revenue**	**Actual total contribution margin**
11	T	AU$ 190	AU$ 155	AU$ 35	30,250	0.55	AU$ 5,747,500	AU$ 1,058,750
12	R	215	165	50	22,000	0.40	4,730,000	1,100,000
13	V	230	205	25	2,750	0.05	632,500	68,750
14	Total				55,000		AU$ 11,110,000	AU$ 2,227,500
15	Budgeted industry unit sales volume				1,375,000			
16	Actual Koala market share				4.0%			
17	* Sales proportion = product unit sales ÷ total unit sales							

Focus on revenue

First we present Koala's sales variance analysis from a sales revenue perspective. The analysis to be conducted is summarized in Exhibit 13.16. Notice that the terms *revenue* or *sales price* preface the name of each variance to make it clear that these variances focus on *sales revenue.*

Koala Camp Gear Company

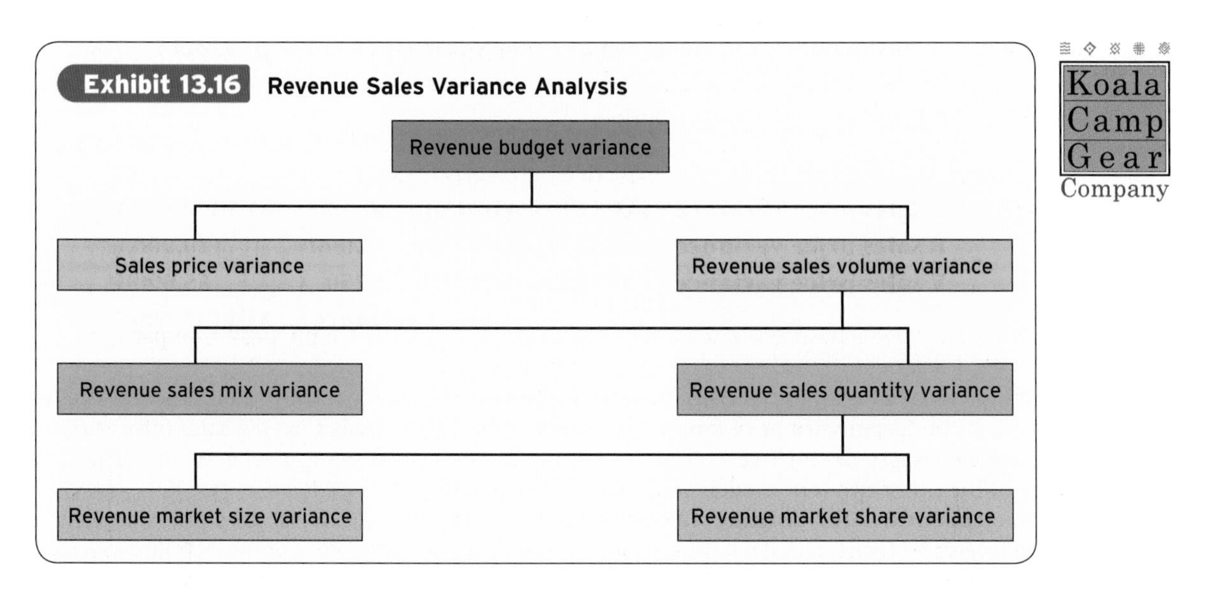

Exhibit 13.16 Revenue Sales Variance Analysis

The **revenue budget variance** is the difference between the actual total sales revenue and the budgeted total sales revenue. It is defined by the following formula. This variance is simply the difference between the actual total sales revenue and the budgeted total sales revenue.

$$\textbf{Revenue budget variance} = \textbf{Sum of revenue budget variances for each product}$$

$$\begin{matrix}\textbf{Revenue}\\ \textbf{budget variance}\\ \textbf{for product } \boldsymbol{i}\end{matrix} = \left(\begin{matrix}\textbf{Actual}\\ \textbf{sales revenue}\\ \textbf{for product } \boldsymbol{i}\end{matrix} - \begin{matrix}\textbf{Budgeted}\\ \textbf{sales revenue}\\ \textbf{for product } \boldsymbol{i}\end{matrix}\right)$$

Applying the formula yields the following results for Koala Camp Gear Company.

T revenue budget variance = **AU\$5,747,500 – AU\$5,400,000**	=	**AU\$347,500 F**
R revenue budget variance = **AU\$4,730,000 – AU\$3,300,00**	=	**AU\$1,430,000 F**
V revenue budget variance = **AU\$632,500 – AU\$1,250,000**	=	**617,500 U**
Revenue budget variance	=	**AU\$1,160,000 F**

An individual component of the revenue budget variance is favourable if the product's actual revenue exceeds its budgeted revenue but is unfavourable if it is less than the budgeted amount. Although Koala's revenue budget variance for Valley model tents is unfavourable, the company's revenue budget variance is favourable overall, AU$1,160,000 F. This result also is apparent from the information given in Exhibit 13.15, since it reveals that Koala's actual total sales revenue of $11,110,000 exceeded budgeted sales revenue of $9,950,000.

What additional insight can management learn about Koala's sales revenue performance? As Exhibit 13.16 shows, the revenue budget variance can be broken down into two variances: the *sales-price variance* and the *revenue sales volume variance.* We next turn our attention to these variances and their interpretations.

The **sales price variance** focuses on the differences between actual and budgeted sales prices while holding constant the sales volume at its actual level. The sales price variance is defined in the following formula.

$$\textbf{Sales price variance} = \textbf{Sum of sales price variances for each product}$$

$$\textbf{Sales price variance for product } i = \left(\textbf{Actual sales price for product } i - \textbf{Budgeted sales price for product } i\right) \times \textbf{Actual sales volme for product } i$$

Using this formula, Koala's sales price variance is computed as follows:

T sales price variance = **(AU\$190 – AU\$180) × 30,250** = **AU\$302,500 F**
R sales price variance = **(AU\$215 – AU\$220) × 22,000** = **110,000 U**
V sales price variance = **(AU\$230 – AU\$250) × 2,750** = **55,000 U**
Sales price variance = **AU\$137,500 F**

Each individual component of the sales price variance is favourable if the product's actual sales price exceeds its budgeted sales price (and unfavourable otherwise). Koala's overall sales price variance is favourable because of the Tree Line tent's higher than expected sales price, even though the sales price of the other two tent models was lower than expected.

The **revenue sales volume variance** holds constant the products' sales prices at their budgeted levels and focuses on deviations between actual and budgeted sales volumes. The revenue sales volume variance is computed as shown in the following formula.

$$\textbf{Revenue sales volume variance} = \textbf{Sum of revenue sales volume variances for each product}$$

$$\textbf{Revenue Sales volume variance for product } i = \left(\textbf{Actual unit sales volume for product } i - \textbf{Budgeted unit sales volume for product } i\right) \times \textbf{Budgeted sales price for product } i$$

Applying the formula yields the following results for Koala Camp Gear Company.

T revenue sales volume variance = (30,250 – 30,000) × AU\$180 = AU\$45,000 F
R revenue sales volume variance = (22,000 – 15,000) × AU\$220 = 1,540,000 F
V revenue sales volume variance = (2,750 – 5,000) × AU\$250 = 562,500 U
Revenue sales volume variance = AU\$1,022,500F

Each individual component of the revenue sales volume variance is favourable if the product's actual sales volume exceeds its budgeted sales volume but unfavourable if it is lower than the budgeted amount. Notice that the higher than expected sales volume for Tree Line tents and River's Edge tents were sufficient to make Koala's overall revenue sales volume variance favourable (AU\$1,022,500 F) even though the Valley model tent experienced disappointing sales volume results.

We can derive more insight into the revenue implications of the sales volume results by breaking down the revenue sales volume variance into two variances: the *revenue sales mix variance* and the *revenue sales quantity variance*, as shown in Exhibit 13.16. Let's now turn our attention to those variances and their interpretation.

The **revenue sales mix variance** focuses on the effects of changes in the sales mix while holding constant the effects of the products' sales prices and the total sales volume. The revenue sales mix variance is computed as shown in the following formula.

$$\text{Revenue sales mix variance} = \text{Sum of revenue sales mix variances for each product}$$

$$\text{Revenue sales mix variance for product } i = \text{Budgeted sales price for product } i \times \left(\text{Actual sales proportion for product } i - \text{Budgeted sales proportion for product } i\right) \times \text{Actual total unit sales volume for all products}$$

Using this formula, Koala's revenue sales mix variance is computed as follows:

T revenue sales mix variance = AU$180 × (0.55 – 0.60) × 55,000 = AU$495,000 U
R revenue sales mix variance = AU$220 × (0.40 – 0.30) × 55,000 = 1,210,000 F
V revenue sales mix variance = AU$250 × (0.05 – 0.10) × 55,000 = 687,500 U
Revenue sales mix variance = AU$27,500 F

Each individual component of the revenue sales mix variance is favourable if the product's actual sales proportion exceeds its budgeted sales proportion but unfavourable if it is lower than the budgeted proportion. Koala's overall favourable revenue sales mix variance (AU$27,500 F) tells us that Koala's actual sales mix differed from its budgeted sales mix in such a way that the effect on overall sales revenue was positive. The higher than expected proportion of sales for the River's Edge tent was sufficiently favourable to overcome the lower proportions of sales for the other two tent models. Note that *it is the overall revenue sales mix variance that conveys a meaningful interpretation for management's analysis, not the individual products' mix variance components.*[37]

The **revenue sales quantity variance** holds constant the sales price and sales mix effects and focuses on the effect of the overall unit sales volume. The revenue sales quantity variance is computed as shown in the following formula.

$$\text{Revenue sales quantity variance} = \text{Sum of revenue sales quantity variances for each product}$$

$$\text{Revenue sales quantity variance for product } i = \text{Budgeted sales price for product } i \times \left(\text{Actual total unit sales volume for all products} - \text{Budgeted total unit sales volume for all products}\right) \times \text{Budgeted sales proportion for product } i$$

The formula yields the following calculation of Koala's revenue sales quantity variance:

T revenue sales quantity variance = AU$180 × (55,000 – 50,000) × 0.60 = AU$540,000 F
R revenue sales quantity variance = AU$220 × (55,000 – 50,000) × 0.30 = 330,000 F
V revenue sales quantity variance = AU$250 × (55,000 – 50,000) × 0.10 = 125,000 F
Revenue sales quantity variance = AU$995,000 F

The revenue sales quantity variance is favourable if actual total sales volume exceeds budgeted total sales volume but is unfavourable if it is lower. Since Koala's actual sales volume, 55,000 units, exceeded the budgeted level of 50,000 units, the company's revenue sales quantity variance is favourable.[38]

Although Koala's actual total sales volume exceeded the budget, did the company maintain its market share? Was the increase in Koala's sales volume due to an industry-wide increase in sales, or did Koala increase its share of a constant or declining market? We can address these questions by decomposing the revenue sales quantity variance into two variances: the *revenue market size variance* and the *revenue market share variance.*

The **revenue market size variance** holds constant the company's market share at its budgeted level and focuses on changes in total industry volume (i.e. market size). The revenue market size variance is computed as shown in the following formula.

$$\textbf{Revenue market size variance} = \textbf{Budgeted weighted-average unit sales price} \times \left(\textbf{Actual total market unit sales volume} - \textbf{Budgeted total market unit sales volume} \right) \times \textbf{Budgeted market share proportion}$$

To apply the formula, we first need to compute Koala's budgeted weighted-average unit sales price. This is equal to the total revenues divided by the total sales volume:

$$\begin{aligned}\textbf{Budgeted weighted-average unit sales price} &= \textbf{AU\$9,950,000} \div \textbf{50,000 units} \\ &= \textbf{AU\$199}\end{aligned}$$

Another way to compute the budgeted weighted-average unit sales price is to weight the three products' budgeted sales prices by their budgeted sales proportions as follows:

$$\textbf{(AU\$180) (0.60) + (AU\$220) (0.30) + (AU\$250) (0.10) = AU\$199}$$

Applying the formula yields the following result for Koala Camp Gear Company.

$$\begin{aligned}\textbf{Revenue market size variance} &= \textbf{AU\$199} \times \textbf{(1,375,000 - 1,000,000)} \times \textbf{0.05} \\ &= \textbf{AU\$3,731,250 F}\end{aligned}$$

Koala's revenue market size variance is favourable simply because the actual total industry sales volume of 1,375,000 units exceeded the expected total industry volume of 1,000,000 units (see Exhibit 13.15). However, did Koala maintain its expected market share in the face of this overall industry expansion?

The **revenue market share variance** holds constant the total industry volume at its actual sales level and focuses on the company's market share. The revenue market share variance is computed as shown in the following formula.

$$\textbf{Revenue market share variance} = \textbf{Budgeted weighted-average unit sales price} \times \left(\textbf{Actual market share proportion} - \textbf{Budgeted market share proportion} \right) \times \textbf{Actual total market unit sales volume}$$

Using this formula, Koala's revenue market share variance is computed as follows:

$$\begin{aligned}\textbf{Revenue market share variance} &= \textbf{AU\$199} \times \textbf{(0.4 - 0.5)} \times \textbf{AU\$1,375,000} \\ &= \textbf{AU\$2,736,250 U}\end{aligned}$$

Although the total industry sales volume was higher than expected, Koala Camp Gear Company's share of the market was lower than expected. Koala garnered only 4 per cent of overall industry volume instead of the anticipated 5 per cent share. This decline in market share is likely to be of considerable concern to Koala's management.

We have completed the revenue sales variance analysis for Koala Camp Gear Company, and our results are summarized in Exhibit 13.17. The exhibit highlights the hierarchical design of the sales

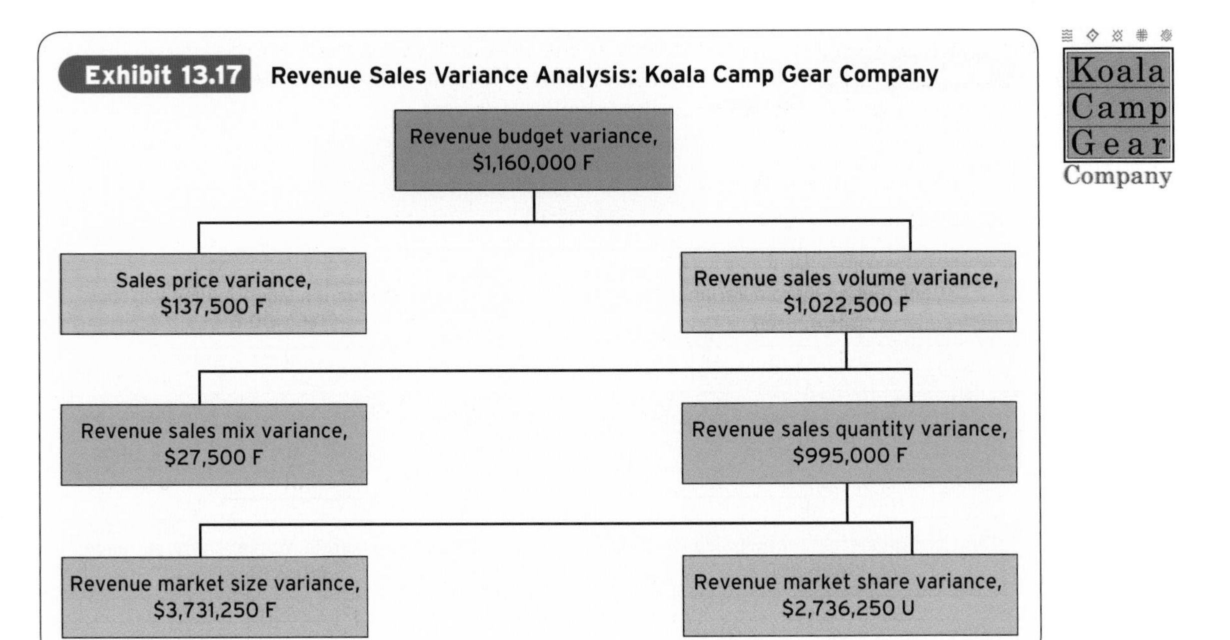

variance analysis for which some variances are decomposed into others to gain additional insight into the phenomena underlying Koala's overall sales revenue performance.

Focus on Contribution Margin

Now we will briefly discuss Koala's sales variance analysis from the contribution margin perspective. The analysis is summarized in Exhibit 13.18 (using the data from Exhibit 13.15, as in the preceding section). Notice that the name of each variance is prefaced by the term *contribution margin* to make clear that the analysis has a contribution margin focus rather than a sales revenue focus. Each variance is analogous to its counterpart in the revenue sales variance analysis. For example, the contribution margin budget variance is calculated in exactly the same way as the revenue budget variance except for the fact that the products' contribution margins are used instead of their sales prices. Moreover, the interpretations of the contribution margin budget variance and the revenue budget variance are analogous. It simply comes down to whether management wants to focus its analysis on sales revenue or contribution margin.

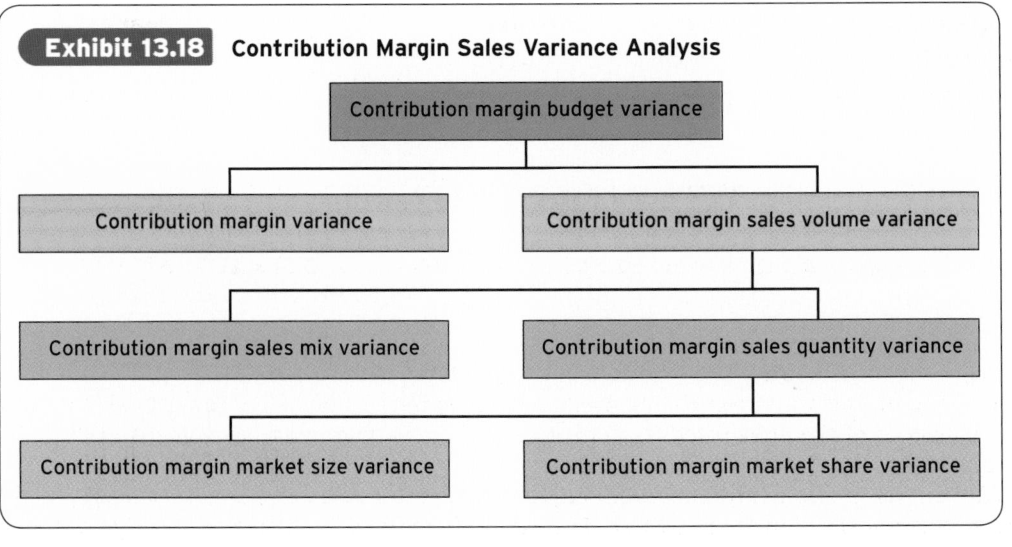

Exhibit 13.19 Contribution Margin Sales Variance Analysis: Koala Camp Gear Company

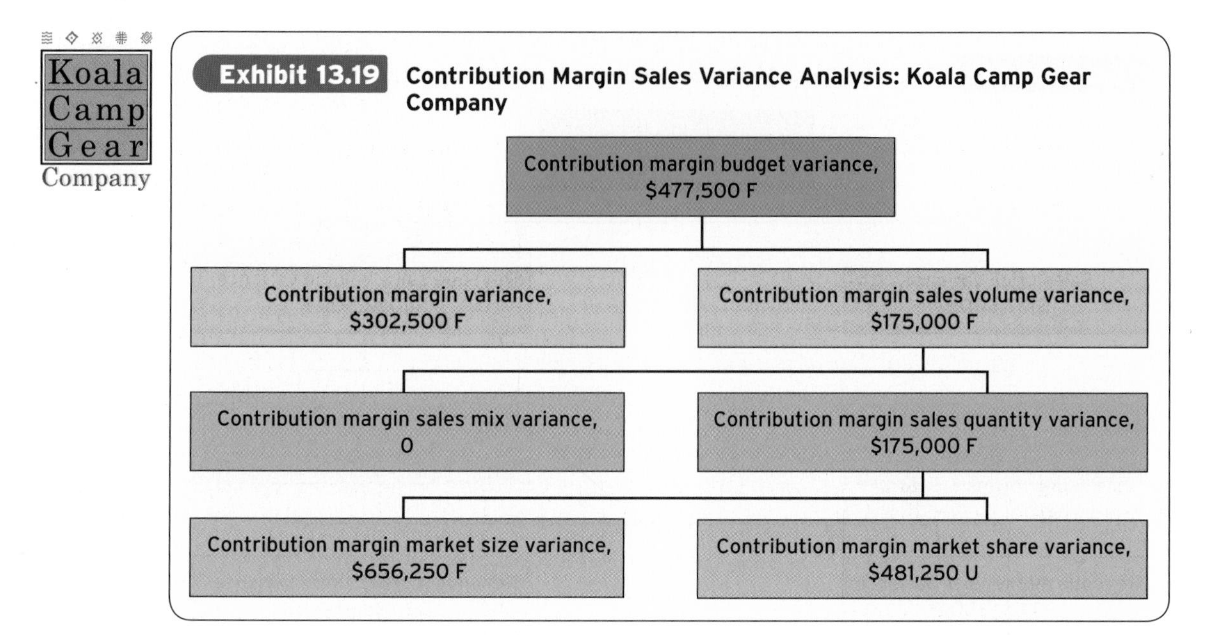

The results of Koala Camp Gear's contribution margin sales variance analysis is shown in Exhibit 13.19. Once again, the exhibit highlights the hierarchical nature of the variance analysis for which certain variances comprise other variances to gain insight into the phenomena underlying a company's sales performance.

Chapter Summary

A standard costing system is a traditional cost management technique with two purposes: cost control and product costing. Accountants work with others in the organization to set standard costs for direct material, direct labour and manufacturing overhead. Budgets are adjusted for the actual production volume (flexible budgeting). For direct costs, this adjustment is straightforward. For overhead costs, this is more complicated, because it is not easy to trace overhead costs to products or services. A conventional flexible overhead budget is based on some activity measure, or cost driver, that varies in a pattern similar to that of variable overhead. Machine hours, process time and direct labour hours are common cost drivers. With an activity-based costing system, the development of an activity-based flexible budget is possible. Such a flexible budget is more accurate than conventional flexible budgets because multiple cost drivers are identified to explain the behaviour of overhead costs.

The cost management analyst uses the standard cost as a benchmark against which to compare actual costs incurred. Managers then use management by exception to determine the causes of significant cost variances. This cost management purpose of the standard costing system is accomplished by computing several different variances:

- Price variances and quantity variances for direct manufacturing costs
- Variable overhead spending variance and efficiency variances
- Fixed overhead budget and volume variances.

Managers determine the significance of cost variances through judgement and rules of thumb. The absolute and relative size of variances, recurrence of variances, variance trends and controllability of variances are all considered in deciding whether variances warrant investigation.

Today's manufacturing environment is changing rapidly due to the influences of worldwide competition, JIT, flexible manufacturing systems and an emphasis on product quality and customer service. As a result, many manufacturers are adapting their standard costing systems to reflect these aspects of the contemporary manufacturing environment. Kaizen costing is the process of cost reduction during the manufacturing phase of a product. *Kaizen* refers to continual and gradual improvement through small betterment activities. Many companies facing global competition find that continual cost reduction is crucial to their survival.

The standard or predetermined overhead rate also is used as the basis for product costing in a standard costing system. Actual costs are entered into Manufacturing overhead and into Work-in-progress inventory. However, these accounts are reduced by the standard direct costs and the standard overhead cost (this equals the standard overhead rate multiplied by the standard amount of the cost driver allowed, or activity base, given actual output). Differences between the actual costs and standard costs show up in these accounts, these are transferred to Owners' equity. Favourable variances increase OE, while Unfavourable variances decrease OE.

Key Terms

For each term's definition, refer to the indicated page, or turn to the glossary at the end of the text.

activity analysis, 627
activity-based flexible budget, 642
budget variance, 630
cost variance, 626
direct labour efficiency variance, 633
direct labour mix variance,* 659
direct labour rate variance, 633
direct labour yield variance,* 659
direct material mix variance,* 659
direct material price variance, 632
direct material quantity variance, 632
direct material yield variance,* 659
favourable, 632
fixed overhead budget variance, 640
fixed overhead volume variance, 654
flexible budget, 630
kaizen costing, 652
management by exception, 626
overhead cost performance report, 641
perfection (or ideal standard), 628

practical (or attainable) standard,	628	standard cost,	626
price variance,	631	standard direct labour quantity,	630
quantity variance,	631	standard direct labour rate,	630
relevant range,	630	standard direct material price,	630
revenue budget variance, **	661	standard direct material quantity,	630
revenue market share variance, **	664	task analysis,	627
revenue market size variance, **	664	unfavourable,	632
revenue sales mix variance, **	662	variable overhead quantity variance,	639
revenue sales quantity variance, **	663	variable overhead spending variance,	638
revenue sales volume variance, **	662	variance analysis,	631
sales price variance, **	661	volume variance,	630

**Terms appear in Appendix 13A.*

***Terms appear in Appendix 13B.*

Review Questions are mostly written at a ***basic*** *level; Critical Analysis questions and Exercises are* ***intermediate****, and Problems and Cases are* ***advanced****.*

Review Questions

13.1 One of the principles espoused by management is that one should manage by exception. How can responsibility reporting systems and/or analysis of variances assist in that process?

13.2 Explain how standard material prices and quantities are set.

13.3 What is the interpretation of the *direct material price variance?* Which manager usually is in the best position to influence the direct material price variance?

13.4 What is the interpretation of the *direct material quantity variance?* Which manager usually is in the best position to influence the direct material quantity variance?

13.5 Describe the factors that managers often consider when determining the significance of a variance.

13.6 What is the interpretation of the *direct labour rate variance?* Which manager generally is in the best position to influence the direct labour rate variance?

13.7 What is the interpretation of the *direct labour efficiency variance?* Which manager generally is in the best position to influence the direct labour efficiency variance?

13.8 Describe how standard costs are used for product costing.

13.9 What is meant by the term *kaizen* costing?

13.10 (Appendix 13A) List four companies that probably use direct material mix and yield variances.

13.11 What is the interpretation of the variable overhead spending variance?

13.12 What is the interpretation of the variable overhead efficiency variance?

13.13 What is the fixed overhead budget variance?

13.14 Distinguish between the control purpose and the product-costing purpose of standard costing and flexible budgeting.

13.15 (Appendix 13B) Into what two variances is a revenue sales volume variance decomposed? What is the purpose of computing these two variances?

Critical Analysis

13.16 Distinguish between *perfection* and *practical* standards. Which type of standard is likely to produce the best motivational effects?

13.17 In a service environment with no inventories, is variance analysis useful? Why or why not?

13.18 Why should management want to divide production cost variances into price and efficiency variances?

13.19 Discuss several ways in which standard costing systems should be adapted in today's advanced manufacturing environment.

13.20 'I don't understand why you accountants want to prepare a budget for a period that is already over. We know the actual results by then – all that flexible budgeting does is increase the controller's staff and add to our overhead.' Comment on this remark.

13.21 Why are flexible overhead budgets based on an activity measure such as machine hours or direct labour hours?

13.22 How does the concept of flexible budgeting reinforce the notion that employees should be held responsible only for what they can control or heavily influence?

13.23 Give one example of a plausible activity base to use in flexible budgeting for each of the following organizations: an insurance company, an express delivery service, a restaurant and a state tax-collection agency.

13.24 Budgets for government units are usually one year in advance of the budget period. Expenditures are limited to the budgeted amount. At the end of the period, performance is evaluated by comparing budget authorizations with actual receipts and outlays. What management control problems are likely to arise from such a system?

13.25 Bodin Company's only variable overhead cost is electricity. Does an unfavourable variable overhead spending variance imply that the company paid more than the anticipated rate per kilowatt hour?

13.26 Does the fixed overhead volume variance represent a difference in the cash outflows for the company when compared to budgeted cash outflows?

13.27 What is the conceptual problem of applying fixed manufacturing overhead as a product cost?

13.28 (Appendix 13B) A company sells three products that must be purchased in a single package. Does computing a sales mix variance provide any benefit under these circumstances?

13.29 (Appendix 13B) How could a CPA firm use a sales mix variance to analyse its revenue?

Exercises

Exercise 13.30 [LO 2] Direct Material Variances: Material Purchased and Material Used are not Equal

Yuriko Company manufactures laboratory glassware in its plant near Kyoto, Japan. The controller recently reported the following information concerning direct material requirements in department 8. (Monetary values given in Japanese yen, ¥.)

Direct material purchased (actual)	¥75,000
Standard direct material cost per unit produced	¥1.31
Standard cost of material purchased	¥62,000
Standard price times actual amount of material used	¥46,000
Actual production	32,000 units

Required

Build a spreadsheet to compute the direct material cost variances for department 8. (See Exhibit 13.5.)

Exercise 13.31 [LO 2] Direct Labour Variances

The standard direct labour cost per unit for Innsbruck Housewares Inc. was €36 (€18 per hour times 2 hours per unit). During the period, actual direct labour costs amounted to €67,800, 3,900 direct labour hours were worked, and 1,900 units were produced.

Required

Build a spreadsheet to compute the direct labour rate and efficiency variances for the period. (See Exhibit 13.5.)

Exercise 13.32 [LO 1, 6] Standard Costs; Ethics

AgriCorp SA, produces items made from local farm products that it distributes to supermarkets and hypermarkets. Because price competition has become increasingly important over the years, Adrienne Prevot, the company's controller, is planning to implement a standard costing system. She asked her cost management analyst, Laurent Moreau, to gather cost information on the production of strawberry jam (AgriCorp's most popular product). Moreau reported that strawberries cost €1.25 per litre, the price he intends to pay to his good friend who has been operating a strawberry farm in the red for the last few years. Due to an oversupply in the market, the prices for strawberries have dropped to €0.95 per litre. Madison is sure that the €1.25 price will be enough to pull his friend's strawberry farm out of the red and into the black.

Required

Is Moreau's behaviour regarding the cost information he provided to Prevot unethical? Explain your answer.

[CMA adapted]

Exercise 13.33 [LO 1] Standards for a New High-tech Product

Several automobile companies have recently developed hybrid vehicles, which run on a combination of gasoline and electricity.

Required

As a group, discuss how companies developing new high-tech products would set standard costs for them. What special challenges might be present in standard setting for the new hybrid automobiles?

Exercise 13.34 [LO 2] Straightforward Computation of Variances

FCB Italia SpA manufactures recyclable soft-drink cans. A unit of production is a case of 12 dozen cans.

Actual material purchases amounted to 240,000 kilograms at €0.80 per kilogram. Actual costs incurred in the production of 50,000 units follow:

Direct labour	€209,990 for 12,650 hours
Direct material	€169,600 for 212,000 kilograms

The following standards have been set by the production-engineering staff and the controller.

Direct material:	Direct labour:
Quantity, 4 kilograms	Quantity, 0.25 hour
Price, €0.79 per kilogram	Rate, €16 per hour

Required

Build a spreadsheet and use the variance formulas to compute the direct material price and quantity variances and the direct labour rate and efficiency variances. Indicate whether each variance is favourable or unfavourable.

Exercise 13.35 [LO 8] Preparation of Journal Entries Under Standard Costing; Posting Journal Entries for Variances

Refer to the data in Exercise 13.34 for FCB Italia SpA.

Required

a. Prepare journal entries to:
  (1) Record the purchase of direct material on account.
  (2) Add direct material and direct labour cost to Work-in-progress inventory.
  (3) Record the direct material and direct labour variances.
  (4) Close these variances to Cost of sales.

b. Set up a spreadsheet, and post the journal entries to the general ledger as in Exhibit 13.12.

Exercise 13.36 [LO 1] Determination of Standard Material Cost

Cleveland Chemical Company manufactures industrial chemicals. The company plans to introduce a new chemical solution and needs to develop a standard product cost. The new chemical solution is made by combining a chemical compound (Lotrel) and a solution (Salex), heating the mixture, adding a second compound (Protet), and bottling the resulting solution in 10-litre containers. The initial mix, which is 11 litres in volume, consists of 10 kilograms of Lotrel and 8.4 litres of Salex. A 1-litre reduction in volume occurs during the boiling process. The solution is cooled slightly before 4 kilograms of Protet is added. The addition of Protet does not affect the total liquid volume.

The purchase price of the direct materials used in the manufacture of this new chemical solution follow:

Lotrel	$1.72 per kilogram
Salex	$1.20 per litre
Protet	$3.00 per kilogram

Required

Determine the standard direct material cost of a 10-litre container of the new product.

[CMA adapted]

Exercise 13.37 [LO 9] Labour Mix and Yield Variances (Appendix 13A)

Fast-food restaurant Kapsalon Patat has two categories of direct labour, unskilled, which costs €8.50 per hour, and skilled, which costs €12 per hour. Management has established standards per 'equivalent meal', which has been defined as a typical meal consisting of a meat item, French fries and a drink. Standards have been set as follows:

Unskilled labour	7.5 minutes per equivalent meal
Skilled labour	3.0 minutes per equivalent meal

During May, Kapsalon Patat sold 38,000 equivalent meals and incurred the following labour costs:

Unskilled labour	4,600 hours	€41,000
Skilled labour	1,800 hours	€20,400

Required

Build a spreadsheet to complete the following requirements:

a. Compute the direct labour rate and efficiency variances.
b. Compute the direct labour mix and yield variances.

Exercise 13.38 [LO 9] Direct Material Mix and Yield Variances (Appendix 13A)

Geneva Gizmos AG has set the following direct material standards for its product, the photon gismo.

Standard costs for one unit of output:
Material I, 10 units of input at CHF 6 per unit
Material II, 20 units of input at CHF 2 per unit

During August, the company had the following results:

Universal gismos produced	2,000 units
Materials purchased and used:	
Material I	22,000 units at CHF 6.25
Material II	38,000 units at CHF 1.80

Required

Build a spreadsheet to complete the following requirements:

a. Compute the direct material price and quantity variances.
b. Compute the direct material mix and yield variances.

Exercise 13.39 [LO 3] Construction of a Flexible Overhead Budget; Hospital

St Bridget's Hospital-Dublin's controller estimates that the hospital uses 30 kilowatt-hours of electricity per patient day, and that the electric rate will be €0.15 per kilowatt-hour. The hospital also pays a fixed monthly charge of €1,450 to the electric utility to rent emergency backup electric generators.

Required

Build a spreadsheet to construct a flexible budget for the hospital's electricity costs using each of the following techniques. (See Exhibit 13.8.)

a. Formula flexible budget.
b. Flexible budget for 30,000, 40,000 and 50,000 patient days of activity. List variable and fixed electricity costs separately.

Exercise 13.40 [LO 1] Sharing Cost-saving Ideas

Anecdotal evidence suggests that workers who devise more efficient work techniques may have an incentive to hide their discoveries from management.

Required

As a group, discuss the preceding phenomenon. Why does it occur? What can be done to mitigate against this behaviour? Is this behaviour ethical?

Exercise 13.41 [LO 3] Straightforward Computation of Overhead Variances

Chongquing Glassware Company has the following standards and flexible budget data. (Monetary values given in Chinese yuan, ¥.)

Standard variable overhead rate	¥36.00 per direct labour hour
Standard quantity of direct labour	2 hours per unit of output
Budgeted fixed overhead	¥600,000
Budgeted output	25,000 units

The company had the following actual results for April:

Actual variable overhead	¥1,965,000
Actual fixed overhead	¥582,000
Actual direct labour	50,000 hours
Actual output	20,000 units

Required

Build a spreadsheet and use the variance formulas to compute the following variances. Indicate whether each variance is favourable or unfavourable where appropriate. (See Exhibit 13.8.)

a. Variable overhead spending variance.
b. Variable overhead efficiency variance.
c. Fixed overhead budget variance.
d. Fixed overhead volume variance.

Exercise 13.42 [LO 3] Variable Overhead Efficiency Variance

You recently received the following note from the production supervisor of the company where you serve as controller. 'I don't understand these crazy variable overhead efficiency variances. My employees are very careful in their use of electricity and manufacturing supplies, and we use very little indirect labour. What are we supposed to do?'

Required

Write a brief memo responding to the production supervisor's concern.

Exercise 13.43 [LO 4, 6] Activity-Based Flexible Budget; Ethics

Refer to Koala Camp Gear's activity-based flexible budget in Exhibit 13.10. Suppose that the company's activity in February is described as follows:

Machine hours	7,500
Production runs	16
Engineering design specs	12
Direct material (sq. metres)	40,000

Required

a. Determine the flexible budgeted cost for each of the following:
  (1) Indirect material (thread)
  (2) Utilities (heat)
  (3) Quality assurance
  (4) Engineering
  (5) Material handling
  (6) Insurance and property taxes

b. Compute the variance for set-up cost during the month assuming that the actual set-up cost was $4,490.
  (1) Using the activity-based flexible budget.
  (2) Using Koala's conventional flexible budget (Exhibit 13.7).

c. Compute the variance for engineering cost during the month assuming the actual engineering cost was $4,540.

   (1) Using the activity-based flexible budget.

   (2) Using Koala's conventional flexible budget (Exhibit 13.7).

d. Comment on the ethical issues in the following scenario: When Koala's director of engineering, John Margrove, was shown a preliminary copy of the February cost variance report, which was based on the activity-based flexible budget, he was dismayed at the unfavourable variance. Refer to your answer to requirement (c).

   The next day, during an afternoon golf outing with his friend Marc Wesley, Koala's controller, Margrove, learned that the reported unfavourable engineering cost variance would have been favourable if the report had been based on the traditional flexible budget instead of the activity-based flexible budget. Margrove was quite annoyed about this, and he began to pressure his friend to use the traditional flexible budget as the basis for the variance report. 'What's the big deal?' pressed Margrove. 'Who's going to know anyway? Just bury that ABC stuff, and use the tried and true method. Nobody will question your methods, and my report will look better'.

   (1) Comment on John Margrove's behaviour.

   (2) How should Marc Wesley respond? What standards of ethical behaviour for management accountants are involved here? (See references to standards provided in Chapter 1.)

Exercise 13.44 [LO 8] Accounting for Variances

Bavaria Leitern manufactures aluminium ladders. Last year, 50,000 units of direct material were acquired for €140,000. The standard price for the material was €2.60 per unit. During last year, 47,000 units of material were used in the production process. Materials are entered into production at the beginning of the process. The standard allowed quantity for the amount of output that was actually produced is 50,000 units. Eighty per cent of the units that used these materials were completed and transferred to Finished goods inventory. Sixty per cent of these units that had been transferred to Finished goods inventory were sold this period. There were no opening inventories.

Required

Prepare journal entries and show the flow of costs through the accounts, as in Exhibit 13.12.

Exercise 13.45 [LO 10] Sales Variances (Appendix 13B)

La Palma Beach Wear manufactures and sells beach T-shirts in the Canary Islands, Spain. The business is very competitive. The budget for last year called for sales of 100,000 units at €12 each. However, as the summer season approached, management realized that the company could not sell 100,000 units at the €12 price but would have to offer price concessions. Budgeted variable cost is €5 per unit. Actual results showed sales of 95,000 units at an average price of €11 each. The actual variable cost was €5 per unit.

Required

Build a spreadsheet and compute the following variances for La Palma Beach Wear: revenue budget variance, sales price variance, and revenue sales volume variance.

Exercise 13.46 [LO 10] Sales Mix and Sales Quantity Variances (Appendix 13B)

Seve Corporation sells two models of golf gloves. The budgeted per-unit price is €10.50 for Recorrido (a basic golf glove) and €25.00 for Gran Premio (a deluxe model). The budget called for sales of 380,000 Recorridos and 150,000 Gran Premios during the current year. Actual results showed sales of 350,000 Recorridos, with a price of €11.00 per unit, and 200,000 Gran Premios, with a price of €26.00 per unit. The standard variable cost is €4 per unit for a Standard and €11 per unit for Ultras.

Required

Compute each of the following variances from a contribution-margin perspective. (*Hint:* Use the formulas given in Appendix 13B but substitute each product's contribution margin for its sales price.) Round monetary amounts to nearest whole number.

a. Sales volume variance.
b. Sales mix and sales quantity variances.

Exercise 13.47 [LO 10] Sales Price, Sales Volume, Market Size and Market Share Variances (Appendix 13B)

Lone Star Condiments Inc. makes bulk artificial seasonings for use in processed foods. A seasoning was budgeted to sell in 21-litre drums at a price of $48 per drum. The company expected to sell 150,000 drums. Budgeted variable costs are $10 per drum. During the year, the company sold 125,000 drums at a price of $47.50.

Required

Lone Star Condiments' cost management staff computes sales variances from a revenue perspective.

a. Compute the sales price and sales volume variances.
b. Assume that the budgeted sales volume was based on an expected 10 per cent share of a total market volume of 1.5 million drums, but the actual results were based on a 12.5 per cent share of a total market of 1 million drums. Compute the market size and market share variances.

Problems

Problem 13.48 [LO 2] Direct Material and Direct Labour Variances

OmniPlay Hong Kong has established the following standards for the prime costs of one unit of its chief product, dartboards.

	Standard quantity	Standard price or rate	Standard cost
Direct material	8.5 kilograms	$14.40 per kilogram	$122.40
Direct labour	0.25 hour	$30.00 per hour	$7.50
Total			$129.90

During May, OmniPlay purchased 160,000 kilograms of direct material at a total cost of $2,380,800. The total wages for May were $168,750, 90 per cent of which were for direct labour. OmniPlay manufactured 19,000 dartboards during May, using 142,500 kilograms of direct material and 5,000 direct labour hours.

Required

Build a spreadsheet and compute the following variances for May, and indicate whether each is favourable or unfavourable.

a. Direct material price variance.
b. Direct material quantity variance.
c. Direct labour rate variance.
d. Direct labour efficiency variance.

[CMA adapted]

Problem 13.49 [LO 2] Direct Material and Direct Labour Variances; Missing Data

Analyse each of the following scenarios independently.

a. Lisbon Company reports the following direct labour information for its primary product for October:

Standard rate	€8.00 per hour
Actual rate paid	€8.25 per hour
Standard hours allowed for actual production	1,400 hours
Direct labour efficiency variance	€650 U

What were the a

b. Information

What was the ac

Problem 13.50 [LO 1, 6] Behavioural Impact of Implementing a Standard Costing System

PrimärPflege AG, a manufacturer of custom-designed home health care equipment, has been in business for 15 years. Last year, to better control the costs of its products, the controller implemented a standard costing system. Reports for tracking performance are issued monthly, and any unfavourable variances are investigated further.

The production manager complained that the standards are unrealistic, stifle motivation by concentrating only on unfavourable variances, and are out of date too quickly. He noted that his recent switch to titanium for the wheelchairs has resulted in higher material costs but decreased labour hours. The net result was no increase in the total cost to produce the wheelchair. The monthly reports continue to show an unfavourable material variance and a favourable labour variance despite indications that the workers are slowing down.

Required

a. Describe several ways that a standard costing system strengthens management cost control.
b. Give at least two reasons to explain why a standard costing system could negatively impact the motivation of production employees.

[CMA adapted]

Problem 13.51 [LO 1, 6, 7] Development of Standard Costs; Causes of Variances; Ethics

Gusto d'Italia is a small producer of fruit-flavoured frozen desserts. For many years, its products have had strong regional sales on the basis of brand recognition. However, other companies have begun marketing similar products in the area, and price competition has become increasingly important. Gianni Costa, the company's controller, is planning to implement a standard costing system and has gathered considerable information on production and materials requirements for Gusto d'Italia's products. He believes that the use of standard costing will allow the company to make better pricing decisions.

Gusto d'Italia's most popular product is raspberry gelato. The gelato is produced in 35-litre batches, and each batch requires 12 litres of good raspberries. The fresh raspberries are sorted by hand before entering the production process. Because of imperfections in the raspberries and normal spoilage, one litre of berries is discarded for every four litres accepted. The standard direct labour time for the sorting required to obtain one litre of acceptable raspberries is 0.75 minutes. The acceptable raspberries are then blended with the other ingredients; blending requires 10 minutes of direct labour time per batch. After blending, the gelato is packaged in 250 ml containers. Costa has gathered the following information from Anna Puglisi, Gusto d'Italia's cost accountant.

- Gusto d'Italia purchases raspberries at a cost of €1.20 per litre. All other ingredients cost a total of €0.20 per litre.
- Direct labour is paid at the rate of €9 per hour.
- The total cost of material and labour required to package the sherbet is €0.41 per litre.

Puglisi has a friend who owns a berry farm that has been losing money in recent years. Because of good crops, an oversupply of raspberries has been available, and prices have dropped to €0.80 per litre. Puglisi has arranged for Gusto d'Italia to purchase raspberries from her friend and hopes that €1.20 per litre will help her friend's farm become profitable again.

Required

a. Develop the standard cost of direct material, direct labour, and packaging for a 35-litre batch of raspberry sherbet. Build a spreadsheet to complete this requirement.

b. As part of the implementation of a standard costing system, Costa plans to train those responsible for maintaining the standards in the use of variance analysis. He is particularly concerned with the causes of unfavourable variances. As his assistant, prepare a page for a company training document that discusses the following:

(1) The possible causes of unfavourable material price variances and the individual(s) who should be held responsible for these variances.

(2) The possible causes of unfavourable labour efficiency variances and the individual(s) who should be held responsible for these variances.

c. Citing the specific ethical standards for management accountants, explain why Puglisi's behaviour regarding the cost information provided to Costa is unethical. (See Chapter 1 for references to examples of ethical standards.)

[CMA adapted]

Problem 13.52 [LO 2, 8] Variances; Journal Entries; Missing Data

Mendocino Surf Designs manufactures fibreglass surfboards in Fort Bragg, California. The standard cost for material and labour is $106.90 per board. This includes 8 kilograms of direct material at a standard cost of $6.50 per kilogram and 4.5 hours of direct labour at $12.20 per hour. The following data pertain to November: (Monetary units given in dollars, $.)

- Purchases of material: 50,000 kilograms for $310,000.
- Total actual labour costs: $381,150.
- Actual hours of labour: 31,500 hours.
- Direct material quantity variance: $1,300 unfavourable.
- Work-in-progress inventory on 1 November: none.
- Work-in-progress inventory on 30 November: 1,000 units (75 per cent complete as to labour; material is issued at the beginning of processing).
- Units completed: 6,150 units.

Required

a. Compute the following amounts. Indicate whether each variance is favourable or unfavourable.

(1) Direct labour rate variance for November.
(2) Direct labour efficiency variance for November.
(3) Actual kilograms of material used in the production process during November.
(4) Actual price paid per kilogram of direct material in November.
(5) Total amounts of direct material and direct labour cost transferred to Finished goods inventory during November.
(6) Total amount of direct material and direct labour cost in the balance of Work-in-progress inventory at the end of November.

b. Prepare journal entries (as in Exhibit 13.12) to record the following:

- Purchasing raw material.
- Adding direct material to Work-in-progress inventory.
- Adding direct labour to Work-in-progress inventory.
- Recording variances.

[CMA adapted]

Problem 13.53 [LO 5] Cost Variance Investigation

British Isles Agribusiness Ltd (BIA) manufactures agricultural machinery in Manchester, England. At a recent staff meeting, the controller presented the following direct labour variance report for the year just ended.

BRITISH ISLES AGRIBUSINESS LTD
Direct Labour Variance Report
(all variances in British pounds sterling)

	Direct labour rate variance		Direct labour efficiency variance	
	Amount	**Standard cost, %**	**Amount**	**Standard cost, %**
January	£800 F	0.16%	£4,900 U	0.98%
February	4,900 F	0.98	6,950 U	1.39
March	100 U	0.02	10,100 U	2.02
April	2,000 U	0.40	13,200 U	2.64
May	3,800 F	0.76	20,100 U	4.02
June	3,900 F	0.78	17,000 U	3.40
July	4,200 F	0.84	28,500 U	5.70
August	5,100 F	1.02	38,000 U	7.60
September	4,800 F	0.96	37,000 U	7.40
October	5,700 F	1.14	42,000 U	8.40
November	4,200 F	0.84	60,000 U	12.00
December	4,300 F	0.86	52,000 U	10.40

BIA's controller uses the following rule of thumb: Investigate all variances equal to or greater than £30,000, which is 6 per cent of standard cost.

Required

a. Which variances would have been investigated during the year? (Indicate month and type of variance.)
b. What characteristics of the variance pattern shown in the report should draw the controller's attention regardless of the usual investigation rule? Explain. Given these considerations, which variances would you have investigated? Why?
c. Is it important to follow up on favourable variances, such as those shown in the report? Why?
d. The controller believes that the firm's direct labour rate variance has a normal probability distribution with a mean of zero and a standard deviation of £5,000. Prepare a statistical control chart and plot the company's direct labour rate variances for each month. The critical value is 1 standard deviation. Which variances would have been investigated under this approach?

Problem 13.54 [LO 7] Kaizen Costing Chart

Brisbane Video Corporation manufactures TV sets in Australia, largely for the domestic market. The company recently implemented a kaizen costing programme with the goal of reducing the manufacturing cost per television set by 10 per cent during 20x7, the first year of the kaizen effort. The cost per TV set at the end of 20x6 was $500. The following table shows the average cost per television set estimated during each month of 20x7.

Month	Cost per set	Month	Cost per set
January	$500	July	$485
February	500	August	470
March	495	September	460
April	492	October	460
May	490	November	450
June	485	December	440

Required

Prepare a kaizen costing chart for 20x7 to show the results of Brisbane Video Corporation's first year of kaizen costing. In developing the chart, use the following steps:

a. Draw and label the axes of the kaizen costing chart.
b. Indicate the current year cost base and the kaizen goal (cost-reduction rate) on the chart.

c. Label the horizontal axis with the months of 20x7. Label the vertical axis with dollar amounts in the appropriate range.
d. Plot the 12 monthly estimates of the average cost per TV set. Then draw a line connecting the cost points that were plotted.
e. Complete the chart with any other labels necessary.
f. Briefly explain the purpose of kaizen costing. How could a continuous quality-improvement programme, coupled with the kaizen costing effort implemented by Brisbane Video Corporation, help the firm begin competing in the worldwide market?

Problem 13.55 [LO 9] Direct Labour Mix and Yield Variances (Appendix 13A)

Zaupne Slovenia Insurance Company compares actual results with standard costs. The standard direct labour rates are established each year when the annual plan is formulated and held constant for the entire year. The standard direct labour rates in effect for the current fiscal year and the standard hours allowed for the actual output of insurance claims for April in the claims department are shown in the following schedule:

	Standard direct labour rate per hour	Standard direct labour hours allowed for actual output
Labour class III	€10.00	500
Labour class II	8.75	500
Labour class I	6.25	500

The wage rates for each labour class increased under the terms of a new contract. The standard wage rates were not revised to reflect the new contract.

The actual direct labour hours worked and the actual direct labour rates per hour experienced for the month of April were as follows:

	Actual direct labour rate per hour	Actual direct labour hours
Labour class III	€10.25	550
Labour class II	8.85	650
Labour class I	6.40	375

Required

a. Build a spreadsheet and calculate the dollar amount of the total direct labour variance for April for Zaupne Slovenia Insurance Company, and break the total variance into the following components:
(1) Direct labour rate and efficiency variances.
(2) Direct labour mix and yield variances.
b. Prepare a variance chart similar to the one in Exhibit 13.14.

[CMA adapted]

Problem 13.56 [LO 2, 3] Manufacturing Variances for Variable Costs; Review of Chapter 13

Thatcher and Blair Ltd manufactures a special type of brass fitting in its plant in London, England. The company prepares its budgets on the basis of standard costs. A monthly responsibility report shows the differences between budgeted and actual costs. Variances are analysed and reported separately. Material price variances are computed at the time of purchase.

The following information relates to the current period.

Standard costs (per unit of output)	
Direct material, 1 kilogram @ £1 per kilogram	£1
Direct labour, 2 hours @ £4 per hour	8
Variable manufacturing overhead (25% of direct labour cost)	2
Total standard cost per unit	£11

Actual costs for the month follow:

Material purchased	3,000 kilograms at £0.95 per kilogram
Output	1,900 units using 2,100 kilograms of material
Actual direct labour cost	3,200 hours at £4.50 per hour
Actual variable overhead	£5,100

Required

Prepare a cost variance analysis for the variable costs (i.e., direct material, direct labour, and variable overhead).

Problem 13.57 [LO 3] Overhead Variances

Vera Forma Metal Stamping, SPA, shows the following overhead information for the current period:

Standard variable overhead rate per direct labour hour	€5
Standard direct labour hours allowed for actual production	3,000 hours
Actual direct labour hours used	2,600 hours
Actual overhead incurred	€20,000, of which €12,500 is variable
Budgeted fixed overhead	€5,000

Required

a. Compute the variable overhead spending and efficiency variances and the fixed overhead budget variance.

b. Interpret each variance.

Problem 13.58 [LO 3] Standard Hours Allowed Flexible Budget; Multiple Products; Insurance Company

Four Corners Insurance Company insures clients in Colorado, New Mexico, Arizona and Utah. The company uses a flexible overhead budget for its application processing department. The firm offers five types of policies. The following number of standard hours are allowed for clerical processing.

Automobile	1.0 hour
Renter's	0.5 hours
Homeowner's	1.5 hours
Health	1.5 hours
Life	4.5 hours

The company processed the following number of insurance applications during July:

Automobile	300
Renter's	220
Homeowner's	130
Health	380
Life	220

Four Corners' controller estimates that the variable overhead rate in the application processing department is $5 per hour and that fixed overhead costs will amount to $2,500 per month.

Required

a. How many standard clerical hours are allowed in July given actual application activity?

b. Why is it not sensible to base the company's flexible budget on the number of applications processed instead of the number of clerical hours allowed?

c. Construct a formula flexible overhead budget for the company.

d. What is the flexible budget for total overhead cost in July?

Problem 13.59 [LO 2, 3] Variance Computations with Missing Data; Review of Chapter 13

The following information is provided to assist you in evaluating the performance of the production operations of Odysseia AE:

Actual costs:	
Direct material purchased and used	€171,600 (104,000 kilograms)
Direct labour	€150,000 (10,600 hours)
Manufacturing overhead	€205,000 (61% is variable)
Standard costs per unit:	
Direct material	€1.65 × 5 kilograms per unit of output
Direct labour	€14 per hour × 1/2 hour per unit
Variable overhead	€11.9 per direct labour hour
Production budget:	
Direct material	€165,000
Direct labour	€140,000
Manufacturing overhead	€199,000

Variable overhead is applied on the basis of direct labour hours. The company's actual production was 21,000 units.

Required

As a group, build a spreadsheet and prepare a complete cost variance report suitable for presentation to the class. Include the following in your report:

- Direct materials price and quantity variances.
- Direct labour rate and efficiency variances.
- Variable overhead spending and efficiency variances.
- Fixed overhead budget and volume variances.

Problem 13.60 [LO 3] Flexible Budget; Performance Report

EduSoft SA distributes educational software packages used in the public schools nationwide. Thomas Maes, president of EduSoft, was looking forward to seeing the performance reports for September because he knew the company's sales for the month had exceeded budget by a considerable margin. The company had been growing steadily for approximately two years. Maes' biggest challenge at this point was to ensure that the company did not lose control of expenses during this growth period. When Maes received the September reports, he was dismayed to see the large unfavourable variance in the company's Monthly Selling Expense Report that follows.

EDUSOFT SA.
Monthly Selling Expense Report
For the Month of September

	Annual budget	September budget	September actual	September variance
Unit sales	2,000,000	280,000	305,000	25,000
Euro sales	€80,000,000	€11,200,000	€12,400,000	€1,200,000
Orders processed	54,000	6,500	5,800	(700)
Sales personnel per month	90	90	96	6
Advertising	€19,800,000	€1,650,000	€1,645,000	(€5,000) F
Staff salaries	1,560,000	130,000	130,000	-
Sales salaries	1,296,000	108,000	117,000	9,000 U
Commissions	3,200,000	560,000	620,000	60,000 U
Per-diem expense	1,782,000	148,500	168,960	20,460 U
Office expenses	4,080,000	340,000	362,300	22,300 U
Shipping expenses	6,750,000	902,500	970,200	67,700 U
Total expenses	€38,468,000	€3,839,000	€4,013,460	€174,460 U

Maes called in the company's new controller, Julie Willems, to discuss the implications of the variances reported for September and to plan a strategy for improving performance. Willems suggested that the company's reporting format might not be giving Maes a true picture of the company's operations. She proposed that EduSoft implement flexible budgeting. Maes offered to redo the Monthly Selling Expense Report for September using flexible budgeting so that Maes could compare the two reports and see the advantages of flexible budgeting.

Willems discovered the following information about the behaviour of EduSoft's selling expenses:

- The total compensation paid to the sales force consists of a monthly base salary and a commission, which varies with sales euros.
- Sales office expense is a semi-variable cost with the variable portion related to the number of orders processed. The fixed portion of office expense is €3,000,000 annually and is incurred uniformly throughout the year.
- Subsequent to the adoption of the annual budget for the current year, EduSoft decided to open a new sales territory. As a consequence, the company hired six additional salespeople effective 1 September. Willems decided that these additional six people should be recognized in her revised report.
- Per-diem reimbursement to the sales force, while a fixed amount per day, is variable with the number of sales personnel and the number of days spent travelling. EduSoft's original budget was based on an average sales force of 90 people throughout the year with each salesperson travelling 15 days per month.
- The company's shipping expense is a semi-variable cost with the variable portion, €3 per unit, dependent on the number of units sold. The fixed portion is incurred uniformly throughout the year.

Required

a. As Willems' assistant, draft a memo for her to send to Maes citing the benefits of flexible budgeting. Explain why EduSoft should use flexible budgeting in this situation.

b. Build a spreadsheet and prepare a revised Monthly Selling Expense Report for September that would permit Maes to more clearly evaluate EduSoft's control over selling expenses. The report should have a line for each selling expense item showing the appropriate budgeted amount, the actual selling expense and the monthly euro variance.

[CMA adapted]

Problem 13.61 [LO 3] Overhead Variances

Meritxell Company developed its overhead application rate from the annual budget, which is based on an expected total output of 720,000 units requiring 3,600,000 machine hours. The company is able to schedule production uniformly throughout the year.

A total of 66,000 units requiring 315,000 machine hours were produced during May. Actual overhead costs for May amounted to €375,000. The actual costs, as compared to the annual budget and to one-twelfth of the annual budget, are as follows:

MERITXELL COMPANY
Annual Budget

	Total amount	Per unit	Per machine hour	Monthly budget	Actual costs for May
Variable overhead:					
Indirect material	€1,224,000	€1.70	€0.34	€102,000	€109,800
Indirect labour	900,000	1.25	0.25	75,000	76,200
Fixed overhead:					
Supervision	648,000	0.90	0.18	54,000	50,100
Utilities	540,000	0.75	0.15	45,000	54,400
Depreciation	1,008,000	1.40	0.28	84,000	84,500
Total	€4,320,000	€6.00	€1.20	€360,000	€375,000

Required

a. Prepare a schedule showing the following amounts for Meritxell Company for May.

(1) Applied overhead costs.
(2) Variable overhead spending variance.
(3) Fixed overhead budget variance.
(4) Variable overhead efficiency variance.
(5) Fixed overhead volume variance.

Where appropriate, be sure to indicate whether each variance is favourable or unfavourable.

b. Draw a graph similar to Exhibit 13.4 to depict the variable overhead variances.

c. Why does your graph differ from Exhibit 13.1 other than the fact that the numbers differ?

[CMA adapted]

Problem 13.62 [LO 10] Sales Price, Sales Volume, Sales Mix and Sales Quantity Variances (Appendix 13B)

Scrooge & Marley is a law firm with partners and staff members. Each billable hour of partner time has a £165 budgeted price and £78 budgeted variable cost. Each billable hour of staff time has a budgeted price of £39 and budgeted variable cost of £21. This month, the partnership budget called for 8,500 billable partner hours and 34,650 staff hours. Actual results follow:

	Revenue	Billable hours	Variable cost
Partner	£1,347,000	8,000 hours	£597,000
Staff	1,281,000	34,000 hours	720,000

Required

Build a spreadsheet and compute the following variances from a revenue perspective:

a. Sales price and sales volume variances.

b. Sales mix and sales quantity variances.

Problem 13.63 [LO 10] Revenue Sales Variance Analysis Using Industry Data and Multiple Product Lines (Appendix 13B)

Dupuis Carpet Company makes three grades of indoor-outdoor carpets. Sales volume for the annual budget is determined by estimating the total market volume for indoor-outdoor carpet and then applying the company's prior year market share, adjusted for planned changes due to company programmes for the coming year. Volume is apportioned for the three grades based on the prior year's product mix, again adjusted for planned changes due to company programmes for the coming year.

The following are the actual and the budgeted results of operations for March (dollar amounts in thousands).

Actual	Grade 1	Grade 2	Grade 3	Total
Sales, units	800 rolls	1,000 rolls	2,100 rolls	3,900 rolls
Sales, dollars	$900	$1,995	$3,004	$5,899
Variable costs	650	1,605	2,324	4,579
Contribution margin	$250	$390	$680	$1,320
Manufacturing fixed cost	210	220	315	745
Product margin	$40	$170	$365	$575
Marketing and administrative costs (all fixed)				275
Operating profit				$300
Budget				
Sales, units	1,000 rolls	1,000 rolls	2,000 rolls	4,000 rolls
Sales, dollars	$1,000	$2,000	$3,000	$6,000

Variable costs	700	1,600	2,300	4,600
Contribution margin	$300	$400	$700	$1,400
Manufacturing fixed cost	200	200	300	700
Product margin	$100	$200	$400	$700
Marketing and administrative costs (all fixed)				250
Operating profit				$450

Industry volume was estimated at 40,000 rolls for budgeting purposes. Actual industry volume for March was 38,000 rolls.

Required

From a revenue perspective:

a. Prepare an analysis to disaggregate the revenue budget variance into the sales price and sales volume variances.
b. Break down the sales volume variance into the parts caused by sales mix and sales quantity.
c. Break down the sales quantity variance into its market size and market share components.
d. Write a memo to the company president that summarizes and comments on the sales variance analysis.
e. Prepare a sales variance chart similar to Exhibit 13.17 to summarize the sales variance analysis for Dupuis Carpet Company.

[CMA adapted]

Problem 13.64 [LO 2, 3] Use of a Flexible Budget; Review of Chapter 13

München-Werkzeugmaschine AG has an automated production process, and production activity is quantified in terms of machine hours. It uses a standard costing system. The annual static budget for 20x6 called for 6,000 units to be produced, requiring 30,000 machine hours. The standard overhead rate for the year was computed using this planned level of production. The 20x6 manufacturing cost report follows.

MÜNCHEN-WERKZEUGMASCHINE AG
Manufacturing Cost Report
For the Year 20x6
(in thousands of dollars)

	Static budget	Flexible budget		
	30,000	31,000	32,000	
Cost item	Machine hours	Machine hours	Machine hours	Actual cost
Direct material:				
T79 aluminum	$252.0	$260.4	$268.8	$273.4
B81 steel alloy	78.0	80.6	83.2	80.0
Direct labour:				
Assembler	273.0	282.1	291.2	287.0
Grinder	234.0	241.8	249.6	250.0
Manufacturing overhead:				
Maintenance	24.0	24.8	25.6	30.0
Supplies	129.0	133.3	137.6	125.0
Supervision	80.0	82.0	84.0	78.0
Inspection	144.0	147.0	150.0	150.0
Insurance	50.0	50.0	50.0	50.0
Depreciation	200.0	200.0	200.0	200.0
Total cost	$1,464.0	$1,502.0	$1,540.0	$1,523.4

München-Werkzeugmaschine develops flexible budgets for different levels of activity for use in evaluating performance. It produced a total of 6,200 units during 20x6, requiring 32,000 machine hours. The preceding manufacturing cost report compares the company's actual cost for the year with the static budget and the flexible budget for two different activity levels.

Required

Compute the following amounts. For variances, indicate favourable or unfavourable where appropriate. Answers should be rounded to two decimal places when necessary.

a. The standard number of machine hours allowed to produce one unit of product.
b. The actual cost of direct material used in one unit of product.
c. The cost of material that should be processed per machine hour.
d. The standard direct labour cost for each unit produced.
e. The variable overhead rate per machine hour in a flexible budget formula. (*Hint:* Use the high-low method to estimate cost behaviour. In the high-low method of cost estimation, the difference between the cost levels at the high and low *activity* levels is divided by the difference between the high and low *activity* levels. This quotient provides a simple estimate of the *variable* cost rate per unit of activity.)
f. The standard fixed overhead rate per machine hour used for product costing.
g. The variable overhead spending variance. (Assume that management has determined that the actual fixed overhead cost in 20x6 amounted to $330,000.)
h. The variable overhead efficiency variance.
i. The fixed overhead budget variance.
j. The fixed overhead volume variance. [Make the same assumption as in requirement (g).]
k. The total budgeted manufacturing cost (in thousands of dollars) for an output of 6,050 units. (*Hint:* Use the flexible budget formula.)

[CMA adapted]

Problem 13.65 [LO 10] Comprehensive Sales Variance Analysis; Revenue Perspective and Contribution Margin Perspective (Appendix 13B)

The Bangalore plant of Hindustan Electronics Ltd (HE) manufactures three styles of clock radio. The basic model (B) targets the teenage market. The standard model (S) is popular with college students. HE's newest product, the deluxe model (D), is designed for home and office use.

For the most recent year, HE's sales manager predicted a total annual industry volume for clock radios of 200,000 units, and the following budget data were compiled by the controller for HE's three products (Monetary units given in Indian rupees, INR).

Model	Budgeted price	Budgeted unit variable cost	Budgeted unit sales volume
Basic	INR 1,350	INR 900	4,000
Standard	2,250	1,350	5,000
Deluxe	4,050	2,250	1,000

When actual results for the year were recorded, the actual industry volume for clock radios was much higher than anticipated, 250,000 units. HE's actual results for the year follow:

Model	Actual price	Actual unit variable cost	Actual unit sales volume
Basic	INR 1,305	INR 630	6,000
Standard	2,295	1,170	5,400
Deluxe	3,960	2,385	600

To help top management understand the year's sales results, HE's controller has asked you, his assistant, to prepare a complete sales variable analysis.

Required

a. Summarize the preceding information for Hindustan Electronics by preparing a table similar to that in Exhibit 13.15.
b. Prepare a complete sales variance analysis from a revenue perspective.
c. Prepare a complete sales variance analysis from a contribution margin perspective.

Cases

Case 13.66 [LO 2, 8] Direct Material and Direct Labour Variances; Job order Costing; Journal Entries

Métro Classique manufactures inexpensive men's dress shirts, which are produced in lots to fill each special order. Its customers are department stores in various cities. Métro Classique sews the particular store's labels on the shirts.

The following information is available:

1. The firm purchased 95,000 m³ of material during June at a cost of €109,250.
2. Direct labour during June amounted to €163,900. According to payroll records, production employees were paid €14.90 per hour.
3. There was no work in progress on 1 June. During June, lots A43 and A44 were completed. All material was issued for lot A45, which was 80 per cent completed as to labour.
4. The standard costs for a box of six shirts are as follows:

Direct material	24 m³ at €1.10	€26.40
Direct labour	3 hours at €14.70	44.10
Manufacturing overhead	3 hours at €12.00	36.00
Standard cost per box		$106.50

5. During June, the company worked on three orders for which the month's job-cost records disclose the following data.

Lot number	Boxes in lot	Material used (m³)	Hours worked
A43	1,000	24,100	2,980
A44	1,700	40,440	5,130
A45	1,200	28,825	2,890

Required

a. Prepare a schedule computing the standard cost of lots A43, A44 and A45 for June.
b. For each lot produced during June, prepare a schedule showing the following:
  (1) Direct material price variance.
  (2) Direct material quantity variance.
  (3) Direct labour efficiency variance.
  (4) Direct labour rate variance.
  Indicate whether each variance is favourable or unfavourable.
c. Prepare journal entries to record each of the following events:
  - Purchase of material.
  - Incurrence of direct labour cost.
  - Addition of direct material and direct labour cost to Work-in-progress inventory.
  - Recording of direct material and direct labour variances.

[CPA adapted]

Case 13.67 [LO 2] Comprehensive Problem on Variance Analysis

Madeiros Guitar Company manufactures top-end acoustic guitars in Espinho, Portugal. The company uses a standard, job-order cost accounting system in two production departments. Highly skilled artisans build the wooden guitars in the construction department and coat them with several layers of lacquer. Then the units are transferred to the finishing department, where the bridge of the guitar is attached and the strings are installed. The guitars are also tuned and inspected in the finishing department. The following diagram depicts the production process:

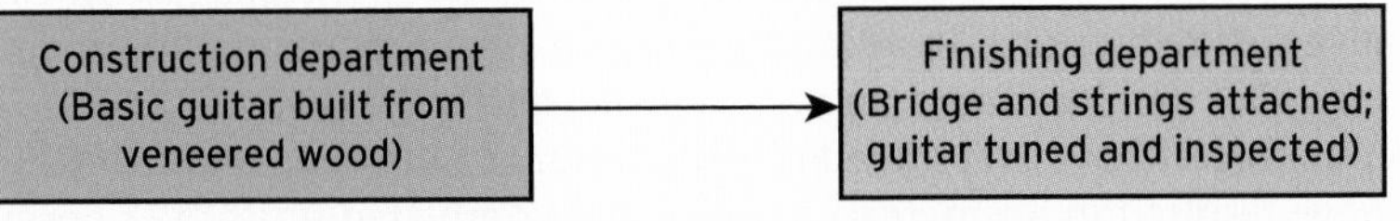

Each finished guitar contains three kilograms of veneered wood. In addition, one-half kilogram of wood is typically wasted in the production process. The veneered wood used in the guitars has a standard price of €25 per kilogram. The other parts needed to complete each guitar, such as the bridge and strings, cost €46 per guitar. The labour standards for Madeiros' two production departments follow: Construction department: 8 hours of direct labour at €30 per hour; Finishing department: 4 hours of direct labour at €20 per hour.

The following additional information pertains to the month of July:

1. Neither production department had any opening or closing Work-in-progress inventories.
2. The company had no opening Finished goods inventory.
3. The company actually produced 200 guitars and sold 100 guitars on account for €1,450 each.
4. The company purchased 1,200 kilograms of veneered wood at a price of €26 per kilogram.
5. Actual usage of veneered wood was 800 kilograms.
6. Enough parts (bridges and strings) to finish 250 guitars were purchased at a cost of €11,500.
7. The construction department used 1,550 direct labour hours. The total direct labour cost in the construction department was €44,950.
8. The finishing department used 850 direct labour hours. The total direct labour cost in that department was €18,700.
9. The finishing department had no direct material variances.

Required

a. Prepare a schedule that computes the standard costs of direct material and direct labour in each production department.
b. Prepare an exhibit that computes the July direct material and direct labour variances in the construction department and the July direct labour variances in the finishing department. (Refer to Exhibit 13.5 for guidance.)

Case 13.68 [LO 8] Journal Entries Under Standard Costing; Continuation of Case

Refer to the preceding case.

Required

Prepare journal entries to record all events listed for Madeiros Guitar Company during July. Specifically, the journal entries should reflect the following events.

1. Purchase of direct material.
2. Use of direct material.
3. Incurrence of direct labour costs.
4. Addition of production costs to the Work-in-progress inventory account for each department.
5. Incurrence of all variances.
6. Completion of 200 guitars.
7. Sale of 100 guitars.
8. Closing all variance accounts to Cost of sales.

Assume that the opening balance in all accounts is zero.

Case 13.69 [LO 2, 3, 6, 10] Comprehensive Review of Variances; Behavioural Effects (Appendix 13B)

This case integrates material from Chapters 9 and 13.

DDN Playmore Corporation manufactures video game machines. Market saturation and technological innovations have caused pricing pressures that have resulted in declining profits. To stem the slide in profits until new products can be introduced, top management has turned its attention to both manufacturing economies and increased production. To realize these objectives, an incentive programme has been developed to reward production managers who contribute to an increase in the number of units produced and achieve cost reductions. In addition, a just-in-time purchasing programme has been implemented, and raw materials are purchased on an as-needed basis.

The production managers have responded to the pressure to improve manufacturing performance in several ways that have resulted in an increased number of completed units over normal production levels. The video game machines put together by the Assembly Group require parts from both the Printed Circuit Boards (PCB) and the Reading Heads (RH) groups. To attain increased production levels, the PCB and RH groups started rejecting parts that previously would have been tested and modified to meet manufacturing standards. Preventive maintenance on machines used in the production of these parts has been postponed with only emergency repair work being performed to keep production lines moving. The Maintenance Department is concerned that there will be serious breakdowns and unsafe operating conditions.

The more aggressive Assembly Group production supervisors have pressured maintenance personnel to attend to their machines at the expense of other groups. This has resulted in machine downtime in the PCB and RH groups which, when coupled with demands for accelerated parts delivery by the Assembly Group, has led to more frequent part rejections and increased friction among departments. DDN operates under a standard costing system. The standard costs are as follows:

	Standard cost per unit		
	Quantity	Cost	Total
Direct material:			
Housing unit, units	1	¥1,600	¥1,600
Printed circuit boards, boards	2	1200	2,400
Reading heads, heads	4	800	3,200
Direct labour (hours):			
Assembly group	2	640	1,280
PCB group	1	720	720
RH group	1.5	800	1,200
Total	4.5		
Variable overhead*		160	720
Total standard cost per unit			¥11,120

*Applied on the basis of direct labour: 4.5 direct labour hours at ¥160 per hour.

DDN prepares monthly performance reports based on standard costs. The following table shows the contribution report for May, when production and sales both reached 2,200 units. The budgeted and actual unit sales price in May were the same at ¥16,000.

DDN PLAYMORE CORPORATION Contribution Report For the Month of May			
	Actual	Budgeted	Variance
Units	2,200	2,000	200 F
Revenue	¥35,200,000	¥32,000,000	¥3,200,000 F
Variable costs:			
Direct material	¥17,632,000	¥14,400,000	¥3,232,000 U

Direct labour	7,344,000	6,400,000	944,000 U
Variable overhead	1,636,800	1,440,000	196,800 U
Total variable costs	26,612,800	22,240,000	4,372,800 U
Contribution margin	¥8,587,200	¥9,760,000	¥1,172,800 U

DDN's top management was surprised by the unfavourable contribution margin variance in spite of the increased sales in May. Takashi Hasegawa, director of cost management, was assigned to report on the reasons for the unfavourable contribution results as well as the individuals or groups responsible. After a thorough review of the data, Hasegawa prepared the following usage report.

DDN PLAYMORE CORPORATION
Usage Report
For the Month of May

Cost Item	Actual quantity	Actual cost
Direct material:		
Housing units, units	2,200	¥3,520,000
Printed circuit boards, boards	4,700	6,016,000
Reading heads, heads	9,200	8,096,000
Direct labour (hours):		
Assembly	3,900	2,464,800
Printed circuit boards	2,400	1,939,200
Reading heads	3,500	2,940,000
Total	9,800	
Variable overhead		1,636,800
Total variable cost		¥26,612,800

Hasegawa reported that the PCB and RH groups supported the increased production levels but experienced abnormal machine downtime, causing idle personnel. This required the use of overtime to keep up with the accelerated demand for parts. The idle time was charged to direct labour. Hasegawa also reported that the production managers of these two groups resorted to parts rejections as opposed to testing and modifying procedures formerly applied. Hasegawa determined that the Assembly Group met management's objectives by increasing production while utilizing lower than standard hours.

Required

As a group, prepare a presentation to the class addressing the following requirements.

a. Calculate the following variances, and explain the ¥1,172,800 unfavourable variance between the budgeted and actual contribution margin during May. Assume that all raw material purchased during May was placed into production.
  (1) Direct labour rate variance.
  (2) Direct labour efficiency variance.
  (3) Direct material price variance.
  (4) Direct material quantity variance.
  (5) Variable overhead spending variance.
  (6) Variable overhead efficiency variance.
  (7) Sales price variance.
  (8) Contribution margin sales volume variance.

b. **(1)** Identify and briefly explain the behavioural factors that could promote friction among the production managers and between the production managers and the maintenance manager.

(2) Evaluate Hasegawa's analysis of the unfavourable contribution results in terms of its completeness and its effect on the behaviour of the production groups.

[CMA adapted]

Solutions to You're the Decision Maker

13.1 Direct Material and Direct Labour Variances, p. 635

The direct material and direct labour variances are computed in Exhibit 13.20.

Exhibit 13.20 **Direct Material Price and Quantity Variances: You're the Decision Maker**

	Flexible budget	Actuals	Variance =	Price Variance +	Quantity Variance
Production volume (tents)		2,000			
Total material usage (m^2)	24,000	24,500			
Total labour hours	4,000	4,200			
Total material costs	AU$192,000	AU$202,125	AU$10,125 U	AU$6,125 U	AU$4,000 U
Total labour costs	AU$72,000	AU$70,350	AU$(1,650) F	AU$(5,250) F	AU$3,600 U
Total direct costs	AU$264,000	AU$272,475			
Price per m^2 of fabric		AU$8.25			
Rate per hour		AU$16.75			

Using Formulas

Materials:

Price variance = $(P_a - P_s)\ Q_a$

= (AU$8.25 – AU$8.00) 24,500

= AU$6,125 Unfavourable

Quantity variance = $(Q_a - Q_s)\ P_s$

= (24,500 – 24,000) AU$8.00

= AU$4,000 Unfavourable

Labour:

Price variance = $(P_a - P_s)\ Q_a$

= (AU$16.75 – AU$18.00) 4,200

= AU$5,250 Favourable

Efficiency variance = $(Q_a - Q_s)\,P_s$

= **(4,200 – 4,000) AU$18.00**

= **AU$3,600 Unfavourable**

Exhibit 13.21 Overhead Cost Variances: You're the Decision Maker

	Original budget	Flexible budget	Actuals	Variance	=	Spending variance	+	Quantity variance
Production volume (tents)			3,600					
Machine hours		5,400	5,700					
Total flexible overhead cost		AU$32,400	AU$37,050	AU$4,650 U		AU$2,850 U		AU$1,800 U
Total fixed overhead costs		AU$30,000	AU$29,000	AU$(1,000) F				
Total overhead costs		AU$62,400	AU$66,050					
Actual overhead cost per machine hour			AU$6.50					
Total variable overhead cost per hour			AU$6.00					

13.2 Overhead Variances p. 640

a. The solution is given in Exhibit 13.21.

b. The fixed overhead budget variance is the difference between actual fixed overhead and budgeted fixed overhead. During December, Koala Camp Gear simply spent less for these cost items than anticipated in the budget.

Variable overhead spending variance = $(R_a - R_s)\,Q_a$

= **(AU$6.50 – AU$6.00) 5,700**

= **AU$2,850 Unfavourable**

Variable overhead quantity variance = $(Q_a - Q_s)\,R_s$

= **(5,700 – 5,400) AU$6.00**

= **AU$1,800 Unfavourable**

Fixed overhead budget variance

= **Actual fixed overhead costs – Budgeted fixed overhead costs**

= **AU$29,000 – AU$30,000**

= **AU$1,000 Unfavourable**

13.3 13.1 and 13.2 Revisited, p. 655

a. The direct material price variance and the direct labour rate variance should be investigated since they exceed 1 standard deviation. The direct material price variance is $6,125 unfavourable, and the direct labour rate variance is $5,250 favourable.

b. There will be no fixed overhead volume variance during a period in which budgeted and applied fixed overhead are equal. This will happen only if the number of standard allowed hours equals the planned monthly activity level of 6,000 machine hours.

Endnotes

1 'Standard' or 'budgeted' or 'allowable' cost are different terms indicating basically the same.

2 The thermostat analogy also demonstrates that a control system based on standard costing only works in specific settings, where objectives are unambiguous and measurable, activities and costs can be modelled quantitatively, and managers have a reasonable understanding of how corrective actions will work out. See Hofstede (1981) who describes control systems in other settings, and see the framework for management control developed by Ferreira and Oltley (2009).

3 Emsley (2001) is one of the few empirical studies about variance analysis. Variance analysis is particularly helpful if it helps managers to direct their attention to the most urgent problems and provides information about the causes of these.

4 The analysis of activities and costs is discussed in more detail in Chapter 4.

5 This is the same problem that faces activity-based management (see Chapter 4) and kaizen costing, which is discussed later in this chapter.

6 Tents also require other direct and indirect materials, such as zippers, fasteners and cords, which we also include as indirect material. We choose to focus on the essential elements of a standard costing system and to keep the example as simple as possible.

7 Chapter 9 is entirely about planning and budgeting.

8 See Chapter 3, which covers cost estimation, for a discussion of the relevant range concept.

9 Cost management analysts typically use the term *variance* when they mean *difference*.

10 The quantity variance is also called efficiency variance. We will use efficiency variance only for direct labour and otherwise talk about the quantity variance. For direct labour, we will also use the term rate variance instead of price variance. The different terminology reflects the customs of many generations of cost analysts.

11 As is immediately apparent from Exhibit 13.4, both variances exactly add up to the total variance. This can also be proven as follows: $(P_a - P_s)\ Q_a + (Q_a - Q_s)\ P_s = P_a\ Q_a - P_s\ Q_a + P_s\ Q_a - P_s\ Q_s = P_a\ Q_a - P_s\ Q_s$ = actual cost – standard costs = variance.

12 This terminology avoids confusion. If, for example, the budget is 800 and actual costs are 950, you could say that the variance is +150 (if the variance is defined as actual – budget), but that can be confusing because then a positive number indicates higher costs and this situation is probably not good for the organization. If the variance would be defined as budget – actual, then the variance is –150, but that is confusing because this is a negative number while costs are *higher*. So using favourable and unfavourable is clearer.

13 Alternative definitions of the variances are possible. For example, the price variance could also be calculated over the actual *quantity purchased* rather than the quantity used in manufacturing. Deviations between the actual and standard price, which are highlighted by the price variance, relate to the purchasing function in the firm. Timely action to follow up a significant price variance will be facilitated by calculating this variance as soon as possible after the material is purchased, instead of when it is used in manufacturing. In this case materials are valued at standard cost in materials inventory. However, a disadvantage of this definition of the price variance is that the price variance and quantity variance do not add up to the total variance, making the results more difficult to interpret for managers.

14 Activity-based budgeting was discussed in more detail in Chapter 9, and activity-based costing has been used throughout this text. Therefore, you may find it easier to read the section called 'Activity-Based Flexible Budget' *first*, and then go back to the sections about less refined budgeting based on a single cost driver.

15 The actual variable overhead rate = actual variable overhead ÷ actual number of hours.

16 In a system of absorption costing, fixed overhead costs are allocated based on actual activity levels using a predetermined rate. This is discussed in Chapter 10, and we will return to this issue later in the present chapter. The key point is that for *cost management* purposes the budget for fixed overhead costs is, as the name suggest, *fixed*.

17 Activity-based costing is covered in Chapter 4.

18 For further reading on this topic, see Malcolm (1991); Mak and Roush (1994) and Kaplan (1994).

19 Standard costing also implies that products are valued on the balance sheet at standard costs, which has implications for the accounting entries. This is briefly discussed later in this chapter and in more detail in Chapter 10. But accounting entries and valuation are of no concern now, when we focus on cost management.

20 Anderson and Sedatole (1998).

21 Early sources discussing changes in manufacturing and accounting due to international competition, especially from Japan, are Kaplan (1990); Johnson (1990); Sukurai (1990). See also the survey about standard costing use by Fry et al. (1998).

22 Some people argue that standard costing systems should even be more or less abolished. Lean accounting advocates a greatly simplified cost accounting system, with a focus on direct cost without overhead allocations, actual costs without standards, and non-financial information visualized on the shop floor. Costing should focus on a smooth flow of production and on groups of products, instead of on the product cost of individual products and activities. See Maskell and Kennedy (2007); and Kennedy and Widener (2008).

23 For example, see Patell (1987) and Schiff (1993).

24 Some companies are developing cost-of-ownership reporting systems. Among them are **Northrop Aircraft Division**, **McDonnell Douglas**, **Texas Instruments**, and **Black & Decker**. See Carr and Ittner (1992) and Ellram (1994).

25 For example, Guerreiro et al. (2008) describe CTS in a Brazilian food company.

26 See Kajüter and Kulmala (2005).

27 Monden and Hamada (1991); Modarress et al. (2005) and Ibusuki and Kaminski (2007).

28 Cooper (1995, pp. 241–42).

29 Cooper (1995, p. 251).

30 Cooper (1995, pp. 240–241).

31 Sako (2004).

32 The kaizen costing chart depicted is based on one used at Daihatsu, a Japanese auto manufacturer owned in part by Toyota. See Monden and Lee (1993).

33 See also Chapter 6 on improvements of quality, time and efficiency in production and service processes.

34 This section is closely related to Chapter 10. In that chapter, an actual costing system is used, which means that the actual cost of direct material and direct labour is accumulated as product costs. Then there will be no variances for direct costs, in contrast to the standard costing system which we used throughout the present chapter.

35 Note that the fixed overhead volume variance only occurs when the firm applies absorption costing. Under absorption costing, the fixed overhead costs are included in the *Cost of Goods Sold* using the predetermined rate. In case of variable costing, the fixed overhead costs are not included in the Cost of Goods Sold. Instead, the fixed overhead costs are treated as *period costs*. However, the other variances can still also apply to direct costing. More details on the journal entries for product costing purposes are explained in Chapter 10.

36 We need a few more digits to avoid rounding errors here.

37 Students who completed Appendix 13A, which covers production mix and yield variances, might notice a conceptual and computational similarity between the revenue sales mix variance and the production mix variance.

38 Students who completed Appendix 13A might notice a conceptual and computational similarity between the revenue sales quantity variance and the production yield variance.

References

Adkins, T. (2006) 'Sierra Trucks: implementing real activity-based budgeting', in T. Adkin (ed.), *Case Studies in Performance Measurements: A Guide from the Experts*, pp. 117–133, John Wiley & Sons, Hoboken, NJ.

Anderson, S.W., and K. Sedatole (1998) 'Designing quality into products: the use of accounting data in new product development', *Accounting Horizons*, vol. 12, no. 3, pp. 213–233.

Carr, L., and C. Ittner (1992) 'Measuring the cost of ownership', *Journal of Cost Management*, Fall, pp. 42–51.

Cooper, R. (1995) *When Lean Enterprises Collide*, Harvard Business School Press, Boston, MA.

Dutta, S.K., R.A. Lawson and D.J. Marcinko (2010) 'A system of cost variances to evaluate sustainability efforts', *Journal of Corporate Accounting and Finance*, March/April, pp. 47–52.

Ellram, L.M. (1994) 'Activity-based costing and total cost of ownership: a critical linkage', *Journal of Cost Management*, Winter, pp. 22–30.

Emsley, D. (2001) 'Redesigning variance analysis for problem solving', *Management Accounting Research*, vol. 12, pp. 157–177.

Ferreira, A., and D. Otley (2009) 'The design and use of performance management systems: an extended framework for analysis', *Management Accounting Research*, vol. 20, pp. 263–282.

Fry, T.D., D.C. Steele and B.A. Saladin (1998) 'The use of management accounting systems in manufacturing', *International Journal of Production Research*, vol. 36, no. 2, pp. 503–525.

Gaffney, K., V. Gladkikh and R.A. Webb (2007) 'A case study of a variance analysis framework for managing distribution costs', *Accounting Perspectives*, vol. 6, no. 2, pp. 167–190.

Guerreiro, R., S. Rodrigues Bio and E. Vazquez Villamor Merschmann (2008), 'Cost-to-serve measurement and customer profitability analysis', *The International Journal of Logistics Management*, vol. 19, no. 3, pp. 389–407.

Hofstede, G. (1981) 'Management control of public and not-for-profit activities', *Accounting, Organizations and Society*, vol. 6, no. 3, pp. 193–211.

Ibusuki, U., and P.C. Kaminski (2007) 'Product development process with focus on value engineering and target costing: a case study in an automotive company', *International Journal of Production Economics*, vol. 105, pp. 459–474.

Johnson, H.T. (1990) 'Performance measurement for competitive excellence', in R.S. Kaplan (ed.), *Measures for Manufacturing Excellence*, pp. 63–90, Harvard Business School Press, Boston, MA.

Kajüter, P., and H. Kulmala (2005) 'Open-book accounting in networks: potential achievements and reasons for failures', *Management Accounting Research*, vol. 16, pp. 179–204.

Kaplan, R.S. (1990) 'Limitations of cost accounting in advanced manufacturing environments', in R.S. Kaplan (ed.), *Measures for Manufacturing Excellence*, pp. 1–14, Harvard Business School Press, Boston, MA.

Kaplan, R.S. (1994) 'Flexible budgeting in an activity-based costing framework', *Accounting Horizons*, vol. 6, pp. 104–109.

Kennedy, F.A., and S.K. Widener (2008) 'A control framework: insights from evidence on lean accounting', *Management Accounting Research*, vol. 19, pp. 301–323.

Krumwiede, K. (2005) 'Rewards and realities of German cost accounting', *Strategic Finance*, April, pp. 27–34.

Krumwiede, K. (2007) 'Getting down to specifics on RCA', *Strategic Finance*, June, pp. 50–55.

Mak, Y.T., and M.L. Roush (1994) 'Flexible budgeting and variance analysis in an activity-based costing environment', *Accounting Horizons*, vol. 6, pp. 93–103.

Malcolm, R.E. (1991) 'Overhead control implications of activity costing', *Accounting Horizons*, vol. 3, pp. 69–78.

Maskell, B.H., and F.A. Kennedy (2007) 'Why do we need lean accounting and how does it work?' *Journal of Corporate Accounting and Finance*, March/April, pp. 59–73.

McKinnon, S.M., and W.J. Bruns, Jr (1992) *The Information Mosaic*, Harvard Business School Press, Boston, MA.

Modarress, B., A. Ansari and D.L. Lockwood (2005) 'Kaizen costing for lean manufacturing: a case study', *International Journal of Production Research*, vol. 43, no. 9, pp. 1751–1760.

Monden, Y., and K. Hamada (1991) 'Target costing and kaizen costing in Japanese automobile companies', *Journal of Management Accounting Research*, vol. 3, pp. 16–17.

Monden, Y., and J. Lee (1993) 'How a Japanese auto maker reduces costs', *Management Accounting*, August, pp. 22–26.

Moscove, S.A. (1998) 'Enhancing detective controls through performance reporting', *Journal of Cost Management*, March/April, pp. 26–29.

Patell, J.M. (1987) 'Cost accounting, process control, and product design: a case study of the Hewlett-Packard personal office computer division', *The Accounting Review*, vol. 62, no. 4, pp. 808–837.

Pitkänen, H., and K. Lukka (2011) 'Three dimensions of formal and informal feedback in management accounting', *Management Accounting Research*, June, pp. 125–137.

Roth, H.P. (2008) 'Using cost management for sustainability efforts', *Journal of Corporate Accounting and Finance*, March/April, pp. 11–18.

Sako, M. (2004) 'Supplier development at Honda, Nissan and Toyota: competitive case studies of organizational capability development', *Industrial and Corporate Change*, vol. 13, no. 2, pp. 281–308.

Schiff, J.B. (1993) 'ABC at Lederle', *Management Accounting*, August, p. 58.

Sharman, P. (2003) 'Bring on German cost accounting', *Strategic Finance*, December, pp. 31–38.

Sharman, P., and K. Vikas (2004) 'Lessons from German cost accounting', *Strategic Finance*, December, pp. 28–35.

Sukurai, M. (1990) 'The influence of factory automation on management accounting practices: a study of Japanese companies', in R.S. Kaplan (ed.), *Measures for Manufacturing Excellence*, pp. 39–62, Harvard Business School Press, Boston, MA.

Van der Veeken, H., and M. Wouters (2002) 'Use of accounting information systems by operations managers in a project company', *Management Accounting Research*, vol. 13, pp. 345–370.

Wouters, M., and D. Roijmans (2011) 'Using prototypes to induce experimentation and knowledge integration in the development of enabling accounting information', *Contemporary Accounting Research*, in press.

CHAPTER

14

Organizational Design, Responsibility Accounting and Evaluation of Divisional Performance

© vernonwiley

Learning Objectives

After completing this chapter, you should be able to:

- **LO 1** Understand the role of responsibility accounting in fostering goal or behavioural congruence.
- **LO 2** Describe the distinguishing characteristics of different kinds of responsibility centres.
- **LO 3** Prepare a performance report and explain the relationships between the reports for various responsibility centres.
- **LO 4** Understand how responsibility accounting influences organizational behaviour.
- **LO 5** Compute an investment centre's return on investment, residual income and economic value added.
- **LO 6** Describe some advantages and disadvantages of return on investment and residual income as performance measures.
- **LO 7** Explain various approaches for measuring a division's income and invested capital.
- **LO 8** Distinguish between accounting performance measures and alternatives to such measures.
- **LO 9** Understand why transfer prices are part of systems for measuring divisional performance.

Outback Outfitters Ltd

10 Woolloomooloo Place

Sydney, New South Wales

AUSTRALIA

PRESS RELEASE

For immediate release; no restrictions.

Contact: Talia Demarest, Media Relations

Outback Outfitters Ltd announces its acquisition of Koala Camp Gear Company. One of Australia's largest retailers of camping equipment and outdoor apparel, Outback Outfitters operates retail outlets throughout Australia, New Zealand and the United Kingdom. Outback also operates a mail-order business from its headquarters in Sydney. Outback's president and CEO, Jack Darwin, made this comment on the acquisition: 'For some time we have been looking to acquire a manufacturing company that could supply us with our own private-label merchandise. In Koala Camp Gear Company, we have found just the right firm. Koala has achieved a reputation around the world for the quality of its products. The Koala Camp Gear and Wallaby Wear product lines are well known from Melbourne to San Francisco to London. With this acquisition, Outback Outfitters will be poised to extend its reach throughout Europe and the United States. We couldn't ask for a better fit between Koala Camp Gear Company and Outback Outfitters. We welcome the folks from Koala into our corporate family, and we look forward to a very prosperous future.'

When an organization begins its operations, it is usually small, and its decision making generally is centralized. It is relatively easy in a small organization for managers to keep in touch with operations through face-to-face contact with employees. A manager's task is increasingly difficult as an organization becomes larger and more complex. For example, as Outback Outfitters grows through the acquisition of Koala Camp Gear Company, as described in the press release on the preceding page, the new company's operations will be more complicated. Managers must make more decisions and manage more employees. Consequently, all but very small organizations delegate managerial duties.

Decentralized Organizations and Responsibility Accounting

LO 1
Understand the role of responsibility accounting in fostering goal or behavioural congruence.

Most large organizations are divided into smaller units, each of which is assigned particular responsibilities. These units are called by various names, including *divisions, segments, business units, work centres* and *departments*. Each department comprises individuals who are responsible for particular tasks or managerial functions. The managers of an organization should ensure that the people in each department are striving toward the same overall goals. **Goal congruence** results when the managers of subunits throughout an organization have a common set of objectives. This occurs when the group acts as a team in pursuit of a mutually agreed upon goal. Individual goal congruence occurs when an individual's personal goals are consistent with organizational goals.

Although complete congruence is rare, in some cases, a strong team spirit suppresses individual desires to act differently. Examples include some military units and some athletic teams. Many companies attempt to achieve this *esprit de corps*. Japanese companies have worked particularly hard to create a strong team orientation among workers that has resulted in considerable goal congruence.

In most business settings, however, personal goals and organization goals differ. Performance evaluation and incentive systems are designed to encourage employees to behave as if their goals were congruent with organization goals. This results in **behavioural congruence;** that is, an individual behaves in the best interests of the organization regardless of his or her own goals.

How can an organization's cost management system promote goal, or at least behavioural, congruence? **Responsibility accounting** refers to the various concepts and tools used to measure the performance of people and departments in order to foster goal or behavioural congruence.

Centralization versus Decentralization

Some organizations are very **centralized;** their decisions are handed down from the top echelon of management and subordinates carry them out. The military is a good example of centralized authority. At the other extreme are highly **decentralized** companies in which *decision rights* are given to many different managers, and consequently many decisions are made at divisional and departmental levels. In many conglomerates, operating decisions are made in the field; corporate headquarters is, in effect, a holding company. The majority of companies fall between these two extremes. At **General Motors,** for example, operating units are decentralized, and the research and development and finance functions are centralized.

Many companies begin with a centralized structure but become more and more decentralized as they grow. Consider the example in Cost Management in Practice 14.1 of a fast-food franchise that started with one hamburger stand.

14.1 Cost Management in Practice

Benefits of Decentralization

We had a counter and 10 stools when we started. When winter came, we had to take out two stools to put in a heating furnace and almost went broke from the loss of revenue! But during the following year, I obtained the statewide franchise for a nationally known barbecue chain, and I expanded my menu.

At first, I did a little of everything - cooking, serving, bookkeeping and advertising. I hired one full-time employee. There was little need for any formal management control system - I made all important decisions, and they were carried out. Soon we had eight outlets. I was still trying to manage everything personally. Decisions were delayed. A particular outlet would receive food shipments, but no one was authorized to accept delivery. If an outlet ran out of supplies or change, its employees had to wait until I arrived to authorize whatever needed to be done. With only one outlet, I was able to spend a reasonable amount of time on what I call high-level decision making - planning for expansion, arranging financing, developing new marketing strategies, and so forth. But with eight outlets, all of my time was consumed with day-to-day operating decisions.

Finally, I realized that the company had grown too big for me to manage alone. So I decentralized, setting up each outlet just like it was an independent operation. Now each outlet manager takes care of day-to-day operating decisions. This not only frees my time for more high-level decision making but also provides a better opportunity for the managers to learn about management, and it gives me a chance to evaluate their performance for promotion to higher management positions, which I intend to create soon.

Source: This example, based on the actual experience of a small company in the USA, came to light during an author's research.

Benefits and Costs of a Decentralized Organization Structure

Most large organizations are decentralized. To better understand the purpose of a responsibility accounting system, it is helpful first to consider the benefits and costs associated with decentralization.

Benefits of decentralization

Decentralization has several positive effects:

- Managers of the organization's subunits are specialists. They have *specialized information and skills* that enable them to manage their departments most effectively.
- Allowing managers some autonomy in decision making provides *managerial training* for future higher-level managers. For example, the manager of a company-owned **Ahold** supermarket in the Netherlands might eventually be promoted to regional supervisor in the company.
- Managers with some decision-making authority usually exhibit more positive *motivation* than those who merely execute the decisions of others.
- Delegating some decisions to lower-level managers provides *time relief to upper-level managers,* enabling them to devote time to strategic planning.
- *Empowering* employees to make decisions draws on the knowledge and expertise of those closest to day-to-day operations.
- Delegating decision making to the lowest level possible enables an organization to give a *timely response* to opportunities and problems as they arise.

Costs of decentralization

Decentralization also has potential negative consequences:

- The performance of managers in a decentralized organization is sometimes *difficult to measure,* especially in terms of overall financial performance. It is always possible to come up with accounting numbers, but what do these really say about how well (or how badly) the manager did? Performance measures need to have certain measurement properties such as: the measure needs to be influenced by the manager's actions (sensitivity), it needs to be not much influenced by factors outside the control of the manager (low noise), and the underlying data need to be reliable.
- The data must also be available on a timely basis, and at a reasonable cost. Also the management cost of dealing with performance measurement and evaluation can be quite high. Some managers complain that they spend more time measuring and evaluating performance than actually performing.

- As a result of the poor measurability of results, managers in a decentralized organization sometimes have a *narrow focus* on their own subunit's performance rather than on the attainment of their organization's overall goals.
- As a result of a narrow focus, managers might tend to *ignore the consequences of their actions on the organization's other subunits.*
- In a decentralized organization, some tasks or *services might be duplicated* unnecessarily. For example, two departments in a decentralized university might both have a computer system (e.g., server and networked personal computers), when one might serve both departments at a lower cost.

The solution to optimizing the costs and benefits of decentralization can be a responsibility accounting system that helps an organization reap the benefits of decentralization while minimizing the costs by fostering goal and behavioural congruence throughout an organization.

Responsibility Accounting

LO 2
Describe the distinguishing characteristics of different kinds of responsibility centres.

A properly designed responsibility accounting system ensures that each manager and employee in an organization is striving to meet the overall goals set by top management. The basis of a responsibility accounting system is the designation of each subunit in the organization as a particular type of *responsibility centre.* A **responsibility centre** is a subunit in an organization whose manager is held accountable for specified financial and non-financial results of the subunit's activities. Five common types of responsibility centres are (1) standard cost, (2) discretionary cost, (3) revenue, (4) profit, and (5) investment.

Responsibility centres differ according to what managers are supposed to focus on, their responsibilities, and their authority to make decisions. These are reflected in the centre's performance measures. The two sides of the measurement coin should be consistent: on the one hand, the type of responsibility centre reflects which decisions a manager can make and which activities he/she manages, and on the other hand, it reflects how that manager is held accountable.

Standard Cost Centre

A **standard cost centre** is an organizational subunit, such as a work centre or department, whose manager is responsible for the cost of an activity for which a well-defined relationship exists between inputs and outputs. Standard cost centre managers are supposed to execute operations efficiently. Standard cost centres are often found in manufacturing operations where inputs, such as direct materials and direct labour, can be specified for each output. The production departments of manufacturing plants are usually standard cost centres. The concept has been applied in non-manufacturing settings as well. In banks, for example, standards can be established for cheque processing, so cheque-processing departments might be standard cost centres. In hospitals, food-service departments, laundries and laboratories are often set up as standard cost centres. Standard costing systems are discussed in Chapter 13.

Discretionary Cost Centre

The cost centres just described require a well-specified relationship between inputs and outputs for performance evaluation. A **discretionary cost centre** is an organizational subunit whose manager is held accountable for costs, but the subunit's input–output relationship is not well specified. Examples of discretionary cost centres might include legal, accounting, research and development, advertising, marketing, and numerous other administrative departments. Discretionary cost centres are also common in government and other non-profit organizations whose budgets are used as a ceiling on expenditures. Managers typically are evaluated on bases other than costs. However, there usually are penalties for exceeding the budget ceiling.

Revenue Centre

The manager of a **revenue centre** is responsible for generating revenues for the organization. Revenue centre managers are supposed to manage the revenue-generating activities effectively and efficiently. They are not responsible for the cost of sales. Consequently they are held accountable for the revenue attributed to the subunit. For example, the reservations department of an airline and the sales department of a manufacturer often are revenue centres. Running such a department and its activities causes costs, such as the labour cost of employees working in the centre, or the cost of the information system. When these costs are deducted from the revenues that the department generates, the revenue centre is also called a *net revenue centre*.

Profit Centre

A **profit centre** is an organizational subunit whose manager is held accountable for profit. Since profit is equal to revenue minus expenses, profit centre managers are held accountable for both the revenue and expenses attributed to their subunits. A profit centre manager is responsible for a wide range of activities that affect both revenues and costs, and the manager can make decisions that involve trade-offs between these. An example of a profit centre is a company-owned restaurant in a fast-food chain. The manager can make decisions about hiring staff, planning staff, local advertising, etc. The manager can make trade-offs, for example to have extra staff during busy hours (extra costs) in order to increase service and revenues.

A few nuances are important to mention. Of course, no profit centre manager has complete freedom for all decisions that affect revenues and costs.[1] For example, the fast-food chain restaurant manager may be bound to company policies regarding the menu, sales prices and restaurant operating procedures.

Some responsibility centres are in between true profit centres and revenue centres. This is the case when standard cost of goods sold are charged to sales-focused entities. A sales department can be considered a profit centre when the cost of sales are deducted from revenues. This makes the sales department focus on the profitability of goods and services sold, rather than just on the revenues (which is easy if they would offer very low prices that generate low profits or even losses, but that still bring in some revenues). However, the sales department cannot make many decisions that affect costs, so it is not a real profit centre in the sense of managing a wide range of activities that stretch both revenues and costs, and that involve trade-offs between these.

Similarly, some responsibility centres are in between true profit centres and cost centres. This is the case when revenues are assigned to cost-focused entities. For example, the standard costs of production (perhaps with a mark-up) can be treated as revenues for a manufacturing site, creating a kind of profit centre. This is basically the same as comparing the actual costs with the standard costs (as discussed in Chapter 13). The manufacturing site manager can do very little to affect these revenues. So this is not a real profit centre from the manager's perspective of responsibility and control, but it is from the perspective of top management that wants to assess whether the centre is sufficiently profitable.

Investment Centre

The manager of an **investment centre** is held accountable for the subunit's profit *and the invested capital* used by the subunit to generate its profit. An investment centre manager is responsible for a wide range of activities that affect revenues, costs and investments, and the manager can make decisions that involve trade-offs between these. A division of a large corporation is typically designed as an investment centre.[2] The manager could for example, invest in a new product line by purchasing specialized equipment and facilities. The revenues that these new products generate should be

Exhibit 14.1 Organization Chart: Outback Outfitters Ltd

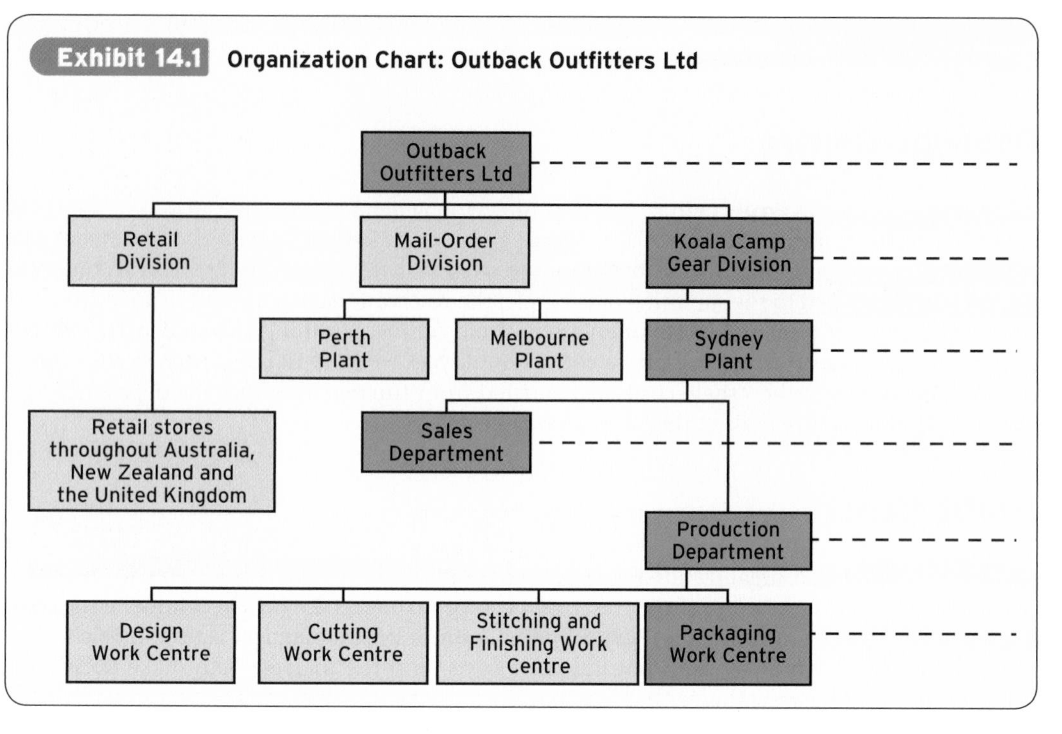

sufficient to not only cover the manufacturing costs (and so to yield a profit), but these should also yield a sufficient return on the investment. In other words, just profit is not good enough; the profit should justify the investments involved.

As with profit centres, the investment centre managers have no complete freedom to make all decisions independently. Apart from the kinds of constraints regarding revenues and costs as mentioned above, there may be extra controls regarding investments. For example, there may be rules about the technology choices in capital investments. Investment centre managers usually need permission in advance before they can make large investments above some threshold. Techniques for evaluating such investment proposals are discussed in Chapter 8.

Illustration of Responsibility Accounting

To illustrate the concepts used in responsibility accounting, we refer again to Koala Camp Gear Company. Margo Hastings' company prospered through its first decade. Hastings added additional products, and the firm grew rapidly. Then Hastings sold her company to Outback Outfitters Ltd, a large Australian retailer specializing in outdoor apparel, camping gear and other outdoor equipment. Hastings retired and now is basking in the sun in Fiji.

Outback Outfitters is a household name throughout Australia, New Zealand and the United Kingdom. The retailer is known for its high-quality outdoor apparel and equipment and its experienced and helpful sales personnel. Outback Outfitters owns retail stores in all the major cities in Australia and New Zealand, as well as in London and Manchester in England, and Glasgow in Scotland. In addition to its retail outlets throughout the world, Outback operates a large mail-order sales operation based in Sydney. Outback's mail-order operation was modelled after the operation of **L. L. Bean**, the highly successful US mail-order company based in Freeport, Maine.

Jack Darwin, Outback's founder and CEO, had long thought that Outback should acquire a high-quality manufacturing company to provide Outback with its own private-label line of outdoor merchandise. Darwin had kept an eye on Koala Camp Gear Company for several years and, when the time seemed right, entered into negotiations with Hastings for the acquisition of the company she founded.

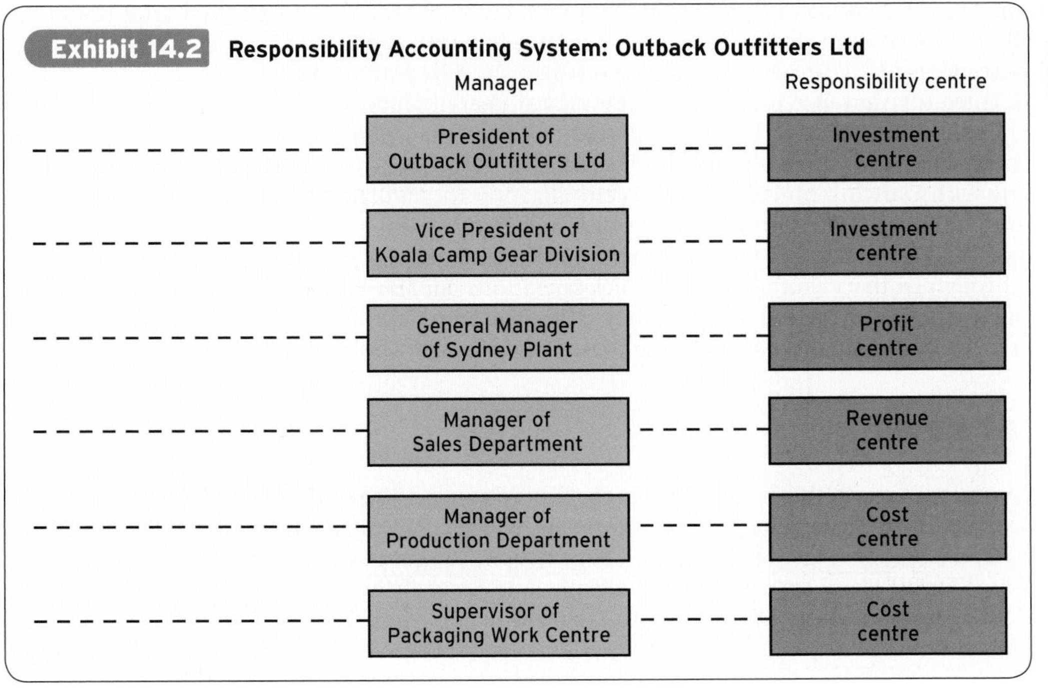

Exhibit 14.2 Responsibility Accounting System: Outback Outfitters Ltd

Outback Outfitters is now organized into three divisions. The Retail Division operates the company's sales outlets in Australia, New Zealand and the United Kingdom. The Mail-Order Division, based in Sydney, is responsible for Outback's global mail-order sales operation. The Koala Camp Gear Division manufactures a wide variety of camping gear and outdoor apparel. The camping gear retains the successful trade name Koala Camp Gear, and the division's outdoor apparel carries the trade name Wallaby Wear.

The Koala Camp Gear Division operates three manufacturing plants, and each plant has a sales department and a production department. The production department in each plant is organized into several work centres.

Exhibit 14.1 shows Outback Outfitter's organization chart, and Exhibit 14.2 depicts the firm's responsibility accounting system. As depicted in Exhibit 14.1, Outback has five levels in its organization chart: corporate, division, plant, department and work centre.

Corporate Level

The chief executive officer of Outback Outfitters Ltd is the company's president. The president, who is responsible to the company's shareholders, is accountable for corporate profit in relation to the capital (assets) invested in the company. Therefore, the entire company is an *investment centre*. The president has the autonomy to make significant decisions that affect the company's profit and invested capital. For example, the president would make the final decision to build a new plant for the Koala Camp Gear Division.

Division Level

Each division is managed by a vice president. The vice president of Koala Camp Gear Division is accountable for the profit it earns in relation to the capital invested in this division. Hence, the Koala Division is an *investment centre*. The vice president has the authority to make significant investment decisions regarding the division, up to a monetary limit specified by Outback Outfitters' CEO. For example, the vice president could decide to invest, but only under particular thresholds (for example, limited investments to buy new production equipment); and above those levels there are separate procedures to ask permission before investments can be made.

All three division vice presidents enjoy a great deal of autonomy in managing their business units. Outback's CEO, Jack Darwin, has said on more than one occasion, 'I hired good people to manage Outback's three divisions, and I'm going to stay out of their way and let them do it.' In keeping with Darwin's philosophy of decentralization for Outback Outfitters, the Retail Division and the Mail-Order Division are free to buy merchandise not only from the Koala Camp Gear Division but also from other manufacturers. Similarly, the Koala Division's goods are marketed not only through Outback Outfitter's retail sales operations but also to retailers throughout the world. Of course, the highly prized brand names of Koala Camp Gear and Wallaby Wear are imprinted only on the higher-quality merchandise that is sold through Outback Outfitters.

Plant Level

The general manager of the Sydney plant in the Koala Camp Gear Division is accountable for the profit the plant earns. The general manager does not have the authority to make major investment decisions but is responsible for operational decisions. For example, the general manager hires the managers and supervisors in the plant, approves salary increases, and generally oversees the plant's operation. Since the plant's general manager has no authority to make major investment decisions, he is held accountable only for the plant's profit, not for the capital invested. Thus, the Sydney plant is a *profit centre.*

Department Level

The Sales Department manager is held accountable for the sales made from the Sydney plant. He has the authority to set sales prices, hire sales personnel, and make other sales-related decisions. Thus, the sales department is a *revenue centre.*

The Production Department is a *standard cost centre*, whose manager is held accountable for the costs incurred in manufacturing the Sydney plant's products. He has the authority to make decisions about purchasing raw materials, hiring production employees, and so forth.

Work Centre Level

Each work centre supervisor is held accountable for the costs incurred in that particular work centre. For example, the supervisor of the Packaging Work Centre has the authority to make decisions about the choice of packaging materials, the scheduling of employees involved in packaging, and the packaging process itself. Hence, the Packaging Work Centre also is a *standard cost centre.* The Cutting and Stitching and Finishing Work Centres are also standard cost centres. The Design Work Centre, however, is a *discretionary cost centre.* In the Design Work Centre, the relationship between inputs and outputs is less definitive than in the other two work centres.

14.2 Cost Management in Practice

Unilever Uses Various Types of Responsibility Centres

Unilever is global company in consumer products, and some of its brands are Dove, Lux, Pond's and Rexona in the deodorant and skin care markets, Lipton's, Brooke Bond, Ben & Jerry's and Heartbrand in the ice cream and beverage markets, and Omo, Surf, Comfort and Cif in the home care market. In 2010 the company's sold in more than 180 countries, total sales were €44.3 billion and the company employed 167,000 people.

The company has simplified its European supply chain to reduce costs and to increase customer service (in particular the availability of products in the stores). The new structure has consequences for responsibility centres.

Previously, the large country-level divisions in Europe were the dominant profit centres that had a large autonomy in marketing, they developed their own products, carried many local brands, and had their own manufacturing sites. The company went for complexity reduction by simplifying the product portfolio and internal supply chain at a European level. This means more commonality across Europe in terms of brands, recipes, packaging, etc. in order to enhance efficiency in production and to reduce complexity in distribution; fewer and more specialized manufacturing sites; fewer and consolidated distribution centres; and shared service centres for back-office processes.

These changes required a new structure. Product development and marketing is now done by the product categories across Europe. For example, new products are introduced in all countries, and a very expensive commercial is used everywhere. Product development may be located in various countries, but this is centrally controlled by the product category. Product categories are profit centres. All manufacturing and distribution sites now fall under the European supply organization. It has closed some sites, made remaining sites more specialized, and it plans production and inventories to optimize European-wide costs. The supply organization is essentially a cost centre. Countries are responsible for sales, and they are profit centres.

Performance measurement has also changed a lot. It is now much more important that performance measures such as market share, profit margins, revenues, brand health, manufacturing costs, safety, quality and service are comparable across markets, countries and sites.

Source: Author's research.

Performance Reports

LO 3
Prepare a performance report and explain the relationships between the reports for various responsibility centres.

Each responsibility centre's performance is summarized periodically on a **performance report**, which shows the budgeted and actual amounts of key financial (or non-financial) results appropriate for the type of responsibility centre involved. For example, a cost centre's performance report concentrates on budgeted and actual amounts for various cost items attributable to the cost centre. Performance reports also typically show the variance between budgeted and actual amounts for the financial results conveyed in the report. The data in a performance report help managers use *management by exception* to control an organization's operations effectively. **Management by exception** means that managers follow up on only the most significant variances between budgeted and actual results. This allows the managers to use their limited time most effectively.[3]

As the organization chart in Exhibit 14.1 shows, Outback Outfitters Ltd is a *hierarchy.* This means that each subunit manager reports to one higher-level manager, from the work centre supervisor all the way up to the president and chief executive officer. Such an organization also has a hierarchy of performance reports since the performance of each subunit constitutes part of the performance of the next higher-level subunit. For example, the cost performance in the Sydney plant's Cutting Work Centre constitutes part of the cost performance of the plant's production department.

Exhibit 14.3 shows the relationships between the March performance reports for several subunits of Outback Outfitters. The Cutting Work Centre is the lowest-level subunit shown. The *total cost* line from the Cutting Work Centre's performance report is included as one line in the performance report of the Production Department. Also included are the total cost figures for the department's other work centres. How is the *total cost* line for the Production Department used in the performance report for the Sydney plant? Follow the relationships in Exhibit 14.3 (the yellow highlights should help you).

The hierarchy of performance reports starts at the bottom and builds toward the top, just as the organization structure depicted in Exhibit 14.1 builds from the bottom upward. Each manager in the organization receives the performance report for his or her own subunit in addition to the performance reports for the major subunits in the next lower level. For example, the general manager of the Sydney plant receives the reports for each of its departments, sales and production. With these reports, the plant's general manager can evaluate her subordinates as well as her own performance. This will help the general manager to improve the plant's performance, motivate employees and plan future operations.

In addition to the financial information in the performance reports, managers at all levels in the organization make significant use of non-financial performance data. See Chapter 16 for discussions

Exhibit 14.3 Performance Reports for Second Quarter: Selected Subunits of Outback Outfitters Ltd

	A	B	C	D	E	F	G	H	I
1		BUDGET		ACTUAL		VARIANCE			
2	Performance Report	Second Quarter	Year to Date	Second Quarter	Year to Date	Second Quarter	*	Year to Date	*
4	**Company**								
5	Retail Division	AU$2,490,000	AU$4,950,000	AU$2,450,000	AU$4,800,000	AU$(40,000)	U	AU$(150,000)	U
6	Mail Order Division	625,000	1,300,000	623,000	1,400,000	(2,000)	U	100,000	F
7	Koala Camp Gear Division	2,419,500	4,457,000	2,533,090	4,500,000	113,590	F	43,000	F
8	Total profit	**5,534,500**	**10,707,000**	**5,606,090**	**10,700,000**	**71,590**	**F**	**(7,000)**	**U**
9									
10	**Koala Camp Gear Division**								
11	Perth Plant	AU$1,150,000	AU$2,050,000	AU$1,130,000	AU$1,946,000	AU$(20,000)	U	AU$(104,000)	U
12	Melbourne Plant	430,000	865,000	445,700	887,000	15,700	F	22,000	F
13	Sydney Plant	839,500	1,542,000	957,390	1,667,000	117,890	F	125,000	F
14	Total profit	**2,419,500**	**4,457,000**	**2,533,090**	**4,500,000**	**113,590**	**F**	**43,000**	**F**
15						*113,590*		*43,000*	
16	**Sydney Plant**								
17	Sales Department (revenues)	AU$3,640,000	AU$7,230,000	AU$3,656,000	AU$7,434,000	AU$16,000	F	AU$204,000	F
18	Production Department (costs)	2,800,500	5,688,000	2,698,610	5,767,000	(101,890)	F	79,000	U
19	Total profit	**839,500**	**1,542,000**	**957,390**	**1,667,000**	**117,890**	**F**	**125,000**	**F**
20						*117,890*		*125,000*	
21	**Production Department**								
22	Design Work Centre	AU$79,000	AU$143,000	AU$7,210	AU$134,000	AU$(71,790)	F	AU$(9,000)	F
23	Cutting Work Centre	1,924,500	3,915,000	1,907,400	3,977,000	(17,100)	F	62,000	U
24	Stitching and Finishing Work Centre	585,000	1,210,000	578,000	1,240,000	(7,000)	F	30,000	U
25	Packaging Work Centre	212,000	420,000	206,000	416,000	(6,000)	F	(4,000)	F
26	Total cost	**2,800,500**	**5,688,000**	**2,698,610**	**5,767,000**	**(101,890)**	**F**	**79,000**	**U**
27						*(101,890)*		*79,000*	
28	**Cutting Work Centre**								
29	Wages	AU$132,000	AU$303,000	AU$134,000	AU$298,000	AU$2,000	U	AU$(5,000)	F
30	Fabric	1,447,000	2,912,000	1,427,000	2,967,000	(20,000)	F	55,000	U
31	Manufacturing overhead						F	-	F
32	Unit level	136,000	283,000	142,000	287,000	6,000	U	4,000	U
33	Batch level	121,500	236,000	117,900	246,000	(3,600)	F	10,000	U
34	Product-sustaining level	88,000	181,000	86,500	179,000	(1,500)	F	(2,000)	F
35	Total expense	**1,924,500**	**3,915,000**	**1,907,400**	**3,977,000**	**(17,100)**	**F**	**62,000**	**U**
36						*(17,100)*		*62,000*	

* F denotes favourable variance; U denotes unfavourable variance. For comparisons between budgeted and actual *profit* amounts, a favourable variance results when actual profit *exceeds* budgeted profit. For comparisons between budgeted and actual cost amounts, a favourable variance results when the actual cost is *lower than* the budgeted amount.

of such non-financial information and the balanced scorecard perspective on performance evaluation.

Budgets, Variance Analysis and Responsibility Accounting

Notice that the performance reports in Exhibit 14.3 make significant use of budgets and variance analysis. Thus, the topics of budgeting, variance analysis and responsibility accounting are closely interrelated. The flexible budget provides the benchmark against which actual revenues, expenses and profits are compared.[4] As you learned in the preceding chapters, the use of a flexible budget is important so that appropriate comparisons can be made. Comparing the actual costs incurred in the Sydney plant's Cutting Department, for example, with the budgeted costs established for a different level of activity is a noisy comparison. This performance measure does not have the required measurement properties discussed earlier in this chapter.

The performance reports in Exhibit 14.3 also show variances between budgeted and actual performance. These variances are often broken down into smaller components to help management pinpoint responsibility and diagnose performance. Variance analysis, which was discussed in detail in Chapter 13, is an important tool in a responsibility accounting system.

How Responsibility Accounting Affects Behaviour

Responsibility accounting systems can influence employee behaviour significantly. Whether the behavioural effects are positive or negative, however, depends on how an organization implements responsibility accounting.

LO 4
Understand how responsibility accounting influences organizational behaviour.

Does It Provide Information or Place Blame?

The proper focus of a responsibility accounting system is *information*. The system should identify the individual in the organization who is in the best position to explain each particular event or financial result. The emphasis should be on providing that individual and higher-level managers with information to help them understand the reasons behind the organization's performance. When properly used, a responsibility accounting system *does not emphasize blame*. If managers believe they are beaten over the head with criticism and rebukes when unfavourable variances occur, they are unlikely to respond in a positive way. Instead, they will tend to undermine the system and view it with scepticism. But when the responsibility accounting system emphasizes its informational role, managers tend to react constructively and strive for improved performance.

Is There Really Cost or Revenue Controllability?

Some organizations use performance reports that distinguish between controllable and uncontrollable costs or revenues. For example, the supervisor of the Cutting Work Centre influences the hours and efficiency of the work centre employees, but this manager probably cannot change the wage rates. A performance report that distinguishes between the financial results influenced by the supervisor and those the supervisor does not influence has the advantage of providing complete information to the supervisor, but the report recognizes that certain results are beyond his or her control.

Identifying costs as controllable or uncontrollable is not always easy. Many cost items are influenced by more than one person. The time frame can also be important in determining controllability. Some costs are controllable over a long time frame, but not within a short time period. To illustrate, suppose that the Cutting Work Centre supervisor has signed a one-year contract with a local fabric supplier. The supervisor can influence the cost of fabric if the time period is a year or more but cannot control the cost on a weekly basis.

How Can Desired Behaviour be Motivated?

Organizations often use the responsibility accounting system to motivate actions that upper-level management considers desirable. Sometimes the responsibility accounting system can solve behavioural problems and promote teamwork. Consider the following scenario, originally reported by Professor R.R. Villers: The production scheduler in a manufacturing firm was frequently asked to interrupt production of one product with a rush order for another product. Rush orders typically resulted in higher costs because more production set-ups were required. Since the production scheduler was evaluated on the basis of costs, he was reluctant to accept rush orders. The sales manager, on the other hand, was evaluated on the basis of sales revenue. By agreeing to customers' demands for rush orders, the sales manager satisfied his customers. This resulted in more future sales and favourable performance ratings for the sales manager.

As the rush orders became more and more frequent, the production manager began to object. The sales manager responded by asking whether the production scheduler wanted to take the responsibility for losing a customer by refusing a rush order. The production scheduler did not want to be blamed for lost sales, so he grudgingly accepted the rush orders. However, considerable ill-will developed between the sales manager and production scheduler.

The company's cost management analysts came to the rescue by redesigning the responsibility accounting system. The system was modified to accumulate the extra costs associated with rush orders and charge them to the sales manager's responsibility centre rather than the production scheduler's centre. The ultimate result was that the sales manager chose more carefully which rush-order requests to make, and the production manager accepted them gracefully.

Clearly, acceptance or rejection of a rush order is a cost–benefit decision.

Potential costs of accepting rush order	Potential benefits of accepting rush order
Disrupted production	Satisfied customers
More set-ups	Increased future sales
Higher costs	
Need to outsource	

The problem described in this scenario developed because two different managers were considering the costs and benefits of the rush-order decision. The production manager was looking only at the costs while the sales manager was looking only at the benefits. The modified responsibility accounting system made the sales manager look at *both the costs and the benefits* associated with each rush order. Then the sales manager could make the necessary trade-off between costs and benefits in considering each rush order. Some rush orders were rejected because the sales manager decided that the costs exceeded the benefits. Other rush orders were accepted when the importance of the customer and potential future sales justified it.[5] This example illustrates how a well-designed responsibility accounting system can make an organization run more smoothly and achieve higher performance.

Responsibility Accounting, Internal Controls and Sarbanes–Oxley

In a broad sense, an organization's responsibility accounting system can be considered part of its internal control system. One of the key goals of an organization's internal control system is to ensure that managers and other employees work toward meeting the objectives of the organization. Responsibility accounting systems specify who is responsible for various aspects of an organization's operations, and therefore the organization's internal controls over financial reporting will be affected by the quality of the responsibility accounting system.

The Sarbanes–Oxley Act, passed by the US Congress in 2002, requires an organization's management to maintain and regularly report on its internal controls over financial reporting. Part of that reporting process would cover various aspects of the organization's responsibility accounting system. See Chapter 1 for further information about the Sarbanes–Oxley Act (often referred to as 'SOX'). This law affects many international non-US companies as well. The UK corporate governance code also requires a report on internal controls, including financial, operational, compliance and risk management, although it is not legislation but voluntary.

Performance Measurement in Investment Centres

LO 5
Compute an investment centre's return on investment, residual income, and economic value added.

How do the top managers of global companies such as **Microsoft, Bosch** and **Shell** evaluate their divisions and other major subunits? The largest subunits within these and similar organizations usually are designated as *investment centres*. The manager of this type of responsibility centre is held accountable not only for the investment centre's *operating profit* but also for the *capital invested* to earn that profit. Operating profit refers to the profit *before* the cost of debt is deducted. Thus far in this chapter, we casually talked about an investment centre's profit, but from this point forward we will be more precise and refer to *operating* profit whenever pertinent. Invested capital refers to assets, such as buildings and equipment, used in a subunit's operations. In this section, we study the methods used to evaluate investment centres and the performance of their managers.[6] This enables us to discuss many topics together that have to do with the evaluation of performance using accounting measures. Some of the topics also apply to the other types of responsibility centres.

Refer again to Outback Outfitters' organization chart (Exhibit 14.1). The Mail-Order Division, Koala Camp Gear Division and the Retail Division are investment centres. This responsibility centre designation is appropriate because each division manager has the authority to make decisions that affect both operating profit and invested capital. For example, the Retail Division manager approves the overall pricing policies in the Retail Division's stores and has the autonomy to sign contracts to buy merchandise for resale. These actions influence the division's operating profit. In addition, the Retail Division manager has the authority to build new Outback Outfitters stores, rent space in shopping centres, or close existing stores. These decisions affect the amount of capital invested in the division.

The primary goals of any profit-making enterprise include maximizing its profitability and using its invested capital as effectively as possible.[7] Cost management analysts use three different measures to evaluate the performance of investment centres: return on investment, residual income and economic value added.[8] We illustrate each of these measures for Outback Outfitters Ltd, using the data about the divisions' performance provided in the table below (Operating income is also found in Exhibit 14.3, cells E5, E6 and E7).

	Sales revenues	Operating income	Invested capital
Mail-Order Division	AU$35,000,000	AU$1,400,000	AU$7,000,000
Koala Camp Gear Division	40,500,000	4,500,000	30,000,000
Retail Division	96,000,000	4,800,000	48,000,000

Why are all three measures to evaluate the performance of investment centres based on **operating income**? While this can be determined in different ways, and we come back to this later in this chapter, the operating income is always *before* subtracting the cost of debt.[9] Operating income is not profit, although the terms are often used rather loosely. You can probably still catch us using the terms profit or income without being explicit about *operating* income. But why is this crucial? The operating income is earned by using the organization's entire invested capital. Some of that operating income goes to investors who provided debt, and this is the *interest*. The remaining income partly goes to government (in the form of *taxation*) and partly goes to investors who provide equity (called *profit after tax*). The definition of income and related capital should be consistent, so the whole operating income is related to the entire invested capital (debt plus equity), the interest is relevant in proportion to the amount of debt, and profit after tax is relevant in proportion to equity.

Cost of Capital

We worry about how effectively each division uses its invested capital, because capital is not free. As we have seen in Chapter 8 on investment decisions, organizations must pay a return to investors who let the organization use their money, either in the form of debt or in the form of equity. The cost of capital plays an important role in evaluating investment proposals. Recall that future cash flows are discounted using the cost of capital and the resulting *net present value* should be greater than zero. Or, future cash flows are discounted such that the net present value becomes zero and the corresponding discount rate, which is called the *internal rate of return*, should exceed the cost of capital.

The same cost of capital is of central importance here, when we are going to evaluate the performance of investment centres. Furthermore, there are some strong parallels with the NPV versus IRR discussion in Chapter 8.

The cost of capital reflects the organization's minimum required rate of return on invested capital. This should be equal to the rate of return on investments of similar risk, because that is the comparable return forgone by investors who are tying up capital in Outback Outfitters Ltd.

Outback Outfitters Ltd has two sources of long-term capital: debt and equity. The cost of issuing debt to Outback Outfitters is the after-tax cost of the interest payments on the debt, considering the fact that the interest payments are tax deductible. The cost of Outback's equity capital is the investment opportunity rate of its investors, that is, the rate they could earn on investments of similar risk to that of investing in Outback Outfitters. The **weighted-average cost of capital (WACC)** is the average of the after-tax cost of debt capital and the cost of equity capital, weighted by the relative proportions of the firm's capital provided by debt and equity.

$$\textbf{Weighted-average cost of capital} = \frac{\begin{pmatrix}\text{After-tax}\\ \text{cost of debt}\end{pmatrix}\begin{pmatrix}\text{Market}\\ \text{value}\\ \text{of debt}\end{pmatrix} + \begin{pmatrix}\text{Cost of}\\ \text{equity}\end{pmatrix}\begin{pmatrix}\text{Market}\\ \text{value}\\ \text{of equity}\end{pmatrix}}{\text{Market value of debt + equity}}$$

The interest rate on Outback Outfitters' AU$40 million debt is 9.00 per cent, and the company's tax rate is 20 per cent. Therefore, Outback's after-tax cost of debt is 7.20 per cent [9% × (1 – 20%)]. Let's assume that the cost of Outback's equity capital is 14 per cent. Moreover, the market value of the company's equity is AU$60 million.[10] The following calculation shows that Outback Outfitters' WACC is 11.28 per cent.

$$WACC = \frac{0.072 \times AU\$40,000,000 + 0.14 \times AU\$60,000,000}{AU\$40,000,000 + AU\$60,000,000} = 0.1128$$

In some firms, the cost of capital that is used for evaluating investment centres is adjusted for the risk of these investments. Thus, divisions that have different levels of risk sometimes are assigned different costs of capital. In other works, the overall cost of capital could be differentiated for different divisions, if their businesses are of significantly different risk. However, we will ignore that for Outback Outfitters Ltd, because many firms do not make such distinctions, and it also is not important for explaining the different accounting performance measures.

Return on Investment as a Performance Measure

Traditionally, the most common investment-centre performance measure is **return on investment (ROI)**, which is defined as the investment centre's operating income divided by its invested capital. The objective of the ROI is that it should be at least equal to the centre's cost of capital.

$$\textbf{Return on investment (ROI)} = \frac{\textbf{Operating income}}{\textbf{Invested capital}}$$

The ROI calculations for Outback Outfitters' three divisions for the most recent year to date are:

$$\frac{\textbf{Operating income}}{\textbf{Invested capital}} = \textbf{Return on investment (ROI)}$$

Mail-Order Division $\dfrac{AU\$1,400,000}{AU\$7,000,000} = 20.00\%$

Koala Camp Gear Division $\dfrac{AU\$4,500,000}{AU\$30,000,000} = 15.00\%$

Retail Division $\dfrac{AU\$4,800,000}{AU\$48,000,000} = 10.00\%$

Note that the ROI calculation for each division considers *both divisional operating income and the capital invested* in the division. Why is this important? Suppose that each division were evaluated only on the basis of its divisional operating income. The Retail Division reported a higher divisional operating income than the Mail-Order Division. Does this mean that the Retail Division performed better than the Mail-Order Division? The answer is no; although the Retail Division's operating income exceeded the Mail-Order Division's operating income, the Retail Division used much more invested capital to earn its operating income. The Retail Division's assets are almost seven times the assets of the Mail-Order Division.

Considering the relative size of the two divisions, we would expect the Retail Division to earn a higher absolute operating income than the Mail-Order Division. The important question is not how much income each division earned but how effectively each division used its invested capital to earn an income.

Note also that the Mail-Order Division and the Koala Camp Gear Division each generates a ROI that is satisfactory because it is above the cost of capital of 11.28 per cent. However, the Retail Division's performance is not satisfactory. Its 10 per cent ROI is below the company's cost of capital.

Factors underlying ROI

We can rewrite the ROI formula as follows:

$$\textbf{Return on investment (ROI)} = \frac{\textbf{Operating income}}{\textbf{Invested capital}} = \frac{\textbf{Operating income}}{\textbf{Sales revenues}} \times \frac{\textbf{Sales revenues}}{\textbf{Invested capital}}$$

Notice that the *sales revenue* term cancels out in the denominator and numerator when the two right-hand fractions are multiplied.

Writing the ROI formula in this way highlights the factors that determine a division's return on investment. Operating income divided by sales revenue is called the **sales margin**, a measure of the percentage of each sales dollar that remains as profit after all expenses are covered. Sales revenue divided by invested capital is called the **capital turnover**; it focuses on the number of sales dollars generated by every dollar of invested capital. The sales margin and capital turnover for Outback Outfitters' three divisions are calculated as follows:

	$\frac{\textbf{Operating income}}{\textbf{Sales revenues}} \times \frac{\textbf{Sales revenues}}{\textbf{Invested capital}}$		= **ROI**
Mail-Order Division	$\frac{\text{AU\$1,400,000}}{\text{AU\$35,000,000}} \times \frac{\text{AU\$35,000,000}}{\text{AU\$7,000,000}}$	= **4.00% , 5.00**	= **20.00%**
Koala Camp Gear Division	$\frac{\text{AU\$4,500,000}}{\text{AU\$40,500,000}} \times \frac{\text{AU\$40,500,000}}{\text{AU\$30,000,000}}$	= **11.11% , 1.35**	= **15.00%**
Retail Division	$\frac{\text{AU\$4,800,000}}{\text{AU\$96,000,000}} \times \frac{\text{AU\$96,000,000}}{\text{AU\$48,000,000}}$	= **5.00% , 2.00**	= **10.00%**

The Retail Division's sales margin is 5 per cent (AU$4,800,000 operating profit ÷ AU$96,000,000 sales revenue). Thus, each dollar of divisional sales resulted in a 5 cent operating profit. The division's capital turnover was 2 (AU$96,000,000 sales revenue ÷ AU$48,000,000 invested capital). Thus, each dollar of capital invested in the division's assets, such as store buildings, display shelves, checkout equipment and inventory, generated AU$2 of sales revenue. This analysis can be expanded to multiple levels of responsibility. This expanded analysis is often termed the DuPont analysis after the company that pioneered it.

Improving a division's ROI

How could the Retail Division manager improve the division's return on investment? Since ROI is the product of the sales margin and the capital turnover, ROI can be improved by increasing either or both of its components. For example, if the Retail Division manager increases the division's sales margin to 7 per cent while holding the capital turnover constant at 2, the division's ROI would climb from 10 per cent to 14 per cent, as follows:

$$\textbf{Retail Division's improved ROI} = \textbf{Improved sales margin} \times \textbf{Same capital turnover}$$

$$\mathbf{14\% = 7\% \times 2}$$

To bring about the improved sales margin, the Retail Division manager would need to increase divisional operating profit to AU$6,720,000 on sales of AU$96,000,000 (U$6,720,000 ÷ AU$96,000,000 = 0.07). How could operating profit be increased without changing total sales revenue? There are two possibilities: (a) increase sales prices while selling less quantity and thereby incurring lower cost of goods sold expense or (b) decrease operating expenses. Neither of these is necessarily easy to do. In increasing sales prices, the division manager must be careful not to lose sales to the extent that total sales revenue declines. Similarly, reducing the expenses must not diminish product quality, customer service or overall store atmosphere. Any of these changes could also result in lost sales revenue.

An alternative way to increase the Retail Division's ROI is to increase its capital turnover. Suppose that the Retail Division manager increased the division's capital turnover to 3 while holding the sales margin constant at 5 per cent. The division's ROI would climb from 10 per cent to 15 per cent:

$$\frac{\textbf{Retail Division's}}{\textbf{improved ROI}} = \frac{\textbf{Improved}}{\textbf{sales margin}} \times \frac{\textbf{Same}}{\textbf{capital turnover}}$$

$$15\% = 5\% \times 3$$

To obtain the improved capital turnover, the Retail Division manager would need to either increase sales revenue or reduce the division's invested capital. For example, the improved ROI could be achieved by reducing invested capital to AU$32,000,000 while maintaining sales revenue of AU$96,000,000 – a very tall order. The division manager can lower invested capital somewhat by reducing inventories and can increase sales revenue by using store space more effectively. Reducing inventories might lead, however, to running out of inventory and lost sales, and crowded aisles could drive customers away.

Improving ROI is a difficult challenge, and it requires the expertise and constant attention of a skilled management team.

Why ROI Can Provide the Wrong Investment Incentives

Although ROI has traditionally been the most popular investment-centre performance measure, it has one major drawback: it can provide the wrong incentives to invest to divisional managers. The ROI performance measure may stimulate managers to *not make* investments that should be made in the interest of the total company, and it may also stimulate managers to *make* investments that should not be made.

When investments should be made

To illustrate, suppose that Outback's Koala Camp Gear Division manager is considering a major investment in computer-integrated manufacturing (CIM) equipment for all three of Koala's plants. The equipment will cost AU$4 million. The investment in the CIM system is expected to result in annual operating savings of AU$500,000 and will therefore increase divisional operating income by AU$500,000. Thus, the return on this new investment is 12.50 per cent (AU$500,000 ÷ AU$4 million).

As we have seen above, it costs Outback Outfitters 11.28 cents for each dollar of capital to invest in operational assets. What is the optimal decision for the Koala Camp Gear Division manager to make, *viewed from the perspective of the company as a whole?* Since it costs Outback Outfitters 11.28 per cent for every dollar of capital and the return on the investment in new equipment is 12.50 per cent, an autonomous division manager should decide to buy the new equipment.

Now consider what is likely to happen. The Koala Camp Gear Division manager's performance is evaluated on the basis of his division's ROI. Without the new equipment, the divisional ROI is 15 per cent (AU$4,500,000 divisional operating income ÷ AU$30,000,000 invested capital). If he purchases the new equipment, his divisional ROI will *decline*:

	Operating income	Invested capital	ROI
Koala Camp Gear Division	AU$4,500,000	AU$30,000,000	15.00%
Investment opportunity	AU$500,000	AU$4,000,000	12.50%
	AU$5,000,000	AU$34,000,000	14.71%

Why did this happen? Although the investment in new equipment earns a return of 12.50 per cent, which is higher than the company's cost of raising capital (11.28 per cent), the return is less than the division's ROI without the equipment (15.00 per cent). Averaging the new investment with that already in place in the Koala Camp Gear Division merely reduces the division's ROI. Since the division manager is evaluated using ROI, he will be reluctant to decide to acquire the new equipment.

A key point to consider is that corporate management probably does not have all the information that the divisional managers have. There is *information asymmetry* between levels of management. If corporate management would also know about this investment opportunity, it could still somehow decide to make this go ahead. But the company decentralized for a good reason: because local managers are closer to decision-making alternatives and their impacts.

When investments should not be made

Now suppose that Outback's Retail Division manager is considering to upgrade several stores, which will cost AU$440,000. The investment is expected to result in extra operating income of AU$4 million. Thus, the return on this new investment is 11.00 per cent, which is below the company's cost of capital of 11.28 per cent. Clearly, this investment should not be made.

However, consider again what is likely to happen. The Retail Division manager's performance is evaluated on the basis of his division's ROI. Without the new equipment, the divisional ROI is 10 per cent (AU$4,800,000 divisional operating income ÷ AU$48,000,000 invested capital). If he purchases the new equipment, his divisional ROI will *increase:*

	Operating income	Invested capital	ROI
Retail Division	AU$4,800,000	AU$48,000,000	10.00%
Investment opportunity	AU$440,000	AU$4,000,000	11.00%
	AU$5,240,000	AU$52,000,000	10.08%

Again, the mechanism is that averaging the old ROI with a higher ROI creates unwanted effects.This time, it makes the ROI go up, even though the investment's ROI is still below the cost capital. In so far as the divisional manager has the authority to make this investment, he could be tempted to go ahead. And even if the investment first needs to be approved by corporate management, information asymmetry is likely to play a role. Obviously, corporate management will not accept an honest investment proposal showing a return on investment of only 11.00 per cent. However, the divisional manager may be tempted to bias the investment proposal and to portray a more optimistic picture that promises an acceptable return on investment.

The problem is that the ROI is a percentage that is the result of averaging the old ROI and the ROI of new investment projects. It ignores the firm's cost of raising investment capital. For this reason, many managers prefer to use different investment-centre performance measures called *residual income* or *economic value added*, instead of ROI. Before turning our attention to these measures, however, let's consider the ethical issues involved in the scenario just described.

Ethical considerations

The manager of the Koala Camp Gear Division and the manager of the Retail Division face a tough decision regarding the investment opportunities. What is in the best interest of the company as a whole, may not work out well for them personally. Purchasing the equipment will lower Koala Camp Gear Division's ROI, and the division manager is evaluated on the basis of divisional ROI. Perhaps his promotion potential, salary increases and bonuses are affected by the division's ROI, to say nothing of similar opportunities for his fellow managers in the Koala Camp Gear Division. The retail division may increase its ROI by upgrading the stores, which may be good for the manager and others in that division, but this is not sensible for the company, and also not for the division in the longer run.

What should these division managers do? Ethical considerations suggest that Koala Camp Gear Division's manager should purchase the CIM equipment, even though this decision could potentially jeopardize his prospects with the company, along with those of his divisional colleagues. The Retail Division manager should not push for upgrading the stores. These division managers, like all managers and employees, are supposed to be looking out for the best interests of the company and its owners. Nevertheless, anecdotal evidence, along with considerations of basic human nature, suggest that it might be unrealistic to expect such a manager to put the interests of corporate shareholders ahead of his own perceived interests, those of his family, and those of his colleagues and their families. What would you do?

Regardless of how you answer this rhetorical question, a very important point for our study of cost management systems is just this: to the extent possible, it is best for all concerned if the performance evaluation system results in goal or (at least behavioural) congruence so that managers have an incentive to make decisions consistent with corporate goals.

Residual Income as a Performance Measure

LO 6 Describe some advantages and disadvantages of return on investment and residual income as performance measures.

The **residual income (RI)** (and its more recent variation EVA, see below) has been recommended as a measure of business-unit performance since at least the 1920s when **General Motors** adopted it.[11] Residual income is a dollar amount, not a ratio like ROI. It is the amount of an investment centre's profit that remains (as a residual) after subtracting an imputed cost of capital.

$$\text{Residual income (RI)} = \text{Operating income} - \left(\text{Cost of captial} \times \text{Invested captial}\right)$$

So the key difference with 'normal' profit, is that not just the cost of debt is included as an expense, but instead a cost of capital is charged for *all assets* employed.

Outback Outfitters' cost of capital has been determined at 11.28 per cent, as we saw earlier. Hence, the RI calculations for Outback Outfitters' three divisions for the most recent year are:

	Operating income	– 11.28% ×	Invested capital	= Residual income (RI)
Mail-Order Division	AU$1,400,000	– 11.28% ×	AU$7,000,000	= AU$610,400
Koala Camp Gear Division	AU$4,500,000	– 11.28% ×	AU$30,000,000	= AU$1,116,000
Retail Division	AU$4,800,000	– 11.28% ×	AU$48,000,000	= AU$(614,400)

Notice that both the Mail-Order Division and Koala Camp Gear Divisions have a positive residual income, which is consistent with what we said earlier, namely that they have an ROI that is above the cost of capital. However, the Retail Division is not doing very well. It has a negative residual income, which corresponds with the fact that it has an ROI that is below the cost of capital.

What happens if the managers of the Koala Camp Gear Division and Retail Division again consider their investment opportunities? As the calculations in the table show, the residual income of Outback's Koala Camp Gear Division with the investment in the new CIM system becomes AU$1,164,800. Notice that the Koala Camp Gear Division's residual income will *increase* if the new equipment is purchased. What will be the division manager's incentive if he is evaluated on the basis of residual income instead of ROI? He will want to make the investment because that decision will increase his division's residual income. Thus, behavioural congruence is achieved when divisional performance is evaluated using residual income.

Notice also that the Retail Division's residual income will *decrease* if the store upgrading investment is pursued. The division manager will not want to make the investment, which is what we also want in the interest of the whole company. Thus, behavioural congruence is achieved.

	Operating Income	Invested capital	ROI	RI
Koala Camp Gear Division	AU$4,500,000	AU$30,000,000	15.00%	AU$1,116,000
Investment opportunity	AU$500,000	AU$4,000,000	12.50%	AU$48,800
	AU$5,000,000	AU$34,000,000	14.71%	AU$1,164,800
Retail Division	AU$4,800,000	AU$48,000,000	10.00%	AU$(614,400)
Investment opportunity	AU$440,000	AU$4,000,000	11.00%	AU$(11,200)
	AU$5,240,000	AU$52,000,000	10.08%	AU$(625,600)

Why does residual income facilitate behavioural congruence while ROI does not? The division's new RI (with the investment) is the *sum* of the current RI + the project RI. So any positive project-RI increases the business unit's total RI. However, the division's new ROI is a weighted *average* of the current ROI and the project ROI. That means that only projects above the current ROI increase the division's total ROI. Because of this underlying mechanism (sums versus averages) ROI wrongly discourages investments that are above the target-ROI but below the business unit's current ROI. Yet, RI correctly encourages any project with a positive RI (which implies a ROI that is above the target). ROI may also wrongly encourage investments that are below the target-ROI as long as they are above the business unit's current ROI. However, RI would not encourage these projects, as they have a negative RI.[12]

In sum, residual income is a desirable performance measure because it increases when investments generate earnings in excess of the cost of capital. RI also increases when companies eliminate investments that earn less than the cost of capital. Thus, residual income should reflect changes in the firm's value.[13]

Unfortunately, residual income also has a serious drawback: it should not be used to compare the performance of different-sized investment centres because it incorporates a bias in favour of the larger investment centre. As we saw in the table above, Koala Camp Gear Division's RI is considerably higher than that of the Mail-Order Division. This is largely due to the much larger size of the Koala Division, as evidenced by its far higher invested capital amount.

Neither ROI nor RI provides a perfect measure of investment-centre performance. ROI can undermine behavioural congruence. Residual income distorts comparisons between investment centres of different sizes. As a result, some companies routinely use both measures for divisional performance evaluation.

14.1 You're the Decision Maker

Evaluating the Success of a Division

One of Koala Camp Gear Division's suppliers, Queensland Fabrics Company, has two divisions, which reported the following results for the most recent year:

	Brisbane division	Cairns division
Operating income	AU$900,000	AU$200,000
Invested capital	6,000,000	1,000,000
ROI	15%	20%

Which was the more successful division for the year? Think carefully about this and back up your answer with a quantitative analysis.

(Solutions begin on page 743.)

Economic Value Added (EVA) as a Performance Measure

The most contemporary measure of investment centre performance is *economic value added (EVA)*. The **economic value added (EVA)** is essentially a residual income measure, but much attention is given to adjustments in the precise ways in which operating income and invested capital are being measured.

One of the selling points for EVA is that it permits multiple adjustments to operating income and invested capital. One of the main adjustments is that *current liabilities* are usually subtracted from total assets for the measure of invested capital used in the EVA measure. But making such adjustments to align incentives with desired behaviour is not new. For many years, companies have adjusted reported earnings in the following ways:

- Capitalize expenditures on research and development in the US, where it must be expensed for financial reporting.
- Capitalize expenditures on customer development, advertising and promotion if these expenditures will benefit future years.
- Capitalize expenditures on employee training that will benefit future years.
- Make general or specific price-level adjustments so assets, revenues and expenses are stated in current year currency values.
- Use gross book values or restated net book values to reflect the assets' actual economic value.
- Restate inventories to replacement cost.
- Do not amortize goodwill, which was required in the US for financial reporting.

Note that this list is neither a recommended guideline nor a complete, current list of adjustments (one consulting company advertises more than 160 adjustments to reported earnings). Each situation is unique and could require its own set of adjustments (or none at all).

A key reason for making these adjustments it to construct a performance measure that is closely related to share price performance. Thus, using EVA as the managerial performance measure should more closely align managers' and shareholders' interest. Recent research partially supports this claim, but at this time the superiority of EVA or RI over reported earnings is open to question (see Research Insight 14.1 for a discussion).

The EVA discussion highlights the need to fine-tune a performance measure for the purpose of assessment of managerial performance. Remember that although components of earnings used in external reports must comply with IFRS or local GAAP, measurements of earnings in managerial performance measures need not. Designers of managerial performance measures should match incentives from earnings numbers to desired behaviour. The right way to measure income and assets for financial reporting may not be the best way to measure how well a manager is doing business. This brings us to the next section, where variations of performance measures are discussed in more detail.

14.1 Research Insight

Does EVA Pay?

Residual income (RI) and economic value added (EVA) have a long history as prescriptions for better performance evaluations. Economic researchers have been interested in finding the conditions when RI or EVA will reflect changes in firm value: if RI or EVA go up, share prices should go up, and vice versa (yes, these conditions might exist). Current accounting and finance research indicates that division managers who evaluated using residual income make investing, financing and operating decisions that should increase share prices. Thus, residual income/EVA might be an effective incentive device. However, the share market does not appear to increase prices of shares of companies when they *adopt* EVA-based incentive plans, but if managers make better decisions, share prices should increase. Perhaps the value of EVA-based plans does not exceed their cost. Furthermore, some research indicates that share price returns are more closely correlated with net income than with EVA. Perhaps net income is a better reflection of changes in firm value than EVA. At this time, we cannot establish a clear link between EVA-based incentives and increased shareholder value. More research is needed in this area.

Sources: Bromwich and Walker (1998); Biddle et al. (1997, 1998); Wallace (1997). For alternative points of view, see Dierks and Patel (1997) and Freedman (1998).

Measuring Invested Capital and Operating Income for EVA, ROI and RI Performance Measures

LO 7
Explain various approaches for measuring a division's operating income and invested capital.

The return on investment, residual income, and economic value added measures of investment centre performance all use operating income and invested capital in their formulas. In particular the proponents of EVA put much emphasis on fine-tuning the precise way in which divisional operating income is measured and invested capital is valued. The financial performance measures commonly include levels or *changes* of the following:

- Revenues
- Costs
- Cash flow
- Operating income (before or after extraordinary items, taxes)
- Invested capital
- Share price.

All of these measures except share price are explicitly based on earnings-related numbers. The last three items are most commonly used to evaluate business unit performance and provide interesting opportunities for the discussion of incentives and motivation. Let's briefly discuss them in this context.[14]

Measuring Invested Capital

We focus on Outback's Koala Camp Gear Division to illustrate several alternative approaches to measuring an investment centre's capital. Exhibit 14.4 lists the assets and liabilities associated with the Koala Camp Gear Division. Notice that Exhibit 14.4 does not constitute a complete balance sheet. First, there are no long-term liabilities, such as bonds payable, associated with the Koala Camp Gear Division. Although Outback Outfitters has long-term debt, assigning portions of that debt to the company's individual divisions is not meaningful. Second, it has no shareholders' equity associated with the Koala Camp Gear Division. The owners of the company own shares in Outback Outfitters, not in its individual divisions.

Exhibit 14.4 Assets and Liabilities Associated with Koala Camp Gear Division

Assets*		
Current assets (cash, accounts receivable, inventories, etc.)		AU$3,400,000
Long-lived assets (land, buildings, equipment, vehicles, etc.):		
Gross book value (acquisition cost)	AU$30,400,000	
Less: Accumulated depreciation	6,400,000	
Net book value		24,000,000
Plant under construction		2,600,000
Total assets		AU$30,000,000
Liabilities*		
Current liabilities (accounts payable, salaries payable, etc.)		AU$500,000

This is not a balance sheet, but a list of the average balances of certain assets and liabilities associated with the Koala Camp Gear Division during the year.

Average balances

ROI, residual income and EVA are computed for a period of time, such as a year or a month. Asset balances, on the other hand, are measured at a point in time, such as 31 December. Since divisional asset balances generally change over time, we use average balances in calculating ROI, residual income and EVA. For example, if the Koala Camp Gear Division's balance in invested capital was AU$29 million on 1 January, and AU$31 million on 31 December, we would use the average invested capital of AU$30 million in the ROI, residual income and EVA calculations.

Should total assets be used?

Exhibit 14.4 shows that during the most recent year the Koala Camp Gear Division had *average balances* of AU$3.4 million in current assets, AU$24 million in net long-lived assets, and AU$2.6 million tied up in a plant under construction. (Outback Outfitters is building a new high-tech plant in Brisbane to manufacture its new line of diving equipment.) In addition, Exhibit 14.4 discloses that the Koala Camp Gear Division's average balance of current liabilities was AU$500,000.

What is the division's invested capital? Consider several possibilities here:

- *Total assets.* The management of Outback Outfitters has decided to use *average total assets* for the year in measuring each division's invested capital. Thus, AU$30 million is the amount used in the ROI, residual income and EVA calculations discussed earlier in this chapter. This measure of invested capital is appropriate if the division manager has considerable authority in making decisions about *all* of the division's assets, *including non-productive assets.* In this case, the Koala Division's partially completed plant is a non-productive asset. Since the division manager had considerable influence in deciding to build the new plant and is responsible for overseeing the project, average total assets provides an appropriate measure.
- *Total productive assets.* In other companies, top management directs division managers to keep non-productive assets, such as vacant land or construction in progress. In such cases, the exclusion of non-productive assets from the measure of invested capital is appropriate. Then *average total productive assets* are used to measure invested capital. If Outback Outfitters had chosen this alternative, AU$27.4 million would have been used in the ROI, residual income and EVA calculations (total assets of AU$30 million less AU$2.6 million for the plant under construction).
- *Total assets less current liabilities.* Some companies allow division managers to secure short-term bank loans and other short-term credit. In such cases, invested capital is often measured by *average total assets less average current liabilities.* This approach encourages investment centre managers to minimize resources tied up in assets and maximize the use of short-term credit to finance operations. If Outback Outfitters had used this approach, the Koala Camp Gear Division's invested capital would have been AU$29.5 million, total assets of AU$30 million less current liabilities of AU$500,000. (*Note:* Current liabilities are typically subtracted from total assets for the measure of invested capital used in the EVA measure.)

Gross or net book value

Another decision to make in choosing a measure of invested capital is whether to use the *gross book value (acquisition cost)* or the *net book value* of long-lived assets. (Net book value is the acquisition cost less accumulated depreciation.) Outback Outfitters' management has decided to use the average net book value of AU$24 million to value the Koala Camp Gear Division's long-lived assets. If gross book value had been used instead, the division's measure of invested capital would have been AU$36.4 million, as the following calculation shows.

Current assets	AU$ 3,400,000
Long-lived assets (at gross book value)	30,400,000
Plant under construction	2,600,000
Total assets (at gross book value)	AU$36,400,000

Advantages are associated with both gross and net book value as a measure of invested capital.

Advantages of net book value

- Using net book value maintains consistency with the statement of financial position prepared for external reporting purposes. This allows for more meaningful comparisons of ROI measures across different companies.
- Using net book value to measure invested capital is also more consistent with the definition of operating income, which is the numerator in ROI calculations. In computing operating income, the current period depreciation on long-lived assets is deducted as an expense.

Advantages of gross book value

- The usual methods of computing depreciation, such as the straight-line and the declining-balance methods, are arbitrary. Hence, they should not be allowed to affect ROI, residual income or EVA calculations.
- When long-lived assets are depreciated, their net book value declines over time. This results in a misleading increase in ROI, residual income and EVA across time. The spreadsheet in Exhibit 14.5 illustrates this phenomenon for the ROI calculated on an equipment purchase under consideration by the Koala Camp Gear Division manager. Notice that the ROI rises steadily across the five-year horizon if invested capital is measured by net book value. However, using gross book value eliminates this problem. The use of an accelerated depreciation method instead of the straight-line method is even more pronounced in the increasing trend in ROI.

Exhibit 14.5 Increase in ROI Over Time (When Net Book Value Is Used)

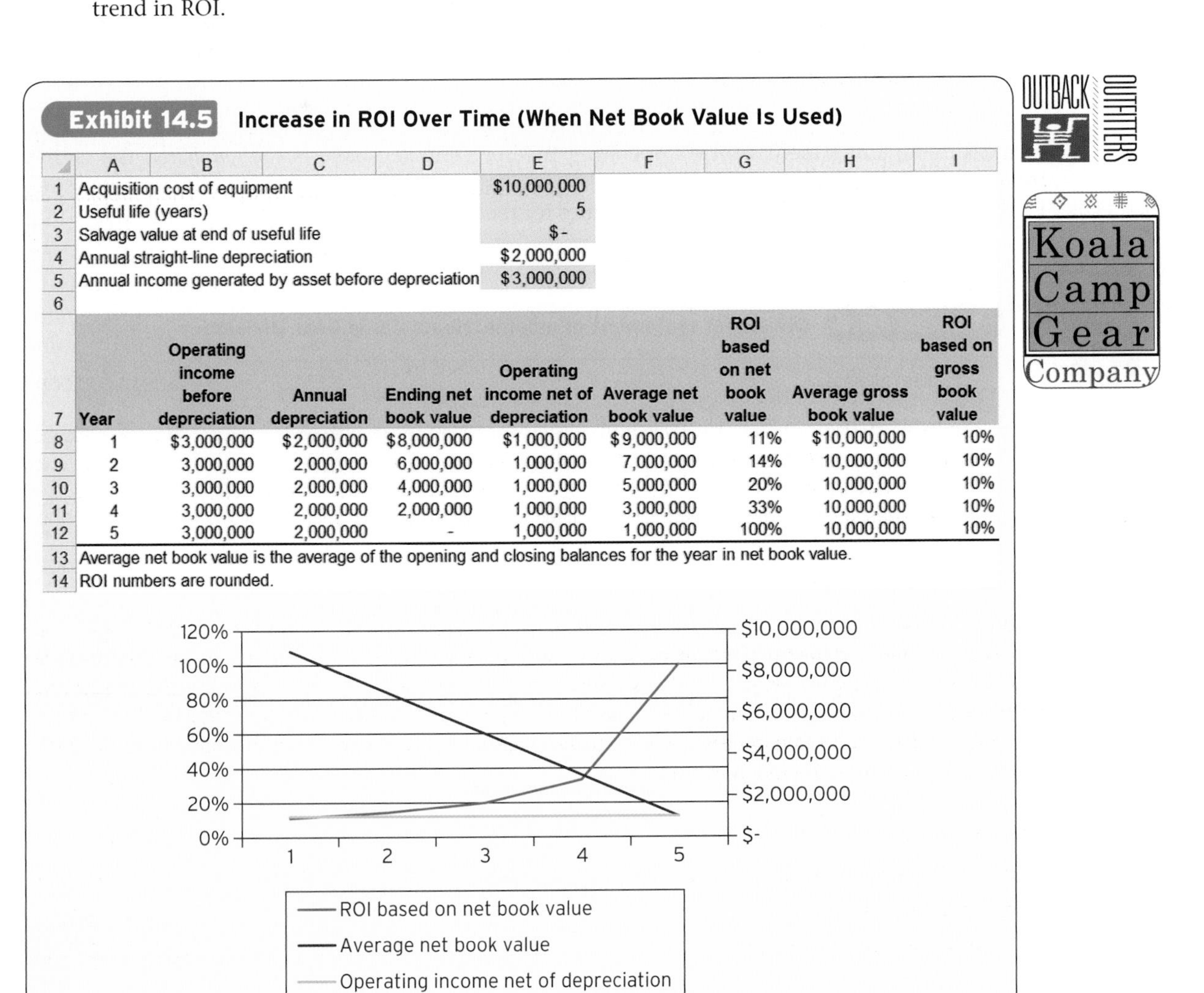

	A	B	C	D	E	F	G	H	I
1	Acquisition cost of equipment				$10,000,000				
2	Useful life (years)				5				
3	Salvage value at end of useful life				$ -				
4	Annual straight-line depreciation				$2,000,000				
5	Annual income generated by asset before depreciation				$3,000,000				
6									
7	Year	Operating income before depreciation	Annual depreciation	Ending net book value	Operating income net of depreciation	Average net book value	ROI based on net book value	Average gross book value	ROI based on gross book value
8	1	$3,000,000	$2,000,000	$8,000,000	$1,000,000	$9,000,000	11%	$10,000,000	10%
9	2	3,000,000	2,000,000	6,000,000	1,000,000	7,000,000	14%	10,000,000	10%
10	3	3,000,000	2,000,000	4,000,000	1,000,000	5,000,000	20%	10,000,000	10%
11	4	3,000,000	2,000,000	2,000,000	1,000,000	3,000,000	33%	10,000,000	10%
12	5	3,000,000	2,000,000	-	1,000,000	1,000,000	100%	10,000,000	10%
13	Average net book value is the average of the opening and closing balances for the year in net book value.								
14	ROI numbers are rounded.								

Dysfunctional behavioural effects

The tendency for net book value to produce a misleading increase in ROI over time can seriously affect the incentives of investment centre managers. Investment centres with old assets show much higher ROIs than investment centres with relatively new assets. This can discourage investment centre managers from investing in new equipment. If this behavioural tendency persists, a division's assets can become obsolete, making the division uncompetitive.

Allocating assets to investment centres

Some companies control certain assets centrally, although these assets are needed to operate the divisions. Common examples are cash and accounts receivable. Divisions need cash to operate, but many companies control cash balances centrally to minimize their total cash holdings. Some large retail firms manage accounts receivable centrally. A credit customer of Outback Outfitters, for example, can make a payment at the local store, mail the payment to corporate headquarters or use a credit card.

When certain assets are controlled centrally, some basis generally is chosen to allocate these asset balances to investment centres for measuring invested capital. For example, cash could be allocated based on the budgeted cash needs in each division or on the basis of divisional sales. Accounts receivable usually are allocated on the basis of divisional sales. Divisions with less stringent credit terms are allocated proportionately larger balances of accounts receivable.

Measuring Investment Centre Operating Income

In addition to choosing a measure of investment centre capital, management must also decide how to measure an investment centre's operating income. The key issue is *controllability*; the choice involves the extent to which uncontrollable items are allowed to influence the income measure. Exhibit 14.6 illustrates six different possibilities for measuring the income of Outback's Koala Camp

Exhibit 14.6 Divisional statement of income: Koala Camp Gear Division

	Sales revenue	AU$40,500,000
	Unit-level, batch-level, product-line-level, and customer-level expenses	27,300,000
(1)	Divisional contribution margin	AU$13,200,000
	General and facility-level expenses controllable by division manager	8,700,000
(2)	Profit margin controllable by division manager	AU$ 4,500,000
	General and facility-level expenses traceable to division but controlled by others	1,500,000
(3)	Profit margin traceable to division	$ 3,000,000
	Common general and facility-level expenses,allocated from company headquarters	500,000
(4)	Divisional operating income before interest and taxes	AU$2,500,000
	Interest expense allocated from company headquarters	1,300,000
(5)	Divisional income before taxes	AU$ 1,200,000
	Income taxes allocated from company headquarters	360,000
(6)	Divisional net income	AU$ 840,000

Gear Division, using the division's revenue and expense data for the most recent year. All of the information in Exhibit 14.6 is derived from data collected by the division's cost accounting system, but notice that some of the numbers require making judgements about controllability, which would be made by the corporate-level cost management staff. For example, the corporate cost management staff makes a judgement regarding how much of the division's general and facility-level expenses is controllable by the division manager and how much of these expenses is controllable by others.

Outback Outfitters' top management uses the *profit margin controllable by division manager*, AU$4.5 million, to evaluate the Koala Camp Gear Division manager. This profit measure is used in calculating ROI, residual income and EVA. Some fixed costs traceable to the division have not been deducted from this AU$4.5 million amount, but the division manager cannot control or significantly influence these costs. Hence, they are excluded from the ROI calculation in evaluating the division manager. In calculating economic value added (EVA), the AU$4.5 million profit-margin amount is converted to an after-tax basis by multiplying by 1 minus the tax rate of 30 per cent.

Managers versus investment centres

A distinction between an investment centre and its manager is important. In evaluating the *manager's* performance, only revenues and costs that the manager can control or significantly influence should be included in the profit measure. The performance measure's overall objective is to provide incentives for goal-congruent behaviour. No performance measure can motivate a manager to make decisions about the costs he or she cannot control. This explains the reliance of Outback Outfitters' top management on the profit margin controllable by the division manager to compute the manager's performance measure (line 2 in Exhibit 14.6).

Evaluating the Koala Camp Gear Division as a viable economic investment is a different matter altogether. In this evaluation, traceability of costs rather than controllability is the issue. For this purpose, Outback's top management uses the profit margin traceable to the division to compute the divisional ROI, residual income or EVA. As Exhibit 14.6 shows (line 3), this amount is AU$3 million.

Other profit measures

Some companies also use the other measures of divisional profit shown in Exhibit 14.6 (lines 4, 5 and 6). The rationale behind these divisional income measures is that all corporate costs must be covered by the operations of the divisions. Allocating corporate costs, interest and income taxes to the divisions makes division managers aware of these costs.

Market Value versus Historical-cost Accounting

Whether measuring investment centre income or invested capital, the impact of price-level changes should not be forgotten. During periods of inflation, historical-cost asset values soon cease to reflect the cost of replacing those assets. Therefore, some managers argue that investment centre performance measures based on historical-cost accounting are misleading. Yet surveys of corporate managers indicate that an accounting system based on current values would not alter their decisions. Most managers believe that measures based on historical-cost accounting are adequate when used in conjunction with budgets and performance targets. As managers prepare those budgets, they build their expectations about inflation (or deflation) into the budgets and performance targets.

Another reason for using historical-cost accounting for internal purposes is that it is required for external reporting. Thus, historical-cost data already are available, while installing current-value accounting would add substantial incremental costs to the organization's information system.

14.2 You're the Decision Maker

Deciding between Alternative Merchandise Inventory Plans

The manager of the Outback Outfitters store in Adelaide is evaluated using ROI. Corporate headquarters requires an ROI of 10 per cent of assets. The manager estimates that for the coming year revenue will be AU$260,000, and cost of goods sold will be AU$163,000. Operating expenses for this level of sales will be AU$26,000. Investment in the store assets throughout the year is AU$187,500 before considering the following proposal.

A representative of Tasmania Trading Company approached the Outback Outfitters manager about carrying its line of camp cookware. This line is expected to generate AU$75,000 in sales in the coming year at the Adelaide store with a cost of merchandise sold of AU$57,000. Annual operating expenses for this additional merchandise line are AU$8,500. To carry the line of goods, an inventory investment of AU$55,000 throughout the year is required.

As an alternative, Tasmania is willing to 'floor plan' the merchandise so that the Adelaide store will not have to invest in any additional inventory. Tasmania's charge for floor planning would be AU$6,750 per year. The floor-planning arrangement with Tasmania would offer two advantages to Outback's Adelaide store. First, Tasmania rather than Outback Outfitters would maintain the AU$55,000 investment in the inventory. Outback would still incur the AU$57,000 annual cost-of-merchandise-sold expense and the AU$8,500 in additional operating expenses, plus the AU$6,750 charge for floor planning. Second, Tasmania would take charge of maintaining floor displays for its merchandise in the Adelaide store, as well as giving Outback's management advice on optimal merchandise placement within the store.

Assume that Outback's cost of capital is 10 per cent.

a. What is the Adelaide store's expected ROI for the coming year if it does not carry Tasmania's cookware in the store?
b. What is the store's expected ROI if the manager invests in the Tasmania inventory and carries the cookware line?
c. What is the store's expected ROI if the manager elects to take the floor-plan option?
d. Would the manager prefer (a), (b), or (c)? Why?

(Solutions begin on page 743.)

Measuring Operating Income and Invested Capital: Summary

To summarize, the primary objective in choosing measures for the evaluation of investment centres and their managers is goal (or at least behavioural) congruence. Cost managers should design investment centre performance measures that reward managers for pursuing the goals of the overall organization.[15]

Photo: Bosch

ROI is the most commonly used measure of business-unit performance. It is straightforward to understand, it can be calculated *without* knowing the appropriate cost of capital (although then there is no benchmark for the ROI), it is a percentage as many other measures (such as return on sales), and it is easy to compare across business units of different sizes. The main disadvantage is that it may provide the wrong incentives to invest. ROI erroneously discourages investments that are above the cost of capital but below the business unit's current ROI. ROI wrongly encourages investments that are below cost of capital but above the business unit's current ROI.

RI and EVA are desirable managerial performance measures because these provide the right incentives to invest. RI and EVA increase when investments generate earnings in excess of the cost of capital. RI and EVA also increase when companies eliminate investments that earn less than the cost of capital. Thus, residual income and economic valued added should reflect changes in the firm's value. However, calculating RI and EVA requires knowing the precise cost of capital, and business units of different sizes are difficult to compare. Residual income and EVA, in some form, are based on a fundamental concept of economic profit generated after considering all costs, including the opportunity cost of capital.

Perhaps more important than the basic choice between ROI, RI and EVA (and why not use them all anyway?) are the specific design choices for how operating income and the investment base are being measured. This may require specific accounting choices, such as about capitalization of particular costs. ROI, RI and EVA allow for the many possible variations of its components (i.e., alternative measures income and investment base).

14.3 Cost Management in Practice

Bosch Uses EVA

The German firm Bosch is a global company that has implemented a form of economic value added since 2000. In 2010, the company generated worldwide sales of €47.3 billion and employed around 285,000 people. The company has almost 300 manufacturing sites around the world. The three main business sectors are Automotive Technology, Industrial Technology, and Consumer Goods and Building Technology, which further comprise of 17 divisions (for example, Automotive Aftermarket, Power Tools and Security Systems), and these consist of around 50 business units. Reporting of financial performance of these units, divisions and business sectors is based on EVA.[a]

The company's shares are not publicly traded. Ninety-two per cent of the share capital of Robert Bosch GmbH is held by Robert Bosch Stiftung GmbH, a charitable foundation. Bosch's objective of EVA is not to maximize shareholder value, but to secure the company's existence and to remain financially independent by offering a market return in the long run.

The starting point for the calculation of the economic value added[b] is the operating profit after tax. The main ingredients of the calculation at Bosch are: a capital charge based on all capital employed (instead of interest paid for debt), and economic depreciation of assets based on annuities (instead of IFRS depreciation).

The capital charge is the investment base × the cost of capital. The investment base consists of fixed assets + current assets − non-interest bearing debt, which is mainly accounts payable, provisions and customer advances. A cost of capital of 8 per cent is used, the same as the discount rate used for investment decisions. Economic depreciation applies to fixed assets such as buildings, machinery, equipment, but also to software and other intangible assets. Economic depreciation avoids that the residual income (and the return on investment) increases over time just because the book value of assets decreases. The depreciation is such that the total of depreciation and capital charge is the same for each period. For example, at 8 per cent and 10 years, the annuity factor is 6.71, and so the depreciation + capital charge remains $1000 \div 6.71 = 149$ over the entire 10-year period.

By rearranging the same data, Bosch also calculates a ROI measure.[c] The capital charge is taken out of the EVA to get the net operating profit again.[d] This is divided by the investment base: ROI = (EVA + Capital charge) ÷ Investment base.

Two types of bonus programmes are based on EVA. A short-term bonus is given if the annual EVA is at least 80 per cent of the planned value. A long-term bonus is provided if, measured over a three-year period, the EVA increase meets 75 per cent of the target EVA increase.

Bosch's experiences with EVA implementation show that communication throughout the company is crucial for the success of the system. Furthermore, EVA has made managers much more sensitive about the efficient employment of capital. The use of EVA as the only performance measure in the incentive systems has quickly brought this into focus at all management levels in the organization.

[a] We use the terms that are used in the main text, but Bosch refers to their performance measurement system as Value-Based Management.
[b] In the Bosch terminology this is called Value Contribution, or Wert Beitrag (WB).
[c] In the Bosch terminology this is called Cash Flow Return on Investment.
[d] Nachhaltiger Cash Flow (NCF) in the Bosch terminology.

Source: Company presentation given at Manufacturing Accounting Conference, Münster, Germany.

Alternatives to Accounting Performance Measures

LO 8
Distinguish between accounting performance measures and alternatives to such measures.

Why use accounting performance measures, if they have the difficulties that we discussed so far? In this section we will discuss alternative approaches, which have considerable limitations, and this helps to understand the pervasive use of accounting performance measures by companies.

Share Price Performance

If an objective is to align managers' interests to those of shareholders, why not use share price performance as the performance evaluation measure? When the share price rises, both managers and shareholders are better off, and vice versa. However, the performance of the company's shares can only be measured at the company level and not per business unit. Therefore, business-unit managers in large companies might see little connection between their actions and the performance of the company's shares. Furthermore, a company's share price can fluctuate widely based on factors over which the manager has no control, including economic and industry trends, interest rates, politics, technology, and customer tastes and preferences. Therefore, tying managers' compensation to share price performance places a good deal of risk on them. Furthermore, this type of risk is not easy for managers to diversify because the performance measure is based on just one share – that of their company.

Despite these problems with share price as a measure of performance, many companies generally provide at least some incentive for managers to be concerned about share performance by rewarding with share awards. Some companies go beyond share awards and require their executives to own shares valued at a multiple of their base pay (for example, one, three or five times, depending on the position). Extensive share ownership gives executives an interest in how well their company's shares are doing even if share price is not an explicit performance measure.

Non-financial Performance Measures

Evidence indicates that the use of non-financial measures of managerial performance is increasing. Of course, organizations have used non-financial measures for managing operations for many years,[16] but including them in incentive plans is an important development.[17]

There is a fundamental trade-off involved between using several non-financial performance measures versus one (or very few) overall financial performance measure. Using an overall financial performance measure such as ROI or EVA means that the manager of the business unit has the authority to make a range of decisions that affect the business and its revenues, costs and investments. It is delegated to the manager to make trade-offs between these and to achieve a good return on the invested capital, as an end result. However, using several non-financial measures means that headquarters is going to be much more involved in how that end result is supposed to be achieved. There is inevitably going to be less delegation of decision rights to the manager.

For example, suppose that Koala Camp Gear Division's manager has specific performance measures with targets for:

- Delivery times
- Customer satisfaction
- Efficiency in manufacturing
- Inventory levels.

Defining the targets for these measures involves making detailed choices for how the business is being run. For example, the business unit can follow very different approaches to how it wants to be able to offer short and reliable delivery times to its customers. The business unit could maintain high inventory levels and optimize production efficiency, or it could invest in a flexible manufacturing system and carry far lower inventories. Companies make these trade-offs in different ways, for example depending on how costly inventories are when considering not only financing, but also the fact that goods may be perishable or go out of fashion, there can be substantial price erosion, and for some goods handling is very expensive.[18] Why would headquarters know about such business choices and be involved in defining targets for separate non-financial measures? Didn't they decentralize for good reasons?[19]

Perhaps the greatest advantages of adding non-financial measures to the incentive system are (1) focus on the drivers of profit and (2) recognition of the time lags between non-financial and financial performance. More on non-financial performance measures in incentive systems can be found in Chapter 16.

Viewing an Investment Centre as a Collection of Investments

ROI, RI and EVA are short-run performance measures. They focus on only one period of time, yet an investment centre is really a collection of assets (investments), each of which has a multiperiod life. To evaluate any one of these individual investments correctly requires a multiperiod viewpoint, which considers the timing of the cash flows from the investment. For example, an investment could start out slowly in its early years but could be economically justified by its expected high performance in later years. Any evaluation of the investment centre in one particular year that ignores the long-term performance of its various investments can result in a misleading conclusion. Thus, single-period performance measures suffer from myopia; they focus on only a short time segment that slices across the division's collection of investments.

To avoid this short-term focus, some organizations downplay such measures as ROI, residual income and EVA in favour of an alternative approach. Instead of relating profit to invested capital in a single measure, these characteristics of investment centre performance are evaluated separately. Actual divisional profit for a time period is compared to a flexible budget, and variances are used to analyse performance. The division's major investments are evaluated through a *postaudit* of the investment decisions.[20] For example, a particular investment could have been undertaken because of expected high performance several years into the future. When that time comes, a review will determine whether the project lived up to expectations.

Evaluating periodic profit through flexible budgeting and variance analysis, coupled with post-audits of major investment decisions, is a more complicated approach to evaluating investment centres. However, it does help management avoid the myopia of single-period measures such as ROI, RI and EVA.

Performance Measurement in Non-profit Organizations

Management control in a non-profit organization presents a special challenge.[21] These organizations are often managed by professionals, such as physicians in a hospital. Moreover, many people participate in a non-profit organization at some personal sacrifice, motivated by humanitarian or public service ideals. Often, such people are less receptive to formal control procedures than their counterparts in business.

The goals of non-profit organizations often are less clear-cut than those of businesses. Public service objectives can be difficult to specify with precision and even more difficult to measure in terms of achievement. For example, one community health centre was established in an economically depressed area with three stated goals:

1. To reduce costs in a nearby hospital by providing a clinic for people to use instead of the hospital emergency room.
2. To provide preventive as well as therapeutic care and establish outreach programmes in the community.
3. To become financially self-sufficient.

These objectives conflict somewhat since goal 2 does not provide revenue to the centre but goals 1 and 3 focus on financial efficiency. Moreover, the health centre was staffed with physicians who could have achieved much higher incomes in private practice. The management control tools described in this and the preceding chapter can be used in non-profit organizations. However, the challenges in doing so effectively often are greater.

Internal Transactions and Transfer Prices

LO 9
Understand why transfer prices are part of systems for measuring divisional performance.

So far we did not consider that in large companies different responsibility centres may also do business with each other. For example, a business unit that sells industrial systems may buy components and individual pieces of equipment from other business units in the same company. For both business units, these internal transactions simply represent revenues (for the selling unit) and expenses (for the buying unit).

Koala Camp Gear's sales are to a large extent to the Mail-Order Division and the Retail Division that are also part of Outback Outfitters Ltd. In fact, such internal transactions do not even constitute revenues at the consolidated level of Outback Outfitters Ltd. Only sales to external customers generate revenues for the company. Nevertheless, the accounting numbers of the Koala Camp Gear Division that were shown in this chapter did not distinguish between internal and external transactions. That is not needed at the divisional level.

However, there is something special about internal transactions. The price used for internal transactions is called the **transfer price**. Transfer prices are the topic of Chapter 15. Briefly, the transfer price is one responsibility centre's sales price and the other centre's purchasing price. And so the transfer price allocates profit between the two divisions. A higher transfer price increases the profit of the selling responsibility centre and by the same amount decreases the buying centre's profit. This is, of course, exactly the same as with any price between two parties that buy and sell. But in contrast to external prices, the company itself governs the transfer prices. Transfer prices often and unavoidably are part of the performance measurement system. The company determines how transfer prices are set and this decision will inherently affect the performance measurement system. Even if the company decides that it will not interfere at all in how prices for internal transactions are set, that is still a decision (namely to do nothing).

Chapter Summary

Responsibility accounting systems are designed to foster *goal* or *behavioural congruence* among the managers in decentralized organizations. Each subunit in an organization is designated as a standard cost centre, discretionary cost centre, revenue centre, profit centre, or investment centre. The cost management team prepares a performance report for each responsibility centre. These reports show the performance of the responsibility centre and its manager for a specified time period. The most effective performance reports include both financial and non-financial information pertaining to performance.

To use responsibility accounting effectively, the emphasis must be on information rather than blame. The intent should be to provide managers with information to help them better manage their subunits. Responsibility accounting systems are also intended to bring about desired behaviour.

The three most common measures of investment centre performance are return on investment (ROI), residual income (RI) and economic value added (EVA). Each of these performance measures relates an investment centre's operating income to the capital invested to earn it. The organization's cost of acquiring capital is considered either as benchmark for the ROI, or by including this as an explicit cost in the RI and EVA calculation. RI and EVA have the advantage of providing the right investment incentives to investment centre managers. ROI, residual income and EVA all require the measurement of a division's operating income and invested capital, and the methods for making these measurements vary in practice.

The primary criterion for judging the effectiveness of performance measures for responsibility centre managers is the extent to which the measures promote goal or behavioural congruence.

Key Terms

For each term's definition, refer to the indicated page, or turn to the glossary at the end of the text.

Term	Page	Term	Page
behavioural congruence,	698	profit centre,	701
capital turnover,	711	residual income (RI),	714
centralized,	698	responsibility accounting,	698
decentralized,	698	responsibility centre,	700
discretionary cost centre,	700	return on investment (ROI),	710
economic value added (EVA),	716	revenue centre,	701
goal congruence,	698	sales margin,	711
investment centre,	701	standard cost centre,	700
management by exception,	705	transfer price,	726
operating income,	709	weighted-average cost of capital (WACC),	709
performance report,	705		

*Review Questions are mostly written at a **basic** level; Critical Analysis questions and Exercises are **intermediate**, and Problems and Cases are **advanced**.*

Review Questions

14.1 Why is goal congruence, or at least behavioural congruence, important to an organization's success?

14.2 Could the type of budget items for which some responsibility centres are accountable differ? That is, might some responsibility centres be responsible only for costs, some only for revenues and some for both? Give examples.

14.3 Accounting is supposed to provide a neutral, relevant and objective measure of performance. Why would problems arise when applying accounting measures in the context of performance evaluation?

14.4 Suppose you overheard this comment: 'This whole problem of measuring performance for segment managers using accounting numbers is so much hogwash. We pay our managers a good salary and expect them to do the best possible job. At least with our system, there is no incentive to play with the accounting data.' Does the comment make sense?

14.5 Define and give examples of the following terms: *standard cost centre, discretionary cost centre, revenue centre, profit centre* and *investment centre*.

14.6 What are the advantages of using an ROI-type measure rather than a division's profit as a performance evaluation technique?

14.7 The production department manager has just received a responsibility report showing a substantial unfavourable variance for overtime premium. The manager objects to the inclusion of this variance because the acceptance of a large rush order by the sales department caused the overtime. To whom should this variance be charged?

14.8 Under what conditions does the use of ROI measures inhibit a division manager's goal-congruent decision making?

14.9 Create an example showing the calculation of residual income. What information is used in computing residual income that is not used in computing ROI?

14.10 Why do some companies use gross book value instead of net book value to measure a division's invested capital?

14.11 Define the term *economic value added (EVA)*. How does it differ from residual income?

14.12 Describe an alternative to using ROI, residual income or EVA to measure investment centre performance.

Critical Analysis

14.13 Under what circumstances is it appropriate to change Outback Outfitters' Sydney plant from a profit centre to an investment centre?

14.14 'Performance reports based on controllability are impossible. Nobody really *controls* anything in an organization!' Do you agree or disagree? Explain your answer.

14.15 Central management of Adler Inc. evaluated divisional performance using residual income (RI) measures. The division managers were ranked according to the RI in each division. All division managers with residual income in the upper half of the ranking received a bonus. The bonus amount was in proportion to the RI amount. No bonus was paid to managers in the lower half of the ranking. What biases might arise in this system?

14.16 Explain why distinguishing between investment centres and their managers is important in performance evaluation.

14.17 Explain how the manager of the automobile division of an insurance company could improve her division's ROI.

14.18 Management of division A is evaluated based on residual income measures. The division can either rent or buy a certain asset. Might the performance evaluation technique have an impact on the rent-or-buy decision? Why or why not?

14.19 What is the chief disadvantage of ROI as an investment-centre performance measure? How does the residual-income measure eliminate this disadvantage?

14.20 Distinguish between the following measures of invested capital and briefly explain when each should be used: (1) total assets, (2) total productive assets, and (3) total assets less current liabilities.

14.21 Bleak Prospects Inc. found that its market share was slipping. Bleak encouraged division managers to maximize ROI and make decisions consistent with that goal. Nonetheless, frequent customer complaints resulted in lost business. Moreover, Bleak depended on an established product line and was unable to find new products for expansion while its competitors seemed to be able to generate new products almost yearly. What would you suggest Bleak Products' management do to improve its situation?

14.22 Why does ROI or residual income typically rise across time in a division? What undesirable behavioural implications could this phenomenon have?

Exercises

Exercise 14.23 [LO 1, 2] Designing Responsibility Centre

For each of the following organizational subunits, indicate the type of responsibility centre that is most appropriate.

a. A cinema in a company that operates a cinemas.
b. A radio station owned by a large broadcasting network.
c. The claims department in an insurance company.

d. The ticket sales division of a major airline.
e. A bottling plant of a soft-drink company.
f. An orange juice factory operated by a large orange grower.
g. The College of Engineering at a large university.
h. The European Division of a multinational manufacturing company.
i. The outpatient clinic in a profit-oriented hospital.
j. The Mayor's Office in a large city.

Exercise 14.24 [LO 6, 7] Return on Investment

Find a recent article in a magazine such as *BusinessWeek, The Wall Street Journal* or the *Financial Times* that describes a large merger or acquisition.

Required

How will the event be likely to change the ROI of the firms involved?

Exercise 14.25 [LO 3] Performance Report; Hotel

The following data for the month of August pertain to the Northern Lights Inn, located in Reykjavík, Iceland. The inn's organization chart shows that the food and beverage department has the following subunits: banquets and catering, restaurants, and kitchen. (Monetary units given in Icelandic króna, kr.)

	Flexible budget: August (in thousands)*	Actual results: August (in thousands)*
Banquets and catering	116,820 kr	118,260 kr
Restaurants	324,180	323,100
Kitchen staff wages.	(15,300)	(15,480)
Food	(124,200)	(124,200)
Paper products	(22,500)	(21,960)
Unit-level (variable) overhead in kitchen.	(13,500)	(14,040)
Facility-level (fixed) overhead in kitchen	(16,200)	(16,740)

*Numbers without parentheses denote profit; numbers with parentheses denote expenses.

Required

Build a spreadsheet and prepare an August performance report for Northern Lights Inn's food and beverage department similar to the lower portion of Exhibit 14.3, which relates to Koala's Production Department and Cutting Work Centre. The report should have three numerical columns instead of six with headings analogous to those in Exhibit 14.3. (Your report will not have any year-to-date columns.) Your performance report should cover only the food and beverage department and the kitchen. Draw arrows to show the relationships between the numbers in the report. Refer to Exhibit 14.3 for guidance.

Exercise 14.26 [LO 1] Responsibility Accounting; Equipment Breakdown

As a group, prepare a report to the class regarding how a responsibility accounting system should handle each of the following scenarios:

a. Department A manufactures a component, which Department B then uses. Department A recently experienced a machine breakdown that held up production of the component. As a result, Department B was forced to curtail its own production, thereby incurring large costs of idle time. An investigation revealed that Department A's machinery had not been properly maintained.
b. Refer to the scenario in requirement (a), but suppose that the investigation revealed that the machinery in Department A had been properly maintained.

Exercise 14.27 [LO 5] Impact of New Project on Performance Measures

Maritza Company manufactures clothing in Buenos Aires, Argentina. The company's outerwear division is considering the acquisition of a new asset that will cost 850,000 pesos and have a cash flow of 325,000 pesos per year for each of the five years of its life. Depreciation is computed on a straight-line basis with no salvage value. (Monetary values given in Argentine pesos, $.)

Required

Build a spreadsheet to complete the following requirements:

a. What is the ROI for each year of the asset's life if the division uses beginning-of-year asset balances and net book value for the computation?
b. What is the residual income each year if the imputed interest rate is 25 per cent?

Exercise 14.28 [LO 5] Impact of New Project on Performance Measures

Sentido SA's Barcelona Division manager is considering the acquisition of a new asset that will increase the division's profit. The division already earns €220,000 on assets of €880,000. The company's cost of capital is 20 per cent. The new investment has a cost of €120,000 and will have a yearly cash flow of €75,000. The asset will be depreciated using the straight-line method over a six-year life and is expected to have no salvage value. Division performance is measured using ROI with beginning-of-year net book values in the denominator.

Required

a. What is the division ROI before acquisition of the new asset?
b. What is the division ROI in the first year after acquisition of the new asset?

Exercise 14.29 [LO 5, 6] Impact of Purchasing versus Leasing on Performance Measures

The Barcelona Division manager in the preceding exercise has the option to lease the asset on a year-to-year lease for €65,000 per year. All depreciation and other tax benefits would accrue to the lessor.

Required

a. What is the division ROI if it leases the asset?
b. What is the division's residual income before considering the project?
c. What is the division's residual income if the asset is purchased?
d. What is the division's residual income if the asset is leased?

Exercise 14.30 [LO 5, 6] Alternative Measures of Division Performance

The following data are available for the two divisions of Great Plains Products Inc.

	East Division	West Division
Division operating income	$42,000	$234,000
Division investment	120,000	900,000

The cost of capital for the company is 21 per cent.

Required

a. As a group, determine which division had the better performance. Explain your answer.
b. Would your evaluation change if the company's cost of capital were 26 per cent? Why?

Exercise 14.31 [LO 5, 6] ROI and Residual Income; Annual Reports; Use of Internet

Select one of the following companies (or any company of your choosing), and use the Internet to explore its most recent annual report.

Apple (www.apple.com)	**Husqvarna** AB (www.husqvarna.com)
Burger King (www.bk.com)	**Pirelli Tyre SPA** (www.pirelli.com)
Carrefour (www.carrefour.com)	**Ryanair** (www.ryanair.com)
Hilton Hotels (www.hilton.com)	

Required

a. Calculate the company's overall return on investment (ROI). Also, calculate the company's overall residual income. (Assume an imputed interest rate of 10 per cent.) List and explain any assumptions you make.
b. Does the company include a calculation of ROI in its online annual report? If it does, do your calculations agree with those of the company? If not, what are some possible explanations?

Exercise 14.32 [LO 5, 7] Compare ROI Using Historical Cost Net Book Value versus Gross Book Value

Liverpool Division of Thompson Metals PLC just started operations. It purchased depreciable assets costing £3 million and having an expected life of four years, after which the assets can be salvaged for £800,000. In addition, the division has £4 million in assets that are not depreciable. After four years, the division will have £4 million available from these non-depreciable assets. In short, the division has invested £7 million in assets that will last four years, after which it will salvage £4.8 million, so annual depreciation is £550,000. Annual cash-operating flows are £2,000,000. In computing ROI, this division uses end-of-year asset values in the denominator. Depreciation is computed on a straight-line basis, recognizing the salvage values noted.

Required

Build a spreadsheet to complete the following requirements:

a. Compute ROI using net book value for each year.
b. Compute ROI using gross book value for each year.
c. Assume the same data except that the division uses beginning-of-year asset values in the denominator for computing ROI.
 (1) Compute ROI using net book value.
 (2) Compute ROI using gross book value.
 (3) How different is the ROI computed using end-of-year asset values from the ROI using beginning-of-year values?

Exercise 14.33 [LO 5] Calculation of Weighted-average Cost of Capital for EVA

Callaghan Construction Associates, a real estate developer and building contractor in Cork, Ireland, has two sources of long-term capital: debt and equity. The firm's cost of issuing debt is the after-tax cost of the interest payments on the debt, considering the fact that the interest payments are tax deductible. Callaghan's cost of equity capital is the investment opportunity rate of Callaghan's investors, that is, the rate they could earn on investments of similar risk to that of investing in Callaghan Construction Associates. The interest rate on Chelsea's €50 million of long-term debt is 10 per cent, and the company's tax rate is 12.5 per cent. Chelsea's cost of equity capital is 14 per cent. Moreover, its market value (and book value) of equity is €100 million.

Required

Calculate Callaghan Construction Associates' weighted-average cost of capital.

Exercise 14.34 [LO 5] Economic Value Added; Continuation of Preceding Exercise

Refer to the data in the preceding exercise for Callaghan Construction Associates. The company has two divisions, real estate and construction. The divisions' total assets, current liabilities, and before-tax operating income for the most recent year follow:

Division	Total assets	Current liabilities	Before-tax operating income
Real estate	£100,000,000	£6,000,000	£20,000,000
Construction	60,000,000	4,000,000	18,000,000

Required

Calculate the economic value added for each of Callaghan Construction Associates' divisions. (You will need to use the weighted-average cost of capital, which was computed in the preceding exercise.)

Problems

Problem 14.35 [LO 1, 2] Responsibility Centres Designation; Hotel

The following partial organization chart pertains to the Estes Park Hotel and Resort, a division of Mountain Resorts Inc. Top management has specified that the hotel is a profit centre, because the hotel's management does not have the authority to make significant investment decisions.

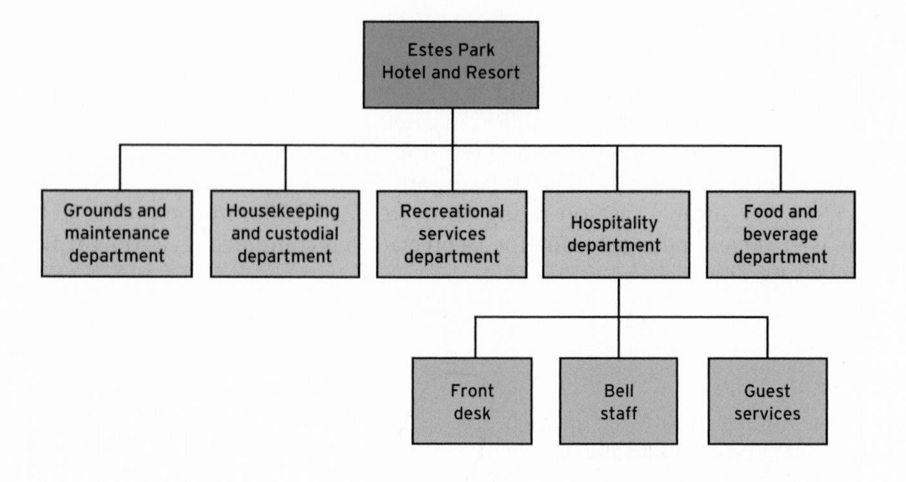

Each of the hotel's main departments is managed by a director (e.g., director of hospitality). The front desk subunit, which is supervised by the front desk manager, handles the hotel's reservations, room assignments, guest payments and key control. The bell staff, managed by the bell captain, is responsible for greeting guests, front-door service, assisting guests with their luggage and delivering room-service orders. The guest services subunit, supervised by the manager of guest services, is responsible for assisting guests with local transportation arrangements, advising guests on tourist attractions, and conveniences such as valet and floral services.

Required

As an outside consultant, write a memo to the hotel's general manager suggesting a responsibility centre designation for each of the subunits shown in the organization chart. Justify your choices.

Problem 14.36 [LO 1, 2] Design of a Responsibility Accounting System

The Albuquerque Medical Equipment Company manufactures a variety of equipment used in hospitals. The company operates in a very price-competitive industry, so it has little control over the price of its products. It *must* meet the market price. To do so, the firm must keep production costs in check by operating as efficiently as possible. Sandra Jefferson, the company's president, has stated that to be successful, the company must provide a very high-quality product and meet its delivery commitments to customers on time. Albuquerque Medical Equipment Company is organized as follows.

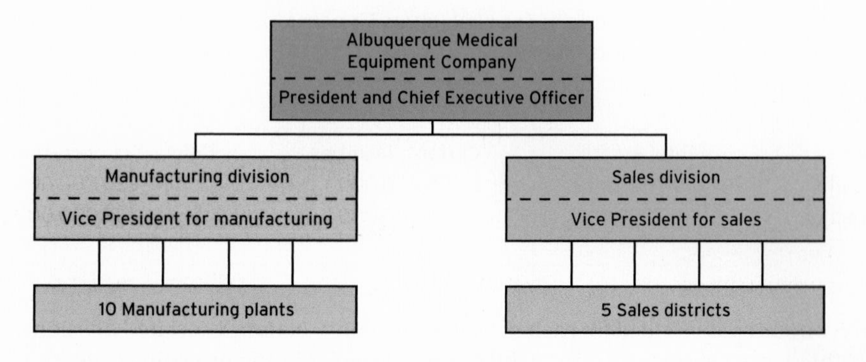

The company's two vice presidents currently disagree regarding the responsibility accounting system. The vice president for manufacturing claims that the 10 plants should be cost centres. He recently expressed the following sentiment: 'The plants should be cost centres because the plant managers do not control the sales of our products. Designating the plants as profit centres would result in holding the plant managers responsible for something they can't control.' The vice president for marketing holds a contrary view. He recently made the following remarks: 'The plants should be profit centres. The plant managers are in the best position to affect the company's overall profit'.

Required

As the company's new controller, you have been asked to make a recommendation to Sandra Jefferson regarding the responsibility centre issue. Write a memo to her making a recommendation and explaining the reasoning behind it. In your memo address the following points.

a. Assuming that Albuquerque Medical Equipment Company's overall goal is profitability, what are the company's critical success factors? A *critical success factor* is a variable that meets these two criteria: it is largely under the company's control, and the company must succeed in this area to reach its overall goal of profitability.
b. Which responsibility accounting arrangement for the plants is most consistent with achieving success on the company's critical success factors?
c. What responsibility centre designation is most appropriate for the company's sales districts?
d. As a specific example, consider the rush-order problem illustrated in the chapter. Suppose that Albuquerque Medical Equipment Company often receives rush orders from its customers. Which of the two proposed responsibility accounting arrangements is best suited to making good decisions about accepting or rejecting rush orders? Specifically, should the plants be cost centres or profit centres?

Problem 14.37 [LO 1, 3] Performance Report Analysis for a Decentralized Organization

Scandinavian Traditions AS manufactures reproduction antique Norwegian and Swedish furniture. The need for a widely based manufacturing and distribution system has led to a highly decentralized management structure. Each division manager is responsible for producing and distributing corporate products in one of eight geographical areas of northern Europe.

Residual income is used to evaluate division managers. The residual income for each division equals its contribution to corporate profits before taxes less a 20 per cent investment charge on a division's investment base. Each division's investment is the sum of its year-end balances of accounts receivable, inventories and net plant fixed assets (cost less accumulated depreciation). Corporate policies dictate that divisions minimize their investments in receivables and inventories. Investments in plant fixed assets are a joint division/corporate decision based on proposals made by division managers, available corporate funds and general corporate policy.

Lars Nilson, division manager for the south-eastern sector, prepared the year 2 and preliminary year 3 budgets for his division late in year 1. Final approval of the year 3 budget took place in late year 2 after adjustments for trends and other information developed during year 2. Preliminary work on the year 4 budget also took place at that time. In early October of year 3, Nilson asked the division controller to prepare the following report, which presents performance for the first nine months of year 3. (Monetary values given in Norwegian krone, kr.)

SCANDINAVIAN TRADITIONS AS
South-eastern Sector
(in thousands)

	Year 3			Year 2	
	Annual budget	Nine-month budget*	Nine-month actual	Annual budget	Actual results
Sales revenue	kr 16,800	kr 12,600	kr 13,200	kr 15,000	kr 14,580
Divisional costs and expenses:					
Direct material and labour	kr 6,384	kr 4,788	kr 5,970	kr 5,400	kr 5,340
Supplies	264	198	210	210	258

Maintenance and repairs	1200	900	360	1050	960
Plant depreciation	720	540	540	660	660
Administration	720	540	540	540	600
Total divisional costs and expenses	kr 9,288	kr 6,966	kr 7,620	kr 7,860	kr 7,818
Divisional margin	kr 7,512	kr 5,634	kr 5,580	kr 7,140	kr 6,762
Allocated corporate fixed costs	2160	1620	1440	2040	1920
Divisional profit	kr 5,352	kr 4,014	kr 4,140	kr 5,100	kr 4,842

	Budgeted balance 31/12/Year 3	Budgeted balance 30/9/Year 3	Actual balance 30/9/Year 3	Budgeted balance 31/12/Year 2	Actual balance 31/12/Year 2
Divisional investment:					
Accounts receivable.	kr 1,680	kr 1,740	kr 1,500	kr 1,500	kr 1,500
Inventories.	3000	3000	3900	2700	2850
Plant fixed assets (net).	7,920	8,100	6,600	6,900	6,600
Total	kr 12,600	kr 12,840	kr 12,000	kr 11,100	kr 10,950

*Scandinavian Traditions' sales occur uniformly throughout the year.

Required

a. Evaluate Lars Nilson's performance for the nine months ending 30 September of year 3. Support your evaluation with pertinent facts from the problem.

b. Identify the features of Scandinavian Traditions' division performance-measurement reporting and evaluation system that need to be revised if it is to be effective.

[CMA adapted]

Problem 14.38 [LO 1, 3] Preparation of Performance Reports; Hospital

Bay State General Hospital serves the metropolitan Boston area. The hospital is a non-profit organization supported by patient billings, county and state funds, and private donations. An organization chart and cost information for August follow.

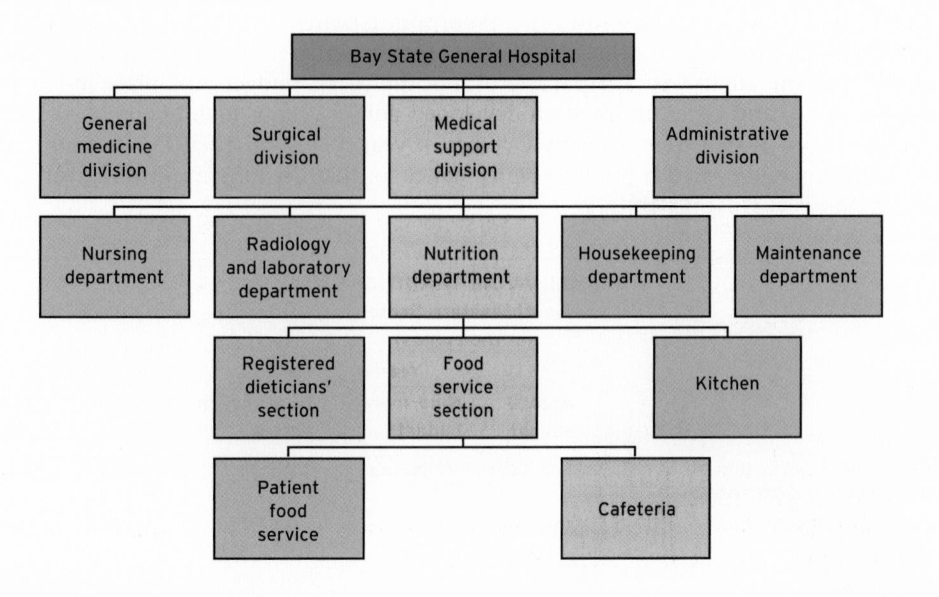

	Actual		Budget	
	August	Year to date	August	Year to date
Cafeteria:				
Food servers' wages	$9,000	$72,000	$8,000	$64,000
Paper products	4,400	36,200	4,500	36,000
Utilities	1,050	8,100	1,000	8,000
Maintenance	100	1,100	400	3,200
Custodial	1,050	8,550	1,050	8,750
Supplies	950	9,650	1,250	9,650
Patient food service	18,500	137,000	17,000	136,000
Registered dieticians' section	7,500	60,000	7,500	60,000
Kitchen	29,400	246,000	31,000	248,000
Nursing department	75,000	580,000	70,000	560,000
Radiology and laboratory department	18,100	144,000	18,000	144,000
Housekeeping department	11,600	86,000	10,000	80,000
Maintenance department	6,000	77,000	13,000	104,000
General medicine division	204,000	1,670,900	210,000	1,680,000
Surgical division	141,000	1,115,800	140,000	1,120,000
Administrative division	53,500	406,000	50,000	400,000

Required

a. Build a spreadsheet and prepare a set of cost performance reports similar to Exhibit 14.3 with six columns. The first four columns will have the same headings as those in the preceding table. The last two columns will have the following headings: Variance – August and Variance – Year to Date.
Since all information in the performance reports for Bay State General Hospital is cost information, you do not need to show these data in parentheses. Use F or U to denote whether each variance in the reports is favourable or unfavourable.

b. Using arrows, show the relationships between the numbers in your performance reports for Bay State General Hospital. Refer to Exhibit 14.3 for guidance.

c. As the hospital's administrator, which variances in the performance reports would you want to investigate further? Why?

Problem 14.39 [LO 5] ROI and Residual Income; Missing Data; Improving ROI

Vins Gravois produces wine in two regions of France: Bordeaux and the Loire Valley. The following data is available for each division. The company's required rate of return on invested capital is 10 per cent.

	Bordeaux division	Loire Valley division
Sales revenue	€12,000,000	?
Income	€3,000,000	€900,000
Average investment	€6,000,000	?
Sales margin	?	20%
Capital turnover	?	1.5
ROI	?	?
Residual income	?	?

Required

a. Supply answers for the question marks in the preceding table.

b. Explain three ways the Bordeaux Division manager could improve her division's ROI. Use numbers to illustrate these possibilities.

c. Suppose the Loire Valley Division's sales margin increased to 25 per cent while its capital turnover remained constant. Compute the division's new ROI.

Problem 14.40 [LO 5, 6] Equipment Replacement and Performance Measures; Ethics

MikroTek SE, a manufacturer of products using the latest microprocessor technology, has appointed you the manager of its Micro Technology Division. Your division has €1,000,000 in assets and manufactures a special chip assembly. On 2 January of the current year, you invested €1 million in automated equipment for chip assembly. At that time, your expected income statement was as follows:

Sales revenue	€4,000,000
Operating costs:	
Unit level (variable)	500,000
Facility level (fixed, all cash)	2,000,000
Depreciation:	
New equipment	300,000
Other	300,000
Division operating income	€900,000

On 25 October, a sales representative from Arktinen Machine Company approached you. For $1.32 million, Arktinen offers a new assembly machine with significant improvements over the equipment you bought on 2 January. The new equipment would expand department output by 10 per cent while reducing cash fixed costs by 5 per cent. The new equipment would be depreciated for accounting purposes over a three-year life. Depreciation would be net of the new machine's €300,000 salvage value. The new equipment meets your company's 20 per cent cost of capital criterion. If you purchase the new machine, it must be installed prior to the end of the year. For practical purposes, though, you can ignore depreciation on the new machine because it will not go into operation until the start of the next year.

The old machine, which has no salvage value, must be disposed of to make room for the new machine.

Your company has a performance evaluation and bonus plan based on ROI. The return includes any losses on disposals of equipment. Investment is computed based on the average balance of assets for the year, net book value.

Required

Build a spreadsheet to complete the following requirements:

a. What is your division's ROI this year if it does not acquire the new machine?
b. What is your division's ROI this year if it does acquire the new machine?
c. If the new machine is acquired and operates according to specifications, what ROI is expected for next year?
d. Is it ethical to decline to purchase the new machine? Explain.

Problem 14.41 [LO 5, 6] Evaluation of Trade-offs in Return Measurement; Continuation of Preceding Problem

Refer to the information given in the preceding problem. As the Micro Technology Division manager, you are still assessing the problem of whether to acquire Arktinen Machine Company's machine. You learn that the new machine could be acquired next year, but it will cost 15 per cent more then. Its salvage value would still be €300,000. Other costs or revenue estimates would be apportioned on a month-by-month basis for the time each machine is in use. (Ignore fractions of months.)

Required

a. When would you want to purchase the new machine if you wait until next year?
b. What are the costs that must be considered in making this decision?

Problem 14.42 [LO 5, 6] ROI Increases over Time; Accelerated Depreciation; Increasing Residual Income over Time

Refer to Exhibit 14.5. Prepare a similar table of the changing ROI, assuming the following accelerated depreciation schedule. Assume income before depreciation of $3,00,000 per year. (If there is a loss, leave the ROIs column blank.)

Year	Depreciation
1	$4,000,000
2	2,400,000
3	1,440,000
4	1,080,000
5	1,080,000
Total	$10,000,000

Required

a. How does your table differ from the one in Exhibit 14.5? Why?
b. What are the implications of the ROI pattern in your table?
c. Prepare a table similar to Exhibit 14.5, which focuses on residual income. Use a 10 per cent rate to compute the imputed interest charge. The table should show the residual income on the investment during each year in its five-year life. Assume income before depreciation of $3,000,000 per year and straight-line depreciation with no salvage value.

Problem 14.43 [LO 5, 6] Impact of Decisions to Capitalize or Expense on Performance Measurement

North Sea Drilling Company is an oil and gas exploration and drilling company operating off the coast of Scotland. Oil and gas companies inevitably incur costs on unsuccessful exploration ventures called *dry holes*. A debate continues over whether those costs should be written off as period expenses or capitalized as part of the full cost of finding profitable oil and gas ventures. Management has been writing these costs off to expense as incurred. However, this year a new management team was hired to improve the profit picture of the firm's Oil and Gas Exploration Division with the provision that it would receive a bonus equal to 10 per cent of any profits in excess of the division's base-year profits. However, no bonus would be paid if profits were less than 20 per cent of end-of-year investment. The following information was included in the division's performance report.

	Base year	This year	Increase over base year
Sales revenue	£12,000,000	£12,800,000	
Costs incurred:			
Dry holes	1,700,000	0	
Depreciation and other amortization	1,200,000	1,600,000	
Other costs	8,000,000	8,500,000	
Division profit	£1,100,000	£2,700,000	£1,600,000
End-of-year investment	£7,200,000	£8,450,000*	

*Includes other investments not at issue here.

During the year, the new team spent £2.2 million on exploratory activities, of which £2 million was for unsuccessful ventures. The new management team has included the £2 million in the current end-of-year investment base because, it states, 'You can't find the good ones without hitting a few bad ones.'

Required

a. What is the ROI for the base year and the current year?
b. What is the amount of the bonus that the new management team is likely to claim?
c. If you were on North Sea Drilling Company's board of directors, how would you respond to the new management's claim for the bonus?

Problem 14.44 [LO 1. 5, 6] Divisional Performance Measurement; Behavioural Issues

Gigantic Corporation's division managers have been expressing growing dissatisfaction with the methods Gigantic uses to measure division performance. Division operations are evaluated every quarter by comparison with the master budget prepared during the prior year. Division managers claim that many factors are completely out of their control but are included in this comparison, resulting in an unfair and misleading performance evaluation.

The managers have been particularly critical of the process used to establish standards and budgets. The annual budget, stated by quarters, is prepared six months prior to the beginning of the operating year. Pressure by top management to reflect increased earnings has often caused divisional managers to overstate revenues and/or understate expenses. In addition, once the budget is established, divisions must 'live with the budget'. Frequently, external factors such as the state of the economy, changes in consumer preferences, and actions of competitors have not been recognized in the budgets that top management supplied to the divisions. The credibility of the performance review is curtailed when the budget cannot be adjusted to incorporate these changes.

Recognizing these problems, top management agreed to establish a committee to review the situation and to make recommendations for a new performance evaluation system. The committee consists of each division manager, the corporate controller and the executive vice president. At the first meeting, one division manager outlined an achievement of objectives system (AOS). In this performance evaluation system, division managers are evaluated according to three criteria:

- *Doing better than last year.* Various measures are compared to the same measures of the prior year.
- *Planning realistically.* Actual performance for the current year is compared to realistic plans and/or goals.
- *Managing current assets.* Various measures are used to evaluate division management's achievements and reactions to changing business and economic conditions.

One division manager believed that this system would overcome many of the current system's inconsistencies because divisions could be evaluated from three different viewpoints. In addition, managers would have the opportunity to show how they would react and account for changes in uncontrollable external factors.

Another manager cautioned that the success of a new performance evaluation system would be limited unless it had the complete support of top management.

Required

a. Explain whether the proposed AOS would improve Gigantic Corporation's evaluation of division performance.

b. Develop specific performance measures for each of the three criteria in the proposed AOS that could be used to evaluate division managers.

c. Discuss the motivational and behavioural aspects of the proposed performance measurement system. Also recommend specific programmes that could be instituted to promote morale and give incentives to divisional management.

[CMA adapted]

Problem 14.45 [LO 1. 5, 6] ROI and Management Behaviour

Montreal Machine Tool Company (MMTC) is a highly diversified and decentralized company. Each division is responsible for its own sales, pricing, production and costs of operations; management of accounts receivable, inventories and accounts payable; and use of existing facilities. Corporate headquarters manages cash.

Division executives present investment proposals to corporate management, who analyse and document them as well as make the final decision to commit funds for investment purposes.

The corporation evaluates divisional executive performance using the ROI measure. The asset base is composed of fixed assets employed plus working capital, exclusive of cash. The ROI performance of a division executive is the most important appraisal factor for salary changes. In addition, each executive's annual performance bonus is based on ROI results, with increases in ROI having a significant impact on the amount of the bonus.

MMTC adopted the ROI performance measure and related compensation procedures about 10 years ago and seems to have benefited from the programme. The corporation's ROI increased during the first years of the programme. Although each division's ROI continued to grow, corporate ROI declined in recent years. The corporation has accumulated a sizeable amount of short-term marketable securities in the past three years.

Corporate management is concerned about the increase in the short-term marketable securities. A recent article in a financial publication suggested that some companies had overemphasized the use of ROI with results similar to those experienced by MMTC.

Required

a. Describe the specific actions that division managers might have taken to cause the ROI to increase in each division but decline for the corporation. Illustrate your explanation with appropriate examples.
b. Using the concepts of goal congruence and motivation of division executives, explain how MMTC's overemphasis on the use of the ROI measure might result in the recent decline in the corporation's ROI and the increase in cash and short-term marketable securities.
c. What changes could be made in MMTC's compensation policy to avoid this problem? Explain your answer.

[CMA adapted]

Problem 14.46 [LO 5] Weighted-average Cost of Capital; Economic Value Added

Nordosten Fischmarkt AG (NF) is a Germany-based seafood restaurant chain operating throughout Europe and the Middle East. The company has two sources of long-term capital: debt and equity. The company's cost of issuing debt is the after-tax cost of the interest payments on the debt, considering the fact that the interest payments are tax deductible. NF's cost of equity capital is the investment opportunity rate of NF's investors, that is, the rate they could earn on investments of risk similar to that of investing in Nordosten Fischmarkt AG. The interest rate on NF's €80 million of long-term debt is 3 per cent, and the company's tax rate is 30 per cent. NF's cost of equity capital is 10 per cent. Moreover, the market value (and book value) of NF's equity is €120 million.

Nordosten Fischmarkt AG consists of two divisions: properties division and food service division. The divisions' total assets, current liabilities and before-tax operating income for the most recent year are as follows:

Division	Before-tax operating income	Total assets	Current liabilities
Properties	€28,900,000	€145,000,000	€3,000,000
Food Service	14,900,000	64,000,000	6,000,000

Required

Build a spreadsheet to complete the following requirements:

a. Calculate the weighted-average cost of capital for Nordosten Fischmarkt AG.
b. Calculate the economic value added (EVA) for each of NF's divisions.

Cases

Case 14.47 [LO 1, 5, 7] Evaluation of Performance Evaluation System; Behavioural Issues

Drawem Company purchased Bildem Company three years ago. Prior to the acquisition, Bildem manufactured and sold electronic products to third-party customers. Since becoming a division of Drawem, Bildem now manufactures electronic components only for products made by Drawem's Macon Division.

Drawem's corporate management gives the Bildem Division management considerable latitude in running the division's operations. However, corporate management retains authority for decisions regarding capital investments, product pricing and production quantities.

Drawem has a formal performance evaluation programme for all divisional management teams that relies substantially on each division's ROI. Bildem Division's income statement provides the basis for the evaluation of its divisional management. (See the following income statement.)

The corporate accounting staff prepares the division's financial statements. Corporate general services costs are allocated on the basis of sales dollars, and the computer department's actual costs are apportioned among the divisions on the basis of use. The net division investment includes division fixed assets at net book value (cost less depreciation), division inventory, and corporate working capital apportioned to the divisions on the basis of sales dollars.

DRAWEM COMPANY
Bildem Division
Income Statement
For the Year Ended June 30
(in thousands)

Sales revenue		$8,000
Costs and expenses:		
Product costs:		
Direct material	$1,000	
Direct labour	2,200	
Manufacturing overhead	2,600	
Total	$5,800	
Less: Increase in inventory	700	5,100
Engineering and research		240
Shipping and receiving		480
Division administration:		
Manager's office	$420	
Cost management	80	
Human services	164	664
Corporate cost:		
General services	$460	
Computer	96	556
Total costs and expenses		$7,040
Divisional operating income		$960
Net plant investment		$3,200
Return on investment		30%

Required

a. As a group, discuss Drawem Company's financial reporting and performance evaluation programme as it relates to the responsibilities of Bildem Division.

b. Based on your response to requirement (a), write a memo to management recommending appropriate revisions of the financial information and reports used to evaluate the performance of Bildem's divisional management. If revisions are not necessary, explain why.

[CMA adapted]

Case 14.48 [LO 1, 2] Budgeting and Responsibility Accounting*

Overview

River Beverages is a food and soft-drink company with worldwide operations. The company is organized into five regional divisions with each vice president reporting directly to the CEO, Cindy Wilkins. Each vice president has an R&D department, controller and three divisions; carbonated drinks, juices and water, and food products. Management believes that the structure works well for River Beverages because different regions have different tastes and the division's products complement each other. River Beverages' company-wide and divisional organization charts are shown here.

Industry

The US beverage industry has become mature with its growth matching population growth. In one recent year alone, consumers drank about 50 billion gallons of fluids. Most of the industry growth has come from the non-alcoholic beverage market, which is growing by about 1.1 per cent annually. In the non-alcoholic

* This integrative case relates to issues from Chapters 9 and 14 and to learning objectives from both chapters.

arena, soft drinks are the largest segment, accounting for 53.4 per cent of the beverages consumed. Americans consume about 26 billion gallons of soft drinks, ringing up retail sales of $50 billion every year. Water (bottled and tap) is the next largest segment, representing 23.7 per cent of the market. Juices represent about 12 per cent of the beverages consumed. The smallest but fastest-growing segment is ready-to-drink teas, which is growing by more than 91 per cent in volume but accounts for less than 1 per cent of the beverages consumed.

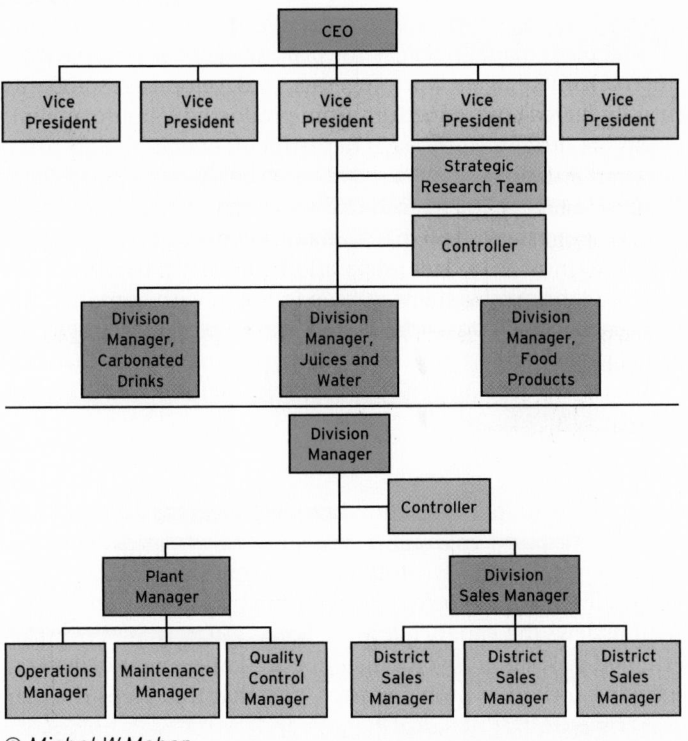

Sales Budgets

Susan Johnson, plant manager at River Beverages' non-carbonated drink plant in St Louis, recently completed the annual budgeting process. According to Johnson, division managers have decision-making authority in their business units except for capital financing activities. Budgets keep the division managers focused on corporate goals.

At the beginning of December, division managers submit a report to the vice president for the region summarizing capital, sales, and income forecasts for the upcoming fiscal year beginning 1 July. Although the initial report is not prepared with much detail, it is prepared carefully because it is used in the strategic planning process.

Next, the strategic research team begins a formal assessment of each market segment in its region. The team develops sales forecasts for each division and compiles them into a company forecast. The team considers economic conditions and current market share in each region. Management believes the strategic research team is effective because it is able to integrate division products and more accurately forecast demand for complementary products. In addition, the team ensures continuity of assumptions and achievable sales goals.

Once the corporate forecast has been completed, the district sales managers estimate sales for the upcoming budget year. The district sales managers are ultimately responsible for the forecasts they prepare. The district sales forecasts are then compiled and returned to the division manager. The division manager reviews the forecast but cannot make any revisions without discussing the changes with the district sales managers. Next, the district sales forecasts are reviewed by the strategic research team and the division controller. Finally, top management reviews each division's competitive position, including plans to increase market share, capital spending and quality improvement plans.

Plant Budgets

After top management approves the sales budget, it is separated into a sales budget for each plant. Plant location is determined by product type and where the product needs to be distributed. The budget is broken down further by price, volume and product type. Plant managers budget contribution margins, fixed costs and pretax income using information from the plant sales budget.

The plants are designated as profit centres. Each plant's budgeted profit is determined by subtracting budgeted variable costs and budgeted fixed costs from the sales forecast. If actual sales fall below forecasts, the plant manager is still responsible for achieving the budgeted profit. One of the most important aspects of the plant budgeting process is that plant managers break the plant budget down into various plant departments.

Operations and maintenance managers work together to develop cost standards and cost-reduction targets for all departments. Budgeted cost reductions from productivity improvements, unfavourable variances and facility-level costs are developed for each department, operation and cost centre in the plant.

Before plant managers submit their budgets, a member of the strategy team and the regional controller visit the plant to keep corporate management in touch with what is happening at the plant level and to help corporate management understand how plant managers determine their budgets. The visits also allow corporate management to provide budget preparation guidance if necessary. The visits are especially important because they force plant management to keep in touch with corporate-level managers.

The final budgets are submitted and consolidated by 1 April. The vice president reviews them to ensure that they are in line with corporate objectives. After all changes have been made by the vice presidents and the chief executive officer (CEO), the budgets are submitted to the board of directors for approval. The board votes on the final budget in early June.

Performance Measurement

The corporate office generates variance reports monthly. River Beverages has a sophisticated information system that automatically generates reports based on input downloaded daily from each plant. Managers in the organization also can manually generate the reports. Most managers generate variance reports several times during the month, allowing them to solve problems before the problems get out of control.

Corporate management reviews the variance reports, looking closely at overbudget variance problems. Plant managers are questioned only about overbudget items. Management believes that this ensures that the plant managers are staying on top of problem areas, and that this keeps the plants operating as efficiently as possible. One week after the variance reports are generated, plant managers are required to submit a response outlining the causes of any variances and how they plan to prevent the problems in the future. If a plant manager has repeated problems, corporate management might send a specialist to the plant to work with the plant manager to solve the problems.

Sales and Manufacturing Relations

'We are expected to meet our approved budget,' remarked Kevin Greely, a division controller at River Beverages. 'A couple of years ago, one of our major restaurant customers switched to another brand. Even though the restaurant sold over one million cases of our product annually, we were not allowed to make revisions to our budget.'

Budgets are rarely adjusted after approval. However, if sales decline early in the year, plant managers might file an appeal to revise the budgeted profit for the year. If sales decline late in the year, management usually does not revise the budgeted amounts but asks plant managers to cut costs wherever possible and delay any unnecessary expenditures until the following year. Remember that River Beverages sets budgets so it is able to see where to make cuts or where it can find any operating inefficiencies. Plant managers are not forced to meet their goals, but they are encouraged to cut costs below budget.

The sales department is primarily responsible for soliciting and accepting orders while plant managers are responsible for overseeing plant operations. As you might imagine, problems occur between plant and regional sales managers from time to time. For example, rush orders could cause production costs to be higher than normal for some production runs. Another problem could occur when a sales manager runs a promotional campaign that causes margins to shrink. In both instances, a plant manager's profit will be affected negatively while a sales manager's sales will be affected positively. Such situations are often passed up to the division level for resolution; however, the customer is always the primary concern.

Incentives

River Beverages' management has devised what it thinks is an effective system to motivate plant managers. First, plant managers are promoted only when they have displayed outstanding performance in their current position. Second, monetary incentives reward plant managers for reaching profit goals. Finally, charts produced monthly display budgeted items versus actual results. Although not required to do so, most plant managers publicize the charts and use them as a motivational tool. The charts allow department supervisors and staff to compare activities in their department to similar activities in other plants around the world.

CEO's Message

Cindy Wilkins, CEO of River Beverages, looks to the future and comments, 'Planning is an important aspect of budget preparation for every level of our organization. I would like to decrease the time spent on preparing the budget, but I believe that it keeps people thinking about the future. The negative aspect of the budgeting process is that sometimes it overcontrols our managers. We need to stay nimble enough to react to customer demands while staying structured enough to achieve corporate objectives. For the most part, our budget process keeps our managers aware of sales goals and alerts them when sales or expenses are off track.'

Required

a. Discuss each step in River Beverages' budgeting process. Begin with the division manager's initial reports and end with the board of directors' approval. Is each step necessary? Explain.

b. Evaluate River Beverages' responsibility accounting system. Specifically, should the plant managers be held responsible for costs or profits? Why?

c. Write a report to River Beverages' management stating the advantages and disadvantages of the company's budgeting process. Start your report by stating your assumption(s) about what River Beverages' management wants the budgeting process to accomplish.

Solutions to You're the Decision Maker

14.1 Evaluating the Success of a Division, p. 715

The answer to the question as to which division is the most successful depends on the firm's cost of capital. To see this relationship, compute the residual income (RI) for each division using various cost of capital rates.

a. Cost of capital of 10 per cent:

	Brisbane division	Cairns division
Divisional profit	AU$900,000	AU$200,000
Less: Imputed interest charge:		
AU$6,000,000 × 10%	600,000	
AU$1,000,000 × 10%		100,000
Residual income	AU$300,000	AU$100,000

b. Cost of capital of 14 per cent:

	Brisbane division	Cairns division
Divisional profit	AU$900,000	AU$200,000
Less: Imputed interest charge:		
AU$6,000,000 × 14%	840,000	
AU$1,000,000 × 14%		140,000
Residual income	AU$60,000	AU$600,000

c. Imputed interest rate of 15 per cent:

	Brisbane division	Cairns division
Divisional profit	AU$900,000	AU$200,000
Less: Imputed interest charge:		
AU$6,000,000 × 15%	900,000	
AU$1,000,000 × 15%		150,000
Residual income	AU$0	AU$50,000

If the firm's cost of capital is 10 per cent, the Brisbane division has a higher residual income than the Cairns division. With a cost of capital of 15 per cent, the Cairns division has a higher residual income. At a 14 per cent cost of capital, the divisions have the same residual income. This scenario illustrates one of the advantages of RI over ROI. Since the RI calculation includes an imputed interest charge reflecting the firm's cost of capital, it gives a more complete picture of divisional performance.

14.2 Deciding between Alternative Merchandise Inventory Plans, p. 722

a. and b. Income statements summarizing the alternatives are as follows:

	Regular merchandise	Camp cookware	Total
Revenue	AU$260,000	AU$75,000	AU$335,000
Cost of goods sold	163,000	57,000	220,000
Gross margin	AU$ 97,000	AU$18,000	AU$115,000
Operating expenses	26,000	8,500	34,500
Operating income	AU$ 71,000	AU$ 9,500	AU$ 80,500
Investment	AU$187,500	AU$55,000	AU$242,500
ROI	37.87%	17.27%	33.20%

Although the camp cookware provides a higher return than the cost of capital, it lowers the status quo ROI.

c. If the floor plan is used, the investment base will remain at AU$187,500 because Outback will not have to carry the additional AU$55,000 inventory investment for the Tasmania product line. Operating income will equal AU$80,500 minus the floor-plan charge of AU$6,750 for a net profit of AU$73,750. The ROI will be 39.33 per cent (AU$73,750 ÷ AU$187,500).

d. The manager would prefer the floor plan because it would raise the store's ROI above the current ROI of 37.87 per cent.

Endnotes

1 A case study by Ahrens and Chapman (2004) provides a rich description and analysis of how profit centre managers deal with both local responsibilities and centrally defined constraints.

2 Although an important conceptual difference exists between profit centres and investment centres, the latter term is not always used in practice. Some managers use the term 'profit centre' to refer to both types of responsibility centres. Hence, when businesspeople use the term 'profit centre', they may be referring to a true profit centre (as defined in this chapter) or to an investment centre.

3 See the preceding chapter for discussion of cost management systems designed to facilitate management by exception in standard cost centres.

4 Flexible budgets are explained in Chapter 13.

5 Customer profitability analysis, which was covered in Chapter 6, can help in making a rush-order acceptance decision when key customers are involved. Also critical to the decision about accepting a rush order are considerations of the impact of accepting the order on production capacity. If accepting the rush order does not affect bottleneck processes, the organization will not incur an opportunity cost by producing the order.

6 Recall that in practice the term profit centre sometimes is used interchangeably with the term investment centre. To be precise, however, the term profit centre should be reserved for a subunit whose manager is held accountable for profit but not for invested capital.

7 In businesses that are not so capital intensive but are people intensive, firms can also use financial performance measures that reflect the effective management of the human resources. See Barber and Strack (2005).

8 EVA is also a registered trademark of the firm Stern Stewart.

9 Another term for the operating income is earnings before interest and taxes, EBIT.

10 The book value of Outback Outfitters' equity is $43 million, but that amount does not reflect the current value of the company's assets or the value of intangible assets such as the Koala Camp Gear and Wallaby Wear brand names.

11 General Electric apparently coined the actual term 'residual income' in the 1950s. See Bromwich and Walker (1998).

12 Note the parallel with what we discussed in Chapter 8 about the comparison of the internal rate of return (IRR) and the net present value (NPV). It is possible that one investment project (A) has a higher IRR but the other

project (B) has a higher NPV. This is called inconsistent ranking. In that situation, only NPV correctly indicates which project is superior. This apparent contradiction happens when the cash flows of project B can be disaggregated into the first project A + an extension of it (project B = project A + extension), and this extension has a positive NPV and an IRR that is lower than that of project A. The IRR of project B is the weighted *average* of the IRR of project A and of the extension, while the NPV of project B is the *sum* of the NPVs of project B and the extension.

13 A number of technical issues must be met to guarantee this relation (e.g., NPV-based depreciation), but most RI and EVA users appear to treat these as minor issues.

14 In this chapter we talk about measuring managerial performance, but the linkage of such performance measures to incentives plans is discussed further in Chapter 16.

15 See Ittner and Larcker (1998) and Merchant (2006) for more review and discussion.

16 See Chapter 6 of this text for examples of commonly used quality, time and productivity measures and Chapter 16 for examples of non-financial performance measures included in performance measurement. See also Ittner et al. (2003), who found that firms making more extensive use of a broad set of financial and (particularly) non-financial measures have higher measurement system satisfaction and share market returns.

17 See Banker et al. (2000) for an example.

18 See Kopczak and Johnson (2003).

19 If headquarters indeed does not want to get involved in separate decisions and only cares about the financial end result, then measures such as ROI and EVA should be able to 'tell the whole story'. These measures should have measurement properties such as high sensitivity and low noise, as mentioned earlier in this chapter. Several recent empirical studies show how performance measurement, delegation and incentives are related; see Abernethy et al. (2004), Moers (2006) and Widener et al. (2008)

20 The evaluation of long-term investment decisions is covered in Chapter 8.

21 Cavalluzzo and Ittner (2004) investigate the implementation of performance measurement in government and they identify several factors that support or hinder such initiatives.

References

Abernethy, M.A., J. Bouwens and L. van Lent (2004) 'Determinants of control system design in divisionalized firms', *The Accounting Review*, vol. 79, no. 3, pp. 545–570.

Ahrens, T., and C. Chapman (2004) 'Accounting for flexibility and efficiency: A field study of management control systems in a restaurant chain', *Contemporary Accounting Research*, vol. 21, no. 2, pp. 271–301.

Banker, R., G. Potter and D. Srinivasan (2000) 'An empirical investigation of an incentive plan that includes non-financial performance measures', *The Accounting Review*, vol. 75, no. 1, pp. 65–92.

Barber, F., and R. Strack (2005) 'The surprising economics of a "people business"', *Harvard Business Review*, June, pp. 80–90.

Biddle, G.C., R.M. Bowen and J.S. Wallace (1997) 'Does EVA beat earnings? Evidence on associations with stock returns and firm values', *Journal of Accounting and Economics*, vol. 24, no. 3, pp. 301–336.

Biddle, G., R. Bowen and J. Wallace (1998) 'Economic value added: some empirical EVAdence', *Managerial Finance*, vol. 24, no. 1, pp. 60–71.

Bromwich, M., and M. Walker (1998) 'Residual income past and future', *Management Accounting Research*, vol. 9, no. 5, pp. 391–419.

Cavalluzzo, K., and C. Ittner (2004) 'Implementing performance measurement innovations: evidence from government', *Accounting, Organizations and Society*, vol. 29, pp. 243–267.

Dierks, P.A., and A. Patel (1997) 'What is EVA and how can it help your company?' *Management Accounting*, vol. 79, no. 5, pp. 52–58.

Freedman, J. (1998) 'New research red flags EVA for stock picks', *Management Accounting*, vol. 79, no. 7, pp. 62–63.

Ittner, C.D., and D.F. Larcker (1998) 'Innovation in performance measurement: trends and research implications', *Journal of Management Accounting Research*, vol. 10, pp. 205–38.

Ittner, C.D., D.F. Larcker and T. Randall (2003) 'Performance implications of strategic performance measurement in financial services firms', *Accounting, Organizations and Society*, vol. 28, pp. 715–741.

Kopczak, L.R., and M.E. Johnson (2003) 'The supply-chain management effect', *MIT Sloan Management Review*, Spring, pp. 27–37.

Merchant, K. (2006) 'Measuring general managers' performances: market, accounting and combination-of-measures systems', *Accounting, Auditing and Accountability Journal*, vol. 19, no. 6, pp. 893–917.

Moers, F. (2006) 'Performance measure properties and delegation', *The Accounting Review*, vol. 81, no. 4, pp. 897–924

Wallace, J.S. (1997) 'Adopting residual income-based compensation plans: do you get what you pay for?' *Journal of Accounting and Economics*, vol. 24, no. 3, pp. 275–300.

Widener, S.K., M.B. Shackell and E.A. Demers (2008) 'The juxtaposition of social surveillance controls with traditional organizational design components' *Contemporary Accounting Research*, vol. 25, no. 2, pp. 605–638.

CHAPTER

15

Transfer Pricing

© IsaacKoval

Learning Objectives

After completing this chapter, you should be able to:

LO 1 Explain the purpose and role of transfer pricing for behavioural congruence.

LO 2 Base a transfer price on a general rule, market prices, costs or negotiations.

LO 3 Understand the drawbacks of interfering in divisional decisions.

LO 4 Discuss the implications of transfer pricing in a multinational company.

LO 5 Discuss the effects of transfer pricing on segment reporting.

Outback Outfitters Ltd
Retail Division
212 Rushcutters Bay Road
Sydney, New South Wales
AUSTRALIA

MEMORANDUM

To: Eric Devon
Vice President, Koala Camp Gear Division

From: Marie Waters
Vice President, Retail Division

Subject: Transfer price for 'RooPacks

We are in the middle of the budgeting process for next year and we are currently planning our purchasing volumes from internal and external suppliers. Of course, in the interest of Outback Outfitters, we consider Koala Camp Gear Division a preferred supplier, and I would like to discuss prices and volumes for next year, in particular for our well-known 'RooPacks. I trust we can come to transfer prices from the Koala Camp Gear Division to enable each of our divisions to make a profit on this product.

Please advise me at your earliest convenience as to when you would like to receive our sales budget numbers and when we could combine our information to calculate transfer prices for next year.

The memo from Marie Waters of Outback Outfitters' Retail Division to Eric Devon of Koala Camp Gear Division (Koala Division) indicates that in this company, as in many others, divisions often exchange products. Internal transfers of products create the need for some pricing mechanism between divisions to accurately reflect the costs and revenues of doing business. The pricing mechanism commonly used to reflect transfers, called a **transfer price**, is the price used for internal transactions, for example, when one division of an organization sells goods or services to another division. In this example, Outback Outfitters' Retail Division is requesting a transfer price from the company's Koala Division for 'RooPacks, one of Outback's most popular items.

Although transfer prices commonly are used in today's organizations, they present some challenges for cost management analysts. For example, when a division of **Bosch** buys parts from another Bosch business unit for the packaging machines that it manufacturers, how does Bosch record this exchange in its accounting records for the two divisions? When an engineering student at the **University of Melbourne** takes an accounting course in the School of Business and Economics, how does the university record this event? At what interest rate does **HSBC** transfer depositors' funds to the loan department? Furthermore, large, global companies such as **Nestlé** nowadays often centralize processes in shared services centres, for example for accounting, IT or human resources management. Such shared services centres also often charge internal 'customers' for the work they do.[1] All of these situations require the transfer of goods or services from one subunit of the organization to another and corresponding transfer prices. Not only manufacturing firms, but also service industry firms and non-profit organizations use transfer pricing when services are transferred between responsibility centres. When responsibility centres are located in different countries, international transfer pricing is involved. This has special problems because it affects the division of taxable profit to these different countries that are regulated by different taxing authorities.

Let's explore some of the challenges that cost management analysts face in determining how to establish transfer prices to represent the substance of the transactions that occur between divisions. First we will derive two principles for creating behavioural congruence through transfer pricing. Then several different transfer pricing methods are explained, such as transfer pricing based on market prices and on costs. After that, we will discuss the dilemma that setting transfer prices may undermine divisional autonomy. International transfer pricing and segment reporting are the final topics in this chapter.

Impact of Transfer Pricing on Organizations

LO 1
Explain the purpose and role of transfer pricing for behavioural congruence.

The transfer price charged when one division of an organization sells goods or services to another division does not affect the overall organization's total profit, *given the internal and external transactions made*. However, the transfer price does affect the profit measurement for both the selling and buying divisions because, in effect, the divisions are completing sales transactions with each other. A high transfer price results in high profit for the selling division but low profit for the buying division. A low transfer price has the opposite effect. Consequently, the transfer-pricing policy *can* affect the *incentives* of autonomous division managers as they decide whether to make the transfer. Exhibit 15.1 depicts this scenario.

If the divisions are evaluated using some investment-centre performance measure (as discussed in Chapter 14), such as return on investment (ROI), residual income (RI), or economic value added (EVA), the transfer price affects each division's reported performance. The higher the transfer price, the more favourable is the performance measure for the selling division and the less favourable is the comparable performance measure for the buying division, all other things being equal.

The Organization as a Whole

What should be management's goal in setting transfer prices for internally transferred goods or services? The starting point is to consider what would be the best decision for the organization in its entirety. Realize that only sales to customers outside the organization and purchases from suppliers outside the organization matter to the entire company's earned (and externally reported) profit. Based

Exhibit 15.1 The Transfer Pricing Scenario

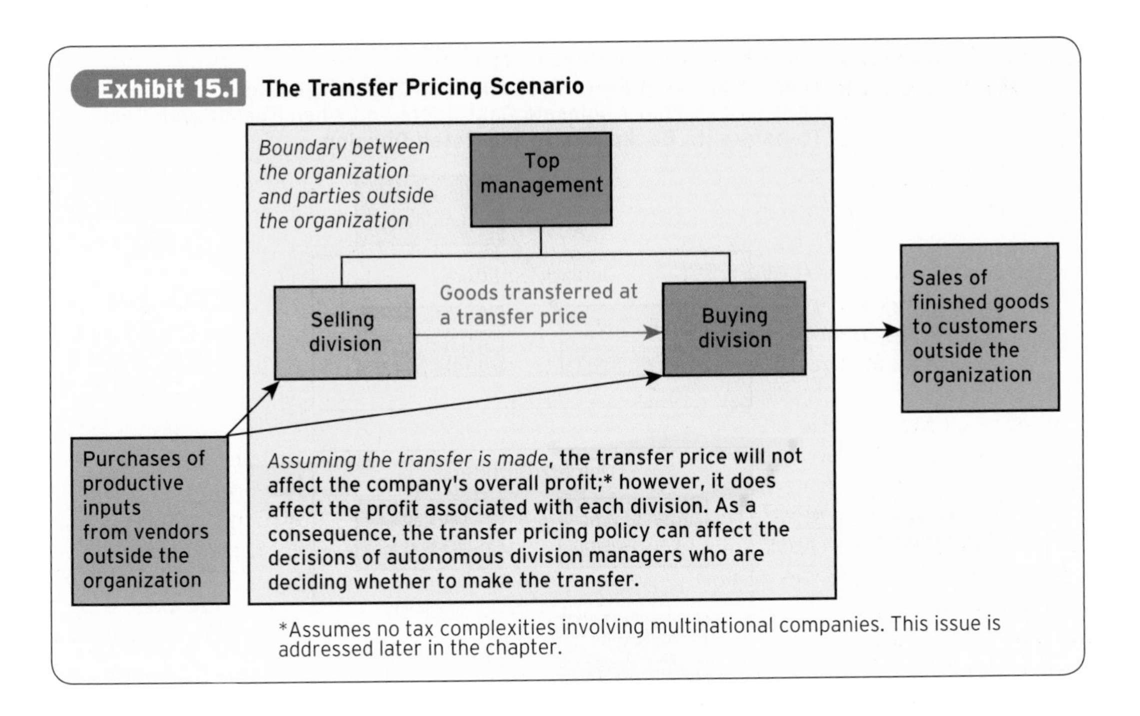
Boundary between the organization and parties outside the organization
Top management
Selling division
Goods transferred at a transfer price
Buying division
Sales of finished goods to customers outside the organization
Purchases of productive inputs from vendors outside the organization
Assuming the transfer is made, the transfer price will not affect the company's overall profit;* however, it does affect the profit associated with each division. As a consequence, the transfer pricing policy can affect the decisions of autonomous division managers who are deciding whether to make the transfer.

*Assumes no tax complexities involving multinational companies. This issue is addressed later in the chapter.

on these external revenues and costs, the best alternative can be identified.

We illustrate this for Outback Outfitters. Its Koala Camp Gear Division manufactures backpacks in its Melbourne plant. The Melbourne plant incurs a unit-variable cost of AU$37 to manufacture a backpack, and AU$1 to ship it to any customer. The Koala Camp Gear Division sells some of its backpacks in the *external* wholesale market to other companies under different labels. Koala incurs a unit-variable sales cost of AU$2 when selling to wholesale customers, for example because of warranty and discounts. The division can also transfer some of its products to the company's Retail Division, saving Koala's unit sales cost.[2] These backpacks carry the brand name 'RooPack and are imprinted with the Koala Camp Gear label. The Retail Division can sell a 'RooPack for AU$70 to consumers, and the Retail Division incurs a unit-level sales cost of AU$6 per backpack when selling to the retail customers, for example for warranty and gifts (such as key cords and drink containers). What is the most profitable transaction for Outback Outfitters as a whole: Koala selling to wholesale customers, or Koala internally supplying the other divisions who, in turn, sell to retail customers? Both alternatives are represented in Exhibit 15.2.[3]

Photo: Bosch

This Bosch packaging machine plant in Hangzhou, China buys parts from several other divisions in the company.

It is clear that for Outback Outfitters, sales to both wholesale customers and retail customers earn a positive contribution margin. If possible, Outback Outfitters would satisfy customers' demand in both markets. It is also clear that the most profitable business is to retail customers. So if production capacity was not enough to supply all customers, Outback Outfitters would prioritize sales to retail customers.

Now suppose that a local organization has made a special offer to the Retail Division manager to buy 800 'RooPacks to sell in a promotional campaign associated with the annual Australia Day celebration. The organization has offered to pay AU$55 per backpack. The contribution margin is shown

Exhibit 15.2 Contribution Margin to Outback Outfitters when Koala Camp Gear Sells to External Wholesale Customers and when Koala Camp Gear Transfers its Backpacks to the Retail Division

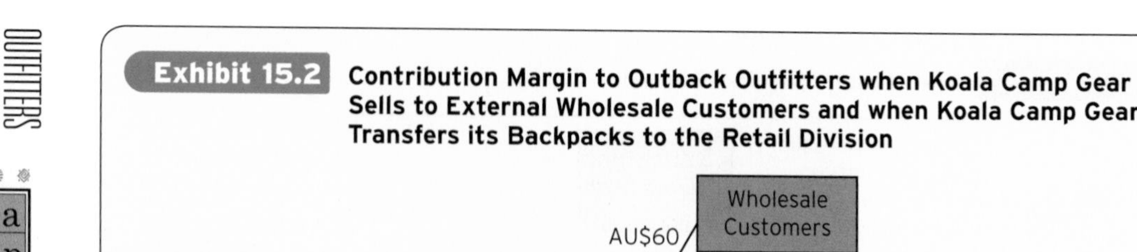

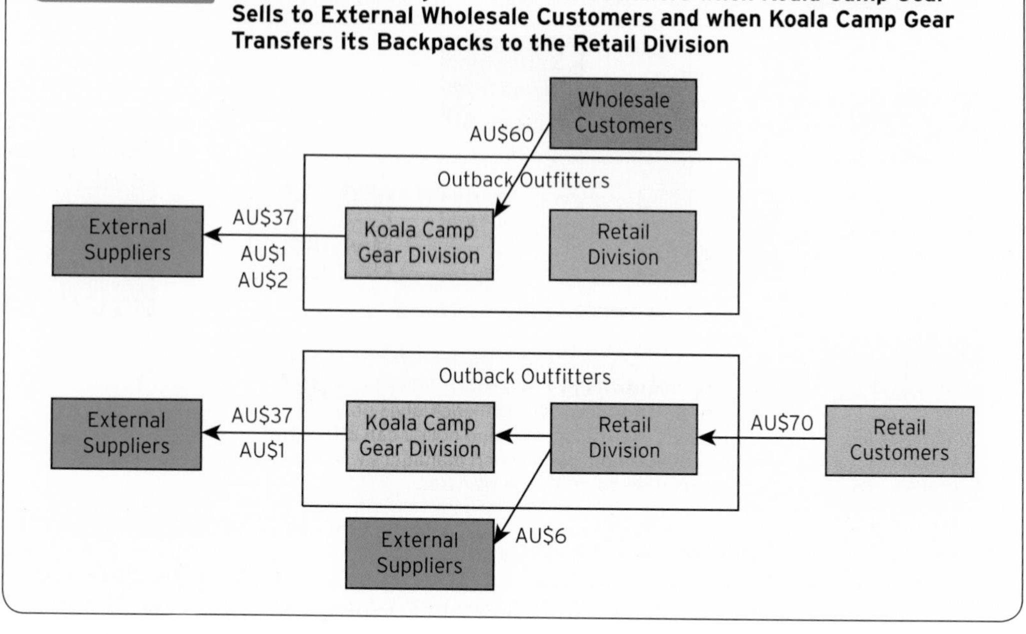

Contribution to Outback Outfitters from sale in external wholesale market		Contribution to Outback Outfitters from transfer to Retail Division	
Wholesale selling price per backpack	AU$60	Retail selling price per backpack	AU$70
Unit-level production cost	37	Unit-level production cost	37
Unit-level sales cost	2	Unit-level sales cost	6
Unit-level shipping cost (from Koala)	1	Unit-level shipping cost (from Koala)	1
Contribution margin	AU$20	Contribution margin	AU$26

in Exhibit 15.3. That calculation assumes that no sales costs are incurred for this special order. The contribution margin is again positive, so Outback Outfitters would like to accept this order. However, the contribution margin is lower than for regular business. Outback Outfitters earns a higher contribution margin if it sells either to other wholesale or retail customers. The contribution margins are AU$20 and AU$26, respectively, as we have just seen. So if Outback Outfitters has to choose between supplying to either wholesale or retail, or accepting this special order, then the latter should be rejected.[4]

More alternatives might be feasible. For example, perhaps the Retail Division could buy backpacks from another supplier instead of from Koala Camp Gear. It does not matter for the principle: what's best for Outback Outfitters depends only on the revenues and cost with external customers. You can look at this situation in more detail in You're the Decision Maker 15.1.[5]

The Divisional Perspective

Once it is clear what is the best alternative for the organization as a whole, the objective of a transfer pricing system is to lead managers of responsibility centres to make decisions that do not distort that decision. The goal in setting the transfer price is to provide incentives for each of these division managers to act in the company's best interests. The transfer price should be chosen so that each

Exhibit 15.3 **Contribution Margin to Outback Outfitters of Special Order**

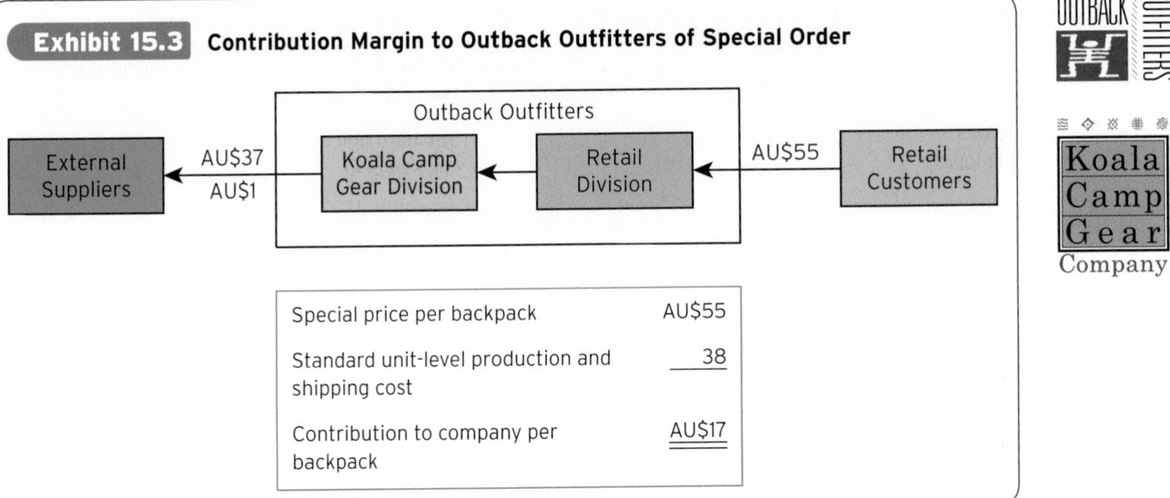

Special price per backpack	AU$55
Standard unit-level production and shipping cost	38
Contribution to company per backpack	AU$17

division manager, when striving to maximize his or her own division's profit, makes the decision that maximizes the company's profit.

Why is that important? In a decentralized organization, the managers of profit centres and investment centres often have considerable autonomy in deciding whether to accept or reject orders and whether to buy from inside or outside the organization. Outback is a decentralized company, and the Retail and Mail-Order Division managers are free to buy goods from either the Koala Camp Gear Division or an outside company. Similarly, the Koala Camp Gear Division manager is free to accept or reject an order for products, at any given price, from the Retail or Mail-Order Divisions.

Now we focus on the separate responsibility units. For them, internal transactions generate divisional revenues as does any other transaction. So by focusing on the revenues and costs at the level of a particular subunit, we can understand which alternative that subunit will prefer. Take Koala Camp

Exhibit 15.4 **Contribution Margin to the Koala Camp Gear Division when it Sells its Backpacks to External Wholesale Customers and when it Transfers Backpacks to the Retail Division**

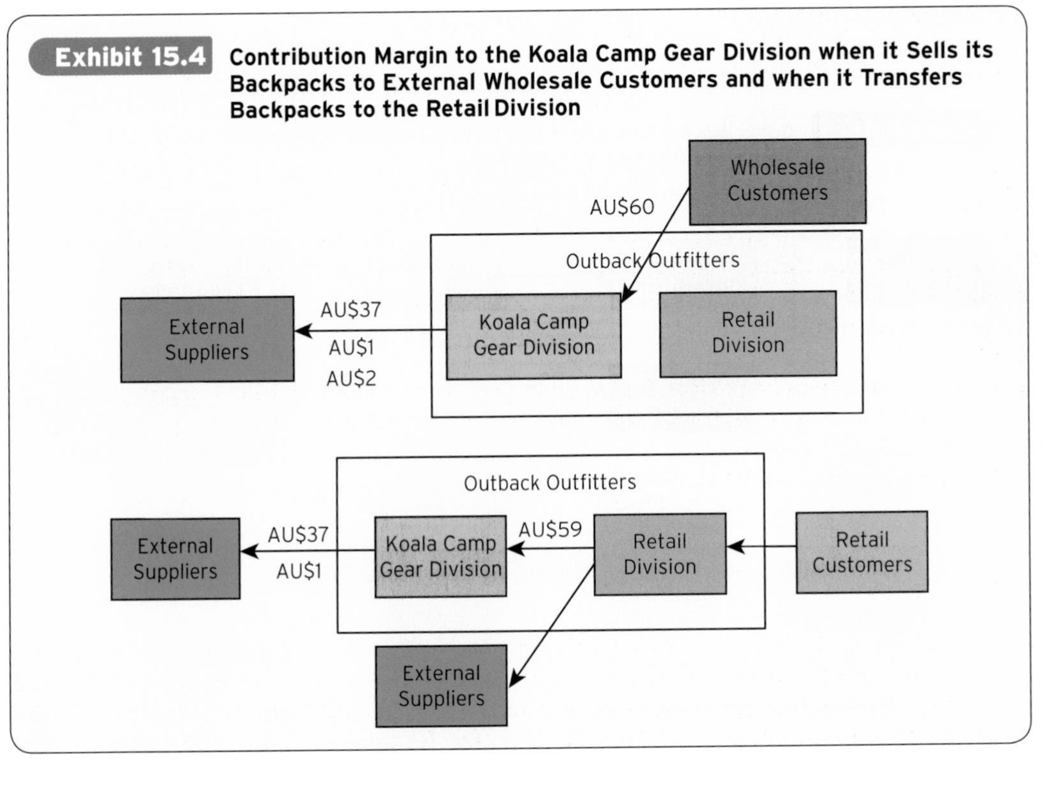

Contribution to Koala Camp Gear from sale in external wholesale market		Contribution to Koala Camp Gear from transfer to Retail Division	
Wholesale selling price per backpack	AU$60	Transfer price per backpack	AU$59
Standard unit-level cost for production, sales and shipping	40	Standard unit-level cost for production and shipping	38
Contribution margin	AU$20	Contribution margin	AU$21

Gear. Suppose the internal transfer price is set at AU$59 (later we will go into setting the transfer price); Koala will make the comparison as shown in Exhibit 15.4. For Koala Camp Gear, for a transfer price of AU$59 selling to the Retail Division is the best alternative. This transfer price creates behavioural congruence between Koala Camp Gear and Outback Outfitters: both prefer the same decision.[6]

How does it look from the Retail Division's perspective? This division will make the comparison as shown in Exhibit 15.5. The Retail Division manager is willing to buy the 'RooPacks because her division will have a contribution margin of AU$5 on each 'RooPack transferred (AU$70 retail sales price minus the AU$59 transfer price minus the AU$6 unit-variable sales costs). The alternative is not buying and selling backpacks, which generates a contribution margin of 0. Again, this transfer price creates behavioural congruence between the Retail Division and Outback Outfitters: both prefer the same decision.

You can verify that the contribution margins of the two divisions (AU$21 and AU$5) indeed add up to the contribution margin to Outback Outfitters as a whole that we calculated earlier.

How will the divisions consider the special order from the local civic organization regarding the purchase of 800 'RooPacks at AU$55 per unit? From Exhibit 15.3 it is clear that the Retail Division will earn a *negative* contribution margin equal to AU$55 less the AU$59 transfer price = –AU$4, while the Koala Camp Gear Division will earn a considerable *positive* contribution margin that is equal to the AU$59 transfer price – AU$38 = AU$21. Hence, the AU$59 transfer price does not create congruence in this case. However, a transfer price of at least AU$38 and at most AU$55 should be acceptable for both divisions. For example, at a transfer price of AU$42, the overall contribution margin of AU$17 on this special order is divided between both divisions as follows: the Retail Division earns AU$55 – AU42 = AU$13, and the Koala Camp Gear Division earns a contribution margin of AU$42 – AU38 = AU$4. Can a single transfer price always create behavioural congruence?

Exhibit 15.5 Contribution Margin to the Retail Division when Koala Camp Gear Transfers Backpacks Internally

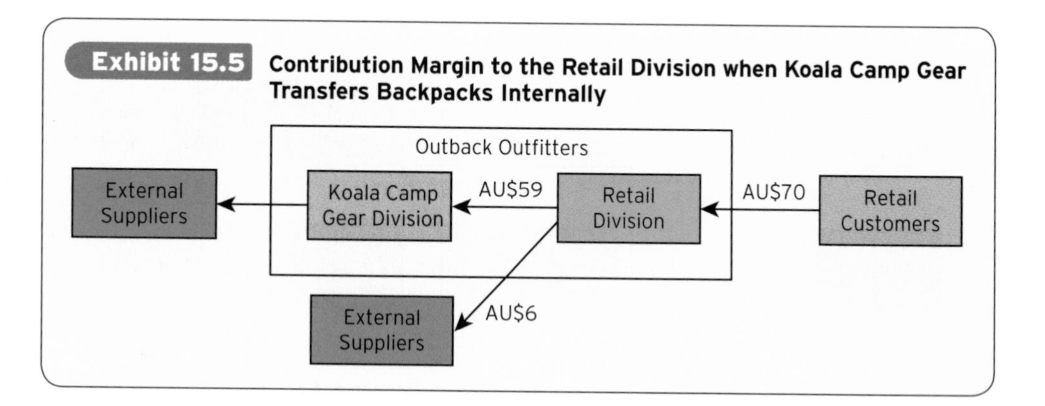

Contribution to Retail Division from buying from Koala Division	
Sales price to retail customers	AU$70
Transfer price per backpack	59
Standard unit-variable cost for sales	6
Contribution margin	AU$5

Creating Behavioural Congruence

So the principles for creating behavioural congruence through transfer pricing are always the same:

1. Determine the preferred alternative for the organization in its entirety. This is based on the incremental cash flows with external suppliers and customers, as done in Exhibit 15.2 for Outback Outfitters. Transfer prices are irrelevant for this analysis.
2. Check that the transfer price makes the preferred alternative also the most attractive alternative for the responsibility centres. This is based on the incremental cash flows each unit has with either external or internal suppliers and customers. In this analysis, transfer prices are treated similarly to external purchase prices and sales prices, as done in Exhibits 15.4 and 15.5 for the Koala Camp Gear Division and the Retail Division.

How are these principles implemented? We will consider several kinds of transfer prices that help to follow these steps.

15.1 You're the Decision Maker

Setting a Transfer Price when Outside Suppliers are also Available

More alternatives could be feasible. For example, maybe the Retail Division could buy backpacks from another supplier instead of from Koala Camp Gear. It does not matter for the principle: what is best for Outback Outfitters depends only on the revenues and cost with external customers.

Suppose the Retail Division could buy the same backpacks from another supplier at a price of AU$57 per unit. The Koala Camp Gear Division does not have excess capacity.

a. What is the preferred alternative for Outback Outfitters?
b. Should Koala also buy from this external supplier instead of producing backpacks itself?
c. What is the range of transfer prices that lead to behaviour congruence for both divisions?

(Solutions begin on page 782.)

Transfer Pricing Methods

LO 2 Explain how to base a transfer price on a general rule, market prices, costs or negotiations.

We will now explain several transfer pricing methods that are often used to set transfer prices in organizations with several responsibility centres. As we will see, several methods provide useful guidance, but actual transfer prices will often be guided by multiple and potentially conflicting objectives. Promoting behavioural congruence can lead to transfer prices based on only variable costs, while transparency and compliance with international transfer pricing principles may lead to full costs. Market prices are often a good starting point, but these need to be adjusted for significant cost differences between external transactions (where market prices truly apply) and internal transactions.

Companies often find that not all transactions between divisions occur as top management prefers. In extreme cases, the transfer pricing problem is so complex that top management reorganizes the company so that buying and selling divisions report to one manager who oversees the transfers.[7]

General Transfer Pricing Rule

A general rule that can provide a starting point for behavioural congruence among the division managers involved in the transfer is as follows:

$$\textbf{Transfer price} = \begin{array}{c}\textbf{Additional } \textbf{\textit{outlay cost}} \\ \textbf{per unit incurred because} \\ \textbf{goods are transferred}\end{array} + \begin{array}{c}\textbf{\textit{Opportunity cost}} \textbf{ per} \\ \textbf{unit to the organization} \\ \textbf{because of the transfer}\end{array}$$

The general rule specifies the transfer price as the sum of two cost components. The first component is the *outlay cost incurred by the division that produces the goods or services* to be transferred. Outlay costs include the direct unit-level costs of the product or service and any other outlay costs incurred as a result of the transfer. The second component in the general transfer-pricing rule is the *opportunity cost incurred by the organization as a whole* because of the transfer. Recall that an opportunity cost is a benefit that is forgone as a result of taking a particular action.

We illustrate the general transfer pricing rule for Outback Outfitters, whereby we distinguish between two different capacity scenarios.

Scenario I: Excess capacity

Suppose that the Koala Division's Melbourne plant has excess production capacity. This means that the total demand for its products from all sources, including the Retail and Mail-Order Divisions and the external market, is less than the plant's production capacity. Under this scenario of excess capacity, what does the general rule specify for an internal transfer price?

Outlay cost per backpack:	
Standard unit-level cost of production	AU$37
Standard unit-level cost of shipping	1
Total outlay cost	AU$38
Opportunity cost (forgone contribution margin from external sale)	AU$0

The general transfer pricing rule yields the following transfer price:

$$\textbf{Transfer price} = \textbf{Outlay cost} + \textbf{Opportunity cost}$$
$$\textbf{AU\$38} = \textbf{AU\$38} + \textbf{AU\$0}$$

The *outlay cost* that the Koala Camp Gear Division incurs to transfer a backpack internally to another division includes the standard unit-level production cost of AU$37 and the standard unit-level shipping cost of AU$1. The *opportunity cost* is zero. There is no opportunity cost to the company when a backpack is transferred to the Retail Division because the Koala Camp Gear Division can still satisfy all of its external demand for backpacks. Thus, the general rule specifies a transfer price of AU$38, the total unit-variable cost of production and shipping.

Does the general transfer pricing rule promote behavioural congruence? We saw earlier that when there is excess capacity, the preferred alternative for Outback Outfitters is that Koala Camp Gear does supply the Retail Division that, in turn, sells to retail customers. The transfer price of AU$38 should make this transfer attractive for both divisions. The alternative is that Koala Camp Gear does not supply and the Retail Division does not sell to retail customers, yielding a contribution margin of AU$0 to both divisions. At the transfer price of AU$38, the divisions earn the following contribution margins:

Koala Camp Gear Transfers to Retail Division	
Contribution to Koala Camp Gear	
Transfer price per backpack	AU$38
Standard unit-level cost for production and shipping	38
Contribution margin	AU$0
Contribution to Retail Division	
Sales price to retail customers	AU$70
Transfer price per backpack	38
Standard unit-variable cost for sales	6
Contribution margin	AU$26

The transfer price of AU$38, according to the general rule is indeed attractive for both the supplying and the buying division. However, notice that the general rule yields a transfer price that leaves the Koala Camp Gear Division manager indifferent to making the transfer. At a transfer price of AU$38, the contribution to the Koala Camp Gear Division is zero (transfer price of AU$38 less outlay cost of AU$38). To avoid this problem, we can view the general rule as providing a lower bound on the transfer price. Some companies allow the producing division to add a mark-up to this lower bound in order to provide a positive contribution margin. This in turn provides a positive incentive to make the transfer.

Scenario II: No excess capacity

Now let's change our basic assumption and suppose that the Koala Camp Gear Division can sell all backpacks it can produce to outside commercial buyers at a wholesale market price of AU$60 each. Since the division can sell all of its production, it has *no excess capacity*.

What transfer price does the general rule yield under this scenario of no excess capacity? The transfer price is determined as follows:

Outlay cost per backpack:	
Standard unit-level cost of production	AU$37
Standard unit-level cost of shipping	1
Total outlay cost	AU$38
Opportunity cost per backpack:	
Wholesale selling price to external market	AU$60
Unit-level cost of production, sales, and shipping	40
Opportunity cost (forgone contribution margin)	AU$20

The general transfer pricing rule yields the following transfer price:

Transfer price = Outlay cost + Opportunity cost
AU$58 = AU$38 + AU$20

The *outlay cost* in the Koala Camp Gear Division's Melbourne plant is still AU$38, since it does not depend on whether there is idle capacity or not. However, the *opportunity cost* incurred by Outback Outfitters when its Koala Division transfers a backpack to the Retail or Mail-Order Division *instead of* selling it in the external market is the forgone contribution margin from the lost external sale. This is now equal to AU$20. This margin is based not only on the unit-level production and shipping cost, but also on the unit-level sales costs that are incurred for external transactions (but not for internal transactions). The company loses a sale in the external market for every backpack transferred to the Retail or Mail-Order Division because the Koala Camp Gear Division has *no excess capacity*. Every backpack transferred to another company division results in one less backpack sold by the Koala Camp Gear Division in the external market.

Does the general transfer pricing rule promote behavioural congruence? We saw earlier that for Outback Outfitters the preferred alternative when there is no excess capacity is that Koala Camp Gear, *instead of selling to outside wholesale customers*, supplies the Retail Division that sells in turn, to retail customers. At the transfer price of AU$58, the divisions earn the following contribution margins:

Koala Camp Gear sells in external wholesale market		Koala Camp Gear transfers to Retail Division	
Contribution to Koala Camp Gear		**Contribution to Koala Camp Gear**	
Wholesale selling price per backpack	AU$60	Transfer price per backpack	AU$58
Standard unit-level cost for production, sales and shipping	40	Standard unit-level cost for production and shipping	38
Contribution margin	AU$20	Contribution margin	AU$20

Contribution to Retail Division		Contribution to Retail Division	
		Sales price to retail customers	AU$70
		Transfer price per backpack	58
		Standard unit-variable cost for sales	6
	AU$0	Contribution margin	AU$6

The Koala Camp Gear Division manager could be willing to transfer 'RooPacks to the Retail Division because the contribution margin is AU$20 in both internal and external transactions (AU$60 – AU$40 = AU$20 for external transactions, and AU$58 – AU$38 = AU$20 for internal transactions). However, a transfer price according to the general rule of just AU$58 leaves the Koala Camp Gear Division manager again indifferent to making the transfer.

The Retail Division manager is willing to buy the 'RooPacks because her division will have a contribution margin of AU$6 on each 'RooPack transferred (AU$70 retail sales price minus the AU$58 transfer price minus the AU$6 unit-level retail sales costs). You can verify that the contribution margins of the two divisions (AU$20 and AU$6) indeed add up to the contribution margin to Outback Outfitters as a whole that we calculated earlier in this chapter.

To conclude, the general transfer pricing rule provides a good starting point for thinking about transfer prices that lead to behavioural congruence. At the resulting transfer price, what is best for the organization as a whole is also the preferred alternative for each division. However, for the supplying division, the resulting transfer price is only the minimally acceptable transfer price. We can consider this transfer price as a lower bound.

Market-based Transfer Price

A common approach is to set the transfer price equal to the price in the external market.[8] When conditions between external and internal transactions are different, the external market price is adjusted to get to the **market-based transfer price**. For example, the producing division could enjoy some cost savings on internal transfers that are not obtained on external sales, such as lower logistics costs, or commissions might not have to be paid to sales personnel on internally transferred products.

In the Outback Outfitters illustration, the Koala Camp Gear Division can obtain AU$60 per 'RooPack, so that is the relevant market price for a market-based transfer price. However, for internal transfers, Koala Camp Gear can avoid a unit-variable sales cost of AU$2, so the comparable market-based transfer price becomes AU$58. In other words, compared to an internal transfer Koala Camp Gear needs to spend AU$2 more to get AU$60. Hence, the equivalent transfer price for Koala Camp Gear is AU$60 – AU$2 = AU$58.

When the producing division has no excess capacity and perfect competition prevails, when no single producer can affect the market price, the general transfer pricing rule and the external market-based transfer price yield the same transfer price. For Outback Outfitters, both rules gave a transfer price of AU$58. In more complicated situations in which the producing division has excess capacity or the external market is imperfectly competitive, the general rule and the external market price might not yield the same transfer price.

If the transfer price is set at the market price, the producing division should have the option to either produce goods for internal transfer or sell them in the external market. The buying division should be required to purchase goods from inside its organization if the producing division's goods meet the product specifications. Otherwise, the buying division should have the autonomy to buy from a supplier outside its own organization. The company should establish an arbitration process to handle pricing disputes that may arise. In other words, transfer prices based on market prices are consistent with the responsibility accounting concepts of profit centres and investment centres. When aggregate divisional profits are determined for the year, and ROI, residual income and EVA are computed, the use of a market-based transfer price helps to assess each division's contributions to overall corporate profits.

Does the market-based transfer price lead to behavioural congruence?

Suppose that the Koala Camp Gear Division of Outback Outfitters transfers backpacks to the Retail Division at a market-based transfer price of AU$58 per unit. We have seen this price earlier when investigating the effects of the general transfer pricing rule.

When there is *no excess capacity*, the best alternative for Outback Outfitters as a whole, is that the Koala Camp Gear supplies to the Retail Division, although this happens at the expense of Koala selling to wholesale customers. For the organization in its entirety, the contribution margin is higher when selling to retail customers through the Retail Division, compared to Koala selling to wholesale customers. As we have seen earlier, a transfer price of AU$58 makes this the preferred alternative for both divisions (or at least: for Koala Camp Gear this is equal to selling externally).

When there is *excess capacity*, the conclusion is slightly different. The best alternative for Outback Outfitters as a whole is that the Koala Camp Gear supplies to the Retail Division, because this does not lower Koala's sales to wholesale customers. For the organization in its entirety, the contribution margin should be greater than 0. At a transfer price of AU$58, both divisions enjoy a positive contribution margin, as we have seen earlier. However, this does not mean that the market-based transfer price will always lead to behavioural congruence in case of excess capacity. You can explore this in You're the Decision Maker 15.2. In that example, there is *excess capacity* and the market-based transfer price happens to be too high. This is because when the supplying unit has excess capacity, the transfer price that is behavioural congruent is lower compared to a situation of no excess capacity. However, this company-specific condition of excess capacity and low opportunity costs may or may not be reflected in the market-based transfer price.

The market-based transfer price can also be too low. Occasionally an industry experiences a period of significant excess capacity and extremely low prices. For example, when gasoline prices soar during political upheavals in oil-producing states, the market prices for recreational vehicles and powerboats can fall (temporarily) to very low levels. Under such extreme conditions, basing transfer prices on market prices can lead to decisions that are not in the best interests of the overall company. Basing transfer prices on artificially low *distressed market prices* could lead the producing division to sell or close the productive resources devoted to producing the product for transfer, and to move the division into a more profitable product line. Although such a decision might improve the division's profit in the short run, it could be contrary to the best interests of the company overall. It might be better for the company as a whole to avoid divesting itself of any productive resources and to ride out the period of market distress. To encourage an autonomous division manager to act in this fashion, some companies set the transfer price equal to the long-run *average external market price* rather than the current (possibly depressed) market price.

To conclude, market prices provide a very useful starting point for setting transfer prices. But it is still important to consider whether these lead to behavioural congruence. There is no guarantee that the market price leads to behavioural congruence under the conditions that are particular for that organization at that point in time.

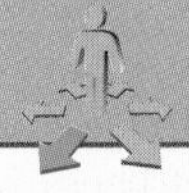

15.2 You're the Decision Maker

Setting a Market-based Transfer Price

The market-based transfer price is still AU$58, and costs are as given earlier. Suppose the Retail Division would be able to sell for AU$63 per unit, and the Koala Camp Gear Division has excess capacity.

a. What is the contribution margin of sales to retail customers for Outback Outfitters as a whole?
b. Will the market-based transfer price lead to behavioural congruence?

(Solutions begin on page 782.)

Cost-based Transfer Prices

Organizations that do not base transfer prices on market prices or negotiations often turn to **cost-based transfer pricing**, which sets the transfer price on the basis of the cost of the product or service transferred.[9]

Unit-variable cost

One cost-based approach is to set the transfer price equal to the standard unit-variable cost. The problem with this approach is that even when the producing division has excess capacity, it is not allowed to show any contribution margin on the transferred products or services. To illustrate, suppose that the Koala Camp Gear Division has excess capacity and the transfer price is set at the standard unit-level cost of AU$40 per backpack. The division has no positive incentive to produce and transfer backpacks to the Retail Division. The Koala Division's contribution margin from a transfer will be zero (transfer price of AU$40 minus unit-level costs of AU$40 equals zero). Some companies avoid this problem by setting the transfer price at standard unit-level cost plus a mark-up to allow the producing division a positive contribution margin.

Absorption or full cost

An alternative cost-based approach is to set the transfer price equal to the absorption, *or* full, cost of the transferred product or service. *Absorption* (or *full*) *cost* equals the product's unit-level cost plus an assigned portion of the higher-level costs (batch-level, product-line-level, customer-level, and general or facility-level costs).

Suppose that for the current year, the Koala Camp Gear Division's Melbourne plant has budgeted higher-level costs totalling AU$1,600,000 and normal production of 100,000 backpacks. The standard fixed cost per unit are, thus, AU$1,600,000 ÷ 100,000 units = AU$16. The full cost per backpack is calculated as follows:

Unit-level production cost (including packaging)	AU$37
Unit-level Sales related costs (only incurred for sales to external customers)	2
Standard unit-level shipping cost	1
Fixed cost per unit	16
Full cost per unit	AU$56

Under this full cost-based approach, the transfer price is set at AU$56 per backpack.

Does the full cost-based transfer price lead to behavioural congruence?

This is unlikely, because full cost-based transfer prices lead the buying division to view those costs that are not unit-variable costs for the entire company as unit-level costs to the buying division. This can cause faulty decision making.

To illustrate, suppose that the Koala Camp Gear Division has *no excess capacity*, and the transfer price of backpacks equals the full cost of AU$56 per pack. Recall that for Outback Outfitters as a whole, the preferred course of action is that the Koala Camp Gear Division supplies the Retail Division given the excess capacity, the sales prices and the unit-variable costs. However, it is easily seen that this will not happen when the transfer price is set at the full cost of AU$56. Both divisions earn the following contribution margins:

Koala Camp Gear sells in external wholesale market		Koala Camp Gear Transfers to Retail Division	
Contribution to Koala Camp Gear		**Contribution to Koala Camp Gear**	
Wholesale selling price per backpack	AU$60	Transfer price per backpack	AU$56
Standard unit-level cost for production, sales, and shipping	40	Standard unit-level cost for production and shipping	38
Contribution margin	AU$20	Contribution margin	AU$18

Contribution to Retail Division		Contribution to Retail Division	
		Sales price to retail customers	AU$70
		Transfer price per backpack	56
		Standard unit-variable cost for sales	6
	AU$0	Contribution margin	AU$8

For Koala Camp Gear the contribution margin is AU$20 per unit when selling to wholesale customers compared to only AU$18 from internal transfers. The transfer price of AU$56 is too low for Koala Camp Gear and this division will prefer selling to its wholesale customers. For Outback Outfitters, however, it would be best if the limited production capacity is allocated differently, such that backpacks are sold to retail customers through the Retail Division. The transfer price does not lead to behavioural congruence.

Why does this happen? In this example, the full cost-based transfer price is too low. It is not sufficient for Koala Camp Gear, the supplying division, because this transfer price deprives the supplying division from profits it can otherwise make. However, the full cost-based transfer price can also be too high. You can explore that in You're the Decision Maker 15.3.

To conclude, although the practice is common, transfer prices should not be based on full cost for proper in-country decision making. The risk is too high that the cost behaviour in the producing division will be obscured. This can all too easily result in decisions in the supplying and buying divisions that are not behavioural congruent. Cost-based transfer prices can either be too high or too low. There is no guarantee that the cost-based transfer price leads to behavioural congruence within the organization under conditions that are particular for that organization at that point in time.[10] However, for international transfer pricing, it might still be best to use full costs – not for decision making but to comply with international transfer pricing rules. International transfer pricing is discussed later in this chapter.

A note on ethics

What are the ethical implications in the situation just discussed? If the Retail Division manager realizes that buying the backpacks from the Koala Division is in the best interests of Outback Outfitters, shouldn't she buy from Koala, even if it hurts her division's performance? Strict adherence to ethical standards suggest that she should. Realistically, however, human nature suggests that we cannot always count on such behaviour to take place. Moreover, most transfer pricing scenarios are much more complicated than the Outback Outfitters' situation. More often than not, a buying division manager does not have enough information to clearly conclude what is in the overall company's best interests. It is important, therefore, to strive to set transfer pricing policies that help to run the business transparently, and that make all divisions at least not worse while improving the efficiency of the company as a whole.

15.3 You're the Decision Maker

Setting a Cost-based Transfer Price

Suppose that the Koala Camp Gear Division has *excess capacity*. Consider the special order from the local civic organization regarding the purchase of 800 'RooPacks at AU$55 per unit. The cost-based transfer price is still AU$56, and costs are as given earlier.

a. What is the contribution margin of this order for Outback Outfitters as a whole?
b. Will the cost-based transfer price lead to behavioural congruence?

(Solutions begin on page 782.)

Standard versus actual costs

Throughout our discussion of transfer prices, we have used *standard costs* rather than *actual costs*. This was true in our discussion of the general transfer pricing rule as well as for cost-based transfer prices. Transfer prices ordinarily should not be based on actual costs because such a practice would allow an inefficient producing division to pass its excess production costs on to the buying division via the transfer price. When standard costs are used in transfer-pricing formulas, the selling division is not forced to pick up the tab for the producer's inefficiency. Moreover, the producing division is given an incentive to control its costs since any costs of inefficiency cannot be passed on.[11]

15.1 Research Insight

Full Cost Transfer Pricing

Professors Jan Bouwens and Bert Steens in the Netherlands studied a company that used actual full costs as transfer prices between production units and sales units in the company. It is often assumed in the literature that using actual costs for transfer pricing purposes stimulates inefficiency, because the internal supplier can shift costs to the internal buyer. However, the authors found that production units often took actions to reduce costs instead of shifting these to buying units. This is understandable, because passing on inefficiencies would threaten the long-term existence of such a production unit in the firm, while reducing costs and transfer prices increased the volume awarded to that unit.

Source: Bouwens and Steens (2008).

Negotiated Transfer Prices

Many companies use **negotiated transfer pricing**. Division managers or their representatives actually negotiate the price at which transfers will be made. Sometimes they start with the external market price and then make adjustments for various reasons, as mentioned earlier, such as different sales and logistics costs. In such cases, a negotiated transfer price could split the cost savings between the producing and buying divisions. In other instances, a negotiated transfer price could be used because no external market exists for the transferred product.

Recall from the previous examples that there will typically be a minimum transfer price that can be acceptable for the supplying division and a maximum transfer price that can be acceptable for the buying division. If this maximum exceeds the minimum, there is a range of acceptable transfer prices, and negotiations will determine the transfer price within this range. Sometimes there is no solution, because the minimum that the internal producer could be willing to accept is higher than the maximum that the internal buyer could be willing to pay. You can see this in You're the Decision Maker 15.1.

Several drawbacks sometimes characterize negotiated transfer prices. First, negotiations can lead to divisiveness and competition between participating division managers. This can undermine the spirit of co-operation and unity that is desirable throughout an organization. If, for example, it would be best for the organization that an internal transfer is made, aggressive negotiations could nevertheless prevent the divisions from reaching agreement, thus frustrating the internal transfers of goods and services. Second, although negotiating skill is a valuable managerial talent, it should not be the sole or dominant factor in evaluating a division manager. If, for example, the producing division's manager is a better negotiator than the buying division's manager, the producing division's profit might look better than it should simply because of its manager's superior negotiating ability. Perhaps the company should use this skilled negotiator elsewhere in the company!

Informational Difficulties in Implementing Transfer Pricing Methods

Setting transfer prices as we have discussed so far requires considerable information. Cost management analysts need to know a lot about opportunity costs, market prices and product costs. Such information is required to understand what is in the best interest of the organization as a whole, and also for setting transfer prices that promote behavioural congruence. However, there can be considerable difficulties regarding the required information.

Unit-variable costs need to be measured for all transferred goods and services. Costing methods need to be comparable and all information must be available from all divisions for central cost management analysts. However, such detailed costing data are often not reported to central analysts, and even company-wide information systems may not allow drilling down to unit-variable cost for individual goods and services within divisions.

Market prices are difficult to measure when transferred goods and services are customized and unique. Sometimes no outside market exists at all. Furthermore, interdependencies among several transferred products or services make it difficult to measure market prices. For example, the producing division might provide design services as well as production of the goods for a buying division. What is the market price associated with each of these related outputs of the producing division?

Market prices are also difficult to measure when selling and buying divisions cannot sell and buy all they want in perfectly competitive markets. Under **perfect competition**, the market price does not depend on the quantity sold by any one producer. However, under **imperfect competition**, a single producer can affect the market price by varying the amount of product available in the market. In such cases, the external market price depends on the producer's production decisions. This in turn means that the opportunity cost the company incurs as a result of internal transfers depends on the quantity sold externally. These interactions could make accurately measuring the opportunity cost caused by a product transfer impossible.

Further difficulties are created when the producing division needs to invest in special equipment to produce the transferred goods, or needs to make other investments that are specific to the transferred goods and services. The organization should consider internal versus external transactions over a longer horizon and not only look at separate transactions.

Opportunity costs are also difficult to measure because these depend not only on market prices, but also on understanding which alternative business could be obtained. Issues involved here we will explore more in the next section.

15.1 Cost Management in Practice

Case Studies of Transfer Pricing Practices

Early case studies started to give more insights in how and why companies adopt particular transfer pricing practices. Gary Colbert and Barry Spicer analyse transfer pricing in four large, vertically integrated high-technology companies in the electronics industry in the USA. One of the main explanations is the extent to which the selling division needs to make high investments specifically for the components that are sold and bought internally (and these assets have considerably lower value for other customers). When more such investments need to be made, manufacturing costs were more important and market prices were less important as the basis for transfer pricing.

Recent case studies provide good illustrations of transfer pricing practices in international companies. Christian Plesner Rossing and Carsten Rohde describe how a Danish company adjusted its central overhead cost allocations and transfer pricing system for central services to comply with new international transfer pricing rules.

In two papers, Martine Cools and co-authors describe how a semiconductor division of a large multinational company adjusted its management control system and transfer pricing to make it more compliant with regulations. In both cases, transfer pricing became more transparent, better documented and more centralized.

Sources: Colbert and Spicer (1995); Rossing and Rohde (2010); Cools et al. (2008); and Cools and Slagmulder (2009).

Undermining of Divisional Autonomy

LO 3
Understand the drawbacks of interfering in divisional decisions.

Suppose the manager of Outback's Koala Camp Gear Division has excess capacity but insists on a transfer price of AU$56 based on full cost. The Retail Division manager is faced with the special offer for backpacks at AU$55 per unit. She does not want to decline the offer because that would reduce her division's profit, and she feels the company's interests would be best served by accepting the offer. She has also looked outside for other suppliers and it would be possible to source externally at competitive prices. If needed, she will go there, but she regrets going outside if it would be in the company's best interest to buy internally. The Retail Division manager calls the company president and explains the situation. She asks the president to intervene and force the Koala Camp Gear Division manager to lower his transfer price.

As the company president, what would you do? If you stay out of the controversy, your company will lose the contribution on the special order. If you intervene, you will run the risk of undermining the autonomy of your division managers. You established a decentralized organization structure for Outback Outfitters and hired competent managers because you believed in the benefits of decentralized decision making.[12]

And there is another consideration. You realize that if the Koala Camp Gear Division sticks to the high price and the Retail Division refuses to buy internally, then Koala Camp Gear will have unused capacity. If opportunity costs are really very low, then *Koala Camp Gear would also be better off accepting a low price for a special order.* Why would Koala Camp Gear not do so? Perhaps their ideas about the opportunity costs are different from what the Retail Division thinks these are (and what the Retail Division wants you as the company president to believe they are). Who knows best? Again, you probably decentralized decision making to the divisions for good reasons. Maybe Koala Camp Gear Division knows the market well and understands the opportunity costs better than you as the company president.

There is no obvious answer to this dilemma. In practice, central managers are reluctant to intervene in such disputes unless the negative financial consequences to the organization are quite large and unambiguous. Most managers believe that decentralized decision making has benefits that are important to protect even if it could result in an occasional dysfunctional decision. You can explore this in more detail in You're the Decision Maker 15.4.

Remedy for Motivational Problems of Transfer Pricing and Profit Centres

For measurement of financial performance of profit centres in the organization, internal transactions based on transfer prices count in the same way as external transactions based on sales prices and purchase prices. However, the cost management analyst should always keep in mind that only external sales are real sales. But if people are going to be evaluated on internal sales, they will act as if these are external sales. It may destroy co-operation, instead of creating value from the fact that divisions are part of the same firm. If divisions would act in exactly the same way as independent organizations, they probably should be that: independent organizations. But then what would be the added value for investors of the divisionalized firm? The challenge for the cost management analysts is making profits centres work together instead of against each other.

When the transfer pricing policy does not give a supplier a margin on the transaction, achieving behavioural congruence is unlikely to be promoted. For example, if transfers are made at differential unit-level costs, the supplier earns no contribution toward overhead or profit on the transferred goods. Then the transfer pricing policy does not motivate the supplier to transfer internally because internal transfers have no likely financial benefit, if that supplier is evaluated as a profit centre. Therefore, a supplier whose transfers are almost all internal usually is organized as a cost centre. The cost centre manager is normally held responsible for costs, not for revenues. Hence, the transfer price does not affect the manager's performance measures. In companies in which such a supplier is, nevertheless, a profit centre, the artificial nature of the transfer price should be considered when evaluating the results of that profit centre's operations.

A supplying centre that does business with both internal and external customers could be set up as a profit centre for external business when the manager has price-setting power and as a cost centre for internal transfers when the manager does not have such power. Performance on external business could be measured as if the responsibility centre were a profit centre; performance on internal business could be measured as if the responsibility centre were a cost centre.

Another possibility is to install a *dual transfer-pricing system* to provide the selling division with a profit but charge the buying division with costs only. A **dual transfer pricing system** charges the buying division for the cost of the transferred product, however the cost might be determined, and credits the selling division with the cost plus some profit allowance. The difference is accounted for in a special centralized account. This system would preserve cost data for subsequent buyer divisions and would encourage internal transfers by providing a profit on such transfers for the selling divisions.

Some companies use dual transfer prices to encourage internal transfers; however, other methods can also encourage internal transfers. For example, many companies recognize internal transfers and incorporate them explicitly in their reward systems. Other companies base part of a supplying manager's bonus on the purchasing centre's profits.

15.4 You're the Decision Maker

Divisional Autonomy and Transfer Pricing Policy

Koala Camp Gear Division was operating below capacity. The Retail Division received a contract for 800 backpacks. Both divisions are decentralized, autonomous profit centres and are evaluated based on operating profits.

The vice president of Koala called the vice president of the Retail Division and made a proposal:

Marie Waters (Retail VP): Look, Eric, I know you're running below capacity out there in your division. I'd like to buy 800 'RooPacks at AU$45 per unit. That will enable you to keep your production lines busy.

Eric Devon (Koala VP): Are you kidding, Marie? I happen to know that it would cost you more, namely AU$49 per backpack if you had to buy these from an outside supplier. We refuse to accept less than AU$56 per unit, which just covers our costs. We are optimistic and we think we can go out and get other orders to 'keep our production lines busy' as you put it. We don't want to block our production with your unprofitable business.

Marie: Eric, we both know that your unit-level costs for each backpack are only AU$38. I realize I'd be getting a good deal at AU$45 compared to the AU$49 that other suppliers would charge me, but so would you. You should treat this as a special order. Anything over your differential costs on the order is pure profit. Look, Eric, if you can't offer me that price, I'll have to go elsewhere. I have to keep my costs down, too, you know.

Eric: The AU$56 per backpack is firm. Take it or leave it!

Put yourself in the place of Outback Outfitters' CEO, Jack Darwin. You are approached by the Retail Division VP to intervene in this situation.

a. Calculate the total contribution margin for Koala Camp Gear if Eric Devon is able to get another order for 800 backpacks at the usual wholesale price of AU$60 (as he claims he will), which he can supply because he refused the internal deal and kept production capacity available. Also calculate the total contribution margin for Outback Outfitters as a whole in this situation.

b. Calculate the total contribution margin for Koala Camp Gear if Eric Devon has accepted the special deal. It turns out that he would have been able to get another order for 800 backpacks at the usual wholesale price of AU$60, but due to the internal deal Koala Camp Gear has no more production capacity available. Also calculate the total contribution margin for Outback Outfitters as a whole in this situation.

c. Calculate the total contribution margin for Koala Camp Gear if Eric Devon has refused the internal deal but he is unable to get a regular outside deal. He was too optimistic. Also calculate the total contribution margin for Outback Outfitters as a whole.

d. Calculate the total contribution margin for Koala Camp Gear if Eric Devon has accepted the special deal and would not have been able to get a regular outside deal. Also calculate the total contribution margin for Outback Outfitters as a whole.

e. What would you do being Jack Darwin? Explain.

(Solutions begin on page 782.)

15.2 Research Insight

Fairness in Transfer Pricing

Economic theory suggests that the outside market price of a product transferred between divisions should be the basis of a negotiated transfer price as long as the selling and buying divisions have options outside the firm for selling and buying the product. In experimental research, however, Professors Luft and Libby found that experienced managers expected the influence of market price to be limited by division managers' concern about how their profits compare with each other. While the market price did affect managers' transfer price estimates, its influence was significantly less when the market price resulted in more unequal (unfair) distribution of profits between divisions. In other words, experienced managers expected that a negotiated transfer price would be less likely to be based on the market price if doing so would result in an unequal (or unfair) distribution of firm profits between the divisions. The Luft and Libby study also concluded that reaching a negotiated agreement on the transfer price would be more difficult to achieve if a market-based transfer price resulted in an unequal (or unfair) distribution of profits.

In a subsequent study, Professors Kachelmeier and Towry cast doubt on whether the managers' *expectations* about the effect of perceived fairness on a negotiated transfer price would actually hold up in an actual transfer price negotiation involving real cash exchanges between parties. This is an area of unresolved research, there is much yet to understand about issues of fairness and efficiency.

Sources: Luft and Libby (1997); and Kachelmeier and Towry (2002).

International Transfer Pricing Practices and Regulations

LO 4
Discuss the implications of transfer pricing in a multinational company.

Recent surveys of international transfer pricing practices[13] report that cost-based transfer prices are used most for tangible goods (30 per cent) and even more for internal services (52 per cent). Market prices are also used often (27 per cent for tangible goods and 21 per cent for internal services). No transfer pricing policy dominates all others. Contrary to earlier in this chapter when we could formulate a general transfer pricing rule, it is not clear what the optimal international transfer pricing rule would be. Pragmatic considerations are clearly important, such as reducing overall taxation but also avoiding that tax authorities do not accept a firm's international transfer prices and impose double taxation. We will address some of these issues in this section.

Multinational Transfer Pricing

In international transactions, transfer prices could affect tax liabilities, import tariffs, royalties, and other payments because laws vary in different countries (or states). Because tax rates vary among countries, companies have incentives to set transfer prices that will increase revenues (and profits) in low-tax countries and increase costs (thereby reducing profits) in high-tax countries. Tax avoidance by foreign companies using biased transfer prices has been a controversial issue for many years. Tax authorities in the US, UK, Australia, China, India and other countries have introduced many new rules for transfer pricing and have started to increase their investigations of companies' transfer pricing practices.[14]

Most tax authorities require internal transfers to be prices based on an '**arm's length transaction**' value, which is the price as if the good or service were sold to an independent party. The Organisation for Economic Co-operation and Development (www.OECD.org/ctp/tp) stimulated the arm's-length standard for establishing the transfer price for goods, services and intangible assets, and the OECD continues to play a significant role in the development and harmonization of international transfer pricing.[15] To find comparable independent transactions, another party should undertake the same function, involving comparable levels of assets and risks. The transfer should represent a real benefit for the recipient that justifies charging a price for it. Transfer pricing methods should be transparent and companies should provide detailed documentation of their methods. The OECD guidelines and the rules specified by tax authorities acknowledge several transfer pricing methods in practice, which aim to follow the arm's-length principle as closely as possible.

Transfer prices and tax effects: an illustration

To understand the effects of transfer pricing on taxes, consider the case of Kaola Camp Gear's Perth Plant. Cost management analysts investigate what would happen if some work is offshored to another country under different transfer prices. Suppose its facility in Country B imports materials from the company's Country S facility.[16] The tax rate in Country B is 70 per cent and in Country S is 40 per cent.[17]

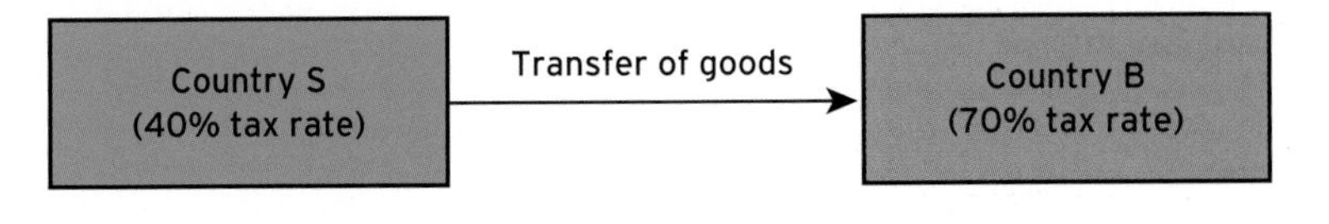

During the current year, the plant incurred production costs of AU$400,000 in Country S. Costs incurred in Country B, aside from the cost of the transferred goods, amounted to AU$1,200,000. (We call these 'third-party costs'.) Sales revenues in Country B were AU$4,800,000. Similar goods imported by other companies in Country B would have cost an equivalent of AU$600,000. However, Koala points out that because of its special control over its operations in Country S and the special approach it uses to manufacture its goods, the appropriate transfer price is AU$2,000,000. What would be the effect on the total tax liability in both jurisdictions if the company used the AU$2,000,00 transfer price instead of the AU$600,000 transfer price?

Assuming that the AU$600,000 transfer price is used, the tax liability is computed in Exhibit 15.6. In contrast, Exhibit 15.7 computes the tax liability assuming the AU$2,000,000 transfer price. Koala Camp Gear can save €420,000 in taxes simply by changing its transfer price![18]

Exhibit 15.6 Tax Liability Assuming a AU$600,000 Transfer Price

	Country S		Country B
Revenue	AU$600,000	←	AU$4,800,000
Third-party costs	(400,000)		(1,200,000)
Transferred goods costs		→	(600,000)
Taxable income	AU$200,000		AU$3,000,000
Tax rate	× 0.40		× 0.70
Tax liability	AU$ 80,000		AU$2,100,000
Total tax liability		AU$2,180,000	

Exhibit 15.7 Tax Liability Assuming a AU$2,000,000 Transfer Price

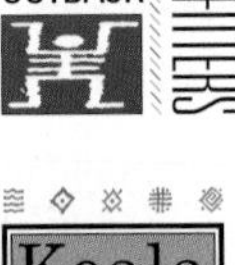

	Country S		Country B
Revenue	AU$2,000,000	←	AU$4,800,000
Third-party costs	(400,000)		(1,200,000)
Transferred goods costs		→	(2,000,000)
Taxable income	AU$1,600,000		AU$1,600,000
Tax rate	× 0.40		× 0.70
Tax liability	AU$ 640,000		AU$1,120,000
Total tax liability		AU$1,760000	

To say the least, international taxing authorities look closely at transfer prices when they examine the tax returns of companies engaged in related-party transactions that cross national boundaries. Companies frequently must provide adequate support for the use of the transfer price that they have chosen for such a situation. Transfer pricing disputes also occur at the state and province levels because of different tax rates.

Import duties

Another international issue that can affect a firm's transfer-pricing policy is the imposition of import duties, or tariffs. These are fees a government charges an importer, generally on the basis of the reported value of the goods being imported. Consider as an example a firm with divisions in Europe and Asia. If the Asian country imposes an import duty on goods transferred in from the European division, the company has an incentive to set a relatively low transfer price on the transferred goods. This minimizes the duty to be paid and maximizes the overall profit for the company as a whole. As in the case of taxation, countries sometimes pass laws to limit a multinational firm's flexibility in setting transfer prices for the purpose of minimizing import duties.

15.5 You're the Decision Maker

Transfer Pricing for Multinational Companies

Refer to the preceding information for Koala Camp Gear's Perth Plant operations. Assume that the tax rate for both countries is 40 per cent.

What would be the tax liability for Koala Camp Gear if the transfer were set at AU$600,000? At AU$2,000,000?

(Solutions begin on page 782.)

15.2 Cost Management in Practice

International Implications of Transfer Pricing

A Japanese motorcycle manufacturer uses just-in-time production for its manufacturing facility in Japan. Its US subsidiary is a distribution company that sells to dealers in the United States. Both the Japanese manufacturing facility and the US distribution subsidiary were profitable as long as demand for the product in the United States remained high.

Eventually, demand in the United States for motorcycles declined. The US subsidiary found itself with lots of inventory, so much that it had more than a year's supply of the product on hand. Meanwhile, the Japanese manufacturing plant was reluctant to reduce production below its efficient operating level and, because it followed the just-in-time philosophy, did not stockpile finished goods inventory in Japan.

As inventories increased at the US subsidiary, so did expenses to store and sell them. The US subsidiary showed declining profits and eventually incurred losses. The US **Internal Revenue Service** claimed that the low profits and losses were the result of the transfer price set by the Japanese manufacturer (which was based on full-absorption manufacturing costs) and the fact that the Japanese manufacturer continued to ship products that the US subsidiary had difficulty selling. Consequently, according to the IRS, the Japanese manufacturer should bear some of the costs of the US subsidiary's high inventory levels, increasing the US division's taxable income.

Source: Based on an author's research.

Segment Reporting and Transfer Pricing

LO 5
Discuss the effects of transfer pricing on segment reporting.

The **International Accounting Standards Board (IASB)** and the **Financial Accounting Standards Board (FASB)** require companies engaged in different lines of business to report certain information about their segments that meet its technical requirements.[19] This reporting requirement is intended to provide a measure of the performance of those segments of a business that are significant to the company as a whole. Specific criteria about revenues, profit or loss, and assets identify reportable segments.

The following are the principal items that must be disclosed about each segment:

- Revenue
- Operating profits or loss
- Interest revenues and interest expense
- Total assets
- Depreciation and amortization
- Material non-cash items other than depreciation and amortization

There are many more requirements. For example, a company has to provide a number of reconciliations (such as the total of the reportable segments' profit or loss to the company's profit or loss) and needs to provide information about its revenues and assets on a geographical basis.

Negotiated transfer prices, which could be useful for internal purposes, are not generally acceptable for external segment reporting. In general, the accounting profession has indicated a preference for market-based transfer prices.[20] This preference arises because the purpose of the segment disclosure is to enable an investor to evaluate a company's divisions as though they were freestanding enterprises. Presumably, sales would be based on market transactions, not on managers' ability to negotiate prices.

Although the conceptual basis for market-based transfer prices is sound in this setting, the practical application can be difficult. Frequently, the segments are really *interdependent*, so market prices might not really reflect the same risk in an intra-company sale that they do in third-party sales.

In addition, in many situations, market prices either are not readily available or might exist for only some products. When these problems arise, management usually attempts to estimate the market price by obtaining market prices for similar goods and adjusting the price to reflect the characteristics of the goods transferred within the company. An alternative is to take the cost of the item transferred and add an allowance to represent the normal (or comparable) profit for the item.

15.3 Cost Management in Practice

Transfer Pricing by Multinational Companies in China

Multinational companies in China now have to 'think local' in the sense of fitting their business to the local situation, but they have to 'act global': their behaviour in China must match their global standards. For transfer pricing, this means that there will be more scrutiny on the practices companies use in China. According to the Chinese tax authorities, transfer pricing mechanisms are now used to take profits out of the country to avoid taxation. Multinational companies will need to follow China's global standards for transparency and documentation also in China.

In many other ways too, companies will need to behave more globally in China. They cannot apply double standards, for example with respect to food safety standards. Even if certain ingredients or doses are legally allowed in China but a company follows more strict standards elsewhere in the world, it could be better to follow the same global practices in China. The Chinese government has been looking at multinational companies to set global standards in China, which is a particularly important contribution at this stage in the development of the country's economy.

Source: Park and Vanhonacker (2007).

Chapter Summary

When products or services are transferred between divisions in the same organization, divisional performance is affected by the transfer price. Creating behavioural congruence through transfer pricing goes in two steps. First, cost management analysts determine the preferred alternative for the organization in its entirety. This is based on the incremental cash flows with external suppliers and customers. Transfer prices are irrelevant for this analysis. Second, cost management analysts check that the transfer price makes the preferred alternative also the most attractive alternative for the individual responsibility centres. This is based on the incremental cash flows of each responsibility centre with either external or internal suppliers and customers. In this analysis, transfer prices are treated similarly to external purchase prices and sales prices.

Organizations can use different methods as a starting point for setting transfer prices. A general rule states that the transfer price should equal the outlay cost incurred to make the transfer plus the organization's opportunity cost associated with the transfer. Furthermore, transfer prices can be based on market prices, costs or negotiations. In some cases, these practical transfer-pricing methods could result in dysfunctional decisions, although that may be difficult to judge for top management. Top management then must weigh the benefits of intervening to prevent suboptimal decisions against the costs of undermining divisional autonomy.

Since tax rates vary in different countries, companies have incentives to set transfer prices to increase revenues (and profits) in low-tax countries and increase costs (thereby reducing profits) in high-tax countries. However, taxing authorities are well aware of these incentives and seek to enforce 'arm's-length transaction'-based transfer prices.

Companies with significant segments are required to report on those segments separately in the financial statements. The accounting profession has indicated a preference for market-based transfer prices when reporting on a segment of a business.

Key Terms

For each term's definition, refer to the indicated page, or turn to the glossary at the end of the text.

arm's length transaction,	764	market-based transfer price,	756
cost-based transfer pricing,	758	negotiated transfer pricing,	760
dual transfer pricing system,	762	perfect competition,	761
imperfect competition,	761	transfer price,	748

Review Questions are mostly written at a ***basic*** *level; Critical Analysis questions and Exercises are* ***intermediate****, and Problems and Cases are* ***advanced****.*

Review Questions

15.1 Why do transfer prices exist even in highly centralized organizations?

15.2 Describe four methods by which transfer prices can be set.

15.3 Why are market-based transfer prices considered optimal under many circumstances?

15.4 What are the limitations to market-based transfer prices?

15.5 What are the advantages and disadvantages of top management's direct intervention in a transfer-pricing dispute?

15.6 Why do companies often use prices other than market prices for interdivisional transfers?

15.7 What is the basis for choosing between actual and standard costs for cost-based transfer pricing?

15.8 Some have suggested that managers should negotiate transfer prices. What are the disadvantages of a negotiated transfer pricing system?

15.9 What is the general transfer pricing rule?

15.10 Explain the effect of import duties, or tariffs, on the transfer pricing policies of multinational companies.

Critical Analysis

15.11 How does the choice of a transfer price affect the operating profits of both segments involved in an intracompany transfer?

15.12 What are some goals of a transfer pricing system in a decentralized organization?

15.13 Division A has no external markets. It produces monofilament used by division B, which cannot purchase this particular type of monofilament from any other source. What transfer pricing system would you recommend for the interdivisional sales of monofilament? Why?

15.14 Refer to Cost Management in Practice 15.2. Why did the Internal Revenue Service dispute the US subsidiary's reported profits and losses?

15.15 When setting a transfer price for goods sold across international boundaries, what factors should management consider?

15.16 Setting transfer prices by negotiation is detrimental to the company. Do you agree or disagree with this statement by the CEO of a midsize manufacturing company? Why?

15.17 'Basing transfer prices on full absorption costs can really screw up decision making in a company!' Explain this remark by a manufacturing vice president, and construct a simple numerical example to make the point.

15.18 In setting transfer prices for multinationals, tax considerations can be the tail that wags the dog. Explain.

15.19 Some observers have suggested that fairness is a criterion that a transfer price should meet. What do you think it means for a transfer price to be 'fair'?

Exercises

Exercise 15.20 [LO 1, 2] Application of Transfer Pricing Rules

Oneida Associates is a real estate company operating in the Finger Lakes region of central New York. Its leasing division rents and manages properties for others, and its maintenance division performs services such as carpentry, painting, plumbing and electrical work. The maintenance division, which has an estimated variable cost of $29 per labour hour, works for both Oneida and other companies. It could spend 100 per cent of its time working for outsiders. Maintenance division charges $71 per hour for labour performed for outsiders, the same rate that other maintenance companies charge. The leasing division complained that it could hire its own maintenance staff at an estimated variable cost of $40 per hour.

Required

a. What is the minimum transfer price that the maintenance division should obtain for its services, assuming that it is operating at capacity?
b. What is the maximum price that the leasing division should pay?
c. Would your answers in requirements (a) or (b) change if the maintenance division had idle capacity? If so, which answer would change, and what would the new amount be?

Exercise 15.21 [LO 1, 2] Transfer Pricing System Evaluation

RechTech's Western Division has an opportunity to transfer component Z50 to the company's Eastern Division. The Western Division, which offers its Z50 product to outside markets for €90, incurs variable costs of €33 per unit and fixed costs of €22,500 per month based on monthly production of 1,000 units.

The Eastern Division can acquire the Z50 product from an alternate supplier for €94.50 per unit or from the Western Division for €90 plus €6 per unit in transportation costs.

Required

a. What are the costs and benefits of the alternatives available to the Western and Eastern Divisions with respect to the transfer of the Western Division's Z50 product? Assume that the Western Division can market all that it can produce.

b. How would your answer change if the selling division had idle capacity sufficient to cover all of the buying division's needs?

Exercise 15.22 [LO 1, 2] General Transfer Pricing Rule

Interlaken Metals SA has two divisions. The fabrication division transfers partially completed components to the assembly division at a predetermined transfer price. The fabrication division, which has a standard variable production cost per unit of CHF 240, has no excess capacity and could sell all of its components to outside buyers at CHF 304 per unit in a perfectly competitive market. (Monetary values given in Swiss francs, CHF.)

Required

a. Determine a transfer price using the general rule.

b. How would the transfer price change if the fabrication division had excess capacity?

Exercise 15.23 [LO 1, 3] Cost-based Transfer Pricing; Ethics

Refer to the preceding exercise. The fabrication division's full (absorption) cost of a component is CHF 272, which includes CHF 32 of applied fixed overhead costs. The transfer price has been set at CHF 300, which is the fabrication division's full cost plus a 10 per cent mark-up.

The assembly division has a special offer of CHF 372 for its product. The assembly division incurs variable costs of CHF 80 in addition to the transfer price for the fabrication division's components. Both divisions currently have excess production capacity.

Required

a. Is the assembly division's manager likely to accept or reject the special offer? Why?

b. Is this decision in the best interests of Interlaken Metals as a whole? Why?

c. Suppose that the assembly division manager decides to reject the special offer. Is the manager acting ethically? Explain.

d. How could the situation be remedied using the transfer price?

Exercise 15.24 [LO 1-3] Transfer Pricing System Evaluation

Edgeworth Box Company has two decentralized divisions, X and Y. Division X always has purchased certain units from division Y at £87 per unit. Because division Y plans to raise the price to £117 per unit, division X desires to purchase these units from outside suppliers for £87 per unit. Division Y's costs follow:

Variable costs per unit	£81
Annual fixed costs	£17,400
Annual production of these units for division X	1,000 units

Required

If division X buys from an outside supplier, the facilities that division Y uses to manufacture these units would remain idle. What would be the result if Edgeworth Box Company enforces a transfer price of £117 per unit between divisions X and Y?

Exercise 15.25 [LO 4] International Transfer Pricing Policy: Use of Internet

Use the Internet to explore international transfer pricing policies by going to the website for the OECD (Organisation for Economic Co-operation and Development) at www.oecd.org. Use the Search OECD Online function and enter *transfer pricing* when prompted for a word or phrase for which to search.

Required

Peruse the OECD transfer pricing guidelines. Choose an issue that interests you and report on it to the class.

Exercise 15.26 [LO 1-3] Transfer Pricing System Evaluation

Memphis Transit Ltd operates a local mass transit system. The transit authority is a governmental agency related to the state government. It has an agreement with the state government to provide rides to senior citizens for $0.50 per trip. The government reimburses Memphis Transit for the 'cost' of each trip taken by a senior citizen.

The regular fare is $1.25 per trip. After analysing its costs, Memphis Transit figured that with its operating deficit, the full cost of each ride on the transit system is $3.00. The number of senior citizens on any route does not affect routes, capacity or operating costs.

Required

a. What alternative prices could be used to determine the governmental reimbursement to Memphis Transit?
b. Which price would Memphis Transit prefer? Why?
c. Which price would the state government prefer? Why?

Exercise 15.27 [LO 1-3] Transfer Pricing System Evaluation

Continentale de L'électronique SA permits its decentralized units to 'lease' space to one another. Division X has leased some idle warehouse space to division Y for €10 per square metre per month. Recently, division X obtained a new five-year contract, which will increase its production sufficiently so that the warehouse space is more valuable to it. Division X has notified division Y that it will increase the rental price to €31.80 per square metre per month. Division Y can lease space at €19.50 per square metre in another warehouse from an outside company but prefers to stay in the shared facilities. Division Y's management states that it prefers not to move. If division X cannot use the space now being leased to division Y, it will have to rent other space for €30 per square metre per month. (The difference in rental prices occurs because division X requires a more substantial warehouse building than division Y.)

Required

As a group, recommend a transfer price and explain your reasons for choosing that price.

Exercise 15.28 [LO 1-3] Transfer Pricing System Evaluation

Invernadero Puerto Morelos (IPM), owned 60 per cent by Pacal Salazar and 40 per cent by Maya Rivera, grows specimen plants for landscape contractors. The wholesale price of each plant is $180. During the past year, IPM sold 5,000 specimen plants.

Of the plants sold last year, 1,000 were sold to Paisajes Cancun (PC). Salazar has a 20 per cent interest in PC, and Rivera has a 60 per cent interest in PC. At the end of the year, Rivera noted that PC was the largest buyer of IPM's plants. She suggested that the plant company give PC a 10 per cent reduction in prices for the coming year in recognition of its position as a preferred customer. (Monetary values given in Mexican pesos, $).

Required

Assuming that Paisajes Cancun purchases the same number of plants at the same prices in the coming year, what effect would the price reduction have on the operating profits that accrue to Salazar and to Rivera for the coming year?

Exercise 15.29 [LO 1, 5] Segment Reporting and Transfer Pricing

Lone Star Homes Inc. has two divisions, building and financing. The building division oversees construction of single-family homes in 'economically efficient' subdivisions. The financing division takes loan applications and packages mortgages into pools and sells them in the loan markets. It also services the mortgages. Both divisions meet the requirements for segment disclosures under accounting rules.

The building division had $75 million in sales last year. Costs, other than those charged by the financing division, totalled $60 million. The financing division obtained revenues of $20 million from servicing mortgages and incurred outside costs of $18 million. In addition, the financing division charged the building division $10 million for loan-related fees. The building division's manager complained to Lone Star's CEO that the financing division was charging twice the commercial rate for loan-related fees and that the building division would be better off sending its buyers to an outside lender.

The financing division's manager stated that although commercial rates might be lower, it was more difficult to service Lone Star mortgages and, therefore, the higher fees were justified.

Required

a. What are the reported segment operating profits for each division, ignoring income taxes and using the $10 million transfer price for the loan-related fees?

b. What are the reported segment operating profits for each division, ignoring income taxes and using a $5 million commercial rate as the transfer price for the loan-related fees?

Exercise 15.30 [LO 4] International Transfer Prices

Western Lumber Corporation has two operating divisions. Its logging operation in Canada mills and ships logs to the United States where the company's building supplies division uses them. Operating expenses amount to $2.5 million in Canada and $7 million in the United States exclusive of the costs of any goods transferred from Canada. Revenues in the United States are $17 million.

If the lumber were purchased from one of the company's US lumber divisions, the costs would be $3.6 million. However, if the lumber had been purchased from an independent Canadian supplier, the cost would be $5 million. Assume that the marginal income tax rate is 60 per cent in Canada and 40 per cent in the United States. (All monetary values given in Canadian dollars, $).

Required

Build a spreadsheet to determine the company's total tax liability to both jurisdictions for each of the two alternative transfer pricing scenarios ~~($3 million and $4 million)~~? Explain.
3.6 million 5 million

Exercise 15.31 [LO 1, 5] Segment Reporting and Transfer Pricing

Down Under Corporation, based in Melbourne, Australia, has two operating divisions, an amusement park in Sydney and a hotel in Brisbane. The two divisions meet the Australian requirements for segment disclosures. Before transactions between the two divisions are considered, revenues and costs were as follows (in thousands of Australian dollars):

	Hotel	Amusement park
Revenue	$32,000	$24,000
Costs	22,000	20,000

The amusement park and the hotel had a joint marketing arrangement by which the hotel gave free passes to the amusement park and the amusement park gave discount coupons good for stays at the hotel. The value of the free passes to the amusement park redeemed during the past year totalled $4,500,000. The discount coupons redeemed at the hotel resulted in a $3,000,000 decrease in hotel revenues. As of the end of the year, all current year coupons have expired.

Required

a. Is there a transfer pricing issue in this exercise? Explain.

b. What are the operating profits for each division, considering the effects of the costs arising from the joint marketing agreement?

Problems

Problem 15.32 [LO 1-3] Analysis of Transfer Pricing Data

Faber Werkzeugmaschine AG is a decentralized organization that evaluates division management based on measures of division contribution margin. Divisions L and N operate in similar product markets. Division L produces a sophisticated electronic assembly that it can sell up to 140,000 units to the outside market for €9.60 per unit per year. These units require 2 direct labour hours each.

If L modifies the units with an additional one-half hour of labour time, it can sell them for €10.80 per unit to N, which will accept up to 120,000 of these units per year.

If N does not obtain 120,000 units from L, it purchases them for €11.10 each from the outside. Division N incurs €4.80 of additional labour and other out-of-pocket costs to convert the assemblies into a home digital electronic radio, calculator, telephone monitor and clock unit. The units can be sold to the outside market for €27 each.

Division L estimates that its total costs are €555,000 for fixed costs and €3.60 per direct labour hour. Its capacity is limited to 400,000 direct labour hours per year.

Required

Determine the following:

a. Total contribution margin to L if it sells 140,000 units to the outside.
b. Total contribution margin to L if it sells 120,000 units to N.
c. The costs to be considered in determining the optimal company policy for sales by division L.
d. The annual contributions and costs for L and N under the optimal policy.

Problem 15.33 [LO 1-3] Transfer Pricing with Imperfect Markets; ROI Evaluation; Normal Costing

Lao Che Corporation's division S has an investment base of ¥3,900,000. The division produces and sells 90,000 units of a product at a market price of ¥65 per unit. Its variable costs total ¥20 per unit. The division also charges each unit with a share of fixed costs. The fixed cost is computed as ¥32.50 per unit, based on planned production of 100,000 units. The budgeted and actual fixed overhead are equal, and any volume variances are closed to Cost of Goods Sold.

Division T wants to purchase 20,000 units from division S but is willing to pay only ¥39 per unit because it has an opportunity to accept a special order at a reduced price. The order is economically justifiable only if division T can acquire the division S output at a reduced price. (Monetary units given in Chinese yuan, ¥).

Required

a. What is the ROI for division S without the transfer to division T?
b. What is division S's ROI if it transfers 20,000 units to division T at ¥39 each?
c. What is the minimum transfer price for the 20,000-unit order that S would accept if it were willing to maintain the same ROI with the transfer as it would accept by selling its 90,000 units to the outside market?

Problem 15.34 [LO 1-3] Transfer Pricing: Performance Evaluation Issues

The Tallahassee Division (TD) of Gulf South Corporation, operating at capacity, has been asked by the Pensacola Division (PD) to supply it with electrical fitting no. 1726. TD sells this part to its regular customers for $15.00 each. PD, which is operating at 50 per cent capacity, is willing to pay $10.00 each for the fitting. It will put the fitting into a brake unit that it is manufacturing on a cost-plus basis for a commercial airplane manufacturer.

TD has a $8.50 variable cost of producing fitting no. 1726. The cost of the brake unit as built by PD follows:

Purchased parts – outside vendors	$45.00
KC fitting no. 1726	10.00
Other variable costs	28.00
Fixed overhead and administration	16.00
Total	$99.00

PD believes that the price concession is necessary to get the job. The company uses ROI and dollar profits to measure divisional and division manager performance.

Required

a. If you were TD's division controller, would you recommend that it supply fitting no. 1726 to PD? Why or why not? (Ignore any income tax issues.)

b. Is it to the short-run economic advantage of Gulf South Corporation for TD to supply PD with fitting no. 1726 at $10 each? Explain your answer. (Ignore any income tax issues.)

c. Discuss the organizational and managerial behaviour difficulties, if any, inherent in this situation. As Gulf South Corporation's controller, what would you advise the corporation's president to do in this situation?

[CMA adapted]

Problem 15.35 [LO 1-3] Comprehensive Transfer Pricing Problem

Solstråle Vinduer A/S manufactures windows for the home-building industry. The frame division produces the window frames. It then transfers the frames to the glass division, which installs the glass and hardware. The company's best-selling product is a 1-by-1.2 metre, double-paned operable window.

The frame division can also sell frames directly to custom homebuilders, which install the glass and hardware. The sales price for a frame is kr 400. The glass division sells its finished windows for kr 950. The markets for both frames and finished windows exhibit perfect competition.

The standard cost of the window is detailed as follows: (Monetary values given in Danish krone, kr).

	Frame division	Glass division
Direct material	kr 75	kr 150*
Direct labour	100	75
Variable overhead	150	150
Total	kr 325	kr 375

*Not including the transfer price for the frame.

Required

a. Assume that the frame division has no excess capacity.

(1) Use the general rule to compute the transfer price for window frames.

(2) Calculate the transfer price if it is based on standard variable cost with a 10 per cent mark-up.

b. Assume that the frame division has excess capacity.

(1) Use the general rule to compute the transfer price for window frames.

(2) Explain why your answers to requirements (a1) and (b1) differ.

(3) Suppose that the predetermined fixed overhead rate in the frame division is 125 per cent of direct labour cost. Calculate the transfer price if it is based on standard full cost plus a 10 per cent mark-up.

(4) Assume that the transfer price established in requirement (b3) is used. The glass division has been approached by the Ministry of Culture with a special order for 1,000 windows at kr 775. From the perspective of Solstråle Vinduer as a whole, should the glass division accept or reject the special order? Why?

(5) Assume the same facts as in requirement (b4). Will an autonomous glass division manager accept or reject the special order? Why?

c. Comment on the use of full cost as the basis for setting transfer prices.

Problem 15.36 [LO 1, 4] International Transfer Prices

Worldwide Merchants Co-op (WMC) operates a fleet of container ships in international trade between Great Britain and Thailand. All of the shipping income (that is, that related to WMC's ships) is deemed as earned in Great Britain. WMC also owns a dock facility in Thailand that services WMC's fleet. Income from the dock facility is deemed earned in Thailand, however. WMC's income attributable to Great Britain is taxed at a 75 per cent rate. Its income attributable to Thailand is taxed at a 20 per cent rate. Last year, the dock facility had operating revenues of £2.4 million, excluding services performed for WMC's ships. WMC's shipping revenues for last year were £15.6 million.

Costs to operate the dock facility were £3 million last year; costs to operate the shipping operation, before deduction of dock facility costs, were £10.2 million. No similar dock facilities in Thailand are available to WMC.

However, a facility in Malaysia would have charged WMC an estimated 1.8 million for the services that WMC's Thailand dock provided its ships. WMC management noted that if the services had been provided in Great Britain, the costs for the year would have totalled £4.8 million. WMC argued to the British tax officials that the appropriate transfer price is the price that would have been charged in Great Britain. British tax officials suggest that the Malaysian price is the appropriate one.

Required

What is the difference in tax costs to WMC for the alternate transfer prices for dock services, that is, its price in Great Britain versus that in Malaysia?

Problem 15.37 [LO 1, 4] Transfer Prices and Tax Regulations

Interglobal Company has two operating divisions in a semiautonomous organization structure. Division X, located in the United States, produces part AB-1, which is an input to division Y, located in the south of France. Division X uses idle capacity to produce AB-1, which has a domestic market price of $50. Its variable costs are $17 per unit. The company's US tax rate is 40 per cent of income.

In addition to the transfer price for each AB-1 received from division X, division Y pays a $12 shipping fee per unit. Part AB-1 becomes a part of division Y's output product. The output product costs an additional $8 to produce and sells for an equivalent $105. Division Y could purchase part AB-1 for $44 per unit from a Paris supplier. The company's French tax rate is 70 per cent of income. Assume that French tax laws permit transferring at either variable cost or market price.

Required

What transfer price is economically optimal for Interglobal Company? Support your answer with an appropriate analysis.

Problem 15.38 [LO 1-3] Transfer Pricing System Evaluation

Waechter Sicherheitssysteme AG (WSAG) consists of three subsidiary divisions – Frankfurt Division, Munich Division and Stuttgart Division – that operate as if they were independent companies. Each division has its own sales force and production facilities. Each division management is responsible for sales, cost of operations, acquiring and financing divisional assets, and working capital management. WSAG corporate management evaluates the performance of the divisions and division managements on the basis of ROI.

Stuttgart Company has just been awarded a contract for a product that uses a component manufactured by outside suppliers and by Munich Company, which is operating well below capacity. Stuttgart used a cost figure of €4.56 for the component in preparing its bid for the new product. Munich supplied this cost figure in response to Stuttgart's request for the average variable cost of the component; it represents the standard variable manufacturing cost and variable marketing costs.

Munich's regular selling price for the component that Stuttgart needs is €7.80. Munich management indicated that it could supply Stuttgart the required quantities of the component at the regular selling price less variable selling and distribution expenses. Stuttgart management responded by offering to pay standard variable manufacturing cost plus 20 per cent.

The two divisions have been unable to agree on a transfer price. WSAG management has never established a transfer price policy. The WSAG vice president of finance suggested a price equal to the standard full manufacturing cost (that is, no selling and distribution expenses) plus a 15 per cent mark-up. The two division managers rejected this price because each considered it grossly unfair.

The unit cost structure for the Munich component and the suggested prices follow.

Costs:	
Standard variable manufacturing cost	€3.84
Standard fixed manufacturing cost	1.44
Variable selling and distribution expenses	0.72
Total	€6.00
Prices:	
Regular selling price	€7.80
Regular selling price less variable selling and distribution expenses (€7.80 – €0.72)	7.08
Variable manufacturing plus 20% (€3.84 × 1.20)	€4.61
Standard full manufacturing cost plus 15% (€5.28 × 1.15)	€6.07

Required

a. Discuss the effect that each proposed price might have on the attitude of Munich's management toward intracompany business.

b. Is the negotiation of a price between the Stuttgart and Munich divisions a satisfactory method to solve the transfer price problem? Explain your answer.

c. As an outside consultant, write a letter to WSAG's management recommending whether it should become involved in this transfer pricing controversy.

[CMA adapted]

Problem 15.39 [LO 1, 5] Segment Reporting and Transfer Pricing

ACE Travel Japan has four operating divisions: airline, hotel, auto rental and travel services. Each division is a separate segment for financial reporting purposes. Revenues and costs for the past year related to outside transactions were as follows (monetary amounts shown in millions, Japanese yen, ¥):

	Airline	Hotel	Auto rental	Travel services
Revenue	¥20,100	¥8,260	¥7,520	¥2,840
Costs	11,900	4,240	5,010	1,870

The airline participated in a frequent stayer programme with the hotel chain. The airline reported that it had traded hotel award coupons during the past year for travel that had a ¥2,080 million retail value, assuming that the travel was redeemed at full airline fares. Auto rental division offered 20 per cent discounts to ACE Travel's airline passengers and hotel guests. These discounts to airline passengers were estimated to have a ¥560 million retail value. ACE Travel hotel guests redeemed ¥240 million in auto rental discount coupons. ACE Travel hotels also provided rooms for flight crews of the airline division, a ¥1,040 million value for the year.

Travel services division booked flights on ACE Travels' airline valued at ¥320 million for the year. This service for intracompany hotel bookings was valued at ¥160 million and for intracompany auto rentals at ¥80 million.

While preparing these data for financial statement presentation, the hotel division's controller stated that the value of the airline coupons should be based on the differential and opportunity costs of the travel awards, not on the full fare for the tickets issued. The fact that a travel award is usually allocated to seats that would otherwise be empty or that are restricted similar to those on discount tickets supported this argument. If the differential and opportunity costs were used for this transfer price, the value would be ¥400 million instead of ¥2,080 million. The airline controller made a similar argument concerning the auto rental discount coupons. If the differential cost basis were used for the auto rental coupons, the transfer price would be ¥80 million instead of the ¥560 million.

ACE Travel Japan, reports assets in each segment as follows:

Airline	¥70,500 million
Hotel	32,000 million
Auto rental	24,600 million
Travel services	7,740 million

Required

Build a spreadsheet to complete the following requirements:

a. Using the retail values for transfer pricing for segment-reporting purposes, what are the operating profits for each of ACE Travel's divisions?
b. What are the operating profits for each division using the differential cost basis for pricing transfers?
c. Rank each division by ROI using the transfer pricing method in (a), as well as using the transfer pricing method in (b). What effect does the transfer pricing system have on the rankings?

Problem 15.40 [LO 1-3] Evaluation of the Profit Impact of Alternative Transfer Decisions

Chasseen SCS manufactures a line of fingernail polish. The manufacturing process entails adding and mixing colouring ingredients; the finished product is packaged in a company-produced glass bottle and packed in cases containing six bottles each. Because the appearance of the bottle highly influences sales volume, the company developed an unusual bottle production process.

The bottle division only produces bottles for the polish division and has no customers outside of the company. Each division is considered a separate profit centre and is evaluated as such. As the new corporate controller, you are responsible for determining the proper transfer price to use for the bottles produced for the polish division.

Bottle division's cost analysis indicates that it can produce bottles at these costs:

Volume (cases)	Total cost	Cost per case
2,000,000	€3,900,000	€1.95
4,000,000	6,400,000	1.60
6,000,000	8,900,000	1.48

These costs include fixed costs of €1.4 million and variable costs of €1.25 per equivalent case. These data have caused considerable corporate discussion as to the proper price to use in the transfer of bottles to the polish division. This interest is heightened because a significant portion of a division manager's income is an incentive bonus based on profit centre results.

The polish division has the following costs in addition to the bottle costs:

Volume (cases)	Total cost	Cost per case
2,000,000	€16,200,000	€8.20
4,000,000	32,200,000	8.05
6,000,000	48,200,000	8.03

At your request, bottle division's general manager asked other bottle manufacturers to quote a price for the number and sizes that the polish division demands. These competitive prices follow:

Volume (equivalent cases)	Total price	Price per case
2,000,000	€3,900,000	€1.95
4,000,000	6,800,000	1.70
6,000,000	9,900,000	1.65

The marketing department provided the following price–demand relationship for the finished product:

Volume (equivalent cases)	Total price	Price per case
2,000,000	€24,500,000	€12.50
4,000,000	45,500,000	11.38
6,000,000	63,800,000	10.63

Required

a. Chasseen SCS has used market-based transfer prices in the past. Using the current market prices and costs and assuming a volume of 6 million cases, calculate operating profits for the:
   (1) Bottle division
   (2) Polish division
   (3) Corporation

b. Is this production and sales level the most profitable volume for the:
   (1) Bottle division
   (2) Polish division
   (3) Corporation

[CMA adapted]

Problem 15.41 [LO 3-5] International Transfer Price and Tax

Stockholm Telecom manufactures telecommunications products in Sweden and has marketing divisions located throughout Europe, Asia and North America. The North American marketing division, located in the United States, imports manufactured products from Sweden. Suppose that Swedish and US tax authorities allow transfer prices between full manufacturing costs and market prices based on comparable imports into the United States. Any US import duty paid in the United States is deductible from US income taxes. The following data have been collected by the cost management team.

Units sold	1,000,000
Sweden's income tax rate on Swedish operating income	50%
US income tax rate on US division's operating income	35%
US import duty based on transfer price	10%
Variable manufacturing cost of product A4	208 kr
Full absorption manufacturing cost of product A4	325
Net selling price in the United States	488
Comparable imported product sales price in the United States	423
Sales price in Sweden	390

Required

Build a spreadsheet to complete the following requirements:

a. Calculate the after-tax profits of the Swedish and US divisions from a transfer of 1,000,000 units of product model A4 at either full manufacturing cost or the comparable import selling price.

b. What transfer price should Stockholm Telecom select to minimize its total import duties and tax liabilities from this transfer? Explain.

c. Suppose that Stockholm Telecom's manufacturing division could sell all of its production of product A4 for 390 kr per unit in Sweden and was free to do so. Suppose also that division managers are paid a bonus based on their division's operating profit after tax. What are the pros and cons of Stockholm Telecom's bonus and transfer pricing policies? What is your recommendation?

Cases

Case 15.42 [LO 1-3] Transfer Pricing; Incentive Issues

'We can't drop our prices below $210 per hundred pounds,' exclaimed Greg Berman, manager of Forwarders, a division of Custom Freight Systems. 'Our margins are already razor thin. Our costs just won't allow us to go any lower. Corporate rewards our division based on our profitability, and I won't lower my prices below $210.'

Custom Freight Systems is organized into three divisions: Air Cargo provides air cargo services; Logistics Services operates distribution centres and provides truck cargo services; and Forwarders provides international freight-forwarding services. Freight forwarders typically buy space on planes from international air cargo companies. This is analogous to a charter company that books seats on passenger planes and resells them to passengers. In many cases, freight forwarders hire trucking companies to transport the cargo from the plane to the domestic destination. The following diagram depicts Custom Freight Systems' operations.

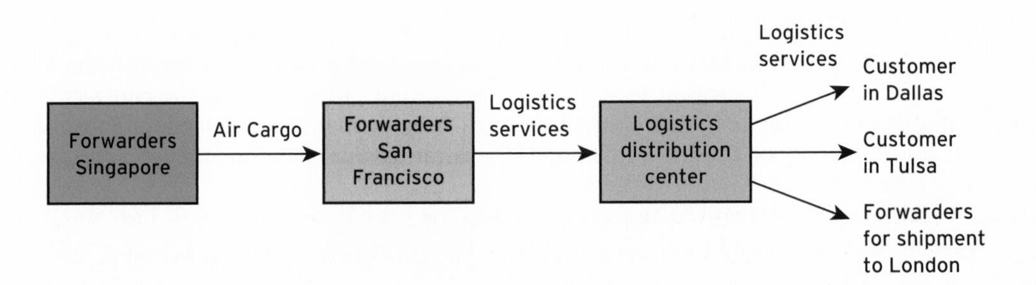

Management believes that the three divisions integrate together well and are able to provide one-stop transportation services to customers. For example, a Forwarders branch in Singapore receives cargo from a shipper, prepares the necessary documentation, and then ships the cargo on Air Cargo to a domestic Forwarders station. The domestic Forwarders station ensures that the cargo passes through customs and ships it to the final destination with Logistics Services as shown in the preceding diagram.

Management evaluates each division separately and rewards division managers based on profit and return on investment. Responsibility and decision-making authority are decentralized. Similarly, each division has a sales and marketing organization. Division salespeople report to the vice president of sales for Custom Freight Systems as well as a division sales manager as depicted in the following organization chart. Custom Freight Systems believes that it has successfully motivated division managers by paying bonuses for high division profits.

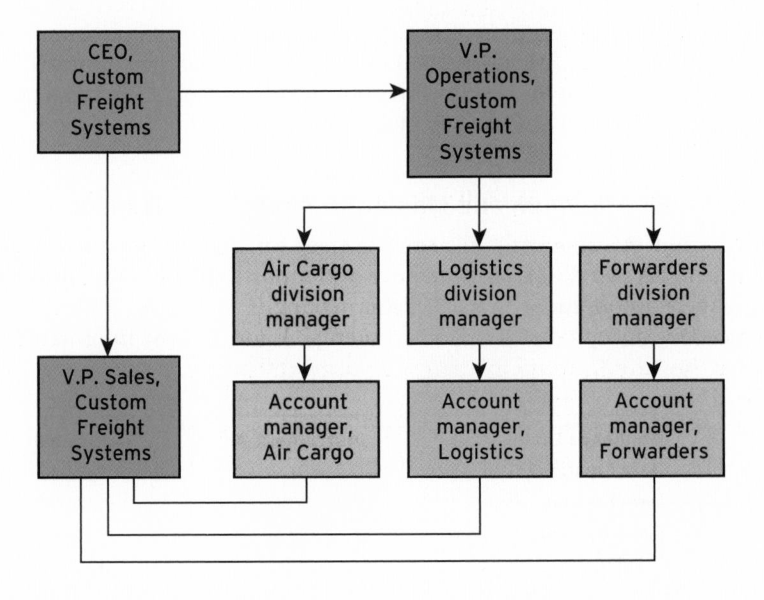

Recently, Logistics Services was preparing a bid for a customer. The customer had freight to import from an overseas supplier and wanted Logistics Services to submit a bid for a distribution package that included providing air freight from the supplier, receiving the freight and providing customs clearance services at the airport, warehousing the shipment and distributing it to customers.

Because this was a contract for international shipping, Logistics Services needed to contact different freight forwarders for shipping quotes. Logistics Services requested quotes from the Forwarders division and United Systems, a competing freight forwarder. Divisions of Custom Freight Systems are free to use the most appropriate and cost-effective suppliers.

Logistics Services received bids of $210 per hundred pounds from Forwarders and $185 per hundred pounds from United Systems. Forwarders specified in its bid that it will use Air Cargo, a division of Custom Freight Systems. Forwarder's variable costs were $175 per hundred pounds, which included the cost of subcontracting air transportation. Air Cargo, which was experiencing a period of excess capacity, quoted Forwarders the market rate of $155; its variable costs typically are 60 per cent of the market rate.

The price difference between the two different bids alarmed Susan Burns, a contract manager at Logistics Services. Burns knows this is a competitive business and is concerned because the difference between the high and low bids was at least $1,000,000 (current projections for the contract estimated 4,160,000 pounds during the first year). Burns contacted Greg Berman, the manager of Forwarders, and discussed the quote. 'Don't you think full mark-up is unwarranted due to the fact that you and the airlines have so much excess capacity?' Burns complained.

She soon realized that Berman was not going to drop the price quote. 'You know how small margins are in this business. Why should I cut my margins even smaller just to make you look good?' Berman asked.

Burns went to Bennie Espinosa, vice president of Custom Freight Systems and chairperson for the corporate strategy committee. 'That does sound strange,' said Espinosa, 'I need to examine the overall cost structure and talk to Berman. I'll get back to you by noon Monday.'

Required

a. Which bid should Logistics Services accept: the internal bid from Forwarders or the external bid from United Systems?
b. What should the transfer price be on this transaction?
c. What should Bennie Espinosa do?
d. Do the reward systems for the division managers support the best interests of Forwarders and of Custom Freight Systems? Give examples that support your conclusion.
e. Assume the same information as given in the case, but instead of receiving one outside bid, Logistics Services receives two. The new bid is from World Services for $195 per hundred pounds. It offered to use Air Cargo for air cargo. Air Cargo will charge World $155 per hundred pounds. The bids from Forwarders and United Systems remain the same as before (i.e., $210 and $185, respectively). Which bid should the Logistics Services take? Explain.

Case 15.43 [LO 1, 2] Minimum and Maximum Acceptable Transfer Prices

Bonn Instrumentarium AG manufactures small gauges for use in household Appliances and Industrial machinery. The firm has two divisions: Appliance and Industrial. The company is decentralized, and each division is completely autonomous in its decision making.

The Appliance Division produces two instruments, A and B. Cost information about these products follows.

Appliance Division	Instrument A	Instrument B
Direct material	€3.00	€2.40
Direct labour	6.00	12.00
Fixed overhead	12.00	28.00
Full cost	€21.00	€42.40

The Appliance Division has no variable overhead. Its direct labour rate is €6 per hour, and a maximum of 10,000 hours is available per year. Fixed overhead is €120,000 per year and is applied on the basis of direct labour hours. The planned activity level is 10,000 direct labour hours per year.

The demand in the external market for instrument A at a price of €27 per unit is unlimited. Anywhere from zero to 3,000 units of instrument B can be sold annually in the external market at a price of 56.40 per unit. The external market has demand for no more than 3,000 units of instrument B per year.

The Industrial Division also has two products, type Y gauges and type Z gauges. Cost information about these products follows.

Industrial Division	Type Y gauges	Type Z gauges
Direct material	€7.20	€4.20
Direct labour	6.00	12.00
Fixed overhead	6.00	12.00
Full cost	€19.20	€28.20

In addition to the costs listed in the preceding table, each type Z gauge unit uses one unit of instrument B, which is produced in the Appliance Division and transferred to the Industrial Division. The costs in the preceding table for type Z gauge are the only costs incurred in the Industrial Division to transform a B instrument into a type Z gauge. They do not include the transfer price of instrument B or the costs of manufacturing instrument B.

The Industrial Division has no variable overhead. The direct labour rate is €6 per hour, and a maximum of 10,000 hours is available per year. Fixed overhead of €60,000 per year is applied on the basis of direct labour hours. The planned activity level is 10,000 hours per year.

The demand for type Z gauges at a fixed price of €154.20 is unlimited. Anywhere from zero to 6,000 units of type Y gauges can be sold annually at a fixed price of €55.20 per unit. Demand for type Y gauges is no more than 6,000 per year.

The labour used in the two divisions is different and is not transferable between them. The situation is summarized in the following diagram.

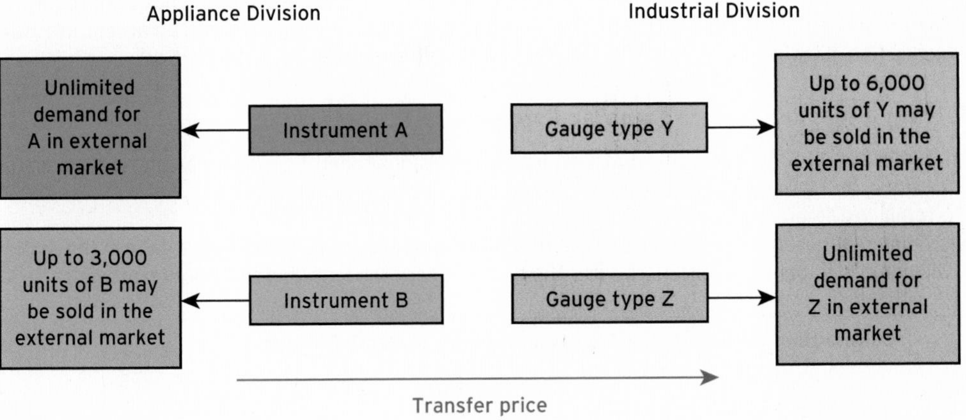

Required

The first four questions refer to the transfer price per unit of instrument B for units transferred. Show calculations. Ignore any long-term or qualitative factors.

a. What is the minimum unit transfer price acceptable to the Appliance Division for any number of units of instrument B transferred in the range zero to 3,000 units?

b. What is the minimum unit transfer price acceptable to the Appliance Division for any number of B units transferred in the range 3,001 to 6,000 units?

c. What is the maximum unit transfer price acceptable to the Industrial Division for any number of B units transferred in the range zero to 3,000 units?

d. What is the maximum unit transfer price acceptable to the Industrial Division for any number of B units transferred in the range 3,001 to 6,000 units?

e. Suppose that the Appliance Division sets the transfer price at its minimum acceptable level in each of the ranges zero to 3,000 units, and 3,001 to 6,000 units. How many units will be transferred? Remember that each division manager has the authority to accept or reject a transfer between the two divisions.

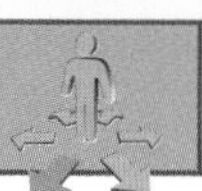

Solutions to You're the Decision Maker

15.1 Setting a Transfer Price when Outside Suppliers are also Available, p. 753

a. The contribution margin for Outback Outfitters from sales to wholesale customers is AU$20 as before. If Koala sells to these customers, then retail has to buy from outside suppliers, which gives a contribution margin for Outback Outfitters of AU$7 per unit. The total contribution margin is thus AU$27 per unit. If Koala instead transfers the backpacks to the Retail Division, the contribution margin is, as before, AU$26. So now the best situation is that Retail buys externally at the given purchase price of AU$57 and Koala sells to wholesale customers.

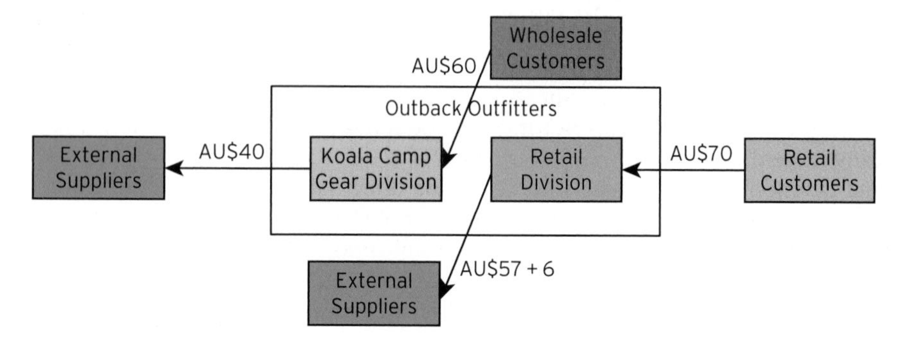

b. Koala should not buy externally, because the price of AU$57 exceeds the unit-variable cost for production of AU$37.

c. For Koala the minimum transfer price is the price that also yields a contribution margin (CM) of AU$20 (the same as external sales). CM = TP - AU$38 ≥ AU$20, so TP ≥ 58. The Retail Division will not want to pay more than the external purchase price of AU$57. Thus, both divisions will not be able to find an acceptable transfer price, which is fine, because the optimal decision is to not have an internal transfer (see a.)

15.2 Setting a Market-based Transfer Price, p. 757

a. Recall that unit-variable costs amount to AU$44 for both divisions together, yielding a contribution margin of AU$19. Hence, for Outback Outfitters there is a positive contribution margin, so in case of excess capacity selling to retail customers at this price is better than not selling at all.

b. However, the market-based transfer price of AU$58, which is based on Koala Camp Gear's sales in the wholesale market, will not lead to behavioural congruence. The divisions earn the following contribution margins:

Contribution to Koala Camp Gear from transfer to Retail Division	
Transfer price per backpack	AU$58
Standard unit-level cost for production and shipping	38
Contribution margin	AU$20
Contribution to Retail Division from buying from Koala Division	
Sales price to retail customers	AU$63
Transfer price per backpack	58
Standard unit-variable cost for sales	6
Contribution margin	(AU$1)

In this example, the market-based transfer price happens to be too high. When the supplying unit has excess capacity, the transfer price that is behavioural congruent is lower compared to a situation of no excess capacity. However, this condition of excess capacity and low opportunity costs is not reflected in the market-based transfer price in this case.

15.3 Setting a Cost-Based Transfer Price, p. 759

a. Recall that the unit-variable costs are AU$38 for the Koala Camp Gear Division and AU$0 for the Retail Division, because there are no sales costs. Hence, Outback Outfitters earns a total contribution margin of AU$55 – AU$38 = AU$17 per backpack.

b. The Retail Division will earn a contribution margin equal to AU$55 – Transfer price, while the Koala Camp Gear Division will earn a contribution margin that is equal to Transfer price – AU$38. So at a transfer price of AU$56, the Retail Division earns AU$55 – AU56 = (AU$1), and the Koala Camp Gear Division earns a contribution margin of AU$56 – AU38 = AU$18. What has happened here? Setting the transfer price equal to the full cost of AU$56 has turned a non-unit-level cost in the Koala Camp Gear Division and, hence a non-unit-level cost for the company as a whole, into a unit-level cost from the viewpoint of the Retail Division manager. The manager would tend to reject the special offer, even though accepting it would benefit the company as a whole.

15.4 Divisional Autonomy and Transfer-Pricing Policy, p. 763

a. If Koala Camp Gear gets an outside wholesale order for 800 backpacks with a regular sales price of AU$60 and a unit-level cost of AU$40, they earn a contribution margin of 800 × (AU$60 - AU$40) = AU$16,000. Outback Outfitters as a whole also earns the contribution margin on the special order, for which the backpacks have been sourced from another suppliers, of 800 × (AU$55 – AU$49) = AU$4,800. Outback Outfitters' total contribution margin earned is therefore AU$20,800.

b. Koala Camp Gear's contribution margin on the special order is 800 × (AU$45 – AU$38) = AU$5,600. For Outback Outfitters as a whole, the contribution margin on this order is 800 × (AU$55 – AU$38) = AU$13,600. There is no other external order in this case.

c. If Koala Camp Gear refuses the special deal and does not obtain an outside order, their contribution margin is 0. Outback Outfitters as a whole earns the contribution margin on the special order, for which the backpacks have been sourced from another suppliers, of 800 × (AU$55 – AU$49) = AU$4,800.

d. The contribution margins are identical to the situation under b.

e. This is a tough call with no clearly correct answer. If another order would be possible, it is better for both Koala Camp Gear and for Outback Outfitters as a whole to not produce the special order internally. You can see this by comparing the results for questions a and b. However, if another order is not possible, it is better for both Koala Camp Gear and for Outback Outfitters as a whole to produce the special order internally. You can see this by comparing the results for questions c and d. Eric Devon is optimistic that he can get another order. Why would you doubt this? On the other hand, if he is wrong, it will cost Outback Outfitters AU$16,000, namely the difference between the contribution margin under a and c.

15.5 Transfer Pricing for Multinational Companies, p. 766

For the AU$600,000 transfer price, the total tax is (0.40 × AU$200,000) + (0.40 × AU$3,000,000) = AU$1,280,000. For AU$2,000,000 transfer price, the total tax is (0.40 × AU$1,600,000) + (0.40 × AU$1,600,000) = AU$1,280,000. With equal tax rates, inflating the transfer price has no advantage.

Endnotes

1 Note that Chapter 12 is about managing and allocating support service costs.

2 Koala Camp Gear also sells to the company's Mail-Order Division, and the principles are exactly the same, but we do not want to make the illustration unnecessarily elaborate.

3 Of course, this kind of representation can be extended to include more than two responsibility centres within the organization and more external suppliers and customers than in this particular example.

4 This conclusion applies if just short-term profits are considered. Perhaps the 'loss' could be thought of as a marketing cost, or a charitable contribution. Both could add to Koala's reputation and increase future sales.

5 If the alternatives have long-term consequences, we might have to consider cash flows of multiple years and discount these, as explained in Chapter 8. For now, the key point is the distinction between external prices and cash flows versus internal transfer prices.

6 Chapter 14 discusses behavioural congruence and goal congruence in more detail.

7 Van Helden et al. (2000) describe how Hoogovens Steel, now owned by Tata Steel, co-ordinated internal transactions and used transfer prices after it introduced a decentralized business unit structure in this highly integrated steel company.

8 Often the term 'comparable uncontrolled price' (CUP) is used to indicate a price that is used with similar independent parties in comparable uncontrolled transactions.

9 The costs of support service activities are discussed extensively in Chapter 12.

10 Much more complex models are described in the literature, often for quite stylized settings, to determine the optimal basis for transfer pricing. See, for example, Pfeiffer et al. (2001), Baldenius et al. (2004) and Göx and Schiller (2006).

11Perhaps *standard* costs are formulated too strictly. Not all organizations use standard costs. In this chapter, we interpret the concept more loosely as the level of costs that are expected, planned or estimated.

12 See the discussion of the costs and benefits of decentralization at the beginning of Chapter 14.

13 Ernst & Young (2010). These findings do not differ much from earlier surveys, see Borkowski (1990). Nearly half of the US companies surveyed used a cost-based transfer pricing system: 33 per cent used a market price-based system and 20 per cent used a negotiated system. Similar results have been found for companies in Canada and Japan. Generally, we find that when negotiated prices are used, the prices negotiated are between the market price at the upper limit and some measure of cost at the lower limit.

14 Ernst & Young (2010).

15 OECD (2010). See also Rossing and Rohde (2010) for more background information on tax regulatory developments.

16 B denotes country with buying division; S denotes country with selling division.

17 These tax rates are unrealistically high, but it makes explaining the principle clearer.

18 This is the AU$1,400,000 that was shifted multiplied by the difference in tax rate, so AU$1,400,000 × (70% – 40%) = AU$420,000.

19 The requirements, which are too detailed to cover here, are specified in IFRS 8, 'Operating Segments', and in FASB, Statement of Financial Accounting Standards No. 131, 'Financial Reporting for Segments of a Business Enterprise'. International Financial Reporting Standards (IFRSs) are formulated by the International Accounting Standards Board (IASB) (www.IFRS.org), which is the independent standard-setting body of the private IFRS Foundation, located in London. The majority of the organization's funding comes through funding regimes managed by official authorities. The Financial Accounting Standards Board (FASB) (www.FASB.org) is the designated organization in the private sector in the US for establishing reporting standards. Those standards are officially recognized by the Securities and Exchange Commission (SEC). The FASB is located in Norwalk, Connecticut, in the USA. The FASB is funded through federally mandated accounting support fees paid by issuers of financial statements. Both organizations are private, not-for-profit organizations that aim to be independent from other business and professional organizations. Standards are developed through an open process with consultative documents for public comment. There are strong developments towards convergence of IFRS and FASB reporting standards, and more countries now accept using either standard.

20 See, for example, FASB (1982), Statement of Financial Accounting Standards No. 69, which specifies the use of market-based transfer prices when calculating the results of operations for an oil and gas exploration and production operation. Note that IFRSs are generally not industry-specific, because these are more principle-based, and provide limited accounting rules per industry.

References

Baldenius, T., N.D. Melumad and S. Reichelstein (2004) 'Integrating managerial and tax objectives in transfer pricing', *The Accounting Review*, vol. 79, no. 3, pp. 591–615.

Borkowski, S. (1990) 'Environmental and organizational factors affecting transfer pricing: a survey', *Journal of Management Accounting Research*, vol. 2, pp. 1–15.

Bouwens, J., and B. Steens (2008) 'The economics of full cost transfer pricing', Working Paper, available on SSRN.

Colbert, G.J., and B.H. Spicer (1995), 'A multi-case investigation of a theory of the transfer pricing process', *Accounting, Organizations and Society*, vol. 20. no. 6, pp. 423–456.

Cools, M., C. Emmanuel and A. Jorissen (2008) 'Management control in the transfer pricing tax compliant multinational enterprise', *Accounting, Organizations and Society*, vol. 33, pp. 603–628.

Cools, M., and R. Slagmulder (2009) 'Tax-compliant transfer pricing and responsibility accounting', *Journal of Management Accounting Research*, vol. 21, pp. 151–178.

Ernst & Young (2010) *Global Transfer Pricing Survey: Addressing the Challenges of Globalization.*

FASB (1976) Statement of Financial Accounting Standards No. 14. 'Financial Reporting for Segments of a Business Enterprise', FASB, Stamford, CT.

FASB (1982) Statement of Financial Accounting Standards No. 69. 'Disclosures About Oil and Gas Producing Activities', FASB, Stamford, CT.

Göx, R., and U. Schiller (2006) 'An economic perspective on transfer pricing', in C.S. Chapman, A.G. Hopwood and M.D. Shields (eds.), *Handbook of Management Accounting Research*, vol. 2, pp. 673–695, Elsevier, Oxford.

Kachelmeier, S., and K. Towry (2002) 'Negotiated transfer pricing: is fairness easier said than done?' *The Accounting Review*, vol. 77, no. 2, pp. 571–593.

Luft, J., and R. Libby (1997) 'Profit comparisons, market prices, and managers' judgments about negotiated transfer prices', *The Accounting Review*, vol. 72, no. 2, pp. 217–229.

OECD (2010) *Transfer Pricing Guidelines for Multinational Enterprises and Tax Administrations 2010*, OECD Publishing.

Park, S.H., and W. Vanhonacker (2007) 'The challenge for multinational corporations in China: think local, act global', *MIT Sloan Management Review*, Summer, pp. W8–W15.

Rossing, C.P., and C. Rohde (2010) 'Overhead cost allocation changes in transfer pricing tax compliant multinational enterprise', *Management Accounting Research*, vol. 21, pp. 199–216.

Pfeiffer, T., U. Schiller and J. Wagner (2011) 'Cost-based transfer pricing', *Review of Accounting Studies*, vol. 16, pp. 219–246.

Van Helden, J., J. Van der Meer-Kooistra and R.W. Scapens (2001) 'Co-ordination of internal transactions at Hoogovens steel: struggling with the tension between performance-oriented business units and the concept of an integrated company', *Management Accounting Research*, vol. 12, pp. 357–386.

CHAPTER 16

Strategy, Balanced Scorecards and Incentive Systems

© bluebird 13

Learning Objectives

After completing this chapter, you should be able to:

- **LO 1** Explain the importance of using leading indicators to build a balanced scorecard for communication, motivation and evaluation.
- **LO 2** Understand how an organization selects related measures for a balanced scorecard.
- **LO 3** Evaluate the benefits and costs of a balanced scorecard.
- **LO 4** Explain how an organization implements a balanced scorecard.
- **LO 5** Understand the key principles of performance-based incentive systems.
- **LO 6** Evaluate the advantages and disadvantages of alternative features of incentive systems.
- **LO 7** Discuss ethical issues of incentive systems.

PRESS RELEASE

Van Coenink Bankiers

Amsterdam, the Netherlands: Van Coenink Bankiers (VCB) President and CEO Johannes van Dijk announced an issuing of new shares that generated €47 million, which was more than the bank and its underwriters had expected.

Speaking to the state's financial press online from bank headquarters, Van Dijk remarked, 'This shows that the market values a successful track record and a bright future. There is abundant capital for good business plans and capable management, and ours are second to none. Van Coenink Bankiers has served an important market niche by providing financial services for fast-growing, well-managed, high-technology firms. They see us as valuable partners, and it definitely helps that we have experienced and overcome the same growing pains that they face.'

Twenty-three investors founded VCB 10 years ago to serve the hot local economy. The founders, some of whom are officers of the bank, now have gained expansion capital and many new shareholders.

The independent five-branch bank specializes in banking with high-technology businesses and professionals such as public accountants, architects and dentists. VCB has dominated its niche based on personal relations and customer service. The bank operates in Amsterdam and also in the high-tech region around Eindhoven. The Eindhoven Region, south of Amsterdam, has long been the industrial centre of the Netherlands, with companies such as **Philips**, **NXP Semiconductors**, **Daf Paccar Trucks** and **ASML**. It is a manufacturing centre in a high-cost country. By focusing on producing high-value, technology-based products, it is in competition with fast-growing manufacturing centres in countries with much lower costs.

VCB's prospectus shows that its balanced scorecard and incentive system resemble those found at many of its high-tech customers. CEO Van Dam emphasized that although unusual for a bank, this performance-based incentive plan is necessary to attract, motivate and retain its highly competent and sought-after employees.

The bank's design of its balanced scorecard and incentive system to align bank employees' fortunes with those of its new shareholders might be another reason for the success of its shares offering.

Van Coenink Bankiers: Ahead of the Competition

Since its founding 10 years ago, Van Coenink Bankiers (VCB) has managed to stay ahead of its competition by consistently creating and designing innovative, reliable services that are first to market. VCB offers commercial-customer services via its website and customer service desk that is available by telephone. Additionally, VCB still puts emphasis on a few, specialized branch banks to meet with customers and better understand their needs. VCB employees also visit customers at their business or at home.

The bank had positioned itself for the success in part by building a **balanced scorecard**, which is a performance measurement system or business model that ties together knowledge of strategy, processes, activities, and operational and strategic performance measures. Balanced scorecard models offer great opportunities and challenges to improve value and performance through better communication, knowledge, and incentives. The bank also created consistent employee incentives that (1) communicate its strategy to employees, (2) attract, motivate and retain excellent employees, and (3) align their interests with the bank's strategy and long-term interests of external stakeholders. In general, an effective **incentive system** communicates strategy, motivates employees and reinforces achievement of organizational goals.

This final chapter presents the design of balanced scorecards and incentive systems as 'capstone' topics of cost management because they bring together concerns about costs, revenues, value and their drivers to devise systems that guide and motivate individuals to create long-term value at lowest cost. First we will explain leading performance indicators, which form the key principle underlying the balanced scorecard. Next, the implementation of a balanced scorecard and the selection of performance measures is addressed. However, there are benefits as well as costs of a balanced scorecard. To complete this topic, the implementation of the balanced scorecard at Van Coenink Bankiers is discussed as an illustration. The second big topic in this chapter is incentive systems, and we will explain some fundamental principles and key features for designing such systems. Finally, ethical aspects of incentives and compensation are important to discuss.

Leading Performance Indicators to Communicate, Motivate and Evaluate

LO 1
Explain the importance of using leading indicators for a balanced scorecard for communication, motivation and evaluation.

VCB identifies and uses its balanced scorecard to communicate plans and results to employees, motivate and evaluate its employees, and evaluate its success at meeting its financial goals. Many of the measures in this balanced scorecard are *leading indicators* of future performance.

Leading Indicators

All indicators report the organization's performance during a past period. In that sense, all indicators look back. But **leading indicators** are measures that identify future non-financial and financial outcomes to guide management decision making. For example, if the organization performed badly towards customers in the past period, this may precede a bad financial period in a future period. We would not know about that if only looking at the financial performance of the past period, because that may still have been acceptable. Leading indicators measure past performance that is predictive of future financial and non-financial outcomes. They are sometimes also called *forward-looking indicators*.

Combining relevant leading indicators into a balanced scorecard makes it a business model of hypothesized cause-and-effect performance measures that reflect key operational and strategic relations. Identifying and measuring reliable leading indicators of performance is an important part of modern cost management because these measures allow employees to plan or gauge their progress toward meeting performance objectives. Employees know, for example, that certain levels of these leading indicators signal desired future cost or profit performance. If, as plans are implemented, the measured leading indicators show that the organization is likely to miss its performance target, employees can take corrective actions in time to get back on course.

Many leading indicators of performance are non-financial in nature and include the following categories of measures:

- *Organizational learning and growth measures*, which describe the way employees and organizations increase their capabilities to develop new products and provide existing products more efficiently.
- *Business and production process efficiency measures*, which describe how efficiently the organization actually transforms resources into products. (*Note:* This can include outsourced processes and processes in the extended value chain.)
- *Customer value measures*, which describe how the organization creates customer satisfaction and loyalty.

Leading indicators are sometimes contrasted to **lagging indicators**, which are measures that reflect the final outcomes of earlier management plans and their execution. For example, when cost management analysts at VCB and other companies report the profits from the products that they have sold in the market, they are said to be reporting lagging indicators. Most financial performance measures show results too late to significantly affect future performance. Financial performance is not so useful for prediction, but reflecting on financial performance can aid learning. However, we should not forget that *all indicators measure past performance*, that is the result of earlier management plans and their execution. The special thing is that some indicators are predictive of other indicators in later periods.

Building leading indicators into a balanced scorecard illustrates relations among performance measures at different stages of an organization's value chain, as shown in Exhibit 16.1. Organizational learning and growth can precede process efficiency; process efficiency can precede customer satisfaction and loyalty, which can lead to subsequent financial outcomes of profit and cash flow. Organizations that monitor and effectively communicate these leading indicators are more likely to (1) consistently and efficiently create valued services and products and (2) generate competitive profit and cash flow.[1]

Exhibit 16.1 Lead and Lag Relations among Indicators of Performance

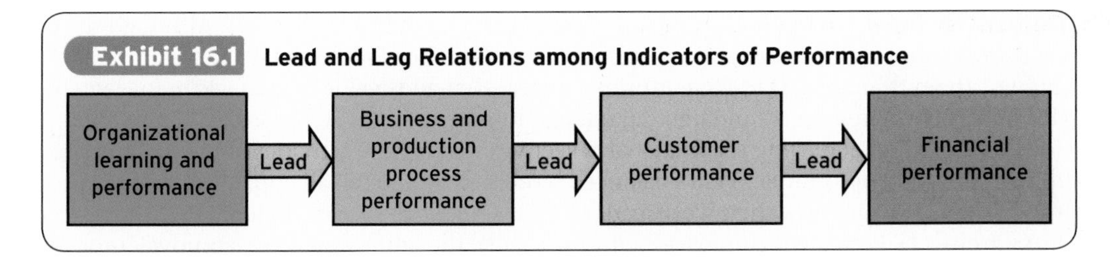

Communicating Strategy to Employees: Strategy Maps

Many employees of an organization do not understand the impacts of their activities on customer value and profitability because their jobs are narrow or they do not interact directly with customers. Communicating leading indicators in a balanced scorecard can make the effects of employees more visible. Once they realize how they affect customer value and financial performance, all employees are more likely to find and support ways to improve activities and processes. The relations among indicators of performance, such as shown in Exhibit 16.1, is a powerful way to communicate the strategy to employees. This is also referred to as the **strategy map**, and this is a visual representation of the company's main objectives and the crucial relationships among them that drive organizational performance.

Not only the performance measures themselves, but also the target levels are important for communicating strategy. The difference between the target level and the currently achieved level of an indicator indicates the organization's ambition: how much improvement on that particular indicator is intended. The organization's strategy makes some areas for improvements more important than others, and therefore the target levels of some indicators will be more ambitious than others. For example, in VCB's strategy attracting the right kind of customers and servicing these customers with products that are highly useful for them and profitable for the bank is more important than growth by itself. For that reason, target levels for customer probability will be more ambitious than target levels for growth.

Furthermore, target setting can be informed by comparisons with other organizations. Such comparisons, often called *benchmarking*, can be done between similar organizations, for example airline companies comparing costs, airplane utilization, or delays of flights. However, comparisons can also be relevant between similar processes of organizations in quite dissimilar businesses. For example, **Nike** could compare efficiency and lead times in distribution processes with clothing companies such as **C&A** and **H&M**. In general, **benchmarking** is a technique for determining an organization's competitive advantage by learning about its own products, services and operations, and compaing them against the best perfomers.

Motivating Employees and Evaluating Performance

Visible leading indicators can contribute to employees' improved motivation and commitment. Simply posting weekly sales or quality charts on the team bulletin board, as many companies do, probably is not enough. Even awarding bonuses for improving leading indicators can backfire if this practice reduces co-operation among individuals or teams in competition for the bonuses. Unless employees know that their efforts to improve processes actually result in improved organizational performance – better customer satisfaction, for example – charts and reports of these leading indicators can recede into background noise. A balanced scorecard can be an effective motivator and trusted evaluation tool because it helps employees understand how their efforts affect performance up and down the value chain.

Modern Origin and Use of Balanced Scorecards

Robert Kaplan and David Norton combined multiple leading indicators of performance into what they have called a *balanced scorecard*.[2] Comparable frameworks exist elsewhere, for example in France the **tableau de bord** is used, as described in Cost Management in Practice 16.1. Although the concept of using leading and lagging indicators is not new, a balanced scorecard is a new way to package and present them that appears to have intuitive appeal that adds value to strategic management.

This approach represents a fundamental change in management style for most companies that previously focused on achieving the financial objectives that lag the activities of most of the organization's employees. For example, VCB's balanced scorecard should tell all employees from janitor to teller to branch manager how their work leads to VCB's financial success. Exhibit 16.2 shows example links from (1) increased employee training to (2) the improved loan approval process to (3) increased customer value to (4) better financial results. The rationale is that if VCB improves customer satisfaction, it is more likely to retain a loyal customer base. A loyal customer base will provide word-of-mouth promotion that will lead to a larger customer base. A larger base of the right customers (see Chapter 5) means more revenue, which should lead to better financial performance. The opposite also is true, but by the time top managers observe poor financial performance, a problem already has occurred and caused damage. Managing drivers of profits can be better for all concerned than correcting problems later.

Exhibit 16.2 **Sequence of Performance from Employee Training to Financial Results**

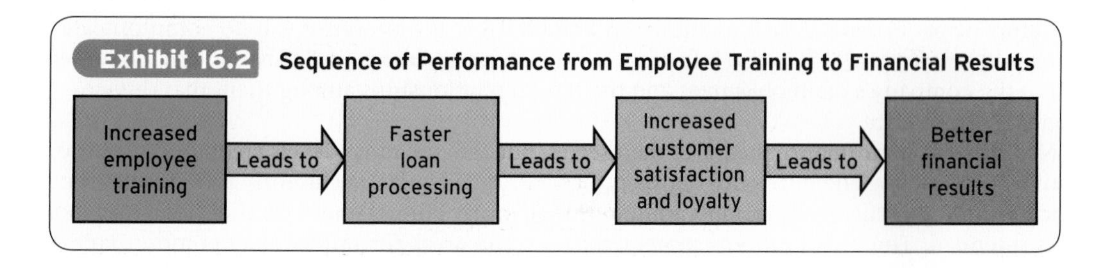

16.1 Cost Management in Practice

Tableau de bord

In France the tableau de bord – literally meaning dashboard – has been used for more than 60 years by a majority of companies. It deserves adoption consideration by non-French companies, too. There are many similarities between the tableau de bord and the later introduced balanced scorecard. The tableau de bord also contains a mix of financial and non-financial performance measures, which are derived from the organization's strategic goals and objectives. The measures are not organized according to specific categories, but in general the tableau de bord contains measures on finance, quality, customer-oriented measures, process measures, human resources and societal measures.

The concept of the tableau de bord was first developed by engineers as a way to think about cause-and-effect relationships in order to improve their production processes. The same principle was then applied to top management level. The tableau de bord should be based on tests of links among performance measures, linking objectives, action variables and action plans. An action variable has to be controllable by the responsible manager, it has to occur in time before the objective should be achieved, and then the probability of achieving that objective should be higher. The tableau de bord for the whole organization can be disaggregated into several tableaux de bord for different responsibility centres. It is then important that these various tableaux are clearly and consistently related. In other words, the action variables at the lower level are the objectives at the higher level.

However, there are also differences between the tableau de bord and the balanced scorecard, which in part have to do with how the system is seen as part of the organization's control system. In the concept of the balanced scorecard, different perspectives are distinguished (such as of the shareholders, customers, internal processes and learning) and it is assumed that these different kinds of objectives reinforce each other. However, in the concept of the tableau de bord it is recognized that tensions can exist between different kinds of objectives. Similarly, the cascading of the tableau to lower levels may not be a mere analytical and hierarchical task, but it may involve interaction and negotiation between the various levels, and managers may have rights in choosing local action variables. Furthermore, in the concept of the tableau de bord there is not much emphasis on incentives for managers.

Sources: Bourguignon et al. (2004) and Epstein and Manzoni (1998).

Balanced Scorecard's Strategic Performance Measures

A balanced scorecard expresses an organization's mission and strategy in the major areas of leading and lagging performance. Kaplan and Norton recommend using the four areas in Exhibit 16.3. This exhibit shows that all four perspectives of performance can interact and reflect the organization's strategy in a more complex way than previously shown in Exhibits 16.1 and 16.2. Each area can be a source of competitive advantage and can affect every other area. A successful balanced scorecard is

Exhibit 16.3 **The Balanced Scorecard: Four Areas of Strategic Action (adapted from Kaplan and Norton, 1996)**

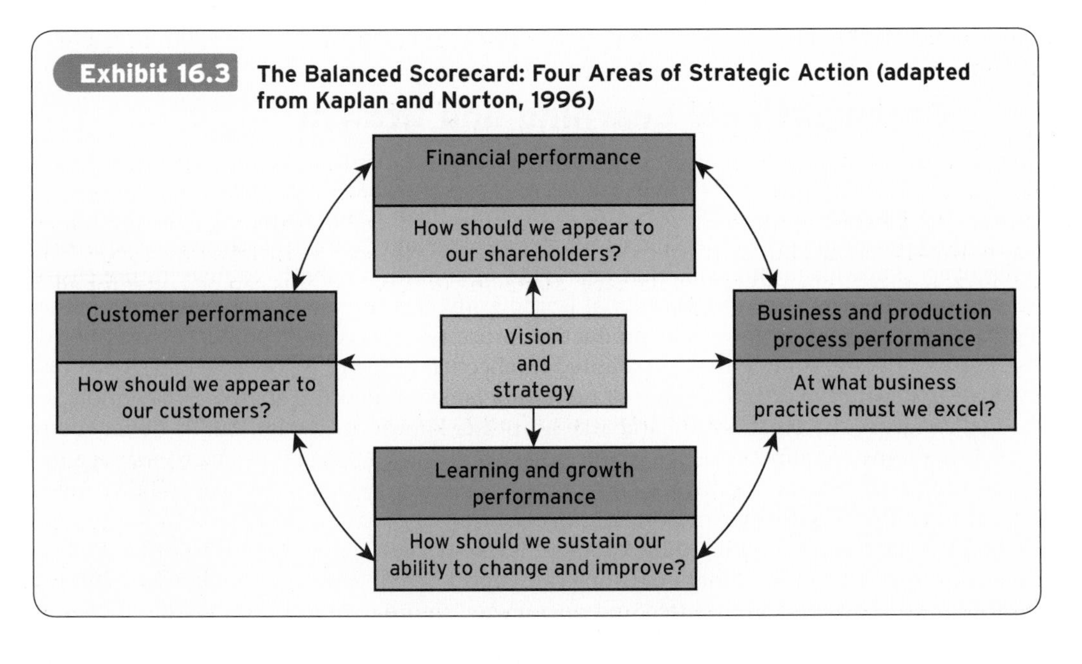

not a random selection of readily available measures of performance. These carefully designed and selected measures reflect the tangible objectives that are consistent with meeting the organization's goals.

The learning and growth perspective indicates how employees' capabilities and the infrastructure for innovation and long-term growth should contribute to strategic goals. In many ways this is the most exciting area because it is the prime source of the organization's future value. The business and production process perspective indicates how process managers should work to add value to customers. The customer perspective indicates how the company's customer-oriented strategy and operations add financial value. Finally, the financial perspective measures the company's success in adding value from the view of shareholders (or other stakeholders). For organizations that do not have shareholders, the financial perspective indicates how well the strategy and operations contribute to improving the organization's financial health.

16.1 You're the Decision Maker

Designing a Balanced Scorecard

Consider the following independent questions.

a. Virtually all companies use financial performance measures to evaluate division and department managers. What are the advantages of focusing also on non-financial performance?

b. You are interviewing for a job. The interviewer says, 'Historically, we have relied just on financial performance measures to evaluate division managers. We know the limitations of relying solely on financial performance measures, but we see a balanced scorecard as being too costly to implement. What do you think we should do?'

c. *Team focus*: You work for an internationally known consulting firm that has been asked by Singapore Airways to design and install a balanced scorecard system. You are starting to assemble a team of airline consultants and employees to work on the project. What characteristics should team members have? What airline departments or segments do you want on the team?

(Solutions begin on page 835.)

Implementation of a Balanced Scorecard

LO 2
Understand how an organization selects related measures for a balanced scorecard.

We now examine how to implement the four typical strategic areas of a balanced scorecard.

Organizational Learning and Growth

Improvements in operating performance result largely from enhancing the capabilities of the organization's employees and motivating them to use those capabilities so that the organization can learn and improve its processes and products. **Employee capabilities** are employees' knowledge and skills that create the organization's ability to meet future customer needs and generate new sales. Organizational learning involves the use of employees' capabilities to create new or improved business and production processes, procedures, products, customer databases, and proprietary, copyrighted or patented intellectual property. Knowledge developed by key individuals to benefit the organization is of no lasting benefit unless it is shared. Furthermore, a key individual can leave the organization and take his or her knowledge, which can be doubly costly if the employee joins a competitor. Like many other companies, VCB uses teams to manage nearly every decision and process. Teamwork encourages employees to share their capabilities and thus transform individual knowledge into organizational knowledge.

Different organizations might require different levels of some employee capabilities, such as education, to prosper. However, all organizations can expect better operating results when employees are well trained, motivated, committed and encouraged to improve processes. VCB sets objectives for a number of measures of employee capabilities, and it regularly monitors employees to encourage improvement. The areas of performance include the following:

- Employee training and education
- Employee satisfaction
- Employee turnover
- Innovativeness
- Opportunities for improvement.

These are shown in the following expansion of Exhibit 16.1 to reflect simplified effects of investments in organizational learning and growth.

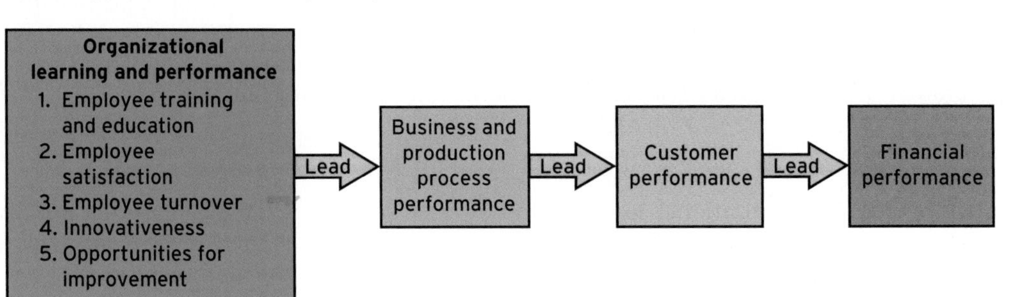

Employee training and education

VCB pays for employee education programmes to motivate employees to improve their individual and team capabilities. Hiring and promotions also depend, in part, on the educational levels achieved by potential or current employees. One top manager at VCB stated the rationale for measuring employee training, 'Yes, we want long-term, loyal employees, but we don't want people who have become uncreative or who lack the drive for constant improvement. By giving managers incentives to send their people to training programmes, the bank should have people who are really up-to-date with the latest ideas. And, frankly, I don't care whether they take classes in virtual banking or foreign language or communications skills, as long as it's expanding their minds and keeping them creative.'

Employee satisfaction

Managing employee satisfaction recognizes that employee morale is important for improving retention, productivity, quality, customer satisfaction and responsiveness to situations. Managers can measure employee satisfaction by taking surveys, interviewing employees or observing employees at work. VCB employs an external consultant to measure employee satisfaction twice a year.

© kupicoo
Educating employees is a major determinant of the success of new strategies and performance measurement.

Employee turnover

Managing employee turnover recognizes that employees develop organization-specific knowledge and are a valuable non-financial asset to the company. Finding and hiring good talent to replace people who leave are costly. A common measure of employee turnover is the percentage of people who leave voluntarily each year because generally these are people the organizations would like to keep.

Innovativeness

Competition in VCB's industry requires continuous innovation and attention to customer needs. New products or improvements to current offerings depend on the ability of an organization's employees to be innovative and translate innovations into new offerings. VCB measures its innovativeness by the percentage of sales generated by new products.

Opportunities for improvement

Organizations can encounter new opportunities to improve processes, products and services. Proactive organizations, however, work to create these opportunities. VCB encourages all employees to make suggestions for innovations and improvements. The bank estimates the value of employee suggestions from cost savings or revenue enhancements. A top manager who proposed the measure stated, 'We'd prefer to have employees come up with one excellent idea a year that had a large impact rather than a hundred trivial ideas that did not amount to much in the end.'

Evaluation of measures of organizational learning and growth

Do investments in organizational learning and growth pay off? Most organizations intuitively believe that they do; however, predicting and measuring the impacts of these investments is particularly difficult. As noted earlier, one complication is that investments in employees can walk out the door if these personnel leave. Another complication is that investments in employees might not result in tangible outcomes for years, and, by then, many other events could have occurred to obscure the impacts of training and education.

Business and Production Process Performance

It is plausible that a cause-and-effect relation exists between improvements in organizational learning and growth and improvements in internal business and production processes. Ideally, a well-trained workforce has the capability to improve internal business processes. If we are very strict, cause-and-effect relations can only be shown if changes of organizational learning measures are correlated with changes in subsequent periods of business and production processes. But by this criterion, it will almost never be possible to validate relationships in the balanced scorecard. Rather, we maintain that BSC relationships might also be logical (that is: consistent with management philosophy and values) and might be correlated with improved financial results. None of these are likely to be valid tests of causality, but probably are the best that cost management analysts can do in many situations.[3]

VCB has learned that the most important areas of process performance are:

- New service development
- Employee productivity and error rates
- Service costs
- Process improvements
- Supplier relations.

The following diagram extends Exhibit 16.1 to show effects of these measures.

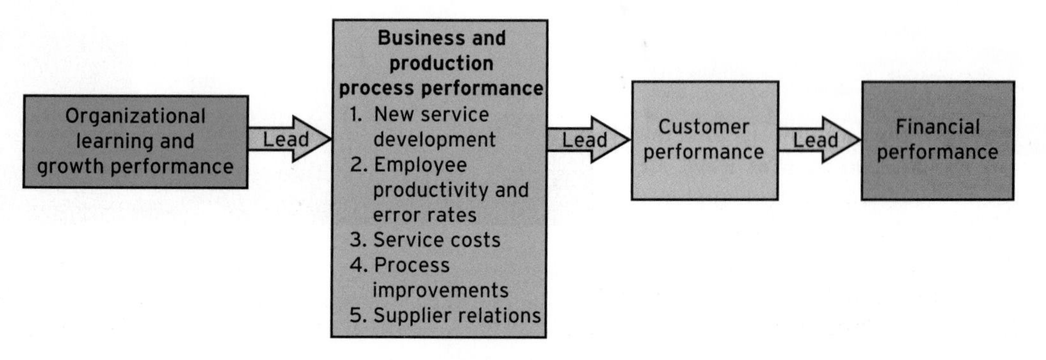

New product development

One of VCB's most important leading indicators of the capability to beat the competition is the average time to develop a new service (from the first team meeting to the delivery of the first service). In part because of innovative suggestions from employees, VCB has reduced the average new-service development time by more than 50 per cent in the past five years. This allows the bank to consistently be early to the market with innovative services. It has also led to VCB's reputation and stature as the premier supplier of financial services to emerging high-technology businesses.

Employee productivity and error rates

Managing productivity recognizes the importance of output from scarce resources (see Chapter 6). Output can be measured in terms of a physical measure, such as miles driven, pages produced or lawns mowed, or as a financial measure, such as revenue per employee or profits per employee. One simple measure of productivity at VCB is the number of loans processed without error per loan officer each month. The bank has similar productivity measures for the other major parts of its business.

Service costs

Similar to many manufacturing and service organizations, VCB regularly computes costs per loan, current account and other services. The bank uses ABC information to effect continuous improvements in these costs without losses in quality or customer service (see Chapters 4 and 5).

Process improvements

VCB once had a problem with the cycle time (see Chapter 6) for processing many loans. Customers complained, and the bank believed that it was about to lose existing and future customers. To remedy this situation, the bank increased the importance of cycle-time management. Performance measures were average cycle time (from application to provision of funds) and percentage of loans completed within one month. As a result of the focus on loan-cycle time, the bank's employees developed Apps for the iPhone, iPad and for other types of smart phones and tablets. In a secure environment, customers can update their files and usually complete their self-correcting loan applications within a few minutes. These innovations in service were possible because bank employees were trained, experienced and sufficiently motivated that they wanted to help their company.

Supplier relations

Supplier relations are becoming increasingly important as companies outsource more business or production activities that the companies once performed internally. Obviously, even though a company has outsourced an internal process, it still must ensure the quality of that process. VCB outsourced its statement preparation for bank accounts and billing for loan payments. Any errors made by the companies performing those services reflected badly on the bank, as if its own employees had performed the services themselves. Therefore, the bank appointed a manager for each outsourced service. The outsourcing contract required the supplier to provide auditable performance statistics, including cycle times and internal error rates, which the bank's manager reviewed daily.

Customer Performance

Successful organizations consistently satisfy customers' expectations. **Customer value** reflects the degree to which products satisfy customers' expectations about price, function and quality. To meet strategic goals of improving customer value, an organization must first define its customers and second identify its customers' expectations (see Chapter 5).

VCB knows that its customers are business owners and professionals who want considerable personal attention and 24-hour service, and they are willing to pay higher fees to get that service. The bank knows that it cannot compete with large interstate banks on price and breadth of services, but it can compete on the basis of the personal attention and availability of service to its customers. The bank uses the following performance measures, among others, to manage customer value:

- Customer satisfaction
- Customer retention and loyalty
- Market share
- Customer risk.

The following figure illustrates how these measures can affect financial performance.

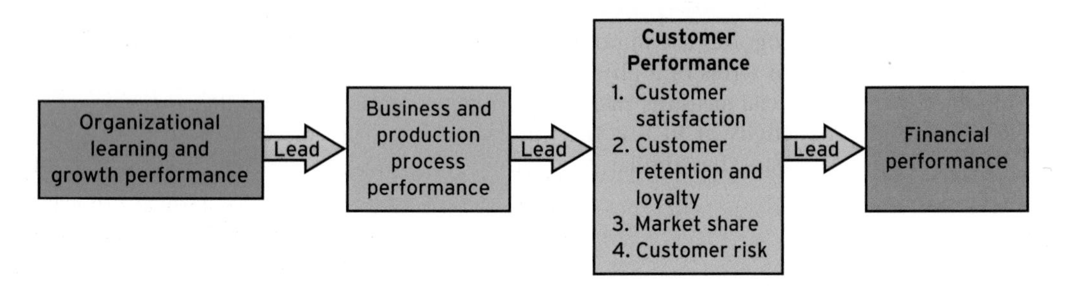

Customer satisfaction

Customer satisfaction measures indicate whether the company is meeting customers' expectations or even delighting them. Customer satisfaction with current products is a leading indicator of future sales. If a company knows that customers are becoming dissatisfied, its alert and well-trained employees are able to take corrective actions in time to prevent loss of future sales. Improvements in customer satisfaction usually lag organizational capabilities and process efficiency. In addition, customer measures can give advance notice about changing customer perceptions and needs, which influence future sales. Some companies wait to see whether customers buy their products. Others, like VCB, are more aggressive and obtain leading indicators of customer satisfaction to help them keep ahead of the competition.

VCB regularly surveys customers randomly to measure their satisfaction with current services. In addition, the bank regularly meets with groups of customers to discuss their future needs. At these meetings, customers also express what they value about the bank's services relative to those provided by competitors. This is valuable information that can help the bank position its current services and design future ones to gain a competitive advantage over its competitors from achieving customer satisfaction measures.

Customer retention

Customer retention (or loyalty) measures how well a company is doing in keeping its customers. Once a firm has a customer, keeping that customer should be much easier than capturing a new one. Satisfied customers, whose needs are met, tend to be loyal or repeat customers and continue to buy existing and probably new products from reliable providers. VCB believes that its high average customer retention rate can be counted as a key leading indicator of future sales from new products.

Market share

Market share measures a company's proportion of the total business in a particular market. Companies typically measure market share as the proportion of dollar sales, unit volume or number of customers. For example, VCB management determined that it served 12 per cent of the small businesses and the professionals in the region. Its goal was to become the dominant bank in that market segment, with 'dominant' defined as securing more than 20 per cent of the small business and professional accounts and loans. Having the largest share of this market would indicate that VCB is the bank of choice for new business and professional customers moving into the region, which should ensure continued sales growth.

Customer risk

Many organizations implicitly loan money to customers by allowing them to buy products on credit. Banks such as VCB do this explicitly and are exposed to more risk (i.e., loan default) because the amounts are larger and terms of the loans usually are longer (i.e., 10 to 30 years rather than the typical 30- or 60-day credit sales terms). Because customers might default on their loan obligations, the bank must also evaluate risk of default. To moderate the incentives created by desires for sales growth and market share, VCB also monitors the risk profiles of its customers using information in new loan applications. Risk information is a leading indicator of future default rates. Although a default rate of zero is undesirable because it implies taking no risks and missing sales opportunities, the bank cannot let the default rate increase to an excessive level without affecting its profitability and its regulatory status. Monitoring the default rate, however, is an important source of feedback on the effectiveness of screening its customers' risk profiles.

Evaluation of measures of customer value

Ideally, improvements in measures of customer value are leading indicators of improvements in financial performance. VCB and other organizations can apply the decision-making and modelling methods described in earlier chapters. Certainly, this application requires valid customer-related measures, which can be difficult to obtain at reasonable cost. Many organizations use customer satisfaction surveys, which – if administered carefully – can illuminate customer problems and opportunities. Consider the following survey results from 100 VCB customers (1 = a very unfavourable evaluation and 5 = a highly favourable evaluation).

	Number of customer responses						
VCB customer satisfaction variable	**1**	**2**	**3**	**4**	**5**	**Total**	**Ave.**
Automated bank services meet customer needs	32	25	22	16	5	100	2.37
Automated services are superior to competitors' services	17	22	20	21	20	100	3.05
Employees can and do respond to special requests	12	20	20	22	26	100	3.30
Employees give prompt service	6	14	22	17	41	100	3.73
Employees are superior to competitors' employees	5	12	20	23	40	100	3.81

What can you infer from these data? If the survey respondents are representative of VCB's preferred customers, the survey data in Exhibit 16.4 reveal both inferior and superior services. Review the charts in Exhibit 16.4. Panel A shows that customers on average have low regard for the bank's automated services but consider them to be comparable to its competitors' automated services. This seems to be an opportunity for VCB to improve its automated bank services and, perhaps, create a competitive advantage. Conversely, the bank appears to have a competitive advantage because of customers' high regard for its employees. The bank should exploit this advantage, perhaps by advertising that features them. Panel B, which shows the frequency of responses, reinforces these conclusions. Note that the unfavourable pattern of responses on the first question regarding VCB's automated services is nearly a mirror image of employee-related responses. VCB should consider the costs and benefits of improving its automated services and exploiting the favourable view of its employees.

Financial Performance

The relations among the leading indicators in the areas of organizational learning and growth, business and production process efficiency, and customer value plausibly result in financial outcomes. This is the compelling 'story' of a balanced scorecard. When organizations use a balanced scorecard as an overall picture of themselves, for example, financial performance might mean customer profitability, net income, return on investment, EVA or share price gains – all of these and others are commonly used. Because this text covers these financial performance measures in detail in Chapter 14, we do not explore them here.

Exhibit 16.4 VCB's Customer Satisfaction

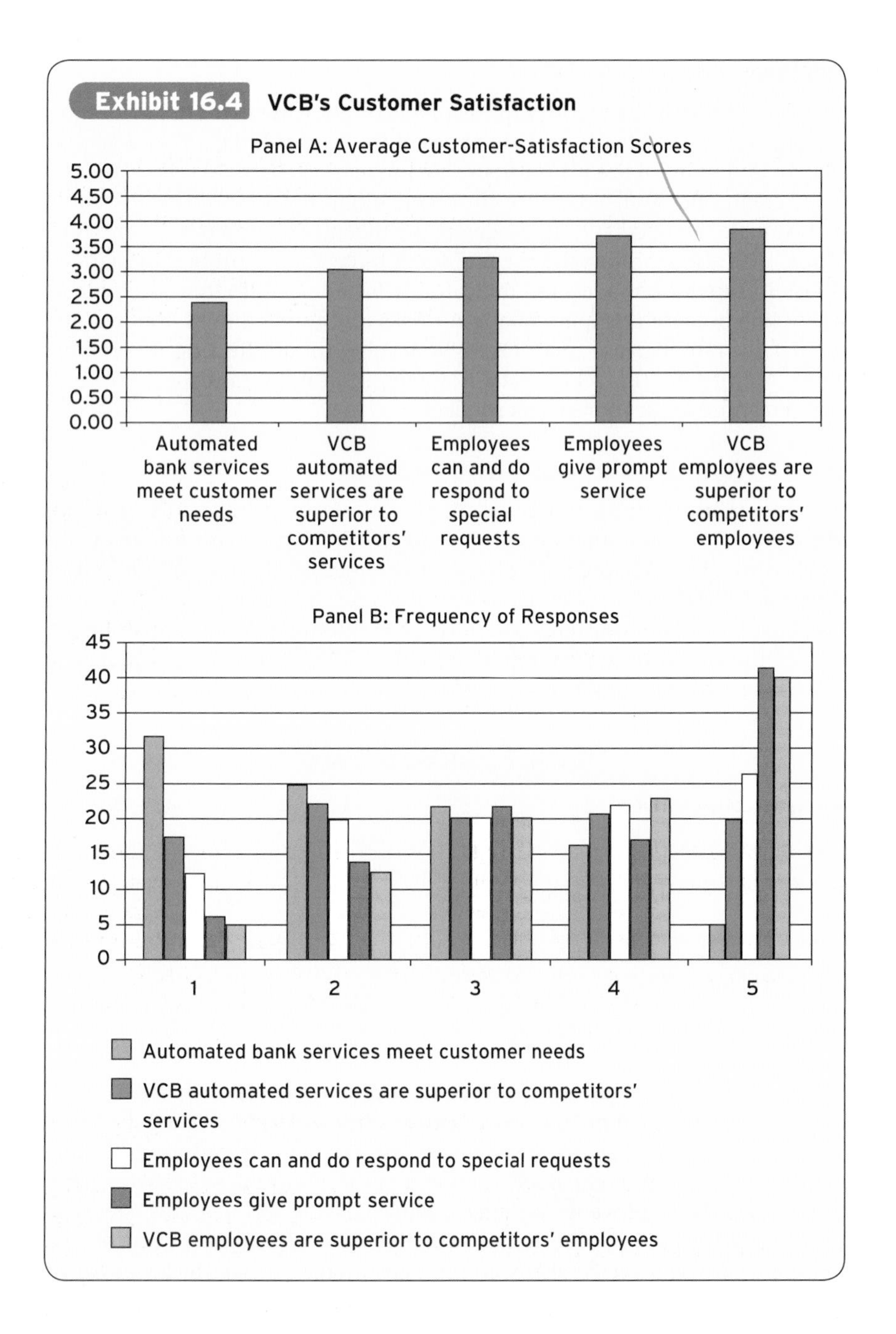

A key point of a balanced scorecard is that financial performance measures are important but are not sufficient guides for organizations to meet their goals. Nor are the lead-indicator measures a replacement for the bottom-line score of financial performance. A balanced scorecard, as the name implies, looks for a *balance* among multiple performance measures, both leading and lagging indicators of performance, to guide organizational performance toward success. Leading indicators point the way to financial success, and lagging indicators, including actual financial performance, provide opportunities for learning about what worked, what did not, and what should be improved.

VCB uses four financial performance measures:

1. *Net interest margin*, the difference between the bank's cost of funds and its average earnings from the use of those funds.
2. *Sales revenue growth*, the percentage change in revenue from one period to the next.

3. *Customer profitability* (see Chapter 5).
4. *Overall return on assets* (see Chapter 14).

Managers had difficulty explaining financial performance, good or bad, with only these measures because they did not fully understand their drivers. However, they now understand that financial success follows good performance on the leading indicators. Poor financial performance can be traced to lapses in leading indicator performance; importantly, managing those leading indicators can prevent poor financial performance. Explaining financial performance provides important feedback, but bank employees know that monitoring and correcting leading indicator performance is an effective way to ensure future financial success – and to avoid unpleasant explanations of financial shortfalls.

The following figure illustrates how other areas of performance affect financial performance.

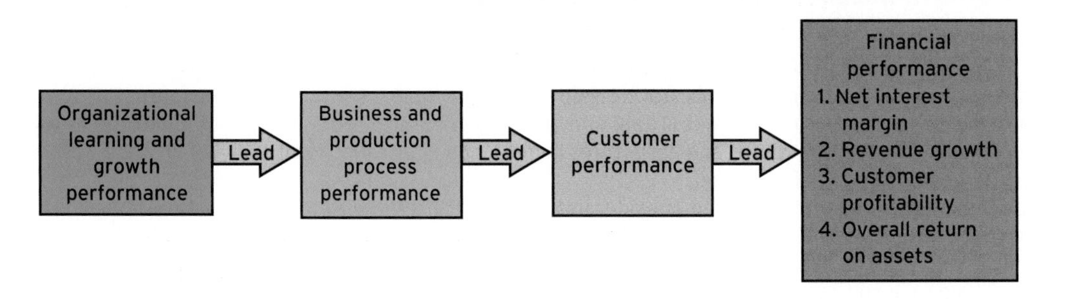

Evaluation of measures of financial performance

Financial measures of performance tend to be the most objective measures because most organizations (and society) have dedicated significant resources (e.g., regulation, auditing and internal controls) to ensure the validity of their financial performance measures. Even so, incidents of financial fraud or earnings manipulation are not rare, necessitating continual reliance on monitoring activities. Although an organization can rate or rank performance fairly objectively, the less objective leading indicators of financial performance are important for evaluating future success.

Benefits and Costs of a Balanced Scorecard

LO 3 Evaluate the benefits and costs of a balanced scorecard.

We have presented four areas of performance and have discussed VCB's related performance measures. There is nothing magic about having four areas of performance; companies have used more or fewer. Organizations should use the areas and performance measures that reflect their critical processes and the links between them. Linking these performance measures distinguishes a balanced scorecard from a list of important or key performance indicators, also known as *critical success factors*.

Benefits of a Balanced Scorecard

A balanced scorecard's greatest value is that it encourages all employees to consider the impacts of their decisions on profitability. A balanced scorecard can be a reliable guide because of its modelled relationships. An example of a leading-indicator relationship included in a balanced scorecard is this: 'Reducing the number of defective products decreases the average production cycle time because there are fewer products to rework.' This clearly demonstrates the importance of controlling the number of defects. A reasonable question is whether the label, format and method of a balanced scorecard are essential to achieving the benefits of modelling cause-and-effect relations among key performance indicators. Can other formulations of cause and effect achieve these benefits? Probably, but little objective research currently exists in this area. Early studies attribute some effects to a balanced scorecard, both favourable and unfavourable.

Another important value of a balanced scorecard is that it appears to work in various types of organizations. Cost Management in Practice 16.2 describes the process and result at **Westside**, the large Indian retailing organization. Other types of organizations, including small companies, government, universities and non-profit hospitals also report successful applications.

16.2 Cost Management in Practice

Westside's Growth Supported by Balanced Scorecard

Westside (www.mywestside.com) is one of India's largest and fastest growing chains of retail stores, and it is part of the **Tata Group**. The 49 Westside stores (in 2011) have departments such as clothing, footwear, cosmetics, perfumes, handbags and household accessories. Tata Group's retail portfolio also includes the hypermarkets Star Bazaar, stores in electronics (Croma), watches (Titan) and jewellery (Tanishq). The company has joined forces with international brands to open Sisley stores and Zara stores in India, and it has launched its new retail brand, Fashion Yatra, for the lower-priced end of the market.

The retail industry in India has changed considerably in recent history with the introduction of new retail formats, such as private-label chains, department stores, hypermarkets, in-house merchandising, etc. Westside is located mainly in malls, which have changed the way people shop in India, making it a form of entertainment that includes buying, a movie and eating at restaurants.

The mission of Westside is to be the most preferred and consistently profitable lifestyle retailer. Its balanced scorecard is a key management instrument for achieving this. The company started in 2001 to develop and implement the balanced scorecard. While the company was successful and growing very strongly, management felt that employees needed to better understand and keep focused on the underlying strategy. Management looked mostly at financial measures and felt it should also monitor other performance measures, such as what customers feel about the company.

The whole process of creating the balanced scorecard was a collaborative effort. Management wanted the process to be inclusive, involving as many people as was possible in co-creating a vision for the organization. In early 2001, they conducted a series of workshops involving the participation of a significant number of people from within the organization, including the heads of departments and middle managers.

In drawing up the strategic goals of the company, the customer's interests were of paramount importance. The company defined its key strategic objective as 'surprisingly affordable style, quality, and a great shopping experience for the entire family'. This embeds all the other strategic objectives. It was in translating this strategic objective into internal business processes, however, that the company faced its first major hurdle: the industry's high attrition rate among entry-level employees. Most jobs of this kind in retail are taken up by people such as college students who don't intend to stay for long in the organization.

The company realized that constantly training people was crucial, otherwise customer service levels would suffer. A coaching programme was developed that they consider to be one of the most successful initiatives to have come out of the balanced scorecard implementation. As part of this programme, the company identifies star employees in each store and designates them as coaches responsible for the training of their own store staff. Today, each store has three kinds of coaches: a customer service coach, an IT skills coach and a product knowledge coach. The success of this programme has made it a benchmark for all Tata Group companies.

Although a friendly staff and an overall pleasant store environment are extremely critical, what customers want most is to walk into a store and find what they want right there on the shelf. Promising this to the customer had clear implications for Westside's performance measurement at the business process level. A central warehousing system that controls products sourced from over 300 vendors, ships merchandise to all of the chain's outlets, and monitors each store's requirements.

Products are updated frequently to stimulate customers to make regular visits to their area stores and to identify successful new products. A good illustration of this is Westside's Gia range of products, aimed at full-bodied women. Today, it is one of the store's fastest growing sections and it came about only because the company was keeping a close watch on which new products were selling well.

In operations, Westside's performance measures concentrate on optimizing costs, tight inventory control and strictly managing ageing merchandise. Cost management is crucial, because rent and property, managerial staff and electricity are increasing very rapidly in urban India, where the majority of modern retail is located.

Westside has introduced a successful loyalty programme with close to a million members, and it offers a 'no questions asked' return policy for ClubWest members.

The company believes that the benefits that have come out of the scorecard's implementation have been enormous. Westside is a highly profitable, rapidly growing retail organization. Customer satisfaction levels are so high that Westside is now considered one of the best companies in the industry in terms of customer service. The reasons for this success, according to the company, is the wholehearted support and participation of the whole top management team, clear articulation of strategy, a clearly laid out action plan and the persistence to stick with it for all these years without faltering.

Source: Company websites, viewed 27 and 29 June 2011.

16.1 Research Insight

Benefits of a Balanced Scorecard

The balanced scorecard is an appealing and popular management tool. Apparently, many managers expect important benefits from balanced scorecard implementation. Some studies have also looked systematically at empirical evidence for such benefits, and many found support for the idea that the balanced scorecard helps to formulate and communicate strategy, and aids managers to act on this strategy.

Some studies are based on investigating companies that have implemented a balanced scorecard, and this allowed collecting information on the effects both across time and by comparing organizational units with and without a balanced scorecard.

Sources: Davis and Albright (2004), Malina and Selto (2001) and Banker et al. (2000).

Other studies are based on survey data among managers from a large sample of companies, asking them about the nature of performance measurement systems used in their companies and about company characteristics. Statistical analyses looked for correlations between the use of balanced-scorecard type performance measurement systems and desirable outcomes (such as flexibility of manufacturing). Yet other studies looked at publicly available data in annual reports and other company information that could be used to assess a company's balanced scorecard adoption. This could then be correlated with publicly available data on these companies' performance (both the performance as reported in annual reports and performance based on the stock market). Some studies have also combined survey data and publicly available data.

Sources: Chenhall (2005), Ittner et al. (2003b) and Said et al. (2003).

Furthermore, experimental studies have been conducted to see how the provision of a broad set of non-financial and forward-looking measures affect how people make decisions. Studies showed that this can make managers look more at the long term, but other studies also showed that it is not easy for managers to consider the overload of diverse information on a balanced scorecard. They do not necessarily make better decisions. Managers can make better decisions, however, if the balanced scorecard is based on an accurate causal model (see also Research Insight 16.2).

Sources: Farrell et al. (2008); Lipe and Salterio (2000); and Vera-Muñoz et al. (2007).

These various kinds of studies show many beneficial consequences of using balanced scorecards. Probably the most difficult aspect to capture in all studies is to understand how this information is actually used, in combination with other kinds of information, and in the interaction between managers.

Costs of a Balanced Scorecard

The value of a balanced scorecard comes with costs. Presently, no studies of the costs to design and implement a balanced scorecard have been published, but these costs surely exist. They include the costs of consultants (if used), measurement, education and use. Some reported and unreported balanced scorecard failures might be attributed to the failure to anticipate these costs. We do know that developing and implementing a balanced scorecard is not an overnight endeavour. Many organizations have spent several years on the process from concept to general use, and subsequent revisions. Furthermore, a balanced scorecard is never completed; it continuously evolves as the organization learns and evolves, so many costs are ongoing.

Measurement costs

Because of the urgency of creating a balanced scorecard, some organizations decide to reuse existing measures and piece together a balanced scorecard. Picking and choosing from an inventory of existing measures can be a first step, but new measures inevitably are necessary. Organizations should resist the temptation to economize by using only currently available measures because some areas of performance probably have no suitable measures available. Each new performance measure has a cost of design, validation, data collection, maintenance and revision, which can be significant. Establishing credible links between measures or areas of performance also is no trivial task. Anticipating the full costs of additional performance measures is more an art than an exact science, but that does not justify ignoring these costs.

Education costs

Just as numbers almost never speak for themselves, creating a balanced scorecard does not ensure that members of the organization understand it or how to use it. Organizations should plan for and not underestimate the education, training, coaching and interpretation activities needed to integrate a balanced scorecard.

Use costs

The costs of using a balanced scorecard also might be significant. Although early studies indicate that information overload is not a problem, assuming that individuals can manage many performance measures simultaneously is unwise, particularly if some measures conflict and require trade-offs. Organizations are learning to assign responsibility or 'ownership' to balanced scorecard measures just as they had for responsibility accounting in the past (see Chapter 14).

Balanced Scorecard Implementation at VCB

LO 4
Explain how an organization implements a balanced scorecard.

Some organizations develop a balanced scorecard at top levels of management and impose it. This approach can be successful, just as top-down management succeeds in some situations, but most observers believe that a participative, bottom-up approach to designing a balanced scorecard improves its acceptance and use by the organization's members. After all, the foundation of a balanced scorecard is learning and growth, reflecting employee capabilities to gain, transfer and apply knowledge. It makes sense to involve them in a balanced scorecard design.[4]

VCB's cost management team sketched the initial balanced scorecard based on its understanding of the bank's strategy and processes and input from key employees. The team then spent more than a year working with employees representing all levels, functions and major activities of the bank to design the scorecard. After more than a year of interaction with other employees, the team unveiled a balanced scorecard using the performance measures previously discussed. Exhibit 16.5 displays VCB's scorecard areas and measures.

Exhibit 16.6 is a graphical representation of part of VCB's balanced scorecard model. The cost management team used this simplified chart to explain several leading/lagging relationships among the four areas of performance. In this simplified model, profitability – VCB's ultimate goal – is achieved, in part, by retaining existing customers through improving loan processing. These links tell the story of VCB's success in its competitive market for banking services. This graphical representation of the bank's strategy was an effective communication and education tool. You should 'walk

Exhibit 16.5 **VCB's Balanced Scorecard Areas and Measures**

Scorecard Areas	Scorecard Performance	Scorecard Measures	Performance Targets
Organizational learning and growth	Employee training and education	Percentage of employees involved in approved training and education	100 per cent
	Employee satisfaction	Employee satisfaction index	Maintain current level
	Employee turnover	Voluntary turnover percentage	Below industry average
	Innovativeness	Percentage of sales from new services	50 per cent
	Opportunities for improvement	Employee suggestions	Estimated value of employee suggestions
Business and production process efficiency	New service development	Average new service development time	Continuous improvement
	Productivity (loans)	Error-free loans processed per employee	Continuous improvement
	Defective service (loans)	Errors per loan officer	Zero
	Service costs	Cost per loan, checking account, and other services	Continuous improvement
	Process improvements	Average process (e.g., loan) cycle time	One week
	Supplier relations	Supplier cycle time, error rates	Below industry averages
Customer value	Customer satisfaction	Customer satisfaction index	Above competitors' average
	Customer retention and loyalty	Customer retention rate	Above industry average
	Sales growth	Account and revenue growth	10 per cent per year
	Market share	Professional and business market share	30 per cent
	Customer risk	Customer risk profiles and loan default rate	Maintain current levels
Financial performance	Service profitability	Net interest margin	5 per cent
	Growth	Revenue growth	Above industry average
	Customer profitability	Percentage of loss customers	Zero
	Competitive return	Return on assets	Above industry average

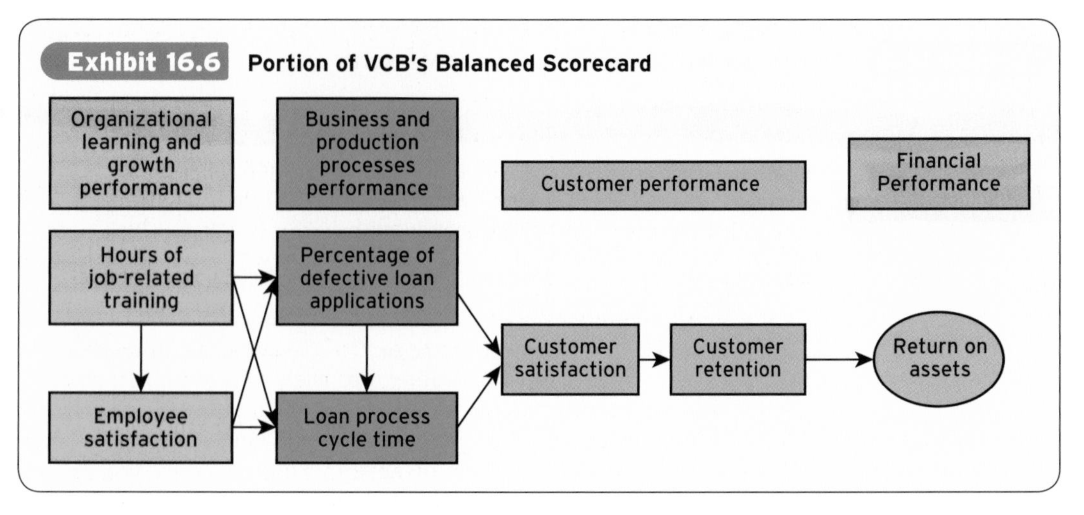

Exhibit 16.6 Portion of VCB's Balanced Scorecard

through' this model carefully, beginning with the hours of job-related training, following the direction of the arrows from one box to the next.

Along with the extensive effort to develop its balanced scorecard, VCB's top management also examined its incentive system for consistency and effectiveness. We now turn to the related topic of incentive systems.

16.2 Research Insight

Causality in a Balanced Scorecard

Ittner and Larcker found that companies in their study 'that adopted nonfinancial measurs and then established a causal link between those measures and financial outcomes produced significantly higher returns on assets and returns on equity over a five-year period than those that did not.' Ittner and Larcker also argue that many firms do not validate their causal model, either because they believe that the cause-and-effect relationships are obvious and need not be verified or the time and cost involved in validating the model are prohibitive. Speckbacher, Bischof and Pfeiffer found in their sample of companies in Germany, Austria and Switzerland that only half of the companies were able to formulate cause-and-effect relationships.

However, case studies have shown that the cause-and-effect relationships expected in the models used by actual organizations might not be empirically supportable (Malina et al., 2007). Establishing causality that is beyond mere correlation between putative cause, *X*, and effect, *Y*, requires time precedence (*X* occurs before *Y*), exclusivity (if *X* does not occur, *Y* also does not), and predictive ability (if *X* is observed, *Y* always follows). These are stringent criteria, but a statistical relationship that fails any of them might be correlation, but not causation. Failure means that the relationship might be spurious and unreliable. Even if these criteria can be met, finding empirical evidence of cause and effect requires stable processes over time, which is unlikely in today's dynamic economy and firms. Furthermore, Malina et al. find that some linkages in balanced scorecards are logical, accounting relationships that cannot be validated by statistical evidence. For example, improving manufacturing efficiency will logically increase profits when cost savings exceed investment costs (*ceteris paribus*). Failing to find a statistically significant link does not invalidate the logical relationship, rather it probably means that *ceteris paribus* conditions were not maintained. Finally, some balanced scorecard links can reflect the company's strategic and operating philosophy that might be effective in unique circumstances, but are not generally valid. For example, increasing market share or customer satisfaction might be successful growth strategies for some firms but they might not lead to financial success for all companies.

These cautions do not mean that firms or researchers should not use balanced scorecards or that they should not look for statistical validation. Perceived benefits have been documented, but convincing statistical validation of causality can be expected to be very difficult.

Sources: Ittner and Larcker (2003), Malina et al. (2007) and Speckbacher et al. (2003).

Fundamental Principles of Incentive Systems

The principle of **pay for performance** is to base at least some portion of a manager's income on measure(s) of organizational performance rather than a guaranteed amount. We will use the term **incentives systems** in this chapter. Incentive systems need to be designed with great care because they have a big impact on the behaviour and decisions of managers, and thereby such systems may either greatly contribute to the success of the organization, or they may be very harmful. Furthermore, managers' incomes, especially of topic executives, is a topic that can create a lot of debate and raise public anger.[5]

LO 5
Understand the key principles of performance-based incentive systems.

Today, many companies and non-profit organizations use incentive systems for executives, managers and, to a lesser degree, employees at all levels. You could easily find yourself eligible for incentive compensation soon after completing your studies. For example, employment with a business assurance or consulting firm might offer you mostly salary with a long-term opportunity of a partnership and profit sharing. A high-technology company, on the other hand, might offer a relatively low initial salary with an early opportunity for share ownership. Similarly, once you are with an organization, you must decide how to attract and retain good employees with different incentives. The structure of incentive systems can matter greatly to employees and employers, and these plans can have a substantial impact on annual pay.

It is interesting to speculate how the different incentive systems might affect managers' behaviour. But, apart from the money, is the 'real world' different from school? If you are currently a student, you already work within a performance-based incentive system; grades in courses can be based on multiple measures of performance. You can easily imagine how differences in the rewards or incentives might alter your motivation and behaviour. Do you study as hard for a course that you take for a pass–fail as for one you take for a grade? Do you concentrate on the same parts of the course if the grade is based on a comprehensive paper versus problem-oriented exams? Variations in incentives and rewards affect student behaviour as they do employees who work for rewards. The key to designing incentive systems is to understand as well as possible which behaviours are desired and how incentives and rewards are likely to influence behaviour. In nearly every case, you get what you measure and reward – even if it is not what you intended.

Two key principles of any incentive system, which are discussed in the remainder of this chapter, are:

1. Measurement of performance
2. Compensation based on measured performance.

Measurement of Performance

The starting point of designing an effective incentive system is knowing the behaviour that the organization wants to motivate, given the organization's goals and objectives. Managers cannot motivate people to 'do the right thing' if no one knows what the right thing is. An effective incentive system should motivate employees to achieve the organization's goals and objectives and reward them if they do.[6]

Unfortunately, translating goals into effective incentive systems is not always as easy as it might seem because sometimes the desired outcome is not easily observed. Here is a seemingly easy question: what is the 'right thing' for a profit-seeking corporation? The standard answer in a market economy is a long-term competitive return for shareholders. In reality, translating even this standard statement into an incentive plan can be a challenge. For one thing, the 'long-term' might be 5 or 10 years from now. A company may wait that long to reward or penalize managers, but what if it needs to reward good managers now or risk losing them to competitors? What is the 'competitive' benchmark? What is the proper measure of 'return'? Are 'shareholders' the only *stakeholders* in the company (that is, those who have an interest in its actions)?

But wait a minute. Didn't we talk a lot about performance measurement in the first part of this chapter? Is the balanced scorecard the starting point for measuring performance as part of an incentive system? That can be the case, but it is not always wise. We will return to these questions at the end of this section.

Early on, VCB also had a problem of measuring the right performance. As a small service-oriented bank, VCB realized the importance of customer relations and relied on satisfying its customers to keep them coming back for more loans and services. The original incentive system, however, emphasized short-term profits and cost minimization, which gave branch managers the incentive to reduce staff. This narrow focus resulted in fewer employees spending less time with customers and lower customer satisfaction. As a result, the bank began to lose some of its key customers because of its incentive system, which it soon revised.

Measurement of performance requires translating the desired behaviour to measurable performance indicators. Such indicators need to have several *measurement properties* to make them effective within incentive systems:

- Performance measures need to be *value relevant*, in the sense of related to the desired goals. In other words, if the performance measure improves, the organization should be closer to achieving its goals and objectives. For example, if the manager improves the division's EVA, this is contributing to one of the organization's goals, namely to increase shareholder value. But shareholder value is clearly not the only goal of many organizations.
- Second, a performance measure needs to be *sensitive* to the manager's actions. In other words, if the manager is actually doing a better job, that should be reflected in an improvement on the performance measure – and the other way around. For example, if a manager takes actions to improve customer service processes, the customer satisfaction index increases. Sometimes it takes a long time before the effects of a manager's action are visible in the performance measures, and that needs to be considered when using the performance measure as part of an incentive plan.
- Third, the performance measure should not be affected much by all kinds of other things happening besides the manager's actions. If there is a lot of *noise*, it means that the performance measure goes up and down regardless of what the manager does. Performance measures in an incentive plan should have low noise.
- Fourth, the performance measure needs to be *accurate, reliable and verifiable*. For example, measurement of the market share needs to be close to the actual market share (which cannot be observed directly), needs to measured consistently, and it should be possible to validate how it has been measured.[7]

Not all measures that are included on an organization's balanced scorecard may have these needed measurement properties. Remember that the primary purpose of a balanced scorecard is to communicate and implement strategy, not to determine bonuses for managers. For example, VCB measures the customer retention rate to understand how it is doing with respect to retaining loyal customers. The measure is based on how many customers take their business away from VCB as part of the total customer base. VCB managers know that this is useful information, but also a crude measure. It does not capture when customers stay at VCB but nevertheless move for some services to another bank. So VCB managers use the customer retention rate to stimulate exchange of ideas about how to really improve customer loyalty (not just how it is measured). That measure is not ideal but still usable for the purpose of communicating and implementing strategy. But if bonuses are attached to it, a measure that lacks solid measurement properties can give rise to unwanted managerial behaviour. It is not always a good idea to use the balanced scored unconditionally as part of incentive systems.

Compensation Based on Measured Performance

The second principle of an incentive system is the linkage between the achieve levels on the performance measures and the resulting compensation. For example, a very straightforward relationship is when a sales agent receives 12 per cent of the gross margin of the sales transactions that she completed. There are many choices that the cost management analyst and others must make about this relationship between measured performance and resulting compensation, and we will discuss those in the next section.

To guide the design of incentive plans, a number of theories are well grounded in observations of individuals and organizations and can provide reliable advice. Not surprisingly, because incentives are so important, researchers have studied the psychology and economics of incentives for many years. Relying on the guidance from this research is an efficient way to begin to design an incentive plan. A key insight from **expectancy theory**[8] is that to motivate people to behave in a particular way, incentive plans must do two things:

1. Provide desirable rewards or undesirable penalties.
2. Provide a high probability that behaving as the organization desires will lead to those rewards or penalties.

That is, the incentive plan provides *expectancy* that desired behaviour leads to desired rewards.[9] From goal-setting theory we can learn:

- Impossible goals all but eliminate motivation because people realize that the desired performance and rewards cannot be achieved, regardless of effort.
- Easy goals reduce motivation to the minimum necessary to achieve them. Easy goals create lost opportunities to create more value at lower cost.
- Difficult but attainable goals consistently create the most motivation, effort, and lead to the highest level of performance compared to either impossible or easy goals.[10]

Incentive plans include mostly extrinsic rewards. **Extrinsic rewards** come from outside the individual from teachers, parents, organizations or partners and include grades, money, praise and prizes. **Intrinsic rewards**, on the other hand, come from within the individual, such as the satisfaction from studying hard, the feeling of well-being from physical exercise, the pleasure from helping someone in need, or the satisfaction of doing a good job. Getting an A on an exam is an extrinsic reward; satisfaction with your performance is an intrinsic reward.

People receive many intrinsic and extrinsic rewards. Teachers and caregivers, such as nurses, often work for wages less than their ability and effort can command because they receive intrinsic rewards from the work. In addition, many people volunteer their services not only because of the intrinsic rewards but also for the extrinsic rewards – praise and gratitude – they receive. These are factors to consider in designing incentive systems. Some jobs inherently have more rewards than others do, and what people consider to be rewards differs. Some are motivated mostly by money; others are more motivated by public praise.

An effective incentive plan considers opportunities for both intrinsic and extrinsic rewards and penalties and allows opportunities for variations, particularly of intrinsic rewards. Effective motivation usually requires a balance between extrinsic and intrinsic rewards, but the balance point varies with the organization and the people it attracts and retains.

Our interpretation of theory and observations of successful practice generate the following guidelines for designing effective incentive plans.

Theory and practice	Guideline
Most individuals are motivated by self-interest	Performance-based rewards must be greater than alternative rewards from non-performance.
Organizations get the behaviour they reward	Performance measures and related rewards must reflect organizational goals.
Effort follows rewards	Employees must believe that their efforts influence performance and will be rewarded.
Difficult but attainable goals motivate best	Impossible goals are de-motivators and so are easy goals. Make goals difficult but not impossible.
Fairness is a basis for sustained motivation	Rewards must be linked to desired performance in a fair and consistent manner.

Manipulation undermines fairness and effort	Performance measures must be observable and verifiable.
Different rewards can motivate effort	Rewards must meet market conditions, and rewards must be available.
Incentive systems involve trade-offs	Minimizing the overall costs of aligning goals and monitoring behaviour is a goal of incentive system design.

Features of Performance-based Incentive Systems

LO 6 Evaluate the advantages and disadvantages of alternative features of incentive systems.

Incentive systems can include many alternative features. We now turn to a number of specific choices that designers of incentive systems must make. Identifying the required trade-offs between effective rewards, goal alignment, monitoring and cost necessitates choosing among many alternative incentive-system configurations and reviewing systems in place to be sure they are still effective.[11]

Exhibit 16.7 displays the many choices that accumulate to create the elements of an effective performance-based incentive system. Designers of incentive systems should consider all of these choices because ignoring any of them can lead to a less-effective system. All of the elements in Exhibit 16.7 speak to this question: *Given the goal(s) of the organization, which alternative incentive(s) will motivate the desired behaviour most effectively?* The answer to that question must be placed in context: *The situation faced by each company determines the answer.* There are no universally right or wrong answers, but there are better or worse answers in a particular situation. Furthermore, many equally effective combinations of incentive plan elements might exist in similar situations. Our aim is to provide an overview of the choices, not to suggest the correct choices for any situation. We discuss each of the boxed alternatives in Exhibit 16.7 in turn.

Exhibit 16.7 **Performance-based Incentive System Choices**

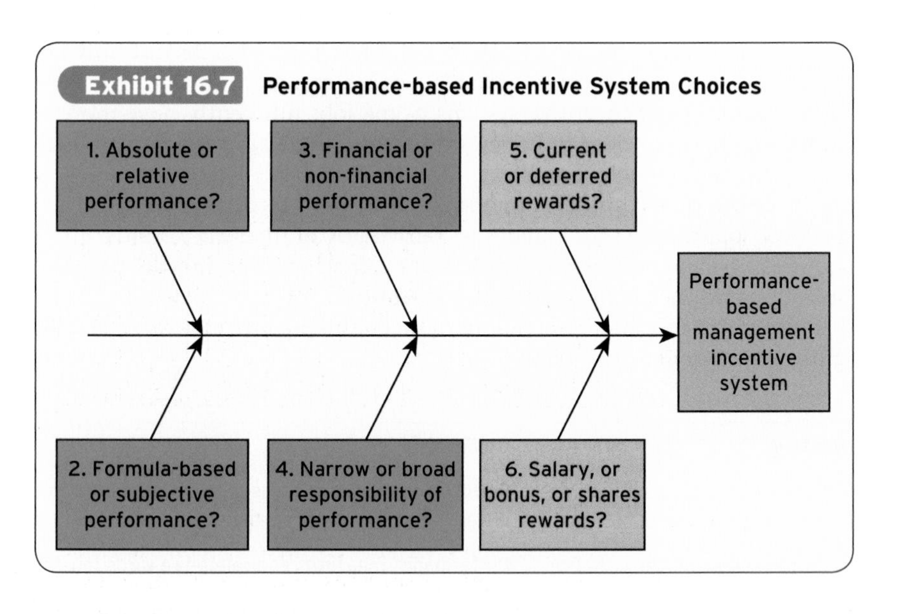

Absolute or Relative Performance

One may evaluate performance against absolute objectives or relative to others' performance. **Absolute performance evaluation** compares individual performance to set objectives or expectations. For example, in classes that use absolute performance evaluation, the instructor grades on an absolute scale, and how well others perform does not affect your grade. For example, panel A of Exhibit 16.8 illustrates a grade distribution that uses absolute cut-offs for how many points you achieved out of the total points that could be obtained (100 per cent < A < 90 per cent; 90 per cent ≤ B < 80 per cent, etc.).[12] **Relative performance evaluation** compares an individual's performance to that of others. In classes that use relative performance evaluation, the instructor grades on the curve; that is, your grade depends on how you perform relative to everyone else. For example, panel B of Exhibit 16.8 reflects a grade distribution relative to an instructor's desired curve of 12.5 per cent As (the top 12.5 per cent of 32 students = 4 students), 50 per cent Bs (the next 50 per cent of 32 = 16 students), 25 per cent Cs (the following 8 students), and 12.5 per cent Ds and Fs (the final 4 students). Both approaches can be effective, but the situation determines the effectiveness. For example, grading on an absolute basis, when exams are extremely difficult, can reduce one's belief that studying can lead to a high grade. Thus, students' effort to study might be less in this situation than if the instructor graded on a relative basis, where final grades reflect relative performance on difficult exams.

Like other companies that use a relative performance evaluation, VCB *benchmarks* branch-bank performance with that of other banks in the same industry.[13] Thus, a branch that generated 3 per cent revenue growth in a market where the average revenue growth was 4.5 per cent might receive a lower evaluation than a VCB branch that earned 3 per cent in a market with 2 per cent average revenue growth. Just as grading on the curve shields students from the risk of an extremely difficult test, relative performance evaluation shields a manager from the risk of managing a division in a market that performs poorly. Relative performance evaluation also motivates high performance if the manager's division is in a market that performs well.

Exhibit 16.8 Absolute versus Relative Grading

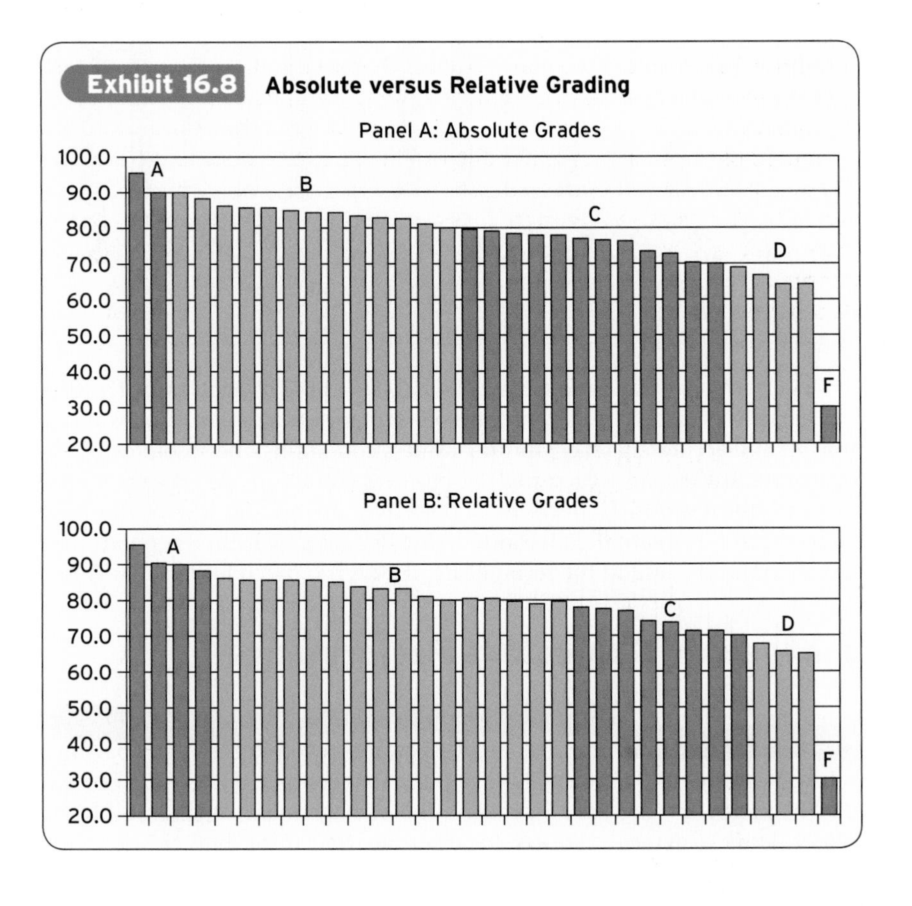

A disadvantage of relative performance evaluation is that it does not provide incentives for managers to move out of poorly performing markets into those that perform well. Why would successful managers in a poor market move to a more competitive market where relative performance evaluation makes the likelihood of rewards low? Furthermore, if good managers decide to move, they might have to work much harder for the same relative performance.

At VCB, top management believes that relative performance evaluation of some aspects of performance is effective. Using relative performance evaluation, top management assesses each branch bank's revenue growth performance relative to each other and to similar banks in the same market. The bank rewards the managers of branches with the highest relative revenue growth. This controls for unforeseen changes in business conditions that might affect all banks' revenue growth. Consider the relative evaluations in Exhibit 16.9. Using a set of comparative banks, VCB branches F, E and B achieved below-average revenue growth, but VCB branches G, D, A and C had above-average revenue growth. Thus, under the same conditions that all faced, branches G, D, A and C outperformed the average.

Exhibit 16.9 **Relative Revenue Growth**

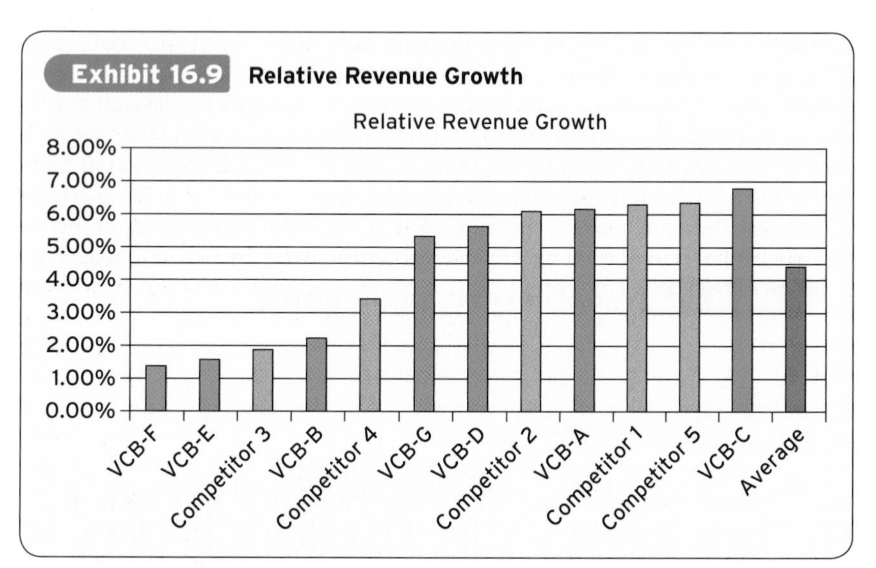

Using relative performance evaluation allows VCB to avoid the difficult task of setting appropriate revenue growth objectives necessary for absolute performance evaluation. Unless the objectives are sufficiently difficult and accurately reflect future business conditions, the absolute objectives might be ineffective motivators. If they are set too high or business conditions deteriorate, managers perceive little chance of earning rewards. Conversely, if objectives are set too low or the business climate improves, managers can easily earn their rewards. In the first case, VCB misses opportunities for growth because managers do not try, and in the second case, it pays too much for less than best efforts.

Formula-based or Subjective Performance

Some companies base rewards on a **performance evaluation formula,** which computes rewards earned for specific achievements. For example, VCB rewards revenue growth by paying branch managers a bonus based on the following explicit formula: for each percentage point by which revenue growth exceeds the market average, say 5 per cent, the manager receives a bonus of 4 per cent of his or her base salary. Thus, a manager knows, for example, that if her branch's revenue growth was 8 per cent for a particular year (that is, three percentage points above the 5 per cent threshold percentage) and her base salary is €100,000 per year, her bonus is €12,000 (three percentage points times 4 per cent per point times €100,000). A manager who did not meet the market average revenue growth rate receives no bonus.

This bonus is in addition to the manager's base salary. VCB included this incentive as part of its formula but rejected a formula-*only* approach to performance evaluation for branch managers as too restrictive to its culture and business climate. One consideration was that using only a formula penalizes managers assigned to problem branches, which VCB management believed is demoralizing and leads to unwanted loss of talented managers. Another factor that limited VCB's enthusiasm for using only an incentive formula was concern about setting the right formula parameters (e.g., average market growth and bonus percentage). Different parameters generate different incentives and might lead to different actions. Having diverse sources of compensation minimizes the risk of incentive-formula mistakes and allows for some experimentation with different formula parameters.

In formula-based evaluations it is even more important that performance measures have all the required *measurement properties* that we discussed in the previous section. For example, inaccurate, unreliable or manipulated measures can create the opportunity for conflict over measured performance and incentives to cheat. Conflict and cheating might encourage eventual measurement improvements but can seriously impair the organization's performance while the inadequate measures are in place. Sometimes taking actions that improve the evaluation numbers but that are detrimental to the organization in the long run is possible (e.g., branch managers can add riskier customers to increase recorded revenues without adjusting for expected future losses). Organizations can also measure some areas of formula-based non-financial performance as reliably as financial performance, but most organizations historically have had more ability and need to measure and verify financial performance because of financial and tax reporting requirements.

Companies also may use **subjective performance evaluation**, which means that the procedure for assessing performance and determining rewards is not completely quantifiable and is also based on personal judgement. The advantage of subjective evaluation is that it considers factors that a formula does not explicitly capture.[14] For example, suppose that the sales growth of one of VCB's branches was below target because it serves a declining market. The bank wants to maintain a presence there, however, because the market area will be the focus of economic redevelopment activities by local and federal governments. Matching the future benefits and opportunity costs of this management decision in an explicit formula can be difficult. Subjective performance evaluation also can eliminate opportunities for 'gaming' formula-based evaluations. Subjective evaluation can counter the tendency to manipulate the numbers in the formula. Recent financial reporting scandals have shown that these gaming motivations can be strong.

The advantage of a formula-based plan is that managers know precisely what is expected of them and what reward they will receive relative to expectations. The subjective approach is a less certain form of incentive plan and can be susceptible to favouritism, political manoeuvring, and even a 'good-old-boys' approach to incentive compensation. Incentive compensation might become a function more of how well superiors like managers than of performance, thus reducing the link between effort and reward. Employees often are comfortable with a subjective approach when they believe in upper management's ability, are willing to take some risks, and trust upper management. Otherwise, employees tend to prefer a formula approach.[15]

Increasing numbers of organizations use elements of both subjective and formula-based incentives. For example, VCB rewards branch managers based on a formula that includes revenue growth, net interest margin and return on net assets as well as subjective evaluation based on industry norms, a manager's level of responsibility and the judged value of a manager's contributions.

Financial or Non-financial Performance

Financial performance reflects the achievement of financial goals, such as cost control, revenue growth, earnings and residual income. Chapter 14 of this text provides extensive discussion of these performance measures, which we do not repeat here. Organizations that ostensibly measure performance with only financial or only non-financial performance measures could be found. Some profit-seeking firms apparently base rewards only on 'bottom-line' financial performance. Some non-profit organizations overtly reward only on the basis of meeting non-financial goals. However, nearly every organization really uses both financial and non-financial measures of performance. For example, in the most bottom-line-oriented corporation, an executive who exceeds financial goals will not last long after being convicted of a serious crime. Furthermore, the most altruistic, non-financial, non-profit organization cannot tolerate an executive who repeatedly fails to operate within the organization's financial means or diverts the organization's funds for personal use. Financial and non-financial performance measurement is not an either-or issue but involves identifying which measures and what balance to use. We next briefly review financial performance measures.

Financial performance: accounting measures or share price?

Financial performance measures commonly include levels or growth of the following:

- Revenues
- Costs

- Cash flow
- Operating income (before or after extraordinary items, taxes)
- Return on investment (total assets, net assets, or equity)
- Residual income or EVA
- Share price.

All of these measures except share price are explicitly based on accounting earnings-related numbers. The last three items are most commonly used to evaluate business-unit performance. VCB uses a mix of financial performance measures in its performance evaluations. Executives are evaluated on residual income, and branch managers are evaluated on net interest margin, return on assets and revenue growth. VCB does not evaluate or provide incentives based on the bank's share price because the bank feels that (1) the share price normally is not directly controllable by managers and (2) basing incentives on share price might cause undesirable consequences if managers tried to manipulate the share price. VCB believes that share price performance will follow financial performance.

Non-financial performance: operational, organizational, social and environmental factors

Evidence indicates that the use of non-financial measures of performance in incentive plans is increasing. Of course, organizations have used non-financial measures for managing operations for many years, but including them in incentive plans is an important development.

Perhaps the greatest advantages of adding non-financial measures to the incentive system are (1) focus on the leading indicators of profit and (2) recognition of the time lags between non-financial and financial performance. Incentives based on non-financial performance direct employees' attention to leading activities more effectively than do indirect incentives based on lagging financial performance alone. Although employees might know that poor quality can surface later as lower profits, for example, the time lag and lack of direct effect can lower the belief that their quality-related actions affect performance. Value Commercial Bank evaluates non-financial performance for compensation, although it does so subjectively.

As with all aspects of incentive plans, however, non-financial performance measures have costs as well as benefits. Costs of including non-financial measures in incentive plans include these:

- Increased cost of performance measurement and supporting information systems.
- Increased cost of reporting and verifying the validity of performance measures.
- Difficulty in determining the proper balance between financial and non-financial measures.
- Danger of 'information overload' from too many measures causing lack of focus on overall performance.
- Increased opportunities for disputes over the validity of performance measures.
- Increased opportunities for manipulating formula-based incentive plans that include multiple measures.

If adding non-financial measures adds problems, why not use financial performance observed over a period of time long enough to capture the effects of non-financial performance?[16] One answer might be that non-financial measures can add value in excess of their costs. Another might be that although competition for managerial talent requires frequent evaluation and payment of compensation, financial performance cannot be matched to efforts in a timely manner. These answers might explain why many organizations have added non-financial performance measures to their incentive systems. For example, **McDonald's** evaluates and compensates many managers on non-financial performance such as customer and employee satisfaction, social responsibility and adoption of technology. The measures to use and the ways to include them in performance-based incentive plans are some of the greatest challenges of incentive system design, and more research is needed in this area.

16.3 Cost Management in Practice

Use of Non-financial Measures of Performance

Professors Ittner and Larcker of the **Wharton School of Business** have reviewed the findings of many international surveys, cases and field studies investigating firms' uses of non-financial measures of performance for both management activities and incentive compensation. They report that as many as 36 per cent of firms explicitly include non-financial measures in executive incentive plans. On average, 37 per cent of the total evaluation was based on these non-financial measures. Firms that use non-financial measures in their incentive plans tend to be more innovative, to have adopted TQM, to have long product-development cycles, to have been more subject to regulation, and to have had 'noisier' financial performance. Thus, factors such as innovativeness and adoption of TQM apparently affect the use of non-financial measures of performance in incentive plans.

Non-financial measures of performance used most commonly in incentive plans include customer satisfaction, productivity, employee performance, community/environmental performance and innovation. But Ittner and Larcker point out that very little objective research reflects whether using these measures in incentive plans results in better *long-term* financial performance. At this point, firms might be reluctant to disclose that they have found successful packages of measures; alternatively, they might include these measures based on the logic of linkages among leading and lagging indicators of performance rather than hard evidence.

Source: Ittner and Larcker (1998b).

Narrow or Broad Responsibility of Performance

An organization can define performance narrowly or broadly. Should a manager's rewards depend on the performance of that individual, of the manager's division, or of the company as a whole? For example, should VCB evaluate its branch managers based on their performance on a set of personal goals, the performance of the manager's branch bank, or the performance of the bank as a whole? Basing compensation on only the performance of the company as a whole gives managers incentives to co-operate, share information, and consider the impact of their actions on the entire organization. This is especially important in large companies whose managers might not see much relationship between their actions and the company's performance.

Incentives work best, however, when individuals see a strong link between their actions and performance results. Moving from incentives based on individual performance to company-wide performance lessens an individual's influence on the performance measure. Many companies reward division managers for both business-unit and company-wide performance, seeking a balance that is appropriate for their situations. VCB rewards *executives* based on overall bank performance. The bank strives to create incentives for co-operation among *branch managers* by linking some of their rewards to the bank's overall economic performance.

Current or Deferred Rewards

Employees prefer rewards sooner than later, but the organization often could benefit from waiting. Rewards for performance can be given now based on current performance or later on sustained performance. Current compensation rewards can be in the form of cash or shares that can be cashed immediately or soon after the award. For example, a manager might be rewarded quickly with a cash bonus if the residual income increases 10 per cent by the end of the year or later on a deferred basis if the residual income increases by an average of 10 per cent per year over the next three years. Thus, the company defers any rewards for the first and second years' performance until after the third year. An alternative is to grant the rewards now but restrict their payment until a future date. These deferred rewards can be cash or shares as well as share options. We defer coverage of shares and option rewards to the next section.

Current rewards

Current rewards have the obvious advantage of being closely linked to current performance. Because uncertainty related to current rewards is low, current rewards should provide strong motivation to improve current performance. The disadvantage of current rewards is that they can induce employees to manipulate the performance measures without concern for future performance or with the expectation of 'cashing out' and leaving the organization before undesirable consequences occur.

Deferred rewards

Advantages of deferred rewards based on sustained performance are that (1) good managers might have incentives to stay with the company (e.g., 'golden handcuffs') and (2) managers have incentives to focus attention on long-term performance. Many commentators argue that managers, particularly in the United States, are too short-term oriented. They take actions now that look good in the short term but are detrimental in the long term. A good example is the failure of some companies to invest in new technology. This 'myopic' view of performance keeps earnings high in the short term by avoiding write-offs or high depreciation expenses but can be detrimental in the long term. Switching to deferred rewards based on sustained financial performance can capture the lagged effects of good or poor non-financial performance and create incentives to make needed improvements.

One mechanism to create deferred incentives is the **bonus bank**. Every year bonuses are added to the bonus bank account, and every year the manager receives part of the total balance that has accumulated in that account. The bonus bank makes it possible to have negative rewards (penalties) in a particular year, which reduces the balance in the bonus bank. When negative rewards are possible, it is possible to create a stronger relationship between the organization's results and the manager's reward. Managers face a symmetric risk compared to shareholders and other stakeholders. If they do well, they get a bonus, but if they destroy shareholder value and negatively affect other stakeholders, they don't lose anything – they just don't get a bonus. In a bonus bank, however, they can actually lose part of their accumulated bonus in the bonus bank account. Note that the balance won't become negative, only the *change of the balance* can be negative. Note also that the manager could still receive a reward based on what has been accumulated in all previous years, because the bonus bank mechanism smooths the payment of bonuses. For example: there is €400,000 in the bonus bank, this year's bonus is –€40,000, so the new balance becomes €360,000. Every year the manager receives 25 per cent of the bonus bank ending balance, so €90,000 in this year. Now suppose this year's results would have been very good and the manager received a bonus of €100,000. The balance would have risen to €500,000 and the manager would receive 25 per cent of that, which is €125,000. For example, the Swiss bank **UBS** has adopted a bonus bank.

A disadvantage of a deferred reward is that managers might view it as coming too far in the future to be motivational. Giving a manager a reward in shares to be paid five years from now is less attractive than giving a payment at the end of the current year. And when results are bad and the bonus bank balance is reduced, then it becomes a disincentive to stay at the company. More generally, a disadvantage of the bonus bank is that it increases the risk for the manager because of the possibility of negative rewards, which could lead to higher expected rewards. The risk-return relationship also works for managerial rewards.

VCB uses a combination of current and deferred awards for top managers but primarily pays current awards for lower-level managers and their subordinates. When making deferred awards to executives, the bank defers the award for three years. This time period appears to be sufficiently long (1) to capture lagged effects of actions and (2) to motivate the managers to think about the future but (3) is not so far in the future that incentive effects of the managers themselves are lost.

Salary, Bonus or Share Rewards

Most management incentive plans include multiple forms of reward, including salary, bonus, shares, share appreciation rights and share options. Organizations design the reward package to address the motivational issues raised earlier in the chapter, within shareholder and taxation guidelines, and many have found that a combination of rewards is more effective than a single form of reward. Most large organizations have compensation committees that design the mix of rewards to reflect the company's compensation philosophy. Some organizations stress salary; others stress performance-based compensation to provide more motivation. For example, VCB states the following:

One of the essential elements of the Bank's compensation policy is to align the interests of the CEO, executive officers, and key employees with the interests of shareholders. . . . The total compensation package is designed to provide a significant percentage of executive compensation from programs such as the bonus plan and share-based long-term incentive programs, which link executive rewards to long-term shareholder rewards.

Salary

Nearly all management employees work in exchange for some salary that is more or less guaranteed. Occasionally, an executive works without salary, but this usually is in exchange for shares or other deferred rewards or as a charitable contribution to a non-profit organization. The typical salary issues are (1) the level of salary and (2) the proportion of compensation that is salary versus performance-based reward. Salary levels often are benchmarked with the organization's industry and the level of responsibility within the organization. At extremes, a manager receives 100 per cent of his compensation from salary, or another manager receives 100 per cent of her compensation based on performance. What difference does the proportion of salary make?

At 100 per cent of compensation, a salary insulates an employee from most risks, so one might think that the employee will be inclined to make risky decisions. In reality, however, such compensation is more likely to attract employees who are not inclined to take risks. Furthermore, fixed compensation can turn away employees who recognize that their compensation has no upside potential regardless of their effort or ability to manage. Because most shareholders can diversify their investments, they prefer that managers take some risks, but they must compensate them for doing so.

One way to motivate risk taking is to shift some compensation from salary and make it depend on performance that is affected by managers' risky decisions. Making all compensation based on performance might not be desirable, however, because, as mentioned earlier, this places all of the risk on managers. The organization might attract only extreme risk takers or those who demand a very large expected reward in exchange for the risk they must bear. Most organizations find a balance between guaranteed salary and performance-based compensation that attracts, retains and motivates employees to make good decisions.

Cash bonuses

Cash bonus awards have the advantage of being liquid and highly attractive because the reward is immediate and unconstrained. Companies usually make cash bonus awards based on the achievement of performance objectives. Often these bonuses have a floor or lower threshold of performance (e.g., a minimum return on investment) before the employee earns any bonus. Many cash bonus incentives also have a ceiling or an upper threshold beyond which no more bonuses can be earned. Much interesting research has focused on the motivational properties of these awards and the incentives they generate to manipulate financial measures of performance.[17]

Share awards

Share awards, in contrast to cash bonuses, might not be redeemable for cash until some time in the future. Some companies have an unwritten rule that managers cannot sell company shares until they leave the firm or retire. Share awards that cannot be immediately sold, while perhaps not as attractive as an equivalent amount of cash, can align the interests of managers with those of shareholders better than cash awards can. For this reason, top-executive compensation often is composed more heavily of shares than of cash bonus or salary.

Share appreciation rights

Share appreciation rights (SARs) confer bonuses to employees based on increases in share prices for a predetermined number of shares. For example, suppose you have been granted 10 SARs and the share price increased €25. Your bonus would be equal to $10 \times €25 = €250$. This incentive combines the immediacy of a cash bonus with the long-term benefit to owners of increases in share prices.

Share options

Share options give an individual the right to purchase a certain number of shares at a specified price over a specified time period. These provide strong incentives for managers to increase share value over the long run.[18] A share option has a lower monetary value than a share, so a company might create more incentive to increase share prices by awarding share options than simply awarding the same value and fewer shares. Managers who receive large awards of share options have much to gain from increases in share prices. This does not mean that managers lose nothing if the share price declines, however, because the value of the options decline and managers suffer the opportunity cost of not increasing share value (or earning an alternative cash bonus). Awards of share options, therefore, have the motivational impact of share grants but at a lower cost to the company. Despite the benefits of share options, their use has declined in the years after the financial bubble burst in 2000 and the financial crisis in 2008.

In addition, sufficient concern now exists that share-option awards give managers too much incentive to manipulate share prices in the short run rather than build the company for the long term. A number of top US executives have tried recently to illegally manipulate share prices but have found that getting caught means losing their reputation, wealth and, in some cases, freedom. Perhaps when a climate of trust has been earned and then returns, firms will again base more compensation on share options. Until then, we should expect more share awards and bonuses based on accounting and operating performance.

VCB rewards its branch managers with cash bonuses for meeting revenue growth, net interest margin, and return on net asset objectives. Executives also earn shares based on meeting overall residual income objectives. The proportions of executive compensation value have averaged 40 per cent salary, 30 per cent cash bonus, and 30 per cent shares. At present, VCB does not extend significant long-term compensation to lower-level managers. Most of their compensation is salary and bonus based.

16.3 Research Insight

International Use of Subjective Evaluations

Objective performance evaluations are those based on performance measures that are compared to a preset performance target, such as a budget. Subjective evaluations, in contrast, are based on the personal judgements of the evaluators. The evaluators may or may not take quantitative performance indicators into consideration when making their evaluative judgements. Subjective performance evaluations are commonly used, and Gibbs et al. used information from automobile dealers in the US to investigate why this is so. The overall idea is that subjective performance evaluations are used to take into account important information that cannot really be incorporated in the formal system or that becomes available after the formal system is set.

More specifically: the results supported that subjective evaluations are used to reward managers for relevant things they did that could not easily be quantified in objective, formula-based systems. For example, an outstanding high quality of repairs and timeliness of service could be included and rewarded. Furthermore, subjective evaluations were used to reduce the problem that objective, formula-based systems can stimulate excessive short-term behaviour. For example, it was found that dealerships that invest more in training (which can be seen as an indication that they invested more for the long-run health of the dealership) also used more subjective evaluations. Moreover, subjective evaluations were used to deter managers from manipulating the numbers. It was clear for managers that if such manipulation would be detected, their evaluation would be effected, even if the numbers would look good. Finally, subjective evaluations helped to reduce risks for the managers when events outside their control would destroy their measured performance. For example, a major price cut by a competitor is something that the dealership needs to deal with as best as possible, but the resulting negative consequences for the dealership's profit is largely outside the control of the manager.

Interestingly, in a study of dealerships in the Netherlands, researchers found very different results. The Dutch firms used incentive compensation for their managers less often, in any form. Where they did offer incentive compensation, the payouts were smaller and their bonus awards were less often based on profit measures of performance. In cases where the Dutch firms did use incentive compensation, the performance-reward functions were more complex.

Sources: Gibbs et al. (2004, 2005); and Jansen et al. (2009).

Incentive Plans in Non-profit Organizations

Non-profit organizations range from small, informal organizations such as sports clubs, student organizations, and parent groups supporting sports and music activities to large, well-established organizations such as the American organization **United Way** (liveunited.org), the **International Committee of the Red Cross** (www.icrc.org), **Médecins Sans Frontières** (www.msf.org), most universities, and government departments and agencies, such as the Danish **Post Danmark** (www.postdanmark.dk), the German **Bundesministerium für Verkehr, Bau und Stadtentwicklung** (www.bmvbs.de) (the department of transportation), and the **Department of Sustainability, Environment, Water, Population and Communities** (www.environment.gov.au) in Australia. By definition, a *non-profit organization* has something other than earning a profit as its primary goal. Thus, effective non-profit incentive systems primarily should create incentives for managers to perform well on non-financial dimensions.[19]

Although non-profits do not try to maximize profits, they must provide services in a cost-effective manner. Non-profits compete for scarce funds and non-monetary support and must be able to show donors and supporters that their contributions are being used effectively. Organizations such as **Charity Navigator** (www.charitynavigator.org) analyse the financial health of a large number of charities in the US. Their aim is to make the evaluations easy to understand and available to the public free of charge, and thus to 'advance a more efficient and responsive philanthropic marketplace'. Thus, a non-profit's concern for creating value at lowest cost can be similar to that of a profit-seeking firm. Non-profit organizations also must demonstrate proper accountability for the use of funds and manage their operations and revenues to ensure that they break even.

Despite differences between for-profit and non-profit organizations, non-profits increasingly use features of executive incentive plans developed in the private sector. These organizations also compete for top management talent and must align executives' interests with those of the organizations. Many non-profit organizations award performance bonuses up to 10 per cent of salary. Some non-profit hospitals offer performance bonuses based on cost savings, health care improvements and other factors. Many organizations, however, decline to develop incentives to retain management talent. It is a difficult dilemma, because they could find that they must pay much more to replace talent lost to the private sector or more aggressive non-profits. For example, the British **BBC** is funded by public money through licence fees, and the organization sells programmes through its commercial arm BBC Worldwide. There is much debate about disclosing and potentially capping salaries. Proponents say that there are many talented people who want to work for a renowned and prestigious organization such as the BBC for an ordinary salary. But opponents say that the BBC will lose heavily against competition from commercial UK stations such as **ITV** if it cannot offer big salaries to star presenters, reporters and senior managers.

Incentive plans also can create difficulties for non-profits. For example, **Harrisburg Hospital** in Pennsylvania, US, lost its non-profit, tax-exempt status in part because the state's courts ruled that its executive compensation plan, which gave cash bonuses for return on equity and revenue performance, clearly was designed to promote the hospital's bottom line. The court observed that, although incentive plans were not contrary to the notion of a non-profit organization, this incentive plan aligned managers' interests more with earning profits than providing charitable health care services. The incentive plan was convincing evidence that the hospital had a strong profit motive.[20]

Ethical Aspects of Incentives and Compensation

LO 7
Discuss ethical issues of incentive systems.

Few people object to the concept and practice of pay for performance. Most people, however, object when pay is inconsistent with performance. For decades, compensation experts have observed that executive pay often rises even in companies whose operating or share price performance has dropped. Add extensive downsizing to this mismatch of pay and performance, and many see high executive pay as unethical and unfair to both shareholders and employees whose returns and pay have decreased. The mismatch of executive pay and firm performance has been widely observed in diverse organizations such as energy firms, telecommunications, charities, investment funds and health care.

How can a mismatch between pay and performance persist? In some cases, the mismatch is the result of poorly designed incentive systems that generate high rewards even when shareholders lose money.[21] In other cases, critics blame rampant CEO greed and lack of oversight by shareholders' representatives on boards of directors.[22] Others like Graef Crystal cite lack of required disclosures and widespread corporate structures that leave compensation decisions in the hands of the CEOs themselves, who cannot be trusted to report performance fairly or be objective critics of their own performance and value to the firm.[23]

Many organizations have restructured their incentive systems to better match pay and performance. Some firms restructured their systems voluntarily, but many others did so in response to the Sarbanes–Oxley Act of 2002.[24] Furthermore, incidents, public outcry and the financial crisis have led to bonuses being lowered or suspended. **BP** lowered bonuses for executives after the oil spill in the Mexican Gulf. **Commerzbank AG**, Germany's second-largest bank, did not pay investment bankers bonuses for 2008 and 2009 when the company posted significant losses. Banker pay became contentious after the financial crisis forced governments to use taxpayer money to support many banks, including Commerzbank and the British **RBS**. However, some other banks in similar situations at the time did pay bonuses. The CEO of Dutch bank **ING** gave up a bonus after public protest and threats of a customer boycott of the bailed-out bank. The CEO of **Dublin Airport Authority** in Ireland rejected a performance-related bonus in light of the country's prevailing national economic circumstances. Sometimes shareholders raise objections, such as in the case of the British-Dutch company **Shell** when the company intended to award millions of pounds of shares to executives despite missing performance targets that should have reduced the payout to zero. It was the second biggest rebellion seen at a FTSE 100 company.

It is likely that regulatory actions will more closely align executive pay and performance, but in the end it is difficult to mandate integrity or ethical behaviour. The least costly economic system would be based on trust and integrity; however, that ideal state is contrary to human nature. The costs of aligning incentives and monitoring behaviour are high, but the opportunity cost of allowing unethical behaviour is higher. Unethical behaviour will be a continuing problem, but the return of investors to the stock market might be a sign of increasing trust in improved pay for performance incentive systems.

16.2 You're the Decision Maker

Designing Incentive Systems

You are a consultant advising VCB about its incentive systems for lower-level managers and employees. Your interviews with branch and department managers inform you that they are satisfied with the new balanced scorecard performance measurement system (see Exhibit 16.6) but believe that they are not rewarded for performing well. Non-management employees likewise enjoy their jobs but do not believe that they have real incentives to work harder or better. At the end of each year, most branch and department managers and employees receive annual salary increases between 4 per cent and 6 per cent. Branch managers also earn bonuses up to 10 per cent of their salary for meeting sales growth and return on asset objectives. Promotions appear to be based on seniority; the longer a person is in a job, the better the person's chances for promotion. Do the interview responses signal a potential problem? If so, what do you think that VCB should do?

(Solution begins on page 835.)

Summary of VCB's Incentive System

Incentive system designers should consider each element of Exhibit 16.7 to ensure that the plan addresses all alternative choices. To sum, VCB seeks to attract, motivate and retain competent employees and to align their interests with shareholders' long-term interests. The bank's incentive system has the following features:

- *Absolute or relative performance.* VCB uses both forms of performance: Residual income and environmental performance are compared to absolute objectives; evaluations of revenue growth, net interest margin and return on assets are based on relative performance of similar business units.

- *Formula-based or subjective performance.* VCB also uses both formula and subjective evaluations. Residual income, net interest margin and return-on-asset incentives for branch managers are formula based, but the bank subjectively evaluates other areas of performance that are measured less reliably (e.g., the value of employee suggestions).
- *Financial or non-financial performance.* As mentioned, VCB uses only financial performance measures in its formula-based incentive plans. The bank understands the value of its non-financial performance for long-term success, but quality of measurement is an issue. If the bank could reliably measure key non-financial performance from its balanced scorecard, it would formally include some of them in its formula-based incentives. Until then, VCB will continue to evaluate non-financial performance subjectively. Top candidates for inclusion in the incentive formula include employee satisfaction, productivity and customer satisfaction because they are based on reliable instruments and can be audited.
- *Narrow or broad responsibility of performance.* VCB evaluates its executives on bankwide performance but its branch managers primarily on branch performance, with a relatively small emphasis on bankwide performance.
- *Current or deferred rewards.* VCB executives receive both current and deferred rewards; lower-level managers receive mostly current rewards.
- *Salary or bonus rewards.* All VCB employees receive a salary, but executives receive most of their compensation from bonus or share rewards. Currently, lower-level managers receive most compensation from salaries, and lower-level employees receive all compensation from salaries.

Although VCB has put much effort into designing its incentive plans, every plan can be improved. The bank's board of directors annually reviews it in light of recent developments and changes in competitive pressures and recommends improvement. Current recommendations include refining some non-financial performance measures for inclusion in the bank's incentive formulas. The bank's president and CEO also serves on the boards of directors of several charitable, non-profit organizations and has been urging their boards to adopt features of the incentive plans of VCB and other successful companies.

Balanced Scorecard-based Incentives at VCB

If the performance measures in Exhibit 16.5 are important to VCB's success, employees should take actions to improve each of them and they should be in the scorecard. The issue is whether employees will do that without explicit incentives attached to each measure. Perhaps, if employees believe the story that a balanced scorecard tells, as discussed earlier, they will manage their activities to improve the measures with or without explicit incentives.

Extending a balanced scorecard to an evaluation and incentive system involves two additional steps:

- Weighting the performance measures
- Tying explicit incentives to measures (individually or in total).

Performance on each measure in the system should have rewards. It does seem likely that no one person or management level should be evaluated on all of the measures, however. A more reasonable approach is to assign responsibility and incentives for the various measures to persons who can best affect or control outcomes. Some organizations also assign overall scorecard incentives to managers at higher levels and more detailed measures and incentives to subordinates who are working to improve the measures they directly control.

Effective incentive systems demand much of the underlying performance measures. These systems require, for example, reliable, objective and verifiable performance measures and clear guidance for evaluating trade-offs. However, not all performance measures on the balanced scorecard may have such solid measurement properties. Remember that the primary purpose of a balanced scorecard is to communicate and implement strategy, not to determine bonuses for managers. Therefore, some companies experienced significant internal conflict when they began to use a balanced scorecard as an incentive device. In a few cases, these companies have dispensed with a balanced scorecard altogether, but in others the conflict has led to compromises and improvements in performance measures and internal auditing procedures.

Because VCB's balanced scorecard had no major surprises and most employees can see the rationale behind each scorecard area and its measures, almost no debate about the scorecard itself occurred. Employees at all levels understand that the scorecard is a balanced set of measures that reflects the bank's strategy to grow and prosper. Bank employees report that they understand why and how their efforts can improve the bank's financial performance. This was a major improvement in the communication of the bank's strategy and led employees to focus on improving the measures that they can influence.

Although none of the performance measures was perfect, top management believed that using them for performance evaluation reinforces the desired behaviour and generates superior profitability. However, many employees express concern about the use of the scorecard as a formula-based evaluation and incentive system because they believe that some measures are too subjective or capable of manipulation. They wonder how they should act when faced with trade-offs between measures that might conflict (e.g., reducing costs or improving customer satisfaction) and whether they will be penalized for making trade-offs. Because VCB's employees trust top management and are comfortable with some subjective evaluations, the bank has been able to co-ordinate its formula-based and subjective evaluations (as discussed earlier) with the use of a balanced scorecard for communication, motivation and evaluation. As in nearly all organizations, VCB's balanced scorecard and incentive system continue to evolve and improve.

Chapter Summary

Leading indicators of performance are early measures of outcomes of activities that allow organizations to predict problems, identify opportunities and prevent mistakes. Leading indicators predict organizational outcomes such as future sales and profit. Employees use leading indicators to manage activities and processes to ensure favourable final outcomes. Employees act to make improvements based on signals from leading indicators rather than wait to see whether final outcomes are favourable or unfavourable before making improvements or corrections.

Organizations use performance measures of (1) organizational learning and growth, (2) business and production processes, and (3) customers as leading indicators of (4) financial performance.

A balanced scorecard or a tableau de bord is a model of cause-and-effect relations among leading and lagging indicators of performance. It is useful for measuring and communicating the effects of activities on organizational performance. A balanced scorecard shows the cause and effect among these four areas of performance. One can think plausibly of performing well on learning and growth as leading to improved business processes and improved customer satisfaction and loyalty, which leads to improved financial performance. Whenever possible, firms should use data to verify their scorecard models and to test which causal links actually exist. Various linkages exist among the four areas, but the point is that performing well on the three leading (usually non-financial) areas should lead to improved financial performance and that financial performance lags non-financial performance. If it is possible to quantify these cause-and-effect relationships, a balanced scorecard can be a valuable financial planning model.

The two key elements of an incentive system are the *measure(s) of performance* and the *method(s) of compensation*. Managers make many choices regarding incentive systems. These choices regarding performance evaluation include whether to rely on measures of current or future performance, whether to use division or company-wide performance measures, whether to base performance on accounting results or share performance, and whether to use absolute or relative performance evaluation. Furthermore, these choices include whether to base rewards on a subjective evaluation or a fixed formula and whether to reward good performance with cash, shares or prizes. The objective of designing incentive plans is to select a package of performance measures and rewards that will attract, motivate and retain good employees and align their interests with those of the organization.

Key Terms

For each term's definition, refer to the indicated page, or turn to the glossary at the end of the text.

Term	Page	Term	Page
absolute performance evaluation,	808	lagging indicator,	789
balanced scorecard,	788	leading indicator,	788
benchmarking,	790	pay for performance,	805
bonus bank,	814	performance evaluation formula,	810
customer retention (or loyalty),	796	relative performance evaluation,	809
customer value,	795	share appreciation rights (SARs),	815
employee capabilities,	792	share options,	816
expectancy theory,	807	strategy map,	789
extrinsic rewards,	807	subjective performance evaluation,	811
incentive system,	788, 805	tableau de bord,	790
intrinsic rewards,	807		

*Review Questions are mostly written at a **basic** level; Critical Analysis questions and Exercises are **intermediate**, and Problems and Cases are **advanced**.*

Review Questions

16.1 Review and define each of the chapter's key terms.

16.2 What is the difference between a *leading* and a *lagging* indicator of performance?

16.3 Is financial performance important to all types of organizations, even non-profits? Explain.

16.4 Explain how an increase in employee capabilities can flow through an organization and how the effects are reflected in a balanced scorecard.

16.5 Why is 'pay for performance' the foundation of incentive systems?

16.6 What are the key elements of an incentive system?

16.7 Explain how an incentive system's design might create disincentives to desired behaviour.

16.8 Contrast absolute and relative performance evaluations.

16.9 What are the advantages and disadvantages of formula-based versus subjective performance evaluations?

16.10 What is the possible relation between a balanced scorecard and the use of financial and non-financial measures of performance?

16.11 What are the advantages and disadvantages of making all rewards immediate and of deferring them?

16.12 What are the different incentive effects of salary, cash bonus, shares, and share options?

16.13 What is an intrinsic reward? How is an intrinsic reward different than an extrinsic reward? Are both necessary?

16.14 How can a bonus bank improve the pay-for-performance relationship?

16.15 What is the disadvantage of adopting a bonus bank?

Critical Analysis

16.16 The chief operating officer of a non-profit organization states, 'It's all very well for a company like Westside to implement a balanced scorecard. It has measures in all four areas of the scorecard and has to satisfy shareholders. Without a profit measure or motive in the last area of the scorecard, I just don't see how or why we should expend the effort to build a partial balanced scorecard.' How do you answer this observation?

16.17 A business executive says, 'The financial area of a balanced scorecard indicates how the organization adds value to shareholders. I am involved with two organizations; a small business that is a partnership with no shareholders, and a church that has no shareholders. A balanced scorecard makes a lot of sense to me, but the financial area is clearly irrelevant for these two organizations.' How do you respond to this statement?

16.18 Respond to the following statement: 'Most measures of performance, such as profits and product costs, are useless for management decision making because they measure what has happened, not what will happen.'

16.19 Until recently the CEO of **Xerox Corporation** prominently stated in his letter to the company's annual reports that Xerox always strives to improve customer satisfaction. Xerox no longer makes this claim so prominently. Is it possible to create too much customer satisfaction? Explain.

16.20 Customers' perceptions of value can differ across cultures. Many people believe that US-based companies are ignorant or arrogant when it comes to appreciating other cultures. Do you think this is true? What are the possible costs of lack of appreciation of other cultures? How can you prepare yourself to contribute value to an organization by appreciating other cultures?

16.21 Some companies formally advertise that its employees are its most important assets. If that is true, why does the balance sheet of these companies not have a category of assets for employees?

16.22 'It is a bigger mistake to develop an unreliable balanced scorecard than never to build one at all.' Do you agree with this statement? Why or why not?

16.23 The manager of an organization is having trouble getting employees to perform adequate work for the organization's benefit. 'I pay them a good salary,' says the manager, 'and I give them big pay increases when I feel generous. I just can't figure out why they won't work harder. Maybe it's this generation of people. You know, when I was a young worker . . .' At this point, your brain shuts down. Using the principles of expectancy theory, explain why the employees might not be working as desired.

16.24 Shauna Dormino is taking a job in a non-profit organization, Freedom from Hunger. Anisa Morenez is taking a job at IBM. The women are equally qualified, each will do the same type of work, and each will put in the same number of hours each week, yet Dormino's job pays $20,000 less than Morenez's job, has fewer benefits, and offers less opportunity for advancement. Why might Dormino take such a job?

16.25 You are offered an executive position at a small high-technology company. The salary is considerably lower than your current salary, but after one year, you will be eligible for many share options. Your only performance measure will be the company's share price. What are the advantages and disadvantages of this incentive plan to you and to the company?

16.26 You are offered the general manager position at a large, mostly autonomous division of a very large company. The company is market driven and has 20 similar divisions in different industries. The division you are offered has performed poorly in the past, but it is in an industry with high profit potential. Describe elements of an incentive plan that induces you to take this job and that the company might accept.

16.27 You are the chair of the board of directors of a large regional charitable organization that has been recognized nationally for outstanding public service. It has just lost its CEO to a profit-seeking firm poised for its initial public offering of shares. You must convene the board to recruit a new CEO and are concerned about attracting, motivating, and retaining a highly competent executive. What major factors should you consider when designing an incentive plan for this executive?

Exercises

Exercise 16.28 [LO 2] Classify Balanced Scorecard Measures

Match each of the following performance measures to one or more of the four areas of a balanced scorecard. Note that a performance measure can relate to more than one area.

Performance measures	Balanced scorecard areas
1. Employee productivity	**a.** Organizational learning and growth
2. Employee satisfaction	**b.** Business and production process efficiency
3. Return on assets	**c.** Customer value
4. Customer satisfaction	**d.** Financial performance
5. Employee turnover	
6. On-time delivery performance from suppliers	
7. Percentage of customers who are repeat customers	
8. On-time delivery performance to customers	
9. Product quality	

Exercise 16.29 [LO 2] Classify Balanced Scorecard Measures

Match each of the following performance measures to one or more of the four areas of a balanced scorecard. Note that a performance measure can relate to more than one area.

Performance measures	Balanced scorecard areas
1. Throughput time	**a.** Organizational learning and growth
2. Return on sales	**b.** Business and production process efficiency
3. Customer satisfaction	**c.** Customer performance
4. Percentage of sales dollars invested in employee training	**d.** Financial performance
5. Ratings of supplier performance	
6. Increase in market share	
7. Employee retention	
8. On-time delivery performance to customers	
9. Product quality	

Exercise 16.30 [LO 1] Match Leading and Lagging Indicators

Arrange the following measures in an order that reflects their possible use as leading or lagging indicators of performance. Note that a measure of performance can itself be a leading indicator of later performance.

Customer satisfaction	Anticipation of customer needs
Acquisition of new customers	Product quality
On-time deliveries	Process efficiency
Customer retention	Employee satisfaction
Customer profitability	Employee skills
Product innovations	Compliance with environmental regulations
Market share	Supplier reliability and quality
Overall profitability	

Exercise 16.31 [LO 2] Describe Measures of Organizational Learning and Growth

Perform an Internet search for a comprehensive article on a real organization's management of organizational learning and growth. Prepare a five-minute presentation (with transparencies or PowerPoint slides) of your findings and how they relate to the chapter's coverage of this topic.

Exercise 16.32 [LO 2] Management of Customer Satisfaction

Review the annual reports for one company from each of the following industries: a tyre manufacturer, an apparel retailer and an airline company. Summarize how each of these organizations manages customer satisfaction.

Exercise 16.33 [LO 2] Management of Customer Satisfaction

Review the annual reports for one company from each of the following industries: car manufacturing, coffee and tea, and life insurance. Summarize how each of these organizations manages customer satisfaction.

Exercise 16.34 [LO 2] Describe Balanced Scorecard Measures

Perform an Internet search for a comprehensive article on an actual organization's management of customer satisfaction or cultural differences. Prepare a five-minute presentation (with transparencies or PowerPoint slides) of your findings and how they relate to the chapter's coverage of this topic.

Exercise 16.35 [LO 2] Prepare Customer Satisfaction Measure

Trust Bank conducts regular customer surveys to assess its customer satisfaction, which is measured by averaging responses (from 1 = highly unfavourable to 5 = highly favourable) on five variables that measure customers' satisfaction with the bank's services. Quantify Trust Bank's recent customer satisfaction from the following information. Do you see a pattern in the scores? If so, what does it tell Trust Bank about its customer satisfaction?

	Number of customer responses				
Customer satisfaction variable response	**1**	**2**	**3**	**4**	**5**
Automated bank services meet customer needs	16	25	22	22	15
Trust Bank services are superior to competitors' services	8	17	24	36	15
Employees give prompt service	6	14	22	41	17
Employees are courteous and friendly	7	12	20	38	23
Employees can and do respond to special requests	12	26	20	21	21

Exercise 16.36 [LO 2] Prepare Customer Satisfaction Measure

Montpelier Co. conducts regular customer surveys to assess customer satisfaction with its products and post-sale services, which is measured by averaging responses (from 1 = highly unfavourable to 5 = highly favourable) on five variables that measure customer satisfaction with the company's products. Quantify Montpelier's recent customer satisfaction from the following information. Do you see a pattern in the scores? If so, what does it tell Montpelier about its customer satisfaction?

	Number of customer responses				
Customer satisfaction variable response	**1**	**2**	**3**	**4**	**5**
Montpelier's products are defect free	20	21	22	22	15
Montpelier's products are superior to competitors' products	8	17	24	36	15
Montpelier's products perform reliably	6	14	22	41	17
Montpelier's repair services are prompt	7	12	20	38	23
Montpelier's warranty is superior to competitors' warranty	12	21	20	26	21

Exercise 16.37 [LO 4] Implementation of Balanced Scorecards

In a small group, conduct an Internet search for an article published in the past three years that describes how a real organization successfully designed and implemented its balanced scorecard. Prepare a five-minute presentation (with transparencies or PowerPoint slides) of your findings and how they relate to the chapter's coverage of this topic.

Exercise 16.38 [LO 4] Implementation of Balanced Scorecards

In a small group, conduct an Internet search for an article published in the past three years that describes how an organization *unsuccessfully* designed or implemented its balanced scorecard. Prepare a five-minute presentation of your findings and how they relate to the chapter's coverage of this topic.

Exercise 16.39 [LO 5] Effects of Performance-based Incentive Plans

Wannabe University (WU) is a medium-size public university with 15,000 students and 1,000 faculty members. The university built its national reputation on the excellence of its teaching and interactions with undergraduate students. Because government support of the university has dropped dramatically, the administration has decided that it must now build the university's reputation on research, which will require obtaining research grants to replace the lost government funding. The university proposes to reward each faculty member with a salary increase that is primarily based on the annual number of articles they publish in high-quality journals. Most faculty members and students were attracted to WU, however, because of its focus on teaching and faculty/student interaction.

Required

In a small group, prepare a brief report or visual presentation to WU's central administration that explains the advantages and disadvantages of its incentive plan proposal.

Exercise 16.40 [LO 6] Alternative Features of Incentive Plans

Magnum Manufacturing rewards its key executives exclusively on return on investment (ROI). The vice president of administration suggests to the CEO that Magnum can increase its ROI by outsourcing most of its manufacturing and logistics activities to business partners and suppliers, thereby greatly reducing its asset base. The CFO/treasurer cautions that although this would reduce the company's asset base, such extensive outsourcing would reduce the company's earnings, cash flow and flexibility. The vice president of manufacturing also warns that the company might outsource its competitive advantage as well.

Required

In a small group, prepare a brief report or visual presentation to Magnum Manufacturing's CEO that evaluates the impact of the company's incentive plan on the recommendation to outsource most activities. What trade-offs should the company's executives consider?

Problems

Problem 16.41 [LO 2] Balanced Scorecard Measures

eToys Inc. had been one of the leading Internet-based retailers of children's toys. However, in 2001 it generated a large loss, its share price plummeted and it declared bankruptcy. **KB Toys** purchased the company's website, a warehouse and its customer list for $15 million. The following table summarizes some of the causes of the eToys financial disaster.

Problem	Solution	Lesson
Loss of control over shipping and late shipments resulting from outsourcing some order fulfilment	Opened two additional warehouses, staffed entirely by eToys employees	Provide the best service to customers by keeping the work in-house
Severe seasonal peaks and drops in revenue	Expanded into baby supplies, party goods and hobbies	Diversify while staying true to the target market
Serious doubts on Wall Street that the company can turn a profit and survive	Held first-ever analysts' conference, committed to profitability by a specific target date	Communicate with the people who hold the purse strings even when the news is not positive

Required

a. In your opinion, what types of employees and what specific skills should KB Toys develop and maintain if it is to avoid the fate of eToys?

b. Write a memo outlining the steps you think KB Toys should take, including the development of leading indicators of employee capabilities.

[Adapted from Weintraub, 2002]

Problem 16.42 [LO 3] Benefits and Costs of Balanced Scorecard Measures

As prices for many items have stabilized because of competition, some Internet-based retailers now are competing on the basis of real-time customer service provided by live company representatives. These e-tailers report improved customer satisfaction, traffic and sales growth that they attribute to real-time customer service. Whether this improved customer satisfaction and sales growth has led to improved profitability is unclear. Consider the following actual and predicted data for HomeMarket.com, which is contemplating adding real-time customer service, through online chat technology:

Current actual data:	
Annual sales	3%
Average cost of sales as percentage of sales	€7,200,000
Sales growth percentage	60%
Predictions related to new customer service:	
Increase in customer satisfaction	3%
Software and training costs for new customer service	5%
Ongoing operating costs for new customer service	€240,000
Cost savings from reduction of email response service	€1,650,000
Additional sales growth	€60,000

Required

a. Identify the costs and benefits of HomeMarket.com's proposed customer service operation. (Ignore taxes.)

b. Build a spreadsheet to thoroughly analyse the profitability of the proposed customer service operation.

[Adapted from Mullaney, 1999]

Problem 16.43 [LO 3] Costs and Benefits of Balanced Scorecard Measures

Bonanza Real Estate is considering enrolling in Rush Corp's Customer Value Seminar, a $2,500 per person, week-long intensive seminar that teaches sales staff to build customer satisfaction and loyalty and to sell products more effectively by understanding customers' needs. Rush Corp advertises a money-back guarantee if its sales seminars do not pay for themselves in increased profits so long as new employees are also trained. Bonanza will send its entire sales force of 100 to the seminar in the current year and its new employees each year thereafter for five years. The company normally experiences annual turnover in sales personnel of 20 per cent; its annual cost of capital is 10 per cent.

Required

What equal, annual net benefit must Bonanza Real Estate experience to validate Rush Corp's money-back guarantee over this six-year period? (Ignore taxes.) Prepare a spreadsheet analysis of the costs and benefits of Bonanza's proposed customer service improvements. Be prepared to present your analysis.

Problem 16.44 [LO 3] Costs and Benefits of Balanced Scorecard Measures

Quattro Drive is considering improvements to its warehousing and distribution operations including a €300,000 purchase of robotic machinery with a useful life of five years. Other improvements entail the installation of new computing equipment and software at a start-up cost of €180,000 and €48,000 per year for the next five years. Employee training costs will increase by €30,000 this year and remain at that level for the next five years. The firm's annual cost of capital is 8 per cent.

Required

What equal, annual net benefit must Quattro Drive experience over the current and next five years to justify the process improvements? (Ignore taxes.) Prepare a spreadsheet analysis of the costs and benefits of Quattro's proposed process improvements. Be prepared to present your analysis.

Problem 16.45 [LO 1, 2] Measuring Leading and Lagging Performance

Ruth Chambers, an executive in a large bank, recently attended a conference on management in the banking industry. At the conference, a **Citibank** manager presented a diagram similar to the one in Exhibit 16.2. Chambers is intrigued by the performance measurement problems posed by the diagram. She asks, 'How do you measure the performance of each step in the sequence from increased employee training to better financial results?'

Required

Using a balanced scorecard as a reference point, write a report to Chambers that explains how to measure performance for each step in the sequence from increased employee training to better financial results.

Problem 16.46 [LO 4] Implementation of Balanced Scorecards

Branford San Miguel, the managing partner of the Melbourne office of the consulting firm of PriceCoopersErnst (PCE) developed a diagram similar to the one in Exhibit 16.2 for a client who owns a small manufacturing company. The diagram had the following links:

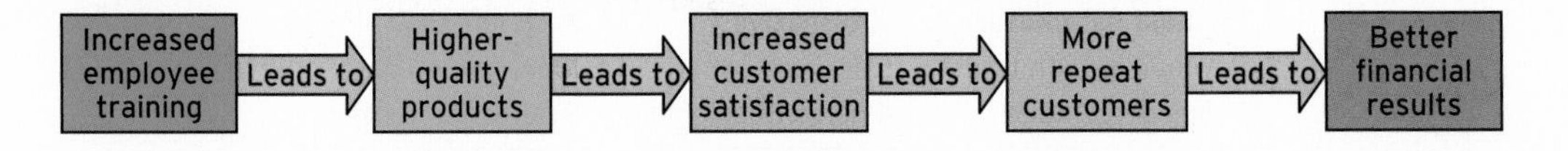

Afterward, San Miguel commented to his fellow consultants, 'I wish I could apply this model to our consulting business. But what we produce is advice, which is not very tangible.'

Required

In a small group and using a balanced scorecard as a reference point, write a report to San Miguel that explains how to implement the model shown in the problem to the consulting business. Be specific in stating how to measure the performance of each step in the sequence from increased employee training to better financial results.

LO 4 Problem 16.47 [LO 4] Implementation of Balanced Scorecards

Sheila Mack, an owner of 42 fast-food franchises, has come to you for advice. She wants to try a balanced scorecard in her stores. She is concerned because some attempts to implement improvements in the past have not been successful. 'I've heard store managers say, "Somebody must have gone to a conference or read some book, because here comes another crackpot idea for us to implement. If we just play along for a while, this too will pass. Then we can get back to business as usual." I don't want store managers to think a balanced scorecard is just another fad. I want them to take it seriously. I want them to give it a fair trial.'

Required

Write a short report to Mack advising her how to implement a balanced scorecard so that her store managers will give it a fair trial.

Problem 16.48 [LO 2] Identify Balanced Scorecard Measures

In a small group, select a real organization of any type for study. Review the organization's website and/or annual report. For each of the four balanced scorecard areas of performance, identify no more than four performance measures. Write a report that states specifically how you plan to measure performance. How might you validate these measures? If possible, you might find it useful to interview a manager in the company that you pick.

Problem 16.49 [LO 3] Leading Indicators of Fraud

One of your suppliers comes to your next meeting in a new Cadillac Escalade, mentions new membership to an exclusive country club, and has started to build a lake house.

Required

Write a memo that explains how to develop leading indicators of problematic supplier relations.

Problem 16.50 [LO 1] Leading and Lagging Indicators of Casualty Losses

Despite conflicting evidence and opinions about the causes of global warming, it is happening. Furthermore, institutional investors and insurers are getting nervous about the environmental disasters that might follow.

Required

Explain how large investors and insurance companies might use leading indicators of global warming to improve investing and managing risks.

Problem 16.51 [LO 6] Analyse Alternative Incentive System Features

Van Coenink Bankiers wants to reward its branch bank managers for exceeding revenue growth targets and is considering alternative incentive formulas that award bonuses as a percentage of salary for each percentage point that actual revenue growth exceeds the target as follows.

Formula parameter	Alternative 1	Alternative 2
Revenue growth target	5%	10%
Bonus percentage	4 percentage points	8 percentage points

Required

a. What are the motivational advantages and disadvantages of each of the four incentive formulas?
b. What are the advantages and disadvantages of the incentive formula approach to motivating revenue growth?

Problem 16.52 [LO 1, 2, 6] Using Performance Measures as Leading Indicators

Van Coenink Bankiers has a criterion to loan only to companies that have an economic value added greater than zero for the past year and for the past three years, on average. Answer the following questions.

a. Build a spreadsheet and solve the following requirement: the bank is considering loaning money to a small company that has the following economic characteristics. Does this company meet the bank's criterion for a positive economic value added?
- Average operating income before tax for the last three years equals €2,000,000 per year.
- The tax rate equals 40 per cent for all three years.
- The appropriate weighted-average cost of capital equals 15 per cent, which is applicable to all three years.
- The average total assets over the past three years equal €8,000,000.
- The average current liabilities over the past three years equal €1,500,000.

b. You work as a loan officer for VCB. A prospective borrower who just graduated from college has come to you for advice. Because her father had been seriously injured in an automobile accident, she is now running the family business, which is a small winery. She wants to borrow money from VCB to buy some wine-processing equipment that will make the company more efficient. The winery had been profitable in the past, but at this point, its economic value added, according to VCB's calculations, is €180,000 for a company that has revenue of €6,000,000 and total assets of

€4,000,000. Ordinarily, the bank will not loan her the money to buy the new equipment. Assume the same cost of capital and tax rates as in part (a). What do you advise?

Problem 16.53 [LO 6, 7] Ethical Impacts of Alternative Incentives

Division managers of Atlantis Ltd have expressed dissatisfaction with the company's division performance measurement system. Division operations are evaluated every quarter by comparing their EVA with the expected EVA identified in the prior year. Division managers claim that many factors are completely out of their control but are included in this comparison, which they say results in an unfair and misleading performance evaluation.

Pressure by top management to reflect increased earnings has often caused division managers to overstate operating income before taxes. In addition, once the EVA target has been set, divisions must live with it; no adjustments for unforeseen events are possible. Frequently, external factors (the economy, competitors' actions and changes in consumer tastes) have not been recognized in the EVA targets that top management supplied to the divisions.

Recognizing these problems, top management agreed to review its procedures. Based on this review, it proposed to change its procedures so division managers have the opportunity to show how they deal with unforeseen events. Top management also agreed to use relative performance evaluation by comparing each division's performance to the performance of other divisions in the same industry and to the performance of outside companies in the same industry.

Required

Write a report to Atlantis top management that explains whether the proposed changes are an improvement over the evaluation of division performance that it now uses. Be sure to address how the company proposes to implement relative performance evaluation.

[CMA adapted]

Problem 16.54 [LO 6, 7] Ethical Impacts of Alternative Incentives

Many critics of business executives complain that they focus on short-term financial results at the expense of investing in the long-term success of their companies. Executives themselves comment that they are constantly pressured to meet annual or even quarterly earnings targets. One executive said, 'If I don't perform well in the short term, I won't be around in the long term.' The critics argue that focusing on the short term means that companies do not invest enough in research and development or new technology, things that might have a negative short-term impact on earnings but might benefit the company in the long run. For purposes of answering these questions, assume that the short term is one year or less, the middle term is one to five years, and the long term is more than five years.

Required

Prepare a written report that addresses the following:

a. Based on library and/or Internet research, indicate whether these organizations appear to be focusing on the short, middle, or the long term: **Toys 'R' Us** (toys), **Cisco** (Internet hardware and software), and **United Way** (charitable non-profit).

b. What is your recommendation for the design of an incentive plan that helps the top executives in requirement (a) to make long-term decisions?

Cases

Case 16.55 [LO 2-4] Implementation of Balanced Scorecard Measures

'I am really confused,' sighed Brian Allen, the CFO of a newly formed biotechnology firm. 'I think we need to build a balanced scorecard to guide our decision making and to help us see whether we are meeting our goals, but everything I have read about balanced scorecards makes me wonder whether we, as a small company, can really build one. I don't think we can afford to waste the time if we can't do it.

'Here's an article in *Fortune* that implies that a balanced scorecard is essential, but professors and businesses using scorecards can't agree whether the relationships must be quantified or not. Professor Shank said great companies 'don't talk profits, they talk key drivers [leading indicators].' He seems to be saying that managing the lead indicators will lead to improved profits but that you don't necessarily need a quantified relationship to know that. On the other hand, Professor Selden says in the article that you have to begin with financial measurements; otherwise, how can you be sure that doing more of something really will add value? And the example companies are all large and well established, like **Shell Oil, Motorola** and **Analog Devices**. If everything has to be quantified, we won't be able to build a useful balanced scorecard. After all, we have existed as a company for only two years, and how much data can we have?'

You reply, 'I've just seen another article by Professor Chow that indicates even small companies can use a balanced scorecard. From the examples in this article, I'm not sure that you have to be able to quantify scorecard relationships to build a useful scorecard. Look at this scorecard for another biotechnology company. I imagine that its information needs must be similar to yours, Brian.'

Refer to the goals and objectives in the following example scorecard.

Example scorecard

Objectives	Measures
Goal: Increase customer value	
New products	Percentage of sales from new products
Early purchase of seasonal products	Percentage of sales that are early purchases
Accurate invoices	Percentage of error-free invoices
Early payment	Percentage of customers that pay early
Product quality	Product performance vs. industry standards
Customer satisfaction	Customer-satisfaction surveys
Goal: Improve business and production Process efficiency	
Low-cost producer	Product cost vs. competitors' product cost
Inventory reduction	Inventory as a percentage of sales
New products	Number of new product introductions
Goal: Leading by innovation	
New active ingredients	Number of new ingredients
Proprietary products and processes	Number of patents
Goal: Financial performance	
Growth	Percentage increase in revenue
Profitability	Return on equity; earnings per share
Industry leadership	Market share

Required

Write a report in which you do the following:

a. Expand on 'your' comment; do balanced scorecard relationships need to be quantified to be useful? Explain.

b. Comment on the completeness of the example scorecard. Can you suggest additions and/or deletions from the objectives and measures? If possible, review websites or annual reports of several biotechnology companies (e.g., **Amgen, Genentech** or other companies that you might find from an Internet search of the keyword 'biotechnology'), and read the letter from the president or the management discussion and analysis to help you. Annual reports are available for many companies on their websites and in several databases.

c. Explain how a balanced scorecard similar to the preceding one can help Allen and his management team to achieve the following objectives:

(1) Develop cost management information to help meet strategic goals.
(2) Analyse and evaluate organizational change.
(3) Evaluate the effects of alternative uses of resources on performance.
(4) Implement and manage change.

[Adapted from Chow et al., 1997]

Case 16.56 [LO 1-4] Analyse Impacts of a Quantified Balanced Scorecard

Part 1

SecondData Corporation provides outsourced data-processing services for large banks, insurance companies and credit-card companies. The president and CEO of SecondData, Christine Howard, recently attended a conference at which Professor Robert Kaplan of the Harvard Business School delivered the keynote address. His speech covered recent innovations in management techniques that, in his opinion, are revolutionizing modern organizations. He spent most of his time explaining the concept of a balanced scorecard, but he also analysed several successful applications of a balanced scorecard for which he had first-hand knowledge.

Howard came away from the conference convinced that the balance scorecard is a powerful concept, but she was sceptical that organizations really can build models of its uses of resources and important outcomes. She wondered whether other respected management 'gurus' were as enthusiastic about a balanced scorecard.

Requirement 1

Write a memorandum (two pages, double-spaced maximum) to Howard describing the concept of a balanced scorecard as explained by Kaplan and Norton and several other authors. Provide references.

Part 2

Howard invited you to attend her next executive committee meeting (attended by senior officers in the firm) to discuss the concept of a balanced scorecard and to generate discussion about whether SecondData Corporation should consider implementing the concept. Following is a partial transcript of that meeting.

Howard:	I'm pleased to welcome one of our bright young staff members, who is going to briefly explain the balanced scorecard I told you about last week. I want us to begin discussions about the concept and move toward deciding whether to implement it.
You:	I'm delighted to be here, and I'm eager to present this exciting concept to you. I hope you will ask lots of questions and all contribute answers. If you think there is more information I should develop, I'll be happy to do so and report back to you as soon as possible.
Marketing VP:	I've heard of this so-called balanced scorecard, and I must say that it sounds like nothing more than the latest management fad. Of course, we should pay attention to our critical variables, inputs and outputs, but do you really think it is possible to build these models? I remember a little of my college statistics, and I particularly remember that statistical modelling is very complex. I suspect that by the time you collected enough data to analyse, it would be obsolete.
CFO:	I'm not sure that statistical analysis is what is called for anyway. Aren't these balanced scorecards just someone's best guess about what variables are important and how they might be connected? I think it's meant to be a way to communicate strategy, not actually manage it. Even then, I worry about whose 'guesses' we will use.
Human Resources Director:	I know that whatever we choose to measure will be the focus of all our division managers' attention. We have 18 divisions that are directly responsible for generating our profits. We had better be careful about what we measure and how we get everyone to buy in. Any suggestions?

Requirement 2

Compose a brief reply (two pages, double-spaced maximum) to these executives' concerns about a balanced scorecard.

Part 3

You decide to talk to several division managers and their key staff members to get their beliefs about key scorecard variables and possible linkages. A transcript of several of these interviews that you believe are representative follows.

Division Manager 1: I'm glad you are taking the time to talk to me and other division managers and division controllers out here on the front lines. I think there has been too much 'top-down' management lately, and I hate to see the executive committee impose a balanced scorecard on us. It doesn't always know what is happening out here. Fire away with your questions; I'll help as much as I can.

You: Can you tell me what you pay most attention to as you manage this division?

Division Manager 1: Well, as one of the oldest and largest divisions in SecondData, I'm very concerned about labour costs and a market that seems more competitive. We also have one of the oldest labour forces, so I am concerned about their skills and education level. I think there is a strong relation between the quality of employees and errors and the time it takes to complete orders. I want to hire some younger employees with more current skills, but I have to wait for attrition.

You: What do you think your customers most want from you?

Division Manager 1: Obviously, they want our service at the lowest price, but they are willing to pay for high quality and orders completed on time. The marketing department developed a customer-satisfaction survey that I have never understood. I suppose it is trying to measure something related to our ability to meet customers' needs.

Division Controller 11: You can talk all you want about fancy new concepts of measurement, but the only measurement that really counts at SecondData is return on assets. (I've learned this the hard way!) I understand that there is talk about using economic value added rather than ROA, but I'm not sure what that will add. It's just a variation on the same theme.

You: Are there process measures that you worry about, too?

Division Controller 11: Yes, we do monitor the number of defects, you know, incorrect billings and such. They really drive up our cycle time, and I am sure our customers are not happy if some of those errors slip by. I also monitor our employee voluntary turnover rate, which is one of the lowest in the company. I think that this reflects good management and our ability to control the quality of our processes.

Division Manager 17: Unfortunately, we have the special difficulty of being in one of the regions with the smallest population. We have to pay higher wages for employees, and we don't have the revenue potential of some of the other divisions. I tell you, it's difficult to meet corporate's profit goals under these conditions. I'll tell you another thing: I think there is a lot of randomness in our environment. I don't think we understand how factors affect each other. Sorting that out will be quite a challenge. Good luck.

Requirement 3

From this interview and your own reasoning, develop a possible balanced scorecard model. Explain how the interviews have influenced your model. Describe each of the measures you have included in your model and explain how they should be causally linked. Prepare a graphical representation of your scorecard model.

Part 4

You have collected the following table of data on each of the 18 business units of SecondData Corporation.

SecondData Corporation

Various Statistics Collected for Domestic Business Units

											($ millions)		
Division	Age of division (years)	Number of employees	Voluntary turnover rate	Average grade level completed	Average hourly wage	Average defects per month	Cycle time per order (hours)	Percentage on-time deliveries	Customer satisfaction score	Regional population (thousands)	Throughput	Operating expense	Assets employed
1	10.1	1,709	4.5%	10.71	$11.11	149.24	61.11	80.6%	78.3	973.0	$3,081	$3,197	$ 6,690
2	7.4	1,220	5.1	11.93	9.49	140.71	55.84	84.5	89.9	872.0	3,073	2,340	11,856
3	7.2	1,169	6.2	11.95	10.11	123.94	57.22	82.1	68.5	556.0	2,952	2,043	8,236
4	11.0	1,726	6.4	10.15	10.13	143.49	51.92	85.2	83.4	760.0	3,140	2,435	7,158
5	7.1	1,567	5.4	11.62	9.89	123.70	53.53	81.6	82.7	676.0	3,259	2,971	5,126
6	6.1	1,314	5.6	10.31	9.59	158.26	69.98	79.1	71.0	862.0	2,920	2,485	10,315
7	10.2	1,136	8.6	11.14	7.59	169.65	76.23	78.9	83.0	618.0	2,778	1,873	8,034
8	8.4	1,108	4.3	11.97	8.35	141.68	50.83	82.2	84.7	593.0	3,383	2,335	10,945

9	7.9	1,815	5.1	10.47	8.02	183.40	67.36	78.3	73.0	539.0	2,762	2,291	7,274
10	9.9	1,655	4.9	11.02	8.65	151.12	58.15	84.8	81.2	946.0	3,108	2,492	3,991
11	10.0	1,076	4.4	10.65	8.66	151.87	55.79	82.2	86.6	731.0	3,409	1,677	4,623
12	9.6	1,248	6.2	10.96	6.42	131.04	61.12	78.9	79.1	814.0	3,291	1,783	9,445
13	8.4	1,563	8.3	10.14	10.13	164.41	55.67	82.2	84.8	831.0	3,392	2,703	5,676
14	10.4	1,210	8.0	10.73	8.71	143.53	52.36	84.9	92.4	517.0	2,647	1,718	4,382
15	8.0	1,133	6.0	10.75	8.09	160.04	54.21	86.1	84.4	598.0	2,431	1,823	7,524
16	11.1	1,954	8.9	10.36	5.72	157.51	62.19	83.8	87.4	948.0	3,215	2,115	4,520
17	6.6	1,401	4.5	11.34	10.59	148.51	72.26	77.0	72.7	515.0	2,825	2,816	12,030
18	10.8	1,141	5.1	10.65	10.31	171.69	59.69	81.6	82.6	507.0	2,427	2,240	8,854

Requirement 4

To the extent possible, use the methods of cost estimation presented in Chapter 3 and these data to test the validity of your proposed balanced scorecard model. Describe which aspects of the model that the analysis supports and which it refutes. Briefly discuss the advantages and disadvantages of using these data to verify the model. What additional data would you like to have? Make recommendations to Howard and the executive committee about whether they should proceed to develop and implement a balanced scorecard. What opportunities and difficulties do you foresee?

Case 16.57 [LO 6] Pay for Performance

Pléthorique SA has hired you to develop a pay-for-performance incentive system based on its four key areas of performance. Pléthorique's CEO ultimately wants each of the company's 20 divisions to perform at the 90th percentile level of the industry for each goal. The company reliably measures performance against each of these goals as follows.

Performance area	Performance measure	Current Pléthorique divisions' average performance	Current industry 90th percentile performance
1. Employee productivity	Sales per employee	€180,000	€200,000
2. Product quality	Customer-found defect rate	2.00%	0.04%
3. Customer satisfaction	Customer satisfaction score (1 to 100)	75	88
4. Profitability	Return on investment	15%	30%

Although each of the 20 divisions performs at different levels, for simplicity, assume that three types of divisions exist: high performers, medium performers and low performers with the following average frequency and performances:

Performance measure	Low performers	Medium performers	High performers
Number of divisions	4	10	6
Sales per employee	€150,000	€180,000	€200,000
Customer-found defect rate	3.33%	2.00%	0.03%
Customer satisfaction score (1 to 100)	60	75	92
Return on investment	-9.50%	20.00%	40%

Required

a. Assume that each division manager is paid an annual salary of €90,000. Suppose if you were to propose an incentive plan that paid 1 per cent of salary as a bonus for exceeding the industry's 90th percentile performance, for each performance measure. What would be the average and total amounts of bonus compensation paid for the current levels of performance?

b. What would be the average and total amounts of bonus compensation paid if two low performers improved to the medium category and two medium performers improved to the high category? What if all divisions were high performers?

c. Do you think the incentive plan in requirements (a) and (b) is a good plan or not? Would an incentive plan that paid bonus compensation for *improvements* in performance be a good idea? Explain.

d. Propose an alternative incentive plan that rewards absolute performance and relative improvement.

Case 16.58 [LO 6, 7] Ethical Impacts of Alternative Incentive System Features: Performance and Measurement at CMP Media

CMP Media is a leading high-technology business-to-business multimedia company that provides information and integrated marketing services to technology and health care professionals worldwide. CMP Media offers marketers and advertisers comprehensive media solutions tailored to meet their individual needs. CMP's diverse products and services include newspapers, magazines, Internet products, research, education and training, trade shows and conferences, direct marketing services and custom publishing.

CMP Media was purchased from the Leeds family in 1999 by the UK firm, **United Business Media.**

Company principles

CMP Media has operated with a set of socially responsible principles for more than 30 years. The company credits these principles with its ability to hire and retain excellent employees, innovate its processes and products, provide exceptional customer value and (until recently) generate consistent financial success.

Financial results at CMP Media

A few years ago, the company continued to suffer the effects of the technology market downturn in which CMP's major customers were cautious in committing their marketing and advertising budgets. Turnover (sales revenues) in this business fell 31.9 per cent to £252.4 million while profits were down 112.5 per cent to an operating loss of £9.9 million. CMP has improved its market leading position. It now has a 29 per cent share of the market for the period, ahead of last year's 25 per cent, and still maintains well over twice the market share of its nearest competitors.

CMP MEDIA
Comparative Operating Results
2009 and 2010
Millions of GBP (£)

	Turnover	**Operating profit**
2002	£252.4	£(9.9)
2001	£370.4	£(8.8)
Percentage change	(31.9)%	(12.5)%
	1 GBP (£) ≈ 1.5 USD ($)	

Performance measurement at CMP Media

CMP Media had been a family-owned business for most of its existence. Most officers and key managers were family members or long-term employees who fully embraced the company's operating principles. Therefore, executives felt no need to formalize the operating principles into the company's incentive system. The company ran smoothly by consensus. Since the purchase of the company by United Business Media and the nearly simultaneous economic downturn in the high-tech sector, the company has felt increased pressure to improve its financial results. Indeed, its two consecutive operating loss years were unprecedented in company history. The company is unwilling, however, to discard any of its operating principles, and the parent company so far agrees.

You (and up to two others) have been retained by CMP Media to design a performance-based incentive system for CMP Media that is consistent with all of its operating principles.

Required

a. Review information about theories of motivation and the elements of performance-based incentive plans.
b. Prepare a report that describes your input to the following table and explains how your choices will effectively motivate employees to achieve the company's goals.
c. Would you recommend any trade-offs among operating principles? Explain.
d. Combine your performance measures into a cause-and-effect, balanced scorecard–type model. Explain how you would establish the validity and usefulness of this performance model.

CMP media's five operating principles	Two objectives for each goal	One performance measure for each objective	Incentives plans for 5 executives, 20 managers, and 400 workers
1. Be a great company to do business with for customers and suppliers. 2. Be an excellent company to work for - able to hire, motivate and develop outstanding, diverse people who work together harmoniously toward a common objective. 3. Provide only superior products and services. 4. Contribute actively to a better social and physical environment. 5. Be profitable to provide the resources for future growth, quality, and financial stability.			

[Information regarding CMP Media was taken from its website (www.cmp.com - now removed) and that of its parent, United Business Media (www.ubm.com)].

Solutions to You're the Decision Maker

16.1 Designing a Balanced Scorecard, p. 792

a. Financial measures indicate how well the organization has done in the past whereas non-financial measures indicate future success. Organizations that perform well on the non-financial performance measures should have financial success in the future. Therefore, directing employee attention to non-financial areas, such as improving business efficiency, should result in future financial success. In addition to these advantages, most employees can relate better to non-financial performance measures. For example, it is easier for a supervisor to think about training employees well and reducing employee turnover than to think about increasing return on investment.
b. The company will incur considerable costs to design and implement a balanced scorecard. The company should specify its vision and strategy (if it has not done so), develop non-financial performance measures, design an information system to collect the non-financial performance data, collect data, use the data to evaluate performance, and provide rewards and penalties based on such performance evaluation. The benefits are improved organizational performance, which might be difficult to measure. Management will have to decide whether the benefits outweigh the costs, which are easier to measure. Note that there is a high start-up cost; the benefits generally come later.
c. You want somebody on the team who is well respected by top management because their buy-in is important. This would be someone who has 'the ear of top management', so to speak. The team should include someone who understands each of the four areas; someone with financial expertise; someone who knows what is needed to generate customer satisfaction; someone who understands the operations of the airline who can improve business processes; and someone who knows how to link learning and growth to the other areas. That team should presumably include people who know both marketing and operations very well. Inclusion of someone

who knows the industry to help benchmark Singapore Airways with competitors will be helpful. The team should include employees who are respected by their peers and who are creative and willing to take risks.

16.2 Designing Incentive Systems, p. 818

This incentive system appears to have a problem. The bank seems to have convinced these employees that a balanced scorecard's measures are appropriate for their activities.

This is an important step in instituting any performance-measurement system. The bank appears not to do well, however, in linking rewards to performance at all levels. Executives can be motivated by overall bank performance and the attendant bonus and share awards, but lower-level employees do not have the same reward system or motivation; the expectancy chain is broken at the link between performance and reward. This can create a problem causing lower-level employees to seek their own rewards in ways that are detrimental to the bank. For example, they might spend excessive time on personal business or surfing the Web when they should be working to improve their knowledge, internal processes or customer satisfaction. They might understand that their actions are detrimental, but they also might believe that out of a sense of fairness, they have a right to steal time and effort from the bank. As long as they do not shirk so much that they get fired, their salaries and annual raises appear to be secure.

You might recommend setting up an incentive plan that provides bonuses for performance on each of a balanced scorecard's measures for lower-level employees who can affect those measures (if appropriate). The bonuses can be cash, prizes or shares (depending on the management level of the individual and the interests of the particular employees). Lower-level employees might be more motivated by prizes; branch and department managers might be more motivated by cash and shares. The bank should include incentives to focus on the future, especially for managers, so at least some of the rewards should be deferred and based on future performance. Overall performance should combine individual and organizational performance so employees see the pay-off of their own individual actions as well as take actions that benefit the organization as a whole.

Endnotes

1 See also Ittner and Larcker (1998a) for an investigation of statistical relations among leading and lagging indicators of performance.

2 See Kaplan and Norton's book *A Balanced Scorecard* (1996) and *The Strategy-Focused Organization* (2000). See also the website of Arthur Schneiderman (www.schneiderman.com) who was involved in the development of one of the first balanced scorecards as an employee at **Analog Devices**, a mid-sized semiconductor company. This early case has later been frequently reported in the literature.

3 See also Research Insight 16.2.

4 Several studies demonstrate how such involvement can be achieved and that it has beneficial effects. See for example Abernethy and Bouwens (2005), Kleingeld et al. (2004), Kruis and Widener (2011) and Wouters and Wilderom (2008).

5 See Dillon (2009).

6 A classic article by Kerr (1975) speaks to fundamental problems with many incentive systems. Designers of incentive plans can be surprised to find that these systems motivate unintended behaviour or create disincentives to desired behaviour.

7 Chapter 8 also talks about the quality of information.

8 Expectancy theory explains that people are motivated to act in ways that they expect to provide them the rewards that they desire and to prevent the penalties that they wish to avoid.

9 Green (1992).

10 Locke and Latham (2002).

11 Personal and corporate income tax regulations can also have major effects on the design of incentive systems.

12 For example, what percentage of your answers were correct, if each question has the same weight.

13 For a field study of companies using relative performance evaluation, see Maher (1987).

14 See Research Insight 16.3.

15 See also Ittner et al. (2003a).

16 Rappaport articulates this question in his book *Creating Shareholder Value* (1997).

17 A classic article is by Healy (1985).

18 A readable article on share options is Hall (2000).

19 For a comprehensive treatment of management control in non-profit organizations, see Anthony and Young (2002).

20 *Harrisburg Hospital* v. *Dauphin County Board of Assessment Appeals* Commonwealth Court of Pennsylvania 708 A. 2d 1284 (1998).

21 For example, see Mathiason (2003).

22 Galloro and Benko (2003).

23 Crystal (1991).

24 See Lo (2003). Interestingly, Lo found that managers of firms whose shareholders had the most to gain from improved incentive systems were most likely in 1991 to lobby against SEC regulations for increased disclosures of their pay.

References

Abernethy, M., and J. Bouwens (2005) 'Determinants of accounting innovation implementation', *Abacus*, vol. 41, no. 3, pp. 217–240.

Anthony, R.N., and D.W. Young (2002) *Management Control in Nonprofit Organizations*, 7th edn, Irwin, Homewood, IL.

Banker, R., G. Potter and D. Srinivasan (2000) 'An empirical investigation of an incentive plan that includes nonfinancial performance measures', *The Accounting Review*, vol. 75, no. 1, pp. 65–92.

Bourguignon, A., V. Malleret and H. Nørreklit (2004) 'The American balanced scorecard versus the French tableau de bord: the ideological dimension', *Management Accounting Research*, vol. 15, pp. 107–134.

Chenhall, R.H. (2005) 'Integrative strategic performance measurement systems, strategic alignment of manufacturing, learning and strategic outcomes: an exploratory study', *Accounting, Organizations and Society*, vol. 30, pp. 395–422.

Chow, C.W., K.M. Haddad and J.E. Williamson (1997) 'Applying the balanced scorecard to small companies', *Management Accounting*, August, pp. 21–27.

Crystal, G. (1991) 'Why CEO compensation is so high', *California Management Review*, Fall, pp. 9–29.

Davis, S., and T. Albright (2004) 'An investigation of balanced scorecard implementation on financial performance', *Management Accounting Research*, vol. 15, no. 2, pp. 135–153.

Dillon, K. (2009) 'The coming battle over executive pay', *Harvard Business Review*, September, pp. 96–103.

Epstein, M., and J.-F. Manzoni (1998) 'Implementing corporate strategy: from tableaux de bord to balanced scorecards', *European Management Journal*, vol. 16, no. 2, pp. 190–203.

Farrell, A.M., K. Kadous and K.L. Towry (2008) 'Contracting on contemporaneous versus forward-looking measures: an experimental investigation', *Contemporary Accounting Research*, vol. 25, no. 3, pp. 773–802.

Galloro, V., and L. Benko (2003) 'Are they worth it?' *Modern Healthcare*, vol. 33, no. 31, pp. 6–8.

Gibbs, M., K. Merchant, W., Van der Stede and M. Vargus (2004) 'Determinants and effects of subjectivity in incentives', *The Accounting Review*, vol. 79, no. 2, pp. 409–436.

Gibbs, M., K. Merchant, W., Van der Stede and M. Vargus (2005) 'The benefits of evaluating performance subjectively', *Performance Improvement*, vol. 44, no. 5, pp. 26–32.

Green, T.B. (1992) *Performance and Motivation Strategies for Today's Workforce: A Guide to Expectancy Theory Applications*, Greenwood, Westport, CT.

Hall, B. (2000) 'What you need to know about stock options', *Harvard Business Review*, March–April, pp. 121–200.

Healy, P. (1985) 'The effect of bonus schemes on accounting procedures and accrual decisions', *Journal of Accounting and Economics*, vol. 7, no. 1/3, pp. 85–107.

Ittner, C., and D. Larcker (1998a) 'Are non-financial measures leading indicators of financial performance?' *Journal of Accounting Research*, vol. 36 (supplement), pp. 1–35.

Ittner, C., and D. Larcker (1998b) 'Innovations in performance measurement: trends and research implications', *Journal of Management Accounting Research*, vol. 10, pp. 205–238.

Ittner, C., and D. Larcker (2003) 'Coming up short on non-financial performance measurement', *Harvard Business Review*, November, pp. 88–95.

Ittner, C., D. Larcker and M.W. Meyer (2003a) 'The use of subjectivity in multi-criteria bonus plans', *The Accounting Review*, vol. 78, no. 3, pp. 725–768.

Ittner, C.D., D.F. Larcker and T. Randall (2003b) 'Performance implications of strategic performance measurement in financial services firms', *Accounting, Organizations, and Society*, vol. 28, pp. 715–741.

Jansen, E.P., K.A. Merchant and W.A. Van der Stede (2009) 'National differences in incentive compensation practices: the differing role of financial performance measurement in the United States and the Netherlands', *Accounting, Organizations and Society*, vol. 34, no. 1, pp. 58–84.

Kaplan, R.S., and D.P. Norton (1996) *The Balanced Scorecard*, Harvard Business School Press, Boston, MA.

Kaplan, R.S., and D.P. Norton (2000) *The Strategy-Focused Organization*, Harvard Business School Press, Boston, MA.

Kerr, S. (1975) 'On the folly of rewarding A, while hoping for B'. *Academy of Management Executive*, vol. 9, no. 1, pp. 7–14.

Kleingeld, A., H. Van Tuijl and J. Algera (2004) 'Participation in the design of performance management systems: a quasi-experimental field study', *Journal of Organizational Behavior*, vol. 25, pp. 831–851.

Kruis, A.-M., and S.K. Widener (2011) 'Managerial influence in performance measurement system design: a recipe for success?' Working Paper, Nyenrode Business University.

Lipe, M.G., and S. Salterio (2000) 'The balanced scorecard: judgmental effects of information organization and diversity', *The Accounting Review,* vol. 75, no. 3, pp. 283–298.

Lo, K. (2003) 'Economic consequences of regulated changes in disclosure: the case of executive compensation', *Journal of Accounting and Economics*, vol. 35, pp. 285–314.

Locke, E.A., and G.P. Latham (2002) 'Building a practically useful theory of goal setting and task motivation: a 35-year odyssey', *American Psychologist*, vol. 57, no. 9, pp. 705–717.

Malina, M., H. Nørreklit and F. Selto (2007) 'Relations among measures, climate of control, and performance measurement models', *Contemporary Accounting Research*, vol. 24, no. 3, pp. 935–982.

Malina, M., and F. Selto (2001) 'Communicating and controlling strategy: an empirical study of the effectiveness of the balanced scorecard', *Journal of Management Accounting Research*, vol. 13, pp. 47–90.

Maher, M. (1987) 'The use of relative performance evaluation in organizations', in W. Bruns and R. Kaplan, (eds.), *Accounting and Management Field Study Perspectives*, pp. 295–315, Harvard Business School Press, Boston, MA.

Mathiason, N. (2003) 'Failing fund men pile on the pounds', *The Observer*, 4 May, business pages: 8.

Mullaney, T.J. (1999) 'Needed: the human touch', *Business Week*, 13 December, pp. 52–54.

Rappaport, A. (1997) *Creating Shareholder Value: A Guide for Managers and Investors,* Free Press, New York.

Said, A.A., H.R. Hassab Elnaby and B. Wier (2003) 'An empirical investigation of the performance consequences of non-financial measures', *Journal of Management Accounting Research*, vol. 15, pp. 193–223.

Speckbacher, G., J. Bischof and T. Pfeiffer (2003) 'A descriptive analysis on the implementation of balanced scorecards in German-speaking countries', *Management Accounting Research*, vol. 14, no. 4, pp. 361–387.

Vera-Muñoz, S.C., M. Shackell and M. Buehner (2007) 'Accountants' usage of causal business models in the presence of benchmark data: a note', *Contemporary Accounting Research*, vol. 24, no. 3, pp. 1015–1038.

Weintraub, A. (2002) 'For creditors, the toy chest is empty', *BusinessWeek*, 23 September.

Wouters, M., and C. Wilderom (2008) 'Developing performance-measurement systems as enabling formalization: a longitudinal field study of a logistics department', *Accounting, Organizations and Society*, vol. 33, pp. 488–516.

Glossary

ABC full costing assigns as many costs to products as can be applied to products

ABC unit-level costing assigns only the costs of unit-level resources to products

abnormal spoilage spoilage from reasons other than the usual course of operations of a process

absolute performance evaluation compares individual performance to set standards or expectations

absorption (accrual, full) costing includes direct material, direct labour, and *both* variable and fixed manufacturing overhead in the costs of products

account analysis method is based on going through the organization's costs accounts to identify the costs of various cost objects and to determine the fixed and variable costs

accrual cost a historical measure of the value of resources used, when reporting results of operations or estimating long-run costs

accurate cost allocation measures the cost of support service resource usage with the least error

accuracy precision in measurement

activity any discrete task (e.g., assembly, testing) that an organization undertakes to make or deliver a good or service

activity analysis see **task analysis**

activity-based analysis four steps to measure the cost of goods and services

activity-based budgeting (ABB) the process of developing a master budget using information obtained from an activity-based costing (ABC) analysis

activity-based costing (ABC) a costing method that, first, *traces* costs to activities, which act as activity-cost pools, and, second, assigns these costs to goods and services based on how much each good or service uses the activities

activity-based flexible budget is based on several cost drivers rather than a single, volume-based cost driver

activity-based management (ABM) evaluates the costs and values of process activities to identify opportunities for improved efficiency

activity dictionary lists activities performed by an organization to build its products

adjusted *R*-square serves the same purpose as the *R*-square but applies a statistical penalty for each added independent variable

administrative costs the costs incurred to manage the organization and provide staff support, including executive and clerical salaries; costs for legal, computing and accounting services; and building space for administrative personnel

annuity a series of the same cash flows per period, and this usually refers to yearly cash flows

applied overhead the amount of manufacturing overhead assigned to Work-in-progress inventory as a product cost. It is calculated by multiplying the predetermined overhead rate by the actual *cost driver* volume.

appraisal (also called *detection* or *inspection*) inspect inputs and attributes of individual units of product or service to detect whether they conform to specifications or customer expectations

arm's length transaction means that the price is the same as if the good or service were sold to an independent party

average cycle time the total processing time for all units divided by good units produced

balanced scorecard is a performance measurement system or business model that ties together knowledge of strategy, processes, activities and operational and strategic performance measures

bar-coding system creates a unique bar code for each batch and order and allows companies to mark and track all batches and orders electronically

batch-level cost cost of resources dedicated to an activity that is performed for every batch of multiple units that receive simultaneous processing

behavioural congruence occurs when an individual behaves in the best interests of the organization regardless of his or her own goals

benchmarking is a technique for determining an organization's competitive advantage by learning about its own products, services and operations and comparing them against the best performers

benefit–cost analysis measures the effects of a plan by comparing its expected benefits and costs

bonus bank a mechanism to create deferred incentives, because every year bonuses are added to the bonus bank account, and every year the manager receives part of the total balance that has accumulated in that account

bottleneck resource the *constraint* or constraining factor limiting production or sales

break-even point the volume of activity that produces equal revenues and costs for the organization

budget a detailed plan, expressed in quantitative terms, that specifies how an organization will acquire and use resources during a particular period of time

budget committee consisting of key senior executives, advises the *budget director* during the preparation of the budget

budget director (or chief budget officer) specifies the process by which budget data are gathered, collects the information, and prepares the master budget

budget manual indicates who is responsible for providing various types of budget information, when the information is required, and what form the information is to take

budget variance the difference between the flexible budget and the actual costs

budgetary slack the difference between the revenue or cost projection that a person provides and a realistic estimate of the revenue or cost

budgeted statement of financial position shows the expected end-of-period balances for the company's assets, liabilities and owners' equity

budgeted financial statements show how the organization's financial statements will appear at a specified time if operations proceed according to plan

budgeted statement of income shows the expected revenue and expenses for a budget period, assuming that planned operations are carried out

budgeted schedule of cost of goods manufactured and sold details the direct materials, direct labour and manufacturing overhead costs to be incurred, and shows the cost of the goods to be sold during a budget period

budgeting system comprises the procedures used to develop a budget

buffer capacity amount of capacity that may be intentionally reserved for unexpected demand

burden indirect or overhead costs that are difficult or impossible to trace to processes and products

business processes support or enable production processes

by-product the output from a joint production process that is minor in quantity and/or NRV when compared to the main products

capital budget is a plan for buying and selling capital assets

capital turnover is sales revenue divided by invested capital

cash budget details the expected cash receipts and disbursements during a budget period

cash (or out of pocket) cost the incremental money price paid by cash or credit to achieve a particular purpose

cash payments budget details the expected cash disbursements during a budget period

cash receipts budget details the expected cash collections during a budget period

cause-and-effect analysis involves formulating diagnostic signals that identify potential causes of product or service defects

centralized means that decisions in the organization are handed down from the top echelon of management and subordinates carry them out

committed cost incurred because of policies or contractual obligations

compensatory method means that the values for all criteria must be converted into a common measurement scale

competitive advantage a resource, process or value chain that enables an organization to provide more value, perhaps at lower cost, than its competitors

consistency of cost allocation the degree to which cost allocation bases fully allocate spending for support services; it is related to accuracy, and is easier to establish than true cost or true cause-and-effect relationships

constant gross margin percentage method allocates joint costs to products in a way that the gross margin as a percentage of revenue is the same for each product

constraint a process or resource in a system that limits the throughput of the system

contribution margin the difference between sales revenue and variable cost of sales that measures the incremental profit earned toward covering fixed costs and desired profits

control chart describes variation in product or service attributes over time by measuring important quality features but additionally compares them to maximum- and minimum-desired levels

conversion cost includes direct labour and manufacturing overhead

cost the sacrifice made, usually measured by the resources given up, to achieve a particular purpose

cost accounting system accumulates, allocates and reports accrual costs for external reporting

cost allocation a systematic process of assigning indirect costs to products or organizational units

cost allocation base a measure that reflects the indirect cost to be allocated

cost allocation rate division of the indirect cost by the amount of the cost allocation base

cost-based transfer pricing sets the transfer price on the basis of the cost of the product or service transferred

cost driver (or cost-driver base) a plausible explanation of the cost to perform an activity

cost-driver rate the cost of resources consumed to perform an activity *per unit of the cost driver*

cost estimation the process of estimating the relation between cost objects, which may be organizational entities, products or inputs to products, and the cost drivers, which are measures of workload or output, that explain those costs

cost of goods sold the cost of the products sold during a specific period of time

cost management an organizational commitment, a professional attitude and a set of techniques to create more value at lower cost

cost management systems represent a set of cost management techniques that function together to support the organization's goals and activities

cost object anything that the cost analyst may want to estimate the cost of, such as products, services, projects, activities, organizational entities or inputs to products

cost-plus contract reimburses the seller for costs incurred plus a profit

cost pools groups or categories of individual cost items that are grouped together because they have a similar function

costs of quality (COQ) costs of activities to *control quality* and the costs of activities to correct a *failure to control quality*

cost reduction target is the difference between the total target cost and the currently feasible total cost

cost reduction target the currently feasible cost less the total target cost

cost variance is the difference between the actual cost and the standard cost

cost-volume-profit (CVP) model is a profit-planning model that reflects the effects of changes in an organization's activities, such as sales volume, and of its prices and costs on profit

criteria the attributes on the basis of which the decision maker compares the decision alternatives and makes a decision

critical success factors the key strengths that are most responsible for making the organization successful

current equivalent units equivalent units added in the current period only for the current layer of inventory, which are calculated by subtracting the equivalent units transferred into the period as opening work-in-progress from the total equivalent units in process

currently feasible cost the total cost *without* improving the efficiency of production or administrative processes

customer-focused quality a broad focus on meeting or exceeding customer expectations

customer-level cost the cost of resources dedicated to an activity that is performed for every unique customer served

customer profitability analysis an application of ABM to processes that serve customers

customer relations management a strategy where the qualitative and quantitative focus of the organization is firmly fixed on the customer

customer response time the amount of time between a customer placing an order for a product or requesting service and the delivery of the product or service to the customer

customer retention (or loyalty) measures how well a company is doing in keeping its customers

customer value reflects the degree to which products and services satisfy customers' expectations about price, function, and quality

decentralized means that in the company decision rights are given to many different managers, and consequently many decisions are made at divisional and departmental levels

decision alternatives the considered alternative courses of action about which a decision is made

decision-making framework consists of five phases and is shown in Exhibit 1.1.

decision tree diagrams decisions and alternative outcomes expected from those decisions in a tree, branch and limb format

decision usefulness (of information) is whether managers make sufficiently better decisions to justify the cost of the information

defect an attribute (tangible or intangible) that falls short of customer expectations

Deming Prize created in Japan by the Japanese Union of Scientists and Engineers, to honour W. Edwards Deming; it is awarded to companies around the world that excel in quality improvement

dependent variables are correlated with independent variables

direct cost cost traceable to a particular cost object

direct labour cost of compensating employees whose work creates the organization's products

direct labour budget shows the number of hours and the cost of direct labour to be used during a budget period

direct labour efficiency variance the difference between the actual hours and the standard hours of direct labour allowed, given actual output, multiplied by the standard hourly labour rate

direct labour mix variance (for a particular type of direct labour), is the difference between the actual and standard input proportions for that type of direct labour multiplied by that labour type's standard rate and multiplied by the actual total quantity of all direct labour used

direct labour rate variance is the difference between the actual and standard hourly labour rate multiplied by the actual quantity of direct labour used

direct labour yield variance (for a particular type of direct labour), is the difference between the actual quantity of all direct labour used and the standard quantity of all direct labour, given actual output, multiplied by the standard rate for that particular type of direct labour and multiplied by the standard input proportion for that type of direct labour

direct material resources such as raw materials, parts and components that one can feasibly observe being used to make a specific product

direct material budget shows the number of units and the cost of materials to be purchased and used during a budget period

direct material mix variance (for a particular direct material) is the difference between the actual and standard input proportions for that direct material multiplied by that material's standard price and multiplied by the actual total quantity of all direct materials used

direct material price variance is the difference between the actual and standard price multiplied by the actual quantity of material used

direct material quantity variance is the difference between the actual quantity and the standard quantity of material allowed, given actual output, multiplied by the standard price

direct material yield variance (for a particular direct material) is the difference between the actual quantity of all direct materials used and the standard quantity of all direct materials, given actual output, multiplied by that particular direct material's standard price and multiplied by that direct material's standard input proportion

direct method (of cost allocation) allocates the costs of support service departments to internal customers *without making allocations among support service departments*. All support service cost allocations go directly to production departments

discount rate measures the opportunity cost of investing and is used to discount future values to their equivalent present values

discounted cash flow (DCF) methods are based on discounting future cash flows to their equivalent present values, using as the discount rate the forgone rate of interest (so an opportunity cost) available from alternative investments with an equal risk

discretionary cost centre is an organizational subunit whose manager is held accountable for costs, but the subunit's input–output relationship is not well specified

dual transfer pricing charges the buying division for the cost of the transferred product and credits the selling division with the cost plus some profit allowance

due diligence is exercising all reasonable care to identify potential problems and opportunities of a proposed investment

economic order quantity (or EOQ) is the order quantity that minimizes the cost of ordering and holding inventory

economic value added (EVA) is essentially a residual income measure, but much attention is given to adjustments in the precise way operating income and invested capital are being measured

employee capabilities are employees' knowledge and skills that indicate the organization's ability to meet future customer needs and generate new sales

engineering estimates measure the work involved in the activities that go into a product then assign a cost to each of those activities

EOQ model a mathematical tool for determining the order quantity that minimizes the cost of ordering and holding inventory

equivalent units the amount of work actually performed on products completed and not yet complete translated to the work required to complete an equal number of whole units

European Quality Award (EQA) examines the impact of quality on a company, its customers, and the company's social and environmental community

excess (or unused) capacity the amount (if any) by which practical capacity exceeds the demand for the output of the process

expectancy theory explains that people are motivated to act in ways that they expect to provide them with the rewards that they desire and to prevent the penalties that they wish to avoid

expected value the value of each possible measure weighted or multiplied by its probability of occurrence

expected value analysis summarizes the combined effects of relevant future events on decision outcomes, weighted by the probabilities or odds that the events will occur

expense the cost incurred when an asset is consumed or sold for the purpose of generating revenue

extended value chain encompasses the ways companies obtain their resources and distribute their products and services, possibly using the services of other organizations

external failure requires activities when defective products or services are detected after being delivered to customers

extrinsic rewards come from outside the individual from teachers, parents, organizations, or partners and include grades, money, praise and prizes

facility-level cost cost of resources dedicated to an activity that is performed for a production facility (e.g., factory)

favourable (variances) when the actual costs are less than the budget, or revenues exceed the budget

feasible solution space the combination of input and output values that satisfy the constraints

final product a product that is ready for sale without further processing

financial and non-financial criteria differ regarding their unit of measurement, whereby financial criteria have a monetary unit of measurement, and non-financial criteria either have a non-monetary but still quantitative unit of measurement, or are expressed qualitatively, so in words.

financial budget shows how the organization will acquire its financial resources

financial model an accurate, reliable and flexible calculation of financial outcomes (such as costs, profit and risk) that exploits (some of) the vast power of current spreadsheet software

financial planning model a set of mathematical relationships that expresses the interactions among the various operational, financial and environmental events that determine the overall results of an organization's activities

financial quantification translating a non-financial criterion into a financial criterion

Finished goods (FG) inventory the cost of products ready for sale or delivery to customers

first-in, first-out (FIFO) costing an inventory method that identifies the first units completed as the first ones sold or transferred out

fixed cost does not change in total within a defined range of underlying productive activity

fixed overhead budget variance the difference between actual fixed overhead and budgeted fixed overhead

fixed overhead volume variance the difference between budgeted fixed overhead and applied fixed overhead

flexible budget is adjusted to the actual activity level and valid for a range of activity levels within which the firm operates

flowchart reflects cause-and-effect and sequential linkages among process activities

further processing costs the costs incurred to make joint products usable or saleable after split-off

Gantt chart depicts the stages required to complete a project and the sequence in which the stages are to be performed

goal congruence results when managers of subunits throughout an organization have a common set of objectives

gross margin ratio a measure of income contributed before period expenses, interest and taxes divided by sales turnover

high-low method estimates a cost function using only the costs at the highest and lowest level of workload and output

histogram a chart that displays the frequency distribution of an attribute's measures – its range and degree of concentration around an average attribute value

idle time time that an employee does not spend productively because of events such as equipment breakdowns or new set-ups of production runs

imperfect competition describes the situation when a single producer can affect the market price by varying the amount of product available in the market

incentive system communicates strategy, motivates employees, and reinforces achievement of organizational goals

inconsistent ranking means that NPV and IRR do not lead to the same conclusion as to which mutually exclusive alternative is the best one

independent variables the cost drivers that the analyst believes are strongly correlated with the dependent variable, costs

indexed cost allocation bases preferable to creating separate cost pools for each type of service activity when resources cannot be easily separated or traced to activities because they recognize that some measures are 'equivalent' to the previous allocation bases that, when added, expand the scope of work performed by each service department

indirect costs costs not feasibly traceable to a particular cost object

indirect labour cost compensation of employees who do not work directly on the product yet are required for the production process

indirect material cost cost of materials that either (1) are not a part of the finished product but are necessary to manufacture it or (2) are part of the finished product but are insignificant in cost

information quality has dimensions of usefulness, subjectivity, objectivity, accuracy, timeliness, cost and relevance for current decisions

intermediate product a product that might require further processing before it is saleable to the ultimate consumer, by either the producer or another processor

internal audit an examination of operations, programmes and financial results performed by independent investigators

internal control a process designed to provide reasonable assurance that an organization will achieve its objectives

internal failure activities required to correct defective processes, products and services that are detected before delivering them to customers

internal rate of return (IRR) the discount rate that would create an NPV of exactly zero for an investment project

intrinsic rewards come from within the individual, such as the satisfaction from studying hard, the feeling of well-being from physical exercise, the pleasure from helping someone in need, or the satisfaction of doing a good job

inventory carrying costs costs of obsolescence, receiving, handling, storing and insuring inventory

investment centre an organizational subunit whose manager is held accountable for the subunit's profit and the invested capital used by the subunit to generate its profit

ISO 9000 a set of international standards for quality management

job-cost record (or file, card, sheet) reports the costs of all production-related resources used on the job to date

job-order costing treats each individual job as the unit of output and assigns costs to each job as resources are used

joint costs the costs to operate joint processes, including the disposal of waste

joint products the products that jointly result from processing a common input

joint production process simultaneously converts a common input into several outputs

just-in-time (JIT) processes to purchase, make and deliver services and products just when needed

kaizen costing the process of cost reduction during the manufacturing phase of a product

lagging indicators measures that reflect the final outcomes of earlier management plans and their execution

lagging indicators of quality measure features of products after exposure or use by customers

lead time the length of time required for the material to be received after an order has been placed

leading indicators measures that identify future non-financial and financial outcomes to guide management decision making

leading indicators of quality measure the features that customers value while manufacturing the product and before shipment or while providing a service but before completion

lean processes *see* **just-in-time (JIT)**

learning curve the mathematical or graphic representation of the systematic relationship between the amount of experience in performing a task and the time required to perform it

learning phenomenon a systematic relationship between the amount of experience in performing a task and the time required to perform it

life-cycle costing tracks costs attributable to each product or service from start to finish

linear programming shows how best to allocate multiple scarce resources among alternative courses of action in the short run when capacity cannot be increased

linear regression analysis (or regression analysis) a statistical method used to create a linear equation relating independent (or *X*) variables to dependent (or *Y*) variables

lower control limit the minimum desired level of product or service feature

main product a joint output that generates a significant portion of the net realizable value from the process

make-or-buy decision any decision an organization makes about acquiring goods or services internally or externally

Malcolm Baldrige National Quality Award created by the US Congress in 1987, recognizes US firms with outstanding records of quality improvement and quality management

management by exception means that managers follow up on only the most significant variances between budgeted and actual results

manufacturing overhead budget shows the cost of overhead expected to be incurred in the production process during the budget period

manufacturing overhead cost (indirect manufacturing costs or burden) indirect resources necessary for the manufacturing process that cannot be easily traced to specific units of product

market-based transfer price is comparable from the external market price, which is adjusted when conditions between external and internal transactions are different

master budget, or profit plan a comprehensive set of budgets covering all phases of an organization's operations for a specified period of time

material requisition form the source document for the transfer of raw material from Raw material inventory to Work-in-progress inventory and to the job-cost record for the production job

maximum quality level is total delight of the customer or zero defects, depending on one's definition of quality

mixed costs have both a fixed and a variable component

model elasticity the ratio of the percentage change in profit divided by the percentage change of an input parameter

multicollinearity the correlation between two or more independent variables in a multiple regression equation

multi-criteria decision making means that alternatives differ on several criteria, typically financial as well as non-financial criteria, which are conflicting and have different units of measurement

multiple regression a regression method that uses more than one independent variable

negotiated transfer pricing means that division managers or their representatives actually negotiate the price at which transfers will be made

net present value (NPV) the present value of a project's future cash flows less its purchase price; it is the economic value of a project at a point in time

net realizable value (NRV) the measure of a product's contribution to profit after the *split-off point* and is computed as sales revenue minus additional processing costs

net realizable value (NRV) method allocates joint costs based on the NRV of each *main product* at the *split-off point*

new product development time the period between the first consideration of a product and its initial sale to the customer

non-compensatory method does not involve a single dimension, and good performance on one criterion cannot compensate for bad performance on another criterion

non-value-added activities do not contribute to customer-perceived value

normal costing system applies manufacturing overhead to jobs using a predetermined overhead rate based on normal production volume

normal production capacity an average of recent periods' production activity supplied

normal spoilage spoiled product that results from the regular operation of the production process

objective function a mathematical relation of inputs and outputs to be maximized or minimized

objectivity describes the degree of consensus about what to measure, how to measure it, what the observed measure is, or whether the measurement is important

operating income gross margin less period expenses, more generally the operating income is the income from normal business operations, before subtracting the cost of debt (interest), and before subtracting taxes. Operating income is also called EBIT (Earnings before Interest and Taxes)

operating leverage reflects the risk of missing sales targets and is measured by the ratio of contribution margin to operating income

operation a standardized method of making a product that is repeatedly performed

operation costing a hybrid of *job-order* and *process costing*, which is used when companies produce batches of similar products with significantly different types of material

operational budgets specify how an organization's operations will be carried out to meet its demand for goods or services

operational performance analysis measures whether the performance of current operations is consistent with expectations

opportunity cost the highest forgone value that could have been obtained from other possible alternatives that are blocked by choosing a particular alternative and using a scarce resource for that

optimum point is the set of inputs and outputs in the feasible solution space that maximizes or minimizes the objective function

outsourcing is acquiring goods or services from an outside provider

overall equipment effectiveness (OEE) a summary measure of the use of process capacity to create good (defect-free) output

over-applied overhead normal overhead applied exceeds overhead incurred

overhead cost performance report shows the actual and flexible budget cost levels for each overhead item, together with the variable overhead spending and quantity variances and the fixed overhead budget variance

overhead variance the difference between the actual and the applied manufacturing overhead amounts

overtime premium the extra hourly compensation paid to an employee who works beyond the time normally allowed by regulation or labour contracts

padding the budget means intentionally underestimating revenue or overestimating costs

Pareto chart prioritizes the causes of problems or defects as bars of varying height, in order of frequency or size

participative budgeting involves employees throughout an organization in the budgeting process

pay for performance bases at least a portion of a manager's income on measure(s) of organizational performance rather than a guaranteed amount

payback period the time necessary to recover the investment cash outflow from discounted or non-discounted cash inflows (these are variations of the method)

perfect competition describes the situation when the market price does not depend on the quantity sold by any one producer

perfection (or ideal) standard one that can be attained only under nearly perfect operating conditions

performance evaluation formula computes rewards earned for specific achievements

performance measure an indicator that allows a person to determine the level of performance according to some critical attribute and to compare performance to expectations

performance report shows the budgeted and actual amounts of key financial (or non-financial) results appropriate for the type of *responsibility centre* involved

period costs non-manufacturing costs that are expensed in the period incurred for external reporting purposes

physical measures (or quantities) method a joint-cost allocation based on the relative volume, weight, energy content or other physical measure of each joint product at the *split-off point*

pilot project is a limited-scope project intended to be a small-scale model of a larger, possibly system-wide, project

plausible correlation the combination of strong statistical correlation and economic rationale

practical capacity (of a process) is the most a resource can be used for normal operations

practical (or attainable) standards are challenging but still are expected to be attained

predatory pricing involves temporarily setting a price below cost to injure competitors that cannot sustain losses and consequently must leave the market

predetermined overhead rate the budgeted fixed manufacturing overhead divided by the budgeted (or normal) level of the cost driver

present value is the equivalent amount that would have to be invested today to generate a future cash flow at a given discount or opportunity rate

prevention refers to activities that seek to prevent defects in the products or services offered to customers

price variance shows to what extent the variance is caused by differences between the actual price and the budgeted price

process a related set of tasks, manual or automated, that transforms inputs into identifiable outputs

process capacity a measure of a process's ability to transform recourses into valued products and services

process costing treats all units processed during a time period as the output to be costed and does not separate and record costs for each unit produced

process costing system accumulates the costs of a production process and assigns them to the products or services that constitute the organization's output

product cost cost assigned to goods that were either purchased or manufactured for resale

product costing system accumulates the costs of a production process and assigns them to the products that constitute the organization's output

product level cost cost of resources dedicated to an activity that is performed for every product line of units produced

product life cycle is the time that elapses from its initial research and development to the point at which customer support is withdrawn

product mix is the relative proportion of each type of product planned or actually sold

production budget shows the number of units of services or goods that are to be produced during a budget period

production cost report summarizes the process costs allocated to final outcomes

production cycle time the time between starting and finishing a production process, including time to correct mistakes

production (or line) departments provide goods and services to customers, clients or public citizens

production processes directly result in the production of products or services provided to external customers

productivity a ratio of outcomes of a process divided by the amount of resources necessary to complete the process

profit centre an organizational subunit whose manager is held accountable for profit

profit plan (or master budget) a comprehensive set of budgets covering all phases of an organization's operations for a specified period of time

qualitative information is descriptive, expressed in words instead of in numbers, and based on characteristics or perceptions, such as relative desirability, rather than quantities

quantitative information is expressed in euros, dollars or another currency (financial information) or in other quantities relating to size, frequency, and so on (non-financial information)

quantity variance shows to what extent the variance is caused by actual quantity used being different from the standard quantity

raw material inventory cost of material that has not yet been entered into production

real option value (ROV) is the difference between the expected NPV of one option form of the investment and the next best option

real option value (ROV) analysis combines analyses of decision trees, expected values and NPV to describe investments as a series of options to change investments

reciprocal method (of cost allocation) recognizes and allocates costs of all services provided by any support service department, including those provided to other support service departments

reciprocal services services provided among multiple support service departments

regression analysis *see* **linear regression analysis**

relative performance evaluation is based on comparing an individual's performance to that of others

relative sales value at split-off method allocates joint costs based on the relative sales values of the joint products at their *split-off point*

relevance refers to whether information is pertinent to a decision

relevant costs and benefits occur in the future and differ among feasible decision alternatives

relevant range the range of activity within which the organization expects to operate and over which assumed cost patterns are reasonably accurate

reserve capacity a set-aside of capacity for flexible or unexpected needs

residual income (RI) the amount of an investment centre's income that remains (as a residual) after subtracting an imputed cost of capital from the operating income

resources supplied commitment to supply a certain level of resources before using them

resources used resources consumed to perform a specific activity

responsibility accounting refers to the various concepts and tools used to measure the performance of people and departments in order to foster goal or behavioural congruence

responsibility centre a subunit in an organization whose manager is held accountable for specified financial and non-financial results of the subunit's activities

return on investment (ROI) (for an *investment centre*) is its operating income divided by its invested capital

return on quality (ROQ) the view that assumes there is a trade-off between the costs and benefits of improving quality

return on sales (or **sales margin) ratio** operating income divided by sales

revenue budget variance the difference between the actual total sales revenue and the budgeted total sales revenue

revenue centre an organizational subunit whose manager is held accountable for generating revenues for the organization

revenue market share variance holds constant the total industry volume at its actual sales level and focuses on the company's market share

revenue market size variance holds constant the company's market share at its budgeted level and focuses on changes in total industry volume

revenue sales mix variance focuses on the effects of changes in the sales mix while holding constant the effects of the products' sales prices and the total sales volume

revenue sales quantity variance holds constant the sales price and sales mix effects and focuses on the effect of the overall unit sales volume

revenue sales volume variance holds constant the products' sales prices at their budgeted levels and focuses on deviations between actual and budgeted sales volumes

risks exposures to loss

rolling (or revolving or continuous) budget is continually updated by periodically adding a new incremental time period

***R*-square (R^2)** the proportion of the variation in the dependent variable explained by the X, or independent, variables

run refers to sequential values above or below the mean or values sequentially increasing or decreasing

run chart shows trends in variation in product or service attributes over time by reflecting measures of important quality features taken at defined points in time

safety inventory the potential excess usage of material when material usage fluctuates during the *lead time*

sales budget displays the projected sales in units and the projected sales revenue

sales forecasting the process of predicting sales of services or goods

sales margin a measure of the percentage of each sales dollar that remains as profit after all expenses are covered

sales mix the relative proportion of each type of product planned or actually sold

sales price variance focuses on the differences between actual and budgeted sales prices while holding constant the sales volume at its actual level

scatter diagram a plot of two measures that could be related

scattergraph plots costs against activity levels

scenario analysis creates realistic combinations of changed parameters

second-stage cost allocation the reallocation of service department costs and direct department costs to products

selling costs sales commissions, sales personnel salaries, and the sales departments' building occupancy costs

selling, general and administrative (SG&A) expense budget shows the planned amounts of expenditures for selling, general and administrative expenses during a budget period

share appreciation rights (SARs) confer bonuses on employees based on increases in share prices for a predetermined number of shares

share options give an individual the right to purchase a certain number of shares at a specified price over a specified time period

shrinkage the cost of unrecovered stolen or mis-shipped finished products

simple linear regression has only one independent variable

special orders are irregular and do not have lasting implications for other products or customers

split-off point the point at which joint products appear in the production process

spoilage effort (materials and conversion) that results in defective outcomes: goods that are damaged, do not meet specifications, or are otherwise not suitable for further processing or sale as good output

standard cost a budget for the production of one unit of product or service

standard cost centre an organizational subunit whose manager is responsible for the cost of an activity for which a well-defined relationship exists between inputs and outputs

standard direct labour quantity the number of labour hours normally needed to manufacture one unit of product

standard direct labour rate the total hourly cost of compensation, including fringe benefits

standard direct material price the total delivered cost after subtracting any purchase discounts

standard direct material quantity the total amount of materials normally required to produce a finished product, including allowances for normal waste or inefficiency

statistical control chart plots *cost variances* across time and compares them with a statistically determined critical value that triggers an investigation

step (semifixed) costs increase in steps as the amount of the cost-driver volume increases

step method (of cost allocation) allocates support-service department costs in ordered, sequential steps to production departments

strategic decision making the process of choosing and implementing actions that will affect an organization's future abilities to achieve its goals

strategic investment a choice among alternative courses of action and the allocation of resources to those alternatives most likely to succeed after anticipating (1) changes in natural, social and economic conditions and (2) actions of competitors

strategic performance analysis measures whether a strategic decision has met expectations

strategy an organization's overall plan or policy to achieve its goals

strategy map a visual representation of the company's main objectives and the crucial relationships among them that drive organizational performance

subjective performance evaluation means that the procedure for assessing performance and determining rewards is not completely quantifiable and is also based on personal judgement

subjectivity describes the degree of disagreement about what to measure, how to measure it, what the observed measure is, or whether the measurement is important

sunk cost cannot be changed by any current or future decision

support service costs the costs of resources supplied by an organization to provide support services

support service (or indirect) departments do not work directly on products but are necessary for the production process to operate by providing services internally within the organization

sustainability means that an organization should not affect the environment in such a way that there are long-term negative economic, ecological or social consequences

tableau de bord a French framework for performance measurement that includes multiple and leading indicators of performance

tangible objectives benchmarks capable of being measured in some manner

target cost the highest cost of a good or service that meets both customer needs and company profit goals

task analysis the technique of setting standards by analysing the process of manufacturing a product to determine what it should cost

theoretical capacity (of a process) the most that the resource could be used for any purpose

Theory of Constraints (TOC) seeks to improve productive processes by focusing on constrained resources

throughput the amount of goods and services produced and delivered to customers during a period of time measured in dollar terms or physical measures

throughput costing assigns only the out-of-pocket spending for direct costs as the cost of products or services

throughput efficiency the relation of throughput achieved to resources used

throughput time ratio the ratio of the time spent adding customer value to products and services divided by total cycle time (also known as the 'ratio of work content to lead time')

time-driven ABC uses the time to complete an activity as its summary cost driver

timeliness means that information is available in time to fully consider it when making a decision

total factor productivity the value of goods and services divided by the total cost of providing them

total quality management (TQM) the view that improvements in quality, as defined by customers, always result in improved organizational performance because improving quality will improve efficiency as problems are identified and eliminated

trace (or track) accurately estimating, in so far as feasible, the costs of resources used to perform a specific activity

transfer price the price used for internal transactions, for example when one division of an organization sells goods or services to another division

***t*-statistic** *t*, is the value of *b*, the coefficient, divided by its standard error

under-applied overhead cost actual, incurred overhead cost that exceeds normal, applied overhead cost

unfavourable (variances) are when the actual costs exceed the budget, or revenues are below budget the budget

unit-level cost cost of resources dedicated to an activity that is performed for every unit of product

upper control limit a maximum desired level of product or service feature

value-added activities enhance the value of products and services in the eyes of the organization's customer while meeting the organization's goals

value-based pricing means setting a price of a market offering based on its value to a target customer

value chain the relationship of an organization's processes that links ideas, resources, suppliers and customers

variable cost changes in total in direct proportion to production volumes

variable costing applies direct materials and direct labour, but only variable manufacturing overhead to products

variable overhead quantity variance the difference between the actual and standard hours of an activity base (or cost driver) multiplied by the standard variable overhead rate

variable overhead spending variance is the difference between the actual and the standard variable overhead rate, multiplied by the standard number of hours (in general, the quantity of an activity base)

variance analysis the investigation of the budget variance with the objective to better understand why budget variances occurred

variances the differences between a plan's actual and expected quantities

volume variance the difference between the original budget and the flexible budget, simply because the budget is adjusted to the actual production volume

waste the cost of unrecovered resources applied to defective products that cannot be sold

weighted-average cost of capital (WACC) the average of the after-tax cost of debt capital and the cost of equity capital, weighted by the relative proportions of the firm's capital provided by debt and equity

weighted-average process costing the method by which the costs and equivalent units of the current efforts applied and the costs of opening WIP are pooled and averaged

weighted-average unit contribution margin (WAUCM) the average of the various products' unit contribution margins weighted by the relative proportion of each product sold

work-in-progress (WIP) inventory the cost of partially completed products in process

zero-base budgeting initially sets the budget for virtually every activity in the organization to zero

Index

Key terms and page numbers for their definitions are shown in **blue**

A

ABC *see* activity-based costing (ABC)
ABC full costing, **162**, **839**
ABC unit-level costing, 162–3, **162**, **839**
abnormal spoilage, **545**, **839**
absolute performance evaluation, 808–9, **808**, **839**
absorption (accrual, full) costing, 495–8, **495**, **839**
account analysis, 93–5, **93**, **839**
accrual cost, **50**, 55–6, **55**, **839**
accuracy, **10**, **597**, **839**
accurate cost allocation, **597**, **839**
activity (ABC costing), **147**, **839**
activity analysis, **627**, **839**
activity dictionary (ABC costing), **147**, **839**
activity-based analysis, **147**, **839**
activity-based budgeting (ABB), 427–8, **428**, **839**
benefits, 433
and the cost hierarchy, 433
activity-based costing (ABC), **147**, **839**
activity-based costing (ABC) analysis, 147–58
step 1: identifying and classifying, 148–51
example activity list, 150–1
hierarchy of resources and activities
1, unit level, 148
2, batch-level, 149
3, product level, 149
4, customer-level, 149
5, facility-level, 149
interview or participative approach, 149
top-down approach, 149
step 2: estimate cost of activities, 151–2
example using activity data sheet, 151–2
step 3: activity cost-driver rates, 152–6
activity levels, 154
cost-driver rate, **148**, **840**
example cost-driver rate measurement, 153–6
normal production capacity, **153**, **845**
practical capacity, **152**, **845**
reserve capacity, **153**, **846**
resources supplied, **153**, **846**
theoretical capacity, **152**, **848**
step 4: assign activity costs to products, 156–8
example assigning, 156–7
practical use, 157–8
activity-based costing (ABC) method/system, 140–66
ABC full costing, **162**, **839**
ABC unit-level costing, 162–3, **162**, **839**
cost/information differences, 163
about ABC costing, 142
activity, **147**, **839**
activity dictionary, **147**, **839**
batch-level cost, **142**, **839**
costs and benefits, 164–5
customer-level cost, **142**, **841**
does ABC improve performance? (study), 165
facility-level cost, **142**, **842**
product-level cost, **142**, **846**
resources used, **147**, **839**
in service and merchandising, 164
time-driven ABC, **164**, **848**
trace (or track), **147**, **848**
unit-level cost, **142**, **848**
see also customer profitability and activity-based costing (ABC); target costing and activity-based costing (ABC); traditional costing system
activity-based costing (ABC) profitability measures, 158–62
example new product cost study, 160–2
example profitability comparisons, 158–60
under-applied overhead cost, **159**, **848**
activity-based costing (ABC) systems, example organisation, 141–4
about the organisation, 141, 143
competitive situation, 143
costing system options, 144
costing system team, 144
products and processes, 143–4
activity-based costing analysis, extended to ABM, 197–201
step 5: customer perceived value, 198–201
non-value-added activities, **198**, **844**
sources, 198
value-added activities, **198**, **848**
identifying and measuring, 199
measures of, 200
step 6: performing the measurement, 200–1
step 7: process improvement using ABM, 201
eliminating non-value-added activities, 201
risks, **201**, **847**
activity-based flexible budget, 642–4, **642**, **839**
conventional flexible budget comparison, 642–3
examples of use, 63, 644
activity-based management (ABM), 188, **198**, 201–5, **839**
customer profitability analysis, **188**, **841**
customer relations management, **188**, **841**
customer value, **188**, **841**
customer-level costs, **188**, **841**
example analysis, 201–5
asking why?, 204–5
bar-coding system, **204**, **839**
estimating the benefits, 203
estimating cost of saved resources, 204, 205
identifying improvement opportunities, 203–4
working from the activity list, 202–3
see also customer profitability and activity-based costing (ABC)
activity-based management (ABM)/costing (ABC) implementation, 205–8
about ABM with ABC, 205
example of customer decisions issues, 208–9
information required, 208
management commitment, 206

personnel/time issues, 207
pilot project, **206**, **845**
resistance to change, 207
effects of culture, 207
responsibility of analysis team, 208
should ABC and ABM be adopted?, 206
technological resources, 207
will ABC and ABM be successful?, 206
adjusted *R*-square, **104**, **839**
administrative costs, **62**, **839**
annuity, **362**, **839**
applied overhead, **490**, **839**
appraisal (for quality), **240**, **839**
arm's length transactions (value), **764**, **839**
attitude, 5
average cycle time, **247**, **839**

B

balanced scorecard, **788**, **839**
about the example bank, 787–9
causality, research insight, 804
origin and use, 790
strategic performance measures, 791–2
tableau de bord, **790**, 791, **848**
balanced scorecards, benefits and costs, 799–802
benefits, 799–800, 801
costs, 801–2
education costs, 802
measurement costs, 802
use costs, 802
critical success factors, 799
balanced scorecards, implementation, 792–9
business/production process performance, 794–5
employee productivity, 795
new product development, 795
process improvements, 795
service costs, 795
supplier relations, 795
customer performance, 795–7
customer retention (or loyalty), **796**, **841**
customer risk, 797
customer satisfaction, 796
customer value, **795**, **841**
customer value evaluation, 797
market share, 796
financial performance, 797–9
evaluation of measures of, 799
learning and growth, 792–4
employee capabilities, **792**, **842**
employee satisfaction, 793
employee training and education, 793
employee turnover, 793
evaluation of learning/growth measures, 794
innovativeness, 794
opportunities for improvement, 794
use at example company, 802–4
business and production, 803
customer value, 803
financial performance, 803
learning and growth, 803
Westside's growth supported by the cards, 800–1
bar-coding system, **204**, **839**
batch-level cost, **142**, **839**
behavioural congruence, **698**, 753, 757, **839**
behavioural issues *see* budgeting, behavioural implications; standard costing, behavioural effects
benchmarking, **790**, **839**
benefit and cost variances, 21–2
benefit-cost analysis, 19–20, **20**, **839**
decision maker issues, 22
bonus bank, **814**, **839**
bottleneck resources, **244**, **839**
break-even point (CVP model), **290**, **839**
budget, **421**, **839**
see also cost variance analysis, flexible overhead budgets; master budget...; responsibility accounting...
budget administration responsibility, 443–4
budget committee, **443**, **839**
budget director (or chief budget officer), **443**, **840**
budget manual, **443**, **840**
budget committee, **443**, **839**
budget director (or chief budget officer), **443**, **840**
budget manual, **443**, **840**
budget variance, 630–1, **630**, **840**
budgetary slack, 444–5, **444**, **840**
budgeted balance sheet, 440–2, **440**, **840**
budgeted financial statements, **422**, **840**
budgeted income statement, **440**, **840**
budgeted schedule of cost of goods manufactured and sold, **439**, **840**
budgeting, behavioural implications, 444–6
beyond budgeting (research insight), 446
key leadership principles, 446
key performance management principles, 446
budgetary slack, 444–5, **444**, **840**
ethical issues, 445
padding the budget, 444–5, **444**, **845**
participative budgeting, **445**, **845**
budgeting research, practice and theoretical approaches, 426–7
budgeting system, **421**, **840**
budgeting systems, purposes, 421–2
allocating resources, 421
budget, **421**, **839**
communication and co-ordination, 421
financial performance management, 422
incentive provision, 422
operational performance management, 422
performance evaluation, 422
planning, 421
see also inventory management; master budget for planning
budgeting systems, types, 422
budgeted financial statements, **422**, **840**
capital budgets, **422**, **840**
financial budgets, **422**, **842**
master budget, or profit plan, **422**, **844**
rolling (or revolving or continuous) budgets, **422**, **847**
zero-base budgeting, **428**, **849**
budgeting/financial planning, example organization, 419–20
buffer capacity, **250**, **840**
Bundeskartellamt (Germany), 310
bundling assets, 377
burden, **48**, **840**
business processes, **247**, **840**
by-product, **538**, **840**

C

capacity *see* process capacity management
capital budget, **422**, **840**
capital budgeting practices, 362
capital turnover (and ROI), **711**, **840**

career perspectives, CFOs, 5
cash budget (combining receipts and payments), 438–9, **438, 840**
cash or out-of-pocket cost, 50, 52, 840
cash outflow, and reporting costs, 58
cash payments budget, 436–8, **436, 840**
cash receipts budget, 435–6, **435, 840**
cause-and-effect analysis/ diagrams, 234–5, **234, 840**
centralized (organizations), **698, 840**
  see also decentralized organizations
change, leading and managing, 17–19
  innovation encouragement, 18–19
  need identification, 17–18
  obstacle removal, 18–19
  performance measure, 18, 845
  reinforce a positive culture, 19
  short-term achievements, 19
  team creation for, 18
  use successes to create opportunities, 19
  vision communication, 18
  vision creation for, 18
chief financial officer (CFO) career perspectives, 5
commitment, 4
committed cost, 53–4, **53, 840**
compensatory method, 371, 840
competitive advantage, 14, 371, 840
competitive advantages, sources, 14–16
  customer services, 15
  design, 14
  distribution, 15
  extended value chain, 15, 842
  marketing, 15
  outsourcing, 15–16, **15, 845**
  processes, 14, 846
  production, 15
  research and development (R&D), 14
  supply, 15
  support services, 15
  value chains, 14, 15–16, **848**
competitive advantages, threats, 16–17
  customer demand and stability, 17
  emerging markets, 17
  existing competitors, 16
  new competitors, 16
  substitute/complementary products, 17
  supplier reliability/quality/ breadth, 17
concepts and measures of cost, 50–6
  accrual cost, 50, 55–6, **55, 839**
    nylon fabric example, 56
  application to decision making, 51–2
    acquiring nylon fabric example, 51
  cash or out-of-pocket cost, 50, 52, 840
    nylon fabric example, 52
  committed cost, 53–4, **53, 840**
  cost, 50, 840
  fixed costs, 54–5, **54, 843**
  opportunity cost, 50, 845
  sunk costs, 55, 848
  variable cost, 53–4, **53, 848**
  see also cost analysis; reporting costs and expenses
concepts and systems, 46–50
  about the example organization, 47
  burden, 48, 840
  direct costs, 48, 841
  example role of cost management, 49–50
  indirect costs, 48, 843
  value chain example, 49
Conseil de la Concurrence (France), 310
consistency of cost allocation, 597–8, **597, 840**
constant gross margin percentage method, 548–9, **548, 840**
constraint, 314, 840
  see also theory of constraints (TOC)
contribution margin, 290, 496, 840
  weighted-average unit contribution margin (WAUCM), 296–7, **296, 849**
control charts, 233–4, **233,** 258–60, **258, 840**
  benefits, 260
  construction and use, 258–60
  patterns of variation, 260
    runs, 260, 847
  statistical control, 258
  statistical control chart, 258, 847
  target control, 258–60
conversion cost, 61, 840
cost, 50, 840
cost accounting system, 57, 840
cost allocation, 166, 578, 840
cost allocation base, 146, 840
cost allocation rate, 146, 840
cost analysis, 58–64
  about cost analysis, 58–60
  analysis example, 58–60
  costs of manufacturing, 60–1
  direct costs, 61, 841
    direct labour, 61, 841
    direct material, 61, 841
  gross margin ratio, 58, 843
  indirect cost, 61–2, **61, 843**
    conversion costs, 61, 840
    idle time, 61, 843
    indirect labour cost, 61, 843
    indirect material cost, 61, 843
    manufacturing overhead cost, 61, 843
    overtime premium, 61, 845
  non-manufacturing costs, 62
    administrative costs, 62, 839
    period costs, 62, 845
    selling costs, 62, 847
  operating income, 59, 845
  return on sales ratio, 59, 847
  see also concepts and measures of cost; goods completed and sold, schedule of costs; production stages and flow of costs
cost of capital, 709
cost driver (or cost driver base), 86, 148, 840
cost estimation, 84–120, **86, 840**
  about the example organization, 85–6
  building cost effective solar power example, 108
  comparison of methods, 108–10
    cost equation choice criteria/ issues, 109
    forecasting problems, 109–10
  cost objects, 86, 840
  cost objects and drivers, 89–90
  cost pattern, 90–1
    mixed costs, 90, 91, **844**
    non-linear behaviour, 91, 92
    relevant range, 90, 846
    step (semi-fixed) cost, 90, 91, **847**
  cost-drivers, 86, 840
  decision making typical questions, 87–8
  example application, 110–13
    high cost model, 110–11
    use of the results, 111–12
  key terms, 120

management for, 87
planning/standard setting, 88
product variety and cost, 92
short-run or long-run incremental cost, 92–3
sticky costs research insight, 112
see also learning curves with cost estimation; regression analysis
cost estimation, **account analysis** method, 93–5, **93**, **839**
about the method, 93
application example, 94
cost estimation, engineering method, 105–8
about the method, 105–6
engineering estimates, **105**, **842**
example application, 106–7
job costs, 107
monthly fixed costs, 107
new-customer costs, 107
new-product costs, 107
unit costs, 106
reverse engineering, 107–8
cost estimation, **high-low method**, **100**, **843**
cost estimation, linear regression analysis method, 95–100, **95**, **844**
application example, 96–9
step 1: identify cost/driver relation, 96–7
step 2: gather data, 97
step 3: apply **scattergraph**, **98**, **847**
step 4: perform regression analysis, 98
step 5: interpret results using ***R*-square**, 98–100, **98**, **847**
dependent variables, **95**, **841**
independent variables, **95**, **843**
simple linear regression, **96**, **847**
simple model, 95–6
cost estimation, **multiple regression** analysis method, 101–5, **101**, **844**
adjusted *R*-square, **104**, **839**
application example, 101–4
step 1: identify cost drivers, 101–2
step 2: gather relevant costs, 102
step 3: plot data, 102–3
step 4: perform regression analysis, 103
step 5: interpret results, 103–4
cautionary note, 104
long-run incremental cost (LRIC), 105
cost management, 4–6, **4**, **840**
about the example organizations, 3
attitude requirement, 5
career perspectives, 5
chief financial officer (CFO) career perspectives, 5
commitment requirement, 4
cost management system, **5**, **841**
Singapore Airlines, 6–7
strategic role, 4–7
techniques, 5
through new product development, 22
see also decision-making framework; plans/outcomes evaluation
cost management analysts, 5–6
cost management system, **5**, **841**
cost object, **86**, **841**
cost pools, **145**, **841**
cost reduction target, **197**, **841**
cost of sales, **57**
cost variance, **626**, **841**
accounting for variances, 653–5
fixed overhead volume variance, 654–5, **654**, **843**
cost variance analysis, direct manufacturing costs, 629–35
about the example organization, 625
actual material/labour costs, 630–1
budget variance, 630–1, **630**, **840**
allowance for defects or spoilage, 634
direct labour variances, 633–4
direct labour efficiency variance, **633**, **841**
direct labour rate variance, **633**, **841**
direct material variances, 632–3
direct material price variance, **632**, **842**
direct material quantity variance, **632**, **842**
direct material/labour standards, 629–30
standard direct labour rate, **630**, **847**
standard direct material price, **630**, **847**
standard direct material quantity, **630**, **847**
standard direct material rate, **630**, **847**
international use of flexible budgeting, 633–4
multiple types of direct material and labour, 634
price and quantity variances, 631–2
favourable (variances), **632**, **842**
price variance, **631**, **846**
quantity variance, **631**, **846**
unfavourable (variances), **632**, **848**
variance analysis, **631**, **849**
standard costs given actual output, flexible budget and volume variance, 630
flexible budget, **630**, **843**
relevant range, **630**, **846**
volume variance, **630**, **849**
see also standard costing systems
cost variance analysis, flexible overhead budgets, 635–42
about flexible overhead budgets, 635
about performance reports, 642
activity-based flexible budget, 642–4, **642**, **839**
budget example, 635–6
choice of activity measure, 636–7
based on input or output, 637
caution with dollar measures, 637
impact of changing technology, 637
example budget, 643
fixed overhead budget variance, **640**, **843**
overhead cost performance report, **641**, **845**
overhead cost variances, 638–40
about spending variance, 639–40
interpretation of quantity variance, 639
variable overhead quantity variance, **639**, **848–9**
variable overhead spending variance, **638**, **849**
cost variances, significant features, 644–6
absolute and relative size, 645
controllability, 646
costs/benefits of investigation, 646
favourable variances, 646
recurring variances, 645
trends, 645–6
cost-based transfer pricing, 758–60, **758**, **840**
cost-driver rate, **148**, **840**
cost-flow information, 482–6
job-cost record (or file, card, sheet), 482–4, **482**, **843**

cost-flow information (*Continued*)
recording job-order costs, 484–6
control accounts, 484
direct labour, 486
indirect labour, 486
material requisition form, 485, 844
opening inventories, 484–5
raw and direct material, 485
subsidiary ledgers, 484
tracking job-order costs, 483–4
using the information, 482–3
WIP and FG inventory accounts, 482–3
cost-flow model, 481–2
basic model, 481
cost flows and jobs, 481
examples, 481–2
cost-plus contracts, 599, 841
cost-volume-profit (CVP) model, 289, 841
cost-volume-profit (CVP) planning model, 289–94
about the CVP model, 289
about the example application, 289–90
break-even point, 290, 839
computer spreadsheet set-up, 293–4
about the spreadsheets, 293
gathering information, 293–4
modelling relations among parameters, 294
separating parameters and formulas, 294
contribution margin, 290, 840
graphical format, 290–1
operating leverage, 292–3, **292, 845**
target income, 291
costing systems *see* activity-based costing (ABC) method/ system; traditional costing system
costs of quality (COQ), 239, 841
costs of time, 245
criteria (decision-making), **8, 841**
critical success factors, 420, 841
balanced scorecards, 799
current equivalent units, 551, 841
currently feasible cost, 197, 841
customer always right study, 199
customer profitability and activity-based costing (ABC)
accuracy/timeliness trade-offs, 196
alternative courses of actions, 195
customer profitability analysis, 188, 841
customer-level cost, 142, 188, 841
effects of profitability analysis study, 194–5
example administrative cost analysis, 192–4
distribution costs, 194
finance and human resources costs, 194
general administration costs, 194
marketing costs, 193–4
selling costs, 192–3
example organization details, 187
example profitability analysis, 191–2
as foundation of process improvement, 190–1
importance of profitability, 188–90
profitability measurement, 188–9
profits and service quality study, 190
qualitative considerations, 189–90
see also activity-based management (ABM)
customer profitability analysis, 188, 841
customer relations management, 188, 841
customer response time, 244–5, **244, 841**
customer retention (or loyalty), 796, 841
customer satisfaction, and quality measurement, 239
customer value, 188, 795, 841
customer-focused quality, 231, 841
customer-level cost, 142, 188, 841

D

decentralized (companies), **698, 841**
decentralized organizations, 698–700
behavioural congruence, 698, 839
centralization versus decentralization, 698
centralized, 698, 840
decentralized, 698, 841
decentralization benefits, 698–9
decentralization costs, 699–700
goal congruence, 698, 843
responsibility accounting, 698, 846
see also responsibility accounting
decision alternatives, 8–9, **8, 841**
decision making, short term *see* cost-volume-profit (CVP) model; financial models/ modelling; modelling; pricing influences and decisions; scarce resource modelling; theory of constraints (TOC)
decision tree, 347–9, **347, 841**
alternative options, 348–9
building steps
display alternatives, 347
measure benefits, 347
trace decision paths, 347
opportunity costs issues, 349
power generation example, 349
decision usefulness, 9, 841
decision-making framework, 7–11, **7, 841**
accuracy, 10, 839
criteria, 8, 841
decision alternatives, 8–9, **8, 841**
decision usefulness, 9, 841
financial and non-financial criteria, 9, 842
financial qualification, 9, 843
information quality, 9–10, **9, 843**
objectivity, 9, 845
relevance, 10, 846
relevant costs and benefits, 10, 846
stages
I: setting goals and objectives, 7–8
II: gathering information, 8–10
III: evaluating alternatives, 10
IV: execution and tracking costs, 11
V: obtaining feedback, 11
subjectivity, 9, 848
sunk costs, 10, 848
tangible objectives, 7, 848
timeliness, 10, 848
decision-making models, 297–9
with multiple cost drivers, 300–3
defect, 229, 841
Delphi technique, 424
Deming Prize, 243, 841
dependent variables, 95, 841
direct cost, 48, 61, 841
direct labour, 61, 841
direct labour budget, 432, **432, 841**
direct labour efficiency variance, 633, 841
direct labour mix variance, 659, 841

direct labour rate variance, **633**, **841**
direct labour yield variance, **659**, **841**
direct material, **61**, **841**
direct material budget, 430–2, **430**, **841–2**
direct material mix variance, **657**, **842**
direct material price variance, **632**, **842**
direct material quantity variance, **632**, **842**
direct material yield variance, **657**, **842**
direct method (of cost allocation), 588–92, **588**, **842**
discount rate, 352–5, **352**, **842**
  about discount rate, 352–3
  effective discount rate and nominal rate, 353
  effective discount rates for different period lengths, 353–4
  inflation effects, 354
  risk issues, 363
  taxation effects, 354–5
discounted cash flow (DCF), **346**, 350–62, **842**
  comparing investment alternatives, 360–2
    annuity, **362**, **839**
    comparing alternatives yearly, 362
    inconsistent ranking, **360**, **843**
    inconsistent ranking of alternatives, 360–1
    independent alternatives, 360
    mutual exclusive alternatives, 360
  discount rate, 352–5, **352**, **842**
  discounting future cash flows, 355–6
  estimating flows for analysis, 350–1
    disinvestment (termination) cash flows, 351
    exclusions, 351
    investment cash flows, 350
    periodic operating cash flows, 350–1
    tax effects, 350
  example illustrating NPV analysis, 351–2
  internal rate of return (IRR), **356**, 358–62, **843**
  net present value (NPV), 356–7, **356**, **844**
  payback period, **356**, 357–8, **845**
  present value, **355**, **845–6**
  risk issues, 353
  timing cash flows, 360
  see also decision tree
discounted cash flow (DCF), other decision applications, 363–9
  add or drop a product, service or business unit, 367–9
    relevant cash flows, 367–9
    unfinished business, 369
  outsourcing or make-or-buy, 364–5
    example outsourcing decision, 365–6
    make-or-buy decision, **364**, **844**
    outsourcing, **364**, **845**
    outsourcing pitfalls, 366–7
  replacement of equipment, 363–4
discretionary cost centre, **700**, **842**
divisional autonomy, and transfer pricing, 761–2
dropping a business, 367–9
dual transfer pricing system, 762–3, **762**, **842**
due diligence, **372**, **842**

E

Easy-Jet, 48
econometric models, 425
economic order quantity (EOQ), **447**, **842**
economic value added (EVA), **716**, **842**
  Bosch use of EVA, 723
  does EVA pay? research insight, 716
  see also invested capital measurement for EVA, ROI and RI; investment centre operating income measurement
emerging markets, competition from, 17
employee capabilities, **792**, **842**
engineering estimates, **105**, **842**
enterprise resource planning (ERP) study, 238
environmental strategic decisions, 26–7
EOQ model, **447**, **842**
equation approach, inventory management, 448
equivalent units, **543**, **842**
ethical issues
  in budgeting, 445
  incentive systems, 817–18
  internal controls, 24–5
  with job costing, 500–1
    about ethics with costing, 500
    charging to wrong job, 500
    fraudulent costs in contracts, 500
    misrepresenting costs, 501
    misstating the stage of completion, 500
    understanding contracts, 501
  with responsibility accounting, 713–14
  strategic investments, 386–7
  support service cost allocations, 600
  in transfer pricing, 759–60
  see also legal and ethical issues in strategic investment analysis
ethical standards issues, 23–6
  bias from personal commitment, 23–6
  codes of ethics, 24
  dilemmas of ordinary people, 23
  fear of loss of prestige, 23
  greed and fraud, 23
  internal auditing to assure compliance, 25–6
  internal controls for asset protection and quality of information, 24–5
  Sarbanes-Oxley Act, 24
    CEOs and CFOs responsibilities, 24
European Quality Award (EQA), **243**, **842**
Excel's Pivot table, 203
excess (or unused) capacity, **250**, 754–5, 757, **842**
expectancy theory, **807**, **842**
expected value, **375**, **842**
expected value analysis, 374–6, **375**, **842**
  expected value, **375**, **842**
  future actions of competitors, 379–80
  investing in high technology, 381–2
  real option value (ROV) analysis, 381–5, **381**, **846**
  scenario analysis, 375
  sensitivity analysis, 375
expense, **57**, **842**
extended value chain, **15**, **842**
external failure (correction), **241**, **842**
extrinsic rewards, **807**, **842**

F

facility-level cost, **142**, **842**
favourable (variances), **632**, **842**
feasible solution space, **317**, **842**

final product, **532**, **428**
Financial Accounting Standards Board (FASB), 766
financial budget, **422**, **842**
financial model, **65**, **286**, **842–3**
financial models/modelling, 64–5, 286–9
  example organization, 285–6
  future and differences only are relevant, 288–9
  kinds of models
    pro forma (budgeted) statements, 287
    relations among costs, revenues and income, 287
    relations between current investments and profitability/value, 287
    specialized models, 287
  objectives, 287–8
    decision making, 287–8
    flexible/responsive analyses, 288
    simulation of factors and relations, 288
  see also cost-volume-profit (CVP) model; multiple cost driver modelling
financial and non-financial criteria (decision-making), **9**, **842**
financial planning model, 442–3, **442**, **843**
financial qualification (decision-making), **9**, **843**
finished goods (FG) inventory, **63**, **843**
first-in, first-out (FIFO) costing, 549–52, **549**, **843**
fixed cost, 54–5, **54**, **843**
fixed manufacturing overheads, 495
fixed overhead budget variance, **640**, **843**
fixed overhead volume variance, 654–5, **654**, **843**
flexible budget, **630**, **843**
flexible budgeting, international use, 633–4
flowchart, 236–7, **236**, **843**
Foreign Corrupt Practices Act, 25
forward-looking indicators, 788
further processing costs (joint products), **535**, **843**

G

Gantt chart, 256–7, **256**, **843**
goal congruence, **698**, **843**
goods completed and sold, schedule of costs, 64–6
  about the schedule, 64
  financial model, 64–5, **65**, **842–3**
  statement of goods completed, 65–6
    example statement, 64
    finished goods, 66
    work in progress, 65
graphical approach, inventory management, 448
gross book value, 718–19
gross margin ratio, **58**, **843**

H

high-low method (cost estimation), **100**, **843**
histogram, 232–3, **232**, **843**

I

idle time, **61**, **843**
imperfect competition, **761**, **843**
incentive plans in non-profit organizations, 817
incentive systems, **788**, 805–8, **805**, **843**
  about incentive systems, 805
  compensation based on measured performance, 806–8
    expectancy theory, **807**, **842**
    extrinsic rewards, **807**, **842**
    guideline design plans, 807–8
    incentive plan design, 807–8
    intrinsic rewards, **807**, **843**
  example system summary, 818–20
  incentives and compensation, ethical aspects, 817–18
  measurement of performance, 805–6
    measurement properties required, 806
  pay for performance (principle), **805**, **845**
incentive systems, performance-based, 808–17
  about performance-based incentives, 808
  absolute performance evaluation, 808–9, **808**, **839**
  current or deferred rewards, 813–14
    bonus bank, **814**, **839**
    current rewards, 813–14
    deferred rewards, 814
  financial or non-financial performance, 811–13
    financial, accounting measures or share price?, 811–12
    non-financial, operational/organizational/social/environmental factors, 812–13
  formula-based or subjective performance, 810–11
    measurement properties required, 811
    performance evaluation formula, **810**, **845**
    subjective performance evaluation, **811**, **848**
  international use of subjective evaluations, 816
  narrow or broad performance responsibility, 813
  relative performance evaluation, 809–10, **809**, **846**
    application example, 810
    benchmarks, 809
    disadvantages, 809
  salary, bonus or share rewards, 814–15
    cash bonuses, 815
    salary, 815
    share appreciation rights (SARs), **815**, **847**
    share awards, 815
    share options, **816**, **847**
inconsistent ranking, **360**, **843**
independent variables, **95**, **843**
indexed cost allocation bases, **586**, **843**
indirect costs, **48**, 61–2, **61**, **843**
indirect labour cost, **61**, **843**
indirect material cost, **61**, **843**
inflation effects, and discount rates, 354
information quality, 9–10, **9**, **843**
information technology (IT) impact, 650
integrity *see* quality and integrity
intermediate product, **532**, **843**
internal audit, **387**, **843**
internal control, **24**, **843**
  for ethical standard issues, 24–5
  Foreign Corrupt Practices Act, 25
  Sarbanes-Oxley Act, 25
internal failure (of quality control), **240–1**, **843**
internal rate of return (IRR), 358–62, **358**, 709, **843**
  spreadsheets for, 358–9
internal transaction and transfer prices, **726**, **848**
  see also transfer pricing...
International Accounting Standards Board (IASB), 766

international transfer pricing *see* transfer pricing: international practices/ regulations
international use of flexible budgeting, 633–4
intrinsic rewards, 807, 843
inventory carrying costs, 250, 843
inventory management, 447–50
 economic order quantity (EOQ), 447–8, **447, 842**
 EOQ model, 447, 842
 equation approach, 448
 graphical approach, 448
 safety stock, 449–50, **450, 847**
 tabular approach, 447–8
 timing of orders, 449
  lead time, 449, 844
 under JIT, 450
invested capital measurement for EVA, ROI and RI, 717–23
 allocating assets, 720
 average balances, 718
 dysfunctional behavioural effects, 720
 summary, 722–3
 use gross or net book value?, 718
  advantages of gross book value, 719
  advantages of net book value, 719
 use total assets?, 718
investment centre, 701–2, **701, 843**
 see also performance measurement in investment centres; performance measures alternatives
investment centre operating income measurement, 720–1
 controllability issue, 720–1
 managers versus investment centres, 721
investment decisions, 344–71
 about investment decisions, 346, 347
 discounted cash flow (DCF), 346, 842
 example organization, 345–6
 see also decision tree
ISO 9000 standard, 243–4, 843

J

job costs/costing, ethical issues, 500–1
job and project management, 256–7
 Gantt charts, 256, 257, **843**
 project cost and time budgets, 256–7
 project scheduling, 256–7
 see also control charts
job-cost record (or file, card, sheet), 482, 843
job-order costs/costing, 479–80, **479, 843**
 about the example organization, 477–9
 applications, 479–80
 appropriate uses, 479
 demonstration of use, 494
 information and decision making, 494–9
 information technology (IT) use with, 495
 job-order costs tracking, 483–4
 operation costing, 480, 552–4, **552, 845**
 process costing comparison, 480
 relevance to value chain, 498–9
 in service organizations, 499
 widespread use, 480
 see also cost-flow information; cost-flow model; ethical issues; product costing systems/methods
joint costs, 532, 843
joint product process, 532, 844
joint product processes, 532–7
 allocation of costs, 538–41
  by-products, 538, 840
  constant gross margin percentage method, 548–9, **548, 840**
  main products, 538, 844
  net realizable value (NRV) method, 539–40, **539, 844**
  for not-for-profit organizations, 541
  not-for-profit organizations, 641
  physical measures (or quantities) method, 539, 845
  relative sales value at split-off method, 548, 846
 example of multiple outputs, 532–3
 example organization, 531
 split off, 532
  final product, 532, 842
  intermediate product, 532, 843
  joint costs, 532, 843
  split-off point, 532, 847
  waste, 532, 849
 see also process costing systems
joint product processes decisions
 which outputs decision, 533–7
  example of timber facility, 534
  further processing costs, 535, 843
  joint product profit estimation, 533–5
 which stage to sell decision, 535–7
  decision tree, 536
  example with timber, 537
  most profitable products, 535
  net realizable value (NRV), 535, 844
joint products, 532, 844
just-in-time (JIT), 250, 844
just-in-time (JIT) or lean process management, 250–6
 inventory carrying costs, 250, 843
 and inventory management, 450
 just-in-time (JIT), 250, 844
  benefits study, 255
 lean processes, 250, 844
  benefits, 251
 traditional processes contrasts, 251–3
  JIT 'pull' manufacturing, 252
  JIT/lean success factors, 253–4
  manufacturing inventory analysis, 252–3, 254
  overall equipment effectiveness (OEE), 252, 845
  traditional 'push' manufacturing, 251–2
 see also time management

K

kaizen costing, 652–3, **652, 844**

L

lagging indicators (performance), **789, 844**
lagging indicators of quality, 232, 844
lead time, 449, 844
leading indicators, 788–9, **788, 844**
 of business/production process efficiency, 789
 of customer value, 789
 of organizational learning and growth, 789
leading indicators of quality, 232, 844
lean processes, 250, 844
 benefits, 251
learning curve, 116, 844
learning curves with cost estimation, 116–19

learning curves with cost estimation (*Continued*)
application to cost management, 118
decision making, 118–19
estimating the curve, 119
learning phenomenon, **116**, **844**
performance evaluation, 119
learning phenomenon, **116**, **844**
least squares regression, how it works, 113–14
legal and ethical issues in strategic investment analysis, 386–7
internal audits, **387**, **843**
internal pressures, 386–7
role of internal controls and audits, 387
life-cycle costing, **310**, **844**
linear programming, 316–20, **317**, **844**
about linear programming models, 317–18
feasible solution space, **317**, **842**
objective function, **317**, **845**
optimum point, 317–18, **317**, **845**
model formulation, 318–19
model solution, 319–20
spreadsheet model, 318–19
linear regression analysis, 95–100
long-run incremental cost (LRIC), 105
lower control limit, **233**, **844**

M

main product, **538**, **844**
make-or-buy decision, **364**, **844**
Malcolm Baldrige National Quality Award, **243**, **844**
management by exception, 626–7, **626**, **705**, **844**
manufacturing overhead budget, 432–4, **432**, **844**
manufacturing overheads, 61, 487–93
about manufacturing overheads, 61, 487
applied overhead, **490**, **839**
fixed, 495
manufacturing overhead budget, 432–4, **432**, **844**
manufacturing overhead cost, **61**, 487–8, **844**
over-applied overhead, **491**, **845**
overhead-variance, 490–3, **491**, **845**
disposition of, 491
periodic operating income, 493
predetermined overhead rate, 488–90, **488**, **845**
prorating a materially large variance, 492
market prices, and pricing decisions, 309
market share, 796
market strategy, for pricing decisions, 308
market value versus historical cost accounting, 721
market-based transfer price, 756–7, **756**, **844**
master budget (profit plan), **422**, **844**
master budget for planning, 422–8
activity-based budgeting (ABB), 427–8, **428**, **839**
benefits, 428
budgeted financial statements, 426
international aspects, 426
for non-profit organizations, 425–6, **425**, 426, **845**
capital budget, 425
cash budget, 425
manufacturing firms, 425
service-industry firms, 425
operational budgets, merchandising firms, 425
sales budget, 422–5
Delphi technique, 424
econometric models, 425
market researchers, 424
sales forecasting, 423–4, **423**, **847**
sales staff, 424
starting point, 422–3
see also budgeting systems...
master budget illustration/example, 429–43
assumptions and predictions, 442
budgeted balance sheet, 440–2, **440**, **840**
budgeted income statement, **440**, **840**
budgeted schedule of cost of goods manufactured and sold, **439**, **840**
cash budget (combining receipts and payments), 438–9, **438**, **840**
cash payments budget, 436–8, **436**, **840**
cash receipts budget, 435–6, **435**, **840**
direct labour budget, 432, **432**, **841**
and cost hierarchy, 432
direct material budget, 430–2, **430**, **841–2**
production/purchasing link, 431–2
financial planning models, 442–3, **442**, **843**
uncollectable accounts expense, 443–4
manufacturing overhead budget, 432–4, **432**, **844**
activity-based budgeting (ABB), 433–4
cost hierarchy, 433
production budget, 429–30, **429**, **846**
sales budget, **429**, **847**
selling, general and administrative (SG&A) expense budget, 434–5, **434**, **847**
material requisition form, **485**, **844**
maximum quality level, **229**, **844**
measures of cost *see* concepts and measures of cost
mixed costs, **90**, 91, **844**
model elasticity, **304**, **844**
modelling
decision-making models, 297–9
decision-making models with multiple cost drivers, 300–3
multiple cost drivers, 299
multiple product modelling, 296–7
multiproduct profit-planning models, 297–9
profit-planning models with multiple cost drivers, 300–3
scarce resource modelling, 306–7
tax modelling, 295–6
see also cost-volume-profit (CVP) model; financial models/modelling
multi-criteria decision making, 370–1, **370**, **844**
multicollinearity, **115**, **844**
multinational transfer pricing, 764–6
multiple cost driver modelling, 299
cost-driver activities, 299
revenue-driver activities, 299
multiple product modelling, 296–7
break-even sales volume, 297

product mix, **296**, **846**
sales mix, **296**, **847**
weighted-average unit contribution margin (WAUCM), 296–7, **296**, **849**
multiple regression, 101–5, **101**, **844**
multiproduct profit-planning models, 297–9

N

negotiated transfer pricing, **760**, **844**
net book value, 718–19
net present value (NPV), 356–7, **356**, **844**
using spreadsheets for, 358–9
net realizable value (NRV), **535**, **844**
net realizable value (NRV) method, **539**, **844**
new product development time, **244**, **844**
non-compensatory method, **371**, **844**
non-financial performance measures, 724–5
non-profit organizations
incentive plans, 817
performance measurement, 725–6
non-value-added activities, **198**, **844**
normal costing system, **488**, **844–5**
normal production capacity, **153**, **488**, **845**
normal spoilage, **545**, **845**
not-for-profit organizations, job cost allocation, 541

O

objective function, **317**, **845**
objectivity (decision-making), **9**, **845**
Office of Fair trading (UK), 310
operating income, **59**, **709**, **845**
measurement for EVA, ROI and RI, 717–23
see also invested capital measurement for EVA, ROI and RI
operating leverage (CVP model), 292–3, **292**, **845**
operation, **845**
operation costing, **480**, 552–4, **552**, **845**
motor scooter illustration, 553–4
operational budgets, 425–6, **425**, **845**
see also master budget for planning
operational performance analysis, **19**, **845**
opportunity cost, **50**, **349**, 754, **845**
optimum point (linear programming), **317**, **845**
outlay cost, 754
outsourcing, **15**, **364**, **845**
pitfalls, 346–7
value chain outsourcing, 15–16
over-applied overhead, **491**, **845**
overall equipment effectiveness (OEE), **252**, **845**
overhead cost performance report, **641**, **845**
overhead-variance, 490–3, **491**, **845**
disposition, 491
overheads *see* manufacturing overheads; predetermined overhead rate
overtime premium, **61**, **845**

P

padding the budget, 444–5, **444**, **845**
Pareto chart, 237–8, **237**, **845**
participative budgeting, **445**, **845**
pay for performance (principle), **805**, **845**
payback period, 357–8, **357**, **845**
perfect competition, **761**, **845**
perfection (or ideal) standard, **628**, **845**
performance evaluation formula, **810**, **845**
performance indicators
communicating strategy to employees, 789–90
benchmarking, **790**, **839**
strategy maps, **789**, **848**
forward-looking indicators, 788
lagging indicators, **789**, **844**
leading indicators, **788**, **844**
motivating employees, 790
performance evaluation, 790
performance measure, **18**, **845**
performance measurement in investment centres, 708–16
about the investment centres, 708–9
cost of capital, 709–10
weighted-average cost of capital (WACC), 709–10, **709**, **849**
economic value added (EVA) as a measure, **716**, **842**
internal rate of return, 709
operating income, **709**, **845**
residual income (RI) as a measure, 714–15, **714**, **846**
return on investment (ROI) as a measure, 710–14, **710**, **847**
capital turnover, **711**, **840**
ethical considerations, 713–14
factors underlying ROI, 711
improving ROI, 711–12
sales margin, **711**, **847**
when not to make investments, 713
when to make investments, 712–13
wrong incentives problem, 712
performance measures alternatives, 724–6
non-financial performance measures, 724–5
non-profit organizations, 725–6
share price performance, 724
view investment centres as collections of investments, 725
performance report (responsibility accounting), 705–6, **705**, **845**
performance reports, research insight, 642
period costs, **57**, **62**, **845**
physical measures (or quantities) method, 539–40, **539**, **845**
pilot project (for ABM with ABC), **206**, **845**
plans/outcomes evaluation, 19–22
benefit and cost variances, 21–2
benefit-cost analysis, 19–20, **20**, **839**
operational performance analysis, **19**, **845**
qualitative information, **20**, **846**
quantitative information, **20**, **846**
strategic performance analysis, **19**, **848**
plausible correlation, **585**, **845**
practical capacity, **152**, 250, **845**
practical (or attainable) standards, 628–9, **628**, **845**
predatory pricing, **311**, **845**

predetermined overhead rate, 488–90, **488**, **845**
normal costing systems, **488**, **844–5**
normal production capacity, **488**, **845**
steps to establish, 488–9
transfers to cost of sales, 490
transfers to goods inventory, 489–90
present value, **355**, **845–6**
prevention (activities for quality), **240**, **846**
price variance, **631**, **846**
pricing influences and decisions, 308–13
about pricing, 308
Bundeskartellamt (Germany), 310
competitor actions, 309
Conseil de la Concurrence (France), 310
costs considerations, 309–10
customer considerations, 309
life-cycle costing, **310**, **844**
market prices, 309
market strategy, 308
Office of Fair trading (UK), 310
politics and image, 311
predatory pricing, **311**, **845**
pricing for the internet, 311
pricing law, 310–11
product life cycle, **310**, **846**
revenue management, 312
special orders, **312**, **847**
relevant costs, 312–13
value-based pricing, 308
process, **14**, **846**
process capacity, **249**, **846**
process capacity management, 249–50
buffer capacity, **250**, **840**
capacity measurement, 250
excess (or unused) capacity, **250**, **842**
practical capacity, 250
process capacity, **249**, **846**
process costing, **480**, **846**
process costing systems, 541–7, **541**, **846**
about the systems, 541
operation costing, 552–4, **552**, **845**
see also joint product processes
process costing systems example 1: no opening WIP or spoilage, 541–4
step 1: summarize flow, 542–3
step 2: compute equivalent number of units, 542–3, 543
equivalent units, **543**, **842**
step 3: accumulate costs, 543–4
step 4: compute costs, 544
step 5: allocate costs, 544
production cost report, **544**, **846**
process costing systems example 2: opening/closing WIP and spoilage, 544–7
abnormal spoilage, **545**, **839**
concepts, 544–5
environmental costs, 545
normal spoilage, **545**, **845**
spoilage measurement, 544–5
spoilage, **544**, **847**
waste, **544**, **849**
step 1: summarize flow, 546–7
step 2: compute units, 547
step 3: accumulate costs, 547
weighted-average process costing, **547**, **849**
step 4: compute costs, 547
step 5: allocate costs, 547
process costing systems example 3: **first-in, first-out (FIFO) costing**, 549–52, **549**, **843**
step 1: summarize flow, 550–1
step 2: compute units, 551
current equivalent units, **551**, **841**
step 3: accumulate costs, 551
step 4: compute costs, 551–2
step 5: allocate costs, 552
process productivity *see* productivity and efficiency management
product cost, **57**, **846**
product costing systems/ methods, 479–80, **479**, **846**
absorption (accrual, full) costing, 495–8, **495**, **839**
misleading issues warning, 498
comparison of absorption/ variable costing, 495–6
contribution margin, **496**, **840**
design issues, 484
absorption costing, 484
job order costing, 484
normal costing, 484
predetermined overhead rate, 484
evaluation of absorption/variable costing, 496–8
pricing decisions, 497–8
product-cost information, 496–7
use of both methods, 498
fixed manufacturing overheads, 495
operation costing, **480**, **845**
process costing, **480**, **846**
throughput costing, **502**, **848**
variable costing, 495–8, **495**, **848**
see also cost-flow information; cost-flow model; job-order costs/costing
product life cycle, **310**, **846**
product mix (multiple products), **296**, **846**
product-level cost, **142**, **846**
production budget, 429–30, **429**, **846**
production cost report, **544**, **846**
production cycle time, **244**, **846**
production mix and yield variances, 656–9
direct material mix variance, **657**, **842**
direct material yield variance, **657**, **842**
multiple direct labour inputs, 658–9
direct labour mix variance, **659**, **841**
direct labour yield variance, **659**, **841**
multiple direct material input example, 656–8
in service organizations, 659
production (or line) departments, **576**, **846**
production processes, **247**, **846**
production stages and flow of costs, 62–4
finished goods (FG) inventory, **63**, **843**
raw material inventory, **63**, **846**
shrinkage, 63–4, **63**, **847**
waste, **63**, **849**
work in progress (WIP) inventory, **63**, **849**
productivity, **247**, **846**
productivity and efficiency management, 247–9
average cycle time, **247**, **839**
measuring, 248
business processes, **247**, **840**
production processes, **247**, **846**
productivity, **247**, **846**
productivity measurement, 247–8
throughput, **247**, **848**
throughput efficiency, **248**, **848**
measuring, 248–9
throughput time analysis, 249
throughput time ratio, **247**, 249, **848**
throughput time ratio, **247**, 249, **848**

total factor productivity, **247, 848**
see also time management
profit centre, **701, 846**
profit plan (master budget), **422, 846**
profit-planning models with multiple cost drivers, 300–3
project management *see* job and project management

Q

qualitative information, **20, 846**
quality improvement methods, 229–31
defects, **229, 841**
maximum quality level, **229, 844**
return on quality (ROQ), 229–30, **229, 847**
total quality management (TQM), **229, 848**
TQM versus ROQ, 230
quality and integrity, 243–4
awards and certificates
Deming Prize, **243, 841**
European Quality Award (EQA), **243, 842**
ISO 9000 standard, **243–4, 843**
Malcolm Baldrige National Quality Award, **243, 844**
ethical behaviour and reputation examples, 243
quality management, 226–62
controlling quality, 240
appraisal activities, **240, 839**
external failure, **241, 842**
internal failure, **240–1, 843**
prevention activities, **240, 846**
costs of quality (COQ), 239, **841**
measuring, 241
reporting, 241–3
example organisation, 227–8
importance of quality, 228–9
quality dimensions, 231–2
customer service, 231–2
customer-focused quality, **231, 841**
return on quality study, 231
strategic effect examples, 228–9
see also just-in-time (JIT) or lean process management; productivity and efficiency management; quality improvement methods; quality management; time management
quality measurement, 232–43
cause-and-effect analysis/diagrams, 234–5, **234, 840**
control charts, 233–4, **233, 840**
and customer satisfaction, 239
diagnostic information, 234–8
enterprise resource planning (ERP) study, 238
flowcharts, 236–7, **236, 843**
histograms, 232–3, **232, 843**
lagging indicators of quality, **232, 844**
leading indicators of quality, **232, 844**
lower control limits, **233, 844**
Pareto charts, 237–8, **237, 845**
quality/price trade-offs, 239
run charts, 233–4, **233, 847**
scatter diagrams, **236, 847**
upper control limits, **233, 848**
variation issues, 232–3
quantitative information, **20, 846**
quantity variance, **631, 846**

R

***R*-square**, **98, 847**
adjusted *R*-square, **104, 839**
raw material inventory, **63, 846**
real option tree analysis by rolling backward, 389–92
imperfect predictive information, 390–2
perfect predictive information, 389–90
real option value, **385, 846**
real option value (ROV) analysis, 381–5, **381, 846**
deferring irreversible decisions, 382–4
real option value, **385, 846**
real option value decision tree, 384
value of option to wait, 385
reciprocal method (of cost allocation), 601–5, **601, 846**
reciprocal services, **596, 846**
regression analysis, 95–100, **95, 846**
regression, technical notes, 113–15
coefficients, confidence in, 114
***t*-statistic**, **114, 848**
least squares regression, how it works, 113–14
multicollinearity, **115, 844**
residuals, 114–15
relative performance evaluation, 809–10, **809, 846**
relative sales value at split-off method, **548, 846**
relevance, **10, 846**
relevant costs and benefits, **10, 846**
relevant range, **90, 630, 846**
reporting costs and expenses, 56–8
cash outflow issues, 58
cost accounting systems, **57, 840**
cost of sales, **57**
expense, **57, 842**
period cost, **57, 845**
product cost, **57, 846**
reserve capacity, **153, 846**
residual income (RI) as a measure, 714–15, **714, 846**
see also invested capital measurement for EVA, ROI and RI; investment centre operating income measurement
residuals, regression
are independent, 115
are normally distributed, 114–15
assumptions about, 114
variance is constant, 115
resources supplied, **153, 846**
resources used, **147, 846**
responsibility accounting, **698**, 700–6, **846**
affect on behaviour, 707–8
cost or revenue responsibility?, 707
motivating the desired behaviour, 707–8
provides information or places blame?, 707
application by Unilever, 704–5
and budgets, 706
discretionary cost centres, 700–1, **700, 842**
investment centres, 701–2, **701, 843**
management by exception, **705, 844**
performance reports, 705–6, **705, 845**
profit centres, **701, 846**
responsibility centres, **700, 846**
revenue centres, **701, 847**
Sarbanes-Oxley Act, 708
standard cost centre, **700, 847**
and variance analysis, 706

responsibility accounting (*Continued*)
see also budget administration responsibility; performance measurement in investment centres
responsibility accounting illustration, 702–5
about the company illustrated, 697–8
about the illustration, 702
corporate level, 702–3
department level, 704
divisional level, 703–4
plant level, 704
work centre level, 704
responsibility centre, **700**, **846**
return on investment (ROI), 710–14, **710**, **847**
see also invested capital measurement for EVA, ROI and RI; investment centre operating income measurement
return on quality (ROQ), 229–30, **229**, **847**
return on sales ratio, **59**, **847**
revenue budget variance, **661**, **847**
revenue centre, **701**, **847**
revenue management, and pricing decisions, 312
revenue market share variance, **664**, **847**
revenue market size variance, **664**, **847**
revenue sales mix variance, 662–3, **662**, **847**
revenue sales quantity variance, **663**, **847**
revenue sales volume variance, **662**, **847**
reverse engineering cost estimation, 107–8
rewards and risks, 12–13
risks
and discounted cash flow, 353
high and low risk strategies, 13
risks (activity-based management), **201**, **847**
rolling (or revolving or continuous) budget, **422**, **847**
run chart, 233–4, **233**, **847**
run (control charts), **260**, **847**

S

safety stock, 449–50, **450**, **847**
sales budget, 422–5, **429**, **847**
see also master budget for planning
sales forecasting, 423–4, **423**, **847**
sales forecasts in retailing, research insight, 306
sales margin (and ROI), **711**, **847**
sales mix (multiple products), **296**, **847**
in practice, 297
sales price variance, 661–2, **661**, **847**
sales variance analysis, 659–66
focus on contribution margin, 665–6
focus on sales revenue, 659, 661–5
revenue budget variance, **661**, **847**
revenue market share variance, **664**, **847**
revenue market size variance, **664**, **847**
revenue sales mix variance, 662–3, **662**, **847**
revenue sales quantity variance, **663**, **847**
revenue sales volume variance, **662**, **847**
sales price variance, 661–2, **661**, **847**
illustration example, 660
Sarbanes-Oxley Act, 24, 708
scarce resource modelling, 306–7
maximization of profit with, 307
see also theory of constraints (TOC)
scatter diagram, **236**, **847**
scattergraph, **98**, **847**
scenario analysis, 305–6, **305**, 375, **847**
research insight, 306
second-stage cost allocation, 591–2, **591**, **847**
selling costs, **62**, **192**, **847**
selling, general and administrative (SG&A) expense budget, 434–5, **434**, **847**
sensitivity analysis, 303–6, 375
model elasticity, **304**, **844**
scenario analysis, 305–6, **305**, **847**
service cost *see* support service costs
service organizations
job-order costing, 499
mix and yield variances, 659
share appreciation rights (SARs), **815**, **847**
share options, **816**, **847**
share price performance, 724
shrinkage, 63–4, **63**, **847**
simple linear regression, **96**, **847**
Singapore Airlines, cost management practice, 6–7
solar power, cost effective, 108
special orders (price decisions), **312**, **847**
split-off point, **532**, **847**
spoilage, **544**, **847**
stages of production *see* production stages and flow of costs
standard cost, **626**, **847**
standard cost centre, **700**, **847**
standard costing, behavioural effects, 646–9
about standard cost with variance analysis, 646–7
interaction among variances, 648
managers' influence on variances, 647
direct labour efficiency variance, 647
direct labour rate variance, 647
direct material price variances, 647
direct material quantity variance, 647
trade-offs among variances, 648–9
standard costing systems, 626–9
cost variance, **626**, **841**
management by exception, 626–7, **626**, **844**
non-manufacturing organizations, use by, 629
perfection versus practical issue, 628–9
perfection (or ideal) standard, **628**, **845**
practical (or attainable) standard, 628–9, **628**, **845**
setting standards
activity analysis, **627**, **839**
analysis of historical data, 627
historical with task analysis, 627
with non-accounting staff, 627–8
staff reluctance problem, 628
task analysis, **627**, **848**
standard cost, **626**, **847**
see also cost variance analysis...
standard costing systems, changing role and adaptation, 649–53
benchmarking, 651
cost drivers, 651
cost of ownership study, 653

emphasis on material and overhead costs, 651
high quality and zero defects, 651
information technology impact, 650
software packages, 650
kaizen costing, 652–3, **652**, **844**
labour standards and variances, reduced importance, 651
non-financial measure for control, 651
open book accounting, 652
shorter product life cycles, 651
total costs of ownership, 651–2
traditional advantages, 649–50
standard direct labour quantity, **630**, **847**
standard direct labour rate, **630**, **847**
standard direct material price, **630**, **847**
standard direct material quantity, **630**, **847**
statistical control chart, **258**, **847**
step method (of cost allocation), 592–6, **592**, **848**
step (semi-fixed) costs, **90**, 91, **847**
strategic decision making, 11–19, **11**, **848**
about strategic decision making, 11–12
environmental strategic decisions, 26–7
missions rewards/risks, 12–13
build, 13
divest, 13
harvest, 13
hold, 13
strategy, **11**, **848**
sustainability, 26–7, **26**, **848**
see also change, leading and managing; competitive advantages...; plans/outcomes evaluation
strategic investment decisions
example analysis of invest now, 388
using financial and non-financial information, 370–1
compensatory methods, **371**, **840**
multi-criteria decision making, 370–1, **370**, **844**
non-compensatory methods, **371**, **844**
see also discounted cash flow (DCF); expected value analysis
strategic investments, 371–9, **371**, **848**
bundling assets, 377
in China and India, 372
due diligence, **372**, **842**
example of forecasts of investment information, 377–9
external events, information sources, 372–3
external factors, uncontrollable, 372
internal information, 376
investments in technology, non-financial benefits, 379
legal and ethical issues, 386–7
uncontrollable future events, identification, 373–4
economic events, 374
natural events, 373–4
social, political and legal events, 374
see also discounted cash flow (DCF); expected value
strategic performance analysis, **19**, **848**
strategic planning for competitive advantage, 420–1
cost control, 420
critical success factors, **420**, **841**
market share, 420–1
strategy, **11**, **848**
strategy map, 789–90, **789**, **848**
subjective performance evaluation, **811**, **848**
subjectivity (decision-making), **9**, **848**
sunk costs, **10**, **55**, **848**
support service costs, 574–606, **576**, **579**, **848**
internal or outsourced services?, 576–7
cost issues, 577
knowledge base, 577
reliability issues, 577
sensitive information issue, 577
production (or line) departments, **576**, **846**
support service costs allocation steps, 583–600
step 1: identify categories and amounts, 584–5
cost pool choice, 584
cost of resources used versus supplied, 584–5
step 2: choose the appropriate allocation base(s), 585–7
indexed cost allocation bases, **586**, **843**
plausible correlation, **585**, **845**
plausible/justifiable bases, 586–7
proportional use of services, 587
step 3: select and use an appropriate method, 587–96
direct method, 588–92, **588**, **842**
application example, 588–90
benefits and limitations, 590–1
reciprocal method, 601–5, **601**, **846**
application examples, 601–5
direct, step, and reciprocal methods comparisons, 605
second-stage cost allocation, 591–2, **591**, **847**
public works department example, 592
step method, 592–6, **592**, **848**
application example, 593–6
benefits and limitations, 596
reciprocal services, **596**, **846**
step 4: are desired results achieved?, 596–600
accuracy, **597**, **839**
accurate cost allocation, **597**, **839**
behavioural effects, 598
consistency of cost allocation, 597–8, **597**, **840**
costs and benefits, 599
effects on cost-plus contracts, **599**, **841**
effects on decision making, 598
effects on distribution of costs, 598
effects on performance evaluation, 598
ethical issues, 600
international tax and customs tariff impacts, 598
support service costs management, 577–83
allocation of costs for
cost-based contracting, 581
decision making, 580–1
influencing behaviour, 582
pricing, 581
profit awareness, 582
required reporting, 582–3
charges recovery approaches

support service costs management (*Continued*)
from general revenues, 577–8
from the providers of the services, 578
cost allocation, 578, 840
deciding who pays, 579–80
distinguishing services from production, 578–9
support service (or indirect) departments, 576, 848
sustainability, 26–7, **26, 848**
sustainability and the Lafuma Group, 27

T

***t*-statistic, 114, 848**
tableau de bord, 790, 791, **848**
tabular approach, inventory management, 447–8
tangible objectives, 7, 848
target cost, 196, 848
target costing and activity-based costing (ABC), 196–7
cost reduction target, 197, 841
currently feasible cost, 197, 841
task analysis, 627, 848
tax modelling, 295–6
theoretical capacity, 152, 848
theory of constraints (TOC), 314–16, **314, 848**
application
1: identify measure of value created, 314–15
2: identify bottleneck, 314, 315
3: use bottleneck(s), 314, 316
4: synchronize to bottleneck(s), 314, 316
5:increase capacity, 314, 316
6:avoid inertia, 314, 316
constraints, 314, 840
throughput, 247, 848
throughput costing, 502, 848
throughput efficiency, 248–9, **248, 848**
throughput time ratio, 247, **249, 848**
time management, 244–7
about time management, 244
bottleneck resources, 244, 839
costs of time, 245
customer response time, 244–5, **244, 841**
new product development time, 244, 844
production cycle time, 244, 846
time-driven ABC, 245–7, **245, 848**
analysis of calling costs, 246
see also job and project management; just-in-time (JIT) or lean process management; productivity and efficiency management; quality management
time-driven ABC, 164, 848
timeliness (decision-making), **10, 848**
total factor productivity, 247, 848
total quality management (TQM), 229, 848
trace (or track), 147, 848
traditional costing system, 145–7
cost allocation base, 146, 840
cost allocation rate, 146, 840
cost pool, 145, 841
example system, 146–7
refining steps, 145–6
under-costing/over-costing example, 145
transfer price (internal transactions), **726, 748, 848**
transfer pricing: impacts on organizations, 748–53
about the example organization, 747
case studies of practices, 761
creating behavioural congruence, 753
divisional autonomy issues, 761–4
about the issues, 761–2
dual transfer pricing system, 762–3, **762, 842**
remedy for motivational problems, 762–3
divisional perspective, 750–3
example scenario, 748–52
fairness in transfer pricing, 763–4
organizational perspective, 748–50
segment reporting, 766–7
Financial Accounting Standards Board (FASB), 766
International Accounting Standards Board (IASB), 766
transfer pricing: international practices/regulations, 764–6
an illustration of the effects, 764–6
import duties, 766
international implications example, 766
multinational companies in China, 767
multinational transfer pricing, 764–6
arm's length transactions, 764, 839
transfer pricing: methods, 753–61
cost-based transfer pricing, 758–60, **758, 840**
absorption or full cost, 758
ethical issues, 759
full cost transfer pricing, 760
helping behavioural congruence?, 758–9
standard versus actual costs, 759–60
unit-variable cost, 758
general rule, 753–6
excess capacity scenario, 754–5
no excess capacity scenario, 755–6
opportunity cost, 74, 75
outlay cost, 754
informational difficulties, 760–1
imperfect competition, **761, 843**
perfect competition, **761, 845**
market-based transfer price, 756–7, **756, 844**
helping behavioural congruence?, 757
negotiated transfer pricing, 760, 844

U

under-applied overhead cost, 159, 848
unfavourable (variances), 632, 848
unit-level cost, 142, 848
upper control limit, 233, 848

V

value chain, 14, 848
value chain example, 49
value chains (for competitive advantage)s, and job-order costing, 498
value-added activities, 198, 848
value-based pricing, 308
variable cost, 53–4, **53, 848**
variable costing, 495–8, **495, 848**

variable overhead quantity variance, **639**, **848–9**
variable overhead spending variance, **638**, **849**
variance analysis, **631**, **849**
  other types of, research insight, 649
  see also cost variance analysis...; sales variance analysis
variances, **21**, **849**
  benefit and cost variances, 21–2
  see also production mix and yield variances
volume variance, **630**, **849**

W

waste, **63**, **532**, **544**, **849**
weighted-average cost of capital (WACC), 709–10, **709**, **849**
weighted-average process costing, **547**, **849**
weighted-average unit contribution margin (WAUCM), 296–7, **296**, **849**
work in progress (WIP) inventory, **63**, 65–6, **849**

Z

zero-base budgeting, **428**, **849**